ANSON'S
LAW OF CONTRACT

ANSON'S
LAW OF CONTRACT

30th Edition

SIR JACK BEATSON

DCL, LLD, FBA

*A Lord Justice of Appeal
sometime Rouse Ball
Professor of English Law, University of Cambridge*

ANDREW BURROWS

DCL, MA, LLM (HARVARD), FBA, QC (HON)

*Professor of the Law of England and
Fellow of All Souls College, University of Oxford*

JOHN CARTWRIGHT

BCL, MA

*Professor of the Law of Contract, University of Oxford
Professor of Anglo-American Private Law, University of Leiden*

OXFORD
UNIVERSITY PRESS

OXFORD

UNIVERSITY PRESS

Great Clarendon Street, Oxford, OX2 6DP,
United Kingdom

Oxford University Press is a department of the University of Oxford.
It furthers the University's objective of excellence in research, scholarship,
and education by publishing worldwide. Oxford is a registered trade mark of
Oxford University Press in the UK and in certain other countries

Twenty-seventh edition 1998
Twenty-eighth edition 2002
Twenty-ninth edition 2010

Impression: 3

Public sector information reproduced under Open Government Licence v2.0
(http://www.nationalarchives.gov.uk/doc/open-government-licence/open-government-licence.htm)

Published in the United States of America by Oxford University Press
198 Madison Avenue, New York, NY 10016, United States of America

British Library Cataloguing in Publication Data
Data available

Library of Congress Control Number: 2015958964

ISBN 978–0–19–873478–9

Printed in Great Britain by
Ashford Colour Press Ltd.

PREFACE

It is almost six years since the last edition of this book. Our intention continues to be to reflect Sir William Anson's approach to provide a clear statement of the basic principles 'which govern the contractual obligation from its beginning to its end', illustrating 'general rules by the most recent or striking decision', and doing so 'in such a way as might best induce the student to refer to cases and to acquire the habit of going to original authorities instead of taking rules on trust'.[1]

This edition has involved more amendment than the last two for two main reasons. The first is that the Courts and the Legislature continue to be active, and both Parliament and the Supreme Court were particularly active in 2015. Indeed we cannot recall a time when there have been so many complex changes in such a short time. The second is that we have sought to reduce the length of the book. The result is that, despite the additions needed, this edition is slightly shorter than the 29th edition.

The significant legislative changes concern consumer and insurance contracts. The poorly drafted and difficult Consumer Rights Act 2015 has made changes to the statutory terms in consumer contracts and remedies for their breach, and has reformed the control of exemption and unfair terms in consumer contracts. The Consumer Protection (Amendment) Regulations 2014, through the Consumer Protection from Unfair Trading Regulations 2008, introduce new remedies for consumers in respect of misleading and aggressive practices by traders. The Consumer Insurance (Disclosure and Representations) Act 2012 and the Insurance Act 2015 have reformed the law on duties of disclosure in insurance contracts. Since *Anson* is a book which deals with the general law of contract, we have sought to deal with the changes introduced by the legislation conceptually rather than treating these two types of contract separately. This has involved significant changes, particularly in the chapters on terms, exemption clauses and unfair terms, and remedies, but also in the chapters on misrepresentation and non-disclosure, and duress, undue influence and unconscionable bargains.

As to the courts, between June and December 2015, the Supreme Court handed down four significant decisions on the law of contract. In June, *Arnold v Britton* provided a restatement of the principles governing the interpretation of a written contract. While seeking to identify the intention of the parties by reference to what a reasonable person having all the background knowledge which would have been available to them would have understood by the language, this focuses more on the natural and ordinary meaning of the words used. In November, the court considered the law on penalties and liquidated damages clauses in *Cavendish Square Holding BV v El Makdessi* and *ParkingEye Ltd v Beavis*. They formulated a new test: whether

---

[1] Preface to 6th edition (1891).

the provision is a secondary obligation which imposes a detriment on the contract-breaker out of all proportion to any legitimate interest of the innocent party in the enforcement of the primary obligation. *ParkingEye* also considered the application of the law on unfair terms.

The Supreme Court's year in contract ended with *Marks & Spencer plc v BNP Paribas Services Trust Co (Jersey) Ltd* in which it reviewed the nature of the requirements which have to be satisfied before a term can be implied by fact into a detailed commercial contract. The judgments discuss 'necessity and obviousness' and the relationship between the process of implying terms into a contract and the interpretation of the contract. We discuss the court's comments about Lord Hoffmann's analysis and formulation in *Attorney General of Belize v Belize Telecom Ltd* in 2009. It was stated that his judgment should not be understood as diluting the requirements which have to be satisfied before a term will be implied. It was also said the suggestion that the process of implying a term is part of the exercise of interpretation could obscure the fact that construing words used and implying additional words are different processes governed by different rules.

We have also sought to deal with all significant decisions in the Court of Appeal and the High Court. We here single out one Court of Appeal decision and one decision at first instance. In 2015, in *Wellesley Partners LLP v Withers LLP* the Court of Appeal decided that, in a claim in respect of economic loss where there are concurrent duties of care owed in contract and tort, the stricter so-called contractual test of reasonable contemplation applies even to the claim in the tort of negligence. The 2013 decision of the High Court in *Yam Seng PTE Ltd v International Trade Corp Ltd* contains an extensive analysis of the truth of the general view that in English contract law there is no legal principle of good faith of general application. It discusses the reasons for that view, and the ways in which a duty to perform in good faith may be implied in fact in commercial contracts.

We have tried to shorten the length of the book without sacrificing any depth of treatment of topics that are central to undergraduate courses. The result is that we have significantly cut the chapters on agency, assignment, and illegality, and reduced the length of the footnotes throughout the book. The focus of the treatment of agency and assignment is now their relationship to the doctrine of privity. We have retained discussion of the general principles governing illegal contracts, and refer to the disagreement between different members of the Supreme Court in no fewer than three cases (albeit in non-contractual contexts) about the effect of illegality, but have shortened what used to be detailed sections covering specific kinds of illegality. At the time of writing, we await the decision of the Supreme Court in *Patel v Mirza*. The chapter on mistake in the last edition analysed the decision of the Court of Appeal in *The Great Peace* which overruled Lord Denning's equitable doctrine of mistake in *Solle v Butcher*, but retained the discussion of the equitable doctrine and the cases applying it, and considered what had been lost as a result of *The Great Peace*. In this edition, we have shortened the treatment of the equitable doctrine.

As in the last edition, Andrew Burrows or John Cartwright undertook the initial drafting of each chapter, and Jack Beatson acted as general editor. We have each read, commented on and discussed all chapters so that the final result remains a collaborative joint enterprise. We are very grateful to friends, colleagues and students for assistance, and for comments on the contents of the 29th edition. The law is stated as at 2 December 2015.

6 March 2016
JB, AB, JC

OUTLINE CONTENTS

PART 5 REMEDIES FOR BREACH OF CONTRACT

PART 6 LIMITS OF THE CONTRACTUAL OBLIGATION

DETAILED CONTENTS

PART 2 CONTENTS OF THE CONTRACT

PART 3 FACTORS TENDING TO DEFEAT CONTRACTUAL LIABILITY

PART 4 PERFORMANCE AND DISCHARGE

PART 5 REMEDIES FOR BREACH OF CONTRACT

PART 6   LIMITS OF THE CONTRACTUAL OBLIGATION

TABLE OF STATUTES

TABLE OF STATUTORY INSTRUMENTS

TABLE OF EUROPEAN
UNION LEGISLATION

TABLE OF INTERNATIONAL AND OTHER NATIONAL LEGISLATION AND RESTATEMENTS

TABLE OF CASES

*(Pages on which the facts of a case are given are printed in **bold**)*

SOME ABBREVIATIONS USED
IN REFERENCE

The Table of Cases contains the English Report references for cases reported in the Nominate Reports

Reports (except the Law Reports, 1865–date: see below, p xcvi)

A & E	Adolphus & Ellis	QB	1834–1840
ALJR	Australian Law Journal Reports	Australia	1927–date
Aleyn	Aleyn	KB	1646–1648
All ER	All England Reports	All	1936–date
ALR	Australian Law Reports	Australia	1973–date
Amb	Ambler	Ch	1737–1783
Anst	Anstruther	Exch	1792–1797
Atk	Atkyns	Ch	1736–1754
B & Ad	Barnewall & Adolphus	KB	1830–1834
B & Ald	Barnewall & Alderson	KB	1817–1822
B & C	Barnewall & Cresswell	KB	1822–1830
B & P	Bosanquet & Puller	CP	1796–1804
B & S	Best & Smith	QB	1861–1869
BCLC	Butterworths Company Law Cases	All	1983–date
Beav	Beavan	Rolls Court	1838–1866
Bing	Bingham	CP	1822–1834
Bing NC	Bingham, New Cases	CP	1834–1840
BLR	Building Law Reports	All	1976–date
Brown, PC	Brown, Parliamentary Cases	HL	1701–1800
Bulst	Bulstrode	KB	1609–1626
Burr	Burrow	KB	1756–1772
C & J	Crompton & Jervis	Exch	1830–1832
C & K	Carrington & Kirwan	Nisi Prius	1843–1850
C & M	Crompton & Meeson	Exch	1832–1834
C & P	Carrington & Payne	Nisi Prius	1823–1841
CB	Common Bench	CP	1845–1856
CBNS	Common Bench, New Series	CP	1856–1865
CLC	CCH Commercial Law Cases	All	1994–date
CLR	Commonwealth Law Reports	Australia	1903–date
CLYB	Current Law Year Book	All	1947–date
CM & R	Crompton, Meeson & Roscoe	Exch	1834–1836
Cab & El	Cababé & Ellis	QB	1882–1885

Camp	Campbell	Nisi Prius	1807–1816
Carth	Carthew	KB	1687–1700
Cl & Fin	Clark & Finnelly	HL	1831–1846
Co Rep	Coke	KB	1572–1616
Colles, PC	Colles	HL	1697–1713
Com Cas	Commercial Cases	All	1895–1941
Con.LR	Construction Law Reports	All	1985–date
Cowp	Cowper	KB	1774–1778
Cox	Cox's Equity	Ch	1783–1796
Cr & Ph	Craig & Phillips	Ch	1840–1841
Cro Eliz	Croke, of the reign of Elizabeth	CP, QB	1582–1603
Cro Jac	Croke, of the reign of James	CP, KB	1603–1625
Dalison	Dalison	CP	1546–1574
DLR	Dominion Law Reports	Canada	1912–date
De G & J	De Gex & Jones	Ch	1857–1859
De G & Sm	De Gex & Smale	Ch	1846–1852
De GF & J	De Gex, Fisher & Jones	Ch	1859–1862
De GJ & S	De Gex, Jones & Smith	Ch	1862–1865
De GM & G	De Gex, Macnaghten & Gordon	Ch	1851–1857
Doug KB	Douglas	KB	1778–1781
Dr & Sm	Drewry & Smale	V-C	1860–1865
Drew	Drewry	V-C	1852–1859
E & B	Ellis & Blackburn	QB	1852–1858
E & E	Ellis & Ellis	QB	1858–1861
EB & E	Ellis, Blackburn & Ellis	QB	1858
EMLR	Entertainment & Media Law Reports	All	1993–date
ECR	European Court Reports	EEC and EU	1954–date
East	East's Term Reports	KB	1800–1812
Eden	Eden	Ch	1757–1766
Esp	Espinasse	Nisi Prius	1856–1857
EG	Estates Gazette	All	1858–date
EGLR	Estates Gazette Law Reports	All	1975–date
Exch	Exchequer Reports	Exch	1862–1865
FLR	Family Law Reports	All	1980–date
F & F	Foster & Finlason	Nisi Prius	1856–1867
H & C	Hurlstone & Coltman	Exch	1862–1866
H & N	Hurlstone & Norman	Exch	1856–1862
H Bl	Henry Blackstone	CP, Exch	1788–1796
HLC	House of Lords Cases	HL	1847–1866
Hare	Hare	V-C	1841–1853
Hob	Hobart	KB	1603–1625
ICR	Industrial Cases Reports	All	1972–date
IRLR	Industrial Relations Law Reports	All	1972–date

Ir Rep	Irish Reports	Ireland	1838–date
Ir CL	Irish Reports, Common Law	Ir QB	1866–1878
J & H	Johnson & Hemming	V-C	1859–1862
J & W	Jacob & Walker	Ch	1819–1821
JP	Justice of the Peace and Local Government Review	All	1837–date
John	Johnson	V-C	1858–1860
K & J	Kay & Johnson	V-C	1854–1858
Keen	Keen	Rolls Court	1836–1838
Keilwey	Keilwey	KB, CP	1496–1531
LGR	Local Government Reports	All	1903–date
LJ CP	Law Journal, Common Pleas	CP	
LJ Ch	Law Journal, Chancery	Ch	
LJ Ex	Law Journal, Exchequer	Exch	1832–1949
LJ QB	Law Journal, Queen's Bench	QB	
LT	Law Times Reports	All	1859–1947
Ld. Raym	Lord Raymond	KB, CP	1694–1732
Lev	Levinz	KB, CP	1660–1697
Ll LR	Lloyd's List Law Reports	All	1919–1950
Lloyd's Rep	Lloyd's (List) Law Reports	All	1951–date
M & G	Manning & Granger	CP	1840–1844
M & S	Maule & Selwyn	KB	1813–1817
M & W	Meeson & Welsby	Exch	1836–1847
Madd	Maddock	V-C	1815–1821
Mer	Merivale	Ch	1815–1817
Mod	Modern Reports	All	1669–1755
My & K	Mylne & Keen	Ch	1832–1835
NZLR	New Zealand Law Reports	NZ	1883–date
Nev & M	Nevile & Manning	KB	1832–1836
Noy	Noy	KB	1559–1649
P & CR	Property, Planning and Compensation Reports	All	1950–date
Peake	Peake	Nisi Prius	1790–1812
Peere Wms	Peere Williams	Ch	1695–1735
Ph	Phillips	Ch	1841–1849
QB	Queen's Bench Reports	QB	1841–1852
RPC	Reports of Patent Cases	Pat Cas	1884–date
Russ	Russell	Ch	1823–1829
SC	Session Cases	Scotland	1906–date
Salk	Salkeld	All	1689–1712
Sid	Siderfin	All	1657–1670
Sim	Simons	V-C	1826–1849
Sm & G	Smale & Giffard	V-C	1852–1857

St Tr	State Trials	—	1163–1820
Stra	Strange	All	1716–1749
Swan	Swanston	Ch	1818–1819
TLR	Times Law Reports	All	1884–1952
Taunt	Taunton	CP	1807–1819
Term R	Term Reports	KB	1785–1800
Ventr	Ventris	All	1668–1691
Ves Jun	Vesey Junior	Ch	1789–1817
Ves Sen	Vesey Senior	Ch	1746–1755
W Bl	William Blackstone	KB	1746–1779
WR	Weekly Reporter	All	1853–1906
Wilmot	Wilmot	All	1757–1770
Wils	Wilson	KB, CP	1742–1774
Y & C Ch	Younge & Collyer (Chancery)	V-C	1841–1843
Y & J	Younge & Jervis	Exch	1826–1830
YB	Year Books (with regnal year)		

Law Reports, 1865–date

LR CP	Common Pleas	
LR Ch App	Chancery Appeals	
LR Eq	Equity Cases	
LR Ex	Exchequer	1865–1875
LR HL	House of Lords, English and Irish Appeals	
LR PC	Privy Council Appeals	
LR QB	Queen's Bench	
LR Sc App	Scottish Appeals	
CPD	Common Pleas Division	1875–1880
Ex D	Exchequer Division	
App Cas	Appeals Cases	
Ch D	Chancery Division	
PD	Probate Division	1875–1890
QBD	Queen's Bench Division	
AC	Appeal Cases	
Ch	Chancery Division	1891–date
KB or QB	King's (Queen's) Bench Division	
P	Probate Division	1891–1971
Fam	Family Division	1972–date
WLR	Weekly Law Reports	1953–date

Neutral Citations

EWCA Civ	England & Wales Court of Appeal, Civil	2000–date
UKHL	United Kingdom, House of Lords	1996–2009
UKPC	United Kingdom, Privy Council	2001–date
UKSC	United Kingdom, Supreme Court	2009–date

Periodicals

ALJ	Australian Law Journal
CLJ	Cambridge Law Journal
CLY	Current Law Yearbook
Can Bar Rev	Canadian Bar Review
Const LJ	Construction Law Journal
Conv (NS)	Conveyancer and Property Lawyer (New Series)
Harv LR	Harvard Law Review
JALT	Journal of the Association of Law Teachers
JBL	Journal of Business Law
JCL	Journal of Contract Law
LMCLQ	Lloyd's Maritime and Commercial Law Quarterly
LQR	Law Quarterly Review
LS	Legal Studies
MLR	Modern Law Review
OJLS	Oxford Journal of Legal Studies
RLR	Restitution Law Review
SALJ	South African Law Journal
SJ	Solicitors' Journal

Other abbreviations

ALI	American Law Institute
CISG	United Nations (Vienna) Convention on Contracts for the International Sale of Goods
CMA	Competition and Markets Authority
CP	Consultation Paper
CPR	Civil Procedure Rules
FCA	Financial Conduct Authority
FSA	Financial Services Authority
OFT	Office of Fair Trading
TEU	Treaty on European Union
TFEU	Treaty on the Functioning of the European Union
WP	Working Paper

1

INTRODUCTION

The principles of the English law of contract are almost entirely the creation of the English Courts, and the legislature has, until recently, played a relatively small part in their development. They are also, for the most part, a development of the last 200 years; for contract law is the child of commerce, and has grown with the growth of Britain from a mainly agricultural into a mainly commercial and industrial nation. In Blackstone's *Commentaries on the Laws of England*, which were first published in 1756, it is significant of the comparative unimportance of the subject that he devoted 380 pages to the law of real property, and only 28 to contract. The industrial revolution, however, brought about a fundamental change in the structure of the British economy. Land was no longer the primary source of wealth. Mills, mines, and factories sprang up and raw materials were converted by process of manufacture into products for sale in the markets of the world. The capital required for these enterprises was beyond the capacity of most private individuals and it was raised by public subscriptions for shares in joint stock companies or by loans from banks and other financial institutions. The growth of international trade further led to the creation of international commodity, shipping, insurance, and money markets, many of which were centred on London. All of these commercial developments depended and still do depend for their successful operation upon contract.

This introductory chapter considers briefly: first, the nature and function of contract; secondly, the history of contractual obligations in English law; thirdly, the content of the contract law as set out in this book which is concerned with the 'general principles' of contract rather than the detailed rules applicable to different types of contracts; fourthly, the location of contract as part of the law of obligations and its relation to other parts of the law of obligations, tort and restitution of an unjust enrichment, and to property law.

1. THE NATURE AND FUNCTION OF CONTRACT

(a) PROMISE OR AGREEMENT

The law of contract may be provisionally described as that branch of the law which determines the circumstances in which a promise shall be legally binding on the person making it. Section 1 of the American Law Institute's *Restatement, Contracts (2d)*[1] gives the following definition:

A contract is a promise or a set of promises for the breach of which the law gives a remedy, or the performance of which the law in some way recognizes as a duty.

This definition is broadly acceptable, provided that it is realized that, in law, a promise may be constituted by an assurance that a thing *has been* or *is* (eg that the engine of a car has been recently overhauled or is now in good mechanical condition) as well as that a thing *will be*, and provided that it is also appreciated that most, but not all, contracts take the form of an agreement by which each party agrees to accept the promise or promises of the other in return for the promise or promises made by itself.[2]

(b) FUNCTIONS OF CONTRACT

The above definition is, however, very much a lawyer's definition and gives little indication of the nature of contract, and still less of its function. Most readers of this book will have some general notion of what a contract is. Indeed, they will enter into a contract very frequently, in some cases almost every day, for example, a contract of carriage (travel by bus or train), or a contract for the sale of goods (the purchase of groceries), or for the supply of services (a haircut), or one involving both sale and the supply of services (having a meal at a restaurant). But the law which will be found in the following pages of this book is law which is derived, for the most part, not from such simple consumer transactions, but from commercial transactions between businesspeople and companies. Commercial transactions involve the exchange of land, goods, or services for money. This exchange is not immediate, as in a supermarket, but is to take place in the future. Contract has an important function of securing that the expectations created by a promise of future performance are fulfilled, or that compensation will be paid for its breach.

Take the example of the construction of an office building. The developer must first purchase the site, and this will often be done with money borrowed from a bank, the developer promising to repay the loan with interest at some future date. It must then engage an architect to design the building, a quantity surveyor to draw up bills of quantities, and a solicitor to do the legal work connected with the development. The building work will be put out to tender and the successful tenderer will be awarded the contract as main contractor. In its turn, the main contractor will often subcontract parts of the work to other contractors. It may be that the developer will put the office space on the market while the building is still under construction and would-be

---

[1] See below, p 23, n 105.

[2] Agreement is unnecessary for the enforcement of a promise in a deed (below, p 33). It is therefore sometimes characterized as a unilateral act, binding by virtue of the formality and not as contract, but this book includes it in the general definition of contract because it is a promise binding in law; see also Supply of Goods and Services Act 1982, s 1(2)(d). Agreement is perhaps not an altogether appropriate description of a unilateral contract, on which see below, pp 32–3, 41, 57.

occupants will agree to take a tenancy once it is completed. All of these relationships will depend on the promise of the participating parties that they will carry out their obligations in the future, whether these consist in the payment of money, or otherwise, and that they will be legally bound to their promised performance. No doubt, as a normal rule, each participant will duly fulfil its promise without the need for any intervention, or threatened intervention, by the law.[3] But, in the last resort, the recipient of the promise (the 'promisee') will rely upon the law to reinforce by appropriate sanctions the promise of performance given. By entering into a contract, the promisee is able to have recourse to those sanctions.

Another important function of contract is a constitutive one: to facilitate forward planning of the transaction and to make provision for future contingencies.[4] The more complex the transaction the greater will be the need for such planning and the more detailed the provisions that are likely to be made. First, and most obviously, contract will normally establish the value of the exchange, that is, how much is to be paid for the land, goods, or services to be provided. In the above example, the developer will need to measure the likely cost of the development against anticipated revenue. While this may to a considerable extent be a matter of estimate, the developer will seek, so far as is practicable, to establish by contract the value of the items that go to make up that cost, for instance, the interest to be paid for the loan and the price to be paid to the main contractor.

Secondly, contract will establish what are the respective responsibilities of the parties and the standard of performance to be expected of them. The building contract will incorporate the specifications for the work, sorting out what is to be done, the nature and quality of the materials to be used, and the date for completion of the work. It will provide for stage payments to be made by the developer. The respective responsibilities of the developer, architect, contractor, and subcontractors will also be established by contract.

Thirdly, contract enables the economic risks involved in the transaction to be allocated in advance between the parties. The building contract may provide, for example, for an increase in the price in the event of an increase in the cost of labour or materials to the contractor, and who is to bear the risk of strikes, bad weather, or fire. The party affected by the risk may then be able to cover it by insurance.

Finally, contract may provide for what is to happen if things go wrong. Suppose that the contractor fails to remedy defects when required to do so by the architect. Or suppose that the developer fails to pay for work which is certified to have been done. The contract can provide for payment in advance,[5] and can determine whether the party not in default is entitled to terminate the contract and on what terms.[6] The contract may also provide for payment by the contractor of a specified sum by way of 'liquidated damages'[7] in the event of delay in completion beyond the date fixed.

---

[3] Macaulay (1963) 28 American Sociological Review 55.   [4] *Ibid.*
[5] See below, pp 607, 624.   [6] See below, p 148.   [7] See below, p 598.

Contract is, in effect, the instrument by which the separate and conflicting interests of the participants can be reconciled and brought to a common goal.[8] The importance accorded by English law to the planning function is shown by its preference for rules that provide certainty, particularly in commercial contracts where speed and certainty have been said to be of paramount importance.[9]

(c) FREEDOM OF CONTRACT

The significance of the role played by contract in any economic system can scarcely be denied. The issue is the extent to which the law does, or should, assume that parties enjoy freedom of economic decision when entering into contracts. The concept of freedom of contract has two meanings. The first is the freedom of a party to choose to enter into a contract on whatever terms it may consider advantageous to its interests, or to choose not to. Contractual obligation is thereby attributed to the will of the parties. This was one of the cornerstones of nineteenth-century *laissez-faire* economics.[10] Adam Smith in his *Wealth of Nations*, published in 1776, offered the first systematic account of economic affairs, championing the cause of freedom of trade against the economic protectionism current at that time, and freedom of contract was taken up as an ideal into classical economic theory.

When, therefore, in 1861, Sir Henry Maine wrote his *Ancient Law*, he postulated that the movement of progressive societies had hitherto been a *movement* from status (with its entrenched protection of privilege by legal and social restrictions) to contract. He considered this movement to be not only desirable, but inevitable. 'Imperative law', he said,[11] 'has abandoned the largest part of the field which it once occupied, and has left men to settle rules of conduct for themselves with a liberty never allowed to them till recently.'

But freedom of contract also referred to the idea that as a general rule there should be no liability without consent embodied in a valid contract. This second and negative aspect of freedom of contract was influential in narrowing the scope of those parts of the law of obligations which deal with liability imposed by law: tort and restitution of an unjust enrichment.[12]

Today the position is seen in a different light. Freedom of contract is generally regarded as a reasonable social ideal only to the extent that equality of bargaining power between contracting parties can be assumed, and no injury is done to the economic interests of the community at large. In the more complicated social and industrial conditions of modern society it has ceased to have much idealistic attraction except, perhaps, to the proponents of a completely free market economy, who have advanced

---

[8] See Gurvitch, *Sociology of Law* (1947).   [9] See below, pp 34–5, 64, 153, 158.
[10] See Friedmann, *Law in a Changing Society* (1959) ch 4; Gilmore, *The Death of Contract* (1977); Atiyah, *The Rise and Fall of Freedom of Contract* (1979); Cornish and Clark, *Law and Society in England, 1750–1950* (1989) 201–3, 226.
[11] *Ancient Law* (1930) ch ix, p 322.   [12] Below, p 18.

it in recent years in a modern and sophisticated way, some using the tools of micro-economic analysis.[13] But whatever its status may be as an ideal, the concept of freedom of contract has suffered severe inroads as the result of developments in modern social life and policy.

(i) Statutory restrictions

In the first place, statute law today interferes at numerous points with inroads into the freedom of the parties to make what contract they like. The relations between employers and employees, for example, have been regulated by statutes designed to ensure that employees are properly protected against redundancy and unfair dismissal, and that they know their terms of service. The public has been protected against economic pressure by such measures as the Rent Acts,[14] the Consumer Credit Act 1974,[15] the Unfair Contract Terms Act 1977,[16] the Consumer Rights Act 2015,[17] and other similar enactments. These legislative provisions will override any contrary terms which the parties may make for themselves. Freedom of contract is also affected by statutorily imposed terms which set the 'default' rule for both consumer and non-consumer contracts, although this can sometimes be varied by the parties in non-consumer contracts.[18] Further, both national[19] and European Union[20] legislation has been enacted to promote competition in industry and to safeguard the interests of consumers, and the Financial Services and Markets Act 2000 (amended by the Financial Services Act 2012) contains provisions to safeguard the interests of investors.

There are also wide-ranging restrictions in the Equality Act 2010 on discrimination on such grounds as disability, race, religion, sex, and age in the provision of goods, facilities, and services, and in the selection of employees and in the terms upon which they are employed. These are a significant departure from the general freedom at common law to refuse to contract.[21] Although they primarily give rise to compensation orders, these statutory provisions can exceptionally lead to specific relief.[22] The

---

[13] Posner, *Economic Analysis of Law* (9th edn, 2014) ch 4; Cooter and Ulen, *Law and Economics* (6th edn, 2011) ch 8. Fried, *Contract as Promise* (2nd edn, 2015) provides a non-economic approach.

[14] In particular the Rent Act 1977 (providing security of tenure and rent control for private residential lettings, as amended by the Housing Acts 1988 and 1996), the Housing Acts 1980 and 1985 (public sector tenants) and the Landlord and Tenant Acts 1985 and 1987 (landlords' duties of information and implied terms as to condition of premises and repair, and tenants' right to buy).

[15] Below, p 232 (as amended by the Consumer Credit Act 2006).

[16] Below, p 208.   [17] In particular, Part 2: below, p 223.

[18] eg Consumer Right Act 2015, ss 9–17, 34–37, 41, 49–52, below, p 178 (consumer contracts); Sale of Goods Act 1979, ss 12–15, below, p 171; Supply of Goods and Services Act 1982, ss 2–5, 7–10, 13–15 (non-consumer contracts).

[19] Fair Trading Act 1973 (now repealed); Restrictive Trade Practices Act 1976 (now repealed); Competition Act 1998, Enterprise Act 2002; Enterprise and Regulatory Reform Act 2013.

[20] Below, p 429. Since 1 December 2009, the European Union has replaced the European Community under the Treaty of Lisbon.

[21] *Timothy v Simpson* (1834) 6 C & P 499. Cf *Constantine v Imperial Hotels Ltd* [1944] AC 693.

[22] Equality Act 2010, s 124.

prohibition on discrimination in the provision of goods, facilities, and services applies where the provision is made to the public or a section of the public.[23]

(ii) Standard form contracts: contracts of adhesion

Most contracts entered into by ordinary people are not in fact the result of individual negotiation. An employee's contract of employment, for example, will often be determined by a collective agreement made between trade unions and employers. Standard form contracts are also frequently used, even between businesses. These will lay down the terms on which the supplier is prepared to do business, or embody or incorporate by reference the terms of a trade association. The freedom of the parties to negotiate is limited by such standard form contracts. Although a party, often a consumer, is free to decide not to deal with a particular retailer and to negotiate prices, delivery dates, and so on, in many areas similar terms will be offered by other retailers so that the individual has either to accept the terms laid down in their totality, or go without. Since, however, it is not feasible to go without many such goods or services, the individual is effectively compelled to adhere to those terms. In certain types of standard form contracts, however, for example those for the charter of ships, the standard form is often extensively modified or supplemented by other terms appropriate to the particular charterparty.

(iii) 'Compulsory' transactions

In the case of utilities such as water or electricity, which are in effect necessities of modern life, but the supplier is a monopoly or near monopoly, there may be a legal compulsion to supply, at least, domestic consumers. Under the legislation regulating such utilities, including electricity and gas where it is now possible to choose an alternative supplier, there is a duty to supply those who wish to be supplied,[24] there are certain prohibitions on undue preference and undue discrimination,[25] and a statutory regulator is given power to control prices and other terms of supply. This may be the modern equivalent of the common law duty on common innkeepers and common carriers to serve all comers on a reasonable basis,[26] probably because of their monopoly or near monopoly position. These common law doctrines have not, however, been developed and the field has been left to the anti-discrimination legislation, and legislation for the control of monopolies and restrictive trade practices, and for regulating utilities. Where

---

[23] Equality Act 2010, ss 29, 31(2).

[24] Gas Act 1986, s 10 (substituted by Gas Act 1995); Electricity Act 1989, s 16 (substituted by Utilities Act 2000). See also Water Industry Act 1991, s 37.

[25] Gas Act 1986, s 9(2) (substituted by Gas Act 1995); Water Industry Act 1991, s 2(3)(b) (substituted by Water Act 2003); see also Telecommunications Act 1984, ss 3, 8(1)(d), and Electricity Act 1989, ss 3(2), 18(4) (now repealed).

[26] *Clarke v West Ham Corp* [1909] 2 KB 858, 879–82. Note that almost all carriers contract out of their common law liability.

there is a statutory obligation to supply and no or little power to negotiate about the incidents of the relationship, the Courts may regard its compulsory nature as incompatible with its being contractual.[27]

(iv) Implied terms and the standard of 'reasonableness'

Finally, the negative aspect of freedom of contract, that there should be no liability without consent embodied in a valid contract, sits uneasily with the practice of implication of terms into the contract, and the use of the standard of 'reasonableness' as a way of dealing with gaps in the contractual language.[28] Terms are implied not only under statute, but also at common law. Although the basis of such implication is said to be 'necessity'[29] or in the case of custom 'presumed consent',[30] in many cases this is rather artificial, and in truth in many standard transactions the implied terms are the legal incidents of the transaction,[31] from which the parties are, subject to statute, often free to deviate although in practice many parties will simply be bound by those implied terms without seeking to negotiate otherwise. Freedom of contract is also difficult to reconcile with the adoption of the 'objective theory' which provides, in essence, that a person (A), whose conduct is such that the other party reasonably believes that A has assented to the terms of a contract, will be bound no matter what A's real intention is.[32] This rule can lead to the imposition of non-consensual obligations, since what creates the obligation is not consent in fact but acting as if consent is being given.

(v) Summary

In many areas of contract, freedom of contract in the classical sense is manifestly lacking. But English law and English judges still to a great extent proceed on the assumption that the parties are free to choose whether or not they will enter into a contract and on what terms. The formulation of the test for implied terms has been noted, and, as recently as 1980, in the House of Lords, Lord Diplock observed:[33] 'A basic principle of the common law of contract . . . is that the parties are free to determine for themselves what primary obligations they will accept'. It may be objected that the general principles of contract law therefore present an inadequate, if not distorted, picture of modern economic life. This may be so, but it is nevertheless the case that the law does still rest on the assumption of freedom of choice, and where a relationship is entered into in which there is no choice, a Court may hold that it is not contractual.[34]

---

[27] *Norweb plc v Dixon* [1995] 1 WLR 636; *Read v Croydon Corp* [1938] 4 All ER 631.

[28] eg *Tillmanns & Co v SS Knutsford Ltd* [1908] AC 406; *Abu Dhabi National Tanker Co v Product Star Shipping Co Ltd (No 2)* [1993] 1 Lloyd's Rep 397, 404.

[29] *Liverpool City Council v Irwin* [1977] AC 239, 254. See below, p 168.

[30] *Produce Brokers Co Ltd v Olympia Oil & Cake Co Ltd* [1916] 1 AC 314, 324. See below, p 170.

[31] *Mears v Safecar Securities Ltd* [1983] QB 54, 78.   [32] Below, pp 34, 274.

[33] *Photo Production Ltd v Securicor Transport Ltd* [1980] AC 827, 848.   [34] Above, pp 6–7.

(d) SANCTITY OF CONTRACTS

Closely associated with the concept of freedom of contract is yet another principle, that of the sanctity of contracts.[35] Businesspeople in particular are concerned to ensure that the parties to a contract keep to their bargain and that as few avenues as possible should be afforded for escape from contractual obligations. In general, English law is reluctant to admit excuses for non-performance. But the Draconian requirements of commercial convenience have to be reconciled with the moral qualifications introduced by the need to discourage the grosser forms of unfair dealing. Thus the common law, and even more so equity, the influence of which has been more apparent in recent times, have admitted defences based on fraud, misrepresentation, mistake, duress (including economic duress), and undue influence, and endeavoured to curb the economic exploitation (in particular) of employees by the doctrine of restraint of trade. Although there is no general principle of 'inequality of bargaining power',[36] Courts take account of this in interpreting the contract and applying these doctrines. Additionally, statutory protection overrides unfair terms in certain types of contracts, for instance those made between consumers and businesses, and employees and employers. It should not be imagined, however, that contractual obligations can be repudiated by one party merely because that party was in the weaker bargaining position. In the 'rough and tumble' of commercial relationships, various types of pressure are frequently brought to bear and terms may be imposed which are, objectively, harsh; but the contract will still bind.

Further, the law will not permit a person of full age and understanding who failed to read the contract or to appreciate its full import and effect to escape from the contract. It will not rewrite a contract for the parties or imply additional provisions merely because it would be reasonable so to do. And it will, in general, give effect to a written contract in accordance with its recorded terms, and not admit evidence to show that one party intended them to be construed in a different way from that which they actually express.

In certain situations, however, the law will pronounce that the parties are relieved from performance of their obligations by reason of a change of circumstances occurring after the contract was made. But this principle—that of 'frustration of the contract'[37]—is very limited in scope, and will not apply, for example, merely because a subsequent event changes the financial equilibrium of the transaction and forces a party who expected to make a profit from the transaction into a position of loss. The event must be of such a serious and fundamental character that to enforce the contract in the changed circumstances would be to enforce a radically different contract from the one which the parties made.

---

[35] See Hughes Parry, *The Sanctity of Contracts in English Law* (1959), and below, p 18.
[36] *National Westminster Bank plc v Morgan* [1985] AC 686, below, p 405.
[37] See below, Chapter 14.

(e) THE INTEREST PROTECTED BY CONTRACT

The entering into of a contract creates an interest in each party that the contract will be performed.[38] The obligation may be strict, for example a seller's undertaking that it has good title to the goods sold, or it may be qualified, for example to use reasonable care, as is the case in many aspects of contracts for services by professionals such as lawyers or surveyors. If one party fails, in whole or in part, to perform the obligations undertaken in the contract, the other party, whose economic, physical, and, in some cases, psychological interests will be affected, will be entitled to redress. But what form will that redress take?

Where the breach of contract consists of a failure to pay money, whether for goods bought and delivered or for services rendered, the redress for breach will often take the form of (direct) specific enforcement of the contract by an action (in debt) for the sum due.[39] Where the breach consists of the failure to render a non-monetary performance, for example, a seller's failure to deliver goods to a buyer, in some cases the injured party will also be entitled to (direct) specific performance of the other party's obligation. Normally, however, the redress will not take the form of specific performance of the contract, but will consist of monetary compensation.[40] How is that compensation to be assessed?

The object of compensatory damages in contract is to put the injured party, from the position it is now in after the breach, into the same position as it would have been had the contract been duly performed. The injured party is entitled to protection of its interest in the performance of the contract. Suppose, for example,[41] a port authority by contract promises a car ferry operator that it will allow it to use the port facilities for car ferry operations during the coming year, but in breach of that contract repudiates the contract almost immediately after it is made. The wasted expenses sustained by the ferry operator may be no more than (say) the trifling expense of having prepared draft timetables of ship movements for the contract period. But it will nevertheless be entitled additionally to be compensated in damages for the profit which it would have made on the car ferry operations during the year in question. Compensation assessed on this basis is, in effect, a substitute for the performance of the other party's obligation, whether by the payment of a debt that has accrued due[42] or by the rendering of other forms of performance.[43] This protection of the 'expectation' or 'performance', interest (these two terms are synonymous) is not peculiar to the English law of contract. It is a consequence of contract in all developed legal systems. Even if the contract is wholly executory, that is to say, nothing has been done by either party under it at the time of its breach, damages for lost performance will be recoverable.[44]

---

[38] See Fuller and Perdue (1936–37) 46 Yale LJ 52, 573; Atiyah (1978) 94 LQR 193; Taylor (1982) 45 MLR 139; Burrows (1983) 99 LQR 217; Friedmann (1995) 111 LQR 628; Coote [1997] CLJ 537.

[39] Below, p 606. Cf p 564.   [40] Below, p 570.

[41] See *Thoresen Car Ferries Ltd v Weymouth Portland BC* [1972] 2 Lloyd's Rep 614.

[42] Below, p 606.   [43] Below, p 608.

[44] But see the criticisms of Atiyah (1978) 94 LQR 193, and in *The Rise and Fall of Freedom of Contract* (1979).

It has sometimes been suggested that, as an alternative to the expectation or performance interest, compensation in contract protects the claimant's 'reliance' and 'restitution' interests.[45] This is misleading. While reliance damages can be awarded for breach of contract, they are best viewed as an alternative way of protecting the claimant's expectation interest and are not protecting a separate reliance interest.[46] Again, restitution of money paid or the value of services rendered can be awarded where a contract has been discharged for breach or frustration or where a contract is ineffective as well as in situations far removed from a contractual context. But that restitution is for the independent cause of action of unjust enrichment at the claimant's expense and is not a remedy *for* breach of contract.[47] Certainly it is true that restitutionary damages or an account of profits can now be awarded, as an alternative to compensatory damages, for breach of contract to remove some or all of the profits made by the contract-breaker. But that is an unusual and relatively rare remedy which has only been fully recognized recently since the decision of the House of Lords in *Attorney-General v Blake*.[48]

2. THE HISTORY OF CONTRACTUAL OBLIGATIONS IN ENGLISH LAW

The modern law of contract contains much which can properly be explained (if at all) only in the light of its history. Hence, even in a book which aims only at stating the principles of the modern law, it is desirable to give some account of how that law came to take the form which has just been indicated in outline. We shall see that it has not been by any process of analysis and elucidation of the essential nature of a contract that the law has been moulded. Indeed, the very idea of enforcing promises or agreements as such, which seems most natural to us, may not be an early one in the history of any legal system. We shall find the key to the story by examining the conditions which the Courts have attached at different stages to the actions which they were willing to admit for the enforcement of the kind of rights which we now regard as contractual. The story can here be given only in the barest outline,[49] and it should be understood that there are some points in it which remain obscure or controversial.

---

[45] Fuller and Perdue (1936–37) 46 Yale LJ 52, 573.   [46] See below, p 573.
[47] See below, p 621.   [48] [2001] 1 AC 268. See below, pp 632–3.
[49] For fuller treatment, see Atiyah, *The Rise and Fall of Freedom of Contract* (1979); Baker, *Introduction to English Legal History* (4th edn, 2002) 317–61; Baker and Milsom, *Sources of English Legal History* (1986) 209–96, 358–505, hereafter 'Baker and Milsom'; Cornish and Clark, *Law and Society in England, 1750–1950* (1989) 197–226; Milsom, *Historical Foundations of the Common Law* (2nd edn, 1981) 243–360; Simpson, *A History of the Common Law of Contract* (1975); Stoljar, *A History of Contract at Common Law* (1975).

(a) THE EARLY ACTIONS

(i) 'Wager of law'

Actions in what we call contract and tort were at first within the jurisdiction of local and manorial courts. The action would commonly end in a general denial of liability, upon which the defendant would 'wage his law', that is undertake to come at the next court day and swear to this denial in the presence of neighbours (their number specified by the Court) who would then swear to their belief in this oath. If on the day all the oaths were made correctly, the defendant won. The efficacy of this depended partly on the fear of damnation for perjury, and partly upon standing among the neighbours (the city of London, for example, which lived by the credit of its citizens, set particular store by this mode of proof). This social sanction would be lost as lawsuits were diverted from the local setting into royal courts in Westminster.

(ii) Trespass

In the field of tort, for which the very rough medieval equivalent is 'trespass', a case would come to a royal court only if there was some royal interest, normally a 'breach of the king's peace'. That allegation had two other effects. It precluded the defendant from answering by wager of law and required the case to go to a jury. And as between the main royal courts, it gave jurisdiction to the King's Bench concurrently with the Common Pleas. The allegation itself became increasingly fictionalized in the early fourteenth century; and around the middle of the century the Chancery began to make writs of trespass returnable into royal courts with no mention of the king's peace. This was the effective beginning of 'actions on the case'; and logically plaintiffs should not have been able to sue in the King's Bench, and defendants should have been permitted to wage their law. But on both points logic was overruled. All actions of trespass and case could go to either of the royal courts, and all went to jury trial; and this was a cause of developments to which we shall come, by which remedies in contract came to be sought by actions in tort.

In the field of contract, jurisdiction as between local and royal courts came to depend upon the amount at stake. From a beginning in the thirteenth century, originally concerned only with the recovery of debts, a general jurisdictional barrier developed at 40 shillings, then a sum so large that very few transactions of ordinary people would reach it. But the amount was never altered, so that a period of rapid inflation in the sixteenth century brought transactions of falling real value to Westminster, and therefore to the modes of proof in use there. In particular, since there had been no equivalent of the king's peace to affect proof as well as jurisdiction, wager of law was often available; but those who swore to the defendant would be not neighbours but persons hired in Westminster. In the old contract actions, therefore, the focus of attention for lawyers and litigants was not some substantive law of contract but modes of proof.

(iii) Covenant

The word 'covenant' (*conventio*, agreement) is the nearest medieval equivalent to our 'contract'. But even in local courts an action for money due under a contract would be called not covenant but debt (or detinue if the action was for a specific chattel lent or bought, for example), so that actions called covenant mainly concern breaches of agreement for services like building or for sales or leases of land. The primary claim was for performance, and in royal courts the action was begun by a writ, known (from its opening word) as a *praecipe* writ,[50] ordering the defendant to keep the agreement; but judgments ceased to order specific performance and damages were awarded instead. Some think that the plaintiff would have to have done his part of the bargain, but we are not informed about the early requirements; and in the royal courts the question was suppressed by a new requirement about proof. Early in the fourteenth century it became settled that the plaintiff was not entitled to an answer unless he could produce a document under the defendant's seal (in illiterate times the equivalent of a signature) setting out the terms of the agreement. Soon after this the action of covenant fell out of use, not because of this requirement but because the kind of sealed document to which we are about to turn proved more effective. But covenant retained a negative importance: parties might contract for the building of a house, for example, not thinking of royal courts or sealing wax, and find the natural remedy barred.

(iv) Debt

Any claim for a fixed sum of money or a fixed quantity of fungible goods would in the royal court be made by the *praecipe* writ of debt. At first even a claim for specific goods would be made by the same writ, so that one who borrowed money and a book was seen to owe the book in the same way that the money was owed; but the separation of detinue need not be discussed here. In royal as in local courts, the defendant could normally answer by wager of law; and one lending a large sum or selling goods for a large price might take precautions, and this led to a separation between two principal uses to which the single writ of debt might be put.

(a) Debt on an obligation The simplest precaution for, say, a lender was to require the borrower to execute a document under seal, a bond. This was evidence not of a promise to pay but of indebtedness itself, and it was conclusive. The defendant could not deny that the debt was owed, though he could deny that the deed was his (*non est factum*).[51] But that was a risky issue to take: it went to a jury, who would compare seals etc; and if they found against the defendant he would go to prison. At law the defendant could not even say that payment had been made; and though he eventually got equitable protection from the Chancery in this situation, that was

[50] Baker, *Introduction to English Legal History* (4th edn, 2002) 57–9.
[51] For the defence of *non est factum* in the modern law, see below, p 279.

only after a long struggle between the competing goods of general certainty and individual justice.

But bonds were put to wider uses than ensuring that a lender or a seller would get the money that was due. One hiring a builder to build a house, for example, would take from him a bond by which the builder would acknowledge that he owed the customer an essentially penal sum, which bond would be void if conditions (written sometimes on the back of the bond, sometimes in a separate indenture) were satisfied; and those conditions specified the site, dimensions, materials, completion date, etc of the house. If the customer sued it would be on the bond for the penalty, and the builder could of course plead that he had satisfied the conditions. Conversely, the builder would take a bond from the customer, commonly for double the agreed price, to be void if the agreed price was duly paid. Such conditional bonds became the principal vehicle for large transactions; and they continued to be so until the Chancery began to relieve against penalties and until *assumpsit*[52] provided a simpler mechanism.

(b) Debt on a covenant   A sealed document was never required in debt as it was in covenant. The lender could always sue for the repayment of the money lent, the seller for the price, and the builder or other provider of services for the agreed payment. But normally this was only possible when the plaintiff had done his part of the bargain, when the defendant had had his *quid pro quo*. And the medieval word 'contract' did not have its modern meaning: it meant precisely the obligation 'contracted' by a debtor who had received his *quid pro quo*. But much of the reality is hidden by the defendant's usual denial by wager of law—not a denial of any specific facts but just that he owed. And the availability of wager had a further consequence. Only the debtor himself could swear that he did not owe: even if the debt had been publicly incurred it might have been privately paid. So the executor of a dead debtor could not wage law, and it was held by a perverse logic that the executor could not be sued. But that applied only to debt on a contract: the executor could be sued if the plaintiff had a bond which would any way exclude wager.

The combined effect of these actions may be described in terms of an agreement to build a house. Well-advised parties would set it up by conditional bonds, so that the party alleged to be in breach would be sued in debt for the penalty and could plead that the conditions had been satisfied. If the agreement was informally made, the builder who had built could sue in debt for the price (normally answerable by wager of law). But the customer could not bring covenant if the builder did not build, because he had no document under seal; and probably he could not even bring debt to recover any money he had paid. This inequity played its part in the rise of *assumpsit*, where the writ asserted that the defendant had 'undertaken' (*assumpsit*) to do something; but it is important not to suppose that from the beginning lawyers saw that *assumpsit* was to become a general contractual remedy.

[52]   Below, pp 14 ff.

(b) ASSUMPSIT

(i) Misfeasance

Among the tort actions which came to royal courts when the need to allege a breach of the king's peace was dropped were some in which there was a contractual background to the wrong. In 1348 a ferry-man was sued: he had undertaken to ferry a horse across the Humber, but so mismanaged it that the horse was drowned.[53] Its owner sued in tort, and the defendant (knowing there was no sealed document) argued that the proper action would be covenant. The action was held to be rightly brought in tort: the plaintiff complained of the killing of his horse, not the failure to transport it; and such claims for 'misfeasance' regularly succeeded.

(ii) Nonfeasance

There was more difficulty if the defendant had made an undertaking but done nothing in the matter at all: this was clearly 'covenant' rather than 'trespass'. Many attempts to get 'trespass' remedies were made, mostly in situations in which performance of the *praecipe* order in covenant would be impossible (eg the date by which the house was to be built has passed) or would be no sufficient remedy (eg timbers have rotted because the roof was not mended as promised). These would have been arguments for not suing in covenant even if the builder or roof-mender had made their promises under seal; and this may have been among the reasons why customers set up their agreements by conditional bonds in which the penalty would cover any consequential damage as well as the value of the performance. And one must remember that all these early attempts to use *assumpsit* for a nonfeasance were by plaintiffs who had omitted the proper formalities. Perhaps they were caught out by the only transaction of a lifetime large enough to come to a royal court. But their hard cases seemed to a judge in 1425 to threaten bad law: 'if this action [against one who had not built a mill as promised] should be maintained . . . then a man would have an action of trespass for every broken covenant in the world'.[54]

He was to be proved a prophet: but his logic was hard to overcome and we cannot be sure how and when it happened. A stage seems to be marked by a case of 1442 in which the defendant agreed to sell and convey land to the plaintiff from whom she took money. But she actually conveyed to a third party; and the plaintiff sued in tort for a deceit.[55] The agreement was made in London about land outside. If the land had been inside the city, the action would have been brought in city courts under the custom of London by which (a) actions in covenant did not require a document under seal, (b) the normal remedy in covenant was an order for performance, and (c) one who had put it out of his power to perform would be sued in deceit and imprisoned until

---

[53] *Bukton v Tounesende, The Humber Ferry Case* (1348), translated in Baker and Milsom, above, n 49, 358.
[54] *Watkins' (or Wykes') Case* (1425) translated in Baker and Milsom, above, n 49, 380, 383 (Martin J).
[55] *Shepton v Dogge (Nos 1 and 2)* (1442), translated in Baker and Milsom, above, n 49, 390–5.

he made fine with the city and repaid the money to his claimant. In London therefore the plaintiff's action would not have been a dodge to get round the absence of a sealed document but the natural remedy, essentially in rescission. In Westminster the logic got the plaintiff a remedy: but the Court could not order imprisonment (and therefore repayment of the money) but only damages.

This looked like enforcement rather than rescission, and the king's courts were left with a distinction without a real difference: the disappointed buyer who had paid for the land could get damages if his seller had conveyed to a third party, but not otherwise. Many approaches were tried; and around 1500 it begins to appear that nonfeasance was becoming remediable, at first only when the claimant had actually paid or there was some other detrimental reliance (and at any period one who has suffered no damage would normally prefer to hire somebody else rather than sue). Mutual promises do not become actionable until later in the century, by equally obscure stages; and the underlying illogicality is increasingly masked by elaborate and unreal allegations of deceit.

(iii) Assumpsit for money

From the use of *assumpsit* in lieu of covenant (where the absence of a sealed document might leave a plaintiff entirely without remedy) we turn to its use in lieu of debt (where the plaintiff always had a remedy, but might be faced by wager of law). But again one must not think that the end was aimed at from the beginning. The beginning is early in the sixteenth century in cases involving not money but fungible goods: a brewer contracts to buy malt or barley, and when it is not delivered has either to buy at a much higher price or to let his brewery go off stream.[56] The substantial claim goes not to the goods themselves but to the damage flowing from reliance upon the promise to deliver them; and this may be reflected in the language of deceit. When money is involved the reliance claim seems first to have appeared in situations involving third parties. Seller sells to Buyer in reliance upon the promise of a third party to pay if Buyer does not. It is Buyer who got the *quid pro quo* and contracted the debt; and any liability of the third party must be on the basis of reliance.[57]

One must not assume that the first use of the same logic as between two parties was intended as a conscious circumvention of debt. Debtor owes Creditor, and when pressed promises to pay the amount at a specified future date. Relying upon this promise, Creditor makes other bargains with third parties. When Debtor does not pay Creditor, Creditor cannot pay the third parties; and, particularly if he is a merchant, this failure so damages his own credit that he is ruined. This consequential damage is the gist of this action, not the original debt, which is not in principle even claimed. But jurors would include the amount of the debt in their assessment of damages; and such actions soon came to be used to recover debts but exclude wager of law.

---

[56] eg see the cases in Baker and Milsom, above, n 49, 406 and 411.
[57] Such cases are cited by Baker and Milsom, above, n 49, 414–15.

Since debt was in the exclusive jurisdiction of the Common Pleas, it was the King's Bench that led in this development and an unseemly difference of practice arose. On the general issue of 'Non assumpsit', where the defendant denied the undertaking, the Common Pleas would direct the jury that if they were to find for the plaintiff they must find both that the defendant was *indebitatus* (indebted) and that he made an express promise to pay the debt, the King's Bench that they need find only the indebtedness (because every debtor could be presumed to promise to pay: every contract executory imports in itself an *assumpsit*). But since the issue would be tried at *nisi prius*,[58] the judge actually directing the jury might not come from the Court in which the action had been begun. It seems clear that in *Slade's Case* the judges at *nisi prius* made a conscious effort to have the matter resolved. The jury was induced to bring in a special verdict that the debt was owed but that there was no subsequent promise to pay it. This was reported to the King's Bench, in which the action had been started; and instead of giving judgment that Court referred it to the Court of Exchequer Chamber, not really a Court but an informal conference of all the judges. That body was unable to agree; the King's Bench gave judgment for the plaintiff in accordance with their own practice; and this result was unwillingly accepted by the Common Pleas.[59]

Various consequences followed. Since the *indebitatus assumpsit* action was formally for reliance damage and not the debt, it now had to be made clear that the debt itself was recoverable as well as any damage, that the actions were alternative, and that the one barred the other. And since formally the reliance damage flowed entirely from the promise to pay the debt, there was no logical need to specify how the debt had arisen; and so a defendant in the *indebitatus* action might not know the actual case he was to answer. The Courts therefore required minimum particulars to be given; and a series of 'common counts' developed stating that the debt was for goods sold and delivered, for work and materials, and so on. More importantly *Slade's Case* marked the effective end of wager of law; and it was necessary to make explicit the important consequence that executors could now be sued for simple contract debts. Nor was the ending of wager unequivocally beneficial: it turned out that jury trial could be manipulated by fraudulent plaintiffs; and in 1677 the Statute of Frauds provided that in certain situations action could be brought only if there was some written evidence signed by the defendant.

With the important exception of agreements supported by sealed documents, in which covenant or debt still could and had to be brought, all contract litigation after *Slade's Case* was brought in *assumpsit*; and it was from this that the modern law of contract developed. It is indeed a general law of contract rather than a law about particular contracts as in Rome.[60] But its beginnings in tort, which remained

---

[58] Baker, *Introduction to English Legal History* (4th edn, 2002) 20–2.   [59] 1602 4 Co Rep 91a.

[60] In Roman law, a promise or agreement was given legal recognition and enforcement as a contract only if it fell within one of a number of particular types for which an action was provided (such as sale, hire, partnership, mandate, loan of a fungible, loan for use, or a unilateral promise made and accepted in a formal oral exchange between the parties): Nicholas, *Introduction to Roman Law* (1975) 165–7. Modern European civil law systems retain the Roman law legacy of a strong doctrine of particular contracts which have special

obvious in the persistent language of deceit until the nineteenth century, inhibited the development of a satisfactory theoretical structure. Instead we have the 'doctrine' of consideration.[61] There has been much speculation about its 'origin', on the basis that it must have developed from some earlier phenomenon. Consideration as detriment to the claimant looks much like the damage he suffered when the case was put in terms of deceit or reliance, and this provides some explanation of the uselessness of past consideration and of the rule that consideration must move from the claimant. Consideration as benefit to the defendant looks much like the *quid pro quo* of debt; and it must be remembered that after *Slade's Case* the debt and therefore the *quid pro quo* was the only issue in *indebitatus*. Other origins have been suggested, such as the canonist idea of *causa* which indeed played some part in the Chancery. But the reality seems to be that sixteenth-century pleadings used the word to mean the reason for which the promise was given, and judges then and later decided which of these were a sufficient basis for legal action. If so, consideration is not so much a 'doctrine' as a considerable body of the substantive rules of contract.

(c) SUBSEQUENT DEVELOPMENTS

There has been much later development, too detailed and perhaps too little explored by historians, to consider in this summary. Lord Mansfield in the eighteenth century and Lord Denning in the twentieth sought to rationalize consideration, but the substantive changes needed were too obtrusive. The English promissory estoppel,[62] for example, is a pale shadow of the American, perhaps because the lesser weight given in the USA to deeds left more obvious injustice when gratuitous promises were relied on. And the American reliance basis for remedy, essentially as alternative to consideration, is a reminder of the mongrel nature of the common law of contract.

The law started with covenant (or contract) as something essentially different from trespass (or tort). That difference was the continuing obstacle in the rise of *assumpsit*; and its overcoming introduced continuing confusion. It was nineteenth-century judges and writers, including Anson, who sought to restore contract law as a thing in itself: rules mostly about the formation of binding agreements, with ancillary rules about the damages recoverable for breach.[63] The impulse may have been partly juristic, partly due to commercial demands for certainty and for more sophisticated rules to deal adequately with the expansion of trade and commerce that resulted from the industrial revolution. Consideration (or a deed) is then represented as something like offer and acceptance: one of the requirements for formation. But it sprang from

---

regulation in their Codes but have also, unlike ancient Roman law, added a general law of contract: see, eg, Bell, Boyron, and Whittaker, *Principles of French Law* (2nd edn, 2008) 297–8.

[61] For consideration in the modern law, see below, Chapter 4.

[62] Below, p 122.   [63] See Simpson (1975) 91 LQR 247.

a law about tort, about damage suffered by the claimant at the end of the story rather than about the beginning of a binding relationship between the parties. Like many mongrels the result may not be elegant; but it is strong.

(i) The nineteenth century

We have noted that the concepts of freedom of contract and sanctity of contract were at their strongest during the nineteenth century. In 1875 Sir George Jessel MR stated:[64]

> if there is one thing which more than another public policy requires it is that men of full age and competent understanding shall have the utmost liberty of contracting, and that their contracts when entered into freely and voluntarily shall be held sacred and shall be enforced by Courts of justice.

This was said to have led to the reduction of supervision over the contractual terms to a bare minimum[65] and the deprivation of the tools available for such control of much of their effectiveness. The doctrine of consideration acquired a predominantly formal meaning, although it was on occasion used to invalidate unfair agreements.[66] A substantial part of the law of contract was attributed to the parties' agreement, and the role of equity, with its discretionary remedies, and its ability to avoid common law rules, was less central.

At the same time, non-contractual liability was kept within narrow boundaries. As regards liability to make restitution of an unjust enrichment (then known as quasi-contract), Bowen LJ's famous statement that '[l]iabilities are not to be forced upon people behind their backs'[67] was profoundly influential. Indeed, Lord Sumner and Sir William Holdsworth argued that all such claims were founded upon an implied contract.[68] If there could not be a contract, there could not be an implied contract; there was no independent non-contractual claim. Tort liability was restricted by what was later called the 'privity of contract' fallacy, that duties which originated in a contract were confined to the parties.[69] It was also mainly concerned with the protection of proprietary interests and with providing a remedy for certain categories of physical injury. Although a number of economic torts were developed, notably deceit, injurious falsehood, inducement of breach of contract, and conspiracy, they required wilful misconduct. There was no liability for pure economic loss which was inflicted negligently.

---

[64] *Printing & Numerical Registering Co v Sampson* (1875) LR 19 Eq 462, 465.

[65] Atiyah, *The Rise and Fall of Freedom of Contract* (1979). But cf Simpson (1979) 46 U Chi L Rev 533; Barton (1987) 103 LQR 118.

[66] *Stilk v Myrick* (1809) 2 Camp 317; 6 Esp 129, below, pp 113–16.

[67] *Falcke v Scottish Imperial Insurance Co* (1886) 34 Ch 234, 248.

[68] *Sinclair v Brougham* [1914] AC 398, 452 (overruled by *Westdeutsche Landesbank Girozentrale v Islington London Borough Council* [1996] AC 669); Holdsworth (1939) 55 LQR 37. Cf Lord Wright (1938) 6 CLJ 305, 312 ff.

[69] *Winterbottom v Wright* (1842) 10 M & W 109.

(ii) The twentieth century

In the modern period there is evidence of the reshaping of contract law accompanied by an expansion of non-contractual obligations in tort, in particular for negligent misrepresentation causing purely economic loss, and in respect of restitution of unjust enrichment. There has been a dilution of formal requirements and increased regard is given to considerations of substantive fairness. The erosion of the doctrine of consideration in the context of contract re-negotiation, and its replacement by rules of equitable estoppel[70] and economic duress is perhaps the most prominent example, but there are others, including an approach to discharge of contract, whether by breach or frustration, that gives greater emphasis to the consequences of an event than to the, often fictional, intentions of the parties.[71] The evolution of new doctrines and approaches has been gradual, and there have been exceptions and inconsistencies. For instance, when, in 1976, economic duress was first recognized as a factor vitiating contract, its theoretical basis was said to be 'coercion of the will', that is, absence of consent. But this was rejected in less than a decade,[72] whereas in the case of frustration, first recognized in 1863, it took almost 100 years for the Courts to turn away from regarding implied contract as the basis of that doctrine.[73]

(iii) Legislation

The last 140 years have also seen a rapid growth in the importance of statute law. There were great codifying Acts of the nineteenth century for particular types of contract, such as the Bills of Exchange Act 1882 and the Sale of Goods Act 1893. We have noted the considerable, and increasing, amount of regulatory legislation, which is designed to protect certain classes of the community or to implement government policy. There are also a number of reforming statutes such as the Law Reform (Frustrated Contracts) Act 1943, the Misrepresentation Act 1967, the Civil Liability (Contribution) Act 1978, the Minors Contracts Act 1987, and the Contracts (Rights of Third Parties) Act 1999 which have been passed to remedy defects or to make good particular deficiencies in the common law. Very significant legislative intervention has been aimed at the protection of consumers, most recently the Consumer Rights Act 2015.

(iv) Codification

In 1872, the Indian Contract Act was enacted, which codified (with some variations) the general English law of contract for use in the Indian sub-continent. But English law remained, and still remains, predominantly judge-made law. In 1965, the Law Commission of England and Wales and the Scottish Law Commission announced their intention to codify the English and Scots law of contract.[74] The code as originally envisaged was to be a uniform body of law applying throughout England and

[70] Below, p 122.   [71] Below, pp 512–13, 549–50.   [72] Below, p 377.
[73] Below, p 510.   [74] Diamond (1968) 31 MLR 361.

Scotland, and it was to embody amendments to the existing law of both countries. Subsequently, however, the Scottish Law Commission withdrew from this enterprise. In 1973, therefore, the Law Commission decided to suspend its work on a contract code.[75] Since then it has examined particular areas of the law of contract, and has either recommended reform, such as in the case of contribution,[76] minors' contracts,[77] implied terms as to quality in the sale of goods,[78] formalities and covenants of title in the sale of land,[79] contributory negligence as a defence in contract,[80] contracts for the benefit of third parties,[81] unfair contract terms,[82] consumer remedies for faulty goods,[83] and insurance contract law,[84] or has concluded that no legislation is necessary, as in the case of the parol evidence rule[85] and illegal contracts.[86] It seems, however, unlikely that the project of codification will be revived. In contrast, there has recently been published *A Restatement of the English Law of Contract*[87] by Burrows assisted by an advisory group of academics, judges, and practitioners.

(v) Extra-judicial controls on contract

The law of contract as presented in this book is that applied by the English courts. It comprises common law and legislation. However, it is important to realize that, in practice, there are controls on contracts other than through the courts. Arbitration is the most obvious example albeit that, if English law applies to the dispute, arbitrators will be seeking to apply the law of contract as presented in this book in the same way as a judge would do. The Competition and Markets Authority and other regulators have an important role in, for example, controlling unfair terms not only by occasionally bringing actions in the courts but also by enforcing them administratively and much more commonly, by informally negotiating with businesses and seeking undertakings from them.[88] There is also, for example, the Financial Ombudsman who has wide powers to make awards, enforceable in the courts, without being bound to apply

---

[75] The draft as it stood when the project was abandoned has since been published: McGregor, *The Contract Code Drawn Up on Behalf of the Law Commission* (1993).

[76] Law Com No 79 (1977), implemented by the Civil Liability (Contribution) Act 1978.

[77] Law Com No 134 (1984), implemented by the Minors Contracts Act 1987, below, p 264.

[78] Law Com No 160 (1987), implemented by the Sale and Supply of Goods Act 1994.

[79] Law Com No 164 (1987) and Law Com No 199 (1991), implemented respectively by the Law of Property (Miscellaneous Provisions) Acts 1989 and 1994.

[80] Law Com No 219 (1993), rejected by the Government.

[81] Law Com No 242 (1996), implemented by the Contracts (Rights of Third Parties) Act 1999, below, p 659.

[82] Law Com No 292 (2005) and Law Commission, 'Unfair Terms in Consumer Contracts: Advice to the Department for Business, Innovation and Skills' (2013), partly implemented in Part 2 of the Consumer Rights Act 2015, below, p 222.

[83] Law Com No 317 (2009).

[84] Law Com No 319, *Consumer Insurance Law: Pre-Contract Disclosure and Misrepresentation* (2009), implemented by the Consumer Insurance (Disclosure and Representations) Act 2012, below, p 361; Law Com No 353, *Insurance Contract Law: Business Disclosure; Warranties; Insurers' Remedies for Fraudulent Claims and Late Payment* (2014), implemented by the Insurance Act 2015 (in force from August 12, 2016), below, p 361.

[85] Law Com No 154 (1986), below, p 147.   [86] Law Com No 320 (2010).   [87] (2016).

[88] Taking over powers formerly exercised by the Office of Fair Trading; see below, pp 223.

the strict rules of contract law.[89] Finally one should bear in mind the increasing encouragement to parties to mediate because it is seen as a relatively inexpensive and quick way of resolving disputes without going to court.[90]

3. EUROPEAN AND INTERNATIONAL INFLUENCES

The English law of contract is exposed to the influence of the European Union and the predominantly civilian systems of its Members because of the perceived importance of its harmonization in the development of the single market. To date the most significant initiatives affecting contract law have been the Directives on Unfair Terms in Consumer Contracts,[91] Consumer Sales,[92] and Unfair Commercial Practices,[93] and those which seek to ensure that there is no discrimination in tendering procedures for major contracts for public works, supplies, and services.[94]

There has also been a movement to develop common principles of European contract law which has resulted in a significant body of academic research comparing the national systems of contract law, and making proposals for possible harmonization.[95] Those who favour this argue that there are many benefits to be derived from a formulation of principles of contract law within Europe. These include the facilitation of cross-border trade, the strengthening of the European single market, the provision of an infrastructure for European Union laws governing contract and of guidelines

---

[89] See Financial Services and Markets Act 2000, Part XVI and Sched 17. For discussion, see Smith, *Atiyah's Introduction to the Law of Contract* (6th edn, 2005) 250–1, 330–1.

[90] Courts now commonly stay proceedings to allow for mediation and there may be cost penalties for a party that refuses to go to mediation. See also Directive 2013/11/EU on alternative dispute resolution for consumer disputes, implemented by SI 2015 No 542.

[91] Council Directive 93/13/EEC, implemented first by Unfair Terms in Consumer Contracts Regulations in 1994 (SI 1994 No 3159), then 1999 (SI 1999 No 2083), and now by Part 2 of the Consumer Rights Act 2015, below, p 222.

[92] Directive 99/44/EC, implemented first by the Sale and Supply of Goods to Consumers Regulations 2002 (SI 2002 No 3045), amending the Sale of Goods Act 1979 and the Supply of Goods and Services Act 1982, and now by the Consumer Rights Act 2015 below, pp 538–40, 610. See also the Package Travel, Package Holidays and Package Tours Regulations 1992 (SI 1992 No 3288), below, pp 232, 349, 372, 677 and the Timeshare Act 1992.

[93] Directive 2005/29/EC, implemented by, inter alia, the Consumer Protection from Unfair Trading Regulations 2008, SI 2008 No 1277, and amended by SI 2014 No 870 to provide consumers' private rights of redress for misleading and aggressive commercial practices: below, p 355.

[94] For the current provisions, see Directive 2014/25/EU, replacing Directive 2004/17/EC which is implemented by the Utilities Contracts Regulations 2006 (SI 2006 No 6), and Directive 2014/24/EU, implemented by the Public Contracts Regulations 2015 (SI 2015 No 102).

[95] See in particular Lando and Beale, *Principles of European Contract Law Parts 1 & II* (2000); Lando, Clive, Prüm, and Zimmermann, *The Principles of European Contract Law Part III* (2003); Research Group on the Existing EC Private Law (Acquis Group), *Principles of the Existing EC Contract Law (Acquis Principles), Contract I: Precontractual Obligations, Conclusion of Contract, Unfair Terms* (2007); Study Group on a European Civil Code and Research Group on EC Private Law (Acquis Group), *Principles, Definitions and Model Rules of European Private Law: Draft Common Frame of Reference (DCFR)* (2009) (covering not only contract law but also other areas of private law such as tort and unjust enrichment).

for national courts and legislatures, and the construction of a bridge between common law and civil law systems. Following the publication of the *Principles of European Contract Law Parts I and II* by the (independent) Commission of European Contract Law,[96] the European Commission produced an Action Plan designed to increase the coherence of the EC *acquis* (existing law) in the area of contract law, to promote the elaboration of EU-wide general contract terms, and to examine whether there should be an 'optional instrument' which contracting parties could choose as their governing terms.[97] The movement towards the drafting of a new instrument to give effect to these aspirations gained significant momentum for a number of years, and resulted in 2011 in the publication by the European Commission of a proposal for a Regulation on a 'Common European Sales Law',[98] including a form of optional instrument based heavily on the text of the Principles of European Contract and the Draft Common Frame of Reference.[99] This did not, however, attract sufficient support and the proposal was withdrawn at the end of 2014. In its place, in 2015 the Commission opened a new consultation on a project of much more limited scope: contract rules for online purchases of digital content and tangible goods (ie internet and other e-commerce transactions). It appears that the idea of a new European Contract Code[100] is no longer on the horizon.

There are wider international initiatives, such as the Unidroit Principles for International Commercial Contracts, the United Nations (Vienna) Convention on Contracts for the International Sale of Goods (the CISG), and growing numbers of international standard form contracts. Renewed consideration has been given to the ratification by the United Kingdom of the CISG[101] which has not yet been ratified because of a perception by some that English contract law is more sophisticated, and fear that uncertainty would result from the broadly formulated provisions of the Convention.[102] Furthermore, the provisions of the European Convention for the Protection of Human Rights, in particular the right to a fair trial under Article 6 and to the protection of property under Article 1 of the First Protocol to the Convention also have an impact on English contract law as a result of the Human Rights Act 1998.[103]

While this book is concerned with English law, the approach of other European systems is mentioned where, as in the case of the use by the Consumer Rights Act 2015

---

[96]   Above, n 95. For the origin, composition and sponsorship of the Commission see Lando and Beale, *Principles of European Contract Law Parts 1 & II*, xi–xvi.

[97]   Communication from the Commission to the European Parliament and the Council: a more coherent European contract law; an action plan: COM(2003) 68 final (12.2.2003), following Communication from the Commission to the Council and the European Parliament on European Contract Law COM(2001) 398 final (11.07.2001).

[98]   COM(2011) 635 final (11.10. 2011).   [99]   Above, n 95.

[100]   Resolution of the European Parliament 26 June 1989, OJ 1989 C 158/400; COM(2001) 398 final (11.07.2001), paras 61–9. In December 2015 the Commission published a proposal for a Directive on contracts for the supply of digital content: COM(2015) 634 (final).

[101]   Moss (2005–06) JL & Com 483.

[102]   Hobhouse (1990) 106 LQR 530. Cf Steyn, in Birks (ed), *The Frontiers of Liability* (vol II) 11.

[103]   *Wilson v First County Trust Ltd (No 2)* [2003] UKHL 40, [2004] 1 AC 816; *Shanshal v Al Kishtaini* [2001] EWCA Civ 264, [2001] 2 All ER (Comm) 601.

of the civilian concept of good faith, these are now directly germane to English law.[104] There are also brief references to European principles and international conventions, as well as to other approaches and developments in common law countries, including the American Law Institute's *Restatement, Contracts (2d)*,[105] where these might be helpful in giving a comparative perspective to problems faced by English law.

4. THE CONTENT OF CONTRACT LAW

(a) A LAW OF CONTRACT OR OF CONTRACTS

The increasingly complex social and commercial relationships of the twentieth century have produced a situation where it is no longer safe to assume that there is a law of contract rather than of contracts. Particular principles and rules of law are applicable, sometimes as the result of statutory definition, say, to contracts of sale of goods, insurance, the carriage of goods by sea, contracts of employment, and consumer contracts, which are peculiar to those contracts. In the past, a number of commercial contexts, such as shipping, insurance, and construction, have been particularly influential in the development of contract law. Some have suggested that they have been disproportionately influential. Whatever the influence of particular contexts, however, apart from statutory intervention the ideology of the common law of contract remains that of a single body of general principles of contract law which apply, with or without modification, across the range of such contracts. It is those general principles of contract law that this book seeks to expound.

The contract law contained in this book follows, for the most part, the subject-matter established by Sir William Anson in the seventh edition of his *Principles of the English Law of Contract and of Agency in its Relation to Contract*. It deals with the Formation of Contract, Performance and Discharge, Remedies for Breach of Contract, and the Limits of the Contractual Obligation (including Agency). It also deals with those factors which tend to vitiate a contract, such as incapacity, mistake, misrepresentation, duress and undue influence, and illegality. A word must be said about these.

(b) EFFECT OF VITIATING FACTORS

Not all the factors that vitiate a contract are uniform in effect. Some of them may render a contract void or illegal, others voidable, while others still may make the contract unenforceable at the suit of one or other of the parties. These terms (void, illegal, voidable, and unenforceable) therefore denote different degrees of ineffectiveness, and

---

[104] Below, p 229.
[105] The ALI Restatement is not a binding legislative text, but a very influential and 'acute interpretation of American case law': Winfield (1929) 11 J Comp Leg 179, 189 (on the first edition).

they are in constant use in the law of contract. They are, however, not infrequently used with insufficient precision,[106] and even the same term may have a different meaning in different situations.

(i)   Void contracts

In the case of a void contract, for example, the basic position is that such a contract is simply one which the law holds to be no contract at all, a nullity from the beginning. The parties would be in the same position as they would have been had the contract never been made. No property would pass under such a contract; so, for example, a third party who purchased goods which had been the subject of a void contract would acquire no title to the goods and have to deliver them up to the true owner.[107] Conversely, money paid in pursuance of a void contract could be recovered from the person to whom it had been paid.[108] This indeed is the meaning of 'void' where a contract is said to be void for mistake. In other cases, however, a void contract may not be so completely without legal effect. A contract for the sale of an interest in land 'can only be made in writing'[109] so that one that is not in writing is not merely unenforceable but void,[110] but, if it is completed in the form required for the transfer of an interest in land, property will nevertheless pass.[111]

(ii)   Illegal contracts

Again, an illegal contract is commonly said to be 'void', but the effects of illegality may vary considerably according to the degree of moral turpitude involved, the culpability of the parties, and whether or not the contract itself is rendered illegal.[112] In this case, the invalidity is imposed by the law, and it is not at the discretion of the contracting parties.

(iii)   Voidable contracts

A voidable contract, however, is a contract which one of the parties has the option to rescind or affirm. If the choice is to affirm the contract, or if the right to rescind is not exercised within a reasonable time so that the position of the parties has, in the meantime, become altered, the option to rescind may be lost and the party who had it will be bound by the contract; otherwise that party is entitled to repudiate its liability. Nevertheless, the contract is not a nullity from the beginning. Until it is rescinded, it is

---

[106]   See Turpin (1955) 72 SALJ 58; Honoré (1958) 75 SALJ 32.

[107]   *Cundy v Lindsay* (1878) 3 App Cas 459; below, p 291.

[108]   *Couturier v Hastie* (1856) 5 HLC 673; below, p 306; *Westdeutsche Landesbank Girozentrale v Islington London Borough Council* [1996] AC 669, below, p 624.

[109]   Law of Property (Miscellaneous Provisions) Act 1989, s 2(1), below, p 88.

[110]   Harpum, Bridge, and Dixon, *Megarry & Wade's Law of Real Property* (8th edn, 2012) 629. See also *United Bank of Kuwait plc v Sahib* [1997] Ch 107, 122 (Chadwick J) and in the Court of Appeal at 136 (Peter Gibson LJ).

[111]   *Tootal Clothing Ltd v Guinea Properties Ltd* (1992) 64 P & CR 452, 455.

[112]   *Aratra Potato Co Ltd v Taylor Joynson Garrett* [1995] 4 All ER 695, 708–10; *Mohamed v Alaga* [2000] 1 WLR 1815. See further below, Chapter 11.

valid and binding. A third party, therefore, who in good faith purchases goods which have been the subject of a voidable contract without notice of the prior defect acquires a good title to the goods and cannot be compelled to surrender them to their former owner.[113]

(iv) Unenforceable contracts

An unenforceable contract is one which is good in substance, though, by reason of some technical defect, one or both of the parties cannot be sued on it. The difference between what is voidable and what is unenforceable is mainly a difference between substance and procedure. A contract may be good, but incapable of enforcement because it is not evidenced by writing as required by statute.[114] But, in some cases, the defect is curable: the subsequent execution of a written memorandum may satisfy the requirements of the law and render the contract enforceable, but it is never at any time in the power of either party to avoid the transaction. The contract itself is unimpeachable, but it cannot be directly enforced in Court.

5. CONTRACT AS PART OF THE LAW OF OBLIGATIONS

The law of obligations has traditionally been divided into contractual obligations, which are voluntarily undertaken and owed to a specific person or persons, and obligations in tort which are primarily based on the wrongful infliction of harm to certain protected interests, primarily imposed by the law, and typically owed to a wider class of persons.[115] Recently it has been accepted that there is a third category, restitutionary obligations, primarily based on the unjust enrichment of the defendant at the claimant's expense,[116] such as where the claimant has mistakenly paid the defendant money or discharged the defendant's debt. Contractual liability, reflecting the constitutive function of contract,[117] is generally for failing to make things better (by not rendering the expected performance), liability in tort is generally for action (as opposed to omission) making things worse, and liability in unjust enrichment is generally for unjustly receiving the benefit of the claimant's money or work. It accordingly follows that it is a defence to a claim for restitution of an unjust enrichment that the defendant has changed its position, for example by incurring expenditure in reliance on a payment received from the claimant, so as to make it inequitable to order that the money be repaid.[118]

---

[113] Sale of Goods Act 1979, s 23; *Car and Universal Finance Co Ltd v Caldwell* [1965] 1 QB 525, below, p 333.
[114] Below, p 84 (contract of guarantee).
[115] Winfield, *Province of the Law of Tort* (1931) 380; Cane, *The Anatomy of Tort Law* (1997).
[116] *Lipkin Gorman v Karpnale Ltd* [1991] 2 AC 548; *Kleinwort Benson Ltd v Glasgow City Council* [1999] 1 AC 153. See Burrows, *A Restatement of the English Law of Unjust Enrichment* (2012).
[117] Above, p 3.   [118] *Lipkin Gorman v Karpnale Ltd*, above, n 116, 579–80.

Although this tripartite division is a useful starting point, as the summary of the history of contract above indicates, it is a rationalization of a less tidy common law. The recent expansion of all these types of obligation also increases the occasions on which the different categories will overlap and it has been argued that the division made between duties which are voluntarily assumed and duties which are imposed by law is an oversimplification.[119] Moreover, care must be taken not to reverse the contractual allocation of risks by non-contractual actions.[120]

(a) CONCURRENCE OF CLAIMS IN CONTRACT AND TORT

Although the Court may decline to find a duty in tort where the parties are in a contractual relationship,[121] or may hold that a term of a contract has excluded or limited what would otherwise be a tortious duty, pre-contractual events, such as misrepresentation, may give rise to an action in tort.[122] Additionally, it is clear that in many cases, exemplified by negligent failure by professionals, such as solicitors and surveyors, to carry out their undertakings to their clients, a defendant may be liable to the same claimant in both contract and in tort.[123] Indeed the fact that tort liability in these contexts may be grounded in an 'assumption of responsibility',[124] means that a negligent breach of contract may often give rise to claims in both contract and tort.[125] Where this is so, the claimant 'can advance his claim, as he wishes, either in contract or in tort, and no doubt he will . . . advance the claim on the basis which is most advantageous to him.'[126] The practical differences between contract and tort include, for example, the measure of recovery,[127] the period of limitation,[128] the relevance of the claimant's contributory fault (it is generally irrelevant in contract but relevant in tort),[129] and assignability, since only a contractual claim can generally be assigned.

(b) CONTRACT AND UNJUST ENRICHMENT

Historically, the effect of the implied term theory was that contract was thought in effect to have swallowed up restitution of an unjust enrichment. While it is now clear that the two are independent of each other and that 'implied contract' is a fictional

---

[119] Atiyah (1978) 94 LQR 193, 223. Cf Burrows (1983) 99 LQR 217.
[120] eg *Marc Rich & Co AG v Bishop Rock Marine Co Ltd* [1996] AC 211, and see below, pp 685–6.
[121] *Tai Hing Cotton Mill v Liu Chong Hing Bank* [1986] AC 80, 107; *Greater Nottingham Co-operative Society v Cementation Piling and Foundations Ltd* [1989] QB 1.
[122] *Hedley Byrne & Co Ltd v Heller & Partners Ltd* [1964] AC 465, below, p 346.
[123] *Midland Bank Trust Co Ltd v Hett, Stubbs and Kemp* [1979] Ch 384; *Henderson v Merrett Syndicates Ltd* [1995] 2 AC 145. Cf *Williams v Natural Life Health Foods* [1998] 1 WLR 830.
[124] Cf *Customs and Excise Commissioners v Barclays Bank plc* [2006] UKHL 28, [2007] 1 AC 181.
[125] *White v Jones* [1995] 2 AC 207, below, p 664, on which see Weir (1995) 111 LQR 357.
[126] *Coupland v Arabian Gulf Oil Co* [1983] 1 WLR 1136, 1153 (Robert Goff LJ). See also Lord Goff's speech in the leading case of *Henderson v Merrett Syndicates* [1995] 2 AC 145, 193–4.
[127] Below, pp 327 and 581 (remoteness of damage).
[128] *Henderson v Merrett Syndicates Ltd* [1995] 2 AC 145, 185.   [129] Below, p 594.

explanation for restitution of an unjust enrichment,[130] it is in the context of money having been paid and services having been rendered under ineffective contracts and contracts discharged by breach or by frustration that many claims in unjust enrichment are made.[131] Sometimes it can be difficult to distinguish the enforcement of a contract or promise from the restitution of an unjust enrichment, as where one person has 'freely accepted' or 'acquiesced' in services rendered by the other.[132] Where there is a contract and it makes provision for repayment or recompense, there will be no claim for restitution of an unjust enrichment.[133] Where, however, it does not, a claim may lie, and, for example, in the case of a contract discharged for breach, the innocent party's claim for restitution of an unjust enrichment may be greater than the contractual claim for damages.[134] We shall also see that a remedy for restitution of an unjust enrichment may be available in respect of work done by one party during pre-contractual negotiations which do not ripen into a contract.[135]

The restitution of an unjust enrichment, independent from contract, is significantly different from restitutionary damages, or an account of profits, given as a remedy *for* breach of contract. The basis of such a restitutionary remedy is the contract and not an independent cause of action in unjust enrichment. Traditionally, such a restitutionary remedy, while available for civil wrongs, such as breach of fiduciary duty and some torts, was not available for breach of contract. But that was departed from by the House of Lords in *Attorney-General v Blake*[136] in which it was accepted that, in exceptional circumstances, an account of profits can be awarded for breach of contract.

6. CONTRACT AND PROPERTY

The law of obligations must be distinguished from the law of property which essentially governs the acquisition and content of the rights persons have in things, which may be land or moveables. In a wider sense, the law of property deals with all assets, including intangibles such as a debt, shares in a company, a beneficiary's right under a trust, or a patent.[137] Whereas a person's property right in a thing is generally valid against the whole world, the rights under the law of obligations, including contract, are personal and valid only against a specific person or persons. Property rights may be *protected* by the law of tort, as where the use and enjoyment of land is protected by the torts of trespass and nuisance, and the right to possession of goods is protected by the tort of conversion. Property rights may be *transferred* by contract, as where A sells goods to B, and the property passes under section 18 of the Sale of Goods Act

---

[130] *Westdeutsche Landesbank Girozentrale v Islington London BC* [1996] AC 669; *Haugesund Kommune v Depfa ACS Bank* [2010] EWCA Civ 579, [2012] 2 WLR 199.

[131] Below, pp 250, 258, 525, 620–30.

[132] See Beatson, *The Use and Abuse of Unjust Enrichment* (1991) ch 2.

[133] *Pan Ocean Shipping Co Ltd v Creditcorp Ltd* [1994] 1 WLR 161.   [134] Below, p 629.

[135] Below, pp 45, 67.   [136] [2001] 1 AC 268. See below, pp 630–7.

[137] Lawson and Rudden, *The Law of Property* (3rd edn, 2003) ch 2.

1979, but they may also be transferred in other ways, for example by delivery with the requisite intention, as where a gift is made. As we have seen, property can pass under voidable and unenforceable contracts as well as valid ones, but not normally under void contracts.[138] Where property has so passed (whether under the contract or by delivery), B may in turn resell the goods and pass the property in them to C, even though B may not have paid A, or may have committed some other breach of contract, but an unpaid seller in possession of goods has the power to dispose of them in certain cases.[139] Where property has not passed to B, B is only able to confer a contractual right to the goods upon C. The position of a person who only has a contractual right to a thing is less secure than that of a person who has a property right since contractual rights may generally only be enforced against the other party to the contract (in our example, B) whereas property rights are generally enforceable against all persons. C would therefore only be able to enforce a contractual right against B, and not against A, or anyone who acquires the goods from A. There is, however, a tendency to reduce the discrepancy between the two and in certain circumstances contractual rights will be protected against third parties.[140]

---

[138] Above, p 24.   [139] See Sale of Goods Act 1979, ss 39(1)(c), 48(3)–(4).
[140] eg *Lumley v Gye* (1853) 3 E and B 216, below, p 689.

PART 1

FORMATION OF CONTRACT

2

THE AGREEMENT

A contract consists of an actionable promise or promises. Every such promise involves at least two parties, a promisor and a promisee, and an outward expression of common intention and of expectation as to the declaration or assurance contained in the promise.

It has been previously pointed out[1] that this outward expression of a common intention and of expectation normally takes the form of an agreement. In most cases, therefore, it will be necessary to ascertain at the outset whether or not an agreement has been concluded.

In this chapter we consider the establishing of an agreement by offer and acceptance; uncertain and incomplete agreements; and the intention to create legal relations.

1. ESTABLISHING AN AGREEMENT

The fact that an agreement has been reached will sometimes be self-evident, since, although as a general rule English law has no requirements of writing or other form,[2] the agreement will be set out in a document signed or initialled by both parties. But where there is no such document, it may be more difficult to discover whether the parties have agreed. The alleged agreement may, in whole or in part, have been concluded by word of mouth or by conduct. Difficulties of proof will then arise and the resultant questions of fact will have to be determined by the trial judge from the evidence given by the parties and their witnesses. We are not, however, here concerned with difficulties of proof, but rather with those problems that occur even where there is no dispute as to what the parties said or did. Such problems are not infrequent in practice, especially when the fact of agreement has to be elicited from correspondence, or from an exchange of other types of communication such as telex messages, fax, or e-mail.

---

[1] See above, p 2.   [2] On such requirements, see below, Chapter 3.

(a) OFFER AND ACCEPTANCE

To determine whether an agreement has actually been concluded, it is normally necessary to inquire whether in the negotiations which have taken place between the parties there has been a definite offer by one party, and an equally definite acceptance of that offer by the other. For most contracts are reducible by analysis to the acceptance of an offer. If, for instance, A and B have agreed that A shall purchase from B a car for £10,000, we can trace the process to a moment at which B must have said to A, in effect, 'Will you give me £10,000 for my car?', and A has replied, 'I will'; or at which A has said to B, 'Will you let me have the car for £10,000?', and B has said, 'I will'. There are, however, cases to which this analysis does not readily apply. These include the signature of a prepared document, the acceptance by two parties of terms suggested by a third, and multiparty agreements.[3] Where, however, a contract is alleged to have been made by an exchange of correspondence between the parties in which the successive communications other than the first are in reply to one another, the Court should look at the correspondence to see whether there is an offer by one party and an acceptance by the other party.[4] It would be a mistake to think that all contracts can thus be analysed into the form of offer and acceptance. The analysis is, however, a working method which, more often than not, enables us, in a doubtful case, to ascertain whether a contract has in truth been concluded, and as such may usefully be retained.

(i) Offer and acceptance in unilateral and bilateral contracts

The process of 'offer and acceptance' may take place in one of two main ways:

(1) In the offer of a promise for an act:[5] as when a person offers a reward for the doing of a certain thing, which being done that person is bound to make good the promise to the doer.

  Illustration: A, who has lost her dog, offers by advertisement a reward of £25 to anyone who will bring the dog safely home; a promise is offered in return for an act; and when B, knowing of the reward, brings the dog safely home, the act is done and A is bound to pay the reward.

(2) In the offer of a promise for a promise: in which case, when the offer is accepted by the giving of the promise, the contract consists of an outstanding obligation on both sides.

  Illustration: C offers to pay D a certain sum of money if D will promise to dig C's garden for him within a certain time. When D makes the promise asked for, he accepts the promise offered, and both parties are bound, the one to do the work, the other to allow the first to do it and to pay for it.

---

[3] *Clarke v Earl of Dunraven, The Satanita* [1897] AC 59, below, p 34.

[4] *Gibson v Manchester City Council* [1979] 1 WLR 294, 297 (Lord Diplock). Cf *Port Sudan Cotton Co v Govindaswamy Chettiar & Sons* [1977] 2 Lloyd's Rep 5.

[5] Or forbearance. See also below, p 108.

It will be observed that case (1) differs from (2) in an important respect. In (1), it is performance on one side which makes obligatory the promise of the other; the outstanding obligation is all on one side. In consequence, such a contract is termed 'unilateral'[6] as only one person is bound. In (2), however, each party is obliged to some act or forbearance which, at the time of entering into the contract, is future; there is an outstanding obligation on each side. This is known as a 'bilateral' contract, and each party is both a promisor and a promisee. It is reasonable to presume in cases of doubt that a bilateral, rather than a unilateral contract has been concluded. Thus if G says to H: 'If you will let me have that table you are making, when it is finished, I will give you £25 for it', and H replies 'All right', there is a bilateral contract and H is bound to deliver the table.[7]

(ii) Promises in deeds

In one exceptional situation, however, it is clear that a contract can come into existence without any need for an 'offer and acceptance'. This is the case of a promise in a deed. For example, if a wealthy person, by a document executed as a deed, promises to pay a college £100,000 in order to establish a scholarship, the promise is binding without any need for an acceptance or even knowledge of the promise by the person to whom the promise is made.[8]

(iii) Inferences from conduct

The description which has been given of the possible forms of offer and acceptance shows that conduct may take the place of written or spoken words either in the offer or in the acceptance.[9] An agreement may also be inferred from conduct alone; the intention of the parties is a matter of inference from their conduct, and the inference is more or less easily drawn according to the circumstances of the case.[10] In day-to-day contracts such inferences are frequent. For example, a person who boards a bus or who hires a taxi thereby undertakes to pay the fare to his destination even though he makes no express promise

---

[6] *GN Ry v Witham* (1873) LR 9 CP 16, 19; *New Zealand Shipping Co Ltd v AM Satterthwaite & Co Ltd* [1975] AC 154, 167–8, 171, 177; *Soulsbury v Soulsbury* [2007] EWCA Civ 969, [2008] Fam 1.

[7] ALI *Restatement, Contracts (2d)* para 31.

[8] Although he cannot be compelled to accept the benefit: *Townson v Tickel* (1819) 3 B & Ald 31. On deeds, see generally below, Chapter 3.

[9] Save in the most exceptional circumstances an offer or acceptance cannot be inferred from inactivity. On acceptance by silence, see below, pp 51–3. On the suggestion that an offer to abandon an arbitration can be inferred, where neither party has taken any steps in the proceedings for a very long time: *Paal Wilson & Co A/S v Partenreederei Hannah Blumenthal* [1981] 2 Lloyd's Rep 438, 439, [1983] 1 AC 854, 865, 885, 914, 916, 924. But the question here is whether a contract to arbitrate disputes between the parties which undoubtedly exists has been modified. Even in that context inactivity on its own, without some overt act, is almost always likely to be insufficient: *Allied Marine Transport Ltd v Vale do Rio Doce Navegacao SA* [1983] 2 Lloyd's Rep 411, 417, [1985] 1 WLR 925, 937; *Yamashita-Shinnihon SS Co Ltd v l'Office Cherifien des Phosphates* [1994] AC 486. For legislative modification see (a) the Arbitration Act 1996, s 41(6) empowering arbitrators to dismiss a claim for want of prosecution, and (b) the Consumer Protection (Distance Selling) Regulations 2000 (SI 2000 No 2334) reg 24 providing that the despatch of goods without any prior request (ie 'inertia selling') may constitute a gift rather than an offer.

[10] Cited with approval in *Wright & Co Ltd v Maunder* [1962] NZLR 355, 358.

to do so.[11] Again, a person who puts a coin in an automatic machine thereby enters into a contract with the supplier although no words have been exchanged on either side.

Sometimes the inference from conduct is not so clear, because the contract has assumed a less simple form. If more than two parties are involved, it may not be particularly helpful to look for a definite offer and acceptance. In *Clarke v Earl of Dunraven, The Satanita*:[12]

The owners of two yachts, the *Satanita* and the *Valkyrie*, entered them in a club regatta. The rules of the regatta bound competitors to make good any damage caused by fouling. While preparing for the start of a race, the *Satanita* fouled and sank the *Valkyrie*.

Although the immediate relationship of each owner was not with the other, but with the secretary of the yacht club, it was held that a contract existed between them, and that the owner of the *Valkyrie* could recover damages. Lord Herschell said:[13]

The effect of their entering for the race, and undertaking to be bound by these rules to the knowledge of each other, is sufficient, where those rules indicate a liability on the part of the one to the other, to create a contractual obligation to discharge that liability.

Similar principles mean that in the case of a company or other corporate entity there will, for certain purposes, be a contract both between the entity and its members and between each of the members themselves.[14]

(b) THE TEST OF INTENTION

In common with most European legal systems,[15] the test of a person's intention is not a subjective, but an objective one; that is to say, the intention which the law will attribute to a person is always that which that person's conduct bears when reasonably construed by a person in the position of the offeree, and not necessarily that which was present in the offeror's own mind. Thus a person may be held to have made an offer although not appreciating that one was being made[16] or not realizing that the terms of the offer embodied a mistake, as where a rent of £65,000 was mistakenly proposed by a landlord instead of £126,000.[17] If a person's words or conduct, when

---

[11] See *Wilkie v London Passenger Transport Board* [1947] 1 All ER 258. See also *Steven v Bromley & Son* [1919] 2 KB 722; *Sullivan v Constable* (1932) 48 TLR 369.

[12] [1897] AC 59.   [13] *Ibid*, 63.

[14] *Rayfield v Hands* [1960] Ch 1 (company); Companies Act 2006, s 33; *JH Rayner (Mincing Lane) Ltd v Department of Trade and Industry* [1989] Ch 72, 190, [1990] 2 AC 413, 515 (international organization whose members were states).

[15] An exception is French law: see Lando and Beale, *Principles of European Contract Law* (2000) 145–6.

[16] *Upton-on-Severn RDC v Powell* [1942] 1 All ER 220. But there the liability (to pay for the provision of fire-fighting services) is probably (see *William Lacey (Hounslow) Ltd v Davis* [1957] 1 WLR 932, 938) best regarded as non-contractual restitution for the value of the services rendered rather than being contractual because neither party believed it was entering into a contract: the fire brigade rendering the services (the 'offeree') believed it was under a duty to provide the service without charge. Cf *Henkel v Pape* (1870) LR 6 Ex 7.

[17] *Centrovincial Estates plc v Merchant Investors Assurance Co Ltd* [1983] Com LR 158. See also *Moran v University College Salford (No 2)*, The Times, 23 November 1993 (mistaken unconditional offer of university

reasonably construed, amount to an offer or to an offer on particular terms, that person will be held to have made that offer provided that the offeree neither knew nor could reasonably have known of the misunderstanding at the time the offer was accepted. The same objective approach applies to an acceptance. Although the approach is objective, the intentions of the parties are not entirely irrelevant so that a contract cannot be formed which is in accordance with the intention of neither party.[18] It has been stated that 'the judicial task is not to discover the actual intentions of each party; it is to decide what each was reasonably entitled to conclude from the attitude of the other'.[19]

2. THE OFFER

An offer is an intimation, by words or conduct, of a willingness to enter into a legally binding contract, and which in its terms expressly or impliedly indicates that it is to become binding on the offeror as soon as it has been accepted by an act, forbearance, or return promise on the part of the person to whom it is addressed.

(a) OFFERS AND INVITATIONS TO TREAT

It is sometimes difficult to distinguish statements of intention which cannot, and are not intended to, result in any binding obligation from offers which admit of acceptance, and so become binding promises. A person advertises goods for sale in a newspaper, or announces that they will be sold by tender or by auction; a shopkeeper displays goods in a shop window at a certain price; or a bus company advertises that it will carry passengers from A to Z and will reach Z and other intermediate stops at certain times. In such cases it may be asked whether the statement or act made is an offer capable of acceptance or merely an invitation to make offers, and do business; one that contemplates that further negotiations will take place. A statement or act of this nature, if it is not intended to be binding, is known as an 'invitation to treat'.

As the classification of any particular act or statement as being either an offer or an invitation to treat depends on intention to be bound rather than upon any *a priori* principle of law, it is not easy to reconcile all the cases or their reasoning. Where the

place); *OT Africa Line Ltd v Vickers plc* [1996] 1 Lloyd's Rep 700 (payment of £150,000 mistakenly offered instead of $150,000). See also below, pp 276–8.

[18] Cf *Upton-on-Severn RDC v Powell* [1942] 1 All ER 220, above, n 16; *Furness Withy (Australia) Pty Ltd v Metal Distributors (UK) Ltd* [1990] 1 Lloyd's Rep 236, 243; *Williston* on Contracts (4th edn, 1991) para 6.58. On the merits and demerits of this 'detached objectivity', see Howarth (1984) 100 LQR 265; Vorster (1987) 104 LQR 274.

[19] *Gloag on Contract* (2nd edn, 1929) 7; approved by Lord Reid in *McCutcheon v David Macbrayne Ltd* [1964] 1 WLR 125, 128. See also *Paal Wilson & Co A/S v Partenreederei Hannah Blumenthal* [1983] 1 AC 854, 924 (Lord Brightman); *ibid*, 914 (Lord Brandon) and cf *ibid*, 916 (Lord Diplock); *Edmonds v Lawson* [2000] QB 501. See generally Spencer [1973] CLJ 104, 106–13; Cartwright, *Unequal Bargaining* (1991) 5–24.

intention is unclear, the Court will take account of the surrounding circumstances and consequences of holding an act or statement to be an offer as well as what is in fact said.

A statement of fact made merely to supply information cannot be treated as an offer, and accepted, so as to create a valid contract. In *Harvey v Facey*:[20]

A telegraphed to B 'Will you sell us Bumper Hall Pen? Telegraph lowest cash price, answer paid'. B replied by telegram, 'Lowest price for Bumper Hall Pen £900'. A telegraphed, 'We agree to buy Bumper Hall Pen for £900 asked by you'. Bumper Hall Pen was a plot of land, and A claimed that this exchange of telegrams constituted a valid offer and acceptance.

The Judicial Committee of the Privy Council pointed out that the first telegram of A asked two questions, (1) as to the willingness of B to sell, and (2) as to the lowest price; and that the word 'telegraph' was addressed to the second question only. It was held that no contract had been made, that B in stating the lowest price for the property was not making an offer but supplying information, that the third telegram set out above was an offer by A—not the less so because he called it an acceptance—and that this offer had never been accepted by B.

In *Gibson v Manchester City Council*:[21]

The city council adopted a policy of selling council houses to its tenants. Gibson, on a printed form supplied by the council, applied for details of the price of the council house he was renting and mortgage terms. The council replied, 'The corporation *may be prepared to sell* the house to you at the purchase price of . . . £2,180.'[22] Gibson thereupon completed and sent off the application form to purchase the house.

The House of Lords held that there was no contract because the council's letter was not an offer to sell (that is, although this terminology was not used, it was merely an invitation to treat). The words italicized were fatal to regarding the letter as an offer.

(i) Advertisements and displays of goods for sale

Generally speaking advertisements in newspapers or periodicals that the advertiser has goods for sale are not offers.[23] Neither are catalogues or price lists.[24] Again, a display of goods marked at a certain price by a shopkeeper in a shop window[25] does

---

[20] [1893] AC 552. See also *Schuldenfrei v Hilton (IT)* [1999] STC 821, 831, 833.

[21] [1979] 1 WLR 294.   [22] Author's emphasis.

[23] *Partridge v Crittenden* [1968] 1 WLR 1204 (advertisement of 'Bramblefinch cocks and hens' for sale). The position is the same in Germany but not in France: Lando and Beale, *Principles of European Contract Law* (2000) 162. But advertisements of a *unilateral* contract are offers: *Carlill v Carbolic Smoke Ball Co Ltd* [1893] 2 QB 49, below, p 41; *Bowerman v ABTA* [1995] 145 NLJR 1815; the 'reward' cases, below, pp 53–4.

[24] *Grainger & Son v Gough* [1896] AC 325 (bookseller's catalogue with prices); *Seacarriers A/S v Aoteraroa International Ltd* [1985] 2 Lloyd's Rep 419 (quotation of freight rates).

[25] *Timothy v Simpson* (1834) 6 C & P 499 (below, n 29); *Fisher v Bell* [1961] 1 QB 394 (on which, see now, Restriction of Offensive Weapons Act 1961, s 1); *Esso Petroleum Ltd v Commissioners of Customs and Excise* [1976] 1 WLR 1 (indication of price at which petrol to be sold at attended service station not an offer).

not bind the shopkeeper to sell at that price or to sell at all. The display is merely an invitation to treat; it is for the customer to offer to buy the goods, and, subject to anti-discrimination legislation,[26] the shopkeeper may choose either to accept or to refuse the offer. One reason given for this conclusion is that otherwise the advertiser, catalogue publisher, and shopkeeper would be obliged to sell to every person who accepted such an 'offer', even where supplies had run out. In the case of displays on shelves in a self-service shop, which are also generally invitations to treat, it is said that if the display were an offer, once an article was selected and placed in the receptacle, the customer would have no right to change his mind.[27] Another reason given is that if a display was an offer a shopkeeper might be forced to contract with his worst enemy: a 'shop is a place for bargains, not for compulsory sales'[28] but this is less convincing in the light of modern regulation of trading practices, for example the prohibition of discrimination on grounds such as disability, race, religion, sex, and age,[29] and the statutory protection of consumers.[30] Where the display clearly states that the goods will be sold to a person who pays the required price it is, however, likely to be held to be an offer. For example, a notice stating 'We will beat any TV HiFi and Video price by £20 on the spot' was held to be 'a continuing offer' and the shop manager was criminally liable for a misleading indication as to the price at which goods may be available.[31]

(ii) Transactions by machine

Different considerations apply where the transaction is effected through a machine,[32] as where the display is on a vending machine or where, as in many self-service petrol stations, the product purchased cannot easily be retrieved from the buyer's property. In such cases the display is likely to be an offer. In *Re Charge Card Services*[33] an open offer to sell at pump prices was held to have been accepted by a motorist putting petrol in the tank.

---

[26] Above, p 5.

[27] *Pharmaceutical Society of Great Britain v Boots Cash Chemists (Southern) Ltd* [1952] 2 QB 795 aff'd [1953] 1 QB 401, criticized by Unger (1953) 16 MLR 369. Note (i) the context was whether the display constituted an unlawful 'sale' of drugs unsupervised by a registered pharmacist under the Pharmacy and Poisons Act 1933, s 18(1), and (ii) in the USA it has been held that there is no acceptance until the goods are presented at the checkout: *Lasky v Economic Stores* 5 NE 2d 305 (1946).

[28] Winfield (1939) 55 LQR 499, 518. See *Said v Butt* [1920] 3 KB 497 (theatre manager refused entry to critic who had got someone else to buy a ticket for him to a first night performance).

[29] Equality Act 2010, above, p 5. See also *Quinn v Williams Furniture* [1981] ICR 328; *Gill v El Vino* [1983] QB 425. Cf *Timothy v Simpson* (1834) 6 C & P 499 (a person who went into a shop asked to pay 7/6d although item was marked at 5/11d and shop assistant said 'don't let him have it, he's only a Jew. Turn him out').

[30] Below, n 31.

[31] *Warwickshire CC v Johnson* [1993] 1 All ER 299, 302; see also Consumer Protection from Unfair Trading Regulations 2008; *Jenkins v Lombard North Central plc* [1984] 1 WLR 307.

[32] *Thornton v Shoe Lane Parking Ltd* [1971] 2 QB 163, 169 (machine controlling entry to car park).

[33] [1989] Ch 497, 512. See also *Chapelton v Barry UDC* [1940] 1 KB 532 (display of deckchairs for hire an offer). On non-self service petrol sales, see above, n 25.

[handwritten marginal note overlapping text: "display of goods marked at certain price – not binding – even when supplies run · Winfield · but misleading indication · transactions by machine = offer · Carriage of persons – offer but x contract"]

(iii) Carriage of persons

The cases differ about the status ~~...~~ ons. A statement in a railway timetab~~...~~ has been said to be an offer capable ~~...~~ ion to buy a ticket,[34] although regula~~...~~ ility is to arise.

(iv) Tenders

An announcement inviting tenders is ~~...~~panied by words indicating that the highest or the lo~~...~~,[36] it is a mere attempt to ascertain whether an acceptable offe~~...~~.[37] In a case where there is no offer to contract with the highest or lowest bidder, if the invitation to tender prescribes a clear, orderly, and familiar procedure, it may be an offer to consider all conforming tenders. Thus, where, a local authority's staff failed to clear a letterbox and the authority did not consider a tender submitted before the deadline, it was held liable for breach of contract.[38] In the case of tenders for major contracts for public works, supplies, and services the freedom to decide which tender to accept has been limited by European Union law.[39]

(v) Auctions

Where goods are put up for sale by auction upon an advertised condition that the sale shall be 'without reserve' the auctioneer thereby indicates to prospective buyers that the bid of the highest *bona fide* bidder will be accepted, and that the goods will not at any stage be withdrawn, for example, on the ground that the reserve price has not yet been reached. An auctioneer who does so withdraw the goods is said to be liable for breach of contract with such a bidder. In *Warlow v Harrison*:[40]

An auctioneer advertised a brown mare for sale by auction 'without reserve'. The owner's name was not disclosed. The claimant bid 60 guineas; the owner bid 61 guineas, and

---

[34] *Denton v Great Northern Railway Co* (1856) 5 E & B 860 (Lord Campbell CJ and Wightman J; Crompton J dissenting). See also *Wilkie v LPTB* [1947] 1 All ER 258 (contract formed when passenger boarded bus, ie running the bus constituted the offer).

[35] Made by the Railways Board and the independent railways contractors under the Transport Act 1962 and the Railways Act 1993. In the context of bus services, see Public Passenger Vehicles Act 1981 and regulations made under it.

[36] *Harvela Investments Ltd v Royal Trust of Canada (CI) Ltd* [1986] AC 207.

[37] *Spencer v Harding* (1870) LR 5 CP 561. Contrast *GN Ry v Witham* (1873) LR 9 CP 16; *Percival Ltd v LCC Asylums etc Committee* (1918) 87 LJ KB 677.

[38] *Blackpool and Fylde Aero Club Ltd v Blackpool BC* [1990] 1 WLR 1195. See below, p 565 on the remedy for breach of this obligation.

[39] See below, pp 245–6.

[40] (1858–59) 1 E & E 295, 309; *Johnston v Boyes* [1899] 2 Ch 73. Contrast *Fenwick v Macdonald, Fraser & Co Ltd* (1904) 6 F 850 (Scotland). By the Sale of Goods Act 1979, s 57(4) the seller is now precluded without notification from the bidding himself or employing anyone to bid for him, and any sale contravening this rule may be treated as fraudulent by the buyer.

the auctioneer knocked down the mare to him. The claimant sought damages from the auctioneer as being the highest *bona fide* bidder.

A majority of the Court of Exchequer Chamber considered that the auctioneer was liable on a contract that the auction sale was to be 'without reserve'.[41] The judgment has, however, been criticized as inconsistent with other principles.

First, it is clear that a bid at an auction is only an offer which can be retracted at any time before the fall of the hammer.[42] This rule is now to be found in section 57(2) of the Sale of Goods Act 1979. No contract for the sale of the goods in the auction, therefore, comes into existence until a bid is accepted by the auctioneer.

Secondly, an advertisement that an auction of certain articles will take place on a certain day does not bind the auctioneer to sell the goods, nor does it make the auctioneer liable upon a contract to indemnify persons who have incurred expense in order to attend the sale.[43] Such an advertisement is an invitation to treat.

So, where goods are advertised for sale without reserve, until the auctioneer accepts by the fall of the hammer, no contract of sale is concluded with the buyer. If, therefore, the auctioneer withdraws the goods prematurely, refusing to knock them down to the highest bidder, there can be no possible action on any *contract of sale* because none has yet come into existence. The Court in *Warlow v Harrison* stated that the claimant was not suing upon the contract of sale (which would at that time have been required by the Statute of Frauds to be evidenced in writing),[44] but upon a different, collateral, contract with the auctioneer. When the auctioneer put up the mare for sale 'without reserve' he contracted that this would be so, that this contract was made with the highest *bona fide* bidder, and it was broken upon a bid being made by or on behalf of the owner.[45]

Several objections have been taken to this analysis.[46] If an advertisement that an auction sale will be held is merely an invitation to treat, how can it be said that a stipulation contained in it that the sale will be 'without reserve' amounts to an offer? Secondly, if a bid may be retracted, or outbid, at any time before it is accepted, how can it be said that it is certain who is the highest bidder? Thirdly, what is the consideration for the promise, since the promisee is not bound to purchase, but may withdraw the bid at any time?

However, while there is a certain artificiality in treating the bidder as having provided consideration by bidding, that is, by exposure to the risk that the bid would be accepted by the auctioneer, this unilateral contract analysis[47] accords with the

---

[41] The minority held that the auctioneer would be liable for breach of warranty of authority: see below, p 731. In fact, a new trial was ordered but never took place.

[42] *Payne v Cave* (1789) 3 Term R 148.   [43] *Harris v Nickerson* (1873) LR 8 QB 286.

[44] See below, p 83.   [45] (1858) 1 E & E 309, 317.

[46] See Slade (1952) 68 LQR 238; Gower (1952) 68 LQR 456; Slade (1953) 69 LQR 21; Cox (1982) 132 NLJ 719.

[47] Above, p 32.

modern approach to similar situations.[48] It was applied in *Barry v Davies*,[49] effectively ending the controversy over *Warlow v Harrison*:

Customs and Excise put up for sale by auction two new engine analyser machines. Each could be obtained from the manufacturers for £14,521 but they were being sold without a reserve price. After the auctioneer failed to obtain bids of £5,000 and £3,000, the claimant bid £200 for each machine. The auctioneer refused to accept these bids and withdrew the machines from the auction. The claimant brought an action against the auctioneer for breach of contract.

The Court of Appeal, applying the majority's view in *Warlow v Harrison*, held that the holding of an auction without reserve is an offer by the auctioneer to sell to the highest bidder so that the auctioneer was indeed contractually bound to sell to the claimant (who was entitled to damages of £27,600).

(b) GENERAL OFFERS

An offer need not be made to an ascertained person,[50] but no contract can arise until it has been accepted by an ascertained person.

This proposition is best understood by an illustration:

An insurance company offers a reward to any person who finds and returns a valuable diamond brooch insured by them. X who knows of the offer, finds and returns the brooch. She is entitled to claim the reward.[51]

An offer, by way of advertisement, of a reward for the rendering of certain services, addressed to the public at large, prima facie creates a power of acceptance in every person to whom it is made or becomes known. But a contractual obligation to pay the reward only comes into existence when an individual person performs the stipulated services, and not before.[52] A general offer may be susceptible of acceptance either by only one person or by a number of persons.

In some cases, such as the offer of a reward for information or the return of a lost possession, the offer is exhausted when once accepted. The offeror clearly does not intend to pay many times over for the same thing. So, where a reward is offered for information and the information asked for reaches the offeror from several sources, it has been held that the person who gave the earliest information is entitled to the reward.[53]

---

[48] See, on tenders, *Harvela Investments Ltd v Royal Trust of Canada (CI) Ltd* [1986] AC 207; *Blackpool and Fylde Aero Club Ltd v Blackpool BC* [1990] 1 WLR 1195.

[49] [2000] 1 WLR 1962.

[50] A proposal not addressed to one or more specific persons is presumptively merely an invitation to treat under the Convention on the International Sale of Goods (CISG) art 14(2) but presumptively an offer under the Italian Civil Code, art 1336(1) and by judicial decision in French law: Nicholas, *The French Law of Contract* (2nd edn, 1992) 63–4.

[51] For the position where X does not know of the offer, see below, p 53.

[52] *New Zealand Shipping Co Ltd v AM Satterthwaite & Co Ltd* [1975] AC 154, 168. See also *Williams v Carwardine* (1833) 4 B & Ad 621, below, p 53.

[53] *Lancaster v Walsh* (1838) 4 M & W 16.

In other cases the nature of the act asked for by the offeror and the circumstances in which the offer is made mean that it remains open for acceptance by any number of persons, such acceptance being signified by performance of its terms. In *Carlill v Carbolic Smoke Ball Co*:[54]

The defendant offered by advertisement to pay £100 to any one 'who contracts the increasing epidemic influenza colds, or any disease caused by taking cold, after having used the ball three times daily for two weeks, according to the printed directions'. It was added that £1,000 was deposited with the Alliance Bank 'showing our sincerity in the matter'. Mrs Carlill used the smoke ball as required by the directions; she afterwards suffered from influenza and sued the company for the promised reward.

The defendant was held liable. It was urged that a notification of acceptance should have been made to it but the Court held that this was one of the class of cases in which, as in the case of a reward offered for information or for the recovery of lost property, there need be no acceptance of the offer other than performance of the condition.[55] The further argument that the alleged offer was merely an advertisement or puff which no reasonable person would take to be serious was rejected because the statement that £1,000 had been deposited to meet demands was regarded as evidence of the sincerity of the offer. The advertisement was an offer which was capable of being accepted by a number of persons, and which had been accepted by Mrs Carlill when she performed the stipulated conditions.

(c) COMMUNICATION OF THE OFFER

In general an offer is effective when, and not until, it is communicated to the offeree. It follows that there can in general be no acceptance in ignorance of an offer, and, despite one somewhat unsatisfactory contrary decision,[56] this seems correct in principle.

(i) Cross-offers

The necessity for the communication of the offer, and for its consequent acceptance, appears to be the reason why two identical cross-offers do not ordinarily make a contract. Two manifestations of a willingness to make the same bargain do not constitute a contract unless one is made with reference to the other.[57] In *Tinn v Hoffman & Co*:[58]

On 28 November 1871, H wrote to T offering to sell him 800 tons of iron at 69*s* per ton, together with a further quantity at the same price. On the same day, T wrote to H offering

---

[54] [1893] 1 QB 256. See also *Bowerman v ABTA* [1995] 145 NLJR 1815.   [55] Below, p 48.

[56] *Gibbons v Proctor* (1891) 64 LT 594, 55 JP 616. For criticism and contrary authority, see below, p 53.

[57] If one is made with reference to the other, there is no reason why a contract should not be held to exist, even though it is expressed to be an 'offer' and not an acceptance: but see *Gibson v Manchester City Council* [1979] 1 WLR 294.

[58] (1873) 29 LT 271, 275, 277, 278, 279; ALI *Restatement, Contracts (2d)* para 23.

to buy 800 tons at 69*s*, together with a further quantity at a lower price. The letters crossed in the post. T contended that there was, at all events, a good contract for 800 tons at 69*s* per ton.

A majority of the Court of Exchequer Chamber expressed the opinion that H would not be bound as a result of the simultaneous offers, each being made in ignorance of the other.

(ii) Offer by rendering services must be communicated

Although conduct such as the rendering of services can constitute an offer, where that offer is not communicated to the party to whom it is intended to be made there is no opportunity of rejection and no presumption of acceptance. Thus, if A does work for B without the request or knowledge of B, A can only sue in contract for the value of the work where there is evidence of a recognition or acceptance of the work by B. This is clearly illustrated by *Taylor v Laird*:[59]

T was engaged to command L's ship and to conduct certain explorers on an expedition up the River Niger. He threw up his command in the course of the expedition, but helped to work the vessel home, though without the knowledge of the defendant. He then claimed to be remunerated for the services thus rendered.

It was held that he could not recover. L never had the option of accepting or refusing the services while they were being rendered; and he repudiated them when he became aware of them. T's offer, being uncommunicated, did not admit of acceptance and could not give him any contractual rights against L. Pollock CB said:[60]

Suppose I clean your property without your knowledge, have I a claim on you for payment? How can you help it? One cleans another's shoes; what can the other do but put them on? Is that evidence of a contract to pay for the cleaning?

In certain circumstances, for instance where the services rendered are necessary services,[61] it may be that there is a liability to make restitution of an unjust enrichment but such liability is not contractual.

3. THE ACCEPTANCE

If a contract is to be made, the offeree must accept the offer. Acceptance of an offer is the expression, by words or conduct,[62] of assent to the terms of the offer in the manner prescribed or indicated by the offeror.

---

[59] (1856) 25 LJ Ex 329. See also *Forman & Co Pty Ltd v Ship Liddesdale* [1900] AC 190.

[60] (1856) 25 LJ Ex 329, 332.

[61] *Jenkins v Tucker* (1788) 1 Hy Bl 90 (burial of the dead); *Re Rhodes* (1890) 44 Ch D 94 (maintenance of a mentally incapable person, although no recovery on the facts because there was no intention to charge).

[62] *Brogden v Metropolitan Railway Co* (1877) 2 App Cas 666, below, p 46; *Day Morris Associates v Voyce* [2003] EWCA Civ 189, [2003] 2 P & CR DG2. See also above, pp 33–4.

(a) OFFER AND ACCEPTANCE MUST CORRESPOND

The intention of the offeree to accept must be expressed without leaving room for doubt as to the fact of acceptance, or as to the coincidence of the terms of the acceptance with those of the offer. These requirements may be summed up in the general rule, sometimes called the 'mirror image' rule, that the acceptance must be absolute, and must correspond with the terms of the offer.

In determining whether or not an acceptance is conclusive, an alleged acceptance must be distinguished from (i) a counter-offer and rejection; (ii) an acceptance with some variation or addition of terms; or (iii) an acceptance which is equivocal, or which is qualified by reference to the subsequent arrangement of terms.

(i) Counter-offer and rejection

A counter-offer amounts to a rejection of the offer, and so operates to bring it to an end. In *Hyde v Wrench*,[63] for example:

W offered to sell a farm to H for £1,000. H said that he would give £950. W refused, and H then said he would give £1,000, and, when W declined to adhere to his original offer, H tried to obtain specific performance of the alleged contract.

The Court held that an offer to buy at £950 in response to an offer to sell for £1,000 was a refusal followed by a counter-offer, and that no contract had come into existence. But making express what would otherwise be implied[64] or inquiring whether the offeror will modify his terms does not necessarily amount to a counter-offer. So in *Stevenson, Jacques & Co v McLean*,[65] the offeree could still accept an offer of a certain quantity of iron 'at 40s. nett *cash* per ton', even though he had telegraphed to the offeror requesting information as to possible terms of credit. It was held that this was not a counter-offer, but was 'a mere inquiry, which should have been answered and not treated as a rejection of the offer'.[66]

(ii) Change of terms

A purported acceptance of an offer may introduce terms at variance with or not comprised in the offer. Although, exceptionally in such a situation the response may be regarded as an acceptance with an offer to enter a further contract,[67] generally, in such cases no contract is made, for the offeree in effect rejects the offer and makes a counter-offer.[68]

In the case of *Jones v Daniel*:[69]

A offered £1,450 for a property belonging to B. In a letter accepting the offer B enclosed a contract for the signature of A. This document contained various terms as to payment of

---

[63] (1840) 3 Beav 334. [64] *Lark v Outhwaite* [1991] 2 Lloyd's Rep 132, 139.

[65] (1880) 5 QBD 346. See also *Brown & Gracie Ltd v FW Green & Co (Pty) Ltd* [1960] 1 Lloyd's Rep 289, 297; *Gibson v Manchester City Council* [1979] 1 WLR 294, 302.

[66] (1880) 5 QBD 346, 350.

[67] *Monvia Motorship Corp v Keppel Shipyard (Private) Ltd* [1983] 1 Lloyd's Rep 356 (PC).

[68] The position is similar in many European systems; see Lando and Beale, *Principles of European Contract Law* (2000) 179.

[69] [1894] 2 Ch 332. See also *Brogden v Metropolitan Ry Co* (1877) 2 App Cas 666, below, p 46. Cf *Global Tankers Inc v Amercoat Europa NV* [1975] 1 Lloyd's Rep 666, 671.

deposit, date of completion, and requirement of title which had never been suggested in the offer.

The Court held that there was no contract; B had not accepted A's offer but made a counter-offer of his own, which was never accepted by A.

(iii) 'Battle of the forms'

In modern commercial practice, a particular problem has arisen which is that of the 'battle of the forms'. A firm may, for example, offer to buy goods from another on a form which contains or refers to its standard conditions of trade. The seller 'accepts' the offer by a confirmation on a form which contains or refers to its (the seller's) standard conditions of trade. These may differ materially from those of the buyer. It may then deliver the goods. Two questions typically arise; is there a contract and, if there is, do the buyer's or the seller's conditions prevail?

One possible solution to this problem is by what might be called the 'first shot' approach. Under this the seller-offeree, by purporting to accept the buyer-offeror's offer, is said to have waived its own conditions of trade, so that the contract is concluded subject to the buyer's conditions.[70] In *Butler Machine Tool Co Ltd v Ex-cell-o Corporation (England) Ltd*,[71] however, a majority of the Court of Appeal (Lawton and Bridge LJJ) applied the 'mirror image' rule and stated that the seller's confirmation amounts to a counter-offer. This is capable of acceptance by the buyer. The buyer may indicate that it accepts the counter-offer made to it by some act or performance; for example, the receipt and acceptance of the goods or by, for instance, the return of an 'acknowledgement' form containing the seller's conditions. This can be called the 'last shot' approach. In our example such an acceptance would conclude a contract subject to the seller's conditions, since it was the seller who fired the 'last shot' in the battle of the forms. Lord Denning MR, while arriving at the same result, advocated a more flexible, but less certain, approach, by which one should look at whether the documents revealed 'an agreement on all material points'.[72] After some doubt, and suggestions made that other more flexible approaches, similar to that advocated by Lord Denning, should be applied,[73] it was confirmed by the Court of Appeal in *Tekdata Interconnections Ltd v Amphenol Ltd*[74] that the majority in *Butler Machine Tool Co Ltd v Ex-cell-o* was correct. Except where there is a long-term clear course of dealing between the parties on particular terms, the normal rules of offer and acceptance must be applied; and, applying those rules, the standard result will be that the party which sends its terms last

---

[70] See also *Chas Davis (Metal Brokers) Ltd v Gilyott & Scott Ltd* [1975] 2 Lloyd's Rep 422, 425 (Donaldson J).

[71] [1979] 1 WLR 401, 406, 407; Rawlings (1979) 42 MLR 715. See also *British Road Services v Arthur Crutchley Ltd* [1968] 1 All ER 811; *A Davies & Co (Shopfitters) v William Old* (1969) 67 LGR 395; *Tekdata Interconnections Ltd v Amphenol Ltd* [2009] EWCA Civ 1209, [2010] 1 Lloyd's Rep 357.

[72] [1979] 1 WLR 401, 404.

[73] See the last edition of this book at p 42 which drew on the Uniform Laws on International Sales Act 1967, Sched 2, art 7(2); CISG art 19; von Mehren (1990) 38 Am J Comp Law 265.

[74] [2009] EWCA Civ 1209, [2010] 1 Lloyd's Rep 357.

(the party which 'fires the last shot') will win because that will be the offer which is regarded as accepted by the other party's conduct. What this approach lacks in flexibility it gains in terms of certainty.

In cases where there is no contract even though services have been rendered or goods delivered, the rendering of services or delivery of goods may give rise to a restitutionary non-contractual obligation in unjust enrichment to pay a reasonable sum.[75] But in such cases, while restitution may protect the performer by the award of the reasonable value of the performance rendered, a recipient, who may have had certain requirements as to the time of performance or its quality, may be unprotected. This is because, in the absence of a contract, the party rendering the services or delivering the goods will not be liable in damages for delay or for defective performance.[76] However, the better view is that this can be satisfactorily dealt with, within the non-contractual law of unjust enrichment, as going to the relevant enrichment of the recipient.[77]

(iv) Equivocal or qualified acceptance

The acceptance must assent unequivocally and without qualification to the terms of the offer. For example, the reply 'Your order is receiving our attention' is too indefinite to amount to an acceptance.[78] The acceptance may also be qualified by reference to the preparation of a more formal contract or by reference to terms which have still to be negotiated. In such a case the agreement is incomplete[79] and there is no binding contract.

(b) COMMUNICATION OF THE ACCEPTANCE

(i) Mental assent insufficient

Acceptance means, in general, communicated acceptance, which must be something more than a mere mental assent. A tacit formation of intention is insufficient.

In an old case in the Year Books[80] it was argued that where the produce of a field was offered to a man at a certain price if he was pleased with it on inspection, the contract was made and the property passed when he had seen and approved of the subject of the sale. But Brian CJ said:

It seems to me the plea is not good without showing that he had certified the other of his pleasure; for it is trite learning that the thought of man is not triable, for the devil himself knows not the thought of man; but if you had agreed that if the bargain pleased then you

---

[75] *Peter Lind & Co v Mersey Docks & Harbour Board* [1972] 2 Lloyd's Rep 234. For the conditions of such liability, see below, pp 67, 71–2.

[76] McKendrick (1988) 8 OJLS 197, 212–13; Ball (1983) 99 LQR 572.

[77] So, eg, goods delivered late to the defendant may not be as valuable to him as goods delivered on time and this will be reflected in measuring the defendant's enrichment: see Burrows, *The Law of Restitution* (3rd edn, 2011) 375.

[78] *Rees v Warwick* (1818) 2 B & Ald 113; ALI *Restatement, Contracts (2d)* para 57.

[79] See below, p 70.   [80] *Anon* (1477) YB Pasch. 17 Edw IV, f 1, pl 2.

should have signified it to such an one, then I grant you need not have done more, for it is matter of fact.

Lord Blackburn approved this decision in *Brogden v Metropolitan Railway Co*:[81]

B (a supplier of coal) altered a draft coal supply agreement sent to him by M and returned it signed and marked 'approved'. M's agent put it in a drawer. The parties appear to have ordered and supplied coal upon the terms stated but, a dispute having arisen, B contended that he was not bound by the agreement.

It was held that there was a contract between the parties. This had not, however, come into existence at the time M's agent acquiesced in the offer by putting the letter in his drawer but later, either when coal was ordered by M or supplied by B.

(ii) Communication to the offeror

Even if there is some overt act or speech to give evidence of the intention to accept, English law stipulates, in addition, that acceptance is normally not complete *unless and until it is communicated to the offeror*. In the words of Lindley LJ: 'Unquestionably, as a general proposition, when an offer is made, it is necessary in order to make a binding contract, not only that it should be accepted, but that acceptance should be notified'.[82] Thus, if an offer is made by telephone, and in the middle of the reply the line goes dead, so that the offeror does not hear the words of acceptance, there is no contract.[83] Again, if a person shouts to another across a river or courtyard, but the offeror does not hear the reply because it is drowned by an aircraft flying overhead, there is no contract at that moment and the offeree must repeat the acceptance in order that it might be effective.

(iii) Communication other than by offeree

The justification for the rule requiring communication is that the offeror is entitled to know whether a binding contract has been concluded by acceptance. In principle, therefore, there would seem to be no reason (other than one of certainty) why a contract should not come into existence if the offeror is made aware or is informed that the offer has been accepted even though the acceptance is not communicated to the offeror by the offeree.[84] *Powell v Lee*,[85] however, appears to hold that it is necessary that the acceptance be communicated by the offeree or by his duly authorized agent.

---

[81] (1877) 2 App Cas 666.

[82] *Carlill v Carbolic Smoke Ball Co* [1893] 1 QB 256, 262. See also *Robophone Facilities Ltd v Blank* [1966] 1 WLR 1428; *Allied Marine Transport Ltd v Vale do Rio Doce Navegacao* [1985] 1 WLR 925, 937; CISG art 23. Cf below, p 51 (no need for communication where offer stipulates a prescribed mode of acceptance).

[83] *Entores v Miles Far East Corporation* [1955] 2 QB 327, 332 (Denning LJ); Winfield (1939) 55 LQR 499, 514; ALI *Restatement, Contracts (2d)* para 65. But cf below, pp 48–51, for the different rule which applies to acceptance by post.

[84] *Levita's Case* (1867) LR 3 Ch App 36. See also *Dickinson v Dodds* (1876) 2 Ch D 463, below, p 60 (third-party notification of revocation of offer effective).

[85] (1908) 99 LT 284.

The managers of a school resolved to appoint the claimant to the headmastership of a school. One of the managers, acting in his individual capacity, informed the claimant of what had occurred. He received no other communication and subsequently the resolution was rescinded.

It was held that there was no concluded contract. It was said: 'the mere fact that the [whole body of] managers did not authorize such a communication, which is the usual course to be adopted, implied that they meant to reserve the power to reconsider the decision at which they had arrived'.[86] In the absence of facts giving rise to such an implication, however, communication by a third party should, it is submitted, suffice.

The general rule that acceptance must be communicated before it can take effect is subject to a number of exceptions, to which we now turn.

(iv) Waiver of communication

The general rule that an acceptance of an offer made ought to be notified to the offeror is for the benefit of the offeror, who may expressly or impliedly waive the requirement of notification and agree that an uncommunicated acceptance will suffice. Thus acceptance may in certain circumstances be held to have been made even though it has not yet come to the notice of the offeror. In such a case two things are necessary. There must be an express or implied intimation from the offeror that a particular mode of acceptance will suffice. And there must be some overt act or conduct on the part of the offeree which is evidence of an intention to accept, and which conforms to the mode of acceptance indicated by the offeror.

In *Carlill v Carbolic Smoke Ball Co*,[87] previously discussed, it will be remembered that the manufacturers of the smoke balls advertised inviting performance of a condition, and it was sufficient for the purposes of binding them that Mrs Carlill had performed the condition without communicating to them the acceptance of the offer. Bowen LJ stated:[88]

The person who makes the offer may dispense with notice to himself if he thinks it desirable to do so, and I suppose there can be no doubt that where a person in an offer made by him to another person, expressly or impliedly intimates a particular method of acceptance as sufficient to make the bargain binding, it is only necessary for the other person to whom such offer is made to follow the indicated mode of acceptance; and if the person making the offer, expressly or impliedly intimates in his offer that it will be sufficient to act on the proposal without communicating acceptance of it to himself, performance of the condition is a sufficient acceptance without notification.

The nature and terms of the offer need to be considered carefully to ascertain whether they entitle the offeree to dispense with notice of acceptance. If A tells B by letter that

---

[86] *Ibid*, 286 (Channell J).   [87] [1893] 1 QB 256, above, p 41.

[88] *Ibid*, 269. Lindley LJ, *ibid*, 262, said such cases were either an exception to the rule or ones in which acceptance need not precede the performance. See also *Manchester Diocesan Council for Education v Commercial & General Investments Ltd* [1970] 1 WLR 241, 245.

he will receive and pay for certain goods if B will send them to him, such an offer may be accepted by sending the goods.[89]

(v) Promise for an act

In the case of general offers and other offers which indicate performance as a mode of acceptance so as to create a unilateral contract, as in *Carlill v Carbolic Smoke Ball Co*, it is performance, not notice of acceptance, that is contemplated. An offer of reward for the supply of information, or for the return of a lost dog, does not contemplate an intimation of acceptance from every person who, on becoming aware of the offer, decides to ascertain the information or to search for the dog.[90] Indeed the offeree may already have the information or have found the dog, and can do no more than send it on to the offeror. The question as to whether it is the commencement of performance, or its completion, that constitutes the acceptance of an offer of a unilateral contract is discussed below in the context of revocation of the offer.[91]

(vi) Acceptance by post

A distinction is drawn between acceptance by instantaneous methods such as telex, telephone, fax, and probably e-mail,[92] and acceptance by non-instantaneous methods such as post.[93] Instantaneous methods, where the acceptor will generally know that his communication has not arrived at once and can try again, are subject to the general requirement that acceptance must be communicated to the offeror.[94] Where, however, it is reasonable for the offeree to notify acceptance by post,[95] the acceptance is completed when the letter is posted.[96] The offeror is bound from that time although the acceptance has not been delivered and may never be delivered.

The postal acceptance rule was laid down in *Adams v Lindsell*:[97]

On 2 September 1817, L wrote offering to sell to A a certain quantity of wool, and added 'receiving your answer in course of post'. If the letter containing this offer had been properly directed, an answer might have been received by the 7th; but it was misdirected and did not

---

[89] *Harvey v Johnston* (1848) 6 CB 295, 304; *Newcomb v De Roos* (1859) 2 E & E 271. Cf *Kennedy v Thomassen* [1929] 1 Ch 426. But cf *Rust v Abbey Life Assurance Co Ltd* [1978] 1 Lloyd's Rep 386, 392 (offer to invest in property bond accepted by allocation of units; no need to send policy to offeror).

[90] *Carlill v Carbolic Smoke Ball Co*, above, n 54, 270.   [91] Below, pp 57–8.

[92] For the view that the same rule should be applied to e-mails as for telex and fax, see Hill (2001) 17 JCL 151; Nolan in Burrows and Peel (eds), *Contract Formation and Parties* (2010) ch 4.

[93] Before they fell out of use, telegrams were treated legally in the same way as letters.

[94] *Entores v Miles Far East Corp* [1955] 2 QB 327 (telex); *Brinkibon Ltd v Stahag Stahl und Stahlwarenhandelsgesellschaft mbH* [1983] 2 AC 34 (telex); *JSC Zestafoni G Nikoladze Ferralloy Plant v Ronly Holdings Ltd* [2004] EWHC 245 (Comm), [2004] 2 Lloyd's Rep 335 (fax).

[95] *Henthorn v Fraser* [1892] 2 Ch 27, 33.

[96] *Dunlop v Higgins* (1848) 1 HLC 381; *Re Imperial Land Co of Marseilles (Harris' Case)* (1872) LR 7 Ch App 587; *Household Fire and Carriage Accident Insurance Co Ltd v Grant* (1879) 4 Ex D 216; *Henthorn v Fraser* [1892] 2 Ch 27; *Port Sudan Cotton Co v Govindaswamy Chettiar & Sons* [1977] 2 Lloyd's Rep 5. For the equivalent rule for telegrams, see *Stevenson, Jacques & Co v McLean* (1880) 5 QBD 346; *Bruner v Moore* [1904] 1 Ch 305, 316.

[97] (1818) 1 B & Ald 681.

reach A until the 5th so that their acceptance, posted the same day, was not received by L until the 9th. On the 8th, however, that is before the acceptance had arrived, L sold the wool to another. A sued for breach of contract.

It was unsuccessfully argued on behalf of L that there was no contract between the parties until the letter of acceptance was actually received. The Court stated:[98]

If that were so, no contract could ever be completed by post. For if [L] were not bound by their offer when accepted by [A] until the answer was received, then [A] ought not to be bound till they had received the notification that [L] had received their answer and assented to it. And so it might go on *ad infinitum*.

The logic of this passage is questionable, but it was undoubtedly necessary for the Court to establish some definite rule as to the time of a postal acceptance.

One of the more obvious consequences of the postal acceptance rule is that the offeror must bear the risk of the letter of acceptance being delayed or lost. In *Household Fire and Carriage Accident Insurance Co Ltd v Grant*:[99]

The defendant offered to buy shares in the claimant company. The claimant sent a letter of acceptance to the defendant but it was lost in the post and never arrived. The liquidator of the company sued the defendant for the money owing for the shares.

The Court of Appeal held that, as an acceptance by post is valid when sent, there was a contract under which the defendant was bound to pay for the shares.

Where, however, the delay or loss is due to the fault of the offeree, as in the case of an acceptance which is improperly addressed or insufficiently stamped, it would seem that it only takes effect if and when it is received by the offeror, provided that this occurs within the time within which a regular acceptance would have been received.[100]

(vii) Place of contracting

Whether the postal acceptance rule applies also determines *where* a contract is made. If the means of communication is by letter, the contract is complete when the letter is posted,[101] and it is there that the contract is made. In other cases the general rule that the contract is made when and where the acceptance is received applies.[102]

---

[98] *Ibid*, 683. The *ratio decidendi* of the case is complicated by the assertion that the delay was caused by the defendants' negligence in misdirecting their offer. The effect of such delay appears to extend the permissible period within which the offer may be accepted (see below, p 62) unless the offeree knows or has reason to know of the delay: ALI *Restatement, Contracts (2d)* para 51.

[99] (1879) 4 Ex D 216.

[100] *Korbetis v Transgrain Shipping BV* [2005] EWHC 1345 (QB). See also *Getreide-Import-Gesellschaft v Contimar SA Compania Commercial y Maritima* [1953] 1 WLR 793; ALI *Restatement, Contracts (2d)* paras 67–8.

[101] *Cowan v O'Connor* (1888) 20 QBD 640.

[102] *Brinkibon Ltd v Stahag Stahl und Stahlwarenhandelsgesellschaft mbH* [1983] 2 AC 34 approving *Entores v Miles Far East Corp* [1955] 2 QB 327 (acceptance by telex from Holland to London held to constitute a contract made in England).

(viii) Rationale of postal rule

Various attempts have been made to justify the postal acceptance rule analytically.[103] One line of reasoning attempts to eliminate any difficulties as to consensus by treating the post office as the agent of the offeror not only for delivering the offer, but for receiving the notification of its acceptance;[104] yet the post office is clearly not an agent to whom acceptance is or could be communicated. Another is based on the fact that posting the acceptance puts it irretrievably out of the offeree's control. The same can, however, be said of communication by telex which is not completed until receipt[105] so this does not explain why posting exceptionally constitutes an acceptance without notification.

The better explanation would seem to be that the rule is based, not on logic, but on commercial convenience.[106] If hardship is caused, as it obviously may be, by the delay or loss of a letter of acceptance, some rule is necessary, and the rule at which the Courts have arrived is probably as satisfactory as any other would be.[107]

First, it is always open to the offeror to secure protection by requiring actual notification of the acceptance.[108] The nature of the offer or the circumstances in which it was made may indicate that notification is required and Courts may be willing to displace what has been termed an 'artificial concept of communication'.[109] Secondly, the rule is a pragmatic way of limiting the power to revoke an offer before acceptance,[110] even where the offeror has promised not to.[111] It also prevents the offeree from being able to nullify the acceptance while it is in transit and thus from speculating by watching the market and deciding whether to send an overtaking rejection.[112] Further, in the event of delay or loss of the letter of acceptance, it is the offeror who is more likely to be the first to enquire why no reply has been received to the offer, rather than the offeree to enquire whether the acceptance has been received.

---

[103] Winfield (1939) 55 LQR 499; Nussbaum (1936) 36 Col L Rev 920.

[104] *Household Fire and Carriage Accident Insurance Co Ltd v Grant* (1879) 4 Ex D 216, 221; *Hebb's Case* (1867) LR 4 Eq 9, 12.

[105] *Entores v Miles Far East Corp* [1955] 2 QB 327.

[106] *Re Imperial Land Co of Marseilles (Harris' Case)* (1872) LR 7 Ch App 587, 594; *Brinkibon Ltd v Stahag Stahl und Stahlwarenhandelsgesellschaft mbH* [1983] 2 AC 34, 41, 48.

[107] Winfield (1939) 55 LQR 499, 506. Three principal systems seem to be in operation in other countries: (i) *information*: when the offeror is actually informed of the acceptance; (ii) *expedition*: when the offeree despatches the letter of acceptance; and (iii) *reception*: when the acceptance is received at its destination, whether the offeror is actually informed or not. See Evans (1966) 15 ICLQ 553. Under CISG arts 18(2), 24, and 21(2) the acceptance becomes effective at the moment the indication of assent is delivered at the address of the offeror; if the letter is lost, there is no contract, but if it is delayed, there is normally a contract, unless the offeror has promptly informed the offeree that he considers his offer as having lapsed.

[108] *Holwell Securities Ltd v Hughes* [1974] 1 WLR 155.

[109] *Ibid*, 157, 158, 161; *New Hart Builders Ltd v Brindley* [1975] Ch 342 (rule displaced where contracts required 'notice to . . .' or 'to notify').

[110] *Re Imperial Land Co of Marseilles (Harris' Case)* (1872) LR 7 Ch App 587, 594.

[111] Below, p 58. Nussbaum (1936) 36 Col L Rev 920, 922–7. The Scottish Law Commission, rejecting the rule (Scot Law Com No 144 (1993) paras 4.4–4.7), did not consider this.

[112] Below, p 55. See also Farnsworth, *Contracts* (4th edn, 2004) §3.22.

The rule has, however, been criticized.[113] The number of different modes of communication now available[114] has been said to give rise to an increasing number of problems of demarcation and it is argued that the law would be much more coherent if there were only one rule for all means of communication. It has also been said that the law should not, as the postal acceptance rule does, favour the offeree because, while the offeror is in ignorance as to the actions of the offeree, the offeree has full knowledge of what the position is. The offeree knows that the acceptance has been posted and knows or ought to know that mail is not infrequently delayed.[115] Nevertheless, the ability of the offeror to control the method of acceptance, the offeror's ability to revoke even a 'firm' offer before acceptance,[116] and the desirability of preventing speculation by the offeree are, it is suggested, good reasons for the rule. It is significant that the Scottish Law Commission's proposal to abolish it was made together with a proposal to prohibit the offeror from revoking a 'firm' offer.[117]

The rule may in any event not be as anomalous as it appears when compared only with the rules governing instantaneous modes of communication. In a previous edition of this work, it was argued that the principles governing postal acceptance were merely examples of a wider principle that where the offeror either expressly or impliedly indicates the mode of acceptance and this, as a means of communication, proves to be nugatory or insufficient, he does so at his own risk.[118] Suppose that A sends an offer to B by messenger across a lake with a request that B, if she accepts, will at a certain hour communicate her acceptance by firing a gun or lighting a fire. Why, it was asked, should B suffer if a storm renders the gun inaudible or a fog obscures the light of the fire? Although, as we have seen,[119] this 'risk' approach does not apply where instantaneous communication is concerned, it is suggested that it has validity in cases where there is bound to be a substantial interval between the time when the acceptance is sent and the time when it is received.[120]

(ix) Acceptance by silence

In principle, it is difficult to see how the silence or inaction of an offeree who fails to reply to an offer can operate as an acceptance, for there will have been no communication of the acceptance to the offeror. Even if the offeror has waived[121] communication by

---

[113] eg by Gardner (1992) 12 OJLS 170; Scot Law Com No 144 (1993) paras 4.4–4.7.

[114] Apart from telex, fax, e-mail, and the various types of electronic document interchange, there are also couriers, private messenger delivery, and document exchange services.

[115] Scot Law Com Memorandum No 36 [1977] para 48, quoted in Scot Law Com No 144 (1993) para 4.5.

[116] Below, p 58.

[117] Prevention of speculation by the offeree, who unlike the offeror has *full* knowledge, does not appear to have been considered by the Scottish Law Commission: Scot Law Com No 144 (1993) paras 4.4–4.7. See also paras 3.10–3.14.

[118] Anson (20th edn, 1952) 36.

[119] *Entores v Miles Far East Corporation* [1955] 2 QB 327; *Brinkibon Ltd v Stahag Stahl und Stahlwarenhandelsgesellschaft mbH* [1983] 2 AC 34, above, p 46.

[120] *Brinkibon Ltd v Stahag Stahl und Stahlwarenhandelsgesellschaft mbH* [1983] 2 AC 34, 48.

[121] See above, p 47.

indicating that acceptance by silence will suffice, it is clear that the offeror cannot confront the offeree with the alternative of either refusing the offer or being subjected to a contractual obligation by reason of the failure to reply. Although a form or time of acceptance may be prescribed, an offeror cannot prescribe the form or time of refusal so as to impose a contract on the other party if the other party does not refuse in some particular way or within some particular time.[122] In *Felthouse v Bindley*, for example:[123]

F offered by letter to buy his nephew's horse for £30 15s, adding, 'If I hear no more about him I shall consider the horse mine at £30 15s'. No answer was returned to this letter, but the nephew told B, an auctioneer, to keep the horse out of a sale of his farm stock, as he intended to reserve it for his uncle F. B sold the horse by mistake, and F sued him for conversion of his property.

The Court held that as the nephew had never signified to F his acceptance of the offer before the auction sale took place, there was no bargain to pass the property in the horse to F, and therefore he had no right to complain of the sale. Willes J said:[124] 'It is clear that the uncle had no right to impose upon the nephew a sale of his horse for £30 15s unless he chose to comply with the condition of writing to repudiate the offer'.

In more modern times this same principle may be illustrated by the practice of sending out unsolicited goods. A publisher may, for example, without previous order, send a book to a prospective customer with a letter saying, in effect, 'If you do not return the book by a certain day, I shall presume that you have bought it'. It is clear that he cannot by these means impose a contract on the unwilling recipient. But persons with no knowledge of the law may well be misled into thinking that they are bound to pay for the book, and the subsequent letters which they receive may frequently be designed to foster this misapprehension. As a result, in 1971, the legislature enacted the Unsolicited Goods and Services Act whereby the recipients of unsolicited goods may, in certain circumstances, treat them as if they were an unconditional gift to themselves, and suppliers may be guilty of a criminal offence if they demand or threaten legal proceedings for payment.[125]

On the other hand, circumstances can arise where acceptance could more legitimately be presumed from silence. Previous dealings between the parties may have been conducted on the basis, for example, that orders for goods have been fulfilled by the seller without any notification of acceptance other than the despatch of the goods, and the offeror has thereby been led to believe that the practice will continue.[126] It is even arguable by analogy with the cases we have noted on waiver by the offeror of the need for communication of acceptance, that, if the offeror stipulates that acceptance

---

[122] Pollock, *Principles of Contract* (13th edn, 1950) 22.

[123] (1862) 11 CBNS 869, aff'd (1863) 7 LT 835. See also *Allied Marine Transport Ltd v Vale do Rio Doce Navegacao SA* [1985] 1 WLR 925, 937. See further Miller (1972) 35 MLR 489.

[124] (1862) 11 CBNS 869, 875.

[125] The Unsolicited Goods and Services Act 1971 has been amended, and partly replaced, by the Consumer Protection (Distance Selling) Regulations 2000 (SI 2000 No 2334).

[126] ALI *Restatement, Contracts (2d)* para 72.

may be constituted by silence or inaction, an unequivocal manifestation of an intention to accept on the part of the offeree (or, possibly, detrimental reliance on the offer by the offeree),[127] should bind the offeror. This, however, would run counter to the decision in *Felthouse v Bindley*, where, it will be noted, the nephew made known his intention to accept his uncle's offer. No doubt, in many cases, silence is ambiguous[128] and therefore cannot constitute an acceptance. But if, as in *Felthouse v Bindley* itself, the necessary intention to accept could be proved, there seems to be no convincing reason why a contract should not come into existence, particularly where the offeree has relied on the terms of the offer and it is the offeror who now denies that there is a contract. More recent *dicta* support this. Thus, it has been stated:[129]

[W]here the offeree himself indicates that an offer is to be taken as accepted if he does not indicate to the contrary by an ascertainable time, he is undertaking to speak if he does not want an agreement to be concluded. I see no reason in principle why that should not be an exceptional circumstance such that the offer can be accepted by silence.

(c) ACCEPTOR MUST HAVE KNOWLEDGE OF OFFER

If A offers a promise for an act and B does the act in ignorance of the offer, can B claim performance of the offer on becoming aware of its existence? As illustrated by the case of cross-offers,[130] the answer appears to be that, if B has not heard of the offer before doing the act, it cannot be accepted.[131] In *Gibbons v Proctor*,[132] however, a Divisional Court held that a police officer was entitled to claim a reward, offered by handbills, for information given to a superintendent of police, although it seems the officer did not know of the handbills before giving the information. The decision, as reported, is an unsatisfactory one, for the facts of the case are by no means clear. Accordingly, it cannot be considered as of compelling authority, and a New York case, *Fitch v Snedaker*,[133] is sometimes cited to the contrary. It was there laid down that a reward cannot be claimed by one who did not know that it had been offered. The latter decision seems correct in principle. A person who does an act for which a reward has been offered in ignorance of the offer cannot say either that there was a consensus of wills with the offeror, or that the act was done in return for or in reliance on the promise offered. If, however, the acceptor knows of the offer, but is inspired to performance by a motive other than that of claiming the reward, such a motive is immaterial. So in

---

[127] Cf *Fairline Shipping Corp v Adamson* [1975] QB 180; *Schuldenfrei v Hilton (IT)* [1999] STC 821, 831, 833. See also, below, p 122 (promissory estoppel).

[128] Above, pp 33–4.

[129] *Re Selectmove Ltd* [1995] 1 WLR 474, 478 (Peter Gibson LJ). See also *Vitol SA v Norelf Ltd* [1996] AC 800, 812.

[130] See *Tinn v Hoffman & Co* (1873) 29 LT 271, above, p 41.

[131] *Taylor v Allon* [1966] 1 QB 304, 311; *Tracomin SA v Anton C Nielsen* [1984] 2 Lloyd's Rep 195, 203.

[132] (1891) 64 LT 594, 55 JP 616. Cf *Neville v Kelly* (1862) 12 CBNS 740. See Hudson (1968) 84 LQR 503.

[133] (1868) 38 NY 248. See also *Bloom v American Swiss Watch Co* 1915 AD 100 (South Africa); *R v Clarke* (1927) 40 CLR 227 (Australia); ALI *Restatement, Contracts* (2d) para 51 and Comment a.

Williams v Carwardine[134] where the claimant, with knowledge of the reward, supplied information leading to the conviction of an assailant for murder, but only did this 'to ease her conscience, and in hopes of forgiveness hereafter', she was held entitled to claim the £20 offered. Her acceptance could be referred to the offer.

(d) PRESCRIBED MODE OF ACCEPTANCE

If the terms or the circumstances of the offer do no more than suggest a mode of acceptance, it seems that the offeree would not be bound to this mode so long as the mode used was one which did not cause delay, and which brought the acceptance to the knowledge of the offeror. A departure from the usual or suggested method of communication would probably throw upon the offeree the risk that the acceptance would be delayed, but, subject to this, an offer delivered by hand could be accepted by post, or an offer made by post could be accepted by telex. Is, however, an offeror who expressly prescribes the method of communication free to treat any departure from this method as a nullity? In the American case, *Eliason v Henshaw*:[135]

E offered to buy flour from H, requesting that an answer should be sent to him at Harper's Ferry by the wagon which brought the offer. H sent a letter of acceptance by mail to Georgetown, thinking that this would reach E more speedily. He was wrong, and the letter arrived after the time that the reply might have been expected.

The Supreme Court of the United States held that E was entitled to refuse to purchase:[136]

It is an undeniable principle of the law of contracts, that an offer of a bargain by one person to another, imposes no obligation upon the former, until it is accepted by the latter, according to the terms in which the offer was made. Any qualification of, or departure from, those terms, invalidates the offer, unless the same be agreed to by the person who made it.

The same rule applies in English law: an offeror, who by the terms of the offer insists upon its acceptance in a particular manner, is entitled to say that he is not bound unless acceptance is effected or communicated in that precise way.[137] Nevertheless, if the stipulation as to the mode of acceptance is inserted at the instance of and for the protection or benefit of the offeror, the offeror may by conduct or otherwise waive strict compliance with it, provided that the offeree is not adversely affected.[138] Moreover, unless as a matter of construction that prescribed mode of acceptance is mandatory, another mode of acceptance which is no less advantageous to the offeror will suffice.[139]

---

[134] (1833) 4 B & Ad 621; the fact of her knowledge is disclosed by the report in (1833) 5 C & P 566; *Lark v Outhwaite* [1991] 2 Lloyd's Rep 132, 140. Cf *R v Clarke* (1927) 40 CLR 227. See Mitchell and Phillips (2002) 22 OJLS 115.

[135] (1819) 4 Wheaton 225.   [136] *Ibid*, 228 (Washington J).

[137] *Manchester Diocesan Council for Education v Commercial & General Investments Ltd* [1970] 1 WLR 241, 246.

[138] *Ibid*; *Carlyle Finance Ltd v Pallas Industrial Finance Ltd* [1999] All ER (Comm) 659.

[139] *Tinn v Hoffman & Co* (1873) 29 LT 271, 274, 278; *Manchester Diocesan Council for Education v Commercial & General Investments Ltd* [1970] 1 WLR 241, 246; ALI *Restatement, Contracts (2d)* paras 29, 68; Winfield (1939) 55 LQR 499, 516.

(e) REVOCATION OF THE ACCEPTANCE

Since the general rule is that acceptance is not complete until it has been communicated to the offeror, it follows that an acceptance can be revoked at any time before this occurs, provided, of course, that the revocation itself is communicated before the acceptance arrives. But what is the position in relation to postal acceptances? Since the acceptance is complete as soon as the letter of acceptance is posted, a telephone call revoking the acceptance would be inoperative, though it reached the offeror before the letter. This, it is argued, is both the logical and fair conclusion; otherwise the offeree could blow both hot and cold, having the benefit of certainty in the postal acceptance, and the opportunity to revoke it if the offer turned out suddenly to be disadvantageous. On the other hand, it is contended that such a revocation can in no way prejudice the offeror, who could not know of the acceptance until it arrived, by which time he would already be aware of the revocation. There is no direct English authority on this point[140] but it is probably the better view that the offeree cannot so revoke.[141] If, for example, shares are offered on a fluctuating market, it would seem unfair if the offeree could bind the offeror by a postal acceptance when the shares advanced in price, but send off a revocation if the market fell. There is no reason why an offeree who chooses to accept by post should have an opportunity of changing his mind which would not have been available if the contract had been made face-to-face.

This solution should not, however, be operated to the detriment of the offeror. If the offeror acts on the purported revocation, for example by selling the shares which are the subject-matter of the offer, the offeree would not be permitted once again to change his mind and rely on the postal acceptance rule in order to claim damages for breach of contract.

4. TERMINATION OF THE OFFER

Once the acceptance has been communicated to the offeror, it cannot be recalled or undone. But until an offer is accepted, it creates no legal rights, and it may be terminated at any time. Termination of the offer may come about in a number of ways: it may be revoked before acceptance, or the offeree may reject the offer. Also, an offer may lapse by the passage of time or be determined by the death of the offeror or offeree.

---

[140] In *Household Fire and Carriage Accident Insurance Co Ltd v Grant* (1879) 4 Ex D 216, Bramwell LJ at 255 was of the opinion that the revocation would be effective. See also *Dick v US* 82 Fed Supp 326 (1949); Ellison Kahn (1955) 72 SALJ 246, 257; Hudson (1966) 82 LQR 169.

[141] In *Countess of Dunmore v Alexander* (1830) 9 S 190 (Scotland), Lord Craigie (dissenting) held that an offeree could not revoke her acceptance, but the majority of the Court treated the case as one of the revocation of an offer. See also *Wenkheim v Arndt* (1873) 1 JR 73 (NZ); *Kinch v Bullard* [1999] 1 WLR 423.

(a) REVOCATION OF THE OFFER

The law relating to the revocation of an offer may be summed up in two rules: (1) an offer may be revoked at any time before acceptance; and (2) an offer is made irrevocable by acceptance.

(i) Revocable before acceptance

The first of these rules may be illustrated by the case of *Offord v Davies:*[142]

D made a written offer to O that, if he would discount bills for another firm, D would guarantee the payment of such bills to the extent of £600 during a period of twelve calendar months. Some bills were discounted by O, and duly paid, but before the twelve months had expired D, the guarantor, revoked his offer and notified O that he would guarantee no more bills. O continued to discount bills, some of which were not paid, and then sued D on the guarantee.

It was held that the revocation was a good defence to the action. The alleged guarantee was an offer, for a period of 12 months, of promises for acts, of guarantees for discounts. Each discount turned the offer into a promise, *pro tanto*, but the entire offer could at any time be revoked except as regards discounts made before notice of revocation.

(ii) Irrevocable after acceptance

The rule that an offer is made irrevocable by acceptance is illustrated by *Great Northern Railway Co v Witham*,[143] which, like that in *Offord v Davies*, involved a continuing relationship:

The GNR company advertised for tenders for the supply of such iron articles as it might require between 1 November 1871, and 31 October 1872. W sent in a tender to supply the articles required on certain terms and in such quantities as the company 'might order from time to time', and his tender was accepted by the company. Orders were given and executed for some time on the terms of the tender but finally W was given an order which he refused to execute. The company sued him for breach of contract in that he had failed to perform this order.

It is important to note the exact relationship of the parties. The company by advertisement invited all dealers in iron to make tenders, that is, to state the terms of the offers which they were prepared to make. W's tender stated the terms of an offer which might be accepted at any time, or any number of times, in the ensuing 12 months. The acceptance of the tender did not in itself make a contract; it was merely an intimation by the company that it regarded W's tender as a standing offer, which on its part it would be willing to accept as and when it required the articles to be supplied. Each fresh order constituted an acceptance of this standing offer. If W wished to

---

[142] (1862) 12 CBNS 748; *Scammell v Dicker* [2001] 1 WLR 631.
[143] (1873) LR 9 CP 16. Contrast *Percival Ltd v LCC Asylums etc Committee* (1918) 87 LJKB 677.

revoke his offer he could have done so, but only as to the future; in the meantime he was bound to perform any order already made. The Court therefore held that he was liable for breach of contract.

(iii) Unilateral contracts

Some difficulty is experienced in the case of 'unilateral' contracts, where an act is done in return for a promise.[144] If one person promises a certain sum to another on performance by that other of a stipulated act, at what point in time is the acceptance of the offer complete? The traditional answer to this question is that the acceptance is complete only when the act has been completely performed. It therefore follows that up to this time the offeror is at liberty to revoke the offer. If, for example, a firm of breakfast food manufacturers were to offer to pay £100 to any person who consumed one hundredweight of their breakfast food within the next three months, they would be able to revoke their offer after two months had elapsed—to the detriment of those who had almost completed their part of the bargain, and with profit to themselves. Or to use a judicial example,[145] if one man offers another £100 if he will go to York, he can revoke when the other is half-way there.

In order to avoid such an inequitable result,[146] Sir Frederick Pollock argued that a distinction should be drawn between the acceptance of the offer and the performance of the stipulated act: the acceptance is complete once the offeree has unequivocally commenced performance (so that the offeror cannot effectively revoke the offer after this time), but the offeror is not bound to pay the £100 until the act has been completely performed.[147] This view has some judicial support. In *Errington v Errington*[148] where a father promised his son and daughter-in-law that a house in which they were living should belong to them as soon as they had paid off the instalments of a mortgage on the premises, and they commenced to pay them to his knowledge, Denning LJ considered that this promise could not be revoked:[149]

The father's promise was a unilateral contractual promise of the house in return for their act of paying the instalments. It could not be revoked by him once the couple entered

---

[144] See above, p 32.

[145] *Rogers v Snow* (1573) Dalison 94; *GN Ry v Witham* (1873) LR 9 CP 16, 19.

[146] It has been contended that there is no injustice, since the offeree is not bound to go to York and may give up at any time. The offeror, it is argued, ought to have a similar right to give up his side of the transaction: Wormser (1916) 26 Yale LJ 136. This reasoning is not attractive.

[147] Pollock, *Principles of Contract* (13th edn, 1950) 19; see also *Offord v Davies* (1862) 12 CBNS 748, 753; Law Revision Committee, Sixth Interim Report (Cmd 5449 1937) para 39; ALI *Restatement, Contracts (2d)* para 45; CISG art 16(2)(b).

[148] [1952] 1 KB 290.

[149] *Ibid*, 295. See also *Daulia Ltd v Four Millbank Nominees Ltd* [1978] Ch 231, 239; *Harvela Investments Ltd v Royal Trust of Canada (CI) Ltd* [1986] AC 207 (submitting bid in response to invitation to tender). For a slightly different view, see *Morrison Steamship Co Ltd v The Crown* (1924) 20 Ll L R 283, 297 where Viscount Cave LC suggested that 'when work is done and expense incurred on the faith of a conditional promise, the promisor comes under an obligation not to revoke his promise, and if he does so he may be sued for damages or on a quantum meruit'. On that view, it would appear that the claimant could not insist on completing performance and claiming the promised sum.

on performance of the act, but it would cease to bind him if they left it incomplete and unperformed.

On this view, the offeror is unable to revoke his offer; but his duty to perform his obligation is conditional upon performance of the stipulated act by the offeree.

Denning LJ's statement was approved by the Court of Appeal in *Soulsbury v Soulsbury*:[150]

The deceased former husband of the claimant promised her that she would receive £100,000 on his death if she did not enforce an order for periodical payments in her favour against him or seek any other order for ancillary relief against him. The question was whether that constituted a binding contract that could be enforced by the claimant against the estate of the deceased.

It was held that there was a binding contract. Although the discussion in the case focused on dismissing policy objections to enforcing this contract (eg that it ousted the jurisdiction of the Courts), Longmore LJ, with whom Smith LJ agreed, pointed out that the facts involved a unilateral contract. Citing Denning LJ in *Errington v Errington*, Longmore LJ said that there could be no revocation once the claimant had refrained from suing for maintenance and that this was a stronger case than *Errington* because here the claimant, on the deceased's death, had completed all possible performance of the act required for enforcement of the deceased's promise.

To overcome the objection that the consideration for the promise (ie what the offeror has bargained for) is the completion rather than the starting of the performance, one might argue that there is a subsidiary unilateral contract under which the offeror promises not to revoke the offer of the main unilateral contract once the offeree has started to perform.

It may well be, of course, that the nature of the offer itself, or the circumstances under which it was made, indicate that it was never intended to be irrevocable by the offeror.[151] But otherwise it is submitted that English law will not deny the offeree a remedy if the offer is revoked after the performance requested has been commenced.

(iv) 'Firm' offers

It will be noted that in *Offord v Davies*, discussed above, the mere fact that the defendants promised to guarantee payment for 12 months did not preclude them from revoking before that period had elapsed.[152] It is a rule of English law that a promise to keep an offer open needs consideration to make it binding. The offeree in such a case is said to 'purchase an option'; that is, the offeror, in consideration usually of a money payment, sometimes nominal,[153] makes a separate contract not to revoke the offer during a stated period. The position is similar where the offeree expressly or impliedly promises

---

[150] [2007] EWCA Civ 969, [2008] Fam 1.   [151] *Luxor (Eastbourne) Ltd v Cooper* [1941] AC 108.
[152] Above, p 56. See also *Dickinson v Dodds* (1876) 2 Ch D 463, below, p 60; *Routledge v Grant* (1828) 4 Bing 653.
[153] *Mountford v Scott* [1975] Ch 258. See further, below, pp 104–6.

to do or refrain from doing something in exchange for the offeror's promise not to revoke the offer. For example, the offeree may promise not to negotiate with anyone else for a fixed period.[154] Again, a builder tendering for a construction contract may have invited quotations for a fixed period (ie firm offers) from electricity or carpentry subcontractors and expressly or impliedly promised to use the figures contained in those offers in its tender. In these cases the offeror by its promise precludes itself from exercising its right to revoke the offer; but where it receives no consideration for keeping the offer open, it says in effect, 'You may accept within such and such a time, but this limitation is entirely for my benefit, and I make no binding promise not to revoke my offer in the meantime'. The Law Revision Committee recommended reform of the law on firm offers so that 'an agreement to keep an offer open for a definite period of time or until the occurrence of some specified event shall not be unenforceable by reason of the absence of consideration'.[155] This has not been implemented.[156]

A firm offer may, moreover, also become irrevocable where the transaction can be characterized as a unilateral contract and the offeree has relied on the offer by embarking on performance of the specified act.[157] We shall see that in its present state of development English law does not recognize a general principle based on the protection of reliance.[158] Unless a unilateral contract can be found or the action in reliance has been requested by the offeror and amounts to consideration, an offeree who relies on a firm offer will not be protected by the law of contract. Similarly there is unlikely to be a remedy in tort for revoking an offer that has been relied on[159] but, where the offeree's action in reliance consists in the rendering of services or the delivery of goods, unless the offeree can be said to have taken the risk that the offer might be withdrawn, as may well be the case in the context of tendering, the offeror may be obliged by the law of unjust enrichment to pay a reasonable sum in respect of the services or goods.[160]

(v) Revocation must be communicated

Revocation, as distinguished from lapse, if it is to be operative, must be communicated. In the case of acceptance we have seen that, in certain circumstances, it is not necessary that the acceptance should have actually come to the notice of the offeror; the posting of a letter, the doing of an act, may constitute an acceptance and make a contract. A revocation of an offer cannot, however, be communicated in the same way, by the posting of a letter of revocation, or by the sale to A of an article offered to B to purchase

---

[154] *Pitt v PHH Asset Management Ltd* [1994] 1 WLR 327, 332, below, p 70 although this is probably better explained as a unilateral contract.

[155] Sixth Interim Report (Cmd 5449, 1937) para 38. CISG art 16(2) provides that an offer indicating that it is irrevocable or one that has been relied on by the offeree cannot be revoked.

[156] An offer in a deed is an exception to the general law on firm offers: *Beesly v Hallwood Estates Ltd* [1961] Ch 105; ALI *Restatement, Contracts (2d)* para 25, Comment c.

[157] Above, pp 57–8.   [158] See below, p 129 ff (the limits of equitable estoppel).

[159] *Holman Construction Ltd v Delta Timber Co Ltd* [1972] NZLR 1081 (negligent pre-contractual statement).

[160] Above, p 45.

but must be brought to the notice of the offeree. The law on this subject was settled by *Byrne & Co v Leon Van Tienhoven & Co*:[161]

VT, writing from Cardiff on 1 October, made an offer to B in New York asking for a reply by cable. B received the letter on the 11th, and at once accepted in the manner requested. In the meantime, however, VT had, on 8 October, posted a letter revoking the offer. This letter did not reach B until the 20th.

Lindley J held, first, that a revocation was inoperative until communicated, and secondly, that the revocation of an offer was not communicated by the mere posting of a letter; therefore B's acceptance on 11 October could not be affected by the fact that VT's letter of revocation was already on its way. He pointed out the inconvenience which would result from any other conclusion:[162]

If [VT's] contention were to prevail no person who had received an offer by post and had accepted it would know his position until he had waited such a time as to be quite sure that a letter withdrawing the offer had not been posted before his acceptance of it. It appears to me that both legal principles, and practical convenience require that a person who has accepted an offer not known to him to have been revoked, shall be in a position safely to act upon the footing that the offer and acceptance constitute a contract binding on both parties.

It has been stated that a revocation must be 'brought to the mind' of the offeree[163] but it is submitted that where it arrives at its address it will be effective when it would, in the ordinary course of business, have come to the offeree's attention.[164] Where the offeree refrains from opening a letter or neglects to pay attention to the telex or fax machine[165] it should, therefore, be effective on arrival. The requirement that a revocation be communicated means that, in law, an offeror may be bound by an agreement which it does not believe itself to have made; but, again, if one of the two parties must suffer, there would seem no good reason why it should be the offeree rather than the offeror.

The case of *Dickinson v Dodds*[166] establishes that an offeree who knows that an offer has been withdrawn cannot accept it even if the communication has not come from the offeror:

On 10 June 1874, Dodds made a written offer to Dickinson to sell certain premises for £800, and stating that this offer would remain open until 9 a.m. on 12 June. On the 11th, however,

---

[161] (1880) 5 CPD 344. See also *Thomson v James* (1855) 18 D 1 (Scotland); *Stevenson v McLean* (1880) 5 QBD 346; *Henthorn v Fraser* [1892] 2 Ch 27. But in *Shuey v United States* 92 US 73 (1875), where a reward was offered in a newspaper, it was held that this offer could be 'withdrawn through the same channel by which it was made', even though the revocation did not come to the notice of the offeree.

[162] (1880) 5 CPD 344, 348.

[163] *Henthorn v Fraser* [1892] 2 Ch 27, 32 (Lord Herschell). See also *ibid*, 37 (Kay LJ) ('actual knowledge', 'actually received').

[164] *Tenax SS Co Ltd v The Brimnes (Owners)* [1975] 1 QB 929, 945, 966, 969 (revocation by telex). See also CISG arts 16(1) and 24 (revocation effective if it 'reaches' the offeree's place of business or mailing address before he has dispatched an acceptance).

[165] *Ibid*. But not where it arrives after or near the close of a working day and is not seen on that day; *ibid*, 970; *Brinkibon Ltd v Stahag Stahl und Stahlwarenhandelsgesellschaft mbH* [1983] 2 AC 34, 42.

[166] (1876) 2 Ch D 463.

he sold the property to a third person without notice to Dickinson. Dickinson had in fact been informed of the sale, though not by anyone acting under the authority of Dodds. Nevertheless before 9 a.m. on the 12th he purported to accept Dodds' offer. He then brought an action for specific performance of the contract.

The Court of Appeal held that there was no contract. James LJ, after stating that a promise to keep the offer open could not be binding, and that at any moment before a completed acceptance of the offer one party was as free as the other, went on to say:[167]

[I]n this case, *beyond all question, the plaintiff knew that Dodds was* no longer minded to sell the property to him as plainly and clearly as if Dodds had told him in so many words, 'I withdraw the offer'.

Is it then the case that information of the offeror's intention to revoke, from whatever source it reaches the offeree, is good notice of revocation? The inconvenience might be grave. Suppose a company receives an offer of a consignment of goods from a distant correspondent, with liberty to reserve an answer for some days. In the meantime an unauthorized person tells the offeree-company that the offeror has sold or promised the goods to another. What is the offeree to do? The informant may be right, and then, if the offeree accepts, the acceptance may be worthless. Or the informant may be a gossip or mischief-maker and if, because of what the offeree has been told, it refrains from accepting it may lose a bargain. The answer might be that it is open to an offeror, who has revoked an offer without direct communication to the offeree, to show that the offeree knew, *from a trustworthy source*, that the offer had been withdrawn.[168] The Court would have to decide every such case on the facts presented, but the onus would be upon the offeror to establish that the information ought reasonably to have been believed.

(b) REJECTION OF THE OFFER

An offer will be held to have terminated once it has been rejected by the offeree.[169] The rejection need not be express, provided that the offeror is justified in inferring that the offeree does not intend to accept the offer.[170] It would seem, therefore, that a rejection would not operate so as to destroy the power of acceptance until it comes to the notice of the offeror:

Suppose that A makes an offer to B by letter. Immediately on receiving the letter B writes a letter rejecting the offer. Before the rejection arrives, B changes her mind and telephones her acceptance.

---

[167] *Ibid*, 472; see also 474 (Mellish LJ).

[168] *Cartwright v Hoogstoel* (1911) 105 LT 628; ALI *Restatement, Contracts (2d)* para 42.

[169] *Hyde v Wrench* (1840) 3 Beav 334 (counter-offer, constituting a rejection, terminates the offer); *Trollope & Colls Ltd v Atomic Power Constructions Ltd* [1963] 1 WLR 333, 337 (counter-offer 'kills' the original offer). Cf *Stevenson, Jacques & Co v McLean* (1880) 5 QBD 346. See above, p 43.

[170] ALI *Restatement, Contracts (2d)* para 37. The position is similar in many European systems, see, eg, Germany, BGB para 146; Lando and Beale, *Principles of European Contract Law* (2000) 168.

There would be a contract between A and B.[171] It should not be supposed, however, that an uncommunicated rejection would always be without effect. It would, in certain circumstances, preclude the operation of the rule that a letter of acceptance is complete when posted:

Suppose that C Ltd makes an offer to D. Immediately on receiving the offer D writes a letter rejecting the offer. Before the rejection arrives, D changes his mind and posts a letter accepting the offer.

Although there is no English authority on this point, it would not seem possible for D to claim that the normal rule as to postal acceptance applied. The letter of acceptance would only create an obligation if received by the offeror before the rejection.[172]

(c) LAPSE OF THE OFFER

An offer may be considered to have lapsed owing to the passing of time.

(i) Offer for a fixed time

The parties may expressly fix a time within which an offer is to remain open. Where the offeror prescribes a specific time limit for acceptance, the offer is conditional upon acceptance within that time.[173] For example, 'This offer to be left open until Friday, 9 a.m. 12 June', allows the offeree to accept the offer, if unrevoked, at any time up to the hour named, after which the offer would lapse.[174] Similarly, an offer to supply goods of a certain sort at a certain price for a year from the present date,[175] or an offer to guarantee the payment of any bills of exchange discounted for a third party for a year from the present date,[176] are offers which may be revoked at any time, except as regards orders already given or bills already discounted, and which will, in any event, lapse at the end of a year from the date of offer.

(ii) No fixed time

In most cases, the offeror will not specify any particular time and it is left to the Court, in the event of litigation, to say what is a reasonable time within which an offer may be accepted. We have already seen that an offer is accepted when acceptance is made in a manner prescribed or indicated by the offeror.[177] If the circumstances of the offer suggest that a reply is required urgently, the offer will be considered to have lapsed if the offeree does not quickly decide whether to accept, or chooses a means

---

[171] Winfield (1939) 55 LQR 499, 513; ALI *Restatement, Contracts (2d)* para 39.

[172] ALI *Restatement, Contracts (2d)* para 39.

[173] The offeror could nevertheless waive this condition, and treat the late acceptance as valid, provided he did not thereby adversely affect the offeree.

[174] *Dickinson v Dodds* (1876) 2 Ch D 463, above, pp 60–1.   [175] *GN Ry v Witham* (1873) LR 9 CP 16.

[176] *Offord v Davies* (1862) 12 CBNS 748.   [177] Above, p 54.

of communication which will delay the notification of the acceptance.[178] In other cases, the effluxion of a reasonable time will terminate the offer. An instance of this is provided by *Ramsgate Victoria Hotel Co v Montefiore*:[179]

The defendant, M, offered by letter dated 8 June to purchase shares in the claimant company. No answer was received by him until 23 November, when he was informed that shares were allotted to him. He refused to accept them.

It was held that M's offer had lapsed by reason of the delay of the company in notifying its acceptance, and that he was not bound to accept the shares.

(iii) Express or implied condition

The terms of the offer may expressly indicate that its continuance is conditional upon the existence of circumstances other than time; and a condition of this nature may also be implied. For example, where the contract requires for its performance the existence of a particular thing, and before acceptance the thing is destroyed or substantially damaged, the offer is terminated unless the offeror has assumed the risk of such mischance.[180] Thus, in *Financings Ltd v Stimson*:[181]

S signed an 'agreement' whereby he undertook to buy a car on hire-purchase terms from F company. The agreement contained a clause which stated that it was to become binding only upon acceptance by signature on F's behalf. Before F signed, the car was stolen by thieves. It was subsequently recovered in a damaged condition.

It was clear that the 'agreement' was in fact only an offer by S since it contemplated acceptance by F. The Court of Appeal held that S's offer was only capable of acceptance if the car remained in substantially the same condition as it was when the offer was made. Since this was not the case, the offer had lapsed and there was no binding contract.

(d) EFFECT OF DEATH

In principle, an offeree cannot accept after being informed of the death of the offeror.[182] An acceptance communicated to the offeror's personal representatives will not bind them, unless the offer is one which could not have been revoked by the offeror during his lifetime.[183] Where the offeree accepts in ignorance of the offeror's death the position is less clear. One view is that the offer is terminated automatically and that knowledge

---

[178] *Quenerduaine v Cole* (1883) 32 WR 185.
[179] (1866) LR 1 Ex 109. See also *Manchester Diocesan Council for Education v Commercial & General Investments Ltd* [1970] 1 WLR 241, 247–9; *Chemco Leasing SpA v Rediffusion Ltd* [1987] 1 FTLR 201.
[180] ALI *Restatement, Contracts (2d)* para 266.
[181] [1962] 1 WLR 1184.   [182] *Coulthart v Clementson* (1870) 5 QBD 42.
[183] *Errington v Errington* [1952] 1 KB 290, 295. Even in this case, death may terminate the offer where it is dependent on the personality of the offeror.

is irrelevant.[184] The alternative, and it is submitted better, view[185] is that an offeree who does not know of the offeror's death should be entitled to accept the offer, unless the offer on its true construction indicates the contrary,[186] for example where the offer is personal to the offeror.

It would seem that an offer is determined by the death of the offeree;[187] his personal representatives could not accept the offer on behalf of the offeree's estate.

5. UNCERTAIN AND INCOMPLETE AGREEMENTS

Although the parties may have reached agreement in the sense that the requirements of offer and acceptance have been complied with, there may be no contract because the terms of the agreement are uncertain or because the agreement is qualified by reference to the need for a future agreement between them. For 'unless all the material terms of the contract are agreed there is no binding obligation. An agreement to agree in future is not a contract; nor is there a contract if a material term is neither settled nor implied by law and the document contains no machinery for ascertaining it'.[188]

The terms of a contract must provide a basis for determining the existence of a breach and for giving an appropriate remedy.[189] Nevertheless, as we shall see, although there are differences of approach in the cases, the law is generally anxious to uphold the contract wherever possible lest it should be criticized as the destroyer of bargains.[190] In addition, where uncertainty or incompleteness prevent an agreement from constituting a contract the factual situation may give rise to liability in tort, for instance for misrepresentation,[191] or in the law of unjust enrichment in respect of benefits received.[192]

(a) CERTAINTY OF TERMS

The law requires the parties to make their own contract; it will not construct a contract for them out of terms which are indefinite or unsettled. A vague or uncertain promise does not accordingly give rise to an enforceable contract. Thus:

C agreed to sell land to D. The agreement provided that the price was to be paid by instalments and that on each payment 'a proportionate part' of the land was to be conveyed. It was held

---

[184] *Dickinson v Dodds* (1876) 2 Ch D 463, 475; ALI *Restatement, Contracts (2d)* para 48.

[185] *Bradbury v Morgan* (1862) 1 H & C 249, often said to support this, was in fact a case where a contract had been concluded before death.

[186] *Harris v Fawcett* (1873) LR 8 Ch App 866, 869; *Coulthart v Clementson* (1870) 5 QBD 42, 46.

[187] *Re Cheshire Banking Co (Duff's Executor's Case)* (1886) 32 Ch D 301; *Reynolds v Atherton* (1921) 125 LT 690, 695, but see (1922) 127 LT 189, 191; *Somerville v National Coal Board* 1963 SLT 334 (Scotland).

[188] *Foley v Classique Coaches Ltd* [1934] 2 KB 1, 13 (Maugham LJ).

[189] ALI *Restatement, Contracts (2d)* para 33(2). See also Lando and Beale, *Principles of European Contract Law* (2000) 146, art 2:103.

[190] *Hillas v Arcos* (1932) 147 LT 503, 512 (Lord Tomlin).

[191] Below, pp 68 and 342–7.   [192] Below, pp 67, 71–2.

that, since the part to be conveyed on each occasion could not be identified, the agreement as a whole was uncertain and unenforceable.[193]

Similarly when a van was to be bought on the understanding that part of the price should be paid on 'hire-purchase' terms,[194] and when woollen goods were to be bought 'subject to war clause',[195] there was no contract in either case, for 'hire-purchase' terms, and 'war clauses' may take many forms, and it is for the parties, and not for the Court, to define them.

On the other hand, in many transactions, particularly those for future performance over a period, the parties may neither be able nor desire to specify all matters. A transaction which at first sight seems to leave some essential term of the bargain undetermined may, by implication, if not expressly, provide some method of determination other than a future agreement between the parties. In that event, since it is a maxim of the law that that is certain which can be made certain, there will be a good contract.[196] In every case the function of the Court is to put a fair construction on what the parties have said and done, though the task is often a difficult one. As Lord Wright stated:[197]

Business men often record the most important agreements in crude and summary fashion; modes of expression sufficient and clear to them in the course of their business may appear to those unfamiliar with the business far from complete or precise. It is accordingly the duty of the Court to construe such documents fairly and broadly, without being too astute or subtle in finding defects; but, on the contrary, the Court should seek to apply the old maxim of English law, *verba ita sunt intelligenda ut res magis valeat quam pereat*.[198]

The line between discovering the agreement of the parties and imposing an agreement on the basis of what the Court considers the parties ought to have intended can be fine. The Court must be satisfied that the parties have in fact concluded a contract, and not merely expressed willingness to contract in the future. It may have regard to what has been said and done, the context in which it was said or done, the relative importance of the unsettled matter, and whether the parties have provided machinery for settling it.

---

[193] *Bushwell Properties Ltd v Vortex Properties Ltd* [1976] 1 WLR 591. See also *Montreal Gas Co v Vasey* [1900] AC 595; *Jacques v Lloyd D George & Partners* [1968] 1 WLR 625; *Stabilad Ltd v Stephens & Carter Ltd (No 2)* [1999] 2 All ER (Comm) 651 (performance left to discretion of promisor).

[194] *G Scammell & Nephews Ltd v Ouston* [1941] AC 251.

[195] *Bishop & Baxter v Anglo-Eastern Trading Co and Industrial Ltd* [1944] KB 12; *British Electrical and Associated Industries (Cardiff) Ltd v Patley Pressings Ltd* [1953] 1 WLR 280.

[196] *Id certum est quod certum reddi potest.* See *Scammell v Dicker* [2005] EWCA Civ 405, [2005] 3 All ER 838 distinguishing *Scammell v Ouston* [1941] AC 251. See generally Fridman (1960) 76 LQR 521; Samek (1970) 47 Can Bar Rev 203.

[197] *Hillas & Co v Arcos Ltd* (1932) 147 LT 503, 514.

[198] 'Words are to be interpreted so as to give effect to the subject matter rather than to defeat it.'

If the contract contains an indefinite, but subsidiary provision, the Courts have felt at liberty to strike it out as being without significance, and to give effect to the rest of the contract without the meaningless term.[199]

(i) Previous transactions; trade custom

In *Hillas & Co v Arcos Ltd*[200] the terms were ascertained from previous transactions between the same parties and the custom of the particular trade:

In 1930, H agreed to buy from A a quantity of Russian softwood timber 'of fair specification'. The contract contained a clause giving to H an option to purchase further timber in 1931, but the option gave no particulars as to the kind or size or quality of the timber, nor of the manner of shipment. When H sought to exercise the option, A pleaded that the clause was too indeterminate and uncertain to indicate an unequivocal intention to be bound, and that it was merely an agreement to negotiate a future agreement.

The House of Lords held that, in the light of the previous dealings between the parties, there was a sufficient intention to be bound: the terms left uncertain in the option could be ascertained by reference to those contained in the original contract and from the normal practice of the timber trade.[201]

(ii) The standard of reasonableness

Alternatively, where the intention to buy and to sell is clear, incidents of the transaction may be determined by the standard of reasonableness, or by rules of law. Thus, in *Hillas v Arcos* the phrase 'of fair specification' was held to mean timber distributed over kinds, qualities, and sizes in fair proportions having regard to the season's output, a matter which, if the parties failed to agree, could be ascertained by the Court determining what was reasonable.[202] Similar principles apply to standards provided in the agreement such as 'market value'[203] 'open market value',[204] and that hire shall be 'equitably decreased'.[205] In the case of price, in transactions for the sale of goods or the supply of services the matter is now governed by statute. By section 8 of the Sale of Goods Act 1979:[206]

(1) The price in a contract of sale may be fixed by the contract, or may be left to be fixed in a manner agreed by the contract, or may be determined by the course of dealing between the parties.

---

[199] *Nicolene Ltd v Simmonds* [1953] 1 QB 543. See also *Adamastos Shipping Co Ltd v Anglo-Saxon Petroleum Co Ltd* [1959] AC 133; *Whitlock v Brew* (1968) 118 CLR 445 (Australia).

[200] (1932) 147 LT 503.

[201] On the terms implied by trade custom see further, below, pp 169–71.

[202] (1932) 147 LT 503, 512, 513, 516. See also *Mamidoil-Jetoil Greek Petroleum Co SA v Okta Crude Oil Refinery AD* [2001] 2 Lloyd's Rep 76, 91 (reasonable fees for services); *Durham Tees Valley Airport Ltd v Bmibaby Ltd* [2010] EWCA Civ 485, [2011] 1 Lloyd's Rep 68 (long-term obligation to fly two planes from an airport held to be sufficiently certain). Cf *Baird Textile Holdings Ltd v Marks & Spencer plc* [2001] EWCA Civ 274, [2002] 1 All ER (Comm) 737 (no long-term contract to be supplied with garments because of lack of certainty consequent on there being no objective criteria by which the Court could assess what would be reasonable for the purchaser to acquire either as to quantity or price).

[203] *Brown v Gould* [1972] Ch 53.   [204] *Gillatt v Sky Television Ltd* [2000] 1 All ER (Comm) 46.

[205] *Didymi Corp v Atlantic Lines and Navigation Co Ltd* [1988] 2 Lloyd's Rep 108.

[206] See also Supply of Goods and Services Act 1982, s 15(1). Cf CISG art 55 ('current trade price').

(2) Where the price is not determined as mentioned in subsection (1) above the buyer must pay *a reasonable price.*

In such cases, the Court will allow an action to recover a reasonable sum for what the goods or services are worth.[207]

It has been held that section 8(2) provides for silence as to the price, and will not apply where an agreement states that the parties will subsequently agree the price to be paid.[208]

(iii) Executed transactions

The Court will also have regard to what has been done by the parties. Where a transaction has been wholly or partially performed it will be:

difficult to submit that the contract is void for vagueness or uncertainty. Specifically, the fact that the transaction is executed makes it easier to imply a term resolving any uncertainty, or, alternatively, it may make it possible to treat a matter not finalised in negotiations as inessential.[209]

In the case of executed transactions, the basis of liability is not, however, always contractual. In some cases the objective test of intention[210] may mean that a contract comes into existence as a result of the performance and liability can be characterized as consensual.[211] In others, however, as noted in the context of 'the battle of the forms',[212] no contractual analysis is possible and, where it is held that there is liability, it is imposed by the Court in the form of an obligation in the law of unjust enrichment to pay a reasonable sum for the work done or the goods received.[213] In determining whether to give a restitutionary remedy, considerations of 'risk' and 'fault' in relation to the reason the transaction fails to come to fruition as a contract are taken into account so that a person who is held to have taken the risk of the transaction failing or to have been responsible for this will not be entitled to recompense for the services rendered.[214]

---

[207] *British Bank for Foreign Trade Ltd v Novinex* [1949] 1 KB 623; *Powell v Braun* [1954] 1 WLR 401 (executed transactions); *Hondly v M'Laine* (1834) 10 Bing 482 (executory transaction).

[208] *May & Butcher v R* [1934] 2 KB 17n; *King's Motors (Oxford) Ltd v Lax* [1970] 1 WLR 426; *Smith v Morgan* [1971] 1 WLR 803. For forceful criticism of *May & Butcher v R,* see *Fletcher Challenge Energy Ltd v Electricity Corp of New Zealand Ltd* [2002] 2 NZLR 433, 466–7.

[209] *G Percy Trentham Ltd v Archital Luxfer Ltd* [1993] 1 Lloyd's Rep 25, 27 (Steyn LJ). See also *F & G Sykes (Wessex) Ltd v Fine Fare Ltd* [1967] 1 Lloyd's Rep 53, 57–8; *Foley v Classique Coaches Ltd* [1934] 2 KB 1.

[210] Above, pp 34–5.

[211] *Foley v Classique Coaches Ltd* [1934] 2 KB 1; *Way v Latilla* [1937] 3 All ER 759. But cf *ibid,* 764–5; *RTS Flexible Systems Ltd v Molerei Alois Muller GmbH & Co KG* [2010] UKSC 14, [2010] 1 WLR 753 at [45]–[56].

[212] Above, p 45.

[213] *British Steel Corp v Cleveland Bridge and Engineering Co Ltd* [1984] 1 All ER 504, 511 in the context of goods delivered under a letter of intent, below, pp 71–2. Birks, *An Introduction to the Law of Restitution* (1985) 271–2 explains *Way v Latilla* [1937] 3 All ER 759 in this way and see *ibid,* 764–5. Cf Dietrich [2001] LS 153.

[214] *Jennings & Chapman Ltd v Woodman, Matthews & Co* [1952] 2 TLR 409; *William Lacey (Hounslow) Ltd v Davis* [1957] 1 WLR 932; *Regalian Properties plc v London Dockland Development Corp* [1995] 1 WLR 212; *Countrywide Communications Ltd v ICL Pathway* [2000] CLC 324.

(iv) Machinery for ascertainment

A contract will not fail for uncertainty even though a material term is to be agreed in future if the contract itself provides machinery for ascertaining it. So, for example, if the contract provides that the parties are to agree a price or quantities for delivery, but also contains an arbitration clause which covers a failure to agree the price or the quantities, the Courts will imply that, in default of agreement, a reasonable price is to be paid, such price to be determined by arbitration.[215] Moreover, in the case of a lease, if premises are let to a tenant for (say) a term of 10 years at a fixed rent for the first five years, but at a rent 'to be agreed' thereafter, the Court will itself determine by inquiry what is a reasonable rent for the premises should the parties fail to agree.[216] Unless the machinery is held to be an essential part of the agreement,[217] the Court will similarly intervene if, for any reason, its operation is stultified, for example, by the refusal of one of the parties to appoint a valuer or an arbitrator.[218]

(v) Agreements to negotiate and not to negotiate

The position of agreements to negotiate and agreements not to negotiate was considered by the House of Lords in *Walford v Miles*:[219]

On 17 March M agreed that, provided that W's bank confirmed that W had the necessary financial resources to purchase M's photographic processing business for £2 million, they would 'break off any negotiations with any third party and would not consider any other alternative and would not accept a better offer but would deal exclusively with W, with a view to concluding the deal as soon as possible after April 6'. M continued to keep in touch with another interested party and on 27 March withdrew from the negotiations with W. M later sold the business to the third party. W sued for breach of contract and for misrepresentation.

It was found that M had represented that they were not in negotiation with the other interested party and W were awarded tortious damages for misrepresentation.[220] The contractual claims, however, failed.

It was held that an agreement to negotiate (a 'lock-in' agreement) is like an agreement to agree and is unenforceable 'simply because it lacks the necessary certainty'.[221] Two reasons have been given in the cases for this conclusion. First, in

---

[215] *Foley v Classique Coaches Ltd* [1934] 2 KB 1; *F & G Sykes (Wessex) Ltd v Fine Fare Ltd* [1967] 1 Lloyd's Rep 53; *Vosper Thornycroft Ltd v Ministry of Defence* [1976] 1 Lloyd's Rep 58; *Queensland Electricity Generating Board v New Hope Collieries Pty Ltd* [1989] 1 Lloyd's Rep 205, 210.

[216] *Beer v Bowden* [1981] 1 WLR 522.

[217] As in *Gillatt v Sky Television Ltd* [2000] 1 All ER (Comm) 46.

[218] *Sudbrook Trading Estate Ltd v Eggleton* [1983] 1 AC 444.   [219] [1992] 2 AC 128.

[220] These amounted to £700 and were in respect of the expenses of the negotiation and the preparation of the contract documents: [1992] 2 AC 128, 135. On damages for misrepresentation, see below, pp 342–7.

[221] [1992] 2 AC 128, 138. See also *Courtney & Fairbairn Ltd v Tolaini Bros (Hotels) Ltd* [1975] 1 WLR 297; *Mallozzi v Carapelli SpA* [1976] 1 Lloyd's Rep 407. Cf *Hillas v Arcos* (1932) 147 LT 503, 515 (Lord Wright).

Walford v Miles, Lord Ackner asked how the Court is to police such an agreement and questioned whether it is possible to tell whether it has been breached:[222] 'How can a court be expected to decide whether, *subjectively*, a proper reason existed for the termination of negotiations?'. The position of parties in negotiations was stated to be adversarial and to entitle them to pursue their own interests so long as they avoided making misrepresentations and, if they so wished, to withdraw from the negotiations at any time and for any reason. It was said not to be possible to cure this uncertainty by asking whether the negotiations have been conducted 'in good faith' because a duty to negotiate in good faith 'is as unworkable in practice as it is inherently inconsistent with the position of a negotiating party'. Secondly, it has been said that 'no court could estimate the damages because no one can tell whether the negotiations would be successful or would fall through: or if successful, what the result would be'.[223]

There are, however, difficulties with those reasons and with this aspect of the decision in *Walford v Miles*.[224] First, it is unlikely to give effect to the reasonable expectations of business people which it is an important object of the law of contract to facilitate.[225] It appears to require a higher degree of certainty and less willingness to use the standard of reasonableness to resolve ambiguity than some of the cases considered above. Secondly, it is not the case that it is a fundamental attribute of a negotiation that the parties should have absolute freedom to walk away from it for any reason or no reason at all. Thirdly, the objection that it would not be possible to assess damages is also open to question. As will be seen, in other contexts in which the transaction contains a large amount of chance, it has been possible to assess damages

---

[222] [1992] 2 AC 128, 138. As Millett LJ explained in *Little v Courage* (1995) P & CR 469, 475 (and see also Andrews J in *Dany Lions Ltd v Bristol Cars Ltd* [2014] EWHC 817 (QB), [2014] 2 All ER (Comm) 403) Lord Ackner's reference to an agreement to use 'best endeavours' being different and sufficiently certain must be read as referring to best or reasonable endeavours to achieve a result other than the conclusion of a contract with the other party (as in *Jet2.com Ltd v Blackpool Airport Ltd* [2012] EWCA Civ 417, [2012] 2 All ER (Comm) 1053 where the obligation to use reasonable endeavours to promote a low-cost airline was held sufficiently certain). There is no real difference between an agreement to negotiate in good faith and an agreement to use best or reasonable endeavours *to agree*. For a decision that an obligation to use best or reasonable endeavours to negotiate is too uncertain, see, eg, *Multiplex Constructions UK Ltd v Cleveland Bridge UK Ltd* [2006] EWHC 1341 (TCC), (2007) 107 Con LR 1.

[223] *Courtney & Fairbairn Ltd v Tolaini Bros (Hotels) Ltd* [1975] 1 WLR 297, 301 (Lord Denning MR).

[224] For persuasive criticism of *Walford v Miles*, see Neill (1992) 108 LQR 405; Berg (2003) 119 LQR 357; Peel in Burrows and Peel (eds), *Contract Formation and Parties* (2010) ch 3. In *Petromec Inc v Petroleo Brasileiro SA Petrobas* [2005] EWCA Civ 891, [2006] 1 Lloyd's Rep 161 at [121] Longmore LJ, *obiter*, suggested that it would be a strong thing to declare unenforceable an express clause to negotiate in good faith. In *Emirates Trading Agency LLC v Prime Mineral Exports Pte Ltd* [2014] EWHC 2104 (Comm), [2015] 1 WLR 1145 an express dispute resolution clause in an otherwise binding contract, requiring the parties to seek to resolve a dispute in good faith and within a limited period of time prior to arbitration, was held enforceable. Note also that in *Queensland Electricity Generating Board v New Hope Collieries Pty Ltd* [1989] 1 Lloyd's Rep 205, 209–10 (PC) an obligation to make reasonable endeavours to agree was implied; and in *Re Debtors* (*Nos 4449 and 4450 of 1998*) [1999] 1 All ER (Comm) 149, 157–8 an obligation to negotiate in good faith was imposed on Lloyds as it was performing functions in the public interest.

[225] FP (1932) 48 LQR 141; Davenport (1991) 107 LQR 366; Lord Steyn (1997) 113 LQR 433.

and the Court has not held that there is no contract.[226] It is unfortunate that Lord Wright's dictum in *Hillas v Arcos*,[227] which recognized a contract to negotiate, has now been rejected by the House of Lords.

An agreement not to negotiate with any third party, a 'lock-out' agreement, has been held not to be enforceable where, as in *Walford v Miles*, it does not specify a time limit for its duration apparently on the ground that it would impose indirectly a duty to negotiate in good faith which, for the reasons given above, could not be a contract.[228] But it was accepted in *Walford v Miles* that such an agreement is sufficiently certain if it is limited to a fixed period.[229] The distinction between these two types of 'lock-out' agreement is difficult to justify. It is submitted that neither indirectly imposes a duty to negotiate in good faith, since the obligation is a negative one and that it should have been possible to resolve the uncertainty of there being no fixed period by applying the standard of a reasonable period.[230]

(b) INCOMPLETE AGREEMENT

The parties may agree on certain points, but nevertheless leave other points unresolved. The question then arises whether or not their agreement is complete. Difficulties of interpretation most frequently arise where there have been lengthy negotiations in correspondence. The parties discuss terms, approach, and recede from an agreement; proposals are made and met by the suggestion of fresh terms. Finally there is a difference, and one party asserts that a contract has been made, and the other that matters have never gone beyond the discussion of terms. Where such a correspondence appears to result, at any moment of its course, in an agreement, it is necessary to ask whether this agreement amounts to a completed agreement, or whether there are other terms of the intended contract, beyond and besides those expressed in the agreement, which are still in a state of negotiation only, and without the settlement of which the parties have no idea of concluding any contract.[231] Where, however, the correspondence shows that the parties have definitely come to terms, even though certain material points may still be left open, a subsequent revival of negotiations cannot, except with the consent of both parties, affect the contract so made.[232]

---

[226] *Allied Maples Group v Simmons & Simmons* [1995] 1 WLR 1602, 1620 and below, p 565.

[227] (1932) 147 LT 503, 515. A majority of the New South Wales Court of Appeal has rejected the view that every promise to negotiate in good faith is unenforceable: *Coal Cliff Collieries Pty Ltd v Sijehama Pty Ltd* (1991) 24 NSWLR 1, 26. In the USA the majority view gives contractual effect to an agreement to negotiate: Farnsworth (1987) 87 Colum L Rev 217, 265–7.

[228] *Walford v Miles* [1992] 2 AC 128, 140.

[229] For an example, see *Pitt v PHH Asset Management Ltd* [1994] 1 WLR 327.

[230] Neill (1992) 108 LQR 405, 413. Bingham LJ, dissenting in the Court of Appeal, was of this view: (1990) 62 P & CR 410. The agreement provided a standard in stating that the transaction was to be concluded as soon as possible after 6 April: [1990] 1 EGLR 212.

[231] *Hussey v Horne Payne* (1879) 4 App Cas 311.

[232] *Perry v Suffields Ltd* [1916] 2 Ch 187; *Mitsui Babcock Energy Ltd v John Brown Engineering Ltd* (1996) 51 Con LR 129, 167, 175, 179.

(i) Effect of reference to further agreement

The classic statement of the issues involved in cases where the agreement is couched in general terms, but reference is made to a contract in which the intentions of the parties may be more precisely stated, is to be found in the judgment of Parker J in *Von Hatzfeldt-Wildenburg v Alexander*:[233]

If the documents or letters relied on as constituting a contract contemplate the execution of a further contract between the parties, it is a question of construction whether the execution of the further contract is a condition or term of the bargain or whether it is a mere expression of the desire of the parties as to the manner in which the transaction already agreed to will in fact go through. In the former case there is no enforceable contract either because the condition is unfulfilled or because the law does not recognize a contract to enter into a contract. In the latter case there is a binding contract and the reference to the more formal document may be ignored.

(ii) Letters of intent

Difficulties frequently arise where parties in negotiations reach 'points of agreement' or have a 'memorandum of understanding' or exchange 'letters of intent' or 'letters of comfort', but nevertheless contemplate that a formal document is later to be drawn up.[234] In such situations the question whether or not a binding contract has been concluded is a matter of interpretation for the Court. While such a letter can have contractual effect where it contains an express promise as to future conduct,[235] the Court may be unwilling to imply such a promise from a statement of present fact because the language is often vague or equivocal or because the surrounding circumstances, including previous negotiations, indicate that all that is assumed is a moral responsibility.[236]

The position may be even further complicated by the fact that the parties often act on their informal agreement pending the execution of a formal contract. Where a formal contract is eventually concluded, the Court may be prepared to imply a term that, although the informal agreement is not legally binding, the formal contract is to have retrospective effect. It will, in consequence, apply to work done and services rendered before it was made.[237] Where no formal contract is concluded, work done or

---

[233] [1912] 1 Ch 284, 288.

[234] See, generally, Mouzat and Furmston [2008] CLJ 37; Furmston (2009) JCL 95; Furmston in Burrows and Peel (eds), *Contract Formation and Parties* (2010) ch 2.

[235] *Chemco Leasing SpA v Rediffusion* [1987] 1 FTLR 201 (comfort letter an offer but lapsed before acceptance). See also Staughton J's judgment quoted in *Kleinwort Benson Ltd v Malaysia Mining Corp Bdh* [1988] 1 WLR 799, 805–6.

[236] *Kleinwort Benson Ltd v Malaysia Mining Corp Bdh* [1989] 1 WLR 379, 388, 391, 393 (letter of comfort not legally binding because it expressed the present policy of the company rather than containing a promise); *Associated British Ports v Ferryways NV* [2009] EWCA Civ 189, [2009] 1 Lloyd's Rep 595 at [24] (per Maurice Kay LJ: 'I regard a letter of comfort, properly so called, as one that does not give rise to contractual liability'). Cf *Wilson Smithett & Cape (Sugar) Ltd v Bangladesh Sugar Industries Ltd* [1986] 1 Lloyd's Rep 378 (letter of intent for the supply of sugar specifying amount, price, and shipping details held to be an acceptance).

[237] *Trollope & Colls Ltd v Atomic Power Construction Ltd* [1963] 1 WLR 333. See Ball (1983) 99 LQR 572.

goods delivered under a letter of intent which is not legally binding may give rise to an obligation in the law of unjust enrichment to pay a reasonable sum for the work or the goods.[238]

(iii) Agreement 'subject to contract'

The initial agreement for the sale or lease of land is usually entered into 'subject to contract' or 'subject to formal contract'. Such an agreement gives rise to no contractual liability.[239] Thus in *Winn v Bull*:[240]

A written agreement was drawn up whereby the defendant agreed to take a lease of a house for a definite period and at a fixed rent, but 'subject to the preparation and approval of a formal contract'.

It was held there was no contract. Jessel MR explained:[241]

It comes, therefore, to this, that where you have a proposal or agreement made in writing expressed to be subject to a formal contract being prepared, it means what it says; it is subject to and is dependent upon a formal contract being prepared.

The insertion of the words 'subject to contract' renders the agreement nugatory in fact, and this is so notwithstanding that a deposit may have been paid.[242] As a normal rule, a binding contract for the sale of land will come into existence only when a formal 'exchange of contracts' contained in writing signed by or on behalf of each party[243] has taken place.[244] Up to this time either party is free to renegotiate the price, or even to withdraw entirely from the transaction and to do so because of movements in the value of property. The express use of the words 'subject to contract' has also been held to preclude a claim in the law of restitution for expenses incurred in respect of the intended contract; the use of those words was said to mean that the parties had in effect expressly agreed that there should be no legal obligation by either party to the other unless and until a formal contract had been entered into.[245] But in other cases, restitutionary

---

[238] *British Steel Corp v Cleveland Bridge & Engineering Co Ltd* [1984] 1 All ER 504. See above, p 67.

[239] See Law Com No 65, '*Subject to Contract' Agreements* (1975) and Law Com No 164, *Formalities for Contracts for Sale etc of Land* (1987) paras 1.4, 4.15.

[240] (1877) 7 Ch D 29. See also *Galliard Homes Ltd v J Jarvis & Sons plc* (1999) 71 Con LR 219, 235–6, 243.

[241] (1877) 7 Ch D 29, 32.

[242] *Coope v Ridout* [1921] 1 Ch 291; *Chillingworth v Esche* [1924] 1 Ch 97; *Eccles v Bryant and Pollock* [1948] Ch 93; *Tiverton Estates Ltd v Wearwell Ltd* [1975] Ch 146.

[243] Law of Property (Miscellaneous Provisions) Act 1989, s 2, on which see below, p 88.

[244] Cf *Alpenstow Ltd v Regalian Properties Ltd* [1985] 1 WLR 721 (exceptionally, agreement 'subject to contract' drawn up by a lawyer after five months of negotiation containing detailed and mandatory provisions of the approval, amendment, and exchange of contracts held binding). In *A-G of Hong Kong v Humphreys Estates (Queens Gardens) Ltd* [1987] 1 AC 114, 127–8, the possibility (said to be unlikely) of the parties being estopped from refusing to proceed was accepted. See also *Akiens v Saloman* (1992) 65 P & CR 364, 370.

[245] *Regalian Properties plc v London Dockland Development Corp* [1995] 1 WLR 212, 225.

remedies for the return of money paid[246] or for the value of work done under anticipated contracts concerning land have been granted.[247]

On the other hand, an agreement for the sale or lease of land will be binding if the terms of the further formal contract are in existence and known to the parties, and not merely in contemplation. For example:

An offer was made to buy land, and 'if offer accepted, to pay deposit and sign contract on the auction particulars'; this was accepted, 'subject to contract as agreed'. The acceptance clearly embodied the terms of the contract mentioned in the offer, and constituted a complete contract.[248]

Further, it has been held that if the parties use the phrase 'a provisional agreement', they then agree to be bound from the beginning, even though they stipulate that a formal document is to be drawn up later on.[249]

(iv) Contracts subject to condition

There are situations which at first sight appear to be cases of incomplete agreement, but really turn out to be cases where there is an immediate binding contract, although some of the parties' rights and obligations may be dependent upon the happening of a particular event.[250] For example, the agreement may contain such a term as 'subject to the purchaser's solicitors approving the title'. Until this approval is given, the contract need not be implemented, although neither party is free to withdraw from it unilaterally. Alternatively, the contract may be fully operative at once, but upon the happening of a particular event it is thereby discharged.[251] The insertion of such conditions produces a quite different effect from a reservation like 'subject to contract' which prevents the formation of any contract at all. They are dealt with in Chapter 5, The Terms of the Contract.[252]

6. INTENTION TO CREATE LEGAL RELATIONS

Although a separate requirement of intention to create legal relations did not exist until the nineteenth century,[253] it is now established that an agreement will not

---

[246] *Chillingworth v Esche* [1924] 1 Ch 97 (restitution of deposit).

[247] *Cobbe v Yeoman's Row Management Ltd* [2008] UKHL 55, [2008] 1 WLR 1752 (quantum meruit for value of work done in obtaining planning permission in respect of an anticipated contract/agreement 'subject to contract').

[248] *Filby v Hounsell* [1896] 2 Ch 737; *Rossiter v Miller* (1878) 3 App Cas 1124.

[249] *Branca v Cobarro* [1947] KB 854. See also *Damon Comp Nav SA v Hapag-Lloyd International SA* [1985] 1 WLR 434, 443, 452; *Global Container Lines Ltd v State Black Sea SS Co* [1999] 1 Lloyd's Rep 127, 156.

[250] *Smith v Butler* [1900] 1 QB 694; *Marten v Whale* [1917] 2 KB 480. Cf *Pym v Campbell* (1856) 6 E & B 370, below, p 151.

[251] *Head v Tattersall* (1871) LR 7 Ex 7, below, p 152.　　　　　　　　　　[252] Below, pp 150–2.

[253] Simpson (1975) 91 LQR 247, 263–5; Hedley (1985) 5 OJLS 391.

constitute a binding contract unless it is one which can reasonably be regarded as having been made in contemplation of legal consequences. A mere statement of intention made in the course of conversation will not constitute a binding promise, though acted upon by the party to whom it was made,[254] and even negotiated agreements do not necessarily give rise to legal obligations. For example, a collective agreement between employers and trade unions is conclusively presumed not to have been intended by the parties to be legally enforceable unless it is in writing and contains a provision stating that the parties intend it to be a legally enforceable contract.[255]

(a) SOCIAL ENGAGEMENTS

Sometimes it is clear from the nature of the agreement that there was no intention to enter into a binding contract. A prime example is a social engagement. This is not always because such engagements are not reducible to a money value, for they often may be. The acceptance of an invitation to dinner or to play in a cricket match,[256] of an offer to share the cost of petrol used on a journey,[257] or to take part in a golf club's competition[258] or between friends relating to musical performances by them[259] form agreements in which the promisee may incur expense in reliance on the promise. The damages resulting from breach might be ascertainable, but the Courts would hold that, if no legal consequences could reasonably have been contemplated by the parties, no action will lie.

In *Balfour v Balfour,* Atkin LJ stated:[260]

It is necessary to remember that there are agreements between parties which do not result in contracts within the meaning of that term in our law. The ordinary example is where two parties agree to take a walk together, or where there is an offer and an acceptance of hospitality. Nobody would suggest in ordinary circumstances that those agreements result in what we know as a contract.

---

[254] *Weeks v Tybald* (1605) Noy 11; *Guthing v Lynn* (1831) 2 B & Ad 232. But these cases appear to turn on uncertainty and vagueness rather than lack of intent. There is a close link between uncertainty and lack of intention to contract.

[255] Trade Union and Labour Relations (Consolidation) Act 1992, s 179, see *NCB v NUM* [1986] ICR 736. The position at common law was similar: *Ford Motor Co Ltd v AUEFW* [1969] 1 WLR 339. See Hepple [1970] CLJ 122.

[256] See Atkin LJ in *Balfour v Balfour*, below, n 260.

[257] *Coward v Motor Insurers' Bureau* [1963] 1 QB 259; *Buckpitt v Oates* [1968] 1 All ER 1145. But see now Road Traffic Act 1988, ss 145, 149.

[258] *Lens v Devonshire Club*, The Times, 4 December 1914 (Scrutton J), referred to in *Rose and Frank Co v JR Crompton & Bros Ltd* [1923] 2 KB 261, 288. Cf *Clarke v Earl of Dunraven* [1897] AC 59, above, p 34 (contract between competitors in yacht club regatta).

[259] *Hadley v Kemp* [1999] EMLR 589, 623.

[260] [1919] 2 KB 571, 578. See also *Vaughan v Vaughan* [1953] 1 QB 762, 765; *Gould v Gould* [1970] 1 QB 275.

(b) FAMILY ARRANGEMENTS

Family arrangements are another category of agreement in which there may be no intention to create legal relations. In *Balfour v Balfour*:

A husband was employed in a government post in Ceylon. He returned with his wife to England on leave, but she was unable to go back to Ceylon with him for medical reasons. He consequently promised orally to make her an allowance of £30 a month until she rejoined him. He failed to make this payment and she sued him.

The Court of Appeal held that, although it was not impossible for a husband and wife to enter into a contract for maintenance, in this case they never intended to make a bargain which could be enforced in law. While that decision has been criticized,[261] agreements between spouses and between parents and children[262] are, as we shall see, presumed not to be enforceable contracts. Thus, it has been said that a parent's promise to pay a child an allowance while at university ordinarily creates only a moral obligation.[263]

(c) DETERMINING INTENTION

The test of an intention to create legal relations is an objective one. It may be that the promisor never anticipated that the promise would give rise to any legal obligation, but if a reasonable person would consider there was an intention so to contract, then the promisor will be bound.[264] It has therefore been contended that the common law does not require any positive intention to create a legal obligation as an element of contract, and that 'a deliberate promise seriously made is enforced irrespective of the promisor's views regarding his legal liability'.[265] This view commands considerable respect, but it is submitted that there are difficulties in the way of its acceptance.

In the first place, the parties to a business transaction may deliberately state that they do not intend to enter into any legal obligation, and the Court will then treat their promises as binding in honour only. Thus in *Appleson v Littlewood Ltd*,[266] it was held that a competitor who claimed to have sent in a successful coupon in a football pool, of which one of the conditions was that the conduct of the pools and

---

[261] Below, p 77.   [262] *Jones v Padavatton* [1969] 1 WLR 328.

[263] *Fleming v Beeves* [1994] 1 NZLR 385, 389 (New Zealand).

[264] *Carlill v Carbolic Smoke Ball Co* [1893] 1 QB 256; *British Airways Board v Taylor* [1976] 1 WLR 13. See above, p 34.

[265] Williston, *Contracts*, vol 1, para 21; Hepple [1970] CLJ 122; Hedley (1985) 5 OJLS 391; ALI *Restatement, Contracts* (2d) para 21B.

[266] [1939] 1 All ER 464. See also *Rose and Frank Co v Crompton & Bros Ltd* [1925] AC 445; *Jones v Vernons' Pools* [1938] 2 All ER 626. Cf *Edwards v Skyways Ltd* [1964] 1 WLR 349 ('*ex gratia*' payment); *Home Insurance Co Ltd v Administratia Asigurarilor* [1983] 2 Lloyd's Rep 674, 677 (agreement to be 'interpreted as an honourable engagement').

everything done in connection therewith was not to be 'attended by or give rise to any legal relationship whatsoever', could have no claim which a Court would enforce. As regards a 'minister' and his church, there is no longer any presumption of there being no intention to create legal relations but the circumstances may indicate that there was no such intention.[267] Moreover, until recently the Crown and civil servants were held not to be in a contractual relationship because the Civil Service Pay and Conditions Code's statement that 'a civil servant does not have a contract of employment enforceable in the courts' meant that the Crown did not have the requisite intention to contract.[268] What was said when the agreement was made,[269] and the vagueness of the language used[270] may be held to be inconsistent with an intent to contract. Where the agreement is made in a commercial context, it has been said there that there is a presumption that there is an intention to create legal relations and that the onus on a party who asserts that an agreement was made without the intent is a heavy one.[271] However, the better view is that that presumption applies only to *express* commercial agreements (that are certain and complete) and that in respect of contracts that are wholly or partly implied from conduct, there is no such presumption so that it is for the party alleging that there is a contract to prove that intention, without the benefit of any presumption.[272] However, where a term is being introduced into a pre-existing contractual relationship, there is a strong presumption that it is intended to be legally binding.[273]

Secondly, where the agreement falls into that class of cases where legal contracts are not normally made, exemplified by social engagements or family arrangements, it will be presumed that no intent to create an enforceable contract is present, even though there may have been an exchange of mutual promises and a 'consideration' moving from the promisee.[274] On the other hand, this presumption may be rebutted

---

[267] See *Preston v President of the Methodist Conference* [2013] UKSC 29, [2013] 2 AC 163 and *President of the Methodist Conference v Parfitt* [1984] QB 368 (no intention to create legal relations). Cf *Percy v Board of National Mission of the Church of Scotland* [2005] UKHL 73, [2006] 2 AC 28; *New Testament Church of God v Stewart* [2007] EWCA Civ 1004, [2008] ICR 282 (in both of which, an intention to create legal relations was found).

[268] *R v Civil Service Appeal Board, ex p Bruce* [1988] ICR 649, [1989] ICR 171; *McLaren v Home Office* [1990] ICR 84; *R v Lord Chancellor's Department, ex p Nangle* [1991] ICR 743; Trade Union and Labour Relations (Consolidation) Act 1992, ss 62(7) and 245.

[269] *Orion Insurance Co plc v Sphere Drake Insurance plc* [1992] 1 Lloyd's Rep 239.

[270] *Vaughan v Vaughan* [1953] 1 QB 762, 765; *Kleinwort Benson Ltd v Malaysia Mining Corp Bdh* [1988] 1 WLR 799, [1989] 1 WLR 379, above, p 71.

[271] *Edwards v Skyways Ltd* [1964] 1 WLR 349, 355; *Esso Petroleum Co Ltd v Commissioners of Customs and Excise* [1976] 1 WLR 1 (World Cup coins given to purchasers of petrol held to be given under a contractual obligation—because of an intention to create legal relations—and not as a gift); *Orion Insurance Co plc v Sphere Drake Insurance plc* [1992] 1 Lloyd's Rep 239, 263, 292.

[272] *Blackpool and Fylde Aero Club v Blackpool BC* [1990] 1 WLR 1195, 1202; *Baird Textile Holdings v Marks & Spencer plc* [2001] EWCA Civ 274, [2002] 1 All ER (Comm) 737 at [62]; *Assuranceforeningen Gard Gjensidig v The International Oil Pollution Compensation Fund* [2014] EWHC 3369 (Comm) at [89]–[103].

[273] *Attrill v Dresdner Kleinwort Ltd* [2013] EWCA Civ 394, [2013] 3 All ER 607.

[274] *Balfour v Balfour* [1919] 2 KB 571, 578; *Buckpitt v Oates* [1968] 1 All ER 1145; *Jones v Padavatton* [1969] 1 WLR 328.

upon proof of the true intention of the parties, which is to be inferred from the language they use and the circumstances in which they use it. Thus in *Parker v Clark*:[275]

The defendants, an elderly couple, agreed with the claimants, who were 20 years younger, that if the latter would sell their cottage and come to live with the defendants, sharing household expenses, the male defendant would leave them a portion of his estate in his will. The claimants sold their cottage and moved in with the defendants. Difficulties developed between the two couples, and the defendants repudiated the agreement by requiring the claimants to find somewhere else to live. The claimants sought damages for breach of contract.

It was argued that the agreement amounted to no more than a family arrangement of the type considered in *Balfour v Balfour*, but Devlin J held that the circumstances indicated that the parties intended to affect their legal relations and that the defendants were therefore liable. Indeed *Balfour v Balfour* has been said to be an extreme example of this presumption,[276] and there are several cases in which it has been held that a husband's promise to his wife, from whom he was about to separate, that she could have the matrimonial home, was enforceable as a contract.[277] Similarly, in *Radmacher v Granatino*[278] a majority of the Supreme Court took the view, in *obiter dicta*, that pre-nuptial agreements are binding contracts. Again, an informal family arrangement, to share the winnings of a football pool entry,[279] was enforceable since the necessary intention was present.

Thirdly, it has been clearly established that the distinction between a warranty, which is a term of a contract, and a 'mere representation' depends upon whether the parties intended the statement to have contractual effect.[280] It would be somewhat curious if contractual intention could be dispensed with in proving the existence of a contract, but not in proving the terms of which it is necessarily composed.

The conclusion is that an intention to create legal relations is essential to the formation of a contract in English law.

---

[275] [1960] 1 WLR 286. Cf *Re Goodchild* [1997] 1 WLR 1216.

[276] *Pettitt v Pettitt* [1970] AC 777, 806, 816.

[277] *Ferris v Weaven* [1952] 2 All ER 233; *Merritt v Merritt* [1970] 1 WLR 1121; *Eves v Eves* [1975] 1 WLR 1338 (cohabitation); *Re Windle* [1975] 1 WLR 1628; *Tanner v Tanner* [1975] 1 WLR 1346 (cohabitation). Cf *Vaughan v Vaughan* [1953] 1 QB 762; *Spellman v Spellman* [1961] 1 WLR 921; *Morris v Tarrant* [1971] 2 QB 143; *Horrocks v Forray* [1976] 1 WLR 230 (cohabitation). See generally Freeman in Halson (ed), *Exploring the Boundaries of Contract* (1996) 68.

[278] [2010] UKSC 42, [2011] 1 AC 534, at [52] (Lord Mance and Baroness Hale dissented on this point). But such agreements cannot oust the jurisdiction of the courts to make orders about the parties' financial arrangements: see analogously the Matrimonial Causes Act 1973, s 34 (maintenance agreements), below p 428.

[279] *Simkins v Pays* [1955] 1 WLR 975.

[280] *Heilbut Symons & Co v Buckleton* [1913] AC 30, 51; *Oscar Chess Ltd v Williams* [1957] 1 WLR 370, 374. See below, pp 142–4.

FURTHER READING

HUDSON, 'Retractation of Letters of Acceptance' (1966) 82 LQR 169

HUDSON, 'Gibbons v Proctor Revisited' (1968) 84 LQR 503

HEPPLE, 'Intention to Create Legal Relations' [1970] CLJ 122, 127–37

MILLER, 'Felthouse v Bindley Revisited' (1972) 35 MLR 489

RAWLINGS, 'The Battle of Forms' (1979) 42 MLR 715

HEDLEY, 'Keeping Contract in its Place—*Balfour v Balfour* and the Enforceability of Informal Agreements' (1985) 5 OJLS 391

GARDNER, 'Trashing with Trollope: a Deconstruction of the Postal Rules in Contract' (1992) 12 OJLS 170

SIMPSON, 'Quackery and Contract Law: *Carlill v Carbolic Smoke Ball Company*' in *Leading Cases in the Common Law* (Oxford: Clarendon Press, 1995) 259

BERG, 'Promises to Negotiate in Good Faith' (2003) 119 LQR 357

PEEL, 'The Status of Agreements to Negotiate in Good Faith' in BURROWS and PEEL (eds), *Contract Formation and Parties* (Oxford: Oxford University Press, 2010) 37

NOLAN, 'Offer and Acceptance in the Electronic Age' in BURROWS and PEEL (eds), *Contract Formation and Parties* (Oxford: Oxford University Press, 2010) 61

3

FORM

1. FORMAL REQUIREMENTS

English law recognizes only two kinds of contract, the contract made by deed, and the simple contract. A contract made by deed derives its validity neither from the fact of the agreement nor because it is an exchange but solely from the *form* in which it is expressed.

A simple contract as a general rule need not be made in any special form, but requires the presence of consideration which, we shall see, broadly means that something must be given in exchange for a promise. The paradigm of the simple contract is thus a bargain but because the requirement of consideration can be satisfied by nominal consideration, such as a peppercorn, it has been argued that consideration is really no more than a requirement of form. In some simple contracts, statute imposes (in addition to the requirement of consideration) the necessity of some kind of form, such as writing, either as a condition of their existence or as a requisite of proving the contract.

In this chapter, we shall therefore examine (1) contracts by deed and (2) (simple) contracts for which writing is required.[1]

Historically, formal requirements played a large role in the English law of contract because the Statute of Frauds 1677 provided that many important and widely used types of contract, in particular contracts for the sale or disposition of an interest in land and, until 1954, contracts for the sale of goods of over £10 in value, were unenforceable unless supported by a note or memorandum in writing.[2]

The significance of formal requirements has now diminished, save in sales of land, guarantees, and a limited number of other types of contract, notably to protect parties (such as tenants, consumers, borrowers, and employees) who are in the weaker bargaining position. Nevertheless, although it has been stated that the advantages of requirements of formality are purely negative in nature and consist in the avoidance of various evils,[3] it should not be forgotten that formality serves a number of useful functions.[4]

---

[1] See Cartwright, *Formation and Variation of Contracts* (2014) Part II.
[2] This requirement was repealed by the Law Reform (Enforcement of Contracts) Act 1954.
[3] Jhering, *Geist des Roemischen Rechts* (4th edn, 1883) vol 2, 480–2.
[4] Law Com No 164, *Formalities for Contracts for Sale etc of Land* (1987) paras 1.4, 2.3–2.11.

First, there is an important evidential function.[5] A requirement such as writing facilitates and renders certain the existence of a transaction and its terms as well as identifying the intention of the parties. The particularly significant issues of authenticity and integrity which arise in the case of contracts made by e-mail can, for example, be addressed by a suitable formal requirement for such transactions.[6] Secondly, there is the paternalistic and cautionary function of helping to ensure that a party deliberately considers whether to contract and to prevent people accidentally binding themselves on impulse or because of improper pressure. For instance, classes of contractors considered to be weaker, such as tenants, employees, borrowers, and consumers, may be protected by requiring a written agreement and clear language.[7] In some such cases, in particular contracts with consumers, there may also be a statutory 'cooling off' period.[8] This is a paternalistic qualification to the substantive requirement of agreement rather than a formal requirement, but the requirement that notice must be given to the protected person of the right to cancel[9] is a requirement of form. The corollary of the evidential and cautionary functions is that formal requirements allow parties to bind themselves with certainty and to know to what they are binding themselves.

As against these useful functions, if the form is complex, it can be inconvenient, mysterious, and inaccessible to ordinary people. Formal requirements may also affront social and commercial attitudes to promises ('my word is my bond') since requiring, for instance, a deed or writing implies mistrust. The result of either or both of these may be that the required form is not used, whether deliberately or by accident, and thus the requirement can have the effect of reducing rather than promoting the security of transactions.

Formal requirements thus prevent impulsiveness, coercion, inadequate evidence, and manufactured evidence. They may, however, undermine security of transactions if either their complexity or social or commercial morality mean they are not observed.

2. CONTRACTS BY DEED

(a) HOW A CONTRACT BY DEED IS MADE

At common law it was often said that a contract by deed was executed by being 'signed, sealed and delivered'. The position is now largely governed by section

---

[5] *Ibid*, para 2.5. See also Holdsworth, *A History of English Law* (7th edn, 1956) 380, 388–90; Simpson, *A History of the Common Law of Contract* (1975) ch XIII.

[6] Below, p 94.

[7] *Writing*: Consumer Credit Act 1974, s 60. *Notice of specified terms*: Landlord and Tenant Act 1985, s 4; Estate Agents Act 1979, s 18; Employment Rights Act 1996, ss 1–2, 4–6.

[8] eg Consumer Credit Act 1974, ss 67–8; Consumer Contracts (Information, Cancellation and Additional Charges) Regulations 2013 (SI 2013 No 3134); Timeshare, Holiday Products, Resale and Exchange Regulations 2010 (SI 2010 No 2960).

[9] eg Consumer Credit Act 1974, s 64.

1 of the Law of Property (Miscellaneous Provisions) Act 1989.[10] To be a deed an instrument must make it 'clear on its face that it is intended to be a deed by the person making it, or as the case may be, by the parties to it (whether by describing itself as a deed or expressing itself to be executed or signed as a deed or otherwise)'.[11] The 1989 Act does not, however, lay down any prescribed manner of making it clear because to do so 'would invalidate what would otherwise be perfectly acceptable deeds merely for failure to include one vital word'.[12]

(i) Signature and attestation

In the case of deeds executed by an individual the requirement of sealing has been abolished.[13] The instrument must either be signed by the person making it in the presence of an attesting witness or, where it is not signed by that person, perhaps because of some physical incapacity, it must be signed at the direction and in the presence of that person and in the presence of two attesting witnesses.[14] In the case of a company incorporated under the Companies Acts either its common seal must be affixed or the instrument must be signed by two directors or one director and the company secretary and expressed to be executed by the company.[15] The requirement of sealing still applies to corporations sole and corporations incorporated under other statutes or by royal charter.[16] In modern times, seals are often very much a legal fiction, being merely an adhesive wafer attached to the document or even a printed circle containing the letters 'LS' (locus sigilli).[17] Even a document bearing no indication of a seal at all will suffice, provided that there is evidence (eg attestation) that it was intended to be executed as a deed.[18] Failure to have a signature witnessed and attested or, where this is still required, to have the document sealed, will not be fatal if the signatory is estopped from denying its validity because another has detrimentally relied on it.[19]

---

[10] Implementing Law Com No 163, *Deeds and Escrows* (1987). Section 1 applies to all deeds, and not just those relating to land, made on or after 31 July 1990; SI 1990 No 1175.

[11] Law of Property (Miscellaneous Provisions) Act 1989, s 1(2)(a). For the similar rule for companies, see Companies Act 2006, s 46(1).

[12] Hansard 1988/89 503 HL Deb 599 (The Lord Chancellor, Second Reading Debate).

[13] Law of Property (Miscellaneous Provisions) Act 1989, s 1(1)(b).

[14] Law of Property (Miscellaneous Provisions) Act 1989, s 1(3)(a). 'Signature' includes making one's mark: *ibid*, s 1(4).

[15] Companies Act 2006, s 44.

[16] Law of Property (Miscellaneous Provisions) Act 1989, s 1(9)–(10).

[17] *First National Securities Ltd v Jones* [1978] Ch 109.

[18] *Ibid; Commercial Credit Services v Knowles* [1978] 6 CL 64. Cf *TCB Ltd v Gray* [1986] Ch 621.

[19] *TCB Ltd v Gray* [1986] Ch 621; Law Com No 163, *Deeds and Escrows* (1987) para 2.15; *Shah v Shah* [2001] EWCA Civ 527, [2002] QB 35 (estoppel in relation to the Law of Property (Miscellaneous Provisions) Act 1989, s 1); *Briggs v Gleeds (Head Office)* [2014] EWHC 1178 (Ch), [2015] Ch 212 (distinguishing *Shah v Shah*).

(ii) Delivery

The 1989 Act preserves the requirement of 'delivery'[20] which, in this context does not signify handing over to the other party, but means an act done or word said so as to make it clear that the person making the deed regards it as binding. Thus, a deed may be 'delivered' even though it is retained in the custody of the grantor.[21]

(iii) Escrow

A deed may be delivered subject to a condition; it then does not take effect until the condition is performed. For example, on a sale of land the vendor does not normally intend the deed to operate until the purchase price has been paid and (where appropriate) the deed has been executed by the purchaser. In such a case, it is termed an *escrow*, but if the condition is fulfilled within a time which is reasonable in all the circumstances,[22] it becomes operative as from the date of its delivery.[23] At one time an escrow could not be handed to one who was a party to it, or else it took effect at once, on the ground that such handing over in fact outweighed oral conditions. But nowadays the intention of the parties prevails if they clearly mean the deed to be delivered conditionally.[24]

(b) WHEN IT IS ESSENTIAL TO CONTRACT BY DEED

Statute sometimes makes it necessary to use an instrument in the form of a deed if the transaction is to be valid. For example, the conveyance of a legal estate in land must normally be made by deed in accordance with the provisions of the Law of Property Act 1925.[25]

Common law requires a deed only in the case of a gratuitous promise, or contract in which there is no consideration for the promise made on one side and accepted on the other. Thus, one of the most common uses today of a deed (outside conveyances of land) is that of a promise to make a payment to a charity.

3. CONTRACTS FOR WHICH WRITING IS REQUIRED

(a) STATUTORY REQUIREMENTS OF WRITING

We have now dealt with the contract which is valid by reason of its form alone, and we pass to the simple contract. Although there is a popular belief that only contracts

---

[20] Law of Property (Miscellaneous Provisions) Act 1989, s 1(3)(b). Authority by a party making a deed to an agent to deliver it need not be given by deed: *ibid*, s 1(1)(c).

[21] *Xenos v Wickham* (1867) LR 2 HL 296; *Macedo v Stroud* [1922] AC 330; *Vincent v Premo Enterprises Ltd* [1969] 2 QB 609; *D'Silva v Lister House Development Ltd* [1971] Ch 17.

[22] *Beesly v Hallwood Estates Ltd* [1961] Ch 105; *Kingston v Ambrian Investment Co Ltd* [1975] 1 WLR 161. Cf *Glessing v Green* [1975] 1 WLR 863.

[23] *Alan Estates Ltd v WG Stores Ltd* [1982] Ch 511.

[24] *London Freehold and Leasehold Property Co v Lord Suffield* [1897] 2 Ch 608, 621; *Glessing v Green* [1975] 1 WLR 863.

[25] ss 52, 54.

in writing are enforceable, this belief is completely illusory and forms no part of the English common law. A simple contract depends for its validity upon the presence of consideration and is in general valid whether in writing or oral.

In certain exceptional cases, however, the law requires writing, sometimes as a condition of the validity of the contract itself, but sometimes only as evidence without which it cannot be enforced. It should be borne in mind that consideration is as necessary in these contracts as in those in which no writing is required: 'If contracts be merely written and not specialties, they are parol, and a consideration must be proved'.[26] The following are examples of contracts which must, by statute, be made in writing:

(1) The Bills of Exchange Act 1882[27] requires that a bill of exchange or promissory note and the acceptance of a bill of exchange must be in writing.

(2) A consumer credit agreement, for example a hire-purchase or loan agreement, must be in writing and be signed by the hirer or debtor and by or on behalf of the owner or creditor. It must also be made in a certain form and contain certain information including prominent notices advising the hirer or debtor of the protection and remedies, including the right to cancel, available under the Act and the annual percentage rate of charge.[28]

(3) A contract for the sale or other disposition of land must be in writing.[29] This is considered in detail below.[30]

Certain other contracts are not required by statute to be made in writing, but merely to be evidenced by writing before they can be enforced. Until 1954 the most frequent examples of such contracts were provided by those specified in the Statute of Frauds 1677, which rendered various contracts unenforceable unless they were supported by a note or memorandum in writing.[31] The object of these statutory requirements was 'for prevention of many fraudulent practices which are commonly endeavoured to be upheld by perjury and subornation of perjury'.[32] But almost from its inception, this requirement that a contract be evidenced by writing exhibited a tendency to encourage, rather than to prevent, dishonest dealing. The attempts of the judges consequently to circumvent the Statute of Frauds, and the niceties of legal learning which resulted, rendered its operation both arbitrary and artificial. By the Law Reform (Enforcement of Contracts) Act 1954,[33] most of its provisions, together with their re-enacting statutes,[34]

---

[26] *Rann v Hughes* (1778) 7 Term R 350n.   [27] ss 3(1), 17(2).

[28] Consumer Credit Act 1974, ss 60, 64; Consumer Credit (Agreements) Regulations 1983 (SI 1983 No 1553).

[29] Law of Property (Miscellaneous Provisions) Act 1989, s 2(1).   [30] Below, p 88.

[31] See also contracts of marine insurance which, by reason of the Marine Insurance Act 1906, s 22, must be evidenced by a written policy.

[32] Statutes of the Realm, vol V, p 840.

[33] See the Sixth Interim Report of the Law Revision Committee (Cmd 5449, 1937), and the First Report of the Law Reform Committee (Cmd 8809, 1953).

[34] Sale of Goods Act 1893, s 4 (writing required for contracts for the sale of goods of over £10 in value).

were repealed. But one important type of contract is still governed by the Statute of Frauds, namely a contract of guarantee. This will now be considered in detail.

(b) CONTRACTS OF GUARANTEE

Section 4 of the Statute of Frauds 1677 provides:

No action shall be brought . . . whereby to charge the defendant upon any special promise to answer for the debt, default, or miscarriage of another person . . . unless the agreement upon which such action shall be brought or some memorandum or note thereof shall be in writing, and signed by the party to be charged therewith or some other person thereunto by him lawfully authorized.

A promise 'to answer for the debt, default or miscarriage or another person' is a contract of guarantee or suretyship. It can usually be reduced to this form: 'Deal with X, and if X does not meet his obligations, I will be answerable'.

(i) Guarantee distinguished from contract of indemnity

A guarantee must be distinguished from a contract of indemnity, which is not subject to any statutory requirement of writing. In a contract of guarantee there must always be three parties in contemplation: a principal debtor (whose liability may be actual or prospective), a creditor, and a promisor (the guarantor) who promises to discharge the debtor's liability *if the debtor should fail to do so*. The guarantor's liability is therefore secondary to that of the principal debtor. In a contract of indemnity, however, the promisor is primarily liable, either alone or jointly with the principal debtor, and undertakes to discharge the liability *in any event* whether or not the principal debtor makes default.[35]

In a contract of guarantee there must, in fact, be an expectation that another person will perform the obligation which the promisor has undertaken. If the promisor is primarily liable the promise is not within the Statute of Frauds, and need not be in writing.[36] The question whether the undertaking is primary or secondary is determined, not merely from the particular words of the promise, but from the general circumstances of the transaction.[37] In the result, the borderline is often very artificial and the subject 'has raised many hair-splitting distinctions of exactly that kind which brings the law into hatred, ridicule and contempt by the public'.[38]

(ii) Nature of liability guaranteed

The liability guaranteed may arise out of tort as well as out of contract.[39] It may also be prospective at the time the promise is made, as, for example, in consideration of

---

[35] *Guild & Co v Conrad* [1894] 2 QB 885, 896; *Pitts v Jones* [2007] EWCA Civ 1301, [2008] QB 706.
[36] *Birkmyr v Darnell* (1704) 1 Salk 27, 28.   [37] *Keate v Temple* (1797) 1 B & P 158.
[38] *Yeoman Credit Ltd v Latter* [1961] 1 WLR 828, 892 (Harman LJ).
[39] *Kirkham v Marter* (1819) 2 B & Ald 613.

a future advance of money; or it may be past, provided some new consideration is given.[40] Yet there must be a principal debtor at some time; if not, there is no contract of guarantee, and the promise though not in writing will nevertheless be actionable. This is illustrated by *Lakeman v Mountstephen*:[41]

M stated that he would construct certain drains provided that L, the Chairman of a local Board of Health or the Board, would become responsible for payment. L responded, 'Go on, [M], and do the work, and I will see you paid'. The Board repudiated liability on the ground that it had never entered into any agreement with L. When sued, L pleaded that his statement was a promise to be answerable for the debt of another and, not being in writing, was unenforceable.

The House of Lords held that M was entitled to succeed. The Board had incurred no liability which could be guaranteed, and there could be no contract of guarantee unless there was a principal debtor. L's words, when properly construed, indicated that he would therefore be liable, not as guarantor, but as sole debtor, by reason of his oral promise to M.

(iii) A continuing liability

The promise must also not effect a release of the original debtor, whose liability must be a continuing liability. If there is an existing debt for which a third party is liable to the promisee, and the promisor undertakes to be answerable for it, there is no guarantee if the terms of the undertaking are such as to extinguish the original liability. If A says to B, 'Give C Ltd a receipt in full for its debt to you, and I will pay the amount', this promise is not a guarantee within the Statute of Frauds, but a substitution of one debtor for another.[42]

(iv) Exceptions

In two exceptional situations a contract of guarantee has been held to fall outside the Statute of Frauds, even though it is a promise to answer for the debt, default, or miscarriage of another.

The first is where the guarantee is merely incidental to a larger contract and not the sole object of the parties to the transaction. So in *Sutton & Co v Grey*,[43] where the defendants entered into an oral agreement with a stockbroker to introduce business to him on the terms that they were to receive half the commissions earned and to pay half the losses in the event of a client introduced by them failing to pay, it was held that their promise to answer for the debt of such a client did not fall within the Statute of Frauds. It was incidental to a wider transaction and did not have to be evidenced in writing.

Secondly, where the main purpose of the guarantor is to acquire or retain property, and the guarantee is given to relieve the property from some charge or incumbrance in

---

[40] *Board v Hoey* (1948) 65 TLR 43.
[42] *Goodman v Chase* (1818) 1 B & Ald 297.

[41] (1874) LR 7 HL 17.
[43] [1894] 1 QB 285.

favour of a third party, it is not within the Statute of Frauds. Thus if A buys goods from B which are subject to a lien in favour of C, and in order to discharge the lien A promises C to pay B's debt if B does not do so, this promise need not be evidenced in writing.[44] But the interest to be acquired or retained must be substantial and proprietary. An oral promise by a shareholder in a company to guarantee the company's debts in order to prevent an execution being levied on its assets does not come within this exception. The interest of a shareholder in the company's assets is purely personal, and is not a proprietary interest.[45]

(v) Criticism of the scope of the Statute of Frauds

These legal niceties on the scope of the requirement of writing for 'guarantees' have nothing to commend them. The administration of justice is not a game. It is a matter for regret that, if special protection is to be afforded by the law to guarantors, it is not embodied in a statute requiring the terms of all contracts of guarantee or indemnity to be set out in a written document,[46] instead of perpetuating subtle distinctions.

(vi) The form required

Until the enactment of the Law Reform (Miscellaneous) Provisions Act 1989 the form required was substantially the same for both contracts of guarantee and contracts for the disposition of an interest in land. The provisions of the Statute of Frauds 1677, which still govern guarantees, were substantially re-enacted as regards sales of land by section 40(1) of the Law of Property Act 1925. Many of the decisions under section 40(1) concerning contracts for the sale of land remain applicable to guarantees.

Under section 4 of the Statute of Frauds, a guarantee does not have to be signed by both parties, but only by the party to be charged or that person's agent.[47] The signature need not be an actual subscription of the party's name as it may be a mark; nor need it be in writing as it may be printed or stamped; nor need it be placed at the end of the document as it may be at the beginning or in the middle.[48]

The parties and the subject-matter of the contract must appear in the note or memorandum. Where the parties are not named they must be so described as to be identified with ease and certainty.[49] All the material terms of the guarantee must be accurately set out in the memorandum, but by section 3 of the Mercantile Law Amendment Act 1856, the consideration need not be stated.

---

[44] *Fitzgerald v Dressler* (1859) 7 CBNS 374.

[45] *Harburg India Rubber Comb Co v Martin* [1902] 1 KB 778.

[46] As in the case of certain contracts of guarantee and indemnity given in relation to regulated consumer credit agreements: Consumer Credit Act 1974, s 105(1).

[47] Above, p 84.

[48] *Leeman v Stocks* [1951] Ch 941. See also *Walker v Copp Clark Publishing Co Ltd* (1962) 33 DLR (2d) 338, 344 (Canada).

[49] *Rossiter v Miller* (1878) 3 App Cas 1124. Cf *Potter v Duffield* (1874) LR 18 Eq 4.

The note or memorandum of a guarantee may consist of various letters and papers, but they must be connected and complete.[50] A sequence of negotiating emails may also satisfy the requirements of writing and signature under the 1677 Act.[51]

(vii) The effect of non-compliance

The effect of a failure to comply with the provisions of the Statute of Frauds is simply that the contract is not void, or voidable, but it cannot be enforced against a party who has not signed a note or memorandum because it is incapable of proof.[52] No action can be brought until the omission is made good. But, provided the note or memorandum acknowledges the existence of the contract,[53] and is signed by the party to be charged or his agent,[54] it may be made at any time before the commencement of the action,[55] and it does not matter that it was never intended to serve as a note or memorandum but was prepared for some entirely different purpose.[56]

The law on claims for restitution of money paid under unenforceable contracts is unclear. Presumably money can be recovered if the payor can establish that there has been a total failure of consideration.[57] But whether the standard ground for restitution of mistake of law (in a situation where the payor can establish that it paid the money mistakenly believing that it could enforce the contract against the payee) applies to money paid under an unenforceable, as opposed to a void, contract is open to debate.[58]

(viii) No evasion by estoppel

It has been held that estoppel, founded on the guarantor's promise and without any additional encouragement or assurance, cannot be invoked as a means of avoiding

---

[50] *Stokes v Whicher* [1920] 1 Ch 411, 418; *Elias v George Saheley & Co (Barbados) Ltd* [1983] 1 AC 646. Cf *Timmins v Moreland Street Property Ltd* [1958] Ch 110; *Moat Financial Services v Wilkinson* [2005] EWCA Civ 1253.

[51] *Golden Ocean Group Ltd v Salgaocar Mining Industries PVT Ltd* [2012] EWCA Civ 265, [2012] 1 WLR 3674.

[52] *Leroux v Brown* (1852) 12 CB 801; *Maddison v Alderson* (1883) 8 App Cas 467, 474.

[53] *Buxton v Rust* (1872) LR 7 Ex 279 (notwithstanding announcement of intention to repudiate contract). See also *Reuss v Picksley* (1866) LR 1 Ex 342; *Parker v Clark* [1960] 1 WLR 286 (written offer containing all material terms suffices though contract concluded by subsequent oral acceptance). Cf *Thirkell v Cambi* [1919] 2 KB 590 (writing denying agreement or a material term insufficient); *Tiverton Estates Ltd v Wearwell Ltd* [1975] Ch 146 (agreement 'subject to contract' insufficient).

[54] *Elpis Maritime Co Ltd v Marti Chartering Co Inc* [1992] 1 AC 21, 28.

[55] *Re Hoyle* [1893] 1 Ch 84; *Elpis Maritime Co Ltd v Marti Chartering Co Inc* [1992] 1 AC 21.

[56] *Jones v Victoria Dock Co* (1877) 2 QBD 314 (entry in company's minute book); *Phillips v Butler* [1945] Ch 358 (receipt for deposit).

[57] Cf *Thomas v Brown* (1876) 1 QBD 714; *Monnickendam v Leanse* (1923) 39 TLR 445.

[58] In the leading case on mistake of law, *Kleinwort Benson Ltd v Lincoln CC* [1999] 2 AC 349, the contract in question was void not unenforceable. For a prior case suggesting that money cannot be recovered under an unenforceable contract, see *Boddington v Lawton* [1994] ICR 478 (Nicholls LJ). See further Burrows, *A Restatement of the English Law of Unjust Enrichment* (2012) s 3(6) and pp 32–5.

section 4 of the Statute of Frauds. In *Actionstrength Ltd v International Glass Engineering SpA:*[59]

An employer in a building project was alleged to have orally promised a sub-contractor to guarantee payments owing to the sub-contractor by the head-contractor in return for the sub-contractor not withdrawing its labour. When the sub-contractor sought to enforce the guarantee, the employer argued that it was unenforceable under section 4 of the Statute of Frauds because it was not supported by a written note or memorandum. In answer to this, the sub-contractor sought to rely on estoppel constituted by its reliance on the oral promise.

The House of Lords held that estoppel could not here succeed because to allow it to do so would entirely undermine section 4. It would contradict section 4 for relied-upon oral guarantees to be routinely enforceable by means of estoppel.

(c) CONTRACTS FOR THE SALE OR OTHER DISPOSITION OF LAND

(i) Scope of the 1989 Act

The most important class of contracts subject to requirements of form are contracts relating to land. The Law Commission considered and rejected the abolition of all formal requirements for such contracts, primarily because of the need for certainty, but also for protective, paternalistic reasons; time to reflect and, if necessary to seek legal advice 'is especially important in the case of contracts dealing with land because they often involve acceptance of a complexity of rights and duties'.[60] Indeed the Commission's recommendations, substantially enacted by the Law of Property (Miscellaneous Provisions) Act 1989 (the '1989 Act'), are in important respects more rigorous than what had hitherto been required.[61] By section 2(1) of the 1989 Act, contracts for the sale or other disposition of an interest in land:

can only be made in writing and only by incorporating all the terms which the parties have expressly agreed in one document or, where contracts are exchanged, in each.

The section applies to a 'disposition'[62] of an interest in land, and 'interest in land' is defined as 'any estate, interest or charge in or over land'.[63] Thus, the section applies to a lease, a mortgage, a release, and a disclaimer. It applies where neither party has any proprietary interest in the relevant property.[64] Contracts for the grant of a lease for a

---

[59] [2003] UKHL 17, [2003] 2 AC 541. Cf n 19, above (estoppel in relation to the Law of Property (Miscellaneous Provisions) Act 1989, s 1); pp 92–3 below (estoppel in relation to the Law of Property (Miscellaneous Provisions) Act 1989, s 2).

[60] Law Com No 164, *Formalities for the Sale etc of Land* (1987) paras 2.7–2.9. For other advantages of formality, see above, pp 79–80.

[61] Contracts made before the 1989 Act came into force on 27 September 1989 had to comply with Law of Property Act 1925, s 40(1) which substantially re-enacted the relevant portion of the Statute of Frauds, s 4. The principles were therefore substantially the same as those for guarantees.

[62] It has the same meaning as in the Law of Property Act 1925: Law of Property (Miscellaneous Provisions) Act 1989, s 2(6).

[63] Law of Property (Miscellaneous Provisions) Act 1989, s 2(6), as amended.

[64] *Singh v Beggs* (1995) 71 P & CR 120.

period not exceeding three years,[65] those made in the course of a public auction, and those regulated under the Financial Services and Markets Act 2000 (for instance unit trusts investing in land) are excluded.[66]

An example of the increased rigour is provided by the position of equitable mortgages by deposit of title deeds. These were previously valid without any writing, but have now been held to be subject to section 2 of the 1989 Act and void if they do not comply with it, because the basis of such equitable mortgage is contract.[67] An option granted by the vendor of land is also a 'contract' within section 2[68] but the subsequent exercise of that option is a unilateral act and not within the section: 'It would destroy the very purpose of the option if the purchaser had to obtain the vendor's countersignature to the notice by which it was exercised'.[69] A 'lock-out' agreement, where the owner of property agrees with a prospective purchaser not to consider any other offers for property for a fixed period, is, however, not subject to section 2 because its negative nature—the vendor cannot sell to a third party but is not committed to a sale to the prospective purchaser—means that there is no disposition of an interest in land.[70] Again, contracts which are preliminary to the acquisition of such an interest, or such as deal with a remote and inappreciable interest, would appear to be outside the section.[71]

In one respect the 1989 Act probably requires a greater degree of formality than the Law Commission recommended. It appears that it is no longer possible to have an enforceable contract by written offer and acceptance in correspondence; there must either be a single document incorporating all the terms agreed and signed by the parties or each party must sign a document incorporating the terms in the expectation that the other has also executed or will execute a corresponding document incorporating the same terms.[72]

Separate supplementary or collateral agreements to contracts relating to land are not within section 2. For instance, in the case of a contract to grant a lease, the agreement by the prospective tenant to carry out certain work on the premises in

---

[65] Contracts to grant leases not exceeding three years need no formality (Law of Property (Miscellaneous Provisions) Act 1989, s 2(5)) because the grant of such a lease itself needs no formality if it takes effect in possession, but contracts to assign such leases are subject to section 2: see Law Com No 164 (1987) para 4.10.

[66] Law of Property (Miscellaneous Provisions) Act 1989, s 2(5)(b), (c), as amended. See Law Com No 164, paras 4.11–4.12.

[67] *United Bank of Kuwait v Sahib* [1997] Ch 107, rejecting the argument that such deposits are equitable charges rather than agreements to mortgage. But cf *Target Holdings Ltd v Priestley* (1999) 79 P & CR 305 (writing not needed for agreement which disposed of a mortgage).

[68] *Spiro v Glencrown Properties Ltd* [1991] Ch 537; Law Com No 164, para 4.3.

[69] *Ibid*, 541 (Hoffmann J). See also *Trustees of the Chippenham Golf Club v North Wiltshire DC* (1991) 64 P & CR 527, 530.

[70] *Pitt v PHH Asset Management Ltd* [1994] 1 WLR 327, above, p 70.

[71] eg *Angel v Duke* (1875) LR 10 QB 174 (agreement to repair house for prospective tenant); *Bligh v Brent* (1836) 2 Y & C 268; *Humble v Mitchell* (1839) 11 A & E 205 (agreement to transfer shares in company possessed of land). Cf *Driver v Broad* [1893] 1 QB 744 (contract to sell debentures of company possessed of land is subject to the statute). These decisions concerned the Statute of Frauds.

[72] *Commission for New Towns v Cooper (Great Britain) Ltd* [1995] Ch 259; *Firstpost Homes Ltd v Johnson* [1995] 1 WLR 1567. NB clause 1(1) of the Draft Bill attached to the Report differs from s 2 and see Law Com No 164, para 4.15. But cf *Hooper v Sherman*, 30 November 1994 (CA), which did not refer to the Act's difference from the Law Commission's Draft Bill and relied on para 4.15.

exchange for payment has been held to be outside it, as long as the non-land elements are independent of the land contract.[73] The line between the contract relating to land and the supplementary or collateral one is, however, not always easy to draw particularly where, as commonly occurs, the contract has been duly signed and is awaiting exchange but a further term is orally agreed immediately prior to exchange. In *Record v Bell*, for instance:[74]

The vendor of property had not received a copy of the entries from the Land Registry by the day before the contract, which had been drawn up, was to be exchanged. He agreed with the purchaser, who was concerned about undisclosed entries, to warrant his title if the purchaser exchanged contracts and this oral agreement was confirmed by letters. Contracts were exchanged and the title was as warranted but the purchaser, whose financial position had deteriorated, refused to complete and relied *inter alia* on non-compliance with section 2 of the 1989 Act, since all the terms were not in either the contracts exchanged or the exchange of letters.

Although the purchaser seemed to be thinking in terms of amending the main contract rather than a separate contract, the agreement was held to be a collateral contract and outside the section:

It would be unfortunate if common transactions of this nature should nevertheless cause the contracts to be avoided. It may, of course, lead to a greater use of the concept of collateral warranties than has hitherto been necessary.[75]

(ii) The form required

Under section 2(1) of the 1989 Act, contracts for the disposition of an interest in land must now be made in writing and not merely evidenced in writing. Furthermore, section 2(3) of the 1989 Act requires all the parties to a contract for the sale or disposition of an interest in land or their agents[76] to sign the document incorporating the terms. The parties must all be identified by their signature and all the express terms must be incorporated in the document.[77] Section 2 does not require the inclusion of implied terms, such as a landlord's covenant of quiet enjoyment,[78] and, if the parties

---

[73] *Tootal Clothing Ltd v Guinea Properties Ltd* (1991) 64 P & CR 452, 455–6 (Scott LJ); cf *Keay v Morris Homes (West Midlands) Ltd* [2012] EWCA Civ 900, [2012] 1 WLR 2855 at [46]–[48]. See also *Record v Bell* [1991] 1 WLR 853; *North Eastern Properties Ltd v Coleman* [2010] EWCA Civ 277, [2010] 1 WLR 2715. For boundary agreements, see *Neilson v Poole* (1969) 20 P & CR 909; *Joyce v Rigolli* [2004] EWCA Civ 79, [2004] 1 P & CR DG22.

[74] [1991] 1 WLR 853; Smith (1992) 108 LQR 217; Harpum [1991] CLJ 399. Cf *McCausland v Duncan Lawrie Ltd* [1997] 1 WLR 38 (a variation of material term had to comply with s 2).

[75] [1991] 1 WLR 853, 862. This was anticipated by the Law Commission, Law Com No 164, para 5.7. On collateral warranties, see below, p 145.

[76] In *Rabiu v Marlbray Ltd* [2013] EWHC 3272 (Ch) one of the contracts was void as against one of the alleged parties because there had been no authority to sign on behalf of that party (and no ratification). For the position where the contract is made by an agent on behalf of an unnamed or undisclosed principal, see below, p 726.

[77] *Francis v F Berndes Ltd* [2011] EWHC 3377 (Ch), [2012] 1 All ER (Comm) 735; *Rabiu v Marlbray Ltd* [2013] EWHC 3272 (Ch).

[78] *Markham v Paget* [1908] 1 Ch 697.

have reached agreement but fail to record all the terms in writing or record one or more of them wrongly, the Court may order the written document to be rectified.[79] Where the written agreement is so rectified, the order does not necessarily have retrospective effect; 'the contract shall come into being . . . at such time as may be specified in the order'.[80] Where contracts are exchanged each document must contain the express terms and be signed by the parties.[81] The incorporation of the express terms in the document can occur either by their being set out or by reference to some other document or documents. Formerly, implied reference in the signed document sufficed[82] but it may well be that express reference is required under the 1989 Act.[83] Where the document has not been incorporated, it may, as we have seen, nevertheless be effective if it is a separate supplementary or collateral agreement.

(iii) The effect of non-compliance

The fundamental change effected by the 1989 Act was that, whereas the form required under the earlier legislation was merely evidentiary and did not go to the *existence* of the contract, the form required by section 2 of the 1989 Act does. That is, the failure to comply with the requirements as to form renders the contract void (ie a nullity) rather than unenforceable.[84] This follows from the wording in section 2(1) that the contract for the disposition of an interest in land 'can only be made in writing and only by incorporating all the [express] terms'.

Thus, whereas a guarantee may be enforceable by having a note or memorandum of the agreement, which could be oral, signed at a later date, an oral agreement subject to section 2 of the 1989 Act cannot be subsequently validated in this way. The Law Commission stated that a regime, such as those under the Statute of Frauds 1677 and the Law of Property Act 1925, section 40(1), which 'allows oral contracts to be binding but unenforceable and which may later become enforceable, but sometimes only against one party, is indefensibly confusing'.[85]

At the heart of the Law Commission's recommendations was the view that the equitable doctrine of part performance should 'no longer have a role to play in contracts concerning land'.[86] Under this doctrine, the Courts, in certain cases, allowed an unenforceable oral contract concerning land to be proved by oral evidence, when the party seeking to enforce the contract had done acts in performance of its obligations under it, provided that the performance was referable to some contract,[87] the acts

---

[79] On rectification see below, pp 282–7. But rectification must not be used to undermine the 1989 Act: *Francis v F Berndes Ltd* [2011] EWHC 3377 (Ch), [2012] 1 All ER (Comm) 735.

[80] Law of Property (Miscellaneous Provisions) Act 1989, s 2(4). See Law Com No 164, para 5.6.

[81] 1989 Act, s 2(1), above, p 88.

[82] Law of Property Act 1925, s 40(1); *Timmins v Moreland Street Property Ltd* [1958] Ch 110.

[83] *Record v Bell* [1991] 1 WLR 853, 859–60. See Cartwright, *Formation and Variation of Contracts* (2014) para 5-21.

[84] *United Bank of Kuwait v Sahib* [1997] Ch 107, 122, 136; Law Com No 164, para 6.4.

[85] Law Com No 164, para 4.2.   [86] *Ibid*, para 4.13.

[87] *Rawlinson v Ames* [1925] Ch 96; *Steadman v Steadman* [1976] AC 536 (mere payment of a sum of money could amount to a sufficient act of part performance, but differing views were expressed as to whether the acts performed must be referable to some contract *concerning land*: [1976] AC 536, 542, 547, 554, 562,

were performed by the person seeking to enforce the contract,[88] and the contract was one which, if properly evidenced, would have been specifically enforceable.[89] This requirement meant the doctrine had no application to contracts of guarantee which equity would not specifically enforce.

Under the new law, although the doctrine of part performance can no longer apply as such, the Commission considered that the parties to an agreement that does not comply with the statutory requirements would not simply be left without a remedy.[90] The use of collateral contracts and the remedy of rectification have been mentioned above.[91] It should also be noted that where the void contract has been performed, for example by the execution of a valid lease or the completion of a conveyance, a property right will have been created and the parties no longer need to rely on the void contract.[92]

But the primary tool the Law Commission anticipated would be used, instead of 'part performance', to enable justice to be achieved between the particular parties is the equitable doctrine of proprietary estoppel. Furthermore, although not mentioned by the Law Commission in its Report, its draft Bill excluded from the formalities required by the Act 'implied, resulting and constructive trusts'. This exclusion (which is also found in relation to trusts of land)[93] is embodied in section 2(5) of the 1989 Act.

(iv) Proprietary estoppel and constructive trusts

Under the doctrine of proprietary estoppel, a party to a transaction who detrimentally relies on the belief (encouraged or acquiesced in by the other party) that he has or will acquire rights in the property of the other will be protected by equity.[94] Thus, the Law Commission pointed to a case in which acquiescence in improvements to a property was held to justify the conveyance of the fee simple[95] and another in which non-contractual assurances that a housekeeper could remain in a house were protected by equitable relief.[96]

Closely akin to proprietary estoppel is a constructive trust based on a common understanding or arrangement relied on by a claimant.[97] Given the explicit exclusion of constructive trusts in section 2(5) of the 1989 Act, it is not surprising that the Courts have sometimes based their decision to give effect to the informal creation of an interest in land by finding a constructive trust rather than by invoking proprietary

---

568–70, on which see *Re Gonin* [1979] Ch 16; *Sutton v Sutton* [1984] Ch 184). Cf *Maddison v Alderson* (1883) 8 App Cas 467.

[88] *Caton v Caton* (1865) LR 1 Ch App 137, 148, aff'd (1867) LR 2 HL 167.
[89] *Britain v Rossiter* (1882) 11 QBD 123; *McManus v Cooke* (1887) 35 Ch D 681, 697.
[90] Law Com No 164, paras 5.1–5.2.   [91] Above, nn 75, 79.
[92] The completion of the contract will give proprietary effect to the transaction, but does not render (non-land) terms of the void contract enforceable: *Keay v Morris Homes (West Midlands) Ltd* [2012] EWCA Civ 900, [2012] 1 WLR 2855 at [46]–[48], rejecting a contrary interpretation of *Tootal Clothing Ltd v Guinea Properties Ltd* (1991) 64 P & CR 452.
[93] Law of Property Act 1925, s 53(2).   [94] Below, pp 133–4.
[95] *Pascoe v Turner* [1979] 1 WLR 431.   [96] *Greasley v Cooke* [1980] 1 WLR 1306.
[97] *Yaxley v Gotts* [2000] Ch 162.

estoppel.[98] But although the view has been expressed that proprietary estoppel, as opposed to a constructive trust, may unacceptably subvert the policy of section 2,[99] the better view, in line with the Law Commission's intentions, is that, even where there is no finding of a constructive trust, proprietary estoppel can be applied to avoid the formal requirements of section 2.[100]

It is apparent that both proprietary estoppel and constructive trusts may provide what in many cases was hitherto provided by the doctrine of part performance: a remedy in a situation in which a party has acted on the void contract. Indeed, there are significant overlaps. Proprietary estoppel, constructive trusts, and part performance can be seen as manifestations of the equitable principle that a person may not rely on strict legal rights where to do so is unconscionable.[101] It has been suggested[102] that the uncertainties of the Statute of Frauds and section 40(1) of the Law of Property Act 1925 stemmed from the tendency of the judges to prevent technical and unmeritorious circumvention of obligations by relying on noncompliance with the statutory requirements. The indications are of a similar approach to the 1989 Act with its new uncertainties. The Law Commission's recognition that it would be necessary to rely on estoppel and collateral contracts 'to do justice between parties in individual otherwise hard cases',[103] in which the strict application of the statutory requirement would result in injustice, accepted this substantial qualification to its stated aim of increasing certainty.

(v) Restitution of unjust enrichment

The parties to an agreement that does not comply with section 2 may also be entitled to a restitutionary remedy. In principle a purchaser of land who has paid a deposit to the vendor under such an agreement, that is, a void contract, may recover it either for total failure of consideration[104] (except where the purchaser has received part of the benefit bargained for in the contract, for example by entering into possession)[105] or for mistake of law.[106]

---

[98] *Ibid*; *Kinane v Mackie-Conteh* [2005] EWCA Civ 45, [2005] 2 P & CR DG3; *Herbert v Doyle* [2010] EWCA Civ 1095, [2011] 1 EGLR 119.

[99] *Godden v Merthyr Tydfil Housing* Association (1997) 74 P & CR D1 (Simon Brown LJ); *Kinane v Mackie-Conteh* [2005] EWCA Civ 45 (Neuberger LJ, who relied, by analogy, on the guarantee case of *Actionstrength Ltd v International Glass Engineering SpA* [2003] UKHL 17, [2003] 2 AC 541; see above p 88); *Cobbe v Yeoman's Row Management Ltd* [2008] UKHL 55, [2008] 1 WLR 1952 at [29] (Lord Scott); *Thorner v Major* [2009] UKHL 18, [2009] 1 WLR 776 at [96] (Lord Neuberger).

[100] *Kinane v Mackie-Conteh* [2005] EWCA Civ 45 (Arden LJ).

[101] *Yaxley v Gotts* [2000] Ch 162, 176–7, 180, 181, 188, 193; *Gillett v Holt* [2001] Ch 210, 225.

[102] Above, p 86.   [103] Law Com No 164, para 5.7. See also *ibid*, paras 5.2, 5.4, 5.8.

[104] See *Rover International Ltd v Cannon Film Sales Ltd (No 3)* [1989] 1 WLR 912, 925, 938; *Westdeutsche Landesbank Girozentrale v Islington LBC* [1996] AC 669. Cf *Sharma v Simposh Ltd* [2011] EWCA Civ 1383, [2012] 1 P & CR 12.

[105] *Linz v Electric Wire Co of Palestine* [1948] AC 371, 377. On what count as such benefits, see below, p 621. Note that the requirement that the failure of consideration be *total* has been put into question, see below, p 623.

[106] *Kleinwort Benson Ltd v Lincoln CC* [1999] 2 AC 349 (mistake of law).

Where services are rendered under an agreement concerning land which does not comply with the requirements of section 2 in the belief that there was a valid contract, the party conferring the services may be able to recover their reasonable value.[107] Thus, for example, restitution should be awarded in respect of alterations to property effected by a lessor or vendor at the request of prospective tenants or purchasers in the belief that there was a valid contract.[108] In principle, restitution should also be awarded in respect of services rendered by the prospective purchaser or lessee, for example improvements to the property and other services rendered at the request of or with the acceptance of the owner of property. As this would be limited to the executed part of the transaction, it would not seem to undermine the policy of section 2, just as restitution in respect of services rendered under contracts unenforceable for non-compliance with the Statute of Frauds and similar provisions has not been held to undermine the policy of those provisions.[109]

(d) ELECTRONIC CONTRACTS

Questions arise in relation to whether the formal requirements of, for example, 'writing' or a 'signature' are satisfied where contracts are made electronically.

It would appear that where contracts are made by e-mail or by trading on a website, any requirement of writing will normally be satisfied.[110] Provided it satisfies the standard common law test of authenticity,[111] it would also appear that the requirement of a signature can be satisfied by, for example, a digital signature[112] or by typing a name into an electronic document.[113]

The EC Directive on Electronic Commerce requires member states to ensure that their legal systems allow contracts to be concluded by electronic means and that such contracts are not deprived of legal effectiveness on account of their being made by electronic means.[114] There are exceptions to this, in particular contracts creating or transferring rights in real estate (except for rental rights), and contracts of guarantee

---

[107] *Rover International Ltd v Cannon Film Sales Ltd (No 3)* [1989] 1 WLR 912, 926–8; *Cobbe v Yeoman's Row Management Ltd* [2008] UKHL 55, [2008] 1 WLR 1752.

[108] By analogy with *Brewer Street Investments Ltd v Barclays Woollen Co Ltd* [1954] 1 QB 428, above, pp 67, 71–2 (anticipated contract which failed to materialize).

[109] *Deglman v Guaranty Trust Co of Canada* [1954] 3 DLR 785 (Canada); *Pavey & Matthews Pty Ltd v Paul* (1986–87) 162 CLR 221 (Australia).

[110] *Pereira Fernandes SA v Mehta* [2006] EWHC 813 (Ch), [2006] 1 WLR 1543; *Golden Ocean Group Ltd v Salgaocar Mining Industries PVT Ltd* [2012] EWCA Civ 265, [2012] 1 WLR 3674.

[111] Under the Electronic Communications Act 2000, s 7, an 'electronic signature' is admissible in evidence. But that in itself does not mean that it is effective as a signature.

[112] See eg the Judicial Studies Board's Digital Signature Guidelines (2000) on public or dual-key cryptography as a method of authenticating electronic communications.

[113] *Pereira Fernandes SA v Mehta* [2006] EWHC 813 (Ch), [2006] 1 WLR 1543 (the actual decision in this case was that the automatic insertion of the name of the person from whom an e-mail has been sent does not constitute a signature); *Golden Ocean Group Ltd v Salgaocar Mining Industries PVT Ltd* [2012] EWCA Civ 265, [2012] 1 WLR 3674.

[114] EC Directive 2000/31, OJ L178/1 17 July 2000.

granted by persons acting outside their trade or business. The Law Commission advised the Government that, with the exception of marine insurance, it would not be necessary to amend statutory requirements of form to enable the use of most current forms of electronic communications in commercial transactions.[115] In line with this, relatively little use has been made of section 8 of the Electronic Communications Act 2000 which, inter alia, empowers the appropriate Minister to modify any enactment for the purpose of authorizing or facilitating the use of electronic communications for the doing of anything which is required to be evidenced in writing or signed or delivered as a deed or witnessed.[116]

---

[115] Law Commission's Advice to Government *Electronic Commerce: Formal Requirements in Commercial Transactions* (December 2001).

[116] s 8(1).

4

CONSIDERATION AND PROMISSORY ESTOPPEL

1. CONSIDERATION

(a) CONSIDERATION DEFINED

Consideration is required in all contracts not made by deed. A promise is not accordingly of itself enforceable in English law. Consideration is the doctrine designed to establish which promises should be legally enforceable.[1] What, then, is it? In *Currie v Misa*[2] Lush J stated:

A valuable consideration, in the sense of the law, may consist in some right, interest, profit, or benefit accruing to the one party, or some forbearance, detriment, loss, or responsibility given, suffered, or undertaken by the other.

This brings out the idea of reciprocity as the distinguishing mark; it is the gratuitous promise that is unenforceable in English law.

We shall, however, see that consideration reflects a variety of policies and serves a number of functions.[3] First, enforceability may depend on the content of the promise or the circumstances in which it was made.[4] Thus, promises to do what one is already obliged to do, particularly where a contract has been renegotiated, have, as we shall see, caused difficulties. Secondly, consideration has been said to identify which promises the parties intend to be legally enforceable. They may so intend either where there is a substantive bargain, or where they have put the transaction into the form of an exchange, for instance by providing that the promisee should pay a nominal price to the promisor. It thus serves an evidential and formal function.[5] Thirdly, consideration is sometimes seen as a requirement which ensures that a

---

[1] See Atiyah, *Essays on Contract* (1986) ch 8; Treitel (1976) 50 ALJ 439; Cartwright, *Formation and Variation of Contracts* (2014) Part III.

[2] (1875) LR 10 Ex 153, 162. See also *Thomas v Thomas* (1842) 2 QB 851, 859; *Bolton v Madden* (1873) LR 9 QB 55, 56.

[3] Llewellyn (1941) 41 Col L Rev 777, 778, 863; Simpson (1975) 9 LQR 247, 263.

[4] Below, pp 109–16, 380–2 (pre-existing duties and duress).

[5] Fuller (1941) 41 Col L Rev 799; Cohen (1933) 46 Harv L Rev 553, 582–3; below, pp 136–8.

promisor has deliberately decided to contract and prevents parties accidentally binding themselves on impulse.[6]

(i) Benefit or detriment

The definition in *Currie v Misa* shows that consideration consists either in some benefit to the promisor or some detriment to the promisee; but there is considerable controversy as to the relative importance of these two factors. It is universally conceded that detriment to the promisee in return for the promise is a good consideration, since detriment is, as Sir Frederick Pollock succinctly stated, 'the price for which the promise of the other is bought'.[7] Yet the element of benefit cannot be entirely disregarded, since there are some cases in which a promise has been held not to be gratuitous on the ground that it secured some benefit to the promisor, though without any real detriment to the promisee. So, for example, there was a contract between a pupil barrister and the chambers whose offer of pupillage she had accepted. Even though no detriment was suffered by her, because she did not undertake to perform any work or services for any member of the chambers, the benefit to the chambers in having a pool of pupil barristers who would compete for recruitment as members of the chambers sufficed.[8]

(ii) Given in return for the promise

The consideration must necessarily be given in return for the promise, and it is usually, although not invariably,[9] given at the request of the promisor. The promisee must, therefore, prove either an exchange of promises (eg a promise to supply goods in return for a promise to pay for them) or some act or forbearance on the part of the promisee in return for the promise made. A benefit conferred or a detriment suffered otherwise than in return for the promise of the other party cannot constitute consideration.[10] In particular, there will be no consideration merely because there is detrimental action by the promisee in *reliance* on the promise, but not in *return* for it. Thus, in *Combe v Combe*,[11] where a husband, upon divorce, promised his wife a permanent allowance of £100 a year, the Court of Appeal refused to hold that a consequent forbearance on the part of the wife to apply for maintenance amounted to consideration. The husband had

---

[6] *Pillans v Van Mierop* (1765) 3 Burr 1663, 1670 (Wilmot J).

[7] *Principles of Contract* (13th edn, 1950) 133 (and earlier editions), approved in *Dunlop Pneumatic Tyre Co Ltd v Selfridge Ltd* [1915] AC 847, 855, and by the Sixth Interim Report of the Law Revision Committee, *Statute of Frauds and the Doctrine of Consideration* (Cmd 5449, 1937) 12. Cf Atiyah, *Essays on Contract* (1986) 183 (consideration is a 'reason for the recognition of an obligation').

[8] *Edmonds v Lawson* [2000] QB 501. See also *Alliance Bank Ltd v Broom* (1864) 2 Dr & Sm 289, below, p 108; *De la Bere v Pearson* [1908] 1 KB 280, below, p 105, n 45; *Ward v Byham* [1956] 1 WLR 496, 498, below, p 110; *Chappell & Co Ltd v Nestlé Co Ltd* [1960] AC 87, below, p 98; *Williams v Roffey Bros & Nicholls (Contractors) Ltd* [1991] 1 QB 1, 15–16, below, p 114.

[9] Goodhart (1951) 67 LQR 456 effectively demonstrates that a request is not essential to a binding obligation provided that the consideration is referable to the promise. Cf Smith (1953) 69 LQR 99. See also *Ball v National and Grindlays Bank Ltd* [1973] Ch 127.

[10] *Wigan v English and Scottish Law Life Assurance Association* [1909] 1 Ch 291.

[11] [1951] 2 KB 215; see below, pp 129–30.

not requested her to forbear, and her action could not be said to have been in return for his promise to pay.

(iii) Consideration and condition

Consideration must also be distinguished from the fulfilment of a condition. If A says to B, 'I will give you £500 if you break your leg', there is no contract, but simply a gratuitous promise subject to a condition.[12] Where the condition consists of the performance of some act by the promisee, the position may be more doubtful. If C says to D, 'You can have my flat if you move in and look after me', there may still be only a conditional gift, unless performance of the stipulation is regarded by the parties as the price to be paid for the promise.[13] This issue was discussed in *Chappell & Co Ltd v Nestlé Co Ltd*:[14]

C were the owners of the copyright of a tune called 'Rockin' Shoes' and N were manufacturers of chocolate. N offered to the public records of this tune in return for 1*s*/6*d* and the wrappers from three bars of their chocolate. Under the statutory provisions then in force[15] any person had an automatic right to use a copyright tune for a record, provided he paid a certain percentage of the 'ordinary retail selling price' of the record to the copyright owner. C contended that N could not rely on the statute, since it contemplated a price consisting of money alone, whereas in this case the consideration for the record included three chocolate wrappers.

In finding for C, the House of Lords, by a bare majority, held that the wrappers formed part of the selling price (consideration) for the record. The object of selling the record was to increase the sales of chocolate and the stipulated evidence of such sales formed part of the consideration. The acquisition of the wrappers was not simply a condition limiting the class of persons qualified to purchase records.

(b) NECESSITY FOR CONSIDERATION

Consideration is necessary for the formation of every simple contract; a promise (unless in a deed) made without consideration is not actionable as a contract[16] in English law.

As we have seen, from the very beginning of the action of *assumpsit*, a claimant who could not produce a sealed instrument had to show that he had contributed to the bargain by furnishing a valuable consideration of some kind.[17] In 1756, however, Lord Mansfield became Chief Justice of the King's Bench, and the doctrine of consideration was attacked by him in two fundamental respects. In the first place, he asserted that consideration was only one of several modes of supplying evidence of the promisor's

---

[12] *Shadwell v Shadwell* (1860) 9 CBNS 159, 177 (Byles J).
[13] *Ellis v Chief Adjudication Officer* [1998] 1 FLR 184 (no intent to contract and condition not performed).
[14] [1960] AC 87.
[15] Copyright Act 1956, s 8. The statutory licence to record was abolished by the Copyright, Designs and Patents Act 1988, s 170 and Sched 1, para 21.
[16] But see Denning (1952) 15 MLR 1, and below, pp 122–4.   [17] Above, pp 14–17.

intention to be bound; and that if the terms of a contract were reduced to writing by reason of commercial custom, or in obedience to statutory requirement, such evidence dispensed with the need for consideration.[18] In *Rann v Hughes*, however, Lord Mansfield's proposal was overruled. Skynner CB stated:[19]

All contracts are by the law of England divided into agreements by speciality and agreements by parol; nor is there any such third class as some of the counsel have endeavoured to maintain as contracts in writing. If they be merely written and not specialties, they are parol, and a consideration must be proved.

Lord Mansfield's second attack was to hold that the existence of a previous moral obligation was sufficient to support an express, but gratuitous, promise.[20] This looser usage of consideration as equivalent to the civilian requirement of 'causa' was finally rejected in *Eastwood v Kenyon*:[21]

E had been guardian and agent of Mrs K while she was a minor, and had incurred expenses in the improvement of her property: he did this voluntarily and, in order to do so, was compelled to borrow money, for which he gave a promissory note. When Mrs K came of age she assented to the transaction and after her marriage her husband promised to pay the note. He was sued upon this promise.

It was held that the moral obligation to fulfil such a promise was insufficient where the consideration was wholly past. 'Indeed', said Lord Denman,[22] 'the doctrine would annihilate the necessity for any consideration at all, inasmuch as the mere fact of giving a promise creates a moral obligation to perform it'.

From that time onwards, every promise not in a deed has been subject to a general and uniform test of actionability. In each case it is necessary to ask whether the promisor gets any benefit or the promisee sustains any detriment, present or future, in respect of the promise. If not, the promise is gratuitous and is not contractually binding. The variety of policies that may be reflected in the doctrine of consideration has been noted. In working out this doctrine to its logical results it has, no doubt, happened from time to time that the Courts have been compelled to hold a promise to be invalid which the parties intended to be binding, or that the slightness of the benefit or detriment which has been held to constitute a consideration has tended to bring the requirement into ridicule. The Courts are reluctant to describe a promise made in a commercial context as gratuitous and it has been said that 'a defence of lack of consideration rarely has merit'[23] and that 'businessmen know their own

---

[18] *Pillans v Van Mierop* (1765) 3 Burr 1663. This is the position in Scotland: Lord Normand (1939) 55 LQR 358.

[19] (1778) 7 TR 350n. It should be noted, however, that the only report of the actual decision of the House of Lords states that the case was decided on the ground of failure to comply with the Statute of Frauds: (1778) 4 Brown PC 27.

[20] *Lee v Muggeridge* (1813) 5 Taunt 36, 46 (Sir James Mansfield CJ, who was Chief Justice of Common Pleas).

[21] (1840) 11 A & E 438.   [22] *Ibid*, 450.

[23] *Thoresen Car Ferries Ltd v Weymouth Portland BC* [1977] 2 Lloyd's Rep 614, 619 (Donaldson J) 619.

business best even when they appear to grant an indulgence'.[24] The doctrine has therefore been the subject of considerable criticism,[25] but it is advisable to reserve a discussion of this until the general rules governing the application of consideration to contracts have been examined.

(c) EXECUTORY AND EXECUTED CONSIDERATION

As far as the relation of the consideration to the promise in respect of time is concerned, a consideration may be *executory*, a promise given for a promise; or it may be *executed*, an act or forbearance given for a promise.

An *executory* consideration consists of a promise to do, forbear, or suffer, given in return for a like promise. Thus mutual promises, for example, a promise to do work in return for a promise of payment, are illustrations of executory consideration. The fact that the promise given for a promise may be dependent upon a condition does not affect its validity as consideration. A promises B to do a piece of work for which B promises to pay if the workmanship is approved by a third party. The promise of B is consideration for the promise of A.

A contract arises upon a present or *executed* consideration when one of the two parties has, either in the act which constitutes an offer or in the act which constitutes an acceptance, done all that party is bound to do under the contract, leaving an outstanding liability on one side only. The case of an act which constitutes an offer may be illustrated by the example of one who offers to do work or provide goods in circumstances that show an obvious expectation that payment be made; the contract arises when the work or goods are accepted by the person to whom they are offered, and that person by accepting them becomes bound to pay a reasonable price. So if a wine merchant sends to a customer a selection of wines, and the customer retains some and returns the rest, the customer will be bound to pay for those retained, since the tender of the wine will be at once the offer and the consideration for the obligation.[26] On the other hand, a contract for which the consideration is the act which constitutes an acceptance is best illustrated by the case of an advertisement of a reward for services, which becomes a binding promise when the service is rendered. In such cases it is not the offeror, but the acceptor, who has performed at the moment when the contract is entered into. If A makes a general offer of reward for information and B supplies the information, A's offer is turned into a binding promise by the act of B, and B simultaneously concludes the contract and furnishes consideration by performance.[27]

---

[24] *Woodhouse AC Israel Cocoa Ltd SA v Nigerian Produce Marketing Co Ltd* [1972] AC 741, 757–8 (Lord Hailsham LC). See also *New Zealand Shipping Co Ltd v Satterthwaite* [1975] AC 154, 157.

[25] See the Sixth Interim Report of the Law Revision Committee (Cmd 5449, 1937).

[26] *Hart v Mills* (1846) 15 M & W 85; cf *Taylor v Laird* (1856) 1 H & N 266; above, p 42.

[27] Above, p 40. See *Carlill v Carbolic Smoke Ball Co* [1893] 1 QB 256.

(d) PAST CONSIDERATION

Executed consideration must be distinguished from *past* consideration which is a mere sentiment of gratitude for benefits received. In the case of executed consideration, both the promise and the act which constitutes the consideration are integral and co-related parts of the same transaction.[28] In the case of past consideration, however, the promise is subsequent to the act and independent of it; they are not in substance part of the same transaction. Thus if A saves B from drowning, and B later promises A a reward, A's action cannot be relied on as consideration for B's promise for it is past in point of time. Past consideration is, in effect, no consideration at all; that is to say it confers no benefit on the promisor, and involves no detriment to the promisee in return for the promise. It is merely an act or forbearance in time past by which a person has benefited without incurring any legal liability. If afterwards, whether from good feeling or interested motives, the person who has benefited makes a promise to the person whose act or forbearance led to the benefit, and that promise is made upon no other consideration than the past benefit, it is gratuitous and cannot be enforced. In *Roscorla v Thomas*[29] this principle was clearly stated:

The claimant purchased a horse from the defendant, who afterwards, in consideration of the previous sale, warranted that the horse was sound and free from vice. It was in fact a vicious horse.

The Court held that the sale itself created no implied warranty that the horse was not vicious. The warranty had therefore to be regarded as independent of the sale and as an express promise based upon a previous transaction. It fell, therefore, 'within the general rule that a consideration past and executed will support no other promise than such as would be implied by law'.

The general rule is, however, subject to certain exceptions.

(i) Previous request of the promisor

A past consideration will, it has been said, support a subsequent promise, if the consideration was given at the request of the promisor. Originally this was an unqualified exception based on the fact that, as was said in 1615 in *Lampleigh v Brathwait*:[30]

the promise though it follows, yet it is not naked, but couples itself with the suit before, and the merits of the party procured by that suit, which is the difference.

In the nineteenth century, however, with the rejection of Lord Mansfield's view that a previous moral obligation might be good consideration,[31] the scope of the exception

---

[28] *Westminster CC v Duke of Westminster* [1991] 4 All ER 136, 145.

[29] (1842) 3 QB 234. See also *Eastwood v Kenyon* (1840) 11 Ad & E 438, above p 99; *Re McArdle* [1951] Ch 669; *Savage v Uwechia* [1961] 1 WLR 455.

[30] (1615) Hob 105, 106 (subsequent promise to pay for requested attempt to obtain pardon held enforceable).

[31] Above, p 99.

was restricted. By the end of the nineteenth century it was clear that a past service performed at the request of the promisor will only amount to consideration if it was assumed at the time that the service was ultimately to be paid for.

In *Re Casey's Patents, Stewart v Casey*,[32] the owners of certain patent rights promised their manager a one-third share of the patents in consideration of his services in having worked for them. The Court of Appeal rejected the argument that this consideration was past. It held that the fact of the services by the manager raised an implication that they were to be paid for; the subsequent promise to pay was then an admission of a bargain and fixed the amount of the remuneration on the basis of which the services were originally rendered.

In *Pao On v Lau Yiu Long*[33] the Judicial Committee of the Privy Council stated the conditions in which this exception will apply as follows:

An act done before the giving of a promise to make a payment or to confer some other benefit can sometimes be consideration for the promise. The act must have been done at the promisor's request, the parties must have understood that the act was to be remunerated either by a payment or the conferment of some other benefit, and payment, or the conferment of a benefit, must have been legally enforceable had it been promised in advance.

In that case the defendant had requested the claimant to promise not to sell certain shares for a year and later promised to indemnify the claimant if the shares fell below a certain price. The defendant contended that the consideration for the indemnity was past but it was held that all three conditions mentioned above were satisfied.

It is arguable, however, that this exception is an apparent rather than a real departure from the general doctrine as to past consideration. When a request is made which is in substance an offer of a promise upon terms to be afterwards ascertained, and an act is done in pursuance of that request, a subsequent promise to pay a fixed sum or to confer some other benefit may be regarded as a part of the same transaction, the effect of the promise being merely to render certain that which was uncertain before.

(ii) An antecedent debt

It has sometimes been thought that the existence of an existing debt is sufficient consideration for a subsequent promise to pay that debt.[34] It should not be supposed, however, that the existence of a debt from A to B will always be consideration for any subsequent promise which A may make to pay that debt. There must be present consideration in the form of a forbearance to sue by the creditor, or else, if a security is given by the debtor, it must be communicated to the creditor and induce such a forbearance.[35]

---

[32] [1892] 1 Ch 104. See also *Kennedy v Broun* (1863) 13 CBNS 677, 740.

[33] [1980] AC 614, 629. See below, p 113, for the facts.

[34] *Slade's Case* (1602) 4 Co Rep 91a, above, p 16. Note that such promises, if in writing, can have the effect of extending the limitation period, below, p 640.

[35] *Wigan v English and Scottish Law Life Assurance Association* [1909] 1 Ch 291.

(iii) Negotiable instruments

By section 27(1) of the Bills of Exchange Act 1882, valuable consideration for a bill may be constituted by: (a) any consideration sufficient to support a simple contract; or (b) an antecedent debt or liability. So if A, whose account at the bank is overdrawn, negotiates to its banker a cheque drawn by a stranger, the banker becomes a holder for value of the cheque, as the antecedent debt of A is consideration for the instrument.[36] This is a genuine exception to the rule that past consideration does not count.

(e) CONSIDERATION MUST MOVE FROM THE PROMISEE

This long-standing maxim is surprisingly ambiguous and confusing.[37] It has three possible meanings.

First, it may mean nothing more than that to be enforceable a promise, not made by deed, must be supported by consideration. If A promises B £1,000, B cannot enforce the promise (unless made by deed) because there is no consideration for A's promise. Although B is a promisee, it has not provided consideration and 'consideration must move from the promisee'. In this sense, the maxim merely restates, and adds nothing to, the requirement of consideration.

Secondly, it may mean that, even though the promise is supported by consideration provided by the promisee, the consideration must move *from the claimant*: that is, the person seeking to enforce the contract must itself have provided the consideration for the promise. So if A promises B to pay C £1,000 in return for B doing work for A, C cannot enforce the contract because the consideration has moved from B and not from C. In this sense the maxim overlaps with, and indeed is indistinguishable from, the doctrine of privity of contract according to which only a party to a contract can enforce it. So in the above example, one would standardly explain the result without referring to the consideration maxim by saying that C cannot enforce the contract between A and B because C is not a party to it. Indeed, the early cases which are now regarded as establishing the privity doctrine were ones in which the reasoning used was that the claimant could not enforce the contract because it had not provided the consideration.[38] It also follows that exceptions to privity,[39] in particular the Contracts (Rights of Third Parties) Act 1999, also constitute exceptions to the need for consideration to move from the claimant.

Thirdly, the maxim may mean that a promisee cannot enforce a promise made to it where the consideration for the promise has been provided by someone else. So if A promises B that in return for C doing work for A, A will pay B £1,000,

---

[36] But see *Oliver v Davis* [1949] 2 KB 727.

[37] Furmston (1960) 23 MLR 373; Smith, *The Law of Contract* (4th edn, 2002) 94–6; Law Revision Committee, Sixth Interim Report (1937) para 37; Law Commission, Law Com No 242 (1996) Part VI.

[38] *Tweddle v Atkinson* (1861) 1 B & S 393; *Dunlop Pneumatic Tyre Co Ltd v Selfridge & Co Ltd* [1915] AC 847. See below, Chapter 21.

[39] See below Chapter 21.

B cannot enforce the promise because, although B is the promisee, C has provided the consideration and 'consideration must move from the promisee'. B has suffered no detriment (unless B impliedly undertook to procure that C would do the work) and, although A has received the benefit, that benefit was conferred by C, and not by B. While used in this sense the maxim has an independent force, separate from the requirement of consideration and the doctrine of privity, the situations where it will apply are extremely rare. So, in the example just considered, unless there is a connection between B and C so that B may itself be providing consideration, it will be very unusual for A to be promising to pay B for work that C does for A. More realistic would be where B and C are joint promisees. Say, for example, A promises B and C to pay B £1,000 if C will do certain work desired by A. If C does the work, and A refuses to pay the £1,000 to B, can B sue A? If not, one might say that, even though B is a party to the contract,[40] because the promise is made to B and C, the reason B cannot enforce A's promise is because it has not provided consideration: consideration must move from the promisee. However, while there is no clear English authority, the High Court of Australia in *Coulls v Bagot's Executor & Trustee Co Ltd*[41] indicated that the joint promisee can enforce a contract in this situation. It is submitted that that ought to be applied in England and, if it were, it would follow that the maxim 'consideration must move from the promisee' in its third independent sense would be rendered inaccurate in relation to its most realistic possible application.

(f) CONSIDERATION NEED NOT BE ADEQUATE

Consideration need not be adequate but it must be of some value in the eye of the law. The Courts will not make bargains for the parties and, if a person gets what has been contracted for, they will not inquire whether it was an equivalent to the promise which was given in return: 'the adequacy of the consideration is for the parties to consider at the time of making the agreement, not for the Court when it is sought to be enforced'.[42] The most trifling detriment or benefit will suffice, and the following cases will show that the Courts have been prepared to find a contract where the consideration was virtually non-existent.

We have already seen that in *Chappell & Co Ltd v Nestlé Co Ltd*[43] wrappers from chocolate bars were held to be part of the consideration for the sale of a record. In

---

[40] This depends on what one means by a 'party' to a simple contract. If one defines a party as someone who has provided consideration, then C would not be a party and would appear to fall foul of the privity doctrine as well as the rule that consideration must move from the promisee.

[41] (1967) 119 CLR 461. See Coote [1978] CLJ 301. Cf *McEvoy v Belfast Banking Co Ltd* [1935] AC 24, 43 (consideration supplied by one of two joint and several promisees).

[42] *Bolton v Madden* (1873) LR 9 QB 55, 57 (Blackburn J).

[43] [1960] AC 87, above, p 98. Cf *Lipkin Gorman v Karpnale Ltd* [1991] 2 AC 548 (gaming chips not consideration, inter alia, because they were 'worthless': but that was in the context not of deciding whether there was an enforceable contract but rather in deciding whether 'value' had been given for the purposes of the defence of being a bona fide purchaser *for value* without notice).

Haigh v Brooks,[44] the consideration of a promise to pay certain bills was the surrender of a document supposed to be a guarantee, which turned out to be of doubtful validity. The worthlessness of the document surrendered was held to be no defence to an action on the promise. The Court was not concerned with the adequacy or inadequacy of the price paid or promised. 'The plaintiffs were induced by the defendant's promise to part with something which they might have kept, and the defendant obtained what he desired by means of that promise'.[45]

The consequence of the rule that the Court is not concerned with the adequacy of consideration is that the requirement can be satisfied by nominal consideration. At common law 'a contracting party can stipulate for what consideration he chooses. A peppercorn does not cease to be good consideration if it is established that the promisee does not like pepper and will throw away the corn'.[46] Statute, however, may make the adequacy of consideration relevant in a particular context. Thus, property legislation distinguishes a transaction for 'nominal' consideration from one for 'valuable' consideration,[47] and the term 'consideration' in the Local Government Act 1972 only includes elements of commercial or monetary value.[48]

In the Roman law of sale, as in certain modern continental systems, the price had to be a serious one—more than just nominal—otherwise the contract could not be characterized as a contract of sale; and in later Roman law the doctrine of *laesio enormis* was developed under which the seller of land could rescind the contract where the price was less than half the value of the land unless the buyer was willing to come up to the fair price.[49] This doctrine of *laesio enormis* forms no part of the English common law. Even where statute has intervened to protect a class of contractor, such as consumers, it does not always require a 'fair' or 'reasonable' or 'market' price.[50] In equity, inadequacy of consideration is treated as relevant in deciding whether there has been undue influence, or whether the bargain is unconscionable, so as to allow the contract to be rescinded.[51] However, it is arguable that mere inadequacy of consideration is not itself a ground on which the equitable remedy of specific

---

[44] (1839) 10 A & E 309; aff'd *sub nom Brooks v Haigh* (1840) 10 A & E 323, where it was said by Maule J that the delivery of the paper alone would suffice. See also *Bainbridge v Firmstone* (1838) 8 A & E 743, 744; *Veitch v Sinclair* [1975] 1 NZLR 264.

[45] (1839) 10 A & E 309, 320 (Lord Denman CJ). See also *De la Bere v Pearson* [1908] 1 KB 280 (possible benefit to newspaper in publishing letter held to be consideration for offer to give financial advice) although liability today would probably lie in tort: *Hedley Byrne & Co Ltd v Heller & Partners Ltd* [1964] AC 465, 527–8.

[46] *Chappell & Co Ltd v Nestlé Co Ltd*, above, n 43, 114 (Lord Somervell). See also above, p 98.

[47] Land Charges Act 1972, s 17(1); Law of Property Act 1925, ss 84(7) and 205(1)(xxi); *Westminster CC v Duke of Westminster* [1991] 4 All ER 136, 146. See also Insolvency Act 1986, s 238 (transactions at undervalue).

[48] *R v Pembrokeshire CC, ex p Coker* [1999] 4 All ER 107.

[49] Nicholas, *Introduction to Roman Law* (1962) 174–5. For modern French law, see Nicholas, *The French Law of Contract* (2nd edn, 1992) 147 (sale at nominal price can be recharacterized as a *donation deguisée*), 137–41 (*lésion*). See also Gordley, *Foundations of Private Law* (2006) 364–6.

[50] Consumer Rights Act 2015, which has a core exclusion as regards price: see below, p 225. Cf Rent Act 1977, s 70(1) (fair rent); Agricultural Holdings Act 1986, s 12, Sched 2, para 1(1) (prudent and willing parties).

[51] Below, pp 392, 402.

performance of a contract will be refused.[52] Thus specific performance was ordered of an option to purchase a house for £10,000 even though the consideration for the grant of the option was the nominal sum of £1.[53]

(g) CONSIDERATION MUST BE REAL

Though consideration need not be adequate, it must be real. It must be 'something which is of some value in the eye of the law'. Thus, 'it is no consideration to refrain from a course of action which it was never intended to pursue'.[54] This section examines those cases where the reality of consideration has been questioned or defined.

(i) Motive and consideration

Motive must be distinguished from consideration. In *Thomas v Thomas*:[55]

A deceased husband's executor promised to allow his widow to occupy a house the deceased had owned in return for her promise to keep it in repair and to pay a ground rent of £1 *per annum*. The executor stated that the agreement was entered into 'in consideration of' the expressed desire of the deceased that his wife should have the use of the house during her lifetime.

It was held that the desire to carry out the wishes of the deceased did not amount to consideration: 'Motive is not the same thing with consideration. Consideration means something which is of some value in the eye of the law, moving from the plaintiff'.[56] In one sense, however, motive is relevant in that the consideration must be given in return for the promise; but the motive of the promisor must be to obtain a legally recognizable return for the obligation incurred, and not something which is of no value in the eye of the law. So, the desire of one member of a pop group to avoid the danger of internal dissention that might result if he had a larger income than others in the group did not constitute consideration for his promise to make payments to the others.[57]

It has already been noted that, at the end of the eighteenth and the beginning of the nineteenth century, the moral obligation to make a return for past benefit was an

---

[52] See, eg, *Coles v Trecothick* (1804) 9 Ves Jun 234, 246 (Lord Eldon). But specific performance will not be ordered of a promise made under deed, and not supported by consideration, applying the maxim that 'equity will not assist a volunteer': *Cannon v Hartley* [1949] Ch 213.

[53] *Mountford v Scott* [1975] Ch 258 (Brightman J). But note that, in contrast to Brightman J, the Court of Appeal in that case regarded the option as having been exercised so that the specific performance related to the contract of sale for £10,000 not the option contract for which the consideration was nominal.

[54] *Arrale v Costain Civil Engineering Ltd* [1976] 1 Lloyd's Rep 98, 106. But an act may be consideration even if it is not solely induced by the promise: *Brikom Investments Ltd v Carr* [1979] QB 467, 490.

[55] (1842) 2 QB 851.

[56] *Ibid*, 859 (Patteson J). The issue arose because the executor had argued that the widow's case was procedurally defective because her declaration referred only to her promise to repair and pay rent and omitted to state part of the consideration, ie the desire of her deceased husband. The Court rejected this and found for the widow.

[57] *Hadley v Kemp* [1999] 2 EMLR 589, 625 (Park J).

equivalent to consideration. But past consideration is no consideration, and what the promisor gets in such a case is the satisfaction of the motive of gratitude. The question was settled once and for all in *Eastwood v Kenyon*,[58] where the final blow was given to the doctrine that consideration for a promise could consist in a motive or moral obligation resting on the promisor.

(ii) Impossibility

Impossibility, either physical or legal, which exists at the time of formation of the contract and is obvious upon the face of it, makes the consideration unreal. The impossibility must be obvious, such as is, 'according to the state of knowledge of the day, so absurd that the parties could not be supposed to have so contracted'.[59] Thus a covenant in a charterparty that a ship would sail on a date which was already past at the time the contract was executed was held to be void for unreality in the consideration furnished.[60] Again, the old case of *Harvy v Gibbons*,[61] where a bailiff was promised £40 in consideration of a promise made by him that he would release a debt due to his master, is an example of legal impossibility. The Court held that the bailiff could not sue; that the consideration furnished by him was 'illegal', for a servant could not release a debt due to his master. By 'illegal' it is plain that the Court meant legally impossible.

(iii) Uncertainty

A promise which purports to be a consideration may be of too vague and insubstantial a character to be enforced. Thus a promise which in terms leaves performance exclusively in the discretion of the promisor will not be enforceable; the consideration being illusory.[62] Again, in *White v Bluett*:[63]

In proceedings by his father's executors on a promissory note, a son alleged that the father had promised to discharge him from liability in consideration of his promise to cease complaining, as he had been used to do, that he had not enjoyed as many advantages as his brothers.

It was said that the son's promise was no more than a promise 'not to bore his father', and was too vague to form a consideration for the father's promise to waive his rights on the note although, in another case, a promise to make a child happy was stated to be part of the consideration.[64] Again, it has been held that a promise to co-operate in the recovery from a joint debtor was sufficiently certain to form a consideration for a forbearance.[65] Other instances of uncertainty have already been given in connection

---

[58] (1840) 11 A & E 438; above, p 99.   [59] *Lord Clifford v Watts* (1870) LR 5 CP 577, 588 (Brett J).
[60] *Hall v Cazenove* (1804) 4 East 477.   [61] (1675) 2 Lev 161.
[62] *Stabilad Ltd v Stephens & Carter Ltd (No 2)* [1999] 2 All ER 651, 660 (Peter Gibson LJ).
[63] (1853) 23 LJ Ex 36.
[64] *Ward v Byham* [1956] 1 WLR 496; below, p 110. See also *Dunton v Dunton* (1892) 18 VLR 114 (Australia); *Hamer v Sidway* 27 NE 256 (1891) (USA).
[65] *Bank of Nova Scotia v MacLellan* (1977) 78 DLR (3d) 1 (Canada).

with incomplete agreements[66] and it is arguable that it is better to view decisions such as *White v Bluett* as turning on there being 'no intention to create legal relations' rather than there being no consideration.

(iv) Forbearance to sue

There is a clear public interest in encouraging the avoidance of litigation and the resolution of disputes by the parties provided that the settlement or compromise is genuine, and entered into freely without the concealment of essential information, the taking of undue advantage,[67] or the exertion of illegitimate pressure.[68] A forbearance to sue, even for a short time, may be consideration for a promise, although there is no waiver or compromise of the right of action. In *Alliance Bank Ltd v Broom*:[69]

The defendants, Messrs Broom were asked to give security for moneys they owed to the bank. They promised to assign the documents of title to certain goods; they failed to do so, and the bank sued for specific performance of the promise.

The Court held that the bank was entitled to this remedy:

Although there was no promise on the part of the plaintiffs to abstain for any certain time from suing for the debt, the effect was that the plaintiffs did, in effect, give, and the defendant received, the benefit of some degree of forbearance; not, indeed, for any definite time, but, at all events, some extent of forbearance . . . The circumstances necessarily involve the benefit to the debtor of a certain amount of forbearance, which he would not have derived if he had not made the agreement.[70]

The consideration in such a case clearly consists in the benefit received by the promisor in that the promise 'stays the hand of the creditor'.[71]

In order that the forbearance should be a consideration, some liability should be shown to exist, or to be reasonably supposed to exist, by the parties. If the claim is not only invalid, but is known by the party forbearing to be so, there is no consideration.[72] It would also seem that the claim must be an honest claim and one which the promisee *bona fide* intends to pursue.[73] Where the claim arises out of an illegal agreement, a forbearance to sue on that claim is not sufficient consideration.[74]

---

[66] See above, p 70.

[67] *Colchester BC v Smith* [1992] Ch 421, 435. Payments made to close a transaction are irrecoverable even if there is no consideration: *Woolwich BS v IRC* [1993] AC 70, 165; Law Com No 227, *Restitution: Mistakes of law and ultra vires public authority receipts and payments* (1994) paras 2.25–2.38.

[68] *Huyton SA v Peter Cremer GmbH* [1999] 1 Lloyd's Rep 620, 629–30. On duress, see below Chapter 10.

[69] (1864) 2 Dr & Sm 289.   [70] *Ibid*, 292.   [71] Cf *Cook v Wright* (1861) 1 B & S 559, 569.

[72] *Wade v Simeon* (1846) 2 CB 548, 564.

[73] *Miles v New Zealand Alford Estate Co* (1886) 32 Ch D 266, 284; *Colchester BC v Smith* [1992] Ch 421, 435. See also *BCCI SA v Ali* [2001] 1 AC 251 (equitable relief against release procured by concealment of facts).

[74] Cf *Poteliakhoff v Teakle* [1938] 2 KB 816; *Hill v William Hill (Park Lane) Ltd* [1949] AC 530; (gaming contracts, although such contracts are no longer illegal: Gambling Act 2005, below, p 414, n 25). But cf below, n 78.

(v) Compromise of a dispute

The same public interest in encouraging the avoidance of litigation and the resolution of disputes applies to a compromise of a dispute, for instance by a promise to pay a proportion of a disputed sum claimed, again provided that it is genuine, and entered into freely without the concealment of essential information, the taking of undue advantage, or the exertion of illegitimate pressure.[75] The difference between forbearance and compromise is that in compromise the debtor does not admit the claim and the creditor promises to abandon the claim. So in the case of forbearance, the offer is in effect, 'I admit your claim but will do or promise something if you will stay your hand'. In the case of a compromise the offer is in effect, 'I do not admit your claim but I will do or promise something if you will abandon it'. It has, however, been argued that if the claim compromised is of an insubstantial character the consideration fails. The answer is to be found in the judgment of Cockburn CJ in *Callisher v Bischoffsheim*:[76]

Every day a compromise is effected on the ground that the party making it has a chance of succeeding in it, and if he *bona fide* believes that he has a fair chance of success, he has a reasonable ground for suing, and his forbearance to sue will constitute a good consideration. When such a person forbears to sue he gives up what he believes to be a right of action, and the other party gets an advantage, and, instead of being annoyed with an action, he escapes from the vexations incident to it . . . It would be another matter if a person made a claim which he knew to be unfounded, and, by a compromise, derived an advantage under it: in that case his conduct would be fraudulent.

In that case, the defendant agreed to deliver to the claimant certain securities in consideration that the claimant would cease to press a claim against the Honduras Government. The claim was worthless, but there was no evidence that the claimant knew this.[77] It was held that there was consideration for the agreement. If, however, one of the parties to the compromise has no case, and knows that there is no case, the agreement to compromise will not be held binding.

As in the case of forbearance, the compromise of a claim arising out of an illegal contract is insufficient as consideration, unless the compromise arises out of a dispute of fact as to whether the contract is in fact illegal.[78]

(h) PERFORMANCE OF, OR PROMISE TO PERFORM, AN EXISTING DUTY

Where what is done, or promised, is no more than that to which the promisee is legally bound, and if nothing is got in return for the promise but that to which the promisor is already legally entitled, the consideration seems unreal.[79] This may occur where the

---

[75] *Huyton v Cremer* [1999] 1 Lloyd's Rep 620, 629–30. [76] (1870) LR 5 QB 449, 452.
[77] See also *Wigan v Edwards* (1973) 1 ALR 497 (Australia) (honest claim sufficient).
[78] *Binder v Alachouzos* [1972] 2 QB 151,158 (Lord Denning MR).
[79] See Davis (1937) 6 CLJ 202; Reynolds and Treitel (1965) 76 Malaya LR 1.

promisee is already under an existing duty to do something and then promises to do that thing. If you have to do an act anyway, how can it be to your detriment to reaffirm your obligation? If the act will be done anyway, how does it benefit me to pay you to do it? The law draws a distinction between the performance of, or promise to perform, a public duty, the performance of, or promise to perform, an existing duty to a third party, and the performance of, or promise to perform, an existing duty owed to the promisor. In the first case the conventional view is that there is no consideration for the promise. In the second the law holds that valuable consideration is present. In the third case it has been held that only where there is, in the particular circumstances, a 'practical' benefit to the promisee is there consideration.

(i) Existing public duty

A conventional view is that, where the promisee is already under an existing public duty, an express promise to perform, or performance of, that duty will not amount to consideration.[80] There will be no detriment to the promisee or benefit to the promisor over and above their existing rights and liabilities. In *Collins v Godefroy*:[81]

The claimant received a subpoena to appear at a civil trial as a witness on behalf of the defendant. The defendant promised him a sum of money for his trouble. A person who receives a subpoena is bound to attend and give evidence.

It was held that there was no consideration for the promise, the claimant being under a public duty to attend.

Where the undertaking is to do more than that to which the promisee is legally bound, this may be consideration, even though it is an act of the same kind as the subject of the obligation. In *Glasbrook Brothers Ltd v Glamorgan County Council*,[82] a police authority sued for the sum of £2,200 promised to it by a colliery company for whose mine the authority had provided a stronger guard during a strike than was in its opinion necessary. It was held that it was entitled to maintain an action on the promise.[83] Again, in *Ward v Byham* it was held that there was consideration for a promise to pay a weekly sum to the mother of an illegitimate child if the mother proved the child was 'well looked after and happy'.[84] Morris LJ considered the mother

---

[80] *Thoresen Car Ferries Ltd v Weymouth Portland BC* [1977] 2 Lloyd's Rep 614, 619. Earlier cases tend to suggest that an agreement of this nature is invalid on grounds of public policy: *Wathen v Sandys* (1811) 2 Camp 640; *Bilke v Havelock* (1813) 3 Camp 374.

[81] (1831) 1 B & Ad 950.

[82] [1925] AC 270. See also *Leeds United FC Ltd v Chief Constable of West Yorkshire Police* [2013] EWCA Civ 115, [2014] QB 168 (police force not going beyond its public duty to maintain law and order in providing policing for football matches on public land away from the football club's stadium).

[83] See also *England v Davidson* (1840) 11 A & E 856; *Neville v Kelly* (1862) 12 CBNS 740 (rewards for police officers) and *Goulden v Wilson Barca* [2000] 1 WLR 167 (payment to expert witness).

[84] [1956] 1 WLR 496. See also *Williams v Williams* [1957] 1 WLR 148 (husband's promise to pay weekly sum to wife who had deserted him, and thus forfeited right to maintenance, if she maintained herself and undertook not to pledge his credit held enforceable: Hodson and Morris LJJ, but not Denning LJ, based their decision only on the wife promising more than her legal duty).

had promised more than her statutory duty to maintain the child. Denning LJ's view[85] was that she was only promising to do what she was bound to do but that this sufficed because it was a benefit to the promisor (the child's father).

More recently *Ward v Byham* has been explained as an instance of the recognition that the mother's promise was a 'practical' benefit to the father which thus amounted to consideration for his promise.[86] It is possible the recognition that such 'practical' benefit can constitute consideration may lead to the reassessment of the general rule but, in the context of pre-existing public duties, it is important to bear in mind that it may be contrary to the public interest to give such recognition to a 'practical' benefit and that this should only be done where 'there is nothing in the transaction which is contrary to the public interest'.[87] For instance, the enforcement of an agreement to make a payment for the performance of a public duty such as the giving of evidence[88] or the renewal of a licence[89] might be thought to be contrary to the public interest in ensuring impartiality in the administration of justice and probity in government and local administration.

(ii) Existing duty owed to a third party

It is now established that consideration which consists in the performance of, or the promise to perform, an existing contract with a third party may be a real consideration. In these cases the promisee obtains the benefit of a direct obligation which can be enforced.[90]

As far as performance of such a duty is concerned, in *Shadwell v Shadwell*:[91]

The claimant was engaged to be married to Ellen Nicholl. His uncle wrote to him stating that he was pleased to hear of the intended marriage and that as he had promised to assist the claimant at starting, would pay him £150 yearly during the uncle's life or until the claimant's income as a Chancery barrister amounted to six hundred guineas. The claimant married Ellen Nicholl. He never earned as much as six hundred guineas. The annuity fell into arrear; the uncle died, and the claimant sued his executors.

A majority of the Court thought that there was a benefit to the uncle in that the marriage was 'an object of interest to a near relative', and a detriment to the claimant because 'he might have made a most material change in his position and have induced the object of his affections to do the same, and might have incurred pecuniary liabilities resulting in embarrassments' if the promised income had been withheld. The majority implicitly accepted that it was no objection to finding consideration for the uncle's

---

[85] [1956] 1 WLR 496, 498. See also *Williams v Williams*, above, n 84, 150.

[86] *Williams v Roffey Bros & Nicholls (Contractors) Ltd* [1991] 1 QB 1, 13 (Glidewell LJ), below, p 114. Cf Purchas LJ at 20.

[87] *Williams v Williams* [1957] 1 WLR 148, 150 (Denning LJ).

[88] *Collins v Godefroy* (1831) 1 B & Ad 590. But see now Senior Courts Act (formerly Supreme Court Act) 1981, s 36(4) (tender of expenses).

[89] *Morgan v Palmer* (1842) 2 B & C 729, 739.

[90] *New Zealand Shipping Co Ltd v AM Satterthwaite & Co Ltd* [1975] AC 154, 168.

[91] (1860) 9 CBNS 159.

promise that the nephew was already engaged to, and therefore under a contractual duty to marry, Ellen Nicholl.[92] Byles J dissented, holding that the claimant had done no more than he was legally bound to do so that his marriage was no consideration for the uncle's promise.

In *Scotson v Pegg*:[93]

S promised to deliver to a third party X, or to his order, a cargo of coal then on board S's ship. X made an order in favour of P. P then made an agreement with S that if S would deliver the coal to him, he would in return unload and discharge the coal at a fixed rate each day from the date when the ship was ready for discharge. When sued for breach, P pleaded that, in delivering the coal to P, S was doing no more than he was bound under his contract with X to do so that there was no consideration for P's promise to unload in the manner specified.

The Court held that P was liable. Wilde B said:[94] 'If a person chooses to promise to pay a sum of money in order to induce another to perform that which he has already contracted with a third person to do, I confess I cannot see why such a promise should not be binding'.

Aspects of these decisions are unsatisfactory. So, in *Shadwell v Shadwell*, as Byles J pointed out, the uncle derived no personal benefit from the marriage; the engagement was in no way induced by his promise, nor was the claimant's subsequent change of position in return for his undertaking. Again, the promise to deliver to P at a fixed rate in *Scotson v Pegg* may have involved duties more onerous than the existing obligation to deliver to X or there may have been some dispute as to P's right to have the coals.[95] Nevertheless, a majority of the Privy Council in *New Zealand Shipping Co Ltd v AM Satterthwaite & Co Ltd, The Eurymedon*,[96] took them as establishing that actual performance of an existing duty to a third party can be sufficient consideration, even though that performance is no additional detriment to the promisee. In *The Eurymedon* the unloading by stevedores of goods from a ship (which the stevedores were bound by a contract with a third party to do) was held to be consideration for a promise to relieve them of the liability for damaging the goods.

The question then arises whether a distinction should be drawn between cases where the consideration alleged is *executed*, that is, by performance of an existing duty to a third party, and cases where the consideration is *executory*, consisting of a promise to perform. In principle a promise to perform an existing duty owed to a third party should also constitute consideration because the person making that promise thereby foregoes the liberty to cancel the contract with the third party by mutual agreement and the person to whom that promise is made has the benefit of a

---

[92] An engagement to marry is no longer a contract: Law Reform (Miscellaneous Provisions) Act 1970, s 1.

[93] (1861) 6 H & N 295.   [94] *Ibid*, 300.   [95] *Ibid*, 299 (Martin B). See above, p 109.

[96] [1975] AC 154. See also *Adams v London Improved Motor Coach Builders Ltd* [1921] 1 KB 495, 501, 504 (trade union's undertaking to pay solicitor the costs of services rendered to a member did not preclude the member from also being liable to the solicitor).

direct obligation.[97] The Judicial Committee of the Privy Council so held in *Pao On v Lau Yiu Long*:[98]

The claimants agreed with a company (Fu Chip) to sell certain shares in return for an allotment to them of 4.2 million shares in Fu Chip. If all the newly allotted shares had been immediately sold in the market, this would have depressed the value of the shares. Accordingly the claimants undertook in their agreement with Fu Chip not to sell or transfer for one year 60 per cent of the allotted shares. Subsequently the claimants refused to complete the agreement unless the defendants (who were the majority shareholders in Fu Chip) promised to indemnify them against any fall in value of the allotted shares during the one year period. The defendants gave that indemnity. The allotted shares fell greatly in value, and, in answer to a claim on the indemnity, the defendants pleaded that there was no consideration for their promise to indemnify.

It was held that the consideration for the indemnity was the promise of the claimants to perform their pre-existing contractual obligations to Fu Chip. 'Their Lordships', said Lord Scarman,[99] 'do not doubt that a promise to perform, or the performance of, a pre-existing contractual obligation to a third party can be a valid consideration'.

(iii) Existing duty owed to the promisor

Where the promisee merely undertakes to fulfil the conditions of an existing contract with the promisor, the perception that it is not detrimental to do what one is obliged to do or beneficial to receive what one is entitled to receive has led to the conclusion that there is no consideration. In this context the need to discourage improper pressure by threatening not to perform one's contract unless the other party offers to pay more has been an important factor, although the pre-existing duty rule was rather a blunt weapon for this since it invalidated non-extortive as well as extortive renegotiations. The regulation of renegotiations was, as we shall see, left to the equitable doctrine of promissory estoppel. Although the development of a concept of economic duress[100] means that the common law now has a more direct and precise method of controlling coercion, normally the performance of, or a promise to perform, a duty owed to the promisor will not be consideration.[101] The general position is illustrated by the old case of *Stilk v Myrick*:[102]

In the course of a voyage from London to the Baltic and back two seamen deserted, and the captain, being unable to replace them, promised the rest of the crew that, if they would work the vessel home, the wages of the two deserters should be divided amongst them.

---

[97] *De Cicco v Schweizer* 221 NY 431 (1917); Hamson (1938) 54 LQR 233, 237.   [98] [1980] AC 614.
[99] *Ibid*, 632.   [100] Below, Chapter 10.
[101] *North Ocean Shipping Co Ltd v Hyundai Construction Co Ltd* [1979] QB 705, 712; *Pao On v Lau Yiu Long* [1980] AC 614, 633; *Vantage Nav Corp v Suhail & Saud Bahwan Building Materials Llc, The Alev* [1989] 1 Lloyd's Rep 138, 147; *Williams v Roffey Bros & Nicholls (Contractors) Ltd* [1991] 1 QB 1, 16, 19, 20, below, p 109.
[102] (1809) 2 Camp 317. But see the report of the same case in 6 Esp 129, and *Harris v Watson* (1791) Peake 102 (promise invalid by reason of public policy). See generally on the two different law reports of *Stilk v Myrick*, Luther (1999) 19 LS 526.

It was held that:

There was no consideration for the ulterior pay promised to the mariners who remained with the ship. Before they sailed from London they had undertaken to do all they could under all emergencies of the voyage . . . The desertion of a part of the crew is to be considered an emergency of the voyage as much as their death; and those who remain are bound by the terms of their original contract to exert themselves to the utmost to bring the ship in safety to her destined port.[103]

The decision would have been otherwise if the existing contract had been rescinded and a new agreement substituted[104] at a higher rate of pay, or if the promise had been made to compromise a dispute,[105] or if uncontemplated risks had arisen.[106] Then the crew would have provided consideration by entering into the new agreement, or forbearing to exercise what were or were believed to be their legal rights or by undertaking to do more than they were contractually bound to do.

Even where the promise is only to perform the existing contractual obligation, the performance may in fact be detrimental to a performing party whose time or money could have been used to greater advantage elsewhere. It may also be beneficial to the promisor because 'a bird in the hand is worth more than a bird in the bush'[107] and because damages for breach of contract might not compensate fully.[108] In *Williams v Roffey Bros & Nicholls (Contractors) Ltd*:[109]

R & N Ltd contracted to refurbish a block of 27 flats. It sub-contracted the carpentry work to W for an agreed price of £20,000. W completed nine of the flats but ran into financial difficulties because the agreed price was too low and because he failed to supervise his workforce adequately. R & N was concerned about delay because the main contract contained a penalty clause. It offered to pay W an additional £10,300 at the rate of £575 for each flat in which the carpentry work was completed. Eight further flats were completed but R & N made only one further payment of £1,500. W ceased work and sued for the additional sum promised. R & N resisted this claim on the ground that W had given no consideration for their promise to pay the additional sum since he was promising to do no more than he was already bound to do by his subcontract.

This defence failed. In the Court of Appeal Glidewell LJ stated:[110]

(i) If A has entered into a contract with B to do work for, or to supply goods or services to, B in return for payment by B; and (ii) at some stage before A has completely performed his obligations under the contract B has reason to doubt whether A will, or will be able to, complete his side of the bargain; and (iii) B thereupon promises A an additional payment in return for A's promise to perform his contractual obligations on time; and (iv) as a result

---

[103] (1809) 2 Camp 317, 319 (Lord Ellenborough CJ).   [104] See below, p 483.
[105] *Wigan v Edwards* (1973) 1 ALR 497; see above, p 109.
[106] *Hartley v Ponsonby* (1857) 7 E & B 872.
[107] *Corbin on Contracts* (1963) para 172. See also *Foakes v Beer* (1884) 9 App Cas 605, 622 (Lord Blackburn).
[108] Below, Chapter 17 (limitations on damages).   [109] [1991] 1 QB 1.
[110] *Ibid*, 15–16. On 'practical benefit', see also *Anangel Atlas Comp Nav SA v Ishikawajima-Harima Heavy Industries Co Ltd (No 2)* [1990] 2 Lloyd's Rep 526, 554–5; *Simon Container Machinery Ltd v Emba Machinery AB* [1998] 2 Lloyd's Rep 429, 435.

of giving his promise, B obtains in practice a benefit, or obviates a disbenefit; and (v) B's promise is not given as a result of economic duress or fraud on the part of A;[111] then (vi) the benefit to B is capable of being consideration for B's promise, so that the promise will be legally binding.

The Court identified several 'practical' benefits to R & N. These were: W's continued performance, avoiding a penalty for delay under the main contract, avoiding the trouble and expense of engaging others to complete the carpentry, and replacing a haphazard method of payment by a more formalized scheme which produced more orderly performance by W and thus enabled R & N to direct its other traders to do work in the completed flats which otherwise would have been held up until W completed his work.[112] It is clear that it was the development of economic duress as a method of controlling improper pressure that enabled the Court to take a more flexible approach to the requirement of consideration:[113]

Now that there is a properly developed doctrine of the avoidance of contracts on the grounds of economic duress, there is no warrant for the court to fail to recognize the existence of some consideration even though it may be insignificant and even though there may have been no mutual bargain in any realistic use of that phrase.[114]

The recognition of 'practical' benefit as consideration could be a significant step towards the overt recognition that all promises to pay more (or to accept less) for performing, or promising to perform, a pre-existing contractual duty owed to the promisor made without duress in a commercial context give rise to enforceable contractual obligations. This derives support from the suggestion in a recent case,[115] involving paying more for performance of a pre-existing duty to the promisor, that *Williams v Roffey* cannot be reconciled with *Stilk v Myrick*; and that the doctrine of consideration no longer needs to be used to protect a participant in such a variation because that role has passed to the law of economic duress which provides a more refined control mechanism.

Several factors, however, make it difficult to assess how radical the impact of *Williams v Roffey* will prove to be. First, the principle in *Stilk v Myrick*, although refined and limited, was not overruled.[116] It appears from this that, where there

---

[111] It is hard to see that Glidewell LJ can have been correct to include this as a requirement for establishing consideration. Duress or misrepresentation operate to make a contract, supported by consideration, voidable.

[112] [1991] 1 QB 1, 11, 19, 20.

[113] *Ibid*, 13–14, 21. See also *Pao On v Lau Yiu Long* [1980] AC 614, 624–35, above, p 113.

[114] *Vantage Navigation Corp v Suhail and Saud Bahwan Building Materials Llc, The Alev* [1989] 1 Lloyd's Rep 138, 147 (Hobhouse J). See also *Huyton SA v Peter Cremer GmbH* [1999] 1 Lloyd's Rep 620, 629–30 (Mance J).

[115] *Adam Opel GmbH v Mitras Automotive (UK) Ltd* [2007] EWHC 3481 (QB) at [42] (David Donaldson QC). Cf *South Caribbean Trading Ltd v Trafigura Beheer BV* [2004] EWHC 2676 (Comm), [2005] 1 Lloyd's Rep 128 at [108] where Colman J said, 'But for the fact that *Williams v Roffey Bros* was a decision of the Court of Appeal, I would not have followed it'.

[116] [1991] 1 QB 1, 16, 19, 20.

is no 'practical' benefit to the promisor, the promise will be 'gratuitous' and unenforceable. Secondly, on the facts of *Williams v Roffey Bros*, although W did not undertake to do any work additional to that which he had originally undertaken to do, one might argue that the institution of and adherence to the new work scheme constituted a different performance so that, applying the traditional approach, there was consideration since he was not obliged to perform in that way.[117] Thirdly, as will be seen, in the context of part payment of a money debt, the Court of Appeal has, since *Williams v Roffey Bros*, declined to have regard to 'practical' benefit.[118]

The notion of 'practical' benefit has been criticized[119] as imprecise, as including the chance of a benefit, as putting into question the adequacy of contract damages, and as undermining the strength of the obligation to perform a contract by recognizing, as Purchas LJ did,[120] that a contracting party can rely upon his own breach to establish consideration. We shall, however, see that rigid adherence to the pre-existing duty rule has also been criticized as invalidating many commercially desirable renegotiations and that, before the development of economic duress, it was necessary to have recourse to equitable promissory estoppel to protect the renegotiated transaction. Now that adequate safeguards exist against improper pressure there would seem to be no very convincing reason why a promise to perform, or performance of, any existing duty, including public duties, should not be sufficient consideration provided that it is not contrary to public policy.[121]

An alternative approach to the problem in *Williams v Roffey*, which would have led to the same result, is to say that consideration is not needed for the variation, as opposed to the formation, of a contract. That was the approach adopted in the United States Uniform Commercial Code.[122] It has also been put forward as an alternative to the *Roffey* approach, but without ultimately making a choice between them, by the New Zealand Court of Appeal.[123]

---

[117] It would appear that this consideration, if valid, would be found in the *performance*; ie the contract was *unilateral*. It is more problematic to argue that there was a new bilateral contract because, although Russell LJ (at 19) considered that 'the terms upon which [W] was to carry out the work were varied', Purchas LJ (at 23) stated that there was 'no obligation added to the contractual duties'. Glidewell LJ did not address the point.

[118] *Re Selectmove Ltd* [1995] 1 WLR 474, 481; *Collier v Wright (Holdings) Ltd* [2007] EWCA Civ 1329, [2008] 1 WLR 643. See below, p 118.

[119] Chen Wishart, in Beatson and Friedmann, eds, *Good Faith and Fault in Contract Law* (1995) ch 5; Coote (1990–91) 3 JCL 23. But Chen Wishart now argues, in Burrows and Peel, eds, *Contract Formation and Parties* (2010) ch 5, that performance of a pre-existing duty does constitute valid consideration for a *unilateral* contract because actual performance, rather than a promise to perform, gives the promisor something more than it previously had which was merely the contractual right to performance.

[120] [1991] 1 QB 1, 23.

[121] *Williams v Williams* [1957] 1 WLR 148, 150 (Denning LJ), above, p 110, n 84; *Huyton SA v Peter Cremer GmbH* [1999] 1 Lloyd's Rep 620, 629–30 (Mance J).

[122] Section 2–209(1).   [123] *Antons Trawling Co Ltd v Smith* [2003] 2 NZLR 23.

(i) DISCHARGE OF A DEBT

The principle that the performance of an existing duty owed to the promisor is an unreal consideration has been applied not only to the creation of a new obligation, but also to the discharge of the existing duty. Thus if A owes B a debt of £200, and B agrees to accept £100 in full satisfaction of the debt, B is not bound by the agreement and may subsequently sue for the whole amount. The payment by a debtor of a smaller sum in satisfaction of a larger is not a good discharge of a debt. Such payment is no more than the promisee is already bound to do, and is no consideration for a promise, express or implied, to forgo the residue of the debt.

(i) The general rule

The rule that the payment of a smaller sum in satisfaction of a larger is not a good discharge of a debt is often known as the rule in *Pinnel's Case*,[124] although it was not part of the *ratio decidendi* of that case.

Pinnel brought an action in debt on a bond against Cole for payment of £8 10s on 11 November 1600. Cole pleaded that, at the instance of Pinnel, he had paid him the sum of £5 2s 2d on 1 October, and that Pinnel had accepted this in full satisfaction of the debt.

The Court of Common Pleas stated that the payment of a lesser sum on the day in satisfaction of a greater was no satisfaction of the whole albeit that, on the facts, that rule did not apply because the debt had been paid and accepted in advance of the due date.

The rule was considered and reaffirmed by the House of Lords nearly three centuries later in *Foakes v Beer*:[125]

Dr Foakes was indebted to Mrs Beer on a judgment for the sum of £2,090. Mrs Beer agreed that if Foakes paid her £500 in cash and the balance of £1,590 in instalments she would not take 'any proceedings whatever' on the judgment. Foakes paid the money exactly as required, but Mrs Beer then claimed an additional £360 as interest on the judgment debt. When sued, Foakes pleaded that his duty to pay interest had been discharged by the promise not to sue.

Their Lordships differed as to whether, on its true construction, the agreement merely gave Foakes time to pay, or was intended to cover interest as well, but they held that, even on the latter construction, there was no consideration for the promise. Foakes therefore remained bound to pay the additional sum. 'It is', said the Earl of Selborne,[126] 'not really unreasonable or practically inconvenient that the law should require particular solemnities to give to a gratuitous contract the force of a binding obligation'.

(ii) Irrelevance of 'practical benefit'

Lord Blackburn recognized that business people 'do every day recognise and act on the ground that prompt payment of a part of their demand may be more beneficial

---

[124] (1602) 5 Co Rep 117a.   [125] (1884) 9 App Cas 605.   [126] *Ibid*, 613.

to them than it would be to insist on their rights',[127] particularly where the credit of the debtor is doubtful, but the House of Lords decided that a practical benefit of that nature is not good consideration. In *Re Selectmove Ltd*[128] it was said in *obiter dicta* that the principle that 'practical' benefit may amount to consideration recognized in *Williams v Roffey Bros & Nicholls (Contractors) Ltd*[129] could not, consistently with the doctrine of precedent, be extended to an obligation to make payment because 'it would in effect leave the principle in *Foakes v Beer* without any application'.

(iii) Any difference in performance suffices

If, however, there is a dispute as to the amount due[130] or the thing done or given by the promisee debtor is different from that which the recipient was entitled to demand,[131] however slight the difference, it will be sufficient consideration for the promise to discharge. Even the performance of the identical obligation will be effective if it is to take place at an earlier date or in a different place.

The Court in *Pinnel's Case* recognized that 'the gift of a horse, hawk or robe, etc. in satisfaction is good' because it 'might be more beneficial to the plaintiff than the money . . . or otherwise the plaintiff would not have accepted it in satisfaction'.[132] Judgment was given for the claimant on a technical point of pleading;[133] but the fact that the payment and the acceptance of part of the money had taken place before the due day would otherwise have resulted in judgment for the defendant, for the difference in time would have constituted sufficient consideration for the promise to discharge the debt.

(iv) Appraisal of rule

It has been argued that the rule in *Pinnel's Case* is supportable on the ground that the law should not favour a person who is excused money which he ought to pay any more than a person who is promised money which has not been earned. On the other hand, it is open to the criticism that it not only runs counter to ordinary commercial practice but that, taken in conjunction with the rule that the law will not inquire into the adequacy of consideration, it may lead to absurd results. 'According to English

---

[127] At *ibid*, 622. See also *ibid*, 630 (Lord Fitzgerald).

[128] [1995] 1 WLR 474, 481 (Peter Gibson LJ). See Peel (1994) 110 LQR 353. See also *Ferguson v Davies* [1997] 1 All ER 315. In *Collier v Wright Holdings Ltd* [2007] EWCA Civ 1329, [2008] 1 WLR 643 the same point was made and was part of the *ratio*.

[129] Above, p 114.   [130] Above, p 109.

[131] Even a negotiable instrument (such as a cheque) for the smaller amount would at one time suffice, provided it was accepted by the creditor in discharge of the obligation (*Goddard v O'Brien* (1882) 9 QBD 37), but this is no longer the case (*D & C Builders Ltd v Rees* [1966] 2 QB 617).

[132] (1602) 5 Co Rep 117a. In *Vanbergen v St Edmund's Properties Ltd* [1933] 2 KB 223, however, it was stated that the new element must not have been introduced merely to oblige the debtor and without any independent benefit to the creditor.

[133] See generally Simpson, *A History of the Common Law of Contract* (1975) 105–6.

Common Law', said Jessel MR,[134] 'a creditor may accept anything in satisfaction of his debt except a less amount of money. He might take a horse, or a canary, or a tomtit if he chose, and that was accord and satisfaction; but, by a most extraordinary peculiarity of the English Common Law, he could not take 19s 6d in the pound'. There is also now a distinction which is difficult to justify in principle between a promise to pay more for the same services, where practical benefit is recognized, and a promise to accept a lesser sum of money owed, where it is not.[135] The rule enables a creditor to go back on an agreement solemnly entered into and intended to affect legal relations; and there are no strong policy considerations which would demand the application of the doctrine of consideration to the discharge, as opposed to the formation, of contracts.[136]

The Law Revision Committee, in 1937,[137] recommended the abolition of the rule in *Pinnel's Case* where the promisee had carried out his side of the agreement, but this reform has never been implemented. It would seem that the best way forward is for the Supreme Court to reconsider the decision of the House of Lords in *Foakes v Beer* in the light of the recognition of 'practical' benefit and other developments, in particular the equitable principle of promissory estoppel in cases where the debtor's position has been altered in reliance on the promise.[138] Before considering the equitable principle we shall consider two common law exceptions to the rule. The first is where a debtor makes a composition with creditors; the second is where part payment of a debt is made by a third party to the contract. It will be seen that these two exceptions are based on reasons of policy rather than on logical evasions of the strict doctrine of consideration.

(v) Compositions with creditors

A composition with creditors (apart from the statutory prohibition of preference by debtors who later become bankrupt)[139] is an exception to the rule, inasmuch as each creditor undertakes to accept a lesser sum than is due in satisfaction of a greater. All are bound, both at common law and by virtue of statute.[140] As far as the common law position is concerned, there is no difficulty as to the consideration between the creditors *inter se*; it is the forbearance on the part of each of them to claim the whole amount of their debt so that no one creditor may gain at the expense of the others. But it is difficult

---

[134] *Couldery v Bartrum* (1881) 19 Ch D 394, 399.

[135] Cf O'Sullivan [1996] CLJ 219.

[136] Sir Frederick Pollock, *Principles of Contract* (13th edn, 1950) 150 (extension of the doctrine from formation to discharge was illegitimate). See also Kötz, *European Contract Law* (1997) 68–71; CISG art 29(1) ('a contract may be modified or terminated by the mere agreement of the parties').

[137] Cmd 5449. In Canada, provincial statutes have now abolished the rule by providing, as the Ontario Mercantile Law Amendment Act RSO 1990, s 16 does, that 'Part performance of an obligation either before or after the breach thereof, when expressly accepted by the creditor in satisfaction or rendered in pursuance of an agreement for that purpose, though without any new consideration, shall be held to extinguish the obligation'.

[138] For the view that promissory estoppel outflanks the rule in *Pinnel's Case*, see *Collier v Wright (Holdings) Ltd* [2007] EWCA Civ 1329, [2008] 1 WLR 643, especially at [42]. See below, p 124.

[139] Insolvency Act 1986, s 340.

[140] Insolvency Act 1986, s 260(2). A voluntary arrangement pursuant to the statute is not a contract with the debtor: *Johnson v Davies* [1999] Ch 117.

to see how the debtor's promise to pay, or the payment of, a portion of the debt can constitute the consideration upon which the creditor renounces the residue.[141]

The consideration must, then, be something other than the payment of a smaller sum in satisfaction of a larger, and it has been suggested that it consists in the procuring of a promise from each creditor to accept less than the full amount of the individual debt, thereby conferring a benefit on the creditors generally.[142] This solution is satisfactory so far as it goes, for there is no doubt that such a consideration would be sufficient, but it cannot apply to a case in which the debtor does not in fact procure the creditors' promises.[143] A more acceptable reason for the existence of this exception would seem to be that a party to such an arrangement cannot claim the original debt because to do so would be to commit a fraud on the other creditors.[144]

(vi) Part payment by third party

The second exception to the general rule, that a creditor who accepts, in full satisfaction, part payment of a debt by a third party cannot later recover the balance from the debtor, is also based on the need to prevent fraud on a third party. In *Hirachand Punamchand v Temple*:[145]

A father wrote to the claimants, his son's creditors, offering to pay part of a debt due on a promissory note in satisfaction of the whole, and enclosing a draft for that amount. The claimants cashed the draft, and then sued the son for the balance.

The Court of Appeal held that the creditors must be deemed to have accepted the draft in full satisfaction, and that the son's debt was extinguished. It approved a *dictum* of Willes J in *Cook v Lister*:[146] 'If a stranger pays part of the debt in discharge of the whole, the debt is gone, because it would be a fraud on the stranger to proceed'.

(j) LETTERS OF CREDIT

The irrevocable letter of credit has often been said to be an example of an exception to the need for consideration.[147] The purpose of such letters of credit is to finance contracts for the sale of goods between buyers and sellers in different countries, particularly where the delay between despatch from the place of manufacture and

---

[141] *Fitch v Sutton* (1804) 5 East 230, 232.

[142] *Good v Cheesman* (1831) 2 B & Ad 328.

[143] Cf *West Yorkshire Darracq Agency Ltd v Coleridge* [1911] 2 KB 326.

[144] *Wood v Roberts* (1818) 2 Stark 417. Another reason (*Corbin on Contracts* (1963) para 190) is that, subject to the statutory prohibition on preferences (Insolvency Act 1986, s 340), the debtor's consideration lies in giving up the opportunity of treating his creditors unequally.

[145] [1911] 2 KB 330. See also *Welby v Drake* (1825) 1 C & P 557.

[146] (1863) 13 CBNS 543, 594, 595. This is not also an exception to the rule that a non-party to a contract (here the debtor) cannot enforce it (below, Chapter 21) because the transaction between the creditor and the person who pays is best seen as an executed (complete) gift to the debtor of the discharge of the debt: see Birks and Beatson (1976) 92 LQR 188, 193–9.

[147] See generally *The Uniform Customs and Practice for Documentary Credits* (2007 Revision, UCP 600); Jack, *Documentary Credits* (4th edn, 2009).

arrival at the destination is a considerable one. It enables short-term credit facilities to be made available, guarantees payment to the seller, and safeguards the parties against currency fluctuations.

There are three stages in the transaction. First, a term is inserted in the contract of sale made between the buyer and the seller whereby the buyer undertakes to furnish an irrevocable letter of credit in favour of the seller.[148] Secondly, the buyer approaches its own banker (usually described as the issuing banker) and instructs it to issue an irrevocable letter of credit, giving the banker details of the transaction. This constitutes a contract between the buyer and the banker. Thirdly, the banker advises the seller that an irrevocable letter of credit has been opened in its favour, that is to say, the banker gives an irrevocable undertaking to pay the seller, or to accept bills of exchange drawn on it, provided the seller tenders the required shipping documents in compliance with the terms of the letter of credit.[149] The seller can then ship the goods in the secure knowledge that it will be paid for them. The shipping documents represent the goods themselves,[150] and they are usually retained by the banker as security against its right to be reimbursed by the buyer.

The irrevocable letter of credit does not fit easily into the common law. If the transaction is regarded simply as a contract between the buyer and its banker, the seller is a third party to this contract and technically would be unable to sue should the banker revoke the letter of credit or for some reason fail to make payment.[151] Nevertheless, it has been established that the banker is legally under an absolute obligation to pay, irrespective of any dispute there may be between the buyer and seller.[152] It has therefore been argued that the irrevocable letter of credit forms an 'exception' to the doctrine of privity of contract; but it seems better to regard the promise of payment given by the banker to the seller as an autonomous undertaking, independent of any other contract. Thus the irrevocable letter of credit is not an exception to privity of contract but to the doctrine of consideration. It is either an irrevocable offer by the banker to the seller (which is accepted by the seller tendering the shipping documents) or a unilateral contract between the banker and the seller to pay on tender of the shipping documents.[153] But on either analysis the essential theoretical problem is that

---

[148] For the effect of a failure to furnish the letter of credit, see below, p 151.

[149] An irrevocable letter of credit may also be 'confirmed' by a banker operating in the seller's country (known as the correspondent banker) who, by confirming the credit, adds to the promise of the issuing banker its own undertaking to ensure payment.

[150] *Lickbarrow v Mason* (1794) 5 TR 683.

[151] In the Sixth Interim Report of the Law Revision Committee, 1937 (Cmnd 5449) para 45, it was pointed out that the liquidator of a bank might be compelled to rely on the defence of privity.

[152] *Urquhart, Lindsay & Co Ltd v Eastern Bank Ltd* [1922] 1 KB 318, 321, 322; *Donald H Scott & Co Ltd v Barclays Bank Ltd* [1923] 2 KB 1, 13; *Trans-Trust SPRL v Danubian Trading Co Ltd* [1952] 2 QB 297, 304–5; *Midland Bank Ltd v Seymour* [1955] 2 Lloyd's Rep 147, 166; *Hamzeh Malas & Sons v British Imex Industries Ltd* [1958] 2 QB 127, 129.

[153] Ellinger (1962) 4 Malaya LR 307. In *Urquhart's* case, above, n 152, 321, Rowlatt J thought that the banker's undertaking took effect once the seller acted on it, eg by commencing performance of their contract with the buyer. Cf *Dexters Ltd v Schenker & Co* (1932) 14 Ll LR 586, 588 (when letter of credit received). On either view there appears to be no consideration (because, eg, acting on a promise does not constitute consideration).

the banker is bound not to revoke even before the seller has tendered the documents and it is therefore hard to see that the tendering of the documents can constitute the consideration. Letters of credit therefore provide an example of a promise in the commercial sphere that, for reasons of commercial convenience, is treated as binding despite there being no consideration.

2. PROMISSORY ESTOPPEL

In practice the most significant limit to the rule in *Pinnel's Case*[154] is to be found in the equitable principle of estoppel, in this context promissory estoppel. Here we consider the extent to which promissory estoppel operates in effect as an alternative to consideration in the discharge or modification of existing duties and its potential to operate in this way in the formation of contracts.[155]

Before turning to the requirements for the establishment of a promissory estoppel, it should be noted that it is only one form of estoppel. We saw in the last chapter that equity may, by the principle of proprietary estoppel, provide a remedy in respect of an agreement for the sale of land that does not comply with statutory requirements of form. Promissory estoppel is one strand in a broader equitable principle whereby parties to a transaction who have conducted their dealings in reliance on an underlying assumption as to a present, past, or future state of affairs, or on a promise or representation by words or conduct, will not be allowed to go back on that assumption, promise or representation when it would be unfair or unjust to do so.[156] The Court will do what is necessary, but not more, to prevent a person who has relied upon such an assumption, promise, or representation from suffering injustice.[157] Promissory estoppel also has similarities to the common law principle of waiver by which the right to performance in accordance with the contract may be lost by a party who in effect promises (albeit without consideration) not to insist on strict adherence to the contract. Common law waiver is considered in the chapter on Discharge by Agreement.[158]

(a) EMERGENCE OF PROMISSORY ESTOPPEL

Promissory estoppel was invoked in *Central London Property Trust Ltd v High Trees House Ltd*:[159]

In 1937 the claimant leased to the defendant a block of flats for a term of 99 years at a rent of £2,500 a year. In 1940, many of the flats were empty, on account of the war,

---

[154] See above p 117.

[155] See Cartwright, *Formation and Variation of Contracts* (2014) Part IV.

[156] Below, pp 132–6. For the relationship between promissory estoppel, proprietary estoppel, and estoppel by convention, see *Baird Textiles Holdings Ltd v Marks & Spencer plc* [2001] EWCA Civ 274, [2002] 1 All ER (Comm) 737; below p 132.

[157] *Crabb v Arun DC* [1976] Ch 179, 198.   [158] Below, Chapter 13.   [159] [1947] KB 130.

and the claimant agreed to reduce the rent to £1,250. By 1945 the flats were again full. In September 1945 the receiver of the claimant demanded full rent for the future and some arrears. Subsequently he brought an action against the defendant claiming the full original rent both for the future and also for the last two quarters of 1945.

Denning J held that the action should succeed. The parties intended the reduction of rent to be a temporary expedient while the flats could not be fully let. This had ceased to be the case early in 1945; therefore the full rent was payable for the last two quarters of 1945, which was all that was actually claimed in the action. The importance of the judgment, however, lies in Denning J's contention that, had the claimant sued for the full rent between 1940 and 1945, it would have been *estopped* by its promise from asserting its legal right to demand payment in full. In other words, the promise to accept less rent while wartime conditions prevailed was binding despite the absence of consideration.

Denning J relied on the decision of the House of Lords in *Hughes v Metropolitan Railway Co*:[160]

H served on M a notice to repair, within six months, houses held on lease from him. Failure to comply with this notice would entitle H to forfeit the lease. The parties then negotiated for the purchase by H of M's lease and these negotiations continued for almost the entire period of the notice. Shortly before the notice was due to expire, H broke off the negotiations, and, upon expiry, brought an action for possession claiming to have forfeited the lease.

The House of Lords held that, by entering into negotiations, H impliedly promised to suspend the notice previously given and that M had acted upon this promise by doing nothing to repair the premises. H was not to be allowed to take advantage of the forfeiture which occurred, and therefore the six months' period was to run only from the breakdown of the negotiations. Lord Cairns described the principle as follows:[161]

If parties who have entered into definite and distinct terms involving certain legal results—certain penalties or legal forfeiture—afterwards by their own act or with their own consent enter upon a course of negotiation which has the effect of leading one of the parties to suppose that the strict rights arising under the contract will not be enforced, or will be kept in suspense, or held in abeyance, the person who otherwise might have enforced those rights will not be allowed to enforce them where it would be inequitable having regard to the dealings which have thus taken place between the parties.

Denning J stated that the application of this principle led logically to the conclusion that 'a promise to accept a smaller sum in discharge of a larger sum, if acted upon, is binding notwithstanding the absence of consideration'.[162]

---

[160] (1877) 2 App Cas 439. See also *Birmingham and District Land Co v L & NW Ry* (1888) 40 Ch D 268. Contrast the view of this case advanced by Gordon [1963] CLJ 222.

[161] (1877) 2 App Cas 439, 448.   [162] [1947] KB 130, 135.

The correctness of Denning J's dictum[163] has, however, been the subject of considerable controversy.[164] In particular, two criticisms have been levelled against it. First, it was argued that the concept of 'promissory' estoppel offends against the rule in *Jorden v Money*[165] in which it was held that only a representation of existing or past fact, and not one relating to future conduct, will ground an estoppel. Estoppel would not therefore apply, as in the *High Trees* case, to a promise as to the future. The rule in *Jorden v Money*, however, is not an absolute one, and it is qualified by a number of exceptions.[166] One of these exceptions is that principle expressed in *Hughes v Metropolitan Railway Co*, which applies where two parties stand together in a contractual or other similar legal relationship, and one of them makes to the other a promise to forbear from enforcing its strict legal rights. To this situation the rule in *Jorden v Money* has no application.

Secondly, it was said that the dictum of Denning J is inconsistent with the decision of the House of Lords in *Foakes v Beer*. But the principle upon which he relied in the *High Trees* case was that of estoppel, which must be specially pleaded. A plea of estoppel was never raised in *Foakes v Beer*. It has recently been boldly stated by Arden LJ, albeit in *obiter dicta* in the context of a decision merely that there was a genuine triable issue on promissory estoppel, that *High Trees* outflanks *Foakes v Beer*. In *Collier v Wright (Holdings) Ltd*[167] she stated:

The facts of this case demonstrate that, if (1) a debtor offers to pay part only of the amount he owes; (2) the creditor voluntarily accepts that offer, and (3) in reliance on the creditor's acceptance, the debtor pays that part of the amount he owes in full, the creditor will, by virtue of the doctrine of promissory estoppel, be bound to accept that sum in full and final satisfaction of the whole debt. For him to resile will itself be inequitable. In addition, in these circumstances, the promissory estoppel has the effect of extinguishing the creditor's right to the balance of the debt. This part of our law originated in the brilliant obiter dictum of Denning J, as he was, in the *High Trees* case. To a significant degree it achieves in practical terms the recommendation of the Law Revision Committee chaired by Lord Wright MR in 1937.

Longmore LJ, however, was more cautious and Mummery LJ expressed no view. Longmore LJ doubted that the agreement could be construed as a permanent surrender of the right to sue for the balance but also stated that, if Arden LJ was correct about the effect of *High Trees*, it was important to construe agreements which are said to have this effect strictly, and referred to the need for meaningful reliance.[168]

---

[163] Being based on hypothetical facts, it is *obiter dictum* and not *ratio decidendi*.

[164] As well as the articles cited below, see Cheshire and Fifoot (1947) 63 LQR 283; (1948) 64 LQR 28; Wilson (1951) 67 LQR 330; Lord Denning (1952) 15 MLR 1; Sheridan (1952) 15 MLR 338; Bennion (1953) 16 MLR 441; Wilson [1965] CLJ 93; Thompson [1983] CLJ 257; McFarlane in Burrows and Peel (eds), *Contract Formation and Parties* (2010) ch 6.

[165] (1854) 5 HLC 185, and applied in *Citizen's Bank of Louisiana v First National Bank of New Orleans* (1873) LR 6 HL 352; *Maddison v Alderson* (1883) 8 App Cas 467, 473.

[166] See Jackson (1965) 81 LQR 84, 223.

[167] [2007] EWCA Civ 1329, [2008] 1 WLR 643 at [42].   [168] *Ibid*, [45]–[47].

(b) SCOPE OF PROMISSORY ESTOPPEL

The recognition of the principle of promissory estoppel in cases since *High Trees*[169] has led to a more precise definition of its essential elements.

(i) A clear promise

The promise must be clear and unequivocal,[170] although it need not be express and may be implied from words or conduct.[171] No estoppel can arise if the language of the promise is indefinite or imprecise and silence and inaction, for example the absence of protest about a breach, will not normally estop a party from relying on the breach.[172] Where, however, the language is clear, no question arises of any particular knowledge by the promisor.[173]

(ii) Inequitable to go back on promise

It must be inequitable for the promisor to go back on the promise and insist on the strict legal rights under the contract. This will not be so where the promise has been induced by intimidation by the promisee. This is illustrated by *D & C Builders Ltd v Rees*:[174]

Mr and Mrs Rees owed £482 to D & C, a small building company, in respect of work done for him. They delayed payment for several months, and then offered D & C £300, stating in effect that if it did not accept this sum it would get nothing. As D & C was in desperate financial straits, it accepted the £300 in full settlement of the debt. It then sued for the balance.

Lord Denning MR saw the case as turning on promissory estoppel. He considered that it was not inequitable for D & C to go back on its promise; the settlement was not truly voluntary as Mr and Mrs Rees had improperly taken advantage of D & C's weak financial situation.[175] Mr and Mrs Rees were therefore liable for the balance. Although there is little other guidance about the types of conduct by the promisee that will make it 'not inequitable' for a person to go back on such a promise, pointers can be found

---

[169] *Tool Metal Manufacturing Co Ltd v Tungsten Electric Co Ltd* (1950) 69 RPC 108 and [1955] 1 WLR 761 was the first case. As well as the cases discussed below, see *Bremer Handelsgesellschaft mbH v Vanden Avenne-Izegem* [1977] 1 Lloyd's Rep 133, 165, aff'd [1978] 2 Lloyd's Rep 109, 127; *The Stolt Loyalty* [1993] 2 Lloyd's Rep 281. Cf *Woodhouse AC Israel Cocoa Ltd SA v Nigerian Produce Marketing Co Ltd*, 758, 762.

[170] *Woodhouse AC Israel Cocoa Ltd SA v Nigerian Produce Marketing Co Ltd* [1972] AC 741, 757, 758, 761, 762, 767–8, 771; *Scandinavian Trading Tanker Co AB v Flota Petrolera Ecuatoriana* [1983] QB 549 (aff'd [1983] 2 AC 694).

[171] *Hughes v Metropolitan Railway Co*, above, n 160. It is unlikely to arise where the negotiations are 'subject to contract': *Attorney-General for Hong Kong v Humphreys Estates (Queen's Garden)* [1987] 1 AC 114.

[172] *Société Italo-Belge pour le Commerce et l'Industrie v Palm & Vegetable Oils (Malaysia) Sdn Bdh* [1982] 1 All ER 19, 25; *Vitol SA v Esso Australia Ltd* [1989] 2 Lloyd's Rep 451, 460.

[173] *Youell v Bland Welch & Co Ltd* [1990] 2 Lloyd's Rep 423, 448–50. (Cf waiver where knowledge of all material facts is required.)

[174] [1966] 2 QB 617. See also *P v P* [1957] NZLR 854.

[175] Cf Danckwerts and Winn LJJ at 626, 632–3, who applied the rule in *Pinnel's Case*.

in the developing doctrine of duress.[176] Misrepresentation by the promisee will also presumably rule out the application of promissory estoppel.

(iii) Alteration of position

It has been said that the promisee must have 'altered his position' in reliance on the promise made,[177] There is, however, some doubt as to what is meant by this requirement. Normally, in order to prove an estoppel, it must be shown that the person to whom the representation is made has acted detrimentally in reliance on it. If these ideas are regarded as fundamentally similar, then the alteration of position which results from the promise must be such that, if the promise is revoked, the promisee will be in a worse position than if the promise had never been made. It is because the position of the promisee has been prejudiced that it is inequitable for the promisor to go back on the promise. In *Hughes v Metropolitan Railway Co* this requirement was clearly satisfied, since M had refrained from carrying out repairs in reliance on the promise and had thus lost the time which it would have enjoyed had the negotiations never taken place. On the other hand, in the *High Trees* case, no evidence was adduced to show any alteration of position by the tenant company, in the sense that it arranged, or omitted to arrange, its affairs any differently as a result of the promise.[178] It appears that the only thing it did in reliance on the promise was to pay part of the debt which it was contractually bound to pay. If the landlord had gone back on its promise, and claimed the full rent between 1940 and 1945, the tenant would have been in no worse position than if the promise had never been made. The *High Trees* case cannot in consequence be regarded as completely identical to *Hughes v Metropolitan Railway Co*. In *WJ Alan & Co Ltd v El Nasr Export and Import Co*[179] Lord Denning MR explicitly stated that for the *High Trees* principle to operate (which he here referred to as the principle of 'waiver') detriment to the promisee was not needed. All that was necessary was for the promisee to have 'acted on the belief induced by the other party'.[180] That is, mere reliance was sufficient.

That reliance will suffice is supported by Lord Cairns's statement of principle in the *Hughes* case.[181] He said that the person seeking to enforce his rights will not be allowed to do so 'where it would be inequitable having regard to the dealings which

---

[176] *Huyton SA v Peter Cremer GmbH* [1999] 1 Lloyd's Rep 620, 629 (Mance J). See also below, Chapter 10.

[177] *Tungsten Electric Co Ltd v Tool Metal Manufacturing Co Ltd* (1950) 69 RPC 108, 112, 115–16; *Tool Metal Manufacturing Co Ltd v Tungsten Electric Co Ltd* [1955] 1 WLR 761, 764, 784; *Ajayi v RT Briscoe (Nigeria) Ltd* [1964] 1 WLR 1326, 1330; *Re Wyvern Developments Ltd* [1974] 1 WLR 1097, 1104.

[178] It could be suggested that the tenant had 'altered its position' by relying on the informal promise and failing to secure a formal release under seal or by refraining from seeking alternative finance or declaring itself bankrupt.

[179] [1972] 2 QB 189, 213. But cf *ibid*, 221 (Stephenson LJ) for the view that, on the facts, there was detrimental reliance. There was detrimental reliance on the facts, in, eg, the following cases: *Combe v Combe* [1951] 2 KB 215, 220, 225; *Tool Metal Manufacturing Co Ltd v Tungsten Electric Co Ltd* [1955] 1 WLR 761, 799 (where, see below, the promisees continued to produce over quota); *Brikom Investments Ltd v Carr* [1979] QB 467, 482; *Youell v Bland Welch & Co Ltd* [1990] 2 Lloyd's Rep 423, 452–4.

[180] These were the words of Lord Cohen in *Tool Metal Manufacturing Co Ltd v Tungsten Electric Co Ltd* [1955] 1 WLR 761, 799.

[181] See above, p 123.

have thus taken place between the parties'. It is therefore arguable that it is for the Court to decide, on the totality of the evidence produced to it, whether the dealings between the parties are such as to render it inequitable for the promisor to go back on the promise. For instance, in *Société Italo-Belge pour le Commerce et l'Industrie v Palm and Vegetable Oils (Malaysia) Sdn Bdh, The Post Chaser*:[182]

The buyers of a cargo of palm oil did not protest about the sellers' failure to make a 'declaration of ship' in writing as soon as possible after sailing and asked the sellers to pass the shipping documents to a sub-buyer, a request that was held to be a representation that they were prepared to accept them and a waiver of any defect in them. The sub-buyer rejected the documents within 2 days and the buyers purported to do so as well.

It was stated that to establish inequity within Lord Cairns's principle, 'it is not necessary to show detriment; indeed the representee may have benefited from the representation, and yet it may be inequitable, at least without reasonable notice, for the representor to enforce his legal rights'.[183] It does not, however, follow that, in every case where there is non-detrimental reliance by the promisee, it will be inequitable for the promisor to enforce the contract. In *Société Italo-Belge pour le Commerce et l'Industrie v Palm and Vegetable Oils (Malaysia) Sdn Bdh* itself, although the sellers had actively relied on the buyers' representation by presenting the documents, the very short time between the representation and the rejection of the documents meant that, in the absence of evidence that the sellers' position had been prejudiced, it was not inequitable for the buyers to enforce their legal right to reject the documents.

The requirement that the promise be 'acted upon' means that there is, in this respect, a further distinction from contracts supported by consideration which are enforceable even if wholly executory.[184]

(iv) Suspensive or extinctive?

It has been suggested that promissory estoppel only serves to suspend, and not wholly to extinguish, the existing obligation; the promisor may, on giving due notice, resume the right which has been waived and revert to the original terms of the contract.[185] Thus in *Tool Metal Manufacturing Co Ltd v Tungsten Electric Co Ltd*:[186]

In 1938 the appellant granted to the respondent a licence to import, make, use, and sell certain hard metal alloys it had patented. The respondent was to pay royalties, and, if the amount of material made exceeded a named quota, 'compensation'. On the outbreak of war,

---

[182] [1982] 1 All ER 19. See also *Scandinavian Trading Tanker Co AB v Flota Petrola Ecuatoriana* [1983] QB 549 (aff'd [1983] 2 AC 694); *Goldsworthy v Brickell* [1987] Ch 378, 411; *Virulite LLC v Virulite Distribution Ltd* [2014] EWHC 366 (QB), [2015] 1 All ER (Comm) 204 at [121].

[183] [1982] 1 All ER 19, 27.

[184] See *Waltons Stores (Interstate) Ltd v Maher* (1988) 164 CLR 387, 406 (Mason CJ and Wilson J), below, p 130. Cf Lord Denning, who has contended extra-judicially that the repudiation of a promise solemnly given, and intended to effect legal relations, is in itself inequitable: (1952) 15 MLR 1, 6–8.

[185] *Birmingham and District Land Co v L & NW Ry* (1888) 40 Ch D 268, 286; *Ajayi v RT Briscoe (Nigeria) Ltd* [1964] 1 WLR 1326, 1330. See also Wilson (1951) 67 LQR 330; [1965] CLJ 93.

[186] [1955] 1 WLR 761.

the appellant agreed to suspend its right to compensation, the parties contemplating that a new agreement would be entered into when the war ended. In 1945, the appellant claimed to have revoked its suspension and to be entitled to compensation from 1 June 1945. This claim failed on the ground that the revocation was premature as no adequate notice had been given to the respondent. In 1950, the appellant brought the present action, claiming compensation from 1 January 1947, at which date the respondent was fully aware that the appellant was determined to revert to the original agreement.

The House of Lords held that the appellant had effectively revoked its promise to suspend its legal rights and that it was entitled to the compensation claimed; the equitable principle enunciated in *Hughes v Metropolitan Railway Co* was applicable to the situation, but here the promisor, on giving adequate notice to the promisee, could resume its rights under the original agreement. As Bowen LJ had said in an earlier case:[187]

If persons who have contractual rights against others induce by their conduct those against whom they have such rights to believe that such rights will either not be enforced or will be kept in suspense or abeyance for some particular time, those persons will not be allowed by a Court of Equity to enforce the rights until such time has elapsed, without at all events placing the parties in the same position as they were before.

The temporary effect of the estoppel raised is, it has been argued, the characteristic of the doctrine and the reason why it should be considered a 'quasi-estoppel' rather than a true example of estoppel in equity or at common law.

It is, however, submitted that this is not a necessary limitation and that promissory estoppel can extinguish, as well as suspend, the promisee's obligations. For example, it is clear that the promise will become 'final and irrevocable if the promisee cannot resume his position'.[188] More generally, the effect of the estoppel will depend on the terms and intent of the promise. No doubt, as a normal rule, where the contract imposes an obligation to make periodic payments of money, such as the 'compensation' in the *Tool Metal* case, rent under a lease,[189] or instalments under a hire-purchase agreement,[190] a promise to waive part of these payments will be construed to mean that the promisor reserves to himself the right, on giving reasonable notice, to demand that future payments be made in full.[191] But it has been assumed, although not decided, that the right to claim the balance of past payments is foregone and is thus extinguished,[192] unless the promise is one which simply allows the promisee to postpone payment but does not extinguish the debt.[193] This assumption seems correct. If the promise is such

---

[187] *Birmingham and District Land Co v L & NW Ry* (1888) 40 Ch D 268, 286.

[188] *Ajayi v RT Briscoe (Nigeria) Ltd* [1964] 1 WLR 1326, 1330. See also *Nippon Yusen Kaisha v Pacifica Navigacion SA* [1980] 2 Lloyd's Rep 245.

[189] *Central London Property Trust Ltd v High Trees House Ltd* [1947] KB 130.

[190] *Ajayi v RT Briscoe (Nigeria) Ltd,* above, n 188.

[191] *Banning v Wright* [1972] 1 WLR 972, 981.

[192] *Central London Property Trust Ltd v High Trees House Ltd* [1947] KB 130; *Tungsten Electric Co Ltd v Tool Metal Manufacturing Co Ltd* (1950) 69 RPC 108; *P v P* [1957] NZLR 854; *Collier v Wright Holdings Ltd* [2007] EWCA Civ 1329, [2008] 1 WLR 643.

[193] *Ledingham v Bermejo Estancia Co Ltd* [1947] 1 All ER 749.

as unequivocally to indicate the intention of the promisor wholly to abandon all right to payment of the money contractually due, whether periodically or as a lump sum, there is no reason why the estoppel should not be held to have permanent effect.[194]

(v) Promissory estoppel not a cause of action

It has been seen that the principle of promissory estoppel has been employed to obviate the necessity for consideration in cases where parties are already bound contractually one to the other and one of them promises to waive, modify, or suspend its strict legal rights. The question therefore arises whether the principle might similarly be employed as a supplement or alternative to consideration as a necessary element in the formation of contracts. If it could be so employed, there would be two routes (apart from making the promise by deed) to the legal enforceability of a promise; first the furnishing of consideration by the promisee in the form of the incurring of detriment or the conferral of benefit in return for the promise, and secondly, where the promise was intended to affect legal relations and to be acted upon by the promisee, where the promisee's position had been altered in reliance on the promise.[195] This has occurred in some jurisdictions[196] but not yet in England where it is thought illegitimate to outflank the requirement of consideration and where the main doctrinal vehicle for reconciling promissory estoppel and consideration has been the rule that promissory estoppel does not create new causes of action where none existed before; it is 'a shield and not a sword'.[197] It has been said 'that it would be wrong to extend the doctrine of promissory estoppel, whatever its precise limits at the present day, to the extent of abolishing in a backhanded way the doctrine of consideration'.[198] Thus in *Combe v Combe*:[199]

A husband, upon divorce, promised his wife £100 a year as a permanent allowance. In reliance upon this promise, the wife forbore to apply to the Courts for maintenance. The husband failed to make the payments, and the wife sued him on the promise.

The Court of Appeal held that there was no consideration for the promise as the wife's forbearance had not been requested and was not in return for the promise made to her; nor could the wife rely on promissory estoppel, for as Denning LJ put it:[200]

Seeing that the principle never stands alone as giving a cause of action in itself, it can never do away with the necessity of consideration when that is an essential part of the

[194] *Brikom Investments Ltd v Carr* [1979] QB 467, 484–5; *Maharaj v Chand* [1986] AC 898, 908; *Sydenham & Co Ltd v Enichem Elastometers Ltd* [1989] 1 EGLR 257; *Virulite LLC v Virulite Distribution Ltd* [2014] EWHC 366 (QB), [2015] 1 All ER (Comm) 204 at [122]–[125], [141]–[145].
[195] See above, p 126. [196] Below, pp 130–1. [197] *Combe v Combe* [1951] 2 KB 215, 224.
[198] *Brikom Investments Ltd v Carr* [1979] QB 467, 486 (Roskill LJ); *Argy Trading Development Corp Ltd v Lapid Developments Ltd* [1977] 1 WLR 444; *Azov Shipping Co Ltd v Baltic Shipping Co (No 3)* [1999] 2 Lloyd's Rep 159, 175; *Thornton Springer v NEM Insurance Co Ltd* [2000] 2 All ER 489, 516.
[199] [1951] 2 KB 215. See also *Morris v Tarrant* [1971] 2 QB 143, 160; *Argy Trading Development Co Ltd v Lapid Developments Ltd* [1977] 1 WLR 444, 457; *Syros Shipping Co SA v Elaghill Trading Co Ltd* [1980] 2 Lloyd's Rep 390, 393; *Hiscox v Outhwaite (No 3)* [1991] 2 Lloyd's Rep 524, 535.
[200] [1951] 2 KB 215, 220.

cause of action. The doctrine of consideration is too firmly fixed to be overthrown by a side-wind. Its ill-effects have been largely mitigated of late, but it still remains a cardinal necessity of the formation of a contract, though not of its modification or discharge.

There are similar statements in other cases[201] and, although some decisions are difficult to reconcile with this restriction,[202] the Court of Appeal in *Baird Textile Holdings Ltd v Marks & Spencer plc*[203] has confirmed that promissory, as opposed to proprietary,[204] estoppel cannot create a cause of action. This marks a distinction, therefore, between the English approach to promissory estoppel and that taken in some other jurisdictions.[205] But it does not mean that promissory estoppel cannot assist a claimant in establishing a cause of action independent of the promise (for example, in tort).[206] Nor does it mean that there must be a pre-existing *contractual* relationship: for example, promissory estoppel has been applied to a relationship derived from statute.[207]

If promissory estoppel were to be developed so as to create a cause of action, the question would arise as to the precise 'interest' that the doctrine would be protecting. Contract law has traditionally protected a promisee's expectations of performance. It has sometimes been suggested that, in contrast, promissory estoppel is concerned merely to protect the promisee's reliance. On that approach, traditional contract law with its requirement of consideration and its protection of expectations could happily coexist with promissory estoppel as a cause of action protecting reliance. In *Waltons Stores (Interstate) Ltd v Maher*:[208]

M was in negotiations with W to whom he hoped to lease premises which were to be demolished and redeveloped to W's specifications. Solicitors had been instructed to prepare formal documents and W's solicitors told M's solicitors that 'we believe approval will be forthcoming. Let you know tomorrow if any amendments not agreed to'. Later M submitted a contract and this was sent to W 'by way of exchange'. W did not respond for 2 months because it was privately reconsidering the whole deal and had instructed its solicitors 'to go slow'. Because it believed exchange would take place shortly and because, if the timetable for occupation specified by W was to be met, there was urgency, M started work. Two months later, when he had demolished the old premises and was well advanced with the new premises, W told him it intended

---

[201] *Argy Trading Development Co Ltd v Lapid Developments Ltd* [1977] 1 WLR 444, 457; *Syros Shipping Co SA v Elaghill Trading Co* [1981] 3 All ER 189.

[202] *Re Wyvern Developments Ltd* [1974] 1 WLR 1097, 1104, noted by Atiyah (1974) 38 MLR 65; *Pacol Ltd v Trade Lines Ltd, The Henrik Sif* [1982] 1 Lloyd's Rep 456, 466–8.

[203] [2001] EWCA Civ 274, [2002] 1 All ER (Comm) 737.

[204] See *Crabb v Arun AC* [1976] Ch 179, below, p 133.

[205] See especially *Waltons Stores (Interstate) Ltd v Maher* (1988) 164 CLR 387 (Australia).

[206] See Halson [1999] LMCLQ 256.

[207] *Robertson v Minister of Pensions* [1949] 1 KB 227 (soldier and military authorities); *Durham Fancy Goods Ltd v Michael Jackson Fancy Goods Ltd* [1968] 2 QB 839 (statutory liability on director).

[208] (1988) 164 CLR 387. See also ALI *Restatement, Contracts (2d)* para 90; *Harris v Harris* [1989] NZ Conv C 190, 406 (New Zealand). See generally Spence, *Protecting Reliance* (1999).

to withdraw. M argued *inter alia* that W was estopped from denying that a concluded contract existed.

The majority of the High Court of Australia held that promissory estoppel could found a cause of action and extended to the enforcement of voluntary promises; W was accordingly estopped. They did not believe this would abolish the doctrine of consideration 'in a backhanded way' because the two protected different interests. An estoppel remedy only seeks to effect the minimum equity needed to avoid the detriment from reliance whereas, where a promise is supported by consideration, the expectations of the promisee are protected even if the promise is entirely executory and there has been no reliance on it.[209]

The step taken in *Walton Stores* has not been taken in England, in part because of the perceived need to protect the doctrine of consideration. For example, in *Johnson v Gore Wood & Co*[210] Lord Goff stated that it was not possible for the test for estoppel by convention—acting on a common assumption—to apply to promises as opposed to existing facts because that would amount to the abandonment of the doctrine of consideration. And in *Baird Textile Holdings Ltd v Marks & Spencer plc*[211] the move to allowing promissory estoppel to be used as a cause of action was not taken even though the claimants confined their claim to damages protecting their reliance interest. However, we have seen that where negotiations have not led to the conclusion of a contract, reliance in the form of the rendering of services or delivery of goods by one party on assumptions created or encouraged by the other may give rise to a restitutionary remedy for the reversal of an unjust enrichment.[212] There are, moreover, examples of reliance generating a contract through unilateral contracts in which promises are rendered legally enforceable by virtue of the performance of an act by the promisee (ie reliance), often where the promisor has not expressly requested the performance of the act[213] and more recently by the recognition that performance of an existing obligation may be a 'practical' benefit.[214] The doctrinal foundations thus exist for it to be held that promissory estoppel is capable itself of creating a cause of action, notwithstanding that the promisee has provided no consideration.[215] It may be that it has not been *necessary* to do so in the cases that have come before the Courts because either a restitutionary remedy could be found or a bargain exchange could be implied. It is, however, arguable that, until this step is taken, it will not be possible to take up the suggestion made by Lord Hailsham LC

---

[209] (1988) 164 CLR 387, 406. On the remedial consequences of this difference, see below, p 570.

[210] [2002] 2 AC 1, 40–1, citing Spencer Bower and Turner, *The Law Relating to Estoppel by Representation* (3rd edn, 1977) 167–8. See also Colman J in *Azov Shipping Co Ltd v Baltic Shipping Co* [1999] 2 Lloyd's Rep 159, 175 and *Thornton Springer v NEM Insurance Co Ltd* [2000] 2 All ER 489, 516.

[211] [2001] EWCA Civ 274, [2002] 1 All ER (Comm) 737.

[212] Above, pp 45, 67, 71–2 and *Brewer St Investments Ltd v Barclays Woollen Co Ltd* [1954] 1 QB 428.

[213] *Warlow v Harrison* (1858) 1 E & E 309, above, pp 38–9; *Carlill v Carbolic Smoke Ball Co* [1893] 1 QB 256, above, p 41; *Collen v Wright* (1857) 8 E & B 647; *Spiro v Lintern* [1973] 1 WLR 1002; *New Zealand Shipping Co Ltd v Satterthwaite & Co Ltd* [1975] AC 154, 167–8.

[214] Above, pp 114–15.   [215] Thompson [1983] CLJ 257; Lunney [1992] Conv 239.

in 1972 and reduce the sequence of cases based on promissory estoppel to a coherent body of doctrine.[216]

It must, however, be emphasized that the neat division suggested by some[217] between, on the one hand, contract, supported by consideration, protecting expectations and, on the other hand, promissory estoppel protecting reliance does not appear to have been borne out by the promissory estoppel cases. In other words, in several cases the Court has concluded that the minimum equity needed to avoid unconscientiousness will not be satisfied by anything short of enforcing the promise. Thus, for instance, the effect of the estoppel in the *High Trees* case would have been to prevent the landlord recovering the full rent between 1940 and 1945 and in *Crabb v Arun DC*[218] (although this is normally viewed as a proprietary estoppel case) the effect of the estoppel was to grant C the right of way the council had undertaken to give him. In *Waltons Stores (Interstate) Ltd v Maher* the effect of the High Court of Australia's ruling that W was estopped from denying that a concluded contract existed appears to have been that M was entitled to damages in lieu of specific performance.[219] In these cases it appears that equitable relief went beyond the protection of reliance.[220]

(c) THREE OTHER TYPES OF ESTOPPEL

Differing views have been expressed by judges as to whether one should regard various similar types of estoppel as underpinned by a single underlying principle. For example, in *Amalgamated Investment & Property Co Ltd v Texas Commerce International Bank Ltd* Lord Denning MR spoke of different estoppels being seen 'to merge into one general principle shorn of limitations'.[221] In contrast, Millett LJ has said, '[the] attempt to demonstrate that all estoppels other than estoppel by record are now subsumed in the single and all-embracing estoppel by representation and that they are all governed by the same requirements has never won general acceptance'.[222] In *Baird Textiles Holdings Ltd v Marks & Spencer plc*[223] the Court of Appeal, while recognizing that estoppel is a flexible concept, accepted that it 'may take different shapes in the context of different fields';[224] and that this made it necessary to continue to distinguish between promissory estoppel, proprietary estoppel and estoppel by convention. For convenience we also deal with another, and newly recognized, type of estoppel, so-called contractual estoppel.

---

[216] *Woodhouse AC Israel Cocoa Ltd SA v Nigerian Produce Marketing Co Ltd* [1972] AC 741, 758.

[217] See, eg, Robertson (1997) 19 Sydney LR 32.   [218] [1976] Ch 179; see below p 133.

[219] The trial judge's decision to this effect was affirmed by the New South Wales Court of Appeal (1986) 5 NSWLR 407, and the High Court of Australia (1988) 164 CLR 387. Such damages are assessed on the same basis as damages at common law: see below, p 619.

[220] Atiyah, *Essays on Contract* (1986) 239–40; Yorio and Thel (1991) 101 Yale LJ 111. For this debate in the Australian courts, see *Commonwealth of Australia v Verwayen* (1990) 170 CLR 394; *Giumelli v Giumelli* (1999) 196 CLR 101.

[221] [1982] QB 84, 122.   [222] *First National Bank v Thompson* [1996] Ch 231, 236.

[223] [2001] EWCA Civ 274, [2002] 1 All ER (Comm) 737.   [224] *Ibid* at [84] (Mance LJ).

(i) Proprietary estoppel

Proprietary estoppel arises where a person acts in reasonable reliance and to his or her detriment on the belief that he or she has or will acquire rights in or over the property of another in circumstances in which it is unconscionable for the property owner to deny the rights. Thus, in *Crabb v Arun DC*:[225]

The council built a road along the boundary between its property and C's and gave C a point of access to the road. Later C wished to divide his land and sell off one portion. For this purpose C needed a second point of access and, at a site meeting with officers of the council at which he said he would need access at an additional specified point, he was assured that that would be acceptable to the council. Later the council fenced off the boundary and erected gates at the two agreed access points. After C sold the front plot without reserving any right of way from the back plot, the council removed the gates at the access point for the back plot and erected a fence, thus leaving the plot landlocked. It then asked C for £3,000 for a right of access. C sought a declaration claiming that he had a right of way over the second point of access.

The Court of Appeal granted the relief sought. There was no consideration for the council's undertaking and the formality requirements for a contract for the transfer of an interest in land had not been satisfied. But the council, at the meeting and by its conduct in putting up the gates, had led C to believe that he had been or would be granted a right of access at the specified point and it was inequitable for it to insist on its strict title.

Cases on proprietary estoppel have often involved improvements to specific property in the mistaken belief that the improver has or will be given ownership with the owner positively encouraging this detrimental reliance[226] or standing by and acquiescing in it.[227] Not all cases, however, involve such improvements; in some, services were rendered in the belief that ownership would be given.[228] This form of estoppel is narrower than promissory estoppel in requiring detrimental reliance[229]

---

[225] [1976] Ch 179, on which see Atiyah (1974) 92 LQR 174; Millett (1974) 92 LQR 342.

[226] *Ramsden v Dyson* (1866) 1 HL 129, 170; *Dillwyn v Llewellyn* (1862) 4 DF & J 517; *Pascoe v Turner* [1979] 1 WLR 431; *Gillett v Holt* [2001] Ch 210. Cf *Blue Haven Enterprises Ltd v Dulcie Ermine Tully* [2006] UKPC 17 (proprietary estoppel not established because the defendant owner did not encourage the claimant's mistaken belief that would be entitled to the land and hence no unconscionability). See generally Allan (1963) 79 LQR 238; Jackson (1965) 81 LQR 84, 223; Moriarty (1984) 100 LQR 376; Gardner (1999) 115 LQR 353.

[227] *Taylors Fashions Ltd v Liverpool Victoria Trustee Co Ltd* [1982] QB 133, 151–2. See also *A-G of Hong Kong v Humphreys Estates (Queen's Gardens)* [1987] 1 AC 114, 124.

[228] *Tanner v Tanner* [1975] 1 WLR 1346 (property management); *Greasley v Cooke* [1980] 1 WLR 1306 (nursing); *Jennings v Rice* [2002] EWCA Civ 159, [2003] 1 FCR 501 (gardening, shopping, and caring); *Thorner v Major* [2009] UKHL 18, [2009] 1 WLR 776 (work on a farm). Cf *Cobbe v Yeoman's Row Management Ltd* [2008] UKHL 55, [2008] 1 WLR 1752 (obtaining planning permission but proprietary estoppel held not to be made out). For the contrast in reasoning of the House of Lords in the last two cases, see McFarlane and Robertson (2009) 125 LQR 535.

[229] Detriment is not a narrow or technical concept and need not consist of quantifiable financial detriment so long as it is something substantial: *Gillett v Holt* [2001] Ch 210, 232 (Robert Walker LJ).

and the belief that a legal right over property[230] has or will be given but broader in not requiring an unequivocal representation and in its ability to create new rights.[231] One reason sometimes given for allowing the creation of new rights is that the legal owner of the property would otherwise be unjustly enriched by getting the benefit of the improved property for nothing. This cannot, however, account for most of the cases. For instance, in *Crabb v Arun DC* the council would not have been unjustly enriched in this way. And even where there has been an unjust enrichment, the remedy for the proprietary estoppel is not concerned to give restitution of the value of that enrichment although there may be a separate claim in the law of restitution.[232] Scarman LJ stated that he did not find the distinction between promissory and proprietary estoppel helpful,[233] but, however tenuous the distinction between the two, they have continued to be treated separately in the subsequent case law.[234]

(ii) Estoppel by convention

When the parties have acted in relation to a transaction upon a shared mistaken[235] assumption (either of fact or law) then, as regards that transaction, each will be estopped against the other from questioning the truth of the facts or of law so assumed where it would be unjust and unconscionable to resile from that shared assumption. In *Amalgamated Investment & Property Co Ltd v Texas Commerce International Bank Ltd*:[236]

AIP negotiated with the TCI bank for a loan to one of its subsidiaries to be secured *inter alia* by a guarantee by AIP. TCI decided to make the loan through Portsoken, a subsidiary company it bought for the purpose, but AIP's guarantee related to *moneys due to you*, ie to loans made by TCI. AIP got into financial difficulties and was wound up. TCI had sold property belonging to AIP and applied $750,000 of the proceeds in payment of the outstanding balance of the loan made through Portsoken. AIP's liquidator sought a declaration that AIP was under no liability for loans made by Portsoken, and that TCI had not been entitled to apply the money in this way.

---

[230] *Western Fish Products Ltd v Penwith District Council* [1981] 2 All ER 204, 217. In principle, property should include all forms of property but the cases, while contemplating property in goods, only provide authority for land.

[231] *Baird Textile Holdings Ltd v Marks & Spencer plc* [2001] EWCA Civ 274, [2002] 1 All ER (Comm) 737.

[232] In *Cobbe v Yeoman's Row Management Ltd* [2008] UKHL 55, [2008] 1 WLR 1752 a quantum meruit for the value of the services in obtaining the planning permission succeeded even though proprietary estoppel was not made out.

[233] [1976] Ch 179, 193.   [234] See especially the *Baird Textile* case, above n 231.

[235] The mistake may be of both parties or of one party acquiesced in by the other: *Republic of India v India Steamship Co Ltd, The Indian Grace (No 2)* [1998] AC 878, 913.

[236] [1982] QB 84, 126, 130; *Lokumal & Sons (London) Ltd v Lotte Shipping Co Pte Ltd* [1985] 2 Lloyd's Rep 28, 34–5 (Kerr LJ); *Hiscox v Outhwaite* [1992] 1 AC 562, 575 (Lord Donaldson MR); *Republic of India v India Steamship Co Ltd, The Indian Grace (No 2)* [1997] 2 WLR 538, 549 (Staughton LJ) and [1998] AC 878, 913 (HL); *The Republic of Serbia v Imagesat International NV* [2009] EWHC 2853 (Comm) at [67]–[71] and [80]–[82]. The estoppel applies only 'for the period of time and to the extent required by the equity which the estoppel has raised': *Troop v Gibson* (1986) 277 EG 1134, 1144.

The Court of Appeal held that the guarantee, on its true interpretation, applied to loans by Portsoken, but also stated that even if it did not, AIP was estopped from denying that by an estoppel by convention: both parties had assumed that the guarantee would cover loans by Portsoken. Brandon LJ stated that while a person 'cannot in terms found a cause of action on an estoppel, he may, as a result of being able to rely on an estoppel, succeed on a cause of action on which, without being able to rely on that estoppel, he would necessarily have failed'.[237] In other words, had the TCI bank been suing on the contractual guarantee, the relevant cause of action would have been a standard contractual cause of action: estoppel by convention would have come in not to found the cause of action but to prevent AIP applying an interpretation of the guarantee that was contrary to both parties' understanding and conduct.

(iii) Contractual estoppel

This type of estoppel has been developed in the specific context of the exclusion of liability for misrepresentation by contractual provisions which provide that a party has not made, or the other party has not relied on, a representation.[238] The explanation for why such a 'no reliance' or 'no representation' clause can contradict the truth that the claimant *has relied on a representation* was said by Moore-Bick LJ in *Peekay Intermark Ltd v Australia and New Zealand Banking Group Ltd*[239] to turn on a 'contractual estoppel'. This type of estoppel does not require reliance or detrimental reliance.

If contractual estoppel is a valid concept, it would appear that it can have importance beyond explaining how 'no reliance' or 'no representation' clauses work and can apply more generally to prevent parties denying the existence of a state of affairs which was the basis of their contract. This is most clearly understood from what Moore-Bick LJ said in the *Peekay* case:[240]

There is no reason in principle why parties to a contract should not agree that a certain state of affairs should form the basis for the transaction, whether it be the case or not. For example, it may be desirable to settle a disagreement as to an existing state of affairs in order to establish a clear basis for the contract itself and its subsequent performance. Where parties express an agreement of that kind in a contractual document neither can subsequently deny the existence of the facts and matters upon which they have agreed, at least so far as concerns those aspects of their relationship to which the agreement was directed. The contract itself gives rise to an estoppel…

This makes clear that the scope of contractual estoppel can extend beyond 'no reliance' and 'no representation' clauses and may apply to all situations in which

---

[237] [1982] QB 84, 132. See also at 122 (Lord Denning MR). Cf Eveleigh LJ at 126.

[238] See below pp 351–2.

[239] [2006] EWCA Civ 386, [2006] 2 Lloyd's Rep 511, at [56]–[57]. This was confirmed in *Springwell Navigation Corp v JP Morgan Chase* [2010] EWCA Civ 1221, [2010] 2 CLC 705 at [165]–[169], [177]. For a sharp denunciation of the notion of 'contractual estoppel', see McMeel [2011] LMCLQ 185.

[240] [2006] EWCA Civ 386, [2006] 2 Lloyd's Rep 511 at [56].

a party has warranted that a certain state of affairs exists. For example, it may be a term of a contract to sell a business that equipment is of a certain age, or that there are no outstanding claims against the business, or that the order books are full. The party providing that warranty cannot then deny that the state of affairs is different than warranted. Indeed one might ask whether there is any need to refer to a contractual estoppel at all since a party denying the state of affairs that it has warranted to be true would be in breach of contract and the other party would be entitled to standard remedies for breach.[241] The fact that one is dealing with breach of a term might explain why, in relation to this type of estoppel, it is irrelevant to consider whether a party relied or detrimentally relied on what was agreed. However, if one were seeking to defend the language of estoppel here, one might say that its importance, going beyond the normal consequences of breach of a term, is that it explains there being a rule of evidence that the party cannot deny that the state of affairs is different than warranted. The ordinary rules as to breach perhaps cannot explain that rule of evidence. However, a contrary, and probably preferable, view is that the language of estoppel here reflects nothing more than the idea that a party may be prevented by a court from being in breach of contract and that the concept of a contractual estoppel is unnecessary and unhelpful.

3. APPRAISAL OF CONSIDERATION AND PROMISSORY ESTOPPEL

Attempts have been made to justify the doctrine of consideration on the ground that it is essential both to the form and the substance of a contract. Consideration, it has been argued, is a formal necessity which serves to distinguish those promises by which the promisor intends to be legally bound from those which are not seriously meant: 'buyers intend business where philanthropists may not'.[242] But English law already requires an intent to create legal relations as a distinct element of a contract. Consideration is cogent evidence of the existence of such an intent, but it is by no means conclusive proof that it is present.[243] The abolition of the doctrine would therefore simply mean that the test of contractual intention would assume a greater significance in the law of contract. Few persons would contend that this constituted an insuperable objection to a change in the law,[244] for civil law systems seem to exist quite happily without the need for consideration.[245]

---

[241] See the analysis by Andrew Smith J in *Credit Suisse International v Stichting Vestia Groep* [2014] EWHC 3103 (Comm) especially at [309].

[242] Smith and Thomas, *A Casebook on Contract* (2nd edn, 1961) 126.

[243] *Balfour v Balfour* [1919] 2 KB 571; *Coward v Motor Insurers' Bureau* [1963] 1 QB 259, above, pp 74–7.

[244] Cf Atiyah, *Consideration in Contracts: A Fundamental Restatement* (1971).

[245] Lando and Beale, *Principles of European Contract Law Parts I and II* (2000) 140–3; cf Chloros (1968) 17 ICLQ 137; Markesinis [1978] CLJ 53.

Similarly, aspects of the doctrine, in particular the pre-existing duty rule, have been justified by the need to discourage improper pressure and coercion, a function now more directly and effectively served by the recent recognition of economic duress as a ground for avoiding a contract.[246]

It has also been argued that English law has made the choice of enforcing bargains (in the sense of exchanges) rather than promises: 'consideration, offer and acceptance are an indivisible trinity, facets of one identical notion which is that of bargain[247] But this does not explain why it is thought better to enforce bargains.[248] Indeed the opposite appears to be the case. Desire to enforce promises has led the Courts on occasion to find a derisory consideration and to construct a bargain where none in fact was present since there was no real exchange. It has been stated that 'ultimately the question of consideration is a formality as in the use of a seal or the agreement to give a peppercorn'[249] and the recognition that a 'practical' benefit will make a promise enforceable[250] makes it difficult to sustain a purely bargain view of contract. Elsewhere, the absence of consideration may enable one of the parties to 'snap his fingers' at a promise deliberately made, and which the person seeking to enforce it has a legitimate interest to enforce.[251] The perception that this is incompatible with such legitimate interests led to the development of promissory estoppel in the context of the part performance of an existing duty. This development makes it difficult to regard bargain as the fundamental principle of contract. When put together with common law 'waiver',[252] it is arguable that consideration has been effectively confined to the formation of contracts and the error in making it also regulate the discharge of contracts[253] has been substantially corrected.

It has been noted that consideration reflects a variety of policies and serves a number of functions. The doctrine has in the past been the Swiss army knife of the law, performing these functions[254] in an ingenious but imperfect way. Professor Simpson has described the identification and separation of these policies and functions and the development in the last 200 years of new, more targeted doctrines.[255] We now have a doctrine of offer and acceptance, a requirement of intention to create legal relations, a concept of economic duress, and a doctrine of privity of contract. There is considerable force in the conclusion of the Law Revision Committee in 1937,[256] which stated that in many cases consideration was a mere technicality, irreconcilable either with business

---

[246] Above, pp 113–16; below, Chapter 10.   [247] Hamson (1938) 54 LQR 233, 234.
[248] It has been said that non-bargain promises are economically sterile (Posner (1977) 6 J Leg Stud 411) and that they should only be enforced if relied upon and only to the extent of the reliance (Eisenberg (1979) 47 U of Chicago LR 1, 3–7).
[249] Vantage Navigation Corp v Suhail & Saud Bahwan Building Materials Llc, The Alev [1989] 1 Lloyd's Rep 138, 147 (Hobhouse J).
[250] Above, pp 114–16.
[251] Above, p 109 (pre-existing duty cases) and, albeit in the context of a contract for the benefit of a third party, Dunlop Pneumatic Tyre Co Ltd v Selfridge & Co Ltd [1915] AC 847, 855 (Lord Dunedin).
[252] Below, p 490.
[253] Pollock, Principles of Contract (12th edn, 1950) 146. See also Kötz, European Contract Law (1997) 68–71.
[254] Above, p 96.   [255] (1975) 91 LQR 247, 263.   [256] Cmd 5449.

expediency or common sense. In *Johnson v Gore Wood & Co*[257] Lord Goff stated that although 'the doctrine of consideration may not be very popular nowadays . . . [it] still exists as part of our law'. It is, however, submitted that its role should be confined to the formation of contracts and that it should be supplemented by the principle of promissory estoppel. Promissory estoppel will only come into play where there has been reliance, whereas if there is consideration the expectations of the promisee are protected even if the promise is entirely executory. Although a promissory estoppel can only be raised where there has been reliance, where it is, as in a number of the cases discussed above,[258] relief may go beyond the protection of that reliance. Although a promissory estoppel remedy only seeks to effect the minimum equity to avoid the detriment from reliance and unconscionable conduct, such cases are arguably explained as ones in which the Court concluded that unconscientiousness could only be prevented by enforcing the promise or otherwise protecting the promisee's expectations.

FURTHER READING

ATIYAH, 'Consideration in Contracts: A Fundamental Restatement' (1971) reprinted (with slight revision) in *Essays on Contract* (Oxford: Clarendon Press, 1986) 179

TREITEL, 'Consideration: A Critical Analysis of Professor Atiyah's Fundamental Restatement' (1976) 50 ALJ 439

ATIYAH, 'When is an Enforceable Agreement not a Contract? Answer: When it is an Equity' (1976) 92 LQR 174

MILLETT, 'Crabb v Arun DC—A Riposte' (1976) 92 LQR 342

BURROWS, 'Contract, Tort & Restitution—A Satisfactory Division or Not?' (1983) 99 LQR 217, 239–44

PEEL, 'Part Payment of a Debt is no Consideration' (1994) 100 LQR 353

O'SULLIVAN, 'In Defence of Foakes v Beer' [1996] CLJ 219

COOKE, 'Estoppel and the Protection of Expectations' (1997) 17 Legal Studies 258

HALSON, 'The Offensive Limits of Promissory Estoppel' [1999] LMCLQ 256

TREITEL, *Some Landmarks of Twentieth Century Contract Law* (Oxford: Clarendon Press, 2002) chapter 1

CHEN-WISHART, 'A Bird in the Hand: Consideration and Promissory Estoppel' in BURROWS and PEEL (eds), *Contract Formation and Parties* (Oxford: Oxford University Press, 2010) 89

CHEN-WISHART, 'In Defence of Consideration' (2013) 13 OUCLJ 209

---

[257] [2002] 2 AC 1, 40. See also the wide-ranging judicial examination of consideration (which reads like a law article) by Andrew Phang Boon Leong JA in *obiter dicta* in *Gay Choon Ing v Loh Sze Ti Terence Peter* [2009] SGCA 3, [2009] 2 SLR 332.

[258] Above, p 132.

PART 2

CONTENTS OF
THE CONTRACT

5

THE TERMS OF
THE CONTRACT

In most cases the contract is composed of a number of contractual terms. This chapter considers the nature and import of those terms and the form which they may take. First, the terms of a contract will be distinguished from representations, which are statements made by one party to the other that are not intended to be an integral part of the agreement. Similarly, collateral warranties, which are preliminary assurances that are contractually binding, but not as part of the principal agreement, will be distinguished from representations that are not contractually binding. Secondly, the importance of different types of terms will be examined by reference to the distinction between conditions, warranties, and innominate terms. Thirdly, the implication of terms into contracts will be explored. Finally, the chapter will look generally at the interpretation or construction of terms.

1. TERMS, COLLATERAL WARRANTIES, AND REPRESENTATIONS

(a) TERMS AND REPRESENTATIONS

During the course of negotiations leading to the conclusion of a binding agreement, one or other of the contracting parties may make a statement or give an assurance calculated to produce in the mind of the other party a belief that facts exist which render the proposed bargain advantageous to the interests of the other party. A Court may later have to decide whether this statement or assurance formed part of the contract, or whether it was merely a 'representation' or inducement, in the sense that the party making it did not undertake to make it good. Although a representation which proves to be false renders the agreement voidable at the suit of the party misled,[1] and may, if made fraudulently or negligently, give rise to damages in tort, nevertheless it cannot of itself give rise to an action for breach of contract.[2]

---

[1] Below, Chapter 9.

[2] *Behn v Burness* (1863) 3 B & S 751, 753.

Such an action will only lie for breach of a contractual term. The question whether a particular statement is a term of the contract or a representation is frequently one of considerable difficulty and the basis of the distinction between the two has been criticized.[3]

(i) Intention to promise

The primary test is of *contractual intention*, that is, whether there is evidence of an intention by one or both parties that there should be contractual liability in respect of the accuracy of the statement.[4] The question therefore is: on the totality of evidence, must the person making the statement be taken to have *warranted* its accuracy, that is, promised to make it good? If the facts of the case are such as to show this intention the Court may construe as a term of the contract a statement or assurance made anterior to the final agreement. In *Bannerman v White*:[5]

B offered hops for sale to W. W asked if any sulphur had been used in the treatment of the year's growth, as brewers were refusing hops contaminated with sulphur. B said 'No'. W said that he would not even ask the price if sulphur had been used. They then discussed the price, and W ultimately purchased by sample B's entire growth. After the hops were delivered he repudiated the contract on the ground that the hops contained sulphur. B sued for their price. It was proved that sulphur had been used on five of B's three hundred acres. B had used it for the purpose of trying a new machine, and had either forgotten the matter or thought it unimportant.

The question whether W was entitled to reject the hops turned upon whether it should be regarded as a condition of the agreement that the hops might be rejected if sulphur had been used. It was argued that 'the conversation relating to the sulphur was preliminary to entering on the contract and no part thereof', but the jury found it was understood and intended by the parties to be part of the contract of sale. The Court of Common Pleas upheld this finding, and said that B's assurance was the condition upon which the parties contracted and the breach of it discharged W from liability to take the hops.[6]

That the test is one of the parties' intentions—and that all evidence is relevant in determining those intentions, rather than there being a decisive secondary test—was shown in the leading case of *Heilbut, Symons & Co v Buckleton*:[7]

B telephoned HS's agent and said 'I understand you are bringing out a rubber company'. The reply was 'We are'. B asked for a prospectus, and was told there were none available. He then asked 'if it was all right', and the agent replied 'We are bringing it out'. On the faith of

---

[3] Williston (1913) 27 Harv L Rev 1; Atiyah, *Essays on Contract* (1986) 275.
[4] *Heilbut, Symons & Co v Buckleton* [1913] AC 30, 51.
[5] (1861) 10 CBNS 844. See also *Schawel v Reade* [1913] 2 Ir R 64.
[6] Contrast *Hopkins v Tanqueray* (1854) 15 CB 130, which was probably wrongly decided.
[7] [1913] AC 30. 38, 42, 49–50 (Lord Haldane LC, Lord Atkinson, and Lord Moulton). See also *Independent Broadcasting Authority v EMI Electronics Ltd* (1980) 14 BLR 1, 22–3, 32, 41 (HL) (in respect of a statement made *long* after the contract).

this, B bought shares which turned out to be of little value. The company was not accurately described as 'a rubber company', although this assurance had not been given in bad faith. B claimed damages for breach of contract.

The House of Lords held that no breach of contract had been committed. There had been merely a representation and no warranty. There was no intention on the part of either or both of the parties that there should be contractual liability in respect of the accuracy of the statement.

Heilbut, Symons & Co v Buckleton has been criticized[8] and, arguably, Courts are no longer as reluctant to find that a pre-contractual statement amounts to a term of the contract.[9]

Certainly, the difficulty of ascertaining intention means that the dividing line between the two categories of statement remains one that is not easy to draw in practice. For example, in *Oscar Chess Ltd v Williams*,[10] a private seller sold a car to a firm of dealers. He told them that the car was a 1948 model, and the car logbook showed that it had been first registered in 1948. In fact it was a 1939 model. The logbook had been altered by some unknown person. The Court of Appeal (Morris LJ dissenting) held that the seller's statement was not a term of the contract, but merely a representation not giving rise to any action for breach of contract. On the other hand, in *Dick Bentley Productions Ltd v Harold Smith (Motors) Ltd*,[11] a statement made by a motor dealer to a private purchaser, based on a reading of the milometer, that a car had done only 20,000 miles, whereas in fact it had done 100,000, was held to be a contractual term. The *Oscar Chess* case was distinguished on the ground that the seller 'honestly believed on reasonable grounds that [the statement] was true', whereas the motor dealer in the latter case 'who was in a position to know, or at least to find out the history of the car', 'stated a fact that should be within his own knowledge. He had jumped to a conclusion and stated it as a fact'.[12]

In endeavouring to reach a conclusion as to the parties' intentions, the Courts can be said to take into account a number of factors, although none of these is in itself decisive. First, they may have regard to the time which elapsed between the time of making the statement and the final manifestation of agreement; if the interval is a long one, this points to a representation.[13] Secondly, they may consider the importance of the statement in the minds of the parties; a statement which is important is likely to be classed as a term of the contract.[14] Thirdly, if the statement was followed by the execution of a formal contract in writing, it is more likely to be

---

[8] Williston (1913) 27 Harv L Rev 1; Greig (1971) 87 LQR 179, Atiyah, *Essays on Contract* (1986) 277–8.

[9] *J Evans & Son (Portsmouth) Ltd v Andrea Merzario Ltd* [1976] 1 WLR 1078, 1081; *Esso Petroleum Co Ltd v Mardon* [1976] QB 801, 817; *Howard Marine and Dredging Co Ltd v A Ogden & Sons (Excavations) Ltd* [1978] QB 574, 590.

[10] [1957] 1 WLR 370. Cf *Beale v Taylor* [1967] 1 WLR 1193.

[11] [1965] 1 WLR 623.　　　　　　　　　　　　　　　　　[12] [1965] 1 WLR 623, 628, 629.

[13] *Routledge v McKay* [1954] 1 WLR 615; *Howard Marine and Dredging Co Ltd v A Ogden & Sons (Excavations) Ltd* [1978] QB 574, 591. Cf *Birch v Paramount Estates Ltd* (1956) 167 EG 396.

[14] *Bannerman v White* (1861) 10 CBNS 844. Cf *Oscar Chess Ltd v Williams*, above, n 10.

regarded as a representation where it is not incorporated in the written document.[15] Finally, where the maker of the statement is, vis-à-vis the other party, in a better position to ascertain the accuracy of the statement or has the primary responsibility for doing this, the Courts will tend to regard it as a contractual term.[16]

(ii) The influence of wider considerations

The precise place in which the dividing line between representations and terms is drawn may have also been affected by two other factors. The first of these was the distorting effect of the rule that, before the decision of the House of Lords in *Hedley Byrne & Co Ltd v Heller & Partners Ltd*[17] in 1963, damages in tort could not be awarded for negligent misstatement. Parties seeking to escape from this much criticized feature of English law would often argue that a statement was a warranty.[18] Although damages for negligent misstatement have been available since *Hedley Byrne*, so that the purpose of making the distinction is no longer to determine whether the maker of the statement is liable in damages, there are still differences between damages in tort and contract. Damages for breach of contract do not depend on establishing negligence and the measure of damages for breach of contract differs from that for misrepresentation.[19]

Secondly, in the past it was generally not possible to adduce extrinsic, for example, oral, evidence to contradict or vary the terms of a written agreement.[20] This 'parol evidence' rule meant that whatever the intention of the parties and however important the oral statement, it could only exceptionally be held to be a term of the contract. Normally therefore, it had to be classified as a representation[21] although, as we shall now see, it might instead be classed as a collateral warranty.

(iii) Information provided by a trader to a consumer

The Consumer Rights Act 2015 provides that a consumer contract for the supply of goods, digital content, or services is to be treated as including as a term certain information provided by a trader to a consumer.[22] In practice, this means that most pre-contractual misrepresentations made by a trader to a consumer become terms

---

[15] *Heilbut, Symons & Co v Buckleton* [1913] AC 30, 50. Cf *Miller v Cannon Hill Estates Ltd* [1931] 2 KB 113, and see below, p 145 (collateral warranty).

[16] *Schawel v Reade*, above, n 5; *Dick Bentley Productions Ltd v Harold Smith (Motors) Ltd*, above, n 11. See also *Harlingdon and Leinster Enterprises Ltd v Christopher Hull Fine Art* [1991] 1 QB 564, 577, 585. Cf *Heilbut, Symons & Co v Buckleton* [1913] AC 30; *Beale v Taylor* [1967] 1 WLR 1193; *Thake v Maurice* [1986] QB 644 (statement that vasectomy was irreversible not a warranty).

[17] [1964] AC 465, below p 346. See also Misrepresentation Act 1967, s 2(1), below, p 347 (non-consumers), and consumers' rights under Consumer Protection from Unfair Trading Regulations 2008, below, p 355.

[18] Cf *Heilbut, Symons & Co v Buckleton* [1913] AC 30, 51 and *Esso Petroleum Co Ltd v Mardon* [1976] QB 801, 817.

[19] Below, pp 344, 347.   [20] Below, p 146.

[21] For a modern example, see *Lambert v Lewis* [1982] AC 225, 263.

[22] Consumer Rights Act 2015, ss 11–12 (goods contracts), ss 36–37 (digital content contracts), and s 50 (services contracts). The information in question is that specified or mentioned in the Consumer Contracts (Information, Cancellation and Additional Charges) Regulations 2013 (SI 2013 No 3134): see below p 370.

of the contract between them. For example, in a consumer contract for the supply of services, anything that is said or written to the consumer, by or on behalf of the trader, about the trader or service, which is taken into account by the consumer when deciding to enter into the contract, is to be treated as included as a term of the contract.[23]

(b) COLLATERAL WARRANTIES

Where a preliminary statement or assurance is not a term of the principal agreement the Courts may be prepared to treat it as a contract or 'warranty', collateral to the principal agreement.[24] In particular, in the past, this device has been used where the principal agreement has been reduced to writing, since the parol evidence rule generally prevented the assurance from constituting a term of that contract. Provided the necessary contractual intention has been present, the Courts have been willing to construe the assurance as a collateral contract or warranty conferring a right to damages.[25] Thus where tenants executed leases upon the oral assurance of the landlord that the drains were in good order,[26] or that the landlord would not enforce a covenant against residing on the premises,[27] the tenant was held entitled to enforce the assurance as a collateral warranty. In particular, a statement was likely to found a warranty where one party refused to enter into a contract unless the other gave it an assurance on a certain point.[28]

In 1913, Lord Moulton said of such collateral warranties that they are 'viewed with suspicion by the law. They must be proved strictly', and that they 'must from their very nature be rare'.[29] Nevertheless, since that time the Courts have showed themselves much more willing to treat pre-contractual statements as collateral warranties, and they are no longer rare.

In *Esso Petroleum Co Ltd v Mardon*,[30] for example:

Esso found a site on a busy main street which it considered suitable for the erection of a petrol filling station. An experienced employee estimated that the throughput of petrol at the station would reach 200,000 gallons in the third year of operation. But the planning authority refused permission for the forecourt and pumps to be sited on the main street and they had to be sited at the rear of the premises where they were only accessible by side streets. M applied for a tenancy of the filling station. He was interviewed by the experienced employee, who gave him the same estimate of throughput but failed to take account of

---

[23] Consumer Rights Act 2015, s 50.   [24] Wedderburn [1959] CLJ 58.

[25] *Morgan v Griffith* (1871) LR 6 Ex 70; *Newman v Gatti* (1907) 24 TLR 18, 20; *Miller v Cannon Hill Estates Ltd* [1931] 2 KB 113; *Birch v Paramount Estates Ltd* (1956) 167 EG 396; *Frisby v BBC* [1967] Ch 932.

[26] *De Lassalle v Guildford* [1901] 2 KB 215.

[27] *City and Westminster Properties (1934) Ltd v Mudd* [1959] Ch 129. See also *Erskine v Adeane* (1873) 8 Ch App 756 (landlord's assurance that the game upon the land would be culled).

[28] *Erskine v Adeane*, above, n 27; *De Lassalle v Guildford* [1901] 2 KB 215; *Couchman v Hill* [1947] KB 554.

[29] *Heilbut, Symons & Co v Buckleton* [1913] AC 30, 47.

[30] [1976] QB 801. Cf *Jonathan Wren & Co Ltd v Microdec plc* (1999) 65 Con LR 157 (Lord Moulton's approach 'applies strongly' where it is sought to make a third party additionally liable for some performance).

the fact that the filling station was now 'back to front'. In reliance on the estimate, M took a 3-year lease of the filling station. Despite his best efforts, the site proved incapable of a throughput of more than 60,000 to 70,000 gallons. In an action by Esso for possession of the station and monies due for petrol supplied, M counterclaimed damages for (inter alia) breach of a collateral warranty.

The Court of Appeal rejected the argument that the estimate could not amount to a warranty because it was a forecast or statement of opinion. It was held that the statement as to potential throughput amounted to a collateral warranty—not in the sense that Esso guaranteed that the throughput would reach 200,000 gallons, but a warranty that the forecast had been prepared with reasonable care and skill. Since Esso negligently made 'a fatal error' in the forecast given to M, and on which he took the tenancy, they were liable to him in damages for breach of contract.

This device of a collateral warranty has also been employed where the principal contract is one to which either the person giving, or the person receiving, the assurance is not a party. In *Shanklin Pier Ltd v Detel Products Ltd*:[31]

The owners (B) of Shanklin Pier in the Isle of Wight consulted Detel (A), a firm of paint manufacturers, about painting the pier. Detel told the owners that its paint was suitable for the purpose. Relying on this statement, the owners caused to be inserted in their agreement with the contractors (C) who were to paint the pier a term requiring the use of Detel's paint. The paint proved unsuitable and the owners sued Detel for breach of warranty.

It was held that the owners were entitled to damages. There was a collateral warranty between the owners (B) and Detel (A), collateral to the purchase of the paint by the contractors (C) from Detel (A), with the consideration for A's promise as to the suitability of the paint being B's instruction to C to buy the paint from A. McNair J said:[32]

I see no reason why there may not be an enforceable warranty between A and B supported by the consideration that B should cause C to enter into a contract with A or that B should do some other act for the benefit of A.

This principle is particularly applicable to cases of hire-purchase where a dealer first sells the article to a hire-purchase finance company which then lets it on hire to the hirer. If the dealer gives a warranty, which induces the hirer to enter into the contract of hire, this warranty is enforceable against the dealer by the hirer, even though the actual contract of hire-purchase is not made between them.[33]

(c) EXTRINSIC EVIDENCE

Where an agreement is contained in a written document, the question arises whether extrinsic evidence may be led to establish the existence of a term. It has often

---

[31] [1951] 2 KB 854. See also *Wells (Merstham) Ltd v Buckland Sand & Silica Co Ltd* [1965] 2 QB 170; *Lambert v Lewis* [1982] AC 225, 263.

[32] [1951] 2 KB 854, 856.

[33] *Andrews v Hopkinson* [1957] 1 QB 229; *Yeoman Credit Ltd v Ogders* [1962] 1 WLR 215.

been said that 'it is firmly established as a rule of law that parol evidence cannot be admitted to add to, vary or contradict a deed or other written instrument', including a contract,[34] although the rule was more favoured in the past than it is now.[35] Its purpose is to promote certainty[36] and to save time in the conduct of litigation,[37] but the large number of exceptions to the rule have resulted in uncertainty. We shall see[38] that extrinsic evidence may sometimes be available to assist with the interpretation of a contract. But it is also admissible to prove the existence of a collateral agreement,[39] to establish implied terms[40] and, more importantly, if it is shown that the document was not intended to express the entire agreement between the parties.[41] It is also admissible to show that the contract is not operative[42] and to impugn the validity of the contract on the grounds of illegality, misrepresentation,[43] mistake, or duress.

The width of the exceptions led the Law Commission to the view that:

although a proposition of law can be stated which can be described as the 'parol evidence' rule it is not a rule of law which, correctly applied, could lead to evidence being unjustly excluded. Rather it is a proposition of law which is no more than a circular statement: when it is proved or admitted that the parties to a contract intended that all the express terms in their agreement should be recorded in a particular document or documents, evidence will be inadmissible (because irrelevant) if it is tendered only for the purpose of adding to, varying, subtracting from or contradicting the express terms of that contract.[44]

The Law Commission concluded[45] that there is no *rule of law* precluding the admissibility of evidence solely because a document exists which looks like a complete contract and that there was accordingly no need for legislation to abrogate the supposed rule as it had provisionally recommended in its Working Paper.[46] The presumption that a document which looks like a contract is the whole contract is only a presumption,[47] and, save where the document states that it contains the entire contract,[48] is unlikely to

---

[34] *Jacobs v Batavia and General Plantations Trust* [1924] 1 Ch 287, 295; *Bank of Australasia v Palmer* [1897] AC 540, 454; *Rabin v Gerson Berger Association Ltd* [1986] 1 WLR 526, 530; *Adams v British Airways plc* [1995] IRLR 577, 583.

[35] Law Com No 154, *The Parol Evidence Rule* (1986) paras 2.3–2.4.

[36] *Shore v Wilson* (1842) 9 CL & F 355, 565–6; *Inglis v John Buttery & Co* (1878) 3 App Cas 552, 577; *Mercantile Agency Co Ltd v Flitwick Chalybeate Co* (1897) 14 TLR 90.

[37] *Prenn v Simmonds* [1971] 1 WLR 1381, 1384.

[38] Below, pp 179–82. [39] Above, p 145.

[40] *Gillespie Bros & Co v Cheney Eggar & Co* [1896] 2 QB 59 (term implied under the Sale of Goods Act 1979); *Hutton v Warren* (1836) 1 M and W 466 (custom).

[41] *Mercantile Bank of Sydney v Taylor* [1893] AC 317, 321; *Gillespie Bros & Co v Cheney, Eggar & Co*, above, n 40, 62; *J Evans & Son (Portsmouth) Ltd v Andrea Merzario Ltd* [1976] 1 WLR 1078, 1083.

[42] *Pym v Campbell* (1856) 6 E & B 370.

[43] *Thomas Witter Ltd v TBP Industries Ltd* [1996] 2 All ER 573, 595.

[44] Law Com No 154 (1986), para 2.7. See generally Wedderburn [1959] CLJ 58.

[45] Law Com No 154 (1986), para 2.17. [46] Law Com WP No 76 (1976).

[47] *Gillespie Bros & Co v Cheney Eggar & Co* [1896] 2 QB 59.

[48] Such an entire agreement clause does not operate to exclude a claim for misrepresentation (although it is commonly combined with a separate clause that does exclude misrepresentation): *McGrath v Shaw* (1987) 57 P & CR 452, 459–60; *Thomas Witter Ltd v TBP Industries Ltd* [1996] 2 All ER 573, 595–7; *Deepak Fertilisers and Petrochemicals Corp v ICI Chemicals & Polymers Ltd* [1999] 1 Lloyd's Rep 387, 395; *Government of*

preclude the receipt of evidence of other terms not included expressly or by reference in the document.

Although the traditional description of a parol evidence *rule* may have a lingering influence,[49] the Law Commission's approach has been judicially approved.[50] It is also attractive from a policy point of view. This is because, although facilitating the parties' intentions is an important function of contract law, regarding the issue as governed by a rule of law can have the effect of excluding much evidence of the intentions of the parties without achieving the certainty which the 'rule' aimed to achieve.

2. CONDITIONS, WARRANTIES, AND INNOMINATE TERMS

(a) INTRODUCTION

In deciding whether a contract can be terminated for breach, or whether the breach merely triggers a right to damages, the Courts have looked at the importance of the term broken as well as the seriousness of the consequences of the breach. This has resulted in the distinction between conditions, warranties, and innominate terms.

One approach, reflected in the Sale of Goods Act 1979,[51] is to classify the term at the time the contract is made as either a condition or a warranty. If the parties regarded the term as essential, it is classified as a *condition*: any breach of a condition gives the innocent party the option of being discharged from further performance of the contract. The innocent party can also claim damages for any loss sustained by the fact that the contract has not been performed. If the parties did not regard the term as essential, but as subsidiary or collateral, it is classified as a *warranty*; its failure gives rise to a claim for such damages as have been sustained by the breach of that particular term, but the innocent party is not given the option of being discharged from further performance. The classification of a term as being either a 'condition' or a 'warranty' will therefore determine the legal remedies available to the innocent party in the event of its breach.

Nevertheless, it is right to observe that the word 'condition' is sometimes used, even in legal documents, to mean simply 'a stipulation, a provision', and does not carry the meaning given to it by lawyers as a term of art.[52] Moreover, in the context of non-consumer sales, statute has restricted the right of a buyer to reject goods by reason of

---

Zanzibar v British Aerospace (Lancaster House) Ltd [2000] 1 WLR 2333; *Axa Sun Life Services Plc v Campbell Martin Ltd* [2011] EWCA Civ 133, [2011] 2 Lloyd's Rep 1.

[49] eg *Perrylease Ltd v Imecar AG* [1988] 1 WLR 463; *AG Securities v Vaughan* [1990] 1 AC 417, 468–9, 475; *Guardian Ocean Cargos Ltd v Banco de Brasil SA* [1991] 2 Lloyd's Rep 68 (but evidence admitted and approach consistent with Law Commission's).

[50] *Wild v Civil Aviation Authority* (CA, 25 September 1987); *Haryanto (Yani) v ED & F Man (Sugar) Ltd* [1986] 2 Lloyd's Rep 44, 46. See also *Rosseel NV v Oriental Commercial and Shipping Co (UK) Ltd* [1991] 2 Lloyd's Rep 625, 628.

[51] See below, p 171.   [52] *LG Schuler AG v Wickman Machine Tool Sales Ltd* [1974] AC 235.

certain implied conditions if the breach is so slight that it would be unreasonable to reject them.[53] The word 'warranty' is also employed in a variety of senses, and in many of the earlier cases and also in insurance law[54] it is not infrequently used simply to mean a term of the contract, whether a warranty proper or a condition. Whether or not the words 'condition' or 'warranty' are employed in their technical sense must, therefore, depend upon the intention of the parties to be ascertained from their agreement and from the subject-matter to which it relates.

Another approach, often seen as more modern but in fact with older roots,[55] rejects the proposition that every term of a contract can be classified as either a condition or a warranty. On this approach there is a third category of *innominate* (or 'intermediate') terms. The legal consequences of the breach of such a term (ie whether or not the innocent party is entitled to treat itself as discharged) do not follow automatically from a prior classification of the undertaking but depend upon the nature and consequences of the breach.

(b) CONDITIONS

(i) Promissory conditions

A condition may be defined as a promise, as to fact or as to future conduct, which forms an essential term of the contract.[56] If the fact proves untrue, or the promise is not fulfilled, the breach may be treated as a repudiation which entitles the innocent party to be discharged from further performance of the contract.

Behn v Burness[57] is an illustration of a promise as to a fact forming a condition. A ship was stated in the contract to be 'now in the port of Amsterdam'. The fact that the ship was not in the port at the date of the contract discharged the charterer from performance. *Glaholm v Hays*[58] is an example of a promise as to conduct forming a condition

A charterparty provided that a vessel was to go from England to Trieste and there load a cargo: 'the vessel to sail from England on or before the 4th day of February next'. The vessel did not sail for some days after 4th February. On its arrival at Trieste the charterers refused to load a cargo and treated the contract as repudiated.

It was held that the charterers were entitled to be discharged from the contract. The Court of Common Pleas stated:[59]

Whether a particular clause in a charter-party shall be held to be a condition, upon the nonperformance of which by the one party, the other is at liberty to abandon the contract,

---

[53] Sale of Goods Act 1979, ss 15A; below, p 156.
[54] Marine Insurance Act 1906, ss 33–41; *Bank of Nova Scotia v Hellenic Mutual War Risks Association (Bermuda) Ltd* [1992] 1 AC 233.
[55] eg *Freeman v Taylor* (1831) 8 Bing 124, 138. See also *Boone v Eyre* (1779) 1 H Bl 273n; *Davidson v Gwynne* (1810) 12 East 381; *Clipsham v Vertue* (1843) 5 QB 265; *McAndrew v Chapple* (1866) LR 1 CP 643, 648.
[56] See also below, Chapter 15.   [57] (1862) 1 B & S 877, (1863) 3 B & S 751.
[58] (1841) 2 M & G 257. See also *Petrotrade Inc v Stinnes Handel GmbH* [1995] 1 Lloyd's Rep 142, 149.
[59] (1841) 2 M & G 257, 266, 268.

and consider it at an end; or whether it amounts to an agreement only, the breach whereof is to be recompensed by an action for damages, must depend upon the intention of the parties to be collected, in each particular case, from the terms of the agreement itself, and from the subject-matter to which it relates . . . [W]e think the intention of the parties to this contract sufficiently appears to have been, to insure the ship's sailing at the latest by the 4th February, and that the only mode of effecting this is by holding the clause in question to have been a condition precedent; which we consider it to have been.

The idea which underlies the use of the word 'condition' in *Glaholm v Hays* is that the term is so vital to the operation of the contract that its fulfilment by one party is a condition precedent to liability on the part of the other. But a condition also means an essential undertaking in the contract which one party *promises* will be made good. If it is not made good, not only will the other party be entitled to treat itself as discharged, but also *to sue for damages for breach*. A condition is therefore a 'promissory' condition, that is to say, the breach of it entitles the innocent party to be released from further performance of the contract and to be compensated by damages.

(ii) Non-promissory conditions

It should be stressed, however, that the meaning of condition so far referred to is to be contrasted with another exceptional meaning of condition where the condition is non-promissory. A condition in this sense may be referred to as a 'contingent' condition. For instance, it may be provided that a contract shall not take effect unless or until the condition is fulfilled or that a particular duty under the contract does not become due unless or until the fulfilment of the condition.[60] The existence or enforceability of the contract or the particular obligation is dependent upon the fulfilment of the condition, but there is no guarantee or promise that it will be fulfilled.

The distinction between promissory conditions and the first type of contingent condition was illustrated by Denning LJ in *Trans Trust SPRL v Danubian Trading Co Ltd*[61] when considering a stipulation in a contract of sale of goods which related to the opening by the buyer of a letter of credit[62] in favour of the seller:

What is the legal position of such a stipulation? Sometimes it is a condition precedent to the formation of a contract, that is, it is a condition which must be fulfilled before any contract is concluded at all. In those cases the stipulation 'subject to the opening of a credit' is rather like a stipulation 'subject to contract'.[63] If no credit is provided, there is no contract between the parties. In other cases, a contract is concluded and the stipulation for a credit

---

[60] ALI *Restatement, Contracts (2d)*, para 224 provides that a condition is 'an event, not certain to occur, which must occur, unless occurrence is excused, before performance under a contract comes due'.
[61] [1952] 2 QB 297, 304.   [62] See above, pp 120–22.
[63] See above, p 72. The parallel is not an exact one, for in the case of an agreement 'subject to contract' there is no obligation at all, whereas in the case of a contingent condition there may be an implied obligation to facilitate, or not to prevent, the fulfilment of the condition: *Dodd v Churton* [1897] 1 QB 562; *MacKay v Dick* (1881) 6 App Cas 251: *Thompson v ASDA-MFI plc* [1988] Ch 241.

is a condition which is an essential term of the contract. In those cases the provision of the credit is a condition precedent, not to the formation of a contract, but to the obligation of the seller to deliver the goods. If the buyer fails to provide the credit, the seller can treat himself as discharged from further performance of the contract and can sue the buyer for damages for not providing the credit.[64]

The examples below show that the insertion of a contingent condition may produce one of several effects.[65]

First, it may prevent the formation of any immediately binding contract, as in *Pym v Campbell*[66] where the parties entered into an agreement for the sale and purchase of part of the proceeds of an invention on the express oral understanding that it should not bind them until a third party approved the invention. In such a situation, either party may withdraw from the transaction at any time before the condition is fulfilled.

Secondly, one party may assume an immediate unilateral obligation, say, to sell or to buy from the other, but subject to a condition. In this case, there is a contract from the start imposing a unilateral obligation from which one party cannot withdraw;[67] but no bilateral contract of sale, binding on both parties, comes into existence until the condition is fulfilled.[68] Many options in leases and hire-purchase agreements are of this nature; in such cases the fulfilment of the condition depends on the will of the option holder.

Thirdly, the parties may enter into an immediately binding contract, the operation of which is suspended pending fulfilment of the condition. So, for example, an agreement 'conditional on the seller securing all relevant approvals from the Secretary of State'[69] is a contract from which neither party can resile until it can be definitely ascertained that the condition will not be fulfilled. Alternatively, while the operation of the contract is not suspended, that of a particular obligation under it is. Thus, the obligation of an insurer to pay does not arise until the occurrence of the loss.

In none of these situations does either party render itself liable in damages to the other in the event of non-fulfilment of the condition. Even if, as is often the case, the Court is prepared to imply a term that one of the parties will use all reasonable endeavours to secure fulfilment of the condition, as, for example, where a sale of land is conditional upon planning permission being obtained,[70] or goods are sold

---

[64] Opening a letter of credit is normally treated as falling within Denning LJ's second category: ie as a promissory, rather than a contingent, condition. See, eg, *UR Power Gmbh v Kuok Oils and Grains Pte Ltd* [2009] EWHC 1940 (Comm), [2009] 2 Lloyd's Rep 495 at [22] (Gross J).

[65] On these effects, see *United Dominions Trust (Commercial) Ltd v Eagle Aircraft Services Ltd* [1968] 1 WLR 74, 82; *Wood Preservation Ltd v Prior* [1969] 1 WLR 1077, 1090; *LG Schuler AG v Wickman Machine Tool Sales Ltd* [1972] 1 WLR 840, 850–1 (CA), [1974] AC 235 (HL).

[66] (1856) 6 E & B 370. See also *Aberfoyle Plantations Ltd v Cheng* [1960] AC 115; *William Cory & Son Ltd v IRC* [1965] AC 1088. Cf *Haslemere Estates Ltd v Baker* [1982] 1 WLR 1109.

[67] *Smith v Butler* [1900] 1 QB 694.

[68] *United Dominions Trust (Commercial) Ltd v Eagle Aircraft Services Ltd* [1968] 1 WLR 74. Cf *Eastham v Leigh, London & Provincial Properties Ltd* [1971] Ch 871.

[69] *Total Gas Marketing Ltd v Arco British Ltd* [1998] 2 Lloyd's Rep 209, 215, 221.

[70] *Hargreaves Transport Ltd v Lynch* [1969] 1 WLR 215.

subject to an import or export licence,[71] the fact that the condition is contingent, and not promissory, will prevent any liability from arising if that party's reasonable endeavours prove unavailing. Although, however, non-fulfilment of a contingent condition does not give rise to a claim in damages, non-fulfilment may, when the time has elapsed for its performance, give either party the right to treat the contract as at an end.[72]

The contingent conditions so far considered have been non-promissory conditions precedent; that is, until the condition has been fulfilled the contract is not binding or the contractual duty is not due. Another sense in which the word 'condition' is used is that of a non-promissory condition subsequent. Here the parties agree that the contract is to be immediately binding, but if certain facts are ascertained to exist or upon the happening of a certain event, then either the contract is to cease to bind or one party is to have the option to cancel the contract. In *Brown v Knowsley BC*[73] a contract of employment provided that a temporary teacher's appointment was to last only as long as sufficient funds were provided either by the Manpower Services Commission or other sponsors. It was held that the contract was terminated when such funds ceased to be provided.

(c) WARRANTIES

Breach of a warranty does not entitle the innocent party to treat the contract as repudiated, but only to claim damages. A warranty has been said to be 'an agreement which refers to the subject-matter of a contract, but, not being an essential part of the contract either intrinsically or by agreement, is collateral to the main purpose of such a contract'.[74] The nature of a warranty is illustrated by the case of *Bettini v Gye*:[75]

B contracted with G, the director of the Royal Italian Opera in London, for the exclusive use of his services as a singer in operas and concerts for a period of 3 months. B undertook, inter alia, that he would be in London at least 6 days before the commencement of his engagement, for rehearsals, but only arrived 2 days beforehand. G refused to go on with the contract and was sued by B for breach.

The Court held that, having regard to the length of the contract and the nature of the performances to be given, the rehearsal clause was not vital to the agreement. It was not a condition but merely a warranty. Accordingly its breach did not entitle G to treat the contract as at an end.

---

[71] *Re Anglo-Russian Merchant Traders Ltd v John Batt & Co (London) Ltd* [1917] 2 KB 679; *Coloniale Import–Export v Loumidis & Sons* [1978] 2 Lloyd's Rep 560.

[72] *Total Gas Marketing Ltd v Arco British Ltd* [1998] 2 Lloyd's Rep 209, 218, 221, 226. But not so as to discharge liabilities which had accrued unconditionally: *Kazakstan Wool Processors (Europe) Ltd v Nederlansche Credietverzekering Maatschappij NV* [2000] 1 All ER (Comm) 708.

[73] [1986] IRLR 102. See also *Head v Tattersall* (1871) LR 7 Ex 7; *Gyllenhammer & Partners International Ltd v Sour Brodogradevna Industrija* [1989] 2 Lloyd's Rep 403.

[74] *Dawsons Ltd v Bonnin* [1922] 2 AC 413, 422 (Lord Haldane). See also Sale of Goods Act 1979, s 61(1).

[75] (1876) 1 QBD 183. Cf *Poussard v Spiers* (1876) 1 QBD 410.

It is reasonable to assume that, in the particular circumstances of *Bettini v Gye*, any breach of the rehearsal clause could have been compensated for by damages. But in most cases it would be misleading to conclude that damages would be a sufficient remedy for every breach of even a seemingly unimportant term. The consequences of the breach of such a term might be so serious as to go to the root of the contract. Unless, therefore, a term has been specifically designated a 'warranty' by statute,[76] or the parties have expressly so provided in their agreement, there are few situations[77] where a Court would be likely to hold, at the present day, that the parties intended that any breach of the term should give rise to a right to claim damages only, and so place the term within this category.

(d) EVALUATION OF THE *AB INITIO* CLASSIFICATION OF TERMS

The dominant approach of the Courts in the 70 years following the enactment of the Sale of Goods Act in 1893 was to classify terms *ab initio* as conditions or warranties. The one clear and obvious advantage in this approach is that of certainty.[78] At least in commercial transactions it is important that parties (or their legal advisers) should be able to know, immediately and unequivocally, what their rights are in the event of a breach by the other party, and to make their decision accordingly. If the term broken is a condition, it will be known with certainty that the breach entitles the innocent party to terminate the contract forthwith.

This certainty is particularly important where the contract is one of a 'string' of contracts under which B buys goods from A and then sells them to C who in turn sells them to D. 'Members of the "string" will have many ongoing contracts simultaneously and they must be able to do business with confidence in the legal results of their actions.'[79] Certainty as to whether there is a right to terminate the contract is also important in cases where it would be difficult for the innocent party to quantify the loss suffered and therefore difficult for the Court to assess damages for a breach of the contract.[80]

On the other hand, the advantage of certainty has to be weighed against the need to reach a fair and just decision in individual cases. Since *any* breach of condition gives rise to a right of termination, the innocent party can refuse to perform the contract even though the breach is trivial in nature, and even though little or no loss has been suffered as a result. For example, it is a condition of a cif contract for the sale of goods that the goods must be shipped within the shipment period specified in the contract.

---

[76] Sale of Goods Act 1979, ss 12(2), (4), (5), and (5A) and 61(1); Supply of Goods (Implied Terms) Act 1973, ss 8(1)(b), (2), and (3).

[77] But see *Anglia Commercial Properties v North East Essex Building Co* (1983) 266 EG 1096 (time limit clause in building contract).

[78] *The Mihalis Angelos* [1971] 1 QB 164, 205; *A/S Awilco of Oslo v Fulvia SpA, The Chikuma* [1981] 1 WLR 314, 322; *Bunge Corp v Tradax Export SA* [1981] 1 WLR 711, 718, 720, 725.

[79] *Bunge Corp v Tradax Export SA* [1981] 1 WLR 711, 720 (Lord Lowry).   [80] *Ibid.*

If the goods are shipped one day later—or even earlier[81]—than the specified shipment period, the buyer is entitled to treat the contract as repudiated and to reject the goods, notwithstanding that the breach has caused no loss. A party may seek to rely on such a trivial breach of condition to get out of a contract which has proved unprofitable, perhaps because of changes in the market.[82] It has been said that 'in principle contracts are made to be performed and not to be avoided according to the whims of market fluctuation and where there is a free choice between two possible constructions . . . the Court should tend to prefer that construction which will ensure performance, and not encourage avoidance of contractual obligations'.[83] Moreover, as noted below, in the context of non-consumer sales, statute has restricted the right of a buyer to reject goods by reason of certain implied conditions if the breach is so slight that it would be unreasonable to reject them.[84]

(e) INNOMINATE TERMS

The distinction between 'conditions' and 'warranties', which placed considerable emphasis on *ab initio* classification of the quality of the term broken, that is to say, whether it was of major or minor importance, and on initial certainty, fell out of favour during the 1960s. Greater emphasis has been given to a more flexible test with roots in older authorities which bases the right of termination on the gravity of the consequences of the breach.[85]

In *Hongkong Fir Shipping Co Ltd v Kawasaki Kisen Kaisha Ltd*, Diplock LJ said:[86]

There are, however, many contractual undertakings of a more complex character which cannot be categorised as being 'conditions' or 'warranties' . . . Of such undertakings all that can be predicated is that some breaches will and others will not give rise to an event which will deprive the party not in default of substantially the whole benefit which it was intended he should obtain from the contract; and the legal consequences of a breach of such undertaking, unless provided for expressly in the contract, depend upon the nature of the event to which the breach gives rise and do not follow automatically from a prior classification of the undertaking, as a 'condition' or a 'warranty'.

The charterers of a ship argued that the shipowners' obligation to provide a seaworthy vessel was a condition, any breach of which entitled them to treat themselves as

---

[81] *Bowes v Shand* (1877) 2 App Cas 455.   [82] *Arcos Ltd v Ronaasen & Son Ltd* [1933] AC 470.
[83] *Cehave NV v Bremer Handelsgesellschaft mbH* [1976] QB 44, 71 (the rejected goods were later bought by the same buyers at a lower price and used for the same purpose). See also *Reardon Smith Line Ltd v Hansen-Tangen* [1976] 1 WLR 989.
[84] Sale of Goods Act 1979, s 15A, below, p 156.   [85] Above, p 149, n 55.
[86] [1962] 2 QB 26, 70. For the facts of this case, see below, p 550. See also *Hardwick Game Farm v Suffolk Agricultural Poultry Producers' Assn* [1966] 1 WLR 287, 341 (aff'd [1969] 2 AC 31). See further Reynolds (1963) 79 LQR 534; Lord Devlin [1966] CLJ 192. The flexible innominate term approach of *Hongkong Fir* has been accepted by the High Court of Australia and the Court of Appeal of Singapore in *Koompahtoo Local Aboriginal Land Council v Sanpine Pty Ltd* [2007] HCA 61 (2007) 241 ALR 88 and *RDC Concrete Pte Ltd v Sato Kogyo (S) Pte Ltd* [2007] SGCA 39, [2007] 4 SLR 413 respectively: see Carter (2008) 24 JCL 226.

discharged. The Court of Appeal rejected this contention. The undertaking as to seaworthiness was not a condition, but an *innominate* term. Breach of such a term would not give rise to a right to treat the charterparty as repudiated unless the conduct of the shipowners, and the actual or anticipated consequences of the breach, were so serious as to frustrate the commercial purpose of the venture. The reason was thus explained by Upjohn LJ:[87]

Why is this apparently basic and underlying condition of seaworthiness not, in fact, treated as a condition? It is for the simple reason that the seaworthiness clause is breached by the slightest failure to be fitted 'in every way' for service . . . If a nail is missing from one of the timbers of a wooden vessel or if proper medical supplies or two anchors are not on board at the time of sailing, the owners are in breach of the seaworthiness stipulation. It is contrary to common sense to suppose that in such circumstances the parties contemplated that the charterer should at once be entitled to treat the contract as at an end for such trifling breaches.

Where a failure of performance is not a breach of condition, but of an innominate term, the right of the innocent party to treat itself as discharged from further performance will depend upon the gravity of the consequences of the breach. Those consequences must be judged at the time of the innocent party's purported termination taking into account what has happened and what is likely to happen.[88] The expressions used to describe the circumstances that justify discharge, are discussed in the chapter on Discharge by Breach.[89] A test frequently applied is whether the failure of performance is such as to deprive the innocent party of substantially the whole benefit which it was intended that it should obtain as the consideration for the performance of its own undertakings.[90] In the *Hongkong Fir* case, which concerned a two-year charterparty, the ship was off hire because of unseaworthiness for all but eight and a half weeks in the first seven months of the charter, but the charterer was held not to be entitled to treat the contract as discharged. Accordingly, in many cases, the innocent party may have to 'wait and see' how serious the consequences of the breach turn out to be.

(f) DISTINGUISHING INNOMINATE TERMS AND CONDITIONS

Whether a term will be classified as a condition depends in part on the Court 'making what is in effect a value judgement about the commercial significance of the term in question'.[91] A term is most likely to be classified as innominate if, as in the *Hongkong Fir* case, it is capable of being broken either in a manner that is trivial and capable of

---

[87] [1962] 2 QB 26, 62.

[88] *Ampurius Nu Homes Holdings Ltd v Telford Homes (Creekside) Ltd* [2013] EWCA Civ 577, [2013] 4 All ER 377 especially at [44] and [64].

[89] See below, Chapter 15.

[90] *Hongkong Fir Shipping Co Ltd v Kawasaki Kisen Kaisha Ltd* [1962] 2 QB 26, 66; see also below, p 549. Cf CISG Art 25.

[91] *State Trading Corp of India Ltd v M Golodetz Ltd* [1989] 2 Lloyd's Rep 277, 283 (Kerr LJ).

remedy by an award of damages or in a way that is so fundamental as to undermine the whole contract. However, the Courts have recognized that the greater flexibility involves more uncertainty and have indicated that in suitable cases they will not be reluctant to hold that an obligation has the force of a condition.[92] In the modern law, it is probably safe to say that any term of a contract will be classified as an innominate term, and not as a condition, unless the Court concludes that it falls within one of the following situations:

(i) Categorization as condition by statute

In non-consumer contracts for the supply of goods,[93] the Sale of Goods Act 1979[94] and the Supply of Goods (Implied Terms) Act 1973[95] expressly define certain implied obligations in contracts of sale of goods or hire-purchase as being 'conditions' or 'warranties'. There can be no doubt that such classification is binding. But in *Cehave NV v Bremer Handelsgesellschaft mbH* [96] the Court of Appeal rejected the argument that the Sale of Goods Act created a statutory dichotomy which divided *all* terms in contracts of sale of goods into conditions and warranties and held that an express term 'shipment to be made in good condition' was an innominate term the breach of which had to be so serious as to go to the root of the contract in order to entitle the buyer to reject the goods.

One should also note that in non-consumer cases, by reason of section 15A of the Sale of Goods Act, if the breach of condition is so slight as to be unreasonable for the buyer to reject the goods, then the buyer can only claim damages and cannot reject the goods.[97] One can argue that, in effect, this comes close to treating conditions as innominate terms where the buyer is not dealing as a consumer.

(ii) Categorization as condition by judicial decision

A particular term may have been categorized as a condition by previous judicial decision. Examples are mainly to be found in certain familiar terms in commercial contracts. Thus stipulations in a voyage charterparty as to the time at which the chartered vessel is expected ready to load,[98] or in a time charterparty as to the date by which hire is to be paid,[99] and stipulations in a cif contract for the sale of goods as to

---

[92] *Bunge Corp v Tradax Export SA* [1981] 1 WLR 711; *Cie Commerciale Sucres et Denrées v Czarnikow Ltd* [1990] 1 WLR 1337; *Petrotrade Inc v Stinnes Handel GmbH* [1995] 1 Lloyd's Rep 142, 149.

[93] In consumer contracts for the supply of goods, the Consumer Rights Act 2015 avoids reference to conditions, warranties or innominate terms: see below, p 478.

[94] See below, pp 171-7.   [95] See below, p 178.

[96] [1976] QB 44. See also *Tradax International SA v Goldschmidt* [1977] 2 Lloyd's Rep 604.

[97] This provision was inserted by the Sale and Supply of Goods Act 1994. The best known case where s 15A would probably now change the result is *Arcos Ltd v Ronaasen & Son* [1933] AC 470. For the equivalent provisions for contracts of hire-purchase, work and materials, and hire, see the Supply of Goods (Implied Terms) Act 1973, s 11A, and the Supply of Goods and Services Act 1982, ss 5A and 10A.

[98] *The Mihalis Angelos* [1971] 1 QB 164. See also *Behn v Burness* (1863) 3 B & S 751, above, p 149.

[99] *Mardorf Peach & Co Ltd v Attica Sea Carriers Corp of Liberia* [1977] AC 850. There is a conflict of views at first instance as to whether a term in a time charterparty requiring the punctual payment of hire is

the time within which the goods must be shipped[100] or a letter of credit opened,[101] have been held to be conditions, any delay in which entitles the other party to treat itself as discharged. It has, however, been stated[102] that a number of previous decisions on such terms are 'excessively technical' and are open to re-examination by the House of Lords.

(iii) Express designation in contract

The parties may have expressly provided in their contract either that a particular term is to be a condition (in the technical sense)[103] or that the consequences of its non-performance by one party are to be that the other party is to have the right to treat itself as discharged. A stipulation expressly stating the time of performance is 'of the essence of the contract' is an example of this.[104] Again, stating that a party 'guarantees' to obtain approval within a specified period has been held to indicate that the term is a condition.[105]

(iv) Implication from nature of contract, subject-matter, or circumstances

Finally, if the nature of the contract or the subject-matter or the circumstances of the case lead to the conclusion that the parties must, impliedly, have intended that the innocent party would be discharged from further performance of its obligations in the event that a particular term was not fully and precisely complied with, that term will be held to be a condition.[106] This is more likely to be the case in single-performance contracts and contracts requiring the performance of particular acts at specified times and in sequence. It is less likely to be the case where the contract is for performance over a long term[107] when substantial performance may have been rendered by the contract-breaker before breach and where the term is of a broad and loose nature. A term is also likely to be held to be a condition where adherence to it is fundamental to the transaction in the sense that it cannot proceed without it and where the term is not one which admitted to different types of breach. So, for example, a stipulation in a conditional sale agreement that the seller was at the date of the agreement the owner of the item sold has been held to be a

---

a condition or not: *Kuwait Rocks Co v AMN Bulkcarriers Inc, The Astra* [2013] EWHC 865 (Comm), [2013] 2 Lloyd's Rep 69 (condition); *Spar Shipping AS v Grand China Logistics Holding (Group) Co Ltd* [2015] EWHC 718 (Comm), [2015] 1 All ER (Comm) 879 (not a condition).

[100] *Bowes v Shand* (1877) 2 App Cas 455.

[101] *Ian Stach Ltd v Baker Bosley Ltd* [1958] 2 QB 130.

[102] *Reardon Smith Line Ltd v Yngvar Hansen-Tangen* [1976] 1 WLR 989, 998 (Lord Wilberforce).

[103] Cf *LG Schuler AG v Wickman Machine Tool Sales Ltd* [1974] AC 235.

[104] *United Scientific Holdings Ltd v Burnley BC* [1978] AC 904, 923, 937, 944; below pp 466–8.

[105] *BS & N Ltd v Micado Shipping Ltd (Malta)* [2001] 1 Lloyd's Rep 341, 349–50.

[106] *United Scientific Holdings Ltd v Burnley BC* [1978] AC 904, 937, 941, 944, 950, 958; *Bremer Handelsgesellschaft mbH v Vanden Avenne-Izegem PVBA* [1978] 2 Lloyd's Rep 109, 133; *Bunge Corp v Tradax Export SA* [1981] 1 WLR 711, 716, 717, 720, 729.

[107] *LG Schuler AG v Wickman Machine Tool Sales Ltd* [1974] AC 235; *Decro-Wall SA v Practitioners in Marketing Ltd* [1971] 1 WLR 361.

condition.[108] If a term would otherwise be an innominate term, a party cannot (absent an express term permitting it) unilaterally turn it into a condition. For example, serving a written notice to complete in a contract for the sale of land does not make 'time of the essence').[109]

In *Bremer Handelsgesellschaft mbH v Vanden Avenne-Izegem PVBA*[110] a term in a contract for the sale of United States soya bean meal, which required the sellers to advise the buyers 'without delay' of impossibility of shipment by reason of a prohibition of export, was held by the House of Lords to be an innominate term, since it did not establish any definite time limit within which the advice was to be given. But further provisions in the same contract, which took effect upon a number of events impeding performance and which established a timetable of fixed periods within which the occurrence was to be notified, an extension of time claimed, and the buyer was to have the option of cancelling the contract, were held to be conditions. Punctual compliance with these stipulations was required as part of a 'complete regulatory code'.

Again in *Bunge Corporation v Tradax Export SA*,[111] a case which also concerned a contract for the sale of soya bean meal:

The sellers were required, by 30 June 1975, to load the goods on board ship at a single United States Gulf port to be nominated by them. The contract further provided that the buyers should give to the sellers 'at least 15 consecutive days' notice of probable readiness of vessel(s) and of the approximate quantity required to be loaded'. The buyers did not give that notice until 17 June, by which time less than 15 days of the loading period remained. The sellers declared the buyers in default and claimed damages for repudiation of the contract on the ground that the term as to notice was a condition.

The House of Lords held that the term, though not expressly stated in the contract to be a condition, was one by implication, so that its breach entitled the sellers to treat themselves as discharged. Their Lordships pointed out that, in general, time was of the essence in mercantile contracts, and in particular in this case where the sellers needed the information to know which loading port they should nominate, so as to ensure that the goods would be available for loading on the ship's arrival at that port before the end of the loading period.

---

[108] *Barber v NWS Bank plc* [1996] 1 WLR 641. Such a condition would otherwise be *implied* by the Sale of Goods Act 1979, s 12, below, p 172.

[109] *Urban 1 (Blonk Street) Ltd v Ayres* [2013] EWCA Civ 816, [2014] 1 WLR 756 at [44].

[110] [1978] 2 Lloyd's Rep 109.

[111] [1981] 1 WLR 711. See also *Toepfer v Lenersan-Poortman NV* [1980] 1 Lloyd's Rep 143; *Bunge GmbH v Landbouwbelang GA* [1980] 1 Lloyd's Rep 458; *Commerciale Sucres et Denrées v C Czarnikow Ltd, The Naxos* [1990] 1 WLR 1337; *Torvald Klaveness A/S v Arni Maritime Corp* [1994] 1 WLR 1465, 1475–6 (redelivery date of chartered ship); *Petrotrade Inc v Stinnes Handel GmbH* [1995] 1 Lloyd's Rep 142. Cf *Universal Bulk Carriers Ltd v Andre et Cie SA* [2001] EWCA Civ 588, [2001] 2 Lloyd's Rep 65 (provision that laydays to be narrowed not a condition).

(g) LOSS OF THE RIGHT OF DISCHARGE

(i) Waiver and affirmation

Where one party has been guilty of a breach of condition, the other party need not necessarily treat itself as discharged. Compliance with the condition can, if the innocent party so wishes, be waived[112] and the contract can be enforced as if it had been omitted. Alternatively, the innocent party can elect to affirm the contract, that is to say, with knowledge of the breach to treat the contract as still binding and to rest content with damages, which are available as a remedy in any event.

These principles, which are of general application in the law of contract, were given statutory force in relation to contracts of sale of goods by section 11(1) of the Sale of Goods Act 1979:

Where a contract of sale is subject to a condition to be fulfilled by the seller, the buyer may waive the condition, or may elect to treat the breach of the condition as a breach of warranty and not as a ground for treating the contract as repudiated.

Part 1 of the Consumer Rights Act 2015, however, provides this is now applicable only to non-consumer sale contracts.

(ii) 'Acceptance' and substantial benefit

Affirmation is voluntary; but an innocent party may, in certain other circumstances, lose the right to discharge the contract for breach of a condition. For example, an innocent party who has taken a substantial benefit under the contract may sometimes be precluded from opting to be discharged by reason of a breach of condition, and have to sue for damages only.[113] In non-consumer contracts for the sale of goods,[114] the Sale of Goods Act 1979 also provides that a buyer cannot treat the contract as repudiated for breach of condition where the goods which are the subject-matter of the sale have been 'accepted'. By section 11(4) of the Act:[115]

where a contract of sale is not severable and the buyer has accepted the goods or part of them, the breach of a condition to be fulfilled by the seller can only be treated as a breach of warranty, and not as a ground for rejecting the goods and treating the contract as repudiated, unless there is an express or implied term of the contract to that effect.

Two points require explanation. In the first place, the word 'accept' in the phrase 'and the buyer has accepted the goods' bears a technical meaning. The buyer is deemed to have accepted the goods when he intimates to the seller that he has accepted them, or when the goods have been delivered and the buyer does any act in relation to them

---

[112] Provided that it is exclusively for its own benefit and not for the benefit of both parties.

[113] *Graves v Legg* (1854) 9 Exch 709, 717; *Pust v Dowie* (1865) 5 B & S 33; *Behn v Burness* (1862) 1 B & S 877; (1863) 3 B & S 751.

[114] Different rules apply to a consumer contract by reason of Part 1 of the Consumer Rights Act 2015.

[115] The terms 'condition' and 'warranty' are used in the Act in the senses given above; see Sale of Goods Act 1979, ss 11(3), 61(1).

which is inconsistent with the ownership of the seller, or when after the lapse of a reasonable time the buyer retains the goods without intimating to the seller that the goods have been rejected.[116] There is no mention of any requirement that the buyer should *know* of the breach of condition before losing the right to reject although, in the case of an intimation of acceptance or an act inconsistent with the seller's ownership, 'acceptance' will not be deemed to have taken place unless and until the buyer has had a reasonable opportunity of examining the goods for the purpose of ascertaining whether they are in conformity with the contract[117] or the buyer has retained the goods during the lapse of a reasonable time without intimating to the seller that he is rejecting them.[118] The availability of a reasonable opportunity of examining goods is a material factor in determining whether a 'reasonable' time has elapsed.[119] Where the buyer has the right to reject goods by reason of a defect that affects all or some of them but accepts some of the goods the right to reject the rest is not lost by that partial acceptance.[120]

Secondly, acceptance does not necessarily have this effect if the contract is severable, for example, if delivery of the goods is to be made by instalments which are to be separately paid for. In such a case the Sale of Goods Act 1979 provides that where 'the seller makes defective deliveries in respect of one or more instalments, or the buyer neglects or refuses to take delivery of or pay for one or more instalments, it is a question in each case depending on the terms of the contract and the circumstances of the case whether the breach of contract is a repudiation of the whole contract or whether it is a severable breach giving rise to a claim for compensation but not to a right to treat the whole contract as repudiated'.[121]

The right of the innocent party to treat itself as discharged may thus be lost either voluntarily or as the result of the operation of a rule of law.

(h) PART 1 OF THE CONSUMER RIGHTS ACT 2015

Part 1 of the Consumer Rights Act 2015 deals with the rights of consumers under consumer contracts for the supply of goods, digital content, or services. The 2015 Act, which applies to contracts made on or after 1 October 2015,[122] does not label certain terms as conditions or warranties (nor is an innominate term approach laid down). Instead the contract is treated as including certain terms[123] and the right of the consumer to 'discharge' the contract for breach of those terms by the trader is laid

---

[116] Sale of Goods Act 1979, s 35, as amended by the Sale and Supply of Goods Act 1994.

[117] Sale of Goods Act 1979, s 35(2).

[118] Sale of Goods Act 1979, s 35(4). See *Clegg v Olle Andersson* [2003] EWCA Civ 320, [2003] 1 All ER (Comm) 721; *J & H Ritchie Ltd v Lloyd Ltd* [2007] UKHL 9, [2007] 1 WLR 670.

[119] Sale of Goods Act 1979, s 35(5).   [120] Sale of Goods Act 1979, s 35A(1).

[121] Sale of Goods Act 1979, s 31(2).

[122] For the previous law, which applies to contracts made before 1 October 2015, see the previous edition of this work at Chapter 5.

[123] See below, p 178.

down in the Act.[124] Although the practical effect is much the same as if, for example, terms as to the quality of goods were 'conditions', that terminology is not used.

3. IMPLIED TERMS

(a) TERMS IMPLIED BY THE COURTS AND BY STATUTE

There may be implied into a contract terms which the parties have not themselves inserted. In some cases, in particular contracts for the sale and supply of goods and services,[125] contracts of employment, and contracts between landlord and tenant, terms are implied by statute. In the absence of statutory provision the cases in which the Courts will imply a term into a contract are strictly limited: it is not their task to make contracts for the parties concerned, but only to interpret the contracts already made.[126] Nevertheless, in certain circumstances the Courts are prepared to imply terms into even a written contract.

A distinction has developed between two broad categories of case where terms are implied by the Courts. First, where it is sought to insert into a particular, sometimes detailed, contract a term that the parties have not expressed. In such cases a strict test is applied. The Courts do not imply terms where it would be reasonable to do so but only where it is necessary to give business efficacy to the contract or where it is obvious that the term was meant to have been included. Such a term is sometimes said to be implied *by fact*. Here the implication of a term depends upon the intention of the parties gleaned from the express terms of the agreement and the surrounding circumstances.[127] Secondly, there are cases in which the Court is considering a common relationship, for example sale, carriage, landlord and tenant, employment, or that between a regulated dominant supplier (eg a telephone or electricity supplier) and its customer, where the parties may have left a lot unsaid. In such cases, when the Court implies a term, it is sometimes laying down a general rule that in all contracts of a defined type some provision is to be implied as an incident of the particular type of contractual relationship unless the parties have expressly excluded it, and it is somewhat artificial to attribute such terms to the intention of the parties.[128] Such terms

---

[124] See especially Consumer Rights Act 2015, ss 19–20 and 42. The Act does not refer to 'discharge' but instead uses the terminology of 'treating the contract as at an end' and by s 19(13) 'treating a contract as at end means treating it as repudiated'. In general, by s 42, there is no such right in relation to a consumer contract for digital content.

[125] But in a consumer contract for the supply of goods, digital content, or services, the Consumer Rights Act 2015 does not refer to implied terms. Instead the terminology used is of a term treated as included in the contract.

[126] *Phillips Electronique Grand Publique SA v BSB Ltd* [1995] EMLR 472, 481 (Sir Thomas Bingham MR).

[127] *Luxor (Eastbourne) Ltd v Cooper* [1941] AC 108, 137; *Shell UK Ltd v Lostock Garages Ltd* [1976] 1 WLR 1187, 1196; *Associated Japanese Bank (International) v Crédit du Nord SA* [1989] 1 WLR 255, 263.

[128] *Liverpool City Council v Irwin* [1977] AC 239, 253–4, and 257–8; *Shell UK Ltd v Lostock Garages Ltd* [1976] 1 WLR 1187, 1196; *Mears v Safecar Security Ltd* [1983] QB 54, 78; *Scally v Southern Health and Social Services Board* [1992] 1 AC 294, 306–7.

are sometimes said to be implied *by law*. A similar process takes place where a term is implied by a trade custom.[129]

(b) TERMS IMPLIED BY THE COURTS

(i) 'Necessary for business efficacy' and the 'officious bystander'

Where the parties to a contract, either through forgetfulness or through bad drafting, fail to incorporate into the contract terms which, had they adverted to the situation, they would certainly have inserted to complete the contract, the Courts may, in order to give 'business efficacy' to the transaction, imply such terms as are necessary to effect that result.

In *The Moorcock*,[130] a shipowner and the owner of a jetty contracted to allow a steamship to be discharged, loaded, and moored at the jetty. The ship was grounded and damaged at low tide. The Court of Appeal held that the parties must have intended to contract on the basis that the owner of the jetty had taken reasonable care to ascertain that the riverbed was safe for the vessel at low tide and therefore a term would be implied to that effect. For a breach of this implied term the defendants were liable.

Bowen LJ said:

Now, an implied warranty, or, as it is called, a covenant in law, as distinguished from an express contract or express warranty, really is in all cases founded on the presumed intention of the parties, and upon reason. The implication which the law draws from what must obviously have been the intention of the parties, the law draws with the object of giving efficacy to the transaction and preventing such a failure of consideration as cannot have been within the contemplation of either side . . . In business transactions such as this, what the law desires to effect by the implication is to give such business efficacy to the transaction as must have been intended to all events by both parties who are business men . . . [131]

The principle in *The Moorcock* is applied where, without the implied term, the contract will not be workable. But the Court is also prepared to imply a term if it was so obviously a stipulation in the agreement that it goes without saying that the parties must have intended it to form part of their contract. This test, which often overlaps with the business efficacy test,[132] is applied by asking whether, if an officious bystander were to suggest some express provision for a matter in the agreement, the parties would testily suppress him with a common 'Oh, of course!'.[133] Such an

---

[129] Below, p 169. [130] (1889) 14 PD 64.

[131] *Ibid*, 68. Cf *Easton v Hitchcock* [1912] 1 KB 535.

[132] eg *Ali SS Corp v Shipyard Trogir* [1999] 1 WLR 314, 326 (Potter LJ); *Codelfa Construction Pty Ltd v State Railway Authority of New South Wales* (1982) 149 CLR 337, 347 (High Court of Australia); *Lymington Marina Ltd v Macnamara* [2007] EWCA Civ 151, [2007] 2 All ER (Comm) 825 at [37], [44].

[133] *Shirlaw v Southern Foundries (1926) Ltd* [1939] 2 KB 206, 227 (MacKinnon LJ). See also *Reigate v Union Manufacturing Co (Ramsbottom) Ltd* [1918] 1 KB 592, 605 (Scrutton LJ); *Liverpool City Council v Irwin* [1977] AC 239, 254; *Alpha Trading Ltd v Dunnshaw-Patten Ltd* [1981] 1 Lloyd's Rep 122, 128; *Equitable Life Assurance Society v Hyman* [2002] 1 AC 408 (implication to give effect to reasonable expectations). See further Phang [1998] JBL 1.

implication will only be made if the Court is satisfied that both parties would, as reasonable persons, have agreed to the term had it been suggested to them, so that the differing commercial motives of the parties will often preclude this type of implication.[134]

Clearly, however, the Court will be reluctant to make such an implication where the parties have entered into a carefully drafted written contract containing detailed terms agreed between them[135] or in a novel or particularly risky contract.[136] It must be possible to formulate the term with a sufficient degree of precision, and without over-complication and artificiality,[137] and the term to be implied must not be inconsistent with the express terms of the contract.[138] For example, where a party taking out insurance is contractually required to provide a correctly completed direct debit mandate to the insurance company, the company will be under an implied duty to implement the direct debit mandate.[139]

In any event, the term to be implied must in all the circumstances be reasonable.[140] But this does not mean that a term will be implied merely because it would be reasonable to do so,[141] or because it would improve the contract[142] or make its performance more convenient.[143] It must be necessary to imply such a term: 'The touchstone is always *necessity* and not merely *reasonableness*'.[144] For example, where parties to a contract are subject to the rules of a regulatory body there is no need to imply those rules into the contract.[145]

---

[134] *Luxor (Eastbourne) Ltd v Cooper* [1941] AC 108; *Attica Sea Carriers Corp v Ferrostaal Poseidon Bulk Reederei GmbH* [1976] 1 Lloyd's Rep 250; *Liverpool City Council v Irwin* [1977] AC 239, 266; *Hughes v Greenwich LBC* [1994] 1 AC 170, 179.

[135] *Shell UK Ltd v Lostock Garages Ltd* [1976] 1 WLR 1187, 1200. See also *Yorkshire Water Services Ltd v Sun Alliance & London Insurance plc* [1997] 2 Lloyd's Rep 21.

[136] *Phillips Electronique Grand Publique SA v BSB Ltd* [1995] EMLR 472, 482–3 (Sir Thomas Bingham MR).

[137] *Ibid*, 497; *Luxor (Eastbourne) Ltd v Cooper* [1941] AC 108, 117 (Viscount Simon LC); *Ashmore v Corporation of Lloyds (No 2)* [1992] 2 Lloyd's Rep 620, 626–9. But note that the term implied may involve a flexible criterion such as to take 'reasonable' care.

[138] *Duke of Westminster v Guild* [1985] QB 688, 700; *Johnstone v Bloomsbury HA* [1992] 1 QB 333, 347 and 350. Browne-Wilkinson V-C stated that powers created by an express term may be qualified by an implied duty to exercise those powers reasonably: *Imperial Tobacco Pension Trust v Imperial Tobacco* [1991] IRLR 66 (employer's power to refuse consent to increases in pensions).

[139] *Weldon v GRE Linked Life Assurance* [2000] 2 All ER Comm 914, 919–21.

[140] *Young & Marten v McManus Childs Ltd* [1969] 1 AC 454, 465; *Liverpool City Council v Irwin* [1977] AC 239, 262; *Wong Mee Wan v Kwan Kin Travel Services Ltd* [1996] 1 WLR 38, 46–7, relying, inter alia, analogically on the Package Travel, Package Holidays and Package Tours Regulations 1992 (SI 1992 No 3288), especially reg 15.

[141] *Reigate v Union Manufacturing Co (Ramsbottom) Ltd* [1918] 1 KB 592, 598; *Liverpool City Council v Irwin* [1977] AC 239.

[142] *Trollope & Colls Ltd v NW Metropolitan Regional Hospital Board* [1973] 1 WLR 601, 609.

[143] *Russell v Duke of Norfolk* [1949] 1 All ER 109.

[144] *Liverpool City Council v Irwin* [1977] AC 239, 266 (Lord Edmund-Davies). See also *Baker v Black Sea & Baltic General Insurance Co* [1998] 1 WLR 974, 980 (Lord Lloyd); *Equitable Life Assurance Society v Hyman* [2002] 1 AC 408, 459; *Mediterranean Salvage & Towage v Seamar Trading and Commerce Inc* [2009] EWCA Civ 531, [2009] 2 Lloyd's Rep 639 (no implied term that nominated berth was safe); Bryan and Ellinghaus (2000) 22 Syd L Rev 636, 644 ('objective necessity').

[145] *Clarion Ltd v National Provident Institution* [2000] 1 WLR 1899, 1896.

In *AG of Belize v Belize Telecom Ltd*[146] Lord Hoffmann, giving the opinion of the Privy Council, offered a refreshing reappraisal of the approach to implying terms.[147]

The question arose as to whether the articles of association of a company impliedly prevented from remaining in office those directors who had been appointed by, and according to the express provisions could only be removed by, those holding specified shares in a situation where there was no longer any holder of such shares.

It was held that there was such an implied term. Although Lord Hoffmann was dealing with the question of whether a term should be implied into the articles of association of a company, rather than into a contract, he was clear that the process was the same for both and indeed for any written instrument. He stressed that the implication of a term is an exercise in the construction of the instrument as a whole so that the central question for the Court is whether the implication 'would spell out in express words what the instrument, read against the relevant background, would reasonably be understood to mean'.[148] He considered that what he had said about interpreting a contract in *Investors Compensation Scheme Ltd v West Bromwich Building Society*[149] applied by parity of reasoning to the implication of a term. 'There is only one question: is that what the instrument, read as a whole against the relevant background, would reasonably be understood to mean?'[150] It followed that the tests traditionally put forward of, for example, business efficacy and the 'officious bystander' should be viewed as merely overlapping ways in which the Courts 'have tried to express the central idea that the proposed implied term must spell out what the contract actually means or in which they have explained why they did not think that it did so'.[151] It was dangerous and incorrect to detach those tests from that underlying objective. In Lord Hoffmann's words, 'There are dangers in treating these alternative formulations of the question as if they had a life of their own'.[152]

Lord Hoffmann's recasting of the law was characteristically bold and had the great merit of supplying a rational underpinning to the application of the traditional 'business efficacy' and 'officious bystander' tests.

However, *Belize Telecom* must now be read in the light of the Supreme Court's judgment in *Marks and Spencer plc v BNP Paribas Services Trust Company (Jersey) Limited*.[153] In this case, a business tenant had exercised its right to terminate a commercial lease under a 'break-clause'. The question at issue was whether a term should be implied into the lease entitling the tenant to repayment of an apportioned

---

[146] [2009] UKPC 10, [2009] 1 WLR 1988: see McCaughran [2011] CLJ 607; Hooley [2014] CLJ 315. In applying *Belize* in *Mediterranean Salvage & Towage v Seamar Trading & Commerce Inc* [2009] EWCA Civ 531, [2009] 2 Lloyd's Rep 639, Lord Clarke MR stated, at [8], 'I predict that [Lord Hoffmann's] analysis will soon be as much referred to as his approach to the construction of contracts in *Investors Compensation Scheme v West Bromwich Building Society* [1998] 1 WLR 896'.

[147] Although the context and his reference to the traditional tests suggest that Lord Hoffmann principally had in mind the sort of implied terms considered so far in this chapter, it may be that, controversially, he regarded his approach as applying to implied terms considered below under the headings 'standardised terms in common relationships' and 'terms implied by custom'.

[148] [2009] UKPC 10, [2009] 1 WLR 1988 at [21].

[149] [1998] 1 WLR 896, 912–13. See below, pp 179–82.

[150] [2009] UKPC 10, [2009] 1 WLR 1988 at [21].

[151] *Ibid* at [27].

[152] *Ibid* at [22].

[153] [2015] UKSC 72, [2015] 3 WLR 1843.

part of the rent (and other charges) for the period between the termination of the lease and the end of the quarter for which the rent (and other charges) had already been paid. In deciding that no such term should be implied, the majority of the Supreme Court thought it important to make clear that Lord Hoffmann's judgment in *Belize* did not change the law and should in no sense be interpreted as loosening the traditional restrictive approach to implying terms by fact.[154] In particular, a term should not be implied on the basis that it is reasonable to do so. The traditional tests of business necessity and obviousness were reaffirmed. The Supreme Court also stressed that there is a difference between interpreting the express terms and deciding whether to imply a term albeit that it accepted that there are factors common to both exercises. In the words of Lord Neuberger (agreed with by Lords Sumption and Hodge):[155]

[T]he factors to be taken into account on an issue of construction, namely the words used in the contract, the surrounding circumstances known to both parties at the time of the contract, commercial common sense, and the reasonable reader or reasonable parties, are also taken into account on an issue of implication. However, that does not mean that the exercise of implication should be properly classified as part of the exercise of interpretation, let alone that it should be carried out at the same time as interpretation.

It would appear that the main target of the critical comments of the majority of the Supreme Court[156] was not so much Lord Hoffmann's words in *Belize* but rather the interpretation that has been given to them by some commentators and judges.[157] With respect, Lord Hoffmann was correct to articulate what lies behind the traditional tests and was also correct that the processes of interpreting the express terms and implying terms are so interconnected that it is artificial to regard them as wholly separate exercises governed by different underlying principles.[158] It is perhaps for these reasons that the Supreme Court chose not to say that Lord Hoffmann was wrong but instead said that his approach was 'quite acceptable'[159] provided it was applied with various factors in mind and that it remained 'a characteristically inspired discussion'[160] albeit that it should not be regarded as 'authoritative guidance on the law of implied terms.'[161]

Finally, we refer to two types of terms implied by fact that are of particular importance in understanding English contract law. First, although English law does not impose a free-standing duty to perform a contract in good faith, it sometimes comes to the same result by implying a term that performance must be carried out in good faith. An example of this is provided by *Yam Seng Pte Ltd v International Trade Corp Ltd*:[162]

---

[154] See above, p 161.   [155] [2015] UKSC 72, [2015] 3 WLR 1843 at [27].

[156] Lords Carnwath and Clarke were both more supportive, than the majority, of Lord Hoffmann's approach.

[157] [2015] UKSC 72, [2015] 3 WLR 1843 at [24].

[158] The Supreme Court was correct to state that one should first interpret the express terms and then consider implied terms. But it is important to bear in mind that the relationship between interpretation and implication is reflexive so that one's view on an implied term may require one to revise one's interpretation of the express words: see the majority's recognition of this at [28], and note that Lord Carnwath at [71] favoured an 'iterative' rather than a 'sequential' process.

[159] [2015] UKSC 72, [2015] 3 WLR 1843 at [23].   [160] *Ibid* at [31].   [161] *Ibid* at [31].

[162] [2013] EWHC 111, [2013] 1 Lloyd's Rep 526. See also *Emirates Trading Agency v Prime Mineral Exports Pte Ltd* [2014] EWHC 2104 (Comm), [2015] 1 WLR 1145 at [51].

The parties entered into a written contract under which the defendant (ITC) granted the claimant (Yam Seng) the exclusive right to distribute certain fragrances bearing the brand name 'Manchester United' in parts of the Middle East, Asia, Africa and Australia. After an initially happy relationship, matters deteriorated and Yam Seng terminated the contract for ITC's alleged repudiatory breach and sought damages.

Leggatt J held that ITC was indeed in repudiatory breach in two respects one of which was that ITC was in breach of an implied term (of fact) to perform in good faith which, more specifically, required ITC not to give false information, knowingly, to Yam Seng. The judgment may be regarded as the most wide-ranging and sophisticated analysis by an English judge of why the standard approach to implying terms by fact is likely to lead to there being an implied term imposing a duty to perform in good faith and more specific implied terms built from it. But it has in general been given a rather lukewarm reception with the courts tending to stress that the context and type of contract are all-important and that one must not undermine the express terms of the contract.[163]

A second significant type of implied term of fact is one that controls express discretion. So in several cases, it has been held that express contractual discretions are subject to an implied term that the discretion must be exercised in good faith and must not be exercised arbitrarily, capriciously, or irrationally.[164]

(ii) Standardized terms in common relationships

In certain types of contract, terms have become standardized, and they will be implied in all contracts of that type in the absence of any contrary intention. For example, if a builder undertakes to build a house for a purchaser, it is an implied term of the contract that the work will be done in a good and workmanlike manner, that the builder will supply good and proper materials, and that the house will be reasonably fit for human habitation when built or completed.[165] Again, if a travel agent undertakes to arrange for services, such as accommodation and excursions, to be provided by others, it is an implied term of the contract that it would use reasonable care and skill in selecting

---

[163] *Mid Essex Hospital Services NHS Trust v Compass Group UK and Ireland Ltd* [2013] EWCA Civ 200, [2013] BLR 265 (although the issue there was how to construe an *express* term requiring performance in good faith); *Hamsard 3147 Ltd v Boots UK Ltd* [2013] EWHC 3251 (Pat) at [86]; *TSG Building Services plc v South Anglia Housing Ltd* [2013] EWHC 1151 (TCC), [2013] BLR 484 at [46]; *Greenclose Ltd v National Westminster Bank plc* [2014] EWHC 1156 (Ch), [2014] 2 Lloyd's Rep 169 at [150]–[151]; *Acer Investment Management Ltd v Mansion Group Ltd* [2014] EWHC 3011 (QB) at [107]–[109]; *Carewatch Care Services Ltd v Focus Caring Services Ltd* [2014] EWHC 2313 (Ch) at [108]–[112]; *Ilkerler Otomotive Sanayai ve Ticaret Anonim Sirketi v Perkins Engines Co Ltd* [2015] EWHC 2006 (Comm) at [22]; *Portsmouth City Council v Ensign Highways Ltd* [2015] EWHC 1969 (TCC) at [91]–[96].

[164] *Paragon Finance Plc v Nash* [2001] EWCA Civ 1466, [2002] 1 WLR 685; *Lymington Marina Ltd v MacNamara* [2007] EWCA Civ 151, [2007] 2 All ER (Comm) 825; *Socimer International Bank Ltd v Standard Bank London Ltd* [2008] EWCA Civ 16, [2008] 1 Lloyd's Rep 558; *British Telecommunications plc v Telefonica O2 UK Ltd* [2014] UKSC 42, [2014] 4 All ER 907 at [37]; *Braganza v BP Shipping Ltd* [2015] UKSC 17, [2015] 1 WLR 1661. See generally Hooley [2013] CLJ 65.

[165] *Miller v Cannon Hill Estates Ltd* [1931] 2 KB 113; *Lynch v Thorne* [1956] 1 WLR 303; *Hancock v Brazier (Anerley) Ltd* [1966] 1 WLR 1317.

the service-providers: but, if the travel agent itself undertakes to supply the services, it is an implied term of the contract that the services themselves will be carried out with reasonable care and skill, even where the agent has arranged for its obligation to be performed by others.[166] Some of these standardized terms have subsequently been codified by statute.[167] Others, as will be seen, continue to emerge by a process of common law development.

In these cases concerning a common relationship, for example sale, carriage, landlord and tenant, or employment, the parties may have left a lot unsaid and the process of implication is different. It involves the Court determining, in the light of general considerations of policy, the standard incidents of the particular type of relationship rather than constructing a hypothetical bargain. Although it has usually been said that the criterion for this form of implication is also 'necessity' rather than 'reasonableness',[168] it does appear that a broader approach is taken. The Courts will consider how the proposed implied term will sit with existing law, the effect on the parties to the relationship, and wider issues of fairness.[169] In Dyson LJ's words in *Crossley v Faithful & Gould Holdings Ltd*, '[R]ather than focus on the elusive concept of necessity, it is better to recognise that, to some extent at least, the existence and scope of standardised implied terms raise questions of reasonableness, fairness and the balancing of competing policy considerations'.[170]

While the parties can exclude or modify the standard incidents of the relationship by express words, unless they do so they will form part of the obligation as a legal incident of the particular kind of contractual relationship.[171] Such standardized terms, implied by law, have been said to 'operate as default rules'.[172] In these cases it has been said[173] that the problem of implication is to be solved by asking:

[H]as the law already defined the obligation or the extent of it? If so, let it be followed. If not, look to see what would be reasonable in the general run of such cases . . . and then say what the obligation shall be.

---

[166] *Wong Mee Wan v Kwan Kin Travel Services Ltd* [1996] 1 WLR 38, 42 and 46–7. In the second situation the contractor may be liable despite the absence of personal negligence.

[167] eg Sale of Goods Act 1979, ss 12–15 (below, p 171); Supply of Goods and Services Act 1982, s 13. Those provisions now apply only to non-consumer contracts but there are similar provisions on consumer contracts, which treat terms as included in the contract, under Part I of the Consumer Rights Act 2015.

[168] *Liverpool City Council v Irwin* [1977] AC 239, 254 (Lord Wilberforce); *Scally v Southern Health and Social Services Board* [1992] 1 AC 294, 307 (Lord Bridge). Cf *Shell UK Ltd v Lostock Garages Ltd* [1976] 1 WLR 1187, 1196 (Lord Denning MR). See also *Lister v Romford Ice & Cold Storage Co Ltd* [1957] AC 555, 576 (Viscount Simonds) and 594 (Lord Tucker).

[169] Peden (2001) 117 LQR 459, 467.   [170] [2004] EWCA Civ 293, [2004] 4 All ER 447 at [36].

[171] *Mears v Safecar Security Ltd* [1983] QB 54, 78.

[172] *Malik v Bank of Credit & Commerce International SA* [1998] AC 20, 45 (Lord Steyn). See also Rakoff, in Beatson and Friedmann (eds), *Good Faith and Fault in Contract Law* (1995) 191; Riley (2000) 20 OJLS 367.

[173] *Shell UK Ltd v Lostock Garages Ltd* [1976] 1 WLR 1187, 1196 (Lord Denning MR). See also *Liverpool City Council v Irwin* [1977] 1 WLR 239, 257–8 (Lord Cross); *Scally v Southern Health and Social Services Board* [1992] 1 AC 294, 307. Cf *Reid v Rush & Tomkins Group plc* [1990] 1 WLR 212 (no such term implied because extent of obligation raised issues of social policy which could only be resolved by the legislature); *Johnson v Unisys Ltd* [2001] UKHL 13, [2003] 1 AC 518 (term not implied where statute provided limited remedy for conduct complained of).

In such cases the contract may be partly but not wholly stated in writing and 'in order to complete it, in particular to give it a bilateral character, it is necessary to take account of the parties and the circumstances', that is the nature of the contract and the relationship established by it.[174] In *Liverpool City Council v Irwin*:[175]

Tenants in a council tower block withheld rent as a protest at conditions in the building. They alleged that the council was in breach of its duty to repair and maintain the lifts, staircases, and rubbish chutes in the common parts of the building which it controlled. There was no formal lease; merely a document entitled 'conditions of tenancy' and the conditions set out only related to the tenants' obligations. They contained nothing about the landlord's obligations.

It was held that the tenants were to have an implied easement over the common parts for access to their premises and to the rubbish chutes and that the landlord was also under an implied obligation to take reasonable care to maintain the common parts in a reasonable state of repair because the contract had not placed the obligation to maintain on the tenants individually or collectively, and the landlord retained control of this essential means of access.

Again, in recent years an implied obligation of mutual trust and confidence has been recognized in contracts of employment by which both employer and employee are obliged not to conduct themselves in a manner calculated and likely to destroy or seriously damage the relationship of confidence and trust between them.[176] It has also been suggested that an apparently unrestricted contractual power to terminate a telephone service on a month's notice should be interpreted as subject to an implied term that the power to terminate should not be exercised without demonstrable reason or cause.[177]

The distinction between terms implied as the incidents of a defined relationship and those implied to give business efficacy to a particular transaction was also applied in *Scally v Southern Health and Social Services Board*:[178]

A contract of employment contained a term giving certain employees the right to acquire a valuable additional pension benefit if they took certain action within a certain time. The term derived from a collective bargain negotiated by the employees' representatives and trade unions. The claimants, employees who had not been informed of this right, claimed damages for, inter alia, breach of contract.

---

[174] *Liverpool City Council v Irwin*, above [1977] AC 239; *Lister v Romford Ice & Cold Storage Ltd* [1957] AC 555, 579.

[175] [1977] AC 239.   [176] *Malik v Bank of Credit & Commerce International* [1998] AC 20.

[177] *Timeload Ltd v British Telecommunications plc* (1995) 3 EMLR 459, 467 (Sir Thomas Bingham MR). Some analogical assistance appears to have been derived from the Unfair Contract Terms Act 1977, s 3; below, p 215.

[178] [1992] 1 AC 294. Cf p 215; *University of Nottingham v Eyett (No 1)* [1999] 2 All ER 437.

It was held that a term obliging the employer to take reasonable steps to inform its employees of this right should be implied into the contract because this term of the contract was not the result of individual negotiation but of a collective bargain and, therefore, the employees could not be expected to be aware of the term unless it was drawn to their attention. The implied obligation to inform employees accordingly did not apply to all contracts of employment. If this is an indication that the categories of defined relationships may be subdivided into smaller and more numerous categories with terms that have a less general application, the distinction between implication of terms in cases concerning a common relationship and implication in those concerning a particular contract may be a fragile one.[179] It has, however, been argued that it can be maintained by having recourse to trade usage in identifying what are the defined types of contractual relationship.[180]

(iii) Terms implied by custom

Another situation in which the Courts lay down a general rule that some provision is to be implied in all contracts of a defined type unless the parties have expressly excluded it is where a term is implied by the custom of a locality or by the usage of a particular trade. Such a custom must be strictly proved. It must be as certain as the written contract, notorious, recognized as legally binding, reasonable, and consistent with the express terms of the contract.[181] Furthermore, the custom must not offend against the intention of any legislative enactment.

In *Hutton v Warren*,[182] a term was implied by the custom of the country into an agricultural tenancy giving the outgoing tenant the right to a reasonable allowance for seeds and labour expended on the land even though the lease contained no express term to this effect. *Harley & Co v Nagata*[183] is an example of a term implied by the usage of a particular trade. It was held that a custom that the commission of the broker who negotiated a time charterparty should be paid out of the hire that was earned, and should not be payable at all unless hire was in fact earned, should be imported into the brokerage contract. Again in *Mount v Oldham Corporation*[184] an obligation to give a term's notice of an intention to withdraw a child from a private school or to pay a term's fees in lieu of notice was implied by custom.

---

[179] See Phang [1993] JBL 242, [1994] JBL 255, and note *Ashmore v Corporation of Lloyd's (No 2)* [1992] 2 Lloyd's Rep 620, 631 (no common relationship in many thousands of contracts between Lloyd's underwriters and the Corporation entered into on the same terms).

[180] Peden (2001) 117 LQR 459, 463.

[181] *Nelson v Dahl* (1879) 12 Ch D 568, 575; *Cunliffe-Owen v Teather & Greenwood* [1967] 1 WLR 1421, 1438–9 (usage of the Stock Exchange).

[182] (1836) 1 M & W 466.   [183] (1917) 23 Com Cas 121.

[184] [1973] QB 309. See also *Lord Eldon v Hedley Brothers* [1935] 2 KB 1.

Certain usages of the mercantile community at large have been codified, for example, those relating to negotiable instruments in the Bills of Exchange Act 1882.

(a) Certainty   A course of conduct which is said to form a custom must be both identifiable and uniform. It is these qualities that give the course of conduct the required certainty. The requirement of uniformity does not require total consistency of conduct. Thus, it has been stated that the continued adherence of 85 per cent of the Lancashire weaving mills to a custom was sufficient to maintain it,[185] although a higher degree of uniformity may be required for the creation of a new custom.[186] Once a custom has been proved in a sufficient number of cases, the Court will take judicial notice of it without the need for further evidence.[187]

(b) Notoriety   To be notorious a custom need not be known to all the world, nor even to both parties to the contract.[188] It must, however, be well known in the market to which it applies and readily ascertainable by any person entering into a contract of which it will form a part.[189]

(c) Recognized as legally binding   The fact that a course of conduct is uniform, certain, and notorious is not, in itself, enough to give rise to a binding custom. It must also be shown that the course of conduct was intended to have a legally binding effect and that compliance with it was the result of a belief in a legal obligation to do so. A custom must therefore be distinguished from a course of conduct that is frequently, or even habitually, followed in a particular commercial community as a matter of grace or commercial convenience.[190] The clearest way of establishing this is to show that the custom has been 'enforced' but this is not necessary and it is sufficient for it to be established that the custom has been acted upon.[191] Where the conduct is required by the rules of a trade or professional association, that will be good evidence that compliance is the result of belief in an obligation to do so.[192]

(d) Reasonableness   Reasonableness is a question of law and, to qualify, a custom must be 'fair and proper and such as reasonable, honest, and fair-minded men would adopt'.[193] Although evidence of the unreasonableness of a course of conduct may

---

[185] *Sagar v H Ridehalgh & Son Ltd* [1931] 1 Ch 310.

[186] *Con-Stan Industries of Australia Pty Ltd v Norwich Insurance (Australia) Ltd* (1985–86) 160 CLR 226 (High Court of Australia), although instances of inconsistency were 'minute': [1981] 2 NSWLR 879, 889–90.

[187] *Universo Insurance Co of Milan v Merchant's Marine Insurance Co Ltd* [1897] 2 QB 93 (judicial notice taken of a broker's liability for unpaid premium in the marine insurance market). See also *JA Chapman & Co Ltd v Kadirga Denizcilik Ve Ticaret* [1998] Lloyd's Rep IR 377.

[188] *Grissell v Bristowe* (1868) LR 3 CP 112, 128, revs'd on the facts of the case (1868) LR 4 CP 36; *Buckle v Knoop* (1867) LR 2 Exch 125, 129, aff'd *ibid*, 333.

[189] *Strathlorne SS Co Ltd v Hugh Baird & Sons Ltd*, 1916 SC (HL) 134, 136 (Lord Buckmaster LC).

[190] *General Reinsurance Corp v Forsakringsaktiebolaget Fennia Patria* [1983] QB 856, 874 (Slade LJ).

[191] *Cunningham v Fonblanque* (1833) 6 C & P 44, 49; *Hall v Benson* (1836) 7 C & P 711; *Johnson v Clarke* [1908] 1 Ch 303, 309. Cf *Sea Steamship Co Ltd v Price, Walker & Co Ltd* (1903) 8 Com Cas 292, 295.

[192] *Cunliffe-Owen v Teather & Greenwood* [1967] 1 WLR 1421 (Stock Exchange rules); *Shearson Lehman Hutton Inc v MacLaine Watson & Co Ltd* [1989] 2 Lloyd's Rep 570 (London Metal Exchange).

[193] *Produce Brokers Co Ltd v Olympia Oil and Cake Co Ltd* [1916] 2 KB 296, 298.

be used to show that it was not generally accepted or known and does not therefore amount to a custom,[194] where a custom has been sufficiently proved, the Courts' tendency to support freedom of bargaining in commercial markets means that it is unlikely to be held to be unreasonable.[195] Where the contracting parties are in a fiduciary relationship, as in the case of an agent or a broker, a stricter approach is taken. The variation, by a trade custom, of a fiduciary duty such as the rule that fiduciaries must not place themselves in a position where their own interest conflicts with that of their customer, is less likely to be held to be reasonable,[196] although in some cases it may be so held.[197]

(e) Consistency with express terms A custom or usage which would otherwise become an implied term of the contract may be expressly or impliedly excluded by the parties. Thus, in *Les Affréteurs Réunis Société Anonyme v Leopold Walford (London) Ltd*[198] the custom that in a time charter the broker's commission was only payable if the hire was earned was excluded by an express provision that 'a commission of 3 per cent on the estimated gross amount of hire is due (to the broker) *on signing this charter*', in other words, whether any hire was earned or not. In *Exxonmobil Sales and Supply Corp v Texaco Ltd*[199] it was held that an entire agreement clause, which included the wording that there was no other usage or course of dealing affecting the contract, excluded the implying of terms based upon usage or custom.

(c) TERMS IMPLIED BY STATUTE

(i) Sale of goods

Contracts for the sale of goods are of such everyday occurrence, and are commonly made with so little consideration of the exact legal results which the parties would desire to produce by it, that if their rights and obligations were to be determined only by what they say or do when they make the contract their reasonable expectations would often be defeated. Consequently certain conditions and warranties are *implied* in a contract of sale, originally by common law, but since 1893 pursuant to sections 12–15 of the Sale of Goods Act 1893, now re-enacted (with amendments) in the Sale of Goods Act 1979.[200] The Consumer Rights Act 2015 has further amended the Sale of Goods Act 1979 so that the statutory implied terms are now only implied into non-consumer contracts. For consumer contracts for the supply of goods (and digital

---

[194] *Bottomley v Forbes* (1838) 5 Bing (NC) 121, 128.

[195] *Moult v Halliday* [1898] 1 QB 125, 130.

[196] *Robinson v Mollett* (1875) LR 7 HL 802; *Anglo-African Merchants Ltd. v Bayley* [1970] 1 QB 311; *North and South Co v Berkeley* [1971] 1 WLR 470.

[197] *Jones v Canavan* [1972] 2 NSWLR 236; *Kelly v Cooper* [1993] AC 205, 214 (although this implication may have been on the ground of business efficacy).

[198] [1919] AC 801, below, p 672.

[199] [2003] EWHC 1964 (Comm), [2004] 1 All ER (Comm) 435.

[200] Amended by, eg, the Sale and Supply of Goods Act 1994, substantially implementing the Report of the Law Commission, *Sale and Supply of Goods* (Law Com No 160, 1987).

content) the equivalent terms (and others) are not implied terms but are rather terms treated as included in the contract.[201]

In principle the statutorily implied terms may be negatived or varied by express agreement, by the course of dealing between the parties, or by a binding usage.[202] This freedom of the parties is, however, made subject to the Unfair Contract Terms Act 1977 which contains significant restrictions so that liability for breach of the statutory implied terms cannot be excluded or restricted or can only be excluded or restricted if the Court is satisfied that the term doing so is reasonable.[203]

(a) Title   By section 12 of the Sale of Goods Act 1979 the following terms are implied:

(1) a condition[204] 'on the part of the seller that in the case of a sale he has a right to sell the goods, and in the case of an agreement to sell he will have such a right at the time when the property is to pass':

(2) a warranty[205] that

'(a) the goods are free, and will remain free until the time when the property is to pass, from any charge or encumbrance not disclosed or known to the buyer before the contract is made, and

(a) the buyer will enjoy quiet possession of the goods except so far as it may be disturbed by the owner or other person entitled to the benefit of any charge or encumbrance so disclosed or known.'

Different and more limited warranties are implied in a contract of sale where 'there appears from the contract or is to be inferred from the circumstances of the contract an intention that the seller should transfer only such title as he or a third person may have'.[206] The seller can, by an express term of the contract, indicate an intention to pass only a limited title and such an intention may also be inferred. Where the goods are sold by an auctioneer[207] the intention of the parties to the contract may be that the buyer should have such title only to the goods, and such right only to take possession of them, as the seller has in fact acquired.[208] But where the seller purports to sell only such title as he or a third person may have, the warranties of freedom from encumbrances and quiet possession are not thereby wholly excluded. The seller must disclose to the buyer, before the contract is made, any known encumbrances, and further warrants that neither he nor anyone claiming under him (or the third person) will disturb the buyer's quiet possession of the goods.[209]

---

[201] Below, p 178.   [202] Sale of Goods Act 1979, s 55.
[203] Unfair Contract Terms Act 1977, s 6, below, p 213.
[204] Sale of Goods Act 1979, s 12(1), (5A).
[205] Sale of Goods Act 1979, s 12(2), (5A).   [206] Sale of Goods Act 1979, s 12(3).
[207] *Niblett v Confectioners' Materials Co Ltd* [1921] 3 KB 387, 401; *Rowland v Divall* [1923] 2 KB 500, 505.
[208] *Bagueley v Hawley* (1867) LR 2 CP 625, 629.   [209] Sale of Goods Act 1979, s 12(4), (5).

The exclusion or restriction of liability for breach of the terms implied by section 12 is absolutely prohibited[210] and they are accordingly a compulsory part of a contract for the sale of goods.

(b) Sale by description   By section 13 of the Act:

(1) In 'a contract for the sale of goods by description', there is an implied condition[211] that 'the goods will correspond with the description'.

(2) 'If the sale is by sample as well as by description it is not sufficient that the bulk of the goods corresponds with the sample if the goods do not also correspond with the description.'

(3) 'A sale of goods is not prevented from being a sale by description by reason only that, being exposed for sale or hire, they are selected by the buyer.'

A sale of goods by description is a sale in which the buyer contracts in reliance on a description, express or implied,[212] even though the buyer has seen the goods[213] and may have selected the goods. Thus, it was held that a person who agreed to buy a second-hand reaping machine described as 'new the previous year and only used to cut 50 acres' was entitled to reject the machine on delivery when he found that it was, in fact, a very old machine.[214] Not all descriptive words are, however, conditions; the words must identify the subject-matter of the contract. So, for instance, words identifying the yard in which a ship that is being sold is to be built are not within section 13.[215]

(c) Satisfactory quality   Ordinarily there is no implied condition or warranty of the quality of goods sold or of their fitness for any particular purpose: *caveat emptor*. But, where goods are sold in the course of a business,[216] the 1979 Act contains important qualifications of this principle. By section 14:

(2)   'Where the seller sells goods in the course of a business', there is an implied condition[217] that 'the goods supplied under the contract are of satisfactory quality.'

(2C) There is no such condition as regards any matter making the quality of the goods unsatisfactory 'which is specifically drawn to the buyer's attention before the contract is made'; or 'where the buyer examines the goods before the contract is made, which that examination ought to reveal.'

---

[210] Unfair Contract Terms Act 1977, s 6(1). But by s 26, UCTA 1977 does not apply to international sale contracts. An express term concerning title will be a condition: *Barber v NWS Bank plc* [1996] 1 WLR 641.

[211] Sale of Goods Act 1979, s 13(1A).   [212] *Wallis, Son & Wells v Pratt & Haynes* [1911] AC 394.

[213] *Grant v Australian Knitting Mills Ltd* [1936] AC 85, 100; *Nicholson & Venn v Smith Marriott* (1947) 177 LT 189.

[214] *Varley v Whipp* [1900] 1 QB 513.

[215] *Reardon Smith Line Ltd v Hansen Tangen* [1976] 1 WLR 989. See also *Ashington Piggeries v Christopher Hill Ltd* [1972] AC 441, 503–4; *Harlingdon & Leinster Enterprises Ltd v Christopher Hull Fine Art Ltd* [1991] 1 QB 564.

[216] This is to be given a broad meaning. There is no restriction that the goods be of a type that the seller deals in: *Stevenson v Rogers* [1999] QB 1028 (fisherman selling boat).

[217] Sale of Goods Act 1979, s 14(6).

Prior to the 1994 amendment the requirement was that the goods be of 'merchantable' quality, a criterion that was criticized[218] as too open-ended, inappropriate for consumer transactions, and as not expressly requiring reasonable durability.[219] The Law Commission had recommended that the criterion be 'acceptable quality'[220] but this was not accepted, inter alia, because of concern that a buyer might decide reluctantly that the goods were of 'acceptable' quality even if, by objective standards the quality was not 'satisfactory'.[221] The new criterion, is 'satisfactory quality' and is defined in section 14 of the Sale of Goods Act 1979:[222]

(2A) Goods are of satisfactory quality 'if they meet the standard that a reasonable person would regard as satisfactory, taking account of any description of the goods, the price (if relevant) and all the other relevant circumstances'.

(2B) The quality of goods 'includes their state and condition and the following (among others) are in appropriate cases aspects of the quality of goods—(a) fitness for all the purposes for which goods of the kind in question are commonly supplied (b) appearance and finish (c) freedom from minor defects (d) safety, and (e) durability'.

The indications are that recourse to decisions on the old law should only be had in exceptional cases[223] but, in the absence of guidance as to what 'satisfactory quality' means, they provide useful indications of what is likely to be required. Thus, in *Rogers v Parish (Scarborough) Ltd*[224] it was said that:

Starting with the purpose for which ['goods of the kind in question'][225] are commonly bought, one would include in respect of any passenger vehicle not merely the buyer's purpose in driving the car from one place to another but of doing so with the appropriate degree of comfort, ease of handling and reliability and, one might add, of pride in the vehicle's outward and interior appearance. What is the appropriate degree and what relative weight is to be attached to one characteristic of the car rather than another will depend on the market at which the car is aimed.[226]

In that case, a new car had been delivered with substantial defects to its engine, gearbox, and bodywork and attempts to rectify these defects over a six-month period had failed. It was held that the car was not of 'merchantable quality' and the buyer was entitled to reject it, even though the defects did not render it unroadworthy.

Again, apart from the factors listed in subsection 2B, the Court is likely to consider the consequences of the defect and the ease or otherwise with which it could be

---

[218] *Cehave NV v Bremer Handelsgesellschaft mbH* [1976] QB 44, 80 (Ormrod LJ); Law Com No 162, *Sale and Supply of Goods* (1987), para 2.9 ff.

[219] But see *Mash & Murrell v Joseph I Emmanuel* [1962] 1 WLR 16; *Lambert v Lewis* [1982] AC 225, 276.

[220] Law Com No 162, above, n 218, paras 3.22, 3.27.

[221] Hansard 237 HC Deb (1993/94), col 633. See further 139 HC Deb (1987/88) WA 705; 165 HC Deb (1989/90), col 1225.

[222] Inserted by the Sale and Supply of Goods Act 1994, s 1(1).

[223] *Rogers v Parish (Scarborough) Ltd* [1987] QB 933, 942–3 (Mustill LJ).   [224] [1987] QB 933.

[225] The bracketed words reflect the 1994 amendments. Before those, s 14(6) referred to 'goods of that kind'.

[226] *Rogers v Parish (Scarborough) Ltd* [1987] QB 933, 944.

remedied. 'In some cases, such as a high-priced quality product, the customer may be entitled to expect that it is free from even minor defects, in other words perfect or nearly so.'[227]

Second-hand goods sold as such and goods sold as 'seconds' or imperfect must still measure up to a reasonable standard, even though not to the standard of a new or perfect article.[228] The price of the goods may frequently be of relevance: a buyer who, for example, buys a cheap carpet cannot expect it to achieve the same quality of resilience or wear as a more expensive one.[229]

The condition as to satisfactory quality extends to 'the goods supplied under the contract' including packaging, containers and extraneous items mixed with the goods sold. Thus, in *Wilson v Rickett, Cockrell & Co Ltd*[230] it was held that a ton of 'Coalite' which contained, unknown to either party, a detonator did not meet the statutory standard. The argument that there was nothing wrong with the 'Coalite' itself was rejected and the defendant was held liable for damage from an explosion caused when a bucketful of the fuel containing the detonator was put on a fire.

The condition is, however, excluded if the defects are pointed out to the buyer before the contract is made; or if, before the contract is made, the buyer examines the goods, then as regards defects which the examination which has been made ought to have revealed.[231]

(d) Fitness for purpose   Section 14(3) of the 1979 Act deals with the fitness for purpose of the goods sold:

(3) Where the seller sells goods in the course of a business and the buyer, expressly or by implication, makes known—

(a) to the seller, or

(b) where the purchase price or part of it is payable by instalments and the goods were previously sold by a credit-broker to the seller, to that credit-broker,

any particular purpose for which the goods are being bought, there is an implied [condition][232] that the goods supplied under the contract are reasonably fit for that purpose, whether or not that is a purpose for which such goods are commonly supplied, except where the circumstances show that the buyer does not rely, or that it is unreasonable for him to rely, on the skill or judgment of the seller or credit-broker.

---

[227] *Clegg v Andersson* [2003] EWCA Civ 320, [2003] 1 All ER (Comm) 721 at [72] (Hale LJ) (purchase of a yacht). For another case, subsequent to the 1994 reform, holding that goods were not of satisfactory quality, see *Britvic Soft Drinks Ltd v Messer UK Ltd* [2002] EWCA Civ 548, [2002] 2 All ER (Comm) 321 (contaminated carbon dioxide). For cases, since the 1994 reform, holding that goods were of satisfactory quality, see, eg, *Jewson Ltd v Boyhan* [2003] EWCA Civ 1030, [2004] 1 Lloyd's Rep 505 (boilers); *Bramhill v Edwards* [2004] EWCA Civ 403, [2004] 2 Lloyd's Rep 653 (motor home).

[228] *Bartlett v Sydney Marcus Ltd* [1965] 1 WLR 1013; *Business Appliance Specialists Ltd v Nationwide Credit Corp Ltd* [1988] RTR 332; *Shine v General Guarantee Corp* [1988] 1 All ER 911.

[229] Cf *BS Brown & Son Ltd v Craiks Ltd* [1970] 1 WLR 752.   [230] [1954] 1 QB 598.

[231] Sale of Goods Act 1979, s 14(2C); *R & B Customs Brokers Co Ltd v United Dominions Trust Ltd* [1988] 1 WLR 321.

[232] Sale of Goods Act 1979, s 14(6).

Although no longer applying to consumer contracts (by reason of the Consumer Rights Act 2015), the application of this subsection is illustrated by two cases concerning the purchase of food. In *Wallis v Russell*[233] the claimant bought from a fishmonger 'two nice fresh crabs for tea' and in *Chaproniere v Mason*[234] the claimant bought a bun from the defendant's baker's shop. The crabs were not fresh and the claimant suffered food poisoning after eating the crabs; the bun contained a stone and the claimant broke a tooth when he bit it. In the first case the claimant expressly made it known through her agent[235] that she required the crabs for eating and relied on the fishmonger to select fresh crabs. In the second case, in buying the bun from a baker, the claimant clearly made it known by implication that he required it for the purpose of eating and relied on the baker's skill and judgement. Both defendants were liable in damages for breach of this implied condition.

Where two business people who are equally knowledgeable are dealing with one another, it may still be that the buyer reasonably relies on the seller's skill or judgement.[236]

It is possible, however, that the reliance will be only partial. If, for example, the buyer procures the seller to manufacture goods in accordance with the buyer's formula or specifications, there will be no implied condition that the formula or specifications will produce goods which are reasonably fit for the purpose made known to the seller by the buyer, yet the buyer may rely on the skill or judgement of the seller to ensure that the materials to be compounded in the formula are not toxic or harmful[237] or there may be an area of expertise outside the specifications in respect of which the skill or judgement of the seller is relied on.[238]

(e) Sections 14(2) and 14(3) compared   The two subsections of section 14, to some extent, overlap, for both the definition of 'satisfactory quality' and section 14(3) refer to fitness for a purpose for which goods are commonly bought or supplied. A buyer who requires the goods for some special or unusual purpose, however, can recover, if at all, only under section 14(3). The special or unusual purpose must be made known to the seller and the buyer must show reliance on the seller's skill and judgement. Under section 14(2) it is not necessary to show such reliance. Where the goods are unfit for a special or unusual purpose, but nevertheless fit for all purposes for which such goods

---

[233] [1902] 2 Ir Rep 585.

[234] (1905) 21 TLR 633. See also *Priest v Last* [1903] 2 KB 148 (hot-water bottle bursts); *Frost v Aylesbury Dairy Co Ltd* [1905] 1 KB 608 (typhoid germs in milk); *St Albans City & DC v International Computers Ltd* [1996] 4 All ER 481, 494 (computer disk with defective program); *Britvic Soft Drinks Ltd v Messer UK Ltd* [2002] EWCA Civ 548, [2002] 2 All ER (Comm) 321 (contaminated carbon dioxide). For cases, where there was held to be no relevant reliance under s 14(3), see, eg, *Jewson Ltd v Boyhan* [2003] EWCA Civ 1030, [2004] 1 Lloyd's Rep 505 (boilers); *Bramhill v Edwards* [2004] EWCA Civ 403, [2004] 2 Lloyd's Rep 653 (motor home).

[235] The purchase was made by the claimant's granddaughter on her behalf. On agency, see below, Chapter 23.

[236] *Henry Kendall & Sons v William Lillico & Sons Ltd* [1969] 2 AC 31. Cf *Slater & Slater v Finning Ltd* [1997] AC 473 (no reliance because of unusual feature in buyer's machinery).

[237] *Ashington Piggeries Ltd v Christopher Hill Ltd* [1972] AC 441.

[238] *Cammell Laird & Co Ltd v Manganese Bronze & Brass Co Ltd* [1934] AC 402.

are commonly supplied, they will still be of 'satisfactory quality' and there will be no breach by the seller of section 14(2).

Where, however, they are only fit for some of the purposes for which such goods are commonly supplied they will not be of 'satisfactory quality'.[239] As amended in 1994, the subsection thus places the risk of unfitness for any of the common purposes on the seller. It is said that the seller who knows that its goods are not fit for one or more of the purposes for which goods of that kind are commonly supplied can protect itself by ensuring that the description of the goods excludes any common purpose for which they are unfit or by otherwise indicating that the goods are not fit for all their common purposes.[240] The amendment has therefore given the characterization of a purpose as 'common' or 'unusual' a new importance.

(f) Sale by sample   In a sale by sample there are two implied conditions. First, that the bulk will correspond with the sample in quality. Secondly, that the goods will be free from any defect making their quality unsatisfactory, which would not be apparent on reasonable examination of the sample.[241] The meaning of this last condition, considered in *Godley v Perry*,[242] is still of relevance in non-consumer contracts but as a result of the Consumer Rights Act 2015 it does not now apply to consumer contracts.

A 6-year-old boy bought a toy catapult from a shop. It was made of brittle polystyrene which fractured while he was using it, blinding him in one eye. He sued the retailer for damages under section 14(2) and (3) of the Sale of Goods Act. The retailer joined the wholesaler from whom he had bought the catapult by sample as a third party and the wholesaler likewise joined the importer who had supplied him.

The retailer was held liable but it was argued that the wholesaler and importer were not liable for breach of the condition as to satisfactory quality in a contract of sale by sample because a reasonable examination of the catapult would have revealed its fragility. Edmund Davies J said:[243]

Counsel . . . suggested that by holding the toy down with one's foot and then pulling on the elastic its safety could be tested and . . . its inherent fragility would thereby inevitably be discovered. True, the potential customer might have done any of these. He might also, I suppose, have tried biting the catapult, or hitting it with a hammer, or applying a lighted match to ensure its non-inflammability, experiments which, with all respect, are but slightly more bizarre than those suggested by counsel.

The phrase 'reasonable examination' was to be construed by the common-sense standards of everyday life: 'Not extreme ingenuity, but reasonableness, is the statutory yardstick'. The wholesaler and importer were held liable.

---

[239] Sale of Goods Act 1979, s 14(2B), above, p 174.
[240] See Law Com No 162, *Sale and Supply of Goods* (1987), para 3.36. Prior to 1994 it was not necessary for the goods to be fit for *all* of their common purposes: *Sumner, Permain & Co Ltd v Webb & Co Ltd* [1922] 1 KB 55; *Aswan Engineering Establishment Co v Lupine Ltd* [1987] 1 WLR 1, *Henry Kendall & Sons v William Lillico & Sons Ltd* [1969] 2 AC 31, 77.
[241] Sale of Goods Act 1979, s 15.   [242] [1960] 1 WLR 9.   [243] *Ibid*, 15.

(ii) Other statutory implied terms

Certain terms are implied by sections 8–11 of the Supply of Goods (Implied Terms) Act 1973 into non-consumer contracts of hire-purchase. These implied terms resemble very closely those implied in contracts of sale of goods, and relate similarly to title, quality, and fitness for purpose, and correspondence with description or sample. Analogous terms are also implied by the Supply of Goods and Services Act 1982 into non-consumer contracts for the hire of goods,[244] and into non-consumer contracts for work and materials in relation to the materials supplied.[245] By sections 13–15 of the Supply of Goods and Services Act 1982, in a non-consumer contract for the supply of services, there are implied terms that the supplier will carry out the service with reasonable care and skill, that (if no time for completion is fixed) the supplier will carry out the service within a reasonable time, and that (if no price is fixed) the party contracting with the supplier will pay a reasonable charge. Finally, the covenants for title which are implied on a disposition of property are set out in Part I of the Law of Property (Miscellaneous Provisions) Act 1994.

(d) PART 1 OF THE CONSUMER RIGHTS ACT 2015: TERMS TREATED AS INCLUDED

In a consumer contract for the supply of goods, digital content, or services, it is no longer the case that there are statutory implied terms as to, for example, title, satisfactory quality, fitness for purpose, and description of the goods or as to the standard of care or timing or price of services. Instead, under the 2015 Act, the contract is to be treated as 'including' terms to that effect.[246] This change of terminology does not in itself effect any real change to the law on the implication of terms so that what has been said above on the statutory implied terms will continue to apply in substance, if not in form, to consumer contracts. As has been noted above, however, the 2015 Act has removed the labelling of the terms as conditions or warranties so that the effect of a breach of those terms on the consumer's right to discharge the contract will now essentially turn on what the statute provides about discharge[247] rather than on the common law.

4. INTERPRETATION OF TERMS

This section deals briefly with certain general principles which govern the interpretation (otherwise referred to as the construction) of terms which have been reduced to writing. The interpretation of a contract is always a matter of law for the Court to determine.

---

[244] Supply of Goods and Services Act 1982, ss 7–10.
[245] Supply of Goods and Services Act 1982, ss 2–5.
[246] Consumer Rights Act 2015, ss 9–18 (goods), 34–41 (digital content), 49–53 (services).
[247] Consumer Rights Act 2015, especially ss 19–20 and 42. See below, pp 538–40.

(a) THE CONTEXTUAL APPROACH

The professed object of the Court in interpreting a written contract is to discover the mutual intention of the parties,[248] the written declaration of whose minds it is. The old approach to construction was that, subject to ambiguity[249] and to some other exceptions (eg the meaning of technical terms, or the avoidance of manifest absurdity[250] or of a very obvious drafting mistake),[251] words were to be interpreted literally—according to their plain meaning—without reference to extrinsic evidence of the background.[252]

In contrast, the modern approach, articulated by Lord Hoffmann in *Investors Compensation Scheme Ltd v West Bromwich Building Society*[253] is that one should always interpret a contract in its context. He said: 'Interpretation is the ascertainment of the meaning which the document would convey to a reasonable person having all the background which would reasonably have been available to the parties in the situation in which they were at the time of the contract'.[254]

He went on to explain that, subject to exceptions (considered below), the background includes 'absolutely anything [relevant] which would have affected the way in which the language of the document would have been understood by a reasonable man';[255] that the literal meaning may be overridden, even though there is no ambiguity because the background makes clear that 'the parties must . . . have used the wrong words or syntax';[256] and that 'the law does not require judges to attribute to the parties an intention which they plainly could not have had'.[257]

This modern contextual approach is to be welcomed as being more likely to reflect the parties' intentions than the literal approach. However, it has been criticized by some[258] as giving rise to greater uncertainty and as increasing the costs of litigation because more material has to be considered by the Courts. It can also

---

[248] *Pioneer Shipping Ltd v BTP Tioxide* [1982] AC 724, 736; *International Fina Services AG v Katrina Shipping Ltd* [1995] 2 Lloyd's Rep 344, 350.

[249] *Shore v Wilson* (1842) 9 Cl & Fin 355, 365 (Tindal CJ).

[250] *Abbott v Middleton* (1858) 7 HLC 68, 69; *River Wear Commissioners v Adamson* (1877) 2 App Cas 743, 746–7 (Lord Blackburn).

[251] *Homburg Houtimport BV v Agrosin Private Ltd, The Starsin* [2004] 1 AC 715; *Littman v Aspen Oil (Broking) Ltd* [2005] EWCA Civ 1579, [2006] 2 P & CR 2; *Dalkia Utilities Services plc v Celtech International Ltd* [2006] EWHC 63 (Comm), [2006] 1 Lloyd's Rep 599.

[252] *Shore v Wilson* (1842) 9 Cl & Fin 355, 365; *Lovell and Christmas Ltd v Wall* (1911) 104 LT 85, 88 (Cozens-Hardy MR).

[253] [1998] 1 WLR 896. This contextual approach was heralded by Lord Wilberforce's speeches in *Prenn v Simmonds* [1971] 1 WLR 1381 and *Reardon Smith Line Ltd v Yngvar Hansen-Tangen* [1976] 1 WLR 989.

[254] [1998] 1 WLR 896, 912.

[255] *Ibid.* The inclusion of the word 'relevant' reflects the qualification made by Lord Hoffmann in *Bank of Credit & Commerce International v Ali* [2001] UKHL 8, [2001] 1 AC 251 at [39].

[256] [1998] 1 WLR 896, 913.

[257] *Ibid.* Lord Hoffmann here referred to Lord Diplock's reference to 'business commonsense' in *Antaios Compania Naviera SA v Salen Rederierna AB* [1985] AC 191, 201. See also *Lord Napier and Ettrick v R Kershaw Ltd (No 2)* [1999] 1 WLR 756, 763 (Lord Steyn).

[258] eg Staughton LJ [1999] CLJ 303; Berg (2006) 122 LQR 354; Calnan, in Burrows and Peel (eds), *Contract Terms* (2007) ch 2.

be argued that a contextual approach produces greater difficulties for third parties who may be assigned the benefit of the contract and yet may be unfamiliar with the background against which the contract was concluded. This concern for third parties presumably lies behind the majority's view in *Cherry Tree Investments Ltd v Landmain Ltd*[259] that the Courts should be more cautious about using background material when interpreting a contract in a public document (in the case itself, a registered legal charge)[260] rather than an ordinary contract.

In the *Investors Compensation Scheme* case:

> A number of investors had been given negligent advice and had claims (in tort or for breach of statutory duty) against their financial advisers, building societies and solicitors. A central scheme was set up by the Securities and Investment Board to ensure compensation was paid to the investors. To be entitled to compensation under that scheme, investors concluded a contract of assignment with the Investors Compensation Scheme (the claimant) whereby they assigned to the ICS their claims against their advisers, building societies and solicitors subject to a clause excluding from the assignment 'Any claim (whether sounding in rescission for undue influence or otherwise)' against a building society which would abate sums otherwise owed to that society. In an action by the ICS against the defendant building society, the central question was whether that clause meant that the investors had retained (ie had not assigned) their rights to claim damages, as well as rescission, against the building societies.

The House of Lords (Lord Lloyd dissenting) held that the right to claim rescission had been retained but that the right to claim damages had been validly assigned. The exclusion from assignment clause, 'Any claim (whether sounding in rescission for undue influence or otherwise)' was interpreted as if it had read, 'Any claim sounding in rescission (whether for undue influence or otherwise)'. This construction meant that only claims for rescission, *and not for damages*, against the building societies were excluded from the assignment.

An acceptance of the modern contextual approach leaves open precisely how much weight is to be given to the words used as against other relevant factors including commercial common sense. In *Rainy Sky SA v Kookmin Bank*,[261] in applying what Lord Hoffmann had said in *Investors Compensation Scheme*, the Supreme Court indicated that, in a commercial context, where there is more than one plausible meaning, the commercially more sensible meaning is to be preferred. Lord Clarke said: 'if the language is capable of more than one construction, it is not necessary to conclude that a particular construction would produce an absurd or irrational result before having regard to the commercial purpose of the agreement.'[262] And earlier his Lordship said: 'The language used by the parties will often have more than one potential meaning... If there are two possible constructions, the court is entitled to

---

[259] [2012] EWCA Civ 736, [2013] Ch 305 (per Longmore and Lewison LJJ, Arden LJ dissenting).

[260] The same argument might be applied to, eg, letters of credit and bills of lading: see Lewison, *The Interpretation of Contracts* (6th edn, 2016) para 3.18; *Re Sigma Finance Corporation* [2009] UKSC 2, [2010] 1 All ER 571 at [37].

[261] [2011] UKSC 50, [2011] 1 WLR 2900.   [262] *Ibid* at [43].

prefer the construction which is consistent with business common sense and to reject the other.'[263]

It has been stressed in cases after *Rainy Sky*[264] that what constitutes the commercially more sensible meaning is often not obvious: it can therefore only be determinative where it can be ascertained by the Court. Moreover, in the latest Supreme Court decision on interpretation, *Arnold v Britton*,[265] which concerned a covenant to pay a service charge in a lease of a holiday chalet, there appears to have been a subtle move to steer interpretation back towards the words used as the primary factor of importance as against, for example, commercial common sense.

Perhaps the most controversial aspect of Lord Hoffmann's restatement was his exclusion from the admissible background of evidence of the previous negotiations of the parties.[266] That traditional exclusionary rule was said to rest on 'reasons of practical policy'.[267] Despite persuasive criticism by numerous commentators,[268] that exclusion was, unfortunately and surprisingly, confirmed, after a detailed examination, by the House of Lords in *Chartbrook Ltd v Persimmon Homes Ltd*.[269]

A dispute arose, in relation to a property development agreement, as to how much was payable by the developers (Persimmon) to the owners of the land (Chartbrook). This turned on the meaning of the term 'additional residential payment'. The developers argued that, on the true construction of the contract, they owed only £897,051. The owners argued that, on the true construction of the contract, they were owed £4,484,862.

The owners succeeded in the lower courts but the developers' appeal was allowed by the House of Lords which held that the smaller sum was due. Their Lordships reached that conclusion because, although the owners' construction was 'in accordance with conventional syntax',[270] it made 'no commercial sense';[271] and, applying the approach in *Investors Compensation Scheme*, this was a case where the background made it clear that something must have gone wrong with the language used.

Although finding for the developers, the House of Lords rejected their argument that one should look at the pre-contractual negotiations which, the developers argued, made it plain that the developers' interpretation was the correct one. While accepting that to allow such evidence did not contradict the objective theory of interpretation,[272]

---

[263] *Ibid* at [21].

[264] *BMA Special Opportunity Hub Fund Ltd v African Minerals Finance Ltd* [2013] EWCA Civ 416 at [24] per Aikens LJ; *Cottonex Anstalt v Patriot Spinning Mills Ltd* [2014] EWHC 236 (Comm), [2014] 1 Lloyd's Rep 615 at [52]–[58] per Hamblen J.

[265] [2015] UKSC 36, [2015] 2 WLR 1593, especially at [14]–[23].

[266] [1998] 1 WLR 896, 913. See also *Prenn v Simmonds* [1971] 1 WLR 1381. Less controversially he also excluded 'declarations of subjective intent'.

[267] [1998] 1 WLR 896, 913.

[268] McLauchlan (2000) 19 NZULR 147; McMeel (2003) 119 LQR 272; Lord Nicholls (2005) 121 LQR 577. Cf Berg (2006) 122 LQR 354.

[269] [2009] UKHL 38, [2009] 1 AC 1101. See the excellent casenote by McLauchlan (2010) 126 LQR 8.

[270] *Ibid* at [11]. [271] *Ibid* at [16].

[272] *Ibid* at [33]. Lord Hoffmann also made reference, at [40], to the argument, often made in support of the exclusionary rule, that to allow in such evidence prejudices third parties who may, eg, take an assignment of the contract. But he accepted that, while in theory removal of the rule would increase the risk for third

Lord Hoffmann, giving the leading speech, reasoned that evidence of pre-contractual negotiations was usually irrelevant; that even if relevant, its inclusion would create greater uncertainty in deciding disputes of interpretation and would add to the cost of advice, litigation, or arbitration; that it would not be easy to distinguish aspiration from provisional agreement; and that, overall, there was no clearly established case (and no empirical evidence) to justify the House of Lords departing from the long-established rule. He also pointed out that there were two legitimate 'safety nets'—rectification[273] and estoppel by convention—which would in most cases prevent injustice.[274] He further recognized that pre-contractual negotiations may be taken into account in establishing that a background fact was known to the parties.[275] In contrast, he thought that the extension of the 'private dictionary' exception, applied in *The Karen Oltmann*,[276] undermined the exclusionary rule and should be overruled.

Although not specifically mentioned by Lord Hoffmann in the *Investors Compensation Scheme* case, it is also clearly established that the subsequent conduct of the parties may not be used as an aid to interpretation of a written contract. This has been said to be because subsequent conduct is equally referable to what the parties intended to agree as to the meaning of what they in fact agreed[277] and because 'otherwise one might have the result that a contract meant one thing on the day it was signed, but by reason of subsequent events meant something different a month or a year later'.[278] Neither reason seems convincing and this exclusion has again been criticized by commentators.[279] In any event, subsequent conduct may be used to show that a contract exists,[280] that there has been a variation of its terms or an estoppel or a waiver,[281] or even to construe an oral, rather than a written, contract.[282]

parties, the same point about prejudicing third parties can be made in respect of the admissibility of any form of background material.

[273] The House of Lords, had they not reached the conclusion they did on construction, would have granted rectification to reach the same result: see below, pp 282–7.

[274] [2009] UKHL 38, [2009] 1 AC 1101 at [47].

[275] It will be rare that a dispute on interpretation will turn on whether the parties did or did not know a particular background fact but where pre-contractual negotiations are admissible under this exception they can include even 'without prejudice' pre-contractual negotiations: *Oceanbulk Shipping and Trading SA v TMT Asia Ltd* [2010] UKSC 44, [2011] 1 AC 662.

[276] *The Karen Oltmann* [1976] 2 Lloyds Rep 708. What is meant by the 'private dictionary exception' is that, where words are used that can have more than one meaning, evidence is admissible to show that the parties have given their own meaning to the words. This exception was applied in, eg, *The Pacific Colocotronis* [1981] 2 Lloyd's Rep 40; *Proforce Recruit Ltd v The Rugby Group Ltd* [2006] EWCA Civ 69.

[277] *Schuler AG v Wickman Machine Tool Sales Ltd.* [1974] AC 235, 261, 263.

[278] *Whitworth Street Estates (Manchester) Ltd v James Miller & Partners Ltd* [1970] AC 583, 603.

[279] See above, n 268. See also *Full Metal Jacket Ltd v Gowlain Building Group Ltd* [2005] EWCA Civ 1809, at [15] (Arden LJ). The exclusion of such evidence has been rejected in New Zealand: *Wholesale Distributors Ltd v Gibbons Holdings Ltd* [2007] NZSC 37.

[280] *Whitworth Street Estates (Manchester) Ltd v James Miller & Partners Ltd* [1970] AC 583; *Wilson v Maynard Shipbuilding Consultants AG Ltd* [1978] QB 665.

[281] Above, p 134; below, p 490.   [282] *Maggs v Marsh* [2006] EWCA Civ 1058, [2006] BLR 395.

(b) PARTICULAR RULES OF INTERPRETATION

While all 'rules' of interpretation must now be read in the light of the modern contextual approach set out in the *Investors Compensation Scheme* case,[283] there are certain 'rules' that can be usefully set out.

(1) Words susceptible of two meanings should be given the meaning which will make the instrument valid rather than void or ineffective.[284] Where a guarantee was expressed to be given to the claimants 'in consideration of your *being* in advance' to JS, it was argued that this showed a past consideration; but the Court held that the words might mean a prospective advance, and be equivalent to 'in consideration of your *becoming* in advance', or '*on condition* of your being in advance'.[285] So strong is this rule in favour of supporting the document that, in suitable cases, the Court is prepared to restrict the written words to those applicable in the agreement, supply obvious omissions, and to transpose or even reject words and phrases if the intention of the parties is clear.

(2) 'An agreement ought to receive that construction which its language will admit, which will best effectuate the intention of the parties, to be collected *from the whole of the agreement*, and greater regard is to be had to the clear intent of the parties than to any particular words which they may have used in the expression of their intent.'[286] The proper mode of interpretation is to take the instrument as a whole, to ascertain the meaning of words and phrases from their general context, and to try and give effect to every part of it.[287]

(3) '[G]reater weight should attach to terms which the particular contracting parties have chosen to include than to pre-printed terms probably devised to cover very many situations to which the particular contracting parties have never addressed their minds.'[288]

(4) Where there is an express mention in the instrument of a certain thing, this will tend to exclude any other thing of a similar nature: *expressio unius est exclusio alterius*.[289] So where a conveyance was made of an iron foundry and two houses, together with the fixtures in the houses, the fixtures in the foundry were held not to pass even though they otherwise would have done so.[290]

---

[283] In Lord Hoffmann's words, 'Almost all the old intellectual baggage of "legal" interpretation has been discarded': [1998] 1 WLR 896, 912.

[284] *Verba ita sunt intelligenda ut res magis valeat quam pereat*: Bac Max 3.

[285] *Haigh v Brooks* (1839) 10 A & E 309; *Steele v Hoe* (1849) 14 QB 431.

[286] *Ford v Beech* (1848) 11 QB 852, 866 (Parke B).

[287] *Ex antecedentibus et consequentibus fit optima interpretatio*: 2 Co Inst 317; *Barton v Fitzgerald* (1812) 15 East 529, 541.

[288] *Homburg Houtimport BV v Agrosin Private Ltd, The Starsin* [2003] UKHL 12, [2004] 1 AC 715, at [11] (Lord Bingham).

[289] Co Litt. 210a.   [290] *Hare v Horton* (1833) 5 B & Ad 715.

(5) The meaning of general words may be narrowed and restrained by specific and particular descriptions of the subject-matter to which they are to apply. Thus in construing a charterparty, where liability to deliver cargo was excluded if through 'war, disturbance, or any other cause' it was not possible to do so, it was held that the words 'any other cause' were restricted to events of the same kind as war and disturbance, and so excluded ice.[291] But this rule (the so-called *ejusdem generis* rule) is again only a canon of construction for the purpose of ascertaining what may be presumed to have been the meaning and intention of the parties to the contract. It is therefore subordinate to the parties' real intention and does not control it. It will have no application if the parties can be shown to have intended a different interpretation to be given to the language which they have used.

(6) The words of written documents are interpreted more forcibly against the party putting forward the document.[292] The rule is based on the principle that a party putting forward the wording of a proposed agreement may be assumed to have looked after its own interests, is responsible for ambiguities in its own expression, and has no right to induce another to make a contract on the supposition that the words mean one thing, and then to argue for a construction by which they would mean another thing, more to its advantage.[293]

(7) The Court of Appeal has recently stated that if one is to exclude a condition implied under the Sale of Goods Act 1979, one must use words which expressly (or perhaps necessarily) refer to conditions.[294] This appears to be an application of the 'intellectual baggage' in older cases which Lord Hoffmann stated has been discarded. One would expect that, if given the opportunity, the Supreme Court will depart from this 'rule'.

(8) By section 69 of the Consumer Rights Act 2015, 'if a term in a consumer contract … could have different meanings, the meaning that is most favourable to the consumer is to prevail'. It is clear that this is a class-protection measure that goes beyond the common law approach to interpretation.[295]

FURTHER READING

PEDEN, 'Policy Concerns Behind Implication of Terms in Law' (2001) 117 LQR 459

McMEEL, 'Prior Negotiations and Subsequent Conduct—the Next Step Forward for Contractual Interpretation' (2003) 119 LQR 272

---

[291] *Tillmanns v SS Knutsford* [1908] 2 KB 385, aff'd [1908] AC 406; *Thorman v Dowgate Steamship Co Ltd* [1910] 1 KB 410.

[292] *Verba chartarum fortius accipiuntur contra proferentem*: Bac Max 3. See below, p 195.

[293] *Tan Wing Chuen v Bank of Credit and Commerce Hong Kong Ltd* [1996] 2 BCLC 69, 77 (Lord Mustill).

[294] *KG Bominflot Bunkergesellschaft für Mineralöle v Petroplus Marketing AG, The Mercini Lady* [2010] EWCA Civ 1145, [2011] 1 Lloyd's Rep 442. Cf *Air Transworld Ltd v Bombardier Inc* [2012] EWHC 243 (Comm), [2012] 1 Lloyd's Rep 349.

[295] Albeit that, in the past, *contra proferentem* interpretation may have produced the same results.

Lord Nicholls, 'My Kingdom for a Horse: the Meaning of Words' (2005) 121 LQR 577

Calnan, 'Construction of Commercial Contracts: a Practitioner's Perspective' in Burrows and Peel (eds), *Contract Terms* (Oxford: Oxford University Press, 2007) 17

McCaughran, 'Implied Terms—the Journey of the Man on the Clapham Omnibus' [2011] CLJ 607

Hooley, 'Controlling Contractual Discretion' [2013] CLJ 65

Hooley, 'Implied Terms after *Belize Telecom*' [2014] CLJ 315

6

EXEMPTION CLAUSES AND UNFAIR TERMS

Written contracts frequently contain clauses excluding or limiting liability.[1] This is particularly so in the case of 'standard form' documents drawn up by one of the parties or a trade association to which one of the parties belongs. At common law there are special rules on the incorporation of exemption clauses (and other onerous terms), special rules of construction applicable to them, and a few miscellaneous other common law rules designed to control them. This chapter considers those common law rules[2] before going on to the legislative control of exemption clauses and unfair terms. That legislative control is now most helpfully understood by separating the control of exemption clauses in non-consumer contracts in the Unfair Contract Terms Act 1977 (and section 3 of the Misrepresentation Act 1967),[3] from that of exemption clauses and unfair terms in consumer contracts, in the Consumer Rights Act 2015.[4] The 2015 Act, which applies to contracts made on or after 1 October 2015, has removed the control of exemption clauses (and indemnity clauses) in consumer contracts that were previously in the Unfair Terms Act 1977 and repealed the Unfair Terms in Consumer Contracts Regulations 1999.[5] In other words, the controls in consumer contracts are now found in a single Act, namely the Consumer Rights Act 2015. The thorny issues raised by exemption clauses and third parties are not discussed in this chapter but are dealt with instead in Chapter 21.

1. STANDARD FORMS OF CONTRACT

One of the most important developments for the law of contract has been the appearance of the standard form of contract.[6] The idea of an agreement freely

---

[1] See generally, Coote, *Exception Clauses* (1964).

[2] For the limited non-statutory control of 'unconscionable bargains', see below, Chapter 10.

[3] Below, Chapter 9.

[4] The 2015 Act partly enacted reforms recommended by the Law Commission in *Unfair Terms in Contracts*, Law Com No 292 (2005).

[5] For the previous law, which is applicable to contracts made prior to 1 October 2015, see the previous edition of this book, Chapter 6.

[6] The standard form contract is sometimes, following the French, referred to as a contract of adhesion: Saleilles, *De la Déclaration de la Volonté* (1901).

negotiated between the parties has given way to a uniform set of printed conditions which can be used time and time again, and for a large number of persons, and at less cost than an individually negotiated contract. Each time an individual travels by air, bus or train, buys a car, takes clothes to the dry-cleaner, buys household goods, or even, in some cases, takes the lease of a house or flat, a standard form contract, devised by the supplier, will be provided which the individual must either accept in whole, or, theoretically, go without. In fact, there is little alternative but to accept; the individual does not negotiate, but merely adheres. In some respects, therefore, it would be more correct to regard the relationship which arises not as one of contract at all, but as one of status. The contracting party has the status of a consumer.

The use of standard terms and conditions is not, however, confined to contracts made with consumers. Many contracts between business people—indeed, perhaps the majority of such contracts—are today entered into on the basis of one person's standard form of agreement or on the basis of a standard form of document, such as an order form, confirmation of order, catalogue or price list, put forward by one party,[7] or which incorporate by reference the standard terms and conditions of trade associations.

The ordinary common law principles of the law of contract may not be capable of providing a just solution for a transaction in which freedom of contract exists on one side only. In particular, the party delivering the document may allocate the risks of non-performance or defective performance to the other party. While such allocation of risks should in principle lead to lower costs, it is only justifiable if at least some of the cost saving is passed on and if the other party is aware of the contractual allocation of risks. In fact the party delivering the document may seek unfair exemption from certain common law liabilities, and thus seek to deprive the other party of the compensation which that person might reasonably expect to receive for any loss or injury or damage arising out of the transaction. Moreover, standard form contracts with consumers are often contained in some printed ticket, or notice, or receipt, which is brought to the attention of the consumer at the time the agreement is made and which a prudent consumer would read from beginning to end. In fact, however, the consumer normally has neither the time nor the energy to do this and, even if this was done, it would be of little assistance for the consumer could not vary the terms in any way. It is not until some dispute arises that the consumer realizes how few are the rights in the contract.

Acting within the limitations imposed on them by the contractual framework of these transactions, the Courts have nevertheless endeavoured to alleviate the position of the recipient of the document by imposing certain requirements for the incorporation into the contract of onerous terms, and by construing the document wherever possible in that person's favour. It has been said that 'the judicial creativity, bordering on judicial legislation' which marked the development of

---

[7] For the 'battle of the forms', see above, p 44.

these rules was a 'desperate remedy to be invoked only if it is necessary to remedy a widespread injustice'.[8] These rules are still important in determining the efficacy of exemption, or other onerous, clauses. But the measure of protection which they offered against unfair clauses is somewhat slender, and the power of the Courts to control such clauses has been greatly increased since the enactment of legislation, such as the Unfair Contract Terms Act 1977.[9]

2. INCORPORATION

(a) SIGNATURE

A person who _signs_ a document which contains contractual terms is normally bound by them even though that person has not read them and is ignorant of their precise legal effect.[10] Three exceptions are first, where the party's signature is induced by misrepresentation;[11] secondly, where _non est factum_ applies;[12] and thirdly, where the document signed does not purport to have contractual effect as, for example, where the signed document was a time sheet.[13]

(b) NOTICE

(i) The notice must be contemporaneous with the contract

Where there is no signature, in order that a term should become binding as part of the contract it must be brought to the notice of the contracting party before or at the time that the contract is made. If it is not communicated until afterwards, it will be of no effect unless there is evidence that the parties have entered into a new contract on a different basis.[14]

An illustration of the necessity for contemporaneity is provided by _Olley v Marlborough Court Ltd_:[15]

O and her husband registered at the defendant's hotel, paid for a week's board and lodging in advance, and then went up to their room. There a notice was exhibited stating: 'The proprietors will not hold themselves responsible for articles lost or stolen, unless handed to the manageress for safe custody'. Owing to the negligence of the hotel staff, a thief gained access to the room and stole some of O's property.

---

[8] _BCCI SA v Ali_ [2001] UKHL 8, [2002] 1 AC 251 at [60] (Lord Hoffmann).

[9] See below, pp 208–22.

[10] _Parker v South Eastern Ry_ (1877) 2 CPD 416, 421; _L'Estrange v F Graucob Ltd_ [1934] 2 KB 394; _Levison v Patent Steam Carpet Cleaning Co Ltd_ [1978] QB 69; Spencer [1973] CLJ 104.

[11] _Curtis v Chemical Cleaning and Dyeing Co Ltd_ [1951] 1 KB 805: see below, p 207.

[12] Below, pp 275–82.   [13] _Grogan v Robin Meredith Plant Hire_ [1996] CLC 1127.

[14] _Levison v Patent Steam Carpet Cleaning Co Ltd_ [1978] QB 69.

[15] [1949] 1 KB 532. See also _Hollingworth v Southern Ferries Ltd_ [1977] 2 Lloyd's Rep 70 (sailing tickets delivered after booking made).

The Court of Appeal held that the notice formed no part of the contract since O could not have seen it until after the contract was made; the defendant was accordingly liable for the loss. Similarly, a customer who parked a car in a garage and received at the entrance a ticket from an automatic machine, was held not to be bound by the conditions printed on the ticket; the machine caused the ticket to be issued when the car was driven to the entrance to the garage, and the customer could not be affected by conditions brought to his notice after this time.[16]

(ii) Reasonably sufficient notice

In what circumstances will a party receiving a ticket, receipt, or common form document at the time the contract is made be bound by the conditions contained in it?

Take the example of a railway or cloakroom ticket, which the person receiving it puts into his pocket unread; three general rules have been laid down to determine whether the traveller or depositor will be bound by the terms contained in the ticket:[17]

(1) A person receiving the ticket who did not see or know that there was any writing on the ticket will not be bound by the conditions.

(2) A person who knows there was writing, and knows or believes that the writing contained conditions, is bound by the conditions.

(3) A person who knows that there was writing on the ticket, but does not know or believe that the writing contained conditions, will nevertheless be bound where the delivery of the ticket, in such a manner that the writing on it could be seen, is reasonable notice that the writing contained conditions.

It is the third of these rules which is the most frequently applied and the most difficult in its application.

It means that a person may be bound by an exemption clause in a standard form document, even though subjectively ignorant of its content, if the party seeking to rely on the clause has done what was reasonably sufficient in the circumstances to bring it to the other party's notice. The principles were discussed in *Parker v South Eastern Railway Co*:[18]

P deposited a bag in the defendant's station cloakroom. He received a paper ticket which said on its face 'See back' and on the back were a number of printed conditions, including a condition excluding liability for any bag with a higher value than £10. P admitted that he knew there was writing on the ticket but stated that he had not read it and did not know or believe that the writing contained conditions. The bag was lost and P claimed £24 10s for its value.

---

[16] *Thornton v Shoe Lane Parking Ltd* [1971] 2 QB 163 (only Lord Denning MR found that the contract was concluded at that moment. Megaw LJ and Sir Gordon Willmer reserved their opinions on this point).

[17] *Parker v South Eastern Ry* (1877) 2 CPD 416, 421, 423; approved in *Richardson, Spence & Co v Rowntree* [1894] AC 217; *Burnett v Westminster Bank* [1966] 1 QB 742.

[18] (1877) 2 CPD 416; *Hood v Anchor Line (Henderson Bros) Ltd* [1918] AC 837.

The jury was directed to consider whether P had read or was aware of the special condition upon which the bag was deposited. It answered this question in the negative and accordingly judgment was entered for P. On appeal by the defendant, the Court of Appeal held that the jury had been misdirected. The real question was whether the defendant had done what was reasonably sufficient to give P notice of the condition. A new trial was ordered.

The question whether all that was reasonably sufficient to give notice was done is a question of fact,[19] and in answering that question the Courts must look at all the circumstances and the situation of the parties.[20] *Thompson v LM & S Railway Co*[21] represents a very liberal approach to what constitutes reasonable notice. There a passenger travelling on an excursion ticket was injured by the alleged negligence of the defendant railway company. It was held that a clause exempting the company from liability,[22] printed in its timetable, was sufficiently, although circuitously, incorporated into the contract since the ticket referred to the timetables and advertisements (the latter also referred to the timetables). But in *Richardson, Spence & Co v Rowntree*,[23] a term limiting the liability of a steamship company to $100 in a steamship ticket was held not to be incorporated. The ticket had been handed to the claimant folded up, and the conditions were obliterated in part by a stamp in red ink. The jury found that, although the claimant knew there was writing on the ticket, she did not know the writing contained conditions, and that reasonably sufficient notice had not been given. The House of Lords refused to upset this finding.

If the notice is otherwise sufficient, the fact that a particular claimant is under some disability (but not constituting incapacity), for example, unable to speak English, or blind,[24] or, as in *Thompson v LM & S Railway Co*, illiterate,[25] will be treated as irrelevant.

If there is no reference on the face of a ticket to the fact that there are conditions printed on the back, the Courts have consistently held that such a notification is defective.[26] Strictly, of course, the issue is one of fact in each particular case but this requirement may fairly be said to be one of law.

---

[19] *Parker v South Eastern Ry* (1877) 2 CPD 416; *Richardson, Spence & Co v Rowntree* [1894] AC 217.

[20] *Hood v Anchor Line (Henderson Bros) Ltd* [1918] AC 837, 844 (Lord Haldane).

[21] [1930] 1 KB 41.

[22] The Unfair Contract Terms Act 1977, s 2(1) and the Consumer Protection Act 2015, s 65 now prevent the exclusion or restriction of liability for death or personal injury resulting from negligence.

[23] [1894] AC 217. See also *Union Steamships v Barnes* (1956) 5 DLR (2d) 535 (Canada).

[24] Cf *Geier v Kujawa, Weston and Warne Bros (Transport) Ltd* [1970] 1 Lloyd's Rep 364, 368 (where the plaintiff's ignorance of English was known). The term there, excluding the liability of a driver of a motor vehicle to a passenger, would now be invalid under the Road Traffic Act 1988, s 149.

[25] However, the ticket had been bought on the plaintiff's behalf by her niece and it was found that the niece's father had ascertained, before the ticket was taken, that there were conditions for excursion tickets.

[26] *Henderson v Stevenson* (1875) LR 2 HL Sc App 470; *White v Blackmore* [1972] 2 QB 651, 664. See also *Poseidon Freight Forwarding Co Ltd v Davies Turner Southern Ltd* [1996] 2 Lloyd's Rep 388 (reference to terms on back of faxed document but terms not communicated).

(iii) Exhibited notices

Printed notices containing conditions, for example, the notices exhibited at the counter of a left-luggage office at a railway station, have been held to become part of the contract where the ticket or receipt refers to the notice[27] and probably even where it does not, provided the notice is sufficiently prominent and can be plainly seen before or at the time of making the contract.[28] But there is also authority for the view that the terms of the notice must be 'brought home' to the party affected and accepted by that party as part of the contract.[29]

(iv) The notice must be in a contractual document

If the document is one which the person receiving it would scarcely expect to contain conditions, for example, if it consisted of the sort of ticket which a reasonable person would suppose to be merely a voucher or receipt, it cannot be said that the notice given was reasonably sufficient in the circumstances. It would be 'quite reasonable that the party receiving it should assume that the writing contained in it no condition, and should put it in his pocket unread'.[30]

In *Chapelton v Barry UDC*:[31]

C wished to hire a beach deck chair. He took two from a pile belonging to the defendant, paying 2*d* for each and receiving two tickets from an attendant. He set the chairs up firmly, sat on one, and went through the canvas. C sued the defendant for personal injuries sustained. The defendant pleaded an exemption clause printed on the back of the ticket: 'The council will not be liable for any accident or damage arising from the hire of the chair'. C had glanced at the ticket but had not realized that it contained conditions.

The Court held that the defendant was not protected. A cheque-book cover[32] and a parking ticket issued by an automatic machine[33] have similarly been held to be non-contractual documents.

(v) Onerous or unusual terms

If the particular condition (whether an exemption clause or not) relied upon by one of the parties is onerous or unusual in that class of contract, special measures may be required fairly to bring it to the notice of the other party. It has even been said that some clauses 'would need to be printed in red ink on the face of the document with a red hand pointing to it before the notice could be held to be sufficient'.[34] In *Interfoto*

---

[27] *Watkins v Rymill* (1883) 10 QBD 178.

[28] *Olley v Marlborough Court Ltd* [1949] 1 KB 532, 549; *Ashdown v Samuel Williams & Sons Ltd* [1957] 1 QB 409.

[29] *Harling v Eddy* [1951] 2 KB 739, 748; *McCutcheon v David Macbrayne Ltd* [1964] 1 WLR 125; *Smith v Taylor* [1966] 2 Lloyd's Rep 231; *Mendelssohn v Normand Ltd* [1970] 1 QB 177, 182.

[30] *Parker v South-Eastern Ry Co* (1877) 2 CPD 416, 422 (Mellish LJ).   [31] [1940] 1 KB 532.

[32] *Burnett v Westminster Bank* [1966] 1 QB 742.

[33] *Thornton v Shoe Lane Parking Ltd* [1971] 2 QB 163.

[34] *J Spurling Ltd v Bradshaw* [1956] 1 WLR 461, 466 (Denning LJ); *Thornton v Shoe Lane Parking Ltd* [1971] 2 QB 163; *Shearson Lehman Hutton Inc v MacLaine Watson & Co Ltd* [1989] 2 Lloyd's Rep 570, 612. Cf

Picture Library Ltd v Stiletto Visual Programmes Ltd which, it should be noted, did not concern an exemption clause:[35]

Interfoto hired 47 transparencies to Stiletto. The transparencies were despatched to Stiletto in a bag containing a delivery note containing conditions printed in small but visible lettering on the face of the document, including condition 2, which stated that 'a holding fee of £5 plus VAT per day will be charged for each transparency which is retained . . . longer than . . . 14 days'. The daily rate per transparency was many times greater than was usual but nothing whatever was done by Interfoto to draw Stiletto's attention particularly to condition 2. Stiletto returned the transparencies 4 weeks later and Interfoto claimed £3,783.50.

The Court of Appeal held that the contract was made when, after the receipt of the transparencies, Stiletto accepted them by telephone. Although, to the extent the conditions were common form or usual terms, they were incorporated into the contract, it was held that condition 2 had not been so incorporated.[36] Bingham LJ stated:[37]

[Stiletto] are not to be relieved of . . . liability because they did not read the condition, although doubtless they did not; but in my judgment they are to be relieved because [Interfoto] did not do what was necessary to draw this unreasonable and extortionate clause fairly to their attention.

In Dillon LJ's words:[38]

[I]f one condition in a set of printed conditions is particularly onerous or unusual, the party seeking to enforce it must show that that particular condition was fairly brought to the attention of the other party.

(c) COURSE OF DEALING

An exception clause will not necessarily be incorporated into a contract by virtue of a *previous* course of dealing between the same parties on similar terms.[39] But such a clause may be incorporated where each party led the other reasonably to believe that it intended that their rights and liabilities should be ascertained by reference to

---

Ocean Chemical Transport Inc v Exnor Craggs Ltd [2000] 1 Lloyd's Rep 446, 454 (red hand approach doubted for commercial contract).

[35] [1989] QB 433.

[36] Interfoto could only recover a holding fee assessed on the basis of a quantum meruit, here £3.50 per transparency per week beyond the 14-day period: [1989] QB 433, 439, 445.

[37] *Ibid*, 445.

[38] *Ibid*, 439. See also *The Northern Progress* [1996] 2 Lloyd's Rep 321; *AEG (UK) Ltd v Logic Resources Ltd* [1996] CLC 265, per Hirst LJ, 273, but cf Hobhouse LJ *ibid*, 277 who took the view that Courts should lean towards treating clauses as incorporated given that, if unreasonable, they can now be struck down under the Unfair Contract Terms Act 1977; *O'Brien v MGN Ltd* [2001] EWCA Civ 1279, [2002] CLC 33 (rule of a competition held to be neither onerous nor unusual).

[39] *Hollier v Rambler Motors (AMC) Ltd* [1972] 2 QB 71 (no incorporation where claimant had signed a form containing exemption clauses on three or four occasions over a five-year period). See also *McCutcheon v David MacBrayne Ltd* [1964] 1 WLR 125. See generally Macdonald (1988) 8 LS 48.

the terms of a document which had been regularly and consistently used by them in previous transactions.[40]

Where the clause is a usual one in the trade, and the parties are of equal bargaining power in the same trade, less will be required in terms of the regularity of the previous course of dealing for it to be included in the contract.[41] Indeed it may be better to regard such a clause as incorporated not so much because of the course of dealing but rather because of the common understanding of the parties based on the practice of the trade to which they belong.[42]

3. INTERPRETATION OF EXEMPTION CLAUSES

Assuming that the terms of a standard form contract have been incorporated, the next issue is the way in which the terms of the document are to be interpreted (or, as one might otherwise say, construed). The disparity between the bargaining power of consumers and large enterprises (both private and public) means that terms have often been imposed upon consumers which are unfair in their application and which exempt the enterprise putting forward the document, either wholly or in part, from its just liability under the contract. This was one of the reasons why, at common law, the Courts evolved certain canons of construction which normally work in favour of the party seeking to establish liability and against the party seeking to claim the benefit of the exemption. However, if the clause is appropriately drafted so as to exclude or limit the liability in question, then the Courts must (subject to the powers conferred on them by the Unfair Contract Terms Act 1977 and the Consumer Rights Act 2015)[43] give effect to it. Moreover, as between businesses, exemption clauses can perform a useful function. They may, for example, anticipate future contingencies which hinder or prevent performance, establish procedures for the making of claims and provide for the allocation of risks as between the parties to the contract. In a business transaction, the effect of an exemption clause may simply be to determine which of the parties is to insure against a particular risk. Exemption clauses in business transactions are not necessarily unfair. But even in business transactions the Courts must be satisfied that the clause, on its wording, does have the effect contended for by the person relying on it, that is, the party seeking to exclude or restrict its liability.

It is a topical question whether the canons of construction for exemption clauses, developed at common law, have been, or should be, loosened not only because of the

---

[40] *Henry Kendall & Sons v William Lillico & Sons Ltd* [1969] 2 AC 31 (incorporation where parties had contracted three or four times a month over a three-year period). See also *J Spurling Ltd v Bradshaw* [1956] 1 WLR 461, 467; *Gillespie Bros & Co Ltd v Roy Bowles Transport Ltd* [1973] QB 400; *Circle Freight International Ltd v Medeast Gulf Exports Ltd* [1988] 2 Lloyd's Rep 427.

[41] *British Crane Hire Corp Ltd v Ipswich Plant Hire Ltd* [1975] QB 303 (usual term incorporated where only two transactions months before).

[42] *Ibid.*

[43] See below, pp 208–32.

statutory controls over unfair terms that now exist but also because of the modern general approach to construction set out in *Investors Compensation Scheme Ltd v West Bromwich Building Society*.[44]

(a) STRICT INTERPRETATION

'If a person is under a legal liability and wishes to get rid of it, he can only do so by using clear words.'[45] The words of the exemption clause must exactly cover the liability which it is sought to exclude. So an exemption clause in a contract excluding liability for 'latent defects' will not exclude the condition as to fitness for purpose implied by the Sale of Goods Act;[46] exclusion of *implied* conditions and warranties will not exclude a term which is actually expressed;[47] and a clause excluding liability for breach of *warranty* will not exclude liability for breach of condition.[48] In *Wallis, Son & Wells v Pratt & Haynes*:[49]

W bought seed from P & H described as 'common English sainfoin' subject to an exemption clause that 'the sellers give no *warranty* express or implied, as to growth, description, or any other matters'. The seed turned out to be giant sainfoin, indistinguishable in seed, but inferior in quality and of less value. W was forced to compensate those to whom it had subsequently sold the seed, and sued to recover the money lost. P & H pleaded the exemption clause.

It was held by the House of Lords that, even though W had accepted the goods and could therefore only sue for breach of warranty *ex post facto*,[50] there was nevertheless originally a breach of the *condition* implied by section 13 of the Sale of Goods Act,[51] and this had not been successfully excluded.

Since the enactment of the Unfair Contract Terms Act 1977, there are indications of a slightly less strict approach to construction. Although 'the reports are full of cases in which what would appear to be very strained constructions have been placed upon exclusion clauses',[52] mainly in consumer contracts and standard form contracts, it has been said that:

in commercial contracts negotiated between businessmen capable of looking after their own interests and of deciding how risks . . . can be most economically borne . . . it is wrong to place a strained construction upon words in an exclusion clause which are clear and fairly susceptible of one meaning.[53]

---

[44] [1998] 1 WLR 896. See above, p 179. See *Bank of Credit and Commerce International SA v Ali* [2002] 1 AC 251 at [62] (Lord Hoffmann).

[45] *Alison (J Gordon) Ltd v Wallsend Shipway and Engineering Co Ltd* (1927) 43 TLR 323, 324 (Scrutton LJ).

[46] *Henry Kendall & Sons v William Lillico & Sons Ltd* [1969] 2 AC 31.

[47] *Andrews Bros Ltd v Singer & Co Ltd* [1934] 1 KB 17.   [48] *Baldry v Marshall* [1925] 1 KB 260.

[49] [1911] AC 394.   [50] See above, p 159.   [51] See above, p 173.

[52] *Photo Production Ltd v Securicor Transport Ltd* [1980] AC 826, 851 (Lord Diplock).

[53] *Ibid*. See also *ibid*, 843.

(b) THE '*CONTRA PROFERENTEM*' RULE

The principle whereby the words of written documents are interpreted more forcibly against the party putting forward the document has been considered above.[54] In the case of exemption clauses this is the party seeking to impose the exemption. This rule of construction is only applied where there is doubt or ambiguity in the phrases used, and provides that such doubt or ambiguity must be resolved against the party proffering the written document and in favour of the other party. In *John Lee & Son (Grantham) Ltd v Railway Executive*:[55]

The lease of a railway warehouse contained a clause exempting the lessors from liability for 'loss damage costs and expenses however caused . . . (whether by act or neglect of the company or their servants or agents or not) which but for the tenancy hereby created . . . would not have arisen'. Goods in the warehouse were damaged by fire owing to the alleged negligence of the lessors in allowing a spark to escape from their railway engines. The lessors claimed that the clause exempted them from liability.

The Court of Appeal held that, applying the *contra proferentem* rule, the operation of the clause was confined by the words 'but for the tenancy hereby created' to liabilities which arose only by reason of the relationship of landlord and tenant created by the lease. Construing the clause against the lessors, they were not protected.

(c) EXCLUSION OF LIABILITY FOR NEGLIGENCE

The ability of contracting parties to exclude their liability for negligence has been substantially restricted by legislation.[56] Apart from statutory restrictions, although it is possible to exclude liability in negligence, the Courts have traditionally approached clauses which are said to exclude such liability on the assumption that it is 'inherently improbable' that the innocent party would have agreed to the exclusion of the contract-breaker's negligence.[57] To have this effect the contractual term in question must exclude liability for negligence clearly and unambiguously. In *Rutter v Palmer*,[58] for example:

R left his car at P's garage to be sold. The contract provided that 'customers' cars are driven by your [P's] servants at customers' sole risk'. The car was taken for a trial run by one of P's drivers, there was a collision and the car was damaged.

---

[54] Above, p 184.

[55] [1949] 2 All ER 581. See also *Adams v Richardson & Starling Ltd* [1969] 1 WLR 1645, 1653 (construction of so-called 'guarantee'); *Tor Line AB v Alltrans Group of Canada Ltd* [1984] 1 WLR 48, 56.

[56] Unfair Contract Terms Act 1977, s 2; Consumer Rights Act 2015, ss 57, 62, and 65.

[57] *Gillespie v Bowles (Roy) Transport Ltd* [1973] QB 400, 419 (Buckley LJ); *Caledonia Ltd v Orbit Valve Co Europe* [1994] 1 WLR 1515, 1523 (Steyn LJ); *Smith v South Wales Switchgear Co Ltd* [1978] 1 WLR 165, 168 (Viscount Dilhorne) (indemnity clause).

[58] [1922] 2 KB 87. See also *Levison v Patent Steam Carpet Cleaning Co Ltd* [1978] QB 69 ('at the owner's risk'); *Thompson v T Lohan (Plant Hire) Ltd* [1987] 1 WLR 649 ('the hirer . . . alone shall be responsible for all claims . . .').

It was held that the clause placed the risk of negligence on R and so his claim failed. Similarly, such phrases as: 'will not be liable for any damage however caused',[59] 'will not in any circumstances be responsible',[60] 'arising from any cause whatsoever'[61] will ordinarily be construed to cover liability for negligence.

On the other hand, there may be some ground of liability (other than negligence) to which the party seeking exemption is subject in respect of the loss or damage suffered, for example a strict liability for breach of contract.[62] If the alternative ground is not so fanciful or remote that he cannot be supposed to have desired protection against it,[63] the exemption clause will be construed as extending to that ground alone, even if the words used are prima facie wide enough to cover negligence.[64] In *Canada Steamship Lines Ltd v The King*:[65]

A lease of a freight shed provided that the lessee should 'not have any claim against the lessor for damage to goods' in the shed. Owing to the negligence of the lessor's employees, a fire broke out and the lessee's goods in the shed were destroyed.

The Privy Council held that a strict liability was imposed upon the lessor by the Civil Code of Lower Canada and the exemption clause should be confined to that head of liability. The lessor was accordingly liable for the negligent destruction of the goods. The decision has been applied many times since, including by the House of Lords,[66] and it has been said that:[67]

Commercial contracts are drafted by parties with access to legal advice and in the context of established legal principles as reflected in the decisions of the courts . . . The parties to commercial contracts must be taken to know what those principles are and to have drafted their contract taking them into account; when the suggested result could have been easily obtained by an appropriate use of language but the parties instead only used general language, the result of the general principle is that the parties will not be taken to have intended to include the consequences of a party's negligence.

---

[59] *Joseph Travers & Sons Ltd v Cooper* [1915] 1 KB 73; *Ashby v Tolhurst* [1937] 2 KB 242; *White v Blackmore* [1972] 2 QB 651. Cf *Bishop v Bonham* [1988] 1 WLR 742.

[60] *Harris Ltd v Continental Express Ltd* [1961] 1 Lloyd's Rep 251; *John Carter (Fine Worsteds) Ltd v Hanson Haulage (Leeds) Ltd* [1965] 2 QB 495.

[61] *AE Farr Ltd v Admiralty* [1953] 1 WLR 965; *Lamport & Holt Lines Ltd v Coubro & Scrutton (M & I) Ltd* [1982] 2 Lloyd's Rep 42.

[62] *White v John Warwick & Co Ltd* [1953] 1 WLR 1285.

[63] *Canada Steamship Lines Ltd v The King* [1952] AC 292; *Smith v South Wales Switchgear Co Ltd* [1978] 1 WLR 165, 178; *Lamport & Holt Lines Ltd v Coubro & Scrutton (M & I) Ltd* [1982] 2 Lloyd's Rep 42.

[64] *Alderslade v Hendon Laundry Ltd* [1945] KB 189, 192; *Canada Steamship Lines Ltd v The King* [1952] AC 292, 208; *Sonat Offshore SA v Amerada Hess Development Ltd* [1988] 1 Lloyd's Rep 145, 157; *Shell Chemicals UK Ltd v P & O Roadtanks Ltd* [1995] 1 Lloyd's Rep 297, 301. Cf *Ailsa Craig Fishing Co Ltd v Malvern Fishing Co Ltd* [1983] 1 WLR 964, 970.

[65] [1952] AC 292.

[66] *Smith v South Wales Switchgear Co Ltd* [1978] 1 WLR 165, 168 (Lord Dilhorne in the context of an indemnity clause).

[67] *Caledonia Ltd v Orbit Valve Co Europe* [1994] 1 WLR 221, 228, 232 (Hobhouse J). See also *Shell Chemicals UK Ltd v P & O Roadtanks Ltd* [1995] 1 Lloyd's Rep 297, 301.

However, the House of Lords in *HIH Casualty and General Insurance Ltd v Chase Manhattan Bank*[68] has since indicated that the *Canada Steamship* principles, while giving helpful guidance, should not be treated as a rigid code. In that case, a generally worded clause excluding all liability of an insured to an insurer for misrepresentation or non-disclosure of its agent was held, on its true construction, not to exclude liability (whether for damages or rescission) for the agent's fraudulent misrepresentation or fraudulent non-disclosure.[69] But as part of the reasoning it was held that the clause did apply to exclude liability for negligent misrepresentation or non-disclosure even though a rigid application of the *Canada Steamship* principles would have led to the contrary result (because liability for innocent misrepresentation or non-disclosure was a realistic possibility).

Where the head of damage in respect of which liability is sought to be imposed by an exemption clause is one which rests on negligence and nothing else, one would expect the clause to be construed as extending to that head of damage, because if it were not so construed 'it would lack subject matter'.[70] However, this conclusion has not always been reached. In *Hollier v Rambler Motors (AMC) Ltd*:[71]

H arranged by telephone to have his car repaired by RM and subsequently sent the car to RM's premises for this purpose. On at least two previous occasions when RM had carried out repairs for him he had signed a form on which appeared the printed words: 'The company is not responsible for damage caused by fire to customer's cars on the premises'. While on the premises, the car was damaged by a fire caused by RM's negligence.

The Court of Appeal held that there was no sufficient previous course of dealing to incorporate the exemption clause into the oral contract;[72] but, in any event, the language of the clause did not exclude liability for negligence. Although the only ground of liability on the part of RM would have been liability in negligence, the clause was not so plain as to indicate that RM was exempting itself in respect of damage caused by fire due to its own negligence. Rather it was a warning to customers as to the legal position where fire was caused without the defendants' negligence.[73] H therefore succeeded in an action against RM for breach of the contract of bailment.

---

[68] [2003] UKHL 6, [2003] 2 Lloyd's Rep 61, applied in *Lictor Anstalt Mir Steel UK Ltd v Morris* [2012] EWCA Civ 1397, [2013] 2 All ER (Comm) 54 when deciding that an indemnity against 'any claim' in respect of certain machinery covered claims for intentional torts such as inducing breach of contract and conspiracy. See also *Greenwich Millennium Village v Essex Services Group plc* [2014] EWCA Civ 960, [2014] 1 WLR 3517.

[69] As a matter of policy, an exemption clause can never exclude liability for personal fraud: *S Pearson & Son Ltd v Dublin Corp* [1907] AC 351; *Armitage v Nurse* [1998] Ch 241.

[70] *Aldersdale v Hendon Laundry Ltd* [1945] KB 189, 192.   [71] [1972] 2 QB 71.

[72] See above, p 192.

[73] It is arguable that, since the enactment of the Unfair Contract Terms Act 1977, such a hostile construction would not be adopted.

(d) LIMITATION CLAUSES

It has been held that a less rigorous approach governs clauses that merely limit the compensation payable but do not totally exclude liability. In *Ailsa Craig Fishing Co Ltd v Malvern Fishing Co Ltd and Securicor (Scotland) Ltd*,[74] a case from Scotland:

S undertook to provide continuous security cover in respect of ACF's fishing vessel in Aberdeen harbour but, by reason of negligence and breach of contract, the vessel fouled the boat berthed next to her and sank. The loss of the vessel cost ACF £55,000. S's standard conditions of contract provided inter alia that its liability 'whether under express or implied terms of the contract, or at common law or in any other way' for any loss or damage was limited to £1,000.

The House of Lords held that, although the *contra proferentem* rule applied to limitation clauses, such clauses were not to be construed by the particularly exacting standards applicable to clauses totally excluding liability and indemnity clauses. According to Lord Fraser, this was because there was a higher degree of improbability that a contracting party would agree to a total exclusion of liability than to a limitation of liability particularly where, as in that case, 'the potential losses that might be caused by the negligence of the proferens or its servants are so great in proportion to the sums that can reasonably be charged for the services contracted for'.[75] In Lord Wilberforce's view, the distinction followed because limitation clauses 'must be related to other contractual terms, in particular to the risks to which the defending party may be exposed, the remuneration which he receives, and possibly also the opportunity of the other party to insure'.[76]

It is, however, somewhat difficult to see why such a clear distinction should be drawn between these two types of exemption clause. In particular, it is not clear why only limitation clauses are 'related to other contractual terms' and to 'the opportunity of the other party to insure'. There may also be practical difficulties. Take the example of first, a clause *excluding* all liability, but not until three months after the delivery of goods,[77] and, secondly, a clause *limiting* liability to £100, but from the start.[78] Which is to be construed more generously? It is submitted that '[t]here is no difference in principle between words which save [contracting parties] from having to pay at all and words which save them from paying as much as they would otherwise have had

---

[74] [1983] 1 WLR 964.

[75] *Ibid*, 970 (Lord Fraser). This statement was approved by the House of Lords in *George Mitchell (Chesterhall) Ltd v Finney Lock Seeds Ltd* [1983] 2 AC 803, 810, 813, 817.

[76] *Ailsa Craig Fishing Co Ltd v Malvern Fishing Co Ltd* [1983] 1 WLR 964, 966 (Lord Wilberforce).

[77] *Atlantic Shipping & Trading Co Ltd v Louis Dreyfus & Co* [1922] 2 AC 250. See also 'cesser' clauses in charterparties excluding the charterer's liability for breach once a cargo is shipped and replacing it with an alternative remedy by way of lien on the cargo: *Overseas Transport Co v Mineralimportexport* [1972] 1 Lloyd's Rep 201.

[78] See the combined operation of the package, unit, and weight limitations of Article IV, r 5, of the Hague/Visby Rules and the one year time bar under Article III, r 6: Carriage of Goods by Sea Act 1971.

to pay'.[79] It has been suggested that the two types of clause should be characterized by reference to the substance of their provisions rather that the particular wording used, and that the more extreme the consequences are, in terms of excluding or modifying the liability which would otherwise arise, the more stringent the Court's approach should be in requiring that the exclusion or liability be clearly and unambiguously expressed.[80]

(e) 'FUNDAMENTAL' TERMS AND 'FUNDAMENTAL BREACH'

(i) Rule of construction not a rule of law

Previously there was considered to be a common law doctrine which seemed to offer some escape from even the most carefully drafted exemption clauses. This was the doctrine of the 'breach of a fundamental term' or of 'fundamental breach'.[81]

There were, it was said, in every contract certain *terms* which were fundamental, the breach of which amounted to a complete non-performance of the contract. A fundamental term was conceived to be something more basic than a warranty or even a condition. It formed the 'core' of the contract and therefore could not be affected by any exemption clause.[82] For example, 'If a man offers to buy peas of another, and he sends him beans, he does not perform his contract; but that is not a warranty; there is no warranty that he should sell him peas; the contract is to sell peas, and if he sends him anything else in their stead, it is a non-performance of it' against which no exemption clause could prevail.[83]

Closely connected was the principle that no party to a contract could exempt himself from responsibility for a fundamental *breach*. Its limits were never precisely defined, but it was said that a party could only claim the protection of an exemption clause 'when he is carrying out his contract, not when he is deviating from it or is guilty of a breach which goes to the root of it'.[84] The two principles were in some cases used interchangeably;[85] and they appeared to establish that, however extensive an exemption clause might be, it could not exclude liability in respect of the breach of a fundamental term or of a fundamental breach. Expressed in this way, the doctrine constituted a substantive rule of law which operated irrespective of the intention of the parties and limited their freedom of contract.

---

[79] *Atlantic Shipping & Trading Co Ltd v Louis Dreyfus & Co* [1922] 2 AC 250, 260 (Lord Sumner). See also *Darlington Futures Ltd v Delco Australia Pty Ltd* (1986) 161 CLR 500, 510 (High Court of Australia), disapproving the statements in *Ailsa Craig Fishing Co Ltd v Malvern Fishing Co Ltd* [1983] 1 WLR 964.

[80] *BHP Petroleum Ltd v British Steel plc* [2000] 2 Lloyd's Rep 277, 285.

[81] See Guest (1961) 77 LQR 98; Reynolds (1963) 79 LQR 534; Lord Devlin [1966] CLJ 192; Jenkins [1969] CLJ 251; Legh-Jones and Pickering (1970) 86 LQR 513; Baker (1970) 33 MLR 441; Weir [1970] CLJ 180; Coote [1970] CLJ 221; Dawson (1975) 91 LQR 380; Coote (1977) 40 MLR 31.

[82] *Smeaton Hanscomb & Co Ltd v Sassoon I Setty, Son & Co* [1953] 1 WLR 1468, 1470.

[83] *Chanter v Hopkins* (1838) 4 M & W 399, 404. See also *Bowes v Shand* (1877) 2 App Cas 455, 480.

[84] *J Spurling Ltd v Bradshaw* [1956] 1 WLR 461, 465 (Denning LJ). See also *Alexander v Railway Executive* [1951] 2 KB 882.

[85] Cf Lord Upjohn in the *Suisse Atlantique* case [1967] 1 AC 361, 421.

The 'rule of law' approach was, however, rejected. In *UGS Finance Ltd v National Mortgage Bank of Greece*[86] Pearson LJ stated:

I think there is a rule of construction that normally an exception or exclusion clause or similar provision in a contract should be construed as not applying to a situation created by a fundamental breach of contract. This is not an independent rule of law imposed by the court on the parties willy-nilly in disregard of their contractual intention. On the contrary it is a rule of construction based on the intention of the contracting parties.

This opinion was subsequently unanimously endorsed by the House of Lords in *Suisse Atlantique Société d'Armement Maritime SA v NV Rotterdamsche Kolen Centrale*.[87] In that case:

SA chartered the *Silvretta* to RKC for a period of 2 years. It was agreed that, in the event of delays in loading or unloading the vessel, RKC would pay to SA $1,000 a day by way of demurrage.[88] Lengthy delays occurred for which SA alleged RKC was responsible, but it nevertheless allowed RKC to continue to have the use of the ship for the remainder of the term. On conclusion of the contract, SA sued RKC for damages, claiming a sum in excess of that stipulated for as demurrage. RKC relied on the demurrage clause as limiting its liability.

It was argued that the breaches would have entitled SA to treat the contract as repudiated; that these breaches amounted to a fundamental breach of contract; and that in consequence RKC could not rely upon the clause which limited their liability to $1,000 a day. The House of Lords rejected this argument. It held that the demurrage clause was not an exemption clause but an 'agreed damages' provision.[89] Nevertheless, even if it had been considered an exemption clause, their Lordships considered that as a matter of construction it covered the breaches which had occurred. Assuming that these breaches amounted to a fundamental breach of contract, in the sense that SA would have been entitled to treat itself as discharged from further performance, there was no rule of law which would prevent the application of an exemption clause to such a breach.

Certain statements in the *Suisse Atlantique* case were nevertheless open to the interpretation that in some situations a substantive doctrine of 'fundamental breach' still existed[90] and the heresy that a 'fundamental breach' of contract deprived the party in breach of the benefit of an exemption clause was not finally laid to rest by the House of Lords until *Photo Production Ltd v Securicor Transport Ltd*:[91]

S agreed to provide a visiting patrol service to PP's factory at a charge of approximately 26p per visit. The contract contained an exemption clause, the most relevant part of which

---

[86] [1964] 1 Lloyd's Rep 446, 450.   [87] [1967] 1 AC 361; noted by Treitel (1966) 29 MLR 546.

[88] Demurrage is a sum agreed by the charterer to be paid to the owner as liquidated damages for delay beyond a stipulated or reasonable time for loading or unloading.

[89] See below, p 598.

[90] [1967] 1 AC 361, 398, 427, 432. See *Harbutt's 'Plasticine' Ltd v Wayne Tank and Pump Co Ltd* [1970] 1 QB 447 (exemption clause did not apply where further performance impossible or innocent party accepted breach as terminating contract). See also *Wathes (Western) Ltd v Austins (Menswear) Ltd* [1976] 1 Lloyd's Rep 14; *Kenyon, Son & Craven Ltd v Baxter Hoare & Co Ltd* [1971] 1 WLR 519.

[91] [1980] AC 827. See also *George Mitchell (Chesterhall) Ltd v Finney Lock Seeds Ltd* [1983] 2 AC 803; *Kenya Railways v Antares Co Pte Ltd* [1987] 1 Lloyd's Rep 424; Unfair Contract Terms Act 1977, s 9.

stated: 'Under no circumstances shall the company [S] be responsible for any injurious act or default by any employee . . . unless such act or default could have been foreseen and avoided by the exercise of due diligence on the part of the company . . .'. An employee of S, while on patrol, deliberately lit a fire in the factory. The fire spread and a large part of the premises was burned down.

The Court of Appeal held that, since S had been engaged to safeguard the factory, the deliberate act of their employee in starting a fire was not covered by the exemption clause. The House of Lords reversed this decision. On the true construction of the clause in the context of the contract, in particular the limited nature of the contractual task, the modesty of the charge, and the ability of the factory owners to insure against fire more economically, the House concluded that the risk assumed by S was a modest one.[92] Accordingly, S had effectively modified its obligation under the contract to the exercise of due diligence in its capacity as an employer, and there was no evidence of any lack of due diligence on its part to foresee or prevent the fire. S was therefore absolved from liability. Their Lordships once again affirmed their opinion that the question whether or not an exemption clause protected a party to a contract in the event of breach, or in the event of what would (but for the presence of the exemption clause) have been a breach, depended upon the construction of the contract. Even if the breach was so serious as to entitle the injured party to treat the contract as repudiated,[93] or to render further performance impossible, the other party was not prevented from relying on the clause.

Any need for a substantive doctrine of fundamental breach has largely been obviated by the enactment of the Unfair Contract Terms Act 1977.[94] In the *Photo Production* case, Lord Diplock stated[95] that, if the expression 'fundamental breach' was to be retained, it should be confined to the ordinary case of a breach of which the consequences are such as to entitle the innocent party to elect to put an end to all primary obligations of both parties remaining unperformed.[96] Similarly it may be supposed that, if the expression 'fundamental term' is to be retained, it should be employed simply as an alternative method of describing a promissory condition.[97] There does not now exist in English law any special rule or rules applicable to cases of 'fundamental breach' where exemption clauses are concerned. No doubt, in deciding whether an exemption clause is, on its true construction, applicable to a particular breach, the Court may reach the conclusion that the parties never intended the clause to apply to the breach in question because its nature or seriousness is such as not to fall within the contemplated ambit of the clause. The parties are less likely to be taken to have agreed that one of them shall be excused in the case of a total non-performance or a performance which is wholly at variance with the object of

---

[92] [1980] AC 827, 846, 851, 852. [93] See below, pp 548–51.

[94] See below, p 192. Certain types of contract are wholly or partly excepted from the operation of that Act: see below, pp 210–11.

[95] [1980] AC 827, 849. [96] See below, pp 548–51.

[97] See *Suisse Atlantique Société d'Armement Maritime SA v NV Rotterdamsche Kolen Centrale* [1967] 1 AC 361, 398, 427, 432–5.

the contract as ascertained from its other terms and the circumstances surrounding it. But there is no separate category of 'fundamental breaches' against which exemption clauses cannot prevail and, if sufficiently clear, they will do so against the most serious and deliberate breach. So, for example, the one-year time bar in the Hague-Visby Rules applies to fundamental and deliberate breaches.[98] Moreover, in Australia it has been held that an exemption clause which stated it applied 'whether or not loss . . . is caused by . . . fundamental breach of contract' prevailed against a fundamental breach.[99]

The view that, whereas a negligent breach could be covered by an exemption clause, a wilful or deliberate breach necessarily fell outside its scope,[100] was also firmly rejected by the House of Lords in the *Suisse Atlantique* case. Lord Wilberforce said:[101]

Some deliberate breaches . . . may be, on construction, within an exceptions clause (for example, a deliberate delay for one day in loading). This is not to say that 'deliberateness' may not be a relevant factor: depending on what the party in breach 'deliberately' intended to do, it may be possible to say that the parties never contemplated that such a breach would be excused or limited . . . but to create a special rule for deliberate acts is unnecessary and may lead astray.

Having established that 'fundamental breach' is now a matter of construction, rather than being a rule of law,[102] it is appropriate to consider the construction of exemption clauses for 'fundamental breaches' in certain familiar types of contract.[103]

(ii) Sale of goods

We have already seen that, in a contract of sale of goods, by reason of the Sale of Goods Act 1979 and the Consumer Rights Act 2015, certain terms as to title, correspondence with description and sample, fitness for purpose, and satisfactory quality are implied into, or are treated as included in, the contract.[104] By virtue of the Unfair Contract Terms Act 1977 and the Consumer Rights Act 2015,[105] the power of a seller to exclude these terms has largely[106] been abrogated, either absolutely or subject to certain qualifications. But at common law, the Courts have refused to

---

[98] *Kenya Railways v Antares Co Pte Ltd* [1987] 1 Lloyd's Rep 424, 429–30; *Comp Portorafti Comm SA v Ultramar Panama Inc* [1990] 1 Lloyd's Rep 310.

[99] *Glebe Island Terminals Pty Ltd v Continental Seagram Pty Ltd* [1994] 1 Lloyd's Rep 213 (New South Wales Court of Appeal), cf Handley JA dissenting, at 230.

[100] eg *Sze Hai Tong Bank Ltd v Rambler Cycle Co Ltd* [1959] AC 576.

[101] [1967] AC 361, 435. See also *ibid*, 394, 414, 415, 429; *Photo Production Ltd v Securicor Transport Ltd* [1980] AC 827; *Comp Portorafti Comm SA v Ultramar Panama Inc* [1990] 1 Lloyd's Rep 310; *China Shipbuilding Corp v Nippon Yusen Kabukishi Kaisha* [2000] 1 Lloyd's Rep 367, 376.

[102] With the demise of the principle of 'fundamental breach', it can no longer be said that the defendant carries the burden of disproving fundamental breach.

[103] For other types of contract, where the courts have construed clauses covering very serious breach, see, eg, *A Turtle Offshore SA v Superior Trading Inc* [2008] EWHC 3034 (Admlty), [2009] 1 Lloyd's Rep 177; *Internet Broadcasting Corp Ltd v MAR LLC* [2009] EWHC 844 (Ch), [2009] 2 Lloyd's Rep 295.

[104] Above, pp 171–8.   [105] See below, pp 213, 222–3.

[106] The Unfair Contract Terms Act 1977 does not apply to, eg, the international sale of goods.

apply an exemption clause covering 'defects in quality' to situations where there was a gross disparity between the goods described in the contract of sale and those delivered, or where the goods were so defective that they were completely unfit for the purpose for which they were required.[107] For example, where copra cake contained so great an admixture of castor beans as to render it dangerous to cattle, a clause disclaiming responsibility for 'defects' was held inapplicable, because what was delivered was not truly copra cake at all.[108] As Lord Wilberforce pointed out in the *Suisse Atlantique* case:[109] 'Since the contracting parties could hardly have been supposed to contemplate such a misperformance, or to have provided against it without destroying the whole contractual substratum, there is no difficulty here in holding exemption clauses to be inapplicable'. But this is a matter of construction only and the construction will be affected by the contractual context. So, 'if an anxious hostess is late in the preparation of a meal, she can perfectly well say: "Send me peas or if you haven't got peas, send beans; but for heaven's sake send something". That would be a contract for peas, beans or anything else *ejusdem generis* and it is a perfectly sensible contract to make'.[110]

(iii) Hire-purchase

The exclusion of terms implied, or treated as included, in hire-purchase contracts is now subject to the Unfair Contract Terms Act 1977 and the Consumer Rights Act 2015.[111] At common law it is governed by similar principles to those in sales. A case of this nature arose in *Karsales (Harrow) Ltd v Wallis*:[112]

W was shown a second-hand Buick motor-car in excellent condition and wished to buy it on hire-purchase. His agreement with the finance company contained an exemption clause excluding liability for breach of conditions or warranties of any description. After the contract had been concluded, the car was towed at night to W's premises in a deplorable state. Many detachable parts had been removed; new parts had been replaced by old; and the engine was now so defective that the car would not go. W refused to accept it and was sued by K, the assignee of the finance company.

The Court of Appeal held that the exemption clause was ineffective because what was contracted for had not been delivered: 'a car that would not go was not a car at all'.[113] On the other hand, a similar clause has been held to cover the delivery of a car which, though unroadworthy and unsafe when hired and in a 'lamentable condition', did still function as a car. These defects were covered by the clause.[114]

---

[107] eg *Munro & Co Ltd v Meyer* [1930] 2 KB 312; *Champanhac & Co Ltd v Waller & Co Ltd* [1948] 2 All ER 724. Cf *Smeaton Hanscomb & Co Ltd v Sassoon I Setty, Son & Co* [1953] 1 WLR 1468; *George Mitchell (Chesterhall) Ltd v Finney Lock Seeds Ltd* [1983] 2 AC 803.
[108] *Pinnock Brothers v Lewis and Peat Ltd* [1923] 1 KB 690.   [109] [1967] 1 AC 361, 433.
[110] Lord Devlin [1966] CLJ 192, 212. On this example, see above, p 199, n 83.   [111] See below, pp 213, 222–3.
[112] [1956] 1 WLR 936. See also *Yeoman Credit Ltd v Apps* [1962] 2 QB 508; *Charterhouse Credit Co Ltd v Tolly* [1963] 2 QB 638; *Farnworth Finance Facilities v Attryde* [1970] 1 WLR 1053.
[113] [1956] 1 WLR 936, 942 (Birkett LJ). See also Parker LJ at 943.
[114] *Handley v Marston* (1962) 106 SJ 327. See also *Astley Industrial Trust Ltd v Grimley* [1963] 1 WLR 584.

(iv) Carriage of goods

It is possible that a version of the fundamental breach rule of law lives on in respect of 'deviation' by a carrier. This has been left open by the House of Lords.[115] Most of the cases concern the carriage of goods by sea but the same principles apply to carriage by land.[116] The basic idea is that a carrier, who deviates without justification from the recognized or agreed route, steps outside the 'four corners' of the contract and cannot claim the benefit of a clause designed to protect only when the carrier is acting in pursuance of its provisions.[117] Put another way, if a ship contracted to carry goods from A to B deviates from her ordinary route, the contract voyage comes to an end, and the shipowner cannot thereafter rely upon an exemption clause in the contract even though the loss or damage to the goods is not attributable to the deviation.[118]

Contracts made between businesses for the carriage of goods by ship fall, as respects loss of or damage to the cargo, outside the Unfair Contract Terms Act 1977,[119] so that the 'deviation cases' continue to be of considerable importance in this context.

What is unclear is whether the non-applicability of an exemption clause where there has been a deviation is a rule of construction based on the parties' intentions that the clause should not apply to a journey not contemplated by the contract; or whether it is a rule of law that applies irrespective of the parties' intentions or the particular wording of the clause in question.

Where a carrier has undertaken to stow cargo below deck but carries it on deck, it has been held to be a question of construction whether an exemption clause applies to such unauthorized deck carriage. Hence a clause limiting liability to a specified sum per package of cargo[120] and a clause requiring all claims to be brought within one year[121] have both been held to apply, as a matter of construction, to unauthorized deck carriage.

Misdelivery of the goods by the carrier may be covered by an appropriately drafted exemption clause.[122] But where the main object and intent of the contract is that delivery should be made to a certain person or persons, the Court may be prepared

---

[115] *Suisse Atlantique Société d'Armement Maritime SA v NV Rotterdamsche Kolen Centrale* [1967] 1 AC 361; *Photo Production Ltd v Securicor Transport Ltd* [1980] AC 827.

[116] *London & North Western Ry v Neilson* [1922] 2 AC 263 (disclaimed liability for loss of goods 'in transit' did not cover deviation).

[117] eg *Cunard SS Co Ltd v Buerger* [1927] AC 1; *Stag Line Ltd v Foscolo, Mango & Co Ltd* [1932] AC 328; *Hain Steamship Co v Tate & Lyle* (1936) 41 Com Cas 350. See *Suisse Atlantique Société d'Armement Maritime SA v NV Rotterdamsche Kolen Centrale* [1967] 1 AC 361, 390, 399, 411, 422, 433; Reynolds, 'The Deviation Problem' (Butterworths Lectures 1990–91) 29; Dockray [2000] LMCLQ 76.

[118] *Joseph Thorley Ltd v Orchis Steamship Co Ltd* [1907] 1 KB 660.

[119] Sched 1, para 2(c).

[120] *Daewood Heavy Industries Ltd v Klipriver Shipping Ltd, The Kapitan Petko Voivoda* [2003] 2 Lloyd's Rep 1 overruling *Wibau Maschinenfabrik Hartman SA v Mackinnon Mackenzie & Co, The Chanda* [1989] 2 Lloyd's Rep 494, 505. See Hague-Visby Rules, Art III, para 5, contained in the Schedule to the Carriage of Goods by Sea Act 1971.

[121] *Kenya Railways v Antares Co Pte Ltd* [1987] 1 Lloyd's Rep 424 (Hague-Visby Rules, Art III, para 6).

[122] *Chartered Bank v British India Steam Navigation Co* [1909] AC 369; *Pringle of Scotland v Continental Express* [1962] 2 Lloyd's Rep 80.

to limit the operation of the clause to the extent that it is inconsistent with that main object and intent. In *Sze Hai Tong Bank Ltd v Rambler Cycle Co Ltd*:[123]

R despatched goods by sea from England to Singapore. The bill of lading required the goods to be delivered 'unto order or assigns' and stated that 'the responsibility of the carrier shall be deemed to cease absolutely after the goods are discharged from the ship'. After the goods were discharged from the ship, the carrier's agents did not deliver them 'unto order or assigns' but released the goods to the consignees without production of the bill of lading, with the result that R was never paid for the goods.

The Privy Council held that, although the exemption, on the face of it, could hardly have been more comprehensive, it did not permit the shipping company deliberately to disregard its obligations as to delivery.[124] To hold otherwise would defeat the main object and intent of the contract. The carrier was therefore liable.

(v) Bailment

As Lord Hodson pointed out in the *Suisse Atlantique* case:[125]

Under a contract of carriage or bailment if the carrier or bailee uses a place other than that agreed on for storing the goods, or otherwise exposes the goods to risks quite different from those contemplated by the contract, he cannot rely on clauses in the contract designed to protect him against liability within the four corners of the contract . . .

It is first, however, necessary to determine what are the 'four corners' of the contract. If, for instance, a railway company contracts to keep an item in a station cloakroom but keeps it elsewhere in the station and it is stolen or damaged, it will not be able to rely on a clause exempting it, for instance, from liability in respect of loss or damage. But if, on its true construction, the contract is not to keep the item necessarily in the cloakroom, but to keep it at the station, reliance can be placed on the clause.[126] Again, it has been held that warehousemen who stored groundnuts in a warehouse otherwise suitable but not rat-proof could rely on a term of the contract excluding liability in the absence of 'wilful neglect or default' when sued in respect of damage to and contamination of the nuts by rats.[127] Although the warehousemen's storage had been negligent, the place where the nuts were stored was one permitted by the contract and the risk to which they were exposed was not one which was wholly uncontemplated by the contract. Since no wilful neglect or default had been proved, the warehousemen were not liable.

The Courts are extremely unlikely to allow a bailee who has converted the goods to shelter under the provisions of an exemption clause, which simply disclaimed liability for loss or damage to the goods bailed, unless the clause specifically authorized the

---

[123] [1959] AC 576. See also *Motis Exports Ltd v Dampskibsselskabet AF 1912 Akt* [2000] 1 Lloyd's Rep 211, 216–17.

[124] In *Suisse Atlantique Société d'Armement Maritime SA v NV Rotterdamsche Kolen Centrale* [1967] 1 AC 361, the decision in *Sze Hai Tong Bank* was said based on construction but the suggestion that a deliberate breach was a fundamental breach which could not be excluded was rejected. See above, p 202.

[125] [1967] 1 AC 361, 412.   [126] *Gibaud v Great Eastern Railway* [1921] 2 KB 426.

[127] *Kenyon, Son & Craven Ltd v Baxter Hoare & Co Ltd* [1971] 1 WLR 519.

bailee to do the act in question, for example to sell the goods in the event that they were not claimed.[128] A simple disclaimer of liability cannot have been intended by the parties to permit the bailee 'to give the goods away to some passerby, or to burn them or throw them into the sea'.[129] Similarly, if a bailee, without authority, subcontracts its obligations to a third party, it will not be protected by an exemption clause, for example for non-delivery, which is intended to apply only while the goods are in its possession and control.[130]

On the other hand, an exemption clause, if appropriately drafted, has been held, at common law, to cover an honest, but negligent, redelivery of the goods to the wrong person.[131]

Contracts of bailment, where the bailor is a consumer or if the goods are bailed on the bailee's written standard terms of business or if the goods are lost or damaged by negligence, are subject to the Consumer Rights Act 2015 and the Unfair Contract Terms Act 1977.[132] By the statutory provisions, the clause will be of no effect unless it satisfies the requirement of fairness or reasonableness.

4. OTHER COMMON LAW RULES CONTROLLING EXEMPTION CLAUSES

The operation of exemption clauses may be further limited by the application of certain other rules of the common law.

(a) EXPRESS UNDERTAKINGS

A collateral oral warranty may be enforced even though it runs counter to the terms (including exemption clauses) of the principal agreement.[133] There is a still more general principle, that is, that where an express undertaking is given which is inconsistent with the printed clauses of a standard form document, the latter must be rejected insofar as they are repugnant to the express undertaking. In *J Evans & Son (Portsmouth) Ltd v Andrea Merzario Ltd*:[134]

E, an importer of machines, arranged the carriage of the machines to England under a contract with AM, a forwarding agent. AM orally assured E that machines shipped in containers would be carried under deck. Nevertheless, eight containers carrying E's

---

[128] *Alexander v Railway Executive* [1951] 2 KB 882, 889; *Garnham, Harris & Elton Ltd v Ellis (Transport) Ltd* [1967] 1 WLR 940, 946.

[129] *Sze Hai Tong Bank Ltd v Rambler Cycle Co Ltd* [1959] AC 576, 587.

[130] *Garnham, Harris & Elton Ltd v Alfred W Ellis (Transport) Ltd* [1967] 1 WLR 940. See also *Davies v Collins* [1945] 1 All ER 247; *The Berkshire* [1974] 1 Lloyd's Rep 185.

[131] *Hollins v J Davy Ltd* [1963] 1 QB 844.   [132] See below, pp 214, 222.

[133] Above, p 145. On the overriding of an exemption clause see *Webster v Higgin* [1948] 2 All ER 127.

[134] [1976] 1 WLR 1078. See also *Couchman v Hill* [1947] KB 544; *Gallagher v British Road Services Ltd* [1970] 2 Lloyd's Rep 440.

machines were subsequently loaded on deck. One container fell overboard and was a total loss. AM denied liability, relying on an exemption clause in the contract of carriage.

It was held that AM's oral assurance overrode the exemption clause, and that it was liable for breach of the warranty given.

Similarly, in *Mendelssohn v Normand Ltd*[135] M parked in N's garage on the terms that N would 'accept no responsibility for any loss or damage sustained by the vehicle its accessories or contents however caused'. M left the car unlocked because one of N's employee's stated that the car must be left unlocked and that the employee would lock it for him. It was held that the loss by theft of valuables in the car was not covered by the exemption clause.

(b) MISREPRESENTATION OR FRAUD

A party who misrepresents (albeit innocently) the contents or effect of a clause inserted by it into a contract cannot rely on the clause in the face of the misrepresentation. So in *Curtis v Chemical Cleaning & Dyeing Co*:[136]

C took a dress to the defendant company for cleaning. She signed a receipt containing a clause exempting the defendant from all liability for damage to articles cleaned after the defendant's servant told her that it would not accept liability for certain specified risks, including damage to the beads and sequins on the dress. When it was returned, the dress was badly stained.

It was held that, as C had been induced to believe that the clause only referred to the beads and sequins, the defendant was not entitled to rely on it in respect of damage by staining. Denning LJ, dealing with the question of exemption clauses generally, said:[137]

Any behaviour, by words or conduct, is sufficient to be a misrepresentation if it is such as to mislead the other party about the existence or extent of the exemption. If it conveys a false impression, that is enough.

It should also be noted that, for reasons of policy, an exemption clause can never exclude liability for personal fraud.[138]

(c) REASONABLENESS AT COMMON LAW?

The theory of freedom of contract presupposed that any party to a contract is free to choose whether or not to enter into it, and regarded a party who chose to enter into a contract which is onerous as only having itself to blame.[139] But the bargaining

---

[135] [1970] 1 QB 177.

[136] [1951] 1 KB 805. See also *Jacques v Lloyd D George & Partners Ltd* [1968] 1 WLR 625.

[137] [1951] 1 KB 805, 808.

[138] *S Pearson & Son Ltd v Dublin Corp* [1907] AC 351; *Armitage v Nurse* [1998] Ch 241; *HIH Casualty and General Insurance Ltd v Chase Manhattan Bank* [2003] UKHL 6, [2003] 2 Lloyds Rep 61.

[139] See above, p 4.

powers of the parties may be so unequal that one can virtually dictate terms to the other. As long ago as 1877 in *Parker v South Eastern Railway Co*,[140] Bramwell LJ asked what the position would be if some unreasonable condition were inserted as, for instance, to forfeit £1,000 if goods in a station cloakroom were not removed within 48 hours. He thought that 'there is an implied understanding that there is no condition unreasonable to the knowledge of the party tendering the document and not insisting on its being read . . .'. Lord Denning MR on numerous occasions[141] maintained that an exemption clause would not be given effect if it was unreasonable, or if it was unreasonable to apply it in the circumstances of the case, for 'there is the vigilance of the common law which, while allowing freedom of contract, watches over to see that it is not abused'.[142] But this approach has not been accepted as part of the common law and it is clear that the Courts have no general power at common law to strike down a contractual term merely because it is unreasonable or unfair.[143] Such a power has, however, been conferred by statute, notably by the Unfair Contract Terms Act 1977 and by the Consumer Rights Act 2015.

5. LEGISLATIVE CONTROL OF EXEMPTION CLAUSES AND UNFAIR TERMS

(a) EXEMPTION CLAUSES IN NON-CONSUMER CONTRACTS: UNFAIR CONTRACT TERMS ACT 1977

The purpose of the Unfair Contract Terms Act 1977[144] which, until the Consumer Rights Act 2015, applied to both consumer and non-consumer contracts,[145] was to limit, and, in some cases, to take away entirely, the right to rely on exempting clauses in certain situations.

---

[140] (1877) 2 CPD 416, 428.

[141] eg *Gillespie Bros & Co Ltd v Roy Bowles Transport Ltd* [1973] QB 400, 416; *Levison v Patent Steam Carpet Cleaning Co Ltd* [1978] QB 69, 161; *Photo Production Ltd v Securicor Transport Ltd* [1978] 1 WLR 856, 865 (revs'd [1980] AC 827).

[142] *John Lee & Son (Grantham) Ltd v Railway Executive* [1949] 2 All ER 581, 584.

[143] *Suisse Atlantique Société d'Armement Maritime SA v NV Rotterdamsche Kolen Centrale* [1967] 1 AC 361, 406; *Photo Production Ltd v Securicor Transport Ltd* [1980] AC 827, 848.

[144] See Coote (1978) 41 MLR 312; Sealy [1978] CLJ 15; Palmer and Yates [1981] CLJ 108; Adams and Brownsword (1988) 104 LQR 94; Macdonald, in Burrows and Peel (eds), *Contract Terms* (2007) ch 8. The Act derives substantially from recommendations made by the Law Commission: Law Com No 69 (1975); Scot Law Com No 39 (1975). See generally *Unfair Terms in Contracts,* Law Com No 292 (2005).

[145] By reason of the Consumer Rights Act 2015, ss 1 and 61, a consumer contract is a contract between a trader and a consumer; and by ss 2 and 76 of the 2015 Act, a 'trader' means 'a person acting for purposes relating to that person's trade, business, craft or profession' and a 'consumer' means 'an individual acting for purposes that are wholly or mainly outside that individual's trade, business, craft or profession'. The distinction between an 'individual' and a 'person' is that an 'individual' means a natural person whereas a 'person' can include a company. The excision of the application of UCTA 1977 to consumer contracts (and the replication in the 2015 Act of the protection for consumers) is effected by, eg, s 31, Part 2 and Sched 4 of the Consumer Rights Act 2015.

(i) Scope of the Act

The title of the Act is somewhat misleading. In the first place, it is not confined to contract terms. The Act also extends to non-contractual notices containing provisions exempting from liability in tort,[146] although this book is concerned solely with contract terms. Secondly, the Act does not confer upon the Courts a general power to strike down any term of a contract on the ground that the term is unfair or oppressive; it applies to terms that 'exclude or restrict liability' (ie exemption clauses). The Act also does not, in general, purport to affect the basis of liability,[147] so that the first enquiry must normally be whether or not the person seeking to rely on the term is in fact under any liability (or obligation), for example, in negligence or for breach of contract. Also logically prior to the application of the Act is the question whether the relevant term has become a term of the contract[148] and, if so, whether on its true construction it applies to the liability which it is sought to exclude or restrict.[149] The tests of incorporation and construction, considered earlier in this chapter, must be applied before considering the Act. It has been said that the existence of the statutory controls makes it unnecessary to apply strict tests of incorporation and construction.[150] But, even accepting that that is true, the application of the Act should not be considered until it has been decided that, applying the tests of incorporation and construction, the exclusion or limitation clause in question forms part of the contract and covers the events that have occurred. If it is either not incorporated or does not cover those events, then, however reasonable the clause, it will not apply.

(ii) Pattern of control

Some of the provisions of the 1977 Act overlap, so that, when applying it to a particular situation, it is often necessary to consider whether more than one section is relevant.[151] The pattern of control is also somewhat complicated. There are three broad divisions of control: first, control over contract terms that exclude or restrict liability for 'negligence'[152] (which includes breach of a contractual duty to exercise reasonable care and skill in the performance of a contract); secondly, control over contract terms that exclude or restrict liability for breach of certain terms implied by statute in contracts of sale of goods, hire-purchase, and in other contracts for the supply of goods;[153] thirdly, control in standard form contracts over terms that exclude or restrict liability for breach of contract.[154]

If the contract term is subject to the control of the Act, the control may assume one of two forms: the restriction or exclusion of liability may be rendered absolutely

---

[146] Unfair Contract Terms Act 1977, s 2.
[147] But see 1977 Act, s 3(2)(b).
[148] 1977 Act, s 11(2). See above, pp 188–93.
[149] See above, pp 193–206.
[150] *Photo Production v Securicor Transport* [1980] AC 827, 843 (Lord Wilberforce); *AEG (UK) Ltd v Logic Resources Ltd* [1996] CLC 265, 277 (Hobhouse LJ).
[151] eg 1977 Act, ss 2, 3, and 7.
[152] Defined in 1977 Act, s 1(1).
[153] 1977 Act, ss 6, 7.
[154] 1977 Act, s 3.

ineffective,[155] or it may be effective only insofar as the term satisfies the requirement of reasonableness.[156]

(iii) 'Business liability'

The 1977 Act is concerned, for the most part,[157] with terms that exclude or restrict 'business liability', that is, 'liability for breach of obligations or duties arising—(a) from things done or to be done by a person in the course of a business (whether his own business or another's), or (b) from the occupation of premises used for business purposes of the occupier'.[158] The word 'business' has, however, been described as 'an etymological chameleon',[159] and it will not always be easy to determine whether or not there is a business liability, for example, in the case of a university or college, since it does not appear necessary for a business that an activity be carried on with a view to profit.[160]

(iv) Excepted contracts

In addition to consumer contacts,[161] certain very important contracts are wholly or partly excepted from the operation of the 1977 Act. These include contracts of insurance,[162] commercial charterparties,[163] contracts between businesses for the carriage of goods by sea,[164] international supply contracts,[165] contracts of employment (except in favour of an employee),[166] and any contract so far as it relates to[167] the creation or transfer of an interest in land,[168] any intellectual

---

[155] 1977 Act, ss 2(1), 6(1), 7(3A).   [156] 1977 Act, ss 2(2), 3, 6(1A), 7(1A), (4).

[157] On the face of it, there is a major exception by reason of the 1977 Act, s 6(4) (exclusion of implied terms in contracts of sale of goods and hire-purchase). But the width of that exception is restricted because certain terms will only be implied if the seller or owner sells or hires the goods in the course of a business: see above, pp 173–7. The consequence is that the only application of UCTA to (non-consumer) contracts where the defendant is *not* acting in the course of a business, so that the liability is not business liability, is in a contract for the sale of goods or hire-purchase where there is an exemption of the implied term as to title (non-excludable) or of the implied term as to the goods' conformity with description or sample (only excludable if reasonable).

[158] 1977 Act, s 1(3).

[159] *Town Investments Ltd v Department of the Environment* [1978] AC 359 383 (Lord Diplock).

[160] See the partial definition in 1977 Act, s 14.

[161] By reason of the reforms made by the Consumer Rights Act 2015, UCTA 1977 now only applies to non-consumer contracts: see Part 2 and Sched 4 of the Consumer Rights Act 2015.

[162] Consumer Rights Act 2015, Sched 1, para 1(a).

[163] Consumer Rights Act 2015, Sched 1, para 2.

[164] Consumer Rights Act 2015, Sched 1, paras 2–3.

[165] Consumer Rights Act 2015, s 26. See *Amiri Flight Authority v BAE Systems plc* [2003] EWCA Civ 1447, [2004] 1 All ER (Comm) 385 (held not to fall within s 26); *Trident Turboprop (Dublin) Ltd v First Flight Couriers Ltd* [2009] EWCA Civ 290, [2010] QB 86 (held to fall within s 26: see also below, p 352).

[166] Consumer Rights Act 2015, Sched 1, para 4.

[167] See *Micklefield v SAC Technology Ltd* [1990] 1 WLR 1002 (share option); *Unchained Growth III plc v Granby Village (Manchester) Management Co Ltd* [2000] 1 WLR 739 (maintenance charge in lease integral to and thus 'relates to' interest in land).

[168] 1977 Act, Sched 1, para 1(b).

property,[169] or the creation or transfer of securities.[170] In some of these, however, there are specific legislative controls on exemption clauses.[171]

Non-Consumer Contracts: Pattern of Control of UCTA

Types of Contract	Type of Liability Excluded/ Restricted	Liability of a Business	Liability of a Non-business
Any contract	Negligent personal injuries	Unexcludable UCTA, s 2(1)	UCTA does not apply
	Negligent loss or damage	Reasonableness UCTA, ss 2(2) and 11(1)	UCTA does not apply
Standard form contract	Any breach of contract	Reasonableness UCTA, ss 3(2) and 11(1)	UCTA does not apply
Sale of goods*	Breach of Sale of Goods Act 1979, s 12, undertakings as to title	Unexcludable UCTA, s 6(1)	
	Breach of Sale of Goods Act 1979, ss 13 and 15, undertakings as to description or sample	Reasonableness UCTA, ss 6(1A), 11 (1)–(2), Sched 2	
	Breach of Sale of Goods Act 1979, s 14, undertakings as to fitness for purpose and satisfactory quality	Reasonableness UCTA, ss 6(1A), 11(1)–(2), Sched 2	Although UCTA on the face of it applies, these terms are implied only where the party relying on the exemption is acting in the course of a business

* Control of terms implied into contracts of hire-purchase follows the same pattern: UCTA, s 6. The control of terms implied into other contracts under which goods pass follows a similar pattern but only for business liability: UCTA, s 7

(v) Varieties of exemption clause

The 1977 Act applies to contract terms 'excluding or restricting' specific types of liability; but by section 13(1) these are extended to include terms:

(a) making the liability or its enforcement subject to restrictive or onerous conditions;

(b) excluding or restricting any right or remedy in respect of liability, or subjecting a person to any prejudice in consequence of his pursuing any such right or remedy;

(c) excluding or restricting rules of evidence or procedure.

---

[169] 1977 Act, Sched 1, para 1(c); Trade Marks Act 1994, s 106(1) and Sched 4, para 1; *Salvage Association v CAP Financial Services Ltd* [1995] FSR 654.

[170] 1977 Act, Sched 1, para 1(d).   [171] Below, p 232.

Section 13 also makes reference to excluding or restricting liability by terms which exclude or restrict the relevant obligation or duty; and section 3(2)(b) refers to a term by which a party claims to be entitled to render a substantially different performance than reasonably expected or no performance at all.[172] The intention is clearly to embrace terms which, though they do not specifically exclude or restrict *liability*, have a similar effect and thus to prevent the evasion of the policy of the Act.[173] For example, terms which require one party to make a claim within a certain time limit,[174] which take away the right to reject defective goods or to withhold payment (because of a set-off),[175] which state that an architect's certificate shall be 'conclusive evidence' that building work has been properly carried out, or which declare that the other party does not 'give any warranty or undertaking, express or implied, in respect of the goods supplied' or accept any responsibility with respect to the accuracy of a property valuation it supplies[176]—all of these are subject to control.

The difficulty, however, is to distinguish such terms from provisions which prevent a contractual duty from arising or circumscribe its extent, or which merely allocate the responsibilities under the contract between the parties[177] or which constitute a compromise or settlement or release or waiver of one's rights.[178] A seller's warning that goods should not be used after a specified time and a statement that the seller of a painting had no expertise in paintings of that type have been held to preclude the implication of obligations of fitness for purpose and correspondence with description under the Sale of Goods Act 1979 and not to exclude or restrict them.[179] It has been stated that the test is one of substance[180] but also that one has to ask whether 'but for' the clause there would be liability;[181] a formal test. It is submitted that, although it has the attraction of certainty, the latter test is too rigid and that the Courts should determine whether a term in a contract 'excludes or restricts' liability by asking whether it deprives a contracting party of the contractual performance which the parties reasonably expected.[182]

---

[172]   See below, p 215.

[173]   Coote, *Exception Clauses* (1964) famously articulated the view that all exclusion clauses are best analysed as merely defining the relevant duty so that there is no breach. But this extreme view has clearly not been accepted in UCTA 1977 which for the most part assumes the validity of the traditional two-stage 'breach and then exemption' analysis.

[174]   *RW Green Ltd v Cade Bros* [1978] 1 Lloyd's Rep 602.

[175]   *Stewart Gill v Horatio Myer & Co* [1992] 1 QB 600; *Skipskredittforeningen v Emperor Navigation* [1998] 1 Lloyd's Rep 66; *Schenkers Ltd v Overland Shoes Ltd* [1998] 1 Lloyd's Rep 498; *United Trust Bank Ltd v Dohil* [2011] EWHC 3302, [2012] 2 All ER (Comm) 765.

[176]   *Smith v Eric S Bush* and *Harris v Wyre Forest DC* [1990] AC 831.

[177]   *Thompson v T Lohan (Plant Hire) Ltd* [1987] 1 WLR 649.

[178]   *Tudor Grange Holdings Ltd v Citibank NA* [1992] Ch 53.

[179]   *Wormell v RHM Agriculture (East) Ltd* [1987] 1 WLR 1091 (1979 Act, s 14(3)); *Harlingdon & Leinster Enterprises Ltd v Christopher Hull Fine Art Ltd* [1990] 1 All ER 737 (1979 Act, s 13). See above, pp 173–6, on these implied terms.

[180]   *Phillips Products Ltd v Hyland* [1987] 1 WLR 659, 666; *Johnstone v Bloomsbury Health Authority* [1992] QB 333, 346.

[181]   *Smith v Eric S Bush* [1990] AC 831, 857 (Lord Griffiths). Note that in the notice there was a non-contractual disclaimer.

[182]   Macdonald [1992] LS 277. See also Law Com No 69 (1975), para 146.

(vi) Liability for negligence

Restrictions are placed by section 2 of the 1977 Act on the power of a party to a contract to secure exemption from business liability for negligence.[183] It is prohibited to exclude or restrict liability for death or personal injury resulting from negligence by reference to any contract term.[184] In the case of other loss or damage, a party to a contract cannot exclude or restrict liability for negligence except in so far as the term satisfies the requirement of reasonableness.[185] Where, in a contract between A and B, a term purports to transfer from A to B responsibility for injury or damage caused to B by A's employees, that term has been held to fall within section 2.[186] But a term requiring B to indemnify A against injury or damage caused to third parties by A's negligence has been held not to fall within section 2 on the ground that it was not an 'exclusion or restriction' of A's liability to the third party victim but an arrangement by A and B as to the responsibility for compensating the victim.[187]

(vii) Sale of goods and hire-purchase

Section 6 of the 1977 Act restricts the ability of sellers of goods to exempt themselves from liability for breach of the stipulations implied in contracts of sale by sections 12–15 of the Sale of Goods Act 1979. In the first place, it prohibits absolutely the exclusion or restriction of liability for breach of the provisions of section 12 of the 1979 Act (stipulations as to title).[188] Secondly, liability for breach of the provisions of sections 13 to 15 of the 1979 Act (conditions as to satisfactory quality, fitness for purpose, and correspondence with description or sample) can be excluded or restricted only in so far as the term satisfies the requirement of reasonableness.[189]

Section 6 of the 1977 Act further contains similar provisions which prohibit, either absolutely or subject to the test of reasonableness, terms excluding or restricting liability for breach of the stipulations implied by the Supply of Goods (Implied Terms) Act 1973 in contracts of hire-purchase.[190]

(viii) Supply contracts

Section 7 of the 1977 Act is concerned with contract terms excluding or restricting business liability for breach of an implied obligation in a contract 'where the possession or ownership of goods passes under or in pursuance of the contract' (other than a contract of sale of goods or hire-purchase). Examples of such contracts are contracts of hire, and contracts for work and materials, such as building and

---

[183] 'Negligence' includes breach of a contractual or common law duty to take reasonable care or to exercise reasonable skill and breach of the duty of care under the Occupiers' Liability Act 1957.

[184] 1977 Act, s 2(1); *Johnstone v Bloomsbury HA* [1992] QB 333, 343, 346.

[185] 1977 Act, s 2(2), (3).

[186] *Phillips Products Ltd v Hyland* [1987] 1 WLR 659; *Flamar Interocean Ltd v Denmore Ltd* [1990] 1 Lloyd's Rep 434 ('deemed servant' clauses).

[187] *Thompson v T Lohan (Plant Hire) Ltd* [1987] 1 WLR 649; *Hancock Shipping Co Ltd v Deacon & Trysail (Private) Ltd* [1991] 2 Lloyd's Rep 550. See also *Neptune Orient Lines Ltd v JCV (UK) Ltd* [1983] 2 Lloyd's Rep 438, 442 (promise not to sue third party).

[188] 1977 Act, s 6(1).   [189] 1977 Act, s 6(1A).   [190] See above, p 178.

engineering contracts. The Supply of Goods and Services Act 1982[191] implies into such contracts terms similar to those implied in contracts of sale of goods in respect of the goods' correspondence with description or sample, or their quality or fitness for purpose. The 1977 Act lays down that liability for breach of these implied terms can be excluded or restricted only in so far as the exempting term satisfies the requirement of reasonableness.[192] Terms excluding or restricting liability for breach of implied terms as to title to or quiet possession of the goods are also subject to the test of reasonableness in contracts of hire[193] but are prohibited absolutely in contracts for work and materials.[194]

(ix) Contractual liability under standard terms of business

A more wide-ranging and general control is effected by section 3 of the 1977 Act, which deals with contractual liability.[195] This section may apply, in addition to sections 6 and 7 mentioned above, to contracts of sale and hire-purchase and supply contracts. But it may also apply to any contract, unless it is of a type expressly excepted by the Act. Thus, it may apply, for example, to a contract for the garaging of a car or for the storage of furniture. The section applies as between contracting parties where one of them deals on the other's written standard terms of business,[196] and the liability which it is sought to exclude or restrict is a business liability. Thus, the many contracts between businesses, made by reference to standard terms and conditions printed in order forms, confirmations of order, or in catalogues or price lists are subject to section 3.

Where a standard form of agreement is used but it has been altered to fit the circumstances of the individual transaction, the question whether section 3 applies has been said to be one of fact and degree.[197] Clearly differences as to price and date of delivery will not prevent the section applying to the rest of the terms. The test has been said to be one of habitual use,[198] and it is submitted that terms may overall be 'standard' even though, for example, a single provision in a standard form has been altered. Where the contract uses model forms drafted by a third party, such as a professional or trade organization, it has been decided controversially that, unless the model form is invariably or at least usually used by a party, it cannot be that party's 'standard' terms of business.[199]

---

[191] Above, p 178.   [192] 1977 Act, s 7(1A).
[193] 1977 Act, s 7(4).   [194] 1977 Act, s 7(3A).
[195] Where there is the breach of a contractual duty of care, s 2 rather than s 3 (which is narrower) will, in practice, be applied.
[196] Prior to the Consumer Rights Act 2015, UCTA 1977, s 3 also applied to where one party was dealing as a consumer: but this was amended, so as to delete the reference to 'as a consumer' by the Consumer Rights Act 2015, Part 2 and Sched 4, para 5.
[197] *Chester Grosvenor Hotel Co Ltd v Alfred McAlpine Management Ltd* (1991) 56 BLR 115, 131–3; *St Albans City & DC v International Computers Ltd* [1996] 4 All ER 481, 491. Cf *Flamar Interocean Ltd. v Denmore* [1990] 1 Lloyd's Rep 434, 438; *Shearson Lehman Hutton Inc v MacLaine, Watson & Co Ltd* [1989] 2 Lloyd's Rep 570, 611; *Salvage Association v CAP Financial Services Ltd* [1995] FSR 654.
[198] *Chester Grosvenor Hotel Co Ltd v Alfred McAlpine Management Ltd* (1991) 56 BLR 115.
[199] *British Fermentation Products Ltd v Compare Reavell Ltd* (1999) 66 Con LR 1.

The control imposed by the section is as follows:[200]

As against that party,[201] the other cannot by reference to any contract term—

    (a) when himself in breach of contract, exclude or restrict any liability of his in respect of the breach; or

    (b) claim to be entitled—

        (i) to render a contractual performance substantially different from that which was reasonably expected of him, or

        (ii) in respect of the whole or any part of his contractual obligation, to render no performance at all,

    except in so far as . . . the contract term satisfies the requirement of reasonableness.

The wording of the first limb (a) of this provision, relating to the exclusion or restriction of liability in respect of breach of contract, is relatively easy to interpret. But the second limb (b) is more difficult to construe. It would appear to be the intention of (b) that it should apply in cases where there is *no breach of contract at all*, but one party claims to rely on a term of the contract which purports to entitle it either to render a contractual performance substantially different from that which was reasonably expected at the time of the contract or in respect of the whole or part of the contractual obligation to render no performance at all.[202]

It has been held that the second limb (b) did not apply to a term permitting an employer to dismiss an employee during the first two years of employment without going through the contractual disciplinary procedure.[203] Although expressed in negative terms, it merely set out the employee's entitlement and the limit of his rights. Similarly a clause in an employment contract by which an employee forfeits its right to earned commission once the contract has been terminated has been held to fall outside section 3(2)(b).[204]

In contrast, examples of the application of the second limb (b) include the following. A holiday cruise line company agrees with a holiday tour operator to provide certain quality and number of cabins for customers of the tour operator. It nevertheless reserves the right, in certain circumstances, to accommodate the customers in lower quality cabins or to switch the customers to a different cruise-liner, or to cancel the cruise in whole or in part.[205] A telephone company reserves the right to disconnect a telephone service without demonstrable reason or cause.[206] Another possible example is a *force majeure* clause excusing a trader

---

[200] 1977 Act, s 3(2).

[201] ie the person dealing on the other's written standard terms of business.

[202] *Shearson Lehman Bros Inc v Maclaine, Watson & Co Ltd* [1989] 2 Lloyd's Rep 570, 612.

[203] *Brigden v American Express Bank Ltd* [2000] IRLR 94. See also *Paragon Finance plc v Nash* [2002] 1 WLR 685.

[204] *Peninsula Business Services Ltd v Sweeney* [2004] IRLR 49.

[205] Cf *Anglo Continental Holidays Ltd v Typaldos Lines (London) Ltd* [1967] 2 Lloyd's Rep 61.

[206] *Timeload Ltd v British Telecommunications plc* (1995) 3 EMLR 459, 468 (Sir Thomas Bingham MR). But cf *Paragon Finance plc v Nash* [2002] 1 WLR 685 at [71]–[77].

from delivering goods to be supplied under the contract, or to suspend or cancel the contract without any further liability on its part upon the happening of events beyond the trader's control such as strikes, war, civil commotion, inability to obtain supplies, etc. However, while in the cases of the holiday cruise line company and the telephone company, it is likely to be held that such provisions do not satisfy the requirement of reasonableness, it seems unlikely that a *force majeure* clause in a commercial agreement would be held to be unreasonable[207] in the absence of special circumstances.[208]

(x) The 'reasonableness' test

Except in those instances where the 1977 Act prohibits absolutely the exclusion or restriction of liability,[209] the contract terms controlled by the Act are subject to the test of reasonableness.[210] The question to be decided by the Court in all cases where the 'reasonableness' test is applied in relation to a contract term is whether the term is a fair and reasonable one to have been included 'having regard to the circumstances which were, or ought reasonably to have been, known to or in the contemplation of the parties when the contract was made'.[211] It is therefore clear that the crucial time is the time of the making of the contract, and not the time at which liability arises.[212] The reasonableness of a contract term is therefore not affected by the nature or seriousness of the loss or damage sustained, except to the extent that it was or ought to have been in contemplation at the time the contract was made. It is also clear that circumstances solely known to one party, that is, the person relying on the exemption clause, such as the experimental nature of the product supplied or the market difficulties involved in procuring it, are to be treated as irrelevant if they were not known, and could not reasonably have been known, to the other party at the time the contract was made.

It has been said that 'it is impossible to draw up an exhaustive list of factors to be taken into account' in assessing the reasonableness of an exemption or limitation clause.[213] In order to assist the Court in determining whether a term satisfies the requirement of reasonableness, the Act sets out five 'guidelines' as to matters to be taken into account.[214] Strictly these guidelines are applicable to the test of reasonableness only in respect of the exclusion or restriction of liability for breach of the implied obligations as to description, sample, quality, and fitness for purpose

---

[207] *Shearson Lehman Hutton Inc v MacLaine, Watson & Co Ltd* [1989] 2 Lloyd's Rep 570, 612. See also *Brigden v American Express Bank Ltd* [2000] IRLR 94, 96.

[208] eg in an exclusive dealing agreement where the supplier is entitled to suspend in the event of *force majeure* but the purchaser is not entitled, during the suspension, to purchase supplies from elsewhere.

[209] 1977 Act, ss 2(1), 6(1), 7(3A).   [210] 1977 Act, ss 2(2), 3(2), 6(1A), 7(1A), (4).

[211] 1977 Act, s 11(1).

[212] *Stewart Gill v Horatio Myer & Co* [1992] 1 QB 600, 607, 608. The reasonableness of a non-contractual notice is determined having regard to the circumstances when the liability arose or would have arisen: 1977 Act, s 11(3); *Smith v Eric S Bush* [1990] AC 831, 848, 857.

[213] *Smith v Eric S Bush* [1990] 1 AC 831, 858.   [214] 1977 Act, s 11(2), Sched 2.

in contracts of sale of goods and hire-purchase,[215] and supply contracts.[216] But 'the considerations there set out are normally regarded as being of general application to the question of reasonableness'.[217] However, even where the guidelines are directly applicable, they are not exhaustive; the Court is required to have regard 'in particular' to those matters, but it can also take account of any other relevant circumstances. The five guidelines are:

(a) the strength of the bargaining positions of the parties relative to each other, taking into account (among other things) alternative means by which the customer's requirements could have been met;

(b) whether the customer received an inducement to agree to the term, or in accepting it had an opportunity of entering into a similar contract with other persons, but without having to accept a similar term;

(c) whether the customer knew or ought reasonably to have known of the existence and extent of the term (having regard, among other things, to any custom of the trade and any previous course of dealing between the parties);

(d) where the term excludes or restricts any relevant liability if some condition is not complied with, whether it was reasonable at the time of the contract to expect that compliance with that condition would be practicable;

(e) whether the goods were manufactured, processed, or adapted to the special order of the customer.

It will be seen that these guidelines could open up quite extensive enquiries, for instance, as to the market position at the time the contract was made. The Court should not, however, be too ready to focus on remote possibilities or to conclude that a clause fails the test by reference to relatively uncommon or unlikely situations.[218]

If a contract term seeks to restrict liability to a specified sum of money (as, for example, in the case of a term which states that a seller's total liability for loss or damage arising from defects in the goods shall be limited to £20,000) and the question arises whether the term satisfies the requirement of reasonableness, the 1977 Act requires that regard is also to be had in particular to (1) the resources which he would expect to be available to him for the purpose of meeting the liability should it arise, and (2) how far it was open to him to cover himself by insurance.[219]

The burden of proving that a contract term satisfies the requirement of reasonableness rests upon the person who claims that it is reasonable.[220]

---

[215] 1977 Act, s 6(1A).

[216] 1977 Act, s 7(1A). By ss 7(4) and 11(2), they also apply to the implied term as to title or quiet possession in contracts of hire.

[217] *Stewart Gill v Horatio Myer & Co* [1992] 1 QB 600, 608 (Stuart-Smith LJ). See also *Flamar Interocean Ltd v Denmore* [1990] 1 Lloyd's Rep 434, 438; *Smith v Eric S Bush* [1990] AC 831, 858 (Lord Griffiths); *Regus (UK) Ltd v Epcot Solutions Ltd* [2008] EWCA Civ 361, [2009] 1 All ER (Comm) 586 at [20] (Rix LJ); *Avrora Fine Arts Investment Ltd v Christie, Manson & Woods Ltd* [2012] EWHC 2198 (Ch), [2012] PNLR 35 at [149] (Newey J).

[218] *Skipskredittforeningen v Emperor Navigation* [1998] 1 Lloyd's Rep 66, 75–6.

[219] 1977 Act, s 11(4).   [220] 1977 Act, s 11(5).

The control of exemption and limitation clauses by a test of reasonableness means that decisions are made on a case by case basis and turn on the type of contract and the precise nature of the relationship between the parties. The consequence is a body of law that is flexible. Decisions of judges at first instance as to whether a clause is reasonable can be seen as broadly similar to exercises of structured discretion.[221] It has been stated that Courts must entertain a wide 'range of considerations, put them into the scales on one side or the other, and decide at the end of the day on which side the balance comes down'.[222] In such circumstances there will be room for a legitimate difference of judicial opinion as to the correct answer, and for this reason the decision of the judge at first instance will be treated 'with the utmost respect' and appellate Courts will 'refrain from interference with it unless satisfied that it proceeded upon some erroneous principle or was plainly and obviously wrong'.[223] An example of such an error was where the trial judge considered the reasonableness of the part of the exemption clause that was in issue, requiring a purchaser to return defective goods at its own expense, separately from the rest of the clause, which in effect excluded all other warranties and conditions including those implied by the Sale of Goods Act.[224]

In practice the decided cases have indicated that the following factors are the most significant.[225]

(1) The relative bargaining strength of the parties.[226] A clause that has been imposed by one side is less likely to be reasonable than one that was the product of negotiations between representative bodies, or had evolved over time as a result of trade practice.[227] The courts have tended to adopt a 'non-interventionist' approach where the contract has been made between commercial parties of

---

[221] In the sense that there is significant scope for setting the reasons and standards (and assessing the relative importance of conflicting reasons and standards) according to which the decision is to be made within a broad but not unlimited statutory framework: see Galligan, *Discretionary Powers* (1986) 21.

[222] *George Mitchell (Chesterhall) Ltd v Finney Lock Seeds Ltd* [1983] 2 AC 803, 816.

[223] *Ibid*, 810 (Lord Bridge). See also *Phillips Products Ltd v Hyland* [1987] 1 WLR 659, 669.

[224] *AEG (UK) Ltd v Logic Resources Ltd* [1996] CLC 265. A rare example of the Court of Appeal overturning the trial judge's assessment of reasonableness is provided by *Watford Electronics Ltd v Sanderson CFL Ltd* [2001] EWCA Civ 317, [2001] 1 All ER (Comm) 696.

[225] As well as decisions on the 1977 Act, guidance is gained from those on the Misrepresentation Act 1967, s 3 (below, p 352, and *Howard Marine and Dredging Co Ltd v A Ogden & Sons (Excavations) Ltd* [1978] QB 574), the Sale of Goods Act 1893, s 55 (as amended by the Supply of Goods (Implied Terms) Act 1973 but now replaced by the Unfair Contract Terms Act 1977, ss 6–7), but see *Rasbora Ltd v JCL Marine Ltd* [1977] 1 Lloyd's Rep 645; *George Mitchell (Chesterhall) Ltd v Finney Lock Seeds Ltd* [1983] 2 AC 803.

[226] *Howard Marine and Dredging Co Ltd v A Ogden & Sons (Excavations) Ltd* [1978] QB 574, 594 (Lord Denning MR); *George Mitchell (Chesterhall) Ltd v Finney Lock Seeds Ltd* [1983] QB 284, 302; *Smith v Eric S Bush* [1990] 1 AC 831, 858; *Singer Co (UK) Ltd v Hartlepool Port Authority* [1988] 2 Lloyd's Rep 164, 169; *St Albans City and District Council v International Computers Ltd* [1995] FSR 686, aff'd [1996] 4 All ER 481; *Balmoral Group Ltd v Borealis (UK) Ltd* [2006] EWHC 1900 (Comm), [2006] 2 Lloyd's Rep 629 at [407]–[409]; *Regus (UK) Ltd v Epcot Solutions Ltd* [2008] EWCA Civ 361, [2009] 1 All ER (Comm) 586 at [40]. Guideline (a) in Sched 2 to the 1977 Act.

[227] *Howard Marine and Dredging Co Ltd v A Ogden & Sons (Excavations) Ltd* [1978] QB 574, 594 (Lord Denning MR); *George Mitchell (Chesterhall) Ltd v Finney Lock Seeds Ltd* [1983] QB 284, 302, 307, 314; [1983] 2 AC 803, 817; *Schenkers Ltd. v Overland Shoes* [1998] 1 Lloyd's Rep 498, 507. Trade practice without negotiation is not a weighty factor.

equal bargaining power. In the words of Tuckey LJ, with whom Hart J and Potter LJ agreed, in *Granville Oil and Chemicals Ltd v Davies Turner and Co Ltd*:[228]

The 1977 Act obviously plays a very important role in protecting vulnerable consumers from the effect of draconian contract terms. But I am less enthusiastic about its intrusion into contracts between commercial parties of equal bargaining strength, who should generally be considered capable of being able to make contracts of their choosing and expect to be bound by their terms.

(2) The question of how far it would have been practicable and convenient to go elsewhere.[229] Similarly, where a party seeking to rely on a clause has given the other party the opportunity to pay more for the contractual performance without the clause, the clause is more likely to be held to be reasonable. For instance, in a number of standard forms governing contracts for the carriage of goods, the liability of the carrier is limited unless the owner of the goods declares their value and pays an increased charge.[230] The size of the limit compared with other limits in widely used standard terms may also be relevant.[231]

(3) The availability of insurance is an important factor, albeit by no means decisive.[232] The statutory requirement that regard is to be had to how far it was open to the party seeking to limit liability to cover itself by insurance[233] was inserted to protect the small business, and possibly also professional persons who might not have the resources to meet unlimited liability should it arise, and who might not be able to obtain insurance cover against such liability. In their case, it might well be reasonable to impose a financial limit to liability. The provision may, however, be held to operate against larger companies with considerable assets, or to render a 'financial limit' clause unreasonable where insurance cover can in fact be obtained. Thus, it has been held that a limitation of liability of £100,000 by a multinational company with insurance cover of £50 million was unreasonable.[234] It is to be noted that the statute makes no reference to the *cost* of such cover, but it has been stated that 'the cost of insurance must be a relevant factor when considering which of two parties should be required to bear the risk of a loss'.[235]

---

[228] [2003] EWCA Civ 570, [2003] 1 All ER (Comm) 819 at [31]. See also *Watford Electronics Ltd v Sanderson CFL Ltd* [2001] EWCA Civ 317, [2001] 1 All ER (Comm) 696.

[229] *Overseas Medical Supplies Ltd v Orient Transport Services Ltd* [1999] 2 Lloyd's Rep 272, 277.

[230] *Gillespie v Roy Bowles Transport Ltd* [1973] QB 400, 446. See, eg, clause 29(A) and (D) of the British International Freight Association's Standard Trading Conditions, 1989 edn. See also Guideline (b) in Sched 2 to the 1977 Act; *Singer Co (UK) Ltd v Hartlepool Port Authority* [1988] 2 Lloyd's Rep 164, 170.

[231] *Overseas Medical Supplies Ltd v Orient Transport Services Ltd* [1999] 2 Lloyd's Rep 272, 277.

[232] *Ibid; Balmoral Group Ltd v Borealis (UK) Ltd* [2006] EWHC (Comm), [2006] 2 Lloyd's Rep 629; *Regus (UK) Ltd v Epcot Solutions Ltd* [2008] EWCA Civ 361, [2009] 1 All ER (Comm) 586 at [41]–[42].

[233] 1977 Act, s 11(4).

[234] *St Albans City & DC v International Computers Ltd* [1995] FSR 686, aff'd [1996] 4 All ER 481, 491. See also *Salvage Association v CAP Financial Services Ltd* [1995] FSR 654.

[235] *Smith v Eric S Bush* [1990] 1 AC 831, 858 (Lord Griffiths). See also *ibid*, 851–4; *George Mitchell (Chesterhall) Ltd v Finney Lock Seeds Ltd* [1983] 2 AC 803, 817.

(4) Negligence on the part of the party seeking to rely on the clause is also an important factor. The Court will take into account whether there has been such negligence, and, if so, whether it was reasonably practicable for the other party to have done anything to avoid the loss.[236] Excluding or limiting liability for negligence may be reasonable provided it is reasonably practicable for the other party to obtain the service from an alternative source, if the task is very difficult with a high risk of failure, or where it would be impossible to obtain adequate insurance cover against a potential liability that would be ruinous without insurance.[237]

(5) The clarity of the clause has been described as an 'overriding' factor; businesses must take the consequences of the uncertainty which their 'small print' has created; 'uncertainty' involves unfairness to the other side.[238] A clause is also less likely to be reasonable if the innocent party has not had an opportunity of discovering the defect or damage. Thus a term in a bulk sale of seed potatoes requiring claims to be made within three days of delivery was held not to protect the seller when the potatoes were infected by virus, a defect not discoverable by inspection.[239]

(6) The relationship between the potential or actual loss and the extent of the limitation is taken into account. That the clause excludes liability altogether, or limits liability to a small amount, compared to a large potential or actual loss, is a factor which leans towards the clause being judged unreasonable.[240] In contrast, the exclusion of damages for negligence (and for liability under section 2(1) of the Misrepresentation Act 1967) was held reasonable where the claimant was, in any event, entitled by an express term of the contract to the refund of the price paid for a painting that was forged.[241]

(7) The magnitude of the damage in relation to the contract price is also of significance. There have been statements that where the price is small but the damages very large this favours a finding of reasonableness.[242]

---

[236] *George Mitchell (Chesterhall) Ltd v Finney Lock Seeds Ltd* [1983] QB 284, 307, 313, [1983] 2 AC 803, 817. See also *Walker v Boyle* [1982] 1 WLR 495, 507; *Smith v Eric S Bush* [1990] 1 AC 831, 858 (non-contractual notice); *Britvic Soft Drinks Ltd v Messer UK Ltd* [2002] EWCA Civ 548, [2002] 2 Lloyd's Rep 368 (exclusion clause failed to pass the reasonableness test in respect of a wholly unexpected manufacturing mishap).

[237] *Smith v Eric S Bush* [1990] 1 AC 831, 858–9.

[238] *George Mitchell (Chesterhall) Ltd v Finney Lock Seeds Ltd* [1983] QB 284, 314 (Kerr LJ); *Monarch Airlines Ltd v London Luton Airport* [1998] 1 Lloyd's Rep 403, 414. Note the overlap with the rules of construction, above, pp 177–190.

[239] *RW Green v Cade Bros Farms* [1978] 1 Lloyd's Rep 602; *R & B Customs Brokers Co Ltd v United Dominions Trust Ltd* [1988] 1 WLR 321.

[240] *St Albans City and District Council v International Computers Ltd* [1995] FSR 686, aff'd [1996] 4 All ER 481; *Balmoral Group Ltd v Borealis (UK) Ltd* [2006] EWHC 1900 (Comm), [2006] 2 Lloyd's Rep 629 at [413] and [424].

[241] *Avrora Fine Arts Investment Ltd v Christie, Mason & Woods Ltd* [2012] EWHC 2198 (Ch), [2012] PNLR 35.

[242] *George Mitchell (Chesterhall) Ltd v Finney Lock Seeds Ltd* [1983] QB 284; [1983] 2 AC 803 (Lord Denning MR and Lord Bridge, cf Kerr LJ). See also *Smith v Eric S Bush* [1990] 1 AC 831, 859–60 (non-contractual notice).

The operation of several of the above factors is well illustrated by *George Mitchell (Chesterhall) Ltd v Finney Lock Seeds Ltd*.[243] But it should be noted that the case concerned the reasonableness test (now repealed) in section 55 of the Sale of Goods Act 1979,[244] which required the Court to consider the reasonableness of *reliance* upon the term and not, as is required by the 1977 Act, whether it is reasonable to include it in the contract. In that case:

GM, a firm of farmers, purchased from F, a seed merchant, a quantity of Dutch winter white cabbage seeds, described as 'Finney's Late Dutch Special' for £201. F negligently supplied seeds of a very inferior variety of autumn cabbage, and as a result the crop failed. GM's loss was £61,513 but F relied on exemption clauses contained in its standard conditions of sale which limited its liability to replacement of the seeds or a refund of the price paid, and excluded any express or implied condition, statutory or otherwise.

The House of Lords held that F could not rely on the clause. Although similar terms were incorporated universally in the terms of trade between seed merchants and farmers, they were never negotiated; the breach was due to negligence for which F was responsible; and seed merchants could insure against crop failure caused by supplying the wrong seeds without materially increasing the price of the seeds. There was also evidence that, in practice, seed merchants always negotiated settlements of claims for damages in excess of the price of seeds if they thought that the claims were 'genuine' and 'justified'. The fact that merchants had not sought to rely on the limitation in the past showed that it would not be reasonable to allow such reliance in this case.[245] Although, under the 1977 Act, reasonableness must be determined at the time of the contract and subsequent reliance is not relevant,[246] it is submitted that it is unlikely to be reasonable to include a term which has never in the past been relied on in a trade, because thought to be unreasonable, and that the absence of such reliance *before* the contract under consideration was made remains relevant under the 1977 Act.

(xi) Powers of the Court

As we have seen, the 1977 Act renders some exclusion or limitation clauses absolutely ineffective (ie void) irrespective of the application of a reasonableness test. Where the reasonableness test is to be applied—and even though the Act uses the words 'except in so far as the term satisfies the requirement of reasonableness'—the powers of the Court are limited to declaring the term either to be effective or of no effect (ie void). It cannot re-write the term or, for example, where the term limited liability to a particular sum, render a 'judgement of Solomon' by raising that sum to an amount which it considers reasonable in the circumstances.[247] Moreover, it has been controversially held that a

---

[243] [1983] 2 AC 803.   [244] The test was set out in para 11 of Sched 1 to the 1979 Act.

[245] Cf *Schenkers Ltd v Overland Shoes Ltd* [1998] 1 Lloyd's Rep 498 where the fact that the clause had not been relied on in the past was not regarded as decisive because the past conduct did not indicate that those in the trade thought the clause was unreasonable.

[246] *Stewart Gill Ltd v Horatio Myer & Co Ltd* [1992] QB 600.

[247] *George Mitchell (Chesterhall) Ltd v Finney Lock Seeds Ltd* [1983] 2 AC 803, 816; *Stewart Gill Ltd v Horatio Myer & Co Ltd* [1992] QB 600.

single term must be declared either valid or void as a whole so that the Courts cannot sever the reasonable from the unreasonable parts, even if the defendant is seeking to rely on merely the (alleged) reasonable part.[248]

(b) UNFAIR TERMS IN CONSUMER CONTRACTS: CONSUMER RIGHTS ACT 2015

(i) Legislation on unfair terms in consumer contracts prior to the Consumer Rights Act 2015

By EEC Council Directive 93/13,[249] a term in a contract between a seller or supplier of goods or services and a consumer which has not been individually negotiated is subjected to a requirement of 'fairness'. The Directive was originally implemented in the Unfair Terms in Consumer Contracts Regulations 1994.[250] These were subsequently replaced by the Unfair Terms in Consumer Contracts Regulations 1999[251] which followed the language of the Directive more closely. The 1999 Regulations have in turn been replaced, for contracts made on or after 1 October 2015, by Part 2 of the Consumer Rights Act 2015. Part 2 of the Consumer Rights Act 2015 largely replicates, albeit with some amendments, the 1999 Regulations. Also within the Consumer Protection Act 2015 are provisions which automatically invalidate (ie without applying a test of fairness) certain exemption clauses in consumer contracts some of which were previously in the Unfair Contract Terms Act 1977. There is therefore no longer an overlap between the application of UCTA 1977 and separate legislation protecting consumers against exemption clauses.

(ii) The Consumer Rights Act 2015: overview

Part 1 of the Consumer Rights Act 2015 deals with consumer contracts (ie contracts between traders and consumers)[252] for goods, digital content, and services. As part of the law governing such contracts, the Act automatically invalidates (ie without applying a fairness test) certain exemption clauses in such contracts. So, for example, by sections 31 and 47, in a contract for the supply of goods or digital content by a trader to a consumer, a term is not binding on a consumer to the extent that it would exclude or restrict the trader's liability for breach of a term that the goods or digital content are of satisfactory quality, or fit for a particular purpose made known by the consumer to

---

[248] *Stewart Gill Ltd v Horatio Myer & Co Ltd* [1992] QB 600. But see *RW Green Ltd v Cade Bros Farms* [1978] 1 Lloyd's Rep 602 (three-day time bar invalid, limitation of damages to contract price valid); *Watford Electronics Ltd v Sanderson CFL Ltd* [2001] EWCA Civ 317, [2001] 1 All ER (Comm) 696 (two separate terms, albeit in a single clause); *Regus (UK) Ltd v Epcot Solutions Ltd* [2008] EWCA Civ 361, [2009] 1 All ER (Comm) 586 at [46].

[249] OJ L 95, 21 April 1993, p 29.   [250] SI 1994 No 3159.

[251] SI 1999 No 2083. See generally, Beale, in Beatson and Friedmann (eds), *Good Faith and Fault in Contract Law* (1995) ch 9; Collins (1994) 14 OJLS 229; Dean (1993) 56 MLR 581; Macdonald [1994] JBL 441; Bright (2000) 20 LS 331; Bright, in Burrows and Peel (eds), *Contract Terms* (2007) ch 9; *Unfair Terms in Contracts*, Law Com No 292 (2005).

[252] Consumer Rights Act 2015, ss 1(1), 2(2), and 2(3).

the trader, or as described, or that the trader has the right to supply the goods or digital content. By section 57, in a contract for the supply of services by a trader to a consumer, a term is not binding on the consumer to the extent that it would exclude or restrict the trader's liability for breach of a term that, for example, the trader must perform the service with reasonable care and skill.

Part 2 of the Consumer Rights Act 2015 largely replicates, albeit with some amendments, the Unfair Terms in Consumer Contracts Regulations 1999; and by section 65 it also automatically invalidates a term by which a trader, in a consumer contract, excludes or restricts liability for death or personal injury resulting from negligence.[253]

(iii) The test of unfairness under Part 2 of the Consumer Rights Act 2015

While it is ultimately for the Courts to decide whether any term is unfair, Part 2 of the Consumer Rights Act may also be enforced administratively by the Competition and Markets Authority (or other named regulator).[254] This was previously a role for the Office of Fair Trading which published guidance as to what it considered fair and unfair.[255]

By section 62(4) of the 2015 Act, a contractual term will be 'unfair' where:

contrary to the requirement of good faith, it causes a significant imbalance in the parties' rights and obligations under the contract to the detriment of the consumer.

Some guidance is provided by section 62(5) and by the 'indicative and non-exhaustive list' of terms in Schedule 2. [256] Section 62(5) provides:

Whether a term is fair is to be determined—(a) taking into account the nature of the subject matter of the contract, and (b) by reference to all the circumstances existing when the term was agreed and to all the other terms of the contract or of any other contract on which it depends.

A term which, in isolation, might appear to be unfair, might thus not be when looked at in the light of the contract as a whole. So while a term may create an imbalance between the parties' rights and obligations, it might be one that is justified as fair (or reasonable) say in a high risk or speculative contract or where a seller is dependent on a third party who may (because of market strength) supply only on very restrictive terms.

Schedule 2 (Part 1) contains 20 categories of term, which 'may' be unfair. These include terms authorizing or enabling the seller or supplier to dissolve the contract on a discretionary basis where the same facility is not given to the consumer,[257] to

---

[253] This provision was previously in UCTA 1977, s 2(1). That provision remains for non-consumer contracts but no longer applies to consumer contracts: see para 4 of Sched 4 to the Consumer Rights Act 2015.

[254] Consumer Rights Act 2015, s 70.

[255] See, eg, *Unfair Contract Terms Guidance* (OFT311) (September 2008).

[256] See also the factors listed in Recital 16 to Directive 93/13 which, by reason of EU law, may be referred to in interpreting the meaning of fairness. These were actually listed in Sched 2 to the 1994 Regulations but were not listed in the 1999 Regulations and are not listed in the Consumer Rights Act 2015.

[257] Consumer Rights Act 2015, Sched 2, para 7.

terminate a contract of indeterminate duration without reasonable notice except where there are serious grounds for doing so,[258] to alter the terms of the contract unilaterally without a valid reason which is specified in the contract,[259] to determine whether goods, digital content, or services supplied are in conformity with the contract,[260] and terms requiring a consumer in breach of contract to pay 'a disproportionately high sum in compensation'[261] or to fulfil all his obligations where the trader does not perform his.[262]

Although there have, as yet, been only a few significant judicial decisions on the meaning of fairness,[263] many of the cases the Office of Fair Trading has considered administratively, as part of the duty to prevent the continued use of unfair terms, have involved 'fairness' and the plainness and intelligibility of the language. For example, following complaints, suppliers have agreed to withdraw or amend certain types of clause. Thus clauses excluding liability for a failure to supply have either been withdrawn or limited to situations in which the failure is beyond the supplier's reasonable control. Clauses excluding delay have either been withdrawn or limited to delay for a reasonable period. Similarly, suppliers have agreed either to withdraw clauses preventing a consumer from withholding any part of the contractual payment where the goods or services are defective or to amend them to prohibit such withholding in the case of a minor defect beyond a proportionate amount of the contractual sum. Suppliers have also agreed to withdraw clauses excluding liability for damage if concerned with death or personal injury or to limit them to damage which has not been caused negligently.[264]

The Office of Fair Trading's guidance stated that its starting point in assessing the fairness of a term was normally to ask what would be the position of a consumer if it did not appear in the contract. It has stated that 'the principle of freedom of contract can no longer be said to justify using standard terms to take away protection consumers would otherwise enjoy. The [legislative provisions] recognize that contractual small print is in no real sense freely agreed with consumers. Where a term changes the normal position seen by the law as striking a fair balance it is regarded with suspicion.'[265] It considered that 'transparency is also fundamental to fairness' and that 'even though a term would be clear to a lawyer, we will probably conclude

---

[258] Consumer Rights Act 2015, Sched 2, para 8.

[259] Consumer Rights Act 2015, Sched 2, para 11.

[260] Consumer Rights Act 2015, Sched 2, para 16.

[261] Consumer Rights Act 2015, Sched 2, para 6. This will normally be void as a penalty at common law: below, p 598.

[262] Consumer Rights Act 2015, Sched 2, para 18.

[263] The most important English cases have been *Director-General of Fair Trading v First National Bank plc* [2001] UKHL 52, [2002] 1 AC 481 (which concerned the 1994 Regulations) and *ParkingEye Ltd v Beavis* [2015] UKSC 67, [2015] 3 WLR 1373 (which concerned the 1999 Regulations).

[264] See Office of Fair Trading Bulletins on *Unfair Contract Terms* (which were published until February 2005) and the individual case summaries on the archived Office of Fair Trading website linked at www.oft. gov.uk/advice_and_resources/publications/guidance/unfair-terms-consumer/

[265] *Unfair Contract Terms* Guidance (OFT311) (September 2008), 10.

that it has the potential for unfairness if it is likely to be unintelligible to consumers and thereby cause detriment, or if it is misleading . . . Moreover, consumers need adequate time to read terms before becoming bound by them, especially lengthy or complex terms, and this can also be a factor in assessing fairness.'[266] The importance of transparency has subsequently been reflected in section 64 of the 2015 Act to which we now turn.

(iv) Exclusion from assessment for fairness: main subject-matter and appropriateness of price provided transparent and prominent

Section 64 of the Consumer Rights Act 2015 contains an important exclusion from the assessment of the fairness of a term. It lays down that, provided a term is 'transparent and prominent',[267] and not a term listed in Part 1 of Schedule 2,[268] it cannot be assessed for fairness to the extent that '(a) it specifies the main subject matter of the contract, or (b) the assessment is of the appropriateness of the price payable under the contract by comparison with the goods, digital content or services supplied under it.'[269]

Section 64 therefore seeks to make a distinction between terms containing the substance of the bargain and other terms. The very similar exclusion from the 1994 and 1999 Regulations, which preceded section 64, has been referred to in shorthand (with some danger of inaccuracy) as excluding the core terms or (and this will here be used) as the 'core exclusion'.[270] The Office of Fair Trading considered that the purpose of the core exclusion was 'to allow freedom of contract to prevail in relation to terms that are genuinely central to the bargain between consumer and supplier' and it saw the core exclusion as 'conditional upon such terms being expressed and presented in such a way as to ensure that they are, or at least are capable of being, at the forefront of the consumer's mind in deciding whether to enter the contract'.[271]

The House of Lords has held that a provision concerning the rate of interest to be paid on a breach of contract neither defined the main subject of the contract nor realistically concerned the adequacy of the price.[272] To construe such a provision as falling within the core exclusion would mean that almost any provision containing any part of the bargain would be capable of falling within the reach of the core exclusion and would leave 'a gaping hole in the system' of protection.[273] Similarly it has been held that an increase in an estate agent's commission if the sum was not paid within ten days of completion of the sale was not within the core exclusion (which was then contained in regulation 6(2) of the 1999 Regulations) so that it could be struck down

---

[266] *Ibid*, 10–11.

[267] Consumer Rights Act 2015, s 64(2).

[268] Consumer Rights Act 2015, s 64(6).

[269] Consumer Rights Act 2015, s 64(1).

[270] *Director-General of Fair Trading v First National Bank plc* [2001] UKHL 52, [2002] 1 AC 481 at [12] (Lord Bingham).

[271] *Unfair Contract Terms Guidance* (OFT311) (September 2008) para 19.13.

[272] *Director-General of Fair Trading v First National Bank plc* [2001] UKHL 52, [2002] 1 AC 481 at [12], [34], [43], [64].

[273] *Ibid* at [34].

by an application of the unfairness test.[274] In Gross J's words, 'Regulation 6(2) must be given a restrictive interpretation; otherwise a coach and horses could be driven through the Regulations'.[275] Again, a narrow interpretation of regulation 6(2) was taken in deciding that a gym membership, requiring a member to pay for a minimum membership period, even though he or she wished to withdraw, was an unfair term under the 1999 Regulations.[276]

In contrast, the Supreme Court in *Office of Fair Trading v Abbey National plc*[277] held that terms levying bank charges on personal current account customers in respect of unauthorized overdrafts fell within regulation 6(2)(b) and (assuming 'in plain, intelligible language')[278] could not therefore be assessed for fairness in terms of the appropriateness of the amount of the charges.[279] This was a somewhat surprising decision because one would have expected the Supreme Court to be anxious not to give the core exclusion a wide meaning so that the unfairness of the charges could be assessed. While accepting the Supreme Court's warning that, especially in the context of regulation 6(2)(b) dealing with price, the shorthand language of 'core terms' was no substitute for construing the words of the regulation directly, the way was open to regard the overdraft charges as not part of the price for banking services because most customers do not incur such charges. For most customers the price provided for banking services is through the use the bank has of the customer's money while paying little interest for it; and charges for unauthorized overdrafts are regarded as ancillary to that. There was no need to regard as relevant that the system of 'free-in-credit' banking is subsidized from unauthorized bank charges (those charges, apparently, amounting to 30 per cent of a bank's revenue stream).

It is not absolutely clear what difference, if any, has been made by the differently formulated core exclusion in section 64 of the 2015 Act although it is understood that the intention was to reverse the *Abbey National* decision. Certainly subsequent to *Abbey National*, the European Court of Justice has taken a narrow view of the core exclusion.[280]

The core exclusion further requires that the term is 'transparent and prominent'.[281] A term is transparent 'if it is expressed in plain and intelligible language and (in the case of a written term) is legible'.[282] A term is prominent 'if it is brought to the consumer's attention in such a way that an average consumer would be aware of the

---

[274] *Bairstow Eves London Central Ltd v Smith* [2004] EWHC 263, [2004] 2 EGLR 25.   [275] *Ibid* at [25].

[276] *Office of Fair Trading v Ashbourne Management Service Ltd* [2011] EWHC 1237 (Ch).

[277] [2009] UKSC 6, [2009] 3 WLR 1215.

[278] There was no additional requirement under the 1994 or 1999 Regulations that the term should be prominent as well as transparent.

[279] The Supreme Court stressed that it was consistent with its decision that the fairness of the bank charges could still be challenged for reasons other than the appropriateness of the amount of the charges. But it is very hard to see what room for challenge was realistically being left open.

[280] C-26/13 *Kásler v OTP Jelzálogbank Zrt* (30 April 2014) [2014] 2 All ER (Comm) 443; C-143/13 *Matei v SC Volksbank România SA* (26 February 2015) [2015] 1 WLR 2385.

[281] Consumer Rights Act 2015, s 64(2).   [282] Consumer Rights Act 2015, s 64(3).

term'.[283] An 'average consumer' means 'a consumer who is reasonably well-informed, observant and circumspect'.[284]

The core exclusion is also inapplicable to a term listed in Part 1 of Schedule 2 to the 2015 Act.[285]

(v) Significant imbalance and good faith: procedural or substantive unfairness?

(a) Significant imbalance. The basic question whether a term causes a significant imbalance in the parties' rights and obligations is primarily concerned with the substantive fairness of the contract.[286] For instance, a term which gives a significant advantage to the seller or supplier without a countervailing benefit to the consumer (such as a price reduction) might fail to satisfy this part of the test of an unfair term. Despite this, it is submitted that, for the reasons given below,[287] the test as a whole will in practice be primarily concerned with procedural fairness, unfair surprise, and the absence of real choice.

The meaning of 'significant imbalance' (under the 1994 Regulations) was considered by the House of Lords in *Director General of Fair Trading v First National Bank plc*. The case concerned the fairness of a term in a bank's loan agreement that, should the borrower default on his repayments, interest would continue to be payable at the contractual rate until any judgment was satisfied. Delegated legislation provided that no statutory interest was payable on a county court judgment given in proceedings to recover money under an agreement regulated by the Consumer Credit Act 1974. It was argued that in these circumstances it was unfair to allow the recovery of contractual interest because that would expose the borrower to further liability after all the instalments the Court ordered him to pay had been paid in full. Lord Bingham stated that:

> the requirement of significant imbalance is met if a term is so weighted in favour of the supplier as to tilt the parties' rights and obligations under the contract significantly in his favour. This may be by the granting to the supplier of a beneficial option or discretion or power, or by the imposing on the consumer of a disadvantageous burden or risk or duty.[288]

The House of Lords upheld the term. It held that the essential bargain in a bank loan is to make available funds which will be repaid with interest until full repayment. There was nothing unbalanced or detrimental to the consumer in requiring interest to be paid after judgment; indeed the absence of such a term would unbalance the contract to the detriment of the lender.[289] Their Lordships considered that any unfairness in exposing the borrower to further liability after judgment was due to the fact that the judgment did not cover the whole of the indebtedness, not from any inherent unfairness in the contractual term.

---

[283] Consumer Rights Act 2015, s 64(4).   [284] Consumer Rights Act 2015, s 64(5).
[285] Consumer Rights Act 2015, s 64(6). See above pp 223–4.
[286] *Director General of Fair Trading v First National Bank plc* [2001] UKHL 52, [2002] 1 AC 481 at [37]
(Lord Steyn).   [287] Below, p 230.
[288] [2001] UKHL 52, [2002] 1 AC 481, at [17].   [289] *Ibid* at [22]–[24], [38], [55]–[57].

(b) Good faith.   The significant imbalance must be contrary to the requirement of good faith. In *Director General of Fair Trading v First National Bank plc* Lord Bingham stated that good faith looked to good standards of commercial morality and practice. The House of Lords held that the requirement of 'good faith' sought to promote fair and open dealing, and to prevent unfair surprise and the absence of real choice. Lord Bingham stated that 'openness requires that the terms should be expressed fully, clearly and legibly, containing no concealed pitfalls or traps',[290] and the Court of Appeal in that case stated that 'terms must be reasonably transparent and must not operate to defeat the reasonable expectations of the consumer' who 'should be put in a position where he can make an informed choice'.[291] While that case was concerned with the 1994 Regulations, the position should be the same under Part 2 of the Consumer Rights Act 2015.

Guidance may also be provided by Recital 16 of the Preamble to the Directive. This states that, in making an assessment of 'good faith', account should be taken of the strength of bargaining positions of the parties, whether the consumer had an inducement to agree to the term, and whether the goods were sold or supplied to the consumer's special order. It would appear that, as a matter of EU law,[292] these factors are useful in applying the test of good faith even though they have not been set out in the Consumer Rights Act 2015.[293] These factors look much like some of the guidelines to the reasonableness test in the 1977 Act.[294]

Recital 16 also states that the requirement of 'good faith' is satisfied where the seller or supplier 'deals fairly and equitably with the other party whose legitimate interests he also takes into account'. The implication is that where the other party's legitimate interests are not taken into account, the requirement will not be satisfied. This is in contrast to the common law position since, as Lord Ackner's speech in *Walford v Miles*[295] shows, parties to a contractual negotiation are generally considered to be in an adversarial relationship in which they are entitled to pursue their own interests so long as they avoid making misrepresentations.

In an important decision, the Court of Justice in *Aziz v Caixa d'Estalvis de Catalunya, Tarragona i Manresa*[296] laid down that 'the national court must assess for those purposes [ie assessing good faith] whether the seller or supplier, dealing fairly and equitably with the consumer, could reasonably assume that the consumer would have agreed to such a term in individual contract negotiations'.[297] In applying the test of fairness in the 1999 Regulations, the Supreme Court in *ParkingEye Ltd v Beavis*[298] relied on that decision of the Court of Justice for guidance. The matter in

---

[290] *Ibid.*   [291] [2000] QB 672, 687.
[292] *Marleasing SA v La Commercial* (Case C-106/89) [1992] 1 CMLR 305 permits reference to be made to the Directive and probably also to the preamble (and hence to the recitals) in interpreting the 2015 Act.
[293] They were set out in the 1994 Regulations but not in the 1999 Regulations.
[294] Above, p 217.
[295] [1992] 2 AC 128, 138, above, p 68.   [296] C-415/11 (March 14, 2013), [2013] 3 CMLR 5.
[297] *Ibid* at [69].   [298] [2015] UKSC 67, [2015] 3 WLR 1373.

issue was the fairness of a clearly displayed charge of £85 for car parking beyond a free period of time. The Supreme Court, in deciding that the term was fair,[299] specifically considered how one should apply the approach in *Aziz* of asking whether the supplier could reasonably have assumed that the consumer would have agreed to such a term had it been negotiated. Lords Neuberger and Sumption concluded as follows: 'a hypothetical reasonable motorist would have agreed to objectively reasonable terms, and these terms are objectively reasonable.'[300] It is noteworthy that much of the more detailed reasoning relied on in deciding that the term imposing the parking charge was fair was similar to that relied on in deciding that the term was not a penalty at common law.[301]

(c) Procedural or substantive fairness?   How should courts in this jurisdiction proceed to put flesh on the bare bones of the elements of 'good faith' and 'significant imbalance', which have been said to overlap substantially?[302] There are a number of possibilities. First, although good faith is not a concept wholly unfamiliar to English lawyers, its conceptual roots lie in the civil law systems and reference might be made to those systems. However, their concepts of good faith differ radically. They range from French law's substantive use of the concept to avoid unreasonable and onerous conditions, to the more procedural notions of unfair surprise and absence of real choice which characterize Dutch and German law.[303] Alternatively, the statutory concept of 'reasonableness' in the 1977 Act might be deployed, perhaps reinforced by support from the equitable concept of unconscionability considered in Chapter 10 below[304] and the rules on penalty and forfeiture clauses considered in Chapter 17 below.[305] This gains some support from the similarity of the guidelines in Recital 16 of the preamble to the Directive to those in the 1977 Act.[306] Finally, an autonomous European Union concept of 'good faith' could be developed.[307] This last appears to have been the favoured approach in *Director General of Fair Trading v First National Bank plc*. It was stated that one of the objectives of the Directive was partially to

---

[299] *Ibid* at [102]–[114], [200]–[213], [289], [291]. Lord Toulson, at [295]–[315], dissented on this point.

[300] *Ibid* at [109].   [301] *Ibid* at [104]. See below pp 598–600.

[302] *Director-General of Fair Trading v First National Bank plc* [2000] QB 672; [2001] UKHL 52, [2002] 1 AC 481 at [37] (Lord Steyn).

[303] Beale, in Beatson and Friedmann (eds), *Good Faith and Fault in Contract Law* (1995) 243–5 cites inter alia, on French law, Ghestin, *Le Contrat: Formation* (2nd edn, 1988) para 608-2; on Dutch law, Storme, *La bonne foi dans la formation des contrats en droit néerlandais* (1992); decision of the Hoge Raad HR 15-11-1957; Art 6.233 of the New Netherlands Civil Code; on German law BGB para 242; Micklitz (1989) 41 Rev int droit comparé 101, 109. See also Lando and Beale, *Principles of European Contract Law Parts I and II* (2000) 116–19.

[304] At pp 400–7.   [305] At pp 598–605.

[306] Unfair Contract Terms Act 1977, s 11 and Sched 2.

[307] See MacNeil (1995) 40 Jur Rev 146, 148, citing *Fiddelaar v Commission* (Case 44/59) [1960] ECR 535, 547; Weatherill, *EC Consumer Law and Policy* (1997) 82. Cf *Chitty on Contracts* (32nd edn, 2015) para 00-000. See also *Principles, Definitions and Model Rules of European Private Law: Draft Common Frame of Reference (DCFR), Outline Edition* (2009) 43–4, 76, 77, 85–7 and arts I.-1:1:102(3)(b), 103 (definition of 'good faith and fair dealing'); cf Whittaker (2009) 125 LQR 616, 640–4.

harmonize the law among all member states of the European Union and that the
language used in expressing the test is clear and not reasonably capable of differing
interpretations.[308]

What then is this autonomous European Union concept of 'good faith'? There is
clearly a substantive component in the test and the controlling concept of 'significant
imbalance' is primarily a substantive one. The fact that some clauses may cause such
a serious imbalance that they should always be treated as being contrary to good
faith,[309] also has a substantive flavour. Moreover, Lord Steyn has stated that 'any purely
procedural or even predominantly procedural interpretation of the requirement of
good faith must be rejected'.[310] Lord Bingham's statement that fair dealing requires that
a supplier should not 'deliberately or unconsciously take advantage of the consumer's
necessity, indigence, lack of experience, unfamiliarity with the subject matter of the
contract, or weak bargaining position'[311] also suggests a substantive concept.

It is, however, submitted that most commentators are correct in considering the test
as a whole to be primarily concerned with procedural fairness.[312] The core exclusion
requiring that terms concerning the price and defining the main subject-matter of the
contract are left out of account (provided they are transparent and prominent) makes
it difficult to regard the test as primarily substantive, because those terms, particularly
'price', are central to substantial fairness.[313] Moreover, the absence of any absolutely
prohibited terms and the fact that 'the indicative and non-exhaustive list of the terms
which may be regarded as unfair' are couched in an open-textured way also suggest
that the test under the 2015 Act is not primarily concerned with substantive fairness
but with the prevention of unfair surprise and the absence of real choice. So the Courts
are likely to be primarily concerned with the requirements of openness which, as
stated by Lord Bingham, are that the terms should be expressed fully, clearly, and
legibly, should contain no concealed pitfalls or traps, and should accord appropriate
prominence to terms which might operate disadvantageously to the customer.[314] This
is also supported by the decision of the Court of Justice in *Aziz v Caixa d'Estalvis de
Catalunya, Tarragona i Manresa*[315] referred to above.

To this extent, the result achieved is not likely to be very different to that under
the 1977 Act albeit in the more limited context of terms excluding or limiting

---

[308] *Director-General of Fair Trading v First National Bank plc* [2001] UKHL 52, [2002] 1 AC 481 at [17].
See also *ibid* at [32], [45]. See also the reliance on *Aziz v Caixa d'Estalvis de Catalunya, Tarragona i Manresa*
C-415/11 (14 March 2013), [2013] 3 CMLR 5 in *ParkingEye Ltd v Beavis* [2015] UKSC 67, [2015] 3 WLR 1373.
[309] Beale, in Beatson and Friedmann (eds), *Good Faith and Fault in Contract Law* (1995) 245. Some of the
terms contained in the indicative list of terms which might be regarded as unfair may fall into this category,
eg excluding or limiting liability for death or personal injury, making the seller or supplier's duty to perform
a matter for its discretion, or giving it the right to determine whether the goods or services are in conformity
with the contract or the exclusive right to interpret any term: see Sched 2 to the 2015 Act.
[310] [2001] UKHL 52, [2002] 1 AC 481 at [36].   [311] *Ibid* at [17].
[312] Beale, in Beatson and Friedmann (eds), *Good Faith and Fault in Contract Law* (1995) ch 9. Cf Smith
(1994) 47 CLP 5, 8.
[313] Collins (1994) 14 OJLS 229, 249.
[314] *Director-General of Fair Trading v First National Bank plc* [2001] UKHL 52, [2002] 1 AC 481 at [17].
[315] C-415/11 (March 14, 2013), see p 228.

liability.[316] The experience of administrative enforcement by the Office of Fair Trading also suggests that there will not be a sharp difference from that previously taken in English law under the 1977 Act. In part this is because of the similarity of the problems, but in part it is because of an understandable tendency to retreat to familiar ground when confronted by unfamiliar concepts on which there is little guidance.

(vi) Effect of term being held to be unfair

An unfair term 'shall not be binding on the consumer'.[317] This means that the term is enforceable by, but not against, the consumer. Moreover, 'the contract continues, so far as practicable, to have effect in every other respect'.[318] This gives the Courts a broad discretion to sever the unfair term but presumably this will not be possible where the unfair term is a 'core term' which has failed the requirement of being transparent and prominent.

(vii) Terms must be transparent

Apart from the role of transparency in relation to the test of fairness (we have already seen in our discussion of the 'core exclusion' that the immunity of a term defining the main subject-matter of the contract or the appropriateness of the price will be lost if it is not transparent and prominent), section 68 of the Consumer Rights Act 2015 separately requires a trader to ensure that any written term of a contract is transparent. This means that it must be expressed in plain, intelligible language and must be legible. Insofar as this is a separate requirement from fairness as assessed by the courts, it is enforceable by the Competition and Markets Authority (and other regulators). It is to enforcement of the Consumer Rights Act 2015 by regulators that we finally turn.

(viii) Prevention of unfair and non-transparent terms

The Consumer Rights Act 2015 gives the Competition and Markets Authority (CMA), a role previously carried out by the Office of Fair Trading and a number of other bodies (eg weights and measures authorities, utility regulators, and the Consumers' Association) power to apply for an injunction to prevent a person using, or recommending the use of, an unfair or non-transparent term in contracts concluded with consumers.[319] Normally, however, cases are resolved by the CMA

---

[316] Dean (1994) 56 MLR 581, 585. For a general view that the common law reaches similar results to those that would be reached in civil law by the application of 'good faith', see Bingham LJ's judgment in *Interfoto Picture Library Ltd v Stiletto Visual Programmes Ltd* [1989] QB 433. See also *Balfour Beatty Civil Engineering v Docklands Light Railway* [1996] CLC 1435, 1442.

[317] Consumer Rights Act 2015, s 62(1).   [318] Consumer Rights Act 2015, s 67.

[319] Consumer Rights Act 2015, s 70 and Sched 3. In *Office of Fair Trading v Foxtons Ltd* [2009] EWCA Civ 288, [2010] 1 WLR 663, it was held (Moore-Bick LJ largely dissenting on this) that, on a general challenge by the Office of Fair Trading, the Office was entitled to an injunction or declaration against an estate agent in respect of an unfair term in existing, as well as future, contracts; and that that relief did not necessarily preclude a judge deciding that that term was fair as between a consumer and the estate agent in an individual challenge.

accepting informal undertakings to amend the offending terms in lieu of Court proceedings. The CMA applies the same test of fairness as a Court but looks forward rather than backwards and considers the circumstances that are generally likely to obtain, not those attending the conclusion of a particular contract.[320] The CMA and the qualifying bodies have wide powers to obtain documents and information.[321] If the CMA considers a relevant complaint but decides not to make an application for an injunction it must give reasons for its decision to the person who made the complaint.[322]

A similar regime is applicable more generally under Part 8 of the Enterprise Act 2002. This gives the CMA and other bodies (eg weights and measures authorities) powers to enforce certain consumer legislation, including the Consumer Rights Act 2015. An 'enforcement order'[323] may be made although it is envisaged that compliance will normally be secured by negotiation[324] and undertakings.[325]

(c) OTHER LEGISLATIVE CONTROLS ON EXEMPTION CLAUSES AND UNFAIR TERMS

The exclusion or restriction of liability for misrepresentation is controlled by section 3 of the Misrepresentation Act 1967 in the case of non-consumer contracts. This is dealt with in Chapter 9.[326] In some other legislation, terms, by which a party purports to contract out of legislative provisions protecting consumers or others, are invalid. Examples of such legislation include, for example, those dealing with consumer credit,[327] product liability,[328] dangerous goods,[329] defective premises,[330] package holidays,[331] timeshare contracts,[332] and carriage by land,[333] sea,[334] or air.[335]

As regards unfair terms apart from exemption clauses, perhaps the most important other legislation (ie aside from the Unfair Contract Terms Act 1977 and the Consumer Rights Act 2015) is the Consumer Credit Act 1974, sections 140A–140D. Those provisions protect against exploitation of the claimant's need for credit by giving the Courts a wide range of remedies to undo credit agreements where the relationship between the creditor and the debtor is unfair to the debtor.[336]

---

[320] eg *Unfair Contract Terms*, Office of Fair Trading Bulletin No 4 (December 1997) 21.

[321] Consumer Rights Act 2015, s 77 and Sched 5.

[322] Consumer Rights Act 2015, Sched 3, para 2(3).   [323] Enterprise Act 2002, ss 214–218.

[324] Enterprise Act 2002, s 214.   [325] Enterprise Act 2002, s 219.   [326] See below, p 352.

[327] Consumer Credit Act 1974, s 173(1).   [328] Consumer Protection Act 1987, s 7.

[329] Consumer Protection Act 1987, s 41(4).   [330] Defective Premises Act 1972, s 6(3).

[331] Package Travel, Package Holidays and Package Tours Regulations (SI 1992 No 3288), reg 15(5).

[332] Timeshare, Holiday Products, Resale and Exchange Contracts Regulations 2010 (SI 2010 No 2960), reg 19.

[333] Carriage of Goods by Road Act 1965; Railways (Convention on International Carriage by Rail) Regulations 2005 (SI 2005 No 2092).

[334] Carriage of Goods by Sea Act 1971; Merchant Shipping Act 1995.

[335] Carriage by Air Act 1961.

[336] See, eg, *Scotland v British Credit Trust Ltd* [2014] EWCA Civ 790, [2015] 1 All ER 708; *Plevin v Paragon Personal Finance Ltd* [2014] UKSC 61, [2014] 1 WLR 4222.

FURTHER READING

ADAMS and BROWNSWORD, 'The Unfair Contract Terms Act: A Decade of Discretion' (1988) 104 LQR 94

BRIGHT, 'Winning the Battle Against Unfair Terms' (2000) 20 LS 331

PEEL, 'Whither Contra Proferentem?' in BURROWS and PEEL (eds), *Contract Terms* (Oxford: Oxford University Press, 2007) 53

BRIGHT, 'Unfairness and the Consumer Contract Regulations' in BURROWS and PEEL (eds), *Contract Terms* (Oxford: Oxford University Press, 2007) 173

BEALE, 'Exclusion and Limitation Clauses in Business Contracts: Transparency' in BURROWS and PEEL (eds), *Contract Terms* (Oxford: Oxford University Press, 2007) 191

PART 3

FACTORS TENDING TO DEFEAT CONTRACTUAL LIABILITY

7

INCAPACITY

1. GROUNDS OF CONTRACTUAL INCAPACITY

The law limits the capacity of certain persons to bind themselves by contract. These persons are:

(1) the Crown and public authorities;

(2) corporations;

(3) minors;

(4) persons lacking mental capacity and drunken persons.

The consequences of contractual incapacity are not identical. In some cases the contract is void, in others voidable, while in others it is unenforceable at the suit of one or both parties.

The underlying policy of rules limiting contractual capacity is to protect those under the incapacity. In the case of public authorities the policy seeks to protect the public finances and taxpayers, and, in the case of companies, investors and creditors. We shall see that this protective policy can inflict hardship upon those who deal with an incapacitated person in good faith and in ignorance of the lack of capacity. Moreover, before the recent recognition of independent restitutionary obligations,[1] an incapacitated party to whom money had been paid or property transferred might have been unjustly enriched at the expense of the other. The practical importance of the limitations on contractual capacity has been reduced. In the case of minors this is the result of the reduction in the age of majority from 21 to 18. In the case of local authorities and companies there has been substantial statutory modification of the *ultra vires* doctrine so as to make many contracts enforceable,[2] thus enhancing security of transactions between local authorities and companies and those who deal with them. Moreover, the development of the law of restitution means that, even where the contract is void or unenforceable, money paid and property transferred

---

[1] *Lipkin Gorman v Karpnale Ltd* [1991] 2 AC 548, above, p 25.
[2] For the principle of the common law that the public authority or company cannot act 'beyond its powers' (*ultra vires*) see below, pp 242, 247.

will, in general, be recoverable, unless this would amount to indirect enforcement of the contract.[3]

2. THE CROWN AND PUBLIC AUTHORITIES

At common law the Crown (acting in its own right or through the agency of others) has unlimited capacity to enter into contracts[4] although, as will be explained below, the peculiar public nature of the Crown affects the scope of obligations undertaken and their enforceability. Other public authorities, however, are created by statute and their capacity to contract depends upon statutory authority, express or implied, while also being subject to special rules of public law.

(a) THE CROWN

(i) Application of public law

Since the passing of the Crown Proceedings Act 1947, actions by or against the Crown or a government department in contract are, for the most part, governed by the same rules of procedure as actions between subjects[5] and the same remedies are available, save that no injunction or order of specific performance can be made against the Crown in 'civil proceedings'.[6] Crown contracts are subject to the procurement procedures and remedies required by European Union law, which are considered later in this chapter.[7]

Although contracts made with government departments or Crown officers are not subject to the *ultra vires* doctrine,[8] rules which arise from the fact that such bodies have statutory and prerogative powers and duties of a public law nature affect contracts made by them. In both Crown contracts and the contracts of public authorities, it is therefore necessary to consider these public law rules as well as the common law and statutory position.

---

[3] *Westdeutsche Landesbank Girozentrale v Islington LBC* [1994] 1 WLR 938, aff'd [1996] AC 669, below, pp 246, 250.

[4] Wade & Forsyth, *Administrative Law* (11th edn, 2014) 180; Turpin, *Government Contracts* (1989) 19.

[5] See generally Wade & Forsyth, *Administrative Law* (11th edn, 2014) 701–6; Arrowsmith, *The Law of Public and Utilities Procurement* (3rd edn, vol 1, 2014; vol 2 expected May 2016).

[6] Crown Proceedings Act 1947, s 21 (the Court may instead make an order declaratory of the rights of the parties). Although injunctive relief may be given in proceedings for judicial review (*M v Home Office* [1994] 1 AC 377), judicial review is not generally available for disputes concerning contracts: *Mercury Energy Ltd v Electricity Corp of New Zealand Ltd* [1994] 1 WLR 521 (New Zealand); cf *Williams Construction Ltd v Blackman* [1995] 1 WLR 102 (Barbados).

[7] Below, pp 245–6.

[8] But the powers of certain Ministers have been defined by statute (eg Supply Powers Act 1975; Ministers of the Crown Act 1975) which may limit the capacity of the Crown (*Cudgen Rutile (No 2) Pty Ltd v Chalk* [1975] AC 520 (Australia)) or the authority of its agents (below, p 242).

(ii) Parliamentary funds

In *Churchward v The Queen*[9] the Admiralty undertook to pay £18,000 a year to C for the carriage of cross-channel mails from Dover to Calais and Ostend. Appropriation of funds for this contract was expressly forbidden by Parliament. C sued for the promised sum but failed on the ground that the contract provided for payment to be 'out of moneys to be provided by parliament' and no such moneys were provided. Shee J went further, stating that 'the providing of funds by parliament is a condition precedent to [the covenant] attaching'. On the basis of this *dictum* it has been said that 'all obligations to pay money undertaken by the Crown are subject to the implied condition that the funds necessary to satisfy the obligation shall be appropriated by Parliament',[10] but the better view is that the Crown is under no antecedent incapacity in this respect. The existence of the contract does not depend upon Parliamentary authority, and the provision of funds is simply a condition to be fulfilled before actual payment by the Crown, a condition that is satisfied where there is a fund in existence out of which payment can lawfully be made.[11]

(iii) Fettering future executive action

It is an important principle of public law that public bodies, including the Crown, should preserve the discretionary powers granted to them by statute or the prerogative, and not divest themselves of those powers.[12] This principle may conflict, however, with the principle of sanctity of contracts. In *Rederiaktiebolaget Amphitrite v The King* Rowlatt J stated that 'It is not competent for the Government to fetter its future executive action, which must necessarily be determined by the needs of the community when the question arises. It cannot by contract hamper its freedom of action in matters which concern the welfare of the State'.[13] In that case:

During the First World War the British legation in Stockholm promised the Swedish owners of the ship *Amphitrite* that, if the ship sailed to England with an approved cargo, she would not be detained. The ship was nevertheless detained and her owners brought a petition of right against the Crown claiming damages for breach of contract.

Rowlatt J held that the guarantee was not a contract for the breach of which damages could be sued for in a court of law; it was merely an expression of intention to act in a particular way in a certain event, because the Crown could not fetter its future executive action by contract.

Rowlatt J's statement has been powerfully criticized on the ground that it is expressed too generally.[14] Three issues must be separated; first, the validity of the contract *ab initio*;

---

[9] (1865) LR 1 QB 173, 210.
[10] *New South Wales v The Commonwealth (No 1)* (1932) 46 CLR 155, 176 (Australia); *A-G v Great Southern and Western Ry Co of Ireland* [1925] AC 754, 773.
[11] *New South Wales v Bardolph* (1934) 52 CLR 455, 502, 514 (Australia).
[12] See below, pp 243–4, and see generally Wade & Forsyth, *Administrative Law* (11th edn, 2014) 259 ff.
[13] [1921] 3 KB 500, 503.
[14] *Robertson v Minister of Pensions* [1949] 1 KB 227, 230 (Denning J); *Ansett Transport Industries (Operations) Pty Ltd v Commonwealth* (1977) 139 CLR 54, 74, 113–14 (Australia); *A v Hayden (No 2)*

secondly, whether, assuming the contract is valid, the Crown is thereafter under a duty to exercise its powers in a manner consistent with it; and thirdly, whether, assuming there is no valid contract, the Crown is nevertheless precluded from exercising its discretion in a particular way by an estoppel or the application of the emerging public law principle of legitimate expectation.[15]

As far as the first issue is concerned, Rowlatt J acknowledged that the Crown can bind itself by a commercial contract.[16] *The Amphitrite* was not such a case, but the distinction between 'commercial' and 'non-commercial' contracts has been criticized as unworkable in practice because commercial contracts tend to conflict with 'governmental' obligations,[17] and it is difficult to see how, for instance, procurement contracts involving large capital expenditure are to be classified.

Where a Crown contract has been validly entered into, the Crown's freedom to exercise its discretionary powers (whether statutory or prerogative) will not, as a matter of construction, be impliedly excluded by the contract. Even in the case of commercial contracts, the Crown must be free to exercise the discretionary powers conferred upon it for the public good. 'No one can imagine, for example, that when the Crown makes a contract which could not be fulfilled in time of war, it is pledging itself not to declare war for so long as the contract lasts.'[18] Thus, it has been held that an *implied* covenant for quiet enjoyment in a Crown lease did not prevent the Crown from requisitioning the premises.[19] The Crown must be at liberty to detain ships, to requisition property, or to perform other essential acts in time of war, and, although the position of an *express* undertaking is less clear,[20] it is submitted that 'no contract would be enforced in any case where some essential governmental activity would be thereby rendered impossible or seriously impeded'.[21] Furthermore, in such cases, a party is unlikely to be able to invoke the principle of estoppel; it is generally recognized that 'estoppel cannot be allowed to hinder the formation of government policy'.[22] Nor can the principle of legitimate expectation be used to fetter the formation or change of policy.[23] The Crown may, however, be vicariously liable for torts committed by its

---

(1984) 56 ALR 82, 86 (Australia). But see *Commissioners of Crown Lands v Page* [1960] 2 QB 274, 287–8 (Lord Evershed MR).

[15] Below, p 244.

[16] [1921] 3 KB 500, 503. An estoppel may arise to prevent both parties from refusing to proceed with such a contract: *A-G of Hong Kong v Humphreys Estate (Queen's Gardens) Ltd* [1987] AC 114, 127–8 (Hong Kong).

[17] Mitchell, *The Contracts of Public Authorities* (1954) 62. See also *Ansett Transport Industries (Operations) Pty Ltd v Commonwealth* (1977) 139 CLR 54, 113 (Aickin J).

[18] *Commissioners of Crown Lands v Page* [1960] 2 QB 274, 292 (Devlin LJ).   [19] *Ibid.*

[20] Devlin LJ, *ibid*, 292 thought nothing turned on this and said that even an express covenant 'must by necessary implication be read to exclude those measures affecting the nation as a whole which the Crown takes for the public good', but Evershed MR and Ormrod LJ reserved their position. Devlin LJ's view is inferentially supported in *Ansett Transport Industries (Operations) Pty Ltd v Commonwealth* (above, n 14).

[21] Mitchell, *The Contracts of Public Authorities* (1954) 7. Cf Holdsworth (1929) 45 LQR 166.

[22] *Laker Airways Ltd v Department of Trade* [1977] QB 643, 709 (Roskill LJ), 728 (Lawton LJ); see also at 680–2, 707.

[23] *Hughes v DHSS* [1985] AC 776; Wade & Forsyth, *Administrative Law* (11th edn, 2014) 319–20.

servants or agents, which will include liability for negligent misstatements, although this does not extend to anything done under the prerogative or statutory powers.[24]

In practice the rule stated in *The Amphitrite* does not often have to be applied since many contracts falling within its scope contain cancellation clauses which usually make provision for compensation.[25]

(iv) Liability of Crown to employees

The general rule is that persons in Crown employment hold office during the pleasure of the Crown, and at common law Crown servants can be dismissed at any time by the Crown and no action lies for wrongful dismissal.[26] In the older cases the reason given for this rule was that the relationship between the Crown and its servants is not one of contract at all, but of status.[27] But more recently it has been said that 'there is nothing unconstitutional about civil servants being employed by the Crown pursuant to contracts of service'.[28] The modern and better view is that there can be a valid contract of employment, although this is always determinable at the pleasure of the Crown.[29] The older cases may reflect the absence of an intention to contract on the part of the Crown. Although it has been held that the use of language of obligation or even of the word 'contract' did not suffice to indicate an intention by the Crown to enter into a contractual relationship,[30] it has been held that a civil servant had a contract of employment, where his appointment was subject to the Civil Service Pay and Conditions of Service Code which stated that 'a civil servant does not have a contract of employment enforceable in the courts but rather a letter of appointment'. Objectively construed, the appointment created a relationship which the Crown must have intended to constitute a contract of employment.[31]

Whether or not the relation is contractual, the power of the Crown to dismiss at pleasure without payment of compensation is now limited by statute. The remedies available for unfair dismissal now contained in the Employment Rights Act 1996 extend to Crown employees, including members of the military services.[32] The Crown is also liable in tort for breach of the duties normally owed by an employer to its servants or agents.[33]

---

[24] Crown Proceedings Act 1947, ss 2(1)(a), 11.   [25] See generally Turpin (above, n 4, 243–6).

[26] *Shenton v Smith* [1895] AC 229; *Dunn v The Queen* [1896] 1 QB 116; *Terrell v Secretary of State for the Colonies* [1953] 2 QB 482; *Riordan v War Office* [1959] 1 WLR 1046; *A-G for Guyana v Nobrega* [1969] 3 All ER 1064. Cf *Reilly v The King* [1934] AC 176, 179; *Terrell v Secretary of State for the Colonies* [1953] 2 QB 482, 498–9 (where the terms of an appointment definitely prescribe a term and expressly provide for a power to determine 'for cause', the implication that the appointment is at pleasure is excluded).

[27] *Shenton v Smith* [1895] AC 229; *Inland Revenue Commissioners v Hambrook* [1956] 2 QB 641.

[28] *R v Civil Service Appeal Board, ex p Bruce* [1988] ICR 649, 660 (May LJ), aff'd [1989] ICR 171.

[29] *Kodeeswaran v A-G of Ceylon* [1970] AC 1111, 1123.

[30] *McClaren v Home Office* [1989] ICR 550, rvsd on different grounds [1990] ICR 824.

[31] *R v Lord Chancellor's Department, ex p Nangle* [1991] ICR 743, 751–2. For general discussion of the requirement of intention to create legal relations see above, pp 73–7.

[32] Employment Rights Act 1996, ss 191, 192. See also Trade Union and Labour Relations (Consolidation) Act 1992, ss 152, 273 (dismissal on grounds of trade union membership, activities, or non-membership).

[33] Crown Proceedings Act 1947, s 2(1)(b).

Although dismissal in breach of the terms of the appointment will not, according to the bulk of the authorities, give rise to a cause of action at common law, it may be susceptible to the public law remedy of judicial review where it is *ultra vires*, an abuse of discretion, or where the principles of procedural fairness have not been observed.[34]

(v) Liability of employees to Crown

Where an intention to contract is established, it is submitted that the Crown can sue its employees for breach of contract.[35] Equitable and restitutionary remedies may also be available against the employees in certain circumstances, such as breach of confidence, or where the employee has profited from a breach of duty.[36]

(vi) Crown agents

If a servant or agent of the Crown enters into an unauthorized contract, the Crown will not be bound unless it has held the agent out to have authority.[37] 'The right to act for the Crown in any particular matter must be established by reference to statute or otherwise.'[38] It is only if the act is within the agent's ostensible authority that the Crown may be estopped from going back on a representation which the agent has made.[39] Furthermore, an agent of the Crown who contracts on behalf of the Crown cannot be sued personally, either on the contract or for breach of warranty of authority.[40]

(b) PUBLIC AUTHORITIES

(i) Doctrine of *ultra vires*

Public authorities whose powers are the product of and defined by statute are subject to the doctrine of *ultra vires*, which is a necessary consequence of the statutory nature of the powers of such authorities. So, at common law the contracts of local authorities will be void unless they relate to functions which the authority is authorized, expressly

---

[34] *R v Secretary of State for the Home Department, ex p Benwell* [1985] QB 554; *Council of Civil Service Unions v Minister for the Civil Service* [1985] AC 374. See also Walsh [1989] PL 131; Fredman and Morris (1991) 107 LQR 298; [1991] PL 485. On estoppel and legitimate expectation, see below, p 244.

[35] Even if there is no contract, the terms are nevertheless deemed to constitute a contract for the purposes of the economic torts: Trade Union and Labour Relations (Consolidation) Act 1992, s 245.

[36] *A-G v Blake* [2001] 1 AC 268; below, p 632.

[37] *A-G for Ceylon v Silva* [1953] AC 461 (Ceylon); *Robertson v Minister of Pensions* [1949] 1 KB 227, 232 (Denning J).

[38] *A-G for Ceylon v Silva*, above, n 37, 479.

[39] *Robertson v Minister of Pensions* [1949] 1 KB 227. But contrast *ibid*, 232, and see *Re L (an infant)* [1971] 3 All ER 743; *Laker Airways Ltd v Department of Trade* [1977] QB 643. See also below, p 244.

[40] *Dunn v Macdonald* [1897] 1 QB 555, criticized by Wade & Forsyth, *Administrative Law* (11th edn, 2014) 700–1. For the position of other agents, see the 29th edition of this work, pp 713, 716.

or impliedly, to perform, or unless the acts are calculated to facilitate, or are incidental to, the discharge of those functions.[41]

The purpose of the *ultra vires* rule is to protect the public funds entrusted to such bodies, in the case of local authorities, by local taxpayers. But it has proved a trap for the unwary and can inflict grave hardship on persons who deal in good faith with an authority in ignorance of its lack of capacity. So banks which participated in housing or recreational schemes by local authorities either as a joint venturer or a guarantor, and other banks which entered into interest rate swaps with local authorities, could not sue on their contracts when they were held to be *ultra vires*.[42] The result was uncertainty and concern that private sector companies would be reluctant to enter into transactions with local authorities.

(ii) Statutory modification of *ultra vires* doctrine

There are two statutory provisions which in substance modify the *ultra vires* doctrine in relation to local authorities. The Localism Act 2011 has the effect of creating a presumption that a local authority has unlimited powers except where there is a specific restriction placed on it by statute.[43] Moreover, in the case of contracts by local authorities for the purposes of or in connection with the discharge of any of their functions which are intended to operate for a period of at least five years, the Local Government (Contracts) Act 1997 provides that where the authority has issued a certificate stating that it has power to enter into the contract and containing information about the statutory provisions conferring the power and the purpose of the contract, the contract has effect 'as if the local authority had had power to enter into it (and had exercised that power properly in entering into it)'.[44] This renders such contracts enforceable, but it is still possible to challenge in judicial review proceedings or an audit of the authority's activities whether the authority had power to enter into a contract or exercised any power properly in entering into a contract.[45]

(iii) Incompatibility with statutory purpose

Those dealing with public authorities may also encounter the rule considered above that a public authority is not competent to fetter a statutory discretion if this would disable it from fulfilling the primary purpose for which it was created: 'if a person or public body is entrusted by the Legislature with certain powers and duties expressly or impliedly for public purposes, those persons or bodies cannot divest themselves of these powers and duties. They cannot enter into any contract or take any action

---

[41] See, eg *Hazell v Hammersmith & Fulham LBC* [1992] 2 AC 1; *Crédit Suisse v Allerdale BC* [1997] QB 306; *Crédit Suisse v Waltham Forest LBC* [1997] QB 362. But see Local Government Act 1972, ss 135, 137.

[42] *Hazell v Hammersmith & Fulham LBC*, above, n 41; *Crédit Suisse v Allerdale BC* and *Crédit Suisse v Waltham Forest LBC*, above, n 41.

[43] Localism Act 2011, s 1 ('A local authority has power to do anything that individuals generally may do'), which is then limited by ss 2–4.

[44] Local Government (Contracts) Act 1997, s 2.   [45] Local Government (Contracts) Act 1997, s 5.

incompatible with the due exercise of their powers or the discharge of their duties'.[46] Thus in *York Corporation v Henry Leetham & Sons Ltd*:[47]

Y entered into a covenant with HL to allow HL to use two rivers which Y maintained and managed under statutory authority in return for an annual payment of £800 in place of the tolls Y that was authorized to charge by the statute.

It was held that this covenant was not one which Y was competent to make because it thereby disabled itself from exercising its statutory powers to increase tolls as necessary in order to perform its statutory duty.

On the other hand, in *Birkdale District Electric Supply Co Ltd v Southport Corporation*:[48]

B, the statutory undertaker for the supply of electricity in Birkdale, was sued by S on an agreement by which B had bound itself not to charge higher prices for electricity than those charged in the borough of Southport. It repudiated this agreement on the ground that it was incompatible with the due discharge of its statutory duties.

The House of Lords held that the agreement was nevertheless binding upon B. It was not wholly incompatible with the fulfilment of the purposes of the statute which empowered B to act as an electricity undertaking. The distinction between this case and the *York Corporation* case is by no means clear but it would seem that a public authority is only incompetent to contract where the contract in question is clearly proved to be incompatible with the full observance of the terms and the full attainment of the purposes for which the statutory powers have been granted. But it possesses contractual capacity where the agreements are mere contracts restricting the undertakers' freedom of action in respect of the business management of their undertaking.[49]

(iv) Estoppel and legitimate expectation

A public authority cannot be estopped by its previous conduct so as to hinder its obligation to carry out its statutory powers or duties. But it has been held that an authority may be estopped in two types of situation. First, where the authority has delegated to its officers the power to determine particular questions, it may be estopped by representations relating to those questions, made by an officer acting within the scope of his ostensible authority, on which another person acts.[50] Secondly, if an authority waives a procedural requirement relating to any application made to it for the exercise of its statutory powers, it may be estopped from relying on lack of formality.[51]

---

[46] *Birkdale District Electric Supply Co Ltd v Southport Corp* [1926] AC 355, 364 (Lord Birkenhead). But see *Lever (Finance) Ltd v Westminster Corp* [1971] 1 QB 222 (estoppel).

[47] [1924] 1 Ch 557. See also *Ayr Harbour Trustees v Oswald* (1883) 8 App Cas 623; *William Cory & Son Ltd v London Corp* [1951] 2 KB 476; *Dowty Boulton Paul Ltd v Wolverhampton Corp* [1971] 1 WLR 204.

[48] [1926] AC 355.   [49] *Ibid*, 369, 370 (Lord Sumner).

[50] *Lever (Finance) Ltd v Westminster Corp* [1971] 1 QB 222 (representation that modification to plan was not material and so did not require further planning permission).

[51] *Western Fish Products Ltd v Penwith DC* [1981] 2 All ER 204, 221 (Megaw LJ: 'The extension of the concept of estoppel beyond these two exceptions, in our judgment, would not be justified').

A public authority may also be under a public law duty to act consistently with an arrangement which does not give rise to a contract or an estoppel, under the principle of legitimate expectation. This is because a person who, as a result of the words or conduct of a public authority, has a legitimate expectation that a benefit will be granted or continue to be enjoyed, may be able to argue that later inconsistent action is an abuse of power and reviewable on the ground of unfairness.[52] Inconsistency is, however, not necessarily unfair, and the Courts will not let an arrangement that has given rise to a legitimate expectation hinder the formation of policy. For example, an authority that has received and resolved to accept a tender from its own workforce might choose to abandon the project or seek fresh tenders.[53]

It has been suggested that, although there is an analogy between a private law estoppel and the public law concept of a legitimate expectation created by a public authority, it is preferable now to rely on the latter, because 'remedies against public authorities also have to take into account the interests of the general public which the authority exists to promote. Public law can also take into account the hierarchy of individual rights which exist under the Human Rights Act 1998'.[54]

(v) Pre-contractual procedures and refusal to contract

Although the general rule, based upon the principle of freedom of contract, is that a person can choose with whom to contract and with whom not to contract,[55] in the case of public authorities this freedom is limited. Both legislation and the regulations implementing European Union Directives on public sector contracts, and the general principles governing the exercise of discretionary powers, may invalidate refusals to contract at all or only on particular terms. Such refusals may be based on a policy that amounts to an improper fetter on an authority's discretion or be 'unfair' in the light of an individual's legitimate expectations. For instance, a decision not to contract with a company in part motivated by the wish to induce it to cease trading with South Africa during the apartheid era was held to be *ultra vires*.[56]

(vi) Statutory and EU controls

Under the Local Government Act 1988, local authorities and certain other public authorities are required to exercise their contracting functions (including

---

[52] *Council for Civil Service Unions v Minister for the Civil Service* [1985] AC 374, 408; *R v North and East Devon Health Authority, ex p Coughlan* [2001] QB 213; Wade & Forsyth, *Administrative Law* (11th edn, 2014) 460–61.

[53] *R v Walsall MBC, ex p Yapp* [1994] ICR 528. See also *Hughes v DHSS* [1985] AC 776 (change in local authority's policy about retirement age).

[54] *R (Reprotech (Pebsham) Ltd) v East Sussex CC* [2002] UKHL 8, [2003] 1 WLR 348 at [34] (Lord Hoffmann, in the context of planning law. See also at [35]: 'public law has already absorbed whatever is useful from the moral values which underlie the private law concept of estoppel and the time has come for it to stand upon its own two feet').

[55] But there may be a requirement to conform to specified tendering requirements; *Blackpool and Fylde Aero Club v Blackpool BC* [1990] 1 WLR 1195, above, p 38. See also *R v Lord Chancellor, ex p Hibbit and Saunders* [1993] COD 326.

[56] *R v Lewisham LBC, ex p Shell UK Ltd* [1988] 1 All ER 938. See also *Mercury Energy Ltd v Electricity Corp of New Zealand Ltd* [1994] 1 WLR 521 (New Zealand) (reviewability of termination of contract).

invitations to tender) without reference to 'non-commercial matters'.[57] Under the Local Government Act 1999 these authorities are required to 'make arrangements to secure continuous improvement in the way in which [their] functions are exercised, having regard to a combination of economy, efficiency and effectiveness'.[58] The Act and any regulations made under it give the government extensive powers to require local and other authorities to achieve 'best value' by a programme of contracting out.[59] The Secretary of State is also empowered[60] to provide that a specified matter cease to be a 'non-commercial matter' for the purposes of section 17 of the Local Government Act 1988.

Public authorities are subject to special rules in awarding major public works, supply, services, and concession contracts which require them normally to publicize through the Publications Office of the European Union their intention to seek offers for the contract. These rules flow from the implementation in the United Kingdom of European Union Directives:[61] standard tendering procedures are required, non-discriminatory specifications and standards must be used, and authorities are required to award the contract on the basis of the 'most economically advantageous' tender. The Court has wide powers to remedy breaches of these requirements, including setting aside decisions of the public authority, and in many cases the public authority must give notice to tenderers after it has made its decision, but before the contract is entered into, to allow a standstill period for any relevant challenge to be made.

(vii) Recovery of payments made under void contracts

Payments made under an *ultra vires* contract with a public authority, whether made to or by the incapacitated party, are recoverable in an action for restitution of an unjust enrichment,[62] although where, as in the interest swaps cases, payments have been made both ways, restitution is only available to a party on the basis that credit is given for what has been received.[63]

---

[57] Local Government Act 1972, s 17. See *R v Islington LBC, ex p Building Employers Confederation* [1989] IRLR 383; *R v Enfield LBC, ex p TF Unwin (Roydon) Ltd* (1989) 46 BLR 1. See also Local Government Act 1972, s 135.

[58] Local Government Act 1972, s 3(1).   [59] Local Government Act 1972, s 18.

[60] Local Government Act 1972, s 19.

[61] Earlier Directives on public procurement and utilities contracts have been replaced by Directives 2014/24/EU (public procurement), 2014/25/EU (utilities), and a new Directive has been added on concession contracts (Directive 2014/23/EU). The public procurement Directive has been implemented by the Public Contracts Regulations 2015 (SI 2015 No 102); the other two Directives are to be implemented by April 2016. See generally Arrowsmith, *The Law of Public and Utilities Procurement* (3rd edn, vol 1, 2014; vol 2 expected May 2016).

[62] *Westdeutsche Landesbank Girozentrale v Islington LBC* [1994] 1 WLR 938, aff'd [1996] AC 669; *Guinness Mahon & Co Ltd v Kensington & Chelsea RLBC* [1999] QB 215; *Kleinwort Benson Ltd v Lincoln City Council* [1999] 2 AC 349.

[63] *Westdeutsche Landesbank Girozentrale v Islington LBC*, above, n 62.

3. CORPORATIONS AND UNINCORPORATED ASSOCIATIONS

(a) CORPORATIONS

(i) Different forms of corporation

A corporation is an artificial person recognized by law and therefore having legal capacity. A corporation may consist of an office occupied by a single individual (a 'corporation sole'), such as the Crown, the vicar of a parish, or the Secretary of State; or a collection of several persons who are united into one body (a 'corporation aggregate'), such as the mayor and corporation of a city, a limited liability company incorporated under the Companies Act 2006, or a limited liability partnership under the Limited Liability Partnerships Act 2000. The key feature of every corporation is that it has legal personality distinct from the individual(s) of whom it is formed.

A corporation can be formed only by charter from the Crown under the Royal Prerogative, or by statute.

(ii) Doctrine of *ultra vires*

At common law the capacity of a corporation to enter into a contract depends upon how the corporation was formed. A corporation created by charter from the Crown has the same unlimited capacity to enter into contracts as a private individual.[64] However, any act done by a corporation incorporated by statute outside its statutory powers is *ultra vires* and void.[65] Since the corporation has no existence independent of the statute which creates the corporation or authorizes its creation, it follows that its capacity is limited to the exercise of such powers as are actually conferred by, or may reasonably be deduced from, the language of the statute. Thus at common law a company is bound by the objects, listed in its constitutional documents,[66] for the purposes of which it is incorporated. The company can make no contracts

---

[64] *Baroness Wenlock v River Dee Co* (1883) 36 Ch D 675n, 685. If it exceeds its powers, the effect is not to avoid the contract, but to give cause for forfeiture of the charter: see Gower (1952) 68 LQR 214; *Jenkin v Pharmaceutical Society* [1921] 1 Ch 392, 398. The Crown itself has unlimited contractual capacity, although the public nature of the Crown affects the scope of obligations undertaken and their enforceability: see above, pp 238–42.

[65] Similarly, public authorities created by statute are subject to the *ultra vires* doctrine, although the public nature of their functions gives a special dimension to the operation of that doctrine: see above, pp 242–4.

[66] Before the reforms made by the Companies Act 2006, the objects were contained in the company's memorandum of association. Now, however, the memorandum is a much simpler document; the principal document within company's 'constitution' is the articles of association; a company's objects are unrestricted unless the articles of association specifically restrict them; and provisions (such as restrictions on objects) which are contained in the memorandum of a company which was incorporated before the coming into force of the 2006 Act are to be treated as provisions of the company's articles: Companies Act 2006, ss 8, 17, 28(1), 31(1).

inconsistent with those objects,[67] and, if it does so, a contract so made is, at common law,[68] void and unenforceable as being *ultra vires*.

In *Ashbury Railway Carriage and Iron Co Ltd v Riche*:[69]

A company was incorporated with the object (set out in the memorandum of association) to make, and sell, or to lend on hire, railway wagons and carriages and other rolling stock. The company contracted to assign to another company a concession which it had bought for the construction of a railway in Belgium.

The House of Lords held that the contract, being related to the actual construction of a railway, as opposed to railway stock, was *ultra vires* the objects in the memorandum and void. Even if the shareholders subsequently ratified the contract, it could not thereby be rendered binding on the company.

The explanation given in this case for the existence of the *ultra vires* rule was not only that it was a necessary consequence of statutory incorporation but also that the rule was required to protect investors in, and creditors of, the company.[70] 'It ensured that an investor in a gold mining company did not find himself holding shares in a fried fish shop, and it gave those who allowed credit to a limited company some assurance that its assets would not be dissipated in unauthorized enterprises'.[71] Nevertheless, the application of the rule not infrequently led to injustice. Persons who entered into an *ultra vires* contract with a company could not enforce it. If they supplied goods to the company or performed services under the contract, they could not obtain payment.[72] If they lent money to the company, and the borrowing was *ultra vires*, then before the recent recognition of independent restitutionary obligations they could not, in general, recover their money.[73] In theory, before entering into the contract with the company, such persons would first scrutinize the memorandum[74] to ascertain the extent of the company's powers. In practice, however, they did not do so, but were nevertheless deemed to have 'constructive notice' of the contents of the memorandum despite the fact that they had no actual knowledge of them. As a result, the doctrine of *ultra vires* proved to be a trap for the unwary and from time to time inflicted grave hardship on persons who dealt in good faith with the company in ignorance of its lack of capacity.[75]

---

[67] Matters which are reasonably incidental to, or consequential upon, that which is authorized by the memorandum are not *ultra vires* unless expressly prohibited: *A-G v Great Eastern Ry Co* (1880) 5 App Cas 473, 478.

[68] For statutory modification of the doctrine to provide protection for third parties, see below, p 249.

[69] (1875) LR 7 HL 653.   [70] *Ibid*, 667–8 (Lord Cairns).

[71] Gower, *The Principles of Modern Company Law* (3rd edn, 1969) 87.

[72] *Re Jon Beauforte (London) Ltd* [1953] Ch 131.

[73] eg *Sinclair v Brougham* [1914] AC 398. But see now *Westdeutsche Landesbank Girozentrale v Islington LBC* [1996] AC 669, above, p 246, below, p 250.

[74] Before the reforms made by the Companies Act 2006, the objects were contained in the company's memorandum of association: above, n 66.

[75] eg *Re Jon Beauforte (London) Ltd*, above, n 72.

(iii) Statutory modification of *ultra vires* doctrine

The *ultra vires* doctrine was criticized by two committees on the reform of company law,[76] and in 1972, although the doctrine was not abolished, statutory protection[77] was given to those dealing with a company[78] in good faith in respect of transactions decided upon by the directors which were within the capacity of the company, although in fact unauthorized. The Companies Act 1989 took the final step of abolishing the restrictions on capacity of companies formed and registered under the Companies Acts,[79] in a provision which is now found in the Companies Act 2006.

Section 39(1) of the Companies Act 2006 provides that the 'validity of an act done by a company shall not be called into question on the ground of lack of capacity by reason of anything in the company's constitution'. The effect of this section is that a transaction entered into by a company cannot be held invalid merely because it falls within any restriction on the objects listed in the company's articles of association.[80]

(iv) Lack of capacity distinguished from excess or abuse of power

An *ultra vires* contract which is 'beyond the capacity of the company and therefore wholly void'[81] should be distinguished from a contract made by the exercise of a power which the company undoubtedly has but for a *purpose* which is unauthorized. Transactions of the latter sort involve an excess or abuse of power rather than a lack of capacity and will be enforceable against the company unless the other party had notice of the excess or abuse of power. At common law, a contract would not bind the company as against person who had actual *or constructive* notice of the excess or abuse of power,[82] but by section 40(2)(b)(i) of the Companies Act 2006,[83] a party to a transaction with a company 'is not bound to enquire as to any limitation on the powers of the directors to bind the company or authorise others to do so'. In effect therefore the doctrine of constructive notice is now a dead letter in this context.

Limited liability partnerships have unlimited capacity, and so have never been subject to the *ultra vires* rule.[84]

---

[76] Cohen Committee (1945, Cmd 6659), para 12; Jenkins Committee (1962, Cmnd 1749), paras 35–42.

[77] European Communities Act 1972, s 9, implementing Art 9 of the first Directive 68/151/EEC on Company Law, 1968 OJ L65/7.

[78] The company itself could not enforce an *ultra vires* contract: *Bell Houses Ltd v City Wall Properties Ltd* [1966] 1 QB 207 (rvsd on other grounds, [1966] 2 QB 656). See Furmston (1961) 24 MLR 715.

[79] Companies Act 1989, s 108, amending Companies Act 1985, s 35.

[80] Before the Companies Act 2006, the objects were set out in the memorandum; under the 2006 Act, however, any restrictions on the company's objects are set out in the articles: above, n 66.

[81] This depends solely upon the true construction of the memorandum of association (now, the articles of association: above, n 66): *Rolled Steel Products (Holdings) Ltd v British Steel Corp* [1986] Ch 246, 303, 306.

[82] *Ibid*, 306–7.

[83] This reform was made by the Companies Act 1989, s 108, introducing Companies Act 1985, s 35B.

[84] Limited Liability Partnerships Act 2000, s 1(3).

(v) Powers of directors

At common law similar limitations existed in respect of contracts which, though within the powers of the company, were entered into by the directors of the company and other officers without authority or in breach of its internal constitution.[85] The Companies Act 2006 requires directors to act in accordance with the company's constitution (and therefore to observe any restrictions on the company's objects contained in the articles of association).[86] But section 40(1) protects those dealing with a company in good faith by providing that 'the power of the directors to bind the company, or authorise others to do so, is deemed to be free of any limitation under the company's constitution'.[87]

(vi) Form of contracts

Since the passing of the Corporate Bodies' Contracts Act 1960 a corporation can, in general, contract in the same manner as any natural person of full age and capacity and is not only bound by contracts made under its corporate seal. The provisions governing contracts made by companies registered under the Companies Acts are contained in the Companies Act 2006.[88]

(vii) Restitution of benefits conferred under an *ultra vires* contract

Payments made to or by a company under an *ultra vires* contract are recoverable in an action for restitution of an unjust enrichment,[89] and a party which has done work under such a contract will be entitled to reasonable remuneration.[90] But, the provisions of section 39 of the Companies Act 2006 mean that restitutionary obligations will be of less significance in the context of companies.

(b) UNINCORPORATED ASSOCIATIONS

(i) Contractual capacity

An unincorporated association has no legal personality. It cannot therefore contract, or sue or be sued in its name, unless such a course is authorized by statute or by rules of Court. But a contract which purports to have been entered into by or with

---

[85] See *Royal British Bank v Turquand* (1856) 6 E & B 327; Campbell (1959) 75 LQR 469; (1960) 76 LQR 115.

[86] Companies Act 2006, s 171.

[87] See Companies Act 2006, s 40(2) for the meaning of 'deals with' and 'good faith'. Cf *ibid*, s 41 in respect of contracts involving directors of the company. This reform was made by Companies Act 1989, s 108, introducing Companies Act 1985, s 35A. For the circumstances in which a limited liability partnership can be bound by an unauthorized act of one of its members acting as the agent of the partnership, see Limited Liability Partnerships Act 2000, s 6.

[88] Companies Act 2006, s 43. On the execution of deeds by companies, see *ibid*, s 44. The provisions of the Companies Act apply also in modified form to contracts made by limited partnerships: Limited Liability Partnerships (Application of Companies Act 2006) Regulations 2009 (SI 2009 No 1804), reg 4.

[89] *Westdeutsche Landesbank Girozentrale v Islington LBC* [1994] 1 WLR 938, aff'd [1996] AC 669; *Rover International Ltd v Cannon Film Sales Ltd* [1989] 1 WLR 912.

[90] *Rover International Ltd v Cannon Film Sales Ltd* [1989] 1 WLR 912.

an unincorporated association is not necessarily invalid. The person or persons who actually made the contract, for example, the secretary or committee of a club, may be held to have contracted personally and be personally liable on the contract.[91] Further, under the rules of agency, they may be held to have contracted on behalf of the members of the association, and, in certain circumstances, a representative action[92] may be brought by or against one or more of the members, including the trustees of the funds of the association,[93] as representing the others, so as to avoid the necessity of joining numerous persons as parties to the action.

(ii) Partnerships

A partnership can normally sue and be sued in the firm's name,[94] and contracts entered into by one of the partners will, as a general rule, bind the firm since each partner has authority to act for the others in the ordinary course of the partnership business.[95]

(iii) Trade unions

A trade union stands juridically in a somewhat anomalous position. Section 10 of the Trade Union and Labour Relations (Consolidation) Act 1992[96] provides that a trade union is not nor is it to be treated as a body corporate, yet it is capable of making contracts,[97] it is capable of suing and being sued in its own name,[98] and a judgment, order, or award made in any proceedings of any description brought against a trade union is enforceable against any property held in trust for it to the same extent and in the same manner as if the union were a body corporate.[99] The same capacity and liability attaches to an employers' association which is an unincorporated association.[100]

4. MINORS

On 1 January 1970, the age of majority was lowered from 21 to 18.[101] All persons under that age are known technically as minors (or infants). On attaining their majority they legally become adults. The rights and liabilities of minors under contracts entered into by them during minority rest upon common law rules as altered by the Minors

---

[91] *Bradley Egg Farm Ltd v Clifford* [1943] 2 All ER 378. See also *Artistic Upholstery Ltd v Art Forma (Furniture) Ltd* [1999] 4 All ER 277.

[92] CPR r 19.6(1).

[93] *Ideal Films Ltd v Richards* [1927] 1 KB 374. But see *News Group Newspapers Ltd v SOGAT 1982* [1986] ICR 716.

[94] CPR r 7.2A; PD7A, para 5A.3.

[95] See below, p 722. For a similar application of agency principles to contracts made by a member of a limited liability partnership (which has separate corporate personality but unlimited capacity), see Limited Liability Partnerships Act 2000, s 6.

[96] It was already clear that a union is capable of being sued for breach of contract in its own name, and that any damages would be recoverable from its funds: *Bonsor v Musician's Union* [1956] AC 104.

[97] 1992 Act, s 10(1)(a).   [98] 1992 Act, s 10(1)(b).   [99] 1992 Act, s 12(2).

[100] 1992 Act, s 127.   [101] Family Law Reform Act 1969, s 1.

Contracts Act 1987.[102] The desire to protect minors on the one hand, and the wish to safeguard the interests of traders on the other, has led to a complicated body of law.

(a) COMMON LAW: INTRODUCTION

At common law, the only class of contract to which minority did not afford some sort of defence was a contract for 'necessaries' in the sense to be explained below. In all other cases, the common law treated a minor's contracts as being either voidable at the option of the minor, either before or after becoming an adult, or unenforceable against him unless he ratified them after attaining majority.

Contracts in which the minor acquired an interest of a permanent or continuous nature, such as a contract to acquire an interest in land, were binding until the minor *disclaimed* them, either during minority or within a reasonable time after becoming an adult. They were therefore voidable by the minor.[103] The common law rule for contracts which were neither contracts for necessaries nor continuous in their operation was that they were not binding on a minor unless ratified within a reasonable time after majority. So, for example, a promise by a minor to perform an isolated act, such as to pay for goods supplied other than necessaries, or for work and labour done, required an express ratification after majority before the minor would be bound. Such contracts were also often referred to as 'voidable', although this is not strictly accurate since the essence of a voidable contract is that it is binding unless rescinded,[104] whereas these contracts were not binding on the minor unless affirmed.

In the case of both these classes of contracts (voidable, and unenforceable unless ratified) there was no objection to the minor enforcing them. But a minor's position differed from that of parties of full contractual capacity in that he or she might recover damages for breach but not obtain specific performance of the contract.[105] Specific performance is granted at the discretion of the Court, which will not grant it where it would not be prepared to enforce the contract at the suit of either party.[106] Since the contract could not be enforced against the minor, equity would not allow the minor to obtain specific performance against the other party.

(b) CONTRACTS FOR NECESSARIES

It has already been stated that, at common law, the only class of contract which was not voidable at the option of a minor was a contract for 'necessaries'.[107] The meaning of the term 'necessaries', however, requires further explanation. We first consider contracts

---

[102] Implementing the recommendations in Law Com No 134, *Minors' Contracts* (1984).
[103] Above, p 24.
[104] Above, p 22.
[105] *Flight v Bolland* (1828) 4 Russ 298.
[106] Cf below, pp 611–12.
[107] But such a contract may be held invalid if the minor was not capable of understanding the nature of the transaction: see *R v Oldham MBC* [1993] 1 FLR 645, 661–2 (Scott LJ). This will vary according to the minor and the nature of the contract: 'at what age a child is able to go to the village shop and enter into an effective contract for the purchase of sweets, I would not wish to guess, but I am sure it would be well under the age of 10 years').

for necessary goods, and then contracts of employment or training, and then other agreements beneficial to the minor.

Part of the common law on this matter has been given statutory form by section 3 of the Sale of Goods Act 1979.[108] This provides:

(1) Capacity to buy and sell is regulated by the general law concerning capacity to contract and to transfer and acquire property.

(2) Where necessaries are sold and delivered to a minor or to a person who by reason of drunkenness is incompetent to contract, he must pay a reasonable price for them.

(3) In subsection (2) above 'necessaries' mean goods suitable to the condition in life of the minor or other person concerned and to his actual requirements at the time of the sale and delivery.

(i) Necessary goods

We must first consider what the word 'necessaries' includes. It has always been held that a minor may be liable for the supply to him or her, not merely of the necessaries of life, but of things suitable to his or her station in life and particular circumstances at the time. Minors are liable for *necessaries*, and not merely for *necessities*.[109] Certain things may be obviously outside the range of possible necessaries. So in *Ryder v Wombwell*:[110]

W, a minor with an income of £500 a year, bought from R a pair of crystal, ruby, and diamond solitaires and an antique goblet in silver gilt.

It was held that neither of these articles could be a necessary, even though W was the son of a deceased baronet and 'moved in the highest society'. Other things may be of a useful character but the quality or quantity supplied may take them out of the character of necessaries. In *Nash v Inman*:[111]

A tailor supplied a Cambridge undergraduate with clothing which included 11 fancy waistcoats at 2 guineas each. It was proved that he had already a sufficient supply of clothing according to his position in life.

The Court of Appeal held that the tailor had failed to prove that the clothing was suitable to the undergraduate's actual requirements at the time of the sale and delivery.

Necessaries also vary according to the minor's station in life or peculiar circumstances at the time of the contract.[112] The Court must take into consideration the character of the goods supplied, the actual circumstances of the minor, and the extent to which the minor was already supplied with them. It is necessary to emphasize the words 'actual circumstances', because a false impression conveyed to the person dealing with the minor as to the station and circumstances of the minor will not affect the minor's

---

[108] Re-enacting Sale of Goods Act 1893, s 2, and amended by Mental Capacity Act 2005.

[109] The Law Commission did not consider that the narrowing of the category in this way was, on balance, desirable: Law Com No 134, *Minors' Contracts* (1984) paras 5.4–5.6.

[110] (1868) LR 3 Ex 90, aff'd (1869) LR 4 Ex 32.

[111] [1908] 2 KB 1. The clothing was 'of an extravagant and ridiculous style having regard to the position of the boy': Buckley LJ at 11.

[112] *Peters v Fleming* (1840) 6 M & W 42.

liability. A shop which supplies expensive goods to a minor thinking that the minor's circumstances are better than they really are, or which supplies goods of a useful class not knowing that the minor is already sufficiently supplied, does so at its peril.[113]

Section 3 of the Sale of Goods Act 1979 also requires that the goods should be necessary to the minor 'at the time of the sale *and* delivery'. This might seem to indicate that the seller would have to prove them to be necessary at both of these times. But, it is probable that this is simply a reference to the action for goods sold and delivered, which is the normal action for a seller who wishes to recover the purchase price.[114] The seller would have to prove them to be necessary at the time of their delivery alone.

(ii) Loans for necessaries

A loan of money to a minor to pay for necessaries was not recoverable at common law, for 'it may be borrowed for necessaries, but laid out and spent at a tavern'.[115] But in equity it was held that if a minor borrowed money to pay a debt for necessaries, and the debt was actually paid with the money, the lender stood in the place of the person paid and was entitled to recover the money lent.[116] This rule is a branch of the equitable doctrine of subrogation. It is not possible, however, to sue a minor on a negotiable instrument given for the price of necessaries, even though it may have been negotiated to a third party.[117] Also, an account stated with a minor is still void although the items in the account may consist of necessaries.[118]

(iii) Contracts of employment and training

A minor may enter into a contract of employment so as to earn a living or into a contract for the purpose of obtaining instruction or education so as to qualify for a suitable trade or profession whereby he or she may profit himself afterwards.[119] Provided that they are beneficial to the minor, these contracts are binding. In *Clements v London and North Western Railway Company*,[120] a minor entered into a contract of employment with a railway company, promising to accept the terms of an insurance against accidents in lieu of his rights of action under the Employers' Liability Act 1880. It was held that the contract, taken as a whole, was for his benefit and that he was bound by his promise.

On the other hand, a contract of this class which is more onerous than beneficial to the minor will impose no liability. So in *De Francesco v Barnum*:[121]

B, aged 14 years, agreed to become De F's apprentice in 'the art of choreography' for 7 years. De F was to teach her stage dancing, and during the period of apprenticeship B was not to

---

[113] The burden of proof is on the supplier: *Nash v Inman*, above, n 111, 5.
[114] Below, p 259. See also Winfield (1942) 58 LQR 82, 90.
[115] *Earle v Peale* (1711) 1 Salk 386 (except where necessaries are purchased at minor's request).
[116] *Marlow v Pitfeild* (1719) 1 P Wms 558.
[117] *Re Soltykoff, ex p Margrett* [1891] 1 QB 413. Cf Bills of Exchange Act 1882, s 22.
[118] *Williams v Moor* (1843) 11 M & W 256.
[119] Co Litt 172a; *Walter v Everard* [1891] 2 QB 369.   [120] [1894] 2 QB 482.
[121] (1890) 45 Ch D 430. See also *Sir WC Leng & Co Ltd v Andrews* [1909] 1 Ch 763.

take any professional engagement without the consent of De F, nor was she to marry. She was to receive certain payments for any performances she might give, but there was no provision for any other remuneration and De F did not undertake to find her any engagements. The effect of the deed was to place B entirely at the disposal of De F.

Fry LJ held that the contract was not beneficial to B and was unenforceable. It should, however, be noted that even though a minor's contract of service contains some terms which are not for the benefit of the minor, the minor cannot necessarily repudiate it, still less select which terms will or will not be followed. 'The Court must look at the whole contract, having regard to the circumstances of the case, and determine . . . whether the contract is or is not beneficial.'[122]

(iv) Other beneficial contracts

The class of contracts for necessaries is not, however, limited to contracts of employment and training. It includes numerous contracts for 'necessaries' other than goods, for example, for medical attendance,[123] for the preparation of a marriage settlement by a solicitor,[124] or the hire of a car to fetch a minor's luggage from the railway station.[125] Provided that these are reasonable and beneficial to the minor, the other party can enforce them. Yet the class does not include ordinary trading contracts, such as the hire-purchase of a motor lorry by a haulage contractor who is a minor.[126] Such contracts may be necessary to the minor's business, and so of benefit to the minor, but they are not binding. Thus, in *Cowern v Nield*,[127] a contract to sell a consignment of hay by a hay and straw dealer who was a minor was held not to be a contract for 'necessaries' because it was a trading contract.

The class is therefore a limited one although the limits are not easy to state. In *Doyle v White City Stadium Ltd*,[128] for instance:

A professional boxer, who was a minor, in consideration of his receiving a licence from the British Boxing Board of Control, agreed to be bound by the rules of the Board in all his professional engagements. A purse of £3,000 was withheld from him by the Board, in accordance with its rules, on the ground that he had been disqualified in a contest for hitting below the belt.

It was held that the agreement was binding on him despite his being a minor. The ground of this decision was that the licence was practically essential in order to enable him to become proficient in his profession, and when the conditions attached to the issue of the licence were incorporated in a particular beneficial contract of employment—in this case, an engagement to box for a heavyweight

---

[122] *Ibid*, 439. See also *Slade v Metrodent Ltd* [1953] 2 QB 112.
[123] *Dale v Copping* (1610) 1 Bulst 39. See also *Gillick v West Norfolk and Wisbech AHA* [1986] AC 112, 166–7, 183, 195 (capacity of girl under 16 to consent to medical treatment, including contraception).
[124] *Helps v Clayton* (1864) 17 CB NS 553.   [125] *Fawcett v Smethurst* (1914) 84 LJ KB 473.
[126] *Mercantile Union Guarantee Corp v Ball* [1937] 2 KB 498.
[127] [1912] 2 KB 419.   [128] [1935] 1 KB 110.

championship—both contracts became binding on the minor, as they were both for his benefit. Also in *Chaplin v Leslie Frewin (Publishers) Ltd*:[129]

C, a minor who was the son of Charlie Chaplin, had been eking out a Bohemian existence in London. In return for an advance of royalties, he assigned to LF publishers the exclusive right to publish an autobiography of himself (entitled *I Couldn't Smoke the Grass on my Father's Lawn*) which was to be written by 'ghost' writers. The completed work, so he alleged, showed him to be 'a depraved creature', and he sought to repudiate the assignment.

The Court of Appeal held that he could not do so. The contract was binding on him since it was one which enabled him to make a start as an author and thus to earn money to keep himself and his wife. It was a beneficial contract, because, as Danckwerts LJ put it,[130] 'The mud may cling but the profits will be secured'.

The judgments in these two cases do not set out to define the contracts which are binding when beneficial to a minor, but they indicate a tendency to enlarge the class by analogy with types of contract which are established as contracts for necessaries. The contracts which the minors had made were arguably merely incidental to the carrying on of a trade or profession and therefore of a kind which had not hitherto been believed to be binding, even when beneficial.

(c) VOIDABLE CONTRACTS

A minor who acquires an interest in permanent property to which obligations attach, or enters into a contract involving continuous rights and duties, benefits and liabilities, and takes some benefit under the contract, will be bound, unless he or she expressly disclaims the contract during the minority or within a reasonable time of coming of age.

Examples of such contracts are the acquisition of an interest in land (such as a lease or tenancy), and of shares in a company. Up to the time that the minor disclaims such a contract he or she will be bound to carry out the obligations under it, provided that these accrue before repudiation. A minor cannot renounce the liabilities until he or she renounces the interest. So a lessee who is a minor is liable for rent until the lease is disclaimed,[131] and if a shareholder, is under a similar liability in respect of calls on the shares until they are expressly repudiated.[132]

---

[129] [1966] Ch 71 (Lord Denning MR dissenting). The Court also held that, even if the contract had been voidable by the minor, it could not have been rescinded because it had been executed by the transfer of the copyright.

[130] *Ibid*, 95.

[131] *Blake v Concannon* (1870) 4 Ir Rep CL 320. By the Law of Property Act 1925, s 1(6) a minor can no longer hold a legal estate in land; but can have an equitable interest, and so be bound in the same way: *Davies v Benyon-Harris* (1931) 47 TLR 424; and a conveyance to a minor operates as a declaration of trust in his or her favour: Trusts of Land and Appointment of Trustees Act 1996, Sched 1, paras 1, 2; *Hammersmith & Fulham LBC v Alexander-David* [2009] EWCA Civ 259, [2010] Ch 272.

[132] There is some doubt as to whether a minor is bound to pay unpaid calls which accrued due before the repudiation, but the better opinion is that the minor is so bound, provided that he cannot plead

(i) Partnership

The position of a member of a partnership who is a minor differs from that of a shareholder. It is true that partnership is a continuous relationship between the partners, but by becoming a partner a minor does not acquire an interest in a subject of a permanent nature to which obligations are attached. During the minority of a partner, the minor is not liable for debts incurred by the partnership; but equally is not entitled to any share of the partnership assets until the firm's debts have been paid.[133] A minor who continues to act as a partner after majority will be liable, equally with the other partners, for the debts subsequently incurred. A minor may also be liable for such debts if, though ceasing to act as a partner, he or she gives no adequate notice of this withdrawal to persons dealing with the firm.[134] The minor's liability in this case, however, merely illustrates a general rule of the law of partnership applicable to any retired partner,[135] and does not depend on any principle peculiar to the law of minors.

(ii) Time of disclaimer

In order that a minor's disclaimer of a permanent interest may take effect, the contract must be repudiated during minority or within a reasonable time of the minor's coming of age. What is a reasonable time will depend upon the circumstances of each particular case. In *Edwards v Carter*[136] the House of Lords held that a minor who entered into a marriage settlement and covenanted to bring into the settlement any property which might come to him under his father's will could not repudiate it nearly five years after coming of age and one year after his father died leaving him property by will.

(iii) Effect of disclaimer

The effect of a valid disclaimer of a contract that binds until repudiated is to release the minor from future obligations under it. A minor who has paid to the other party in the mistaken belief that the contract is enforceable may be able to recover the payment.[137] But in the absence of such a mistake the minor will not be able to recover anything unless there has been a total failure of the consideration for which the money has been paid. Where, for example shares have been allotted to the minor, money paid for them will be irrecoverable whether or not a dividend has been paid or any other real advantage received.[138] The minor will have received something which had a marketable value and which was the very consideration for which he or she had bargained.

---

total failure of consideration: *Steinberg v Scala (Leeds) Ltd* [1923] 2 Ch 452. See also *Cork & Bandon Ry Co v Cazenove* (1847) 10 QB 935; *North Western Railway Co v M'Michael* (1850) 5 Exch 114; *Newry and Enniskillen Ry Co v Coombe* (1849) 3 Exch 565.

[133] *Lovell and Christmas v Beauchamp* [1894] AC 607.
[134] *Goode v Harrison* (1821) 5 B & Ald 147.   [135] Partnership Act 1890, s 36.
[136] [1893] AC 360. See also *Carnell v Harrison* [1916] 1 Ch 328.
[137] *Kleinwort Benson Ltd v Lincoln CC* [1999] 2 AC 349.
[138] *Steinberg v Scala (Leeds) Ltd* [1923] 2 Ch 452. See also *Holmes v Blogg* (1818) 8 Taunt 508 (premium paid by minor for lease not recoverable).

(d) OTHER CONTRACTS: UNENFORCEABLE UNLESS RATIFIED

As explained above, a contract which is not for necessaries, and is not for an interest in permanent property to which obligations attach, nor involves continuous rights and duties, will not bind the minor at common law unless ratified by the minor within a reasonable time after attaining majority. Until the Minors' Contracts Act 1987 came into force this common law rule was displaced by the Infants Relief Act 1874 which made it impossible for a person of full age to be sued on a contract entered into during minority, even though he or she had ratified such a contract and even though there was some new consideration for the ratification.[139] However, this did not stop the minor enforcing the contract against the other party. The repeal of the 1874 Act means that the common law rule as it existed prior to that legislation has again become the law.

(e) THE NATURE OF THE LIABILITY OF MINORS

Where there is an enforceable obligation against a minor, for example, for necessaries, it remains to characterize that obligation. Two theories have been put forward.

(i) Liability in unjust enrichment

The first is that the liability arises in unjust enrichment rather than contract. The obligation is imposed by the law because the minor has actually received the benefit of performance, and not consensually as a result of entering a valid contract. This was the view taken by Fletcher Moulton LJ in *Nash v Inman*:[140]

An infant, like a lunatic, is incapable of making a contract of purchase in the strict sense of the words; but if a man satisfies the needs of the infant or lunatic by supplying to him necessaries, the law will imply an obligation to repay him for the services so rendered, and will enforce that obligation against the estate of the infant or lunatic. The consequence is that the basis of the action is hardly contract. Its real foundation is an obligation which the law imposes on the infant to make a fair payment in respect of needs satisfied.

(ii) Liability in contract

The second theory is that the liability is contractual. The minor can, it is said, enter into a valid contract for necessaries just like any other person. 'The plaintiff', said Buckley LJ in *Nash v Inman*:[141]

when he sues the defendant for goods supplied during infancy, is suing him in contract on the footing that the contract was such as the infant, notwithstanding infancy, could

---

[139] See Infants Relief Act 1874, s 2 (repealed by Minors' Contracts Act 1987, s 4(1)) discussed in Guest, *Anson's Law of Contract* (26th edn, 1984) 184–92.

[140] [1908] 2 KB 1, 8; *Elkington v Amery* [1936] 2 All ER 86, 88. For the application of this to contracts with those lacking mental capacity, see *Re Rhodes* (1890) 44 Ch D 94, 105; *Re J* [1909] 1 Ch 574, 577.

[141] [1908] 2 KB 1, 12. See also *Gillick v West Norfolk and Wisbech AHA* [1986] AC 112, 169 (Lord Fraser: child could enter into a 'contract').

make. The defendant, although he was an infant, had a limited capacity to contract. In order to maintain his action the plaintiff must prove that the contract sued on is within that limited capacity.

The problem is not academic since, unless the liability is contractual in nature, the minor will not be liable where the contract is executory. In the case of necessary goods, section 3 of the Sale of Goods Act 1979 indicates that the obligation is restitutionary. It deals only with 'necessaries sold and delivered', and says nothing of necessaries sold to a minor and not delivered, that is to say, of a contract of sale which is still executory.[142] There does not seem to be a single case since the seventeenth century[143] in which a minor has been held liable for the non-acceptance of necessaries or on a contract for necessaries bargained and sold but not delivered. Since necessity is in part determined at the time of delivery, it is in fact difficult to know whether an executory contract is or is not one for necessaries.[144] Moreover, even if the goods are delivered, the plaintiff will not necessarily recover the contractual price but only 'a reasonable price for them'. This does not suggest a consensual contract.[145]

Contracts of employment, apprenticeship, and the like, provided that they are beneficial to the minor, have, however, always been regarded as merely one variety of contracts for 'necessaries',[146] and there seems to be no authority for regarding the nature of the liability which they create as resting on a different basis from that of contracts for the supply of necessary goods. Nevertheless in *Roberts v Gray*:[147]

G, a minor, entered into a contract by which he agreed to join R, a famous billiard player, in a world tour as 'professional billiardists'. R incurred certain necessary expenses as a result of preparations for the tour, but, before the tour began, G repudiated the contract.

The Court of Appeal held that to play in company with a noted billiard player such as R was instruction of the most valuable kind for a minor who wished to make billiard playing his occupation, and they upheld an award of £1,500 damages for the breach. They rejected the view that a contract for necessaries in this wider sense was not binding on a minor while it was still executory. 'I am unable to appreciate', said Hamilton LJ,[148] 'why a contract which is in itself binding, because it is a contract for necessaries not qualified by unreasonable terms, can cease to be binding merely because it is still executory'. This decision and that in *Doyle v White City Stadium Ltd*,[149] considered above, imply that when the minor is liable the nature of the liability

---

[142] Cf the wording of the Infants Relief Act 1874 (repealed by Minors' Contracts Act 1987, s 4(1)), s 1 of which might have suggested the contrary: 'contracts . . . for goods supplied *or to be supplied* (other than contracts for necessaries)'. See generally Winfield (1942) 58 LQR 82.

[143] *Ive v Chester* (1619) Cro Jac 560; *Delavel v Clare* (1652) Latch 156.

[144] *Benjamin's Sale of Goods* (9th edn, 2014) para 2–032.

[145] *Pontypridd Union v Drew* [1927] 1 KB 214, 220 (Scrutton LJ). See also Birks, *An Introduction to Restitution* (1985) 436.

[146] *Walter v Everard* [1891] 2 QB 369; above, p 254.

[147] [1913] 1 KB 520. See also *Hamilton v Bennett* (1930) 94 JPN 136.

[148] [1913] 1 KB 520, 530.   [149] [1935] 1 KB 110; above, p 255.

does not differ from that of a contracting party of full capacity; that it is, in fact, a true contractual liability and not restitutionary.

In principle, there is much to be said for the contractual explanation. The law governing minors' contracts is based on the principle of 'qualified unenforceability';[150] the minor has a limited capacity to contract, and within that limited capacity, there is no reason to deny the contractual nature of liability. Moreover, the other party is liable for non-delivery and other non-performance,[151] and it has been argued that section 3 of the Sale of Goods Act 1979 does not exclude the possibility of liability being contractual. This is because a contract for necessaries only binds a minor where it is not, on balance, onerous to the minor. Thus a minor 'will not, in any case, be bound by a contract for necessaries for which more than a reasonable price is charged', a position unaffected by the Sale of Goods Act, the provisions of which 'are consistent with the view that a minor may be liable on an executory contract for necessaries, provided that the terms are not onerous to him'.[152] But in the present state of the authorities it is difficult to state the nature of the minor's liability with certainty.

(iii) Liability for voidable and unenforceable covenants

If the contract is a voidable contract not disclaimed in time, or an unenforceable contract which has been ratified, it is clear that it may be enforced as a contract. The real issue, however, concerns the non-contractual liability of the minor. That is, the tortious or restitutionary liability of the minor in the case where a voidable contract has been disclaimed or an unenforceable contract has not been ratified. On what basis may the minor be liable? This is addressed below.

(f) LIABILITY OF MINORS IN TORT

A minor is generally liable for torts that he or she has committed, but a breach of contract may not be treated as a tort so as to make the minor liable. The tort must be more than a misfeasance in the performance of a contract, and must be separate from and independent of it, otherwise the policy of the law of contract to protect the minor could too easily be subverted by switching to a claim in tort.

For instance, in *Jennings v Rundall*[153] where a minor hired a mare to ride and injured her by over-riding, it was held that he could not be made liable by framing an action really arising out of contract as an action in tort. And in *Fawcett v Smethurst*,[154] it was said that a minor who hired a car to take his luggage from the station would be under no liability in tort if he used the car to drive several miles further than the station, and

---

[150] Law Com No 134 (1984) para 1.12.

[151] *Farnham v Atkins* (1669) 1 Sid 446; *Bruce v Warwick* (1815) 6 Taunt 118.

[152] Mitchell, Mitchell, and Watterson, *Goff and Jones on the Law of Unjust Enrichment* (8th edn, 2011) para 24–16. But note the difficulty of ascertaining this at that stage, above, p 259.

[153] (1799) 8 Term Rep 335.

[154] (1914) 84 LJ KB 473, although in that case the minor did not, in fact, commit any tort.

there met with an accident. Minors who obtain a loan by falsely representing their age cannot be made to repay the amount of the loan in the form of damages for deceit,[155] nor can minors who buy goods on credit be forced to pay for them by charging them with conversion:[156] 'one cannot make an infant liable for the breach of a contract by changing the form of action to one *ex delicto*.'[157]

But this is not to say that every tort of a minor which originates in a contract is not actionable. If the wrongful action is of a kind not contemplated by the contract,[158] the minor may be exposed to tortious liability. So in *Burnard v Haggis*:[159]

A minor hired a mare for riding. He was given strict instructions 'not to jump or lark with her'. He lent her to a friend who jumped and killed her.

It was held that the minor was liable, for, as Willis J said:[160]

It appears to me that the act of riding the mare into the place where she received her death-wound was as much a trespass, notwithstanding the hiring for another purpose, as if, without any hiring at all, the defendant had gone into a field and taken the mare out and hunted her and killed her. It was a bare trespass, not within the object and purpose of the hiring.

In a more modern case,[161] a minor was successfully sued for the non-return of a microphone and amplifier which he had hired and improperly parted with to a friend. The Court of Appeal held that 'the circumstances in which the goods passed from his possession and ultimately disappeared were outside the purview of the contract of bailment altogether',[162] and the minor was liable. In considering the extent of the contract, it seems that the terms of the agreement, the presence or absence of an express prohibition, and the nature of the subject-matter of the contract must all be considered to be relevant, although not necessarily determining, factors.

(g) LIABILITY OF MINORS IN UNJUST ENRICHMENT

(i) Common law

Where, overall, a contract for necessaries is not beneficial to the minor and is not therefore binding, the minor will nevertheless be liable to pay a reasonable price for any necessaries supplied.[163] But a claimant who seeks restitution of money paid or benefits in kind conferred on the minor under a contract cannot simply rely on the normal grounds for restitution of an unjust enrichment, in particular mistake and

---

[155] *Johnson v Pye* (1665) 1 Sid 258; *Stikeman v Dawson* (1847) De G & Sm 90; *R Leslie Ltd v Sheill* [1914] 3 KB 607.

[156] *Manby v Scott* (1659) 1 Sid 109, 129.

[157] *Burnard v Haggis* (1863) 32 LJ CP 189, 191 (Byles J, cited by Lord Sumner in *R Leslie Ltd v Sheill* [1914] 3 KB 607, 611).

[158] *Burnard v Haggis* (1863) 14 CBNS 45, 53 (Willis J); *Fawcett v Smethurst* (1914) 84 LJ KB 473, 475 (Atkin J); *R Leslie Ltd v Sheill* [1914] 3 KB 607, 620 (Kennedy LJ); *Ballett v Mingay* [1943] KB 281, 283 (Lord Greene MR).

[159] (1863) 14 CBNS 45.   [160] *Ibid*, 53.   [161] *Ballett v Mingay* [1943] KB 281.

[162] *Ibid*, 283.   [163] Above, p 253.

failure of consideration. This is because the Court will take care not to grant restitution where this would amount to indirectly enforcing the void contract, as it would be if, for example, the minor is ordered to repay a loan. There is authority to the effect that a minor can only be made liable in restitution if it can be shown that a wrong quite independent of the contract has been committed,[164] and that otherwise minority affords a good defence.[165] Thus in *Cowern v Nield*[166] a hay and straw dealer who was a minor was held entitled to retain money paid to him as the price of a consignment of hay which he had failed to deliver in accordance with his contract. But these decisions reflect the now discredited 'implied contract' theory of liability in such cases, and their reasoning should be rejected now that it has been accepted that the basis of restitutionary liability is the unjust enrichment of the defendant, here the minor.[167] There is force in the argument that a restitutionary claim against a minor should be allowed unless it would contravene the policy underpinning the rule that invalidates the contract.[168]

(ii) Equitable relief against a fraudulent minor

Minors who fraudulently represent themselves to be of full age and thereby induce other persons to enter into contracts, are nevertheless not liable under the contracts despite the fraud. Equity, however, will, in certain circumstances, intervene in order to prevent minors from taking advantage of their own deceit. 'Minors', said Lord Chancellor Hardwicke,[169] 'are not allowed to take advantage of infancy to support a fraud'. This equitable intervention is distinct and separate from the contract. The principle was succinctly stated by Lord Sumner in *R Leslie Ltd v Sheill*:[170]

When an infant obtained an advantage by falsely stating himself to be of full age, equity required him to restore his ill-gotten gains, or to release the party deceived from obligations or acts in law induced by the fraud, but scrupulously stopped short of enforcing against him a contractual obligation, entered into while he was an infant, even by means of a fraud.

The exact extent of such equitable relief is the subject of some dispute. It is clear that a minor who obtains property, whether consisting of goods or money or any other security, by means of a false representation of full age, can be compelled to restore that property to the person deceived, provided that it is identifiable and still in the minor's possession. It is equally clear that it is impossible to make the minor repay a loan of money which has been borrowed by such a fraud and subsequently spent. In the words

---

[164] *Cowern v Nield* [1912] 2 KB 419.
[165] *R Leslie Ltd v Sheill* [1914] 3 KB 607, below, p 263; *Thavorn v Bank of Credit & Commerce International SA* [1985] 1 Lloyd's Rep 259.
[166] [1912] 2 KB 419.   [167] *Lipkin Gorman v Karpnale Ltd* [1991] 2 AC 548.
[168] Mitchell, Mitchell, and Watterson, *Goff and Jones on the Law of Unjust Enrichment* (8th edn, 2011) para 34-04.
[169] *Earl of Buckinghamshire v Drury* (1760) 2 Eden 60, 71.
[170] [1914] 3 KB 607, 618; Atiyah (1959) 22 MLR 273.

of Lord Sumner in *R Leslie Ltd v Sheill*:[171] 'Restitution stops where repayment begins.' In that case:

L were a firm of registered moneylenders, and they sued S, to whom they had made two loans of £200 each, to recover £475, being the amount of the loans with interest. At the time of obtaining the loans, S was a minor, but he had falsely represented to L that he was of full age.

The Court of Appeal held that no action could be maintained for the recovery of the money. The loan was rendered void by the Infants Relief Act 1874 then in force[172] and the minor could not be forced to repay:[173]

The money was paid over in order to be used as the defendant's own and he has so used it and, I suppose, spent it. There is no question of tracing it, no possibility of restoring the very thing got by the fraud, nothing but compulsion through a personal judgment to pay an equivalent sum out of his present or future resources, in a word nothing but a judgment in debt to repay the loan. I think this would be nothing but enforcing a void contract.

Once the identity of the property has been lost because it has been dissipated, it is no longer possible to invoke the aid of the equitable doctrine of restitution.

So much is clear; the difficulty arises when the minor has parted with the property obtained by the fraud, but stands possessed of other money or property which represents it. Suppose, for example, that a minor obtains certain goods by the misrepresentation, and then sells the goods and stands possessed of the proceeds of sale. Is it possible to claim that the money represents the goods and so ought to be restored to the person deceived? In *Stocks v Wilson*:[174]

W, a minor, by falsely representing himself to be of full age, induced S to sell and deliver to him certain goods for which he promised to pay £300. The goods were not necessaries. He subsequently sold some of the goods for £30, and granted a bill of sale over the remainder as security for the sum of £100 lent to him by a third party. These goods were later sold by him to the grantee of the bill of sale. S claimed, by way of equitable relief, the value of the goods.

Lush J held that S was not entitled to recover the value of the goods from W as this would be to enforce a void contract. Equity, however, had the power to prevent a minor from retaining the benefit of what had been obtained by reason of his fraud, and since W had obtained the sum of £130 by parting with the goods, he was liable to account to S for this sum. This decision was criticized, but not overruled, by the Court of Appeal in *R Leslie Ltd v Sheill* on the ground that Lush J had proceeded on the false assumption that a minor who had obtained money by a false representation of full age could be compelled to refund it. This may, perhaps, be reconciled with *Stocks v Wilson* on the assumption that it is possible for the party defrauded to 'trace' the value of the goods into the proceeds of their sale.[175] If this is so, then the defrauded

---

[171] [1914] 3 KB 607.   [172] Above, p 258.
[173] [1914] 3 KB 607, 619 (Lord Sumner).   [174] [1913] 2 KB 235.
[175] *R Leslie Ltd v Sheill* [1914] 3 KB 607, 618. See also *Thavorn v Bank of Credit & Commerce International SA* [1985] 1 Lloyd's Rep 259, 264; Atiyah (1959) 22 MLR 273. *Stocks v Wilson* may fairly be criticized, since

party's right is similar to that of a beneficiary in respect of a trust fund in the hands of a trustee.[176] It is possible to trace so long as there is an identifiable fund in existence against which the defrauded party can enforce its claim *in rem*; but, once the fund has been dissipated, it is no longer possible to obtain a judgment *in personam* against the infant for the amount.

Equity will also relieve the deceived party of obligations imposed upon that party by the minor's fraud. Thus it has ordered the setting aside of a lease[177] and the giving up of promissory notes[178] obtained by false representation of age. The Court scrupulously refrained from enforcing the contracts, and merely restored the status quo affected by the minor's fraud. For example, a claim by the lessor for damages for use and occupation of the premises was dismissed as being inconsistent with this relief.

Where a person is induced to lend money by a false misrepresentation of age by the minor, after the minor comes of age the lender is entitled to prove in any bankruptcy proceedings against the minor.[179] The reason seems to be that the lender has a claim, not against the minor personally, but against the minor's assets in competition with the other creditors.[180]

(iii) Minors' Contracts Act 1987

In addition to rights to restitution that may arise at common law and in equity, there is a statutory scheme allowing for restitution. Section 3 of the Minors' Contracts Act 1987[181] provides:

> (1) Where—
>
> > (a) a person ('the plaintiff') has after the commencement of this Act entered into a contract with another ('the defendant'), and
> >
> > (b) the contract is unenforceable against the defendant (or he repudiates it) because he was a minor when the contract was made,
>
> the court may, if it is just and equitable to do so, require the defendant to transfer to the plaintiff any property acquired by the defendant under the contract, or any property representing it.

The provision leaves the issue of restitution to the discretion of the Court. There is no requirement of fault or fraud. It is also only concerned with property acquired under the contract (or property acquired in exchange for property acquired under the contract) and not property gained in any other way. It appears that money is included within this notion of property. The Law Commission's policy was to extend the equitable

---

it appears that judgment was given *in personam* against the minor and without any proper inquiry as to whether the money had been spent.

[176] The representation of full age might be considered to raise an 'equity' in the defrauded party similar to that possessed by a beneficiary of a fiduciary relationship.

[177] *Lemprière v Lange* (1879) 12 Ch D 675.   [178] *Clarke v Cobley* (1789) 2 Cox 173.

[179] *Re King, ex p Unity Joint Stock Mutual Banking Association* (1858) 3 De G & J 63; *Re Jones, ex p Jones* (1881) 18 Ch D 109, 125.

[180] *R Leslie Ltd v Sheill* [1914] 3 KB 607, 616.   [181] See Law Com No 134, *Minors' Contracts* (1984).

remedy available against a fraudulent minor to a case where the minor, though not guilty of fraud, had failed to pay for goods obtained on credit.[182] That equitable relief extended, as in *Stocks v Wilson*[183] and as recognized by the Law Commission, to money which was the proceeds of the property sold to the minor and resold by him or her. But if property delivered to a minor has been consumed or lost, there will be no remedy under the 1987 Act. The Law Commission considered that to order the minor to pay to the seller a sum equivalent to the purchase price or the value of the property 'would amount to the enforcement of the contract' against the minor.[184]

(h) RESTITUTION IN FAVOUR OF MINORS

In order for the minor to recover money paid to the other party under a contract which does not bind the minor, a ground for restitution making the enrichment unjust must be established, that is, that the money was paid by mistake, under compulsion, or that there has been a failure of consideration. Where the ground of recovery is failure of consideration, in the present state of the authorities it would appear that what is required is a *total* failure of consideration, so that, as noted above,[185] receipt by the minor of any part of the other party's performance will be fatal. But, as will be seen,[186] the indications are that the requirement of totality is being reconsidered, and it is submitted that the authority of the cases requiring it in this context has been fatally undermined. Provided the minor can return what has been received or give recompense for it in a way that does not amount to indirect enforcement of the contract, the minor should, in principle, be able to recover money paid.

(i) THIRD PARTIES

An interesting question arises as to the effect the invalidity of a minor's contract has on third parties. So far, we know that although a minor may enforce a contract the other party to the contract can only enforce it if it is a valid contract for necessaries or if it is a voidable contract that has not been disclaimed or another (unenforceable) contract that has been ratified. If the contract is not enforceable, what is the position of, say, a guarantor of the minor's obligations? Section 2 of the Minors' Contracts Act 1987 provides:

Where—

(a) a guarantee is given in respect of an obligation of a party to a contract made after the commencement of this Act, and

---

[182] *Ibid*, para 4.21. [183] [1913] 2 KB 235, above, p 263.

[184] Law Com No 134 (1984), para 4.23.

[185] Above, p 257. On the recovery of property, see *Pearce v Brain* [1929] 2 KB 310 but cf *Chaplin v Leslie Frewin (Publishers) Ltd* [1966] Ch 71, above, p 256.

[186] Below, pp 623–4.

(b) the obligation is unenforceable against him (or he repudiates the contract) because he was a minor when the contract was made,

the guarantee shall not for that reason alone be unenforceable against the guarantor.[187]

5. PERSONS LACKING MENTAL CAPACITY AND DRUNKEN PERSONS

The Mental Capacity Act 2005 set up a new framework within which the Court or other designated persons can take decisions on behalf of a person who lacks capacity, and for the supervision of such a person. A person must be assumed to have capacity unless it is established that he or she lacks capacity;[188] and the lack of capacity is no longer defined as a general disability but as the inability to make a decision in relation to a particular matter, at a particular time, because of permanent or temporary impairment of, or disturbance in the functioning of, the mind or brain.[189] For this purpose a person is unable to make a decision for himself if he is unable: (a) to understand the information relevant to the decision; (b) to retain that information; (c) to use or weigh that information as part of the process of making the decision; or (d) to communicate his decision (whether by talking, using sign language or any other means).[190]

A person who does not lack capacity within the meaning of the Mental Capacity Act 2005 may, however, still be vulnerable and deprived of the capacity to take relevant decisions, or disabled from making a free choice, or incapacitated or disabled from giving or expressing a real and genuine consent by reason of such things as constraint, coercion, undue influence or some other vitiating factor.[191] A contract entered into in such circumstances may be voidable on the grounds of duress or undue influence.[192] However, the court also has a protective inherent jurisdiction to make orders in support of the vulnerable person.[193]

---

[187] Cf the position under the Infants Relief Act 1874, s 1 (repealed by Minors' Contracts Act 1987, s 4(1): above, p 258, n 139) which rendered loans to infants void rather than unenforceable: see *Coutts & Co v Browne-Lecky* [1947] KB 104. See also Law Com No 134 (1984) para 4.15.

[188] 2005 Act, s 1(2).

[189] 2005 Act, s 2(1). Cf *Dunhill v Burgin (Nos 1 and 2)* [2014] UKSC 18, [2014] 1 WLR 933 at [13] (Baroness Hale: 'the general approach of the common law, now confirmed in the Mental Capacity Act 2005, is that capacity is to be judged in relation to the decision or activity in question and not globally'). The law on mental (in)capacity was formerly contained in the Mental Health Act 1983, consolidating major revision made by the Mental Health Act 1959. The language has changed over the years, and the 2005 Act has abandoned such old terms as 'lunatic' or 'person of unsound mind' (Lunacy Act 1890), 'mentally defective', 'idiot', 'imbecile', or 'feeble-minded person' (Mental Deficiency Act 1913), and 'mentally disordered patient' (1959 and 1983 Acts).

[190] 2005 Act, s 3(1).

[191] *Re L (Vulnerable Adults with Capacity: Court's Jurisdiction) (No 2)* [2012] EWCA Civ 253, [2013] Fam 1 at [10].

[192] Below, Chapter 10.

[193] *Re L (Vulnerable Adults with Capacity: Court's Jurisdiction) (No 2)*, above, n 191.

The contract of a person lacking mental capacity or a drunken person is not binding if it can be shown that at the time of making the contract he or she was incapable of understanding the general nature of what was being done, and that the other party was aware[194] of this incapacity. This principle was established by Lord Esher MR in *Imperial Loan Co v Stone*:[195]

When a person enters into a contract, and afterwards alleges that he was so insane at the time that he did not know what he was doing, and proves the allegation, the contract is as binding upon him in every respect, whether it is executory or executed, as if he had been sane when he made it, unless he can prove further that the person with whom he contracted knew him to be so insane as not to be capable of understanding what he was about.

Authority for the view that, even if the condition of person lacking mental capacity was not known to the other party, the contract may be set aside if it was 'unfair' or 'unconscionable' in its terms[196] was disapproved by the Judicial Committee of the Privy Council in *Hart v O'Connor*.[197] Lord Brightman said:[198]

the validity of a contract entered into by a lunatic who is ostensibly sane is to be judged by the same standards as a contract by a person of sound mind, and is not voidable by the lunatic or his representatives by reason of 'unfairness' unless such unfairness amounts to equitable fraud which would have enabled the complaining party to avoid the contract even if he had been sane.

Lack of mental capacity therefore operates differently from minority, where the overriding policy is to protect the minor even if the person dealing with him or her does not know of the minority.[199] A party dealing with the person who lacks mental capacity, by contrast, is protected if he or she did not know of the lack of capacity. The basis on which the contract with a person lacking mental capacity, as also the contract with a drunken person,[200] is voidable is that the other party has improperly taken advantage of the weaker person. Such forms of 'procedural impropriety', 'equitable fraud', or 'unconscionable bargains' are discussed later.[201]

A contract made in such circumstances is voidable at the option of the incapacitated person, who can elect either to avoid the contract or to affirm it, in which case it is binding. Thus in *Matthews v Baxter*:[202]

B, while drunk, agreed at an auction sale to purchase from M certain houses and land. Afterwards, when sober, B affirmed the contract and then repented of his bargain. When

---

[194] But cf Lady Hale's statement in *Dunhill v Burgin (Nos 1 and 2)*, above, n 189 at [25] that it is 'generally accepted' that it is sufficient if the other party 'ought to have known' of the incapacity.

[195] [1892] 1 QB 599, 601; *York Glass Co Ltd v Jubb* (1925) 134 LT 36; *Hart v O'Connor* [1985] AC 1000. See also Law Com No 231, *Mental Incapacity* (1995) paras 3.5–3.6, 3.16–3.19.

[196] *Molton v Camroux* (1848) 2 Exch 487, 503 (aff'd (1849) 4 Exch 17); *Archer v Cutler* [1980] 1 NZLR 386 (New Zealand). For similar cases in relation to drunkenness, see *Cooke v Clayworth* (1811) 18 Ves 12; *Wiltshire v Marshall* (1866) 14 LT (NS) 396; *Blomley v Ryan* (1956) 99 CLR 362 (Australia).

[197] [1985] AC 1000.   [198] *Ibid*, 1027.   [199] Above, p 252.

[200] Or a contract with a person incapacitated by drugs: *Irvani v Irvani* [2000] 1 Lloyd's Rep 412.

[201] Below, pp 400–3.   [202] (1873) LR 8 Ex 132.

sued on the contract, he pleaded that he was drunk at the time he made it, and to M's knowledge.

The Court held that although B had once an option in the matter and might have avoided the contract, he was now bound by his affirmation of it. 'I think', said Martin B[203] 'that a drunken man when he recovers his senses, might insist on the fulfilment of his bargain, and therefore that he can ratify it, so as to bind himself to a performance of it'. It will be seen from this case that the contract of a mentally disordered or drunken person is voidable at the option of the incapacitated person and not completely void. Therefore if property is transferred as the result of such a contract and subsequently passes to a purchaser in good faith for value, it seems that the innocent purchaser would acquire a good title.[204]

Section 3 of the Sale of Goods Act 1979, which has already been quoted in respect of minors' contracts for necessaries, provides that 'where necessaries are sold and delivered to a person who by reason of drunkenness is incompetent to contract, he must pay a reasonable price for them'. The Mental Capacity Act 2005 makes a similar provision for contracts for necessary goods or services supplied to a person who lacks capacity to contract for the supply.[205] There is little doubt that the liability arises in restitution[206] and that an executory contract for necessaries, if avoided by the party lacking capacity, would be unenforceable.

---

[203] At 134.   [204] Above, pp 24–5.

[205] 2005 Act, s 7, replacing a provision for persons with mental incapacity in Sale of Goods Act 1979, s 3, above, p 253.

[206] *Re Rhodes* (1890) 44 Ch D 94. See also Winfield (1942) 58 LQR 82, 87.

8

MISTAKE

1. INTRODUCTION

This chapter is concerned with the circumstances in which a contract will be held to be defective if one or both of the parties enter into it under some misapprehension or misunderstanding but would not have done so had they known the true position.[1] Where one party's misunderstanding was caused by the words or conduct of the other party, the mistaken party will normally challenge the validity of the contract not by asserting that he made a mistake but by basing his claim on the other party's *misrepresentation* because, as we shall see, the scope of the doctrine of mistake is narrow and rather uncertain, but a claimant may obtain a wider range of remedies for misrepresentation.[2] There are, however, situations in which it is advantageous to a party to seek a remedy based on his or both parties' mistake, even where the mistake was induced by misrepresentation, because on the facts an appropriate remedy for misrepresentation is not available.[3] Moreover, if the claimant cannot establish a misrepresentation, he will be driven to base his claim on his own mistake.

Mistake is one of the most difficult topics in the English law of contract. The principles have never been precisely settled, the decided cases are open to a number of varying interpretations and the position is complicated by the fact that there have been distinct changes in the attitude of the judges to the question of mistake during the last 150 years.[4] A doctrine of mistake was first recognized in the English law of contract in the nineteenth century, under the influence of Roman law and modern civil law (and in particular French law).[5] There was a time when, in reliance on the *consensus* theory of contract and influenced by the eighteenth-century French jurist Pothier, the Courts were more readily disposed to hold that, where there was

---

[1] See Cartwright, *Misrepresentation, Mistake and Non-Disclosure* (3rd edn, 2012) Part 2.

[2] Misrepresentation is discussed in Chapter 9.

[3] eg rescission of a contract which is *voidable* for misrepresentation is barred by lapse of time or intervening third-party rights: below, p 337; but the claimant can assert that it is *void* for mistake: below, p 290.

[4] Cartwright, 'The Rise and Fall of Mistake in the English Law of Contract' in Sefton-Green (ed), *Mistake, Fraud and Duties to Inform in European Contract Law* (2005) 65.

[5] Simpson (1975) 91 LQR 247; Ibbetson, *A Historical Introduction to the Law of Obligations* (1999) ch 12; MacMillan, *Mistakes in Contract Law* (2010).

no 'true, full and free' consent, there was no valid contract.[6] At the present time, however, the Courts are very reluctant to intervene in this manner and the role of mistake is narrower than in many European legal systems.[7]

The reasons for this change are first that, at common law, if a contract is entered into under a legally operative mistake, it is void *ab initio*; it has no legal effect whatever. Consequently, if the subject-matter of the contract consists of goods, no property in the goods will pass under the contract. A third party will acquire no title to the goods even if he takes them in good faith and for value.[8] Secondly, there is a feeling that, once the parties are ostensibly in agreement in the same terms and upon the same subject-matter, they ought to be held to their bargain; they must rely on the terms of the contract for protection from the effect of facts unknown to them.[9] This has led to increased use of the objective test under which matters are judged by the external standard of the reasonable person,[10] a test which tends to protect a third party who relies in good faith on the apparent position. This promotes the certainty and finality of transactions which has been the hallmark of the English law of contract. Thirdly, there is a fear that parties to a contract will plead mistake to get out of a bad bargain or to reallocate the risks and consequently undermine the sanctity of contract.[11] This is coupled with a perception, also used to justify the absence of a general duty of disclosure, that if a person who has acquired expertise in the subject-matter of the contract could be deprived of the benefit of a bargain made with an uninformed counter-party it might imperil the market system.[12] By contrast, where there is no contractual bargain to set aside, the common law recognizes a broader role for mistake. Thus any (non-contractual) payment caused by a mistake is prima facie recoverable,[13] and a voluntary disposition may be rescinded in equity on the basis of mistakes that would be insufficient to render a contract void.[14]

Nevertheless, cases will undoubtedly arise in which it would be unjust to hold the parties strictly to their contract. Such cases will occur quite independently of any warranty or misrepresentation or fraud, and relief must be sought, if at all, on the ground of mistake. The Courts have displayed a mixed response to this problem. In 1932 Lord Atkin took a strict approach, and said that it was each party's responsibility

---

[6] Pothier, *Traité des Obligations* (1761) para 19 (discussing mistake of identity) was cited in *Smith v Wheatcroft* (1878) 9 Ch D 223, 230; *Gordon v Street* [1899] 2 QB 641, 647; *Phillips v Brooks* [1919] 2 KB 243, 248; *Said v Butt* [1920] 3 KB 497, 501; *Lake v Simmons* [1927] AC 487, 501; *Sowler v Potter* [1940] 1 KB 271, 274. Cf *Solle v Butcher* [1950] 2 KB 671, 692 (Denning LJ); *Lewis v Averay* [1972] 1 QB 198, 206 (Lord Denning MR).

[7] Lando and Beale, *Principles of European Contract Law Parts I and II* (2000) 235.

[8] *Cundy v Lindsay* (1878) 3 App Cas 459, below, p 291; cf *Shogun Finance Ltd v Hudson* [2003] UKHL 62, [2004] 1 AC 919, below, p 292 at [13], [35], [60], [82] (Lord Nicholls and Lord Millett (both dissenting)).

[9] *Bell v Lever Brothers Ltd* [1932] AC 161, 224 (Lord Atkin).

[10] *Smith v Hughes* (1871) LR 6 QB 597, below, p 277. See above, p 34.

[11] eg *Tamplin v James* (1880) 15 Ch D 215, 221; *Riverlate Properties Ltd v Paul* [1975] Ch 133, 140–1; *Associated Japanese Bank (International) Ltd v Crédit du Nord SA* [1989] 1 WLR 255, 264.

[12] *Smith v Hughes* (1871) LR 6 QB 597, 604, 606. See generally Kronman (1978) 7 JLS 1. On the absence of a general duty of disclosure, see below, pp 318, 358.

[13] *Kleinwort Benson Ltd v Lincoln CC* [1999] 2 AC 349.

[14] *Pitt v Holt* [2013] UKSC 26, [2013] 2 AC 108 at [114]–[115].

to check the facts which were significant for him in relation to the contract, or at least to ask for confirmation or a warranty from the other party in relation to significant facts.[15] However, taking the lead from an important judgment of Denning LJ in 1949[16] the Courts, side by side with their insistence that at common law the doctrine of mistake of facts is extremely narrow (if it exists at all), developed the use of certain equitable remedies which are, in some ways, more satisfactory as they are discretionary and, further, do not render the contract void *ab initio* but only voidable.[17] Moreover, it appeared that, again under the influence of Lord Denning, the Courts were moving away from the traditional approach under which a mistake made by one party about the identity of the other party can render the contract void, and preferred to find the contract only voidable[18] with the result that, as in the position of a contract vitiated by fraud, misrepresentation or duress, the position of third parties who take goods in good faith is protected.[19]

However, more recently the Court of Appeal has rejected Lord Denning's equitable doctrine of mistake of facts and has asserted that only the narrow common law doctrine of mistake can be relied upon in the absence of other vitiating factors such as misrepresentation or any statutory protection of the disadvantaged party.[20] In addition, the House of Lords has (by a bare majority) reasserted the traditional view that mistake of identity, even though it may occur relatively rarely, renders the contract void.[21] Later in this chapter we shall consider what has been lost in the latest reversion by the Court of Appeal back to the narrower common law doctrine of mistake of facts,[22] and the reassertion by the House of Lords of the traditional common law doctrine of mistake of identity.[23]

2. CATEGORIZING MISTAKES

For the purposes of understanding the law on mistake, it is possible to categorize the cases in various different ways. Sometimes it can be helpful to distinguish between a mistake made by only one of the parties ('unilateral') and a mistake shared by both parties (which has been called 'mutual',[24] but is nowadays generally labelled by the Courts as a 'common' mistake).[25] Sometimes we may distinguish

---

[15] *Bell v Lever Brothers Ltd* [1932] AC 161, 224 (Lord Atkin); below, p 301.

[16] *Solle v Butcher* [1950] 1 KB 671; below, p 312.

[17] *Associated Japanese Bank (International) Ltd v Crédit du Nord SA* [1989] 1 WLR 255, 267–8.

[18] *Solle v Butcher*, above, n 16, 692–3 (Denning LJ); *Lewis v Averay* [1972] 1 QB 198, 207 (Lord Denning MR). See also *Ingram v Little* [1961] QB 31, 73–4 (Devlin LJ); *Shogun Finance Ltd v Hudson* [2003] UKHL 62, [2004] 1 AC 919 at [33]–[35] and [61] (Lord Nicholls and Lord Millett, dissenting).

[19] Above, pp 24–5.

[20] *Great Peace Shipping Ltd v Tsavliris Salvage (International) Ltd, The Great Peace* [2002] EWCA Civ 1407, [2003] QB 679; below, p 314.

[21] *Shogun Finance Ltd v Hudson*, above, n 18; below, p 397.

[22] Below, pp 315–16.　　　　　　　　　　　　　　　　　　　　[23] Below, pp 297–8.

[24] eg *Bell v Lever Bros Ltd* [1932] AC 161 and in earlier editions of the present work.

[25] eg *Solle v Butcher* [1950] 1 KB 671, 693; *The Great Peace* [2002] EWCA Civ 1407, [2003] QB 679 at [32].

between the different effects of mistakes on the formation of the contract: some mistakes 'negative' the parties' consent, in the sense of preventing there being a sufficient agreement between the parties to bring the contract into existence; other mistakes do not operate to negative the consent but render the contract void by 'nullifying' it.[26] Sometimes we may separate out the effects of mistakes under the common law (under which an operative mistake renders the contract void) and in equity (which may provide different remedies: rescission of a (voidable) contract, refusal of specific performance even if the contract is valid at common law; rectification of the contract). In the following sections of this chapter, however, a different categorization is adopted—according to what the mistake is *about*. A party may make a mistake about the *terms* of the contract; the *identity* of the other contracting party; or *facts or law* relating to the *subject-matter* of the contract or to the *circumstances* surrounding the formation of the contract. Examining the cases by reference to these different categories helps to understand the approaches of the Courts to mistakes in different circumstances. However, in the course of this examination, we shall also see the relevance of whether the mistake is unilateral or shared; the impact on the formation of the contract; and the range of remedies at both common law and equity.

3. MISTAKES ABOUT THE TERMS OF THE CONTRACT

(a) 'SUBJECTIVE' AND 'OBJECTIVE' AGREEMENT IN THE FORMATION OF A CONTRACT

This section is concerned with that form of mistake which invalidates a contract because, although to all outward appearances the parties are agreed on the terms of their contract, there is in fact no sufficient agreement between them and the law therefore does not regard a contract as having come into existence. Such cases must be distinguished from cases in which there is not even the outward semblance of agreement because offer and acceptance never coincided in their respective terms.[27] However, these different cases are closely related. It follows from the essential nature of a contract that if there is no agreement between the parties, or, as is commonly said, if the parties are not *ad idem*, there is no contract. This is only another way of saying that offer and acceptance must correspond exactly, or no contract will ensue. Therefore, if the offeree thinks that the terms proposed by the offeror are other than those actually proposed, and if she accepts on that mistaken assumption, it is clear that there is no real agreement, for the offer which she has accepted is not the offer made by the other party.

---

[26] *Bell v Lever Bros Ltd* [1932] AC 161, 217 (Lord Atkin).   [27] Above, p 43.

If the test for the formation of a contract were whether the parties have both actually agreed on the existence and terms of the contract—that is, both parties not only intend to contract with each other but also have in their minds the same terms of the contract—then any mistake by either party about the terms of the contract would prevent the formation of the contract. That would be a *subjective* test for the formation of a contract which would have the merit that a party would be bound only to contracts which she genuinely intended to enter into. But it would also give great scope for a party to avoid being bound by the contract by simply showing that she misunderstood the terms proposed by the other party, and this could have the effect of undermining the security of contracts. English law has rejected the purely subjective test, and provides that a party may nevertheless be held to have agreed with the other party if an agreement can reasonably be inferred from objective facts.

We have already seen in Chapter 2, The Agreement[28] and Chapter 5, The Terms of the Contract[29] that, as a general rule, the intentions of the parties must be construed objectively. However, the meaning of 'objectivity' varies from one situation to another. Where the question is how to construe a *written* contract, the Courts normally discover the parties' common intentions from the document alone: the words are interpreted as a reasonable reader of the document would have understood them. The actual (subjective) intentions of the parties are in principle irrelevant to the question of construction, although as we shall see they may be relevant to the question of whether the document can be *rectified*.[30] However, where the question is how to construe the communications between parties who are negotiating a contract—the offer, counter-offers, and acceptance—the Courts have generally rejected a test based on 'detached objectivity' and the intentions of each party are interpreted from the perspective of the reasonable person in the position of the other party.[31] This is the general 'objective test' which will be discussed in the following section. Issues relating to written contracts will be considered later in this chapter.[32]

(b) THE 'OBJECTIVE TEST'

The general test used to ascertain the intentions of the parties was set out by Blackburn J in *Smith v Hughes*:[33]

if one of the parties intends to make a contract on one set of terms, and the other intends to make a contract on another set of terms, or, as it is sometimes expressed, if the parties are not ad idem, there is no contract, unless the circumstances are such as to preclude one of the

---

[28] Above, p 34.   [29] Above, p 179.   [30] Below, p 282.
[31] Above, p 34; Spencer [1973] CLJ 104, 106–13; Vorster (1987) 104 LQR 274, criticizing Howarth (1984) 100 LQR 265; Cartwright, *Unequal Bargaining* (1991) 5–24.
[32] Below, p 279.
[33] (1871) LR 6 QB 597, 607. For details of the case, see below, p 277. See also *The Hannah Blumenthal* [1983] 1 AC 854, 914, 915–16, 924; *Centrovincial Estates plc v Merchant Investors Assurance Co Ltd* [1983] Com LR 158; *OT Africa Line Ltd v Vickers plc* [1996] 1 Lloyd's Rep 700.

parties from denying that he has agreed to the terms of the other . . . If, whatever a man's real intention may be, he so conducts himself that a reasonable man would believe that he was assenting to the terms proposed by the other party, and that other party upon that belief enters into the contract with him, the man thus conducting himself would be equally bound as if he had intended to agree to the other party's terms.

This makes clear that the fact that the parties are not in real (subjective) agreement does not necessarily prevent the contract being formed, if one party has led the other party reasonably to believe that he was agreeing. In the vast majority of cases the operation of this objective test will exclude the plea that the parties were not in agreement. So the cases in which mistake affects a contract must be considered to be the rare exceptions to this general rule. Parties are bound by agreements to which they have expressed a clear assent. If they exhibit all the outward signs of agreement the law will hold that they have agreed.

Nevertheless it may happen that, although at first sight a contract appears perfectly valid, the law regards it as void because there was no agreement even when the parties' communications are assessed by reference to the objective test. This may occur in any of four situations:

(1) where, despite outward appearances, there is no coincidence between the terms of the offer and those of the acceptance because when each is tested objectively they conflict;

(2) where there is a mistake about the promise, or terms of the contract, which is known to the other party;

(3) where there is a mistake in relation to a written document;

(4) where there is a mistake about the identity of the person with whom the contract is made.

We shall here consider (1), (2), and (3). Mistakes about the identity of the other party raise particular difficulties and are considered separately in the next section.[34]

(i) Offer and acceptance not coincident

It may happen that, owing to a mistake, an offer may be innocently accepted in a different sense from that in which it was intended by the offeror, and the terms in which the contract is expressed may suffer from such latent ambiguity that it is impossible to say that the conduct of the parties points to one solution rather than another. In such a case one party may say that she did not attach the same meaning to the terms as the other party, and it will be impossible to say that her conduct would have induced a reasonable person to make one deduction rather than the other. The contract will be void because the terms of the offer and the acceptance did not coincide.[35]

---

[34] Below, p 289.   [35] Cited with approval in *Alampi v Swartz* (1963) 38 DLR (2d) 300 (Canada).

If, for example, two things have the same name, and A makes an offer to B referring to one of them, which offer B accepts thinking that A is referring to the other, then provided there is nothing in the terms of the contract to identify one or other as its subject-matter, evidence may be given to show that the mind of each party was in fact (and subjectively) directed to a different object: that A offered one thing and B accepted another. Where a reasonable person in each of A and B's positions would also have come to different conclusions about the parties' intentions, there is a (subjective) misunderstanding which cannot be resolved by an application of the objective test. So in *Raffles v Wichelhaus*:[36]

W agreed to buy from R 125 bales of cotton 'to arrive [in Liverpool] *ex Peerless* from Bombay'. There were two ships called *Peerless*, and both sailed from Bombay, but W meant the *Peerless* which sailed in October, and R the *Peerless* which sailed in December.

It was held that there was no contract. There was nothing in the agreement which would point to one or other of the vessels as being the one identified in the contract; the offer and acceptance did not coincide.

Similarly, if A makes to B an offer which is ambiguous in its terms, or is rendered ambiguous by the circumstances surrounding it, and B accepts the offer in a different sense from that in which it is meant, then unless an objective construction requires otherwise, B may effectively maintain that there is no binding contract. In *Scriven Bros & Co v Hindley & Co*:[37]

S instructed an auctioneer to sell certain bales of hemp and tow. These bore the same shipping mark and were described in the auction catalogue as so many bales in different lots with no indication of the difference in their contents. H's manager examined samples of the hemp before the sale intending to bid for the hemp alone. At the auction, the tow was put up for sale, and H's buyer, believing it to be hemp, made a bid which was a reasonable one if it had been intended for hemp, but an excessive one for tow. This bid was accepted by the auctioneer, who did not realize the buyer's mistake, but merely thought the bid an extravagant one for tow. S sought to enforce the contract by suing for the price.

It was clear that offer and acceptance did not coincide. S intended to sell tow; H's buyer, misled by the auction catalogue, intended to buy hemp. The Court held that there was nothing in H's conduct which would estop it from pleading that the parties were not in agreement as to the subject-matter of the sale—or, to put it in the language of the objective test set out by Blackburn J in *Smith v Hughes*,[38] H had not so conducted itself that a reasonable man would believe that it was assenting to S's terms. Accordingly, no contract had come into existence, and H was not liable.

It has been said that these are not truly cases of mistake rendering the contract void, but rather cases where there is no concurrence between the terms of the offer

---

[36] (1864) 2 H & C 906. See Simpson, *Leading Cases in the Common Law* (1995) ch 6. See also *Thornton v Kempster* (1814) 5 Taunt 786; *Henkel v Pape* (1870) LR 6 Ex 7; *Falck v Williams* [1900] AC 176; *Lloyds Bank plc v Waterhouse* (1991) 10 Tr LR 161, 185, 191.

[37] [1913] 3 KB 564.   [38] Above, p 274.

and those of the acceptance: no agreement, and therefore never a contract at all.[39] This is true, but it is important to see them in the context of the application of the objective test to override subjective misunderstandings, since the essential question is whether the offer and acceptance, objectively construed, can be taken to match. They also illustrate the point that proof of a mistake must be adduced before a flaw can be found in an ostensible agreement.

It is also important to realize the limits of these decisions. Where A sues B under an alleged contract but it is shown that there was no subjective agreement between the parties, and A cannot establish that B has so conducted himself as to entitle A reasonably to believe that B was agreeing to A's intended terms, then A's claim against B fails. But that outcome does not necessarily establish whether B (had he so wished) could have established that A's conduct had led B reasonably to believe that A was agreeing with B's intended terms. That is, just because A fails to establish a contract on A's terms does not mean that B could not establish a contract on B's terms. In every case the question is whether the party seeking to establish a contract can do so on the evidence of what the parties intended, and what the defendant's conduct had led the claimant reasonably to believe. If both parties were equally reasonable (or unreasonable) in their different understandings of the agreed terms, then there will be an ambiguity which cannot be resolved, and neither can establish a contract.[40] But if the misunderstanding was a result of the fault of one party, which was not known to the other party, it may often be the case that the latter can establish a contract on the basis of the terms as he understood them.

(ii) Mistake about the promise, or terms, which is known to the other party

In entering into contracts people must use their own judgement or, if they cannot rely upon their judgement, must take care that the terms of the contract secure to them what they want. *Caveat emptor* is a general rule of the law of contracts. One party is not bound to disclose to the other all material facts or circumstances which might affect the bargain and which are known to that party alone. Even if one party knows that the other party is contracting under a misapprehension about the facts, the general rule is that she has no duty to disillusion the mistaken party.[41] The law imposes certain particular duties of disclosure of material facts, where it is required by the particular type of contract[42] or the relationship between the parties (eg a fiduciary relationship).[43] Active concealment may constitute misrepresentation.[44] Save in these cases, however, mere silence will not constitute a misrepresentation and there is no duty of disclosure, and each party must protect itself from the consequences of its own mistake.

---

[39] *Statoil ASA v Louis Dreyfus Energy Services LP* [2008] EWHC 2257 (Comm), [2008] 2 Lloyd's Rep 685 at [87].

[40] Vorster (1987) 103 LQR 274, 286.   [41] Below, pp 358–9.   [42] Below, p 360.

[43] Below, p 364.   [44] Below, p 321.

Nevertheless a mistake about the terms of the contract is different from a mistake about the facts or the circumstances surrounding the formation of the contract.[45] The law will not allow one party to hold the other to a contract where that party knows that the other does not intend to agree on the same terms—for example, where A purports to accept B's offer knowing that B does not intend it in the sense that A claims to be entitled to interpret it. A cannot, as it is sometimes said, 'snap up' B's offer.[46] Moreover, a mistake by one party of which the other ought reasonably to have known will suffice.[47] This follows from the application of the objective test set out in *Smith v Hughes*.[48] Blackburn J said:

> If, whatever a man's real intention may be, he so conducts himself that *a reasonable man would believe* that he was assenting to the terms proposed by the other party, *and that other party upon that belief enters into the contract with him*, the man thus conducting himself would be equally bound as if he had intended to agree to the other party's terms.

The italicized words show that A can hold B to A's offer only if it was *reasonable* for him to believe that B was agreeing with the terms of the offer as A understood them, and only if A *in fact* believed it. So a party can never enforce a contract on terms which he did not in fact himself intend at the time of the formation of the contract.

In *Smith v Hughes*:[49]

S sued H for the price of oats sold and delivered, and for damages for not accepting the oats. S had offered to sell to H, by sample, a parcel of oats at 35s a quarter. According to H, S described the oats as 'good *old* oats', but S denied that the word 'old' had been used. This offer was rejected by H's counter-offer of 34s a quarter, which in turn was accepted by S's delivery of the oats. When they were delivered, they were found to be new oats, and unsuitable for S's purpose.

The trial judge directed the jury to consider:

(1) whether the word 'old' had been used by S or H in making the contract. If so, they were to give a verdict for H;

(2) if the word 'old' had not been used, whether they were of the opinion that S believed H to believe, or to be under the impression, that he was contracting for the purchase of old oats. If so, they were to give a verdict for H.

The jury found for H without stating on which ground they had based their verdict. On a motion for a new trial, the majority of the Court of Queen's Bench were of the

---

[45] *Smith v Hughes* (1871) LR 6 QB 597, 606, 607, 610–11; *Bell v Lever Brothers Ltd* [1932] AC 161, 218. On mistakes about facts and circumstances, see below, pp 298 ff.

[46] *Tamplin v James* (1880) 15 Ch D 215, 221; *Hartog v Colin & Shields* [1939] 3 All ER 566, 567.

[47] *Centrovincial Estates plc v Merchant Investors Assurance Co Ltd* [1983] Com LR 158; *OT Africa Line Ltd v Vickers plc* [1996] 1 Lloyd's Rep 700, 703. See also *Mannai Investment Co Ltd v Eagle Star Life Assurance Co Ltd* [1997] AC 749; *Homburg Houtimport BV v Agrosin Private Ltd, The Starsin* [2003] UKHL 12, [2004] 1 AC 715 at [73]–[76] (interpretation of written document by reference to the reasonable reader). Cf the test for rectification in cases of unilateral mistake, below, p 286.

[48] Above, p 274.   [49] (1871) LR 6 QB 597.

opinion that the second of these two directions would not sufficiently bring to the minds of the jury the distinction between agreeing to take the oats under the belief that they were old, and agreeing to take the oats under the belief that S *contracted* that they were old.[50] Hannen J said:[51]

> If, therefore, in the present case, [S] knew that [H], in dealing with him for oats, did so on the assumption that [S] was contracting to sell him old oats, he was aware that [H] apprehended the contract in a different sense to that in which he meant it, and he is thereby deprived of the right to insist that [H] shall be bound by that which was only the apparent, and not the real bargain.

But H might merely have been mistaken as to the age of the oats, and not as to the plaintiff's promise. If such were the case, the contract would be valid, and a verdict should have been given for S:[52]

> In order to relieve [H], it was necessary that the jury should find not merely that [S] believed [H] to believe that he was buying old oats, but that he believed [H] to believe that he, [S], was contracting to sell old oats.

Accordingly, a new trial was ordered.

The same rule was applied in different circumstances in *Hartog v Colin & Shields*:[53]

C & S offered to sell to H 3,000 Argentine hare skins, but by a mistake they offered them at so much per *pound* instead of so much per *piece*. H accepted the offer. It was shown that it was the usual practice of the trade to charge on a per piece basis and that the written and oral negotiations leading up to the sale had proceeded throughout on a price per piece. As a pound contained on average three pieces the price under the agreement was roughly one-third of what it would have been on a per piece basis. H sought to enforce the sale in the terms of the offer, and sued for non-delivery.

Singleton J held that H could not reasonably have supposed that that offer contained C & S's real intention. Indeed, he held that H did in fact know that C & S were under a mistake. The *apparent* agreement (ie so much per pound) was therefore void. However, the Judge did not consider whether C & S could enforce the intended contract (ie so much per piece) but both principle and the analogy of rectification in cases of unilateral mistake[54] suggest that they might have been able to do so.[55]

---

[50] *Ibid*, 608 (Blackburn J).   [51] *Ibid*, 610.

[52] *Ibid*, 611 (Hannen J); ie, a mere unilateral mistake about the facts relating to the subject-matter is insufficient to render the contract void: below, p 300.

[53] [1939] 3 All ER 566, followed in *McMaster University v Wilchar Construction Ltd* (1971) 22 DLR (3d) 9 (Canada), aff'd (1973) 69 DLR 3d 410; *Chwee Kin Keong v Digilandmall.com Pte Ltd* [2005] 1 SLR 502 (Singapore, but drawing a different distinction: actual knowledge of the other party's mistake about the terms is renders the contract void at common law; constructive notice renders it voidable in equity).

[54] Below, p 286. See also *Commission for the New Towns v Cooper (Great Britain) Ltd* [1995] Ch 259 (false and misleading statements made to divert mistaken party's attention).

[55] *Chitty on Contracts* (31st edn, 2012) para 5-081, citing *Ulster Bank Ltd v Lambe* [2012] NIQB 31.

(c) MISTAKE IN RELATION TO A WRITTEN DOCUMENT

We now deal with two remedies for mistakes about the terms of the contract which are peculiar to written contracts. First, there is the common law defence of *non est factum* which permits one who has signed a written document, which is essentially different from that which he intended to sign, to plead that, notwithstanding his signature, the legal position is that 'it is not his deed'.[56] The term properly applies to a deed but is equally applicable to other written contracts. Secondly, there is the equitable remedy of rectification of the contract, by which the Court can order that the written contract be given effect in terms other than those of the actual document in order to remedy the mistake of one or both parties about the terms of the contract.

Written contracts are different because the parties have taken the step of agreeing a text containing the terms of the contract, and the Courts therefore look for the agreed terms in the document itself. The interpretation of the document, although it takes into account the context of the transaction and the person to whom the document was addressed, is entirely objective. 'The question is what a reasonable person having all the background knowledge which would have been available to the parties would have understood them to be using the language in the contract to mean.'[57] In consequence, the Courts are not easily persuaded that the parties' apparent contract, as set out in the document, should be held to be void or rectified.

(i) *Non est factum*

The effect of a successful plea of *non est factum* is that the transaction contained in the document is not merely voidable against the person who procured its execution, but is entirely void into whosesoever hands the document may come.

It must be emphasized that *non est factum* is a narrow defence. A party is normally bound by the terms of a document which he has signed,[58] and those too lazy or too busy to read through it before signing it cannot plead *non est factum*. Nor can those who sign a document containing objectionable terms or terms the legal effect of which they are unaware. As Donovan LJ explained in *Muskham Finance Ltd v Howard*:[59]

Much confusion and uncertainty would result in the field of contract and elsewhere if a man were permitted to try to disown his signature simply by asserting that he did not understand that which he had signed.

In *Blay v Pollard & Morris*,[60] the defendant signed a document which he knew to relate to the dissolution of a partnership of which he was a member. Unknown to him, the document contained a term which had not been mentioned in a previous oral

---

[56] *Scriptum predictum non est factum suum.* See *Thoroughgood's Case* (1582) 2 Co Rep 9a; Holdsworth, *HEL* viii, 50; Simpson, *A History of the Common Law of Contract* (1975) 98.

[57] *Chartbrook Ltd v Persimmon Homes Ltd* [2009] UKHL 38, [2009] 1 AC 1101 at [14]; *Investors Compensation Scheme Ltd v West Bromwich Building Society* [1998] 1 WLR 896, 912–13. On interpretation generally, see above, p 178.

[58] Above, p 188.   [59] [1963] 1 QB 904, 912.   [60] [1930] 1 KB 628.

agreement, and which made him liable to indemnify his fellow partner in respect of certain partnership liabilities. It was held that he was bound by his signature and the defence of *non est factum* was rejected.

The narrowness of *non est factum* is also explained by the fact that it can be invoked against third parties:

Where a fraudster has tricked, first, the signer of the document, in order to induce the signature, and then some third party, who is induced to rely on the signed document, which of the two victims is the law to prefer? The authorities indicate that the answer is, almost invariably, the latter. The signer of the document has, by signing, enabled the fraud to be carried out, enabled the false document to go into circulation.[61]

(a) Essentially different transaction   In order for the defence to succeed, the person executing the document must show[62] that the transaction which the document purports to effect is essentially different in substance or in kind from the transaction intended. At one time it was thought that the plea of *non est factum* would not succeed if the mistake was as to the contents of a document, as opposed to its essential nature or character.[63] This distinction between contents and character is not an intelligible one,[64] for a document takes its character from its contents and in *Saunders v Anglia Building Society*,[65] it was rejected by the House of Lords in favour of a more flexible test: that there must be a 'radical' or 'essential' or 'fundamental' or 'serious' or 'very substantial' difference between the document signed and the document which the person signing intended to sign. If, for example, a person signs a guarantee for £10,000 believing it to be a guarantee of a lesser sum, it will depend on the amount of the lesser sum and the surrounding circumstances of the case whether or not the difference between the two transactions is sufficient to satisfy this test. The question is one of degree.

In *Saunders v Anglia Building Society*[66] the House of Lords held that the test had not been satisfied:

The appellant, an elderly widow, gave the title deeds of her house to her nephew, intending to make a gift to him of the house in order that he could borrow money on the security of the property. It was a condition of the gift that he was to permit her to reside there for the rest of her life. She was subsequently requested by a friend of her nephew, whom she knew to be assisting him to obtain a loan, to sign a document. The friend told her that it was 'to do with the gift by deed to Wally [her nephew] for the house'. As she had broken her spectacles, she signed the document without reading it. The document was in fact a deed conveying

---

[61] *Norwich and Peterborough BS v Steed (No 2)* [1993] Ch 116, 125 (Scott LJ).

[62] The burden of proof lies on the person wishing to establish the defence of *non est factum*: *Saunders v Anglia Building Society* [1971] AC 1004, 1016, 1019, 1027, 1038; *Crédit Lyonnais v PT Barnard & Associates Ltd* [1976] 1 Lloyd's Rep 557; *Norwich and Peterborough BS v Steed (No 2)* [1993] Ch 116.

[63] *Howatson v Webb* [1907] 1 Ch 537, aff'd [1908] 1 Ch 1.

[64] See Glanville Williams (1945) 61 LQR 179, 194; *Gallie v Lee* [1969] 2 Ch 17, 31, 41, 43; on appeal as *Saunders v Anglia Building Society* [1971] AC 1004, 1017, 1022, 1025, 1039.

[65] [1971] AC 1004, 1017, 1019, 1021, 1026, 1039.   [66] *Ibid.*

the house on sale to the friend. The friend did not pay the appellant or her nephew, but subsequently mortgaged the house to the respondents.

The plea of *non est factum* failed. At first sight there might seem to be an essential difference between a gift of the house to the nephew and a sale of the house to his friend. But, as Russell LJ pointed out in the Court of Appeal,[67] the appellant intended to transfer the house so that the transferee could raise money on it, and she knew that her nephew and his friend were engaged jointly on this project. The 'object of the exercise' might well have been achieved by means of a sale if the friend had been honest and paid the nephew. Although their Lordships were by no means unsympathetic to the appellant's situation,[68] they held that the document which she had executed was not of a fundamentally different nature from the document which she believed she was signing. The building society could therefore enforce the mortgage.

(b) Absence of negligence of party signing   In *Saunders v Anglia Building Society*[69] it was held that, even if the document signed is essentially different from that which the person signing it intended to sign, as against a third party he will not be entitled to disown his signature unless he proves that he exercised reasonable care. What is reasonable care will depend on the circumstances of the case and the nature of the document being signed. If one of two innocent parties is to suffer for the fraud of a third, the sufferer should be the one whose negligence has contributed to the loss suffered.

As a normal rule, therefore, if a person of full understanding and capacity forbears, or carelessly omits, to read what he signs, the defence of *non est factum* will not be available.[70] However, as Lord Wilberforce pointed out in *Saunders'* case:[71]

There remains a residue of difficult cases. There are still illiterate or senile persons who cannot read, or apprehend, a legal document; there are still persons who may be tricked into putting their signature on a piece of paper which has legal consequences totally different from anything they intended . . . Accepting all that has been said by learned judges as to the necessity of confining the plea within narrow limits, to eliminate it altogether would, in my opinion, deprive the courts of what may be, doubtless on sufficiently rare occasions, an instrument of justice.

An example of a case where the defence succeeded is *Foster v Mackinnon*:[72]

Mackinnon, 'a gentleman far advanced in years', was fraudulently induced to indorse a bill of exchange for £3,000 on the assurance that it was a guarantee of a similar nature to one

---

[67] *Gallie v Lee* [1969] 2 Ch 17, 40–1.

[68] The building society, in fact, undertook not to evict the appellant during her lifetime.

[69] [1971] AC 1004, 1019, 1023, 1027, 1037–8. *Carlisle and Cumberland Banking Co v Bragg* [1911] 1 KB 489, criticized by Anson (1912) 28 LQR 190 and Guest (1963) 79 LQR 346, was overruled.

[70] Cf Stone (1972) 88 LQR 190; Spencer [1973] CLJ 104.

[71] [1971] AC 1004, 1025–6. See also *Petelin v Cullen* (1975) 132 CLR 355 (Australia); *Lloyds Bank plc v Waterhouse* [1993] 2 FLR 97.

[72] (1869) LR 4 CP 704. See also *Lewis v Clay* (1897) 67 LJQB 224; and for a recent case *Trustees of Beardsley Theobalds Retirement Benefit Scheme v Yardley* [2011] EWHC 1380 (QB) at [53]–[55].

which he had previously signed. Later the bill was indorsed for value to Foster, who took it in good faith.

It was held that the defence of *non est factum* was available to Mackinnon, as he never intended to make such a contract, and had been guilty of no negligence.

Where a person signs a document in blank, leaving it to another to fill in the terms of the contract in accordance with an oral agreement reached between them, it would seem that he could in theory rely on the defence of *non est factum* if the terms inserted render the transaction essentially different in substance or in kind from the transaction intended. However, unless there are exceptional circumstances present, a person who signs a document in blank accepts responsibility for it; and he takes the risk if, through fraud or error, the document is filled in in some different way.[73] He cannot therefore avoid his liability as against an innocent third party.

There is support in other jurisdictions for the view that, where no third party is involved, negligence is irrelevant.[74] But it has also been suggested that in two party cases remedies for fraud, misrepresentation, or unilateral mistake should be used rather than *non est factum*.[75]

(ii) Rectification of written contracts

(a) Rectification contrasted with interpretation   Rectification and interpretation fulfil different purposes. Interpretation discovers the meaning which the law will give to the document as written; rectification changes the document.[76] However, a party who admits that the written document does not appear by its language to reflect his intentions may claim, first, that it should be interpreted so to give effect to those intentions; and secondly, if such an interpretation is not possible, that the document should be rectified to reflect his intentions. In some cases, therefore, a mistake in the document may effectively be remedied by interpretation without the need to have recourse to rectification.[77]

(b) Rectification for common mistake   Where a contract has been reduced to writing, or a deed executed, and the writing or deed fails to express the concurrent intentions of the parties at the time of its execution, the Court may rectify the document in accordance with their intentions.

---

[73] *United Dominions Trust Ltd v Western* [1976] QB 513. Cf *Mercantile Credit Co Ltd v Hamblin* [1965] 2 QB 242. See Allcock (1982) 45 MLR 18.

[74] *Petelin v Cullen* (1975) 132 CLR 355, 360; *Bradley West Solicitors Nominee Co Ltd v Keenan* [1994] 2 NZLR 111, 118.

[75] *Lloyds Bank plc v Waterhouse* [1993] 2 FLR 97, 117, 122–3.

[76] The rules relating to interpretation have been discussed above, pp 178 ff.

[77] eg *Chartbrook Ltd v Persimmon Homes Ltd* [2009] UKHL 38, [2009] 1 AC 1101 (decision based on interpretation, so rectification not necessary); *Littman v Aspen Oil (Broking) Ltd* [2005] EWCA Civ 1579, [2006] 2 P & CR 2; cf *KPMG v Network Rail Infrastructure Ltd* [2007] EWCA Civ 363, [2008] 1 P & CR 11 (no ground for rectification, but omission in document corrected by interpretation). See also Burrows, in Burrows and Peel (eds), *Contract Terms* (2007) 77; cf *Cherry Tree Investments Ltd v Landmain Ltd* [2012] EWCA Civ 736, [2013] Ch 305 at [122] (rectification, not interpretation, appropriate where third parties may be affected).

In *Craddock Brothers v Hunt*,[78] for example:

A vendor agreed orally to sell to a purchaser a certain piece of property. By a mistake, the written contract embodying this agreement included an adjoining yard which the parties had excluded from the sale and the subsequent conveyance actually conveyed this land to the purchaser.

The Court ordered that the conveyance should be rectified to bring it into line with the parties' oral agreement.

In *Swainland Builders Ltd v Freehold Properties Ltd*[79] Peter Gibson LJ set out the requirements for rectification for common mistake:

The party seeking rectification must show that:

(1) the parties had a common continuing intention, whether or not amounting to an agreement, in respect of a particular matter in the instrument to be rectified;

(2) there was an outward expression of accord;

(3) the intention continued at the time of the execution of the instrument sought to be rectified;

(4) by mistake the instrument did not reflect that common intention.

(1) *Common intention.* The document which it is sought to rectify must fail to express the common intentions and outward accord of the parties. Such accord cannot be shown where there is confusion as to what has been agreed[80] or where a matter is omitted from a document as a result of forgetfulness; an absence of intention does not suffice.[81] The accord need not, however, as some older cases suggested, amount to a complete concluded contract in advance of the execution of the written document.[82] It is now clearly established that there is jurisdiction to rectify where the parties have made a mistake in their attempt to embody in the document their concurrent intentions in regard to a particular term which existed at the time it was put into writing or executed.[83] A concluded contract need not be shown. There must, however, be evidence of the parties' 'common intention'. Until recently the cases had suggested that this referred to a common *subjective* intention of the parties,[84] and that the 'outward expression of accord' was a matter of evidence rather than a formal requirement.[85] However, Lord

---

[78] [1923] 2 Ch 136. See also *USA v Motor Trucks Ltd* [1924] AC 196, 202.

[79] [2002] EWCA Civ 560, [2002] 2 EGLR 71 at [33], approved in *Chartbrook Ltd v Persimmon Homes Ltd* [2009] UKHL 38, [2009] 1 AC 1101 at [48].

[80] *Cambro Contractors Ltd v John Kennelly Sales Ltd*, The Times, 14 April 1994 (CA).

[81] *Olympia Sauna Shipping Co SA v Shinwa Kaiun Kaisha* [1985] 2 Lloyd's Rep 364, 370; *Kemp v Neptune Concrete* (1989) 57 P & CR 369, 377, 379–80.

[82] *Mackenzie v Coulson* (1869) LR 8 Eq 368, 375; *Faraday v Tamworth Union* (1916) 86 LJ Ch 436, 438; *Higgins (W) Ltd v Northampton Corp* [1927] 1 Ch 128, 136; *USA v Motor Trucks Ltd* [1924] AC 196, 200.

[83] *Crane v Hegemann-Harris Co Inc* [1939] 1 All ER 662, 664, aff'd [1939] 4 All ER 68; *Joscelyne v Nissen* [1970] 2 QB 86, 98; *Chartbrook Ltd v Persimmon Homes Ltd* above, n 79 at [59].

[84] *Agip SpA v Navigazione Alta Italia SpA* [1984] 1 Lloyd's Rep 353, 359 (the 'true agreement'); *Kemp v Neptune Concrete*, above, n 81, 377 ('the subjective intention of the party seeking relief').

[85] *Munt v Beasley* [2006] EWCA Civ 370, [2006] All ER (D) 29 (Apr) at [36].

Hoffmann has said that the existence of a common intention before the document was executed should be tested objectively by reference to what the reasonable observer would have thought the intentions of the parties to be.[86] This influential *obiter dictum* has been followed,[87] and sometimes approved[88] but also criticized.[89] It is submitted that Lord Hoffmann's statement should not be followed. The purpose of rectification is to bring the written document into line with the parties' agreement as it stood immediately before the execution of the document. In referring to the parties' agreement (their 'common intention') Lord Hoffmann used the perspective of the 'detached' objective observer, which is appropriate in the case of written documents[90] but not in interpreting the communications between the parties, where the question is how a reasonable person placed in the position of each party would have understood the other, and how each party also in fact understood the other since a party cannot hold the other to an agreement on terms which he knows the other did not intend.[91] A party should succeed in a claim for rectification only where the Court is satisfied that he in fact believed that the terms of the contract were those into which he claims that the document should be rectified. Morgan J stated:[92]

The law as stated by Lord Hoffmann appears to mean that a court can rectify a contract even though one party to the contract (even the party seeking rectification) fully intended, subjectively, to be bound by that contract, if the court is able to find that the final expression of consensus in the contract as executed differs from an earlier expression of consensus in a communication passing during the negotiations between the parties.

Rectification on the basis of common mistake should therefore be limited at least to the case where the document fails to reflect the parties' agreement as it would be determined on an analysis of their communications leading up to the execution of the document.[93] However, there is only a common 'mistake' where both parties in fact make the same mistake, and therefore the remedy should allow only the *actual* shared intentions of the parties as to the terms of the contract to override the written document.[94] If the parties did not in fact share the same understanding as to the terms of the contract, the claim for rectification may be based on a unilateral mistake.[95]

---

[86] *Chartbrook Ltd v Persimmon Homes Ltd* above, n 79 at [60].

[87] *Daventry DC v Daventry & District Housing Ltd* [2011] EWCA Civ 1153, [2012] 1 WLR 1333; *Ahmad v Secret Garden (Cheshire) Ltd* [2013] EWCA Civ 1005 at [30]; *Scottish Widows Fund and Life Assurance Society v BGC International* [2012] EWCA Civ 607, (2012) 142 Con LR 27 at [46]. In support of an objective test, see also Smith (2007) 123 LQR 116.

[88] *Daventry DC v Daventry & District Housing Ltd*, above, n 87, at [89] (Etherton LJ, going so far as to say at [80] that the 'outward expression of accord' and 'common continuing intention' are not separate conditions but two sides of the same coin).

[89] *Daventry DC v Daventry & District Housing Ltd*, above, n 87, at [176] (Toulson LJ); *Crossco No 4 Unlimited v Jolan Ltd* [2011] EWHC 803 (Ch), [2011] All ER (D) 13 (Apr) at [253]; *Tartsinis v Navona Management Co* [2015] EWHC 57 (Comm), [2015] All ER (D) 110 (Jan) at [90]; Davies (2012) 75 MLR 412; *Chitty on Contracts* (31st edn, 2012) para 5-119.

[90] Above, p 179.   [91] Above, pp 33, 273.

[92] *Crossco No 4 Unlimited v Jolan Ltd*, above, n 89 at [253]. See similarly *Tartsinis v Navona Management Co* above, n 89 at [90] (Leggatt J).

[93] McLaughlan (2014) 130 LQR 83.   [94] Davies (2012) 75 MLR 412.

[95] Below, p 285; *Chitty on Contracts* (31st edn, 2012) para 5-119A.

(2) *Continuing intention*. The intention of the parties as expressed in the prior accord must have continued unchanged up to the time of the execution of the written instrument.[96] If there is no clear evidence to this effect, the document (in its different terms) would indicate that the parties had changed their intentions by the time of the execution of the written document.

(3) *Document must fail to represent the common intention*. The party seeking to have a document rectified must adduce convincing evidence that its terms do not accurately record the common intention of the parties at the time.[97] However, rectification is not an appropriate remedy where the mistake relates to the transaction itself rather than to the document which purports to record it. Accordingly, there must be a literal disparity between the terms of the agreement and the document. Proof of an inner misapprehension is insufficient. In *Frederick E Rose (London) Ltd v William H Pim Jnr & Co Ltd*:[98]

Rose received from its Middle East associates an order for up to five hundred tons of 'Moroccan horsebeans described here as feveroles'. Rose did not know what feveroles were, and asked Pim. Pim replied that they were simply horsebeans, and so Rose orally contracted to buy from Pim a quantity of horsebeans to meet this order. A subsequent written agreement embodied the same terms. In fact, however, feveroles were quite another type of bean, and Rose claimed to have the written agreement rectified to read 'feveroles', intending to claim damages on the agreement if so rectified.

The Court of Appeal refused rectification. Both the oral and the written contracts were for horsebeans. There was no literal disparity between them. The only mistake was in the minds of the parties at the time. As Denning LJ put it:[99]

Rectification is concerned with contracts and documents, not with intentions. In order to get rectification it is necessary to show that the parties were in complete agreement on the terms of their contract, but by an error wrote them down wrongly; and in this regard, in order to ascertain the terms of their contract, you do not look into the inner minds of the parties—into their intentions—any more than you do in the formation of any other contract.

It has, however, been held that, where the parties have expressly agreed what is the meaning of particular words used in a written contract, the contract can be rectified to make it clear that the words bear the meaning agreed.[100]

(c) Rectification for unilateral mistake The remedy of rectification was originally granted only in cases of common mistake, to correct the erroneous expression of the

---

[96] *Fowler v Fowler* (1859) 4 De G & J 250.

[97] *Joscelyne v Nissen* [1970] 2 QB 86, 98; *Luk Leamington Ltd v Whitnash plc* [2002] 1 Lloyd's Rep 6. In order to establish the intention, parol evidence is admissible even where the contract is one which is required to be in writing: *Craddock Bros v Hunt* [1923] 2 Ch 136; *USA v Motor Trucks Ltd* [1924] AC 196; or where evidence of the communications between the parties during the negotiations would not be admissible to interpret the written contract: *Chartbrook Ltd v Persimmon Homes Ltd*, above, n 79; above, p 181.

[98] [1953] 2 QB 450. See also *Agip SpA v Navigazione Alta Italia SpA* [1984] 1 Lloyd's Rep 353, 359; *Ets Georges et Paul Levy v Adderley Navigation Co Panama SA* [1980] 1 Lloyd's Rep 67, 72.

[99] At 461.

[100] *London Weekend Television Ltd v Paris and Griffith* (1969) 113 SJ 222; *Joscelyne v Nissen* [1970] 2 QB 86, 98; *Re Butlin's Settlement* [1976] Ch 251.

common intentions of *both* parties. But it has been extended to cases of unilateral mistake, where the document fails to reflect the intention of only one of the parties at the time of its execution.[101] If, however, the mistake is unilateral, it is more difficult to establish that the document should be rectified because rectification is a 'drastic' remedy[102] which deprives the non-mistaken party of the benefit of the document in the terms which he intended and which were apparently agreed by the party who claims that he made a mistake.[103] The knowledge or conduct of the party who was not mistaken must be such as to make it inequitable for that party to object to rectification.

The Court will not order rectification for unilateral mistake unless three conditions are satisfied.[104] First, the other party must have actual knowledge of the mistaken party's intentions and of the mistake.[105] In this context the knowledge of an agent will not suffice[106] but a party who has wilfully shut his eyes to the obvious, or wilfully and recklessly failed to make such inquiries as an honest and reasonable person would have made, will be taken to have actual knowledge.[107] Secondly, the party not under a mistake must have failed to draw the mistaken party's attention to the mistake. Thirdly, the mistake must be such that the party not under a mistake would derive a benefit,[108] or the mistaken party would suffer a detriment,[109] if the inaccuracy in the document were to remain uncorrected. Previously there was some authority for the view that the conduct of the party who was not mistaken had to amount to fraud,[110] or at least involve a degree of sharp practice on his part;[111] but this is not required.[112] The question is whether the non-mistaken party's conduct is unconscionable so that he cannot insist on performance in accordance to the strict letter of the contract.[113] Nevertheless, it is clear that if a party executes a document

---

[101] *Roberts & Co Ltd v Leicestershire CC* [1961] Ch 555; *Riverlate Properties Ltd v Paul* [1975] Ch 133, 140; *Thomas Bates & Son Ltd v Wyndham's (Lingerie) Ltd* [1981] 1 WLR 505.

[102] *Agip SpA v Navigazione Alta Italia SpA* [1984] 1 Lloyd's Rep 353, 365 (Slade LJ); *George Wimpey UK Ltd v VI Construction Ltd* [2005] EWCA Civ 77, [2005] BLR 135 at [75]. Cf, however, McLaughlan (2008) 124 LQR 608 (not really 'drastic' at all, but a routine application of the objective principle); McLauchlan (2014) 130 LQR 83; Cartwright, *Unequal Bargaining* (1991) 53–7.

[103] Where rectification is sought of a voluntary disposition rather than a contract, the remedy is more readily available. What is important is the subjective intention of the settlor rather than the requirement in the case of a contract of outward expression of objective communication of that intention: *Day v Day* [2013] EWCA Civ 280, [2014] Ch 114 at [22]. Similarly, for rescission of a voluntary disposition entered into under a unilateral mistake, see *Pitt v Holt* [2013] UKSC 26, [2013] 2 AC 108 at [114]–[115], above, p 270.

[104] *Thomas Bates and Son Ltd v Wyndham's (Lingerie) Ltd*, [1981] 1 WLR 505, 515–16, 520–1.

[105] *Riverlate Properties Ltd v Paul* [1975] Ch 133, 140; *Agip SpA v Navigazione Alta Italia SpA*, above, n 102, 365.

[106] *Kemp v Neptune Concrete* (1989) 57 P & CR 369.

[107] *Commission for the New Towns v Cooper (GB) Ltd* [1995] Ch 259.

[108] *Thomas Bates and Son Ltd v Wyndham's (Lingerie) Ltd* [1981] 1 WLR 505, 516.

[109] *Ibid*, 521.   [110] *May v Platt* [1900] 1 Ch 616, 623.

[111] *Riverlate Properties Ltd v Paul* [1975] Ch 133, 140.

[112] *Thomas Bates and Son Ltd v Wyndham's (Lingerie) Ltd* [1981] 1 WLR 505.

[113] *Commission for the New Towns v Cooper (GB) Ltd*, above, n 107, 280; *Littman v Aspen Oil (Broking) Ltd* [2005] EWCA Civ 1579, [2006] 2 P & CR 2 at [18]–[26].

in ignorance that the other party is under a mistake, the remedy of rectifi
be denied.[114]

(d) Limits on the remedy of rectification   The award of the remedy of rectification
within the discretion of the Court. As an equitable remedy, it is barred not only by the
mistaken party waiving his claim to the remedy, but also by the equitable doctrine of
laches—that is, where the other party would be prejudiced by the delay in bringing
the claim. Rectification may also not be ordered if it would prejudice the rights of an
innocent third party.[115]

(e) Nature of the remedy of rectification   The court order of rectification itself changes
the terms of the contract, and the parties do not need to execute a new document.[116]
The effect of the court order is normally retrospective to change the terms of the
document with effect from the formation of the contract.[117]

(d) EQUITABLE REMEDIES FOR MISTAKES ABOUT THE TERMS

The Courts of Equity developed their own remedies in favour of a party who
had made a mistake.[118] We have already seen that equity would rectify a written
document in order to give effect to the true agreement between the parties.[119] Two
other remedies are also relevant: specific performance, which may be refused where
there has been a mistake; and rescission.

(i) Refusal of specific performance

In the case of breaches of contracts for the sale or transfer of land, the common
law remedy is damages but equity would normally compel the transfer of the
land by means of an order for specific performance.[120] Specific performance is a
discretionary remedy[121] and the Court will not order it where it would cause undue
hardship in the circumstances of the case. Mistake of a type which is insufficient to
render the contract void at law may be a ground for resisting specific performance
where it would be harsh to enforce performance of a contract against one who has
entered into it under a mistake. Specific performance may be refused not only where
the mistake is about the facts relating to the land but also where mistake relates to
the terms of the contract itself such as the term which identifies the property that

---

[114] *Riverlate Properties Ltd v Paul* [1975] Ch 133; *Agip SpA v Navigazione Alta Italia SpA* [1984] 1 Lloyd's Rep 353, 362.

[115] The right to rectification is an 'equity'. For the nature of an equity and the circumstances in which the right to rectify a contract relating to land will bind a purchaser of a legal or equitable interest in the land, see Burn and Cartwright, *Cheshire and Burn's Modern Law of Real Property* (18th edn, 2011) 903–6.

[116] *White v White* (1872) LR 15 Eq 247.

[117] *Malmesbury v Malmesbury* (1862) 31 Beav 407, 418. Cf Law of Property (Miscellaneous Provisions) Act 1989, s 2(4) (such time as stated in Court's order).

[118] See also below, p 312.   [119] Above, pp 282 ff.   [120] Below, p 611.

[121] See below, pp 608 ff.

the purchaser has agreed to buy. In *Malins v Freeman*[122] where a purchaser bid for and bought one lot of land at an auction in the belief that he was buying a wholly different lot, the Court refused to order specific performance of the contract. The defendant's mistake was due to his own carelessness and to no fault of the claimant, but the Court was prepared to exercise its discretion in his favour, leaving the claimant to claim damages at law. On the other hand, in *Tamplin v James*,[123] the defendant bid for and bought an inn and outbuildings in the mistaken belief that the lot also included two attached pieces of garden. There was little excuse for this misapprehension as the plans of the property to be sold were exhibited at the sale. The Court made an order for specific performance of the agreement.

(ii) Rescission

It has sometimes been said that, where a contract is binding at law, a party who made a mistake about the terms may be able to obtain rescission in equity;[124] or that, in cases of unilateral mistake in written contracts, equity might give the defendant the option of accepting rectification or having the contract rescinded.[125] However, such statements must now be viewed with caution, and there appears not to be any general equitable discretion to grant rescission for mistake about the terms of a contract which is valid at law. On one view, there must be fraud or misrepresentation on the part of the other party before rescission is available.[126] On another, somewhat wider, view, which formed the basis of the decision in *Solle v Butcher*,[127] it is sufficient if the Court 'is of the opinion that it is unconscientious for [the other party] to avail himself of the legal advantage which he has obtained' by the contract.[128] However, the approach of Denning LJ in *Solle v Butcher* was rejected in *The Great Peace*[129] where the Court of Appeal held that there is no equitable jurisdiction to rescind a contract for a common mistake of fact where the mistake is not sufficient to render the contract void at common law, on the basis that 'the premise of equity's intrusion into the effects of the common law is that the common law rule in question is seen in the particular case to work injustice, and for some reason the common law cannot cure itself'.[130] A similar

---

[122] (1837) 2 Keen 25. The Courts in such cases do not always consider explicitly whether the mistake is about a term of the contract, or only about the facts relating to the subject-matter. See also *Wood v Scarth* (1855) 2 K & J 33; *Denny v Hancock* (1870) LR 6 Ch App 1; *Burrow v Scammell* (1881) 19 Ch D 175, 182. In *Webster v Cecil* (1861) 30 Beav 62 the contract would have been void at common law because the claimant knew or ought to have known about the mistake.

[123] (1880) 15 Ch D 215.

[124] *Solle v Butcher* [1950] 1 KB 671, 692–3; *OT Africa Line Ltd v Vickers plc* [1996] 1 Lloyd's Rep 700, 704.

[125] *Garrard v Frankel* (1862) 30 Beav 445; *Paget v Marshall* (1884) 28 Ch D 255; *Harris v Pepperell* (1867) LR 5 Eq 1; *Bloomer v Spittle* (1872) LR 13 Eq 427; *May v Platt* [1900] 1 Ch 616, 623.

[126] *May v Platt* [1900] 1 Ch 616, 623; *London Borough of Redbridge v Robinson Rentals* (1969) 211 EG 1125; *Riverlate Properties Ltd v Paul* [1975] Ch 133.

[127] [1950] 1 KB 671.   [128] *Torrance v Bolton* (1872) LR Ch App 118, 124.

[129] [2002] EWCA Civ 1407, [2003] QB 679; below, p 303.

[130] *Ibid* at [156]; applied to unilateral mistakes of fact in *Statoil ASA v Louis Dreyfus Energy Services LP* [2008] EWHC 2257 (Comm), [2008] 2 Lloyd's Rep 685 at [105].

argument should apply to a mistake about the terms. The objective test applied by the common law already prevents a party who makes a mistake about the terms of the contract from being bound where the other party knew, or ought to have known, about the mistake.[131] No further role is needed for equity. Indeed, this appears to be the approach taken by the Court of Appeal in *Riverlate Properties Ltd v Paul*.[132] The Court of Appeal held that there was no power to grant equitable relief on the grounds of mere unilateral mistake unless the party against whom relief is sought was aware, at the time of the transaction, that the other party was contracting under a mistake. Russell LJ stated:[133]

Is the lessor entitled to rescission of the lease on the mere ground that it made a serious mistake in the drafting of the lease which it put forward and subsequently executed, when (a) the lessee did not share the mistake, (b) the lessee did not know that the document did not give effect to the lessor's intention, and (c) the mistake of the lessor was in no way attributable to anything said or done by the lessee? . . . If reference be made to principles of equity, it operates on conscience. If conscience be clear at the time of the transaction, why should equity disrupt the transaction? If a man may be said to be fortunate in obtaining a property at a bargain price, or on terms that make it a good bargain, because the other party unknown to him has made a miscalculation or other mistake, some high-minded men might consider it appropriate that he should agree to a fresh bargain to cure the miscalculation or mistake, abandoning his good fortune. But if equity were to enforce the views of those high-minded men, we have no doubt that it would run counter to the attitudes of much the greater part of ordinary mankind (not least the world of commerce), and would be venturing on the field of moral philosophy.

4. MISTAKES ABOUT THE IDENTITY OF THE PERSON WITH WHOM THE CONTRACT IS MADE

Mistakes of this sort can occur only where A contracts with B, believing B to be C: that is, where a party has in contemplation a definite and identifiable person with whom he intends to contract. Further, at the time when the contract is made, one party must regard the identity of the other party as a matter of vital importance.[134] One who, for example, accepts a bid at a public auction cannot normally allege that he is concerned with the identity of the person who makes the bid.[135]

---

[131] Above, p 277. Cf the different approach in Singapore, where actual knowledge of the other party's mistake about the terms renders the contract void at common law; constructive notice renders it voidable in equity: *Chwee Kin Keong v Digilandmall.com Pte Ltd* [2005] 1 SLR 502; above, p 278, n 53. See also *Taylor v Johnson* (1983) 151 CLR 422 (High Court of Australia).

[132] [1975] Ch 133.   [133] *Ibid*, 140–1.

[134] *Ingram v Little* [1961] 1 QB 31, 57; *Lewis v Averay* [1972] 1 QB 198, 209; *Shogun Finance Ltd v Hudson* [2003] UKHL 62, [2004] 1 AC 919 at [48], [178], [191].

[135] *Dennant v Skinner* [1948] 2 KB 164.

Mistake about identity has posed particular difficulties for the Courts because often the issue of its effect on an apparent agreement arises not as between the parties to the agreement but in determining which of two innocent people defrauded by a third party is to bear the loss. In many of the reported cases A was induced to enter into a contract of sale of goods by a fraudulent misrepresentation by B about his identity; but by the time A had discovered the truth B had sold and delivered the goods to C. The fraudulent misrepresentation would render the contract between A and B voidable, but rescission is no longer possible once the goods have passed into the hands of an innocent purchaser, C,[136] who can therefore keep the goods and leave A to his remedy in damages against B (if he can find him, and if B is solvent). But if A can show that there was a mistake of identity which rendered his contract void, then B acquired no title to the goods and so could not transfer title to C:[137] C must therefore return the goods or pay damages in the tort of conversion to A.[138] Some of the disagreement between the judges in the cases reflects different policies as to the incidence of loss between the innocent parties. Many of the issues relating to mistake about identity have been settled by the House of Lords in *Shogun Finance Ltd v Hudson*[139] but even there the House was divided as to the proper approach to be taken. The minority (Lord Nicholls and Lord Millett) would have overruled many of the older cases in order to achieve the result that a contract entered into under a mistake of identity is normally only voidable and not void, thus protecting the innocent third-party purchaser.[140] However, the majority affirmed the existing authorities, and held that a contract may be void for mistake of identity. Even under the approach approved by the majority in *Shogun*, however, such an operative mistake will be relatively rare.

(a) AN OFFER CAN BE ACCEPTED ONLY BY THE PERSON TO WHOM IT IS ADDRESSED

A person cannot constitute himself a contracting party with one whom he knows or ought to know has no intention of contracting with him: an offer can be accepted only by the person to whom it is addressed. In *Boulton v Jones*:[141]

B had taken over the business of one Brocklehurst, with whom J had been used to deal. J had a running account with Brocklehurst and was entitled to a set-off in respect of sums

---

[136] Below, p 337.   [137] Above, p 270.

[138] It is the tort of conversion (rather than the law of property) that protects the right to possession of goods; and where the defendant does not return the goods the normal remedy is damages, rather than an order for specific recovery: Peel and Goudkamp, *Winfield & Jolowicz on Tort* (19th edn, 2014) para 18-050; Bridge, *Personal Property Law* (4th edn, 2015) 120–121.

[139] [2003] UKHL 62, [2004] 1 AC 919. Strictly, the *ratio* relates only to contracts in writing: below, p 295, but there was also significant discussion about the approach to be taken in the case of unwritten contracts: below, p 297.

[140] *Ibid* at [35] and [84], approving the discussion in the 28th edn of this book, p 332.

[141] (1857) 2 H & N 564. Boulton had been Brocklehurst's foreman, and from the report of this case in (1857) 6 WR 107 it appears that Boulton knew the existence of the set-off. It is, however, an unusual case in that Jones's mistake was not induced by a fraudulent misrepresentation by Boulton.

owed to him by Brocklehurst. J sent an order for goods addressed to Brocklehurst, which B supplied without informing J that the business had changed hands. When J learned that the goods had not come from Brocklehurst, he refused to pay for them, and was sued by B for the price.

It was held that he was not liable to pay for the goods. Pollock CB said:[142]

It is a rule of law, that if a person intends to contract with A, B cannot give himself any right under it. Here the order in writing was given to Brocklehurst. Possibly Brocklehurst might have adopted the act of [B] in supplying the goods, and maintained an action for their price. But since [B] had chosen to sue, the only course [J] could take was to plead that there was no contract with him.

Nevertheless it must be remembered that offer and acceptance must here, as elsewhere, be understood in an objective sense. The test is not merely 'Did the offeror intend to contract with the person to whom the offer was made?' but also 'How would a reasonable person in the position of the offeree have interpreted the offer?'[143] So if A makes an offer to B in mistake for C, and B, reasonably believing that the offer is intended for him, accepts, then A is bound even though he can prove that he had made a mistake. An extreme application of this principle can be seen in *Upton-on-Severn RDC v Powell*:[144]

The defendant sent for the Upton fire brigade in mistake for the Pershore fire brigade, in whose area he was, and the call was accepted in good faith by the Upton brigade.

It was held that the defendant was contractually bound to pay for their services despite his mistake and despite the fact that neither party thought they were entering a contract; the defendant thought he was calling the brigade the services of which he was entitled to without charge, and the fire brigade thought they were answering a call within their area for which there would be no charge.[145]

But no contract will be formed if a person accepting an offer believes on reasonable grounds that he is accepting an offer from someone other than the person by whom it has in fact been made, and this fact is known to the offeror. In *Cundy v Lindsay*:[146]

L received an order for goods from one Blenkarn, who gave as his address '37 Wood Street, Cheapside'. He imitated the signature of a respectable firm named Blenkiron & Co, who were known by reputation to L and who carried on business at 123 Wood Street. L were thus fraudulently induced to send the goods to Blenkarn's address, which goods he afterwards sold to C. L sued C for conversion of the goods.

---

[142] *Ibid*, 565.   [143] *Shogun Finance Ltd v Hudson*, above, n 139 at [123]–[125] (Lord Phillips MR).
[144] [1942] 1 All ER 220.
[145] It is not clear whether the plaintiff would have been contractually liable if he had cancelled the call before the services were rendered: it is preferable to regard the liability for the services rendered as based on restitution (reasonable recompense for services rendered) rather than on contract. See also above, p 34, n 16.
[146] (1878) 3 App Cas 459.

If the contract between L and Blenkarn was merely voidable for fraudulent misrepresentation, C would be entitled to retain the goods as they had taken them in good faith and for value. If the contract was void for mistake, Blenkarn had acquired no title to the goods from L, and so could pass no title to C.[147] The House of Lords held that L were entitled to succeed. Lord Cairns said:[148]

> Of him [Blenkarn] they knew nothing, and of him they never thought. With him they never intended to deal. Their minds never, even for an instant of time rested upon him, and as between him and them there was no *consensus* of mind which could lead to any agreement or any contract whatever. As between him and them there was merely the one side to a contract, where, in order to produce a contract, two sides would be required.

When his offer was accepted, Blenkarn knew that L thought they were entering into a contract with Blenkiron & Co. The contract was therefore void *ab initio*. Again, in *Shogun Finance Ltd v Hudson*[149] a finance company agreed to sell a car on hire purchase terms to a fraudster who then sold it on to the defendant. Under section 27 of the Hire-Purchase Act 1964 a private purchaser of a motor vehicle from the debtor under a hire-purchase agreement can acquire title to the vehicle as long as he purchases in good faith and without notice of the hire-purchase agreement. The defendant's claim to title therefore turned on the validity of the hire-purchase agreement. If the agreement was only voidable for fraud, the defendant would obtain good title. But if it was void for mistake about the fraudster's identity, the fraudster would not be a 'debtor' under a 'hire-purchase agreement' and the defendant would not be protected. As proof of identity the fraudster had produced a genuine but unlawfully-obtained driving licence in the name of a Mr Patel, and the company had checked Mr Patel's credit rating. It was held by the majority of the House of Lords that the hire-purchase agreement was void. It could have been made only between the company and Mr Patel, and this was not possible because Mr Patel knew nothing of it and had not signed the agreement.[150] Accordingly the defendant did not obtain title to the car and the finance company was entitled to it.

(b) THE NEED FOR AN IDENTIFIABLE THIRD PERSON

If A's mistake is not about the *identity* of the other party, then the fact that he would not have entered into the contract if he had not been labouring under some mistake regarding the personality of the other party will not prevent the formation of a contract. It is sometimes said that mistake as to *attributes* is insufficient.[151] The

---

[147] Above, p 290.   [148] (1878) 3 App Cas 459, 465.   [149] [2003] UKHL 62, [2004] 1 AC 919.
[150] The majority (Lord Hobhouse, Lord Phillips, and Lord Walker) held that since the contract was in writing, the identity of the parties could be determined only by reference to the written document, but they also considered that the agreement was void because the company intended to contract only with Mr Patel and so there was no *consensus*. Lord Nicholls and Lord Millett dissented, considering the agreement to be only voidable because a contract is normally entered into between the persons who in fact deal with each other (here, the fraudster and the claimant) even if it may then be voidable for fraud.
[151] *Whittaker v Campbell* [1984] QB 318, 329.

examples given of mistakes as to 'attributes' include those about the solvency or social position of that person or whether that person holds a driving licence. While the case law draws a distinction between *identity* and *attributes*, there is arguably, in principle, no more intrinsic validity in that distinction than that, as we shall see,[152] between *substance* and *qualities* of the subject-matter of a contract. As Lord Denning MR observed, '[a] man's very name is one of his attributes. It is also the key to his identity'.[153] The law does, however, conveniently distinguish between cases where there are two individuals in the picture (ie A contracts with B in mistake for C) and cases where there is only one (ie A contracts with B in the belief that B is not B). Glanville Williams stated cogently:[154]

The conclusion is that a so-called 'error of identity' consists in misapprehending (the attributes of) two or more persons. An 'error of attributes' consists in misapprehending (the attributes of) a single person.

In *King's Norton Metal Co Ltd v Edridge, Merrett & Co Ltd:*[155]

KN, a metal manufacturer, received a letter purporting to come from 'Hallam & Co' in Sheffield asking for quotations for metal wire. On the letterhead was a picture of a large factory and a list of overseas depots. KN replied, and Hallam & Co ordered the wire. In fact, the firm of 'Hallam & Co' consisted solely of a fraudulent person named Wallis. The letters had been written, and the writing paper prepared, by him. Wallis subsequently sold the wire to the defendant. KN sued the defendant, contending that the contract with Hallam & Co was void, and that the wire was therefore still its property.

The Court of Appeal held that KN had intended to contract with the writer of the letter. Although it would not have done so if it had known what sort of a person the writer was, and that he was using an alias, a contract had been made which was not void on the ground of mistake, but only voidable for fraud. Consequently the property in the goods delivered had passed under it to Wallis, and an innocent purchaser from him acquired a good title to them. AL Smith LJ put the question as follows:[156]

With whom, upon this evidence, which was all one way, did [KN] contract to sell the goods? Clearly with the writer of the letters. If it could have been shown that there was a separate entity called Hallam & Co and another entity called Wallis then the case might have come within the decision in *Cundy v Lindsay*.

Therefore, in order to establish mistake as to identity, the party contracting must prove not merely that she did not intend to contract with the person with whom the

---

[152] Below, p 308.
[153] *Lewis v Averay* [1972] 1 QB 198, 206. See also the similar view of the minority in *Shogun Finance Ltd v Hudson*, above, n 149 at [5], [60], [73]–[74].
[154] (1945) 23 Can Bar Rev 278. Cf Wilson (1954) 17 MLR 515, and the reply by Unger (1955) 18 MLR 259.
[155] (1897) 14 TLR 98. Cf *Newborne v Sensolid (Great Britain) Ltd* [1954] 1 QB 45.
[156] (1897) 14 TLR 98, 99.

apparent contract was concluded, but also that there was a third identifiable person with whom there was an intention to contract.[157]

Where A contracts with B in the belief that B is not B, and B knows of this error, it might be thought that the situation is no different from that where A contracts with B in mistake for C, and B realizes the mistake. There is in fact a considerable difference.[158] In the latter situation the contract is void because B cannot accept an offer which he knows is not intended for himself but for C. In the former, there is no third person to whom the offer is really addressed: it is addressed to B, even though A mistakenly believes that he is not B. B is not, therefore, prevented from accepting an offer addressed to himself, and the contract will be valid and binding.

In certain circumstances, however, the offer made by A may expressly or impliedly contain a stipulation that excludes B. These are the terms upon which A is prepared to contract, and, as we have seen,[159] it is not possible for an offeree to accept an offer which he knows is made to him in different terms from those in which he purports to accept it. B cannot, therefore, accept such an offer. For example, the offer may be made to a limited class of persons, such as the members of a club or college, of whom B is not one. B may know, by reason of a previous refusal, that he is a person with whom A is unwilling to contract: a drama critic who is refused a ticket for a theatre performance cannot conclude a contract by going to the box office in disguise, or by employing a friend to buy a ticket for him.[160]

The difficulty is to know in what circumstances such a term is to be *implied* into the offer. In *King's Norton Metal Co Ltd v Edridge, Merrett & Co Ltd*,[161] the mistaken claimant was unable to satisfy the Court that such an implication should be made. This decision does not appear to have been cited in the case of *Sowler v Potter*[162] in which it was held that the identity of the tenant was a vital element in a tenancy contract and that therefore *any* mistake with regard to her identity rendered the contract void *ab initio*. But this does not constitute a sound positive test of mistake in English law. The proper approach in such a case as *Sowler v Potter* would be to inquire whether a stipulation could be implied into the offer that the offer excluded the particular person as a tenant, and whether this stipulation was known to the offeree. The answer is clear: no such stipulation could be implied, and the contract should not have been held to be void. The decision in *Sowler v Potter* has incurred almost unanimous disapproval, and must now be taken to have been overruled.[163]

---

[157] See also *Citibank NF v Brown Shipley & Co Ltd* [1991] 2 All ER 690, 702 (mistake as to identity of messenger insufficient). See generally Goodhart (1941) 57 LQR 228; Unger (1955) 18 MLR 259. Cf Wilson (1954) 17 MLR 515.

[158] This section relies heavily on the convincing argument of Professor Goodhart in (1941) 57 LQR 228, 241 ff.

[159] Above, p 277.

[160] *Said v Butt* [1920] 3 KB 497 (this case was primarily concerned with the question of an undisclosed principal and not with mistake).

[161] Above, p 293.   [162] [1940] 1 KB 271.

[163] *Solle v Butcher* [1950] 1 KB 671, 691; *Gallie v Lee* [1969] 2 Ch 17, 33, 41, 45 aff'd [1971] AC 1004; *Lewis v Averay* [1972] 1 QB 198, 206; *Shogun Finance Ltd v Hudson* [2001] EWCA Civ 1000, [2002] QB 834 at [34] (Dyson LJ, approving the suggestion as to the proper approach in previous editions of this book. *Sowler v Potter* was not discussed in the opinions on appeal to HL). Cf *Gordon v Street* [1899] 2 QB 641.

(c) WRITTEN CONTRACTS

In the case of a contract wholly in writing, the identity of the parties is established by the names in the written contract. In *Shogun Finance Ltd v Hudson*[164] the majority of the House of Lords based their decision on the fact that the contract was in writing, and therefore the only person who could have been a party to the hire-purchase agreement with Shogun Finance was Mr Patel whose driving licence had been used as the basis of the credit check. Because it was not Mr Patel who had signed the agreement, it was void. Lord Hobhouse said:[165]

The agreement is a written agreement with Mr Durlabh Patel. The argument seeks to contradict this and make it an agreement with the rogue. It is argued that other evidence is always admissible to show who the parties to an agreement are. Thus, if the contents of the document are, without more, insufficient unequivocally to identify the actual individual referred to or if the identification of the party is non-specific, evidence can be given to fill any gap. Where the person signing is also acting as the agent of another, evidence can be adduced of that fact . . . But it is different where the party is, as here, specifically identified in the document: oral or other extrinsic evidence is not admissible. Further, the rogue was no one's agent (nor did he ever purport to be). The rule that other evidence may not be adduced to contradict the provisions of a contract contained in a written document is fundamental to the mercantile law of this country; the bargain is the document; the certainty of the contract depends on it.[166]

(d) TRANSACTIONS CONCLUDED IN THE PARTIES' PRESENCE

Where the parties do not conclude their contract in writing, nor through communications at a distance from one another, but deal face to face, there is a presumption that each intended to deal with the other and not with someone else. In *Phillips v Brooks Ltd*:[167]

A man, North, called at P's shop and selected some pearls and a ring. He wrote out a cheque for £3,000, saying 'I am Sir George Bullough' (a person of credit whose name was known to P) and giving Sir George Bullough's address. P, finding on reference to a directory that Sir George lived at that address, allowed North to take away the ring which North then pledged to the defendants for £350. The defendants had no notice of the fraud. P sued for the return of the ring, or its value, alleging that he had never parted with the property in it.

Horridge J held that, although the claimant believed that the person to whom he was handing the ring was Sir George Bullough, he in fact contracted to sell and

---

[164] [2003] UKHL 62, [2004] 1 AC 919, above p 292. See also *Hector v Lyons* (1988) 58 P & CR 156.

[165] [2003] UKHL 62, [2004] 1 AC 919 at [94]. See also Lord Phillips at [154], [161], [178] and Lord Walker at [192].

[166] For the general (wholly objective) approach to the interpretation of written contracts, and operation of the parol evidence rule, see above, pp 179 ff, 279 ff. For support of the majority decision, see Stevens, in Burrows and Peel (eds), *Contract Terms* (2007) ch 6.

[167] [1919] 2 KB 243, criticized by Goodhart (1941) 57 LQR 228, 241.

deliver it to the person who came into his shop. His intention was 'to sell to the person present and identified by sight and hearing'.[168] The contract, therefore, was not void on the ground of mistake, but only voidable on the ground of fraud, and the defendants had acquired a good title to the ring. It does not follow from this decision that there can be no operative mistake as to identity where the parties are in each other's presence, although there is a strong presumption against the mistake being operative.[169]

Two further cases illustrate the difficulty of deciding whether a contract is void for mistake as to identity, or merely voidable for fraud. In *Ingram v Little*:[170]

Miss Elsie Ingram, Miss Hilda Ingram and Mrs Mary Ann Maud Badger advertised their car for sale. A rogue who called himself Hutchinson visited them and offered to buy the car. When he made as if to pay them by cheque, they refused to accept it and insisted on payment in cash. He then gave his initials and an address, describing himself as a respectable businessman living in Caterham. One of the Ingrams went to the local post office and ascertained from the telephone directory that there was such a person living at that address. They then allowed the rogue to take away the car in return for a worthless cheque and the rogue sold the car to the defendants who took it in good faith.

The Court of Appeal held by a majority that the contract between the ladies and 'Hutchinson' was void for mistake and that the vehicle was still their property. Although in a face-to-face contract there is a presumption that the contract is not void for mistake of identity, the circumstances (particularly the investigation of the telephone directory) indicated that it was with Hutchinson that the claimants intended to deal and not with the rogue who was physically present before them. The presumption was therefore rebutted.

On the other hand, in *Lewis v Averay*:[171]

L, a post-graduate chemistry student, advertised his car for sale. A rogue, posing as the well-known television actor Richard Greene, called on L and offered to buy the car. L accepted the offer, and the rogue wrote out a cheque, signing it 'R.A. Green'. The rogue wished to take away the car at once, but L was not willing for him to have it until the cheque had been cleared. At L's request the rogue produced 'proof' that he was Richard Greene in the form of a special pass of admission to Pinewood studios bearing the name 'Richard A. Green' and an address, a photograph of the rogue and an official stamp. L was satisfied on seeing this pass

---

[168] Adopting *Edmunds v Merchant Despatch Co* (1883) Mass 283, 286 (Morton CJ).

[169] Cf *Lake v Simmons* [1927] AC 487 where Viscount Haldane distinguished *Phillips v Brooks* and thought that a jeweller did not enter into a contract with a customer (a woman who claimed that she was Mrs Van de Borgh) who was physically present in the shop because he 'thought that he was dealing with a different person, the wife of Van der Borgh, and it was on that footing alone that he parted with the goods. He never intended to contract with the woman in question' (at 500). However, this was an individual approach and has been disapproved: *Shogun Finance Ltd v Hudson* [2003] UKHL 62, [2004] 1 AC 919 at [141]. Cf *Citibank NA v Brown Shipley & Co Ltd* [1991] 2 All ER 690, 700. See also *Hardman v Booth* (1863) 1 H & C 803.

[170] [1961] 1 QB 31 (Devlin LJ dissenting). Cf *Fawcett v Star Car Sales Ltd* [1960] NZLR 406.

[171] [1972] 1 QB 198.

and allowed the rogue to have the car. The cheque was worthless and the rogue sold the car to A, a music student, who bought it in good faith.

The Court of Appeal held that A intended to contract with the person actually present before him. The contract was therefore merely voidable for fraud, and in consequence A acquired the property in the car as against L.

Although *Shogun Finance Ltd v Hudson*[172] did not involve a contract concluded between parties who were physically present, guidance on the issue was given in two of the majority opinions. Both Lord Phillips and Lord Walker accepted that contracts concluded face to face raise different questions from both contracts concluded at a distance, and written contracts; but they also agreed that in a face-to-face transaction each party is presumed to have intended to deal with the person physically present. This presumption is a 'strong' presumption;[173] perhaps so strong that it can be rebutted only in exceptional cases, such as physical impersonation.[174]

(e) THE CURRENT STATE OF THE LAW; CRITIQUE

The decision of the majority of the House of Lords in *Shogun Finance Ltd v Hudson*[175] rested on the fact that the contract there was in writing, and the identity of the parties to the contract was therefore to be determined by an objective interpretation of the document itself. However, all members of the House discussed in general terms the issues raised by mistakes about identity. Lord Nicholls and Lord Millett, in the minority, proposed a radical reconsideration of the law, which would have overruled many of the older cases and would have resulted in a rule by which a mistake of identity would normally render a contract at most voidable, and not void. However, the majority declined to overturn the established authorities. In contracts which are not in writing but formed through offer and acceptance between the parties, such as by an exchange of letters, the intentions of each party as to the person with whom he is willing to contract is determined by an objective test of the communications, and a party who knows (for example) that he is not the intended recipient of the offer cannot claim to have entered into a contract by accepting it. An apparent contract may therefore still, after *Shogun*, be void for mistake of identity, as it was in *Cundy v Lindsay*.[176] In principle, a contract may even be void for mistake where the parties meet face to face, since it is still said in *Shogun*, following the earlier cases, that there is a presumption that the contract is valid. But it will be very rare that this presumption can in fact be rebutted.

---

[172] Above, p 292.

[173] [2003] UKHL 62, [2004] 1 AC 919 at [170] (Lord Phillips), [187] (Lord Walker).

[174] *Ibid* at [187] (Lord Walker, who also at [185] thought that the presumption was not rebutted in *Ingram v Little*, above, n 170, which was therefore wrongly decided).

[175] Above, p 292.

[176] (1878) 3 App Cas 459; see [2003] UKHL 62, [2004] 1 AC 919 at [55], [170]. Lord Nicholls and Lord Millett would have departed from *Cundy v Lindsay*: [2003] UKHL 62, [2004] 1 AC 919 at [35], [110].

The result of the decision in *Shogun* is, however, unsatisfactory. We have seen that the significance of a contract being void is that it can prejudice an innocent third party who purchases property which was delivered under the contract.[177] Lord Millett considered that, of the two 'innocent' parties—the original owner and the later purchaser—the latter was the more innocent:[178]

Of course, someone has to bear the loss where there is fraud, but it is surely fairer that the party who was actually swindled and who had an opportunity to uncover the fraud should bear the loss rather than a party who entered the picture only after the swindle had been carried out and who had none.

He went on to point out that in such cases English law is out of step with its continental neighbours, because civilian systems such as Germany provide protection to a purchaser who can acquire good title by purchasing property in good faith from a non-owner.[179] The approach taken in English law is to link the passing of title (and therefore the third party's rights) to the validity of the earlier contract.[180] However it would be preferable if effect were given to a recommendation made by the Law Reform Committee in 1966[181] that, where goods are sold under a mistake as to the buyer's identity, the contract should, so far as third parties are concerned, be considered voidable and not void. In the light of the decision in *Shogun* the Law Commission included this topic in its list of possible projects for reform,[182] but it has since decided not to pursue it.[183]

5. MISTAKES OF FACT OR LAW ABOUT THE SUBJECT-MATTER OF THE CONTRACT OR THE SURROUNDING CIRCUMSTANCES

This section is concerned with the situation where the parties have agreed on the terms of the contract, and neither makes an operative mistake about the other's identity,

---

[177] Above, p 290.

[178] *Shogun*, above, n 173 at [82]. Cf however Lord Walker at [181]–[182]. The difficulties encountered are compounded because of the difficulty, absent a requirement to have an identity card (see Identity Documents Act 2010, ss 1–3), of proving identity, and because a person can freely change his or her name: Halsbury's Laws, vol 88 (2012), para 326.

[179] *Shogun*, above, n 173 at [84]–[85].

[180] For a robust defence of the English position, however, see Lord Hobhouse in *Shogun*, above, n 173 at [55]. See also Stevens, in Burrows and Peel (eds), *Contract Terms* (2007) ch 6. The third party is protected in English law only where the original possessor's right to claim in the tort of conversion is barred (and his title is extinguished) by the expiry of the six-year period of limitation from the first purchase in good faith: Limitation Act 1980, ss 3, 4.

[181] Twelfth Report of the Law Reform Committee (Cmd 2958, 1966) 15.

[182] Law Commission Ninth Programme of Law Reform, Law Com No 293 (2005), paras 1.16, 3.51–3.57.

[183] Law Commission Eleventh Programme of Law Reform, Law Com No 330 (2011), paras 3.4–3.6.

but one or both of the parties have contracted in the mistaken belief that some fact which lies at the root of the contract is true, either a fact about the subject-matter of the contract, or a fact relating to the circumstances surrounding the formation of the contract, which was relevant to the claimant's decision to enter into the contract. We shall see that it is very rare for such a mistake to satisfy the very narrow test set down by the Courts in this area, but if it does, the mistake renders the contract void. It is sometimes said that this form of mistake invalidates a contract by nullifying consent.[184]

Until recently, for such a mistake to be operative and to invalidate a contract it had to be one of fact and not of law.[185] However, it was held by the House of Lords in 1999, in the context of claims for the recovery of money paid under a mistake, that a distinction should no longer be made between mistakes of law and mistakes of fact.[186] Similar reasoning has now also been applied to cases of mistake in contract.[187]

It has been argued[188] that there is a close relationship between mistake of fact, which is concerned with misapprehensions or misunderstandings at the time of the formation of an apparent contract, and the doctrine of frustration, which concerns uncontemplated events occurring after that time. Both mistake and frustration are concerned with the allocation of risk in which the construction of the contract is central, and the Courts are conscious that both may be pleaded to get out of a bad bargain or to reallocate the risks.[189] Moreover, the two situations may appear factually similar, particularly where it is an accident whether the uncontemplated event occurred before or after the making of the contract.[190] But it is important to remember that they are 'different juristic concepts'.[191] Mistake relates to the formation of a contract and, where operative, renders the whole contract void *ab initio*, whereas frustration relates to its termination and only discharges obligations which would have been due to be performed after the time of the frustrating event. Frustration is considered in Chapter 14.

---

[184] *Bell v Lever Brothers Ltd* [1932] AC 161, 217.

[185] *British Homophone Ltd v Kunz* (1932) 152 LT 589.

[186] *Kleinwort Benson Ltd v Lincoln CC* [1999] 2 AC 349.

[187] *Brennan v Bolt Burdon* [2004] EWCA Civ 1017, [2005] QB 303. Similarly, misrepresentations of law may now be remedied on the same basis as misrepresentations of fact: *Pankhania v Hackney LBC* [2002] EWHC 2441 (Ch), [2002] All ER (D) 22 (Aug); below, p 324.

[188] *Associated Japanese Bank (International) Ltd v Crédit du Nord SA* [1989] 1 WLR 255, 264–5, 268; *William Sindall plc v Cambridgeshire CC* [1994] 1 WLR 1016, 1039–40; *Great Peace Shipping Ltd v Tsavliris Salvage (International) Ltd, The Great Peace* [2002] EWCA Civ 1407, [2003] QB 679 at [61], [73]–[75], [82]–[85]. See generally McKendrick, *Contract Law* (11th edn 2015) 244–5, 266–7; Smith (1994) 110 LQR 400, 403. Cf Peel, *Treitel's Law of Contract* (13th edn 2011) paras 19.121–19.123.

[189] *Amalgamated Investment & Property Co Ltd v Walker & Sons Ltd* [1977] 1 WLR 164, 172. See also above, p 270, n 11.

[190] *Ibid.* Compare also the facts of *Griffith v Brymer* (1903) 19 TLR 434 (below, p 311, n 270) and *Krell v Henry* [1903] 2 KB 740 (below, p 502).

[191] *Joseph Constantine Steamship Line Ltd v Imperial Smelting Corp Ltd* [1942] AC 154, 186.

(a) UNILATERAL MISTAKES OF FACT OR LAW

A unilateral mistake of fact or law does not render the contract void. We have already seen that the Court in *Smith v Hughes*[192] drew a clear distinction between a unilateral mistake about the terms of the contract, which may prevent there being a contract unless the objective test can override the absence of subjective agreement, and a unilateral mistake about the facts relating to the subject-matter of the contract, which is irrelevant even if the other party knows about the mistake. The mistaken party will have a remedy if the other party gave a warranty in the contract about the subject-matter, or if the mistake was induced by the other party's misrepresentation.[193] Blackburn J said:[194]

[O]n the sale of a specific article, unless there be a warranty making it part of the bargain that it possesses some particular quality, the purchaser must take the article he has bought though it does not possess that quality. And I agree that even if the vendor was aware that the purchaser thought that the article possessed that quality, and would not have entered into the contract unless he had so thought, still the purchaser is bound, unless the vendor was guilty of some fraud or deceit upon him, and that a mere abstinence from disabusing the purchaser of that impression is not fraud or deceit; for, whatever may be the case in a court of morals, there is no legal obligation on the vendor to inform the purchaser that he is under a mistake, not induced by the act of the vendor.

It has recently been held that the correctness of the decision in *Smith v Hughes*, and the analysis in it, has 'never been doubted'.[195] Nor is there a jurisdiction in equity for a Court to set aside a contract on the basis of a unilateral mistake of fact.[196]

(b) COMMON MISTAKES OF FACT OR LAW

Where both parties make the same mistake of fact or law relating to the subject-matter or the facts surrounding the formation of the contract, the contract may be void. However, the Courts have developed a very narrow test for such mistakes, emphasizing that the parties are normally expected to provide in the contract for the allocation of the risk of unknown facts, and that a party should be entitled to rely on the doctrine of mistake only in exceptional cases. There is a clear line of authorities relating to common mistakes which may render a contract void at common law. As we shall see, between 1949 and 2002 there was also a line of cases in which the Courts held that, even if the common mistake was not sufficient to render the contract void at common law, it might satisfy a less strict test under which the contract would be

---

[192] (1871) LR 6 QB 597; above, p 277.   [193] For misrepresentation, see Chapter 9.
[194] (1871) LR 6 QB 597, 606–7.
[195] *Statoil ASA v Louis Dreyfus Energy Services LP* [2008] EWHC 2257 (Comm), [2008] 2 Lloyd's Rep 685 at [88] (Aikens J). See also *Bell v Lever Bros* [1935] AC 161, 218.
[196] *Statoil ASA v Louis Dreyfus Energy Services LP*, above, n 195 at [105], because, in light of the decision in *The Great Peace*, below, n 197 and p 314, that there is no equitable jurisdiction to rescind for common mistake, one cannot logically devise a rationale for an equitable jurisdiction for cases of unilateral mistake.

voidable in equity at the discretion of the Court. However, in *The Great Peace*[197] the Court of Appeal rejected this wider equitable jurisdiction.

(i) Common mistake at common law

The leading case is *Bell v Lever Brothers Ltd*,[198] which was decided by the House of Lords in 1931. The facts of the case are fairly simple, but the opinions are difficult to interpret, and this has led to a variety of theories about the scope of the doctrine of common mistake. In 2002 the Court of Appeal sought in *The Great Peace*[199] to give an authoritative interpretation of the doctrine, but this latest decision can be understood only by reference to the decision in *Bell v Lever Brothers Ltd* as well as other cases which had been decided on the basis of common mistakes.

(a) Bell v Lever Brothers Ltd   In this case:

L entered into two agreements with B and with S. The first agreements were service contracts by which B and S were appointed to the Board of the Niger Company, a subsidiary of L, for a period of five years at salaries of £8,000 and £6,000 a year respectively. The second were compensation contracts by which L, in consideration of their retiring within the service period, later promised to pay B £30,000 and S £20,000.

While they were acting under their appointments, both B and S had secretly entered on their own account into speculative transactions in cocoa, a course of conduct which would have given L the right to dismiss them summarily and without compensation. L had entered into the compensation contracts, and paid the sums promised, in ignorance of this fact. L now sought rescission of the compensation contracts and recovery of the money on the ground that it had been paid under a mistake of fact.

The jury found that B and S had been guilty of no fraud and that, at the time they entered into the compensation contracts, they did not have in mind their breaches of duty. The case must therefore be considered as one of *common* mistake,[200] that is, one where the parties had both contracted under the same mistaken assumption. L would never have entered into the contract had it known the true state of affairs, and it therefore alleged that the contract was a nullity from the beginning. Wright J and the Court of Appeal[201] upheld this contention; but the House of Lords, by a bare majority, held that the contract was valid and binding.

There has been considerable discussion as to what this case in fact decided. Lord Blanesburgh, while stating that he was in accord with the other majority opinions, based his own decision mainly on a point of pleading.[202] The other two majority

---

[197] [2002] EWCA Civ 1407, [2003] QB 679.
[198] [1932] AC 161. Cf MacMillan (2003) 119 LQR 625.   [199] Above, n 197; below, pp 304 ff.
[200] In *Bell v Lever Brothers Ltd* the term used for a shared mistake is 'mutual' mistake, but the more modern term ('common' mistake) is used here; cf above, p 271.
[201] [1931] 1 KB 557.
[202] He also pointed out (at 180–1, 183, 197) that the payments made to B and S were, at any rate in part, voluntary payments because their agreement was with the Niger Company not Lever Brothers, and so could not be recovered as money paid under a mistake: see *Morgan v Ashcroft* [1938] 1 KB 49, 66, 71, 77.

members, Lord Atkin and Lord Thankerton, formulated in the course of their speeches a number of propositions which, although directed to the same end, tend not to be easily reconcilable one with another. The speeches therefore provide support for a variety of conflicting interpretations of the doctrine of common mistake.

First, it has been said that the case establishes that there is no doctrine of mistake, rendering the contract void *ab initio*, in English law.[203] In *Solle v Butcher*, for example, Denning LJ said:[204]

> The correct interpretation of [*Bell v Lever Brothers Ltd*], to my mind, is that, once a contract has been made, that is to say, once the parties, whatever their inmost states of mind, have to all outward appearances agreed with sufficient certainty in the same terms on the same subject matter, then the contract is good unless and until it is set aside for failure of some condition on which the existence of the contract depends, or for fraud, or on some equitable ground. Neither party can rely on his own mistake to say that it was a nullity from the beginning, no matter that it was a mistake which to his mind was fundamental, and no matter that the other party knew that he was under a mistake. A fortiori, if the other party did not know of the mistake but shared it.

Some support for this contention can be found in the speech of Lord Atkin,[205] but both he and other members of the House of Lords assume throughout that certain types of mistake will avoid a contract, although they differ as to the circumstances in which it will do so and it has been said that Denning LJ's interpretation does not do justice to the speeches of the majority.[206] Nevertheless, it is clear that the effect of the decision in *Bell v Lever Brothers* is to confine the doctrine of common mistake within the most narrow limits; it is only in the most extreme cases that the Court will intervene.

Secondly, it has been said that the case establishes that a contract is void at law only if some term can be implied in both offer and acceptance which prevents the contract from coming into operation. Lord Atkin expressly stated that this is a proposition to which few would demur,[207] but cogently went on to point out that it does not take us very far in the inquiry how to ascertain whether the contract does contain such a term.

An example is provided by *Associated Japanese Bank (International) Ltd v Crédit du Nord SA*:[208]

> A fraudulent party purported to sell to AJB and lease back from it certain machines which in fact did not exist. CN guaranteed the fraudulent party's obligations under the sale and lease-back. When the fraudulent party was adjudged bankrupt, AJB sued on the guarantee.

---

[203] Slade (1954) 70 LQR 385; Shatwell (1955) 33 Can Bar Rev 164; Smith (1994) 110 LQR 400.

[204] [1950] 1 KB 671, 691, below, p 312. Bucknill and Jenkins LJJ did not mention *Bell v Lever Brothers Ltd*.

[205] *Bell v Lever Brothers Ltd* [1932] AC 161, 224.

[206] *Associated Japanese Bank (International) Ltd v Crédit du Nord SA* [1989] 1 WLR 255, 267 (Steyn J, approved in *The Great Peace* [2002] EWCA Civ 1407, [2003] QB 679 at [92]–[93]). But cf Smith (1994) 110 LQR 400, 412–13.

[207] [1932] AC 161, 225. See also *Whittaker v Campbell* [1984] QB 318, 327; Goldberg and Thomson [1978] JBL 150.

[208] [1989] 1 WLR 255.

It was held that as the guarantee provided that substitution of the subject of the contract, that is, the machines, could be made only with the guarantor's consent, it was subject to an express condition precedent that the lease related to existing machines. Alternatively, it was stated that the contextual background and the fact that both parties were informed that the machines existed meant that such a condition could be implied.[209]

However, just as the Courts have now rejected as artificial the old view that frustration of a contract depended on the implication of a term into the contract,[210] so it is not possible to base the doctrine of common mistake on implied terms. In *The Great Peace*[211] the Court of Appeal said:

[T]he theory of the implied term is as unrealistic when considering common mistake as when considering frustration. Where a fundamental assumption upon which an agreement is founded proves to be mistaken, it is not realistic to ask whether the parties impliedly agreed that in those circumstances the contract would not be binding.

Thirdly, it has been suggested that the application of the doctrine of common mistake depends upon the true construction of the contract made between the parties.[212] As a general rule, one or other of them will be considered to have assumed the risk of the ordinary uncertainties which exist when an agreement is concluded. Normally, because of the principle *caveat emptor*, the buyer is held to have taken the risk that property sold might prove defective or might be in some way different from that which the parties believed it to be. Alternatively, this risk will have been assumed by the seller if there was an express or implied warranty as to quality or description in the contract. A common misunderstanding will not therefore normally nullify the contract.

The construction of the contract is certainly critical to any claim of mistake. It is only where the terms of the contract, construed in the light of the nature of the contract and of the circumstances believed to exist at the time it was made,[213] show that it was never intended to apply to the situation which in reality existed at that time, and the risk of the relevant mistake has not been allocated to one of the parties, that the contract can be held void.[214] On the other hand, it is not sufficient to say that the doctrine of common mistake rests on construction of the contract. If the contract expressly or by implication allocates the risk of the unknown fact to one or other of the parties, then there is no mistake: the contract provides for the situation. But a test is needed for those cases where the unknown fact is not dealt with expressly or impliedly in the

---

[209] *Ibid*, 263. See also *Financings Ltd v Stimson* [1962] 1 WLR 1184.

[210] Below, p 510. For the link between mistake and frustration, see above, p 299.

[211] [2002] EWCA Civ 1407, [2003] QB 679 at [73].

[212] Atiyah (1957) 73 LQR 340; Atiyah and Bennion (1961) 24 MLR 421; McTurnan (1963) 41 Can Bar Rev 1.

[213] Extrinsic evidence is admissible to assist for this purpose in the construction of the contract: *Pritchard v Merchants' and Tradesmen's Life Assurance Society* (1858) 3 CB (NS) 622.

[214] *Associated Japanese Bank (International) Ltd v Crédit du Nord SA* [1989] 1 WLR 255, 268; *William Sindall plc v Cambridgeshire CC* [1994] 1 WLR 1016, 1035, 1039; *The Great Peace* [2002] EWCA Civ 1407, [2003] QB 679 at [75], [82], [84]; *Amalgamated Investment & Property Co Ltd v John Walker & Sons Ltd* [1977] 1 WLR 164, and below, pp 306–7 and cf *Gamerco SA v ICM/Fair Warning (Agency) Ltd* [1995] 1 WLR 1226.

contract itself, to determine whether the mistake is sufficient to render the contract void. The Court of Appeal in *The Great Peace*[215] said that the doctrine of mistake:

fills a gap in the contract where it transpires that it is impossible of performance without the fault of either party and the parties have not, expressly or by implication, dealt with their rights and obligations in that eventuality.

(b) The facts and decision in The Great Peace   In this case:

The defendant urgently required the use of a vessel in order to carry out salvage services for another ship which was in distress. The defendant was told by a reputable shipping organisation that the claimant's vessel, *The Great Peace*, was in the vicinity, and contacted the claimant's manager in the middle of the night to ask to hire the vessel. A contract was entered into for a minimum five-day hire, both parties believing that *The Great Peace* was 35 miles away from the distressed ship. The information about the location of *The Great Peace* was wrong, however, and she was in fact 410 miles away. After discovering the truth, the defendant waited two hours in order to find another vessel closer to the distressed ship, and then cancelled the contract and argued that it was not required to pay the five days' hire because the contract was void for common mistake about the location of *The Great Peace*.

Toulson J and the Court of Appeal held that the contract was valid, and the defendant was liable to pay the hire charge. They reviewed the authorities, in particularly the decisions in *Bell v Lever Brothers Ltd*[216] and *Associated Japanese Bank (International) Ltd v Crédit du Nord SA*[217] and drew on the related doctrine of frustration of a contract in order to explain the doctrine of mistake, and to articulate it in language which is sometimes also used in relation to frustration.[218] The Court of Appeal suggested that the following elements must be present if common mistake is to avoid a contract:[219]

(i) there must be a common assumption as to the existence of a state of affairs; (ii) there must be no warranty by either party that that state of affairs exists; (iii) the non-existence of the state of affairs must not be attributable to the fault of either party; (iv) the non-existence of the state of affairs must render performance of the contract impossible; (v) the state of affairs may be the existence, or a vital attribute, of the consideration to be provided or circumstances which must subsist if performance of the contractual adventure is to be possible.

The third element listed by the Court of Appeal (absence of fault) was not discussed in *Bell v Lever Brothers Ltd*. However, in the High Court of Australia in *McRae v Commonwealth Disposals Commission* it was said:[220]

[A] party cannot rely on mutual[221] mistake where the mistake consists of a belief which is, on the one hand, entertained by him without any reasonable ground, and, on the other hand, deliberately induced by him in the mind of the other party.

---

[215] [2002] EWCA Civ 1407, [2003] QB 679 at [80].
[216] [1932] AC 161; above, p 301.   [217] [1989] 1 WLR 255; above, p 302.
[218] For frustration of the 'contractual adventure', see *Jackson v Union Marine Insurance Co Ltd* (1874) LR 10 CP 125; below, p 500.
[219] [2002] EWCA Civ 1407, [2003] QB 679 at [76]. This test been applied in a number of later cases: see, eg, *Perpetual Trustee Co Ltd v BNY Corporate Trustee Services Ltd* [2009] EWCA Civ 1160, [2010] Ch 347 at [109]; *Acre 1127 Ltd v De Montfort Fine Art Ltd* [2011] EWCA Civ 87, [2011] All ER (D) 111 (Feb) at [38].
[220] (1950) 84 CLR 377, 408 (Dixon and Fullagar JJ).   [221] ie, common mistake: see above, p 271.

In *Associated Japanese (International) Bank Ltd v Crédit du Nord SA*[222] Steyn J accepted this qualification of the positive rules regarding mistake, and this was confirmed by the Court of Appeal in *The Great Peace*.[223]

The contract in *The Great Peace* was not void, because performance of the contract—the 'contractual adventure'—was not impossible.[224] *The Great Peace* could still be used for the defendant's salvage operation, even though it would have taken longer to reach the distressed ship and therefore it would have been less useful. Moreover, the fact that the defendant delayed before cancelling the contract showed that *The Great Peace* would have been of some use.[225]

(c) Examples of situations considered by the Courts   Relatively few reported cases have been argued, and even fewer have succeeded, on the basis of common mistake. We have already noted that many mistakes will be caused by misrepresentations, and that it will often be better for a claimant to seek a remedy for misrepresentation rather than mistake.[226] The narrow test for common mistake, and the attendant uncertainties of its application, no doubt discourage its use. However, we can see its application by considering a number of factual situations which have been considered by the Courts:

(1)   mistake as to the existence of the subject-matter of the contract;

(2)   mistake as to title to property;

(3)   mistake as to the quality or the substance of the thing contracted for;

(4)   a false and fundamental assumption going to the root of the contract, or impossibility of performance of the contract.

The first three are distinct types of situation; the fourth sets out more compendious tests for the doctrine generally.

(1) *Mistake as to the existence of the subject-matter of the contract.* If the subject-matter of the contract is what is sometimes called a *res extincta*, that is, at the time of the contract, and unknown to the parties, it has ceased to exist, or if it has never been in existence, then the contract may be void for common mistake.

In a contract for the sale of specific goods, for example, the non-existence of the goods will produce a situation not contemplated by the contract and to which it cannot apply.[227] It is also enacted in section 6 of the Sale of Goods Act 1979[228] that, where there

---

[222] [1989] 1 WLR 255, 268. The qualification was said to rest on policy and good sense rather than principles such as estoppel or negligence. Cf also the requirement of absence of fault in the test in equity under *Solle v Butcher* [1950] 1 KB 671, 693; below, p 313.

[223] Above, n 219 at [78]–[79].

[224] Cf Reynolds (2003) 119 LQR 177, 178 (doubting whether there was a common mistake at all: 'the owners of the *Great Peace* surely did no more than think, correctly, that the salvors had reason to believe that the *Great Peace* was the nearest ship').

[225] *Great Peace* [2002] EWCA Civ 1407, [2003] QB 679 at [165].

[226] Above, p 269.   [227] *Bell v Lever Brothers Ltd* [1932] AC 161, 217.

[228] See *Barrow, Lane, and Ballard Ltd v Phillip Phillips & Co* [1929] 1 KB 574 (subject-matter of sale stolen prior to it). But cf s 55(1) of the Act which, it has been argued, enables contractual variation of this rule: Atiyah (1957) 73 LQR 340, 348–9; Adams and MacQueen, *Atiyah's Sale of Goods* (12th edn, 2010) 99–104.

is a contract for the sale of specific goods, and the goods without the knowledge of the seller have perished at the time when the contract is made, the contract is void. As well as physical destruction, 'perishing' includes cases in which the goods are so damaged that they become for business purposes something other than the description under which they were sold.[229]

The leading case is *Couturier v Hastie*:[230]

A contract was made for the sale of a cargo of corn, which the parties believed was being shipped from Salonica to England. Before the date of sale the corn had, in fact, deteriorated and had been unloaded at Tunis and sold. The buyer contended that, since the cargo of corn was not in existence, he was not bound to pay the price. But the seller argued that, on the true construction of the contract, 'this was not a mere contract for the sale of an ascertained cargo, but that the purchaser bought the adventure, and took upon himself all risks from the shipment of the cargo'.

The House of Lords held that the purchaser was not liable to pay for the corn. The contract contemplated a sale of existing goods. Neither Coleridge J, who delivered the judgment of seven judges in the Exchequer Chamber,[231] nor Lord Chancellor Cranworth in the House of Lords, actually mentioned the word 'mistake', for they considered the case purely as one of the construction of the contract; but they intimated that the contract would be void, inasmuch as 'it plainly imports that there was something which was to be sold at the time of the contract, and something to be purchased', whereas the object of the sale had ceased to exist.[232]

Similarly, in *Strickland v Turner*,[233] S bought and paid for an annuity on the life of a man who was, unknown to both parties, already dead. He was able to recover the purchase money as the annuity had ceased to exist at the time of sale.

In these cases it is not difficult to see that the non-existence of the subject-matter of the contract gave rise to a total failure of consideration.[234] If a cargo does not exist, it cannot be delivered; if an annuity is purchased on the life of a dead person, the purchaser gets nothing for his money. It does not matter whether the contract is valid or void. In neither case can the seller claim to recover, or retain, the purchase money. The consideration for the contract has totally failed. It is only when the buyer brings an action for *damages* for non-delivery that the crucial question of the validity of the contract will arise. The mere fact that the subject-matter does not exist does not render the contract void: one party may have undertaken in

---

[229] *Asfar & Co v Blundell* [1896] 1 QB 123; *Oilfields Asphalts v Grovedale Coolstores (1994) Ltd* [1998] 3 NZLR 479 (account taken of contemplated use or purpose for goods).

[230] (1856) 5 HLC 673. See also Atiyah (1957) 73 LQR 340.

[231] (1853) 9 Exch 102, reversing the Court of Exchequer at (1852) 8 Exch 40.

[232] (1856) 5 HLC 673, 681. Ibbetson, *A Historical Introduction to the Law of Obligations* (1999) 228 states that the 'reanalysis' of this decision was 'pivotal' to the rooting of mistake in English law.

[233] (1852) 7 Exch 208. See also *Hitchcock v Giddings* (1817) 4 Price 135.

[234] Consideration refers here to *performance* of the contractual promise, and total failure of consideration on one side of the contract gives rise to recovery of money paid (or release from the duty to pay) on the other side: below, pp 621–4.

the contract the risk of its existence.[235] So in *McRae v Commonwealth Disposals Commission*:[236]

The Commonwealth Disposals Commission invited tenders for the purchase of a wrecked vessel described as 'an oil tanker lying on Jourmaund Reef, which is approximately 100 miles North of Samarai' in New Guinea. M's tender was accepted, and he thereupon fitted out a salvage expedition at considerable expense. In fact there was no oil tanker in the locality indicated, nor was there even such a reef as Jourmaund Reef. M claimed damages against the Commission for the loss sustained by him in the expedition.

The Commission, whose conduct was described by the High Court of Australia as 'reckless and irresponsible', resisted the claim to damages on the ground that the contract was void *ab initio*. It relied on *Couturier v Hastie* for the proposition that common mistake as to the existence of the subject-matter of a contract nullifies consent and avoids the contract. The Court did not, however, accept this argument, considering that the question of the validity of the contract had never arisen in that case; it was merely concerned with the failure of the consideration. If it had arisen, the decision would have depended upon whether the contract was subject to an implied condition precedent that the cargo existed at the time of the contract. No such condition could, in any event, be implied in the case before the Court, for the Commission had clearly contracted that there was a tanker in the position specified, and they must be held liable for breach.

It has been argued that the reasoning of the High Court of Australia in *McRae's* case negatives the existence of any doctrine of common mistake; indeed, it is said that a contract concerning subject-matter which is non-existent is always valid and binding, unless a term can be implied to the contrary.[237] It is submitted, however, that this is not the case. The merit of the decision in *McRae v Commonwealth Disposals Commission* is that it shows that invalidity is not an invariable consequence of such a contract. The question is one of the construction of the agreement.

When properly construed, the contract may indicate that the seller assumed responsibility for the non-existence of the subject-matter. This was so in *McRae's* case, where the seller was held to have guaranteed the existence of the tanker.[238] Alternatively the contract may indicate that the buyer took the risk that the subject-matter might not exist and undertook to pay in any event. This was the point at issue in *Couturier v Hastie*, where the House of Lords was called upon to decide whether or not the buyer had purchased merely the expectation that the cargo would arrive, and the securities (ie the shipping documents) against the contingency of its loss. There is therefore no absolute rule that a contract for the sale of a *res extincta* is necessarily void in English law. But if the true construction of the contract is that the parties entered into it on the footing that the subject-matter was in existence, and neither of

---

[235] Above, p 303.   [236] (1951) 84 CLR 377, noted (1952) 15 MLR 229.

[237] Slade (1954) 70 LQR 385. See also Smith (1994) 110 LQR 400, 402.

[238] (1951) 84 CLR 377, 407. See also *Barr v Gibson* (1838) 3 M & W 390; *Tommey v Finextra* (1962) 106 SJ 1012.

them undertook in the contract the risk that this might not be so, then the contract is void for common mistake.[239]

(2) *Mistake as to title to property.* Where a person agrees to purchase property which, unknown to himself and the seller, is already owned by the buyer (sometimes called in the older cases a *res sua*), the contract may be void.

In *Bell v Lever Brothers*, Lord Atkin said:[240]

Corresponding to mistake as to the existence of the subject-matter is mistake as to title in cases where, unknown to the parties, the buyer is already the owner of that which the seller purports to sell to him. The parties intended to effectuate a transfer of ownership: such a transfer is impossible.

So if A agrees to take from B a lease of land of which, contrary to the belief of both parties at the time of the contract, A is already tenant for life, the contract is void at common law.[241] But this principle must not be applied too widely. Normally a seller is taken to warrant title to the property sold; even though the parties both contract under a mistaken belief as to the title of the seller, there is a valid contract, and the seller may be made liable in damages. It is only where the buyer happens to purchase his own property, and where no warranty can be implied, that the contract is a nullity from the beginning. For both parties must necessarily have accepted in their minds as an essential and integral element of the subject-matter of the transaction that the seller was, and that the buyer was not, entitled to the property.[242]

(3) *Mistake as to the quality or the substance of the thing contracted for.* This has proved to be one of the most contentious categories in the law of common mistake. In *Bell v Lever Brothers*, Lord Atkin said:[243]

Mistake as to quality . . . will not affect assent unless it is the mistake of both parties, and is as to the existence of some quality which makes the thing without the quality *essentially different* from the thing as it was believed to be.

In reliance on this statement, it has been suggested that while a mistake as to *quality* (or attributes) will not avoid the contract, a mistake as to *substance* (or essence) will.[244]

Some support may be gained from *Kennedy v Panama, New Zealand, and Australian Royal Mail Co Ltd*:[245]

K was induced to take shares in a further issue of capital by the defendant company by a statement in the prospectus that the new capital was required to carry out a contract

---

[239] See also *The Great Peace* [2002] EWCA Civ 1407, [2003] QB 679 at [77]–[80].

[240] [1932] AC 161, 218.

[241] *Cooper v Phibbs* (1867) LR 2 HL 149, a case in equity where the contract was rescinded for mistake; but see the views of Lord Atkin in *Bell v Lever Brothers* at 218, and Lord Thankerton at 236, on its validity at common law. Cf Matthews (1989) 105 LQR 599.

[242] [1932] AC 161, 235, 236 (Lord Thankerton).

[243] *Ibid*, 218 (emphasis added).   [244] Tylor (1948) 11 MLR 257.

[245] (1867) LR 2 QB 580 (a common law case), expressly approved throughout the opinions in *Bell v Lever Brothers Ltd*. Cf *Emmerson's Case* (1866) LR 1 Ch App 433 (company in liquidation).

recently entered into with the New Zealand government for the carriage of mails. The contract, which the company believed to be valid, had been made with an unauthorized agent of the New Zealand government and the government refused to ratify it. The shares fell greatly in value and K claimed to return the shares and recover back the purchase price.

The Court of Queen's Bench refused to allow K to do so. It held that the shares which he received were far from being of no value, and were not different in substance from those which the company had contracted to deliver. Blackburn J, delivering the judgment of the Court, referred to the Roman Digest of Civil Law[246] which distinguished substance and quality. He considered that the principle of English law was the same as that of Roman law,[247] and that 'the difficulty in every case is to determine whether the mistake or misapprehension is as to the substance of the whole consideration, going, as it were, to the root of the matter, or only to some point, even though a material point, an error as to which does not affect the substance of the whole consideration.'[248]

A mistake as to quality will not generally avoid the contract. We may give some examples, both actual and hypothetical:[249]

A agrees to buy from B a certain parcel of oats which both believe to be old oats. They are in fact new oats, and unsuitable for the purpose for which A wants them. There is a valid contract despite the mistake.[250]

C buys from D a picture which both believe to have been painted by Constable. Several years later, when C tries to sell the picture, he finds that it was not painted by Constable at all. The mistake does not avoid the contract.[251]

E agrees to buy from F '100 bales of Calcutta kapok, Sree brand'. The sale is by sample, but both parties believe that this particular brand of kapok is pure kapok, consisting of tree cotton, whereas it in fact contains an admixture of bush cotton and is a commercially inferior product. The contract is valid.[252]

G buys from H a car which both believe to be a 1948 model. It is actually a 1939 model, and worth very much less. There is no mistake at common law.[253]

---

[246] (1867) LR 2 QB 580, 588. Digest, 18.1.9, 10, 11.   [247] Cf Lawson (1936) 52 LQR 79.

[248] (1867) LR 2 QB 580, 588. In this case the mistake was induced by a misrepresentation in the prospectus, but there was no fraud and at common law there was no remedy for innocent misrepresentation: below, p 330.

[249] See also *Solle v Butcher* [1959] 1 KB 671 (mistake about whether structural alterations to flat rendered it a 'new' dwelling and therefore not subject to rent control), *Frederick E Rose (London) Ltd v William H Pim Junior & Co Ltd* [1953] 2 QB 450, above, p 285 (parties contracted to buy and sell 'horsebeans', in the belief that they were the same as 'feveroles', an entirely different sort of bean), and *Grist v Bailey* [1967] Ch 532 (mistake as to whether property to be sold was occupied by secure tenant) where the mistakes were said not to be sufficient to make the contract void at common law. However, these were decisions during the period when the Courts applied a wider test for common mistake in equity: below, p 312 ff.

[250] Cf *Smith v Hughes* (1871) LR 6 QB 597 where, however, the mistake was unilateral: above, p 300.

[251] *Leaf v International Galleries* [1950] 2 KB 86; below, p 337; *Bell v Lever Brothers Ltd* [1932] AC 161, 224.

[252] *Harrison & Jones Ltd v Bunten and Lancaster Ltd* [1953] 1 QB 646.

[253] *Oscar Chess Ltd v Williams* [1957] 1 WLR 370, 373 (Denning LJ); above, p 143.

It is evident that there is no clear rule that a mistake as to the substance of the thing contracted for will avoid the contract. The distinction between substance and quality is at best an arbitrary one, for there is no metaphysical 'substance' independent of qualities.[254] Moreover, 'the principle enunciated in *Bell v Lever Brothers Ltd* is markedly narrower in scope than the civilian doctrine' and 'it is therefore no longer useful to invoke the civilian distinction'.[255] However, where the mistake is as to 'an essential and integral element in the subject-matter of the bargain'[256] so that it renders the subject-matter 'essentially and radically different from the subject matter which the parties believed to exist'[257] the contract will be void. Accordingly, the following contracts of sale have been held to be void: of a quantity of Georgian table linen erroneously described in the particulars of sale as 'the authentic property' of Charles I and as bearing the arms of that unhappy monarch;[258] of a breeding cow which was mistakenly believed to be a sterile cow and sold by the pound for beef;[259] and of a plot of land, zoned as building land, for which, however, due to the absence of sewage facilities, it was impossible to obtain a building permit.[260]

(4) *A false and fundamental assumption; impossibility of performance of the contract.* A contract may be void where the parties contract under a false and fundamental assumption, going to the root of the contract, and which both of them must be taken to have had in mind at the time they entered into it as the basis of their agreement; or where performance of the contract, as both parties understood it, is impossible. These categories are not separate and distinct from those categories of mistake already mentioned, but rather act as more general tests, which will cover cases of non-existence of the subject-matter, mistakes as to title, and mistakes as to quality or substance, but will also cover other situations. The test based on a 'fundamental assumption' received approval in *Bell v Lever Brothers Ltd*,[261] although some doubts were expressed as to its value owing to the necessary vagueness of its formulation. It was also referred to by the Court of Appeal in *The Great Peace*, drawing an analogy with similar ideas in the doctrine of frustration.[262] As we have seen, the Court of Appeal in that case

---

[254] Glanville Williams (1945) 61 LQR 293. Cf Tylor (1948) 11 MLR 257.

[255] *Associated Japanese Bank (International) Ltd v Crédit du Nord SA* [1989] 1 WLR 255, 268 (Steyn J). The original Roman ('civilian') notion of mistake was developed in some modern continental civilian systems, and particularly in the French civil code, where it fits more naturally: above, p 269. For a significantly wider interpretation to the notion of 'substance' and 'substantial qualities' in contemporary French Law, see Nicholas, *The French Law of Contract* (2nd edn, 1992) 85–90.

[256] *Bell v Lever Brothers Ltd* [1932] AC 161, 236 (Lord Thankerton).

[257] *Associated Japanese Bank (International) Ltd v Crédit du Nord SA* [1989] 1 WLR 255, 264 (Steyn J), approved in *The Great Peace* [2002] EWCA Civ 1407, [2003] QB 679 at [91].

[258] *Nicholson and Venn v Smith Marriott* (1947) 177 LT 189 (the decision was however based on an implied condition as to description under Sale of Goods Act 1893 (now 1979), s 13).

[259] *Sherwood v Walker* 33 NW 919 (1887) (Michigan).

[260] *Alessio v Jovica* (1974) 42 DLR (3d) 242 (Canada). Cf *Amalgamated Investment & Property Co Ltd v John Walker & Sons Ltd* [1977] 1 WLR 164.

[261] [1932] AC 161, 208, 225, 236; cf [1931] 1 KB 557, 564 (Wright J: 'the underlying assumption without which the parties would not have made the contract they did').

[262] [2002] EWCA Civ 1407, [2003] QB 679 at [73], [76], [82].

has suggested that the core of the doctrine of common mistake, like the doctrine of frustration, is that the contract—or the 'contractual adventure'—cannot be performed: a test of impossibility of performance, although this must be interpreted as not limited to physical impossibility but extending to commercial impossibility: the shared purpose of the contract cannot be fulfilled, through no fault of the either party and where neither party has undertaken the risk of non-performance.[263]

However, this test is still narrow, and will not easily be satisfied. It is certainly not sufficient for one party to establish that the mistake was as to the effect or commercial consequences of the contract,[264] or that, had the true facts been known, that party would never have entered into the bargain. Indeed, there may be assumptions regarded by one or both of the parties as, in some sense, 'fundamental'—for example, that a picture is the work of an old master, or that a flat is free from rent control. Yet the contract will still bind. As Lord Thankerton pointed out:[265]

The phrase 'underlying assumption by the parties', as applied to the subject-matter of a contract . . . can only properly relate to something which both must have necessarily accepted in their minds as an essential and integral element of the subject-matter.

In *Bell v Lever Brothers Ltd* itself, this requirement was not fulfilled. On its true construction, the agreement to pay compensation applied notwithstanding the fact that the contract of service had been broken:

The contract released is the identical contract in both cases, and the party paying for release gets exactly what he bargains for. It seems immaterial that he could have got the same result in another way, or that if he had known the true facts he would not have entered into the bargain.[266]

Nor was the test satisfied in *The Great Peace*: because of its distant position, the vessel was much less useful than both parties had expected. But it was not impossible still to use it for the salvage operation.[267]

It is not surprising that the strictness of the test for common mistake has resulted in a dearth of cases on the subject. In *Scott v Coulson*,[268] however, a contract for the assignment of a policy of life insurance was made upon the basis of an erroneous belief, shared by both parties, that the assured was still alive. It was held that the vendor was entitled to the return of the policy and also the moneys payable under it. Similarly the following have been held to be void: a separation deed entered into by a husband and wife on the erroneous assumption that their marriage was valid;[269] a contract for the hire of rooms to watch a coronation procession made in ignorance that the procession had already been cancelled;[270] a contractual licence to cut and

---

[263] *Ibid* at [76]; above, p 304.

[264] *Clarion Ltd v National Providential Institution* [2000] 1 WLR 1888, 1899.

[265] [1932] AC 161, 235.   [266] *Ibid*, 223 (Lord Atkin). Cf *Horcal v Gatland* [1984] IRLR 288.

[267] [2002] EWCA Civ 1407, [2003] QB 679 at [165].   [268] [1903] 2 Ch 249.

[269] *Galloway v Galloway* (1914) 30 TLR 531.

[270] *Griffith v Brymer* (1903) 19 TLR 434, discussed in *The Great Peace* [2002] EWCA Civ 1407, [2003] QB 679 at [67]. Cf *Krell v Henry* [1903] 2 KB 740 (frustration of purpose), below, p 502.

facture all sisal grown on a particular estate, in return for payment and the delivery of a monthly quantity of sisal which the estate was not in fact capable of producing;[271] and an agreement as to the amount due under two contracts of sale entered into in the erroneous belief that the results in the two certificates of analysis had been transposed.[272]

(ii) Common mistake in equity

The effect of a mistake at common law, if it operates at all, is to render the contract void *ab initio*; but there are circumstances in which equity may be prepared to grant relief where the common law refuses to intervene. For example, we have already seen that although a written contract may be valid at common law, equity may grant rectification of the written document, or may refuse to grant specific performance of a contract that is binding at law.[273] In Chapter 9 we shall see that, although the common law allowed rescission of a contract for misrepresentation only in the case of fraud, in equity an innocent misrepresentation sufficed to render the contract voidable. The question here is whether equity will allow rescission of a contract on the basis of common mistake where the mistake is not sufficient to render the contract void under the principles set out in *Bell v Lever Brothers Ltd*[274] and the other cases discussed in the previous section. In *Solle v Butcher*[275] Denning LJ set out an equitable doctrine of common mistake which expanded the range of circumstances in which the Court, in its discretion, could set aside a contract—a doctrine which over a period of 50 years came to be regarded as good law and 'on occasion the passport to a just result'.[276] However, this equitable doctrine was emphatically rejected by the Court of Appeal in *The Great Peace*.[277]

(a) *The equitable doctrine set out in Solle v Butcher.* Cases can certainly be found in which the Courts, exercising their equitable jurisdiction, set aside contracts or other instruments on the basis of common mistake,[278] although it is not clear that in any of these cases the mistake would have been insufficient to satisfy the common law test for

---

[271] *Sheikh Brothers Ltd v Ochsner* [1957] AC 136 (Privy Council, on appeal from Kenya under Indian Contract Act 1872, s 20 which provided: 'Where both the parties to an agreement are under a mistake as to a matter of fact essential to the agreement, the agreement is void'). See also *Clifford v Watts* (1870) LR 5 CP 577; *Associated Japanese Bank (International) Ltd v Crédit du Nord SA* [1989] 1 WLR 255, 269, above, p 302 (guarantee of machine lease agreement said to be void because machines did not exist); cf *Marquis of Bute v Thompson* (1844) 13 M & W 487; *Jefferys v Fairs* (1876) 4 Ch D 448.

[272] *Grains & Fourrages SA v Huyton* [1997] 1 Lloyd's Rep 628.

[273] Above, pp 282, 287. The equitable remedies in respect of contracts are only one aspect of a much wider equitable jurisdiction to relieve from the consequences of mistake, a jurisdiction which extends to gifts and is less concerned with the nature of the mistake: eg mistake of law was not a bar in equity even before the general recognition of remedies for mistakes of law (above, p 299): *Gibbon v Mitchell* [1990] 1 WLR 1304, 1309.

[274] [1932] AC 161; above, p 301.   [275] [1950] 1 KB 671; below, p 313.

[276] *West Sussex Properties Ltd v Chichester DC* [2000] NPC 74 at [42] (Sir Christopher Staughton).

[277] [2002] EWCA Civ 1407, [2003] QB 679; below, p 314.

[278] eg *Cooper v Phibbs* (1867) LR 2 HL 149, above, p 308 (lease); *Huddersfield Banking Co Ltd v Henry Lister & Son Ltd* [1895] 2 Ch 273 (consent order).

common mistake.[279] In *Solle v Butcher*,[280] however, such cases were used by Denning LJ as the basis of a new and general doctrine of mistake in equity. He based his doctrine on the proposition that the court 'had power to set aside the contract whenever it was of opinion that it was unconscientious for the other party to avail himself of the legal advantage which he had obtained',[281] and stated the principle as follows:

A contract is . . . liable in equity to be set aside if the parties were under a common misapprehension either as to facts or as to their relative and respective rights, provided that the misapprehension was fundamental, and that the party seeking to set it aside was not himself at fault.

Denning LJ stated that the Court would grant relief if the mistake was *fundamental*, and the party seeking rescission was *not at fault*. Despite this requirement of 'fundamentality', the cases which applied Denning LJ's principle showed that that the category of operative common mistake was broader in equity than at common law,[282] and there was little guidance as to how to apply the requirement that the claimant be not 'at fault'.[283] The approach of the Courts was also open to the criticism that insufficient attention was paid to the question of contractual allocation of risk.[284] As in the case of common law,[285] an express or implied allocation of a particular risk should generally preclude rescission of the contract for mistake.

Two further points should be noted about the doctrine of mistake in equity, as stated by Denning LJ, which made it more attractive than the narrower, common law doctrine. First, the remedy was said to be at the discretion of the Court, and the discretion extended to the imposition of terms for the setting aside of the contract.[286] Secondly in equity the contract was voidable, rather than void, as a result of the mistake. This not only gave a more nuanced remedy, allowing the mistaken parties to affirm the contract, and allowing the Court to exercise more control over the remedy, but it would also protect third parties since, as we have seen in other contexts, a voidable contract cannot be rescinded if it would prejudice an innocent third party such as the purchaser of property delivered pursuant to the contract.[287]

[279]   See *Bell v Lever Brothers Ltd* [1932] AC 161, 218 (Lord Atkin: contract in *Cooper v Phibbs* was void); *Huddersfield Banking Co Ltd v Henry Lister & Son Ltd*, above, n 278, 280–1 (Lindley LJ, discussing common law cases with cases decided in equity).

[280]   [1950] 1 KB 671. For criticism, see Goodhart (1950) 66 LQR 169; Slade (1954) 70 LQR 385, 407; Atiyah and Bennion (1961) 24 MLR 421, 440–1; Cartwright (1987) 103 LQR 594.

[281]   *Torrance v Bolton* (1872) LR 8 Ch App 118, 124, (James LJ), above, p 288.

[282]   *Solle v Butcher*, above, n 280; *Grist v Bailey* [1967] Ch 532, 541 (mistake as to value of subject-matter); *Magee v Pennine Insurance Co Ltd* [1969] 2 QB 507 (Winn LJ dissenting on the ground that the case was indistinguishable from *Bell v Lever Brothers Ltd*).

[283]   *Solle v Butcher*, above, n 280, 684, 694; *Grist v Bailey*, above, n 282, 542; *Laurence v Lexcourt Holdings Ltd* [1978] 1 WLR 1128, 1137–8.

[284]   *William Sindall plc v Cambridgeshire CC* [1994] 1 WLR 1016, 1035, criticizing the decisions in *Grist v Bailey*, above, n 282, and *Laurence v Lexcourt Holdings Ltd*, above, n 283. See also *Associated Japanese Bank (International) Ltd v Crédit du Nord SA* [1989] 1 WLR 255, 268.

[285]   Above, p 307.

[286]   *Solle v Butcher*, above, n 280, 695–6; *Grist v Bailey*, above, n 282, 543. See also *Cooper v Phibbs*, above, n 278. See also *Bingham v Bingham* (1748) 1 Ves Sen 126; *Earl Beauchamp v Winn* (1873) LR 6 HL 223.

[287]   Cf above, pp 290, 298 (mistake of identity).

(b) Rejection of the equitable doctrine by The Great Peace.   In *The Great Peace*[288] the Court of Appeal roundly rejected Denning LJ's approach and held that *Solle v Butcher* was not good law,[289] on the basis that it was contrary to the binding authority of *Bell v Lever Brothers Ltd*,[290] and was contrary to principle.

We have already seen[291] that the Court explained the common law doctrine of mistake, for which *Bell v Lever Brothers Ltd* is the principal authority; but that it also emphasized that mistake was a narrow doctrine, designed for only exceptional cases. As Lord Atkin said in *Bell v Lever Brothers*:[292]

> it is of paramount importance that contracts should be observed, and that if parties honestly comply with the essentials of the formation of contracts—ie, agree in the same terms on the same subject-matter—they are bound, and must rely on the stipulations of the contract for protection from the effect of facts unknown to them . . . Nothing is more dangerous than to allow oneself liberty to construct for the parties contracts which they have not in terms made by importing implications which would appear to make the contract more businesslike or more just.

Before *Solle v Butcher*, there was no evidence in the case law of an equitable jurisdiction to rescind a contract for a common mistake which would not render the contract void under the common law test: Lord Atkin's narrow test for mistake in *Bell v Lever Brothers Ltd* reflected also the circumstances where equity had intervened.[293] The Court of Appeal considered that the test proposed by Denning LJ in *Solle v Butcher* was not only uncertain in its scope and placed too much power into the hands of the Court to exercise its discretion,[294] but also, by allowing a broader test for mistake, had undermined the policy of the common law in setting narrow limits for the doctrine of mistake:[295]

> [T]he premise of equity's intrusion into the effects of the common law is that the common law rule in question is seen in the particular case to work injustice, and for some reason the

---

[288] [2002] EWCA Civ 1407, [2003] QB 679; above, p 304.

[289] The Court of Appeal held that it had power to depart from its own previous decision: *ibid* at [160], although this has been doubted: Midwinter (2003) 119 LQR 180; Sheehan [2003] RLR 26, 33. However, cases have assumed that *The Great Peace* is authoritative; see, eg, *Islington LBC v Uckac* [2006] EWCA Civ 340, [2006] 1 WLR 1303 at [20]–[21]; *Smithson v Hamilton* [2007] EWHC 2900 (Ch), [2008] 1 WLR 1453 at [118]; *Statoil ASA v Louis Dreyfus Energy Services LP* [2008] EWHC 2257 (Comm), [2008] 2 Lloyd's Rep 685 at [105]; *Qayyum v Hameed* [2009] EWCA Civ 352, [2009] 3 FCR 545 at [37].

[290] [1932] AC 161, above, p 301.   [291] Above, p 304.

[292] [1932] AC 161, 224, 226, quoted in *The Great Peace* [2002] EWCA Civ 1407, [2003] QB 679 at [48]. See also *Associated Japanese Bank (International) Ltd v Crédit du Nord SA* [1989] 1 WLR 255, 268 (Steyn J: 'The first imperative must be that the law ought to uphold rather than destroy apparent contracts'), approved in *The Great Peace* at [90]–[91].

[293] *The Great Peace* [2002] EWCA Civ 1407, [2003] QB 679 at [118].

[294] *Ibid* at [131], [154] (uncertainty over meaning of 'fundamental' in equity compared with common law test); [138] (application depends on consideration of what is 'fair'). For the strongest criticism, see Toulson J at first instance in *The Great Peace* [2001] All ER (D) 152 (Nov) at [120]: 'Bluntly, the difficulty about this form of the doctrine [ie, giving the court a discretion to decide whether to rescind the contract] is that it puts palm tree justice in place of party autonomy'.

[295] [2002] EWCA Civ 1407, [2003] QB 679 at [156].

common law cannot cure itself. But it is difficult to see how that can apply here. Cases of fraud and misrepresentation, and undue influence, are all catered for under other existing and uncontentious equitable rules. We are *only* concerned with the question whether relief might be given for common mistake in circumstances wider than those stipulated in *Bell v Lever Bros Ltd*. But that, surely, is a question as to where the common law should draw the line; not whether, given the common law rule, it needs to be mitigated by application of some other doctrine. The common law has drawn the line in *Bell v Lever Bros Ltd*. The effect of *Solle v Butcher* is not to supplement or mitigate the common law: it is to say that *Bell v Lever Bros Ltd* was wrongly decided.

(c) Critique. The decision of the Court of Appeal in *The Great Peace* was emphatic and uncompromising: there is no place in the law of contract for a broader doctrine of common mistake in equity than the limited common law doctrine; and there is no place for a judicial discretion in remedying mistake because it would undermine the security of contracts. However, it is not obvious that the equitable jurisdiction set out in *Solle v Butcher* would in any event have been exercised in *The Great Peace* to rescind the contract, since the defendants' mistake about the location of the vessel, even though they then shared it with the claimants, surely fell firmly within the scope of risk borne by the defendants under the contract for the hire of the vessel—a risk allocation which would be respected not only by the common law, as made clear by the Court in *The Great Peace*, but which also could equally be protected by an appropriate application of the equitable test.[296] The Court of Appeal, following the lead of Toulson J at first instance, appeared to be using the case as a vehicle to review this difficult area of jurisprudence.[297]

One ought, however, to reflect on what has been lost by the rejection of the equitable doctrine of common mistake.[298] It should be noted that other jurisdictions in the common law world have adopted it and have applied the approach set out by Denning LJ in *Solle v Butcher*, and some may well be much more reluctant than the English Court of Appeal to wind back the clock in order to restore the law on mistake as it stood before this infusion of equity.[299] The advantages which it appears that Denning LJ sought through the development of his doctrine in *Solle v Butcher* were that a contract would be voidable for mistake (rather than void), thereby

---

[296] Reynolds (2003) 119 LQR 177, 178–9.

[297] Cf *The Great Peace* [2002] EWCA Civ 1407, [2003] QB 679 at [2].

[298] Tettenborn (2011) 27 JCL 91.

[299] See, eg, *Chwee Kin Keong v Digilandmall.com Pte Ltd* [2005] 1 SLR 502 at [56] ff, especially at [77] (Singapore: mistake about the terms, but rejecting narrow *Great Peace* approach generally: 'Equity is dynamic. A great attribute, thus an advantage, of equity, is its flexibility to achieve the ends of justice'); *Miller Paving Ltd v B Gottardo Construction Ltd* (2007) 285 DLR (4th) 568 at [26] (Gouge JA in CA Ontario: '*Great Peace* appears not yet to have been adopted in Canada and, in my view, there is good reason for not doing so. The loss of the flexibility needed to correct unjust results in widely diverse circumstances that would come from eliminating the equitable doctrine of common mistake would, I think, be a step backward'); cf *Australia Estates Pty Ltd v Cairns CC* [2005] QCA 328 at [52] (Atkinson J: *Great Peace* should be followed in Queensland in preference to *Solle v Butcher*), although differing views have been expressed amongst the courts of the States and Territories within Australia.

protecting the rights of innocent third parties to property delivered pursuant to the contract; and that the Court would have greater control over the remedy, both as to whether rescission should be granted at all, and also as to whether it should be granted only on terms set by the Court. Furthermore, the scope of actionable mistakes in equity could be less restricted than under the common law doctrine. This doctrine therefore moved the Courts closer towards exercising a power over the terms of the contract, particularly in cases where the effect of the mistake was to impose hardship on one of the parties. This was one of the objections raised by the Court of Appeal in *The Great Peace*:[300]

A common factor in *Solle v Butcher* and the cases which have followed it can be identified. The effect of the mistake has been to make the contract a particularly bad bargain for one of the parties. Is there a principle of equity which justifies the court in rescinding a contract where a common mistake has produced this result?

However, even that Court recognized that there might have been some merit in Denning LJ's endeavour, but considered that any intervention should be by statute, rather than by the common law:[301]

We can understand why the decision in *Bell v Lever Bros Ltd* did not find favour with Lord Denning MR. An equitable jurisdiction to grant rescission on terms where a common fundamental mistake has induced a contract gives greater flexibility than a doctrine of common law which holds the contract void in such circumstances. Just as the Law Reform (Frustrated Contracts) Act 1943 was needed to temper the effect of the common law doctrine of frustration, so there is scope for legislation to give greater flexibility to our law of mistake than the common law allows.

Relatively few cases were decided in England on the basis of the equitable doctrine of *Solle v Butcher* during the 50 years when it was treated as good authority.[302] There are also relatively few reported cases based on the common law doctrine of common mistake of fact or law. No doubt this is in part because of the expressly limited scope of the common law doctrine. But it may also be because, although there are many cases involving common mistakes where one of the parties seeks to avoid the contract, they result from misrepresentations made by the other party to the contract. An innocent misrepresentation of fact or law gives rise to a common mistake, since the first party shares the incorrect information with the other, and therefore makes the mistake common. As long as the remedies for misrepresentation are sufficient for the claimant, he will in practice base his claim not on mistake, but on the defendant's misrepresentation. It is to the remedies available for misrepresentation that we now turn.

---

[300] [2002] EWCA Civ 1407, [2003] QB 679 at [155].

[301] *Ibid* at [161]. For a similar preference of the Courts to rely on statute to deal with exclusion clauses and other unfair terms, see *National Westminster Bank plc v Morgan* [1985] AC 686, 708; below, p 405.

[302] *Ibid* at [153].

FURTHER READING

GOODHART, 'Mistake as to Identity in the Law of Contract' (1941) 57 LQR 228

SLADE, 'The Myth of Mistake in the English Law of Contract' (1954) 70 LQR 385

ATIYAH and BENNION, 'Mistake in the Construction of Contracts' (1961) 24 MLR 412

ATIYAH, 'Judicial Techniques and Contract Law' in *Essays on Contract* (Oxford: Clarendon Press, 1986) 244

CARTWRIGHT, '*Solle v Butcher* and the Doctrine of Mistake in Contract' (1987) 103 LQR 594

SMITH, 'Contracts—Mistake, Frustration and Implied Terms' (1994) 110 LQR 400

MACMILLAN, 'How Temptation Led to Mistake: an Explanation of *Bell v Lever Bros Ltd*' (2003) 119 LQR 625

HARE, 'Identity Mistakes: A Missed Opportunity?' (2004) 67 MLR 993

MACMILLAN, 'Rogues, Swindlers and Cheats: The Development of Mistake of Identity in English Contract Law' [2005] CLJ 711

BURROWS, 'Construction and Rectification' in Burrows and Peel (eds), *Contract Terms* (Oxford: Oxford University Press, 2007) 77

STEVENS, 'Objectivity, Mistake and the Parol Evidence Rule' in Burrows and Peel (eds), *Contract Terms* (Oxford: Oxford University Press, 2007) 101

McLAUCHLAN, 'The "Drastic" Remedy of Rectification for Unilateral Mistake' (2008) 124 LQR 608

TETTENBORN, 'Agreements, Common Mistake and the Purpose of Contract' (2011) 27 JCL 91

McLAUCHLAN, 'Refining Rectification' (2014) 130 LQR 83

9

MISREPRESENTATION AND NON-DISCLOSURE

1. INTRODUCTION

This chapter is concerned with relief for misrepresentation and for the exceptional cases in which there may be relief for non-disclosure.[1] Although, as we shall see, there is some overlap between these two vitiating factors in cases in which there has been partial disclosure, the rationale for the intervention of the law where a false or misleading statement is made is fundamentally different from that for imposing a duty upon a party to disclose to the other party information about the subject-matter of the proposed contract.

The general rule of the common law is that a person contemplating entering a contract with another is under no duty to disclose information to that other. 'Ordinarily the failure to disclose a material fact which might influence the mind of a prudent contractor does not give the right to avoid the contract.'[2] The parties must look out for their own interests and ensure that they acquire the information necessary to avoid a bad bargain. We have already seen in Chapter 8 that the law is reluctant to allow a party to avoid a contract on the basis of his mistake about the facts relating to the subject-matter of the contract or its surrounding circumstances, and the reluctance to impose duties of disclosure is in tune with this. Thus, a person who visits an antiques shop and sees a rare George II table being sold as a nineteenth-century piece need say nothing to the seller before buying it. The seller's mistake does not affect the validity of the contract, and the fact that the buyer realizes that the seller has made a mistake does not impose upon him a duty to disclose information to correct the mistake. Nor does the oil prospector who discovers that there is oil under a given piece of land have to inform the land owner. There are, however, exceptions to the general rule, both at common law and by statute, which impose duties to disclose and where failure to do so makes the contract voidable or may give rise to other remedies.

---

[1] See Cartwright, *Misrepresentation, Mistake and Non-Disclosure* (3rd edn, 2012) Parts 1 and 3; Handley, *Spencer Bower and Handley on Actionable Misrepresentation* (5th edn, 2014); Spencer Bower, Turner, and Sutton, *Actionable Non-Disclosure* (2nd edn, 1990).

[2] *Bell v Lever Bros Ltd* [1932] AC 161, 227 (Lord Atkin).

A misleading statement made during the negotiations leading to a contract—a misrepresentation—is, however, viewed quite differently. The party making the misrepresentation has induced the other party to enter into the contract on the basis of false information, and this displaces the normal rule that each party takes responsibility for acquiring information relevant to the bargain. The effect of a misrepresentation, subject to certain limitations, is to render the agreement voidable at the suit of the misled party. A person who has been induced to enter into a contract by reason of a misrepresentation can refuse to carry out the undertaking, resist any claim for specific performance, and, if necessary, have the contract set aside by means of the remedy of *rescission*. In addition, the misled party will sometimes be entitled to claim *tortious damages* in respect of loss sustained by reason of the misrepresentation. If the misrepresentation was made fraudulently, damages in the tort of deceit can be recovered. If it was made without reasonable care being taken to ascertain its truth, the misled party may recover damages by virtue of statute, or at common law in the tort of negligence. Where the party making the misrepresentation believed, and had reasonable ground to believe, that the facts represented were true, although the contract is still voidable at the suit of the misled party, tortious damages cannot be claimed but damages may sometimes be awarded in lieu of rescission.

Moreover, the facts which give rise to a remedy for misrepresentation may also give rise to other remedies. Where the misrepresentation has been incorporated as a term of the contract, the misled party may, instead of relying on the misrepresentation to obtain a remedy, choose instead to rely on the breach of contract and claim *damages,* or sometimes *discharge of the contract, for breach.* The circumstances in which a misrepresentation will be so incorporated were dealt with in Chapter 5. Sometimes a misrepresentation made by a trader which induces a consumer to enter into a contract will also constitute a 'prohibited practice' under the Consumer Protection from Unfair Trading Regulations 2008, which will give the consumer 'rights to redress' under the Regulations: to 'unwind' the contract, or to a discount or damages.

2. MISREPRESENTATION

(a) PUFFS, REPRESENTATIONS, AND TERMS

A misleading statement made during the negotiations leading to a contract may fall into one of three categories. First, it may be a mere 'puff', a commendatory expression which by virtue of its vagueness or extravagance would not be expected to and does not ground any form of liability. Secondly, the preliminary statement may be intended by neither party to have contractual effect, but nevertheless may affect the inclination of one party to enter into the contract. It is then known as a 'representation'. If it proves false, the misled party will not be entitled to claim damages for breach of contract, for no contractual stipulation has been broken; but will be entitled to claim the relief accorded by the law in the case of misrepresentation. Thirdly, the preliminary statement may be a term of the contract, or constitute a warranty collateral to the contract, if the party making the statement undertakes or guarantees that it is true.[3] There is an overlap between the second and third categories because a statement that is a misrepresentation may also become a term of the contract. In such cases there will be a choice of remedy since the misled party will be entitled to claim damages for breach of contract or relief for misrepresentation.

(b) REQUIREMENTS FOR RELIEF FOR MISREPRESENTATION

An operative misrepresentation consists in a false statement of existing or past fact or law made by one party (the 'representor') before[4] or at the time of making the contract, which is addressed to the other party (the 'representee') and which induces the other party to enter into the contract.

(i) There must be a false representation

Mere silence does not constitute a misrepresentation.[5] There must be some positive statement, or some conduct from which a statement can be implied, in order to amount to an operative misrepresentation. With regard to conduct, 'a nod or a wink, or a shake of the head, or a smile' may suffice,[6] as may a photograph.[7] It has been held that the participation by the Spice Girls in the making of a commercial to be shown in the future constituted a representation by conduct that none of the group had an existing declared intention to leave the group before it was shown.[8] And the use of a credit card or cheque implies that such use is authorized by the credit card company and that the state of facts existing when a cheque is handed over is that it will be honoured when presented.[9]

In assessing whether a complex pre-contractual document contains a misrepresentation, it has been suggested that it is preferable to look at the matter broadly and to assess whether overall the statements in the document are substantially correct rather than to focus 'more and more microscopically so as to concentrate on each sentence, phrase or word'.[10]

---

[3] See above, pp 141–5.

[4] *Cramaso LLP v Ogilvie-Grant* [2014] UKSC 9, [2014] AC 1093 at [16], [57].

[5] *Keates v Lord Cadogan* (1851) 10 CB 591.

[6] *Walters v Morgan* (1861) 3 De GF & J 718, 724 (Lord Campbell). See also *R v Charles* [1977] AC 177; *R v Lambie* [1982] AC 449 (on the meaning of 'deception' in the criminal law).

[7] *Atlantic Estates plc v Ezekiel* [1991] 2 EGLR 202.

[8] *Spice Girls Ltd v Aprilia World Service BV* [2000] EMLR 478, aff'd on this point [2002] EWCA Civ 15, [2002] EMLR 27.

[9] *R v Charles* [1977] AC 177; *R v Gilmartin* [1983] QB 953 (criminal offence of deception).

[10] *Avon Insurance plc v Swire Fraser Ltd* [2000] 1 All ER (Comm) 573, 632 (Rix J).

(ii) Partial non-disclosure and active concealment

A partial non-disclosure may constitute a misrepresentation. Suppression of material facts can render that which is stated false, as where a seller of land told a purchaser that the land had recently been occupied at a particular rent (which was true) but omitted to inform him that more recently he had failed to find a new tenant except at a lower rent, which therefore created the false impression that the land still had the higher value.[11]

There is also authority for the view that if a person does some positive act in order to conceal defects in the subject-matter of the contract, as where the seller of a ship takes the vessel from the slipway into the water in order to conceal its rotten hull,[12] such active concealment will constitute a misrepresentation. The question is whether the person, by his words or actions, has misled the other.

(iii) Change in facts

To constitute a *mis*representation, the representation must be false; and for the purposes of the various remedies for pre-contractual misrepresentation this means that it must be false at the time when the representee enters into the contract in reliance upon it. If the representor makes a representation which is true at the time when it is made, but which subsequently becomes false, it constitutes a misrepresentation at least where the representor knows about the change of facts which render it now false.[13] In such cases the Courts say either that it is treated as a continuing representation (which is therefore a misrepresentation at the critical time, when the contract is entered into) or that the representor is bound to disclose the change in circumstances to the other party.[14]

(iv) Representations of opinion normally insufficient

A mere expression of opinion, which turns out to be unfounded, will not invalidate a contract. There is a wide difference between the seller of property saying that it is worth so much, and a statement that the seller gave so much for it. The first is an opinion

---

[11] *Dimmock v Hallett* (1866) LR 2 Ch App 21. See also *Nottingham Patent Brick and Tile Co v Butler* (1886) 16 QBD 778; *South Western General Property Co v Marton* [1982] 263 EG 1090.

[12] *Schneider v Heath* (1813) 3 Camp 505. See also *Gordon v Selico Co Ltd* [1985] 2 EGLR 79, 83 (landlord's agents covered up dry rot in flat); *Cottee v Douglas Seaton (Used Cars) Ltd* [1972] 1 WLR 1408, 1417 (plastic filler to cover up rust in car).

[13] Cf Bigwood [2005] CLJ 94 (arguing that unknown change of facts is not tantamount to innocent misrepresentation because 'misrepresentation' is an agency-responsible act).

[14] *Davies v London & Provincial Marine Insurance Co* (1878) 8 Ch D 469, 475 (duty to disclose known change of facts); *With v O'Flanagan* [1936] Ch 575, 582–4 (duty to disclose or continuing representation); *Dietz v Lennig Chemicals Ltd* [1969] 1 AC 170 (innocent misrepresentation on basis of changed facts); *Traill v Baring* (1864) 4 De GJ & S 318 (duty to communicate change of intention); cf *Wales v Wadham* [1977] 1 WLR 199 (where *Traill v Baring* was not cited); *Cramaso LLP v Ogilvie-Grant* above, n 4 at [22] (continuing effect of pre-contractual representation). See also Misrepresentation Act 1967, s 2(1) (representor liable 'unless he proves that he had reasonable ground to believe and did believe *up to the time the contract was made* the facts represented were true').

which the buyer may or may not choose to adopt; the second is an assertion of fact which, if false to the knowledge of the seller, is also a fraudulent misrepresentation.[15] Thus in *Bisset v Wilkinson*:[16]

W agreed to purchase from B certain land at Avondale, in the Southern Island of New Zealand, for the purpose of sheep-farming, in reliance on B's statement that his 'idea was that [the land] would carry two thousand sheep'. W was aware that neither B nor other person had at any time carried out sheep-farming on the land in question. When B claimed the balance of the purchase price, W counter-claimed rescission of the contract on the ground of misrepresentation.

The Judicial Committee of the Privy Council held that the statement was merely of an opinion which B honestly held and accordingly the claim for rescission failed. Again, in *Economides v Commercial Union Assurance Co plc*[17] a statement that the cost of replacing the contents of a flat was £16,000, made to an insurance company by a 21-year-old student with no special knowledge, was a statement of opinion. It should not be assumed, however, that what appears to be simply a statement of opinion can never constitute a representation of fact. In one sense it always does so, for it asserts that the opinion is actually held. A statement of opinion which is not in fact held is therefore a fraudulent misrepresentation. Also an opinion will usually be based upon facts; so the person making the representation may impliedly state that facts are known which justify that opinion. This is especially the case where the situation is such that the representor must know the facts much better than the other party. If it is shown that the representor had no reasonable grounds for that opinion, or failed to investigate the facts which gave rise to it, there may well be an actionable misrepresentation. For example, in *Smith v Land and House Property Corporation*:[18]

L bought a hotel as an investment at auction from S, who had stated in the auction particulars that it was let to 'a most desirable tenant'. However, the tenant was in significant financial difficulty and had paid his last quarter's rent only 'by driblets under pressure'. S claimed specific performance of the contract, and L counter-claimed for rescission.

It was held that the statement about the tenant was a misrepresentation and L's claim to rescind the contract succeeded. The statement amounted at least to an assertion that nothing had occurred in the relations between the landlords and the tenant which could be considered to make the tenant an unsatisfactory one.

---

[15] Cf *Lindsay Petroleum Co v Hurd* (1874) LR 5 PC 221, 243–4.

[16] [1927] AC 177. See also *Anderson v Pacific Fire and Marine Insurance Co* (1872) LR 7 CP 65.

[17] [1998] QB 587 (discussing Marine Insurance Act 1906, s 20(3), (4), (5) which has now been repealed and superseded by Consumer Insurance (Disclosure and Representations) Act 2012 and (from 12 August 2016) Insurance Act 2015).

[18] (1884) 28 Ch D 7. See also *Brown v Raphael* [1958] Ch 636; *Sirius International Insurance Corp v Oriental Insurance Corp* [1999] 1 All ER (Comm) 699.

(v) Mere commendatory 'puffs' insufficient

Commendatory expressions, such as advertisements to the effect that a certain brand of beer 'refreshes the parts that other beers cannot reach', or that a perfume will irresistibly attract members of the opposite sex, are not treated in law as representations of fact. A similar latitude is allowed to a person who wants to gain a purchaser, though it must be admitted that the borderline of permissible assertion is not always easily discernible. At a sale by auction, land was stated to be 'fertile and improvable'; it was in fact partly abandoned and useless. This was held to be 'a mere flourishing description by an auctioneer'.[19] But, as we have seen, the statement in auction particulars that the property was let to 'a most desirable tenant', was not a mere commendatory puff but a representation.[20]

(vi) Expression of intention or prediction normally insufficient

An expression of the speaker's intention, a promise, and a prediction about the future are not normally misrepresentations. None of these can be regarded as true or false at the time when it is made, except insofar as a person may misrepresent the state of his or her own mind or power to bring an event to pass.[21] Thus there is a distinction between a promise which the promisor intends to perform and one which the promisor intends to break or knows cannot be performed. In the first case the representation is truly one of an intention that something shall take place in future, and is binding only if it fulfils the requirements of a contractual promise. In the second case there is a misrepresentation of the representor's existing intention: not only is a promise made which is ultimately broken, but when it is made, the representor's ability to perform or state of mind is represented to be something other than it really is. Such a misrepresentation is one of fact. Bowen LJ said:[22]

the state of a man's mind is as much a fact as the state of his digestion. It is true that it is very difficult to prove what the state of a man's mind at a particular time is, but if it can be ascertained it is as much a fact as anything else. A misrepresentation as to the state of a man's mind is, therefore, a misstatement of fact.

Thus it has been held that a person makes a fraudulent misrepresentation where he buys goods having at the time no means to pay or having formed an intention not to pay for them.[23] There may also be a misrepresentation of fact behind a negligent misprediction. Thus a prediction by a bank manager that the granting of a loan

---

[19] *Dimmock v Hallett* (1866) LR 2 Ch App 21, 27. See also *Lambert v Lewis* [1982] AC 225, 262–3.

[20] *Smith v Land and House Property Corp*, above, n 18.

[21] *R v Sunair Holidays Ltd* [1973] 1 WLR 1105, 1109; *British Airways Board v Taylor* [1976] 1 WLR 13, 17, 21, 23, 27. See also *R v Gilmartin*, above, n 9.

[22] *Edgington v Fitzmaurice* (1885) 29 Ch D 459, 483. See also *Goff v Gauthier* (1991) 62 P & CR 388.

[23] *Ex p Whittaker* (1875) LR 10 Ch App 446; *DPP v Ray* [1974] AC 370. On cheques and credit cards, see above, p 320, n 9.

facility would be a formality once supported by insurance from the Export Credit Guarantee Department has been held to contain a statement of fact as to the existing policy of the bank.[24]

(vii) Representation of law

Until recently it was held that a misrepresentation of law did not render the contract voidable by the representee.[25] It was, however, often difficult to distinguish between a representation of law and one of fact. Many statements of fact contain implicit propositions of law and vice versa. If a dwelling-house is represented to be a 'new' dwelling-house for the purposes of the Rent Acts, is this a representation of fact or of law?[26] A misrepresentation that planning permission exists for the business use of premises has been treated as a representation of fact,[27] as have misrepresentations as to private rights (as distinct from the general law)[28] or as to the content or effect of documents.[29] A misrepresentation of foreign law has also been treated as a representation of fact.[30] And there is no good reason why a *wilful* misrepresentation of law should not be treated in the same way as a statement of opinion which is not actually held:[31] misrepresentation of law has sometimes been treated as similar to misrepresentation of opinion.[32]

But the law has now moved on. It was held by the House of Lords in 1999, in the context of claims for the recovery of money paid under a mistake, that a distinction should no longer be made between mistakes of law and mistakes of fact.[33] Similar reasoning has also been applied to cases of mistake[34] and misrepresentation[35] in contract and therefore in principle misrepresentations of law are now capable of remedy on the same basis as misrepresentations of fact.

(viii) The representation must be addressed to the misled party

The representation must have been addressed by the representor (or by someone on his behalf) to the misled party with the intention that he act on it.[36] In *Peek v Gurney*:[37]

The promoters of a company were sued by P who had purchased shares on the faith of false statements contained in a prospectus issued by them. P was not a person to whom shares had

---

[24] *Box v Midland Bank Ltd* [1979] 2 Lloyd's Rep 391, 399; [1981] 1 Lloyd's Rep 434. Cf *Esso Petroleum Co Ltd v Mardon* [1976] QB 801.

[25] Cf *Beattie v Lord Ebury* (1872) LR 7 Ch App 777.   [26] *Solle v Butcher* [1950] 1 KB 671, 695.

[27] *Laurence v Lexcourt Holdings Ltd* [1978] 1 WLR 1128.

[28] *Cooper v Phibbs* (1867) LR 2 HL 149, above, p 308.

[29] *Hirshfeld v London Brighton and South Coast Railway Co* (1876) 2 QBD 1; *Wauton v Coppard* [1899] 1 Ch 92; *Re Roberts* [1905] 1 Ch 704; *Horry v Tate & Lyle Refineries Ltd* [1982] 2 Lloyd's Rep 416.

[30] *Andre & Cie SA v Ets Michel Blanc & Fils* [1979] 2 Lloyd's Rep 427.

[31] *West London Commercial Bank v Kitson* (1884) 13 QBD 360, 362.

[32] *Beattie v Lord Ebury*, above, n 25, 802.   [33] *Kleinwort Benson Ltd v Lincoln CC* [1999] 2 AC 349.

[34] *Brennan v Bolt Burdon* [2004] EWCA Civ 1017, [2005] QB 303.

[35] *Pankhania v Hackney London Borough Council* [2002] EWHC 2441 (Ch), [2002] All ER (D) 22 (Aug).

[36] (2015) 131 LQR 275 (Handley).

[37] (1873) LR 6 HL 377, applied in *Al Nakib Investments Ltd v Longcroft* [1990] 1 WLR 1390.

been allotted on the first formation of the company; he had merely purchased shares from such allottees.

The House of Lords held that the prospectus was only addressed to the first applicants for shares; that it could not be supposed to extend to others than these; and that on the allotment 'the prospectus had done its work; it was exhausted'.

A statement made directly to the misled party is clearly addressed to that party; but will also be held to have been so addressed where the person is one to whom the representor intended the statement to be passed on.[38] If this fact is established, it is immaterial that the misled party is merely one of a class of persons, even of the public at large.[39]

(ix) The representation must induce the contract

The representation must form a material inducement to the party to whom it is addressed, although the courts have held that for remedies at common law or in equity[40] it need only be *an* inducement for the party to enter into the contract, not the sole or predominant or decisive inducement.[41] Thus a person who bought shares in a company on the faith of fraudulent statements contained in a prospectus, but also in the erroneous belief that he would be entitled to the benefit of a charge on the company's assets, was able to claim that he had been materially misled by the statements.[42] Whether or not a person who has entered into a contract was induced to do so by a particular representation is in each case a question of fact.

The burden of proving that the representation induced the contract rests upon the misled party.[43] But such inducement may be inferred. Thus it was said by Lord Blackburn:[44]

I think that if it is proved that the defendants with a view to induce the plaintiff to enter into a contract made a statement to the plaintiff of such a nature as would be likely to induce

---

[38] *Commercial Banking Co of Sydney Ltd v RH Brown & Co* [1972] 2 Lloyd's Rep 360 (Australia); *Smith v Eric S Bush* [1990] 1 AC 831. Cf *Gross v Lewis Hillman Ltd* [1970] Ch 445.

[39] *Andrews v Mockford* [1896] 1 QB 372 (prospectus part of wider scheme of fraud).

[40] Legislative remedies for misrepresentation may have different rules: see, eg, Consumer Protection from Unfair Trading Regulations 2008 (below, p 328), reg 27A(6) ('significant factor'); Consumer Insurance (Disclosure and Representations) Act 2012, Sched 1, paras 5, 6, 7 (insurer would not have entered into consumer insurance contract on any terms, or would have entered it but on different terms). Cf *Raiffeisen Zentralbank Osterreich AG v Royal Bank of Scotland Plc* [2010] EWHC 1392 (Comm), [2011] 1 Lloyd's Rep 123 at [195] (for Misrepresentation Act 1967, s 2, the test is whether, had the representation not been made to him, the representee would not have contracted, not whether he might not have done so), criticized (2015) 131 LQR 275 (Handley).

[41] *Attwood v Small* (1838) 6 Cl & Fin 232, 502; *Reynell v Sprye* (1852) 1 De GM & G 660, 708; *Assicurazioni Generali SpA v Arab Insurance Group* [2002] EWCA Civ 1642, [2003] 1 All ER (Comm) 140 at [59], [218]. Cf *Raiffeisen Zentralbank Osterreich AG v Royal Bank of Scotland Plc*, above, n 40 at [197]–[199] (test in fraud and non-fraud cases may be different), relying on *Barton v Armstrong* [1976] AC 104, 119 (duress).

[42] *Edgington v Fitzmaurice* (1885) 29 Ch D 459.

[43] *Arkwright v Newbold* (1880) 17 Ch D 301, 324. See also *Bristol & West BS v Mothew* [1998] Ch 1.

[44] *Smith v Chadwick* (1884) 9 App Cas 187, 196. See also *Mathias v Yetts* (1882) 46 LT 497, 502 (Jessel MR); *Barton v County Natwest Ltd* [1999] Lloyd's Rep (Bank) 408.

a person to enter into a contract, and if it is proved that the plaintiff did enter into the contract, it is a fair inference of fact that he was induced to do so by the statement.

It will not be inferred that a representation induced the contract where it would not have induced a reasonable person to contract but, in such a case, a representee who proves that he or she was in fact so induced will be entitled to relief.[45]

On the other hand a person who was not actually influenced by a false representation cannot be said to have been induced to enter a contract by it. The representation may have been immaterial, in the sense that the representee's judgment was never affected[46] or the representee did not become aware, until after the conclusion of the contract, that a representation had been made.[47] In *Horsfall v Thomas*,[48] for example:

T bought a cannon which had been manufactured for him by H. The cannon had a defect which made it worthless, which H had endeavoured to conceal by inserting a metal plug into the weak spot in the gun. T never inspected the gun and upon using it the gun burst.

It was held that, the attempted concealment having had no operation upon T's mind or conduct, he could not successfully set up a plea of fraud. 'If the plug, which it was said was put in to conceal the defect, had never been there, his position would have been the same; for, as he did not examine the gun or form any opinion as to whether it was sound, its condition did not affect him.' [49]

(x) Opportunities for inspection

The mere fact that the misled party has had the opportunity of investigating and ascertaining whether the representation is true or false will not necessarily deprive that person of the right to claim to have been deceived by it and therefore to avoid the contract,[50] although if the circumstances are suspicious and he has information which ought to put him on inquiry he may not be able to rely on the misrepresentation to claim a remedy.[51] If, however, the representee does investigate, and consequently relies not upon the misrepresentation but upon the accuracy of those investigations, the action will fail, as it can no longer be said that the representation was a reason for entering the contract.

---

[45] *Museprime Properties Ltd v Adhill Properties Ltd* (1991) 61 P & CR 111, 124; cf *Goff v Gauthier* (1991) 62 P & CR 388, 397–8.

[46] *Smith v Chadwick* (1884) 9 App Cas 187; *JEB Fasteners v Marks, Bloom & Co* [1983] 1 All ER 583.

[47] *Re Northumberland and Durham District Banking Co* (1858) 28 LJ Ch 50.

[48] (1862) 1 H & C 90. Cf *Smith v Hughes* (1871) LR 6 QB 597, 605.

[49] (1862) 1 H & C 90, 99 (Bramwell B).

[50] *Central Ry Co of Venezuela v Kisch* (1867) LR 2 HL 99, 120 (fraudulent misrepresentation); *Redgrave v Hurd* (1881) 20 Ch D 1 (non-fraudulent misrepresentation); *Laurence v Lexcourt Holdings Ltd* [1978] 1 WLR 1128. Contributory negligence is a (partial) defence to a claim for damages in the tort of negligence, but not in the tort of deceit: *Standard Chartered Bank v Pakistan Shipping Co (Nos 2 and 4)* [2002] UKHL 43, [2003] 1 AC 959.

[51] *Redgrave v Hurd*, above, n 50, 23; *New Brunswick and Canada Railway Co v Conybeare* (1862) 9 HLC 711, 743.

(c) REMEDIES FOR MISREPRESENTATION: AN OVERVIEW

Once it has been established that there is an operative misrepresentation, the next step is to identify the remedies available to the representee. The circumstances in which the different remedies can be obtained will be explained in more detail below[52] but, in outline, they are as follows.

(i) Rescission of the contract

Misrepresentation renders the contract voidable at the instance of the misled party, and rescission is the remedy by which the representee obtains the retrospective avoidance of the contract. Both parties' obligations under the contract are set aside *ab initio* and the parties must normally return the benefits which they received from each other under the contract. For example, when a contract of sale is rescinded either by the buyer or by the seller, the buyer must return the goods and the seller must repay the price.

Where a contract is rescinded, the representee may also sometimes be able to obtain an 'indemnity' against obligations which have been incurred in favour of third parties under the terms of the contract. Where the misrepresentation was made otherwise than fraudulently, the Court has a discretion under section 2(2) of the Misrepresentation Act 1967 to refuse rescission and to award damages in lieu.

(ii) Damages in tort

If the representor committed a tort in making the misrepresentation, the representee may sue for damages in tort. If the misrepresentation was made fraudulently, the representor may be liable in the tort of deceit. If it was made negligently—without reasonable care—the representor may be liable in the tort of negligence or in a special statutory claim under section 2(1) of the Misrepresentation Act 1967. Deceit and negligence are general torts which are not limited to pre-contractual misrepresentations. The statutory claim was devised specially for pre-contractual misrepresentations, although it does not apply where the representee is a consumer who has a right to redress under Part 4A of the Consumer Protection from Unfair Trading Regulations 2008 in respect of the conduct constituting the misrepresentation.[53]

Damages in tort are calculated to compensate the loss which the claimant suffers as a result of the tort. In the context of misrepresentation, this means the amount by which the claimant is worse off as a result of entering into the contract in reliance on the misrepresentation. This may include consequential losses, but not the profits which the claimant hoped to make from the contract. That would be a claim for 'expectation' measure damages which are available only in a claim for breach of contract.[54]

---

[52] Below, pp 332 ff.   [53] Below, pp 328, 355. An award of damages under s 2(2) is similarly excluded.
[54] An example illustrating the difference between tort and contract measure damages is set out below, p 329.

(iii) Remedies for breach of contract

If the misrepresentation became a term of the contract, or constituted a warranty collateral to the contract, the claimant may claim not for the misrepresentation but for breach of contract. Damages are calculated to put the claimant into the financial position in which he would have been if the contract had not been broken. If the representor warranted that his representation was true, this means putting the claimant into the position as if it had been true.[55]

If the truth of the representation was a condition of the contract, or if the fact that it is false is a fundamental breach of contract, the representee may also be able to discharge the contract for breach. These remedies for breach of contract are not discussed in detail in this chapter.[56]

(iv) Consumers' rights to redress

If a consumer enters into a contract with a trader, and the trader (or, in certain circumstances, the producer of goods) has made a misrepresentation which constitutes a 'prohibited practice' under the Consumer Protection from Unfair Trading Regulations 2008 and which is a significant factor in the consumer's decision to enter into the contract, the consumer may have additional rights to redress. He may have a right to 'unwind' the contract, under which the contract comes to an end, and the trader must give a refund to the consumer and the consumer must make any goods which he received under the contract available for collection by the trader (or, where the consumer transferred goods to the trader under the contract, he has a right to return of the goods but he must repay any amount paid by the trader). If the consumer has not exercised the right to unwind, he may have the right to a discount in respect of the payments made or due to be made under the contract. And if he has incurred consequential financial loss, or has suffered alarm distress or physical inconvenience or discomfort, he may have a right to damages. Where the consumer has a right to redress under the 2008 Regulations he is not entitled to be paid damages under section 2(1) of the Misrepresentation Act 1967, although in many cases the loss that would have been covered under that section will in substance be covered by exercising the rights to a discount and to damages under the Regulations.[57]

(v) Defence to a claim under the contract

The representee may also be able to raise the misrepresentation as a defence to a claim by the representor under the contract; for example as a defence to a claim for specific performance of the contract, even in a case where the representee could not obtain rescission of the contract. Specific performance is a discretionary remedy and it will

---

[55] If the warranty was not that that the representation was true, but only that the representor was exercising reasonable case in making it, the measure of damages (even in contract) is similar to damages in the tort of negligence: *Esso Petroleum Co Ltd v Mardon* [1976] QB 801, 820.

[56] See below, Chapter 15 (discharge for breach); Chapter 17 (damages for breach of contract).

[57] See below, p 357.

be refused where it would be inequitable for one party to insist on performance of the contract by the other. Thus it will be refused where the party against whom it is sought would not have entered into the contract but for the misrepresentation.[58]

(vi) Choice between remedies

Sometimes the representee can establish a successful claim to more than one remedy. In such a case he will make a choice between the available remedies based on the benefit which each would give him; and sometimes he is able to obtain two remedies simultaneously, whereas other remedies are mutually inconsistent and he must choose between them.

For example, the representee may obtain at the same time both rescission of the contract and damages in tort (in deceit, negligence or under section 2(1) of the Misrepresentation Act 1967, as the case may be) because the underlying purpose of these remedies is essentially the same: to restore the position as if the contract had not been entered into, either by setting aside the obligations (rescission) or through a monetary award (damages in tort). If the representee takes both remedies, the rescission of the contract will reduce much of the loss since it involves each party returning what he received from the other, but if after the rescission the representee will still have out-of-pocket losses which fall within a possible tort claim, he is entitled to make that claim.[59] However, the representee cannot at the same time obtain rescission of the contract and damages for breach, since the latter remedy presupposes the continuing existence of the obligations under the contract.

The rights to redress provided by the Consumer Protection from Unfair Trading Regulations 2008 constitute a further route for a consumer to seek a remedy where the misrepresentation constitutes conduct to which the Regulations apply, although the consumer must choose between claims and cannot be compensated both under the Regulations and under any other rule of law or equity or under any enactment in respect of the conduct.[60] The representee must choose between damages for breach of contract and damages in tort, since their purpose is different. The measures of damages will often be different, even where the claims arise from the same misrepresentation, and the facts will determine which is better for the representee. Take an example:[61]

A sells a car to B, and makes a misrepresentation, which he also warrants to be true, about the age of the car. The car is really 10 years old, but A says that it is 7 years old. B pays £1,000 for the car. The market value of a 7-year-old car (with, apart from the age, the same characteristics as this car) is £1,200; but the actual value of this 10-year-old car is £700.

---

[58] *Lamare v Dixon* (1873) LR 6 HL 414.   [59] *Archer v Brown* [1985] QB 401, 415.

[60] Consumer Protection from Unfair Trading Regulations 2008 (SI 2008 No 1277, as amended by SI 2014 No 870), reg 27L. There is no choice between claiming damages under Misrepresentation Act 1967, s 2 and a right to redress under the Regulations in respect of conduct constituting a misrepresentation, since the consumer who has a right to redress is not entitled to be paid damages under Misrepresentation Act 1967, s 2 in respect of that misrepresentation: Misrepresentation Act, s 2(4), below, p 357.

[61] Cartwright, *Unequal Bargaining* (1991) 106.

If B sues in tort, he claims to be put back into the position in which he would have been if he had not been induced by the misrepresentation to buy the car. He would still have his £1,000. But since he has exchanged that money for a car which is worth only £700, he has lost £300. On the other hand, if he sues for breach of contract, B claims to be put into the position in which he would have been if the representation were true—that is, he would have a seven-year-old car, which would be worth £1,200. So, since the car is in fact worth only £700 his 'loss' is £500. On these facts, the damages in contract are higher than the damages in tort. But this is only because the bargain (apart from the misrepresentation) was good: if the representation had been true, B was getting a good deal in paying only £1,000 for a car which should have been worth £1,200. But if the bargain had been bad, and B was paying too much for the car even if it had been only seven years old, the contract measure would be less generous than the tort measure.

(d) 'FRAUDULENT', 'NEGLIGENT', AND 'INNOCENT' MISREPRESENTATIONS

In the modern law misrepresentations may be categorized as fraudulent, negligent, or innocent. This section outlines the different remedies available in these categories, and the details of each of the remedies is given in the following sections.

(i) Categorization of misrepresentations in the older cases

Before 1963, the significant difference was between fraudulent misrepresentations for which the contract could be set aside (ie 'rescinded') and for which damages were available in the tort of deceit, and non-fraudulent misrepresentations (known as 'innocent misrepresentations') for which only rescission was available.[62]

The explanation for this lay in the distinction between common law and equity, and the historical development of the law of tort. In equity a contract could be rescinded for non-fraudulent misrepresentation, but damages, a common law remedy, was not available in the Court of Chancery. By contrast, the common law courts awarded damages for fraud in the tort of deceit, and for the breach of a contractual term, but they gave no remedy for a non-fraudulent misrepresentation which merely induced the formation of a contract.[63] The Judicature Act 1873[64] enabled equitable remedies to be granted in any division of the High Court, but did not affect the substantive rule that damages in addition to rescission cannot be awarded for innocent misrepresentation. The important developments were the decision of the House of Lords in 1963 in *Hedley Byrne & Co Ltd v Heller & Partners Ltd*,[65] which first extended the tort of negligence

---

[62] *Heilbut Symons & Co v Buckleton* [1913] AC 30, 48–9; *Gilchester Properties Ltd v Gomm* [1948] 1 All ER 493.

[63] *Kennedy v Panama, New Zealand, and Australian Royal Mail Co Ltd* (1987) LR 2 QB 580, 587.

[64] 1873 Act, ss 24(1), (2), and 25(11). See now the Senior Courts Act 1981 (formerly Supreme Court Act 1981), s 49.

[65] [1964] AC 465, below, p 346; extended to pre-contractual misrepresentations in *Esso Petroleum Co Ltd v Mardon* [1976] QB 801.

to cover claims for economic loss caused by reliance on a negligent misstatement, and the enactment of the Misrepresentation Act 1967, which created a special remedy for negligent pre-contractual misrepresentations. Since then, therefore, it has become usual to use the label 'innocent' (or, sometimes, 'wholly innocent') to refer to misrepresentations which are made neither fraudulently nor negligently. But it is important to understand that judges in the cases before 1963 did not make this distinction, and therefore applied the label 'innocent' also to misrepresentations which would now be classified as negligent.

(ii) The remedies available in the modern law for fraudulent, negligent, and innocent misrepresentations

At common law a *fraudulent* misrepresentation not only renders the contract voidable, and therefore allows the representee to obtain rescission of the contract, but also gives rise to an action for damages in tort in respect of the deceit.[66] If, therefore, the misrepresentation was made fraudulently, the injured party will be entitled to choose either to affirm the contract and recover damages in respect of any loss which may have been suffered by reason of the fraud, or to rescind the contract and recover damages in respect of any loss which will remain after rescission has been effected.[67]

A person who has been induced to enter into a contract as the result of a *negligent* misrepresentation made to him by the other party to the contract is entitled to rescind as in the case of fraud, although here the Court has a discretion under section 2(2) of the Misrepresentation Act 1967 to refuse rescission and award damages in lieu. The representee may also be able to claim damages in the tort of negligence or under section 2(1) of the Misrepresentation Act 1967.[68] Again, he has the choice between affirming the contract and claiming damages in negligence or under section 2(1) for all his loss, and rescinding the contract and claiming damages for any loss which will remain following rescission. If the Court refuses rescission and awards damages in lieu under section 2(2) of the 1967 Act, the representee may claim any additional losses in negligence or under section 2(1).[69] Where the claimant is a consumer who has a right to redress under the Consumer Protection from Unfair Trading Regulations 2008, however, he is not entitled to be paid damages under section 2 of the Misrepresentation Act 1967, although he may claim the right to redress under the Regulations (the rights to unwind, to a discount and/or to damages). His claim

---

[66] In many circumstances a fraudulent misrepresentation will also constitute a criminal offence: eg Fraud Act 2006, s 2; Financial Services Act 2012, Part 7. The Court convicting a defendant for a criminal offence may in some cases also make a compensation order: Powers of Criminal Courts (Sentencing) Act 2000, s 130. There are also statutory remedies in respect of certain fraudulent statements: eg Financial Services and Markets Act 2000, s 382 (restitution order where profits made or losses inflicted by contravention of certain requirements, including Financial Services Act 2012, Part 7).

[67] *Archer v Brown* [1985] QB 401.

[68] For the difference between what has to be established under these claims, and the difference between the damages awarded under them, see below, pp 348–51.

[69] 1967 Act, s 2(3).

to the general remedies of rescission and/or damages in the tort of negligence are, however, unaffected.

A person who has been induced to enter into a contract as the result of an *innocent* misrepresentation made to him by the other party to the contract is entitled to the remedy of rescission; but, in contrast with cases of fraudulent or negligent misrepresentation, cannot obtain damages in addition to rescission, only an indemnity. However, the Court has a discretion under section 2(2) of the Misrepresentation Act 1967 to refuse rescission and award damages in lieu.

(e) RESCISSION OF THE CONTRACT

Rescission is, in principle, available for all classes of operative misrepresentation.[70] At common law a contract was voidable for misrepresentation only if it was made fraudulently. But there was no such limitation in equity, and the rules of equity now prevail.[71] When a person has been induced to enter into a contract by a misrepresentation of any description, the effect on the contract is not to make it void, but to give the misled party an option either to avoid it or, alternatively, to affirm it. A party who is misled and elects to avoid the contract may take steps to have it set aside by the Court, or may resist an action for specific performance or for damages brought by the representor, and rescind by way of counterclaim.[72] Rescission, however, is not merely a judicial remedy. The misled party can rescind without seeking the assistance of a Court,[73] and any property transferred to the representor under the contract will revest in the party who has so rescinded the contract.[74]

---

[70] There are, however, special rules for insurance contracts, where the common law remedies for misrepresentation by an insured before the insurance contract is entered into have been replaced for consumer insurance contracts by the Consumer Insurance (Disclosure and Representations) Act 2012, and will be replaced for non-consumer insurance contracts by the Insurance Act 2015 (in force from 12 August 2016). The insurer may avoid the contract in case of a *deliberate or reckless* misrepresentation (and retain any premiums paid except, in the case of a consumer insurance contract, to the extent (if any) that it would be unfair to the consumer to retain them). Where the misrepresentation was only *careless* (or, in the case of non-consumer insurance contracts, was neither deliberate nor reckless, ie *careless or innocent*) the insurer may avoid the contract only if it would not have entered into the contract on any terms in the absence of the misrepresentation; if it would have entered into the contract but on different terms or would have charged a higher premium, the terms of the contract or the premium may be varied if the insurer so requires: Consumer Insurance (Disclosure and Representations) Act 2012, Sched 1, Part 1; Insurance Act 2015, Sched 1, Part 1 (in force from 12 August 2016). There is no remedy against a consumer insured who exercises reasonable care not to make a misrepresentation to the insurer: 2012 Act, s 2.

[71] *Redgrave v Hurd* (1881) 20 Ch D 1, 12–13; Supreme Court of Judicature Act 1873, s 25(11). See now Senior Courts Act (formerly Supreme Court Act) 1981, s 49.

[72] The setting up of the misrepresentation by way of defence has in some instances been treated as equivalent to rescission: *Clough v London & NW Ry* (1871) LR 7 Ex 26.

[73] *TSB Bank Plc v Camfield* [1995] 1 WLR 430, 438. Cf, however, O'Sullivan [2000] CLJ 509.

[74] If the nature of the property is such that a particular formality is required to revest the title (eg land or shares), the representor holds the legal title on constructive trust for the representee: *Alati v Kruger* (1955) 94 CLR 216, 224.

(i) Mode of rescission

As a normal rule, rescission must be communicated to the other party.[75] But where a seller of goods has a right to avoid the contract for the buyer's misrepresentation, it suffices if the seller, even without the buyer's knowledge, retakes possession of the goods.[76] The Courts have even been prepared to accept that, at least in the case of a fraudulent misrepresentation, it is sufficient for the seller to take all possible steps to regain the goods. In *Car and Universal Finance Co Ltd v Caldwell:*[77]

C was fraudulently induced to sell a motor car to a purchaser in return for a bad cheque. When the cheque was dishonoured, C immediately informed the police and the Automobile Association, but the purchaser had deliberately absconded and could not be found. The purchaser sold the car to a person who had notice of the fraud, but it was later sold on to another person who had no such notice. Eventually, it came into the hands of the claimant who bought it in good faith.

The Court of Appeal held that C had rescinded the contract even though he had not communicated his rescission to the purchaser. The title to the car had revested in the defendant on rescission and so the claimant had no title to the vehicle. It is not, however, clear whether anything less than communication to the purchaser or re-taking the goods would be sufficient to effect rescission in the case of a non-fraudulent misrepresentation.[78]

(ii) No power to award partial rescission

Notwithstanding the flexibility of equity, it was held in *TSB Bank plc v Camfield*[79] that because, save as otherwise provided by statute, the right to rescind is that of the representee and not of the Court, there is no power to order partial rescission. In that case, as a result of an innocent misrepresentation, a woman charged her interest in a house to a bank to secure the debts of her husband's business believing that the maximum liability under the charge was £15,000 when it was in fact unlimited. Despite her willingness at the outset to charge the property for £15,000, the charge was set aside in its entirety. This result has not been followed in Australia[80] and was left open by the Privy Council in an appeal from New Zealand,[81] but is settled law in England unless it is reviewed by the Supreme Court.[82] The approach in the English

---

[75] *Scarf v Jardine* (1882) 7 App Cas 345, 360, 361.

[76] *Car and Universal Finance Co Ltd v Caldwell* [1961] 1 QB 525, 554–5, 558; *Re Eastgate* [1905] 1 KB 465.

[77] Above, n 76. Cf *Newtons of Wembley Ltd v Williams* [1965] 1 QB 560.

[78] *Car and Universal Finance Co Ltd v Caldwell*, above, n 76, 551–2, 555, 558–9.

[79] [1995] 1 WLR 430. This case is in the line of cases following *Barclays Bank Plc v O'Brien* [1994] 1 AC 180, in which the misrepresentation is made by a third party (here, the husband) to induce the misled party (the wife) to enter into a contract with a bank. For third-party misrepresentations, see below, pp 397–400.

[80] *Vadasz v Pioneer Concrete (SA) Pty Ltd* (1995) 184 CLR 102.

[81] *Far Eastern Shipping Co Public Ltd v Scales Trading Ltd* [2001] 1 All ER (Comm) 319, 326. The New Zealand Court of Appeal had expressed a strong preference for the flexible approach of *Vadasz*'s case (above, n 80).

[82] *De Molestina v Ponton* [2002] 1 Lloyd's Rep 271, 288 (Colman J), on the basis that *Vadasz* is inconsistent with the decision of HL in *Barclays Bank Plc v O'Brien*, above, n 79. Cf *Kennedy v Kennedy* [2014] EWHC

cases follows from the fact that (apart from the Court's power to award damages in lieu of rescission under section 2(2) of the Misrepresentation Act 1967)[83] rescission for misrepresentation is not a discretionary remedy. In this, it is in marked contrast to the approach of equity in analogous situations. Thus, mortgagees' claims have been upheld only to the extent of the other party's understanding of the amount of the mortgage.[84] Again, in rescission for undue influence, the Court is concerned to achieve 'practical justice' for both parties. We shall see that the party seeking rescission may be required to pay the other reasonable remuneration for beneficial services rendered,[85] and, where the market value of property transferred has fallen, to bear a proportionate part of the loss.[86] Where the objectionable parts of a transaction can be severed without rewriting it, setting aside is, moreover, not invariably an 'all or nothing process'.[87] The misled party may also sometimes be able to seek rectification of the contract if (as in *TSB Bank plc v Camfield*) the misrepresentation relates to a term of the contract, and if he wishes to enforce the contract on the basis of the terms as he believed them to be.[88] But if he wishes to avoid the whole transaction on the basis of the misrepresentation, then, unless the Court exercises its power under section 2(2) of the Misrepresentation Act 1967, he may do so.[89]

(iii) Indemnity alongside rescission

When a contract is rescinded, each party is entitled to be relieved of the obligations under the contract and to recover any benefit which has been conferred upon the other party. The object of rescission is to restore the position as it was before the contract was entered into, and with this end in view the misled party can claim an indemnity against any obligations which may be incurred, or which have been incurred, as a result of the contract.

In *Newbigging v Adam*:[90]

N entered into a partnership with A and provided £10,000 of new capital. He was induced to enter into the partnership agreement by a material non-fraudulent misrepresentation as

---

4129 (Ch), [2015] BTC 2 at [46] (Etherton C: the rejection of partial rescission makes sense for contract, but does not apply to a self-contained and severable part of a *non-contractual* voluntary transaction). See, however, Poole and Keyser (2005) 121 LQR 273.

[83] Below, p 339.

[84] *Bristol & West BS v Henning* [1985] 1 WLR 778 and *Skipton BS v Clayton* (1993) 66 P & CR 233. See Ferguson (1995) 111 LQR 555.

[85] *O'Sullivan v Management Agency and Music Ltd* [1985] 1 QB 428, below, p 395.

[86] *Cheese v Thomas* [1994] 1 WLR 129. See also Jones and Goodhart, *Specific Performance* (2nd edn, 1996) 293 (purchaser's action for specific performance with compensation).

[87] *Barclays Bank plc v Caplan* [1998] 1 FLR 532, 546.

[88] For rectification, see above, pp 282–7.

[89] In *TSB Bank plc v Camfield* the bank conceded that it could not invoke s 2(2) directly and since an award of damages against the husband would have been an empty remedy no Court could have formed the view that it would be equitable to exercise its power under s 2(2).

[90] (1886) 34 Ch D 582, aff'd as *Adam v Newbigging* (1888) 13 App Cas 308.

to the capacity of certain machinery. The business failed, and N sued for rescission of the agreement, for recovery of his capital, and for an indemnity against all claims which might be made against him by virtue of his having become a partner.

The Court of Appeal agreed that N was entitled to the relief for which he asked, that the right to an indemnity must be less extensive than the right to damages, and that the principle underlying the award of an indemnity is to restore the misled party to his old position. But they differed in their conclusion as to how the pre-contract position should in general be achieved. Fry LJ was inclined to hold that the misled party 'is entitled to an indemnity in respect of all obligations entered into under the contract when those obligations are within the necessary or reasonable expectation of both of the contracting parties at the time they made the contract'.[91] But an award made on this basis would not differ from damages. A narrower and more satisfactory test was propounded by Bowen LJ when he said the misled party 'is not to be replaced in exactly the same position in all respects, otherwise he would be entitled to recover damages, but he is to be replaced in his position so far as regards the rights and obligations which have been *created by the contract* into which he has been induced to enter'.[92] Cotton LJ similarly said that 'the indemnity to which he is entitled is only an indemnity against the obligations which he has contracted under the contract which is set aside'.[93]

The distinction between damages and an indemnity as it works out in practice may be illustrated by the case of *Whittington v Seale-Hayne*,[94] where the Court adopted the narrower principle suggested by Bowen LJ:

Poultry farmers had been induced to take a lease by the defendant's non-fraudulent misrepresentation that the premises were sanitary. This was not the case, and in consequence of the contamination of the water supply, their manager fell ill and the poultry died. They claimed rescission of the lease, and an indemnity to cover the value of the stock, loss of profit on sales, loss of breeding season, medical expenses of the manager, rates, rent, and money spent on outbuildings, etc. They had also been compelled by the local council to renew the drains, and this item, too, was included.

It was held that the poultry farmers were entitled to have the lease rescinded, and to recover what they had spent on rent, rates, and the renewal of the drains, since these were expenses incurred under the covenants in the lease or arising necessarily out of the occupation of the property, and thus 'obligations created by the contract'. Their claim for payment in respect of the other items of loss was not allowed, since these were damages, there being no obligation to carry on a poultry farm on the leased premises.

In practice, an indemnity is a useful remedy only where the misrepresentation is wholly innocent. In cases of fraudulent or negligent misrepresentation the claimant may claim damages on the tort measure, in addition to rescinding the contract.[95]

---

[91] (1886) 34 Ch D 582, 596.   [92] *Ibid*, 592–3 (emphasis added).
[93] *Ibid*, 589.   [94] (1900) 82 LT 49.   [95] Above, p 329.

Damages will be at least as extensive as the indemnity. Thus it is generally only where there is no claim for damages that the claimant has an interest in pursuing an indemnity.

(iv) Limitations on the right to rescind

In a number of situations, the misled party may be precluded from rescinding the contract. It is important to note, however, that the loss of the remedy of rescission will not prevent a claim for damages in the tort of deceit or the tort of negligence or under section 2(1) of the Misrepresentation Act 1967. The right to damages, where this exists, is independent of the claim to rescind and still survives. Nor does the loss of the right to rescind prevent a consumer bringing a claim to enforce the rights to redress under the Consumer Protection from Unfair Trading Regulations 2008 which is also independent of rescission.

There are five limitations on the right to rescind.

(a) Affirmation   If after becoming aware of the misrepresentation the representee affirms the contract either by express words or by an act which shows an intention to affirm it, rescission cannot be obtained. So, for example, if persons who have purchased shares on the faith of a misrepresentation subsequently become aware of its falsity, but act inconsistently with rescission of the contract such as by accepting dividends or attempting to sell the shares,[96] they will not be permitted to avoid the contract. In *Long v Lloyd*:[97]

Long was induced to purchase a lorry by Lloyd's representation that it was in 'exceptional' and 'first class' condition. On the first journey after the sale, the dynamo broke and Long noticed several other serious defects. Lloyd was informed of these and offered to pay half the cost of some of the repairs. On the next long journey, the lorry broke down completely and Long realized that it was in a deplorable condition. He claimed to rescind the contract.

The Court of Appeal held that, although the first journey did not amount to an affirmation of the contract as it had been undertaken merely to test the truth of Lloyd's representation, the second journey did constitute such an affirmation since Long then had knowledge that the representation was untrue.

It has been held that the right to rescind will not be lost by affirmation unless the representee has knowledge both of the facts and that these give rise to the right to rescind.[98] Where there is no such knowledge, however, the conduct of the representee may, if relied on by the representor, give rise to an estoppel precluding rescission.[99] The position thus differs from that concerning the right to reject for breach of condition in contracts for the sale of goods which may be lost by 'acceptance' without such

---

[96] *Scholey v Central Ry Co of Venezuela* (1867) LR 9 Eq 266; *Re Hop and Malt Exchange and Warehouse Co* (1866) LR 1 Eq 483.

[97] [1958] 1 WLR 753.   [98] *Peyman v Lanjani* [1985] Ch 457, 486–7, 494, 500.

[99] *Ibid*, 488, 493, 501; *Motor Oil Hellas (Corinth) Refineries SA v Shipping Corp of India* [1990] 1 Lloyd's Rep 391, 398–9 (Lord Goff).

knowledge.[100] In *Long v Lloyd*, where there may not have been such knowledge, the Court may have considered that rescission for misrepresentation should be barred where the right to reject for breach of condition has been lost.[101]

(b) Lapse of time   Lapse of time may in certain circumstances bar the right to rescind. It may be treated as evidence of affirmation where the misled party fails to exercise the right to rescind for a considerable time after discovering the representation to be untrue.[102] But, since knowledge is required for affirmation, mere lapse of time does not normally have this effect.[103] And where the misrepresentation was fraudulent, time does not run against the representee until he has discovered the fraud (or, at least, should have discovered it).[104] Where the misrepresentation was not fraudulent, however, the passage of time may operate so as to preclude rescission even though the representee has no knowledge of the untruth of the representation. It then depends upon whether, on the facts, the representee has failed to rescind within a 'reasonable' time from the contract. In *Leaf v International Galleries*:[105]

L bought from IG a picture of Salisbury Cathedral which IG innocently represented to him at the time of the purchase to have been painted by Constable. Five years later, when he tried to sell it, he discovered this was not the case. He endeavoured to return the picture and recover the price. IG refused, whereupon he brought an action claiming rescission of the contract of sale.

The Court of Appeal held that the right to rescind had been lost. Jenkins LJ said:[106]

contracts such as this cannot be kept open and subject to the possibility of rescission indefinitely . . . it behoves the purchaser either to verify or, as the case may be, to disprove the representation within a reasonable time, or else stand or fall by it. If he is allowed to wait five, ten, or twenty years and then reopen the bargain, there can be no finality at all.

(c) Rights of third parties   Since the contract is not void but voidable, being valid until rescinded, if third parties in good faith ('*bona fide*') without notice and for value acquire rights in the subject-matter of the contract, those rights are valid against the misled party, provided that the contract has not before that time been rescinded.[107] Thus a shareholder who wishes to rescind a contract to take up shares in a company must do so before winding-up, for once winding-up commences the rights of the creditors become fixed, since they stand in the position of *bona fide* purchasers for value.[108]

---

[100] Sale of Goods Act 1979, s 35 as amended by the Sale and Supply of Goods Act 1994 (which now applies only to non-consumer contracts for the sale of goods by reason of amendment of the 1979 Act by the Consumer Rights Act 2015). See generally above, pp 159–60.

[101] See *Leaf v International Galleries* [1950] 2 KB 86, 91; Atiyah (1959) 22 MLR 76; Davies (1959) 75 LQR 32.

[102] *Clough v L & NW Ry* (1871) LR 7 Ex 26, 35. Cf *Allen v Robles* [1969] 1 WLR 1193.

[103] *Armstrong v Jackson* [1917] 2 KB 822, 830.

[104] *Rolfe v Gregory* (1865) 4 De GJ & S 576, 579; *Redgrave v Hurd* (1881) 20 Ch D 1, 13.

[105] [1950] 2 KB 86. See also *Salt v Stratstone Specialist Ltd* [2015] EWCA Civ 745 at [34] (Longmore LJ, doubting the reasoning in *Leaf* which linked the test for lapse of time to that for acceptance of goods under Sale of Goods Act 1893, s 35).

[106] [1950] 2 KB 86, 92.   [107] *Babcock v Lawson* (1880) 5 QBD 284.

[108] *Oakes v Turquand* (1867) LR 2 HL 325.

Also where goods are obtained by means of a misrepresentation, a third party who, before rescission, acquires the goods in good faith and for value from the fraudulent purchaser cannot be displaced by the representee.[109]

(d) Inability to make restitution   It has been said that when a party 'exercises his option to rescind the contract, he must be in a state to rescind; that is, he must be in such a situation to be able to put the parties into their original state before the contract'.[110] Each must give back what has been transferred. But the purpose of this limitation is to prevent the unjust enrichment of the party seeking to rescind[111] and it should not be too strictly construed. Thus the mere fact that the subject-matter of the contract may have deteriorated before the truth is discovered is not sufficient to prevent a party making restitution and so to destroy the right to rescind a contract.[112] In Adam v Newbigging[113] rescission was granted of a partnership agreement even though the partnership business was then 'worse than worthless'. It has been suggested that rescission of a contract of sale of quoted shares ought still to be possible even after the purchaser has sold the shares, since he could purchase other identical shares and can offer substantial restitution,[114] although this idea of making restitution by handing over an equivalent thing, rather than the actual subject-matter of the contract, has not been developed. Nor has English law contemplated the approach taken by some legal systems which allow the misled party, who has sold the goods, to avoid the contract on restoring to the other party not the goods themselves, but the money which he has obtained through the sale.[115]

The Courts have refrained from defining the scope of this equitable remedy by any rigid rules; as a condition of rescission there must be restitution, but at the same time the Court has full power to make all just allowances. It was said by Lord Blackburn in Erlanger v New Sombrero Phosphate Co[116] that the practice had always been for a Court of Equity to give relief by way of rescission whenever by the exercise of its powers it can do what is practically just by directing accounts, ordering equitable compensation,[117]

---

[109] Sale of Goods Act 1979, s 23; Phillips v Brooks Ltd [1919] 2 KB 243. This rule is a reason why a misled party may seek to argue that the original contract of sale was void for mistake, rather than only voidable for misrepresentation: Shogun Finance Ltd v Hudson [2003] UKHL 62, [2004] 1 AC 919, above, p 290. Cf Car and Universal Finance Co Ltd v Caldwell (above, p 333), where the goods were purchased by an innocent third party only after rescission had already been effected.

[110] Clarke v Dickson (1858) EB & E 148, 154 (Crompton J; see also in argument at 152: 'you cannot both eat your cake and return your cake').

[111] MacKenzie v Royal Bank of Canada [1934] AC 468 (Canada); Bouygues Offshore v Owner of the M/T Tigr Ultisol Transport Contractors Ltd [1996] 2 Lloyd's Rep 153, 159 (South Africa).

[112] Armstrong v Jackson [1917] 2 KB 822, 829; Lagunas Nitrate Co v Lagunas Syndicate [1899] 2 Ch 392; Alati v Kruger (1955) 94 CLR 216 (Australia).

[113] (1888) 13 App Cas 308, above, p 334.

[114] Smith New Court Securities Ltd v Citibank NA [1997] AC 254, 263.

[115] Restitution 'by value' rather than in kind: Lando and Beale, Principles of European Contract Law Parts I and II (2000) 277-9.

[116] (1878) 3 App Cas 1218, 1278.

[117] See Mahoney v Purnell [1996] 3 All ER 61 (undue influence).

and making allowances, though it cannot restore the parties precisely to the state they were in before the contract.

How this goal of doing 'what is practically just' may be reached depends on the circumstances of the case. For instance, the Court may think that justice requires the making of some allowance for the deterioration, or the improvement, as the case may be, of the subject-matter of the contract. Again, it may require compensation for losses incurred by the representor[118] or recompense for services rendered to the representee.[119] The Court will be more drastic in exercising its discretionary powers in a case of fraud than in a case where no fraud is present; it will be 'less ready to pull a transaction to pieces where the defendant is innocent, whereas in the case of fraud the Court will exercise its jurisdiction to the full in order, if possible, to prevent the defendant from enjoying the benefit of his fraud at the expense of the innocent plaintiff'.[120] But, even in a case of fraud, rescission will not be ordered where it is not possible to achieve a broadly just result by orders for monetary adjustment to reflect benefits and detriments which have accrued under the contract since to do so would unjustly enrich the defrauded party.[121]

(e) Damages in lieu of rescission   Except in cases of fraud and cases where the claimant is a consumer who has a right to redress under the Consumer Protection from Unfair Trading Regulations 2008,[122] the Court has a discretion to refuse to allow rescission and to award damages in lieu of this remedy. This power is conferred by section 2(2) of the Misrepresentation Act 1967, which states:

Where a person has entered into a contract after a misrepresentation has been made to him otherwise than fraudulently, and he would be entitled, by reason of the misrepresentation, to rescind the contract, then, if it is claimed, in any proceedings arising out of the contract, that the contract ought to be or has been rescinded, the court or arbitrator may declare the contract subsisting and award damages in lieu of rescission, if of opinion that it would be equitable to do so, having regard to the nature of the misrepresentation and the loss that would be caused by it if the contract were upheld, as well as to the loss that rescission would cause to the other party.

The reason for this provision is that rescission in some situations may be too drastic a remedy; for example, a car might be returned to the seller because of a trifling misrepresentation about the mileage done since the engine was last overhauled.[123] Section 2(2) requires the Court to take into account the relative importance or unimportance of the facts which have been misrepresented, as well as the relationship

---

[118] *Spence v Crawford* [1939] 3 All ER 271, 283 (Lord Thankerton) (loss to representor from sale by bank of shares held as security conceded to be recoverable). See also *Cheese v Thomas* [1994] 1 WLR 129 (undue influence).

[119] *Atlantic Lines & Navigation Co Inc v Hallam Ltd* [1983] 1 Lloyd's Rep 188, 202 (Mustill J) (services of chartered ship); *O'Sullivan v Management Agency and Music Ltd* [1985] 1 QB 428 (undue influence).

[120] *Spence v Crawford* [1939] 3 All ER 271, 288 (Lord Wright).

[121] *Society of Lloyd's v Wilkinson (No 2)* (1997) 6 Re LR 214, 222, 289, 296.

[122] Misrepresentation Act 1967, s 2(4), inserted by SI 2014 No 870. For the right to redress under the 2008 Regulations, see below, p 355.

[123] See the Tenth Report of the Law Reform Committee (Cmnd 1782, 1962) para 11.

between the loss caused to the representee by the misrepresentation and the loss which would be caused to the representor if the contract is rescinded. Where the former is significantly less than the latter it is likely that damages in lieu of rescission will be awarded.[124]

(i) *Unavailable where rescission barred.* Is there power to award damages of this nature where the right to rescind, though once in existence, has become barred by reason of affirmation, lapse of time, the intervention of third-party rights, or an inability to make restitution? The sub-section and its legislative history are ambiguous,[125] but no such power was proposed by the Law Reform Committee on whose recommendations the 1967 Act was based.[126] Divergent views at first instance in the cases[127] have been resolved by the Court of Appeal deciding that the court cannot award damages in lieu of rescission if it has become barred:[128]

The words of the statute are 'if it is claimed ... that the contract ought to be or has been rescinded the court ... may declare the contract subsisting and award damages in lieu of rescission'. No doubt a claimant can be said to make a claim even if he is subsequently held not to be entitled to do so. But the words 'in lieu of rescission' must, in my view, carry with them the implication that rescission is available (or was available at the time the contract was rescinded). If it is not (or was not available in law) because eg the contract has been affirmed, third party rights have intervened, an excessive time has elapsed or restitution has become impossible, rescission is not available and damages cannot be said to be awarded 'in lieu of rescission'.

(ii) *Measure of damages.* The measure of damages to be awarded under this subsection is the loss caused by the misrepresentation as a result of the refusal to allow rescission of the contract, not the loss caused by entering into the contract.[129] In a contract for the sale of land, for example, this would be the difference in value between what the representee was misled into thinking was being bought and the value of what was received. Broadly, therefore, this follows the contractual measure of damages, rather than the tort measure.[130] However, it is not a claim for damages for breach of contract, and it has been stated that the damages under the sub-section should never exceed

---

[124] *William Sindall plc v Cambridgeshire CC* [1994] 1 WLR 1016, 1038 (loss to representee £18,000 to divert a sewer; loss to representor some £6 million in return of purchase price and interest for land the value of which had substantially fallen).

[125] Atiyah and Treitel (1967) 30 MLR 369, 375–9.

[126] Tenth Report (Cmnd 1782, 1962) para 27.

[127] eg *Atlantic Lines and Navigation Co Inc v Hallam Ltd* [1983] 1 Lloyd's Rep 188, 202; *Government of Zanzibar v British Aerospace (Lancaster House) Ltd* [2000] 1 WLR 2333, 2343 (s 2(2) not available where rescission has become barred); cf *Thomas Witter Ltd v TBP Industries Ltd* [1996] 2 All ER 573, 590 (Jacob J: s 2(2) still available, relying on a statement of the Solicitor-General on the third reading of the Bill (741 HC Deb, col 1387, 20 February 1967) but cf the Lord Chancellor and Viscount Colville of Culross (274 HL Deb, col 929, 17 May 1966; 277 HL Deb, col 53, 18 October 1966) and see further Beale (1995) 111 LQR 385).

[128] *Salt v Stratstone Specialist Ltd* [2015] EWCA Civ 745 at [17] (Longmore LJ). However, on the facts, restitution was not impossible and therefore rescission was not barred.

[129] *William Sindall plc v Cambridgeshire CC* [1994] 1 WLR 1016. See also *UCB Corporate Services Ltd v Thomason* [2005] EWCA Civ 225, [2005] 1 All ER (Comm) 601 at [37] (loss includes financial loss, which may be loss of a chance).

[130] For the difference, see above, pp 329–30.

what the claimant would have got had the representation been a term. As section 2(2) was enacted because it was thought it might be a hardship to the representor to be deprived of the whole of the benefit of the bargain on account of a minor misrepresentation, 'it could not possibly have been intended the damages in lieu be assessed on a principle which would invariably have the same effect'.[131] Moreover, account is not taken of losses due to a general fall in market values after the contract is made. Where a misrepresentation is made without reasonable ground for belief in its truth, damages can be claimed under section 2(1) of the 1967 Act, and the measure of these damages is that applicable in tort.[132] In certain transactions there may be no difference between the damages recoverable under section 2(1) and section 2(2); but since consequential damage can be recovered under section 2(1)[133] and account may be taken of losses due to a general fall in the market after the contract,[134] damages under that sub-section will in many cases be more extensive than those recoverable under section 2(2). Although awards can be made under both section 2(1) and section 2(2), it is not possible to recover damages twice over, for the Act provides that any award under section 2(2) shall be taken into account in assessing the liability of the representor under section 2(1).[135]

Where the misrepresentation is innocent, but the Court refuses rescission, the representee is, of course, not entitled to an indemnity in addition to damages under section 2(2). An indemnity is attached to the remedy of rescission and is awarded in order to achieve the restoration of the representee's financial position before the contract.[136] Since, however, the representee would have been entitled to an indemnity had rescission been granted, the Court should, in assessing the damages under section 2(2), take account of any sum recoverable as an indemnity in computing the loss which has been suffered as a result of the refusal of rescission.

(v) Limitations removed by the 1967 Act

Before 1967 it was said that there were two further limitations on the remedy of rescission. These were removed by the Misrepresentation Act 1967.

(a) Executed contracts   In the case of innocent misrepresentation, there was authority that there could be no rescission of a contract after it had been executed by the transfer of property under it.[137] The extent of this rule was somewhat uncertain and it was the subject of much criticism,[138] for in many cases the falsity of a misrepresentation cannot be discovered until, for example, a lease of a house has been executed and the tenant has moved into occupation of the premises. Section 1(b) of the Act therefore provides that a contract is to be capable of rescission notwithstanding that it has been

---

[131] *William Sindall plc v Cambridgeshire CC*, above, n 129, 1038 (Hoffmann LJ).
[132] See below, p 349.
[133] *Davis & Co (Wines) Ltd v Afa-Minerva (EMI) Ltd* [1974] 2 Lloyd's Rep 27.
[134] Below, pp 344–5, 349.   [135] 1967 Act, s 2(3).   [136] Above, p 334.
[137] *Seddon v NE Salt Co Ltd* [1905] 1 Ch 326; *Angel v Jay* [1911] 1 KB 666.
[138] See eg *Lever Bros Ltd v Bell* [1931] 1 KB 557, 588 (aff'd [1932] AC 161); *Leaf v International Galleries* [1950] 2 KB 86, 90, 91, 95; Tenth Report of the Law Reform Committee (Cmnd 1782, 1962) paras 6–10.

performed. This does not affect the other bars to rescission, and the circumstances in which a Court will exercise its discretion under section 2(2) of the 1967 Act are more likely to be present when a contract has been executed than when it is still executory.

(b) Incorporation as term   If a misrepresentation is also incorporated as a term of the contract, it was previously believed that the right to rescind was lost: the situation was treated simply as involving the breach of a contractual term, for 'the representation becomes merged in the higher contractual right'.[139] This rule was criticized because the representee would be worse off if the misrepresentation were incorporated in the contract as a mere warranty, since the representee would then have no right to rescind the contract but only to claim damages.[140] Section 1(a) of the 1967 Act now provides that rescission is still open notwithstanding that the misrepresentation has become a term of the contract. The present rule is: 'once a misrepresentation, always a misrepresentation'. The representee must choose between the remedies, however: he cannot both rescind the contract for misrepresentation and claim damages for breach of a contractual term, since, by rescinding it, the contract is effectively set aside for all purposes, including the right to claim damages for the breach of it.

(f) DAMAGES FOR FRAUDULENT MISREPRESENTATION: THE TORT OF DECEIT

(i) Elements of the claim in deceit

In order to succeed in a claim the tort of deceit, the representee must show that the representor made a misrepresentation; that the representation was made fraudulently; that the representor intended that he (or someone in his position) should act upon it; and that he did act upon it and suffered loss by so doing.[141]

As with other remedies for misrepresentation, the representation may be by words or conduct, including partial non-disclosure or active concealment which misleads the representee, but it cannot normally be by silence.[142] And the test for whether the representee acted upon the misrepresentation is the same here as in the other remedies where the misrepresentation must have induced the contract.[143] The elements peculiar to this remedy are the requirement of fraud, and the measure of damages.

(ii) The meaning of fraud

The meaning of fraud was laid down by the House of Lords in *Derry v Peek*:[144]

A company obtained a statutory right to run trams by animal power or, if the consent of the Board of Trade was obtained, by steam or mechanical power. The directors believed that the

---

[139] *Pennsylvania Shipping Co v Compagnie Nationale de Navigation* [1936] 2 All ER 1167, 1171.

[140] For remedies for breach of warranty (contrasted with breach of a condition of the contract, or a fundamental breach), see above, pp 148–58.

[141] *Bradford Third Equitable Benefit Building Society v Borders* [1941] 2 All ER 205, 211.

[142] Above p 320. For cases which allow a claim in the tort of deceit for fraudulent breach of a duty of disclosure, see below, pp 367–8.

[143] *Smith v Chadwick* (1884) 9 App Cas 187, 196; above, p 325.   [144] (1990) 14 App Cas 337.

Board would give this consent as a matter of course, as they had already submitted plans to the Board without any objection being made. They therefore issued a prospectus saying that the company had the right to run trams by steam or mechanical power. Peek took up shares in the company on the faith of the representation. The Board of Trade ultimately refused its consent, and the company was wound up.

Peek sued in tort for deceit. Lord Herschell said:[145]

First, in order to sustain an action of deceit, there must be proof of fraud, and nothing short of that will suffice. Secondly, fraud is proved when it is shewn that a false representation has been made (1) knowingly, or (2) without belief in its truth, or (3) recklessly, careless whether it be true or false. Although I have treated the second and third as distinct cases, I think the third is but an instance of the second, for one who makes a statement under such circumstances can have no real belief in the truth of what he states.

Lord Herschell went on to point out that making a false statement through want of care falls far short of fraud; so too does a false representation honestly believed, though on insufficient grounds. However, evidence of the reasonableness of the belief, and of the information available to the representor, will be relevant in the Court's assessment of whether the claimant has established his case that the representor did not honestly believe his representation.[146] In the present case, there were obviously reasons which had led the directors to make the untrue statement, and they 'honestly believed what they stated to be a true and fair representation of the facts'.[147] Peek's action therefore failed.

Derry v Peek thus established that a negligent misrepresentation will not amount to deceit, however gross the negligence may be.[148] Nothing short of fraud will suffice. On the other hand, it also shows that, to constitute fraud, it is not necessary that there should be a clear knowledge that the statement made was false. What is essential is the absence of an honest belief in its truth. Further, the motive of the person making the representation is irrelevant. It is no justification to show that the representation was made without criminal dishonesty, bad motive, or that there was no intention to cheat or cause loss to another by the deception.[149]

The elements of the tort of deceit must be established at the moment when the representee acts upon the representation.[150] That is the moment at which the representation must be false, and the representor must be fraudulent. A

---

[145] *Ibid*, 374.   [146] *Ibid*, 375.   [147] *Ibid*, 376.

[148] *Angus v Clifford* [1891] 2 Ch 449, 464; *Thomas Witter Ltd v TBP Industries Ltd* [1996] 2 All ER 573, 587–8. The effect of the decision in *Derry v Peek* was reversed for the particular case of misrepresentations in company prospectuses by Directors Liability Act 1890, but no general remedy in damages was created for non-fraudulent pre-contractual misrepresentation until the development of the tort of negligence by *Hedley Byrne & Co Ltd v Heller & Partners Ltd* [1964] AC 465 (below, p 346) and Misrepresentation Act 1967, s 2(1) (below, p 347).

[149] *Bradford Third Equitable Benefit Building Society v Borders* [1941] 2 All ER 205, 211; *Brown Jenkinson & Co Ltd v Percy Dalton (London) Ltd* [1957] 2 QB 621.

[150] *Briess v Woolley* [1954] AC 333, 353.

statement which is believed to be true when made and which is subsequently discovered by the representor to be false, will be considered to be fraudulent if the mistake is not communicated to the other person before that person acts on it.[151]

(iii) Measure of damages

Damages in deceit are designed to compensate the person who is deceived by the misrepresentation, and are assessed in accordance with the tortious measure; that is, in the context of a fraudulent pre-contractual misrepresentation, the amount by which the claimant is worse off as a result of entering into the contract in reliance on the misrepresentation.[152] A wider liability is imposed upon an intentional wrongdoer than a negligent or innocent one in order to deter fraud, and because 'moral considerations militate in favour of requiring the fraudster to bear the risk of misfortunes directly caused by his fraud'.[153] Accordingly, all actual losses directly flowing from the fraud are recoverable even if they could not reasonably have been foreseen[154] and, as contributory negligence is not a defence to fraud, damages will not be reduced on this ground.[155] The defrauded party is, however, required to mitigate the loss once aware of the fraud[156] but where it is claimed that there has been a failure to mitigate the burden lies on the wrongdoer to show both that the defrauded party has failed to act reasonably and that the failure in fact resulted in an increased loss.[157]

The measure of damages can be illustrated by an example loosely based on the facts in *Smith New Court Securities Ltd v Citibank NA* in which the House of Lords stated the applicable principles.[158]

Suppose a person has been fraudulently induced to buy shares for £24 million. They are in fact worth £12 million at the date of the contract. If the representation had been true they would have been worth £26 million.

The injured party will be entitled to recover the amount by which it is out of pocket (£12 million), but not for the loss of the bargain (£14 million).[159] The injured party must give credit for any benefits received as a result of the transaction, including, as

---

[151] *Davies v London and Provincial Marine Insurance Co* (1878) 8 Ch D 469, 475.

[152] Above, p 330.

[153] *Smith New Court Securities Ltd v Citibank NA* [1997] AC 254, 279–80 (Lord Steyn).

[154] *Doyle v Olby (Ironmongers) Ltd* [1969] 2 QB 158; *Smith New Court Securities Ltd v Citibank NA* (above, n 153), 267, 279.

[155] *Standard Chartered Bank v Pakistan National Shipping Co (Nos 2 and 4)* [2002] UKHL 43, [2003] 1 AC 959.

[156] *Smith New Court Securities Ltd v Citibank NA* (above, n 153) 266.

[157] *Standard Chartered Bank v Pakistan National Shipping Corp* [2001] EWCA Civ 55, [2001] 1 All ER (Comm) 822.

[158] [1997] AC 254, 267 (Lord Browne-Wilkinson).

[159] See also the illustration of the difference between contract and tort measure damages above, pp 329–30.

a general rule, the market value of the property acquired. Account will not generally be taken of a fall in the market value after the date of the contract unless, as in the case of *Smith New Court Securities Ltd*, the fraudulent misrepresentation continued to operate after that date or the misled party is unable to sell the property because of the fraud.[160] On the other hand, the misled party can undoubtedly recover in respect of consequential damage, such as injury to the person or property, or, say, the expense involved in moving into a house which that party has been fraudulently induced to buy,[161] or even for distress caused by the fraud.[162] The misled party may also recover in respect of opportunities foregone as a result of entering the contract. Thus, in *East v Maurer*,[163] the purchasers of a hair salon bought in reliance on a fraudulent representation that the seller had no intention of regularly working at another salon he owned in the same town recovered, inter alia, the profit they would have made if the false representation had not been made, that is, the profit they might have been expected to make in another hairdressing business bought for a similar sum. As Sedley LJ noted in a later case, 'it does not follow that the proper mode of ascertaining damage in certain cases of tort may not mimic reasoning more familiar in contract'.[164]

Damages in tort are calculated principally to compensate the claimant's losses, not to deprive the representor of any profits he has made from his fraud. In principle a Court may award punitive or exemplary damages in any tort, including deceit, where the defendant's conduct was calculated by him to make a profit for himself which may well exceed the compensation payable to the claimant.[165] However, although there is evidence of the courts having awarded exemplary damages in deceit,[166] most deceits will be punishable by the criminal law, in which case it may be better to leave punishment to the criminal process.[167] Moreover, although there are some situations in which the representee may be able to obtain restitution of benefits made by the defendant committing the tort of deceit, such a claim is not a claim in tort but in unjust enrichment, and may be limited, for example, to cases where the fraud is committed concurrently with a breach of fiduciary duty.[168]

---

[160] [1997] AC 254, 267 (Lord Browne-Wilkinson).

[161] *Doyle v Olby (Ironmongers) Ltd* [1969] 2 QB 158.

[162] *Shelley v Paddock* [1979] QB 120, aff'd [1980] QB 348; *Archer v Brown* [1985] QB 401.

[163] [1991] 1 WLR 461. See also *Smith New Court Securities Ltd v Citibank NA* (above, n 153), 282; *Clef Aquitaine SARL v Laporte Ltd* [2001] QB 488 (though transaction not loss-making, a more profitable one would have been entered into but for defendant's deceit).

[164] *Clef Aquitaine SARL v Laporte Materials (Barrow) Ltd* [2001] QB 488, 513.

[165] *Rookes v Barnard* [1964] AC 1129, 1226; *Kuddus v Chief Constable of Leicestershire Constabulary* [2001] UKHL 29, [2002] 2 AC 122.

[166] cf *Parabola Investments Ltd v Browallia Cal Ltd* [2009] EWHC 901 (Comm), [2009] 2 All ER (Comm) 589 at [205].

[167] *Archer v Brown*, above, n 162.

[168] *Murad v Al-Saraj* [2005] EWCA Civ 959, [2005] WTLR 1573.

(g) DAMAGES FOR NEGLIGENT MISREPRESENTATION: THE TORT OF NEGLIGENCE OR SECTION 2(1) MISREPRESENTATION ACT 1967

(i) Common law: the tort of negligence

Before the passing of the Misrepresentation Act 1967 there was no clear entitlement to claim damages for a non-fraudulent misstatement in the absence of a fiduciary relationship.[169] In 1963, in the case of *Hedley Byrne & Co Ltd v Heller & Partners Ltd*[170] the House of Lords extended liability in damages in tort to negligent misstatement and held that a duty of care could exist where there was an assumption of responsibility creating a 'special relationship' between the person making the statement and the person to whom it was made. The effect of this decision on pre-contractual statements and the law relating to misrepresentation was not directly considered,[171] nor were the tests advanced by their Lordships for determining the existence of this special relationship uniform in their terminology.[172] Nevertheless, it was later made clear that the existence of a contract between the parties does not exclude a parallel or concurrent duty of care in tort.[173] Moreover, it has been held that a negligent misrepresentation made by one party to the other, preparatory to entering into a contract, can give rise to an action for damages in tort for negligent misstatement if the person making it has or professes to have special knowledge or skill in respect of the facts stated[174] or if the representation, in the context in which it is made, is to be regarded as neither casual nor unconsidered, but to be relied on.[175] The burden of proving negligence—both the duty of care and breach of that duty—rests on the party alleging it, that is, on the representee.

The tort measure of damages applies, but for a negligent misstatement the representor is liable only for the losses which he could reasonably have foreseen. The policy which we have seen in the tort of deceit, that the fraudulent defendant should be made to pay for all the loss which he caused through his dishonesty,[176] gives way in the tort of negligence to a policy which holds the defendant liable only for foreseeable losses because the basis of the imposition of the duty of care is that the defendant should, as a reasonable man, have foreseen the consequences of his actions.[177]

---

[169] On the liability and more rigorous duties of a fiduciary, see *Nocton v Lord Ashburton* [1914] AC 932, 954 and below, p 365.

[170] [1964] AC 465.   [171] But see Lord Pearce, *ibid*, 539.

[172] [1964] AC 465, 486, 503, 514, 528, 529.

[173] *Henderson v Merrett Syndicates Ltd* [1995] 2 AC 145, 186–91 (Lord Goff).

[174] *Esso Petroleum Co Ltd v Mardon* [1976] QB 801; *Cornish v Midland Bank plc* [1985] 3 All ER 513; *Gran Gelato Ltd v Richcliff (Group) Ltd* [1992] Ch 560. McNair J in *Oleificio Zucchi SpA v Northern Sales Ltd* [1965] 2 Lloyd's Rep 496, 519 had assumed that *Hedley Byrne* did not apply as between contracting parties.

[175] *Howard Marine and Dredging Co Ltd v A Ogden & Sons (Excavations) Ltd* [1978] QB 574, 592, 600.

[176] Above, p 344.

[177] *Overseas Tankship (UK) Ltd v Morts Dock & Engineering Co Ltd, The Wagon Mound* [1961] AC 388, 422–3.

Thus the common law draws distinctions to reflect moral differences between the fraudulent representor and the negligent representor.[178]

The measure of loss in a claim in the tort of negligence will also depend upon the scope of the duty of care undertaken by the representor. If he undertakes a general duty to advise the representee about the transaction, his duty may extend to the consequences generally of the representee having entered into the contract, which could include losses flowing from fluctuations in the market in a case where, for example, the advice induces the representee to enter into a contact to purchase property. But where the duty is not to advise but is only to take care that specific information is correct, for example the valuation of a property by a surveyor or information given by a solicitor to a client, it has been held that a valuer is only liable for the foreseeable loss of the information being wrong, so that the damages are the difference between the valuation given and the true value of the property at the time of the breach.[179] This has been criticized as inappropriately capping the tort measure by reference to the contractual bargain[180] and as redefining 'duty' in a way that prevents inquiry into the other legal issues; namely causation, remoteness, and measure of damages.[181]

(ii) Misrepresentation Act 1967

Section 2(1) of the Misrepresentation Act 1967[182] establishes a statutory right to damages:

Where a person has entered into a contract after a misrepresentation has been made to him by another party thereto and as a result thereof he has suffered loss, then, if the person making the misrepresentation would be liable to damages in respect thereof had the misrepresentation been made fraudulently, that person shall be so liable notwithstanding that the misrepresentation was not made fraudulently, unless he proves that he had reasonable ground to believe and did believe up to the time the contract was made that the facts represented were true.

The use of the words 'reasonable ground to believe' in the closing words of the sub-section might suggest that the duty imposed upon the representor is equivalent to the

---

[178] Ibid; *Smith New Court Securities Ltd v Citibank NA* [1997] AC 254, 279–80.

[179] *South Australia Asset Management Corp v York Montague Ltd* [1997] AC 191. See also *Bristol & West BS v Mothew* [1998] Ch 1; *Swindle v Harrison* [1997] 4 All ER 705 (breach of fiduciary duty). Cf *Aneco Reinsurance Underwriting Ltd v Johnson & Higgins Ltd* [2001] UKHL 51, [2002] 1 Lloyd's Rep 157 (duty to advise).

[180] Stapleton (1997) 113 LQR 1. See also McLaughlan *ibid*, 421; [1997] JCL 114, cf Dugdale [1995] JBL 533; Burrows, *Remedies for Torts and Breach of Contract* (3rd edn, 2004) 109–22.

[181] *Kenny & Good Pty Ltd v MGICA (1992) Ltd* (1999) 163 ALR 611, 634–5 (Gummow J) (Australia).

[182] Implementing the Tenth Report of the Law Reform Committee (Cmnd 1782, 1962) para 17. The precedent for s 2(1) was in s 43 of the Companies Act 1948 (itself based originally on the Directors Liability Act 1890; above, p 343, n 148). See now Financial Services and Markets Act 2000, s 90, below, p 349. On the Misrepresentation Act, see generally Atiyah and Treitel (1967) 30 MLR 369. In relation to contracts entered into on or after 1 October 2014, s 2(4) (added by SI 2014 No 870) excludes the entitlement to damages under s 2 where the conduct constituting the misrepresentation gives rise to a right to redress under Part 4A of the Consumer Protection from Unfair Trading Regulations 2008: below, p 355.

duty of care in negligence. In general terms, it is appropriate to classify the remedy under section 2(1) as being for 'negligent' misrepresentation,[183] since it does not require proof of fraud, yet does not impose liability if the defendant is able to show that he had reasonable ground to believe his statement (broadly speaking, that he was not negligent).[184] But there are significant differences in the scope of liability under the section 2(1) and the tort of negligence. In *Howard Marine and Dredging Co Ltd v A Ogden & Sons (Excavations) Ltd*:[185]

O entered into a charterparty by which it chartered from HM two barges. In the course of negotiations leading to the contract, HM's manager represented to O that the barges had a payload of 1,600 tonnes. He based this figure on his recollection of a statement in Lloyd's Register that the deadweight capacity of the barges was 1,800 tonnes. That statement was in fact erroneous and the German shipping documents (which the manager had seen) relating to the barges gave the true deadweight capacity at 1,055 tonnes. O refused to pay the agreed hire charges and HM withdrew the barges and sued for the balance due. O counterclaimed £600,000 on the grounds of misrepresentation, being the loss which it alleged it had sustained because of the low carrying capacity of the barges.

The Court of Appeal was divided as to whether the circumstances were such as to impose a duty of care in negligence at common law.[186] But a majority of the Court held[187] that HM was liable under section 2(1), since the sub-section goes further than the common law, does not require a special relationship or special skill and does not depend upon the representor being under a duty of care the extent of which may vary according to the circumstances in which the representation is made. The statute imposes an absolute obligation not to state facts which the representor cannot prove it had reasonable ground to believe were true. The burden thus lies on the representor and not, as at common law, on the representee and it may be a heavy one to discharge, particularly since reasonable ground for belief in the truth of the statement must be shown to exist up to the time the contract is made.

It should, however, be noted that the sub-section is narrower than the common law because it only applies where a person has (a) entered into a contract after a misrepresentation has been made to that person and (b) the misrepresentation is made by another party to the contract, and not by a third party. Thus if A enters into a contract with B as a result of a misrepresentation made to B by C, no action will lie under the subsection unless C is B's agent; nor will C be liable to A under this provision, though

---

[183]   eg *HIH Casualty and General Insurance Ltd v Chase Manhattan Bank* [2003] UKHL 6, [2003] 1 All ER (Comm) 349 at [5] (Lord Bingham).

[184]   If the misrepresentation is made by an agent of the contracting party, thus rendering the contracting party liable under s 2(1) (*Resolute Maritime Inc v Nippon Kaiji Kyokai* [1983] 1 WLR 857), it may be that the principal is liable unless both the agent can show that he had reasonable ground to believe his statement and the principal had no means of knowledge of facts which would show the representation to be untrue.

[185]   [1978] QB 574.

[186]   Lord Denning MR and Shaw LJ. Bridge LJ expressed no concluded view on this issue.

[187]   Bridge and Shaw LJJ (Lord Denning MR dissenting).

C might be liable under a collateral warranty,[188] or in tort for negligent misstatement if a special relationship of care or reliance is shown to exist.[189]

Section 2(1) of the Misrepresentation Act 1967 is a general remedy for pre-contractual misrepresentations.[190] In addition, there are other statutes which impose liability in damages in respect of negligent statements in particular contexts: prospectuses and listing particulars issued in support of the public issue of company securities,[191] and misleading information in literature concerning package holidays.[192] There are also certain criminal offences involving the making of false statements in particular contexts,[193] although in most such cases there will be no claim for damages by reason only of the commission of the offence.[194]

The effect of section 2(1) of the 1967 Act is to confer upon the representee a right to damages for misrepresentation in circumstances in which there would have been such a right had the misrepresentation been fraudulent. It is now clear that the measure of damages is the tortious measure, that is, so as to put the representee in the position he would have been in had he never entered into the contract.[195] But the equation with fraud has given rise to certain problems. Most importantly, it appears that under the sub-section it is the fraud measure (that is, the measure in the tort of deceit) which applies, rather than that for negligent misstatement at common law. This allows the recovery of all losses directly flowing from the misrepresentation even if not foreseeable.[196] In *Royscot Trust Ltd v Rogerson*:[197]

A finance company was induced to advance a greater sum than it would otherwise have done by a car dealer's misrepresentation that a 20 per cent deposit had been paid by a prospective hire-purchaser of a car. The hire-purchaser later ceased to pay the instalments due and

---

[188] Above, p 145.   [189] *Resolute Maritime Inc v Nippon Kaiji Kyokai* [1983] 1 WLR 857.

[190] It does not, however, apply as between a consumer and a trader where the conduct constituting the misrepresentation gives the consumer a right to redress under Part 4A of the Consumer Protection from Unfair Trading Regulations 2008: below, p 355.

[191] Financial Services and Markets Act 2000, s 90. To avoid liability, those responsible must show they reasonably believed that the statement was true and not misleading: *ibid*, Sched 10, para 1. The origin of this provision is the Directors Liability Act 1890, above, p 343, n 148, which was also the inspiration for Misrepresentation Act 1967, s 2(1): above, n 182.

[192] Package Travel, Package Holidays and Package Tours Regulations 1992 (SI 1992 No 3288) implementing Council Directive 90/314/EC.

[193] Cf p 331, n 66, above (criminal liability for fraudulent misrepresentation, and power to award damages under Powers of Criminal Courts (Sentencing) Act 2000, s 130); Business Protection from Misleading Marketing Regulations 2008 (SI 2008 No 1276); Consumer Protection from Unfair Trading Regulations 2008 (SI 2008 No 1277).

[194] Cf, however, consumers' rights to redress under Part 4A of the Consumer Protection from Unfair Trading Regulations 2008, below, p 355.

[195] *Sharneyford Supplies Ltd v Edge* [1986] Ch 128, 149 (rvsd on different grounds [1987] Ch 305), disapproving the earlier statement in *Watts v Spence* [1976] Ch 165, 178 that the contractual measure ('loss of bargain') applied; *André & Cie SA v Ets Michel Blanc & Fils* [1977] 2 Lloyd's Rep 166, 181; *Naughton v O'Callaghan* [1990] 3 All ER 191, 196–8; *Royscot Trust Ltd v Rogerson* [1991] 2 QB 297, 304–5.

[196] Above, pp 344 (deceit), 346 (negligence).

[197] [1991] 2 QB 297. See also *William Sindall plc v Cambridgeshire CC* [1994] 1 WLR 1016, 1037; *South Australia Asset Management Corp v York Montague Ltd* [1997] AC 191, 216.

dishonestly sold the car. It was held that whether or not the sale by the hire-purchaser was foreseeable, the loss to the finance company of the unpaid instalments was recoverable from the car dealer under section 2(1) of the 1967 Act.

The argument that as a matter of policy it was undesirable to adopt the fraud measure for what is basically negligence liability, since fools should not be treated as if they were rogues,[198] was rejected by the Court of Appeal as incompatible with the literal words of the statute. Indeed, it appears that this literal reading may be what was originally intended by the legislature, because at the time when the proposal for section 2(1) was devised the distinction between the measure of damages in deceit and in negligence was not yet fully developed,[199] and the Law Reform Committee[200] did not think that it was 'in general the function of the civil law to grade the damages which an injured person may recover in accordance with the moral guilt of the defendant'.

However, the law of tort has moved on, and there is now a reluctance to apply the fraud measure for what is in essence only a negligent misrepresentation or, indeed, a misrepresentation which may not even be negligent but where the defendant cannot discharge the burden of proving that he had reasonable ground for his belief.[201] The point is, moreover, not beyond argument. First, it was not necessary in *Royscot*'s case to choose between the fraud and negligence measures. This was because the act of disposing of the car by the hire-purchaser was held to be foreseeable so the unpaid instalments would have been recoverable in any event. Secondly, it is already established that not all the consequences of fraud follow in the case of liability under section 2(1) of the 1967 Act. Damages under section 2(1) may be reduced for contributory negligence where the loss was partly the fault of the representee[202] although, as has been seen,[203] damages for fraudulent misrepresentation in the tort of deceit may not be reduced for contributory negligence. Again, the extended limitation period which applies in an action of deceit[204] will not apply to liability under section 2(1) because the statutory claim is not in fact

---

[198] Cf Fairest [1967] CLJ 239, 244; Hooley (1991) 107 LQR 547, 549–51. See also Atiyah and Treitel (1967) 30 MLR 369, 373; Cartwright, *Unequal Bargaining* (1991) 131–2.

[199] The Law Reform Committee (above, n 182) reported in 1962, after the Privy Council in *The Wagon Mound* (above, n 177) had laid down the test of remoteness of damage in the tort of negligence, but before the House of Lords in *Hedley Byrne* extended the tort of negligence to misrepresentations, and long before *Hedley Byrne* was extended to pre-contractual misrepresentations in *Esso Petroleum Co Ltd v Mardon* (above, n 174). The natural point of reference for the new statutory liability during the formulation of the proposals was therefore the tort of deceit. See also Cartwright [1987] Conv 423.

[200] Above, n 182, para 22.

[201] *Howard Marine and Dredging Co Ltd v A Ogden & Sons (Excavations) Ltd*, above, n 175. Cf *Avon Insurance plc v Swire Fraser Ltd* [2000] 1 All ER (Comm) 573, 633 (at the margin, 'a misrepresentation should not be too easily found' if the decision in *Royscot*'s case has to be applied).

[202] *Gran Gelato Ltd v Richcliff (Group) Ltd* [1992] Ch 560, 574. Nicholls V-C stated at 573 that 'in short liability under the Misrepresentation Act 1967 is essentially founded on negligence' and see Cane (1992) 108 LQR 539, 544.

[203] Above, p 344.

[204] Limitation Act 1980, s 32(1)(a): in an action 'based on the fraud of the defendant' the limitation period does not begin to run 'until the plaintiff has discovered the fraud . . . or could with reasonable diligence have discovered it'.

based on the defendant's fraud. There are, moreover, indications that the Sup̲
Court would be reluctant to find that what Lord Steyn described as 'the rather loo̲
wording' of the statute 'compels the court to treat a person who was morally innocent̲
as if he was guilty of fraud when it comes to the measure of damages'.[205]

(h) EXCLUSION AND LIMITATION OF LIABILITY

Chapter 6 contains a detailed account of the approach of the common law to the incorporation and interpretation of exclusion and limitation clauses, and the statutory control of such clauses. Here we consider particular issues which arise with regard to clauses which seek to exclude or limit a contracting party's liability for misrepresentation—and 'liability' is used here in the broadest sense, including any of the remedies for misrepresentation. Thus a clause may exclude all remedies for misrepresentation; or may exclude or limit damages; or may exclude the right to rescind the contract.

(i) Common law

At common law, a party to a contract is entitled, by means of an appropriately drafted clause, to limit or exclude his liability for misrepresentation, except in cases of personal fraud. 'It is clear that the law, on public policy grounds, does not permit a contracting party to exclude liability for his own fraud in inducing the making of the contract.'[206] It may, however, be possible to exclude liability for the fraud of an agent or employee, but if such an exclusion is possible, it must be done 'in clear and unmistakeable terms on the face of the contract'.[207]

Two common forms of clause should be noted in particular. First, a party may seek to avoid liability by providing in the contract that he has not made any representations during the negotiations, or that the other party has not relied on any representations that have been made. If there is no representation, or no reliance, there can be no remedy for misrepresentation.[208] There has been some uncertainty in the cases as to how such a clause operates,[209] although it is now settled at the level of the Court of Appeal[210] that by agreeing to such a clause the parties have established a contractual

---

[205] *Smith New Court Securities Ltd v Citibank NA* [1997] AC 254, 283. See also at 267 (Lord Browne-Wilkinson).

[206] *HIH Casualty and General Insurance Ltd v Chase Manhattan Bank* [2003] UKHL 6, [2003] 2 Lloyd's Rep 61 at [16] (Lord Bingham); see also at [76], [121]–[122]. See also *S Pearson & Son Ltd v Dublin Corp* [1907] AC 351, 353, 362.

[207] *HIH Casualty and General Insurance Ltd v Chase Manhattan Bank*, above, n 206 at [16] (Lord Bingham); see also differing views at [76]–[82] (Lord Hoffmann), [98] (Lord Hobhouse), [122] (Lord Scott).

[208] Above, p 325.

[209] Cf *Watford Electronics Ltd v Sanderson CFL Ltd* [2001] EWCA Civ 317, [2001] 1 All ER (Comm) 696 at [39]–[40]; Cartwright in Burrows and Peel (eds), *Contract Terms* (2007) 222–225; Trukhtanov (2009) 125 LQR 648.

[210] *Axa Sun Life Services plc v Campbell Martin Ltd* [2011] EWCA Civ 133, [2011] 1 CLC 312 at [93]. See also *Prime Sight Ltd v Lavarello* [2013] UKPC 22, [2014] AC 436 at [47].

:ludes the claimant from asserting that he was induced to enter
misrepresentation.[211] However, it is unlikely that a Court would
operate to exclude personal fraud.[212] Even a successful clause of
ct to the statutory control of section 3 of the Misrepresentation
:e it constitutes an attempt to exclude or restrict liability for a
was in fact made.[213]

common clause is one which provides that a written contract constitutes the 'entire agreement' between the parties. Such a clause does not, however, exclude remedies for pre-contractual misrepresentation: it is interpreted as providing only that the totality of the parties' *contractual* obligations are to be found in the written document and not, for example, in any collateral contract.[214]

(ii) Statute

The Misrepresentation Act 1967, the Unfair Contract Terms Act 1977, and the Consumer Rights Act 2015 restrict the freedom to exclude liability for misrepresentation. The 1967 and 1977 Acts apply only to non-consumer contracts and notices; the 2015 Act applies only to consumer contracts and notices.

(a) Misrepresentation Act 1967   Section 3 of the 1967 Act provides:

(1) If any contract contains a term which would exclude or restrict:

   (a) any liability to which a party to a contract may be subject by reason of any misrepresentation made by him before the contract was made; or

   (b) any remedy available to another party to the contract by reason of such a misrepresentation,

   that term shall be of no effect except in so far as it satisfies the requirement of reasonableness as stated in section 11(1) of the Unfair Contract Terms Act 1977; and it is for those claiming that the term satisfies that requirement to show that it does.[215]

(2) This section does not apply to a term in a consumer contract within the meaning of Part 2 of the Consumer Rights Act 2015 (but see the provision made about such contracts in section 62 of that Act).[216]

---

[211] *Peekay Intermark Ltd v Australia and New Zealand Banking Group Ltd* [2006] EWCA Civ 386, [2006] 2 Lloyd's Rep 511 at [56]; *Springwell Navigation Corp v JP Morgan Chase* [2010] EWCA Civ 1221 at [165]–[169], [177]. See further above, p 133.

[212] *S Pearson & Son Ltd v Dublin Corporation*, above, n 206, 353–4 (Lord Loreburn LC: 'it seems clear that no one can escape liability for his own fraudulent statements by inserting in a contract a clause that the other party shall not rely upon them'); but cf *Smith v Chadwick* (1882) 20 Ch D 27, 44–5 (Jessel MR).

[213] Below; *Springwell Navigation Corp v JP Morgan Chase Bank*, above, n 211 at [181].

[214] *Deepak Fertilisers and Petrochemicals Corp v ICI Chemicals & Polymers Ltd* [1999] 1 Lloyd's Rep 387, 395.

[215] Substituted by the Unfair Contract Terms Act 1977, s 8(1). See also *Trident Turboprop (Dublin) Ltd v First Flight Couriers Ltd* [2009] EWCA Civ 290, [2010] QB 86 at [19] (reference to Unfair Contract Terms Act 1977 renders that Act the controlling instrument, and therefore international supply contracts are excluded from scope of the Misrepresentation Act, s 3 by the Unfair Contract Terms Act, s 26).

[216] Inserted by Consumer Rights Act 2015, Sched 4, para 1.

This provision regulates clauses in contracts, except consumer contracts,[217] which seek to exclude or limit liability or any remedy for pre-contractual misrepresentation: that is, where the misrepresentation is the gist of the claim, such as rescission, or a claim under section 2(1) of the Misrepresentation Act 1967. A non-consumer clause or notice which excludes or limits liability at common law for a negligent misstatement[218] is regulated by section 2 of the Unfair Contract Terms Act 1977,[219] but may also, where the misstatement is made by a party to the contract, be regulated by section 3 of the Misrepresentation Act 1967.[220]

Under the 1967 Act the clause which seeks to exclude or limit liability or any remedy for misrepresentation is prima facie invalid, unless the representor can show that it was a fair and reasonable term to be included in the contract having regard to all the circumstances which were, or ought reasonably to have been, known to or in the contemplation of the parties when the contract was made.[221] A clause purporting to exclude liability for fraudulent misrepresentation, even if it is valid at common law (such as a clause excluding liability for an agent's fraud),[222] will generally not be held to be reasonable.[223] Since a clause which is not proved to be reasonable is ineffective for all purposes, and the Court has no power to rewrite it so as to limit it to such an exclusion as would have been reasonable,[224] there is a risk that an over-wide exclusion clause which might also have covered fraud will be held ineffective, although the Courts are likely for this reason not to interpret clauses as covering fraud unless they clearly so provide.[225]

The question arises whether it is possible to avoid the application of section 3 of the 1967 Act by means of a contract term, for example, that statements made are 'not to be construed as assertions of fact', or that they are 'statements of opinion or belief only', or that no representations have been made, or that no representation has been relied on. In *Cremdean Properties Ltd v Nash*,[226] the

---

[217] For consumer contracts, see below, p 355.

[218] *Hedley Byrne & Co Ltd v Heller & Partners Ltd* [1964] AC 465; above, p 346.

[219] Below, p 354.

[220] cf Cartwright, *Misrepresentation, Mistake and Non-Disclosure* (3rd edn, 2012) para 9.23.

[221] Unfair Contract Terms Act 1977, s 11(1); see above, p 216. For illustrations, see *Walker v Boyle* [1982] 1 WLR 495 (condition 17 of the National Conditions of Sale not reasonable); cf *McCullagh v Lane Fox & Partners* (1996) 49 Con LR 124 (estate agent's disclaimer about size of plot reasonable); *Cleaver v Schyde Investments Ltd* [2011] EWCA Civ 929, [2011] 2 P & CR 21 at [43] (distinguishing *Walker v Boyle* on the basis that the limitation of the right to rescind in the modern standard conditions of sale are far less draconian); *Lloyd v Browning* [2013] EWCA Civ 1637, [2014] 1 P & CR 11.

[222] Above, n 207.

[223] *Thomas Witter Ltd v TBP Industries* [1996] 2 All ER 573, 598; *South West Water Services Ltd v International Computers Ltd* [1999] BLR 420.

[224] *Skipskredittforeningen v Emperor Navigation* [1998] 1 Lloyd's Rep 66, 75; *Stewart Gill Ltd v Horatio Myer & Co Ltd* [1992] QB 600, above, p 222.

[225] *Government of Zanzibar v British Aerospace (Lancaster House) Ltd* [2000] 1 WLR 2333, 2346-7 (disapproving *Thomas Witter Ltd v TBP Industries Ltd*, above, n 223); *HIH Casualty and General Insurance Ltd v Chase Manhattan Bank* [2003] UKHL 6, [2003] 2 Lloyd's Rep 61 at [16], [68], [97].

[226] (1977) 244 EG 547.

defendants, by whom it was alleged a misrepresentation had been made, relied on
the following clause:

These particulars are prepared for the convenience of an intending purchaser or tenant and
although they are believed to be correct their accuracy is not guaranteed and any error,
omission or misdescription shall not annul the sale or the grounds on which compensation
may be claimed and neither do they constitute any part of an offer of a contract. Any
intending purchaser or tenant must satisfy himself by inspection or otherwise as to the
correctness of each of the statements contained in these particulars.

The Court of Appeal rejected the defendants' argument that the effect of this clause was
to bring about a situation as if no representation at all had been made. The Court further
doubted whether, even if the defendants' argument were correct, it would be possible
thus to defeat the application of section 3 of the 1967 Act. This has been confirmed
in more recent cases where the Court has accepted that a 'no representation' or 'non-
reliance' clause can in principle create a contractual estoppel,[227] but has also indicated
that, if a representation has in fact been made, a contract term which purports to deny
one or more of the conditions to be fulfilled before a representation is effective will be
subject to section 3, and to the test of reasonableness provided for in that section: the
question is one of substance rather than form.[228]

In *Overbrooke Estates Ltd v Glencombe Properties Ltd*,[229] on the other hand:

An auctioneer sold property belonging to O to G, and in the course of so doing made a
misrepresentation as to local authority plans with respect to the property. G refused to
proceed with the sale because of the misrepresentation and O brought an action for specific
performance of the contract. O relied upon a term in the conditions of sale which stated
that the auctioneer had no authority to make any representation in relation to the property.

Brightman J held that section 3 of the 1967 Act did not operate to qualify the right of
a principal publicly to limit the authority of an agent and was therefore inapplicable.
Where, despite a term limiting an agent's actual or ostensible authority, the principal
expressly authorizes the agent to make the representation in question, section 3 should
apply.[230] The cases permitting the limitation of an agent's authority concern auctioneers
and estate agents, and it is not clear whether an employer could rely on a term limiting an
employee's actual or ostensible authority in order to avoid the operation of section 3.[231]

(b) Unfair Contract Terms Act 1977   Where a claim for misrepresentation is based
on the defendant's breach of a duty of care in the tort of negligence, a non-consumer

---

[227]   Above, p 133.

[228]   *Raiffeisen Zentralbank Osterreich AG v Royal Bank of Scotland Plc* [2010] EWHC 1392 (Comm), [2011]
1 Lloyd's Rep 123 at [314]–[315]; *Springwell Navigation Corp v JP Morgan Chase Bank* [2010] EWCA Civ 1221,
[2010] 2 CLC 705 at [181].

[229]   [1974] 1 WLR 1355. This decision was accepted as correct by Bridge LJ in *Cremdean Properties Ltd v
Nash* (above, n 226) 549. See also *Collins v Howell-Jones* (1980) 259 EG 331.

[230]   *Museprime Properties Ltd v Adhill Properties Ltd* (1991) 61 P & CR 111. Cf *Collins v Howell-Jones*
(1980) 259 EG 331, 332; but note Murdoch (1981) 97 LQR 518, 524.

[231]   Cf *Mendelssohn v Normand Ltd* [1970] 1 QB 177, above, p 207.

clause or notice seeking to exclude or limit the defendant's liability will be regulated by section 2 of the Unfair Contract Terms Act 1977.[232] This provides that a person cannot by reference to a contract term or notice exclude or restrict his business[233] liability for death or personal injury resulting from negligence nor (except in so far as the term or notice satisfies the requirement of reasonableness) for any other loss or damage. The operation of section 2 and of other related provisions of the 1977 Act was considered in Chapter 6 above.[234]

(c) Consumer Rights Act 2015   Part 2 of the Consumer Rights Act 2015,[235] which applies to all unfair terms and not only to exclusion or limitation clauses, will also affect clauses excluding or restricting a consumer's remedies for misrepresentation. A term which has the object of effect of limiting the trader's obligation to respect commitments undertaken by his agents is one of those included in the indicative and non-exhaustive list of terms of consumer contract terms which may be regarded as unfair[236] and it therefore appears that clauses such as that in *Overbrooke Estates Ltd v Glencombe Properties Ltd* will be effective only if they satisfy the tests of good faith and absence of a significant imbalance in the parties' rights to the detriment of the consumer in the Act.[237]

3. CONSUMERS' RIGHTS TO REDRESS UNDER THE CONSUMER PROTECTION FROM UNFAIR TRADING REGULATIONS 2008

Part 4A of the Consumer Protection from Unfair Trading Regulations 2008[238] provides remedies ('rights to redress') for consumers in circumstances which include cases where the consumer has entered into the contract in reliance on the other party's misrepresentation. If a consumer enters into a contract with a trader, either for the sale or supply by the trader to the consumer of a 'product' (widely defined and including goods, services, and digital content),[239] or for the sale of goods by the consumer to the trader, and the trader engages in a 'prohibited practice' (a misleading action or an aggressive commercial practice)[240] in relation to

---

[232] Amended by Consumer Rights Act 2015, Sched 4, para 4.

[233] 1977 Act, s 1(3).   [234] Above, p 208.

[235] Replacing the Unfair Terms in Consumer Contracts Regulations 1999 (SI 1999 No 2083), and reimplementing the Directive on Unfair Terms in Consumer Contracts 93/13/EEC, as to which see above, pp 222 ff.

[236] 2015 Act, Sched 2, para 17.   [237] 2015 Act, s 62; above, p 223.

[238] SI 2008 No 1277, inserted by Consumer Protection (Amendment) Regulations 2014 (SI 2014 No 870), as regards contracts entered into on or after 1 October 2014. For the background, see Law Com No 332 (2012). The 2008 Regulations provided criminal sanctions for unfair commercial practices and regulatory enforcement but (until the amendment in 2014) no private law remedies.

[239] Consumer Protection from Unfair Trading Regulations 2008, as amended, reg 2(1). Immoveable property is within the definition of 'product', but for the purposes of the rights to redress under Part 4A, this includes only certain residential leases: s 27C.

[240] *Ibid*, reg 27B.

the product,[241] and the prohibited practice is a significant factor in the consumer's decision to enter into the contract,[242] the consumer has a right to redress:[243] the right to unwind in respect of the contract or, in certain circumstances, the right to a discount or the right to damages. A misrepresentation will often constitute a 'misleading action',[244] which is defined as including a commercial practice[245] which contains false information and is therefore untruthful in relation to certain matters relating to the product, such as its existence, its nature, and its main characteristics, and it causes or is likely to cause the average consumer to take a transactional decision he would not have taken otherwise.[246]

Where the consumer has contracted for the supply of a product by the trader, the consumer has the 'right to unwind' by clearly rejecting the product (by words or conduct) with a period of 90 days from the contract (or sometimes from a later date, such as the delivery of the goods or the first performance of services under the contract), and as long as the product can still be rejected and the consumer has not exercised the right to a discount.[247] The effect of the consumer's exercising this right is that the contract comes to an end so that both parties are released from their obligations under it, the trader must give the consumer a refund and (in the case of contracts for the supply of goods) the consumer must make the goods available for collection by the trader.[248] Where the consumer has contracted to sell goods to the trader, the consumer exercises the right to unwind by indicating clearly to the trader (by words or conduct) that the contract is ended, and the consumer then has a right to the return of the goods (and the duty to repay the price paid by the trader) or, if the goods cannot be returned in the same condition, a right to payment of the amount by which the market value exceeded the price when it was paid by the trader.[249]

The consumer's right to a discount involves the return of a proportion of payments already made (or the reduction of payments due) calculated by reference to the seriousness of the prohibited practice,[250] except where the amount payable for the

---

[241] Or, in the case of a contract for goods or digital content, the *producer* engages in such a practice of which the trader is aware or could reasonably be expected to be aware: *ibid*, reg 27A(4)(b). The 'producer' is the manufacture, the importer into the European Economic Area or an 'own-brander' of the goods or digital content: *ibid*, reg 27A(5).

[242] Note that this is a stronger test of causation than generally adopted in the remedies for misrepresentation: above, p 325.

[243] Consumer Protection from Unfair Trading Regulations 2008, reg 27A.

[244] Conduct which can be characterized as duress or undue influence may constitute an 'aggressive commercial practice': below, p 403.

[245] 'Any act, omission, course of conduct, representation or commercial communication (including advertising and marketing) by a trader, which is directly connected with the promotion, sale or supply of a product to or from consumers, whether occurring before, during or after a commercial transaction (if any) in relation to a product': Consumer Protection from Unfair Trading Regulations 2008, as amended, reg 2(1).

[246] Consumer Protection from Unfair Trading Regulations 2008, reg 5. For the purposes of the rights to redress under Part 4A, a 'transactional decision' means the consumer's decision to enter into the contract with a trader: reg 27B(2).

[247] *Ibid*, reg 27E.   [248] *Ibid*, reg 27F.   [249] *Ibid*, reg 27G.

[250] 25% if it is more than minor; 50% if it is significant; 75% if it is serious; 100% if it is very serious. The seriousness is assessed by reference to the behaviour of the person who engaged in the practice, the impact of the practice on the consumer and the time that has elapsed since the prohibited practice took place: *ibid*, reg 27I(1)–(5).

product under the contract exceeds £5,000 and the market value was less than the contract price at the time of the contract, in which case the discount is based on the difference between the market price and the contract price[251]—in effect, depriving the trader of his profit over the market price.

The consumer's right to damages covers financial loss, and any alarm, distress, or physical inconvenience or discomfort, which would not have occurred if the prohibited practice had not taken place, but does not include the right to be paid damages in respect of the difference between the market price of the product and the contract price[252]—that is, it is not a remedy aimed at covering the core measure of loss covered by an action in tort[253] but other, consequential losses. However, the damages are limited to losses that were reasonably foreseeable at the time of the prohibited practice, and there is no right to damages where the trader proves (inter alia) that his misrepresentation was due to a mistake or reliance on information supplied by another person, and he took all reasonable precautions and exercised all due diligence to avoid the occurrence of the prohibited practice.[254]

The rights to redress under Part 4A of the Consumer Protection from Unfair Trading Regulations 2008 will sometimes arise concurrently with claims under the general law for remedies for misrepresentation discussed earlier in this chapter. With one very significant exception, the Regulations are intended to provide additional remedies for consumers, allowing choice between claims under the Regulations and under the general law, and even allowing concurrent claims as long as the consumer does not obtain double compensation.[255] There is therefore no obstacle to the consumer rescinding the contract in equity (rather than exercising the right to unwind under the Regulations) whilst claiming damages for consequential loss under the Regulations. The choice of remedy will no doubt depend on the circumstances, and sometimes one will be more easily available, or more advantageous, than another. For example, the right to unwind under the Regulations is exercisable for a fixed period of 90 days from (normally) the contract,[256] whereas (depending on the circumstances) there may be an earlier bar to rescission based on lapse of time;[257] and a claim in the tort of deceit allows recovery of unforeseeable consequential losses,[258] whereas damages under the Regulations are limited to reasonably foreseeable losses.[259]

The very significant exception, however, is that a consumer who has a right to redress under Part 4A of the 2008 Regulations is not entitled to be paid damages under section 2 of the Misrepresentation Act 1967 in respect of the conduct constituting the misrepresentation.[260] The consumer has no choice: if there is a right to redress under the Regulations, section 2 of the 1967 Act is disapplied and so the consumer cannot

---

[251] *Ibid*, reg 27I(6), (7).　　　[252] *Ibid*, reg 27J(1)–(3).　　　[253] Above, p 330.

[254] Consumer Protection from Unfair Trading Regulations 2008, reg 27J(4), (5). Cf the defence to the general claim of damages under Misrepresentation Act 1967, s 2(1), above, p 347; and the fact that the claim for consequential loss under s 2(1) extends to unforeseeable losses: above, p 349.

[255] *Ibid*, reg 27L.　　　[256] *Ibid*, reg 27E.　　　[257] Above, p 337.　　　[258] Above, p 344.

[259] Consumer Protection from Unfair Trading Regulations 2008, reg 27J(4).

[260] Misrepresentation Act 1967, s 2(4), inserted by SI 2014 No 870.

claim damages on that basis. This has the curious effect of reducing the consumer's protection in relation to unforeseeable consequential losses since, as we have seen, the claimant under section 2(1) may recover the same damages as if there were fraud.[261]

4. NON-DISCLOSURE

(a) NO GENERAL DUTY TO DISCLOSE

We have noted that silence does not normally amount to a misrepresentation and that at common law there is in general no duty of disclosure of material facts before the contract is made; and that this is consistent with the reluctance of the common law to allow a party to avoid a contract on the basis of his own mistake.[262] The examples were given of the person who visits an antiques shop and sees a rare George II table being sold as a nineteenth-century piece and the oil prospector who discovers that there is oil under a given piece of land. Neither has to inform the other party. Nor does a bank have to inform its customer that a more attractive rate of interest is available in a different account.[263] There is not even a duty on one party to disclose where he realizes that the other party is making a mistake about some relevant fact.[264] This reflects a major difference between English law and civil law systems since in most civil law systems not only is a greater place found for mistake as a ground of vitiation of contracts, but also a party who deliberately does not disclose a relevant fact to the other party may be liable for fraud.[265] The justification for the common law rule is said to be the need to give people an incentive to invest in the acquisition of skill and knowledge and consequently to allow 'good deals' to the more intelligent or the hard-working.[266] Even in civil law systems there is no duty to disclose information 'which is the product of one's own efforts in evaluating market conditions or ascertaining the attributes of property which enhance its value'.[267] This economic argument does not apply to information which has been acquired by pure chance or without any investment. Nor can it be conclusive where the information is acquired by a method regarded by the law as illegitimate—for example where it is 'insider' information about the position of a company. There may also be situations where it may be economically efficient to

---

[261] Above, p 349. If he can prove the trader's fraud, however, the consumer may still bring a claim in the tort of deceit.

[262] Above, p 318. See *Bell v Lever Bros Ltd* [1932] AC 161, 227 (Lord Atkin); *Banque Keyser Ullmann SA v Skandia (UK) Insurance Co Ltd* [1990] 1 QB 665, 798–9, aff'd [1991] 2 AC 249; *Clarion Ltd v National Provident Institution* [2000] 1 WLR 1888, 1905.

[263] *Suriya & Douglas v Midland Bank* [1999] 1 All ER (Comm) 612.

[264] *Smith v Hughes* (1867) LR 6 QB 597, 603–4, 607, 610–11, above, p 300; *Davies v London and Provincial Marine Insurance Co* (1878) 8 Ch D 468, 474.

[265] Lando and Beale, *Principles of European Contract Law Parts I and II* (2000) 256.

[266] See generally Duggan, Bryan, and Hanks, *Contractual Non-Disclosure* (1994); Kronman (1978) 7 JLS 1; Nicholas, in Harris and Tallon (eds), *Contract Law Today* (1989); Fried, *Contract as Promise* (1981) 77 ff; Trebilcock, *The Limits of Freedom of Contract* (1993) 106 ff.

[267] Kötz, *European Contract Law* (1997) 201.

impose a duty of disclosure. In the case of house sales, the absence of a duty of disclosure means that generally it is the intending purchaser who commissions the survey and where several people are interested in a property each will have to invest in the search for information, whereas if sellers were obliged to disclose key elements concerning the state of their houses to all potential buyers, the cost of surveying would in many cases be incurred only once.[268] Less compellingly, the rule has also been justified by the great difficulty in imposing any sensible limits on a duty of disclosure,[269] because the information which had to be disclosed may be unreliable or doubtful or inconclusive, and because disclosure may expose the informer to criticism or litigation.[270]

As well as the exceptions to the general rule, discussed below, there may be situations in which English law affords similar protection by the use of implied terms, such as the implied term that goods should be of satisfactory quality and fit for purpose:[271] even if the seller has no duty to disclose information about what he sells, he has an incentive to do so in order to avoid the implication of a contractual term about it.[272] Moreover, as we have seen, where A knows that B has misunderstood the *terms* of an offer made by A, no contract will be formed if A does not inform B of its true nature.[273] In this section, we are concerned with the duty to disclose *facts* which are relevant to the other party's decision to enter into the contract.

(b) PARTICULAR DUTIES OF DISCLOSURE

Although there is no general duty to disclose information during the negotiations for a contract, English law recognizes particular duties of disclosure. Two reasons account for most situations where, at common law or in equity, or by statute, parties negotiating a contract have been held to be subject to a duty of disclosure. The first is that, in certain classes of contract, one of the parties is presumed to have means of knowledge which are not accessible to the other, either at all or only by incurring disproportionately high costs. The party who is presumed to have the information is bound to disclose everything which may be supposed likely to affect the judgment of the other party. At common law such contracts have been labelled contracts *uberrimae fidei* (contracts 'of utmost good faith'), although in reality the label is not helpful to identify what has to be disclosed for each of the limited classes of contract which carry

---

[268] Fabre-Magnan, in Beatson and Friedmann (eds), *Good Faith and Fault in Contract Law* (1995) 117–18.

[269] *Laidlaw v Organ* 15 US 178, 194 (1817).

[270] *Banque Financière de la Cité SA v Westgate Insurance Co Ltd* [1991] 2 AC 249, where a narrower range of policy issues relevant to the imposition of a duty of disclosure were addressed in the leading speech by Lord Templeman who concluded at 274 that 'A professional should wear a halo but need not wear a hair shirt'.

[271] Zimmermann and Whittaker, *Good Faith in European Contract Law* (2000) 194–7, above, pp 161 ff.

[272] Cartwright, *Misrepresentation, Mistake and Non-disclosure* (3rd edn, 2012) para 17–40. There are no such wide-ranging statutory terms in contracts for the sale of land, but the seller has a duty to convey the property as contracted which may best be characterized as an implied term that there are no undisclosed latent defects in the title—in effect, a duty of disclosure as defects in the title is imposed indirectly on the seller: see generally Harpum (1992) 108 LQR 280, 320–33; Cartwright, para 17–41.

[273] *Hartog v Colin & Shields* [1939] 3 All ER 566, above, p 278.

duties of disclosure. Moreover, the principal use of this label was in relation to the contract of insurance, which was commonly identified, even by statute, as a contract *uberrimae fidei*—of utmost good faith;[274] but the rule that a contract of insurance is a contract based on utmost good faith has been, in effect, abolished.[275] The second reason for imposing a duty of disclosure is that, in certain situations, the relationship between the contracting parties during the negotiations is not a pure arm's length commercial relationship but one of trust and confidence or one of dependence which imposes upon the party in whom confidence is reposed a duty to make disclosure. The clearest examples of such situations arise where there is a fiduciary relationship.

The remedies available for breach of duties of disclosure vary, and depend upon the source of the duty to disclose. Rescission is the most generally available remedy; but sometimes damages are available in tort or by statute.

(c) DUTIES OF DISCLOSURE GIVING RISE TO RESCISSION

(i) Contracts of insurance

At common law, before a contract of insurance is made, the intending assured was under an obligation to disclose to the insurer all material information affecting the risk.[276] This duty to disclose was mutual, based on the fact that the contract of insurance was a contract of 'utmost good faith', and so the insurer was also required to disclose all material information although disclosure by the insurer was in practice rare because the material circumstances are normally known only to the intending assured.[277] The common law duty of disclosure was codified in section 18 of the Marine Insurance Act 1906, one of a group of sections which were held to apply not just to marine insurance but to all classes of insurance because they codified the common law.[278]

If there had been non-disclosure by one party, whether the non-disclosure was fraudulent, negligent or wholly innocent, the other party was entitled to avoid the contract if it had been induced to enter into the policy on the relevant terms,[279] but breach of the duty of disclosure did not of itself give rise to a claim for damages.[280]

---

[274] Marine Insurance Act 1906, s 17. Cf, however, *Carter v Boehm* (1766) 3 Burr 1905, 1910 where Lord Mansfield referred only to 'good faith'; 'utmost' good faith is a later refinement: *Manifest Shipping Co Ltd v Uni-Polaris Insurance Co Ltd* [2001] UKHL 1, [2003] 1 AC 469 at [44].

[275] Formally it was only modified by Consumer Insurance (Disclosure and Representations) Act 2012, s 2(5) (for consumer insurance contracts) and then by Insurance Act 2015, s 14(2) (for all insurance contracts, in force from 12 August 2016), but the legal significance of the label *uberrimae fidei* was that non-observance of the utmost good faith allowed the other party to avoid the contract, and, while the label survives, that rule will be abolished for insurance contracts by the Insurance Act 2015, s 14(1): see below, pp 361–2.

[276] *Carter v Boehm* (1766) 3 Burr 1905.

[277] *Banque Keyser Ullman SA v Skandia (UK) Insurance Co Ltd* [1990] 1 QB 665, 770, [1991] 2 AC 249, 268, 281.

[278] *PCW Syndicates v PCW Reinsurers* [1996] 1 WLR 1136, 1140; *Pan Atlantic Insurance Co Ltd v Pine Top Insurance Co Ltd* [1995] 1 AC 501, 541.

[279] *Pan Atlantic Insurance Co Ltd v Pine Top Insurance Co Ltd* [1995] 1 AC 501; *St Paul Fire & Marine Insurance Co (UK) Ltd v McConnell Dowell Constructors Ltd* [1996] 1 All ER 96, 112.

[280] *Banque Keyser Ullman SA v Skandia (UK) Insurance Co Ltd* [1990] 1 QB 665, 801.

In practice, however, insurance companies frequently inserted a 'basis of the contract' clause in the proposal form by which the proposer was made to warrant the accuracy of the information supplied by him to the company, with a proviso that the company might avoid the contract and forfeit the premium if any part of the information proved untrue. The assured was thus compelled to assume responsibility for the truth of even non-material facts,[281] and of facts which he did not know, or did not appreciate, were false.[282] Such provisions could work injustice to the assured by conferring on insurers a discretion to repudiate the policy on technical grounds alone. Lord Greene MR described them as 'particularly vicious' and 'mere traps' which should be construed strictly[283] and the insurance industry's statements of practice provided, inter alia, that insurers should not repudiate liability on grounds of non-disclosure of a fact which the assured could not reasonably be expected to disclose.

The law has now been changed very significantly by two Acts which implement recommendations of the Law Commission. In relation to 'consumer insurance contracts'[284] the consumer's duty of disclosure was removed by the Consumer Insurance (Disclosure and Representations) Act 2012,[285] and replaced by a duty to take reasonable care not to make a misrepresentation to the insurer.[286] In relation to 'non-consumer insurance contracts',[287] the Insurance Act 2015[288] removed the common law duty of disclosure, abolished the associated right for a party to avoid the contract on the ground that the utmost good faith has not been observed by the other party,[289] and repealed section 18 and related provisions of the Marine Insurance Act 1906;[290] but introduced a new duty on the insured to make to the insurer a 'fair presentation of the risk', which still includes a duty of disclosure. Each Act, for its separate area of operation, abolished 'basis of the contract clauses'.[291]

---

[281] *Thomson v Weems* (1884) 9 App Cas 671, 689; *Dawsons Ltd v Bonnin* [1922] 2 AC 413.

[282] See, eg, *Kumar v Life Insurance Corp of India* [1974] 1 Lloyd's Rep 147 (insurance company entitled to avoid policy of life insurance where applicant declared that she had not had any 'operation' when, in fact, she had given birth to a child by Caesarian section).

[283] *Zurich General Accident and Liability Insurance Co Ltd v Morrison* [1942] 2 KB 53, 58. See also *Joel v Law Union and Crown Insurance Co* [1908] 2 KB 863, 885.

[284] 'a contract of insurance between (a) an individual who enters into the contract wholly or mainly for purposes unrelated to the individual's trade, business or profession, and (b) a person who carries on the business of insurance and who becomes a party to the contract by way of that business (whether or not in accordance with permission for the purposes of the Financial Services and Markets Act 2000)': Consumer Insurance (Disclosure and Representations) Act 2012, s 1.

[285] See Law Com No 319, *Consumer Insurance Law: Pre-Contract Disclosure and Misrepresentation* (2009). The Act came fully into force on 6 April 2013.

[286] 2012 Act, s 2.

[287] 'a contract of insurance that is not a consumer insurance contract' [within the meaning of the 2012 Act]: Insurance Act 2015, s 1.

[288] See Law Com No 353, *Insurance Contract Law: Business Disclosure; Warranties; Insurers' Remedies for Fraudulent Claims and Late Payment* (2014). The 2015 Act comes into force on 12 August 2016.

[289] 2015 Act, s 14.   [290] 2015 Act, s 21(2).

[291] 2012 Act, s 6 (consumer insurance contracts); 2015 Act, s 9 (non-consumer insurance contracts).

The duty of disclosure which now exists is therefore only on the insured under a non-consumer insurance contract, and its scope (and the remedies for breach of the duty) are defined by the Insurance Act 2015. That Act requires:[292]

(a) disclosure of every material circumstance which the insured knows or ought to know, or

(b) failing that, disclosure which gives the insurer sufficient information to put a prudent insurer on notice that it needs to make further enquiries for the purpose of revealing those material circumstances

in a manner which would be reasonably clear and accessible to a prudent insurer but, in the absence of enquiry, it does not require the insured to disclose a circumstance if it diminishes the risk, the insurer knows it, the insurer ought to know it, the insurer is presumed to know it, or it is something as to which the insurer waives information.

The insurer has a remedy against the insured for breach of the duty of fair presentation only if it shows that, but for the breach, it would not have entered into the insurance contract at all, or would have done so only on different terms.[293] Where the insurer shows that the breach was deliberate (ie the insured knew that it was in breach of the duty of fair presentation) or reckless (ie the insured did not care whether or not it was in breach of the duty)[294] the insurer may avoid the contract and refuse all claims, and need not return any of the premiums paid.[295] In the case of other breaches, however, the remedy depends on whether, in the absence of the breach, the insurer would have entered into the contract not at all, or only on different terms. In the former case, the insurer may avoid the contract and refuse all claims, but must return the premiums paid (ie in effect this is rescission of the contract with restitution as the common law used to provide for breach of the general duty of disclosure). But in the latter case, the insurer's remedy is limited to requiring the contract to be treated as if it had been entered into on the terms which the insured would have accepted (with a proportionate reduction in the payment of claims if the premium would have been higher).[296]

(ii) Partnership contracts

It has long been established that, once a partnership has been formed, each partner is bound to exercise good faith in all that relates to their common business.[297] However, it has recently been settled that mutual duties of good faith and disclosure arise also between persons who are negotiating their entry into partnership, so that each party

---

[292] 2015 Act, s 3. See also ss 4–6 for further definitions of what constitutes 'knowledge' of the insured and of the insurer, and s 7 for what constitutes a 'material circumstance'.

[293] 2015 Act, s 8(1).   [294] 2015 Act, s 8(5).

[295] 2015 Act, Sched 1, para 2.   [296] 2015 Act, Sched 1, paras 3–6.

[297] The duties of partners are, however, for the most part regulated by the provisions of the Partnership Act 1890, ss 28–30. See also *F & C Alternative Investments (Holdings) Ltd v Barthelemy (No 2)* [2011] EWHC 1731 (Ch), [2012] Ch 613 (no fiduciary duties between members of a limited liability partnership).

owes a duty to the other negotiating parties to disclose all material facts of which he has knowledge and of which the other parties may not be aware.[298]

(iii) Contracts of suretyship or guarantee

A contract of suretyship (or guarantee) is one under which the surety (or guarantor) undertakes to the creditor to pay the debt, or satisfy some other obligation of his debtor, in the event of the debtor's default. Such contracts are not *uberrimae fidei* and therefore do not carry the same general duty of disclosure of material facts at common law as contracts of insurance or partnership contracts. However, the Courts regard surety contracts as different from normal commercial contracts, and although a surety is expected to inform himself about the risks he is undertaking in favour of the creditor, the creditor is required to disclose to the surety any unusual feature of the contract between the creditor and the debtor, or between the creditor and other creditors of the debtor, which makes it materially different in a potentially disadvantageous respect from what the surety might naturally expect.[299] Where the creditor is in breach of this duty, and the surety is thereby induced to enter into the surety contract,[300] the surety may rescind (subject to the usual bars to rescission).

Nevertheless it is not always easy in practice to draw the line between contracts of guarantee in the strict sense of contracts to answer for the debt, default, or miscarriage of another and contracts of insurance taking the form of contracts to indemnify against some risk stated in the contract.[301] It was pointed out by Romer LJ in *Seaton v Heath*[302] that many contracts may with equal propriety be called contracts of insurance or contracts of guarantee, and that whether a contract requires *uberrima fides* or not depends not upon what it is called, but upon its substantial character and how it came to be effected. Generally, in a contract of insurance the person desiring to be insured has means of knowledge of the risk which the insurer does not possess, and he puts the risk before the insurer as a business transaction. In a contract of guarantee, on the other hand, the creditor does not as a rule go to the surety, explain the risk, and ask the surety to undertake it. The surety is often a friend or relation of the debtor and knows the risk to be undertaken, or the circumstances indicate that as between the creditor and the surety it is contemplated that the surety will ascertain what the risk is. Only in the exceptional cases when a contract of guarantee has the characteristics which occur normally in a contract of insurance is the former a contract *uberrimae fidei*.

Accordingly, it is settled that there is no duty of full disclosure where a surety guarantees to a bank the account of one of the bank's customers.[303] On the other hand,

---

[298] *Conlon v Simms* [2006] EWHC 401 (Ch), [2006] 2 All ER 1024 at [196]–[199], aff'd [2006] EWCA Civ 1749, [2008] 1 WLR 484 at [127] (Jonathan Parker LJ). See also *Bell v Lever Bros Ltd* [1932] AC 161, 227 (Lord Atkin).

[299] *Royal Bank of Scotland Plc v Etridge (No 2)* [2001] UKHL 44, [2002] 2 AC 773 at [81], [114], [186]–[188]; *North Shore Ventures Ltd v Anstead Holdings Inc* [2011] EWCA Civ 230, [2012] Ch 31 at [31].

[300] *North Shore Ventures Ltd v Anstead Holdings Inc*, above, n 299 at [33].

[301] *Trade Indemnity Co Ltd v Workington Harbour and Dock Board* [1937] AC 1.

[302] [1899] 1 QB 782, 792–3.

[303] *National Provincial Bank v Glanusk* [1913] 3 KB 335; *Cooper v National Provincial Bank* [1946] KB 1.

when an employer takes a bond from a surety for the 'fidelity', that is, honesty, of an employee, he must disclose to the surety any previous acts of dishonesty of the employee within his knowledge,[304] and even any subsequent acts of dishonesty which would entitle the surety to withdraw the guarantee.[305] Similarly, where the creditor is put on inquiry that the surety may be subjected to undue influence or misrepresentation by the principal debtor, as is the case where the relationship between the surety and the debtor is non-commercial such as spouses or cohabitees, the creditor will be unable to enforce the surety contract if it has not taken steps to satisfy itself that the surety entered into the obligation freely and in knowledge of the true facts.[306]

(iv) Contracts of compromise and family settlements

Parties who are negotiating the compromise of a disputed claim do not generally owe duties to disclose to each other information relating to the claim or its validity.[307] However, the House of Lords has considered, but not yet decided, whether there is a duty on one party to disclose the existence of claims which will be covered by a compromise but of which he knows that the other party is unaware.[308]

One form of compromise or settlement in which it is, however, established that there is a duty of disclosure is the contract for a family settlement, under which members of a family compromise a dispute such as the division of property. Such a contract requires full disclosure of all material facts within the parties' knowledge. Thus in *Gordon v Gordon*,[309] a family arrangement entered into without a secret marriage being disclosed by one side to the other was set aside under this principle. Parties who are divorcing and make an agreement about the division of the property which is to be embodied in a Court order are under an obligation to make a full and frank disclosure *to the Court which made the order*. But, although the duty is owed to the Court and not to the other party it has been held that a party affected by such non-disclosure could rely on it as a ground for setting the order (and therefore the agreement) aside.[310]

(d) CONTRACTS BETWEEN THOSE IN A FIDUCIARY RELATIONSHIP

A fiduciary relationship imposes a duty on one party to the relationship (or, sometimes, both parties)[311] to make full disclosure of all material facts which might be considered likely to affect a transaction with the other to whom the duty is owed. This is a

---

[304] *London General Omnibus Co Ltd v Holloway* [1912] 2 KB 72.

[305] *Phillips v Foxall* (1872) LR 7 QB 666.

[306] *Barclays Bank plc v O'Brien* [1994] 1 AC 180; *Royal Bank of Scotland v Etridge (No 2)* [2001] UKHL 44, [2002] 2 AC 773, below, pp 398–400.

[307] *Turner v Green* [1895] 2 Ch 205.

[308] *Bank of Credit and Commerce International SA v Ali* [2001] UKHL 8, [2002] 1 AC 251 at [32]–[33] (Lord Nicholls), [69]–[70] (Lord Hoffmann).

[309] (1821) 3 Swan 400.   [310] *Livesey v Jenkins* [1985] AC 424, 439–40.

[311] eg partnerships.

component of wider and rigorous equitable obligations. While not all fiduciaries owe the same duties in all circumstances,[312] they are broadly obliged to act in good faith, not to place themselves in a position where their duty and their interest may conflict, or to act for their own benefit or the benefit of a third person without the informed consent of those to whom the duty is owed.[313] Breach of these duties is sometimes, rather misleadingly, called 'equitable' or 'constructive' fraud.

(i) Who is a fiduciary?

By contrast to a contractual relationship where, subject to the terms of the contract, the parties may legitimately act for their own interests, albeit sometimes in cooperation with the other party, the key feature of fiduciary relationships is a duty to act in the interests of another.[314] Fiduciary relationships can be divided into two categories, those that are status-based and those that are fact-based.[315] Examples of the former include principal and agent, solicitor and client, guardian and ward, and trustee and beneficiary.

The second category arises where, in the absence of an inherently fiduciary status, the factual situation of the particular relationship between the parties gives rise to a fiduciary relationship.[316] The relationship of the parties may be contractual but a contractual relationship gives rise to particular fiduciary obligations only where specific contractual obligations have been undertaken which place one party in the position in which equity imposes its rigorous duties on that party in addition to the contractual obligations.[317] While fiduciary duties should not be superimposed on common law contractual duties simply to improve the nature or extent of the remedy available,[318] they may arise where one party is in a position of influence over another,[319] is in receipt of information imparted in confidence by the other, or has undertaken to act in the interests of another or placed himself or herself in a position where he or she is obliged so to act.[320] In such cases the fiduciary obligation is, however, circumscribed by the contractual terms: equity cannot alter the terms of a contract validly undertaken.[321] Examples of such fact-based

---

[312] *Henderson* v *Merrett Syndicates Ltd* [1995] 2 AC 145, 206 (Lord Browne-Wilkinson).

[313] *Bristol and West BS* v *Mothew* [1998] 1 Ch 1, 18. See generally Finn, *Fiduciary Obligations* (1977); Hanbury & Martin, *Modern Equity* (20th edn, 2015) paras 22.017–22.025. Fiduciaries are also under a duty to use care and skill: *Nocton v Lord Ashburton* [1914] AC 932, 954.

[314] *Bristol and West BS* v *Mothew* [1998] 1 Ch 1, 18.   [315] Flannigan (1989) 9 OJLS 285.

[316] *Reading v Attorney-General* [1951] AC 507; *Hospital Products Ltd v United States Surgical Corp* (1984) 156 CLR 41 (High Court of Australia).

[317] *Nottingham University v Fishel* [2000] ICR 1462, 1491 (contract of employment, not otherwise typically fiduciary: see below, p 366).

[318] *Norberg v Wynrib* (1992) 92 DLR (4th) 449, 481.

[319] eg where one reposes trust and confidence in the other so as to give rise to a presumption of undue influence: below, p 388; *Royal Bank of Scotland Plc v Etridge (No 2)*, above, n 299 at [36] (husband's 'duty of candour and fairness' to wife); *Hewett v First Plus Financial Group plc* [2010] EWCA Civ 312, [2010] 2 P & CR 22.

[320] Millett (1998) 114 LQR 214.

[321] *Nottingham University v Fishel*, above, n 317, 1491; *Hospital Products Ltd v United States Surgical Corp*, above, n 316, 97. See also *Kelly v Cooper* [1993] AC 205.

fiduciary relationships may be seen in certain joint ventures[322] and employment relationships.[323]

(ii) Examples of duties of disclosure

The duty to disclose all material facts which might be considered likely to affect a transaction can be illustrated by examples. Thus a broker who is employed to buy shares for a client cannot sell his own shares to the client unless a full and accurate disclosure of this fact is made to the client and the client's consent is obtained.[324] Again, the promoters of a company, who stand in a fiduciary relationship with the company, are required to make a full disclosure of their interest either to an independent board of directors or to the intended shareholders.[325] In some situations, all that equity requires is disclosure of material facts. In others, however, where the fiduciary relationship gives rise to a presumption of undue influence[326] disclosure in itself may be insufficient, and it must be shown that the transaction is the result of the act of a free and independent mind of the party to whom the duty is owed.

(iii) Employment

The relationship between an employer and employee is not inherently 'fiduciary' but it may be the foundation for a fiduciary relationship as a result of the terms of the particular contract or where, for example, the employee is in receipt of confidential information. There is an implied term of fidelity, giving rise to duties of loyalty and good faith, in the contract between employee and employer, but this is not to be equated with a fiduciary obligation.[327] An employee is not, however, under a duty to disclose his own misconduct. In *Bell v Lever Brothers Ltd*[328] the respondent, Lever Brothers, had entered into a contract with two of its employees whereby it promised to pay, and did in fact pay, considerable sums to them in compensation for the premature termination of their contracts of employment. This contract, however, was strictly unnecessary, for during their employment the two men had been guilty of certain breaches of duty which would have entitled Lever Brothers to dismiss them immediately. When Lever Brothers discovered this fact, it claimed to avoid the contract and recover the money paid on the ground, inter alia, that the employees were bound to disclose to them these breaches

---

[322] *Lac Minerals Ltd v International Corona Resources Ltd* [1989] 2 SCR 574 (Supreme Court of Canada). Cf also *Yam Seng Pte Ltd v International Trade Corp Ltd* [2013] EWHC 111 (QB), [2013] 1 All ER (Comm) 1321, above, pp 165–6 (*implied term* of good faith in 'relational contracts').

[323] *Nottingham University v Fishel*, above, n 317.

[324] *Armstrong v Jackson* [1917] 2 KB 822. For other agents, see *Regier v Campbell-Stuart* [1939] Ch 766; *English v Dedham Vale Properties Ltd* [1978] 1 WLR 93. For contractual modification of fiduciary duty see *Kelly v Cooper* [1993] AC 205.

[325] *Erlanger v New Sombrero Phosphate Co* (1878) 3 App Cas 1218; *Lagunas Nitrate Co v Lagunas Syndicate* [1899] 2 Ch 392; *Gluckstein v Barnes* [1900] AC 240. See now Financial Services and Markets Act 2000, ss 80–82, 90, below, p 369.

[326] See below, p 389.

[327] *Nottingham University v Fishel*, above, n 317, 1491; *Helmet Integrated Systems Ltd v Tunnard* [2006] EWCA Civ 1735, [2007] IRLR 126 at [36].

[328] [1932] AC 161, above, p 301.

of duty. No member of the House of Lords was prepared to accept this contention,[329] and Lord Atkin said[330] that he was aware of no authority which placed contracts of service within the limited category of contracts *uberrimae fidei*. Nevertheless, it has subsequently been held that in certain circumstances an employee may be under a duty to report to the employer misconduct on the part of fellow employees.[331]

(iv) Special relationships

We have seen that, under the principle enunciated in *Hedley Byrne & Co Ltd v Heller & Partners Ltd*,[332] a special relationship, giving rise to a duty of care in the tort of negligence, may arise between parties negotiating a contract. That duty may be more extensive than merely to refrain from making negligent misstatements, and may impose upon the party in whom confidence is reposed an obligation to disclose to the other party information relevant to the contract[333] or to provide an adequate explanation of the contract into which the other party is about to enter.[334] Prima facie the breach of such a duty would give rise to an action in damages in tort only,[335] and not to a claim that the contract be rescinded. But it could be argued that, at least in some situations, the facts giving rise to such a duty also evidence a relationship between the parties imposing a duty of disclosure the breach of which would entitle the party to whom the duty was owed to avoid the contract.

(v) Remedies for breach by a fiduciary of the duty of disclosure

Breach of the fiduciary's duty to make full disclosure will entitle the innocent party to rescind the contract or transaction, to be restored to the pre-contractual position, and to recover any profit made by the other party as a result of the breach. In awarding these remedies, it is well established that equity takes a strict approach, and does not draw a distinction between fraudulent, negligent and wholly innocent breaches of duty, although there have been some suggestions that the liability to account for profits is too stringent and should not be applied to the fiduciary who acted in good faith.[336]

(e) LIABILITY IN TORT FOR NON-DISCLOSURE

It has generally been said that there is no liability in the tort of deceit for non-disclosure, because deceit requires an active misrepresentation, or at least a partial or fragmentary statement which misleads the representee.[337] Following this approach,

---

[329] Although it was accepted by the Court of Appeal: [1931] 1 KB 337.   [330] [1932] AC 161, 227.
[331] *Swain v West (Butchers) Ltd* [1936] 1 All ER 224; *Sybron Corp v Rochem Ltd* [1984] Ch 112.
[332] [1964] AC 465, above, p 346.
[333] *Al-Kandari v JR Brown & Co* [1988] QB 665, 674; *Banque Keyser Ullman SA v Skandia (UK) Insurance Co Ltd* [1990] 1 QB 665, 790–805; aff'd on other grounds [1991] 2 AC 249. Cf *Dillingham Construction Pty Ltd v Downs* [1972] 2 NSWR 49 (Australia). See also *Horry v Tate & Lyle Refineries Ltd* [1982] 2 Lloyd's Rep 416.
[334] *Rust v Abbey Life Assurance Co Ltd* [1982] 2 Lloyd's Rep 386, 391; aff'd [1979] 2 Lloyd's Rep 334.
[335] Below, p 368.   [336] *Murad v Al-Saraj* [2005] EWCA Civ 959, [2005] WTLR 1573 at [74], [82]–[83].
[337] *Peek v Gurney* (1873) LR 6 HL 377, 403; see also Lord Chelmsford at 390–1; *Arkwright v Newbold* (1881) 17 Ch D 301, 318, 320; *Bradford Third Equitable Building Society v Borders* [1941] 2 All ER 205. Cf, however, *Browlie v Campbell* (1880) 5 App Cas 925, 950.

the Court of Appeal has also rejected the argument that the tort of deceit applies in the case of an intentional breach of the duty of disclosure in a contract *uberrimae fidei*.[338] However, it has recently been held that where there is a duty to disclose, and the failure to disclose is fraudulent, there can be an action in deceit on the basis that 'non-disclosure where there is a duty to disclose is tantamount to an implied representation that there is nothing relevant to disclose'.[339] This new approach was adopted without discussion of the older authorities which had assumed that there is no liability for pure non-disclosure, even where there is a duty of disclosure. But if it is confirmed, it may also overturn the existing case-law which has held that section 2(1) of the Misrepresentation Act 1967[340] does not apply in its terms to cases of non-disclosure because it imposes liability only where a 'misrepresentation has been made'.[341]

The tort of negligence can in principle apply to non-disclosure because a claim in negligence does not require a 'misrepresentation', but a breach of a duty of care.[342] To find a duty to take care to provide information requires either some prior conduct by the defendant evidencing his assumption of responsibility towards the claimant in relation to the provision of information, or some pre-existing relationship between the parties giving rise to a duty.[343] However, the Courts are careful not to use the tort of negligence to create duties to provide information or advice which undermine the general principle that there is no duty of disclosure between parties negotiating an ordinary commercial contract;[344] and the mere fact that there is a duty of disclosure for the purpose of the remedy of rescission (eg in negotiations for a contract of insurance) does not automatically give rise to a concurrent duty of care in tort.[345]

(f) STATUTORY DUTIES OF DISCLOSURE

Certain statutes impose duties of disclosure in relation to particular contracts, and also define the remedy which will be awarded for breach of the duty.

---

[338] *Banque Keyser Ullmann SA v Skandia (UK) Insurance Co Ltd* [1990] 1 QB 665, 788.

[339] *Conlon v Simms* [2006] EWCA Civ 1749, [2008] 1 WLR 484 at [130] (Jonathan Parker LJ, approving [2006] EWHC 401 (Ch), [2006] 2 All ER 1024 Lawrence Collins J at [201]). See also *HIH Casualty and General Insurance Ltd v Chase Manhattan Bank* [2001] EWCA Civ 1250, [2001] 2 Lloyd's Rep 483 at [48], [164], [168] and [2003] UKHL 6, [2003] 2 Lloyd's Rep 61 at [21], [75].

[340] Above, p 347.

[341] *Banque Keyser Ullman SA v Skandia (UK) Insurance Co Ltd* [1990] 1 QB 665, 789, aff'd on other grounds [1991] 2 AC 249. Cf *Stratwell Ltd v Energie Golbal Brand Management Ltd* [2015] EWHC 421 (QB) (Warbey J: it seems questionable whether an implied representation arising from non-disclosure is one that is 'made' within s 2(1)).

[342] *Hedley Byrne & Co Ltd v Heller & Partners Ltd* [1964] AC 465, 511; *Banbury v Bank of Montreal* [1918] AC 626, 713.

[343] *Banque Keyser Ullmann SA v Skandia (UK) Insurance Co Ltd*, above, n 341, 794–5; *Al-Kandari v JR Brown & Co* [1988] QB 665; *Hamilton v Allied Domecq plc* [2007] UKHL 33, 2007 SC(HL) 142 at [19]–[23].

[344] *Banque Keyser Ullmann SA v Skandia (UK) Insurance Co Ltd*, above, n 341, 798–9.

[345] *Ibid*, 801.

(i) Contracts for the allotment of shares

Promoters and directors of a company have information at their disposal which is not available to the general public, although at common law they have no duty of disclosure akin to parties negotiating a contact of insurance,[346] nor is there any fiduciary relationship between those issuing the prospectus and the public.

Protection to persons applying for shares is, however, afforded by the Financial Services and Markets Act 2000. In relation to prospectuses and listing particulars issued in support of the public issue of company securities, this imposes a general duty of disclosure of specified information that investors and their advisers would reasonably require and reasonably expect.[347] The remedy provided by the statute is the right to compensation from those responsible to persons who have acquired securities to which the prospectus or listing particulars apply, and have sustained loss in respect of them as a result of the omission of information required to be included, unless those responsible can show that up to the time of the allotment they had reasonable ground to believe and did believe that the information was properly omitted.[348]

The Financial Services and Markets Act 2000 also established a regulatory regime over those conducting investment business in order to protect the purchasers of the products of the financial services industry, namely insurance policies, investments, and advice. This regime was amended significantly by the Financial Services Act 2012. Detailed treatment of this area would be out of place in the present textbook,[349] but it should be noted that protection is achieved by a licensing system and by close control of the way those licensed conduct their businesses, including statutory 'cooling-off' periods after an agreement has been made. Many financial services practitioners, will be in a fiduciary relationship with their clients and therefore Equity will sometimes provide a remedy.[350] The 2000 Act replaced specific requirements in the Financial Services Act 1986[351] with a general rule-making power of the Financial Services Authority,[352] which was replaced by the 2012 Act by new general rule-making powers of the Financial Conduct Authority (the renamed Financial Services Authority) and the new Prudential Regulation Authority.[353] Practitioners continue to be obliged to subordinate their interests to those of their clients, and to make proper provision for disclosure of interests and facts material to transactions entered into or advice given, and the basis, method and frequency of payment by the customer and in certain cases termination provisions.[354] Private investors are given a right to damages for contravention of regulatory rules.[355]

---

[346] *Aaron's Reefs Ltd v Twiss* [1896] AC 273, 287.

[347] Financial Services and Markets Act 2000, ss 80–82.

[348] Financial Services and Markets Act 2000, s 90(1), Sched 10. For the similar liability for untrue or misleading statements in prospectuses and listing particulars, see above, p 349, n 191.

[349] See generally Lomnicka and Powell, *Encyclopedia of Financial Services Law*.

[350] Above, p 365.   [351] Sched 8.   [352] ss 138–140.

[353] 2012 Act, s 24, introducing a new Part 9A into the 2000 Act.

[354] See FCA *Conduct of Business Sourcebook*, sections 5–6.

[355] 2000 Act, s 138D (introduced by the 2012 Act, s 24 (replacing original provisions in the 2000 Act, s 150).

(ii) Consumer contracts

In recent years, duties have been imposed on persons who supply goods or services to consumers to provide particular information to consumers before they enter into the contract. These duties have often been imposed in order to implement EU Directives, and the most comprehensive duties are now owed under the Consumer Contracts (Information, Cancellation and Additional Charges) Regulations 2013.[356] The Regulations apply to most 'on-premises', 'off-premises', and 'distance' contracts between a trader and a consumer.[357] The information to be provided is more extensive for off-premises contracts and distance contracts[358] than for on-premises contracts,[359] and the duty does not extend to an on-premises contract which involves a day-to-day transaction and is performed immediately at the time when the contract is entered into. But for all three types of contract, where the duty arises it requires the trader to give information in a clear and comprehensible manner about such things as the main characteristics of the goods, services or digital content to which the contract relates, and the price. The failure to provide the required information does not give the consumer the right to rescind the contract or claim damages,[360] but in the case of an off-premises or distance contract the consumer has a right to cancel the contract within a period of 14 days from the date of the contract (or, in a contract for the supply of goods, from the date on which the consumer received the goods).[361] Where the supplier fails to provide the information required by the regulations the cancellation period is extended, and the right of cancellation is exercisable by the consumer until 14 days after the day on which supplier provides the information or, if he fails to provide it for 12 months, the long-stop cancellation period is 12 months and 14 days from the day on which the contract was concluded (or the consumer received the goods).[362] In addition, the contract is treated as including a term that the trader has complied with the regulations requiring information to be provided,[363] therefore providing the consumer with a claim for breach of contract in cases where the information has not in fact been provided.

---

[356] SI 2013 No 3134, implementing Directive 2011/83/EU, and replacing the Consumer Protection (Distance Selling) Regulations 2000 (SI 2000 No 2334), which implemented Council Directive 97/7/EC. For similar provisions in relation to contracts for the distance marketing of consumer financial services, see Financial Services (Distance Marketing) Regulations 2004 (SI 2004 No 2095), implementing Directive 2002/65/EC.

[357] In essence, an 'off-premises' contract is one formed when, or after, the trader and consumer were physically present together during the negotiations but away from the trader's business premises (sometimes referred to as a 'doorstep contract'); a 'distance' contract is one formed without the parties being physically present together and exclusively through distance communications; and an 'on-premises' contract is one which is neither a distance contract nor an off-premises contract: 2013 Regulations, reg 5. All forms of contracts are therefore, in principle, included; there are some exceptions in regs 6 and 7, such as off-premises contracts under which the payment to be made by the consumer is not more than £42: reg 7(4).

[358] 2013 Regulations, regs 10 and 13 and Sched 2.   [359] 2013 Regulations, reg 9 and Sched 1.

[360] The 'prohibited practices' giving rise to rights to redress under Part 4A of the Consumer Protection from Unfair Trading Regulations 2008 (above, p 355) do not extend to misleading *omissions* under reg 6: see reg 27B(1).

[361] 2013 Regulations, reg 30.   [362] 2013 Regulations, reg 31.   [363] 2013 Regulations, reg 18.

(g) THE FUTURE

There has been no challenge to the general common law rule of non-disclosure, but questions may be asked about its scope. Should a more liberal approach be taken to the exceptions? Are they too narrow? Take the case of the couple who are divorcing and make an agreement about the division of the property. If the negotiations prior to the agreement proceeded on the basis of the husband's belief, based on the wife's conscientious and religious objections to divorce, that the wife would never remarry, is the agreement vitiated by the failure of the wife to disclose that she had earlier become engaged to be married? On pure common law analysis, on such facts, after considering whether any of the common law and equitable exceptions applied, it has been held that none did and there was no duty to disclose.[364] Although, as we have seen, the common law position has been affected by statute where the property settlement is embodied in a Court order, it was said that this *contractual* aspect of the decision is not open to criticism in any way.[365] But is it right in principle that there should be no duty to disclose in such a case? The economic arguments do not appear applicable, let alone compelling, and it was certainly very difficult and probably impossible for the husband to acquire the information from another source. One commentator who supports the general rule has described the decision as 'repugnant to an ordinary sense of fairness'.[366]

The position might have been different if a broader view had been taken of the concept of 'fiduciary' relationship or if it had been possible to look at the statutory as well as the common law exceptions to the rule and from them find particular analogies or even a general principle which could provide the Courts with a broader, principled basis for exceptions to the general rule of non-disclosure. The common law develops by analogy from case to case and sometimes more radically by finding underlying general principles for a whole area of the law.[367] But this approach is taken only for developments of the common law itself; traditionally, statutory provisions have been regarded as isolated irruptions into the body of the common law and have not been seen as expressing a policy from which a principle could be synthesized.[368]

There has, however, been recent significant development by the legislature of duties of disclosure. We have mentioned particular statutory duties of disclosure in the Financial Services and Markets Act 2000 and the rules made under it, and

---

[364] *Wales v Wadham* [1977] 1 WLR 199.

[365] *Livesey v Jenkins* [1985] AC 424, 439. But in *Wales v Wadham, Traill v Baring* (1864) 4 De GJ & S 318 (duty to communicate change of intention) was not cited; above, p 321.

[366] Smith, *Atiyah's Introduction to the Law of Contract* (6th edn, 2005) 246. The decision, but not the reasoning, may, however, be justified on the merits since the husband had not made a full disclosure of his assets.

[367] Cartwright, *Contract Law: an Introduction to the English Law of Contract for the Civil Lawyer* (2nd edn, 2013) 33–42.

[368] Nicholas, in Harris and Tallon (eds), *Contract Law Today* (1989) 178; Cartwright, above, n 367, 27–33. Cf the different approach in France, in relation in particular to duties of disclosure: Ghestin, in Harris and Tallon (eds), *Contract Law Today* (1989) 153–5. See also Legrand (1986) 6 OJLS 322.

the Consumer Contracts (Information, Cancellation and Additional Charges) Regulations 2013. Other earlier examples are to be found in the Consumer Credit Act 1974,[369] the Hallmarking Act 1973,[370] the Housing Act 1985,[371] the Energy Act 1976,[372] and the Package Travel, Package Holiday and Package Tours Regulations 1992.[373] The financial services and consumer credit statutes reflect a legislative decision that consumers buying on credit and the purchasers of the products of the financial services industry require protection. Although there are many differences between the financial services and the consumer credit regimes, they have similar disclosure and 'cooling-off' provisions. Both regimes also exercise close control over the content of advertisements. The fact that the legislative schemes are so detailed means that it is not unreasonable to see them as self-contained codes and that no common law duty should be superimposed on them.[374] However, that part of the regimes which relates to disclosure might arguably be of wider significance. In both contexts the relationship is one of inequality; in financial services (and probably in consumer credit) there is also imbalance of information in the sense that the professional has information that the client cannot acquire from any other source—or cannot do so without incurring considerable expense. We have noted that this imbalance is also at the root of the duty of disclosure in contracts *uberrimae fidei* and the other non-statutory exceptions. The most recent, broader imposition of duties of disclosure in favour of consumers under the Consumer Contracts (Information, Cancellation and Additional Charges) Regulations 2013 reinforces this argument.

It is arguable that the fact that the legislature has imposed a duty of disclosure in the specified cases can be seen, alongside the cases in which a duty exists at common law, as an indication of the underlying rationale and principle of such a duty. If so, such legislative duties could assist a Court which is considering the scope of the exceptions or the extension of the duty to a new fact situation.[375] Such an approach would bring English law closer to its continental neighbours.[376] However, it would

---

[369] s 55, and Consumer Credit (Disclosure of Information) Regulations 2004 (SI 2004 No 1481), both amended by SI 2010 No 1010, implementing Directive 2008/48/EC. See also s 60 of the 1974 Act and SI 1983 No 1553, amended by SI 2004 No 1482, which require credit agreements subject to the Act to contain specific information.

[370] s 11 (disclosure by dealer of information explaining hallmarks).

[371] s 125(4A), added by Housing and Planning Act 1986 (disclosure by landlord of known structural defects where secure tenant exercises right to buy landlord's interest)

[372] s 15(3) (disclosure of results of passenger car fuel consumption tests).

[373] SI 1992 No 3288, regs 7–8.

[374] *Aldrich v Norwich Union Life Assurance Co Ltd* [1999] 2 All ER (Comm) 707 (Financial Services Act 1986, s 47); *Payne v Barnet LBC* (1998) 30 HLR 295 (Housing and Planning Act 1986, s 125(4A)).

[375] See *Timeload Ltd v British Telecommunications plc* (1995) 3 EMLR 459, 468 (Bingham MR); *Malik v Bank of Credit & Commerce International SA* [1998] AC 20, 52–53 (Lord Steyn); Beatson (2001) 117 LQR 247. Cf the different approach in *Banque Financière de la Cité SA v Westgate Insurance Co Ltd* [1991] 2 AC 249, 273–4 (Lord Templeman).

[376] Study Group on a European Civil Code and Research Group on EC Private Law (Acquis Group), *Principles, Definitions and Model Rules of European Private Law: Draft Common Frame of Reference (DCFR)* (2009), arts II.-3:101–105; II.-7:201, 205; Lando and Beale (eds), *Principles of European Contract Law Parts I and II* (2000) 256; Ghestin, in Harris and Tallon, above, n 368.

not only go beyond the current position, but would also in large measure revert to a general approach which was proposed by Lord Mansfield in 1766, but which was later rejected as a universal proposition and limited to particular classes of contract (notably, insurance contracts):[377]

The governing principle is applicable to all contracts and dealings.

Good faith forbids either party by concealing what he privately knows, to draw the other into a bargain, from his ignorance of that fact, and his believing the contrary.

But either party may be innocently silent, as to grounds open to both, to exercise their judgment upon.

The objection may be raised that English law does not recognize a general principle of good faith, and so cannot use such a principle to define duties of disclosure in contracts generally.[378] However, as we have seen, the Courts and the legislature have been able to define many particular circumstances in which duties of disclosure arise, and it is submitted that these could serve as analogies for the definition of other particular duties based on a general principle.

FURTHER READING

ATIYAH and TREITEL, 'The Misrepresentation Act 1967' (1967) 30 MLR 369

KRONMAN, 'Mistake, Disclosure, Information and the Law of Contracts' (1978) 7 JLS 1

CARTWRIGHT, 'Damages for Misrepresentation' [1987] Conv 423

BROWN and CHANDLER, 'Deceit, Damages and the Misrepresentation Act 1967, s 2(1)' [1992] LMCLQ 40

O'SULLIVAN, 'Rescission as a Self-Help Remedy: a Critical Analysis' [2000] CLJ 509

CARTWRIGHT, 'Excluding Liability for Misrepresentation' in Burrows and Peel (eds), *Contract Terms* (Oxford: Oxford University Press, 2007) 213

[377] *Carter v Boehm* (1766) 3 Burr 1905, 1910; *Manifest Shipping Co Ltd v Uni-Polaris Insurance Co Ltd* [2001] UKHL 1, [2003] 1 AC 469 at [42]–[45]. The common law duties of disclosure in insurance contracts have now been removed by statute (above, p 361) but this is not inconsistent with the argument presented here, since the common law in fact operated against the interests of, especially, the consumer: cf Law Com No 319, *Consumer Insurance Law: Pre-Contract Disclosure and Misrepresentation* (2009); (2012) 75 MLR 1099 (Lowry and Rawlings).

[378] *Walford v Miles* [1992] 2 AC 128, 138. But cf Steyn (1997) 113 LQR 433, 439; *Director-General of Fair Trading v First National Bank plc* [2002] 1 AC 481 at [17]; *Yam Seng Pte Ltd v International Trade Corp Ltd* [2013] EWHC 111 (QB), [2013] 1 All ER (Comm) 1321 at [120]–[154], above, p 166.

10

DURESS, UNDUE INFLUENCE, AND UNCONSCIONABLE BARGAINS

1. INTRODUCTION

This chapter considers three vitiating factors based on the improper conduct of one party, the vulnerability of the other, or a combination of the two.[1] Because of their narrow scope these were, in the past, considered to be relatively unimportant in the law of contract, but they are of more significance in the modern law.

Duress and undue influence occur where one party to a contract has coerced the other or exercised such domination that the other's independence of decision was substantially undermined. Although in some respects undue influence is the equitable equivalent of common law duress, in equity relief was granted in cases of pressure or coercion where the common law provided no remedy.[2] Moreover, in some cases the primary concern of equity is to protect certain relationships and it does so by a presumption of undue influence. Since the Judicature Act 1873, it has been the duty of the Courts to apply the common law and equitable rules concurrently, and in the event of any conflict or variance between them, the equitable rules are to prevail. The common law and equitable rules have, therefore, now to be treated in the light of their combined effect.[3] Duress, like misrepresentation, is primarily concerned with the process by which the contract was made (procedural unfairness or impropriety) rather than whether the terms of the contract are in fact harsh or unconscionable (substantive unfairness or impropriety). Undue influence, especially in cases of overt acts of improper pressure or coercion, is also said to be primarily concerned with procedural unfairness, but because it also has a role in protecting the excessively vulnerable the position is more complicated and it has significant substantive aspects.

---

[1] See Enonchong, *Duress, Undue Influence and Unconscionable Dealings* (2nd edn, 2012).

[2] *Royal Bank of Scotland plc v Etridge (No 2)* [2001] UKHL 44, [2002] 2 AC 773 at [6]–[8], [103]. Cf Burrows (2002) 22 OJLS 1, 6.

[3] *United Scientific Holdings Ltd v Burnley BC* [1978] AC 904.

In the limited category of cases in which the doctrine of unconscionable bargains operates, it is necessary to show not only that the process by which the contract was made was unfair but that there is contractual imbalance, that is, the doctrine extends to the actual substance of the contract and the fairness of its terms. The role of unconscionability was restricted in the nineteenth century by the assumption that parties enjoy freedom of economic decision when entering into contracts which enables them to choose to enter into a contract on whatever terms they may consider advantageous to their interests, or to choose not to,[4] and more recently by the view that the task of limiting such freedom so as to relieve inequality of bargaining power is essentially a legislative task for Parliament.[5] In the case of consumer contracts there has been significant statutory intervention to protect consumers against unfair terms.[6] Employment and landlord and tenant relationships are also regulated by statute so as to protect employees and tenants from unfairness.[7] As in the case of statutory duties of disclosure,[8] it is arguable that to the extent that the statutory regimes can be seen as expressing a policy from which a principle can be derived they may be of some analogical assistance in developing the common law.[9]

We saw in Chapter 9 that a misrepresentation made by a trader which induces a consumer to enter into a contract may also sometimes constitute a 'prohibited practice' under the Consumer Protection from Unfair Trading Regulations 2008, which will give the consumer 'rights to redress' under the Regulations.[10] Similarly, conduct which constitutes duress or undue influence may constitute an 'aggressive commercial practice' under those Regulations, and may offer the consumer an additional choice of remedies.[11]

2. DURESS

(a) NATURE OF DURESS

A contract which has been induced by unlawful or other illegitimate forms of pressure or intimidation is voidable[12] on the ground of duress.[13] A restitutionary claim lies

---

[4] Above, p 4.   [5] *National Westminster Bank plc v Morgan* [1985] AC 686, 708 (Lord Scarman).
[6] Above, pp 222, 232.   [7] Above, p 5.   [8] Above, p 372.
[9] *Timeload Ltd v British Telecommunications plc* (1995) 3 EMLR 459, 468; *Malik v Bank of Credit & Commerce International SA* [1998] AC 20, 52–3. See generally Beatson (2001) 117 LQR 247; Burrows (2012) 128 LQR 232.
[10] Above, p 355.   [11] Below, p 403.
[12] Coke 2 Inst 483; *Whelpdale's Case* (1605) 5 Co Rep 119a; *North Ocean Shipping Co Ltd v Hyundai Construction Co Ltd* [1979] QB 705; *Pao On v Lau Yiu Long* [1980] AC 614; *Universe Tankships Inc of Monrovia v International Transport Workers Federation, The Universe Sentinel* [1983] 1 AC 366. Cf *Barton v Armstrong* [1976] AC 104, 120 (declaration that the contracts 'are void'; but this may only be describing the contract *after* it has been rescinded). Cf Lanham (1966) 29 MLR 615, contending that duress renders the contract void.
[13] Beatson, *The Use and Abuse of Unjust Enrichment* (1991) ch 5; Cartwright, *Unequal Bargaining* (1991) ch 7; Dawson (1947) 45 Mich L Rev 253; Hale (1943) 43 Col L Rev 603; Halson (1991) 107 LQR 649; Smith [1997] CLJ 343.

for the recovery of money paid under duress, and in many cases the duress will also be tortious and give rise to an action for damages, for example for assault, wrongful interference with property and, in the case of economic duress, intimidation.[14] Where duress by a trader induces a consumer to enter into a contract, the consumer may also have remedies under Part 4A of the Consumer Protection from Unfair Trading Regulations 2008: the right to 'unwind' the contract, or to a discount, or to damages.[15]

(i) 'Unlawful' pressure and 'illegitimate' pressure

The modern cases generally define the sort of pressure which constitutes duress as 'illegitimate' pressure.[16] This emphasizes that the law must distinguish between pressures to which a contracting party is not expected to submit without having a remedy, and other ('legitimate') pressures which the law does not take into account.

Some forms of pressure which constitute duress are unlawful; but others, though not unlawful, are still illegitimate. Unlawful pressure occurs where the coercive party threatens to do something that is a breach of a common law or statutory duty. The act may be a crime, a tort or, subject to the qualifications set out below, a breach of contract. Where an unlawful act is threatened, provided it induces the contract, in principle the contract may be set aside by the other party. In the words of Lord Devlin, '[a]ll that matters to the plaintiff is that, metaphorically speaking, a club has been used. It does not matter to the plaintiff what the club is made of—whether it is a physical club or an economic club, a tortious club or an otherwise illegal club'.[17]

The position is different where what is threatened is not an unlawful act. Ordinarily it is not duress to threaten to do that which one has a legal right to do, for instance to refuse to enter into a contract or to terminate a contract lawfully. But exceptionally such a threat may constitute duress when coupled with a demand. Although such pressure is not unlawful, it is still 'illegitimate'.

(ii) Categorization of types of duress

Traditionally, duress has been categorized according to the form of the threat. As we shall see, the Courts first recognized threats to the person, and only later threats to property and finally threats of economic harm. Now that they have unified duress as involving 'illegitimate' pressure one might expect that the different categories of threat could be abandoned. However, there appear still to be differences between them, such as in the rules of causation,[18] and for the purpose of analysis it is also preferable to consider the different types of duress separately.[19]

---

[14] *The Universe Sentinel*, above, n 12, 385, 400; *Rookes v Barnard* [1964] AC 1129; *Kolmar Group AG v Traxpo Enterprises Pvt Ltd* [2010] EWHC 113 (Comm), [2010] 1 CLC 256. The duress need not constitute a tort: *Dimskal Shipping Co SA v International Transport Workers Federation, The Evia Luck* [1992] 2 AC 152, 169.

[15] Below, p 403.   [16] *The Universe Sentinel*, above, n 12, 384, 401.

[17] *Rookes v Barnard* [1964] AC 1129, 1209, discussing the tort of intimidation.

[18] In duress to the person, the threat need only be 'a' cause, and may be inferred: *Barton v Armstrong* [1976] AC 104; in economic duress the threat must be a significant cause and must be proved: *Huyton SA v Peter Cremer GmbH & Co* [1999] 1 Lloyds Rep 620; below, p 379.

[19] Below, pp 377 ff.

(iii) Juridical basis of duress

It used to be said that a contract could be set aside for duress only if the will of the victim was coerced so as to vitiate his consent.[20] But this was misleading, because it was interpreted as saying not simply that the victim's consent was defective, but that his entry into the contract was not a voluntary act.[21] The fallacy of this approach was exposed in *The Universe Sentinel*.[22] A person subjected to duress is fully aware of the nature and terms of the contract which is thus entered. The victim still intends to contract, though his freedom to choose whether to enter into the contract is vitiated.[23] 'The classic case of duress is . . . not the lack of will to submit but the victim's intentional submission arising from the realization that there is no other practical choice open to him.'[24] The rationale of duress is thus not lack of knowledge or consent but illegitimate pressure which means that the victim's apparent consent is treated in law as revocable, unless approbated expressly or by implication after the pressure has ceased to operate on the victim's mind.[25]

(b) UNLAWFUL PRESSURE

(i) Types of duress

(a) Duress of the person. It has long been established that duress can vitiate a contract where it consists of actual or threatened violence to the person,[26] for example threats to kill the party to the contract or perhaps a close relative.[27] How serious the action threatened must be in order to render the contract voidable will depend upon the ability of the person threatened to resist the pressure improperly brought to bear.[28] But once it is established that the threats contributed to the decision of the person threatened to enter into the contract, that person is entitled to relief, even though the contract might well have been entered into all the same if no threats had been made.[29]

At common law, a threat of lawful imprisonment, for example a criminal prosecution, would not ordinarily amount to duress, but in equity a threat by one party to prosecute

---

[20] *Occidental Worldwide Investment Corp v Skibs A/S Avanti, The Siboen and The Sibotre* [1976] 1 Lloyd's Rep 293, 336; *North Ocean Shipping Co Ltd v Hyundai Construction Co Ltd* [1979] QB 705, 717; *Pao On v Lau Yiu Long* [1980] AC 614, 635. See also *Barton v Armstrong* [1976] AC 104, 121; *Alec Lobb (Garages) Ltd v Total Oil Great Britain Ltd* [1983] 1 WLR 87, 93.

[21] *Pao On v Lau Yiu Long* [1980] AC 614, 636.

[22] *Universe Tankships Inc of Monrovia v International Transport Workers Federation* [1983] 1 AC 366. See also *Lynch v DPP of Northern Ireland* [1975] AC 653, 670, 675, 680, 690–1, 695, 703, 709 (duress as a defence in criminal law); Atiyah (1982) 98 LQR 197, (1983) 99 LQR 353; Beatson (1976) 92 LQR 496, *The Use and Abuse of Unjust Enrichment* (1991) 113–17; *Dimskal Shipping Co SA v International Transport Workers Federation, The Evia Luck* [1992] 2 AC 152, 165–6.

[23] Cartwright, *Unequal Bargaining* (1991) 160–3.

[24] [1983] 1 AC 366, 400 (Lord Scarman).   [25] *Ibid*, 384 (Lord Diplock).

[26] Co 2 Inst 483; Co Litt 253b; 1 Roll Abr 687, pl 5, 6; *Skeate v Beale* (1841) 11 A & E 983.

[27] *Barton v Armstrong* [1976] AC 104.   [28] *Scott v Sebright* (1886) 12 PD 21, 24.

[29] *Barton v Armstrong* [1976] AC 104, 118–19.

the other for a criminal offence could constitute a ground on which the contract would be set aside for undue influence,[30] and today the equitable rule prevails.[31]

(b) Duress of goods.   It used to be uncertain whether a contract entered into as the result of actual or threatened violence to or the illegal seizure of goods or other property could be set aside on the ground of duress,[32] but it is now established that it can.[33] Older authority to the contrary can possibly be explained as the voluntary compromise of a claim,[34] or as involving facts in which the degree of coercion applied was in fact insufficient to constitute duress.[35] It was in any event inconsistent with authority granting the recovery of money paid under protest for the release of goods from unlawful detention.[36]

(c) Economic duress.   It is also now established that, in certain circumstances, a contract can be set aside for economic duress, that is, the threat of such serious financial consequences as give the threatened party no practical choice but to enter into the contract.[37] So it has been held that an unlawful threat by a trade union to continue the 'boycotting' of a ship[38] and a threat to break an existing contract[39] can be a sufficient ground to render voidable a contract, supported by consideration, entered into as a result of its pressure. In particular, one party may threaten to break an existing contract unless the contract is renegotiated in its favour, and the other party may accede to this demand in order to avoid the adverse financial consequences which would ensue from the threatened breach.[40] In *Atlas Express Ltd v Kafco (Importers and Distributors) Ltd*:[41]

K had agreed to supply basketware to a chain of retail shops and made a contract for its delivery with A, a carrier. A had erroneously estimated that each load would contain over

---

[30]   *Williams v Bayley* (1886) LR 1 HL 200.

[31]   *Mutual Finance Ltd v John Wetton & Sons Ltd* [1937] 2 KB 389.

[32]   There were cases of successful claims for restitution of money paid under duress: *Astley v Reynolds* (1731) 2 Str 915; *Maskell v Horner* [1915] 3 KB 106; but not of avoidance of contracts, for which duress to the person was generally thought to be required: see Guest, *Anson's Law of Contract* (24th edn, 1975) 259–60.

[33]   *Vantage Navigation Corp v Suhail & Saud Bahwan Building Materials Llc, The Alev* [1989] 1 Lloyd's Rep 138. See also *Lloyds Bank Ltd v Bundy* [1975] QB 326, 337; *Occidental Worldwide Investment Corp v Skibs A/S Avanti* [1976] 1 Lloyd's Rep 293, 335–6; *North Ocean Shipping Co Ltd v Hyundai Construction Co Ltd* [1979] QB 705, 715; *Pao On v Lau Yiu Long* [1980] AC 614, 635; *The Universe Sentinel* [1983] 1 AC 366.

[34]   *Occidental Worldwide Investment Corp v Skibs A/S Avanti*, above, n 33; Beatson, *The Use and Abuse of Unjust Enrichment* (1991) 105–6. On compromises, see above, p 109.

[35]   *Skeate v Beale* (1840) 11 A & E 983, 990.

[36]   Above, n 33. Cf Burrows, *The Law of Restitution* (3rd edn, 2011) 259–60.

[37]   *Occidental Worldwide Investment Corp v Skibs A/S Avanti*, above, n 33, 336; *North Ocean Shipping Co Ltd v Hyundai Construction Co Ltd*, above, n 33; *Pao On v Lau Yiu Long*, above, n 33, 635; *The Universe Sentinel*, above, n 22, 383, 391, 397, 400; *Alec Lobb (Garages) Ltd v Total Oil Great Britain Ltd* [1983] 1 WLR 87, 93.

[38]   *The Universe Sentinel*, above, n 22; *Dimskal Shipping Co SA v International Transport Workers Federation, The Evia Luck* [1992] 2 AC 152.

[39]   *North Ocean Shipping Co Ltd v Hyundai Construction Co Ltd*, above, n 33; *Pao On v Lau Yiu Long*, above, n 33. See also *Occidental Worldwide Investment Corp v Skibs A/S Avanti*, above, n 33 (threat to put company into liquidation). Cf McKendrick, in Burrows and Rodger (eds), *Mapping the Law: Essays in Memory of Peter Birks* (2006) 181, 188 (threatened breach of contract is always illegitimate).

[40]   On the distinction between a 'threat' and a 'warning', which will not suffice, see below, p 381.

[41]   [1989] QB 833.

400 cartons and, on this basis, had agreed a price of £1.10 per carton. The first load was for a smaller number of cartons, and A, believing that carrying such a load at the agreed rate was not financially viable, said that it would not perform unless K agreed to pay a minimum of £440 a load. Because K's commercial survival depended on the contract with the retail chain and it could not find an alternative carrier, it agreed to A's demand but then refused to pay.

It was held that the new terms were agreed under economic duress. In that case there was a direct threat to repudiate the contract, but the threat may be indirect. Thus, in *B & S Contracts and Design Ltd v Victor Green Publications Ltd* an indication by a party to a contract that it was prepared to allow its workers to strike unless the other party agreed to make a payment in addition to the contract price was held to be a veiled threat and to constitute duress because the other party had no other practical choice open to it but to agree to pay.[42] Good faith in the sense that the contractual difficulty is not the fault of the party seeking to renegotiate does not preclude a finding of economic duress.[43]

(ii) Causation

There must be a sufficient causal link between the duress and the contract. In cases of duress of the person it needs only be shown that the duress was 'a' cause of the contract, and the Court may be willing to infer, in the absence of evidence to the contrary, that the duress induced the contract.[44] But in cases of economic duress, it is for the party seeking to have the contract set aside to establish that the duress was a significant cause of the contract: 'but for' the illegitimate pressure, the agreement would not have been made either at all or, at least, in the terms in which it was made.[45]

Not every threat to break a contract unless its terms are renegotiated will amount to duress. It is also necessary for the threat to induce the renegotiation, and in this context a number of factors will be taken into account. These include the availability of an adequate alternative remedy, whether there has been a compromise or a submission to a claim made in good faith, and whether the victim has protested or taken independent advice. Thus, in *Pao On v Lau Yiu Long*,[46] where one party was coerced into accepting the renegotiation of a business transaction by a threat by the other party to break an existing contract, but did so with legal advice and without protest, and after a considered appraisal of the risk involved, it was held by the Privy

---

[42] [1984] ICR 419, 426, 428.

[43] *Huyton SA v Peter Cremer GmbH & Co* [1999] 1 Lloyd's Rep 620, 629.

[44] *Barton v Armstrong* [1976] AC 104, 118–9,120. Cf the similar willingness of the Courts to infer reliance on a misrepresentation: above, pp 325–6.

[45] *Huyton SA v Peter Cremer GmbH & Co* [1999] 1 Lloyds Rep 620, 636, 638–9. Cf *Crescendo Management Pty Ltd v Westpac Banking Corp* (1998) 19 NSWLR 40, 46 (McHugh JA). Cf McKendrick in Burrows and Rodger, above, n 39, 181, 187.

[46] [1980] AC 614, above, p 113. See also *Alec Lobb (Garages) Ltd v Total Oil Great Britain Ltd* [1983] 1 WLR 87.

Council that the renegotiated agreement would not be set aside on the ground of economic duress.

(iii) Alternative remedies

A person threatened with duress of goods or a breach of contract can stand up to the threat and, if the other party breaches the contract, sue for damages. In the context of duress of goods the presence of an alternative remedy, such as an action in tort for wrongful interference with goods, is not necessarily a bar to relief; the threatened party might have had 'such an immediate want of his goods that [such an action] would not do'[47] and in any event there is no *right* to recover the goods themselves as opposed to damages in an action in tort.[48]

In the case of duress by threatened breach of contract, although damages and, where available, specific relief may be adequate, there will be situations in which such remedies do not adequately protect the victim, for example where it is imperative that there be no interruption in performance[49] or where, as in *Atlas Express Ltd v Kafco (Importers and Distributors) Ltd*, it is not possible to obtain the contractual services from another source. The existence and adequacy of an alternative remedy is taken into account in such cases. There is some support for treating this as purely evidential and not conclusive, that is, one of the factors (with protest and independent advice) which the Court takes into account in determining whether the victim was in fact coerced by the threat.[50] But it is submitted that, since the basis of the doctrine of duress is the absence of a practical alternative on the part of the victim to submission to the threat, the better view is that the existence of an adequate alternative remedy goes to the essence of and precludes a finding of duress.[51]

(c) DURESS DISTINGUISHED FROM LEGITIMATE RENEGOTIATION

We noted in Chapter 4 of this book that it may well be reasonable for a party to seek to renegotiate a contract and that one of the functions of promissory estoppel is to protect reasonable renegotiations. Where the party seeking to renegotiate honestly believes that in the circumstances it is entitled not to perform, we have seen that the result

---

[47] *Astley v Reynolds* (1731) 2 Str 915, 916; *Maskell v Horner* [1915] 3 KB 106, 122. See also *Kanhaya Lal v National Bank of India* (1913) 29 TLR 314. Cf *Vantage Navigation Corp v Suhail & Saud Bahwan Building Materials Llc, The Alev* [1989] 1 Lloyd's Rep 138, 146–7.

[48] By the Torts (Interference with Goods) Act 1977, ss 3(2)(a), 3(3)(b) an order for delivery of the goods may be made at the discretion of the Court.

[49] *Kolmar Group AG v Traxpo Enterprises Pvt Ptd* [2010] EWHC 113 (Comm), [2010] 1 CLC 256.

[50] *Pao On v Lau Yiu Long*, above, n 33, 635, 640; *Huyton SA v Peter Cremer GmbH & Co* [1999] 1 Lloyd's Rep 620, 638; *Kolmar Group AG v Traxpo Enterprises Pvt Ptd*, above, n 49 at [92].

[51] *Vantage Navigation Corp v Suhail & Saud Bahwan Building Materials Llc, The Alev*, above, n 47; *Hennessy v Craigmyle & Co Ltd* [1986] ICR 461; *DSND Subsea Ltd v Petroleum Geo Services ASA* [2000] BLR 530 at [131]; *Borrelli v Ting* [2010] UKPC 21 at [31] ('Put colloquially James Henry Ting had the Liquidators over a barrel').

will generally be a binding compromise.[52] But where it does not, the development of duress makes it important that parties who genuinely face difficulties if they complete performance on the contract terms and wish to renegotiate know what is and what is not permissible conduct.

(i) Was there a threat?

In *Williams v Roffey Bros & Nicholls (Contractors) Ltd*[53] R & N, noticing their carpentry subcontractor's difficulties, offered an additional payment which, as we have seen, was held binding. But surely the renegotiation would not automatically have been vitiated by duress if it was the subcontractor who had taken the initiative. It should not necessarily be seen as a threat to point out that without renegotiation it will not be possible to continue performance,[54] provided that this is so in fact. This is particularly so where, as in the *High Trees* case,[55] changes of circumstances have affected the risks originally undertaken.[56] It must be recalled that, save for specifically enforceable contracts, it is open to a party to a contract to be in deliberate breach of contract in order to cut its losses commercially.[57] We have seen that the good faith—*bona fides*—of the person making a demand is relevant in determining whether there is a compromise or whether the doctrine of promissory estoppel applies.[58] It should also be relevant in determining whether there is duress.[59] Thus, in *B & S Contracts and Design Ltd v Victor Green Publications Ltd*, considered above,[60] it seems that the fact that the contractor had not made reasonable efforts to avoid a strike by its workers before demanding an additional payment from the other party to the contract was a factor in the conclusion that the demand was a veiled threat.

(ii) Is it commercially reasonable to renegotiate?

One way to determine what is permissible is by a test, similar to that in paragraph 176(2) of the American Law Institute's *Restatement, Contracts (2d)*, which would ask whether it was commercially reasonable to seek to renegotiate and whether the renegotiated terms are 'fair and equitable'. But it is difficult to see how the Courts

---

[52] Above, p 109.

[53] [1991] 1 QB 1, above, p 114. Cf *Adam Opel GmbH v Mitras Automotive (UK) Ltd* [2007] EWHC 3481 (QB) (threat to stop supplies constituted duress and rendered renegotiated contract voidable).

[54] See, on the difference between a 'threat' and a 'warning' in the context of economic torts, *Conway v Wade* [1909] AC 506, 510; *Rookes v Barnard* [1964] AC 1129, 1166; *Camellia Tanker Ltd SA v International Transport Workers Federation* [1976] ICR 274, 284, 296. See also *Hodges v Webb* [1920] 2 Ch 70; Beatson, *The Use and Abuse of Unjust Enrichment* (1991) 118–20; Smith [1997] CLJ 343, 346–50.

[55] [1947] KB 130, above, pp 122–3.

[56] See *Watkins & Sons Inc v Carrig* 21 A 2d 591 (1941) (hard rock unexpectedly struck during excavations) but cf *North Ocean Shipping Co Ltd v Hyundai Construction Co Ltd* [1979] QB 705, 714; *Williams v Roffey Bros & Nicholls (Contractors) Ltd*, above, n 53, 20.

[57] *Williams v Roffey Bros & Nicholls (Contractors) Ltd*, above, n 53, 23.

[58] *Callisher v Bischoffsheim* (1870) LR 5 QB 449, above, p 109; *D & C Builders v Rees* [1966] 2 QB 617, above, p 125.

[59] *CTN Cash and Carry Ltd v Gallaher Ltd* [1994] 4 All ER 714 (lawful act duress; see below, pp 382–3).

[60] [1984] ICR 419, above, p 379.

could do this without becoming more involved in an examination of the fairness of both the original contract and the renegotiation than they have hitherto been.[61] It is, however, equally difficult to see any way of distinguishing permissible and impermissible conduct during renegotiations that does not ultimately involve some monitoring of the substantive fairness of the contract, although this should be kept to the absolute minimum by emphasizing that duress is primarily a doctrine of *procedural* impropriety focusing on conduct.

(d) THREATS OF LAWFUL ACTION

(i) Ordinarily not duress

It is not ordinarily duress to threaten to do that which one has a right to do, for instance to refuse to enter into a contract or to terminate a contract lawfully.[62] In the cut-and-thrust of business relationships various types of pressure may be brought to bear in differing situations. Where there are shortages in goods or services the person who wishes to acquire them has little choice. Thus a private person or undertaking is generally permitted to refuse to deal with another at all or except on specified terms,[63] and the poor person who has to agree to pay a high rent to get a roof over his head is nevertheless bound. 'No bargain will be upset which is the result of the ordinary interplay of [market] forces'[64] and a contracting party will not be permitted to escape from its contractual obligations merely because it was coerced into making a contract by fear of the financial consequences of refusing to do so.[65] In *CTN Cash & Carry Ltd v Gallaher Ltd* it was held that a wholesale buyer of cigarettes who, following an honest but mistaken demand by the seller, paid a sum not due because the seller had threatened, as it was entitled to do, to withdraw credit facilities from the buyer, could not recover it on the ground of duress:[66]

We are being asked to extend the categories of duress of which the law will take cognisance. That is not necessarily objectionable, but it seems to me that an extension capable of covering the present case, involving 'lawful act duress' in a commercial context in pursuit of a bona fide claim, would be a radical one with far-reaching implications. It would introduce a substantial and undesirable element of uncertainty in the commercial bargaining process. Moreover, it will often enable bona fide settled accounts to be reopened when parties to

---

[61] Beatson, *The Use and Abuse of Unjust Enrichment* (1991) 126–9, 135; Michell, Mitchell and Watterson, *Goff & Jones on the Law of Unjust Enrichment* (8th edn, 2011) para 10–43.

[62] *Leyland DAF Ltd v Automotive Products plc* [1994] 1 BCLC 245, 249–50, 257; *Smith v William Charlick Ltd* (1923) 34 CLR 38, 56, 64–5 (Australia). See also *A-G v R* [2003] UKPC 22, [2003] EMLR 24 (threat to return member of SAS Regiment to his former regiment if he did not sign a lifelong confidentiality agreement was a lawful threat, and the demand supported by the threat was justified).

[63] For the position of a public body see *R v Lewisham LBC, ex p Shell UK Ltd* [1988] 1 All ER 938 and the statutory controls discussed above, pp 245–6.

[64] *Lloyds Bank Ltd v Bundy* [1975] QB 326, 336 (Lord Denning MR).

[65] *Hardie and Lane Ltd v Chilton* [1928] 2 KB 306; *Eric Gnapp Ltd v Petroleum Board* [1949] 1 All ER 980.

[66] [1994] 4 All ER 714, 719 (Steyn LJ), and see Birks, *An Introduction to the Law of Restitution* (1985) 177. See also *Leyland DAF Ltd v Automotive Products plc* [1994] 1 BCLC 245.

commercial dealings fall out. The aim of our commercial law ought to be to encourage fair dealing between parties. But it is a mistake for the law to set its sights too highly when the critical inquiry is not whether the conduct is lawful but whether it is morally or socially unacceptable.

Although this approach leaves many forms of socially objectionable conduct unchecked, as a general rule the determination of when socially objectionable conduct which is not in itself unlawful should be penalized is for the legislature rather than the judiciary.

(ii) Exceptional cases: 'lawful act' duress?

Exceptionally a threat of lawful action may constitute duress and render a contract voidable.[67] It has been said that the threat, if not wrongful, must be immoral or unconscionable.[68] We have seen that a threat by one party to prosecute the other for a criminal offence could constitute a ground on which the contract would be set aside in equity for undue influence.[69] Again, it is inconceivable that the Courts would give effect to an agreement obtained by threats amounting to blackmail, although in one sense the blackmailer may only be threatening to do some act which he is lawfully entitled to do, such as to tell a wife of her husband's adultery, or to appoint a receiver.[70] Such a threat may now be categorized not only as undue influence but also as duress:[71]

Duress can, of course, exist even if the threat is one of lawful action: whether it does so depends upon the nature of the demand. Blackmail is often a demand supported by a threat to do what is lawful, eg to report criminal conduct to the police.

In the typical case of blackmail, the blackmailer has no economic interest in the outcome apart from getting what has been demanded, and it is for this reason that the threat is regarded as illegitimate. Where the person making the threat has some economic or other interest in the outcome apart from getting what has been demanded, the question will be whether the demand is 'unwarranted' in the sense of being unrelated to any 'legitimate' interest of the party making the demand. It is submitted that, as in the criminal law, a demand will not be unwarranted where the person making it believes that there are reasonable grounds for making it and that the use of the menaces is a proper means of reinforcing the demand.[72] In the

---

[67] Cf Ahdar [2014] CLJ 39, 44–7, criticizing the commercial uncertainty created by the courts' unwillingness to rule out 'lawful act' duress.

[68] *Alf Vaughan & Co Ltd v Royscot Trust plc* [1999] 1 All ER (Comm) 856, 863, following Goff and Jones, *The Law of Restitution* (5th edn, 1998) 309–10 (see now *The Law of Unjust Enrichment* (8th edn, 2011) paras 10-03, 10-42, 10-86); *Progress Bulk Carriers Ltd v Tube City IMS LLC, The Cenk Kaptanoglu* [2012] EWHC 273 (Comm), [2012] 1 Lloyd's Rep 501 at [35].

[69] *Mutual Finance Co Ltd v John Wetton & Sons Ltd* [1937] 2 KB 389.

[70] *Westpac Banking Corp v Cockerill* (1998) 152 ALR 267.

[71] *Universe Tankships Inc of Monrovia v International Transport Workers Federation, The Universe Sentinel* [1983] 1 AC 366, 401 (Lord Scarman); see also Lord Diplock, *ibid*, 385. See further *Dimskal Shipping Co SA v International Transport Workers Federation, The Evia Luck* [1992] 2 AC 152.

[72] Theft Act 1968, s 21(1); Criminal Law Revision Committee, Eighth Report (1966, Cmnd 2977); *Thorne v Motor Trade Association* [1937] AC 797, 822; *R v Harvey* (1980) 72 Cr App R 139.

typical case of coercion by the threat of a lawful act concerning an existing or future contractual relationship, the threatener will have a direct economic interest, and therefore the demand will, in the majority of cases, be 'legitimate'.[73] The tort of 'lawful means conspiracy' provides a useful guide. In that context the pursuit of more profit, of a larger share of the market, price stability, and of higher wages have all been held to be legitimate purposes.[74] For these reasons, while in principle a threat to do what is lawful can constitute duress, this form of pressure is unlikely to have much practical impact save where the relationship between the parties is one accorded special protection by the law.[75] There appears, however, to be no clear reported case of duress by threat of 'lawful act' which did not also involve some form of unlawful or illegitimate threat, either at the time when the (voidable) contract is entered into or in the past which forms part of a course of conduct driving the victim into a position where it has no realistic alternative but to enter into the contract.[76]

(e) RESCISSION

Duress renders the contract voidable, and the remedy by which the contract is avoided is rescission. Although there are few cases which explore the details of the remedy, in principle it should be no different from rescission for other vitiating factors such as misrepresentation and undue influence.[77] Therefore rescission can be obtained only if restitution can be made to restore both parties to their positions as they were before the contract;[78] and will be barred by affirmation[79] or, presumably, if the subject-matter of the contract has passed into the hands of a purchaser in good faith for value and without notice of the defect in the contract.[80]

---

[73] For a possible example of an unwarranted demand, see *Norreys v Zeffert* [1939] 2 All ER 187.

[74] *Mogul Steamship Co Ltd v McGregor, Gow & Co* [1892] AC 25; *Thorne v Motor Trade Association* [1937] AC 797; *Crofter Hand Woven Harris Tweed Co Ltd v Veitch* [1942] AC 435. See Carty, *An Analysis of the Economic Torts* (2nd edn, 2010) 140–4.

[75] See below, pp 388 (presumed undue influence) and 400 (unconscionability) for consideration of such relationships.

[76] *Progress Bulk Carriers Ltd v Tube City IMS LLC*, above, n 68 at [39] (prior repudiatory breach of contract); *Borrelli v Ting* [2010] UKPC 21 (course of conduct including forgery and the provision of false evidence); cf Ahdar [2014] CLJ 39, 46–7.

[77] *Halpern v Halpern (Nos 1 and 2)* [2007] EWCA Civ 291, [2008] QB 195 at [70]–[76], rejecting the argument that since a contract is voidable for duress at common law (rather than in equity) the nature of the remedy and its limitations are different. For rescission for misrepresentation, see pp 332 ff, above; for rescission for undue influence, see pp 394 ff, below.

[78] *Ibid.* cf *Borrelli v Ting*, above, n 76 at [38]–[39] (rejecting the 'unacceptable proposition' that rescission was not available where parties cannot be restored to the position created by the illegitimate means).

[79] *North Ocean Shipping Co Ltd v Hyundai Construction Co Ltd* [1979] QB 705.

[80] Cf *White v Garden* (1851) 10 CBNS 919 (third-party rights were a bar to rescission for fraud at common law).

3. UNDUE INFLUENCE

We have already seen that the term 'fraud' was used in a sense wider and less precise in the Court of Chancery than in the common law courts.[81] It was often used in equity in the sense of unconscientious dealing although, in the words of Lord Haldane, a great equity lawyer, this was unfortunate.[82] One such form of dealing is commonly described as 'undue influence'. The nature and operation of undue influence in the modern law was considered by the House of Lords in eight appeals heard together and reported as *Royal Bank of Scotland plc v Etridge (No 2)*.[83] The principles are set out in the speech of Lord Nicholls with whom, although there are some differences of expression and approach, the other members of the Appellate Committee agreed.[84]

(a) NATURE OF UNDUE INFLUENCE

The term 'undue influence' has sometimes been used by the Courts to describe the equitable doctrine of coercion referred to above,[85] but it also includes, and it would perhaps be more helpful to confine it to, forms of pressure much less direct or substantial than those already discussed. It may also arise where the parties are in a relation of confidence or dependence which puts one of them in a position to exercise over the other an influence which may be perfectly natural and proper in itself, but is capable of being unfairly used.[86] A finding of undue influence does not depend upon a conclusion that the victim made no decision of her own, or that her will was overborne: a conscious exercise of will may be vitiated by undue influence.[87] 'The question is, not, whether she knew what she was doing, had done, or proposed to do, but how the intention was produced: whether all that care and providence was placed round her, as against those, who advised her, which, from their situation and relation with respect to her, they were bound to exert on her behalf'.[88] The undue influence may consist not only in the positive application of pressure, directly or

---

[81] Above, p 365. [82] *Nocton v Lord Ashburton* [1914] AC 932, 953.
[83] [2001] UKHL 44, [2002] 2 AC 773. [84] *Ibid* at [3]. See also [91], [100], [192].
[85] *Mutual Finance Co Ltd v John Wetton & Sons Ltd* [1937] 2 KB 389; *Royal Bank of Scotland plc v Etridge (No 2)*, above, n 2 at [7]–[8].
[86] Winder (1939) 3 MLR 97. See also Cartwright, *Unequal Bargaining* (1991) ch 8; *A-G v R* [2003] UKPC 22, [2003] EMLR 24 at [21] (undue influence has concentrated on unfair exploitation of a relationship of ascendancy or influence); *National Commercial Bank (Jamaica) Ltd v Hew* [2003] UKPC 51 at [32]–[33]. Cf Birks and Chin in Beatson and Friedmann (eds), *Good Faith and Fault in Contract Law* (1995) ch 3 (undue influence is about impaired consent, not exploitation); Chen-Wishart, in Burrows and Rodger (eds), *Mapping the Law: Essays in Memory of Peter Birks* (2006) 201 and [2006] CLP 231; *Pesticcio v Huet* [2004] EWCA Civ 372, [2004] WTLR 699 at [20] (Mummery LJ: basis of court's intervention is not the commission of a dishonest or wrongful act by the defendant).
[87] *Hewett v First Plus Financial Group plc* [2010] EWCA Civ 312, [2010] 2 P & CR 22 at [25].
[88] *Huguenin v Baseley* (1807) 14 Ves Jun 273, 300 (Lord Eldon).

indirectly, but also in the failure to fulfil a duty of candour and fairness arising from the relation of confidence or dependence, involving misrepresentations or the failure to disclose relevant information.[89] Depending on the circumstances, there is therefore potential for overlap of claims for undue influence with claims for duress, misrepresentation, or non-disclosure because the facts which justify a finding of undue influence may also give rise to these other claims.

Courts, including the House of Lords in *Etridge*'s case, have been careful not to define precisely the sort of influence which will be regarded as 'undue'.[90] Nevertheless, it is accepted that equity identified broadly two forms of unacceptable conduct, which Lord Nicholls described as follows:[91]

The first comprises overt acts of improper pressure or coercion such as unlawful threats . . . The second form arises out of a relationship between two persons where one has acquired over another a measure of influence, or ascendancy, of which the ascendant person then takes unfair advantage . . . In cases of this latter nature the influence one person has over another provides scope for misuse without any specific overt acts of persuasion. The relationship between two individuals may be such that, without more, one of them is disposed to agree a course of action proposed by the other. Typically, this occurs when one person places trust in another to look after his affairs and interests, and the latter betrays this trust by preferring his own interests. He abuses the influence he has acquired.

The first type of case, the direct analogue of common law duress, has been called 'actual' undue influence. The second type of case, where the parties are in a relationship in which duties of care and confidence are imposed on one party towards the other, has been called 'presumed' undue influence.

It is often said that, in the first type of case, evidence of express influence must be adduced by the party seeking to impeach the transaction, whereas, in the second, undue influence is presumed in the absence of evidence to the contrary.[92] While this is true, it can be somewhat misleading, as the burden of proof of undue influence rests upon the person who claims to have been wronged, although once the claimant has shown that the defendant was in a position to exercise undue influence over the other, and that the transaction between the parties calls for explanation, the burden of proof may be discharged unless the defendant adduces sufficient evidence to the contrary.[93]

---

[89] *Hewett v First Plus Financial Group plc*, above, n 87 at [24] (husband's concealment of affair from his wife amounted to exercise of undue influence against her).

[90] *Royal Bank of Scotland plc v Etridge (No 2)*, above, n 2 at [11]; *National Westminster Bank plc v Morgan* [1985] AC 686, 709; *Allcard v Skinner* (1887) 36 Ch D 145, 183.

[91] *Ibid* at [8]–[9]. See also at [103]–[105] (Lord Hobhouse) and [151]–[158] (Lord Scott). But Lord Clyde, at [92] questioned the wisdom of attempting to make classifications of cases of undue influence.

[92] *Allcard v Skinner* (1887) 36 Ch D 145, 181 (Lindley LJ).

[93] *Royal Bank of Scotland plc v Etridge (No 2)*, above, n 2 at [13]–[14]; below, p 389. See *Annulment Funding Co Ltd v Cowey* [2010] EWCA Civ 711, [2010] BPIR 1304 (defendant relied on presumed undue influence, but judge entitled to find actual undue influence on facts).

(b) ACTUAL UNDUE INFLUENCE

Where one party exercised such domination over the mind and will of the other that the latter's independence of decision was substantially undermined, and this domination brought about the transaction, the victim will be entitled to relief on the ground of undue influence:[94]

It is an equitable wrong committed by the dominant party against the other which makes it unconscionable for the dominant party to enforce his legal rights against the other.

There is no need for any special relationship (of the type mentioned below) to exist between the parties, although, of course, it may do so. The mere fact that domination was exercised is sufficient; no abuse of confidence need be proved. In *Smith v Kay*,[95] for example, a young man, only just of age, incurred liabilities to the appellant by the contrivance of an older man who had acquired a strong influence over him, and who professed to assist him in a career of extravagance and dissipation. It was held that influence of this nature, though in no way 'fiduciary', entitled the young man to the protection of the Court. Similarly, in *Morley v Loughnan*[96] executors sued to recover £140,000 paid by the deceased to a member of the 'Exclusive Brethren' in whose house he had lived for some years, and under whose religious influence he had been. Wright J, in giving judgment for the claimants, said that it was unnecessary to decide whether or not any special relationship existed between the deceased and the defendant, for he 'took possession, so to speak, of the whole life of the deceased, and the gifts were not the result of the deceased's own free will, but the effect of that influence and domination'.[97]

Many older cases on this point have concerned spiritual 'advisers' who have used their expert knowledge of the next world to obtain material advantages in this. In more recent times the cases have often concerned men who have put pressure on their wives or partners to secure business debts by mortgaging the family home.[98] While heavy family pressure will not in itself suffice to constitute domination, in one case wounding and insulting language, and demeaning comparisons between what a husband characterized as his wife's disloyalty and his relations' loyalty, amounted to moral blackmail and coercion.[99]

Actual undue influence itself suffices for relief. It is not necessary that the transaction induced by it be not readily explicable or be manifestly disadvantageous to the victim:[100]

Actual undue influence is a species of fraud. Like any other victim of fraud, a person who has been induced by undue influence to carry out a transaction which he did not freely and knowingly enter into is entitled to have that transaction set aside as of right . . . A man guilty of fraud is no more entitled to argue that the transaction was beneficial to the person

---

[94] *Ibid* at [103].   [95] (1859) 7 HLC 750.   [96] [1893] 1 Ch 736.
[97] *Ibid*, 756.   [98] eg *CIBC Mortgages plc v Pitt* [1994] 1 AC 200.
[99] *Bank of Scotland v Bennett* [1997] 1 FLR 801, 822–7, one of the cases on appeal to HL in *Etridge's* case: see [2002] 2 AC 773 at [312]–[315].
[100] *CIBC Mortgages plc v Pitt*, above, n 98, 209 (Lord Browne-Wilkinson).

defrauded than is a man who has procured a transaction by misrepresentation. The effect of the wrongdoer's conduct is to prevent the wronged party from bringing a free will and properly informed mind to bear on the proposed transaction which accordingly must be set aside in equity as a matter of justice.

It has been said, however, that in the nature of things questions of undue influence will not usually arise where the transaction is innocuous.[101]

(c) PRESUMED UNDUE INFLUENCE

Even if it cannot be proved that the claimant's mind was a 'mere channel through which the will of the defendant operated',[102] relief may be given if there existed between the parties some special relationship of confidence which the defendant has abused:

Wherever two persons stand in such a relation that, while it continues, confidence is necessarily reposed by one, and the influence which naturally grows out of that confidence is possessed by the other, and this confidence is abused, or the influence is exerted to obtain an advantage at the expense of the confiding party, the person so availing himself of his position will not be permitted to retain the advantage, although the transaction could not have been impeached if no such confidential relation had existed.[103]

Prior to *Etridge*'s case Slade LJ[104] had divided presumed undue influence into two classes, an approach approved by the House of Lords in *Barclays Bank plc v O'Brien*.[105] The first (class 2A) was where the duties of care and confidence arose as a matter of law by virtue of the relationship between the parties. The second (class 2B) was said to occur where the duties arose in the special circumstances of the parties' association with each other, that is, because on the facts of the particular case the claimant placed trust and confidence in the other party and the transaction between the parties was one calling for an explanation.

    In *Etridge*'s case, however, their Lordships considered that it was only in class 2A cases that there is a true presumption of influence, arising from the law's 'sternly protective attitude towards certain types of relationship'. In such cases the claimant 'need not prove he actually reposed trust and confidence in the other party. It is sufficient for him to prove the existence of the relationship'.[106] However, it is important to notice that even in such cases all that is presumed is the *influence*—that the defendant was in a position to exercise influence over the claimant. It is not automatically presumed that the influence was *undue*—that the defendant abused the relationship—although this may be established on the evidence by the claimant showing that the transaction

---

[101] *Royal Bank of Scotland plc v Etridge (No 2)*, above, n 2 at [12].
[102] *Tufton v Sperni* [1952] 2 TLR 516, 530.
[103] *Tate v Williamson* (1866) LR 2 Ch App 55, 61 (Lord Chelmsford).
[104] *Bank of Credit and Commerce International SA v Aboody* [1990] 1 QB 923, 953.
[105] [1994] 1 AC 180, 189–90.
[106] [2002] 2 AC 773 at [18] (Lord Nicholls). See also *ibid* at [107], [161].

between the parties called for explanation and no explanation is forthcoming from the defendant.[107]

In class 2B cases, however, although described by generations of equity lawyers as cases in which a presumption of undue influence arises, there is no true presumption but only a shift in the evidential onus on a question of fact. The burden of proving undue influence rests on the claimant, but will normally be discharged by proof that he or she placed trust and confidence in the other party and that the transaction between the parties is one which calls for explanation. Proof of those two facts is prima facie evidence that the defendant abused the influence he or she acquired in the relationship, and it is then for the defendant to counter the inference which should otherwise be drawn. Accordingly, a claimant who succeeds does so because he or she has established a case of undue influence.[108] Analytically, the general burden of proof remains on the claimant, but this can be discharged by establishing a sufficient prima facie case. Despite this difference, since there is a shift in the evidential onus and since the requirement that the transaction must be one calling for explanation is relevant in both categories of case, the two different types of presumption are considered in this section. In both there are two components required for the establishment of a situation in which undue influence will be presumed. The first is the nature of the relationship, and the second is the nature of the transaction, which must be one calling for explanation; that is, not be readily explicable by the relationship of the parties, but also, less satisfactorily, sometimes described as one that is 'manifestly disadvantageous' to the victim.

(i) The nature of the relationship

A true presumption that one party acquires influence over another who is vulnerable is made as a matter of law in respect of certain relationships. In other situations, proof that on the particular facts trust and confidence has been reposed by one party in the other is necessary.

(a) True presumption raised as a matter of law.   It is not every fiduciary relationship that as a matter of law raises a presumption of undue influence.[109] It must be one of a limited class which the Courts regard as suggesting undue influence. While it has been stated that the relations which fall into this category cannot be listed exhaustively,[110] they include those between parent (or person *in loco parentis*) and child,[111] solicitor and client,[112] doctor and patient,[113] trustee and beneficiary,[114] and spiritual adviser and any person to whom that person stands in that relationship.[115] It has been held in the past that the relationship of fiancé and fiancée also raises the presumption,[116]

---

[107] *Ibid* at [104].   [108] *Ibid* at [13]–[14].   [109] *Re Coomber* [1911] 1 Ch 723.

[110] *Royal Bank of Scotland plc v Etridge (No 2)* [2002] 2 AC 773 at [10].

[111] *Bainbrigge v Browne* (1881) 18 Ch D 188; *Archer v Hudson* (1844) 7 Beav 551.

[112] *Wright v Carter* [1980] 1 Ch 27.   [113] *Mitchell v Homfray* (1881) 8 QBD 587.

[114] *Beningfield v Baxter* (1886) 12 App Cas 167.

[115] *Huguenin v Baseley* (1807) 14 Ves Jun 273; *Allcard v Skinner* (1887) 36 Ch D 145.

[116] *Re Lloyds Bank Ltd* [1931] 1 Ch 289, 302 (Maugham J: 'In most cases [a young woman engaged to be married] does not interest herself in her future pecuniary position as between herself and her husband.

but a different view is now taken of the relationship between an engaged couple, and the existence of influence is no longer assumed automatically, but will depend on the facts.[117] The relationship of husband and wife is certainly not one to which this presumption applies as a matter of law.[118]

As mentioned earlier, it is important to note that the presumption is that one party has acquired influence over the other, it is not a presumption that the influence has been abused. If all that has happened is that a client has left a small bequest to his family solicitor, no inference of abuse or unfair dealing will arise.[119]

(b) Shift in the evidential onus as a result of the facts of the particular case.   Where, as in the case of husband and wife, the presumption does not apply as a matter of law, one of the parties may nevertheless be able to demonstrate that on the facts of the particular case he or she placed trust and confidence in the other. In such a case, the degree of trust may be such that (provided, as discussed below, that the transaction is one that calls for explanation) the Court can infer, in the absence of a satisfactory explanation, that the transaction can only have been procured by undue influence.[120] In such cases there is a rebuttable evidential presumption of undue influence. In the case of wives, it has been stated that 'this special tenderness of treatment' is attributable to the fact that in many cases a wife is able to demonstrate that she placed trust and confidence in her husband in relation to her financial affairs and because 'the sexual and emotional ties between the parties provide a ready weapon for undue influence: a wife's true wishes can easily be overborne because of her fear of destroying or damaging the wider relationship between her and her husband if she opposes his wishes'.[121] Similar principles apply to all other cases where there is an emotional relationship between unmarried cohabitees.[122] The trust and confidence may arise generally from the nature of the relationship: for example, trust and confidence by the wife in the husband's conduct of the family's financial affairs, but it may also arise, or be intensified, in the course of the impugned transaction itself.[123]

The list of situations in which such a relationship exists on the facts of the particular case is not a closed one. The principle applies to every case where influence is acquired and abused, where confidence is reposed and betrayed.[124] All the circumstances have to be considered to determine whether such a relationship exists,[125] and it is not

---

In general, she reposes the greatest confidence in her future husband; otherwise she would not marry him. In many, if not most, cases she would sign almost anything he put before her').

[117] *Zamet v Hyman* [1961] 1 WLR 1442, 1446. An 'engaged couple' may now be of the same sex: Marriage (Same Sex Couples) Act 2013.

[118] *Barclays Bank plc v O'Brien* [1994] 1 AC 180; *Etridge*, above, n 2 at [19]. Cf *Backhouse v Backhouse* [1978] 1 WLR 243, 251.

[119] *Etridge*, above, n 2 at [104].   [120] *Ibid* at [14].

[121] *Barclays Bank plc v O'Brien*, above, n 118, 190–1, 196 (Lord Browne-Wilkinson).

[122] *Ibid*, 198. See also *Etridge* [2002] 2 AC 773 at [47].

[123] *Turkey v Awadh* [2005] EWCA Civ 382, [2005] 2 P & CR 29 at [9]–[10]; *Thompson v Foy* [2009] EWHC 1076 (Ch), [2010] 1 P & CR 16 at [100]; *Hewett v First Plus Financial Group plc* [2010] EWCA Civ 312, [2010] 2 P & CR 22 at [27]–[30].

[124] *Smith v Kay* (1859) 7 HLC 750, 779 (Lord Kingsdown).

[125] *Lloyds Bank Ltd v Bundy* [1975] QB 326, 342.

necessary to show that it is one of domination. It suffices that the party in whom trust and confidence is reposed is in a position to exercise influence over the party who reposes it. Thus in *Tate v Williamson*:[126]

An undergraduate, T, aged 23 years, was being pressed to pay his college debts, which amounted to some £1,000. Being estranged from his father, he asked his great-uncle to advise him how he should find the means to pay. The great-uncle was unable to advise in person owing to ill health, but he deputed the defendant, his nephew, to do so. Conversations took place between T and the defendant in which T expressed the desire to sell part of his estate, upon which the defendant offered to buy it for £7,000. Before the sale was completed, the defendant obtained a report from a surveyor on the property, and this valued it at £20,000. The defendant did not disclose this fact to T, but proceeded with the purchase. Excessive drinking led to T's death one year later. It was held that the purchase must be set aside. The defendant, having been asked to give advice, stood in a confidential relationship to T, and this prevented him from becoming a purchaser of the property without the fullest communication of all material information which he had obtained as to its value.

Similarly, in *Tufton v Sperni*,[127] the situation was such that a confidential relationship arose:

T and S were fellow members of a committee formed to establish a Moslem cultural centre in London, it being understood that T would provide the funds for the centre. S induced T to buy his (S's) own house for the purpose at a price which grossly exceeded its market value.

The Court of Appeal set the contract aside. The situation was not one which was comprehended by the established categories, nor was there any domination of T by S; yet, as Evershed MR pointed out:[128]

If a number of persons join together for the purpose of furthering some charitable or altruistic objective, it would seem not unreasonable to conclude that in regard to all matters

[126] (1866) LR 2 Ch App 55. See also *Cheese v Thomas* [1994] 1 WLR 129 (great nephew and aged great-uncle); *Grosvenor v Sherratt* (1860) 28 Beav 659 (executor and young woman); *Re Craig* [1971] Ch 95 (secretary-companion and man of 84 years); *Goldsworthy v Brickell*, below, n 128 (85-year-old farmer and farm manager; contrast *Evans v Lloyd* [2013] EWHC 1725 (Ch) at [58] (70-year-old residential ex-farm worker not 'dependent' for purposes of undue influence)); *Lloyds Bank Ltd v Bundy*, above, n 33 (banker and customer) but cf *National Westminster Bank plc v Morgan* [1985] 1 AC 686; *Horry v Tate & Lyle Refineries Ltd* [1982] 2 Lloyd's Rep 416 (employer's insurers and injured employee); *O'Sullivan v Management Agency and Music Ltd* [1985] QB 428 (internationally recognized manager and unknown pop musician); *A-G v R* [2003] UKPC 22, [2003] EMLR 24 at [24] (commanding officer and soldier, in context of military hierarchy and strong regimental pride); *Macklin v Dowsett* [2004] EWCA Civ 904, [2004] 2 EGLR 75 (owners of property and rent-free life tenant who granted option to surrender life tenancy; contrast *Birmingham CC v Beech* [2014] EWCA Civ 830, [2015] 1 P & CR 1 (no relationship of trust and confidence between local authority landlord's agent and elderly tenant who signed notice to quit); *Smith v Cooper* [2010] EWCA Civ 722, [2010] 2 FCR 551 (cohabitees, where man acquired position of ascendancy over the woman because of her mental condition, his awareness of it, and his decision to run her finances). Perhaps the high watermark is *Credit Lyonnais Bank Nederland NV v Burch* [1997] 1 All ER 144 (employer and employee), recognized in *Etridge* [2002] 2 AC 773 at [83], [86], [89] but which is perhaps better regarded (see Chen-Wishart [1997] CLJ 60) as a case of unconscionability, on which see below, p 400.

[127] [1952] 2 TLR 516. See also *Roche v Sherrington* [1982] 1 WLR 599.
[128] *Ibid*, 523. See also *Goldsworthy v Brickell* [1987] 1 Ch 378.

related to that objective, each 'necessarily reposes confidence' in the others and each possesses accordingly that 'influence which naturally grows out of confidence'.

(ii) A transaction which is not readily explicable by the relationship and calls for explanation

In *Goldsworthy v Brickell*, drawing on Lindley LJ's classic nineteenth-century formulation in *Allcard v Skinner*,[129] Nourse LJ stated:

[T]he presumption is not perfected and remains inoperative until the party who has ceded the trust and confidence makes a gift so large, or enters a transaction so improvident, as not to be reasonably accounted for on the ground of friendship, relationship, charity or other ordinary motives on which ordinary men act. Although influence might have been presumed beforehand, it is only then that it is presumed to have been undue.[130]

The reason for this requirement is to prevent the presumption applying to obviously innocuous transactions between those in a relationship of trust and confidence, such as a moderate gift as a Christmas present by a child to a parent, an agreement by a client to pay the reasonable fees to a solicitor, or a moderate bequest to one's doctor.[131]

In *National Westminster Bank plc v Morgan*[132] Lord Scarman stated that the transaction must be 'manifestly disadvantageous' to the influenced person. This formulation has been widely criticized because its primary focus appears to be financial, that is, the adequacy of the consideration given in exchange for the money paid or property transferred. 'Manifest disadvantage' can generally be shown where a person agrees to guarantee the debts of another and is, of course, an inherent feature of gifts, which have been the subject of many cases of undue influence.[133] It would also exist where a charge over a matrimonial home secured not only money borrowed under the proposed transaction but also any other transaction entered into by the debtor. But in the case of a guarantee of the debts of a business it may be more difficult to determine whether the transaction is 'manifestly disadvantageous'. In the sense that the guarantor undertakes a serious financial obligation with no personal financial return it is disadvantageous. But where the guarantor has an interest in the business, as in the case of a shareholder or a wife where the business is the source of the family income, it may not be.[134] Moreover, the formulation does not readily allow non-financial factors to be taken into account. Where the requisite relationship of trust and confidence exists between two persons, the fact that an offer by one to buy land or a valuable oil painting from the other is for the full or even an enhanced market price should not necessarily prevent the transaction being presumed to be vitiated by undue influence. The person subjected to the influence should not be presumed to wish to sell a family home or business, or an item of particular sentimental value, even for the

---

[129] (1887) 36 Ch D 145, 185.
[130] [1987] Ch 378, 401. This requirement does not apply to cases of 'actual' undue influence, above, p 387.
[131] *Royal Bank of Scotland plc v Etridge (No 2)* [2002] 2 AC 773 at [24], [104], [156].
[132] [1985] AC 686.   [133] eg *Allcard v Skinner* (1887) 36 Ch D 145, below, p 395.
[134] *Royal Bank of Scotland plc v Etridge (No 2)*, above, n 2 at [28]–[29].

full market price. A relationship and the influence resulting from it may be abused 'even though the transaction is, on the face of it, one which, in commercial terms, provides reasonably equal benefits for both parties'.[135] In *Etridge*'s case it was accepted that the label 'manifest disadvantage' can give rise to misunderstanding and should be discarded. Lord Nicholls stated that the better approach was to adhere more directly to the classic test which asks whether the transaction can be 'reasonably accounted for on the ground of friendship, relationship, charity or other ordinary motives' as well as whether it is 'improvident'.[136] The core question is whether the nature of the transaction was such as to give rise to an inference that it was obtained by an unfair exploitation of the relationship.[137]

(iii) Rebutting the presumption

Where influence is shown to exist, the presumption of its undue exercise can be rebutted only by proof that the party reposing the confidence has been 'placed in such a position as will enable him to form an entirely free and unfettered judgment, independent altogether of any sort of control'.[138] The most obvious way of establishing this is to show that the party reposing the confidence received independent legal advice and took it. In some (possibly extreme) cases, very cogent evidence has been required to be adduced by the defendant to prove that the significance of the advice was brought home to the other party. In *Powell v Powell*:[139]

A settlement was executed by a young woman, under the influence of her stepmother, by which she shared her property with the children of the stepmother's second marriage. She received some independent advice from a solicitor, but he was acting for some of the other parties to the settlement as well as for the claimant. It appeared that, although he had expressed disapproval of the transaction, he had not carried his disapproval to the point of withdrawing his services.

It was held that the settlement should be rescinded. And in *Huguenin v Baseley*, where a woman made over her property to a clergyman in whom she reposed confidence, Lord Eldon said:[140]

The question is, not, whether she knew what she was doing, had done, or proposed to do, but how the intention was produced: whether all that care and providence was placed round her,

---

[135] *National Westminster Bank plc v Morgan* [1983] 3 All ER 85, 92 (Slade LJ). Although the House of Lords disagreed ([1985] AC 686, 704), see *Barclays Bank plc v Coleman* [2001] QB 20, 31 (Nourse LJ).

[136] [2002] 2 AC 773 at [28]–[29]. See also *ibid* at [104], [156].

[137] *A-G v R* [2003] UKPC 22, [2003] EMLR 24 at [24] (lifelong confidentiality agreement signed by serving member of SAS was one which anyone who wished to serve could reasonably have been required to sign); *Turkey v Awadh* [2005] EWCA Civ 382, [2005] 2 P & CR 29 at [22]–[23].

[138] *Archer v Hudson* (1844) 7 Beav 551, 560 (Lord Langdale MR). See also *Zamet v Hyman* [1961] 1 WLR 1442, 1446; *Re Craig* [1971] Ch 95, 105; *Goldsworthy v Brickell* [1987] 1 Ch 378, 408–9; *Smith v Cooper* [2010] EWCA Civ 722, [2010] 2 FCR 551 at [71] (trial judge failed to consider whether presumption rebutted).

[139] [1900] 1 Ch 243.

[140] (1807) 14 Ves Jun 273, 300. See also *Credit Lyonnais Bank Nederland NV v Burch* [1997] 1 All ER 144, 155–6 (Millett LJ: independent advice 'is neither always necessary nor always sufficient. It is not a panacea').

as against those, who advised her, which, from their situation and relation with respect to her, they were bound to exert on her behalf.

But this is not the only way of rebutting the presumption. The essential thing is to show that the transaction was 'the result of the free exercise of independent will'.[141] If this is established, the transaction will be upheld despite the absence of independent advice.[142] On the other hand, such advice will not necessarily rebut the presumption. There must be a full appreciation of the facts. In *Tate v Williamson*, for example, the young man, T, was referred to independent solicitors, but such fair dealing in other respects was, said Lord Chelmsford, 'of no consequence, when once it is established that there was a concealment of a material fact, which the defendant was bound to disclose'.[143]

(d) RESCISSION

The right to rescind contracts and to revoke gifts made under undue influence is similar to the right to rescind contracts induced by misrepresentation. The conditions for and bars to rescission considered in Chapter 9 above in principle apply here.[144]

(i) The need for restitution

If the transaction is to be set aside, the parties must be restored to their original positions.[145] Each must give back what has been received, although here too the flexibility of equity means that the impossibility of restoring the parties precisely to their original position will not bar the remedy.[146] The Court will grant relief whenever, by directing accounts and making allowances, it can do what is practically just. Moreover, since it is restitution that has to be made, not damages paid,[147] when reversing a transaction under which both parties had made a financial contribution to the acquisition of an asset from which they were both to benefit but the value of which has fallen, if the conduct of the party presumed to have exercised influence was not morally reprehensible, the Court may order the loss in the value of the asset to be borne by the parties in proportion to their contributions to the purchase price.[148] However, the rescission of a property transaction entered into between cohabiting parties in the course of their relationship requires a focus on that transaction, and that the transaction be reversed, in effect and in substance, not that the parties be put

---

[141] *Inche Noriah v Shaik Allie Bin Omar* [1929] AC 127, 135.

[142] *Re Brocklehurst* [1978] Ch 14; *A-G v R* [2003] UKPC 22, [2003] EMLR 24.

[143] (1866) LR 2 Ch App 55, 65.

[144] There is, however, no statutory discretion to refuse rescission for undue influence and award damages in lieu; cf Misrepresentation Act 1967, s 2(2), above, p 339. Delay may be evidence of affirmation or acquiescence (below, p 395) but is not generally recognized as an independent bar to rescission.

[145] *Dunbar Bank plc v Nadeem* [1998] 3 All ER 876 (party setting aside transaction required to restore beneficial interest in lease).

[146] *Cheese v Thomas* [1994] 1 WLR 129. See above, pp 338–9.

[147] *Ibid*, 135 (Nicholls V-C).   [148] *Ibid*. See Chen-Wishart (1994) 110 LQR 173.

back into the position as if they had never had a relationship, nor that all the parties' financial contributions during the course of their relationship be taken into account.[149]

Another example of equity's flexibility where complete restitution is impossible is provided by *O'Sullivan v Management Agency and Music Ltd*.[150] In that case a management agreement between an inexperienced pop musician and an internationally known firm of managers, presumed to have been entered as a result of undue influence, was set aside although the parties could not be restored to their original position, inter alia, because the musician had since achieved considerable fame. The managers were ordered to account for the profit they had made from the agreement, but were also held to be entitled to reasonable remuneration for their skill and work in promoting the musician and making a significant contribution to his success. Where taking an account of profits will not do justice, the defendant may be ordered to pay equitable compensation to the claimant.[151]

(ii) Severance

A finding of undue influence normally vitiates effective consent, so that it will rarely be possible to sever the objectionable parts of the transaction leaving the parts uncontaminated by undue influence enforceable. But, where a person's consent can be regarded as having been freely given in relation to part of the transaction and it is possible to sever that part without rewriting the contract, this will be possible.[152]

(iii) Affirmation of transaction

The right to rescind may be lost by affirmation, and so as soon as the undue influence is withdrawn, the action or inaction of the party influenced may constitute evidence that he or she intended to affirm the transaction. Thus in *Mitchell v Homfray*[153] a jury found as a fact that a patient who had made a gift to her physician determined to abide by her gift after the confidential relationship of physician and patient ceased, and the Court of Appeal held that the gift could not be impeached. Also in *Allcard v Skinner*:[154]

A was introduced by her spiritual adviser and confessor to S who was the lady superior of a Protestant community called 'The Sisters of the Poor'. A subsequently became a professed member of the community and bound herself to observe rules of poverty, chastity, and

---

[149] *Smith v Cooper*. above, n 138 at [101]. See also at [110] (Lloyd LJ): 'On the basis of a finding of undue influence, and consequently of setting aside the transactions, it is not appropriate to ask whether the ultimate result corresponds with the parties' intentions. It is relevant to consider whether the result does practical justice between the parties, in the light of the principles enunciated in *Cheese v Thomas*'; cf the valuation of cohabiting parties' interests in the family home under a 'common intention' constructive trust, which does take into account the 'whole course of dealings' between the parties in relation to the property: *Jones v Kernott* [2011] UKSC 53, [2012] 1 AC 776.

[150] [1985] QB 428.   [151] *Mahoney v Purnell* [1996] 3 All ER 61. See Heydon (1997) 113 LQR 8.

[152] *Barclays Bank plc v Caplan* [1998] 1 FLR 532. Cf *Allied Irish Bank plc v Byrne* [1995] 2 FLR 325 and the position concerning rescission for misrepresentation, above, p 333. Cf also *Yorkshire Bank plc v Tinsley* [2004] EWCA Civ 816, [2004] 1 WLR 2380 (undue influence rendering mortgage voidable also extends to replacement mortgage).

[153] (1881) 8 QBD 587.   [154] (1887) 36 Ch D 145.

obedience. The rule of poverty bound her to relinquish all earthly possessions, and the rule of obedience not to seek the advice of anyone outside the community without permission. In 1872 she came into possession of certain stocks, which she transferred to S as superior of the community; she also made a will in S's favour. In 1879, she left the sisterhood. She immediately revoked the will, but took no steps to retrieve the property which she had conveyed to S until some 6 years had elapsed.

It was held that, by her inactivity after she had been freed from the spiritual influence of S, she had acquiesced in the gift, and her claim was barred by this acquiescence.[155]

Affirmation will not bar the right to rescind unless there is an entire cessation of the undue influence which had brought about the contract or gift. The necessity for such a complete relief of the will of the injured party from the dominant influence was stated in *Moxon v Payne*:[156]

Frauds or impositions of the kind practised in this case cannot be condoned; the right to property acquired by such means cannot be confirmed in this Court unless there be full knowledge of all the facts, full knowledge of the equitable rights arising out of those facts, and an absolute release from the undue influence by means of which the frauds were practised.

The same principle is applied where someone parts with a valuable interest under pressure of poverty and without proper advice: an 'unconscionable bargain'.[157] Acquiescence is not presumed from delay alone; on the contrary, 'it has always been presumed, that the same distress, which pressed him to enter into the contract, prevented him from coming to set it aside'.[158]

(iv) Rights of third parties

As transactions affected by undue influence are voidable, not void, third parties who acquire some interest in the subject-matter of the contract in good faith without notice and for value cannot be displaced by the person seeking rescission.[159] 'Notice' in this context includes imputed and constructive notice.[160] A transaction into which a person has been induced to enter by the exercise of undue influence may therefore be set aside, not only as against the person exercising the influence, but also as against a third party having notice of the fact that the compulsion or influence was used. Money or property transferred can be recovered from such a

---

[155] See also *Nicholl v Ryder* [2000] EMLR 632 (acquiescence based on solicitor's knowledge which was imputed to defendant).

[156] (1873) LR 8 Ch App 881, 885 (James LJ). See also *Re Pauling's Settlement Trusts* [1964] Ch 303; *Goldsworthy v Brickell* [1987] 1 Ch 378, 410 (uncertainty whether knowledge of the right to rescind is needed; cf above, p 336 (affirmation of right to rescind for misrepresentation); below, p 536 (affirmation of right to terminate for breach)).

[157] Below, p 400.   [158] *Fry v Lane* (1888) 40 Ch D 312, 324 (Kay J).

[159] *Bainbrigge v Browne* (1881) 18 Ch D 188.

[160] *Ibid*, 197 (Fry J: 'notice of the circumstances from which the Court infers the equity [ie, the right to rescind for undue influence]').

person, and from a person who, even though ignorant of the undue influence, has furnished no consideration: 'Let the hand receiving it be ever so chaste, yet, if it comes through a polluted channel, the obligation of restitution will follow it.'[161]

(e) UNDUE INFLUENCE BY A THIRD PARTY TO THE CONTRACT

The principles which we have discussed so far in this chapter cover the situation where undue influence is exercised over the claimant by the other contracting party. In such cases it is clearly right that the influenced party should have the right to rescind the contract against the party who was responsible for the influence. If, however, it was a third party, rather than the other contracting party, who exercised the influence it is less clear that the contracting party should have a right to rescind. The interference with his freedom to decide, free of undue pressure or influence, whether to enter into the contract, is identical in both situations. However, where the source of the influence is a third party, the other contracting party does not deserve to have his security of contract undermined, unless he is in some way affected by the third party's misconduct. However, if the party who has been unduly influenced by a third party cannot rescind the contract, he will be left to his remedy against the third party personally, such as if the third party's conduct constitutes a tort.

If the third party is acting as the other contracting party's agent, no question arises: the influence of the agent is attributed to the principal.[162] In other circumstances in which a third party might exercise undue influence, the third party will generally have something to gain from the contract being concluded. In recent years, largely as a result of the change in the nature of ownership of the family home,[163] many such cases have involved one co-owner of the property (typically, the husband) putting pressure on the other (typically, the wife) to enter into a contract with a bank to guarantee a business loan. Such cases are not limited to married couples,[164] and are not simply a recent phenomenon.[165] But there has been a very significant rise in cases involving guarantees relating to the family home where there were claims that one partner had unduly influenced the other to give the guarantee,[166] and we have already seen that

---

[161] *Bridgeman v Green* (1757) Wilmot 58, 65 (Wilmot J).

[162] *Barclays Bank Plc v O'Brien* [1994] 1 AC 180, 191.

[163] *Royal Bank of Scotland plc v Etridge (No 2)* [2002] 2 AC 773 at [34].

[164] Guarantors in other relationships include employees (*Credit Lyonnais Bank Nederland NV v Burch* [1997] 1 All ER 144) and friends (*Banco Exterior Internacionale SA v Thomas* [1997] 1 WLR 221).

[165] See, eg, *Lancashire Loans Ltd v Black* [1934] 1 KB 380 (mother influencing daughter to sign promissory note and execute charge over property in favour of moneylender).

[166] See, eg, *Barclay's Bank plc v O'Brien* [1994] 1 AC 180 185–6 (Lord Browne-Wilkinson: there had been eleven reported cases in CA in the last eight years); *Royal Bank of Scotland plc v Etridge (No 2)* [2002] 2 AC 773 (HL heard appeals in eight separate cases). There have been many further similar cases since *Etridge*'s case. Where the guarantee is voidable, a replacement guarantee will also be voidable, at least if it is taken out as a condition of discharging the earlier guarantee: *Yorkshire Bank plc v Tinsley* [2004] EWCA Civ 816, [2004] 1 WLR 2380 at [19].

the law takes notice of the need to protect the weaker party within married or other emotional relationships.[167]

(i) Actual and constructive notice

In *Royal Bank of Scotland plc v Etridge (No 2)* the House of Lords gave guidance on how to deal with cases involving third parties. Lord Nicholls[168] drew a distinction between the 'traditional view of equity', under which a party who is subjected to undue influence or other misconduct by a third party will be relieved of the bargain only if the other party *knew* of the third party's conduct; and the new principle, introduced by the House of Lords in *Barclays Bank plc v O'Brien*,[169] under which, in certain circumstances, a party to a contract may lose the benefit of it if he *ought to have known* that the other's concurrence had been procured by the misconduct of a third party. That is, in an 'O'Brien' case—a bank guarantee where the relationship between the surety (guarantor) and the debtor is non-commercial[170]—constructive notice of the third party's influence is sufficient; in other cases, actual notice is required. This distinction does not however appear to be sound, because although there are cases, some of which were referred to by Lord Nicholls, where the Courts appear to have required 'knowledge' of a third party's wrong,[171] it is not clear that the Courts in using such language had intended to limit such 'knowledge' to actual knowledge of the third party's conduct.[172] It is submitted that the better view is that a party to a contract can avoid a contract for undue influence exercised by a third party if the other contracting party knew or ought to have known that he was entering into the contract under that influence.

(ii) Surety cases: putting the lender 'on inquiry'

The House of Lords in *Barclays Bank plc v O'Brien*[173] and *Royal Bank of Scotland plc v Etridge (No 2)*[174] defined both the circumstances in which a lender, taking a guarantee, is to be taken to have constructive notice of the risk that the surety is acting under undue influence from the debtor, and the steps that the lender should take in order to minimize the risk of having the contract set aside.

The lender will have constructive notice where it knows of facts which 'put it on inquiry' that there is a risk of undue influence,[175] but the lender is put on inquiry by a

---

[167] Above, p 390. For a sociological analysis of the law and practice relating to surety wives and partners, see Fehlberg, *Sexually Transmitted Debt* (1997).

[168] [2002] 2 AC 773 at [40]–[41].   [169] Above, n 166.

[170] *Royal Bank of Scotland plc v Etridge (No 2)*, above, n 2 at [87].

[171] *Cobbett v Brock* (1855) 20 Beav 524, 528 (fraud and undue influence); *Kempson v Ashbee* (1874) LR 10 Ch App 15, 21. See also *Talbot v Von Boris* [1911] 1 KB 854, 863 (duress); *Lynde v Anglo-Italian Hemp Spinning Co* [1896] 1 Ch 178, 183 (misrepresentation).

[172] Cf *Bainbrigge v Browne* (1881) 18 Ch D 188, 197 (which was also cited by Lord Nicholls in *Etridge*'s case). See also *Lancashire Loans Ltd v Black* [1934] 1 KB 380, 416–7 (which is, however, in substance an 'O'Brien' case, although it pre-dates O'Brien's case by 60 years).

[173] Above, n 166.   [174] Above, n 166.

[175] The burden of proof lies on the party claiming to have been subjected to undue influence by the third party: *Barclays Bank plc v Boulter* [1999] 1 WLR 1919, 1925.

combination of two factors: first, that the relationship between the third-party debtor and the surety is non-commercial; and, secondly, that the transaction is on its face not to the financial advantage of the wife, as where she guarantees the husband's business debts,[176] but not where there was nothing to indicate to the lender that the transaction was anything other than a normal advance of funds to the husband and wife for their joint benefit.[177] In the case of a family company where the wife who is a guarantor has an interest in the business, the lender will be put on notice where the security given is out of all proportion to the interest in the company.[178]

(iii) Surety cases: steps the lender should take

If the guarantor (in our scenario the wife) shows that the lender was put on inquiry of the risk of undue influence, the burden is then upon the lender to show that it took reasonable steps to satisfy itself that her consent was properly obtained. Normally it will be able to do so by warning the person entering the transaction, in our example the wife, at a meeting not attended by the principal debtor, of the amount of the existing indebtedness and of the proposed new loan, of the potential liability and of the risks involved, and advising her to take independent legal advice.[179] The lender will not, however, have to take these steps where it has a reasonable belief that legal advice has been given to the guarantor by a lawyer acting for her who has knowledge of the amount of the existing indebtedness and of the proposed new loan. If so, the lender is entitled to assume that the legal adviser has carried out its professional duty to advise the guarantor.[180] Provided the legal adviser is acting for the wife, this will be so even where the adviser is also the debtor's lawyer, where the legal adviser has agreed to act as the lender's agent on completion, or where the lender instructed the legal adviser to explain the transaction to the guarantor and to confirm that she appeared to understand it.[181] Unless the legal adviser is acting for the lender, the lender is not fixed with constructive notice of what the legal adviser learns in the course of advising the guarantor since such knowledge is not acquired in the adviser's capacity as the lender's lawyer.[182] Where the lender is put on inquiry, it has no duty to ask about the guarantor's motives.

---

[176] *Royal Bank of Scotland plc v Etridge (No 2)*, above, n 2 at [44], [46], [109]–[113], [163]–[165]. See also *Barclays Bank plc v O'Brien*, above, n 118, 196.

[177] *CIBC Mortgages plc v Pitt* [1994] 1 AC 200, 211 (advance to enable parties to purchase shares); *Chater v Mortgage Agency Services Number Two Ltd* [2003] EWCA Civ 490, [2004] 1 P & CR 4 (application for loan by mother and son living in same house, to be secured on house owned by the mother, appeared 'perfectly ordinary', and bank did not know that the money was for son's business).

[178] *Bank of Scotland v Bennett* [1997] 1 FLR 801 (one of the cases on appeal to HL in *Royal Bank of Scotland plc v Etridge (No 2)* [2002] 2 AC 773, where it was decided on a different ground); *Credit Lyonnais Bank Nederland NV v Burch* [1997] 1 All ER 144. Cf *Britannia Building Society v Pugh* [1997] 2 FLR 7.

[179] *Barclays Bank plc v O'Brien*, above, n 118, 196. See also *Credit Lyonnais Bank Nederland NV v Burch*, above, n 178.

[180] *Royal Bank of Scotland plc v Etridge (No 2)*, above, n 2 at [56] [114], [171].

[181] *Ibid* at [69]–[74], [115], [173]–[174]. See also *Banco Exterior Internacional SA v Thomas* [1997] 1 WLR 221; *Kapoor v National Westminster Bank* [2010] EWHC 2986 (Ch).

[182] *Royal Bank of Scotland plc v Etridge (No 2)*, above, n 2 at [77], [115], [180]. See also *Halifax Mortgage Services Ltd v Stepsky* [1996] Ch 207; *National Westminster Bank plc v Beaton* (1997) 30 HLR 99.

(iv) Application of the O'Brien and Etridge principles to other vitiating factors

The principles discussed in *Barclays Bank plc v O'Brien* and *Royal Bank of Scotland plc v Etridge (No 2)* in relation to third-party wrongdoing are not limited to claims of undue influence, but also apply to other forms of conduct which render a contract voidable. Many of the cases involving undue influence, including *O'Brien*'s case itself, have also involved misrepresentations, and so it is clear that these decisions of the House of Lords constitute direct authority for the avoidance of a contract as a result of a third-party misrepresentation of which the other contracting party knows or ought to know.[183] In an '*O'Brien* case'—a non-commercial bank guarantee—this will extend to the lender being put on inquiry about the risk of misrepresentation. The discussion in *Etridge*'s case is also sufficiently wide to cover duress, and in principle a party to a contract who is subjected to duress by a third party can avoid the contract if, but only if, the other party knows or ought to know of it.[184]

4. UNCONSCIONABLE BARGAINS

There is another class of cases in which equity also throws the burden of justifying the fairness of a bargain on the party who claims the benefit of it. Lord Selborne describes these cases in *Earl of Aylesford v Morris*[185] as cases:

which, according to the language of Lord Hardwicke,[186] raise, 'from the circumstances or conditions of the parties contracting—weakness on one side, usury on the other, or extortion, or advantage taken of that weakness'—a presumption of fraud. Fraud does not here mean deceit or circumvention, it means an unconscientious use of the power arising out of these circumstances and conditions; and when the relative position of the parties is such as *prima facie* to raise this presumption, the transaction cannot stand unless the person claiming the benefit of it is able to repel the presumption by contrary evidence, proving it to have been in point of fact fair, just, and reasonable.

Thus although equity will not normally intervene to protect a contracting party against the consequences of his or her own folly, some protection is offered to poor and ignorant persons who are overreached in the absence of independent advice. This ground of relief differs from undue influence in that it is concerned with 'the nature and circumstances of the bargain' whereas undue influence is concerned 'with the

---

[183] *Annulment Funding Co Ltd v Cowey* [2010] EWCA Civ 711, [2010] BPIR 1304 at [64].

[184] eg *Royal Bank of Scotland plc v Etridge (No 2)*, above, n 2 at [40] (Lord Nicholls: 'misconduct of a third party'). For an example, see *Talbot v Von Boris* [1911] 1 KB 854. Cf Consumer Protection from Unfair Trading Regulations 2008, above, pp 355 (misrepresentation), 403 (duress and undue influence), reg 27A(4)(b) (consumer has right to redress not only where trader engages in prohibited practice but also where trader is aware of, or could reasonably be expected to be aware of, prohibited practice by producer of the product).

[185] (1873) LR 8 Ch App 484, 490. See also *Hart v O'Connor* [1985] AC 1000, 1024.

[186] *Earl of Chesterfield v Janssen* (1751) 2 Ves Sen 125, 157.

prior relationship between the parties and with whether that was the motivation or reason for which the bargain was entered into'.[187]

A particular case of the application of this principle was the protection given by equity to 'expectant heirs', that is, to those persons who have expectations (in the popular sense) of succeeding to property on the death of another.[188] But this is just one illustration, and the principle also applies generally to what have been called 'catching bargains', that is to say, whenever the parties 'meet under such circumstances as, in the particular transaction, to give the stronger party dominion over the weaker'.[189]

In ordinary cases each party to a bargain must take care of his own interest, and it will not be presumed that undue advantage or contrivance has been resorted to on either side; but in the case of the 'expectant heir', or of persons under pressure without adequate protection, and in the case of dealings with uneducated ignorant persons, the burden of shewing the fairness of the transaction is thrown on the person who seeks to obtain the benefit of the contract.[190]

Thus in *Fry v Lane*[191] it was held that when a purchase had been made from a poor and ignorant man at a considerable undervalue, the vendor having had no independent advice, equity would set aside the transaction. At common law, the nearest analogue is to be found in the cases on salvage, in which a refusal to rescue a vessel in distress or those on board save on extortionate terms has led to the resulting contract being set aside.[192]

The cases suggest that three elements are necessary if the Court is to intervene.[193] First, one party must be at a serious disadvantage to the other through, for example poverty, ignorance, or lack of advice. Secondly, this weakness must be exploited by the other party in some morally culpable manner; and thirdly, the resulting transaction must be, not merely harsh or improvident, but overreaching and oppressive. The last requirement means that, in the case of a sale by the disadvantaged party, the sale must not merely be at an undervalue, but at a *substantial* undervalue which 'shocks the conscience of the court'.[194] And the second requirement means that a gross disparity in the price does not alone suffice, however serious the disadvantage of the weaker party. In *Hart v O'Connor*[195] it was held by the Judicial Committee

---

[187] *Irvani v Irvani* [2000] 1 Lloyd's Rep 412, 424 (Buxton LJ).

[188] By the Law of Property Act 1925, s 174, a bargain with an expectant heir, made in good faith, and without unfair dealing, is not to be set aside merely on the ground of undervalue. But the jurisdiction of the Court to set aside or modify unconscionable bargains is not affected.

[189] *Earl of Aylesford v Morris* (1873) LR 8 Ch App 484, 491 (Lord Selborne LC).

[190] *O'Rorke v Bolingbroke* (1877) 2 App Cas 814, 823 (Lord Hatherley).

[191] (1888) 40 Ch D 312. See also *Cresswell v Potter* [1978] 1 WLR 255n; *Boustany v Piggott* (1993) 69 P & CR 298.

[192] *The Port Caledonia* [1903] P 184 ('£1,000 or no rope'). See also *The Rialto* [1891] P 175 (agreement to pay £6,000 when proper sum was £3,000).

[193] *Alec Lobb (Garages) Ltd v Total Oil (Great Britain) Ltd* [1983] 1 WLR 87, 94–5 (Peter Millett QC). This aspect of his judgment was not varied by the Court of Appeal: see [1985] 1 WLR 173, 182–3.

[194] *Alec Lobb (Garages) Ltd v Total Oil (Great Britain) Ltd* [1983] 1 WLR 87, 95.

[195] [1985] AC 1000, 1018 (there must be 'unconscionable dealing').

of the Privy Council that a contract made with a person who, although apparently of full capacity, was mentally disordered, could not be set aside as unconscionable unless the other party was aware of the mental disorder at the time the contract was made.[196] More recently, in *Portman Building Society v Dusangh*[197] the Court of Appeal held that a mortgage entered into by the 72-year-old defendant, who had a low income, was illiterate, and whose understanding of spoken English was poor, where the purpose of the mortgage was to raise money to assist the defendant's son in a business, could not be set aside because 'the building society did not act in a morally reprehensible manner. The transaction, although improvident, was not "overreaching and oppressive". In short, the conscience of the court is not shocked'.[198] So, for relief to be granted, both procedural and substantive unconscionability must be shown.

Although there have been expressions of support for a wider role for this doctrine,[199] particularly by giving a broad meaning to the elements of the doctrine,[200] there has been no fundamental change. The fact that procedural unconscionability must be present means that there will often be an overlap with the doctrines of duress and undue influence, and some cases which would perhaps have been best regarded as cases of unconscionability have been treated as cases of duress or undue influence.[201] This is in contrast to the position in other common law jurisdictions, particularly Australia and the USA, where a general doctrine of unconscionability has been developed.[202]

---

[196] *Fineland Investments Ltd v Pritchard* [2011] EWHC 113 (Ch) at [77] (the law of unconscionable bargain requires the knowing taking advantage by one party of another).

[197] [2000] 2 All ER (Comm) 221.

[198] *Ibid*, 229 (Simon Brown LJ). The son did not exert undue influence over the father, and therefore the principles set out in *Royal Bank of Scotland plc v Etridge (No 2)* [2002] 2 AC 773, above, p 398, did not apply. See also *Fineland Investments Ltd v Pritchard*, above, n 196 (no unconscionable bargain because no unfair treatment); *Minder Music Ltd v Sharples* [2015] EWHC 1454 (IPEC) (settlement agreement not imposed in morally reprehensible manner).

[199] See, eg, *A Schroeder Music Publishing Ltd v Macaulay* [1974] 1 WLR 1308, 1315 (Lord Diplock); *Alec Lobb (Garages) Ltd v Total Oil (Great Britain) Ltd* [1985] 1 WLR 173; Waddams (1976) 39 MLR 369; Bamforth [1995] LMCLQ 538; and for criticism, Trebilcock (1976) 26 U of Tor LJ 359.

[200] *Cresswell v Potter* [1978] 1 WLR 255n, 257 (Megarry J: 'the euphemisms of the 20th century may require the word "poor" to be replaced by "a member of the lower income group" or the like, and the word "ignorant" by "less highly educated"'); *Backhouse v Backhouse* [1978] 1 WLR 243; *Watkin v Watson-Smith*, The Times, 3 July 1986 (elderly man, incapacitated in judgement and desirous of a quick sale). Cf, however, *Portman Building Society v Dusangh*, above.

[201] *Credit Lyonnais Bank Nederland NV v Burch* [1997] 1 All ER 144 (undue influence, but see Chen-Wishart [1997] CLJ 60); *CTN Cash and Carry Ltd v Gallaher Ltd* [1994] 4 All ER 714, 720 (Sir Donald Nicholls V-C) (and see Carter and Tolhurst [1996] 9 JCL 220).

[202] *Commercial Bank of Australia Ltd v Amadio* (1983) 151 CLR 447; *Louth v Diprose* (1992) 175 CLR 621; *Garcia v National Australia Bank Ltd* (1998) 194 CLR 395 (Australia); Uniform Commercial Code section 2–302 (USA); *Paris v Machnik* (1972) 32 DLR (3d) 723 (Canada); Capper (2010) 126 LQR 403. For the approach in continental European jurisdictions to avoidance of the contract on the basis of one party's taking advantage of the other's weakness or necessity, see Lando and Beale, *Principles of European Contract Law Parts I and II* (2000) 261–5.

An unconscionable bargain is not void but, as in the case of undue influence, voidable by the weaker party for whose protection equity intervenes. The bars to rescission discussed above in relation to undue influence[203] apply equally here.

5. CONSUMERS' RIGHTS TO REDRESS UNDER THE CONSUMER PROTECTION FROM UNFAIR TRADING REGULATIONS 2008

We saw in Chapter 9[204] that Part 4A of the Consumer Protection from Unfair Trading Regulations 2008[205] provides remedies ('rights to redress') for a consumer who enters into a contract with a trader, either for the sale or supply by the trader to the consumer of a 'product' (widely defined and including goods, services and digital content),[206] or for the sale of goods by the consumer to the trader, and the trader engages in a 'prohibited practice' (a misleading action or an aggressive commercial practice)[207] in relation to the product,[208] and the prohibited practice is a significant factor in the consumer's decision to enter into the contract. Conduct which constitutes duress or undue influence, or which gives rise to an application of the equitable rules governing unconscionable bargains, may constitute an 'aggressive commercial practice', defined as a commercial practice which, taking account of all of its features and circumstances, (a) significantly impairs or is likely significantly to impair the average consumer's freedom of choice or conduct in relation to the product concerned through the use of harassment, coercion or undue influence; and (b) thereby causes or is likely to cause him to take a transactional decision he would not have taken otherwise.[209] 'Coercion' includes the use of physical force,[210] and 'undue influence' is defined as exploiting a position of power in relation to the consumer so as to apply pressure, even without using or threatening to use physical force, in a way which significantly limits the consumer's ability to make an informed decision.[211] In determining whether a commercial practice uses harassment, coercion, or undue influence, account is to be taken of such things as the use of threatening or abusive language or behaviour, any threat to take any action which cannot legally be taken,[212] and the exploitation by the trader of any specific misfortune or circumstance of such

---

[203] Above, pp 394–7.   [204] Above, pp 355–8.

[205] SI 2008 No 1277, inserted by Consumer Protection (Amendment) Regulations 2014, SI 2014 No 870, as regards contracts entered into on or after 1 October 2014.

[206] Consumer Protection from Unfair Trading Regulations 2008, as amended, reg 2(1). Immoveable property is within the definition of 'product', but for the purposes of the rights to redress under Part 4A, this includes only certain residential leases: s 27C.

[207] 2008 Regulations, reg 27B.

[208] Or, in the case of a contract for goods or digital content, the *producer* engages in such a practice of which the trader is aware or could reasonably be expected to be aware: 2008 Regulations, reg 27A(4)(b). The 'producer' is the manufacture, the importer into the European Economic Area or an 'own-brander' of the goods or digital content: 2008 Regulations, reg 27A(5).

[209] 2008 Regulations, reg 7(1).   [210] 2008 Regulations, reg 7(3)(a).

[211] 2008 Regulations, reg 7(3)(b).   [212] 2008 Regulations, reg 7(2)(b), (e).

gravity as to impair the consumer's judgment, of which the trader is aware, to influence the consumer's decision with regard to the product.[213]

The consumer's rights to redress are the right to unwind in respect of the contract or, in certain circumstances, the right to a discount or the right to damages.[214] These have been explained above.[215] They constitute additional remedies for consumers who have choice between claims under the Regulations and under the general law in respect of conduct constituting duress, undue influence or under the equitable rules governing an unconscionable bargain, including concurrent claims as long as the consumer does not obtain double compensation.[216]

6. INEQUALITY OF BARGAINING POWER?

The intervention of common law and equity in all these cases of coercion, undue influence, and unconscionable bargains, and also in certain other cases such as unfair salvage agreements,[217] has been stated by Lord Denning MR[218] to be grounded upon the same general principle: that of 'inequality of bargaining power'. In *Lloyds Bank Ltd v Bundy*:[219]

B, an elderly farmer, and his only son, had been customers of the bank for many years. The son founded a company which banked at the same bank. In 1966, B guaranteed the company's overdraft for £1,500 and charged his farm to the bank to secure that sum. Subsequently the overdraft was increased and the bank sought further security. In May 1969, B, having taken legal advice, signed a further guarantee in favour of the bank for £5,000 and a further charge for £6,000. In December 1969, the bank manager visited B and indicated to him that continuance of the company's overdraft facility was dependent upon B executing in favour of the bank a further guarantee for £11,000 and a further charge for £3,500. The bank manager did not advise B to seek independent advice, and B signed the required guarantee and charge without such advice.

The Court of Appeal held that this last guarantee and charge should be set aside for undue influence, since a special relationship of confidence existed between B and the bank in the particular circumstances of the case. But Lord Denning MR also considered that the guarantee and charge were voidable on the larger ground of inequality of bargaining power:[220]

There are cases in our books in which the courts will set aside a contract, or a transfer of property, where the parties have not met on equal terms—when the one is so strong in

---

[213] 2008 Regulations, reg 7(2)(c).   [214] 2008 Regulations, reg 27A.   [215] Above, p 356.
[216] 2008 Regulations, reg 27L. Cf above, p 357 (claim under Misrepresentation Act 1967, s 2 for damages for *misrepresentation* disapplied where the consumer has a right to redress; in the case of duress, there is a free choice between the remedies under the general common law and under the Regulations).
[217] Above, p 401.   [218] *Lloyds Bank Ltd v Bundy* [1975] QB 326, 339.   [219] *Ibid.*
[220] *Ibid*, 336–7. See also *Clifford Davis Management Ltd v WEA Records Ltd* [1975] 1 WLR 61, 64–5; *Arrale v Costain Civil Engineering Ltd* [1976] 1 Lloyd's Rep 98, 102; *Backhouse v Backhouse* [1978] 1 WLR 243, 252. Cf *Alec Lobb (Garages) Ltd v Total Oil Great Britain Ltd* [1985] 1 WLR 173, 181–3, 188–9.

bargaining power and the other so weak—that, as a matter of common fairness, it is not right that the strong should be allowed to push the weak to the wall.

His Lordship nevertheless pointed out that no bargain should be upset which was the result of the ordinary interplay of economic forces, but only 'where there has been inequality of bargaining power, such as to merit the intervention of the court'. He went on to state his principle in the following terms:[221]

English law gives relief to one who, without independent advice, enters into a contract upon terms which are very unfair or transfers property for a consideration which is grossly inadequate, when his bargaining power is grievously impaired by reason of his own needs or desires, or by his own ignorance or infirmity, coupled with undue influences or pressures brought to bear on him by or for the benefit of the other.

When stated in these terms as a detailed test, however, such a general principle goes too far.[222] It appears to require both substantive unfairness ('terms which are very unfair') and procedural unfairness ('undue influences or pressures'), whereas we have seen that duress and actual undue influence require only procedural impropriety;[223] and the role of substantive unfairness in 'presumed' undue influence is to throw onto the stronger party an evidential burden of justifying the contract, precisely where there is no actual evidence of undue influence or pressure.[224]

Moreover, Lord Denning's principle has not been accepted by the English Courts, which have generally regarded it as involving undue uncertainty. Indeed, on two occasions Lord Scarman spoke emphatically against it. In *National Westminster Bank plc v Morgan*,[225] he questioned the need for such a general principle on the basis, first, that the doctrine of undue influence was adequate to deal with cases in which remedies are required and, secondly, that the task of restricting freedom of contract was essentially a legislative rather than a judicial task, and one that Parliament has undertaken in legislation protecting, for example, consumers, employees, tenants, and investors.[226] And in *Pao On v Lau Yiu Long*,[227] giving the opinion of the Privy Council, Lord Scarman rejected the idea that English law should adopt a general rule of public policy to the effect that contracts entered into following the unfair use of a dominant bargaining position are void, on this occasion emphasizing that the doctrine of duress was adequate to deal with cases which called for remedy,[228] and

---

[221] *Lloyds Bank Ltd v Bundy*, above, n 218, 339.   [222] Cartwright, *Unequal Bargaining* (1991) 216–19.

[223] Above, pp 374, 387.   [224] Above, p 389.

[225] [1985] AC 686, 708. See also *Horry v Tate & Lyle Refineries Ltd* [1982] 2 Lloyd's Rep 416, 423.

[226] He cited as examples Supply of Goods (Implied Terms) Act 1973, Consumer Credit Act 1974, Consumer Safety Act 1978, Supply of Goods and Services Act 1982, and Insurance Companies Act 1982. See now Consumer Protection Act 1987 (repealing Consumer Safety Act 1978), Financial Services and Markets Act 2000 as amended (repealing Insurance Companies Act 1982), Consumer Credit Act 2006, ss 19–21 (replacing Consumer Credit Act 1974, ss 137–140 with new ss 140A–140C). The most general provisions are contained in the Consumer Rights Act 2015, Part 2, above, pp 223 ff; and the Consumer Protection from Unfair Trading Regulations 2008, below. See also above, pp 5–6.

[227] [1980] AC 614, 634.

[228] *Pao On* is one of the cases which recognized the recent expansion of the doctrine of duress to cover economic duress: above, p 378.

that such a rule would be uncertain and would undermine contractual negotiations between commercial parties:

[W]here businessmen are negotiating at arm's length it is unnecessary for the achievement of justice, and unhelpful in the development of the law, to invoke such a rule of public policy . . . It is unnecessary because justice requires that men, who have negotiated at arm's length, be held to their bargains unless it can be shown that their consent was vitiated by fraud, mistake or duress . . .

Such a rule of public policy as is now being considered would be unhelpful because it would render the law uncertain. It would become a question of fact and degree to determine in each case whether there had been, short of duress, an unfair use of a strong bargaining position.

At present, therefore, a contract can be avoided at common law or in equity only if the elements of one of the established categories of vitiation can be shown: duress, undue influence, or the rather limited doctrine of unconscionable bargains. Development of the law in this area has rested on two distinct approaches. Rather than generalize a single common law doctrine of inequality of bargaining, the Courts have preferred to develop each of the separate doctrines, such as the significant development in the law of duress to cover economic duress.[229] In other respects, the development of protection of weaker contracting parties has been left to statutory intervention, particularly in the field of consumer contracts, often in response to European Directives, the most significant of which have been the Directives on Unfair Terms in Consumer Contracts,[230] on the Sale of Consumer Goods and Associated Guarantees,[231] on Unfair Commercial Practices[232] and on Consumer Rights.[233] Parliament has not limited intervention to that required by Directives, but has sometimes gone beyond those requirements,[234] or has set its own rules designed to protect consumers.[235]

---

[229] Above, p 378.

[230] Directive 93/13/EEC, now implemented in Part 2 of the Consumer Rights Act 2015, replacing earlier implementations in the Unfair Terms in Consumer Contract Regulations 1994 (SI 1994 No 3159) and 1999 (SI 1999 No 2083): see above, pp 222 ff.

[231] Directive 1999/44/EC, now implemented in Part 1 of the Consumer Rights Act 2015, replacing earlier implementation in the Sale and Supply of Goods to Consumers Regulations 2002 (SI 2002 No 3045, amending the Sale of Goods Act 1979, the Supply of Goods and Services Act 1982 and the Supply of Goods (Implied Terms) Act 1973).

[232] Directive 2005/29/EC, implemented in (inter alia) the Consumer Protection from Unfair Trading Regulations 2008 (SI 2008 No 1277).

[233] Directive 2011/83/EC, replacing Directive 97/7/EC on the protection of consumers in respect of distance contracts and Directive 85/577/EEC to protect consumers in respect of contracts negotiated away from business premises; implemented in (inter alia) the Consumer Contracts (Information, Cancellation and Additional Charges) Regulations 2013 (SI 2013 No 3134), above, p 370.

[234] eg Consumer Rights Act 2015, which goes beyond the Consumer Sales Directive, for instance by providing the right not only to repair or replacement of good but also to repeat performance of services (above, p 610); and in going beyond the Consumer Rights Directive by providing *private* rights to redress under Part 4A of the Consumer Protection from Unfair Trading Regulations 2008 (above, pp 355, 403).

[235] eg Unfair Contract Terms Act 1977 (above, p 208); and the Consumer Credit Act 1974, ss 140A–140C (inserted by Consumer Credit Act 2006, ss 19–21), which protect against the claimant's need for credit by

We have seen that, in the context of duress, undue influence, and unconscionable bargains, the most significant of these legislative interventions is the provision of private rights to redress in Part 4A of the Consumer Protection from Unfair Trading Regulations 2008 which, although not defined by reference to the common law and equitable doctrines, in practice overlap significantly with them by the definition in the Regulations of 'aggressive commercial practices'.[236] Whether the Courts might yet be willing themselves to take the step of unifying the doctrine of duress, undue influence, and unconscionable bargains, as Lord Denning sought to do, remains uncertain. We have noted elsewhere that there are examples of statutory regimes, which express a policy from which a principle can be derived, being used analogically in developing the common law.[237] This has not, however, yet occurred in the context of duress, undue influence and unconscionable bargains. But in *Timeload Ltd v British Telecommunications plc*[238] Sir Thomas Bingham MR said, in relation to section 3 of the Unfair Contract Terms Act 1977, that it was arguable that 'the common law could, if the letter of the statute does not apply, treat the clear intention of the legislature expressed in the statute as a platform for invalidating or restricting the operation of an oppressive clause'.

FURTHER READING

ATIYAH, 'Economic Duress and the Overborne Will' (1982) 98 LQR 197

THAL, 'The Inequality of Bargaining Power Doctrine: the Problem of Defining Contractual Unfairness' (1988) 8 OLJS 17

BEATSON, 'Duress, Restitution, and Contract Renegotiation' in *The Use and Abuse of Unjust Enrichment* (Oxford: Clarendon Press, 1991) 95

BAMFORTH, 'Unconsionability as a Vitiating Factor' [1995] LMCLQ 538

BIRKS and CHIN, 'On the Nature of Undue Influence' in Beatson and Friedmann (eds), *Good Faith and Fault in Contract Law* (Oxford: Clarendon Press, 1995) 57

BIGWOOD, 'Undue Influence: "Impaired Consent" or "Wicked Exploitation"?' (1996) 16 OJLS 503

SMITH, 'Contracting Under Pressure: A Theory of Duress' [1997] CLJ 343

CAPPER, 'Undue Influence and Unconscionability: A Rationalisation' (1998) 114 LQR 479

---

giving the Court a wide range of remedies to undo credit agreements where the relationship between the creditor and the debtor is unfair to the debtor.

[236] Above, pp 355, 403.

[237] Above, pp 372–3; see Beatson (2001) 117 LQR 247. See also Collins (2010) 75 MLR 89, 113–14 for discussion of whether the Courts might develop the common law in directions that harmonize the rules regarding the invalidity of contracts in the laws of misrepresentation, duress, and undue influence with the prohibitions contained in the Consumer Protection from Unfair Trading Regulations 2008.

[238] (1995) 3 EMLR 459, 468.

CHEN-WISHART, 'Undue Influence: Beyond Impaired Consent and Wrongdoing towards a Relational Analysis' in Burrows and Rodger (eds), *Mapping the Law: Essays in Memory of Peter Birks* (Oxford: Oxford University Press, 2006) 201

McKENDRICK, 'The Further Travails of Duress' in Burrows and Rodger (eds), *Mapping the Law: Essays in Memory of Peter Birks* (Oxford: Oxford University Press, 2006) 181

CAPPER, 'The Unconscionable Bargain in the Common Law World' (2010) 126 LQR 403

11

ILLEGALITY

1. INTRODUCTION

Public policy imposes certain limitations upon the freedom of persons to contract. An ostensibly valid contract may be tainted by illegality.[1] The source of the illegality may arise by statute or by virtue of the principles of common law. In some instances the law prohibits the agreement itself and the contract is then by its very nature illegal, but in the majority of cases the illegality lies in the object which one or both parties have in mind or in the method of performance. As a general rule, although all the other requirements for the formation of an agreement are complied with, an agreement that is illegal in one of these ways will not be enforceable.

The subject of illegality is one of great complexity and the effects of illegality are by no means uniform. This is because the seriousness of the illegality varies. Illegal objects may range from those tainted with gross moral turpitude, for example murder, to those where the harm to be avoided is relatively small, for example breach of licensing requirements or cases in which a person commits an unlawful act in order to escape danger to his or her life or the life of a third party.[2] It is not surprising, therefore, that there are differences in the attitude of the judges to those who have an illegal object in view or are parties to an illegal transaction. Attempts have been made to distinguish between 'illegal' contracts and those which are 'nugatory' or 'void'. In the former case, it is said that the law will refuse to aid in any way a person whose cause of action is founded upon such a contract; in the latter case, the law simply says that the contract is not to have legal effect. While some contracts can be classified in this way, it is both impracticable and impossible to apply this classification over the whole field of the subject. Moreover, confusion is created by the fact that the judges have on many occasions treated the terms as interchangeable. It seems better to use the single word 'illegality' to cover the multitude of instances where the law, for

---

[1] See Buckley, *Illegality and Public Policy* (3rd edn, 2013). This chapter is concerned with initial illegality and illegality in performance and not with supervening illegality which is dealt with in Chapter 14, Discharge by Frustration. The illegality is tested at the time when the contract is formed, even if the law is later changed to render future similar contracts lawful: *Westlaw Services Ltd v Boddy* [2010] EWCA Civ 929, [2011] PNLR 4 at [47]; see also *Commercial Plastics Ltd v Vincent* [1965] 1 QB 623, 644 (time for assessment of reasonableness of restrictive covenant, below, p 431, is the time of the making of the contract).

[2] *Howard v Shirlstar Container Transport Ltd* [1990] 1 WLR 1292.

some reason of public policy or as a result of a statutory prohibition, denies to one or both of the parties the rights under the contract to which he or she would otherwise be entitled.

It should be noted at the outset that some key aspects of the law on illegality are presently in a state of uncertainty as a result of series of decisions in which the Supreme Court has not spoken with one voice,[3] and has even made clear that further argument is necessary to establish authoritatively the basis of the illegality defence. Lord Neuberger PSC said in 2015:[4]

[T]he proper approach which should be adopted to a defence of illegality ... is a difficult and important topic on which, as the two main judgments in this case show, there can be strongly held differing views, and it is probably accurate to describe the debate on the topic as involving something of a spectrum of views. The debate can be seen as epitomising the familiar tension between the need for principle, clarity and certainty in the law with the equally important desire to achieve a fair and appropriate result in each case.

Although these cases in the Supreme Court have not concerned the effect of illegality on contracts, similar arguments have arisen in the lower courts in the context of claims arising under contracts[5] and it is likely that the strongly held different views of the Justices of the Supreme Court would extend to such cases. Until resolved by the Supreme Court, this difference of opinion at the highest level will cause uncertainty in all areas of the law where illegality may be in issue, including in contract law.[6]

2. STATUTORY ILLEGALITY

(a) EXPRESS PROHIBITION: CONTRACT ILLEGAL

The nature and effects of statutory illegality may vary considerably. A statute may declare that a certain type of contract is expressly prohibited. There is then no doubt of the intention of the legislature that such a contract should not be enforced. 'What is done in contravention of the provisions of an Act of Parliament

---

[3] *Hounga v Allen* [2014] UKSC 47, [2014] 1 WLR 2889; *Les Laboratoires Servier v Apotex Inc* [2014] UKSC 55, [2015] AC 430; *Bilta (UK) Ltd v Nazir (No 2)* [2015] UKSC 23, [2015] 2 WLR 1168.

[4] *Bilta (UK) Ltd v Nazir (No 2)*, above, n 3 at [13], suggesting at [15] that the issue needs to be addressed by a panel of seven or conceivably nine Justices. See also Lord Mance JSC at [34] and Lord Toulson and Lord Hodge JJSC at [174]. The particular focus of the debate is the (re-)assessment of the earlier decision of the House of Lords in *Tinsley v Milligan* [1994] 1 AC 340, below, p 437. Permission has been granted for the appeal to the Supreme Court in another case involving an illegal contract, albeit the case raises again different issues: see *Patel v Mirza* [2014] EWCA Civ 1047, [2015] Ch 271.

[5] The most recent decision is *ParkingEye Ltd v Somerfield Stores* [2012] EWCA Civ 1338, [2013] QB 840, below, p 438.

[6] Cf *Sharma v Top Brands Ltd* [2015] EWCA Civ 1140 at [37]–[39] (not, however, a case of contractual illegality).

cannot be made the subject-matter of an action.'[7] Thus, in *Re Mahmoud and Ispahani*:[8]

A wartime statutory order prohibited the purchase or sale of linseed oil without a licence from the Food Controller. M held a licence to sell to other licensed dealers. I falsely assured him that he had a licence and M agreed to sell a quantity of linseed oil to I. I later refused to accept the oil on the ground that he had no licence. M brought an action for damages for non-acceptance.

The Court of Appeal rejected M's claim even though he was ignorant, at the time the contract was made, of the facts which brought it within the statutory prohibition. 'The Order', said Bankes LJ,[9] 'is a clear and unequivocal declaration by the Legislature in the public interest that this particular kind of contract shall not be entered into'.

(b) IMPLIED PROHIBITION: CONTRACT ILLEGAL

The position is the same where the contract is impliedly prohibited by statute. The statute is to be construed in the ordinary way. The Courts must determine whether the statutory words, construed in context including the purpose of the statute, prohibit and penalize only the prescribed conduct or whether they additionally prohibit the contract.[10] If, for example, the purpose of the statute is to protect the public from injury or fraud the inference is likely to be that contracts made in contravention of its provisions are prohibited.[11] Again,

if a contract has as its whole object the doing of the very act which the statute prohibits, it can be argued that you can hardly make sense of a statute which forbids an act and yet permits to be made a contract to do it.[12]

But, in the absence of a clear implication, the following pages show that Courts are cautious in construing a statute in this way, in part because 'so much of commercial life is governed by regulations of one sort or another; which may easily be broken without wicked intent'.[13] Thus, the fact that the purpose of a statute is to limit the scope of companies' commercial activities does not mean that every contract entered into in a prohibited sphere should be invalidated.[14] The absence of a criminal sanction and the presence of a wide array of regulatory remedies indicate that such contracts are not prohibited.[15]

---

[7] *Langton v Hughes* (1813) 1 M & S 593, 596 (Lord Ellenborough CJ).

[8] [1921] 2 KB 716. See also *Chai Sau Yin v Liew Kwee Sam* [1962] AC 304; *Wilson, Smithett & Cope Ltd v Terruzzi* [1976] QB 683; *Hughes v Kingston upon Hull CC* [1999] QB 1193; *RTA (Business Consultants) Ltd v Bracewell* [2015] EWHC 630 (QB), [2015] Bus LR 800.

[9] [1921] 2 KB 716, 724.

[10] *St John Shipping Corp v Joseph Rank Ltd* [1957] 1 QB 267, 283, 287. See generally Buckley (1975) 38 MLR 535.

[11] *Anderson v Daniel* [1924] 1 KB 138.

[12] *St John Shipping Corp v Joseph Rank Ltd* [1957] 1 QB 267, 288 (Devlin J); *Mohamed v Alaga & Co* [2000] 1 WLR 1815, 1824.

[13] *St John Shipping Corp v Joseph Rank Ltd* [1957] 1 QB 267, 288 (Devlin J). See also *Shaw v Groom* [1970] 2 QB 504, 522.

[14] *Fuji Finance Inc v Aetna Life Insurance Co Ltd* [1997] Ch 173, 193–4.   [15] *Ibid.*

(c) ILLEGAL PERFORMANCE

Statutory illegality may also arise in connection with the performance of a contract which is not in itself illegal. The method of performance adopted by one of the parties may violate some statutory prohibition, for example, the vendor of goods may deliver them to a purchaser without the required statutory invoice.[16] In such a situation the party in default will not be able to enforce any claim based on its own illegal performance. But since such a contract is lawful in its inception, notwithstanding that it has been performed in an unlawful manner, there is no reason why the other party, if *innocent*, should not be able to sue. The innocent party does not have to rely on the illegal performance in order to establish a cause of action. Thus in *Marles v Philip Trant & Sons Ltd*:[17]

PT, a firm of seed merchants, bought a quantity of wheat described as 'spring wheat' from a third party. It sold this wheat to various farmers, including M, but the wheat was found not to be spring wheat and the crops failed. M claimed damages from PT for breach of warranty. PT, as it was entitled to do, brought in the third party to the action, claiming from him an indemnity in respect of M's claim, and damages. The third party, however, raised the defence that PT had not, at the time of the sale, delivered to M certain particulars in writing as required by section 1(1) of the Seeds Act 1920. He contended that he was not bound to indemnify PT, as he could not be made liable on a contract which was illegal.

A majority of the Court of Appeal held that the contract between PT and M was not illegal from the beginning, but was only rendered illegal later by the method of performance which did not comply with the statutory requirements. M could recover damages for breach of warranty from PT, since the warranty was given on the lawful stage of the agreement. The third party's contention that he was not liable to compensate PT in respect of its liability under this head therefore failed.[18]

On the other hand, if the other party participates in, or assents to, the illegal performance, it will likewise be unable to sue. In *Ashmore, Benson, Pease & Co Ltd v AV Dawson Ltd*:[19]

The defendant, a road haulage company, contracted with ABP to carry two 25-ton tube banks to a port. ABP's transport manager and his assistant watched the tube banks being loaded onto two lorries whose lawful maximum load was 20 tons. ABP sued the defendant in respect of damage to one of the tubes when the lorry carrying it toppled over.

The Court of Appeal found that ABP's manager must have realized that the lorries were overloaded, and that he had participated in the defendants' illegal performance

---

[16] *Anderson Ltd v Daniel* [1924] 1 KB 138.

[17] [1954] 1 QB 29. See also *Archbolds (Freightage) Ltd v Spanglett Ltd* [1961] 1 QB 374, below, p 441.

[18] Singleton and Denning LJJ. Hodson LJ, dissenting, stated (at 42) that the defendants 'cannot rely upon the breach of warranty by a third party to prove their damages when those damages are to be measured by reference to a contract illegally performed by them'.

[19] [1973] 1 WLR 828.

of the contract by sanctioning the loading of the two vehicles with a load in excess of the statutory maximum. ABP's claim therefore failed.

(d) STATUTE ONLY IMPOSES A PENALTY

Although the fact that a statutory offence has been committed in the course of performance of a contract may render the contract unenforceable, it will not necessarily have this effect.[20] For the law to prescribe that the commission of any unlawful act in the course of performing a contract should inevitably deprive the wrongdoer of all contractual remedies might well inflict on the wrongdoer a loss far in excess of the statutory penalty. This would be unreasonable. For example, a road haulier might be unable to claim freight simply on the ground that the driver of the vehicle had exceeded the speed limit or the permitted driving hours or on the ground that the vehicle did not have the appropriate licence.[21] It is therefore necessary, in all cases of statutory illegality to have regard to the statutory language and to its scope and purpose. Was the statute intended to interfere with the contract under consideration, to render it unenforceable at the suit of a party who performs it illegally, or merely to impose a penalty on the offender?[22] Where the purpose of the statute is simply to impose a penalty, even the 'guilty' party can sue. Thus in *St John Shipping Corporation v Joseph Rank Ltd*:[23]

St J, shipowners, contracted to carry a load of grain but overloaded the ship contrary to the Merchant Shipping (Safety and Load Line Conventions) Act 1932. The master was prosecuted and fined for this offence. JR, the consignee of part of the cargo, withheld a proportion of the freight due, ie a sum equivalent to the freight on the excess cargo carried.

Devlin J held that JR was not entitled to do so. The Act did not render unlawful the contract of carriage, but merely imposed a penalty in respect of its infringement. Similarly, a landlord who fails to provide a tenant with a proper rent-book is exposed to a criminal penalty, but is not precluded from recovering the rent.[24]

(e) VOID CONTRACTS

A statute may also declare a contract, or a particular kind of term, to be void, that is, a nullity, and may also prescribe the consequences of the contract or the term being void. Statutory provisions of this nature are numerous and are often (but by no means

---

[20] Sometimes the statute is explicit: below, n 32.

[21] See the facts of *Archbolds (Freightage) Ltd v Spanglett Ltd* [1961] 1 QB 374, 385, 390, below, p 441.

[22] *Hughes v Asset Managers plc* [1995] 3 All ER 669, 673–4, 'applauded' by the Law Commission in Consultation Paper No 189, *The Illegality Defence: A Consultative Report* (2009), para 3.101; *Nelson v Nelson* (1995) 132 ALR 133 (High Court of Australia), below, p 453.

[23] [1957] 1 QB 267. See also *Cope v Rowlands* (1836) 2 M & W 149.

[24] *Shaw v Groom* [1970] 2 QB 504.

invariably)[25] connected with a failure to register the agreement[26] or to comply with certain requirements of form.[27] A party to such a contract cannot enforce it, but may be able to recover money or property transferred under it,[28] provided that this is not precluded by the express words of the statute[29] or by judicial interpretation.[30]

(f) CONTRACT UNENFORCEABLE BY ONE PARTY

Frequently, a statute will in express terms or on its true construction render a contract unenforceable only by the party whose duty it is to observe the statutory requirement. In such a case, if that party contravenes the provisions of the statute, the contract will be unenforceable by him or her but may be enforced by the other party.[31]

(g) CONTRACT NOT VOID OR UNENFORCEABLE

Finally, where a contract is not directly contrary to the provisions of a statute by reason of any express or implied prohibition or even where the statute expressly states that a breach of its prohibition does not render any contract void or unenforceable,[32] the Court may still refuse to enforce the contract because this could lead to the Court assisting in something illegal or because the contract is associated with or furthers an illegal purpose.[33] This, however, is a question of illegality at common law, which is considered in Section 3 of this chapter.

[25] See, eg, Gaming Act 1845, s 18 (contracts of 'gaming or wagering' null and void; repealed by Gambling Act 2005 under which the fact that a contract relates to gambling does not prevent its enforcement unless it is otherwise illegal: s 335); Marine Insurance Act 1906, s 4(1) (every contract of marine insurance by way of gaming or wagering is void: this is unchanged by Gambling Act 2005); Equality Act 2010, ss 142–144 (unlawfully discriminatory term in a collective agreement is void, but term in a contract is not void but only unenforceable against the victim of the discrimination or by the person in whose favour it purports to operate).

[26] Bills of Sale Act 1878, s 8; Companies Act 2006, s 859H, inserted by SI 2013 No 600 and replacing similar provision originally contained in s 874 (unregistered company charge is void, but without prejudice to contract for repayment of money secured by the charge which becomes immediately repayable).

[27] Bills of Sale Act (1878), Amendment Act 1882, s 9 (bill of sale void if not in required form); Marine Insurance Act 1906, s 22 (marine insurance inadmissible in evidence if not embodied in a marine policy); see above, p 83.

[28] *North Central Wagon Finance Co Ltd v Brailsford* [1962] 1 WLR 1288 (bill of sale).

[29] This was the position under Gaming Act 1845, s 18, above, n 25.

[30] See, eg, Life Assurance Act 1774, s 1; *Harse v Pearl Life Assurance Co* [1904] 1 KB 558. See below, p 444.

[31] *Cope v Rowlands* (1836) 2 M & W 149; *Victorian Daylesford Syndicate Ltd v Dott* [1905] 2 Ch 624; Consumer Credit Act 1974, ss 55 (amended by SI 2010 No 1010), 65; Equality Act 2010, s 144; Financial Services and Markets Act 2000, ss 26, 27 (amended by Financial Services Act 2012). See *Group Josi Re v Walbrook Insurance Co Ltd* [1996] 1 WLR 1152 on the similarly worded Financial Services Act 1986, s 132.

[32] See, eg, Trade Descriptions Act 1968, s 35; Business Protection from Misleading Marketing Regulations 2008 (SI 2008 No 1276) reg 29; Consumer Protection from Unfair Trading Regulations 2008 (SI 2008 No 1277) reg 29, amended by SI 2014 No 870.

[33] See *Chase Manhattan Equities Ltd v Goodman* [1991] BCLC 897, 931–4, and below, p 435; *Nelson v Nelson* (1995) 132 ALR 133, 143, 178 (High Court of Australia). See also Gambling Act 2005, s 335 (gambling contract not unenforceable, but without prejudice to unenforceability for unlawfulness other than a rule relating specifically to gambling).

3. ILLEGALITY AT COMMON LAW

There are a number of situations where the policy of the common law means that a contract cannot be enforced even though it is not expressly or impliedly prohibited by statute. The origins of the concept of the policy of the law, or public policy, are ancient and obscure. By the beginning of the nineteenth century the lack of definition and consequent uncertainty of the concept led to judicial statements against the extension of public policy which was described as 'a very unruly horse'.[34] The view was also expressed that it was not the function of the Courts to create new law, but to interpret and elucidate existing principles,[35] and that there was a public interest in upholding freedom of contract. The effect of the nineteenth-century emphasis on freedom of contract was reluctance to interfere with a contract on the ground of public policy.[36] It is in reconciling this freedom of contract with other public interests that the difficulty arises.

By the second half of the twentieth century, however, the positive function of the Courts in matters of public policy was increasingly recognized. As Lord Denning MR said: 'With a good man in the saddle, the unruly horse can be kept in control. It can jump over obstacles'.[37] Moreover, some flexibility is clearly desirable in matters of public policy which cannot remain immutable.[38] Most recently it has been said that, apart from criminal acts, the ex turpi causa principle is concerned only with claims founded on dishonesty or corruption, some anomalous categories of misconduct (such as prostitution) which without themselves being criminal are contrary to public policy and involve criminal liability on the part of secondary parties, and the infringement of statutory rules enacted for the protection of the public interest and attracting civil sanctions of a penal character. However, torts (other than those of which dishonesty is an essential element), breaches of contract, statutory and other civil wrongs are not included because they offend against interests which are essentially private, not public.[39]

Certain aspects of public policy are more susceptible to change than others, though the policy of the law has, on some subjects, been worked into a set of tolerably definite rules. The principles applicable to agreements in restraint of trade, for example, have on a number of occasions been modified or extended to accord

---

[34] *Richardson v Mellish* (1824) 2 Bing 229, 252 (Burrough J).

[35] *Re Mirams* [1891] 1 QB 594, 595; *Mogul Steamship Co v McGregor, Gow & Co* [1892] AC 25, 45.

[36] Above, pp 4, 17 and see especially *Printing and Numerical Registering Co v Sampson* (1875) LR 19 Eq 462, 465 (Jessel MR).

[37] *Enderby Town FC Ltd v Football Association Ltd* [1971] Ch 591, 606.

[38] *Nagle v Feilden* [1966] 2 QB 633, 650 (Danckwerts LJ).

[39] *Les Laboratoires Servier v Apotex Inc* [2014] UKSC 55, [2015] AC 430 at [25], [28]. This case decided that the breach of a foreign patent right was not within the scope of the illegality principle.

with prevailing economic conditions,[40] and this process still continues.[41] So too the principles applicable to transactions between cohabiting couples have been modified to accord with prevailing social conditions,[42] as have those concerning the financing of litigation.[43] For the rest, the application of canons of public policy to particular instances necessarily varies with the progressive development of public opinion and morality, but like any other branch of the common law is governed by the judicial use of precedents.[44]

Contracts which the Courts will not enforce because they are contrary to public policy may be arranged under certain heads.

(a) AGREEMENTS TO COMMIT A CRIME OR CIVIL WRONG, OR TO PERPETRATE A FRAUD

(i) Agreements to commit a crime

The Courts will not enforce an agreement which has as its object the deliberate commission of a criminal offence (whether by statute or at common law),[45] although the fact that an offence is committed in the course of an otherwise legal agreement will not necessarily render the contract unlawful.[46]

(ii) Agreement to commit a civil wrong or fraud

The Courts will not enforce an agreement to commit a tort. An agreement to commit an assault has therefore been held to be void, as in *Allen v Rescous*,[47] where one of the parties undertook to beat up someone. So too has an agreement involving the publication of a libel,[48] or deceit,[49] or the perpetration of a fraud.[50] In *Mallalieu v Hodgson*[51] a secret agreement by which a debtor agreed to pay M part of his debt in full, when the debtor had agreed to pay all his other creditors was held to be a fraud on the other creditors, each of whom had promised to forgo a portion of his debt in consideration that the others would forgo a similar proportion of their debts. The agreement to prefer one creditor was unenforceable.[52] Similarly, an agreement by the promoters of a company to defraud prospective

---

[40] See below, p 430.   [41] See below, pp 430, 433.

[42] Below, p 425.

[43] *Thai Trading Co v Taylor* [1998] QB 781, but cf *Sibthorpe v Southwark LBC* [2011] EWCA Civ 25, [2011] 1 WLR 2111; below, pp 423–4.

[44] Lord Wright, *Legal Essays and Addresses* (1939) 76, 78.

[45] See, eg *Levy v Yates* (1838) 8 A & E 129; *Bigos v Bousted* [1951] 1 All ER 92, below, p 446; *Tinsley v Milligan* [1994] 1 AC 340.

[46] See above, p 412.   [47] (1677) 2 Lev 174.   [48] *Clay v Yates* (1856) 1 H & N 73.

[49] *Brown Jenkinson & Co Ltd v Percy Dalton (London) Ltd* [1957] 2 QB 621.

[50] *Willis v Baldwin* (1780) 2 Doug KB 450.   [51] (1851) 16 QB 689.

[52] *Ibid*, 711 (Erle J) ('altogether void'). See also Insolvency Act 1986, ss 339–40.

shareholders,[53] or to rig the market for shares,[54] has been held to be fraudulent and unenforceable.

(iii) Agreements to defraud the revenue

One of the most common types of illegal agreement is one to defraud the revenue, whether that of the central or local government. In *Alexander v Rayson*:[55]

A let a flat in Piccadilly to R at a rent of £1,200 a year. The transaction was effected by two documents: (1) a lease of the flat at a rent of £450 a year, covering certain services to be rendered by the lessor A, and (2) an agreement to render services (which were substantially the same) in consideration of an extra £750 a year. A dispute having arisen, R declined to pay an instalment due under the agreement. When sued by A, R pleaded that the object of the two documents was that only the lease was to be disclosed to the local authority in order to deceive them as to the true rateable value of the premises.

The Court of Appeal held that, if the documents were to be used for this fraudulent purpose, A was not entitled to the assistance of the law in enforcing either the lease or the agreement.

(iv) Contracts of indemnity

An indemnity against civil or criminal liability resulting from the deliberate commission of a crime by the person to be indemnified is not enforceable by the criminal or his representatives,[56] although it has been held that a motorist may recover under a policy of insurance against third party risks even if the motorist's own gross or criminal negligence caused the loss.[57]

The mischief to which this rule of public policy is directed does not, however, cover agreements concluded after the criminal event, in relation to civil proceedings arising out of it. It is therefore lawful for one of the two joint tortfeasors to agree to pay the costs of the other in defending the claim or satisfying the judgment if that defence is unsuccessful.[58]

---

[53] *Begbie v Phosphate Sewage Co Ltd* (1876) 1 QBD 679.

[54] *Scott v Brown, Doering, McNab & Co* [1892] 2 QB 724.

[55] [1936] 1 KB 169; see also *Miller v Karlinski* (1945) 62 TLR 85; *Napier v National Business Agency Ltd* [1951] 2 All ER 264; *Corby v Morrison* [1980] IRLR 218; *Tinsley v Milligan* [1994] 1 AC 340, below, p 452 (social security authorities). Cf *21st Century Logistic Solutions Ltd v Madysen Ltd* [2004] EWHC 231 (QB), [2004] 2 Lloyd's Rep 92 (contract not unenforceable where claimant's illegal intention is too remote from the contract).

[56] *Brown Jenkinson & Co Ltd v Percy Dalton (London) Ltd* [1957] 2 QB 621; *Hardy v Motor Insurers' Bureau* [1964] 2 QB 745; *Gray v Barr* [1971] 2 QB 554; *Geismar v Sun Alliance and London Insurance Ltd* [1978] QB 383; *Charlton v Fisher* [2001] EWCA Civ 112, [2002] QB 578; cf *Lancashire CC v Municipal Mutual Insurance Ltd* [1997] QB 897 (exemplary damages not excluded).

[57] *Tinline v White Cross Insurance Co Ltd* [1921] 3 KB 327. See also *Hardy v Motor Insurers' Bureau*, above, n 56; *Cooke v Routledge* [1998] NILR 174.

[58] *Mulcaire v News Group Newspapers Ltd* [2011] EWHC 3469 (Ch), [2012] Ch 435 at [45].

(b) AGREEMENTS WHICH INJURE THE STATE IN ITS RELATIONS WITH OTHER STATES

(i) Contracts with an alien enemy

Contracts with alien enemies are illegal in time of war and it is unlawful to enter into or to perform such a contract, even one made before war broke out.[59] Further, a contract which expressly provides for the suspension of all rights and obligations arising under it during a war may yet be held to be void on grounds of public policy as tending, merely by its continued existence, to promote the economic interests of the enemy state or to prejudice those of the United Kingdom.[60]

(ii) Contracts hostile to a friendly state

An agreement which contemplates action hostile to a friendly foreign government cannot be enforced.[61] It is also contrary to public policy to allow the enforcement in English Courts of agreements to be performed in a foreign state in breach of the laws of that state. 'This country', it has been said,[62] 'should not assist or sanction the breach of the laws of other independent States'. Thus the Court of Appeal has refused to entertain an action arising out of certain transactions which had for their object the importation of whisky contrary to the prohibition laws of the United States of America.[63]

This does not, however, mean that the Court must necessarily refuse to enforce a contract merely because its performance will involve a foreign defendant in a breach of its own law.[64] A foreign law that is repugnant to English conceptions of liberty or freedom of action will not be enforced here. Examples of such laws include those involving persecution of such a character that an agreement to break the law would be regarded as meritorious[65] or imposing a contractual incapacity which is foreign to the ideas of English law.[66] Although the same principle has been said to apply to the penal, political, or revenue laws of other countries,[67] this formulation is too wide; the

---

[59] *Potts v Bell* (1800) 8 Term R 548; *Kuenigl v Donnersmarck* [1955] 1 QB 515; Trading with the Enemy Act 1939. For the contractual incapacity of an alien enemy, see *Porter v Freudenberg* [1915] 1 KB 857.

[60] *Ertel Bieber & Co v Rio Tinto Co Ltd* [1918] AC 260.

[61] *De Wütz v Hendricks* (1824) 2 Bing 314, 316.

[62] *Ralli Brothers v Compañia Naviera Sota y Aznar* [1920] 2 KB 287, 304 (Scrutton LJ). See also *Libyan Arab Foreign Bank v Bankers Trust Co* [1989] QB 728, 743–6 (Staughton J); *Soleimany v Soleimany* [1999] QB 785.

[63] *Foster v Driscoll* [1929] 1 KB 470.

[64] *Kleinwort Sons & Co v Ungarische Baumwolle Industrie AG* [1939] 2 KB 678; *British Nylon Spinners Ltd v ICI Ltd* [1953] Ch 37; *Toprak Mahsulleri Ofisi v Finagrain Compagnie Commerciale Agricole et Financière* [1979] 2 Lloyd's Rep 98.

[65] *Regazzoni v KC Sethia (1944) Ltd*, below, n 69, 325. See also *Lemenda Trading Co Ltd v African Middle East Petroleum Co Ltd* [1988] QB 448, 461. Cf *Westacre Investments Inc v Jugoimport-SPDR Holding Co Ltd* [1999] QB 740, 801, aff'd [2000] QB 288.

[66] *Re Selot's Trust* [1902] 1 Ch 488.

[67] *Holman v Johnson* (1775) 1 Cowp 341, 343; *Government of India Ministry of Finance v Taylor* [1955] AC 491; *Brokaw v Seatrain UK Ltd* [1971] 2 QB 476; *A-G of New Zealand v Ortiz* [1982] QB 349; cf [1984] AC 1, 46.

Court is not prepared to disregard them altogether.[68] And if two people knowingly contract to *break* such a law, they cannot expect the Court to enforce their agreement. In *Regazzoni v KC Sethia (1944) Ltd*:[69]

S agreed to sell and deliver to R at Genoa in Italy a quantity of jute bags to be shipped from India. At that time the government of India was in dispute with the South African government over the treatment of Indian nationals in South Africa and had prohibited the direct export of jute to South Africa, and also imposed penalties on any indirect shipments. Both S and R knew that the jute bags were to be shipped to South Africa in violation of the Indian prohibition. The bags were not delivered and R brought an action for non-delivery.

The House of Lords held that, since the contract required the export of goods from India in breach of the law of that country, it could not be enforced in this country, even though the law might be classed as a political law. R accordingly failed.

(c) AGREEMENTS WHICH TEND TO INJURE GOOD GOVERNMENT

(i) Sale of offices

The public has an interest in the proper performance of their duty by public servants, and is entitled to be served by the fittest persons procurable. Contracts which have for their object the sale of public offices are illegal.

(ii) Assignment of public salaries

An agreement to assign the salary of a public officer is also illegal based on a somewhat different principle. The rule has been explained on the ground that 'it is fit that the public servants should retain the means of a decent subsistence, without being exposed to the temptations of poverty'.[70]

(iii) Other contracts injurious to the public service

The law will not uphold a contract whereby one of the parties agrees to use influence or position for the purpose of securing a title, contract, or some other benefit from the government for the other;[71] or an agreement whereby a member of Parliament in consideration of receiving a salary from a political association agreed to vote on every subject in accordance with the directions of the association;[72] or an agreement

---

[68] *Re Emery's Investment Trusts* [1959] Ch 410; *Empresa Exportadora De Azucar v Industria Azucarera Nacional SA* [1983] 2 Lloyd's Rep 171. Cf *Re Helbert Wagg & Co Ltd's Claim* [1956] Ch 323, 352.

[69] [1958] AC 301. Cf *Pye v BG Transport Service Ltd* [1966] 2 Lloyd's Rep 300; *Fielding & Platt Ltd v Najjar* [1969] 1 WLR 357.

[70] *Wells v Foster* (1841) 8 M & W 149, 151 (Lord Abinger CB). See also *Roberts v Roberts* [1986] 1 WLR 437 (statutory prohibition of assignment of soldiers' pay and benefits). Cf *Re Mirams* [1891] 1 QB 594 (assignment of salary of chaplain to workhouse not void: 'To make the office a public office, the pay must come out of national and not out of local funds, and the office must be public in the strict sense of that term' (Cave J at 596)).

[71] *Montefiore v Menday Motor Components Co* [1918] 2 KB 241.

[72] *Osborne v Amalgamated Society of Railway Servants* [1910] AC 87.

whereby a donation to a charity is made in consideration of a promise to secure the donor a knighthood.[73] The public has a right to demand that public officials shall not be induced merely by considerations of personal gain to act in a manner other than that which the public interest demands, and that no-one shall enter or refrain[74] from entering the public service for the same reason.

But agreements that may influence the proceedings before a public official are not necessarily against the public interest. Thus, it has been held not to be against public policy for a party to a commercial transaction involving the disposition of an interest in land to enter into a covenant to support and not to oppose a planning application by the other party.[75]

(d) AGREEMENTS WHICH TEND TO PERVERT THE COURSE OF JUSTICE

(i) Agreements not to disclose wrongdoing

The Courts will normally refuse to enforce an undertaking not to disclose misconduct which is of such a nature that it ought in the public interest to be disclosed to others who have a proper interest to receive it.[76] Nevertheless, a promise not to disclose the fact that a crime has been committed may still be lawful. In *Howard v Odhams Press Ltd* Greene LJ stated 'It may well be permissible for a person against whom frauds have been and are intended to be committed to give a promise of secrecy in order to obtain information relating to them which will enable him, by taking steps himself, to prevent the commission of future frauds'.[77] But such a promise is void if its effect is not merely to enable the protection of the party to whom the information is given, but to preclude that party from disclosing information as to frauds committed or contemplated against others to whom such information would be of use in preventing the commission of such frauds.

(ii) Compromise of criminal offences

Before 1967, although the compromise of a prosecution for a misdemeanour which was of a private character, for example assault or libel, was permissible,[78] an agreement not to prosecute a felony or a misdemeanour of a public nature was not enforceable,[79] and the compounding of a felony was itself a criminal offence.[80]

---

[73] *Parkinson v College of Ambulance Ltd* [1925] 2 KB 1.

[74] *Re Beard* [1908] 1 Ch 383 (armed forces).

[75] *Fulham Football Club Ltd v Cabra Estates plc* [1994] 1 BCLC 363, 390–1.

[76] *Initial Services Ltd v Putterill* [1968] 1 QB 396; *Lion Laboratories Ltd v Evans* [1985] 1 QB 526. See also *A-G v Guardian Newspapers Ltd (No 2)* [1990] 1 AC 109, 268–9.

[77] [1938] 1 KB 1, 42.

[78] *Baker v Townsend* (1817) 7 Taunt 422; *Fisher & Co v Apollinaris Co* (1875) LR 10 Ch App 297. See also *Keir v Leeman* (1844) 6 QB 308, 321, aff'd (1846) 9 QB 371.

[79] *Windhill Local Board of Health v Vint* (1890) 45 Ch D 351 (obstruction of highway); *Clubb v Hutson* (1865) 18 CBNS 414 (obtaining by false pretences).

[80] It was also probably an offence to compound a misdemeanour of a public nature.

The Criminal Law Act 1967 abolished the distinction between felonies and misdemeanours and further provided that the compounding of an offence (other than treason) was no longer to be criminal by English law.[81] Section 5 of the Act, however, established a new crime of concealing an arrestable offence[82] which is committed if a person accepts as the price of not disclosing such an offence any consideration other than the making good of loss or injury occasioned by the offence, or the making of any reasonable compensation for that loss or injury. The effect of this provision in the law of contract is enigmatic. It can be argued that, subject to the rules of duress,[83] an agreement to compromise a prosecution is now legal and enforceable, provided that it is not one which is rendered criminal by the Act of 1967. The better view, however, is that the abolition of the offence of compounding did not in itself affect the rules of public policy administered by the Courts, for these were not dependent upon the fact that the agreement itself constituted a crime. Further, an agreement to compromise a criminal offence may, in certain circumstances, expose one (or possibly both) of the parties to a charge of attempting or conspiring to pervert the course of justice,[84] and the agreement will in consequence be illegal in that event.

(e) AGREEMENTS WHICH TEND TO ABUSE THE LEGAL PROCESS

(i) The policy against speculative litigation

Agreements encouraging speculative litigation are contrary to public policy and unlawful. It is not thought right that a person should buy an interest in another's quarrel, or should incite another to litigation by offers of assistance for which there is an expectation of payment. Someone who does this might be tempted, for personal gain, to inflame the damages, to suppress evidence, or even to suborn witnesses.[85] This head of public policy, which rests on the perceived need to protect the integrity of public justice,[86] has, however, not been static. In the last century, as much litigation became supported by some association or other, for example by trade unions or insurance companies, its operation was progressively redefined and narrowed in scope. It was also significantly altered by the Courts and Legal Services Act 1990, as amended by the Access to Justice Act 1999 and the Legal Aid, Sentencing and Punishment of Offenders Act 2012. The legislation constitutes recognition by Parliament that where legal aid is not available certain agreements which would have been illegal at common law confer a benefit to the public by increasing access to justice.

---

[81] s 5(5).
[82] Amended by Serious Organised Crime and Police Act 2005 to simply a 'relevant' offence, but still defined as an offence the sentence for which is fixed by law or for which a person may be sentenced to imprisonment for five years: Criminal Law Act 1967, s 4(1A), inserted by the 2005 Act.
[83] See above, p 375.   [84] *R v Grimes* [1968] 3 All ER 179; *R v Panayiotou* [1973] 1 WLR 1032.
[85] *Re Trepca Mines Ltd (No 2)* [1963] Ch 199, 219–20 (Lord Denning MR: champerty).
[86] *Giles v Thompson* [1993] 3 All ER 321, 328 (Steyn LJ); [1994] 1 AC 142, 164 (Lord Mustill).

(ii) Maintenance and champerty

Maintenance and champerty are the names given to agreements which may contravene the policy against the encouragement of speculative litigation. Maintenance occurs where a person supports litigation in which he has no legitimate concern without just cause or excuse.[87] Champerty occurs where it is agreed that the person who maintains another's litigation is to receive a share of the proceeds of the litigation.[88] Champerty has been said to be an aggravated form of maintenance.[89] The Courts, until recently, looked with particular disfavour upon champertous agreements between solicitors and their clients under which the solicitor is to receive a share of the proceeds of the client's litigation.[90]

Agreements which 'savour of champerty' will also be struck down. It is not unlawful to agree to supply information which will enable property to be recovered, in consideration of receiving a part of the property when recovered;[91] but if the person giving such information is to recover the property or actively to assist in the recovery by procuring evidence or other means, the arrangement is contrary to the policy of the law and void.[92] The question to what extent the purchase of a right of action already accrued is obnoxious to the rules against champerty is considered later in connection with the subject of assignment of choses in action.[93]

Maintenance and champerty were both torts and crimes at common law. Both criminal liability and tortious liability were abolished by the Criminal Law Act 1967.[94] But section 14(2) of the Act expressly provides that this abolition is not to affect cases in which a contract is to be treated as contrary to public policy or otherwise illegal.

(iii) Just cause or excuse

The concept of what is a just cause or excuse widened considerably as the operation of this head of public policy narrowed during the time that maintenance and champerty were still criminal and civil wrongs.[95] For example, as a general rule it came to be legitimate for litigation to be supported by trade unions or insurance companies. Again, it was held not to be maintenance where an employer supported an action for libel brought by an employee to protect his reputation attacked by reason of acts

---

[87] *Hill v Archbold* [1968] 1 QB 686, 694.

[88] *Re Trepca Mines Ltd (No 2)*, above, n 85, 219 (Lord Denning MR: 'Champerty is derived from campi partitio (division of the field). It occurs when the person maintaining another stipulates for a share of the proceeds').

[89] *Giles v Thompson* [1993] 3 All ER 321, 328 (Steyn LJ).

[90] *Wild v Simpson* [1919] 2 KB 544; *Re Trepca Mines Ltd (No 2)* [1963] Ch 199. See also Solicitors Act 1974, s 59; *Wallersteiner v Moir (No 2)* [1975] QB 373 (contingency fees); *Aratra Potato Co Ltd v Taylor Joynson Garrett* [1995] 4 All ER 695 (acceptance of a lower fee for lost cases).

[91] *Rees v De Bernardy* [1896] 2 Ch 437.

[92] *Stanley v Jones* (1831) 7 Bing 369. See also Theft Act 1968, s 23.

[93] See below, p 709.   [94] ss 13, 14.

[95] See the historical survey in *Giles v Thompson* [1993] 3 All ER 321, 328–33 (Steyn LJ), approved [1994] 1 AC 142, 164.

done by him in the course of his employment,[96] and where a national anglers' society provided funds for an action by a riparian owner against a company alleged to be polluting a particular river.[97] A genuine commercial interest might also suffice.[98] But the legitimacy of the interest of the person supporting the action had to be distinct from the benefit which that person sought to derive from the agreement to support it.[99]

Where a person with a legitimate interest in maintaining an action agrees to do so, but does not agree to pay the costs of action if the action of the person supported does not succeed, the better view is that an agreement by a person with a legitimate interest in maintaining the action will not be illegal solely on the ground that it makes no provision for the maintainer to pay the costs if the action does not succeed.[100]

(iv) Conditional fee agreements and damages-based agreements

Section 58 of the Courts and Legal Services Act 1990 permitted certain speculative actions undertaken on a 'no win, no fee' basis, and validated certain agreements between lawyers and their clients for a percentage uplift in the fees in the event of success.[101] 'Contingency fees', calculated as a percentage of monies recovered in the claim but with no fee payable if the client loses, used not generally to be permitted,[102] but the Legal Aid, Sentencing and Punishment of Offenders Act 2012 amended the 1990 Act to permit 'damages-based agreements' subject to specified conditions.[103] However, a damages-based agreement which does not satisfy the conditions is unenforceable.[104]

There have been different views about the effect of the legislation on further common law development of the head of public policy against speculative litigation. In 1998, the Court of Appeal in *Thai Trading Co v Taylor* had to consider the enforceability at common law of an agreement by a solicitor only to charge his client if she succeeded in litigation. It took the view that the progressive narrowing by the Courts of this head of public policy during the previous half-century meant that, if

---

[96] *Hill v Archbold*, above, n 87. See also *Bourne v Colodense Ltd* [1985] ICR 291 (support by trade union). Cf *Neville v London Express Newspaper Ltd* [1919] AC 368 (support by newspaper).

[97] *Martell v Consett Iron Co Ltd* [1955] Ch 363.

[98] *British Cash and Parcel Conveyors Ltd v Lamson Stores Service Co Ltd* [1908] 1 KB 1006; *Bourne v Colodense Ltd*, above, n 96; *Trendtex Trading Corp v Crédit Suisse* [1980] 1 QB 629, 668, [1982] AC 679; *Giles v Thompson* [1994] 1 AC 142, 164; *Camdex International Ltd v Bank of Zambia* [1998] QB 22; *Norglen Ltd v Reeds Rains Prudential Ltd* [1999] 2 AC 1.

[99] *Giles v Thompson* [1994] 1 AC 142, 163.

[100] *Hayward v Giffard* (1838) 4 M & W 194, 196; *Shah v Karanjia* [1993] 4 All ER 792; *Murphy v Young & Co's Brewery plc* [1997] 1 Lloyd's Rep 236; *Tharros Shipping Co Ltd v Bias Shipping Ltd (No 3)* [1997] 1 Lloyd's Rep 246, 250. Cf *Hill v Archbold*, above, n 87, 694–5; *McFarlane v EE Caledonia Ltd (No 2)* [1995] 1 WLR 366.

[101] See also Access to Justice Act 1999, ss 27–28; Conditional Fees Agreements Order 2013 (SI 2013 No 689); Legal Aid, Sentencing and Punishment of Offenders Act 2012, amending the 1990 Act to provide that the success fee chargeable by the claimant's lawyer can no longer be recoverable against an unsuccessful defendant.

[102] Courts and Legal Services Act 1990, s 58AA, added by Coroners and Justice Act 2009, allowed damages-based agreements but only in relation to employment matters.

[103] Implementing Jackson LJ's *Review of Civil Litigation Costs: Final Report* (2009), ch 12. See also CPR r 44.18; Damages-Based Agreements Regulations 2013 (SI 2013 No 609).

[104] Courts and Legal Services Act 1990, s 58AA(2).

Parliament wished to freeze further common law development, it had to do so more directly. The agreement was held not to be contrary to public policy.[105] Millett LJ stated that the policy which had invalidated such agreements in the past was formed in an age when litigation was regarded as an evil and to be discouraged. 'It rings oddly in our ears today when access to justice is regarded as a fundamental human right which ought to be readily available to all.' He considered that current attitudes are exemplified by the passage into law of the Courts and Legal Services Act 1990 which showed that 'the fear that lawyers may be tempted by having a financial incentive in the outcome of litigation to act improperly is exaggerated, and that there is a countervailing public policy in making justice readily accessible to persons of modest means'.[106] But this was not followed by the Court of Appeal in subsequent cases. In *Awwad v Geraghty & Co*[107] the Court was of the view that the carefully crafted legislative scheme shows and defines the extent to which Parliament has decided to make such agreements enforceable. May LJ stated that where Parliament has by successive enactments 'modified the law by which any arrangement to receive a contingency fee was impermissible, there is no present room for the court, by an application of what is perceived to be public policy, to go beyond that which Parliament has provided'.[108] More recently the Court of Appeal has again rejected the views expressed by Millett LJ in the *Thai Trading* case, and has said that the common law of champerty remains unchanged.[109]

(f) AGREEMENTS WHICH ARE CONTRARY TO GOOD MORALS

Although it has sometimes been said that contracts *contra bonos mores*—contrary to good morals—are void, the only aspect of immorality with which Courts of law have actually dealt is sexual immorality.[110] Formerly the Courts generally refused to enforce any contract which directly or indirectly promotes sexual immorality. Thus a promise by a man to pay a woman money if she would become his mistress has been held to be illegal and unenforceable.[111] And a landlord who let premises to a woman who was, to the knowledge of the landlord's agent, the kept mistress of a man who was in the

---

[105] [1998] QB 781, overruling the earlier contrary decisions of *British Waterways Board v Norman* (1993) 26 HLR 232 and *Aratra Potato Co Ltd v Taylor Joynson Garrett* [1995] 4 All ER 695.

[106] *Ibid*, 786, 790.   [107] [2001] QB 570.

[108] *Ibid*, 600. See also at 593 (Schiemann LJ). *Thai Trading* may be also open to question on other grounds: see *Thomas Hughes v Kingston upon Hull CC* [1999] QB 1193; *Mohamed v Alaga & Co* [2000] 1 WLR 1815, but notice that leave to appeal was refused by HL in *Thai Trading*: see *Awwad v Geraghty & Co*, above, n 107, 588–9.

[109] *Sibthorpe v Southwark LBC* [2011] EWCA Civ 25, [2011] 1 WLR 2111 at [39] (Lord Neuberger MR: 'although the trenchant judgment of Millett LJ is powerful and deserves respect, it was clearly per incuriam'). See also *R (Factortame) v Secretary of State for Transport, Local Government and the Regions (No 8)* [2002] 2 EWCA Civ 932, [2003] QB 381.

[110] *Coral Leisure Group Ltd v Barnett* [1981] ICR 503, 506.

[111] *Walker v Perkins* (1764) 1 W Bl 517; *Benyon v Nettlefold* (1850) 3 Mac & G 94. But a promise made in consideration of past illicit cohabitation merely lacks consideration, and is not illegal: *Beaumont v Reeve* (1846) 8 QB 483.

habit of visiting her there, and who was expected to pay the rent, was not permitted to recover the rent reserved in the lease.[112]

The Courts today, however, are unlikely to adopt the same attitude to agreements involving extra-marital cohabitation.[113] As an Australian judge has said: 'The social judgments of today upon matters of "immorality" are as different from those of the last century as is the bikini from a bustle'.[114] The law has come to terms with the fact that a man and woman, or two persons of the same sex, may set up home together in a stable relationship, and has afforded to unmarried partners certain rights in the 'quasi-matrimonial home'.[115] Such rights (which may sometimes be contractual in origin) have not been denied on the ground of immorality. And the Court of Appeal has held that an agreement to advertise telephone sex lines is not unenforceable on the grounds of immorality.[116]

On the other hand, it seems unlikely that an agreement which involves prostitution would be enforced. An action cannot be maintained to recover the rent of premises knowingly let for the purposes of prostitution,[117] or upon a contract of employment which requires the employee to procure prostitutes for customers of the employer.[118] Also in *Pearce v Brooks*:[119]

P, a firm of coach-builders, agreed with B, a prostitute, to hire to her an ornamental brougham of an intriguing design, with the knowledge that it was to be used by her in the furtherance of her trade. She failed to pay the hire, and P brought an action to recover the money.

It was held that P could not recover.

(g) AGREEMENTS WHICH AFFECT THE FREEDOM OR SECURITY OF MARRIAGE OR THE DUE DISCHARGE OF PARENTAL DUTY

(i) Restraint of marriage

Agreements which restrain the freedom to marry are contrary to policy as injurious to the moral welfare of the citizen. Thus a promise under seal not to marry any person

---

[112] *Upfill v Wright* [1911] 1 KB 506.   [113] See Dwyer (1977) 93 LQR 386.

[114] *Andrews v Parker* [1973] Qd R 93, 104 (Stable J).

[115] *Eves v Eves* [1975] 1 WLR 1338; *Tanner v Tanner* [1975] 1 WLR 1346; and for modern leading cases, see *Stack v Dowden* [2007] UKHL 17, [2007] 2 AC 432; *Jones v Kernott* [2011] UKSC 53, [2012] 1 AC 776. See also Part IV of the Family Law Act 1996, especially s 62 (defining cohabitants), as amended by Civil Partnership Act 2004; *Davis v Johnson* [1979] AC 264; *Tinsley v Milligan* [1994] 1 AC 340, below, p 452 (where what made the agreement illegal was that its purpose was to defraud the social security, rather than that it concerned lesbian cohabitees); *Barclays Bank plc v O'Brien* [1994] 1 AC 180, 198. Cf Law Com No 304, *Cohabitation: The Financial Consequences of Relationship Breakdown* (2007) which did not equate cohabiting couples fully with married couples.

[116] *Armhouse Lee Ltd v Chappell*, The Times, 7 August 1996.

[117] *Girardy v Richardson* (1793) 1 Esp 13.

[118] Cf *Coral Leisure Group Ltd v Barnett* [1981] ICR 503.

[119] (1866) LR 1 Ex 213. See also *Armhouse Lee Ltd v Chappell*, above, n 116 (agreements to promote sex dating probably illegal).

besides the promisee, and on breach to pay the promisee £1,000, was held void, as there was no promise of marriage on either side and the agreement was purely restrictive.[120]

(ii) Marriage brokage

Promises made upon the consideration of procuring a marriage between two persons, are held illegal 'not for the sake of the particular instance or the person, but of the public, and that marriages may be on a proper foundation'.[121] It has been held that an agreement to introduce a person to others of the opposite sex with a view to marriage is invalid, even where there is a choice given of a number of persons, and not an effort to bring about marriage with a particular person.[122] However, it is submitted that decisions such as these require reconsideration in the light of modern conditions. If they remain good law the transactions between the many marriage bureaux and dating agencies and their clients may be unenforceable.

(iii) Agreements for separation

Agreements providing for the separation of husband and wife are valid if made in prospect of an immediate separation; but it is otherwise if they contemplate a possible separation in the future, because they then give inducements to the parties not to perform their matrimonial duties, in the fulfilment of which society has an interest.[123]

(iv) Parental duty

For the same reason a parent cannot by contract transfer to another his or her rights and duties in respect of a child, because the law imposes such duties in respect of the minor and for his or her benefit.[124] In a proper case, however, an adoption order can be obtained from the Court under the Adoption and Children Act 2002. Statute expressly provides that a surrogacy arrangement, that is, one made by a woman with a view to carrying a child and to handing the child over to, and parental responsibility being met by, another person, is unenforceable.[125]

---

[120] *Lowe v Peers* (1768) 4 Burr 2225.   [121] *Cole v Gibson* (1750) 1 Ves Sen 503, 506 (Lord Eldon).
[122] *Hermann v Charlesworth* [1905] 2 KB 123. Note, however the liberal approach to the restitution of money paid under such an agreement after substantial performance, below, p 446, and compare the general approach, below, p 444.
[123] *Cartwright v Cartwright* (1853) 3 De GM & G 982.
[124] *Humphrys v Polak* [1901] 2 KB 385. See also Children Act 1989, s 2 (defining which parent has responsibility) and see s 2(9) (person who has parental responsibility for a child may not surrender or transfer any part of that responsibility to another but may arrange for some or all of it to be met by one or more persons acting on his behalf).
[125] Surrogacy Arrangements Act 1985, s 1A, inserted by Human Fertilisation and Embryology Act 1990. See also *Re P (Minors) (Wardship: Surrogacy)* [1987] 2 FLR 421.

(h) AGREEMENTS WHICH OUST THE JURISDICTION OF THE COURTS

At common law an agreement which purports to oust the jurisdiction of the Courts is contrary to public policy and void.[126] It is the policy of the common law that citizens have the right to have their legal position determined by the ordinary tribunals. In the case of arbitration, the common law position has been substantially modified by statute, particularly in the case of arbitrations involving foreign nationals and companies.

(i) Arbitration clauses

There is no objection at common law to contract clauses to the effect that any dispute or difference between the parties is to be referred to and settled by arbitration.[127] An arbitration clause which requires as a condition precedent to the accrual of any cause of action that the arbitrator shall have made an award is not contrary to public policy. Such a clause is common in arbitration agreements and is known as a 'Scott v Avery' clause.[128] It does not oust the jurisdiction of the Court but merely provides that the cause of action shall not be complete until the arbitration award is made. A similar provision known as an 'Atlantic Shipping' clause is also frequently inserted, and this provides that no claim shall arise unless it is put forward in writing and an arbitrator appointed within a limited period.[129] Its validity rests upon the same foundation.

Provision is made in the Arbitration Act 1996 for an appeal to the Court on points of law arising out of an arbitrator's award.[130] There are, however, a number of limits on this right. For example, unless all the parties agree to the appeal, leave of the Court is required.[131]

(ii) Foreign jurisdiction clauses

The Courts will normally uphold a clause in a contract whereby any dispute between the parties is to be referred to the exclusive jurisdiction of a foreign Court.[132] But such

---

[126] *Czarnikow v Roth Schmidt* [1922] 2 KB 478. But cf *Jones v Sherwood Computer Services plc* [1992] 1 WLR 277; Kendall (1993) 109 LQR 385 (question remitted to expert); *West of England Shipowners Mutual Insurance Association v Crystal Ltd* [1996] 1 Lloyd's Rep 370 (a chosen tribunal may be the final arbiter on questions of fact).

[127] An arbitration clause in a consumer contract may however be an unfair term within Part 2 of the Consumer Rights Act 2015, Sched 2, Part 1, para 20: above, p 223; and is unfair where it relates to a claim for a pecuniary remedy not exceeding £5,000: Arbitration Act 1996, s 91; SI 1999 No 2167, art 3.

[128] *Scott v Avery* (1855) 5 HLC 811. Cf Arbitration Act 1996, s 9(4)–(5).

[129] *Atlantic Shipping and Trading Co v Louis Dreyfus & Co* [1922] 2 AC 250. But see Arbitration Act 1996, s 12.

[130] Arbitration Act 1996, s 69(1). See also ss 70 and 71.   [131] Arbitration Act 1996, s 69(2)–(3).

[132] *Donohue v Armco Inc* [2001] UKHL 64, [2002] 1 Lloyd's Rep 425 at [24] (Lord Bingham: the contractual bargain should be given effect 'in the absence of strong reasons for departing from it').

a clause is not absolutely binding, and the Court has a discretion to override it if the claimant establishes good cause for bringing the claim in England.[133]

(iii) Maintenance agreements

Another example of an agreement which ousts the jurisdiction of the Courts is one in which a wife contracts not to apply to the Courts for maintenance in return for a promise by the husband that he will make her a definite allowance.[134] The right of the Court to award maintenance cannot be ousted, although the financial arrangements are not thereby rendered void or unenforceable.[135]

(i) AGREEMENTS IN RESTRAINT OF TRADE

The common law does not favour agreements that prohibit or restrain a person in the exercise of a lawful trade, employment, or profession. It protects the right of individuals to work and prevents them from disabling themselves from earning a living by an unreasonable restriction by the doctrine of restraint of trade. Not all restraints of trade, however, are contrary to public policy. For example, the public interest does not necessarily suffer if a person who sells the goodwill of a business undertakes an obligation not to enter into immediate competition with the buyer. An agreement prima facie in restraint of trade is enforceable if it is established that the restrictions in it are reasonable in the interests of the parties and of the public.

(i) Restraint of trade defined

An agreement in restraint of trade has been defined as 'one in which a party (the covenantor) agrees with any other party (the covenantee) to restrict his liberty in the future to carry on trade with other persons not parties to the contract in such a manner as he chooses'.[136] This definition is adequate provided it is not applied too literally. In one sense, all commercial contracts restrain trade; for when one person binds another by contract, say to sell a rare Sheraton writing table or a particular cargo of oil, the seller's future liberty to deal lawfully in that subject-matter with persons not parties to the contract is restricted. Yet ordinary commercial contracts are clearly not tainted with invalidity. The issue is how to determine which agreements are 'in restraint of trade'.

Two categories of agreement have long been recognized as 'in restraint of trade'. First, agreements between employers and employees, whereby the employees

---

[133] *The Fehmarn* [1958] 1 WLR 159; *The Eleftheria* [1970] P 54; *The Adolf Warski* [1976] 1 Lloyd's Rep 107, aff'd [1976] 2 Lloyd's Rep 241. But see the Civil Jurisdiction and Judgments Act 1982, Sched 1, art 17, and Council Regulation (EC) 44/2001 (Brussels 1) art 23.

[134] *Hyman v Hyman* [1929] AC 601. See Cretney, in Rose (ed), *Consensus ad idem* (1996) 269–74.

[135] Matrimonial Causes Act 1973, s 34. Cf *Sutton v Sutton* [1984] Ch 184. A financial agreement which is then embodied in a consent order will bar further application to the Court: *De Lasala v De Lasala* [1980] AC 546, 560.

[136] *Petrofina (Great Britain) Ltd v Martin* [1966] Ch 146, 180 (Diplock LJ, adopted by Lord Hodson in *Esso Petroleum Co Ltd v Harper's Garage (Stourport) Ltd* [1968] AC 269, 317. See also *ibid*, 307 (Lord Morris).

covenant not to set up business on their own account on leaving the employers' service or to enter into employment with a rival firm. Secondly, agreements between the buyer and seller of a business together with its goodwill, whereby the seller covenants not to carry on a business which will compete with that of the buyer.

Apart from these types of agreement, there is no definitive way of determining whether or not an agreement is in restraint of trade. As noted above, asking whether a person has agreed to give up some freedom which he or she otherwise had could bring in all commercial contracts. The difficulty is not met by asking whether the agreement only regulates normal commercial relations because this too begs the question. Lord Wilberforce has said:[137]

[I]t would be mistaken, even it were possible, to try to crystallise the rules of this, or any, aspect of public policy into neat propositions. The doctrine of restraint of trade is one to be applied to factual situations with a broad and flexible rule of reason.

The factual situations which invite the application of the doctrine will change with prevailing economic and social conditions, and it is important to bear in mind that those referred to later in this chapter are not exhaustive: 'the classification must remain fluid and the categories can never be closed'.[138] But today, when economic theory indicates that a competitive economy produces more beneficial results—from the point of view of the public—than a non-competitive economy, it is tempting to define a contract in restraint of trade as being one which is designed to restrict competition,[139] although it must be admitted that there is no judicial authority for this formulation and it has been authoritatively stated that the reason for the Courts' intervention in cases of restraint of trade is simply to protect the weaker party against oppression.[140]

The law concerning restraint of trade has also changed from time to time, both in form and in spirit, in response to changes in conditions of trade. In modern law the operation of the common law doctrine, particularly concerning agreements for exclusive dealing and market-sharing, has been significantly overtaken by both national and European Union legislative provisions which seek to control anti-competitive practices, which are of wider application than the common law doctrine and which are primarily administered by regulatory authorities.[141]

---

[137] *Esso Petroleum Co Ltd v Harper's Garage (Stourport) Ltd*, above, n 136, 331.

[138] *Ibid*, 337. See also *Proactive Sports Management Ltd v Rooney* [2011] EWCA Civ 1444, [2012] FSR 16 at [93] (contract restricting footballer's exploitation of his image rights subject to restraint of trade doctrine, although ancillary to his primary activity as footballer).

[139] Guest (1968) 2 JALT 3. Contrast *Texaco Ltd v Mulberry Filling Station Ltd* [1972] 1 WLR 814, 827; Heydon (1969) 85 LQR 229.

[140] *A Schroeder Music Publishing Co Ltd v Macaulay* [1974] 1 WLR 1308, 1315–16 (Lord Diplock).

[141] See arts 101 and 102 of the TFEU (formerly EEC Treaty, arts 85 and 86, later EC Treaty, arts 81 and 82); and in domestic legislation the Competition Act 1998, the Enterprise Act 2002, and the Enterprise and Regulatory Reform Act 2013; Whish and Bailey, *Competition Law* (8th edn, 2015) and Rodger and MacCulloch, *Competition Law and Policy in the EC and UK* (5th edn, 2014).

(ii) The modern law

The foundation of the modern law on restraint of trade is contained in the speech of Lord Macnaghten in *Nordenfelt v Maxim Nordenfelt Guns and Ammunition Co Ltd*:[142]

N was a maker and inventor of guns and ammunition. He sold his business to the MN company for £287,500 and entered into a covenant (later to be repeated in a contract of service) that he would not for 25 years 'engage . . . either directly or indirectly in the trade or business of a manufacturer of guns, gun mountings or carriages, gunpowder explosives or ammunition, or in any business competing or liable to compete in any way with that for the time being carried on by the company', but expressly reserved the right to deal in explosives other than gunpowder, in torpedoes or submarine boats, and in metal castings or forgings. After some years N entered into a business with a rival company dealing with guns and ammunition, and MN sought an injunction to restrain him from so doing.

The House of Lords was of the opinion that the covenant not to compete with the company 'in *any* business competing or liable to compete in any way with that for the time being carried on by the company' was unreasonable, as it attempted to protect not only the business as it was when sold, but any future activities of the company. It was therefore void; but this clause was distinct and severable from the rest of the agreement.[143] As for the remainder of the restraint, insofar as it protected the business actually sold, it was reasonable between the parties, because N not only received a large sum of money, but also by his reservation retained scope for the exercise of his inventive and manufacturing skill. Moreover, the wide area over which the business extended necessitated a restraint co-extensive with that area for the protection of the respondents. Finally it could not be said to be contrary to the public interest since it transferred to an English company the making of guns and ammunition for foreign lands. The restraint was therefore valid.

As a result of this decision and later cases in which it has been elucidated, certain propositions of law can be stated:

(1) All restraints of trade, in the absence of special justifying circumstances, are contrary to public policy and do not give rise to legally binding obligations, and in that sense are void.[144] But in this context being void does not mean that the agreement will be disregarded for all purposes, and it has been said that a contract in restraint of trade should more properly be spoken of as one 'which the law will not enforce'.[145] It is not unlawful for the parties to agree to implement it, and if the parties do so the Courts will not later allow them to recover sums paid under the agreement or property transferred on the basis that the agreement is of no effect whatsoever.[146] But, as we shall see, in certain situations it is the effect of an agreement

---

[142] [1894] AC 535.

[143] For severance, see below, p 455.

[144] *Mason v Provident Clothing & Supply Co Ltd* [1913] AC 724.

[145] *Joseph Evans & Co Ltd v Heathcote* [1918] 1 KB 418, 431 (Bankes LJ).

[146] *Boddington v Lawton* [1994] ICR 478, 491–3 (Nicholls V-C). See also *Joseph Evans & Co Ltd v Heathcote* [1918] 1 KB 418; *Esso Petroleum Co Ltd v Harper's Garage (Stourport) Ltd* [1968] AC 269, 297; *A Schroeder Music Publishing Co Ltd v Macaulay* [1974] 1 All ER 174, 181, aff'd [1974] 1 WLR 1308.

on third parties which renders the agreement in unreasonable restraint of trade, and, in such cases, the third parties may be able to challenge the agreement.[147]

(2) It is a question of law for the decision of the Court whether the special circumstances adduced do or do not justify the restraint; and if a restraint is not justified, the Court will, if necessary, take the point, since it relates to a matter of public policy, and the Court does not enforce agreements which are contrary to public policy.[148]

(3) A restraint can only be justified if it is reasonable (a) in the interests of the contracting parties, and (b) in the interests of the public.[149]

(4) The onus of showing that the restraint is reasonable between the parties rests upon the person alleging that it is so, that is to say, upon the covenantee.[150] The onus of showing that, notwithstanding that a covenant is reasonable between the parties, it is nevertheless injurious to the public interest and therefore void, rests upon the party alleging it to be so, that is to say, usually upon the covenantor.[151] But once the agreement is before the Court it is open to scrutiny in all its surrounding circumstances as a question of law.[152]

(5) Covenants in restraint of trade are construed (a) with reference to the object sought to be obtained, that is the protection of one of the parties against competition in trade, and (b) in their context and in the light of the factual matrix when the agreement was made.[153]

Reasonableness as a test for the validity of a restraint, however, requires further consideration.

(iii) Reasonableness in the interests of the parties

The application of this test will depend on the answers to two questions: what is it that the covenantee is entitled to protect, and how far can such protection extend? A covenant cannot be considered reasonable unless it is designed to protect the legitimate interests of the covenantee.[154] The issue of whether a covenant in restraint of

---

[147] Below, p 434.

[148] *Wyatt v Kreglinger and Fernau* [1933] 1 KB 793, 806; *North Western Salt Co Ltd v Electrolytic Alkali Co Ltd* [1914] AC 461, 470.

[149] *Proactive Sports Management Ltd v Rooney*, above, n 138 at [93] (Arden LJ: 'Public policy is concerned with the manner in which a person may properly realise his potential, not only for the good of that individual but for the economic benefit of society generally').

[150] *Mason v Provident Clothing & Supply Co Ltd* [1913] AC 724, 733; *Herbert Morris Ltd v Saxelby* [1916] 1 AC 688, 700; *Attwood v Lamont* [1920] 3 KB 571, 587.

[151] *Herbert Morris Ltd v Saxelby*, above n 150, 700, 708; *A-G of Commonwealth of Australia v Adelaide Steamship Co Ltd* [1913] AC 781, 795.

[152] *Esso Petroleum Co Ltd v Harper's Garage (Stourport) Ltd* [1968] AC 269, 319.

[153] *Clarke v Newland* [1991] 1 All ER 397, 402; *Commercial Plastics Ltd v Vincent* [1965] 1 QB 623, 644.

[154] The restraint must be reasonable for *both* parties: *Herbert Morris Ltd v Saxelby* above n 150, 707 (Lord Parker), and the reasonableness is assessed at the time when the covenant is entered into; cf, however, *Shell UK Ltd v Lostock Garage Ltd* [1976] 1 WLR 1187 (Lord Denning MR, not supported by Ormrod and Bridge LJJ).

trade is reasonable ultimately falls to be decided by reference to the legitimate interests that are sought to be protected and not by a classification of the relationship between the parties.[155] But the nature of the interests recognized as legitimate by the law will vary according to the subject-matter and nature of the contract.

The different approaches of the Courts can be illustrated by comparing restraints on the seller of a business and those on former employees.[156] The buyer of a business with its goodwill is entitled to prevent the seller from competing with the business sold. The buyer has acquired a business which, from the nature of the case, has been immune from competition by the person who has sold it, and the goodwill of that business is an interest which the buyer is legitimately entitled to protect.[157] A different set of considerations comes into play in the case of restraints upon former employees. An employer cannot prevent competition by a former employee, or restrict the use by the employee of personal skill and knowledge acquired in the course of the employment. The employer is entitled only to protect its trade secrets, and to prevent the use by the employee of influence acquired over its clients or customers.[158]

Where the covenantee has a legitimate interest which it is entitled to protect, the restriction must not be longer in point of time, or wider in area, or otherwise be more extensive in scope than is necessary to protect that interest. The answer to this question in any individual case, however, must necessarily depend upon the interest to be protected, the nature of the contract and the relative positions of the contracting parties.[159]

The quantum of the consideration which the covenantor has received in exchange for the restraint is relevant to the determination of the reasonableness of the contract.[160]

(iv) Reasonableness in the interests of the public

Cases in which a restraint has been held void as not being reasonable in the interests of the public are not common. Indeed, in 1913, the Judicial Committee of the Privy Council observed that 'their Lordships are not aware of any case in which a restraint though reasonable in the interests of the parties has been held unenforceable because it involved some injury to the public',[161] and it was further said that 'if once the Court is satisfied

---

[155] *Bridge v Deacons* [1984] 1 AC 705, 714.

[156] For other contexts, see *Esso Petroleum Co Ltd v Harper's Garage (Stourport) Ltd*, above, n 136 ('solus tie' for purchase of petrol); *A Schroeder Music Publishing Co Ltd v Macaulay* [1974] 1 WLR 1308 ('exclusive services' agreement between young and unknown song-writer and music publishing company).

[157] *Herbert Morris Ltd v Saxelby* [1916] 1 AC 688, 713.

[158] *Faccenda Chicken Ltd v Fowler* [1987] Ch 117, 137.

[159] eg *Esso Petroleum Co Ltd v Harper's Garage (Stourport) Ltd*, above, n 136 (covenant for four years and five months was reasonable; covenant for 21 years was unreasonable); *Mason v Provident Clothing & Supply Co* [1913] AC 724 (covenant for three years within 25 miles of London was unreasonable); cf *Foster & Sons Ltd v Suggett* (1918) 35 TLR 87 (covenant extending to the whole of the UK was reasonable); *Bromley v Smith* [1909] 2 KB 235 (restriction on baker from opening restaurant was unreasonable).

[160] *Nordenfelt v Maxim Nordenfelt Guns and Ammunition Co Ltd* [1894] AC 535, 565; *Esso Petroleum Co Ltd v Harper's Garage (Stourport) Ltd* [1968] AC 269, 300, 318, 323; *Allied Dunbar (Frank Weisinger) Ltd v Weisinger* [1988] IRLR 60.

[161] *A-G of Commonwealth of Australia v Adelaide Steamship Co* [1913] AC 781, 795.

that the restraint is reasonable as between the parties this onus [of proving injury to the public] will be no light one'.[162] More recently, however, in relation to certain types of restrictive trading agreements there has been a distinct shift of emphasis in favour of recognizing the importance of the interests of the public.[163] Such agreements are, as a general rule, freely entered into between traders who are perfectly capable of deciding for themselves what is reasonable in their own interests. So the real point at issue is whether the maintenance of the restraint is detrimental to the interests of the public.

Even where cases are decided on the basis of reasonableness between the parties, it is *ultimately* on the ground of public policy that the Court will decline to enforce an unreasonable restraint. As Lord Pearce has said: 'There is not, as some cases seem to suggest, a separation between what is reasonable on grounds of public policy and what is reasonable as between the parties. There is one broad question: is it in the interests of the community that this restraint should, as between the parties, be held to be reasonable and enforceable?'[164]

(v) Cartel agreements

Business organizations frequently enter into cartels, that is to say, agreements to regulate the production and marketing of the commodities manufactured by them, and to maintain prices and standards in relation to those commodities. Similarly, employers may enter into agreements attempting to regulate labour and to impose mutual restrictions upon the re-employment of former employees. The rules of professional organizations also restrict professionals such as lawyers or doctors as to how they may work, for instance, by restricting advertising or controlling the charges for services. Cartel agreements are, like all other agreements in restraint of trade, prima facie void at common law and must be justified as being reasonable in the interests of the parties and of the public.

In this type of agreement, which is generally freely negotiated, the parties can be regarded 'as the best judges of what is reasonable between themselves'.[165] They are entered into for the purpose of avoiding undue competition and carrying on trade without excessive fluctuations or uncertainty. As a result, it is difficult for a Court to say that they are unreasonable between the parties, and in fact the Courts have only done so if an agreement contains no provision, or virtually no provision, for voluntary withdrawal.[166]

---

[162] *Ibid*, 797.

[163] *Esso Petroleum Co Ltd v Harper's Garage (Stourport) Ltd* [1968] AC 269, 300–1, 318–19, 321, 324, 330, 340–1. See also *Dickson v Pharmaceutical Society of Great Britain* [1970] AC 403, 441. But cf the more cautious approach adopted by Ungoed-Thomas J in *Texaco Ltd v Mulberry Filling Station Ltd* [1972] 1 WLR 814, 826–9. See also *Alec Lobb (Garages) Ltd v Total Oil (Great Britain) Ltd* [1985] 1 WLR 173, 191.

[164] *Esso Petroleum Co Ltd v Harper's Garage (Stourport) Ltd*, above, n 163, 324.

[165] *North Western Salt Co v Electrolytic Alkali Co Ltd* [1914] AC 461, 471 (Viscount Haldane LC); *English Hop Growers v Dering* [1928] 2 KB 174, 180.

[166] *McEllistrim v Ballymacelligott Co-operative Agriculture and Dairy Society Ltd* [1919] AC 548; *J Evans & Co v Heathcote* [1918] 1 KB 418; *Bellshill and Mossend Co-operative Society v Dalziel Co-operative Society* [1960] AC 832.

The position adopted by the common law has been to regard many cartels at least as being not injurious to the public,[167] and in some cases even as positively beneficial.[168] Indeed, the Courts virtually excluded the possibility that a cartel should be held contrary to the public interest by requiring it to be one which was calculated to produce 'a pernicious monopoly, that is to say, a monopoly calculated to enhance prices to an unreasonable extent'.[169] The effect was that in this context the common law did not promote competition. Even if the Courts had, in fact, adopted a different economic attitude, the doctrine of restraint of trade could not have been employed to any real effect in the suppression of cartels, since, save in exceptional circumstances, a cartel agreement would only have come before the Courts if one of the parties failed to perform it and was sued for the breach.

The exception concerns agreements between employers which attempt to regulate labour and to impose mutual restrictions upon the re-employment of former employees. These may be struck down as being employer–employee covenants in disguise or as being contrary to the public interest.[170] So, in *Eastham v Newcastle United Football Club Ltd*[171] a professional football player, who could be debarred by rules in an agreement between his club and the Football Association from playing for any other club, was entitled to a declaration that the rules were invalid. Wilberforce J accepted that some restriction was required for the proper and stable organization of the game of football in England, but concluded the rules were more restrictive on the player's liberty of employment than was necessary to protect this interest. He therefore granted a declaration that the system was invalid, not only against the defendant club, but also in respect of the rules of the Football Association. Although these rules constituted an agreement between employers only, they were calculated to affect the employees' freedom of employment and so could be challenged by the player on the same grounds as if they had been contained in an agreement between him and his employer. Similarly, in *Greig v Insole*[172] Slade J held void as being in unreasonable restraint of trade resolutions of the International Cricket Conference and the Test and County Cricket Board disqualifying from playing in test and county matches any player who took part in a match arranged by a private promoter (Mr Kerry Packer) during a certain period.

---

[167] *A-G of Commonwealth of Australia v Adelaide Steamship Co* [1913] AC 781.

[168] *North Western Salt Co Ltd v Electrolytic Alkali Co Ltd* [1914] AC 461.

[169] *A-G of Commonwealth of Australia v Adelaide Steamship Co*, above, n 167, 796.

[170] *Mineral Water Bottle Exchange and Trade Protection Soc v Booth* (1887) 36 Ch D 465; *Kores Manufacturing Co Ltd v Kolok Manufacturing Co Ltd* [1959] Ch 108; *Esso Petroleum Co Ltd v Harper's Garage (Stourport) Ltd* [1968] AC 269, 300, 319. But see Trade Union and Labour Relations (Consolidation) Act 1992, s 128 (purposes of employers' associations, defined in s 122, not unlawful or unenforceable by reason only that they are in restraint of trade).

[171] [1964] Ch 413, 432. See also *Buckley v Tutty* (1971) 46 ALJR 23; *Hall v Victorian Football League* [1982] VR 64 (Australia).

[172] [1978] 1 WLR 302.

The common law doctrine of restraint of trade also extends to cover the rules of professional bodies. Thus the Court of Appeal refused to strike out a claim that a rule of the Jockey Club preventing a woman from holding a trainer's licence was invalid,[173] and a rule of the Pharmaceutical Society restricting the types of goods in which their members might deal has been held invalid.[174] The doctrine may even apply to the rules of professional bodies the members of which do not technically engage in 'trade',[175] though possibly not to those rules which are related solely to the maintenance of professional honour or standards.[176] But the basis upon which a person who is not a member of the relevant professional body, and thus a party to the restrictive agreement, can challenge it, has been put into question[177] and in practice the field has largely been left to modern legislation promoting competition or proscribing certain forms of discrimination.[178]

4. THE EFFECT OF ILLEGALITY

(a) THE FUNDAMENTAL PRINCIPLE OF POLICY

It has already been pointed out that the single word 'illegal' may embrace varying degrees of impropriety,[179] and it should not be supposed that the effect of illegality is always identical.

In some cases, the law adopts a very severe attitude and refuses to assist a person implicated in the illegality in any way whatsoever. In others, public policy does not require that such a person should be so completely denied a remedy. Money paid or property transferred may be recoverable;[180] collateral transactions may not be tainted;[181] and the Court may be prepared to sever the illegal part of the contract from that which is legal, and enforce the legal part alone.[182] In this section, however, unless otherwise stated, we shall be dealing with those situations where the law rigorously discourages the claims of those who found their cause of action upon an illegal transaction. Even in these situations, there is some variation in the rules to be applied.[183] Moreover, in some instances, the Courts will refuse their aid only to a party who intends to break the law; in others, the contract is unlawful *per se*.[184]

---

[173] *Nagle v Feilden* [1966] 2 QB 633. See also *Greig v Insole* [1978] 1 WLR 302; *Adamson v NSW Rugby League Ltd* (1991) 103 ALR 319.

[174] *Pharmaceutical Society of Great Britain v Dickson* [1970] AC 403.

[175] *Ibid*, 420, 427, 430, 436, 441.   [176] *Ibid*, 421, 436.

[177] Privity of contract precludes an action in contract at common law (see below, Chapter 21), and in *R v Disciplinary Committee of the Jockey Club, ex p Aga Khan* [1993] 1 WLR 909 it was said by Hoffmann LJ at 933 that gaps in private law remedies should not be filled by subjecting them to public law and the judicial review procedure. Where there is unlawful discrimination or the restriction seeks to prevent those subject to the rules from dealing with a non-party, there may be a remedy: *Cutsforth v Mansfield Inns Ltd* [1986] 1 WLR 558.

[178] Above, n 141.   [179] See above, p 410.   [180] See below, pp 445, 447.

[181] See below, p 454.   [182] See below, p 455.   [183] See below, pp 444, 447.

[184] See below, p 442.

Thus, although general rules can be set out, each case must be examined in order to discover the precise effect of the illegality.

The fundamental principle upon which the Courts will act when they have to deal with an illegal contract was long ago explained by Lord Mansfield:[185]

The objection, that a contract is immoral or illegal as between plaintiff and defendant, sounds at all times very ill in the mouth of the defendant. It is not for his sake, however, that the objection is ever allowed; but is founded in general principles of policy, which the defendant has the advantage of, contrary to the real justice, as between him and the plaintiff, by accident, if I may so say. The principle of public policy is this: *ex dolo malo non oritur actio.* No Court will lend its aid to a man who founds his cause of action upon an immoral or an illegal act. If, from the plaintiff's own stating or otherwise, the cause of action appears to arise *ex turpi causa*, or the transgression of a positive law of this country, there the Court says he has no right to be assisted. It is upon that ground the Court goes; not for the sake of the defendant, but because they will not lend their aid to such a plaintiff. So if the plaintiff and defendant were to change sides, and the defendant was to bring his action against the plaintiff, the latter would then have the advantage of it; for where both are *equally* at fault, *potior est conditio defendentis.*[186]

It has been said that:

the principle is not a principle of justice: it is a principle of policy, whose application is indiscriminate and so can lead to unfair consequences as between the parties to litigation. Moreover the principle allows no room for the exercise of any discretion by the court in favour of one party or the other.[187]

In other words, on one view, the doctrine of illegality is not concerned with balancing the interests or rights of the parties, but is a rule of judicial abstention, given effect in the public interest:[188]

[R]ather than regulating the consequences of an illegal act (for example by restoring the parties to the status quo ante, in the same way as on the rescission of a contract) the courts withhold judicial remedies, leaving the loss to lie where it falls. This is so even in a contractual context, when the court is invited to determine the financial consequence of a contract's voidness for illegality. The ex turpi causa principle precludes the judge from performing his ordinary adjudicative function in a case where that would lend the authority of the state to

---

[185] *Holman v Johnson* (1775) 1 Cowp 341, 343. See also Glanville Williams (1942) 8 CLJ 51; Grodecki (1955) 71 LQR 254; *Stone & Rolls Ltd v Moore Stephens* [2009] UKHL 39, [2009] 1 AC 1391 at [20]–[26], [128]–[141].

[186] The maxim is '*in pari delicto* potior est conditio defendentis': where both are equally at fault, the defendant's position is the stronger.

[187] *Tinsley v Milligan* [1994] 1 AC 340, 355 (Lord Goff). But cf Case C-453/99 *Courage Ltd v Crehan* [2002] QB 507 (where EC competition law renders agreement illegal a national rule barring relief to an innocent party is precluded by art 81 EC Treaty (now art 101 TFEU)).

[188] *Les Laboratoires Servier v Apotex Inc* [2014] UKSC 55, [2015] AC 430 at [23] (Lord Sumption JSC). See also *Hounga v Allen* [2014] UKSC 47, [2014] 1 WLR 2889 at [56]; *Bilta (UK) Ltd v Nazir (No 2)* [2015] UKSC 23, [2015] 2 WLR 1168 at [60].

the enforcement of an illegal transaction or to the determination of the legal consequences of an illegal act.

The consequence is that, subject to exceptions, discussed below, no person who is aware of the illegal nature of a contract can enforce it, or recover money or property transferred under it.

Since the justification for the rule that an illegal contract cannot be enforced by a guilty party is not to protect the defendant but because the Courts will not lend their aid to such a claimant, it does not matter that the defendant shares the guilt. But questions of illegality involve varying degrees of impropriety, of participation and responsibility, of injustice because of unjust enrichment, and of relationship between the illegality and the claim.[189] This, as well as the harshness of the consequences of the application of the *ex turpi causa* maxim, led to the adoption in some decisions of an approach, originating in cases concerned with the effect of illegality on a claim in tort,[190] whereby the Courts would help such a claimant unless to do so 'would be an affront to public conscience'.[191] However, the 'public conscience' test was rejected by the House of Lords in *Tinsley v Milligan*, where their Lordships stated that it was 'inconsistent with numerous authorities' and with Lord Mansfield's principle, it was 'imponderable', and that its adoption would replace a system of rules by a discretionary balancing operation.[192] Lord Goff considered that to introduce a system of discretionary relief is a matter for the legislature after a full inquiry rather than for a Court. However, after a lengthy review of the law on illegality, the Law Commission concluded that there should be no legislation in this area because it would be difficult to define the ambit of a statutory discretion in a way that did not cause further problems.[193] Rather, the Courts should develop the law in ways that would render it clearer, more certain, and less arbitrary, basing their decisions in individual cases directly on the policies that underlie the illegality defence.[194]

---

[189] Tan (1988) 104 LQR 523, 526. See also above, p 409, below, pp 439, 444–5; Buckley (1994) 110 LQR 3; Rose (1996) JCL 271; *Les Laboratoires Servier v Apotex Inc*, above, n 3 at [22] (Lord Sumption JSC: 'The application of the ex turpi causa principle commonly raises three questions: (i) what acts constitute turpitude for the purpose of the defence? (ii) what relationship must the turpitude have to the claim? (iii) on what principles should the turpitude of an agent be attributed to his principal, especially when the principal is a corporation?').

[190] *Thackwell v Barclays Bank plc* [1986] 1 All ER 676; *Saunders v Edwards* [1987] 1 WLR 1116. On the test in tort, see further *Gray v Thames Trains Ltd* [2009] UKHL 33, [2009] 1 AC 1339; *Hounga v Allen* [2014] UKSC 47, [2014] 1 WLR 2889; Peel and Goudkamp, *Winfield and Jolowicz on Tort* (19th edn, 2014) 26-062–26-067; *Clerk & Lindsell on Torts* (21st edn, 2014) 3-02–3-46.

[191] *Euro Diam Ltd v Bathurst* [1990] QB 1, 35. See also *Howard v Shirlstar Container Transport Ltd* [1990] 1 WLR 1292, although *Tinsley v Milligan* (above, n 4) 360 explained this case as an example of the principle stated in *St John Shipping Corp v Rank* [1957] 1 QB 267, above, p 413.

[192] [1994] 1 AC 340, respectively at 358 and 361 (Lord Goff), 369 (Lord Browne-Wilkinson), and 358 and 363–4 (Lord Goff). This decision is open to criticism on other grounds; below, p 453.

[193] See, however, the New Zealand Illegal Contracts Act 1970 and NZ Law Commission Report No 25 *Contract Statutes Review* (1993) 21, 173 ('in practice [this statute] has worked reasonably well').

[194] Consultation Paper No 189, *The Illegality Defence: A Consultative Report* (2009), confirmed in the final report, Law Com No 320, *The Illegality Defence* (2010). They identified the policies as including (a)

The decision in *Tinsley v Milligan* remains authority,[195] and has received some further recent support in the Supreme Court[196] but has also been questioned,[197] and is likely to be subject to review as soon as the opportunity arises.[198] The debate continues to be between a 'rule-based' approach to this issue,[199] and a discretionary approach which balances the relevant factors on the facts of the case in hand.[200] The decisions of the Supreme Court have not yet addressed the effects of illegality on claims in contract, but in that context in *ParkingEye Ltd v Somerfield Stores Ltd*[201] the Court of Appeal applied the 'balance of factors' approach, adopting a statement from Etherton LJ in an earlier case. Toulson LJ stated:[202]

This is not to suggest that a list of policy factors should become a complete substitute for the rules about illegality in the law of contract which the courts have developed, but rather that those rules are to be developed and applied with the degree of flexibility necessary to give proper effect to the underlying policy factors. The decision in *Les Laboratoires Servier v Apotex Inc*[203] provides a good example. I would particularly endorse Etherton LJ's statement at para 75:

'what is required in each case is an intense analysis of the particular facts and of the proper application of the various policy considerations underlying the illegality principle so as to produce a just and proportionate response to the illegality. That is not the same as an unbridled discretion.'

In some parts of the law of contract it is necessary in the interests of commercial certainty to have fixed rules, sometimes with exceptions. But in the area of illegality, experience has shown that it is better to recognise that there may be conflicting considerations and that the rules need to be developed and applied in a way which enables the court to balance them fairly.

---

furthering the purpose of the rule which the illegal conduct has infringed; (b) consistency; (c) that the claimant should not profit from his or her own wrong; (d) deterrence; and (e) maintaining the integrity of the legal system: Consultation Paper No 189, paras 2.5–2.35, and that only if depriving the claimant of his or her rights is a proportionate response should the defence succeed: *ibid*, para 3.142. Cf Consultation Paper No 154, *The Effect of Illegality on Contracts and Trusts* (1999).

[195] *Les Laboratoires Servier v Apotex Inc*, above, n 3 at [19], [64]; *Bilta (UK) Ltd v Nazir (No 2)*, above, n 3 at [62], [99] (Lord Sumption JSC).

[196] *Les Laboratoires Servier v Apotex Inc*, above, n 3 at [20] (Lord Sumption JSC, with whom Lord Neuberger PSC and Lord Clarke JSC agreed); *Bilta (UK) Ltd v Nazir (No 2)*, above, n 3 at [99]; see also Fisher (2015) 78 MLR 854.

[197] *Bilta (UK) Ltd v Nazir (No 2)*, above, n 3 at [173] (Lord Toulson and Lord Hodge JJSC).

[198] *Bilta (UK) Ltd v Nazir (No 2)*, above, n 3 at [13]–[17] (Lord Neuberger PSC); above, p 410.

[199] Favoured by Lord Sumption JSC, above, n 196.

[200] Favoured by Lord Toulson and Lord Hodge JJSC, above, n 197; see also *Hounga v Allen* [2014] UKSC 47, [2014] 1 WLR 2889.

[201] [2012] EWCA Civ 1338, [2013] QB 840. See also *Patel v Mirza* [2014] EWCA Civ 1047, [2015] Ch 271 at [63]–[64] (Gloster LJ)); Buckley (2015) 131 LQR 341.

[202] [2012] EWCA Civ 1338, [2013] QB 840, at [53]–[54]; see also Sir Robin Jacob at [39].

[203] [2012] EWCA Civ 593, [2013] Bus LR 80 at [75]. For the decision of the Supreme Court in this case, see above, n 282.

(b) THE INTENTION OF THE PARTIES AND ENFORCEABILITY OF THE CONTRACT

Most contracts are not legal or illegal in the same way that eggs are good or bad. The effect of illegality will in most cases turn on the intention of the parties, that is, whether one or both of them entered into the contract intending to do an act forbidden by the law. Their rights and remedies will depend upon whether they knew of or participated in the illegal intention.

(i) Guilty parties

A party who enters into a contract for an illegal purpose or intending to perform it in an illegal manner, or a contract which to the knowledge of that party involves or has as its object the commission of an illegal act, cannot bring any action upon the contract or enforce it in any way.[204] And if both parties share the unlawful intention, as in *Pearce v Brooks*,[205] where both knew that the brougham was to be used for the purpose of prostitution, no action can be maintained by either party.

(ii) Innocent parties

A party who is innocent of any illegal intention is not without remedy. A number of situations must be distinguished.

(a) Lawful act intended to further illegal purpose. If the contract is one to do something which is lawful in itself, but which one of the parties intends to use for the furtherance of some illegal purpose or to perform in an illegal manner, the agreement can be the subject-matter of an action *at the suit of the innocent party*. Provided that there was no knowledge of the illegal intention of the other party, the innocent party is entitled to recover what may be due under the contract, or to obtain damages in full.[206] An innocent party who becomes aware of the illegality before the transaction is completed or while it is still executory, may refuse to perform the contract. Thus in *Cowan v Milbourn*:[207]

M agreed to let a set of rooms to C for certain days; then he discovered that it was proposed to use the rooms for the delivery of lectures which were unlawful because blasphemous within the meaning of a statute. M refused to carry out the agreement.

---

[204] *Alexander v Rayson* [1936] 1 KB 169, 182. Cf *Edler v Auerbach* [1950] 1 KB 359. On the attribution of knowledge to a company, see *Meridian Global Funds Management Asia Ltd v Securities Commission* [1995] 2 AC 500. See further *Selangor United Rubber Estates Ltd v Cradock (No 3)* [1968] 1 WLR 1555, 1654–5.

[205] (1866) LR 1 Ex 213, above, p 425. See also *Alexander v Rayson*, above, n 417; *Corby v Morrison* [1980] IRLR 218; *Anglo Petroleum Ltd v TFB (Mortgages) Ltd* [2007] EWCA Civ 456, [2007] BCC 407 at [79] (Toulson LJ: shared purpose can be inferred, eg, from letting of a flat to a prostitute at a rent beyond normal commercial rent).

[206] *Mason v Clarke* [1955] AC 778, 793, 805. See also *Fielding & Platt Ltd v Najjar* [1969] 1 WLR 357; *Newland v Simons and Willer (Hairdressers) Ltd* [1981] ICR 521.

[207] (1867) LR 2 Ex 230. The definition of blasphemy in this case must be revised in the light of *Bowman v Secular Society Ltd* [1917] AC 406.

It was held that he was entitled to do so. But should the illegal purpose be discovered before it is carried into effect, an innocent party who allows it to proceed none the less cannot recover. In *Cowan v Milbourn*, M could not have recovered the rent of his rooms if, having let them in ignorance of C's intentions, he had allowed the rooms to be used after he had learned of the illegal purpose which his tenant contemplated.

(b) Commission of illegal act.   The same principle applies where the contract is not unlawful *'per se'*[208] and one party is unaware that it involves or has as its object the commission of an illegal act. The contract itself is still valid, and an innocent party who was ignorant of the facts which constitute the illegality can enforce it. In *Bloxsome v Williams*:[209]

B contracted with W on a Sunday for the purchase of a horse, W warranting that the horse was not more than 7 years old and sound. Unknown to B, W was a horse-dealer and the Sunday Observance Act 1677 imposed a penalty on a horse-dealer for exercising his trade on a Sunday. The horse was 17 years old and unsound, and B sued for damages for breach of warranty.

The Court of King's Bench held that the illegality was no defence to the action for breach of contract as B was ignorant of the fact that W was a horse-dealer. It is also possible for an innocent party who has executed part of such a contract before discovering the illegality to recover reasonable remuneration for the work already done in a restitutionary action. So in *Clay v Yates*[210] a printer was able to recover the value of work done towards the publication of a treatise which, after the major part of it had been printed, he found to contain defamatory material.

(c) Legal formation but illegal performance.   Different considerations, however, apply where there is no illegal intention at the time the contract is entered into, but one party subsequently performs the contract in an illegal manner. Normally that party will be precluded from enforcing any claim which requires reliance on its own illegal performance.[211] But this is not necessarily the case. As we have seen, if a statutory offence is committed in the course of performing a contract, the intention of the statute may simply be to impose a penalty, and not to prevent the party in default from asserting civil remedies.[212] There may also be other situations where public policy does not require that the commission of an unlawful or immoral act in the course of performance should deprive the 'guilty' party of recourse to the Courts.[213]

---

[208]   See below, p 442.

[209]   (1824) 3 B & C 232 (the defendant in this case could not have sued: *Fennell v Ridler* (1826) 5 B & C 406). See also *Shaw v Shaw* [1954] 2 QB 429; *Bank für Gemeinwirtschaft v City of London Garages Ltd* [1971] 1 WLR 149 and the cases cited above, p 412. Cf *Phoenix General Insurance Co of Greece SA v Halvanon Insurance Co Ltd* [1988] QB 216 (effect reversed by the Financial Services Act 1986, s 132; now replaced by Financial Services and Markets Act 2000).

[210]   (1856) 1 H & N 73. Cf *Taylor v Bhail* [1996] CLC 377, 383 (no such remuneration for guilty party) and *Aratra Potato Co v Taylor Joynson Garrett* [1995] 4 All ER 695, 709–10 (no quantum meruit for work done under champertous agreement).

[211]   *Anderson Ltd v Daniel* [1924] 1 KB 138; *B & B Viennese Fashions v Losane* [1952] 1 All ER 909.

[212]   See above, p 413.   [213]   *Coral Leisure Group Ltd v Barnett* [1981] ICR 503.

In any event, the normal contractual remedies are available to the innocent party. In *Archbolds (Freightage) Ltd v Spanglett Ltd*:[214]

S agreed with A to carry a consignment of whisky from Leeds to London docks in one of its vans. Unknown to A, the vehicle to be used for this purpose did not possess an 'A' licence entitling it to carry the goods of other persons for reward. Owing to the driver's negligence, the whisky was stolen *en route* and A claimed damages for its loss. S contended that it was not liable as the contract was illegal.

The Court of Appeal refused to accept this contention. The contract was not one prohibited by statute; and it was not rendered illegal merely by the fact that one of the parties (S) had performed it in an unlawful manner. Thus, even though S might not have been able to enforce the contract, A was ignorant of the illegality and was entitled to damages. In such cases the illegal performance of the contract will not render it unenforceable unless, in addition to knowledge of the facts which make the performance illegal, the party seeking to enforce it actively participates in the illegal method of performance.[215]

(d) Ignorance of law generally no defence. There is, however, an important qualification which must be made to the principles stated above. A party to a contract who has full knowledge of the facts which constitute the illegality, but is ignorant of the law, will not be held to be innocent, for, in the context of enforcement, ignorance of the law is no defence. In *JM Allan (Merchandising) Ltd v Cloke*[216] the claimant sued the defendant for rentals payable in respect of a roulette table hired to the defendant and designed for the playing of 'Roulette Royale', a game which was at that time unlawful by virtue of the Betting and Gaming Act 1960.[217] At the time the parties entered into the hiring agreement, neither knew that the game was illegal, and the claimant pleaded that it had no 'wicked intention to break the law'. The Court of Appeal rejected this plea and held that ignorance of the law was no answer to the charge of illegality so as to permit the claimant to enforce the agreement.

(e) Ignorance of law a defence where performance legal. In *Cloke*'s case, the parties intended from the beginning that the subject-matter of the contract should be used for an unlawful purpose (the playing of 'Roulette Royale'), and this fact was held to render the contract illegal in its formation. On the other hand, in *Waugh v Morris*:[218]

M chartered a ship belonging to W to take a cargo of hay from Trouville to London, the cargo to be unloaded alongside ship in the river. M subsequently instructed the master to land the hay at a wharf at Deptford Creek, and the master agreed to do so. Unknown to the

---

[214] [1961] 1 QB 374.

[215] *Ashmore, Benson, Pease & Co Ltd v AV Dawson Ltd* [1973] 1 WLR 828; above, p 412; *Hall v Woolston Hall Leisure Ltd* [2001] 1 WLR 225, 236, 246; *Wheeler v Quality Deep Ltd* [2004] EWCA Civ 1085, [2005] ICR 265 at [71] (foreigner with limited knowledge of English language and tax and national insurance provisions).

[216] [1963] 2 QB 340. See also *Nash v Stevenson Transport Ltd* [1936] 2 KB 128; *Miller v Karlinski* (1945) 62 TLR 85. Cf *Shelley v Paddock* [1980] QB 348.

[217] The Act has now been repealed.   [218] (1873) LR 8 QB 202.

parties an Order in Council (made before the charterparty was entered into) had forbidden the *landing* of French hay in order to prevent the spread of disease among animals. M, on hearing this, took the cargo from alongside the ship without landing it, and exported it, thus avoiding a breach of the Order in Council. The return of the vessel was delayed, and W sued for damages arising from the delay.

M pleaded as a defence that the charterparty contemplated an illegal act, the landing of French hay contrary to the Order in Council. This defence did not prevail. The charterparty itself merely provided that the hay should be taken and delivered alongside, but not landed; and the Court found as a fact that W never contemplated or believed that M would violate the law. In his judgment, however, Blackburn J said:[219]

[W]here a contract is to do a thing which cannot be performed without a violation of the law it is void, whether the parties knew the law or not. But we think, that in order to avoid a contract which can be legally performed, on the ground that there was an intention to perform it in an illegal manner, it is necessary to show that there was the wicked intention to break the law; and, if this be so, the knowledge of what the law is becomes of great importance.

It is submitted that Blackburn J did not intend, by these words, to lay down a general rule that, when a contract is not illegal in its formation, but the illegality resides only in its performance, a party may be excused by ignorance of the law. The principle is more narrow: that if one or both parties contemplate a method of performance which is, unknown to them, illegal, they will not be shut out from their contractual remedies if, on their discovering the illegality, the contract is lawfully performed.[220]

(c) CONTRACTS UNLAWFUL '*PER SE*'

If a contract is expressly or by implication forbidden by statute or by public policy, then it is void and unenforceable, though the parties may have been ignorant of the facts constituting the illegality and did not intend to break the law. Such contracts are unlawful *per se*[221] and the intention of the parties is irrelevant. The situation in which a contract is forbidden by statute has been discussed above.[222] An example of a contract forbidden by public policy is one which necessarily involves trading with an alien enemy in time of war. No rights of action will arise, even though one party at the time of the agreement is ignorant of the fact that war has broken out or that the other party has the status of an enemy.[223] The agreement itself is prohibited and cannot be enforced in any way.

It is clear that considerable difficulty may be experienced in deciding whether a particular head of public policy renders the contract unlawful *per se* or merely prevents

---

[219] *Ibid*, 208.
[220] See also *Hindley & Co Ltd v General Fibre Co Ltd* [1940] 2 KB 517; *Anglo Petroleum Ltd v TFB (Mortgages) Ltd* [2007] EWCA Civ 456, [2007] BCC 407 at [56]–[64]. Cf *Reynolds v Kinsey* 1959 (4) SA 50 (South Africa).
[221] ie unlawful *in itself; intrinsically.*   [222] Above, p 410.
[223] *Sovfracht (v/o) v Van Udens Scheepvaart en Argentuur Maatschappij (NV Gebr)* [1943] AC 203.

a guilty party from suing on it. The modern tendency is to hold that a contracting party who has not participated in the unlawful intention should not be denied relief. The state of mind of the parties is the crucial factor. Unless it is clear that public policy demands that the contract be prohibited altogether, the innocent party can sue on the agreement.

Moreover, even if the contract is one which is unlawful *per se*, the innocent party is not necessarily without remedy. If the innocent party has been induced to enter into the contract by a misrepresentation or assurance by the other party, then damages can be recovered for breach of a collateral warranty if such has been given,[224] or for fraud if there is fraud,[225] provided that the conduct of the innocent party is not itself sufficiently culpable to bar that remedy.[226] So in *Strongman (1945) Ltd v Sincock*[227] a builder recovered damages for the breach of a collateral assurance by his client that he would obtain the necessary licences to enable the work to be carried out, even though a contract to build without a licence was absolutely prohibited by statute. And in *Shelley v Paddock*[228] a woman who was fraudulently induced to agree to buy a house in Spain in ignorance of the fact that the purchase was in breach of the Exchange Control Act 1947 was held entitled to recover damages for the fraud.

(d) BENEFIT FROM ILLEGAL CONTRACTS

It is sometimes said to be a rule of law that no person can take any benefit from a contract, either directly or through a personal representative, when that benefit results from the performance by *that person* of an illegal act.[229] In *Beresford v Royal Insurance Co Ltd*:[230]

R insured his life with the defendant company for £50,000. A few minutes before the policy was due to lapse, he committed suicide. The policy contained a term avoiding it in the event of suicide within a year of its commencement, but the suicide occurred after the policy had run for some years.

The House of Lords held that the insurance company had agreed to pay in this event, but that the claim was contrary to public policy as the deceased's personal

---

[224] *Strongman (1945) Ltd v Sincock* [1955] 2 QB 525, 536, 539; *Gregory v Ford* [1951] 1 All ER 121.

[225] *Burrows v Rhodes* [1899] 1 QB 816; *Road Transport & General Insurance Co v Adams* [1955] CLY 2455; *Shelley v Paddock* [1980] QB 348. Rescission on the ground of fraud may also be available: see *Hughes v Clewley, The Siben (No 2)* [1996] 1 Lloyd's Rep 35 (not available in that case), above, pp 331, 332.

[226] *Askey v Golden Wine Co Ltd* [1948] 2 All ER 35.   [227] [1955] 2 QB 525.

[228] [1980] QB 348. See also *Hughes v Clewley, The Siben (No 2)* [1996] 1 Lloyd's Rep 35, 63 and *Saunders v Edwards* [1987] 1 WLR 1116, the result, but not the reasoning of which was said to be 'unassailable' by Lord Goff in *Tinsley v Milligan* [1994] 1 AC 340, 360.

[229] *Cleaver v Mutual Reserve Fund Life Association* [1892] 1 QB 147; *In the Estate of Crippen* [1911] P 108, 112; *Archbolds (Freightage) Ltd v Spanglett Ltd* [1961] 1 QB 374, 388; *Re Giles* [1971] Ch 544; *Davitt v Titcumb* [1990] 1 Ch 110. But see the Forfeiture Act 1982; *Re K* [1985] Ch 85; *Re S* [1996] 1 WLR 235.

[230] [1938] AC 586. See also *Prince of Wales etc Association v Palmer* (1858) 25 Beav 605. Cf *White v British Empire etc Assurance Co* (1868) LR 7 Eq 394.

representatives could not obtain any benefit from the assured's illegal act. The case would certainly not be decided the same way at the present day, for suicide is no longer a crime,[231] and the rule itself is probably too widely stated. It is submitted that it will only apply where the statute or head of public policy is such as to require that the offender be deprived of the fruits of the illegal act.[232] Thus, although it has been held that no recovery would be allowed under a policy of insurance when the insured goods had been deliberately imported without payment of customs duty,[233] the same considerations would not apply in the case of unintentional importation or the innocent possession of uncustomed goods.[234] Similarly, in principle no remuneration in the form of a restitutionary quantum meruit will be given for work done pursuant to an illegal contract where that would amount to indirect enforcement of the contract.[235]

(e) RECOVERY OF MONEY PAID OR PROPERTY TRANSFERRED

(i) Generally not recoverable

It is scarcely surprising that the Courts will refuse to enforce an illegal agreement at the suit of a person who is implicated in the illegality. But it is also a rule of English law that money paid or property transferred by such a person cannot be recovered. This is a consequence of the view that the doctrine of illegality is a rule of judicial abstention, given effect in the public interest.[236] It is also often expressed in the maxim *in pari delicto potior est conditio defendentis*[237] and it may be illustrated by the case of *Parkinson v College of Ambulance Ltd*:[238]

The secretary of a charitable organization promised P that he would secure for him a knighthood if P made a sufficient donation to the organization's funds. In consideration of this promise, P paid over £3,000 and promised more when he should receive the honour. The knighthood never materialized, and P sued for the return of his money.

Although, there was 'a total failure of consideration', which, but for the illegality, would have grounded a restitutionary claim for the return of the money, it was held that the action must fail as it was founded upon a transaction which was illegal at common law.

---

[231] Suicide Act 1961.

[232] *Marles v Philip Trant & Sons Ltd* [1954] 1 QB 29, 39; *St John Shipping Corp v Joseph Rank Ltd* [1957] 1 QB 267, 292; *R v Chief National Insurance Commissioner* [1981] QB 758, 765; *Gardner v Moore* [1984] AC 548; *Thorne v Silverleaf* [1994] 1 BCLC 637.

[233] *Geismar v Sun Alliance and London Insurance Ltd* [1978] QB 383.   [234] *Ibid*, 395.

[235] *Aratra Potato Co v Taylor Joynson Garrett* [1995] 4 All ER 695, 709–10 (champertous agreement). But, in the case of statutory illegality, there is an issue whether the test is whether the statute bars restitution as well as enforcement of the executory contract; see by analogy *Scott v Pattison* [1923] 2 KB 723; *Pavey & Matthews Pty Ltd v Paul* (1986–87) 162 CLR 221 (unenforceable contracts).

[236] Above, p 436.   [237] Cf above, n 186.

[238] [1925] 2 KB 1. See also *Shaw v Shaw* [1965] 1 WLR 937. For a criticism of the maxim, see Grodecki (1955) 71 LQR 254.

But there are exceptional cases in which a person will be relieved of the consequences of an illegal contract which that person has entered—cases to which the maxim just quoted does not apply. They fall into three classes: (i) where the illegal purpose has not yet been carried into effect before it is sought to recover the money paid or goods delivered or other property transferred in furtherance of it; (ii) where the party seeking recovery is not *in pari delicto* with the party resisting recovery; (iii) where the claimant does not have to rely on the illegal contract to make out the claim, but can establish an independent claim, such as one based on a legal or equitable property right. Each of these exceptions will be considered in turn.

(ii) Illegal purpose not yet carried into effect

The first exception relates to cases where money has been paid, or goods delivered, or other property transferred for an unlawful purpose which has not yet been carried into effect because the claimant withdrew in time.[239] The law is not quite satisfactorily settled on this point,[240] and the authorities are difficult to reconcile, but its present condition would seem to demand that two conditions be satisfied. First, the party seeking to recover must withdraw from the transaction before the illegal purpose is executed in whole or in part. Secondly, the withdrawal must be voluntary, although no genuine repentance is required. It is, however, highly unlikely that the Courts would allow any opportunity for a withdrawal or change of mind in the most serious cases of moral reprehensibility, as for example, where money is paid to another to commit murder.[241]

(a) Time of withdrawal from the illegal transaction. While the illegality is still completely executory, the parties are allowed an opportunity for repentance or change of mind, a *locus poenitentiae*. But some doubt exists as to when this privilege ceases. In *Taylor v Bowers*[242] it was said by Mellish LJ that:

If money is paid or goods delivered for an illegal purpose, the person who had so paid the money or delivered the goods may recover them back *before the illegal purpose is carried out*; but if he waits till the illegal purpose is carried out, or if he seeks to enforce the illegal transaction, in neither case can he maintain an action.

The facts of the case to which these words applied were as follows:

T, a debtor, had made a fictitious assignment of his goods to one A in order to defraud his creditors. Two meetings of creditors were then called, but no composition was reached as only one creditor turned up. A had in the meantime, without T's consent, parted with the goods under a bill of sale to the defendant, who was one of the creditors and knew of the fraudulent assignment. T sued the defendant for the recovery of the goods.

---

[239] See Beatson (1975) 91 LQR 313; Merkin (1981) 97 LQR 920.
[240] The most recent general discussion is found in *Patel v Mirza* [2014] EWCA Civ 1047, [2015] Ch 271; permission has been given for an appeal to the Supreme Court.
[241] *Kearley v Thomson* (1890) 24 QBD 742, 747; *Tappenden v Randall* (1801) 2 B & P 467; *Patel v Mirza*, above, n 240 at [75], [117].
[242] (1876) 1 QBD 291, 300.

It was held that he was entitled to succeed. It could be contended that, in this case, the illegal purpose was still entirely executory, for no creditor had actually been defrauded.[243] But it is difficult to see the fictitious assignment as anything but a part-performance of the illegal purpose, since at the two creditors' meetings the creditors would clearly have been less likely to have pressed their claims in view of the assignment. If this is so, then the facts in *Taylor v Bowers* support the principle stated by Mellish LJ, that recovery is possible at any time before the illegal purpose is carried out, that is, completed.[244]

Subsequent cases, however, do not endorse this formulation. In *Kearley v Thomson*,[245] for instance:

The defendants, a firm of solicitors acting for a petitioning creditor of one Clarke, a bankrupt, agreed with K, a friend of Clarke, that in consideration of the payment of their costs they would not appear at the public examination of Clarke, nor oppose the order for his discharge. They carried out the first part of the agreement, but before any application was made for Clarke's discharge, K changed his mind and sought to recover the money which he had paid.

K's action failed. It was held that the agreement was illegal as tending to pervert the course of justice, and that recovery was precluded as the illegal purpose had already been partly executed. The principle as formulated by Mellish LJ in *Taylor v Bowers*, and even the case itself, might, said the Court, require reconsideration.[246] In any event, the case before the Court was distinguishable as there had been 'a partial carrying into effect of an illegal purpose in a substantial manner'.[247] Although the matter is not free from doubt,[248] the position now seems to be that money paid or goods delivered in pursuance of an illegal purpose cannot be recovered where that purpose has been executed *in whole or in part*.[249]

(b) Withdrawal must be voluntary.   What the law allows in these cases is a *locus poenitentiae*, and therefore, whilst it will help one who repudiates, it will not help a person who has abandoned the illegal purpose only because that purpose has been frustrated by the failure of the other contracting party to fulfil his side of the illegal contract. So, in *Bigos v Bousted*:[250]

In breach of the provisions of the Exchange Control Act 1947, A entered into an agreement with B whereby B agreed to make available £150 worth of Italian currency to enable A's

---

[243] *Tinsley v Milligan* [1994] 1 AC 340, 374; *Tribe v Tribe* [1996] Ch 107, 121–2, 124, 132–3. See also *Perpetual Executor & Trustees Assoc v Wright* (1917) 23 CLR 185, 193 (Australia).

[244] See also *Singh v Ali* [1960] AC 160, 167.   [245] (1890) 24 QBD 742.

[246] See Millett LJ's doubts in *Tribe v Tribe* [1996] Ch 107, 125. But the decision was cited without disapproval in *Tinsley v Milligan* [1994] 1 AC 340, 374.

[247] (1890) 24 QBD 742, 747 (Fry LJ). See also *Apthorp v Neville & Co* (1907) 23 TLR 575; *Re National Benefit Assurance Co Ltd* [1931] 1 Ch 46; *Parker (Harry) Ltd v Mason* [1940] 2 KB 590.

[248] Cf Lord Browne-Wilkinson's formulations (whether illegal purpose 'put into operation' and whether it was 'carried through') in *Tinsley v Milligan*, above, n 4, 374.

[249] *Tribe v Tribe* [1996] Ch 107, 122, 124, 133; cf at 134; *Patel v Mirza*, above, n 240 at [24], [115].

[250] [1951] 1 All ER 92. But see *Shelley v Paddock* [1980] QB 348.

wife and daughter to travel in Italy. As security, A deposited with B a share certificate. The promised money was never forthcoming, and A sued B to recover the certificate.

It was pleaded on A's behalf that he was entitled to a *locus poenitentiae* as the illegal contract had not been performed, but this contention was rejected by Pritchard J. He held that there was no true withdrawal on A's part; the contract had merely been frustrated by B's failure to supply the money.

But although the withdrawal must be voluntary, it is not necessary that there be genuine repentance. Thus in *Tribe v Tribe*:[251]

A father transferred shares to his son on trust so that they would not be the subject of claims made against him by creditors but the illegal purpose of defrauding the creditors was not carried out because the claims settled. The son refused to transfer the shares back to his father.

The Court of Appeal held that the father was entitled to the benefit of the *locus poenitentiae* doctrine. Millett LJ stated that 'genuine repentance is not required . . . voluntary withdrawal from an illegal transaction when it has ceased to be needed is sufficient'.[252] This was followed in *Patel v Mirza*[253] where an agreement for the defendant to use the claimant's money to bet on the movement of shares on the basis of inside information[254] could not be carried out because the expected insider information was not forthcoming. The claimant was entitled to recover the money he had paid, even though his withdrawal was not because of a change of mind that he no longer wished to participate in the illegal agreement, but because the agreement was no longer capable of being performed at all: if such a distinction were to be drawn it would call for proof of a true sense of penitence, which is not required.[255]

(c) Marriage brokage contracts. Marriage brokage contracts are an exception to the general rule. In *Hermann v Charlesworth*,[256] a woman who had paid £52 to the proprietor of a newspaper, *The Matrimonial Post and Fashionable Marriage Advertiser*, with a view to obtaining by advertisement an offer of marriage, successfully recovered the money after advertisements had appeared, and several prospective suitors had been introduced, but before any marriage had been arranged.

(iii) Parties not '*in pari delicto*'

Where the parties are not *in pari delicto* the less guilty party may be able to recover money paid, or property transferred, under the contract. This possibility may arise in two basic situations. The first is where the contract is rendered illegal by statute in order to protect a class of persons of whom the claimant is one. The second is where

---

[251] [1996] Ch 107.   [252] *Ibid*, 135.
[253] Above, n 240 at [45], [97], [113]. The decision in *Bigos v Bousted*, above, n 250, was doubted by Gloster LJ at [96], but distinguished by Rimer LJ at [41] and by Vos LJ at [117].
[254] Contrary to the prohibition on insider dealing in Criminal Justice Act 1993, s 52.
[255] Above, n 240 at [45], [96]. Vos LJ took the strongest view that the reason for the claimant's withdrawal is not material: at [113].
[256] [1905] 2 KB 123. Cf above, p 426 doubting that such contracts should be unenforceable.

the nature of the restitutionary cause of action shows that the claimant was ignorant or innocent of the illegality.

(a) Class-protecting statutes.   First, the case of a contract made illegal by statute in the interests of a particular class of persons of whom the claimant is one. As Lord Mansfield explained in *Browning v Morris*:[257]

where contracts or transactions are prohibited by positive statutes, for the sake of protecting one set of men from another set of men; the one, from their situation and condition, being liable to be oppressed or imposed upon by the other; there, the parties are not *in pari delicto*; and in furtherance of these statutes, the person injured, after the transaction is finished and completed, may bring his action and defeat the contract.

The Rent Acts have furnished an illustration of this type of case. The Rent Act 1977 provides that, where under any agreement a premium is paid which could not lawfully be required or received, the premium is to be recoverable by the person by whom it is paid.[258] But even in the absence of any such express statutory provision, it has been held that a tenant or assignee of a lease, though a willing party to the evasion of the Rent Acts, may recover an illegal premium paid, since the Acts were passed for the protection of such persons.[259]

The intention of the statute is one of prime importance. In *Green v Portsmouth Stadium Ltd*:[260]

G, a bookmaker, alleged that, over a long period of time, he had been overcharged by the defendants for admission to a greyhound track run by them. The Betting and Lotteries Act 1934, section 13(1), allowed a charge to be made to bookmakers not exceeding five times the highest fee for the public at large, but G had been compelled to pay considerably more. He claimed the excess from the defendants in an action for money had and received.

The Court of Appeal held that the action must fail. The Act was designed to regulate racecourses; it was not a bookmakers' charter. The statute was not passed 'to protect one set of men from another set of men', at any rate, not so as to give bookmakers the right to bring civil proceedings for the recovery of their money.

(b) Fraud.   Where a person has been induced to enter into the contract by fraud, recovery will be allowed. In *Hughes v Liverpool Victoria Legal Friendly Society*:[261]

H took up five insurance policies with the defendants on the lives of persons in which she had no insurable interest. She was induced to do so by a fraudulent misrepresentation on the part of the defendants' agent that the policies were valid and would be paid. They were in fact illegal and void.

It was held that she was entitled to recover the premiums which she had paid.

---

[257] (1778) 2 Cowp 790, 792.   [258] Rent Act 1977, s 125. See *Farrell v Alexander* [1977] AC 59.
[259] *Gray v Southouse* [1949] 2 All ER 1019; *Kiriri Cotton Co Ltd v Dewani* [1960] AC 192. See also *Ailion v Spiekermann* [1976] Ch 158.
[260] [1953] 2 QB 190.
[261] [1916] 2 KB 482. Cf *Harse v Pearl Life Assurance Co* [1904] 1 KB 558 where there was no fraud. See also *Reynell v Sprye* (1852) 1 De GM & G 660. See also above, p 443 (*damages* for fraud).

(c) Oppression and duress. The position is the same where a person has been induced to enter into the contract by improper pressure. In *Atkinson v Denby*:[262]

A, a debtor, offered his creditors a composition of 5 shillings in the pound. The defendant, an influential creditor, refused to assent to the composition unless A would make him an additional payment of £50 in fraud of the other creditors. This was done and the composition arrangement was carried out. A then sued to recover the £50 on the ground that it was a payment made by him under oppression.

It was held that he could recover. The Court of Exchequer Chamber, affirming the judgment of the Court of Exchequer, observed that the parties were not equally to blame:[263]

It is said that both parties are *in pari delicto*. It is true that both are *in delicto*, because the Act is a fraud upon the other creditors, but it is not *par delictum*, because one has the power to dictate, the other no alternative but to submit.

(d) Mistake. Where money is mistakenly paid under an invalid or ineffective contract, the payer may recover it subject to defences in the law of restitution such as change of position. This has long been the case for mistakes of fact, even where the contract is illegal. In *Oom v Bruce*[264] insurance premiums paid by the agent of a Russian in ignorance of the outbreak of war between the United Kingdom and Russia (a matter making the contract illegal) were held to be recoverable. Until recently, as a general rule, money paid under a mistake of law was irrecoverable. The rule had been subject to much criticism, and, in 1960, in the context of an illegal contract, Lord Denning had suggested that money paid under a mistake of law should be recoverable whenever the payee is primarily responsible for the mistake.[265] By 1994, when the Law Commission recommended its abolition,[266] the rule was clearly 'on the turn',[267] and, in 1998 the House of Lords, in *Kleinwort Benson Ltd v Lincoln CC*,[268] held that it was not part of English law. In that case KB sought to recover payments made to the defendant under interest rate swaps contracts believed to be binding but subsequently held *ultra vires*. In principle, the position should be the same in the case of money paid under an illegal contract.

(e) Fiduciary duty. There is some authority for the view that a person who is under a fiduciary duty to the claimant may not be allowed to retain property, or to refuse to account for monies received, on the ground that the property or the monies have come into his hands as the proceeds of an illegal transaction. In *Re Thomas*,[269] where a client sought to recover from his solicitor money paid in pursuance of a champertous

---

[262] (1861) 6 H & N 778, aff'd (1862) 7 H & N 934. On duress, see above, p 375.

[263] (1862) 7 H & N 934, 936. [264] (1810) 12 East 225.

[265] *Kiriri Cotton Co Ltd v Dewani* [1960] AC 192, 204.

[266] Law Com No 227, *Mistakes of Law and Ultra Vires Public Authority Receipts and Payments* (1994), paras 3.7–3.12.

[267] *Friends Provident Life Office v Hillier Parker* [1997] QB 85, 97 (Auld LJ). [268] [1999] 2 AC 349.

[269] [1894] 1 QB 747. But cf *Kearley v Thomson* (1890) 24 QBD 742; *Palaniappa Chettiar v Arunasalam Chettiar* [1962] AC 294.

agreement between them, it was held that he was entitled to do so. 'Is every rascally solicitor', said Lindley LJ,[270] 'to invoke his own rascality as a ground of immunity from the jurisdiction of the Court?' It may also be that an agent who receives money from a third party under an illegal contract is bound to account to the principal for the proceeds.[271] But this exception is by no means clearly established, and it is probable that recovery will be denied where the agency is itself illegal.[272]

(f) Critique.   It will be seen from this discussion that until recently only a limited number of situations in which one of the parties will be held not to be *in pari delicto* with the other were recognized. The removal of the bar on recovery of money paid under a mistake of law is an important liberalizing development. But there is also a case for going further, and applying a test similar to that in the *St John Shipping Corp* case in the context of enforcement of the contract,[273] that is, weighing up the comparative merits of the parties in the light of the statutory purposes and policies, and allowing the recovery of money or property when to do so would not undermine them.[274]

(iv) Claimant not relying on the illegal contract

It is settled law that the ownership of property can pass under an illegal contract if the parties so intend, as in the case of goods sold to a buyer under an illegal contract of sale.[275]

Where, however, only a limited interest is transferred, as under a contract of bailment or a lease, or a trust, it is equally well established that the owner of the property who is not forced to found the claim on the illegal contract,[276] but simply relies on his or her title to the property, can recover it from the bailee or lessee.

This principle is extremely difficult to apply since it is frequently hard to determine whether a claimant is relying upon title, or upon the contractual provisions of the illegal agreement.[277] For example, it seems probable that a landlord can recover premises let to a tenant under an illegal agreement once the term of years has expired; but it is a matter of doubt whether the landlord could recover them in the meantime

---

[270] [1894] 1 QB 747, 749.

[271] *Tenant v Elliott* (1797) 1 B & P 3; *Farmer v Russell* (1798) 1 B & P 296; *Bone v Eckless* (1869) 5 H & N 925. See also *Bridger v Savage* (1884) 15 QBD 363.

[272] *Harry Parker Ltd v Mason* [1940] 2 KB 590.   [273] [1957] 1 QB 267, above, p 382.

[274] See *Nelson v Nelson* (1995) 132 ALR 133, below, p 453.

[275] *Scarfe v Morgan* (1838) 4 M & W 270, 281; *Elder v Kelly* [1919] 2 KB 179; *Singh v Ali* [1960] AC 167; *Kingsley v Sterling Industrial Securities Ltd* [1967] 2 QB 747, 782, 783; *Belvoir Finance Co Ltd v Stapleton* [1971] 1 QB 210; *Tinsley v Milligan* [1994] 1 AC 340, 374 (Lord Browne-Wilkinson); *Aratra Potato Co v Taylor Joynson Garrett* [1995] 4 All ER 695, 710. Cf *Amar Singh v Kulubya* [1964] AC 142 (transfer prohibited). See also Higgins (1962) 25 MLR 149.

[276] *Amar Singh v Kulubya*, above, n 275; *Tinsley v Milligan*, above, n 4.

[277] Cf *Patel v Mirza* [2014] EWCA Civ 1047, [2015] Ch 271 at [22], [102] (claimant seeking restitution of money paid under illegal contract engaged the illegality principle by pleading that the illegal purpose had not been carried out; cf Gloster LJ at [79]: illegality principle not engaged unless it was objectively an essential element of his cause of action).

under a covenant which provided for forfeiture for non-payment of rent.[278] Would the landlord be relying on his independent right of ownership, or (more probably) upon the contractual provisions of the illegal lease?

(a) Claims based on legal title. In the case of chattels, it has been held that the termination of the bailment puts the bailor in the more favoured position. In *Bowmakers Ltd v Barnet Instruments Ltd*:[279]

The defendant entered into a contract whereby it agreed to hire-purchase from Bowmakers certain machine tools. Such an agreement was rendered illegal by a government order which prohibited the disposition of machine tools without a licence from the Ministry of Supply. The defendant failed to make the agreed payments for hire. It further sold some of the tools and refused to deliver up to Bowmakers others still in its possession. Bowmakers sued for damages for conversion.

It was contended on behalf of the defendant that since the contract of hire-purchase was illegal, Bowmakers could have no remedy on it. It pointed to the case of *Taylor v Chester*[280] where a man failed to recover half of a £50 bank note deposited by him to secure the payment of money for a night's debauch in a brothel. To this the claimant replied that it was not relying on the contract, but upon its paramount right of ownership, the bailment having come to an end; the case of *Taylor v Chester* was distinguishable because the pledge had not been redeemed, whereas in *Bowmakers'* case all possessory rights of the defendant had been extinguished. This latter argument was adopted by the Court of Appeal. Du Parcq LJ said:[281]

In our opinion, a man's right to possess his own chattels will as a general rule be enforced against one who, without any claim of right, is detaining them, or has converted them to his own use, even though it may appear either from the pleadings, or in the course of the trial, that the chattels in question came into the defendant's possession by reason of an illegal contract between himself and the plaintiff, provided that the plaintiff does not seek, and is not forced, either to found his claim on the illegal contract or to plead its illegality in order to support his claim.

This case has been criticized[282] on the ground that, although the possessory rights of the defendants in the tools *sold* had come to an end,[283] this was not so in the case of the tools *retained*. Insofar as the Court allowed the claim to these latter in pursuance of the terms of the agreement, it was in effect permitting the enforcement of the

---

[278] *Jaijbhay v Cassim* 1939 AD 537 (South Africa); *Gas Light & Coke Co v Turner* (1839) 5 Bing NC 666, 677 (Tindal CJ); *Alexander v Rayson* [1936] 1 KB 169, 186 (*per curiam*).

[279] [1945] KB 65. See also *Tinsley v Milligan* [1994] 1 AC 340.

[280] (1869) LR 4 QB 309.   [281] [1945] KB 65, 71.

[282] Hamson (1949) 10 CLJ 249; Paton, *Bailment in the Common Law* (1952) 34; *Miles v Watson* [1953] NZLR 958. For wider criticism, see *Nelson v Nelson* (1995) 132 ALR 133, 176, 189–90, below, p 453. The case is stoutly defended by Coote (1972) 35 MLR 38.

[283] An act inconsistent with the bailment, such as pledging or selling the goods bailed, automatically determines the bailment and the immediate right to possession re-vests in the bailor.

provisions of an illegal agreement. Nevertheless, the principle has been accepted,[284] even if its application is a matter of dispute.

It seems probable that, if the property were of such a kind that it would be absurd to encourage litigation concerning its ownership, such as housebreaking instruments, obscene books, or controlled drugs, the Court would not countenance recovery in any event.[285] But it is difficult to see how a principle that entitles parties to recover their property can properly make a distinction of this sort.[286]

(b) Claims based on equitable interests.   In *Tinsley v Milligan*[287] the principle in the *Bowmakers* case was applied to a claim based upon an equitable interest.

T and M purchased a house with funds generated by a joint business venture on the understanding that they had equal interests in it, but registered it in T's name so that M was able to make fraudulent claims for benefit from the Department of Social Security. Later, after the parties had quarrelled, T asserted her legal title and M, who had confessed her wrongdoing and made amends to the Department, counterclaimed for a declaration that T held the house on trust for the parties in equal shares.

Where two parties have contributed to the acquisition of property which is conveyed into the name of one alone, that party may in certain circumstances hold the property on trust—either a resulting trust or a constructive trust—for both parties;[288] in the case of a resulting trust, the parties' shares are proportionate to their contributions to the price. Such a resulting trust arose in the case of the purchase of the house by T and M, and a majority of the House of Lords[289] held that the counterclaim by M did not therefore rely on the illegality but on her equitable interest. Lord Goff and Lord Keith dissented on the ground that, as M did not have 'clean hands' she could not assert an equitable interest, and that the rule in the *Bowmakers* case is not applicable where equitable relief is sought.[290] But the majority thought that if the law is that a party is entitled to enforce a proprietary right acquired under an illegal transaction, the same rule ought to apply to any property right so acquired, whether such right is legal or equitable.

The limited scope and procedural nature of the decision in *Tinsley v Milligan* can be illustrated by comparing the facts of that case with those in *Tribe v Tribe*, considered above,[291] where a father voluntarily transferred shares to his son, and the presumption of resulting trust did not apply. In such cases there is a presumption

---

[284]   *Belvoir Finance Co Ltd v Stapleton* [1971] 1 QB 210.

[285]   *Bowmakers Ltd v Barnet Instruments Ltd*, above, n 281, 72; *Taylor v Chester*, above, n 280; *Webb v Chief Constable of Merseyside Police* [2000] QB 427.

[286]   *Tinsley v Milligan* [1994] 1 AC 340, 362 (Lord Goff). See also *R v Lomas* (1913) 9 Cr App Rep 220, as explained in *R v Bullock* [1955] 1 WLR 1.

[287]   [1994] 1 AC 340. See Buckley (1994) 110 LQR 3; Enonchong (1995) 111 LQR 134.

[288]   *Stack v Dowden* [2007] UKHL 17, [2007] 2 AC 432 (constructive trust; cf Lord Neuberger at [110] preferring resulting trust as the default analysis); cf *Laskar v Laskar* [2008] EWCA Civ 347, [2008] 1 WLR 2695 (joint names purchase for investment; resulting trust).

[289]   Lord Browne-Wilkinson, Lord Jauncey, and Lord Lowry.

[290]   [1994] 1 AC 340, 362.   [291]   Above, p 447.

of advancement, that is, equity presumes an intention to make a gift so that the person who has transferred property or allowed it to be registered in the name of another will have no equitable interest to assert unless the presumption is rebutted. Lord Browne-Wilkinson in *Tinsley v Milligan* considered this would be difficult for the transferor in such a case to do without pleading or leading evidence that would reveal the illegal aspect of the transaction, so that the transferor's claim would fail.[292] In *Tribe v Tribe* the Court of Appeal was troubled by this consequence of the decision of the House of Lords[293] but was able to avoid it because the father fell within the *locus poenitentiae* principle,[294] which M did not in *Tinsley v Milligan* because the illegal purpose had been carried into effect. So, if T had been M's wife or child, so that the presumption of advancement applied, M's claim would have failed.

(c) Critique of the proprietary based approach. The rule established in the *Bowmakers* case and extended to equitable interests in *Tinsley v Milligan* is a manifestation of judicial concern, where there is no question of enforcing the *executory* provisions of an illegal contract or transaction, that people should not be unnecessarily precluded by illegality from enforcing rights already acquired under the completed provisions of such a contract or transaction.[295] But it is submitted that it is open to a number of objections. First, it avoids confronting the issue of illegality, the underlying policy issues, and the merits of the parties, and relies instead on the mechanical application of highly technical and procedural concepts.[296] Secondly, to the extent that the parties can, in their illegal contract, determine who owns the property that is its subject-matter, parties who know that the contract is illegal and nevertheless enter into it may be able to insulate themselves from the consequences of the *in pari delicto* rule. Furthermore, where the illegality consists, as it often does in modern conditions, in the contravention of a statute, the property-based approach takes no account of the statutory purposes.

In *Nelson v Nelson*,[297] where a mother provided the purchase money for a house that was transferred into the names of her two children to enable her unlawfully to obtain a subsidized advance from a governmental body on another property, the High Court of Australia disapproved of both the proprietary based approach of the majority in *Tinsley v Milligan* and the unremitting application by the minority of the rule laid down in *Holman v Johnson*.[298] It applied a similar test to that in

---

[292] [1994] 1 AC 340, 372. Equality Act 2010, s 199 abolishes the presumption of advancement, but this provision has never been brought into force. See also *Barrett v Barrett* [2008] EWHC 1061 (Ch), [2008] 2 P & CR 17, distinguished in *Davies v O'Kelly* [2014] EWCA Civ 1606, [2015] 1 WLR 2725 at [33].

[293] [1996] Ch 107, 118, 134. See also *Nelson v Nelson* (1995) 123 ALR 132, 148, 165–6 and Davies, in Oakley (ed), *Trends in Contemporary Trust Law* (1996) ch 2.

[294] Above, pp 445–7.

[295] *Tinsley v Milligan* [1994] 1 AC 340, 366 (Lord Jauncey). See also *Nelson v Nelson* (1995) 132 ALR 133, 176 (Toohey J) (Australia); *Stone & Rolls Ltd v Moore Stephens* [2009] UKHL 39, [2009] 1 AC 1391 at [21].

[296] Cf *Stone & Rolls Ltd v Moore Stephens* [2009] UKHL 39, [2009] 1 AC 1391 at [25], [129]–[131].

[297] (1995) 132 ALR 133.   [298] (1775) 1 Cowp 341, above, p 436.

the *St John Shipping Corp* case in the context of enforcement of the contract,[299] and asked whether the policy of the statute precluded the claim made. McHugh J stated:[300]

[T]he sanction imposed should be proportionate to the seriousness of the illegality involved ... The statute must always be the reference point for determining the seriousness of the illegality; otherwise the courts would embark on an assessment of moral turpitude independently of and potentially in conflict with the assessment made by the legislature.

Secondly, the imposition of the civil sanction must further the purpose of the statute and must not impose a further sanction for the unlawful conduct if Parliament has indicated that the sanctions imposed by the statute are sufficient to deal with conduct that breaches or evades the operation of the statute and its policies.

The Court concluded that the policy of the statute did not preclude the claim made, and awarded the mother the relief sought on the condition that she made appropriate recompense to the body that had given her the subsidy.

(f) COLLATERAL TRANSACTIONS

(i) Securities

A transaction which is collateral to an illegal agreement may also be affected by taint of illegality.[301] Any security given to secure payment under, or performance of, an illegal contract is itself illegal, even though not given in pursuance of the contract. Thus in *Fisher v Bridges*[302] a deed executed to secure the payment of the price for land conveyed to the defendant for an illegal purpose was held to be illegal and unenforceable. Jervis CJ, said that the deed:[303]

springs from, and is a creature of, the illegal agreement; and, as the law would not enforce the original illegal contract, so neither will it allow the parties to enforce a security for the purchase money, which by the original bargain was tainted with illegality.

(ii) Bills of exchange

Similarly, if a bill of exchange is made and given to secure payment of money due or about to become due upon an illegal agreement, the rule that a subsequent holder is presumed to be a holder in due course does not apply; the holder can only recover by proving that consideration has been given either by himself or some immediate holder, and without notice of the illegality.[304] Money knowingly lent for the purpose of financing an illegal agreement is also, in principle, irrecoverable.[305]

---

[299] [1957] 1 QB 267, above, p 413.
[300] (1995) 132 ALR 133, 192. See also *ibid*, 146, 149, 167 and McCamus (1987) 25 Osgoode Hall LJ 787.
[301] *Heald v O'Connor* [1971] 1 WLR 497 (guarantee).   [302] (1854) 3 E & B 642.
[303] *Ibid*, 649.   [304] Bills of Exchange Act 1882, s 30(2).
[305] *Cannan v Bryce* (1819) 3 B & Ald 179; *Spector v Ageda* [1973] Ch 30.

(iii) No tainting

Not all collateral transactions are necessarily tainted. As noted above, an innocent party may have an action for breach of a collateral warranty.[306] And securities given in respect of an agreement which is not strictly illegal, but merely nugatory and void, can be enforced if supported by independent consideration.[307]

5. SEVERANCE

(a) INTRODUCTION

The same contract may contain both legal and illegal terms. In such a case it has long been established that an illegal term, or an illegal part of a term, can in certain circumstances be 'severed', leaving the remainder of the contract in force.[308] In *Pickering v Ilfracombe Railway Co* Willes J stated:[309]

The general rule is that, where you cannot sever the illegal from the legal part of a covenant, the contract is altogether void; but, where you can sever them, whether the illegality be created by statute or by the common law, you may reject the bad part and retain the good.

This does not indicate the circumstances in which it is, or it is not, possible to sever the illegal from the legal parts of the contract; nor does it indicate that differing criteria have been adopted from time to time by the Courts. For example, in recent years the Courts have moved away from the nineteenth-century requirement that an illegal promise could only be severed if it was supported by separate consideration.[310] Emphasis has now shifted to the nature of the illegality involved and whether it accords with public policy that severance should be allowed. Nevertheless, the Courts have to bear in mind that it is not their task to force on the parties an entirely different contract.[311] Before severance is permitted, certain conditions must be satisfied in order to ensure that the elimination of the offending clause still leaves substantially the same agreement.

(b) PUBLIC POLICY

Where there are legal and illegal terms which are capable of severance, the jurisdiction to enforce the legal terms will only be exercised if the severance is in accordance with public policy.

---

[306] Above, p 443. [307] *Lilley v Rankin* (1887) 56 LJQB 248.

[308] *Henry Pigot's Case* (1614) 11 Co Rep 27b. See Marsh (1948) 64 LQR 230, 347, and (1953) 69 LQR 111.

[309] (1868) LR 3 CP 235, 250.

[310] *Waites v Jones* (1835) 1 Bing NC 646, 662; *Walrond v Walrond* (1858) 28 LJ Ch 97; *Lound v Grimwade* (1888) 39 Ch D 605; *Kearney v Whitehaven Colliery Co* [1893] 1 QB 700; *Kuenigl v Donnersmarck* [1955] 1 QB 515, 537; below, p 456.

[311] *Putsman v Taylor* [1927] 1 KB 637, 639.

(i) Illegal conditions

If a stipulation involves a serious element of moral turpitude—if, for example, it is one which has as its object the deliberate commission of a criminal offence—it will so infect the rest of the contract that the Courts will refuse to give any effect to the agreement,[312] at least at the suit of one who knew of or participated in the illegality. Thus in *Napier v National Business Agency Ltd*:[313]

The defendant agreed to employ N at a salary of £13 a week, with a further £6 a week for 'expenses'. In fact, N's expenses were nowhere near that sum, and this further provision was merely a device to defraud the income tax authorities. N brought an action to recover his salary, abandoning his claim to the expense allowance.

The Court of Appeal held that the provision as to expenses was contrary to public policy. Its inclusion vitiated the whole agreement and no severance could be allowed. Similarly relief will be refused if severance would be inconsistent with the policy of the Courts or of Parliament to discourage contracts containing an illegal element of the type sought to be severed. Thus, in *Kuenigl v Donnersmarck*,[314] McNair J refused to sever certain clauses in an agreement which involved dealings with an alien enemy.

On the other hand, if a provision in a contract is illegal by virtue of a statute passed for the protection of a class of persons,[315] there is no ground of public policy to prevent the Court from severing the illegal provision and giving effect to the remainder of the contract in an action brought by a member of the protected class.[316]

(ii) Unenforceable provisions

Public policy does not prevent the severance of provisions that are merely void or unenforceable,[317] and, in particular, of covenants in unreasonable restraint of trade, or clauses which oust the jurisdiction of the Courts. Such stipulations are not illegal in the strict sense, and will not taint the entire agreement in which they are contained. Provided that certain requirements are satisfied, they may be severed from the rest of the agreement. As Denning LJ pointed out in *Bennett v Bennett*:[318]

The presence of a void covenant of this kind does not render the deed totally ineffective . . . The party who is entitled to the benefit of the void covenant, or rather who would have been entitled to the benefit of it if it had been valid, can sue upon the other covenants of the deed which are in his favour; and he can even sue upon the void covenant, if he can sever the good from the bad, even to the extent of getting full liquidated damages for a breach of the good part. So also the other party, that is, the party who gave the void covenant and is not bound by its restraints, can himself sue upon the covenants in his favour, save only when the void covenant forms the whole, or substantially the whole, consideration for the deed.

---

[312] *Bennett v Bennett* [1952] 1 KB 249, 254.
[313] [1951] 2 All ER 264. See also *Kenyon v Darwen Manufacturing Co Ltd* [1936] 2 KB 193; *Miller v Karlinski* (1945) 62 TLR 85; and *Hyland v JH Barker (North West) Ltd* [1985] ICR 861.
[314] [1955] 1 QB 515.   [315] See above, p 448.   [316] *Ailion v Spiekermann* [1976] 1 Ch 158.
[317] *Bennett v Bennett* [1952] 1 KB 249, 254.   [318] [1952] 1 KB 249, 260; below, p 458.

There is no clear delimitation of the types of illegal stipulation which can be severed in this way, but whether or not a particular stipulation can be severed will depend upon considerations of public policy.

(iii) Extent of severance

Public policy may also affect the extent of the severance to be allowed. As we have already seen, the law dislikes employer–employee covenants in restraint of trade and will be zealous to see that freedom of contract is not abused. The question, therefore, arises whether an employer should be permitted to bluff (whether intentionally or not) the employee into accepting a covenant which is unreasonably wide, and, then, when the bluff is called, to make use of the principle of severance to carve out of that void covenant the maximum of what might validly have been required. In *Mason v Provident Clothing and Supply Co Ltd*,[319] Lord Moulton expressed the view that, in such cases, the excess which it is sought to delete must be 'merely trivial'.

More recently, however, in *T Lucas & Co Ltd v Mitchell*,[320] the Court of Appeal held that an unreasonable restraint, if it can be regarded as intended by the parties to be separate and separable from a valid restraint,[321] is capable of being severed notwithstanding that it is contained in an agreement between employer and employee. It may be that, in modern times, an employee needs less protection than formerly. But as Lord Moulton pointed out:[322] 'It must be remembered that the real sanction at the back of these covenants is the terror and expense of litigation, in which the servant is at a great disadvantage, in view of the longer purse of his master'.

(c) REQUIREMENTS

Assuming that severance of the contract is in accord with public policy, certain requirements must still be satisfied. The formulation of these requirements has been the subject of much speculation and contradiction, but at present the situation would appear to be as follows.

(i) The 'blue pencil' rule

In the first place, the illegal portion of the contract must be capable at least of being verbally separated from the remainder of the agreement. This is generally known as the 'blue pencil' rule, that is, 'severance can be effected when the part severed can be removed by running a blue pencil through it'[323] without affecting

---

[319] [1913] AC 724, 745. See also *Attwood v Lamont* [1920] 3 KB 571, 593. Cf *Nevanas & Co v Walker* [1914] 1 Ch 413; *Putsman v Taylor* [1927] 1 KB 637.

[320] [1974] Ch 129. See also *Scorer v Seymour Jones* [1966] 1 WLR 1419; *Beckett Investment Management Group Ltd v Hall* [2007] EWCA Civ 613, [2007] ICR 1539.

[321] See below, p 458.

[322] [1913] AC 724, 745. A similar concern also affects the construction of such clauses: *JA Mont (UK) Ltd v Mills* [1993] IRLR 173.

[323] *Attwood v Lamont* [1920] 3 KB 571, 578 (Lord Sterndale MR). See also *Business Seating (Renovations) Ltd v Broad* [1989] ICR 729, 734 and *Ginsberg v Parker* [1988] IRLR 483.

the meaning of the part remaining. The rule in practice can be seen in *Goldsoll v Goldman*:[324]

The defendant sold his jeweller's business in New Bond Street, London to Goldsoll, who was also a jeweller, and covenanted that he would not for the period of 2 years 'either solely or jointly . . . carry on the business of a vendor of or dealer in real or imitation jewellery in the county of London, England, Scotland, Ireland, Wales, or any part of the United Kingdom . . . or in France, the United States of America, Russia, or Spain, or within 25 miles of Potsdamerstrasse, Berlin, or St Stefans Kirche, Vienna'. The defendant joined a rival firm of jewellers in New Bond Street, and Goldsoll sought an injunction to restrain breach of the covenant.

The Court of Appeal held that, as Goldsoll's business was chiefly confined to imitation jewellery, the covenant was unreasonably wide, and that it was also too wide in area. But it was possible to excise the words 'real or' and also the references to foreign countries, and so to limit the covenant to dealing in imitation jewellery within the United Kingdom. In this form the covenant was unexceptionable and could be enforced. The reason for this somewhat technical rule is that the Court is not prepared to rewrite the agreement for the parties.

(ii) Illegal promise must not form main consideration

Secondly, the illegal promise must not form the whole or the main consideration for the contract. It must go only to a part, and a subsidiary part, of the consideration provided.[325] Otherwise one party would be compelled to perform a promise, the consideration for which would be far less than was ever contemplated when the promise was made. In *Bennett v Bennett*:[326]

A wife entered into a deed with her husband by which she covenanted not to apply to the Court for maintenance for herself or for her children, to maintain the younger herself, and to indemnify her husband against any legal expenses arising out of the deed. The husband undertook to pay his wife and son an annuity, and to convey to her certain property. The husband failed to make the promised payments and was sued by his wife.

It was held that the covenant by the wife not to apply to the Court for maintenance was contrary to public policy and void. Since it formed the main consideration for the contract, it could not be severed from the rest of the agreement. The wife was therefore unable to enforce her claim to the annuity since it was founded upon a consideration which was void. On the other hand, in *Goodinson v Goodinson*:[327]

A husband promised to pay his wife a weekly sum if she would indemnify him against any debts incurred by her, not pledge his credit for necessaries, and forbear to bring any matrimonial proceedings against him.

---

[324] [1915] 1 Ch 292. See also *Putsman v Taylor* [1927] 1 KB 637; *Ronbar Enterprises Ltd v Green* [1954] 1 WLR 815.

[325] See *Carney v Herbert* [1985] 1 AC 301 (illegal ancillary provision for the exclusive benefit of the plaintiff).

[326] [1952] 1 KB 249. This decision was effectively reversed by the Matrimonial Causes Act 1965, s 23(1), now the Matrimonial Causes Act 1973, s 34; above, p 428. See also *Triggs v Staines UDC* [1969] 1 Ch 10.

[327] [1954] 2 QB 118.

He fell into arrears with the payments and was sued by her. It was held that there was ample consideration to support the agreement apart from the covenant not to sue, and so the husband was liable.

(iii) Illegal promise must not alter agreement

Thirdly, the Court will not permit severance where the offending provisions are 'inextricably interwoven with the other promises in the agreement'[328] so that severance would 'alter entirely the scope and intention of the agreement'.[329] This is a sensible rule, for the mechanical deletion of an offending clause could affect the whole nature of the contract. Nevertheless, it is extraordinarily difficult to apply, and the understanding of its application is by no means increased by a study of its leading illustration. In *Attwood v Lamont*:[330]

A was the proprietor of a general outfitter's business. L had been employed as a tailor and cutter in one of A's departments. He was not concerned with any of the other departments. In his contract of service he had bound himself, after the termination of his employment, not to be concerned in the trade or business of a tailor, dressmaker, general draper, milliner, hatter, haberdasher, gentlemen's, ladies', or children's outfitter within 10 miles of his employer's place of business at Kidderminster.

The Court of Appeal held that this covenant was too wide. It attempted to protect against competition all departments of the employer's business, and not merely tailoring. The Divisional Court had found that the covenant was severable by striking out the other trades except that of tailor. The Court of Appeal reversed this finding. Both Lord Sterndale MR and Younger LJ considered that severance was only permissible in a case where the covenant to be severed was 'not really a single covenant, but was in effect a combination of several distinct covenants',[331] and the latter said:[332]

Now, here, I think, there is in truth but one covenant for the protection of the respondent's entire business, and not several covenants for the protection of his several businesses. The respondent is, on the evidence, not carrying on several businesses but one business, and, in my opinion, this covenant must stand or fall in its unaltered form.

It may be presumed that their Lordships intended simply to say that the deletion of the offending trades altered the *nature*, and not merely the *extent*, of the original covenant.[333] But the distinction drawn between 'single' and 'several' covenants is somewhat unprofitable, and cannot easily be applied to covenants such as that in *Goldsoll v Goldman*.[334] It seems better to say that the question of altering the scope and

---

[328] *Kuenigl v Donnersmarck* [1955] 1 QB 515, 538.

[329] *Attwood v Lamont* [1920] 3 KB 571, 580 (Lord Sterndale MR). See also *Routh v Jones* [1947] 1 All ER 179, 758; *Marshall v NM Financial Management Ltd* [1995] 1 WLR 1461; *Crehan v Courage (No 1)* [1999] Eu LR 834.

[330] [1920] 3 KB 571. Cf *Putsman v Taylor* [1927] 1 KB 637; *T Lucas & Co Ltd v Mitchell* [1974] Ch 129 (reversing the decision of Pennycuick J [1972] 1 WLR 938).

[331] They differed, however, as to how this test should be applied.   [332] [1920] 3 KB 571, 593.

[333] See Lord Sterndale MR at 578.   [334] See above, p 458.

intention of the agreement is one which depends upon the true construction of the covenant and agreement rather than upon this difficult and elusive distinction.

(d) EFFECT OF SEVERANCE

The effect of severance is not uniform in all cases.

(i) True severance

If the illegal and legal undertakings are distinct and separate, each being supported by its own consideration, the Court will strike out the offending conditions, together with the consideration, leaving the rest unimpaired.

Suppose that Government regulations prohibit building on a single property in excess of £1,000 without a licence. A builder undertakes to execute a number of unlicensed works on a single property on a 'cost plus' basis, ie the individual items being executed and paid for as required.[335]

Any work ordered or executed within the £1,000 limit will be legal and must be paid for. Work ordered in excess of this limit will be illegal, but it can be severed from the rest of the agreement. Neither a promise to do such work, nor a promise to pay for it, will be enforceable. The illegal part is truly and completely severed.

(ii) One-sided severance

On the other hand, the Court may strike out one or more of the promises on one side, while leaving the consideration on the other side unaffected. *Goldsoll v Goldman*[336] and *Goodinson v Goodinson*,[337] are examples of 'one-sided' severance.[338] The Court excised the offending provisions, but did not interfere with the consideration given for them. The severance was on one side only.

(iii) Restitution

If severance would substantially alter the nature of the contract, and neither party is willing to accept the contract in its severed form, the Court may order restitution of benefits obtained under the contract.[339] In *South Western Mineral Water Co Ltd v Ashmore*:[340]

A wished to purchase from SWMW a controlling interest in a company. It was agreed that he should pay £6,000 and be given an option to purchase the assets of the company for £36,500 to be secured by a debenture over the assets. A was let into possession of the company's premises and took delivery of all the assets. It was subsequently realized

---

[335] *Frank W Clifford Ltd v Garth* [1956] 1 WLR 570.
[336] See above, p 458.   [337] See above, p 458.
[338] A term suggested by Somervell LJ in *Bennett v Bennett* [1952] 1 KB 249, 260.
[339] Provided that recovery is not precluded by the maxim *in pari delicto potior est conditio defendentis* (see above, p 444) if the contract as a whole is tainted.
[340] [1967] 1 WLR 1110.

that the proposed debenture was illegal as it infringed a provision of the Companies Act 1948.

Cross J held that the stipulation for an illegal debenture did not render the whole agreement void. The agreement could be enforced by SWMW if they waived the security or by A if he tendered immediate payment. But as neither party was willing to accept an agreement in these terms, SWMW was to return the £6,000 and A was to give up possession of the premises and restore the assets received.

FURTHER READING

WINFIELD, 'Public Policy in the English Common Law' (1928) 42 Harv LR 76

GLANVILLE WILLIAMS, 'The Legal Effect of Illegal Contracts' (1942) 8 CLJ 51

GRODECKI, 'In Pari Delicto Potior Est Conditio Defendentis' (1955) 71 LQR 254

SUMPTION, 'Reflections on the Law of Illegality' [2012] RLR 1

PART 4

PERFORMANCE AND DISCHARGE

12

PERFORMANCE

1. PERFORMANCE MUST BE PRECISE AND EXACT

(a) STANDARDS OF CONTRACTUAL DUTY

The general rule is that performance of a contract must be precise and exact. That is, a party performing an obligation under a contract must perform that obligation exactly within the time frame set by the contract and exactly to the standard required by the contract. Sometimes that standard will be strict. This is so in the case of many common law obligations such as a seller's obligation to load cargo,[1] not to ship dangerous cargo,[2] and to obtain an export licence.[3] It is also so in the case of the statutory implied terms of title and quality in contracts for the sale and supply of goods.[4] Sometimes, as in the case of contracts for services, it will only require the exercise of reasonable care[5] or due diligence.[6] Whether the alleged performance satisfies this criterion is a question to be answered by construing the contract, so as to see what the parties meant by performance, and then by applying the ascertained *facts* to that construction, to see whether that which has been done corresponds to that which was promised.

---

[1] *Kurt A Becher GmbH & Co KG v Roplak Enterprises SA, The World Navigator* [1991] 2 Lloyd's Rep 23.

[2] *The Anathanasia Cominos* [1990] 1 Lloyd's Rep 277, 282.

[3] *Pagnan SpA v Tradax Ocean Transportation SA* [1987] 3 All ER 565.

[4] Non-consumer goods contracts: Sale of Goods Act 1979, ss 12, 14 (as amended), above, pp 171–7; Supply of Goods and Services Act 1982, ss 2, 4, 7, and 9; Supply of Goods (Implied Terms) Act 1973, ss 8, 10 (hire-purchase); consumer goods contracts: Consumer Rights Act 2015, ss 9, 17, above, p 178. See also Consumer Rights Act 2015 ss 34, 41 (consumer contracts to supply digital content).

[5] eg *Lister v Romford Ice and Cold Storage Co Ltd* [1957] AC 555 (driving lorry); *Thake v Maurice* [1986] QB 644, 684–7, cf 677–8 (medical treatment); *Smith v Eric S Bush* [1990] 1 AC 831, 843 (surveying house); *Henderson v Merrett Syndicates Ltd* [1995] 2 AC 145, 176 (managing agents of Lloyd's underwriters). See also Supply of Goods and Services Act 1982, s 13 (non-consumer services contracts); Consumer Rights Act 2015, s 49 (consumer services contracts). Cf *Samuels v Davis* [1943] 1 KB 526 (contract to supply services and materials in finished product).

[6] Carriage of Goods by Sea Act 1971, s 3 (seaworthiness); *Union of India v NV Reederij Amsterdam* [1962] 2 Lloyd's Rep 233 (HL).

(b) DEVIATION FROM CONTRACTUAL TERMS

If there is the slightest deviation from the terms of the contract, the party not in default will be entitled to say that the contract has not been performed, and will be entitled to sue for damages for breach and, in certain cases, to elect to be discharged. Thus in *Re Moore & Co and Landauer & Co:*[7]

D agreed to buy from P 3,000 tins of canned fruit from Australia to be packed in cases containing 30 tins. When the goods were tendered it was found that a substantial part of the consignment was packed in cases containing 24 tins.

D was entitled to reject the whole consignment. Even if the performance effected is commercially no less valuable than that which was promised, there is a default in performance. So a contract to ship goods direct from Singapore to New York was held not to have been performed by shipping them to the American Pacific Seaboard and thence to New York by train.[8]

Only if the deviation is 'microscopic' will the contract be taken to have been correctly performed, for *de minimis non curat lex.*[9] A party who does not render precise and exact performance of a contract is nevertheless exceptionally treated as having performed to some extent where that party has attempted (tendered) performance but the other party has prevented that performance, and in certain cases where there has been partial performance of an entire obligation.

2. TIME OF PERFORMANCE

(a) STIPULATIONS AS TO TIME AT COMMON LAW

Where a time was fixed for the performance of an undertaking by one of the parties to the contract, the common law as a general rule held this to be 'of the essence of the contract'. This phrase is often used but is capable of causing confusion because the question relates not to the contract as a whole but to the particular term which has been breached.[10] If the condition as to time was not fulfilled, the other party might treat the contract as broken and elect to terminate it.[11] For instance, in a contract for the sale of a flat where time was stated to be of the essence, the vendor was entitled to terminate when the purchaser tendered the price 10 minutes late.[12]

---

[7] [1921] 2 KB 519.   [8] *Re L Sutro & Co and Heilbut Symons & Co* [1917] 2 KB 348.

[9] *Arcos Ltd v EA Ronaasen & Son* [1933] AC 470, 479, 480 (Lord Atkin).

[10] *British and Commonwealth Holdings plc v Quadrex Holdings Inc* [1989] QB 842, 857 (Browne-Wilkinson V-C).

[11] *United Scientific Holdings Ltd v Burnley BC* [1978] AC 904, 940–1 (Lord Simon). Cf *ibid*, 927–8 (Lord Diplock). See further, above, pp 149, 156 (conditions).

[12] *Union Eagle Ltd v Golden Achievement Ltd* [1997] AC 514 (express termination and forfeiture clause). See also *Compagnie Commerciale Sucres et Denrées v C Czarnikow Ltd* [1990] 1 WLR 1337, 1347. But cf Sale of Goods Act 1979, s 10(1), below, p 468.

(b) STIPULATIONS AS TO TIME IN EQUITY

Equity did not regard a condition as to time as of the essence. Where it could do so without injustice to the contracting parties it decreed specific performance notwithstanding failure to observe the time fixed by the contract for completion, and as an incident of specific performance relieved the party in default by restraining proceedings at law based on such failure.[13]

(c) LAW OF PROPERTY ACT 1925, SECTION 41

Since the passing of the Judicature Acts, the rules of common law and equity have been fused,[14] and section 41 of the Law of Property Act 1925[15] provides:

Stipulations in a contract, as to time or otherwise, which according to rules of equity are not deemed to be or to have become of the essence of the contract, are also construed and have effect at law in accordance with the same rules.

But this relief is not available in three instances:

(1) where the agreement expressly states that time is of the essence of the contract;[16]

(2) where time was not of the essence of the contract, but upon a breach by one party,[17] the other has given notice requiring performance of the contract within a reasonable time.[18] This has often been referred to incorrectly as the service of a notice 'making time of the essence' of the contract, although strictly one party cannot unilaterally transform an innominate term into a condition;[19]

(3) where from the nature of the contract, its subject-matter, or the circumstances of the transaction, time must be taken to be of the essence of the agreement. The most common examples of this are provided by mercantile contracts, considered below, but, although time is prima facie not of the essence in sales of land,[20] or provisions in leases, such as rent review clauses,[21] in certain cases it will

---

[13] *United Scientific Holdings Ltd v Burnley BC* [1978] AC 904, 942. See also *Stickney v Keeble* [1915] AC 386, 415.

[14] *United Scientific Holdings Ltd v Burnley BC* [1978] AC 904, 924–5, 926–7, 940, 956–7, 964.

[15] Re-enacting the Judicature Act 1873, s 25(7). Cf *Raineri v Miles* [1981] AC 1050 (damages available).

[16] *Steedman v Drinkle* [1916] 1 AC 275; *Union Eagle Ltd v Golden Achievement Ltd*, above, n 12.

[17] *Behzadi v Shaftesbury Hotels Ltd* [1992] Ch 1; *British and Commonwealth Holdings plc v Quadrex Holdings Inc* [1989] 1 QB 842, 857–8; *Ramlal v Chaitlal* [2003] UKPC 12, [2004] 1 P & CR 1 (party giving notice must not be in default).

[18] *Stickney v Keeble*, above, n 13; *Behzadi v Shaftesbury Hotels Ltd*, above, n 17; *Finkielkraut v Monohan* [1949] 2 All ER 234. See also Stannard (2004) 120 LQR 137. On 'reasonableness', see also *Oakdown Ltd v Berstein and Co* (1985) 49 P & CR 282.

[19] *Urban 1 (Blonk Street) Ltd v Ayres* [2013] EWCA Civ 816, [2014] 1 WLR 756 at [44].

[20] *Webb v Hughes* (1870) LR 10 Eq 281; *Chancery Lane Developments Ltd v Wade's Department Stores Ltd* (1986) 53 P & CR 306, 312.

[21] *United Scientific Holdings Ltd v Burnley BC*, above, n 13.

be. Thus, in the case of the sale of a public-house as a going concern,[22] or of a leasehold house required for immediate occupation,[23] or of an option to acquire property,[24] or the power under a 'break' clause in a lease to determine the lease prematurely,[25] time may well be of the essence and, if so, no relief is permitted. Similarly, failure to make timely payment of a deposit normally constitutes a repudiatory breach and any presumption that time is not of the essence is rebutted.[26]

(d) MERCANTILE CONTRACTS

In mercantile contracts, time will readily be assumed to be of the essence of the contract. For example, if a contract to purchase shares provides for payment by a fixed date, payment must be made on or before that date, and in default the seller can treat the contract as discharged.[27] Similarly, time is of the essence for payment under a time charterparty of a ship if the owner is given the right to withdraw the vessel in default of 'punctual payment' of hire.[28] However, section 10(1) of the Sale of Goods Act 1979 provides that, unless a different intention appears from the terms of the contract, stipulations as to time of *payment* are not of the essence of a contract of sale of goods. The unpaid seller may, however, give notice of his intention to re-sell perishable goods and, if payment is not tendered within a reasonable time thereafter, re-sell and recover damages for any loss.[29] Whether or not any other stipulation as to time is of the essence of a contract of sale of goods depends upon the terms of the contract;[30] but it is very often held to be so.[31]

Where a person is required to perform on or before a particular date, the performance may normally be carried out during the whole of that day.[32] Thus if payment of hire under a time charterparty is due on 14 June, the charterer has (regardless of banking hours) until midnight on 14/15 June to make the payment, and the shipowner cannot withdraw the ship for non-payment before that time.[33]

---

[22] *Tadcaster Tower Brewery Co v Wilson* [1897] 1 Ch 705.

[23] *Tilley v Thomas* (1867) LR 3 Ch App 61.   [24] *Hare v Nicoll* [1966] 2 QB 130.

[25] *United Scientific Holdings Ltd v Burnley BC*, above, n 13, 929; *Coventry City Council v J Hepworth & Sons Ltd* (1982) 46 P & CR 170. But cf *Metrolands Investments Ltd v JH Dewhurst Ltd* [1986] 3 All ER 659.

[26] *Samarenko v Dawn Hill House Ltd* [2011] EWCA Civ 1445, [2013] Ch 36.

[27] *Hare v Nicoll*, above, n 24. See also *Union Eagle Ltd v Golden Achievement Ltd*, above, n 12.

[28] *Scandinavian Trading Tanker Co AB v Flota Petrolera Ecuatoriana, The Scaptrade* [1983] 2 AC 694.

[29] Sale of Goods Act 1979, s 48(3).

[30] Sale of Goods Act 1979, s 10(2). But see *Hartley v Hymans* [1920] 3 KB 475, 483.

[31] *Reuter v Sala* (1879) 4 CPD 239, 246, 249; *Hartley v Hymans*, above, n 30, 484; *Finagrain SA Geneva v P Kruse Hamburg* [1976] 2 Lloyd's Rep 508; *United Scientific Holdings Ltd v Burnley BC* [1978] AC 904, 924, 937, 944, 950, 958; *Bunge Corp v Tradax Export SA* [1981] 1 WLR 711, above, p 158; *Compagnie Commerciale Sucres et Denrées v C Czarnikow Ltd* [1990] 1 WLR 1337, 1347.

[32] Contrast Sale of Goods Act 1979, s 29(5) (demand or tender of delivery may be treated as ineffectual unless made at a reasonable hour).

[33] *Afovos Shipping Co SA v Pagnan* [1983] 1 WLR 195.

Where no time is fixed by the contract for performance, it must normally be performed within a reasonable time.[34]

3. PLACE OF PERFORMANCE

The place of performance depends upon the express or implied intentions of the parties, judged from the nature of the contract and the surrounding circumstances. If no place of performance is specified even by implication, then in a non-consumer contract for the sale of goods it is basically the duty of the buyer to collect the goods rather than the seller to send them,[35] although in a consumer sales contract it is the trader's duty to deliver the goods to the consumer buyer;[36] and in contracts to pay money it is basically the debtor's duty to pay the creditor at the creditor's place of business or residence.[37]

4. ORDER OF PERFORMANCE

Where the contract makes no express provision, the order of performance depends on whether the obligation of one party to perform is interdependent on or independent of the other's obligation. The obligations may be interdependent in one of two ways. The obligation of one to perform may either be conditional upon performance by the other or concurrent with the obligation of the other. The determination of this is a matter of intention, and thus of the construction of the contract. The distinction between interdependent obligations (ie conditions precedent and concurrent obligations), and independent promises is discussed in Chapters 5 and 15.[38] In a contract of sale, unless the contract provides otherwise, payment and delivery are treated as due simultaneously and as concurrent,[39] but in a contract of employment the general rule is that the performance of the work is a condition precedent to the obligation to pay. The order of performance determines whether one party has to extend credit to the other and whether failure to perform is a breach of contract,[40] and, if so, whether the innocent party is entitled to be discharged from its obligations. The position at common law differs from that in many civil law countries where a party may withhold performance until the other party performs, not only in cases of concurrent obligations but also where the other party has to perform first.[41]

---

[34] *Postlethwaite v Freeland* (1880) 5 App Cas 599; Sale of Goods Act 1979, s 29(3) (non-consumer sales contracts); cf Consumer Rights Act 2015, s 28(3) (consumer sales contract: unless time or period agreed, trader must deliver goods without undue delay, and in any event not more than 30 days after day of contract).

[35] Sale of Goods Act 1979, ss 29(1) (2). See also CISG, art 31.

[36] Consumer Rights Act 2015, s 28.

[37] *Charles Duval & Co Ltd v Gans* [1904] 2 KB 685; *Fowler v Midland Electricity Corporation for Power Distribution Ltd* [1917] 1 Ch. 656 (debenture). On payment through the banking system, see below, p 470.

[38] Above, p 150; below, p 547.   [39] Sale of Goods Act 1979, s 28.   [40] Below, Chapter 15.

[41] Lando and Beale, *Principles of European Contract Law Parts I and II* (2000) 407.

5. PAYMENT

(a) INTRODUCTION

One mode of complete performance of an obligation is by payment of a money obligation. No request or demand for payment is normally necessary[42] unless the contract so provides.[43]

There is a common, but mistaken, belief that payment of a debt can be proved only by the production of a written receipt. But payment may be proved by any evidence,[44] and a receipt is only prima facie evidence that a debt has been paid.[45]

Payment normally means payment in cash. The parties may, however, agree, expressly or impliedly, that payment may be made in some other manner, and, in the absence of any express stipulation, the method of payment may be determined by course of dealing between the parties or by trade custom. If the parties are dealing together on a regular basis, it may be agreed that, at periodic intervals, sums due from one party shall be set off against sums due to that party by the other, and such set-off is then equivalent to an actual cash payment.[46]

(b) INTERBANK TRANSFERS

Nowadays payment is frequently made by use of the banking system. The debtor instructs its bank to pay a specified sum to the account of the creditor at another bank. The transfer may be effected by letter, telex, or nowadays generally electronically from the one bank to the other. Such payment, when made, 'is the equivalent of cash, or as good as cash' for the purposes of a contract that requires payment in cash.[47] But difficulties can arise. If payment has to be made by a certain date, does the receipt of the payment order by the creditor's bank constitute payment? Or is payment only made when the order has been processed and the amount credited to the creditor's account? In *Mardorf Peach & Co Ltd v Attica Sea Carriers Corporation of Liberia*,[48] where the evidence was that the system of processing might take up to 24 hours before the account was credited, members of the House of Lords expressed differing opinions. Lord Salmon[49] and Lord Russell[50] were inclined to the view that, since a payment order was as between banks the equivalent of cash, it should suffice for punctual payment that such cash equivalent was tendered in due time to the creditor's bank to be credited

---

[42] *Bell & Co v Antwerp, London & Brazil Line* [1891] 1 QB 103, 107 (Lord Esher MR); *Carne v Debono* [1988] 1 WLR 1107, 1112.

[43] *Libyan Arab Foreign Bank Co v Bankers Trust Co* [1989] 1 QB 728, 748–9. On the need for notice by a tenant of want of repair before landlord's obligation to repair is due, see *Calabar Properties Ltd v Stitcher* [1984] 1 WLR 287, 298; *British Telecommunications plc v Sun Life Assurance Society plc* [1996] Ch 69.

[44] *Eyles v Ellis* (1827) 4 Bing 112. See also Cheques Act 1957, s 3.

[45] *Wilson v Keating* (1859) 27 Beav 121.   [46] *Larocque v Beauchemin* [1897] AC 358, 365–6.

[47] *A/S Awilco of Oslo v Fulvia SpA di Navigazione of Cagliari, The Chikuma* [1981] 1 WLR 314, 320.

[48] [1977] AC 850.   [49] *Ibid*, 880.   [50] *Ibid*, 889.

to its account.[51] But Lord Fraser[52] was of the opinion that payment would not take place until the creditor's bank acted on the request in the order and credited the amount to the creditor's account. However, in *A/S Awilco of Oslo v Fulvia SpA di Navigazione of Cagliari, The Chikuma*:[53]

R chartered A's vessel *Chikuma*. Failing punctual payment of hire in cash in American currency monthly in advance, A was entitled to withdraw the vessel from service. Payment of one instalment of hire fell due on 22 January. On 21 January R instructed its Norwegian bank to make the required payment by credit transfer. By a telex message before noon on the 22nd there was a credit transfer to A's bank in Italy of the sum due. The bank credited this on the same day to A's account. By Italian banking law, however, although A would have immediate access to the money, interest would not start to be paid by the bank until 26 January, and if A had withdrawn the sum credited it would probably have incurred liability to the bank to pay interest for those 4 days. A withdrew the vessel for default in punctual payment.

The House of Lords upheld their right to do so. The payment on 22 January was not equivalent to cash for it could not be used to earn interest, for example by immediate transfer to a deposit account. The fact that A could withdraw the money, but subject to payment of interest, did not make the payment equivalent to cash, since the arrangement amounted in substance to an overdraft facility.

(c) PAYMENT BY NEGOTIABLE INSTRUMENT OR DOCUMENTARY CREDIT

A negotiable instrument such as a bill of exchange, cheque, or promissory note may, by agreement, be given and accepted in payment. But the presumption where a negotiable instrument is taken in lieu of a money payment is that the parties intend it to be a conditional discharge only:[54]

Suppose that A, being owed a sum of money by B, agrees to take a cheque in payment of the sum due.

So far, B has satisfied the debt.[55] But if the cheque is dishonoured when presented for payment, A's right to sue on the debt revives and A's original rights are restored.[56] Exceptionally, however, a negotiable instrument may be given and accepted as absolute payment. In such a case, in the example given above, B's debt would then be wholly discharged. A would have to rely upon the rights conferred by the cheque, and, if the

---

[51] In the case of a transfer between branches of the same bank, *Momm v Barclays Bank International Ltd* [1977] QB 79 held that payment was effected when the staff of the bank received the debtor's instructions and set in motion the bank's internal procedures for crediting the creditor's account.

[52] [1977] AC 850, 885.   [53] [1981] 1 WLR 314 (criticized by Mann (1981) 97 LQR 379).

[54] *Re Romer and Haslam* [1893] 2 QB 286, 296, 300, 303.

[55] *Sayer v Wagstaff* (1844) 5 Beav 415, 423; *Hadley & Co Ltd v Hadley* [1898] 2 Ch 680; *Bolt & Nut Co (Tipton) Ltd v Rowlands, Nicholls & Co Ltd* [1964] 2 QB 10.

[56] *Sayer v Wagstaff*, above, n 55; *Re Romer and Haslam*, above, n 54.

cheque is dishonoured, A must sue on it, and cannot revert to the original claim for the debt.[57] Similar principles apply to payment by documentary credit.[58]

(d) PAYMENT BY CREDIT OR CHARGE CARD

By contrast, payment by a credit or charge card is an unconditional and absolute payment unless the contract provides otherwise. So, the liability of a cardholder who has paid for goods or services in this way is discharged and the cardholder will not be liable to the seller or supplier if the credit or charge card company fails to pay the seller or supplier the amount charged to the card.[59]

6. VICARIOUS PERFORMANCE

There may be circumstances which make it permissible for a contracting party to perform his side of the contract by getting someone else to do in a satisfactory fashion the work for which the contract provides.[60] A contract may be vicariously performed where this is expressly permitted by the contract,[61] or, from the terms of the contract, its subject-matter, and surrounding circumstances, it may properly be inferred that it is a matter of indifference whether the performance is that of the contracting party or his nominee. Thus it has been held that a contract to let out railway wagons and keep them in repair could be vicariously performed.[62] The repairs were 'a rough description of work which ordinary workmen conversant with the business would be perfectly able to execute'.[63] If, however, the person employed has been selected with reference to his individual skill, competence, or other personal qualification, that person is not entitled to sub-contract the performance of the contract to another. Thus it has been held that personal care and skill is an ingredient in contracts by a warehouseman for the storage of furniture,[64] by a publishing firm for the publication of a book,[65] and by an architect in the design of a building.[66] Such contracts cannot be vicariously performed without the consent of the promisee. Contracts of service are normally personal to the contracting parties.[67] Furthermore, payment of a debt

---

[57] *Sard v Rhodes* (1836) 1 M & W 153; *Sibree v Tripp* (1846) 15 M & W 23; *Re Romer and Haslam*, above, n 54, 296, 300.

[58] *WJ Alan & Co Ltd v El Nasr Export and Import Co* [1972] 2 QB 189, 209–12; *Re Charge Card Services Ltd* [1989] Ch 497, 511.

[59] *Re Charge Card Services Ltd* [1989] Ch 497; *Customs & Excise Commissioners v Diners Club Ltd* [1989] 1 WLR 1196.

[60] See below, p 712, for the distinction between vicarious performance and assignment.

[61] eg *Société Commerciale de Réassurance v ERAS International Ltd* [1992] 1 Lloyd's Rep 570, 596.

[62] *British Waggon Co v Lea & Co* (1880) 5 QBD 149.

[63] *Ibid*, 153 (Cockburn CJ).   [64] *Edwards v Newland & Co* [1950] 2 KB 534.

[65] *Griffith v Tower Publishing Co Ltd* [1897] 1 Ch 21.

[66] *Moresk Cleaners Ltd v Hicks* [1966] 2 Lloyd's Rep 338.

[67] *Nokes v Doncaster Amalgamated Collieries Ltd* [1940] AC 1014 (rights). But note the Transfer of Undertakings (Protection of Employment) Regulations 2006 (SI 2006 No 246), reg 4(1), below, p 711.

which is made by a person other than the debtor or the debtor's agent will not be effective to discharge the debt.[68]

Even where the contract may not, in principle, be vicariously performed, if the promisee in fact agrees to it being performed by a non-party and accepts such performance, the contract will be discharged.[69]

7. ALTERNATIVE MODES OF PERFORMANCE

A contract can provide for alternative modes of performance in one of two ways.[70] First, it may provide for performance in a particular way, for instance a shipper's obligation to load a cargo of wheat, but give that party the option to perform in an alternative way, for instance, to change to a cargo of barley. Secondly, it may permit one party to choose[71] between alternative modes of performance without specifying one as the primary mode, for instance, a shipper's obligation to load a full cargo in the month of September or October.

(a) CONTRACT OPTION

In the first situation, once the option is exercised, the contractual obligation is varied; in the example above, the contract ceases to be one to load wheat and becomes one to load barley. The option must be exercised within a reasonable time and this must be communicated to the other party;[72] if it is not exercised it is lost. But, in considering whether to exercise the option, the promisee is not generally bound to consider the interests of the other party.[73] For example, if the primary mode of performance becomes impossible, the option-holder is not obliged to exercise it in order to avoid the contract being frustrated.[74] But, in the case of a non-consumer contract, an attempt to rely on the exercise of such an option to render a contractual performance substantially different from that which was reasonably expected may be ineffective against a party dealing on the other's written standard terms of business,[75] and in a consumer contract such an option may be an unfair term and therefore not binding on the consumer.[76]

---

[68] See *Belshaw v Bush* (1851) 11 CB 191; *Walter v James* (1871) LR 6 Ex 124; *Owen v Tate* [1976] 1 QB 402. See generally Beatson and Birks (1976) 91 LQR 188; Beatson, *The Use and Abuse of Unjust Enrichment* (1991) ch 7; Friedmann (1983) 99 LQR 534.

[69] *Belshaw v Bush*, above, n 68; *Hirachand Punamchand v Temple* [1911] 2 KB 483, above, p 120.

[70] See generally Treitel, *Frustration and Force Majeure* (3nd edn, 2014) ch 10.

[71] If the contract does not specify which party has the option, it will be the one who has to do the first act: *Reed v Kilburn Co-operative Society* (1875) LR 10 QBD 264.

[72] *Reardon Smith Line Ltd v Ministry of Agriculture, Fisheries & Food* [1963] AC 691, 731.

[73] *Ibid*, 719–20, 730. See also *Thompson v ADSA-MFI Group Plc* [1988] Ch 241, 251, 266–7 (no general principle that a party cannot take advantage of own acts to avoid obligations under the contract).

[74] On frustration, see further Chapter 14.   [75] Unfair Contract Terms Act 1977, s 3(2)(b).

[76] Consumer Rights Act 2015, ss 62, 63 and Sched 2, Part 1, paras 2, 3, 11, 13, 15. See generally above, pp 215, 223.

(b) PERFORMANCE OPTION

In the second situation there is a truly alternative obligation. The promisor is obliged to perform in any of the authorized modes. If, prior to a choice being made, one mode ceases to be available, that simply narrows the scope of contractually authorized performance.[77] So, in the example given above, if access to the loading port is impossible due to strikes or bad weather during September, that does not affect the obligation to ship a full cargo; the shipper remains liable to load a full cargo in October, even if the shipper had planned to do so in September. But once a party chooses the alternative to be performed, that choice binds.[78]

8. RIGHT OF PARTY IN BREACH TO CURE BAD OR INCOMPLETE PERFORMANCE

We have seen that English law treats a serious misperformance, such as incomplete delivery or delivery of goods that are not of satisfactory quality, as the standard example of a breach entitling the innocent party to treat the contract as discharged.[79] Unlike the position in some other systems, the innocent party is not required to serve notice requiring the other party to perform in a stated time[80] and there is only a limited right to cure defective performance.[81] If, however, a bad or incomplete performance is tendered before the time of performance has arrived, the promisor is not generally prevented from making another tender of performance within time that does comply. The promisee would have to accept this fresh tender unless the first amounted to a repudiation which the promisee had already acted upon and terminated the contract.[82] One situation in which the defective performance will be treated as a repudiation is where the defective performance has destroyed the confidence of the promisee.[83]

---

[77] *Reardon Smith Line Ltd v Ministry of Agriculture, Fisheries & Food* [1963] AC 691, 717, 720, 730; *Atlantic Lines & Navigation Co Ltd v Didymi Corp, The Didymi* [1984] 1 Lloyd's Rep 583, 587; *Libyan Arab Foreign Bank v Bankers Trust Co* [1989] QB 728, 766; *J Lauritzen AS v Wijsmuller BV, The Super Servant Two* [1990] 1 Lloyd's Rep 1, 9.

[78] *Schneider v Foster* (1857) 2 H & N 4; *Gath v Lees* (1865) 3 H & C 558. But authority (*Brown v Royal Insurance Co* (1859) 1 E & E 853) suggesting the party remains bound even where it is no longer possible to perform the contract in that way is doubtful since it pre-dates the development of the doctrine of frustration, on which see below, Chapter 14.

[79] Above, pp 148–9, 154 (conditions and innominate terms). See further below, Chapter 15.

[80] Treitel, *Remedies for Breach of Contract* (1988) 327–34 (*Nachfrist* in German law, *délai de grâce* in French law).

[81] *Ibid*, 371–4; CISG art 48; ALI *Restatement, Contracts (2d)* para 237 (serious breach initially only justifies suspension of performance by innocent party).

[82] *Borrowman, Phillips & Co v Free & Hollins* (1878) 4 QBD 500; *Motor Oil Hellas (Corinth) Refineries SA v Shipping Corporation of India, The Kanchenjunga* [1990] 1 Lloyd's Rep 391, 399.

[83] On repudiation, see further below, Chapter 15.

9. TENDER

Tender is attempted performance; and the word is applied to attempted performance of two kinds, dissimilar in their results. It is applied to a performance of a promise to do something, and of a promise to pay something. In each case the performance is prevented by the act of the party for whose benefit it is to take place.

(a) TENDER OF ACTS

Where one party is obliged by the contract to perform a promise to do something, but the other party refuses to accept the performance when tendered,[84] the promisor is discharged from performing that obligation and may sue for damages. In addition, if the promisee commences an action against the promisor for failure to perform the obligation, the promisor is entitled to set up the refusal to accept the tender as a defence.[85] The promisor will not, however, be treated as having performed the obligation. If the refusal to accept the tender amounts to a repudiation of the contract the promisor can elect to terminate the contract and sue for damages.[86] Although such a refusal does not always have this effect,[87] if it is absolute and unqualified it entitles the promisor to elect to be discharged. For example, section 37 of the Sale of Goods Act 1979 provides that when the seller is ready and willing to deliver the goods and requests the buyer to take delivery, the buyer must do so within a reasonable time or become liable for any loss occasioned to the seller by the buyer's neglect. But this does not affect the rights of the seller where the non-acceptance amounts to a repudiation of the contract.

(b) TENDER OF PAYMENT

Where, however, the performance due consists of the payment of a sum of money, a tender by the debtor, though refused by the creditor, does not discharge the debtor from the obligation to pay the debt. The debtor is bound in the first instance 'to find out the creditor and pay him the debt when due';[88] if the creditor will not take payment when tendered, the debtor must nevertheless continue to be ready and willing to pay the debt. Then, the debtor, if sued, can plead that a tender had been made, but must pay the money into Court.[89] If the debtor proves this plea, the creditor gets nothing but the money originally tendered, that is, no interest or damages, while the debtor

---

[84] Tender must be in strictly accordance with the terms of the contract. In the absence of express terms a tender of goods must be made at a reasonable hour: Sale of Goods Act 1979, s 29(5).

[85] *Startup v Macdonald* (1843) 6 M & G 593.　　　　　　　　　　　　　　　　　　[86] *Ibid.*

[87] See, eg, Sale of Goods Act 1979, s 31(2) (non-consumer sales contracts); Consumer Rights Act 2015, s 26(3), (4) (consumer goods contracts); above, p 160.

[88] *Walton v Mascall* (1844) 13 M & W 452, 458 (Parke B).　　　　　　　　　　　[89] CPR r 37.2.

gets judgment for the costs of the action, and so is placed in as good a position as at the time of the tender. Tender of payment, to be a valid performance to this extent, must observe exactly any special terms which the contract may contain as to time, place, and mode of payment. The nineteenth-century authorities further prescribe extremely strict requirements for a valid tender: it must be unconditional and it must be in legal currency.[90] There must be an offer of money produced and accessible to the creditor, not necessarily of the exact sum, but of such a sum as will allow the creditor to take exactly what is due without being called upon to give change.[91] Finally, it was necessary for the cash to be produced to the creditor in person. 'Great importance', it was said,[92] 'was attached to the production of money, as the sight of it might tempt the creditor to yield'. But these requirements may be dispensed with expressly or impliedly by the creditor,[93] and the requirement of payment in cash must be interpreted against the background of modern commercial practice. In commercial transactions, it would appear that any commercially recognized method of transferring funds, the result of which is to give the transferee the immediate use of the funds transferred, will nowadays suffice.[94]

(c) EARLY TENDER

A promisee need not, moreover, accept an early tender, but, as we have seen, if a bad tender is made before the time of performance has arrived, it does not generally prevent the promisor making another tender within time that does comply with the contract.[95]

10. PARTIAL PERFORMANCE

(a) ENTIRE AND DIVISIBLE OBLIGATIONS

Since the performance of a contractual obligation must be precise and exact, where one party's performance is made conditional on complete and entire performance by the other party,[96] at common law[97] the general rule is that the other can recover

---

[90] The Currency and Bank Notes Act 1954, the Coinage Act 1971, and the Currency Act 1983 define legal tender.

[91] *Betterbee v Davis* (1811) 3 Camp 70.

[92] *Finch v Brook* (1834) 1 Bing NC 253, 257 (Vaughan J).

[93] *Farquharson v Pearl Assurance Co Ltd* [1937] 3 All ER 124.

[94] *Tenax Steamship Co Ltd v The Brimnes (Owners)* [1975] 1 QB 929, 963; *Mardorf Peach & Co Ltd v Attica Sea Carriers Corp of Liberia* [1977] AC 850, 880, 885, 889; see above, p 470; *Libyan Arab Foreign Bank Co v Bankers Trust Co* [1989] 1 QB 728, 749–50.

[95] Above, p 475.

[96] See Williams (1941) 57 LQR 373; Treitel (1967) 30 MLR 139, 141ff; Law Com No 121, *Pecuniary Restitution on Breach of Contract* (1983). Mr Brian Davenport QC dissented and the government rejected the report: 19th Annual Report (1983–84) Law Com No 140, para 2.11.

[97] For statutory exceptions, see Apportionment Act 1870, s 2 (rents, annuities, dividends, and other periodic payments in the nature of income prima facie considered as accruing from day to day); Law Reform (Frustrated Contracts) Act 1943, below, p 525.

nothing for incomplete performance. It is immaterial how the failure to effect complete performance comes about. It may be due to a deliberate abandonment of the contract, to a negligent act or omission, or to a simple misfortune occurring without any fault. In *Cutter v Powell*,[98] for example:

A seaman was engaged to act as second mate on a voyage from Jamaica to Liverpool. He was to be paid 30 guineas, almost four times the going rate, in a single payment upon completion of the voyage. Nineteen days out from Liverpool, when the voyage was nearly completed, he died. His widow sued to recover a proportion of the agreed sum.

Her action failed. The seaman's obligation was construed as an entire contract or, more accurately, an entire obligation, that is to say, if the voyage was completed he was to receive the stipulated sum, but, if it was not, he was to receive nothing. As Sir George Jessel MR said: 'if a shoemaker agrees to make a pair of shoes, he cannot offer you one shoe, and ask you to pay one half the price'.[99]

The reason it is inaccurate to refer to 'entire contracts' is that it is very unlikely that complete performance of each and every obligation in a contract by one party is a condition precedent to the liability of the other. The contract may, for example, be a complex one, composed of a number of undertakings differing in character or importance; or it may be a promise to do a number of successive acts; or to do a single act which can be partly or defectively performed.[100] Very often a contract may be entire as to one aspect but 'divisible' or 'severable' (in the sense that the right to payment accrues incrementally as the performance is rendered) as to another. For example, in *Cutter v Powell*, although the seaman's obligation to complete the voyage was entire, his obligation to exercise reasonable care in the performance of his duty was unlikely to be entire, so that, had he completed the voyage, but had performed his duty badly, it seems he would have been able to recover his wages, subject to a claim against him for poor work.[101] Again, in contracts for the carriage of goods by sea, whereas the obligation to deliver the cargo to the stipulated port is entire, so that no freight at all is payable if delivery is made at an intermediate port,[102] the obligations with respect to the quantity or condition of the cargo are not, so that, if half the cargo is delivered, half the freight is payable,[103] and if all the cargo arrives damaged (but still of the same

---

[98] (1795) 6 Term R 320; Stoljar (1956) 34 Can Bar Rev 288. But the effect of this decision has been alleviated by statute: see the Law Reform (Frustrated Contracts) Act 1943, below, p 525, and what is now the Merchant Shipping Act 1995, s 38.

[99] *Re Hall & Barker* (1878) 9 Ch D 538, 545.

[100] See the discussion in *Baltic Shipping Co v Dillon* (1993) 176 CLR 344, 350, 384 (High Court of Australia).

[101] Law Com No 121, *Pecuniary Restitution on Breach of Contract* (1983) para 2.12, citing Somervell LJ in *Hoenig v Isaacs* [1952] 2 All ER 176, 178.

[102] *St Enoch SS Co Ltd v Phosphate Mining Co* [1916] 2 KB 624; *Metcalfe v Britannia Iron Works Co* (1877) 2 QBD 423.

[103] *Ritchie v Atkinson* (1808) 10 East 295, 530. But where there is a stipulation for lump freight or freight to be computed on loading, the carrier will be entitled to full freight: *Aires Tanker Corp v Total Transport Ltd, The Aires* [1977] 1 WLR 185; *Colonial Bank v European Grain & Shipping Ltd, The Dominique* [1989] AC 1056. See further *Scrutton on Charterparties* (22nd edn, 2011) Ch 15.

commercial description), freight will be payable subject to a counterclaim against the carrier for damages.[104]

Because the consequences can be draconian, Courts are reluctant to construe an obligation as 'entire'.[105] But where the payment for the performance was to be a lump sum to be paid after completion they have generally done so, so that the promisee cannot recover anything until the work is completely executed.[106] Thus, apart from *Cutter v Powell*, this construction has been put on obligations by a builder to build two houses and stables for a client,[107] and by a plumber to supply and install a combined central heating and hot water system in a private house.[108]

(i) Rationale of rule

The general rule has been justified in a number of ways.[109] First, the recipient of the performance has not contracted to buy part of the performance for a proportionate part of the price and should not be compelled to pay for performance that is different from that agreed and, in some cases, insisted upon.[110] Where, like the seaman in *Cutter v Powell*, the performer is to be paid significantly more than the going rate for the job, it can also be said that he has accepted the risk of incomplete or defective performance. Secondly, the rule holds people to their contracts and gives them a strong incentive to complete.[111] It is particularly important where there is inequality of bargaining power or scope for opportunistic behaviour, as there often is in contracts for small building works on private houses. It is all too common for a builder not to complete one job before moving on to the next, and the rule enables the householder to withhold all payment unless the job is finished.[112] Thirdly, the losses the innocent party suffers may be ones for which the law finds it difficult to compensate.[113]

(ii) Critique of rule

The principle precluding recovery, however, if rigorously applied, could be productive of great injustice. It is hard to contend, for example, that even the most trivial defect

---

[104] *Dakin v Oxley* (1864) 15 CB(NS) 646, 667. See further *Scrutton on Charterparties*, above, n 103.

[105] *Button v Thompson* (1869) LR 4 CP 330, 342.

[106] *Appleby v Myers* (1867) LR 2 CP 651, 660–1, *The Madras* [1898] P 90, and *Sumpter v Hedges* [1898] 1 QB 190, below, p 481, appear to adopt this as a general rule. For criticism, see below.

[107] *Sumpter v Hedges*, above, n 106.   [108] *Bolton v Mahadeva* [1972] 1 WLR 1009.

[109] See generally, Waddams, in Reiter and Swan (eds), *Studies in Contract Law* (1980) 163 ff; Law Com No 121, *Pecuniary Restitution on Breach of Contract* (1983) paras 2.24–2.26.

[110] *Wiluszynski v Tower Hamlets LBC* [1989] ICR 493; *Miles v Wakefield MBC* [1987] AC 539, below, p 481; *British Telecommunications plc v Ticehurst* [1992] ICR 383.

[111] *Munro v Butt* (1858) 8 E & B 735, 754; Law Com No 121, *Pecuniary Restitution on Breach of Contract* (1983) para 2.25.

[112] Law Com No 121, *Pecuniary Restitution on Breach of Contract* (1983) 37 (Mr BJ Davenport QC's dissent). A builder may protect itself by requiring payments before the completion of performance, which (below, pp 621, 625) will generally be irrecoverable. Note that in contracts for the sale of goods, consumers have wider power of rejection than non-consumers: Sale of Goods Act 1979, ss 15A(1), 30(2A), below, n 127.

[113] As in the case of non-pecuniary loss (*Vigers v Cook* [1919] 2 KB 475; and see below, p 567) or loss to a third party (below, p 653).

of workmanship in the decoration of a flat,[114] or some momentary slip or inefficiency on the part of an employee,[115] should entitle the 'injured' party to refuse all payment save where the injured party has made it absolutely clear that the trivial defect or breach will have this effect.[116] It should not, accordingly, be inferred, as it has been,[117] that such penal consequences follow from the mere postponement of payment of a lump sum by one party until after the other party has completely performed.[118] Such postponement may be prompted by a number of other reasons, including easing the 'cash-flow' of the party who will have to pay, and protecting that party from the risk that the other may become insolvent. Moreover, the application of the principle would often result in the unjust enrichment of the injured party if that party could retain the benefit of the incomplete performance without the necessity of paying for it. A general acceptance of the risk of incomplete performance by the part performer may not extend to a situation where the other party is incontrovertibly benefited, and a restitutionary remedy does not necessarily constitute a redistribution of risks allocated by the contract.[119]

The unpalatable consequences that can follow have led Courts to seek to avoid construing an obligation as entire. Broadly speaking this can properly be done in two situations; where the injured party has *accepted* the partial performance, and, although this is not so clearly established, where the part performer can establish that the services rendered or the work done has *incontrovertibly benefited* the other party so as to give rise to a claim for restitution of the unjust enrichment. The underdevelopment until recently of the law of restitution for unjust enrichment, and the tendency to construe an obligation as 'entire' simply because the contract provides for a lump sum has, however, also led to authority favouring a remedy in a third situation; where the part performer has *substantially performed* the 'entire' obligation.

(b) DOCTRINE OF 'SUBSTANTIAL PERFORMANCE'

Where the contract is *substantially* performed, there is authority that the injured party is not discharged from the obligation to pay, but is protected by a counterclaim or set-off for any loss which may have been sustained by reason of the incomplete or defective

---

[114] *Hoenig v Isaacs* [1952] 2 All ER 176 (contract price £750, defects remedied for £55).

[115] *Ibid*, 178.

[116] *Miles v Wakefield MBC* [1987] AC 539, 551, 561, 568; *Wiluszynski v Tower Hamlets LBC* [1989] ICR 493, 500, 503.

[117] Above, n 106.

[118] Law Com No 121, *Pecuniary Restitution on Breach of Contract* (1983) paras 2.11, 2.27, and 2.67; Williams (1941) 57 LQR 373, 389 ff.

[119] Although it *might* do so; see Beatson, *The Use and Abuse of Unjust Enrichment* (1991) ch 4, and *Wiluszynski v Tower Hamlets LBC* [1989] ICR 493, below, p 481. Cf McFarlane and Stevens (2002) 118 LQR 569, supporting the decision in *Sumpter v Hedges* [1898] 1 QB 673, below, p 481, on the basis that a party in breach should have no claim for value of services rendered or goods supplied unless he has an accrued *contractual* right to payment.

performance.[120] A Court will hold a contract to have been substantially performed if the actual performance falls not far short of the required performance, and if the cost of remedying the defects is not too great in amount in comparison with the contract price.[121] In *H Dakin & Co Ltd v Lee*:[122]

D were builders who had contracted to execute certain repairs to L's premises for £1,500. They carried out a substantial part of the contract, but failed to perform it exactly in three unimportant respects (which could have been rectified at a cost of £80). The official referee appointed by the parties held that D were consequently not entitled to recover any part of the contract price.

On appeal, it was held that this finding was erroneous. The contract had been substantially, if not precisely, performed. Pickford LJ stated that the fact that the work was done badly did not mean that it had not been performed at all.[123] D was accordingly entitled to recover the price less a reduction for the breach. In the USA a more flexible approach has been taken whereby the Court may look at the quality of performance so that, even if the cost of compliance is great, there may still be substantial performance if the work that is done is of the same quality as that contracted for. In *Jacob & Youngs Inc v Kent*[124] the New York Court of Appeals held that a builder who failed to use galvanized piping of 'Reading manufacture' for the plumbing in a building had substantially performed the contract; the pipes in fact used were of the same quality as those specified and the defect could only be remedied by demolishing a substantial part of the building. There are indications that this approach may also be taken in English law.[125]

Since the basis of the rules governing entire obligations is that the parties have made *complete* and *precise* performance by one party a condition to entitlement to performance by the other, it is submitted that it is logically difficult to justify applying a principle of substantial performance to such obligations. To do so is to set aside the contractual allocation of risks. But the cases which have construed an obligation as entire simply because the contract provided for a lump sum to be paid after the completion of performance provide some pragmatic justification, since this fact alone may not truly indicate that the risks of any trivial incompleteness in performance are to lie with the part performer. On principle, however, the correct approach is

---

[120] *Boone v Eyre* (1779) 1 H Bl 273; *Broom v Davis* (1794) 7 East 480n; *Bolton v Mahadeva* [1972] 1 WLR 1009, 1015; *Sim v Rotherham Metropolitan Borough Council* [1987] Ch 216, 253; *Wiluszynski v Tower Hamlets LBC* [1989] ICR 493, 499; *Williams v Roffey Bros & Nicholls (Contractors) Ltd* [1991] 1 QB 1, 8–10, 17.

[121] Compare *Hoenig v Isaacs* [1952] 2 All ER 176 (cost of remedying defects was 7.3 per cent of contract price) and *Bolton v Mahadeva* [1972] 1 WLR 1009 (no substantial performance where cost of remedying defects was 31 per cent of contract price).

[122] [1916] 1 KB 566, 579. Note Greer LJ's criticism in *Eshelby v Federated European Bank Ltd* [1932] 1 KB 423, 431 and cf *Vigers v Cook* [1919] 2 KB 475; *Bolton v Mahadeva* [1972] 1 WLR 1009.

[123] This suggests that on true analysis the obligation concerning the *quality* of the work may not have been entire. See Williams (1941) 57 LQR 373, 386–7, and see above, p 477.

[124] 129 NE 889 (1921).

[125] In *Ruxley Electronics Ltd v Forsyth* [1996] 1 AC 344 (below, p 571, but not involving an entire obligation), *Jacob & Youngs Inc v Kent*, was approved at 363 in a slightly different context.

greater caution in the categorization of an obligation as entire, and development of the emerging restitutionary principles to which we now turn.

(c) ACCEPTANCE OF PARTIAL PERFORMANCE BY INNOCENT PARTY

A party who renders incomplete performance of an entire contract may nevertheless claim remuneration where the other party has freely accepted such partial performance or otherwise waived the need for complete performance. So, if the customer of Sir George Jessel's shoemaker had accepted one shoe he would have been obliged to pay for the shoe he accepted.[126] In the case of the sale of goods, where the seller delivers to the buyer a quantity of goods less than he contracted to sell, the buyer may reject them, but if the buyer accepts the goods so delivered he must pay for them at the contract rate.[127]

In most cases, such a claim will arise upon a quantum meruit, that is to say, for a reasonable sum in respect of the services rendered or the work done by the partial performance. But it will do so only if the party not in default has the option whether to accept or to refuse the partial performance. Thus in *Sumpter v Hedges*:[128]

S agreed to erect two houses and stables on H's land for £565. He failed to complete the contract. H thereupon completed the buildings himself, using the materials left on the site by S. S brought an action to recover the value of the work done before he abandoned the contract, and also claimed in respect of the building materials used.

It was held that S was entitled to recover the value of the materials left which H used, for H had the choice whether or not to use these to complete the building. But S could not recover for the work he had done, for H had no option but to accept the partly-erected building which was on his land. Similarly, an employer who told employees working 'to rule' and not carrying out part of their contractual services not to come to work at all unless they were prepared to work normally, was not held to have 'accepted' the partial performance simply because it did not send them home; 'a person is not treated by the law as having chosen to accept that which is forced down his throat despite his objections'.[129]

---

[126]   Above, p 477. See also *Baltic Shipping Co v Dillon* (1993) 176 CLR 344, 378.

[127]   Sale of Goods Act 1979, s 30(1) (non-consumer sale of goods contracts); Consumer Rights Act 2015, s 25(1) (consumer goods contracts). But a non-consumer may not reject where the shortfall, or the breach of the conditions implied by ss 13–15 of the 1979 Act, is so slight that it would be unreasonable for him to do so: 1979 Act, ss 30(2A), and 15A, inserted by the Sale and Supply of Goods Act 1994.

[128]   [1898] 1 QB 673. See also *Munro v Butt* (1858) 8 E & B 738; *Forman & Co Proprietary Ltd v Ship 'Liddesdale'* [1900] AC 190; McFarlane and Stevens (2002) 118 LQR 569.

[129]   *Wiluszynski v Tower Hamlets LBC* [1989] ICR 493, 504 (Nicholls LJ), but see Mead (1990) 106 LQR 192. In *Miles v Wakefield MBC* [1987] AC 539, 553, 563, two of their Lordships suggested that, if the employer has not made it clear that reduced or inefficient work will not be accepted, the employee will be entitled to a reasonable sum for that reduced work. But, as the contract had not been discharged, there are formidable difficulties with any restitutionary claim: below, pp 628–9. Cf Lord Bridge's doubts, *ibid*, 552. Lord Brandon and Lord Oliver reserved their opinions.

Originally the basis of this liability was said to be that acceptance of partial performance implies a fresh agreement between the parties to pay for the work already done or goods supplied[130] but the implication of such a contract can be fictional, and, in such cases, it is better to regard the obligation to pay as restitutionary arising from the operation of the principle of unjust enrichment.[131]

(d) INCONTROVERTIBLE BENEFIT

The failure of the claim in respect of the partially erected building in *Sumpter v Hedges* shows that the mere fact that a person appears to have benefited from the part performance of an entire obligation, does not suffice to ground a claim for restitution.[132] This is because in the law of unjust enrichment, objective benefits may be 'subjectively devalued' by the defendant.[133] But, where it can be shown that the recipient of the part performance has gained a readily realizable financial benefit or has been saved expense which he must have incurred, there is some support for the view that the part performer would be entitled to restitution[134] save where the parties have made it clear that the risk of non-completion is to be borne by the part performer even where there is such a benefit.[135]

---

[130] *Sumpter v Hedges*, above, n 106; *Steele v Tardiani* (1946) 72 CLR 386, 394, 402 (High Court of Australia).

[131] *Baltic Shipping Co v Dillon* (1993) 176 CLR 344, 374, 385 (High Court of Australia). For the recognition of unjust enrichment in England, see *Lipkin Gorman v Karpnale* [1991] AC 548, above, p 25.

[132] See also *Bolton v Mahadeva* [1972] 1 WLR 1009.

[133] *Benedetti v Sawiris* [2013] UKSC 50, [2014] AC 938; Birks, *Unjust Enrichment* (2nd edn, 2005) ch 3; Burrows, *The Law of Restitution* (3rd edn, 2010) ch 3.

[134] *Hain SS Co Ltd v Tate & Lyle Ltd* (1936) 41 Com Cas 350, 358 (Lord Atkin), 367–8 (Lord Wright MR), and 373 (Lord Maugham); *Procter & Gamble Philippine Manufacturing Corp v Peter Cremer GmbH & Co, The Manila* [1988] 3 All ER 843, 855; *Miles v Wakefield MBC*, above, n 110, 553, 563. See also *Britton v Turner* 6 NH 481 (1834) (New Hampshire). Cf Beatson (1981) 98 LQR 389, 411, 413.

[135] Law Com No 121, *Pecuniary Restitution on Breach of Contract* (1983) paras 2.66–2.69, 2.73, and see above, n 129.

13

DISCHARGE BY AGREEMENT

1. INTRODUCTION

Contract rests on the agreement of the parties: as it is their agreement which binds them, so by their agreement they may be discharged. And this mode of discharge may occur by release under seal; by accord and satisfaction; by rescission or variation; or by the operation of some provision contained in the contract itself.

Two sources of difficulty, however, exist which render the topic of discharge by agreement one of considerable artificiality and refinement.

(a) CONSIDERATION APPLIES TO DISCHARGE

The first is that the doctrine of consideration applies to the discharge as well as to the formation of a contract.[1] As a result, a distinction has to be drawn between those situations where the contract is still *executory* on both sides, and those where the contract has been *executed* on one side. In the case of an executory contract, the consideration for the discharge by agreement is found in the relinquishment by each promisee of its right to performance. Where, however, the contract has been wholly executed by one party, leaving the other party still to perform its side of the obligation, as, for example, where A has sold and delivered goods to B, but B has not yet paid for them, any release of B would be purely gratuitous since A would not receive any benefit, nor would B suffer any detriment, by this action. This distinction was emphasized by Parke B in *Foster v Dawber*, when he said:[2]

It is competent for both parties to an executory contract, by mutual agreement, without any satisfaction, to discharge the obligation of that contract. But an executed contract cannot be discharged except by release under seal, or by performance of the obligation, as by payment, where the obligation is to be performed by payment.

The agreement to discharge must therefore be under seal, or be supported by some other consideration ('accord and satisfaction') on the part of the person seeking to be released.

---

[1] See above, p 117.

[2] (1851) 6 Exch 839, 851.

(b) CONTRACTS EVIDENCED BY WRITING

The second source of difficulty is that certain contracts are required by law to be in writing, or to be evidenced by writing,[3] and any subsequent variation of such a contract must also be in writing, or proved by writing.[4] But writing is not required for the rescission by agreement of such a contract, nor for the waiver of a term contained in it.[5] The distinction between rescission, variation, and waiver is, as we shall see, a fine one, and there is much artificiality in the lines to be drawn between almost identical cases. The occasions on which this difficulty can arise have declined greatly since writing is a requirement for very few types of contract.[6] But writing is still required for contracts for the sale or other disposition of land and contracts of guarantee, so that it cannot be said that the difficulties have entirely disappeared.

2. FORMS OF DISCHARGE BY AGREEMENT

(a) RELEASE

The right to performance of a contract can be abandoned by release contained in a deed.[7] If a deed is employed, it is immaterial that the contract has been executed on one side, for the deed dispenses with the need for consideration. A release not contained in a deed requires consideration. The agreement is then discharged by accord and satisfaction. A release is construed in the same way as any other contract. It has been held that a general release could not be interpreted as covering rights which the parties had no idea existed.[8]

An agreement not to sue in perpetuity amounts to a release[9] but, at common law, an agreement not to sue for a limited period merely gave rise to a cross-action for damages.[10] Equity, however, would restrain the promisor from suing within that time,[11] and today the equitable rule prevails[12] so that the agreement acts as a bar to the original action.

---

[3] See Chapter 3.

[4] eg *McCausland v Duncan Lawrie Ltd* [1997] 1 WLR 38 (variation of material term in a contract for sale or other disposition of an interest in land must comply with Law of Property (Miscellaneous Provisions) Act 1989, s 2).

[5] *Morris v Baron & Co* [1918] AC 1, below, p 487; *McCausland v Duncan Lawrie Ltd*, above, n 4, 48.

[6] See Chapter 3.   [7] For the requirements of a deed, see above, p 80.

[8] *BCCI SA v Ali* [2001] UKHL 8, [2002] 1 AC 251 (Lord Hoffmann dissenting). It did not release rights to stigma damages (below, p 569) which the law did not recognize at the time of the release.

[9] *Hodges v Smith* (1599) Cro Eliz 623. See, however, *Cutler v McPhail* [1962] 2 QB 292, 298.

[10] *Ford v Beech* (1848) 11 QB 852.   [11] *Beech v Ford* (1848) 7 Hare 208.

[12] Senior Courts Act (formerly Supreme Court Act) 1981, s 49.

(b) ACCORD AND SATISFACTION

Discharge of a contract in return for a consideration which consists in some satisfaction other than the performance of the original obligation is termed 'accord and satisfaction':

Accord and satisfaction is the purchase of a release from an obligation whether arising under contract or tort by means of any valuable consideration, not being the actual performance of the obligation itself. The accord is the agreement by which the obligation is discharged. The satisfaction is the consideration which makes the agreement operative.[13]

It is effective to discharge any contract, whether executory or executed, and even if the original contract was contained in a deed.[14]

(i) Executory satisfaction

Formerly, a contractual obligation, or cause of action arising from the breach of a contract, was not discharged so long as the satisfaction remained executory, that is, so long as the agreement to furnish new consideration had not been carried out.[15] As it was said in an old case:[16] 'Accord executed is satisfaction; accord executory is only substituting one cause of action in the room of another, which might go on to any extent'. But the question is now regarded as one of the construction of the agreement; and the promise only, as distinct from the actual performance of it, may be a good satisfaction and discharge the original obligation, if it clearly appears that the parties so intended.[17] The original obligation or claim is then discharged from the date the promise is accepted. If the promisor fails to perform its promise, the promisee's only remedy is to sue for breach of the promise, and it cannot return to the original obligation or claim.[18]

It must be remembered, however, that the rule in *Pinnel's Case*[19] prescribes that the payment of a smaller sum in satisfaction of a larger is not a good discharge of a debt. So if B owes A the sum of £50 for goods sold and delivered, and A agrees to excuse him £45 out of this amount, the debt is not discharged by the payment of £5. But the receipt by A of some satisfaction different in kind, or of a fixed sum instead of an uncertain sum, or of a lesser sum at an earlier date or in a different place than that required by the contract, is sufficient. Compromises of a disputed claim,[20] compositions with creditors,[21] and payments by a third party,[22] also afford exceptions to this rule.

---

[13] *British Russian Gazette and Trade Outlook Ltd v Associated Newspapers Ltd* [1933] 2 KB 616, 643–4 (Scrutton LJ).

[14] *Steeds v Steeds* (1889) 22 QBD 537.   [15] *Peytoe's Case* (1612) 9 Co Rep 79b.

[16] *Lynn v Bruce* (1794) 2 H Bl 317, 319 (Eyre LCJ).

[17] *Good v Cheesman* (1831) 2 B & Ad 328; *Morris v Baron & Co* [1918] AC 1, 35; *British Russian Gazette and Trade Outlook Ltd v Associated Newspapers Ltd*, above, n 13, 650, 654–5; *Jameson v Central Electricity Generating Board* [1998] QB 323, 335.

[18] *British Russian Gazette and Trade Outlook Ltd v Associated Newspapers Ltd*, above, n 13, 644, 654; *Green v Rozen* [1955] 1 WLR 741.

[19] (1602) 5 Co Rep 117a; above, p 117; *Ferguson v Davies* [1997] 1 All ER 315.

[20] Above, p 109, and see *Kitchen Design & Advance Ltd v Lea Valley Water Co* [1989] 2 Lloyd's Rep 221.

[21] Above, p 119.   [22] Above, p 120.

(ii) Promissory estoppel

Accord without satisfaction is not contractually binding, and it is still not certain whether the principle of promissory estoppel considered above in Chapter 4 could be successfully relied upon to obviate the necessity for consideration where the accord involves the permanent abandonment by one party of his right to performance by the other. The view has been advanced that promissory estoppel serves only to suspend, and not totally to extinguish, existing rights,[23] although it is probable that this is not a necessary limitation on the doctrine. As we have seen, there is in particular an unresolved question about whether a debt can be extinguished through the operation of promissory estoppel.[24]

(iii) Bills of exchange

One important exception does, however, exist. It was a rule of the law merchant, imported into the common law, that no satisfaction was required for the discharge of a bill of exchange or promissory note. Section 62 of the Bills of Exchange Act 1882 gives statutory force to this rule, but subject to the provision that the discharge must be in writing, or the bill delivered up to the acceptor.

(c) RESCISSION

(i) By agreement

A contract which is executory on both sides may be discharged by agreement between the parties that it shall no longer bind them. This is commonly referred to as a rescission of the contract, although whether it rescinds the obligations under the contract *ab initio* or merely discharges the parties from their outstanding obligations will depend on the parties' agreement. Such an agreement is formed of mutual promises, and the consideration for each promise of each party is the abandonment by the other of its rights under the contract.

(ii) Abandonment

The Court can infer from a long period of delay or inactivity that the parties have agreed to abandon their contract. It must be shown that one party conducted itself in such a way that the other party reasonably assumed that it was agreed that the contract was abandoned.[25] Courts have come close to inferring an offer to abandon a contract from mere silence, although some overt act is almost always likely to be required.[26] In the case of arbitration, legislation now gives arbitrators the power to dismiss a claim where there has been inordinate and inexcusable delay on the part of

---

[23] Above, p 127.   [24] Above, p 128.

[25] *Paal Wilson & Co A/S v Partenreederei Hannah Blumenthal, The Hannah Blumenthal* [1983] 1 AC 854, 865, 885, 914, 916, 924.

[26] On arbitration, see above, p 33, n 9. On landlord and tenant, see *Collin v Duke of Westminster* [1985] 1 QB 581.

the claimant in pursuing his claim, irrespective of whether the arbitration contract has been abandoned.[27]

(iii) Substituted contract

Rescission of a contract may also take place by such an alteration in its terms as substitutes a new contract for the old one. The old contract may be expressly discharged in the new one, or discharge may be implied by the introduction of new terms or new parties. This method of discharge is therefore a form of rescission with a new contract superadded.

An example of the discharge of a contract by the substitution of new terms is provided by *Morris v Baron & Co*:[28]

A dispute had arisen out of a contract for the sale of cloth and an action had been begun. Before the case came on for trial the parties made an oral arrangement of which the chief terms were that the action and counterclaim were to be withdrawn, an extension of credit was to be given to the buyer for a sum admittedly due from him under the old contract, and, as regards the balance of goods contracted for but undelivered, there was to be substituted for a firm contract of sale an option for the buyer to take them if he pleased.

The House of Lords held that in these circumstances it must be concluded that the parties had agreed to abrogate the old contract and substitute a new one for it.

Similarly, the introduction of new parties[29] may impliedly rescind an existing contract and substitute a new one for it:

Suppose A has entered into a contract with B and C, and that B and C agree among themselves that C shall retire from the contract and cease to be liable upon it.

A may of course insist upon the continued liability of C; but if A continues to deal with B after becoming aware of the retirement of C, A's conduct will probably justify the inference that a new contract to accept the sole liability of B has been made, and A cannot then hold C to the original contract. 'If one partner goes out of a firm, and another comes in, the debts of the old firm may, by the consent of all three parties—the creditor, the old firm, and the new firm—be transferred to the new firm',[30] and this consent may be implied by conduct, if not expressed in words or writing.

(iv) Form of discharge by agreement

As regards the form needed for the expression of an agreement which purports to rescind an existing contract, the old rule of the common law was that a contract under seal could only be discharged by agreement expressed under seal. But, in equity, an agreement to rescind which was not under seal afforded a defence to an action on the

---

[27] Arbitration Act 1996, s 41(3).   [28] [1918] AC 1.   [29] See also 'novation', below, p 712.
[30] *Hart v Alexander* (1837) 2 M & W 484, 493 (Parke B). In the case of partnership, these rules are substantially embodied in the Partnership Act 1890, s 17(3).

deed. Since the Judicature Acts the rule of equity prevails, and a contract contained in a deed may be rescinded by a parol contract (a simple contract, oral or in writing) as well as by deed.[31]

A parol or simple contract, whether in writing or not, may be discharged by a subsequent agreement, either written or oral. Even when the original agreement is one required by statute to be in or evidenced by writing, as in the case of contracts for the sale or other disposition of land, or contracts of guarantee,[32] there is no need for a written discharge since there is no requirement that they shall be dissolved in writing. In *Morris v Baron & Co*,[33] for example, the original contract for the sale of cloth was one which was required by section 4 of the Sale of Goods Act 1893 (now repealed) to be evidenced by writing. The substituted contract was itself unenforceable because it did not comply with that section. Nevertheless, it operated as a discharge of the old contract with the result that the buyer, who claimed damages for non-delivery of the goods alternatively under the original and under the substituted agreement, was unable to succeed on either ground.

Rescission of an agreement by substitution of new terms must, however, be distinguished in form and in effect from (i) variation, and (ii) forbearance or waiver.

(d) VARIATION

The parties to a contract may effect a variation of the contract by modifying or altering its terms by mutual agreement, but without intending to rescind it and to substitute a wholly new contract for it.[34] A contract may also give one of the parties the power unilaterally to vary the obligations, for example by a price variation clause, as long as it is clear.[35] In the case of consumer contracts, however, this power has been restricted by legislation.[36]

(i) Form of variation

A contract under seal may be varied, as it may be rescinded, by a parol contract.[37] A simple contract, again, whether in writing or not, may be varied by a subsequent agreement either written or oral. This in no way conflicts with the rule that extrinsic evidence is not admissible to vary or add to the contents of a written document, for that principle merely refers to the ascertainment of the *original* intention of the parties. It has no application to the case of a *subsequent* variation.[38] But a contract required by

---

[31] *Berry v Berry* [1929] 2 KB 316; Senior Courts Act 1981 (formerly Supreme Court Act 1981), s 49.

[32] See Chapter 3.   [33] [1918] AC 1, above n 28.

[34] *British and Beningtons Ltd v North Western Cachar Tea Co Ltd* [1923] AC 48; Stoljar (1957) 35 Can Bar Rev 485; Dugdale and Yates (1976) 39 MLR 680.

[35] *Lombard Tricity Finance Ltd v Paton* [1989] 1 All ER 916; *Amberley (UK) Ltd v West Sussex CC* [2011] EWCA Civ 11.

[36] Consumer Rights Act 2015, ss 62, 63 and Sched 2, above, p 223, replacing similar provisions in Unfair Terms in Consumer Contracts Regulations 1999 (SI 1999 No 2083).

[37] *Berry v Berry* [1929] 2 KB 316.   [38] *Goss v Lord Nugent*, below, n 39, 64.

law to be in writing, or to be evidenced by writing, must be varied in writing. In *Goss v Lord Nugent*:[39]

By an agreement in writing G had contracted to sell to N several lots of land and to make good title to them. It was afterwards discovered that a good title could not be made to one of the lots, and N orally agreed not to insist on a good title to that lot. N later, relying on the defective title, refused to pay the purchase money.

The contract, being one for the sale of land, was at that time required to be evidenced in writing.[40] The promise to accept the defect in title would operate to vary that contract. But the Court held that G could not rely on this variation as it was merely oral, and N was therefore entitled to succeed on the ground that a good title had not been made.

Whether there has been a mere variation of terms or a rescission must depend upon the intention of the parties in each particular case and the question is often not an easy one to determine; but the following test has been suggested by Lord Dunedin:[41]

In the first case [variation] there are no such executory clauses in the second arrangement as would enable you to sue upon that alone if the first did not exist; in the second [rescission] you could sue on the second arrangement alone, and the first contract is got rid of either by express words to that effect, or because, the second dealing with the same subject-matter as the first but in a different way, it is impossible that the two should be both performed. When I say you could sue on the second alone, that does not exclude cases where the first is used for mere reference, in the same way as you may fix a price by a price list, but where the contractual force is to be found in the second by itself.

The changes must go to the 'very root' of the original agreement,[42] and 'there should have been made manifest the intention in any event of a complete extinction of the first contract, and not merely the desire of an alteration, however sweeping, in terms which leave it still subsisting'.[43]

(ii) Consideration for variation

A variation involves a definite alteration, *as a matter of contract*, of contractual obligations by the mutual agreement of both parties.[44] It must be supported by consideration. In most cases, consideration for the variation can be found in a mutual abandonment of existing rights or the conferment of new benefits by each party on the other.[45] Alternatively, consideration may be found in the assumption of additional

---

[39] (1833) 5 B & Ad 58. See also *Noble v Ward* (1867) LR 2 Ex 135; *United Dominions Corp (Jamaica) Ltd v Shoucair* [1969] 1 AC 340; *New Hart Builders Ltd v Brindley* [1975] Ch 342.

[40] See now Law of Property (Miscellaneous Provisions) Act 1989, s 2, above, p 88 (contract must be *in writing*); *McCausland v Duncan Lawrie Ltd* [1997] 1 WLR 38.

[41] *Morris v Baron & Co* [1918] AC 1, 26.

[42] *British and Beningtons Ltd v North Western Cachar Tea Co Ltd* [1923] AC 48, 68 (Lord Sumner).

[43] *Morris v Baron & Co*, above, n 41, 19 (Lord Haldane).

[44] *Besseler Waechter Glover & Co v South Derwent Coal Co* [1938] 1 KB 408, 416 (Goddard J).

[45] *Re William Porter & Co Ltd* [1937] 2 All ER 361; *W J Alan & Co Ltd v El Nasr Export and Import Co* [1972] 2 QB 189.

obligations or the incurring of liability to an increased detriment.[46] Although an agreement whereby one party undertakes an additional obligation, but the other party is merely bound to perform its existing obligations, will, as a general rule, not be effective to vary a contract, as no consideration is present,[47] it has been held that the contract may exceptionally be varied where the Court can identify a 'practical' benefit to the party undertaking the additional obligation.[48] And if one party merely agrees not to enforce one of the terms of the contract to be performed by the other, this does not constitute a variation. Such an agreement may, however, be binding as a waiver[49] or in equity.[50]

(e) WAIVER

A party who voluntarily agrees to forbear from insisting on the mode of performance or time of performance fixed by the contract, or forbears from so insisting, will be held to have waived the right to require that the contract be performed by the other party in accordance with its terms.[51] But 'waiver' is a term which bears many meanings, has been criticized as a 'slippery word worn smooth with overuse',[52] and, as we shall see, is also used to refer to an election between inconsistent rights. Waiver is relevant where difficulties of form or absence of consideration mean that there is no variation of the contract. Waiver was developed by the common law mainly as a device for evading the formal requirements of the Statute of Frauds, but because, as we have noted, formal requirements are much less important in the modern law, this aspect is now of less importance, although still relevant for certain types of contract, such as contracts for the sale of land and guarantees.[53]

(i) Form of waiver

Where a contract has to be by deed, or in, or evidenced by, writing, an oral agreement to forbear, for example by acceding to a request to extend the time of performance, might be met by the plea that the contract had been discharged by an alteration

---

[46] *North Ocean Shipping Co Ltd v Hyundai Construction Co Ltd* [1979] QB 705.

[47] *Stilk v Myrick* (1809) 2 Camp 317; *Syros Shipping Co SA v Elaghill Trading Co* [1980] 2 Lloyd's Rep 390; see above, pp 113–16.

[48] *Williams v Roffey Bros & Nicholls (Contractors) Ltd* [1991] 1 QB 1; *Anangel Atlas Compania Naviera SA v Ishikawajima-Harima Heavy Industries Co Ltd (No 2)* [1990] 2 Lloyd's Rep 526, above, p 114. Cf *Re Selectmove Ltd* [1995] 1 WLR 474; *Collier v Wright (Holdings) Ltd* [2007] EWCA Civ 1329, [2008] 1 WLR 643, above, pp 117–18.

[49] See below.   [50] Equitable, or promissory, estoppel: see above, p 122; below, p 493.

[51] See Phipps (2007) 123 LQR 286 for a valuable discussion of waiver and forbearance at common law. 'Waiver' is also used in a different sense, where a party is entitled either under the terms of the contract or by the general law to choose between alternative and inconsistent rights, eg the right of one party to treat itself as discharged by reason of a repudiatory breach by the other, below, p 536; or to terminate a contract for breach under an express contractual provision to that effect, below, p 552.

[52] Roscoe Pound's forward to Ewart, *Waiver Distributed* (1917) vi. See also Carter (1991) 4 JCL 59.

[53] Above, p 488, and see generally Chapter 3.

of the time of performance, that a new contract was thereby created, and that the new contract was not binding or was unenforceable for non-compliance with the statutory requirements as to form.[54] Alternatively, the party which agreed to extend the time for performance, if sued by the other party, might plead that the other party was never ready and willing to perform within the time originally fixed for performance. A party thus given more time for performance, could not rely on the assent of the other to this, as this constituted a variation of the contract which was nugatory since it was not in writing.[55]

(ii) Variation and waiver distinguished

In order to overcome these difficulties, and so that statutory requirements of formality might not become a cloak for fraud, the Courts showed themselves willing to draw a distinction between variation on the one hand and mere waiver or forbearance on the other. Whereas the former might, in the cases previously mentioned, be required to be in writing, an oral waiver would be efficacious although not in the statutory form. In *Levey & Co v Goldberg*,[56] for example:

G agreed in writing to buy from L certain cloth over £10 in value, delivery to be made within a specified time. At the request of G, L orally consented to withhold delivery during that period. Subsequently, however, before delivery was made, G sought to terminate the contract claiming that L had repudiated the contract by not being ready and willing to deliver the cloth within the contract time or within a reasonable time, and pleading the Sale of Goods Act 1893, section 4,[57] as a defence to L's subsequent action for non-acceptance of the goods.

It was held that the forbearance by L at the request of G to deliver within the defined period did not constitute a variation but was a valid and effective waiver although not in writing. G was therefore liable for his failure to accept the cloth. The distinction between variation and waiver has been said to depend upon the intention of the parties;[58] for there to be a variation the parties must intend permanently to alter the contractual obligation; if the party forbearing wishes to preserve the possibility of reverting to the contract, it is at most a waiver. The distinction is difficult to apply in practice,[59] and, although now much less important in respect of formal requirements, it is still important in commercial transactions.

---

[54] *Stead v Dawber* (1839) 10 A & E 58.   [55] *Plevins v Downing* (1876) 1 CPD 220, 225.
[56] [1922] 1 KB 688.
[57] Sale of Goods Act 1893, s 4, required the contract to be evidenced by writing. Cf Sale of Goods Act 1979, s 4 (contract of sale may be made in writing, with or without seal, or by word of mouth, or partly in writing and partly by word of mouth, or may be implied from the parties' conduct).
[58] *Stead v Dawber* (1839) 10 A & E 57; *Tallerman & Co Pty Co Ltd v Nathan's Merchandise (Vic) Pty Ltd* (1954) 91 CLR 288, 297 (High Court of Australia). Dugdale and Yates (1976) 39 MLR 680 distinguish pre-breach statements which are likely to be variations from post-breach ones, which are not.
[59] Compare, eg *Goss v Lord Nugent* (1833) 5 B & Ad 58 with *Hickman v Haynes* (1875) LR 10 CP 598.

(iii) Waiver does not require consideration

Waiver is important because it is an extremely common occurrence in commercial transactions. It is, however, open to the technical objection that it ought to have no binding force since it is gratuitous and made without consideration. As it benefits only the promisee, without any corresponding benefit to the promisor, the element of consideration is lacking. It should therefore be without legal effect. But the Courts have not hesitated to hold that the waiver of a contractual stipulation is valid and binding even though there is no consideration. The party granting the indulgence cannot go back on the promise and require strict adherence to the contract.[60] However, in cases of postponement of performance, if no period of postponement is fixed, that party may give reasonable notice to the other party requiring the contract to be performed within a certain time, and the contract must then be performed within that time.[61] Similarly, in cases of the waiver of other types of contractual term, the party granting the indulgence may as a general rule, upon reasonable notice, require the other party to comply with the original contractual stipulation; but cannot treat the forbearance as of no effect. In *Panoutsos v Raymond Hadley Corporation of New York*:[62]

P contracted to buy from RH 4,000 tons of flour which RH was to ship to Greece, by means of separate shipments. The contract required payment to be effected by P opening a bankers' confirmed letter of credit in RH's favour. P did open a letter of credit, but it was not 'confirmed'. RH made some shipments and received payment for these by this letter of credit. Subsequently, however, RH summarily terminated the remainder of the contract on the ground that the letter of credit was not in accordance with the contractual stipulation. P sued for breach.

It was held that RH, by its acceptance of payment by means of the unconfirmed letter of credit, had impliedly waived this condition in the contract. This, however, did not mean that it was consequently bound to accept that letter of credit until the end of the contract; it might, by giving reasonable notice, insist on the strict contractual terms. But it was not entitled to cancel the contract in a summary manner.

(iv) Risk borne by party requesting forbearance

The party to whom the forbearance is granted is also bound by its terms.[63] Moreover, if that party asks to have the performance of the contract postponed, it does so at its own risk. For if that party subsequently refuses to accept the goods, and the market value of the goods which it should have accepted at the earlier date has altered at the later date, the measure of damages may be increased as against it by the addition of damages consequent on the delay.[64]

---

[60] *Leather Cloth Co v Hieronimus* (1875) LR 10 QB 140; *Bruner v Moore* [1904] 1 Ch 305; *Besseler Waechter Glover & Co v South Derwent Coal Co* [1938] 1 KB 408; *Tankexpress A/S v Compagnie Financière Belge des Petroles SA* [1949] AC 76.

[61] *Charles Rickards Ltd v Oppenhaim* [1950] 1 KB 616.   [62] [1917] 2 KB 473.

[63] *Hickman v Haynes* (1875) LR 10 CP 598; *Levey & Co v Goldberg* [1922] 1 KB 688.

[64] *Levey & Co v Goldberg*, above, n 63.

(v) Promissory estoppel and waiver distinguished

In developing waiver mainly as a common law device for evading the formalities required by the Statute of Frauds, little attempt was made to explain why a gratuitous promise should thus be binding. If it is to be justified analytically, it may be more satisfactory to regard waiver as a species of estoppel. It will be remembered that equity, by use of the principle of promissory estoppel,[65] is also prepared to give effect to a promise made in similar circumstances:

If persons who have contractual rights against others induce by their conduct those against whom they have such rights to believe that such rights will either not be enforced or will be kept in suspense or abeyance for some particular time, those persons will not be allowed by a Court of Equity to enforce the rights until such time has elapsed, without at all events placing the parties in the same position as they were before.[66]

The party who has waived strict performance may be said to be estopped from going back on the promise or representation to do so, at any rate without giving fair and adequate notice to the promisee.

The similarity between waiver and estoppel was noted by Denning LJ in *Charles Rickards Ltd v Oppenhaim*:[67]

CR contracted with O to build a body on a Rolls Royce car chassis, and to deliver the completed car to O by 20 March 1948 at the latest. On that day it was still not completed, but O continued to press for delivery. On 29 June, however, he wrote to CR stating he would not take delivery after 25 July. CR still having failed to deliver the car, O treated the contract as repudiated.

The Court of Appeal held that he was entitled to do so. Although by his conduct he had impliedly waived the original stipulation as to time, he had given reasonable notice of his intention to reimpose a new time limit. CR having failed even then to perform, the contract was clearly discharged by its breach. Denning LJ said of O's consent to postponement:[68]

Whether it be called waiver or forbearance on his part, or an agreed variation or substituted performance, does not matter. It is a kind of estoppel. By his conduct he evinced an intention to affect their legal relations. He made, in effect, a promise not to insist on his strict legal rights. That promise was intended to be acted on, and was in fact acted on. He cannot afterwards go back on it.

The analogy, however, is not exact: promissory estoppel may be more limited than waiver. For an estoppel to become binding, it has been said that the promisee must

---

[65] See above, p 122.

[66] *Birmingham and District Land Co v London and North Western Railway Co* (1888) 40 Ch D 268, 286 (Bowen LJ).

[67] [1950] 1 KB 616; cf Stoljar (1957) 35 Can Bar Rev 485. For more recent discussion on waiver in the sense of estoppel see *Motor Oil Hellas (Corinth) Refineries SA v Shipping Corp of India, The Kanchenjunga* [1990] 1 Lloyd's Rep 391; *Commonwealth of Australia v Verwayen* (1990) 170 CLR 394.

[68] [1950] 1 KB 616, 623. Cf Phipps (2007) 123 LQR 286, 298–9.

alter its position in reliance on the promise,[69] but when waiver is used in the sense of estoppel, the focus of the law is on whether the dealings between the parties and the prejudice to the party who has been told that strict performance is not required are such as to render it inequitable for the other party to go back on its promise or representation.[70] The requirement of reliance has not been strictly enforced for waiver,[71] although in cases of waiver of a time fixed for performance (but not in the case of waiver of other types of stipulation) it will usually be satisfied.

(f) PROVISIONS FOR DISCHARGE CONTAINED IN THE CONTRACT ITSELF

A contract may contain within itself the elements of its own discharge, in the form of provisions, express or implied, for its determination or termination in certain circumstances. Apart from the statutory protection given to non-consumers dealing on the other party's written standard terms of business[72] and to consumers,[73] and the power of the Court to give equitable relief against forfeiture,[74] there is no requirement that a party act reasonably when deciding to exercise a contractual power to terminate.[75]

The parties may expressly provide that, upon the happening of a certain event, either the contract shall automatically determine,[76] or that, on the occurrence of that event, one party is to have the option to cancel the contract.[77]

(i) Automatic termination

Where the event is one over which the parties have no control and cannot bring about themselves, then effect will generally be given to a provision that the contract is automatically to cease to bind.[78] But if the relevant event is a breach of contract the Courts are likely to interpret the contract as nevertheless requiring an election by the

---

[69] Above, p 126. [70] See above, p 125.

[71] *WJ Alan & Co Ltd v El Nasr Export and Import Co Ltd* [1972] 2 QB 189, 213, but cf *ibid*, 221; *Finagrain SA Geneva v P Kruse Hamburg* [1976] 2 Lloyd's Rep 508.

[72] Unfair Contract Terms Act 1977, s 3(2)(b)(ii); above, p 215.

[73] Consumer Rights Act 2015, ss 62, 63 and Sched 2, Pt 1, especially paras 7, 8, replacing similar provisions in Unfair Terms in Consumer Contracts Regulations 1999 (SI 1999 No 2083); Consumer Credit Act 1974, ss 76, 86B, 86D, 86E, 87, 88, 98 (amended by Consumer Credit Act 2006).

[74] This is considered below, pp 625–7. See also Law of Property Act 1925, s 146 (forfeiture of lease).

[75] In some legal systems, a party is required to exercise its rights and remedies, including the right to terminate, in good faith: Lando and Beale, *Principles of European Contract Law Parts I and II* (2000) 117–19 or (in particular) to give notice requiring the other party to perform before terminating the contract: above, p 474, n 80. Cf *Union Eagle Ltd v Golden Achievement Ltd* [1997] AC 514, 519 Lord Hoffmann: 'The existence of an undefined discretion to refuse to enforce the contract on the ground that this would be "unconscionable" is sufficient to create uncertainty').

[76] *Continental Grain Export Corp v STM Grain Ltd* [1979] 2 Lloyd's Rep 460.

[77] *Head v Tattersall* (1871) LR 7 Ex 7; *Brown v Knowsley BC* [1986] IRLR 102, above, p 152. For the contractual right of a party to terminate for the other party's breach, see below, p 552.

[78] *New Zealand Shipping Co v Société des Ateliers et Chantiers* [1919] AC 1, 15 (Lord Wrenbury); *Gyllenhammar & Partners International Ltd v Sour Brodogradevna Industrija* [1989] 2 Lloyd's Rep 403, 413 (Hirst J).

innocent party before holding that the contract is terminated. This is an application of the principle that a party may not rely on its own breach to bring the contract to an end;[79] that is, a party may not take advantage of his or her own wrong.[80] The better view is that this is not an independent rule of law,[81] but a principle of construction reflecting the presumed intention of the parties, and which may be rebutted by the express terms of the contract.[82] Moreover, even if the event triggering the automatic termination provision is not a breach of contract, a party will not be able to take advantage of that provision if its wrongful action gave rise to the event upon which the automatic termination provision is based.[83]

(ii) Termination on notice

More often, a provision is inserted making the contract terminable at the option of one or both of the parties upon notice. This right of termination may be exercisable upon a breach of the contract by one party (whether or not the breach would amount to a repudiation of the contract),[84] or upon the occurrence or non-occurrence of a specified event other than breach,[85] or simply at the will of the party upon whom the right is conferred. For example, the contract may be terminable 'by three months' notice in writing on either side'. A similar provision may be incorporated by implication, or by the usage of trade. At common law,[86] for instance, a contract of employment may be terminated by reasonable notice by either party, the length of the notice depending upon the nature of the employment and the intervals at which remuneration is to be paid. Moreover, even where the duration of a written contract is on the face of the instrument indefinite and unlimited, such a provision may sometimes be implied from the nature of the contract,[87] particularly where the

---

[79] The principle does not apply if breach is of a duty owed to a person who is not a party to the contract: *Cheall v Association of Professional Executive Clerical and Computer Staff* [1983] 2 AC 180, 189 (Lord Diplock) and *Thompson v ASDA-MFI Group plc* [1988] 1 Ch 241, 266.

[80] *Alghussein Establishment v Eton College* [1988] 1 WLR 587; *Cheall v Association of Professional Executive Clerical and Computer Staff*, above, n 79; *Brown v Knowsley BC* [1986] IRLR 102.

[81] *New Zealand Shipping Co v Société des Ateliers et Chantiers*, above, n 78; *Alghussein Establishment v Eton College*, above, n 80; *Cheall v Association of Professional Executive Clerical and Computer Staff*, above, n 79.

[82] See, eg *Gyllenhammar & Partners International Ltd v Sour Brodogradevna Industrija* [1989] 2 Lloyd's Rep 403, 416 (Hirst J).

[83] See *Cheall v Association of Professional Executive Clerical and Computer Staff*, above, n 79, 189 (Lord Diplock). This principle means that even where such a provision declares that the contract is to be 'void', it is not absolutely so: *New Zealand Shipping Co v Société des Ateliers et Chantiers*, above, n 78, 15 (Lord Wrenbury). See also below, p 518 (self-induced frustration).

[84] But cf *Laing Management Ltd v Aegon Insurance Co (UK) Ltd* (1998) 86 BLR 70 (reliance on contractual right to terminate did not constitute acceptance of repudiatory breach, although this may be questioned).

[85] *Mannai Investment Co Ltd v Eagle Star Life Assurance Co Ltd* [1997] AC 749 ('break' clause in lease). See also *Head v Tattersall* (1871) LR 7 Ex 7 and above, p 152 (condition subsequent).

[86] But see now Employment Rights Act 1996, s 86 (minimum periods of notice by employer).

[87] *Crediton Gas Co v Crediton UDC* [1928] 1 Ch 447; *Winter Garden Theatre (London) Ltd v Millennium Productions Ltd* [1948] AC 173; *Re Spenborough UDC's Agreement* [1968] Ch 139. Cf *Kirklees Metropolitan BC v Yorkshire Woollen District Transport Co* (1978) 77 LGR 448 (fixed-term agreement could not be terminated by notice). See also Carnegie (1969) 85 LQR 392.

contract is for a fixed price[88] or is a commercial contract.[89] Thus a partnership for no fixed time is terminable by notice.[90]

Any notice given must be clear and unambiguous in its terms, and if it is to be given in a certain form, for example in writing, or within a certain time, or if a specified period of notice must be given, these requirements must normally be strictly complied with, otherwise the notice will be of no effect.[91] Notwithstanding this prima facie rule, in interpreting a clause in a contract which lays down a procedure for the termination of the contract, the Court will have regard to the commercial purpose served by the clause.[92]

[88] *Staffordshire Area Health Authority v South Staffs Waterworks Co* [1978] 1 WLR 1387, on which see below, p 518. Where there are price variation provisions, such an implied term is unlikely: *The Queensland Electricity Generating Board v New Hope Collieries Pty Ltd* [1989] 1 Lloyd's Rep 205; *Watford Borough Council v Watford Rural Parish* (1987) 86 LGR 524, 528.

[89] *Martin-Baker Aircraft Co Ltd v Canada Flight Equipment Ltd* [1955] 2 QB 556, 577; *Re Spenborough UDC's Agreement* [1968] Ch 139; *Watford Borough Council v Watford Rural Parish*, above, n 88, 532.

[90] Partnership Act 1890, s 26.

[91] *Afovos Shipping Co SA v Pagnan* [1983] 1 WLR 195. Cf *Bremer Handelsgesellschaft mbH v Vanden Avenne-Izegem PVBA* [1978] 2 Lloyd's Rep 109, above, p 158.

[92] *Mannai Investment Co Ltd v Eagle Star Life Assurance Co Ltd* [1997] AC 749 (minor misdescription did not preclude notice from being effective where, construed in its contractual setting, it would unambiguously inform a reasonable recipient how and when it was to operate); *Ellis Tylin Ltd v Co-operative Retail Services Ltd* [1999] BLR 205.

14

DISCHARGE BY FRUSTRATION

1. INTRODUCTION

Some legal systems accept that changes of circumstances may justify modifying a contract where to maintain the original contract would produce intolerable results incompatible with justice.[1] But many legal systems, including English law, concerned that modification would undermine certainty and alter the risks allocated by the contract, make provision for the discharge of a contract only where, after its formation, a change of circumstances makes contractual performance illegal or impossible. In English law, such a situation is provided for by the doctrine of frustration.[2] Originally, this term was confined to the discharge of maritime contracts by the 'frustration of the adventure', but it has now been extended to cover all cases where an agreement has been terminated by supervening events beyond the control of either party.[3] But the doctrine is not simply one of supervening impossibility; some kinds of impossibility may in some circumstances not discharge the contract at all, while 'impossibility' does not accurately describe the cases of frustration of a commercial purpose where the fundamentally different situation which has unexpectedly occurred means that performance would be, as a matter of business, radically different from the contractually stipulated performance.[4] In these cases the contract is discharged although performance is not literally impossible.

The defining characteristics of the doctrine of frustration that have emerged from the case law have been summarized by Bingham LJ[5] in the following terms:

The doctrine of frustration was evolved to mitigate the rigour of the common law's insistence on literal performance of absolute promises . . . The object of the doctrine

---

[1] Lando and Beale, *Principles of European Contract Law Parts I and II* (2000) 328.

[2] See Treitel, *Frustration and Force Majeure* (3rd edn, 2014).

[3] Initial impossibility and misunderstandings that exist at the time of the formation of the contract, sometimes referred to as 'pre-contractual frustration', are considered above, in Chapter 8. See especially p 299, and note that care should be taken not to treat such cases as frustration; cf *Gamerco SA v ICM/Fair Warning (Agency) Ltd* [1995] 1 WLR 1226, where it may have been wrongly so treated; see Carter and Tolhurst (1996) 10 JCL 264, 265–6. For discussion of the relationship between frustration and common mistake see above, pp 299, 310–11.

[4] *Joseph Constantine Steamship Line Ltd v Imperial Smelting Corp Ltd* [1942] AC 154, 164 (Viscount Simon). See also *Jackson v Union Marine Insurance Co Ltd* (below, p 500) and *Krell v Henry* (below, p 502). In the US common law, 'impossibility' (or 'impracticability' of performance) and 'frustration of purpose' are separate doctrines: A Farnsworth, *Contracts* (4th edn, 2004) §§9.6, 9.7.

[5] *J Lauritzen AS v Wijsmuller BV, The Super Servant Two* [1990] 1 Lloyd's Rep 1, 8. For the facts, see below, p 519.

was to give effect to the demands of justice, to achieve a just and reasonable result, to do what is reasonable and fair, as an expedient to escape from injustice where such would result from enforcement of a contract in its literal terms after a significant change in circumstances . . . Since the effect of frustration is to kill the contract and discharge the parties from further liability under it, the doctrine is not to be lightly invoked, must be kept within narrow limits and ought not to be extended . . . Frustration brings the contract to an end forthwith, without more and automatically . . . The essence of frustration is that it should not be due to the act or election of the party seeking to rely on it . . . A frustrating event must be some outside event or extraneous change of situation . . . A frustrating event must take place without blame or fault on the side of the party seeking to rely on it.

In this chapter we trace the history of the doctrine and examine the scope of its present application. It should, however, be noted that as the doctrine has developed, so too has the use, particularly in standard form contracts and negotiated commercial contracts, of so-called *force majeure* clauses, which entitle one or both of the parties to be excused (in whole or in part) from performance of the contract. Such clauses may cover non-frustrating events and may provide for more flexible remedies than total discharge. For instance they may entitle a party to suspend performance, to claim an extension of time for performance, or to be compensated for performance which will be more onerous.[6] They cannot, however, impose on the parties a duty to renegotiate the terms of the contract in the light of changed circumstances, because the duty to renegotiate, like the duty to negotiate, has been held to be too uncertain to be enforced in English law.[7]

2. EMERGENCE OF THE DOCTRINE

Before 1863 it was a general rule of the law of contract that a person was absolutely bound to perform any obligation which had been undertaken, and could not claim to be excused by the mere fact that performance had subsequently

---

[6] On such clauses, which fall outside the scope of this book, see generally, *Channel Island Ferries Ltd v Sealink UK Ltd* [1988] 1 Lloyd's Rep 323; Treitel, *Frustration and Force Majeure* (3rd edn, 2014) ch 12; McKendrick, *Force Majeure and Frustration of Contract* (2nd edn, 1994), especially chs 1 and 3. For one other advantage, see below, p 520. 'Force majeure' is a term of art in French and Belgian law, but has no clear meaning in English law: *Matsoukis v Priestman & Co* [1915] 1 KB 681, 685–6; *Thomas Borthwick (Glasgow) Ltd v Faure Fairclough Ltd* [1968] 1 Lloyd's Rep 16, 28. Cf *Thames Valley Power Ltd v Total Gas & Power Ltd* [2005] EWHC 2208 (Comm), [2006] 1 Lloyd's Rep 441 ('*force majeure*' defined in the contract).

[7] *Walford v Miles* [1992] 2 AC 128, 138; above, p 68. Cf *Petromec Inc v Petroleo Brasilieiro SA* [2005] EWCA Civ 891, [2006] 1 Lloyd's Rep 161 at [121]; Cartwright, in Cartwright, Vogenauer, and Whittaker (eds), *Reforming the French Law of Obligations* (2009) ch 3; Peel, in Burrows and Peel (eds), *Contract Formation and Parties* (2010) ch 3.

become impossible; for 'where there is a positive contract to do a thing, not in itself unlawful, the contractor must perform it or pay damages for not doing it, although in consequence of unforeseen accidents, the performance of his contract has become unexpectedly burdensome or even impossible'.[8] So in *Paradine v Jane* in 1647:[9]

P sued J for rent due upon a lease. J pleaded 'that a certain German Prince, by name Prince Rupert, an alien born, enemy to the King and kingdom, had invaded the realm with an hostile army of men; and with the same force did enter upon the defendant's possession, and him expelled, and held out of possession . . . whereby he could not take the profits'. This plea was in substance a plea that the rent was not due because the lessee had been deprived, by events beyond his control, of the profits from which the rent should have come.

The Court held that this was no excuse:[10]

When the party by his own contract creates a duty or charge upon himself, he is bound to make it good, if he may, notwithstanding any accident by inevitable necessity, because he might have provided against it by his contract. And therefore if the lessee covenant to repair a house, though it be burnt by lightning, or thrown down by enemies, yet he ought to repair it.

It has always, however, been open to the parties to introduce an express provision into their agreement that the fulfilment of a condition or the occurrence of an event should discharge one or both of them from some or all of their obligations under it;[11] and just as the parties may expressly discharge their obligation to perform a contract, so there are cases in which a contract, though containing no express provision, will be interpreted by the Courts as containing such a provision by implication. An implication of this nature would, it might be thought, readily be made where, without the fault of either party, an event occurs which renders the contract not merely more onerous, but completely impossible of performance.

This was the device[12] used by the Court of Queen's Bench in 1863 in the case of *Taylor v Caldwell*[13] in order to introduce an exception into the existing law:

C agreed with T to hire to him a music-hall and gardens for the purpose of entertainment. Before the day of performance arrived, the music-hall was destroyed by fire. T sued C for damages for breach of the contract which C, through no fault of his own, was unable to perform.

---

[8] *Taylor v Caldwell* (1863) 3 B & S 826, 833 (Blackburn J).
[9] (1647) Aleyn 26 and Style 47. On the antecedents of this decision, see Ibbetson, in Rose (ed), *Consensus ad Idem* (1996) ch 1.
[10] (1647) Aleyn 26, 27.   [11] See above, p 152.   [12] See Trakman (1983) 46 MLR 39.
[13] (1863) 3 B & S 826.

C was held not liable to pay, for 'the contract is not to be construed as a positive contract, but as subject to an implied condition that the parties shall be excused in case, before breach, performance becomes impossible from the perishing of the thing without default of the contractor'.[14] Blackburn J said:[15]

The principle seems to us to be that, in contracts in which the performance depends on the continued existence of a given person or thing, a condition is implied that the impossibility of performance arising from the perishing of the person or thing shall excuse the performance. In none of these cases is the promise in words other than positive, nor is there any express stipulation that the destruction of the person or thing shall excuse the performance; but that excuse is by law implied, because from the nature of the contract it is apparent that the parties contracted on the basis of the continued existence of the particular person or chattel.

From this time onwards the Courts showed themselves prepared to hold that, unless a contrary intention appears, the continuance of a contract was conditional upon the possibility of its performance.

It was not long, however, before the new doctrine was extended outside the sphere of literal impossibility to situations where there had been a 'frustration of the adventure'. Most of the early frustration cases arose out of delay, attributable to the fault of neither party, in the carrying out of charterparties; and they seem at first to have been treated as raising a question which was regarded as connected, rather than identical, with that raised by the cases of impossibility.

In *Jackson v Union Marine Insurance Co Ltd*:[16]

J's ship had been chartered to proceed in January to Newport to load a cargo of iron rails for San Francisco. On the way to Newport she ran aground and it took over a month to refloat her. She was then taken into Liverpool and underwent lengthy repairs lasting until August. In the meantime the charterers had chartered another ship. J claimed from the defendant insurance company for a total loss, by perils of the sea, of the freight to be earned under the charterparty.

The question whether or not there had been such a loss depended for the answer on the question whether or not the charterers had been justified in throwing up their contract with J instead of waiting until the ship was repaired and then loading her. The jury found that the time necessary to get the ship off, and to repair her so that she might become a cargo-carrying ship, had been so long as to put an end in a commercial sense to the speculation entered into by J and the charterers; and on this finding the Court held that a voyage undertaken after the ship had been repaired would have been an adventure different from that which both parties had contemplated at the time of the contract. It was, they said, an implied term of the contract that the ship should arrive at Newport within a reasonable time, and her inability to arrive put an end to it. 'The adventure', said Bramwell B,[17] 'was frustrated by perils of the seas, both parties were

---

[14] *Ibid*, 833.   [15] *Ibid*, 839.   [16] (1874) LR 10 CP 125.   [17] *Ibid*, 148.

discharged, and a loading of cargo in August would have been a new adventure, a new agreement'.

The dislocation of business caused by the war with Germany from 1914 to 1918 brought a large number of frustration cases into the Courts, and it soon became clear that they raised the same questions as those raised by cases previously considered under the head of impossibility. 'When this question arises in regard to commercial contracts', said Lord Loreburn,[18] 'the principle is the same, and the language used as to "frustration of the adventure" merely adapts it to the class of cases in hand'. 'The doctrine of frustration is only a special case of the discharge of contract by an impossibility of performance arising after the contract was made.'[19] The modern practice is to use the term 'frustration' to cover cases of both classes.

3. INSTANCES OF FRUSTRATION

Before turning to the theoretical basis of the doctrine of frustration, we consider examples of factual situations in which the Courts have been ready to infer, from the nature of the contract and from the circumstances surrounding it, that it has been frustrated by the happening of a subsequent event. While the reasoning in some of these examples is based on the 'implied term' theory of frustration, which, as we shall see, is now discredited, they remain useful illustrations of situations in which a contract may be frustrated.

(a) DESTRUCTION OF SUBJECT-MATTER OF CONTRACT

The most simple case is probably that where the performance of the contract is made impossible by the destruction of a specific thing *essential* to that performance, for example, the destruction of the music-hall in *Taylor v Caldwell*. So if A agrees with B to supply and install certain machinery in B's factory premises, and the premises are destroyed by fire, the contract will be frustrated.[20] But if the machinery only is destroyed, leaving the premises untouched, then it is still possible to obtain other machinery and A must do the work over again: the contract will not be discharged.[21] Where an agreement for the sale of specific goods has been made and, before the risk passes to the buyer, without any fault on the part of the seller or buyer, the goods perish, the agreement is avoided.[22]

---

[18] *FA Tamplin Steamship Co Ltd v Anglo-Mexican Petroleum Products Ltd* [1916] 2 AC 397, 404.
[19] *Joseph Constantine Steamship Line Ltd v Imperial Smelting Corporation Ltd* [1942] AC 154, 168 (Viscount Maugham).
[20] *Appleby v Myers* (1867) LR 2 CP 651; below, p 524.   [21] *Ibid*, 660.
[22] Sale of Goods Act 1979, s 7. See further below, pp 530–2 (effect of frustration and partial perishing of goods).

(b) NON-OCCURRENCE OF A PARTICULAR EVENT

The principle of frustration has also been held to apply to cases concerning the cancellation of an expected event. In the so-called 'Coronation cases', which arose out of the postponement of the coronation of King Edward VII owing to his sudden illness, it was applied to contracts the performance of which depended on the existence or occurrence of a particular state of things forming the basis on which the contract had been made. In *Krell v Henry*,[23] for instance:

H agreed to hire a flat from K during the daytime of 26 and 27 June 1902; the contract itself contained no express reference to the coronation processions, but K had advertised that the windows of the flat were to be let to view the processions which would pass the flat on those days, and H had entered into the contract after reading the advertisement. The processions were cancelled.

Two-thirds of the rent had not been paid when the processions were abandoned and the Court of Appeal held that K could not recover it. The Court considered that the processions and the relative position of the flat lay at the foundation of the agreement. The contract was therefore discharged.

It should not be imagined, however, that failure before performance of the factor which induced the parties to enter into the agreement will necessarily discharge the contract; for 'it may be that the parties contracted in the expectation that a particular event would happen, each taking his chance, but that the actual happening of the event was not made the basis of the contract'.[24] In *Herne Bay Steamboat Co v Hutton*:[25]

The defendant chartered from the claimant the SS *Cynthia* for 28 and 29 June 1902, for the express purpose of taking paying passengers to see the Coronation naval review at Spithead and to tour the fleet. The review was cancelled, but the fleet remained.

The Court of Appeal, composed of the same judges as in *Krell v Henry*, refused to hold the defendant discharged. They did so, partly on the ground that a tour of the fleet was still possible, but mainly because they considered that it was the defendant's own venture and it was at his risk. The Court pointed out that if the existence of a particular state of things is merely the motive or inducement to one party to enter into the contract, as distinct from the basis on which both contract, the principle cannot be applied. In both *Krell v Henry*[26] and *Herne Bay Steamboat Co v Hutton*[27] the example was given of the hire of a vehicle to take the hirer to Epsom to view the races on Derby day; the hirer will not be discharged if the races are cancelled, for the hirer's purpose is not the common foundation of the contract to hire the vehicle.

---

[23] [1903] 2 KB 740. See also *Chandler v Webster* [1904] 1 KB 493 (below, p 524). Cf *Griffith v Brymer* (1903) 19 TLR 434 (mistake, rather than frustration, because the parties made the contract in ignorance of the fact that the coronation had already been cancelled; above, p 311).

[24] *Larrinaga & Co Ltd v Société Franco-Américaine des Phosphates de Medulla, Paris* (1923) 39 TLR 316, 318 (Lord Finlay).

[25] [1903] 2 KB 683.   [26] [1903] 2 KB 740, 750-1.   [27] [1903] 2 KB 683, 689.

(c) DEATH, OR INCAPACITY FOR PERSONAL SERVICE

Where performance of obligations under a contract for personal services is rendered impossible or radically different by the death or incapacitating illness of the promisor, the contract will be frustrated. In *Stubbs v Holywell Railway Co*[28] it was held that a contract for personal services was put an end to by the death of the party by whom the services were to be rendered. And in *Robinson v Davison*:[29]

D's wife, an eminent piano player, promised see to perform at a concert, but was prevented from doing so by a dangerous illness. An action was brought against D claiming damages for breach of contract.

It was held that the contract was discharged by D's wife's illness, and it was not therefore broken by her failure to perform, nor, on the other hand, could she have insisted on performing when she was unfit to do so as frustration is not brought about by an act of election.[30] These are examples of cases where performance by the relevant party is personal and cannot be carried out by anyone else so that death or illness gives rise to frustration.[31] Similar decisions have been reached in the case of the discharge of a seaman's contract of service by his internment,[32] and of that of a music-hall artist, by his call-up for service in the army.[33] However, absence—even prolonged absence—through illness will not necessarily determine a contract of employment. A number of factors must be considered: the terms of the contract (including any sick pay provisions), the nature and the expected duration of the employment, the period of past employment, and the nature and duration of the illness and the prospects for recovery.[34] In *Marshall v Harland & Wolff Ltd*[35] the test for frustration of a contract of employment was formulated as follows, 'Was the employee's incapacity . . . of such a nature, or did it appear likely to continue for such a period, that further performance of his obligations in the future would either be impossible or would be a thing radically different from that undertaken by him and agreed to be accepted by the employer under the agreed terms of his employment?'. The application of the doctrine of frustration to employment contracts can give rise to results that may appear harsh. In *Notcutt v Universal Equipment Co (London) Ltd*[36] frustration was held to have occurred when it became apparent to the parties that an employee who had suffered a heart attack would never work again. This had the effect of automatically terminating the contract of employment and thereby releasing the employer from the contractual provisions

---

[28] (1867) LR 2 Ex 311.   [29] (1871) LR 6 Ex 269.   [30] Below, p 518 ff.

[31] If performance is not of a personal character then the contract is not necessarily frustrated by death or incapacity: *Phillips v Alhambra Palace Co Ltd* [1901] 1 QB 59.

[32] *Horlock v Beal* [1916] 1 AC 486.   [33] *Morgan v Manser* [1948] 1 KB 184.

[34] *Marshall v Harland & Wolff Ltd* [1972] 1 WLR 899, 903–5. Note that an employee who is suspended from work on medical grounds is entitled to be paid by the employer for up to 26 weeks: Employment Rights Act 1996, s 64.

[35] [1972] 1 WLR 899, 903 (Donaldson J). But see *Hart v AR Marshall & Sons (Bulwell) Ltd* [1977] 1 WLR 1067 ('key' worker replaced); *Egg Stores (Stamford Hill) Ltd v Leibovici* [1977] ICR 260, 264. See also *FC Shepherd & Co Ltd v Jerrom* [1987] 1 QB 301 (imprisonment of employee).

[36] [1986] 1 WLR 641.

which required that notice be given before terminating the contract and the statutory obligation to pay the employee during the period of notice.

(d) REQUISITIONING OF SHIPS AND INTERFERENCES WITH CHARTERPARTIES

A number of cases have arisen concerning charterparties, and these provide some of the most important instances of the application of the doctrine.

In wartime, ships are often requisitioned for such time and for such purposes as the Government may require them. If the ship is under charterparty the question will arise whether or not the requisitioning operates so as to frustrate the rights of the shipowners and charterers under the agreement. In *FA Tamplin Steamship Co Ltd v Anglo-Mexican Petroleum Products Co Ltd*:[37]

The steamship *FA Tamplin* was chartered by a time charterparty for 5 years from 4 December 1912, to 4 December 1917. In February 1915 the Government requisitioned the ship for use as a troopship and made certain structural alterations to her for this purpose. The charterers were willing to go on paying the agreed freight under the charterparty, but the owners claimed that the contract had been frustrated by the requisition as they wished to obtain a larger amount of compensation from the Crown.

The House of Lords, by a bare majority, held that the contract still continued. The interruption was not of sufficient duration to make it unreasonable for the parties to go on. There might be many months during which the ship would be available for commercial purposes before the five years expired.

In *Bank Line Ltd v Arthur Capel & Co*,[38] on the other hand:

In February 1915, BL chartered the steamship *Quito* to C for a period of 12 months from the time the vessel should be delivered. It was provided in the charterparty that (i) if the steamer had not been delivered by 30 April 1915, C, the charterers, were to have the option to cancel the contract or to proceed with it, and (ii) 'Charterers to have option of cancelling this charterparty should steamer be commandeered by Government during this Charter'. The steamer was not delivered by 30 April, and, on 11 May, before delivery, she was commandeered by the Government and not released until September. She was then sold by BL, and C sued for non-delivery, having never exercised their options to cancel.

The House of Lords held that the contract had been frustrated. The clauses in the charterparty were not intended to place the shipowners indefinitely at the charterers' mercy, to oblige them to deliver however long the delay. They merely gave to the charterers the option to cancel the contract without the necessity of proving frustration:

A contingency may be provided for, but not in such terms as to show that the provision is meant to be all the provision for it. A contingency may be provided for, but in such a way

---

[37] [1916] 2 AC 397.   [38] [1919] AC 435.

as shows that it is provided for only for the purpose of dealing with one of its effects and not with all.[39]

Lord Haldane, who dissented, was of the opinion that there was no frustration: the requisition was not of such a permanent character as to make the terms of the charterparty wholly inapplicable.

These differences of opinion within the highest tribunal show that cases of frustration raise most difficult questions of fact and principle. In the *Bank Line* case Lord Loreburn stated[40] that 'the main thing to be considered is the probable length of the total deprivation of the use of the chartered ship compared with the unexpired duration of the charterparty'. On this basis, the two decisions can perhaps be reconciled without undue difficulty, since the *Bank Line* charter was of one year's duration only, whereas that in the *Tamplin* case had still nearly three years to run at the time the requisitioning took place. But it is by no means certain that Lord Loreburn's test is the correct one to apply.[41]

Events other than the seizure or requisitioning of the ship may also frustrate a charterparty. It has already been seen that, in *Jackson v Union Marine Insurance Co Ltd*,[42] the charterparty was frustrated by the stranding of and damage to the ship. In a number of cases a charterparty has been held to have been frustrated by the inability of the ship to leave port, due, for example, to the refusal of a foreign government to allow the ship to depart,[43] or to the outbreak of hostilities, as happened in 1980 when some sixty ships were trapped in the Shatt-el-Arab river upon the outbreak of war between Iran and Iraq,[44] or to the arrest of the ship.[45] More difficulty, however, arises where strikes prevent the loading or unloading of the ship. The charterer of a ship usually undertakes in the contract to load and unload the cargo within a specified number of days, and, in default, to pay a certain sum of money to the shipowner by way of 'demurrage'. If strikes occur at the port of loading or discharge, this does not (in the absence of any express provision to the contrary) absolve the charterer from his liability to pay demurrage in respect of the delay.[46] However, a prolonged strike may in exceptional circumstances frustrate a charterparty, that is if the delay

---

[39] *Ibid*, 456 (Lord Sumner).   [40] *Ibid*, 454. See also the *Tamplin* case, above, n 37, 405.
[41] *International Sea Tankers Inc v Hemisphere Shipping Co Ltd* [1982] 1 Lloyd's Rep 128, 131, 133, 135. The alternative tests were discussed by Diplock J in *Port Line Ltd v Ben Line Steamers Ltd* [1958] 2 QB 146. Cf also *Edwinton Commercial Corp v Tsavliris Russ, Worldwide Salvage & Towage Ltd (The Sea Angel)* [2007] EWCA Civ 547, [2007] 2 Lloyd's Rep 517 at [117]–[120]. See also below, p 512.
[42] (1874) LR 10 CP 125, above, p 500.
[43] *Embiricos v Sydney Reid & Co* [1914] 3 KB 45; *Scottish Navigation Co v Souter* [1917] 1 KB 222; *Lloyd Royal Belge v Stathatos* (1917) 34 TLR 70.
[44] *International Sea Tankers Inc v Hemisphere Shipping Co Ltd* [1983] 1 Lloyd's Rep 400; *Kodros Shipping Corp of Monrovia v Empresa Cubana de Fletes* [1983] 1 AC 736; *Finelvet AG v Vinava Shipping Co Ltd* [1983] 1 WLR 1469.
[45] See *Adelfamar SA v Silos E Mangimi Martini SpA, The Adelfa* [1988] 2 Lloyd's Rep 466.
[46] *Budgett & Co v Binnington & Co* [1891] 1 QB 35.

is such as to make further performance something radically different from that which was undertaken in the contract.[47] Prolongation of a voyage by interruption of the contemplated route might also bring about frustration, but did not do so, for example, where the blocking of the Suez Canal necessitated a voyage round the Cape, since the alternative route was not fundamentally different, but merely longer and more expensive.[48]

(e) SALE AND CARRIAGE OF GOODS

Similar principles have been applied to contracts for the sale of goods to be carried by sea. In *Nickoll v Ashton Edridge & Co*,[49] for example, a cargo sold by the defendants to the claimants was to be shipped 'per steamship *Orlando* . . . during the month of January'. Without default on the defendant's part the ship was so damaged by stranding as to be unable to load in January. It was held that in these circumstances the contract must be treated as at an end.

The Anglo-French invasion of Egypt in 1956 and the consequent closure of the Suez Canal led to a number of cases concerning the frustration of cif contracts[50] for the sale of goods. Among these was the case of *Tsakiroglou & Co Ltd v Noblee Thorl GmbH*:[51]

T agreed to sell to NT a quantity of groundnuts to be shipped from the Sudan to Hamburg during November or December 1956. On 2 November, the Suez Canal was closed and remained closed for the next 5 months. The price of the groundnuts cif Hamburg was clearly calculated on the basis of shipment via the canal, but the contract contained no term to this effect. T refused to perform the contract, claiming that it had been frustrated by the closure of the canal.

The House of Lords held there was no frustration, since it would still be possible to ship the nuts to Hamburg around the Cape of Good Hope. Such a journey would not be commercially or fundamentally different from that by the canal, but merely more expensive. Their Lordships also pointed out that the contract was one of sale of goods, the transport of which is normally of no direct concern to the buyer. Nevertheless, they indicated that, if the goods had been perishable or if a definite date had been fixed for delivery, the contract might possibly have then been frustrated by the necessity for the longer Cape route.

---

[47] *The Penelope* [1982] P 180; *Pioneer Shipping Ltd v BTP Tioxide Ltd* [1982] AC 724.

[48] *Ocean Tramp Tankers Corp v V/O Sovfracht, The Eugenia* [1964] 2 QB 226, overruling *Société Franco Tunisienne D'Armement v Sidermar SpA* [1961] 2 QB 278. See also *Palmco Shipping Inc v Continental Ore Corp* [1970] 2 Lloyd's Rep 21.

[49] [1901] 2 KB 126.

[50] 'Cif' stands for cost, insurance, and freight. In a cif contract the price will be agreed on the basis that it includes insurance of the goods while in transit and the expenses of carriage (freight) to the port of destination.

[51] [1962] AC 93, overruling *Carapanayoti & Co Ltd v ET Green Ltd* [1959] 1 QB 131.

(f) BUILDING CONTRACTS

Further instances of the doctrine of frustration are provided by a group of cases concerning building or construction contracts. Events may occur which hold up completion of the works. Such delays inevitably increase the contractor's costs. If the contract is a fixed-price contract, the contractor may lose the profit which it expected to gain, or even be forced into loss. In *Davis Contractors Ltd v Fareham UDC*:[52]

In July 1946, D entered into a contract with Fareham UDC to build 78 houses for a fixed sum of £94,424 within eight months. Owing to the unexpected shortage of skilled labour and of certain materials the contract took 22 months to complete, and cost some £115,000. D contended that the contract had been frustrated and that they were entitled to claim on a quantum meruit for the cost actually incurred.

The House of Lords refused to accept this contention. The mere fact that unforeseen circumstances had delayed the performance of the contract, and rendered it more onerous to the appellants, did not discharge the agreement. The ultimate situation was still within the scope of the contract; the thing undertaken was not, when performed, different from that contracted for.

These strict requirements were, however, fulfilled in the case of *Metropolitan Water Board v Dick, Kerr & Co Ltd*:[53]

DK & Co contracted with the MWB to construct a reservoir within 6 years. Two years elapsed when the Minister of Munitions, acting under statutory powers, required them to cease work on their contract and to remove and sell their plant. The MWB brought an action claiming that the contract still continued.

The House of Lords held that the interruption created by the prohibition was of such a character and duration as to make the contract, if resumed, in effect a different contract, and that the original contract was therefore discharged.

(g) CHANGE IN THE LAW

The performance of a contract may be made legally impossible either by a change in the law or by a change in the operation of the law by reason of new facts supervening. The law may actually forbid the doing of some act undertaken in the contract;[54] or it may take from the control of the promisor something in respect of which it has contracted to act or not to act in a certain way, as, for example, where a piece of land subject to a restrictive covenant against building is compulsorily acquired and built upon by Act of Parliament.[55] Such cases are explained by policy and 'the elementary proposition

---

[52] [1956] AC 696. [53] [1918] AC 119.

[54] *Denny, Mott & Dickson Ltd v James B Fraser & Co Ltd* [1944] AC 265.

[55] *Baily v De Crespigny* (1869) LR 4 QB 180. See also *Brown v London Corp* (1862) 13 CBNS 828; *Studholme v South Western Gas Board* [1954] 1 WLR 313; *Hildron Finance Ltd v Sunley Holdings Ltd* [2010] EWHC 1681 (Ch), [2010] 3 EGLR 1 (contract to sell long lease of porter's flat in block of flats frustrated by introduction of right to collective enfranchisement by tenants of the block).

that if further performance of a contract becomes impossible by legislation having that effect the contract is discharged'.[56]

For there to be frustration, the change in the law must be such as to strike at the root of the agreement, and not merely to suspend or hinder its operation in part. So it has been held that a nine-year building lease was not frustrated by Government restrictions on building for only a small part of the term,[57] and that the rights of a payee of a cheque drawn on a bank in Holland were not discharged by an enemy invasion and occupation of that country rendering presentation for payment there illegal, but not elsewhere.[58] Lesser interruptions may, however, be covered by provisions in the contract, for instance clauses providing a seller with an excuse for non-performance in the event of 'prohibition of export . . . preventing fulfilment',[59] although, as will be seen, the presence of such a clause may preclude the application of the doctrine of frustration.

The outbreak of war is another event which, by changing the operation of the law, may have the effect of abrogating obligations outstanding under a contract by reason of supervening illegality, if one of the parties resides in this country and the other in enemy or enemy-occupied territory, and the contract is one which involves commercial dealings with the enemy.[60] So strong are the public policy considerations in this situation that the contract will be wholly frustrated, even though the parties themselves provide that their obligations shall be merely postponed.[61]

(h) PERFORMANCE OF ONLY ONE PARTY AFFECTED

The illustrations above show that, save in cases of supervening illegality, a frustrating event often affects the ability of only one of the parties to perform, while the other party, who usually has to pay money, is still capable of performing. So, in the requisitioning cases considered above, the charterers were able to pay the hire, and may have been willing to do so notwithstanding the non-availability of the ship, since the rate paid by the Government for requisitioned ships was higher

---

[56] *Reilly v The King* [1934] AC 176, 180 (Lord Atkin). On the implications for the theoretical basis of the doctrine, see below, pp 509–14.

[57] *Cricklewood Property and Investment Trust Ltd v Leighton's Investment Trust Ltd* [1945] AC 221; below, p 521. See also *Libyan Arab Foreign Bank v Bankers Trust Co* [1989] QB 728, 772 (Staughton J).

[58] *Cornelius v Banque Franco-Serbe* [1942] 1 KB 29. See also *Arab Bank Ltd v Barclays Bank* [1954] AC 495 (accrued rights not destroyed).

[59] On such clauses, see *Bremer Handelgesellschaft mbH v Vanden Avenne-Izegem PVBA* [1978] 2 Lloyd's Rep 109; *Bremer Handelgesellschaft mbH v C Mackprang Jr* [1979] 1 Lloyd's Rep 221; *Bremer Handelgesellschaft mbH v Westzucker GmbH (No 3)* [1989] 1 Lloyd's Rep 198, and Treitel, *Frustration and Force Majeure* (3rd edn, 2014) paras 12–020 ff.

[60] *Ertel Bieber & Co v Rio Tinto Co Ltd* [1918] AC 260; *Fibrosa Spolka Akcyjna v Fairbairn Lawson Combe Barbour Ltd* [1943] AC 32 (below, p 525); McNair and Watts, *The Legal Effects of War* (4th edn, 1966) ch 3.

[61] *Ertel Bieber & Co v Rio Tinto Co Ltd*, above, n 60.

than that payable under the charter.[62] Nevertheless, if the event is a frustrating one, it excuses both parties even where this may be to the advantage of the party who is unable to perform.

4. THE THEORETICAL BASIS OF FRUSTRATION

Considerable judicial attention has been paid to the theoretical basis on which the doctrine of discharge of a contract by frustration rests, perhaps because of a perceived need to explain why a finding of frustration does not constitute a reallocation of risks nor permit an escape from a bad bargain.[63]

Successive pronouncements of the House of Lords have set out a number of learned, but often contradictory, opinions concerning this issue and a number of theories have been put forward at various times. Since there is now general agreement on the appropriate test to be applied, it is necessary to refer only briefly to the four principal tests or 'theories' which have been advanced.[64]

(a) IMPLIED TERM

At one time the preponderance of judicial opinion favoured the view that frustration of a contract depended upon the implication of a term although, as we have noted, this did not explain discharge where the performance of the contract is made *legally* impossible by a change in the law or its operation.[65] Lord Loreburn's speech in *FA Tamplin Steamship Co Ltd v Anglo-Mexican Petroleum Products Co Ltd*[66] contains the classic exposition of the reasons on which the implied term theory of frustration was based:

[A] Court can and ought to examine the contract and the circumstances in which it was made, not of course to vary, but only to explain it, in order to see whether or not from the nature of it the parties must have made their bargain on the footing that a particular thing or state of things would continue to exist. And if they must have done so, then a term to that effect will be implied, though it be not expressed in the contract . . . Sometimes it is put that performance has become impossible and that the party concerned did not promise to perform an impossibility. Sometimes it is put that the parties contemplated a certain state of things which fell out otherwise. In most of the cases it is said that there was an implied condition in the contract which operated to release the parties from performing it, and in

---

[62] *FA Tamplin Steamship Co Ltd v Anglo-Mexican Petroleum Products Co Ltd* [1916] 2 AC 397, 405, 410, 422; *Bank Line Ltd v Arthur Capel & Co* [1919] AC 435, above, p 504.

[63] *Pacific Phosphates Co Ltd v Empire Transport* (1920) 4 LLR 189, 190.

[64] In *National Carriers Ltd v Panalpina (Northern) Ltd* [1981] AC 675, 687, Lord Hailsham LC stated there were at least five theories; in addition to those considered below, he referred to and rejected one based on total failure of consideration.

[65] In the heyday of the implied contract theory legal impossibility was sometimes said to differ from other categories of frustration: *Joseph Constantine SS Line Ltd v Imperial Smelting Corp Ltd* [1942] AC 154, 163.

[66] [1916] 2 AC 397, 403–4; see above, p 504, for the facts. For recent support for this theory, see Smith (1994) 110 LQR 400, 403.

all of them I think that was at bottom the principle upon which the Court proceeded. It is in my opinion the true principle, for no Court has an absolving power, but it can infer from the nature of the contract and the surrounding circumstances that a condition which was not expressed was a foundation on which the parties contracted . . . Were the altered conditions such that, had they thought of them, they would have taken their chance of them, or such that as sensible men they would have said, 'If that happens, of course, it is all over between us'?

A contract would therefore be frustrated if a term could be implied that, in the events that subsequently happened, the contract would come to an end. The expression 'an implied term' is, however, ambiguous. It may be used in a subjective sense, that is to say, it may mean a term which the Court reads into the contract in order to give effect to what it regards as the parties' real intention at the time of contracting. As was said in a later case[67] 'the law is only doing what the parties really (though subconsciously) meant to do for themselves'. To such an implied term a number of objections may be raised. The general test for implication of terms on the facts is not subjective but objective.[68] In any event, it is difficult to see how the parties could be taken, even impliedly, to have provided for something which never occurred to them.[69] Moreover, had it occurred to them, it is unlikely that they would have agreed that the contract was to come to an end. Lord Wright said:[70]

It is not possible, to my mind, to say that if they had thought of it, they would have said: 'Well, if that happens, all is over between us'. On the contrary, they would almost certainly on the one side or the other have sought to introduce reservations or qualifications or compensations.

That this is so is shown by the widespread use of so-called *force majeure* clauses which specify what is to happen on the occurrence of an event which affects one or both parties' performance.[71]

On the other hand, the implied term may be formulated more objectively. It may mean a term which, in the light of the events which have actually arisen, the parties *as reasonable people* would have imported into the contract to deal with that possibility.[72] When used in this sense, the implied term is betrayed by a similar artificiality. The 'reasonable person' has no real existence and represents 'no more than the anthropomorphic conception of justice'; an opinion ascribed to such a person is, in fact, that of the Court, which is and must be the spokesman of the fair and reasonable person.[73] An implied term of this sort is no more than a fiction, something added to the contract by the law.

---

[67] *Hirji Mulji v Cheong Yue SS Co Ltd* [1926] AC 497, 504.   [68] Above, pp 161–71.

[69] *Davis Contractors Ltd v Fareham UDC* [1956] AC 696, 728. Also see the example given by Lord Sands in *James Scott & Sons Ltd v Del Sel* 1922 SC 592, 597: 'A tiger has escaped from a travelling menagerie. The milkgirl fails to deliver the milk. Possibly the milkman may be exonerated from any breach of contract: but, even so, it would seem hardly reasonable to base that exoneration on the ground that "tiger days excepted" must be held as if written into the milk contract'. See further, *FC Shepherd & Co Ltd v Jerrom* [1987] 1 QB 301, 322 (Mustill LJ).

[70] *Denny, Mott & Dickson Ltd v James B Fraser & Co Ltd* [1944] AC 265, 275.

[71] On '*force majeure*' clauses, see above, p 498, n 6.

[72] *Dahl v Nelson, Donkin & Co* (1881) 6 App Cas 38, 59.

[73] *Davis Contractors Ltd v Fareham UDC* [1956] AC 696, 728 (Lord Radcliffe).

(b) 'JUST AND REASONABLE RESULT'

In truth, the discharge of a contract by frustration occurs, not because of the actual or imputed will of the parties, but by operation of law. The doctrine of frustration is, as Lord Sumner pointed out, 'a device, by which the rules as to absolute contracts are reconciled with a special exception which justice demands'.[74] In declaring a contract to have been frustrated, the Court exercises a positive function: it releases the parties from further performance of the obligations which they would otherwise be bound to perform.

Recognition of these facts led certain of the judges (and notably Lord Wright and Lord Denning) to the conclusion that the basis of the doctrine of frustration was the desire of the Courts to reach a just and reasonable result.[75] 'The truth is', Lord Wright said,[76] 'that the Court or jury as a judge of fact decides the question in accordance with what seems just and reasonable in its eyes'. This view, however, might be taken to suggest that a Court had the power to release the parties from their obligations whenever it was just and reasonable to do so,[77] even, for example, where the only effect of the subsequent event had been to render the contract financially more onerous than the parties had anticipated. But it is clear that the circumstances in which a contract will be held to have been frustrated are far more limited in scope.[78]

(c) FOUNDATION OF THE CONTRACT

Some test was, therefore, required which would recognize that frustration did not depend on the intentions of the parties, but which would not permit contracts to be too easily discharged. The first such test to be formulated was that of the 'disappearance of the foundation of the contract'. The question to be asked was whether the events that had occurred were of a character and extent so sweeping as to cause the foundation of the contract to disappear.[79] It was adopted, for example, by Goddard J in *WJ Tatem Ltd v Gamboa*:[80]

During the Spanish Civil War, T chartered to G, acting on behalf of the Republican Government of Spain, a steamship, for 30 days from 1 July 1937. The ship was to be used for the evacuation of refugees from Northern Spain to French ports. The hire was to be at the rate of £250 a day and was payable until the ship was returned to T. On 14 July, the ship was

---

[74] *Hirji Mulji v Cheong Yue SS Co Ltd* [1926] AC 497, 510.

[75] *Joseph Constantine Steamship Line Ltd v Imperial Shipping Corp Ltd* [1942] AC 154, 186.

[76] *Legal Essays and Addresses* (1939) 259. See also *Denny, Mott & Dickson Ltd v James B Fraser & Co Ltd* [1944] AC 265, 274–6.

[77] *British Movietonews Ltd v London and District Cinemas Ltd* [1951] 1 KB 190, 201–2 (Denning LJ, disapproved on appeal: [1952] AC 166).

[78] See *Notcutt v Universal Equipment Co (London) Ltd* [1986] 1 WLR 641, 646–7, where the Court of Appeal rejected an argument to the effect that, before a Court could determine that a contract was frustrated, it must be shown that it would be unjust to hold the parties to the contract.

[79] *FA Tamplin Steamship Co Ltd v Anglo-Mexican Petroleum Products Co Ltd* [1916] 2 AC 397, 406.

[80] [1939] 1 KB 132.

seized by the Nationalists and detained in the port of Bilbao until 11 September. In answer to T's claim for hire, G pleaded that the contract had been frustrated.

Goddard J was prepared to assume that the circumstances of the contract (including the very high rate of hire) showed that the parties contemplated that seizure and detention of the vessel might occur. He nevertheless held that the contract was frustrated: the foundation of the contract was destroyed by the seizure, as G thereafter no longer had the use of the vessel. The expression 'foundation' of the contract is, however, imprecise, and it leaves open the question what is the foundation of the contract in a particular case. Moreover, the test is difficult to apply to situations other than those in which the subject-matter of the contract ceases to be available. It has, therefore, been rejected by the House of Lords.[81]

(d) RADICAL CHANGE IN THE OBLIGATION

There is now general agreement that the appropriate test to apply to determine whether a contract has been frustrated is that of a 'radical change in the obligation'. In *Davis Contractors Ltd v Fareham UDC*, Lord Radcliffe said:

[F]rustration occurs whenever the law recognizes that without default of either party a contractual obligation has become incapable of being performed because the circumstances in which performance is called for would render it a thing radically different from that which was undertaken by the contract. Non haec in foedera veni. It was not this that I promised to do.[82]

This test has been adopted by the House of Lords in several cases,[83] and was reformulated by Lord Simon in *National Carriers Ltd v Panalpina (Northern) Ltd*:[84]

Frustration of a contract takes place when there supervenes an event (without default of either party and for which the contract makes no sufficient provision) which so significantly changes the nature (not merely the expense or onerousness) of the outstanding contractual rights and/or obligations from what the parties could reasonably have contemplated at the

---

[81] *National Carriers Ltd v Panalpina (Northern) Ltd* [1981] AC 675.

[82] [1956] AC 696, 729; for the facts, see above, p 507. The Latin phrase is said to be drawn from Virgil's *Aeneid*, Book 4, lines 338–9: see Sir John Megaw, letter to *The Times*, 20 December 1980 and *Edwinton Commercial Corp v Tsavliris Russ (Worldwide Salvage & Towage) Ltd, The Sea Angel* [2007] EWCA Civ 547, [2007] 2 Lloyd's Rep 517 at [84] n 1 (Rix LJ: 'It is ironic that Aeneas's shabby excuse to Dido has become the watchword of the modern doctrine of frustration'). But whether the relationship between Aeneas and Queen Dido was affected by a supervening event (Mercury's intervention) or an initial mistake (as to the nature of the relationship) is not entirely clear. Neither is it clear that Aeneas's 'excuses' for his planned desertion of Queen Dido, were as shabby as many (from Ovid to Sir John Megaw) consider them to be; see Williams, *Tradition and Originality in Roman Poetry* (1968) 378–6 and John Sparrow, Jackson Knight Memorial Lecture, *Dido v Aeneas: the case for the defence* (1973).

[83] *Tsakiroglou & Co Ltd v Noblee Thorl GmbH* [1962] AC 93, 131; *Pioneer Shipping Ltd v BTP Tioxide Ltd* [1982] AC 724, 744, 745, 751; *Paal Wilson & Co A/S v Partenreederei Hannah Blumenthal* [1983] 1 AC 854, 909, 918. See also *William Sindall plc v Cambridgeshire County Council* [1994] 1 WLR 1016, 1039.

[84] [1981] AC 675, 700. See also *ibid*, 688, 717. For the facts, see below, p 512.

time of its execution that it would be unjust to hold them to the literal sense of its stipulations in the new circumstances; in such a case the law declares both parties to be discharged from further performance.

This approach has sometimes been called the 'construction' theory, because it requires the Court first to construe the terms of contract in the light of its nature and the relevant surrounding circumstances when it was made. The original obligation undertaken by the parties can thus be determined. The Court must then consider whether there would be a radical change in that obligation if performance were enforced in the circumstances which have subsequently arisen. A mere rise in cost or expense will not suffice. 'It is not hardship or inconvenience or material loss itself which calls the principle of frustration into play. There must be as well such a change in the significance of the obligation that the thing undertaken would, if performed, be a different thing from that contracted for.'[85] However, the Court of Appeal has emphasized that the application of this test cannot safely be performed without the consequences of the decision being measured against the demands of justice since, among other considerations, the frustration of a contract may well mean that the contractual allocation of risk is reversed.[86]

(i) Application of test

The test is clearly meant to be a difficult one to satisfy. It is, moreover, easier to state than to apply. 'The data for decision are, on the one hand, the terms and construction of the contract, read in the light of the then existing circumstances, and on the other hand the events which have occurred.'[87] If the parties have themselves provided for the situation that has arisen the contract governs and there is no frustration. If they have not provided for it then the new situation must be compared with the situation for which they did provide to see how different it is.[88] The comparison is between the rights and obligations of the parties after the event, assuming the contract still binds them, and what their rights and obligations would have been had the event not occurred. We have noted the factors taken into account in contracts of employment.[89] In contracts for the carriage of goods by sea and charterparties, account may be taken of the extent to which the goods carried or to be carried are liable to damage or to deterioration,[90] or are subject to a seasonal market,[91] and the extent to which the vessel and crew are fit to proceed in the new circumstances. To constitute frustration, the event or events must make performance of the contract a thing 'radically' or 'fundamentally'

---

[85] *Davis Contractors Ltd v Fareham UDC*, above, n 52, 729 (Lord Radcliffe). See also *Tsakiroglou & Co Ltd v Noblee Thorl GmbH* [1962] AC 93.

[86] *Edwinton Commercial Corp v Tsavliris Russ (Worldwide Salvage & Towage) Ltd, The Sea Angel* [2007] EWCA Civ 547, [2007] 2 Lloyd's Rep 517 at [112].

[87] *Denny, Mott & Dickson Ltd v James B Fraser & Co Ltd* [1944] AC 265, 274–5 (Lord Wright).

[88] *Ocean Tramp Tankers Corporation v V/O Sovracht, The Eugenia* [1964] 2 QB 226, 239.

[89] Above, p 503.

[90] *Tsakiroglou & Co Ltd v Noblee Thorl GmbH* [1962] AC 93, 115, 118, and 123. See also *Jackson v Union Marine Insurance* (1874) LR 10 CP 125, 146 (carriage of ice would be frustrated by shorter delay than carriage of iron rails).

[91] *Jackson v Union Marine Insurance* (1874) LR 10 CP 125, 115. See also *ibid*, 146.

different in a commercial sense from that undertaken by the contract. These concepts are elusive and the Courts recognize that it is often difficult to draw the line[92] and that the question is one of degree.[93] It is, however, clearly more difficult to frustrate a long-term contract than a short-term one.[94]

(ii) Similarity to test for discharge for breach

The terms 'radical' and 'fundamental' are also used to determine whether a contract may be discharged for breach of an innominate term.[95] In *Hongkong Fir Shipping Co Ltd v Kawasaki Kisen Kaisha Ltd*[96] Diplock LJ stated that *Jackson v Union Marine Insurance Co Ltd*[97] was seeking to apply to frustrating events the same standard as if they had arisen by a breach by one of the parties. For the purpose of determining whether a contract may be discharged it is the happening of the event and not whether the event was the result of a breach that is crucial.[98] Despite this, in practice it is more likely than not that there will be differences between cases of frustration and cases of breach because in the context of breach, factors other than the ratio of failure to the performance undertaken are relevant to the question of whether the breach is fundamental.

(iii) Question of law

The application of the 'radical change in the obligation' test is a matter of law; but once it is shown that a judge or arbitrator has correctly applied the test to the facts found by him, an appellate Court should be slow to differ from his conclusion.[99]

5. INCIDENCE OF RISK

The doctrine of frustration is principally concerned with the incidence of risk—who must take the risk of the happening of the supervening event? The Courts have therefore to determine whether the contract, on its true construction, has made provision for that risk. We have noted that increased expense, even if caused by wholly abnormal

---

[92] *Ocean Tramp Tankers Corp v V/O Sovracht, The Eugenia* [1964] 2 QB 226, 239.

[93] *National Carriers Ltd v Panalpina (Northern) Ltd* [1981] AC 675, 688; *Pioneer Shipping v BTP Tioxide, The Nema* [1982] AC 724, 744. See also *Edwinton Commercial Corp v Tsavliris Russ (Worldwide Salvage & Towage) Ltd, The Sea Angel* [2007] EWCA Civ 547, [2007] 2 Lloyd's Rep 517 at [111] (Rix LJ: application of doctrine of frustration requires 'multi-factorial approach'), applied in *Islamic Republic of Iran Shipping Lines v Steamship Mutual Underwriting Association (Bermuda) Ltd* [2010] EWHC 2661 (Comm), [2010] 2 CLC 524 at [105]; *ACG Acquisition XX LLC v Olympic Airlines SA* [2012] EWHC 1070 (Comm), [2012] 2 CLC 48 at [178].

[94] *Lord Strathcona Shipping Co Ltd v Dominion Coal Co Ltd* [1926] AC 108, 115; *National Carriers Ltd v Panalpina (Northern) Ltd* [1981] AC 675, 691 (Lord Hailsham LC). See also *Larrinaga & Co v Société Franco-Américaine des Phosphates de Medulla, Paris* (1922) 28 Com Cas 1, 5.

[95] Below, p 549 ff. See also above, p 155.

[96] [1962] 2 QB 26, on which see below, p 549.   [97] Above, p 500.

[98] [1962] 2 QB 26, 49, 68. See also, in the same context, *The Hermosa* [1980] 1 Lloyd's Rep 638, 649 (delay by a variety of events, some the consequences of breach and some not).

[99] *Pioneer Shipping Ltd v BTP Tioxide Ltd* [1982] AC 724, 738, 752–3.

fluctuations in prices, does not frustrate.[100] In this connection, the cases show that a number of difficult questions may arise.

(a) EXPRESS PROVISION

Except in certain cases of illegality[101] there is little doubt that it is open to the parties to provide that the contract shall continue, or be merely suspended, and not discharged, upon the occurrence of a particular event, or to allocate the risks attendant upon that event. Where the contract makes provision (that is, full and complete provision, so intended) for a given contingency, this will preclude the Court from holding that the contract is frustrated.[102] But the parties may fail to make complete provision, as happened in the *Bank Line* case,[103] where the option given to one party, that is, the charterers, to cancel or continue with the charterparty if the ship should be requisitioned, was held not to be intended to apply to requisitioning of so long a duration as to make the charter, as a matter of business, a wholly different thing. And a provision in a building contract, for example, that the contractor is to be allowed an extension of time in the event of 'delays', may be construed as inapplicable to a situation where the delay which occurs is such as to bring about a radical change in the obligation.[104] In this type of case, the contract can still be frustrated.

It is also open to the parties to provide that the contract is to be suspended or discharged by a non-frustrating event.[105] There are, for example, difficulties in determining whether a given delay or prospective delay frustrates a contract.[106] As a matter of interpretation the Court may conclude that the parties preferred the certainty of termination after a specified period of delay, pursuant to a contractual term, to the uncertainty of possible discharge under the doctrine of frustration.[107]

(b) FORESEEN EVENTS

The second question is whether events which were foreseen by the parties at the time of contracting can be relied upon to establish frustration. In many of the

---

[100] Above, p 507: *Davis Contractors Ltd v Fareham UDC* [1956] AC 696, 724 (Lord Reid) and *Tsakiroglou & Co Ltd v Noblee Thorl GmbH* [1962] AC 93. But note that in the latter case at 118 Lord Reid reserved his position on an increase which reached a wholly astronomical figure, and cf *William Cory v LCC* [1951] 1 KB 8, aff'd [1951] 2 KB 476.

[101] See above, p 507.

[102] *Bank Line Ltd v Arthur Capel & Co* [1919] AC 435, 455; *Joseph Constantine Steamship Line Ltd v Imperial Smelting Corporation Ltd* [1942] AC 154, 163. See also *Bangladesh Export Import Co Ltd v Sucden Kerry SA* [1995] 2 Lloyd's Rep 1.

[103] [1919] AC 435, above, p 504. See also *Jackson v Union Marine Insurance Co Ltd* (1874) LR 10 CP 125 (clause excusing one party only from liability in a given contingency).

[104] *Metropolitan Water Board v Dick, Kerr & Co Ltd* [1918] AC 119, above, p 507.

[105] Above, pp 494, 498.   [106] Below, p 517.

[107] *Total Gas Marketing Ltd v Arco British Ltd* [1998] 2 Lloyd's Rep 209, 222 (Lord Steyn).

cases reference is made to the occurrence of an 'unforeseen' or 'unexpected' or 'uncontemplated' event, and it may be argued that the parties must be taken to have assumed the risk of an event which was present in their minds at the time the contract was made. It is, however, a question of construction of the contract whether it was intended to continue to be binding in that event,[108] or whether, in the absence of any express provision, the issue has been left open,[109] so as to allow the incidence of risk to be determined by the law relating to frustration. In *WJ Tatem Ltd v Gamboa*,[110] for example, the fact that seizure of the ship was within the contemplation of the parties did not preclude the operation of frustration since the contract made no express provision for the contingency.

(c) PREVENTION OF PERFORMANCE IN MANNER INTENDED BY ONE PARTY

The third question is whether a contract will be frustrated by an event which prevents performance in a manner intended by one party alone. In *Blackburn Bobbin Co Ltd v TW Allen & Sons Ltd*:[111]

A agreed to sell and deliver to BB at Hull a quantity of Finnish birch timber. A found it impossible to fulfil this contract because the outbreak of war cut off its source of supply from Finland. BB was unaware that timber from Finland was normally shipped direct from a Finnish port to England, and that timber merchants did not, in practice, hold stocks of it in England.

The Court of Appeal held that there was no frustration. What had happened was merely that an event had occurred which rendered it practically impossible for the defendants to deliver: that event might have been, but was not, provided for in the contract. To free A from liability, it would have to be shown that the continuance of the normal mode of shipping the timber from Finland was a matter which *both* parties contemplated as necessary for the fulfilment of the contracts. Since this was not the case, A bore the risk.

---

[108] *Larrinaga & Co v Société Franco Américaine des Phosphates de Medulla* (1923) 39 TLR 316; *Maritime National Fish Ltd v Ocean Trawlers Ltd* [1935] AC 524; *Chandler Bros Ltd v Boswell* [1936] 3 All ER 179; *Paal Wilson & Co A/S v Partenreederei Hannah Blumenthal, The Hannah Blumenthal* [1983] 1 AC 854, 909.

[109] *WJ Tatem Ltd v Gamboa* [1939] 1 KB 132, 138; *Ocean Tramp Tankers Corporation v V/O Sovfracht, The Eugenia* [1963] 2 QB 226, 239; *The Nile Co for the Export of Agricultural Crops v H & JM Bennett (Commodities) Ltd* [1986] 1 Lloyd's Rep 555, 582; *Adelfamar SA v Silos E Mangimi Martini SpA, The Adelfa* [1988] 2 Lloyd's Rep 466, 471. See also *Edwinton Commercial Corp v Tsavliris Russ (Worldwide Salvage & Towage) Ltd, The Sea Angel* [2007] EWCA Civ 547, [2007] 2 Lloyd's Rep 517 at [99]–[103].

[110] [1939] 1 KB 132; above, p 511.

[111] [1918] 2 KB 467. It was also said in this case that there could never be frustration of a contract for the sale of unascertained goods, but this is probably too wide: see *Re Badische Co Ltd* [1921] 2 Ch 331; *Tsakiroglou & Co Ltd v Noblee Thorl GmbH* [1962] AC 93; above, p 506; *CTI Group Inc v Transclear SA, The Mary Nour* [2008] EWCA Civ 856, [2008] 2 Lloyd's Rep 526.

(d) DELAY

Frequently, as we have seen, a subsequent event causes delay[112] in the performance of the contract, bringing financial loss to one of the parties. But the risk of delay is one which has to be accepted in commercial transactions. Lord Sumner said:[113]

Delay even of considerable length and of wholly uncertain duration is an incident of maritime adventure, which is clearly within the contemplation of the parties . . . so much so as to be often the subject of express provisions. Delays such as these may very seriously affect the commercial object of the adventure, for the ship's expenses and overhead charges are running on . . . None the less this is not frustration.

The delay must be such as 'to render the adventure absolutely nugatory',[114] 'to make it unreasonable to require the parties to go on',[115] 'to destroy the identity of the work or service when resumed with the work or service when interrupted',[116] 'to put an end in a commercial sense to the undertaking'.[117] It may, however, be difficult for the parties to determine whether, at any particular point of time, the delay is of this nature. On this point, Lord Roskill, in *Pioneer Shipping Ltd v BTP Tioxide Ltd*,[118] provided guidance:

[I]t is often necessary to wait upon events in order to see whether the delay already suffered and the prospects of further delay from that cause, will make any ultimate performance of the relevant contractual obligations 'radically different'. . . from that which was undertaken by the contract. But, as has often been said, business men must not be required to await events too long. They are entitled to know where they stand. Whether or not the delay is such as to bring about frustration must be a question to be determined by an informed judgment based upon all the evidence of what has occurred and what is likely thereafter to occur.

While, therefore, it is for the tribunal to whom the issue has been referred to decide as a question of law whether or not the contract has been frustrated, 'that conclusion is almost completely determined by what is ascertained as to mercantile usage and the understanding of mercantile men'[119] about 'the significance of the commercial differences between what was promised and what in the changed circumstances would now fall to be performed'.[120]

Even where the delay is prima facie sufficient, where one or both parties are responsible for it, the rule that reliance cannot be placed on a self-induced frustration will preclude discharge.[121]

---

[112]   See Stannard (1983) 46 MLR 738.

[113]   *Bank Line Ltd v Arthur Capel & Co* [1919] AC 435, 458–9.

[114]   *Bensaude & Co v Thames and Mersey Marine Insurance Co* [1897] 1 QB 29, 31 (Lord Esher), [1897] AC 609, 611, 612, 614.

[115]   *Metropolitan Water Board v Dick, Kerr & Co Ltd* [1918] AC 199, 131 (Lord Atkinson); *FA Tamplin Steamship Co Ltd v Anglo-Mexican Petroleum Products Co Ltd* [1916] 2 AC 397, 405 (Lord Loreburn).

[116]   *Metropolitan Water Board v Dick, Kerr & Co Ltd*, above, n 115, 128 (Lord Dunedin); *Bank Line Ltd v Arthur Capel & Co* [1919] AC 435, 460 (Lord Sumner).

[117]   *Jackson v Union Marine Insurance Co Ltd* (1874) LR 10 CP 125.   [118]   [1982] AC 724, 752.

[119]   *Tsakiroglou & Co Ltd v Noblee Thorl GmbH* [1962] AC 93, 124.

[120]   *Pioneer Shipping Ltd v BTP Tioxide Ltd*, above, n 118.

[121]   *Paal Wilson & Co A/S v Partenreederei Hannah Blumenthal* [1983] 1 AC 854. See below, p 518.

(e) INFLATION

Finally, some mention must be made of the effects of inflation. In *Staffordshire Area Health Authority v South Staffordshire Waterworks Co*[122] a contract was entered into in 1929 under which the defendants agreed 'at all times hereafter' to supply water to a hospital at a fixed price of seven (old) pence per 1,000 gallons. By 1978 the equivalent cost of supplying the water was some 20 times the contract price. The Court of Appeal held that the contract was, on its true construction, terminable by the defendants upon reasonable notice.[123] But Lord Denning MR expressed the opinion[124] that, by reason of 50 years of continuing inflation, a fundamentally different situation had emerged in which the contract had ceased to bind. His reasoning was not, however, accepted by the other members of the Court of Appeal, and the orthodox view is that any depreciation in the purchasing power of sterling,[125] or the devaluation of a foreign currency in which a debt is expressed,[126] is a risk which must be borne by the creditor. If the creditor does not wish to bear this risk, provision may be made in the contract. In certain contexts, for example leases, it is not unusual for the terms of the contract to provide for modification of the price to take account of inflation.

6. SELF-INDUCED FRUSTRATION

It is well established that a party whose act or election has given rise to the event which is alleged to have frustrated the contract cannot invoke the doctrine of frustration; reliance cannot be placed upon a self-induced frustration.[127] In *Maritime National Fish Ltd v Ocean Trawlers Ltd*:[128]

OT chartered to MNF a steam trawler fitted with an otter trawl. Both parties knew at the time of the contract that it was illegal to use an otter trawl without a licence from

---

[122] [1978] 1 WLR 1387.

[123] On the implication of a term to this effect (less likely where there is a price variation clause), see above, pp 495–6.

[124] [1978] 1 WLR 1387, 1397–8. He did not, however, hold that the contract was terminated automatically (see below, p 523), but only on reasonable notice.

[125] *Wates Ltd v GLC* (1987) 25 BLR 1, 35.

[126] *British Bank for Foreign Trade Ltd v Russian Commercial and Industrial Bank* (1921) 38 TLR 65; *Re Chesterman's Trusts* [1923] 2 Ch 466.

[127] *J Lauritzen AS v Wijsmuller BV, The Super Servant Two* [1990] 1 Lloyd's Rep 1, 8. A party cannot rely on its own self-induced frustration to say that the contract is not frustrated: *FC Shepherd & Co Ltd v Jerrom* [1987] 1 QB 301, below, p 524. But where the relevant act is caused by a third party for whose action the party claiming frustration is not responsible the result is not considered to be self-induced frustration: *Adelfamar SA v Silos E Mangimi SpA, The Adelfa* [1988] 2 Lloyd's Rep 466, 471.

[128] [1935] AC 524 (see [1934] 1 DLR 621, especially at 623 and [1934] 4 DLR 288, especially at 299 for a full statement of the facts). See also *Bank Line Ltd v Arthur Capel & Co* [1919] AC 435, 452; *Ocean Tramp Tankers Corp v V/O Sovfracht, The Eugenia* [1964] 2 QB 226, 237; *Denmark Productions Ltd v Boscobel Productions Ltd* [1969] 1 QB 699, 725, 736–7; *Paal Wilson & Co A/S v Partenreederei Hannah Blumenthal* [1983] 1 AC 854.

the Canadian Government. Some months later MNF applied for licences for five trawlers which it was operating, including OT's trawler and three trawlers owned directly or indirectly by MNF. It was informed that only three licences would be granted, and was requested to state for which of the three trawlers it desired to have licences. It named two trawlers that it owned directly or indirectly and a third chartered from a person other than OT, and then claimed that it was no longer bound by the charterparty as its object had been frustrated.

The Judicial Committee of the Privy Council held that the failure of the contract was the result of MNF's own election, and that since 'reliance cannot be placed upon a self-induced frustration' there was no frustration. Similar conclusions have been reached where, in breach of contract, a charterer of a ship allowed the ship to enter a war-zone, where she was trapped,[129] and where parties to arbitration proceedings were in breach of their mutual contractual obligations to apply to the arbitral tribunal for directions to prevent delay in the conduct of the arbitration.[130]

(a) CHOOSING BETWEEN DIFFERENT CONTRACTS

The position is more complicated where a party enters into a number of contracts and the supervening event means that, while it is possible to perform one or more of the contracts, it is not possible to perform them all. This was the position in *J Lauritzen AS v Wijsmuller BV, The Super Servant Two*:[131]

In July 1980 W contracted with L to carry a drilling rig from Japan to a location off Rotterdam using, at its option, either the *Super Servant One* or the *Super Servant Two*. It also entered into two contracts with third parties containing similar substitution clauses, one before the contract with L and one afterwards. In its internal schedules W planned to use the *Super Servant Two* for L's contract and the *Super Servant One* for the other two contracts, but, prior to the time set for performance, the *Super Servant Two* sank. W informed L that it would not transport the rig with either the *Super Servant One* or the *Super Servant Two*, but the parties agreed, without prejudice to their rights under the contract, that the drilling rig would be transported by another, more expensive, method. In answer to L's claim for the losses suffered, W counterclaimed *inter alia* that the sinking of the *Super Servant Two* frustrated the contract.

The Court of Appeal held that the contract was not frustrated. Even if the sinking of the *Super Servant Two* occurred without any fault on the part of W, it was not the cause

---

[129] *Ocean Tramp Tanker Corporation v V/O Sovfracht, The Eugenia*, above, n 128.

[130] *Paal Wilson & Co A/S v Partenreederei Hannah Blumenthal*, above, n 128. The position in arbitration caused difficulties in commercial practice; see above, p 33, n 9 for another, only partially successful, attempt to deal with the problem of stale arbitrations, which has now been addressed by legislation empowering the arbitrator to dismiss a claim in the case of inexcusable and inordinate delay where the delay results in a substantial risk that it would not be possible to have a fair resolution of the issues or of serious prejudice to the respondent: Arbitration Act 1996, s 41 and *L'Office Cherifien Des Phosphates v Yamashita-Shinnihon Steamship Co Ltd* [1994] 1 AC 486.

[131] [1990] 1 Lloyd's Rep 1, affirming [1989] 1 Lloyd's Rep 149.

of the inability to perform. The real cause was said to be W's election not to use the *Super Servant One*, something which it would have been physically possible for it to do. It was said that that exercise of choice meant that W had accepted the risk of the *Super Servant Two* being unable to perform with the result that its unavailability gave rise to a breach not a frustrating event. Moreover, to allow W to rely on the unavailability of the *Super Servant One* as a frustrating event would allow it to rely on its own act of election whereas frustration in theory occurs automatically.

The reasoning in this case has been criticized[132] for not taking sufficient account of the fact that, in the *Maritime National Fish* case, it was possible for OT to perform all contracts made with third parties, and because the rule that frustration is automatic is not an absolute one.[133] W's 'election' was only as to which contract it was not going to perform and it is submitted that the decision is likely to lead to practical difficulties. It would appear to mean, for instance, that where a farmer agrees to sell to A 250 tons of a crop to be grown on specific land which normally yields over 500 tons, and 250 tons to B, but there is a poor harvest and the yield is only 250 tons, neither contract would be frustrated. But this result is difficult to reconcile with cases, apparently not considered in *The Super Servant Two*, in which neither party to a contract for the sale of a specific crop was held to be liable if the crops failed to materialize.[134] It is also difficult to reconcile with cases in which a seller who, following a partial failure of supply, delivered to other customers or delivered the available supply to all customers on a *pro rata* basis, was held entitled to rely on a *force majeure* clause.[135] In the present state of the law, however, a promisor who wishes protection in the case of a partial failure of supply 'must bargain for the inclusion of a suitable *force majeure* clause in the contract'.[136]

(b) NEGLIGENT ACTS

Where the act of the party pleading frustration was inadvertent and merely negligent the position is not altogether clear. Although there have been frequent statements to

[132] Treitel, *Frustration and Force Majeure* (3rd edn, 2014) para 14–025. Treitel's earlier arguments on the issue were considered and rejected by the Court: [1989] 1 Lloyd's Rep 148, 152–3, 154, 158; [1990] 1 Lloyd's Rep 1, 9, 13–14.

[133] See below, p 523.

[134] eg *Howell v Coupland* (1876) 1 QBD 258; *HR & S Sainsbury Ltd v Street* [1972] 1 WLR 834, on which see below, pp 531–2.

[135] *Intertradex SA v Lesieur Tourteaux SARL* [1978] 2 Lloyd's Rep 509, 513; *Bremer Handelgesellschaft mbH v Mackprang Jr (No 2)* [1979] 1 Lloyd's Rep 221; *Bremer Handelgesellschaft mbH v Continental Grain Co* [1983] 1 Lloyd's Rep 169, 292; *Bremer Handelgesellschaft mbH v Vanden Avenne-Izegem PVBA* [1978] 2 Lloyd's Rep 109. In *The Super Servant Two* the *force majeure* cases were said to be of no assistance in the context of frustration: [1989] 1 Lloyd's Rep 148, 158; [1990] 1 Lloyd's Rep 1, 9. For a different view, see Hudson (1968) 31 MLR 535.

[136] *J Lauritzen AS v Wijsmuller BV, The Super Servant Two* [1989] 1 Lloyd's Rep 148, 158 (Hobhouse J), although the distinction from frustration may be put into question since his Lordship also accepted that protection might be afforded by an implied term. On '*force majeure*' clauses, see above, p 498, n 6.

the effect that the frustrating event must occur without the 'default' of either party, this point has never been expressly decided. It was discussed by the House of Lords in *Joseph Constantine Steamship Line Ltd v Imperial Smelting Corporation Ltd*, where Lord Russell, commenting on the kind or degree of fault which might debar a party from relying on a self-induced frustration, said:[137]

The possible varieties are infinite, and can range from the criminality of the scuttler who opens the sea-cocks and sinks his ship, to the thoughtlessness of the prima donna who sits in a draught and loses her voice. I wish to guard against the supposition that every destruction of corpus for which a contractor can be said, to some extent or in some sense, to be responsible, necessarily involves that the resultant frustration is self-induced within the meaning of the phrase.

In that case:

JC chartered to ISC its steamship *Kingswood* to proceed to Australia and load a cargo there. Before this could be done, a violent explosion occurred in the boiler of the ship which resulted in such a delay as would discharge the contract. The cause of the explosion was never ascertained, but ISC alleged that JC had first to establish that it occurred without its fault before it could rely on the doctrine of frustration and so not be liable for breach of contract.

It was not necessary for the House of Lords to decide whether mere negligence would suffice, for it held that the burden of proving that the event which causes the frustration is due to the act or default of a party lies on the party alleging it to be so. Since ISC failed to satisfy the Court on this point, the contract was discharged. It would appear logical, however, for a finding of negligence to prevent a party claiming that the contract was frustrated where that negligent act caused the alleged frustrating event.[138]

7. LEASES AND CONTRACTS FOR THE SALE OF LAND

There was at one time considerable doubt as to whether the doctrine of frustration applied to leases of land. In 1945, in *Cricklewood Property and Investment Trust Ltd v Leighton's Investment Trust Ltd*[139] the House of Lords held unanimously that, since wartime restrictions preventing the performance of a building lease covered only a small part of the 90 years remaining on the lease, it had not been frustrated. But on the question whether a lease could in any circumstances be terminated by frustration the House was evenly divided. Viscount Simon and Lord

---

[137] [1942] AC 154, 179.
[138] See *J Lauritzen AS v Wijsmuller BV, The Super Servant Two* [1990] 1 Lloyd's Rep 1, 10.
[139] [1945] AC 221.

Wright considered that, on very rare occasions, frustration could occur, giving as illustrations some vast convulsion of nature which might sweep the property into the sea, or the frustration of a building lease by a perpetual statutory prohibition on building for the remainder of the term. Lord Russell and Lord Goddard took the contrary view. A lease was more than a contract: it vested an estate in land in the lessee, and the contractual obligations which it contained were merely incidental to the relationship of landlord and tenant. If all or some of these should become impossible of performance, the lease would remain.[140] The estate in the land would still be vested in the tenant. Lord Porter, the fifth member of the House, refused to express an opinion.

In 1981, this question was reconsidered by the House of Lords in *National Carriers Ltd v Panalpina (Northern) Ltd*:[141]

P let a warehouse to NC for 10 years from 1 January 1974. NC covenanted that it would not without P's consent use the premises for any purpose other than that of warehousing in connection with its business, or assign, underlet, or part with possession. In May 1979, the local authority temporarily closed the street which provided the only vehicular access to the warehouse. The closure lasted for 20 months and during this period the warehouse could not be used for the purpose contemplated by the lease. In answer to a claim for rent, NC counterclaimed that the lease had been frustrated.

Their Lordships unanimously held that there was no frustration. A majority,[142] however, agreed with Viscount Simon and Lord Wright in the *Cricklewood* case that, in principle, the doctrine of frustration was applicable to leases. 'Coastal erosion as well as the "vast convulsion of nature" . . . can . . . cause houses, gardens, even villages and their churches, to fall into the North Sea.'[143] However, the view was expressed[144] that in practice the doctrine would 'hardly ever' apply. In the present case, having regard to the nature and length of the interruption, and in particular to the fact that the lease would still have some three years to run after the interruption came to an end, it could not be said that the lease had been frustrated.

There appears to be no reported English case in which it has been held that a lease has been frustrated.[145] The reason for this may be the relative indestructibility of land. But the absence of cases of frustration is more likely to be due to the fact that the events which are most likely to occur, for example, fire,[146] are normally expressly provided for in the lease, and the incidence of the risk of less common events (such

---

[140] But there may be excuses for non-performance of covenants short of frustration: *ibid*, 233–4 (Lord Russell); *John Lewis Properties plc v Viscount Chelsea* [1993] 2 EGLR 77, 82.

[141] [1981] AC 675. For criticism see Price (1989) 10 JLH 90, 101–3.

[142] Lord Russell of Killowen dissenting.

[143] [1981] AC 675, 691 (Lord Hailsham LC). See also *Holbeck Hall Hotel Ltd v Scarborough BC* (1998) 57 Con LR 113, 152–3 (point not considered by CA: [2000] QB 836).

[144] [1981] AC 675, 692, 697, 717.

[145] Cf *Rom Securities Ltd v Rogers (Holdings) Ltd* (1967) 205 EG 427 (agreement for a lease). Contrast *Tay Salmon Fisheries Co Ltd v Speedie* 1929 SC 593 (Scotland).

[146] Cf *National Carriers Ltd v Panalpina (Northern) Ltd* [1981] AC 675, 690.

as requisitioning)[147] may be held to have been assumed by the tenant and not by the landlord. It is also very improbable that some personal incapacity which prevents the tenant from using the premises would be sufficient to terminate the lease,[148] at least if the tenant's personal occupation was not the common basis of the venture.[149] But if commercial premises are let (particularly for a short term) for one principal purpose known to the lessor, and one which gives to the premises a large part of its rental value, the failure of that purpose by legal prohibition or otherwise might be sufficient to bring about the radical change in the obligation required to frustrate the lease.

Similar problems arise in relation to contracts for the sale of land where a change of circumstances occurs after exchange of contracts but before completion. The risk that the premises may be destroyed or damaged, for example, by fire, is one which must be borne by the purchaser, and in respect of which it is usual to insure.[150] It has further been held that such a contract was not frustrated when the land agreed to be sold was made the subject of a compulsory purchase order[151] and where a building intended for development was listed as being of historic or architectural interest.[152] The position is in doubt, but the answer to the question whether a contract of sale of land can be frustrated would again appear to be 'hardly ever' rather than 'never'.[153]

8. EFFECTS OF FRUSTRATION

(a) COMMON LAW

(i) Contract generally determined automatically

Generally, the contract is not merely dischargeable at the option of one or other of the parties; it is brought to an end forthwith and automatically. In *Hirji Mulji v Cheong Yue Steamship Co Ltd*:[154]

In November 1916 CY chartered its ship, the *Singaporean*, agreeing that it should be placed at HM's disposal on 1 March 1917, for 10 months. Shortly before this date the ship was requisitioned by the Government. Believing that she would soon be released, CY asked if HM would be willing to take up the charter. HM said that they would. The ship was, however, not released until February 1919, and HM then refused to accept her.

---

[147] *Whitehall Court Ltd v Ettlinger* [1920] 1 KB 680; *Matthey v Curling* [1922] 2 AC 180; *Swift v Mackean* [1942] 1 KB 375. See also (before the *National Carriers* case) *Simper v Coombs* [1948] 1 All ER 306; *Redmond v Dainton* [1920] 2 KB 256 (destruction of premises).

[148] *London and Northern Estates Co v Schlesinger* [1916] 1 KB 20 (internment of tenant). See also *Youngmin v Heath* [1974] 1 WLR 135 (death).

[149] See *Sumnall v Statt* (1984) 49 P & CR 367, and above, p 502.

[150] Cheshire and Burn's *Modern Law of Real Property* (18th edn, 2011) 979–81.

[151] *Hillingdon Estates Co v Stonefield Estates Ltd* [1952] Ch 627; *E Johnson & Co (Barbados) Ltd v NSR Ltd* [1997] AC 400.

[152] *Amalgamated Investment & Property Co Ltd v John Walker & Sons Ltd* [1977] 1 WLR 164.

[153] See also *Denny, Mott & Dickson Ltd v James B Fraser & Co Ltd* [1944] AC 265, 274–6 (option to purchase land).

[154] [1926] AC 497. See also *J Lauritzen AS v Wijsmuller BV, The Super Servant Two* [1990] 1 Lloyd's Rep 1, 8.

The shipowners contended that HM had so conducted themselves as to oust the doctrine of frustration. But the House of Lords held that frustration, unlike breach, brings the contract to an end automatically, and could not be waived in this manner.[155]

The rule precluding a party relying on a self-induced frustration, considered above, shows that the rule that discharge is automatic is not absolute. We have seen that the party whose act or default has caused the frustrating event is not entitled to treat himself as discharged. But *FC Shepherd & Co Ltd v Jerrom*,[156] shows that this will not affect the position of the other party, for whom the event is not 'self'-induced. In that case:

An employee was sentenced to a term of detention, and his employer stated that it would not take him back on his release. Once released, he instituted proceedings for unfair dismissal, which the employer defended inter alia on the ground that the contract had been frustrated by the imposition of the sentence of imprisonment.

Although it was clear that the employee could not rely on his detention as frustrating the contract of employment, it was held that the employer could.

(ii) Future obligations discharged

The effect of frustration *at common law* is to release both parties from any further performance of the contract. All obligations falling due for performance after the frustrating event occurred are discharged. In *Appleby v Myers*,[157] for example:

A undertook to erect certain machinery upon M's premises, the agreement providing that the work was to be paid for on completion. While the work was in progress, and before it was completed, the premises and the machinery already erected were wholly destroyed by fire.

The contract was frustrated, but since it had been agreed that payment was to be made only on completion, A could recover nothing for the work already done.

(iii) Accrued obligations remain

Legal rights or obligations already accrued and due, before the frustrating event occurred, are left undisturbed. In *Chandler v Webster*:[158]

C agreed to hire from W a room in Pall Mall to watch the Coronation procession. The price for the hire was to be £141, payable immediately. C paid £100 of this sum, but before he paid the balance, the procession was cancelled. He claimed to recover back the money paid.

It was held not only that he could not recover the £100 already paid, but that he was also liable to pay the other £41 as this obligation had fallen due before the frustrating event

---

[155] [1926] AC 497, 509 (Lord Sumner). See also *BP Exploration (Libya) Co Ltd v Hunt* [1979] 1 WLR 783, 809 (waiver or estoppel could not prevent reliance on frustration).

[156] [1987] 1 QB 301. See also *Joseph Constantine Steamship Line Ltd v Imperial Smelting Corp Ltd* [1942] AC 154, 199–200 (Lord Porter); *Notcutt v Universal Equipment Co (London) Ltd* [1986] 1 WLR 641.

[157] (1867) LR 2 CP 651. See also *Compania Naviera General SA v Kerametal Ltd* [1983] 1 Lloyd's Rep 373.

[158] [1904] 1 KB 493.

occurred. In part because of the underdevelopment of restitutionary principles at that time, the Court of Appeal rejected C's argument that he was entitled to recover the £100 in restitution as money paid under a consideration which had totally failed. The effect of the frustration was not to wipe out the contract altogether but only to release the parties from further performance, so it could not be said that the 'consideration' had failed completely.

(iv) Development of a restitutionary response

The harshness of the decision in *Chandler v Webster*, which allocated all the risks of the frustrating event on to C, excited considerable criticism,[159] and in 1942 it was overruled by the House of Lords in *Fibrosa Spolka Akcyjna v Fairbairn Lawson Combe Barbour Ltd*:[160]

The respondent contracted with the appellant, a Polish company, to manufacture certain machinery and deliver it to Gdynia. Part of the price was to be paid in advance, and the appellant accordingly paid £1,000. The contract was frustrated by the occupation of Gdynia by hostile German forces in September 1939. The appellant thereupon requested the return of the £1,000. This request was refused on the ground that considerable work had been done, and expense incurred, under the contract.

Under the rule in *Chandler v Webster* this money would have been irrecoverable, as it had already been paid at the time the frustrating event occurred. The House of Lords, however, allowed the appellants to recover. It was pointed out that an action for the recovery of the sum paid was not an action on the contract, which *ex hypothesi* had ceased to exist, but an action in restitution to recover money paid on a consideration which had totally failed.[161] The House held that, in the context of a claim to recover money paid, the term 'consideration' should be understood not in the sense of the consideration which is necessary to the formation of a contract, but rather in the sense of the performance of an obligation already incurred. A party who has paid money but has received no part of the bargained-for performance, is entitled to recover it, for the consideration has totally failed.

(b) LAW REFORM (FRUSTRATED CONTRACTS) ACT 1943

(i) Underlying principle

The law as the *Fibrosa* case left it was still not satisfactory, for the party who had to return the pre-payment might have incurred expenses for the purpose of the performance of the contract, or might be left with goods which were made valueless by the failure of the contract.[162] Moreover, the insistence that the failure of consideration

---

[159] *Cantiare San Roco SA v Clyde Shipbuilding & Engineering Co Ltd* [1924] AC 226, 257.
[160] [1943] AC 32.   [161] See below, p 621.
[162] This was probably not a problem in *Fibrosa* since, although the sellers had done a considerable amount of work in manufacturing the machines ([1942] 1 KB 12, 14), it was accepted that they could be resold without loss: [1943] AC 32, 49.

be total[163] meant that if the party seeking recovery of the money had received any part, however small, of the performance of the contract, the *Fibrosa* case did not apply, and the money was irrecoverable. It was to remedy this situation that the Law Reform (Frustrated Contracts) Act 1943 was passed.[164]

It has been stated that the 'fundamental principle underlying the Act . . . is prevention of the unjust enrichment of either party to the contract at the other's expense' and not the apportionment of the loss caused by the frustrating event between the parties.[165] Although it has been argued that the law is defective in not providing for such loss-apportionment,[166] especially since the line between action in reliance on a contract which results in a benefit, and action which does not, can be very fine,[167] the case for a financial adjustment is stronger where such pre-frustration action has resulted in a benefit to one of the parties. But in the present state of the law, it is important not to allow an over-wide interpretation of 'enrichment' or 'benefit' to operate as loss-apportionment by subsuming virtually all action taken by a contracting party in reliance on the contract. The Act does not apply if there is a provision to the contrary in the contract.[168]

(ii) Money paid or payable

By section 1(2) of the 1943 Act:

All sums paid or payable to any party in pursuance of the contract before the time when the parties were so discharged (in this Act referred to as 'the time of discharge') shall, in the case of sums so paid, be recoverable from him as money received by him for the use of the party by whom the sums were paid, and, in the case of sums so payable, cease to be payable:

Provided that, if the party to whom the sums were so paid or payable incurred expenses before the time of the discharge in, or for the purpose of, the performance of the contract, the court may, if it considers it just to do so having regard to all the circumstances of the case, allow him to retain or, as the case may be, recover the whole or any part of the sums so paid or payable, not being an amount in excess of the expenses so incurred.

A careful reading of this subsection reveals that it has two effects.

In the first place, it embodies the rule in the *Fibrosa* case, although it is now no longer necessary to prove a total failure of consideration. So if A agrees to manufacture

---

[163] See below, p 621.

[164] See Williams, *Law Reform (Frustrated Contracts) Act 1943* (1944); Mitchell, Mitchell, and Watterson, *Goff and Jones on the Law of Unjust Enrichment* (8th edn, 2011) ch 15; McKendrick, *Force Majeure and Frustration of Contract* (2nd edn, 1994) ch 11; Treitel, *Frustration and Force Majeure* (3rd edn, 2014) paras 15–049 ff.

[165] *BP Exploration (Libya) Co Ltd v Hunt (No 2)* [1979] 1 WLR 783, 799–800 (Robert Goff J). Cf Lawton LJ in CA at [1981] 1 WLR 232.

[166] Williams, *Law Reform (Frustrated Contracts) Act 1943* (1944) 35; McKendrick, 'Frustration, Restitution and Loss Apportionment' in Burrows (ed), *Essays on the Law of Restitution* (1991) 147; cf Posner and Rosenfield (1977) 6 JLS 83, 112 ff (part-performer can generally evaluate the risk better and insure more cheaply than the other party); Stewart and Carter [1992] CLJ 66, 86–9, 109–10; Burrows, *The Law of Restitution* (3rd edn, 2010) ch 15.

[167] Below, pp 621–2.

[168] 1943 Act, s 2(3). Cf *BP Exploration (Libya) Ltd v Hunt* [1983] 2 AC 352, 372, 373.

and deliver to B certain machinery, B promising to pay £10,000 down and the balance on completion, then even if A has delivered part of the machinery to B before the frustrating event occurs, B can recover the £10,000, if paid, and, if not paid, it ceases to be payable.[169]

(iii) Expenses incurred by payee

The Act goes further than the *Fibrosa* case in that it gives to the Court a discretionary power to allow the payee to set off against the sum so paid or payable a sum not exceeding the value of any expenses which the payee has incurred in or for the purpose of performing the contract before the frustration.[170] So if, in the above example, A has incurred expenses totalling, say, £6,000, then the Court has power to permit A to recover or retain the whole or part of this sum from the £10,000 due from B under the contract. But expenses can only be set off against 'the sums so paid or payable', that is, those due before frustration, so that if the expenses amounted to, say, £12,000, it would not be possible to charge the £2,000 in excess of £10,000 against the unpaid balance due after the frustrating event occurred.

In *Gamerco SA v ICM/Fair Warning (Agency) Ltd*[171] Garland J considered three methods by which the Court should exercise its discretion; allowing the payee to retain all the expenses incurred[172] as a statutory recognition of the defence of change of position,[173] equal division of the loss caused by the frustrating event,[174] and a broad discretion to do what the Court considers just, 'having regard to all the circumstances of the case'.[175] His Lordship favoured the third, concluding that the task of the Court 'is to do justice in a situation which the parties neither contemplated nor provided for, and to mitigate the possible harshness of allowing all loss to lie where it has fallen'.[176] In *Gamerco*'s case:

$775,000 was payable by the promoters of a pop concert to the defendant group, Guns N' Roses, at the time the contract was frustrated, $412,500 of which had been paid. Both parties had incurred expenses before the date of frustration which were wholly wasted: the defendant $50,000, and the promoters $450,000. Neither party was left with any residual benefit or advantage.

In these circumstances, and having particular regard to the promoters' loss, and his view that there was no question of any change of position by the defendant as a result

---

[169] A's position may be protected by s 1(3), on which see below.

[170] 'Expenses' include a reasonable sum in respect of overhead expenses: s 1(4), and the onus of proof lies on the payee: *Gamerco SA v ICM/Fair Warning (Agency) Ltd* [1995] 1 WLR 1226, 1235. See also *Lobb v Vasey Housing Auxiliary (War Widows Guild)* [1963] VR 239 (Victoria, Australia).

[171] [1995] 1 WLR 1226.

[172] This was favoured by the Law Revision Committee (Cmd 6009, 1939) 7.

[173] As suggested in *BP Exploration Co (Libya) Ltd v Hunt (No 2)* [1979] 1 WLR 783, 800. Note that this decision was substantially approved by the House of Lords: [1983] 2 AC 352.

[174] Williams, *Law Reform (Frustrated Contracts) Act 1943* (1944) 35–6.

[175] Treitel, *Frustration and Force Majeure* (3rd edn, 2014) paras 15-075–15-076.

[176] [1995] 1 WLR 1226, 1237.

of the promoters' advance payment,[177] his Lordship made no deduction under the proviso and ordered repayment of the $412,500.

(iv) Obligations other than to pay money

Section 1(3) of the 1943 Act provides for the adjustment of the financial relations of the parties:

Where any party to the contract has, by reason of anything done by any other party thereto in, or for the purpose of, the performance of the contract, obtained a valuable benefit (other than a payment of money to which the last foregoing subsection applies) before the time of discharge, there shall be recoverable from him by the said other party such sum (if any) not exceeding the value of the said benefit to the party obtaining it, as the court considers just, having regard to all the circumstances of the case and, in particular—

    (a) the amount of any expenses incurred before the time of discharge by the benefited party in, or for the purpose of the performance of the contract, including any sums paid or payable by him to any other party in pursuance of the contract and retained or recoverable by that party under the last foregoing subsection, and

    (b) the effect, in relation to the said benefit, of the circumstances giving rise to frustration of the contract.

The result is that recompense may be awarded in respect of a valuable benefit conferred by either party upon the other party in pursuance of the contract. In *BP Exploration Co (Libya) Ltd v Hunt (No 2)*[178] Robert Goff J pointed out that the subsection must be applied in two distinct stages. The first is the identification and valuation of the benefit. The second stage is for the Court to assess what sum (not exceeding the value of the benefit) it considers just to award to the party by whom the benefit has been conferred.

With regard to the identification and valuation of the benefit, there are three situations to be considered. The first is where the performance rendered results in the delivery of an item which is unaffected by the frustrating event. If, for example, in the illustration set out above, A has delivered to B some of the machinery, the machinery so delivered could constitute a benefit to B. The value of that benefit will ordinarily be its value to B at the date of frustration. This may be more or less than the expenses incurred by A in manufacturing and delivering that machinery. It was stated by Robert Goff J that as a matter of construction 'benefit' in the subsection normally meant the end product of services rather than the services themselves.[179]

The second is where, although the performance results in the delivery of an item or an end product, in our example the machinery, the event which frustrates the

---

[177] The decision may be questioned: see *Lipkin Gorman v Karpnale Ltd* [1991] 2 AC 548; Carter and Tolhurst (1996) 10 JCL 265.

[178] [1979] 1 WLR 783 (aff'd by the Court of Appeal [1981] 1 WLR 232, and by the House of Lords [1983] 2 AC 352). For the facts, see below, pp 529–30.

[179] *BP Exploration Co (Libya) Ltd v Hunt (No 2)* [1979] 1 WLR 783, 801–2.

contract (as in *Appleby v Myers*),[180] destroys it or renders it useless and of no value to B without delivery of the remainder. Under paragraph (b) of the subsection regard is to be had to 'the effect, in relation to the . . . benefit, of the circumstances giving rise to the frustration of the contract'. The interpretation of this provision is problematic. Robert Goff J stated[181] that 'benefit' in section 1(3)(b) clearly refers to the end product of the services, rather than the services themselves, and that the subsection 'makes it plain that the plaintiff [the party conferring the benefit] is to take the risk of depreciation or destruction by the frustrating event'. If this view is correct,[182] then the value of the benefit in such a case will be nil, and no award could be made in favour of A under the subsection.

The third situation is where the performance rendered is a 'pure' service, without any end product, such as gardening, surveying, or transporting goods.[183] Here, Robert Goff J stated that the 'benefit' in the subsection was the services themselves,[184] and it is these that must be valued. In such cases care must be taken not to cross the line between restitution in respect of a benefit conferred, which is permitted by the subsection, and recompense for action taken by one party in reliance on the contract: 'if in fact the performance of services has conferred no benefit on the person requesting them, it is pure fiction to base restitution on a benefit conferred'.[185]

The second stage is for the Court to assess what sum (not exceeding the value of the benefit) it considers just to award to the party by whom the benefit has been conferred. This has been termed the 'just sum'. The purpose of the award has been said to be to prevent the unjust enrichment of the other party at his expense.[186] In the example given above, if the machinery delivered remained of value to B after the frustrating event, the just sum would probably be assessed as the reasonable value of that machinery,[187] or a rateable part of the contract price.

The principles were applied in *BP Exploration Co (Libya) Ltd v Hunt (No 2)*:[188]

BP entered into a contract to explore and develop an oil concession in Libya owned by H. BP was to make initial payments and a transfer of oil to Hunt, and in return was to get a 50 per cent share in the concession and 'reimbursement oil' calculated by a formula. A significant oil field was discovered and oil was produced and transferred under the contract for four

---

[180] (1867) LR 2 CP 651, above, p 524. See also *Parsons Bros Ltd v Shea* (1965) 53 DLR(2d) 86 (Canada).

[181] *BP Exploration Co (Libya) Ltd v Hunt (No 2)* [1979] 1 WLR 783, 803. Contrast Williams, *Law Reform (Frustrated Contracts) Act 1943* (1944) 48–51.

[182] Cf Treitel, *Frustration and Force Majeure* (3rd edn, 2014) para 15-068 (s 1(3) applies where a valuable benefit has been obtained 'before the time of discharge' and subparagraphs (a) and (b) are relevant to the assessment of the just sum, not the identification of the benefit); Birks, *An Introduction to the Law of Restitution* (1985) 253.

[183] See eg *Angus v Skully* 44 NE 674 (1900) (USA) and the facts of *Cutter v Powell* (1795) 6 TR 320, above, p 477.

[184] *BP Exploration Co (Libya) Ltd v Hunt (No 2)*, above, n 181, 803.

[185] *Coleman Engineering v North American Airlines* 420 P 2d 713 (1966) 729 (Traynor CJ) (California).

[186] *BP Exploration Co (Libya) Ltd v Hunt (No 2)*, above, n 181, 805.   [187] *Ibid*, 805–6.

[188] [1979] 1 WLR 783 (aff'd by the Court of Appeal [1981] 1 WLR 232, and by the House of Lords [1983] 2 AC 352).

and a half years, but the contract was then frustrated when both parties' interests were expropriated by the Libyan Government, which paid some compensation to H. BP claimed under section 1(3) of the 1943 Act.

It was held that, under section 1(3), the 'valuable benefit' had to be not the work exploring and extracting oil but the end product of that work, the enhancement of the value of H's concession. But the effect of the frustrating event was to make this valueless and unrealizable by H, and subparagraph (b) required this to be reflected in the valuation of the benefit. But H had received considerable amounts of oil produced prior to the expropriation, and compensation thereafter, and half the value of this ($85 million) was held to be the benefit obtained from BP's exploration and development, and the upper limit of any award.[189] The 'just sum' was determined by taking account of the cost to BP of the work done for H and the oil it initially transferred to H reduced by the amount of the 'reimbursement oil' it had received. This amounted to just under $35 million. Since this was in effect the value of 'reimbursement oil' due to BP but not transferred at the date of frustration, the remedy given approximately corresponded to a scaled-down contract price, that percentage of the contract price which the part-performer had 'earned' by performance before the frustrating event.

Neither under subsection (2) nor under subsection (3) can any allowance be made for the time-value of money, that is to say, for the fact that money may have been paid, or expenses incurred, long before the date of frustration.[190]

(v) Carriage of goods by sea and voyage charters

The Act does not apply to contracts for the carriage of goods by sea or a charterparty (other than a time charterparty or a charterparty by way of demise).[191] This recognizes a well-established custom, which has become part of the business practice of shipowners and insurers, that freight paid or payable in advance under such contracts is not recoverable even though the completion of the voyage is frustrated.[192]

(vi) Sale of goods and insurance

The Act is also not applicable to contracts of insurance[193] and certain contracts for the sale of goods.

The exclusion of contracts for the sale of goods is complex in its drafting, but its effect is to exclude all contracts for the sale of specific goods, where the frustration occurs by reason of the perishing of the goods. By section 2(5)(c) the Act does not apply to:

any contract to which section 7 of the Sale of Goods Act 1979 (which avoids contracts for the sale of specific goods which perish before the risk has passed to the buyer) applies or to any

---

[189] The other half was attributed to Hunt's ownership of the concession prior to the exploration and development under the contract.

[190] *BP Exploration Co (Libya) Ltd v Hunt (No 2)* [1979] 1 WLR 783, 800.   [191] 1943 Act, s 2(5)(a).

[192] *Compania Naviera General SA v Kerametal Ltd* [1983] 1 Lloyd's Rep 372.

[193] 1943 Act, s 2(5)(b).

other contract for the sale, or for the sale and delivery, of specific goods, where the contract is frustrated by reason of the fact that the goods have perished.

The first part of this subsection (exclusion by reference to section 7 of the 1979 Act) covers contracts where the goods perish before the risk has passed to the buyer. If the goods then perish without the fault of either party, the contract is *avoided* by section 7 of the Sale of Goods Act 1979 and the 1943 Act does not apply. The general rule in the case of the non-consumer sale of goods is that they are at the risk of the person whose property they are: *res perit domino*.[194] Where there is a sale of *specific* goods property in the goods normally passes to the buyer at the time the contract is made,[195] and so it follows that they are also at the buyer's risk. In the case, however, of a consumer sale, the goods remain at the trader's risk until they come into the physical possession of consumer or his or her agent.[196] But the second part of the subsection quoted above also exempts cases where there is a contract for the sale, or sale and delivery, of specific goods and the goods perish but which are not covered by section 7 of the 1979 Act. This will apply to cases where the risk has passed to the buyer. In such circumstances the buyer will bear the loss resulting from the perishing of the goods.

These exclusions relate only to contracts for specific goods, which are defined by section 61(1) of the Sale of Goods Act 1979 as 'goods identified and agreed on at the time a contract of sale is made'. Goods which are unascertained at this time do not therefore come within the exclusion, although it must be noted that the doctrine of frustration rarely then applies. If A agrees to sell to B 'six hundred tons of coal', there can normally be no frustration of this contract. Even though A may have had in mind a particular source, this assumption is not common to both parties. The contract can be fulfilled at any time and A must obtain sufficient coal from another source or be liable for breach.[197] On the other hand, if the goods, though unascertained, are to come from a source which is specifically defined, for example, 'six hundred tons of coal from the ship *Rose Marie* now in dock', and subsequently the ship and cargo are destroyed by fire, this contract is clearly capable of frustration, but there is some doubt as to whether or not it falls outside the 1943 Act. In one case,[198] goods of this nature were held not to be specific goods for the purposes of section 52 of the Sale of Goods Act 1979 (specific performance), and it is submitted that, for the purposes of frustration, the goods are likewise not specific goods and so are subject to the provisions of the 1943 Act.[199]

A similar problem may arise in the type of situation exemplified by *Howell v Coupland*:[200]

C agreed to sell to H 200 tons of potatoes to be grown on a particular field. The crop failed, so that C was able to deliver only 80 tons. In answer to H's claim for non-delivery of the other

---

[194] Sale of Goods Act 1979, s 20.   [195] Sale of Goods Act 1979, s 18, Rule 1.
[196] Consumer Rights Act 2015, s 29.
[197] *Blackburn Bobbin Co Ltd v TW Allen & Sons Ltd* [1918] 2 KB 467, above, p 516; *CTI Group Inc v Transclear SA, The Mary Nour* [2008] EWCA Civ 856, [2008] 2 Lloyd's Rep 526 at [23]. Cf *Re Badische Co Ltd* [1921] 2 Ch 331; see above, p 516.
[198] *Re Wait* [1927] 1 Ch 606.   [199] See also Hudson (1968) 31 MLR 535.   [200] (1876) 1 QBD 258.

120 tons, C pleaded that he had duly delivered all that it was possible for him to deliver and that he was excused from delivering the remainder.

It was held that C was not liable. Mellish LJ said:[201]

This is not like the case of a contract to deliver so many goods of a particular kind, where no specific goods are to be sold. Here there was an agreement to sell and buy 200 tons of a crop to be grown on specific land, so that it is an agreement to sell what will be and may be called specific things; therefore neither party is liable if the performance becomes impossible.

Despite the use by Mellish LJ of the word 'specific' in this case, it is clear that the potatoes were not 'specific goods' within the meaning of the Sale of Goods Act. Nevertheless this is not a situation to which the provisions of the 1943 Act would appear to apply. It has been held[202] that a contract of sale of this nature is subject to a condition. Depending on the intention of the parties, the condition which will be implied may be one that neither party shall be liable if any part of the promised goods fails to materialize;[203] alternatively, it may, as in *Howell v Coupland*, be a condition that the buyer can require such performance as remains possible, but the seller is excused from delivering the remainder of the goods.[204]

Then exclusion of contracts for the sale of goods from the operation of the 1943 Act only applies where the frustration occurs by reason of the perishing of the goods. Other grounds of frustration, such as the performance of the contract becoming illegal, are not covered and the 1943 Act would then apply.

FURTHER READING

POSNER and ROSENFIELD, 'Impossibility and Related Doctrines in Contract Law: An Economic Analysis' (1977) 6 JLS 83

McKENDRICK, 'Frustration, Restitution and Loss Apportionment' in BURROWS (ed), *Essays on the Law of Restitution* (Oxford: Clarendon Press, 1991) 147

SMITH, 'Contracts—Mistake, Frustration and Implied Terms' (1994) 110 LQR 400

McKENDRICK, 'Force Majeure and Frustration—Their Relationship and a Comparative Assessment' in McKendrick (ed), *Force Majeure and Frustration of Contract* (2nd edn, London: Lloyd's of London Press, 1995) 33

McKENDRICK, '*Force Majeure* Clauses: the Gap between Doctrine and Practice' in Burrows and Peel (eds), *Contract Terms* (Oxford: Oxford University Press, 2007) 233

---

[201] *Ibid*, 262.

[202] *HR & S Sainsbury Ltd v Street* [1972] 1 WLR 834. See also *Re Wait* [1927] 1 Ch 606, 631.

[203] See the Sale of Goods Act 1979, s 5(2) (condition precedent). The sale might also be subject to a condition subsequent: above, pp 152, 494–6.

[204] *HR & S Sainsbury Ltd v Street*, above, n 202.

15

DISCHARGE BY BREACH

If one of the parties to a contract breaches an obligation which the contract imposes, that party is in breach of contract. The breach may consist in the non-performance of the relevant obligation, or its performance in a manner or at a time which fails to comply with the requirements of the contract. English law does not generally distinguish between these different forms of breach of contract, but applies the same remedial regime to them all, and as soon as the party is in breach a new obligation will in every case arise by operation of law—an obligation to pay damages to the other party in respect of any loss or damage sustained by the breach. However, the duty to perform the contractual obligation normally remains unchanged, although there are circumstances under which the breach not only gives rise to a right of action for damages but also gives the innocent party the right to decide not to render further performance under the contract and to discharge both parties from their obligations under the contract—that is, to terminate the contract.[1] The remedy of damages is discussed in detail in Chapter 17. Here we consider only the circumstances in which the contract may be discharged following a breach of contract, and we shall see that the breach may give rise to discharge only if it is sufficiently serious in its effects (a breach which 'goes to the root of the contract', or a 'repudiation' of the contract) or if it is a breach of a sufficiently serious term of the contract (breach of 'condition'). These rules were devised by the common law to provide the innocent party with a general remedy for serious breaches, or breaches of serious terms, of the contract. Under the Consumer Rights Act 2015, however, the consumer's common law right to treat a contract to supply goods or digital content as at an end for breach is substantially modified.[2]

1. DISCHARGE AT OPTION OF THE INJURED PARTY

It is common to speak of the contract as having been 'discharged by the breach'. The phrase, though convenient, is not strictly accurate. A breach does not, of itself,

---

[1] *Photo Production Ltd v Securicor Transport Ltd* [1980] AC 827, 849–50 (Lord Diplock, who labels the obligations contained in the contract, express or implied, 'primary' obligations, and the obligation to pay damages for the loss or damage caused by the breach or by the termination of the contract 'secondary' obligations); see also *Moschi v Lep Air Services Ltd* [1973] AC 331, 350 (Lord Diplock), below, p 537. On the terminology of 'discharge', 'termination', and 'rescission' for breach, see below, p 553.

[2] See below, p 539.

effect a discharge;[3] what it may do is to justify the innocent party, if that party so chooses, in regarding itself as absolved or discharged from further performance of the contract. It does not automatically terminate the innocent party's obligation since that party has the option either to treat the contract as still continuing or to regard itself as discharged by reason of the breach of the contract by the other party. An acceptance of a breach, in order to discharge the contract, must be clear and unequivocal,[4] although the innocent party has a reasonable period to make up his mind what to do, and if he does nothing for too long there may come a time when the law will treat him as having affirmed.[5] Once the option is exercised to either keep the contract on foot or terminate it, the decision is not revocable.[6] A fresh option may arise, however, if the breach continues, or there is another separate breach, sufficient to justify the innocent party terminating the contract.

(a) EFFECT OF UNACCEPTED REPUDIATION

In principle, an innocent party who does not 'accept' a repudiation[7] is entitled to continue to insist on performance because the contract remains in full effect. Thus in *White and Carter (Councils) Ltd v McGregor*:[8]

W & C, an advertising contractor, agreed with McG, a garage proprietor, to display advertisements for his garage for 3 years. On the same day, McG refused to perform the agreement and requested W & C to cancel the contract. W & C refused to do so, and elected to treat the contract as still continuing. It made no effort to relet the space, displayed advertisements as agreed, and sued for the full amount due.

It was contended on behalf of McG that, since he had renounced the agreement before anything had been done under it, W & C was not entitled to carry out the agreement and sue for the price: its remedy, if any, lay in damages. A bare majority of the House of Lords rejected this contention and held that W & C was entitled to the full contract sum.

The decision has been criticized as encouraging wasteful and unwanted performance. The criticisms are considered in the context of specific remedies.[9]

---

[3] See below, pp 534, 536–7, 552.

[4] *Vitol SA v Norelf Ltd* [1996] AC 800, 810–11 (Lord Steyn). See also *Heyman v Darwins Ltd* [1942] AC 356, 361; *Northwest Holt Group Administration Ltd v Harrison* [1985] ICR 668; *Bliss v South East Thames Regional Health Authority* [1987] ICR 700, 716–17; *State Trading Corp of India Ltd v M Golodetz Ltd* [1989] 2 Lloyd's Rep 277, 286; *Geys v Société Générale, London Branch* [2012] UKSC 63, [2013] 1 AC 523 at [17].

[5] *Stocznia Gdanska SA v Latvian Shipping Co (No 2)* [2002] EWCA Civ 889, [2003] 1 CLC 282 at [87]; *White Rosebay Shipping SA v Hong Kong Chain Glory Shipping Ltd* [2013] EWHC 1355 (Comm), [2013] 2 CLC 884.

[6] *Motor Oil Hellas (Corinth) Refineries SA v Shipping Corp of India, The Kanchenjunga* [1990] 1 Lloyd's Rep 391 398 (Lord Goff); *Peyman v Lanjani* [1985] Ch 457.

[7] See below, p 540.

[8] [1962] AC 413, on the facts of which, see Rodger (1977) 93 LQR 168. See also Liu (2011) 74 MLR 171.

[9] Chapter 18.

It is in any event clear from the speeches of the majority in this case that the party not in breach will not always thus be entitled to complete the contract and sue for the contract price. In the first place, if the contract cannot be carried out without the co-operation of the party who has refused to perform, and such co-operation is withheld, the innocent party's only remedy is to sue for damages and not for the price.[10] So an employee who is wrongfully dismissed from employment can only claim damages. The employee cannot claim the salary payable after dismissal on the ground that he is ready, able, and willing to serve the employer if only the employer would allow him to do so.[11] Secondly, the rule in *White and Carter (Councils) Ltd v McGregor* does not apply 'if it can be shown that a person has no legitimate interest, financial or otherwise, in performing the contract rather than claiming damages',[12] in which case a claimant may be compelled to resort to the remedy of damages, provided the damages are an adequate remedy for any loss suffered.

The need for acceptance of a repudiation for the contract to be discharged led to Asquith LJ's famous and influential aphorism that 'an unaccepted repudiation is a thing writ in water'.[13] But an unaccepted repudiation is not altogether without effect. An innocent party who remains ready and willing to perform[14] can rely on the unaccepted repudiation as a defence in an action brought by the guilty party.[15] Again, while the suggestion that contracts of employment are an exception to the normal rule and are discharged by a unilateral repudiation by the employer, without the need for acceptance by the employee, has been rejected,[16] it has been held that an employee's right to damages following an unlawful dismissal does not continue beyond the time at which the employer could have lawfully brought the contract to an end.[17]

---

[10] [1962] AC 413, 430, 432, 439.

[11] *Vine v National Dock Labour Board* [1956] 1 QB 658, 674; *Denmark Productions Ltd v Boscobel Productions Ltd* [1969] 1 QB 699; *Hill v CA Parsons & Co Ltd* [1972] Ch 305, 314; *Gunton v Richmond LBC* [1980] ICR 755. Cf *Boyo v Lambeth LBC* [1994] ICR 727, 742–4, 747.

[12] *White and Carter (Councils) Ltd v McGregor* [1962] AC 413, 431 (Lord Reid); *Attica Sea Carriers Corp v Ferrostaal Poseidon Bulk Reederei GmbH, The Puerto Buitrago* [1976] 1 Lloyd's Rep 250; *Gator Shipping Corp v Trans-Asiatic Oil Ltd SA* [1978] 2 Lloyd's Rep 357, 372–4; *Stocznia Gdanska SA v Latvian SS Co* [1996] 2 Lloyd's Rep 132, [1998] 1 WLR 574; *Reichman v Beveridge* [2006] EWCA Civ 1659, [2007] 1 P & CR 20; *MSC Mediterranean Shipping Co SA v Cottonex Anstalt* [2015] EWHC 283 (Comm), [2015] 2 All ER (Comm) 614. On the action for the agreed sum, and its contrast with a claim for damages, see further pp 606–8, below.

[13] *Howard v Pickford Tool Co Ltd* [1951] 1 KB 417, 421. See also *Fercometal SARL v Mediterranean Shipping Co SA, The Simona* [1989] AC 788, 800; *State Trading Corp of India Ltd v M Golodetz Ltd* [1989] 2 Lloyd's Rep 277, 285.

[14] *Fercometal SARL v Mediterranean Shipping Co SA, The Simona* [1989] AC 788.

[15] *Peter Turnbull & Co Pty Ltd v Mundus Trading Co (Australasia) Pty Ltd* (1954) 90 CLR 235, 245, 251; *Foran v Wight* (1989) 168 CLR 385, 438 (Australia). See further Carter, *Breach of Contract* (2nd edn, 1991) 242 ff.

[16] *Geys v Société Générale, London Branch* [2012] UKSC 63, [2013] 1 AC 523, approving *Gunton v Richmond LBC* [1980] ICR 755.

[17] *Boyo v Lambeth LBC* [1994] ICR 727.

(b) FAILURE OF PERFORMANCE

In cases of a failure of performance by one party which goes to the root of the contract,[18] the contract is likewise not determined by the breach,[19] and it is open to the innocent party to treat the contract as continuing or to accept the defective performance when tendered. An innocent party who adopts this course is sometimes said to have elected to *affirm* the contract, that is, to have waived the right to be treated as discharged, although the right to claim damages for the breach is still retained.[20] Affirmation may be express or implied. Affirmation will be implied if, to the knowledge of the party in default, the innocent party does some unequivocal[21] act which shows an intention to go on with the contract regardless of the breach or from which it may be inferred that the right to be treated as discharged will not be exercised.[22] And affirmation must be total. A contracting party cannot affirm part of the contract and disaffirm the rest, for that would be to make a new contract.[23]

(c) AFFIRMATION OF CONTRACT

Affirmation is a voluntary act, and requires knowledge. Although old authorities to the contrary can be found, the traditional position was that a party need only have knowledge of the facts which give rise to the right to affirm or terminate.[24] Recent cases go further and suggest that a party cannot be called upon to make an election or be held to have made an election, unless, in addition to knowledge of the relevant facts, that party has knowledge of the right to elect.[25] Despite this debate, as we have seen,[26] there are circumstances where the innocent party will be deprived of the right to be treated as discharged even though that party has no knowledge of the breach. There may also be cases where an innocent party who has led the party in default to believe that it will not exercise that right will be estopped from exercising it.[27]

---

[18] See below, p 549.

[19] *Photo Productions Ltd v Securicor Transport Ltd* [1980] AC 827 (overruling *Harbutt's 'Plasticine' Ltd v Wayne Tank and Pump Co Ltd* [1970] 1 QB 447).

[20] See below, p 563.

[21] *China National Foreign Trade Transportation Corp v Evlogia Shipping Co SA of Panama* [1979] 1 WLR 1018; *Yukong Line Ltd of Korea v Rendsburg Investments Corp of Liberia* [1996] 2 Lloyd's Rep 604 (very clear evidence required).

[22] *Bentsen v Taylor, Sons & Co* [1893] 2 QB 274; *Hain SS Co Ltd v Tate & Lyle Ltd* (1936) 41 Com Cas 350, 355, 363; *Suisse Atlantique Société d'Armement Maritime SA v NV Rotterdamsche Kolen Centrale* [1967] 1 AC 361.

[23] *Suisse Atlantique Société d'Armement Maritime SA v NV Rotterdamsche Kolen Centrale*, above, n 22, 398.

[24] *Matthews v Smallwood* [1910] 1 Ch 777, 786; *Kammins Ballrooms Co Ltd v Zenith Investments (Torquay) Ltd* [1971] AC 850, 877–8, 883.

[25] *Peyman v Lanjani* [1985] Ch 457; *Sea Calm Shipping Co SA v Chantiers Navals de L'Esterel* [1986] 2 Lloyd's Rep 294. See also *Kendall v Hamilton* (1879) 4 App Cas 504, 542. Cf *Motor Oil Hellas (Corinth) Refineries SA v Shipping Corp of India, The Kanchenjunga* [1990] 1 Lloyd's Rep 391, 398.

[26] See above, p 494 (waiver).

[27] The incidence of estoppel in this situation depends upon interpretation of the difficult case of *Panchaud Frères SA v Établissements General Grain Co* [1970] 1 Lloyd's Rep 53 (especially at 57–8) and cases consequent thereon.

(d) EFFECT OF ELECTION TO ACCEPT BREACH

If the innocent party decides to accept the breach, this discharges all the future contractual obligations of that party which have not already been performed. At the same time, the primary obligations of the party in default to perform any of that party's contractual promises which remain unperformed are likewise discharged.[28] However, in the case of the party in default, in place of the primary obligations imposed by the contract there arises a secondary obligation to pay damages for the breach. This point was clearly made in *Moschi v Lep Air Services Ltd*:[29]

R Ltd was indebted to L Ltd, the respondent, in the sum of £40,000, which it agreed to pay to L Ltd at the rate of not less than £6,000 per week. M, the appellant, guaranteed to L Ltd the performance by R Ltd of its obligation to make these payments. R Ltd defaulted from the outset and, after 3 weeks, paid only some £10,000 of the £18,000 then due. L Ltd elected to treat this default as a repudiation of the contract which it accepted. R Ltd went into liquidation and L Ltd sued M in respect of both the accrued and future instalments unpaid.

M argued that, since the repudiation had been accepted, the obligation of the company to pay the outstanding instalments due after that time came to an end, and in consequence his obligation as guarantor also came to an end. The House of Lords found little difficulty in disposing of this argument and held that he was liable on the guarantee. In the first place, upon acceptance of the repudiation, although the company's primary obligation to pay the future instalments came to an end, it was replaced, by operation of law, by a secondary obligation to pay damages for the breach. This secondary obligation was just as much an obligation arising from the contract as were the primary obligations it replaced. Secondly, M had undertaken that R Ltd would perform its contract and so was in breach of his contract of guarantee. The damages which R Ltd had not paid constituted the loss flowing from M's breach of contract for which M was liable.

(e) NO REASON OR BAD REASON FOR CLAIMING TO BE DISCHARGED

Where one party refuses to go on with the contract, giving no reason for this refusal or the wrong or an inadequate reason, the action can still be justified if (even if this is unknown to that party) the other party had at the time committed a breach of contract which would have provided a good reason.[30] So, for example, if

---

[28] For the terminology of 'primary' and 'secondary' obligations see above, p 533, n 1. It may, however, be the intention of the parties that certain primary obligations, eg, an arbitration or jurisdiction clause, should continue notwithstanding that their other primary obligations have come to an end: see *Heyman v Darwins Ltd* [1942] AC 356; *Moschi v Lep Air Services Ltd* [1973] AC 331, 350. See also above, pp 200–2 (exemption clauses); below, p 554.

[29] [1973] AC 331. See also *Photo Production Ltd v Securicor Transport Ltd* [1980] AC 827, 849.

[30] *Taylor v Oakes Roncoroni & Co* (1922) 127 LT 267, 269; *British & Beningtons Ltd v NW Cachar Tea Co* [1923] AC 48, 71; *The Mihalis Angelos* [1971] 1 QB 164, 195, 200, 204; *Scandinavian Trading Co A/B v Zodiac Petroleum SA* [1981] 1 Lloyd's Rep 81; *Sheffield v Conrad* (1987) 22 Con LR 108.

an employer dismisses an employee without giving any reason at all, the employer can justify the dismissal should it subsequently be discovered that, prior to the dismissal, the employee had been guilty of dishonesty which would have entitled the employer to dismiss the employee.[31] Similarly if a buyer of goods rejects the goods on the erroneous ground that they are defective in quality, that rejection will still be lawful should the goods turn out not to have been in conformity with the contract description—a breach of contract which would have justified rejection. This rule, though well established, could be criticized on the ground that it allows a party to a contract to 'blow hot and cold', first alleging one reason then in fact relying on another. There is some authority[32] for the view that a party will be estopped from relying on a ground which was not specified at the time of the refusal to perform if that party has thereby led the other party to believe that no reliance would be placed on that ground and it would be unfair or unjust now to allow such reliance.

Where, however, a party purports to terminate by accepting a breach which does not in law justify termination, it risks being itself in repudiatory breach of contract, although the Courts are reluctant so to hold as long as the purported termination was done in good faith, honestly (if mistakenly) believing that there was a right to terminate.[33]

(f) CONSUMER SALE AND SUPPLY CONTRACTS: INTERACTION WITH OTHER REMEDIES

Until 1 October 2015 the common law remedy of termination of the contract, set out above and in the following sections of this chapter, applied equally to consumer and non-consumer sale contracts, although in the case of contracts for the sale or supply of goods to consumers there was a special additional remedial regime for non-conforming goods, giving the consumer in certain circumstances the right to repair or replacement of the goods, reduction of the price, or rescission of the contract.[34] These remedies, introduced in order to implement the Consumer Sales Directive,[35] were in addition to the right to reject the goods for breach of a condition

---

[31] *Ridgway v Hungerford Market Co* (1835) 3 A & E 171, 177, 178, 180; *Boston Deep Sea Fishing & Ice Co v Ansell* (1888) 39 Ch D 339, 352, 364; *Cyril Leonard & Co v Simo Securities Trust* [1972] 1 WLR 80, 85, 87, 89. But the rule does not apply to cases of unfair dismissal under statute: *W Devis & Co v Atkins* [1977] AC 931.

[32] *Panchaud Frères SA v Établissements General Grain Co* [1970] 1 Lloyd's Rep 53, 57–8. See also *Heisler v Anglo-Dal Ltd* [1954] 1 WLR 1273, 1278.

[33] *Woodar Investment Development Ltd v Wimpey Construction UK Ltd* [1980] 1 WLR 277, where HL was divided on this issue; but see Lord Wilberforce at 283.

[34] Sale and Supply of Goods to Consumers Regulations 2002 (SI 2002 No 3045), introducing new provisions into Sale of Goods Act 1979 (Part 5A); Supply of Goods and Services Act 1982 (Part 1B) which have now been removed and replaced by provisions of the Consumer Rights Act 2015, below.

[35] Directive 1999/44/EC.

as to description, quality or conformity with sample implied by sections 13 to 15 of the Sale of Goods Act 1979.[36]

The complex overlap of remedies in this area was reviewed by the Law Commission in 2009,[37] and with effect from 1 October 2015, Part 1 of the Consumer Rights Act 2015 amends significantly the special remedial regime for consumer contracts, replacing the earlier implementation of the Consumer Sales Directive and in certain respects going beyond its provisions, in relation to contracts between a trader and a consumer for the trader to supply goods, digital content, or services.[38]

A particularly significant change is that the consumer no longer has the common law right to treat a contract to supply goods as at an end where the breach is of a term required by the 2015 Act to be treated as included in the contract,[39] but instead the consumer has new statutory remedies to reject the goods and to treat the contract as at an end for breach of the statutory terms as to quality, fitness for purpose, description, and matching a sample or model.[40] There is a *short-term right to reject* (and to treat the contract as at an end) which may generally be exercised during the 30 days after the later of the transfer of ownership or possession of the goods to the consumer, delivery of the goods, and installation of the goods;[41] and a *final right to reject* (and to treat the contract as at an end) which may be exercised if the consumer has instead claimed the right to repair or replacement of the non-conforming goods and after one repair or one replacement the goods still do not conform to the contract, or the trader has failed to repair or replace the goods within a reasonable time and without significant inconvenience to the consumer, or if the consumer cannot require repair or replacement because it is impossible or disproportionate.[42] In all cases the right to reject is exercised by the consumer clearly indicating (by words or conduct) to the trader that he or she is rejecting the goods and treating the contract as at an end,[43] and the trader then generally has a duty to give the consumer a refund and the consumer has a duty to make the goods available for collection by the trader, at the trader's cost.[44]

In the case of consumer contracts to supply digital content, the common law remedy of termination is similarly excluded in the case of non-conformity with the terms treated as included in the contract, but in this case there is no statutory right

---

[36] For the terms implied by the Sale of Goods Act 1979 and their classification as conditions, see above, pp 171–7.

[37] Law Com No 317, *Consumer Remedies for Faulty Goods* (2009).

[38] Consumer Rights Act 2015, s 1(1).

[39] Consumer Rights Act 2015, s 19(12), also excluding the case where the goods do not conform to the contract by reason of defective installation (s 15) or non-conforming digital content (s 16). Cf s 28 (non-exclusive right to treat the contract as at an end for late delivery of goods).

[40] Consumer Rights Act 2015, s 19(3). For these statutory terms see further above, p 178.

[41] Consumer Rights Act 2015, ss 20, 22.

[42] Consumer Rights Act 2015, ss 20, 24. In such circumstances the consumer may claim either the final right to reject or reduction of the price, but not both: *ibid*, s 24.

[43] Consumer Rights Act 2015, s 20(5), (6). For rejection of part of the goods under a severable contract, see s 20(20), (21); and for partial rejection of non-conforming goods see s 21.

[44] Consumer Rights Act 2015, s 20(7), (8).

of rejection but there are rights to repair or replacement, or price reduction, as well as other common law remedies such as damages and specific performance.[45] In the case of contracts for the supply of services, the common law remedy of termination is unchanged.[46]

2. FORMS OF BREACH WHICH JUSTIFY DISCHARGE

The right of a party to be treated as discharged from further performance may arise in any one of three ways: the other party to the contract (a) may renounce its liabilities under it, (b) may by its own act make it impossible to fulfil them, (c) may fail to perform what it has promised.[47] Of these forms of breach the first two may take place not only in the course of performance but also while the contract is still wholly executory, that is, before either party is entitled to demand a performance by the other of the other's promise. In such a case the breach is usually termed an 'anticipatory breach'.[48] The last can only take place at or during the time for performance of the contract.

(a) RENUNCIATION

Renunciation (often termed 'repudiation') occurs where one of the parties evinces an intention not to go on with the contract. If there is an express and unqualified refusal to perform, this intention will, of course, be clear and obvious.[49] But it can also be evinced by conduct.

(i) By conduct

The test of whether an intention to renounce a contract is evinced by conduct is 'whether the party renunciating has acted in such a way as to lead a reasonable person to the conclusion that he does not intend to fulfil his part of the contract'.[50] Acts or omissions from which renunciation can be inferred may also entitle the injured party to be treated as discharged on one or both of the two other grounds previously mentioned.[51] But if the injured party relies upon renunciation as a ground for discharge, they must

---

[45] Consumer Rights Act 2015, s 42.   [46] Consumer Rights Act 2015, s 54(7)(f).

[47] This statement of the law was approved by Lord Porter in *Heyman v Darwins Ltd* [1942] AC 356, 397 and by Devlin J in *Universal Cargo Carriers Corp v Citati* [1957] 2 QB 401, 436 (aff'd in part [1957] 1 WLR 979 and revs'd in part [1958] 2 QB 254).

[48] See below, pp 542–4; Dawson [1981] CLJ 83.

[49] A party who makes his performance dependent on a discretion to be exercised by a third party is not ipso facto deemed to be evincing an intention not to perform: *Geden Operations Ltd v Dry Bulk Handy Holdings Inc, The Bulk Uruguay* [2014] EWHC 885 (Comm), [2014] 2 All ER (Comm) 196.

[50] *Universal Cargo Carriers Corp v Citati* [1957] 2 QB 401, 436 (Devlin J). See also *Forslind v Becheley Crundall* 1922 SC (HL) 173; *The Hermosa* [1982] 1 Lloyd's Rep 570; *Nottingham Building Society v Eurodynamics plc* [1995] FSR 605, 611–12; *Eminence Property Developments Ltd v Heaney* [2010] EWCA Civ 1168, [2011] 2 All ER (Comm) 223 at [61].

[51] *Mersey Steel and Iron Co v Naylor, Benzon & Co* (1884) 9 App Cas 434, 441 (renunciation) and 444 (failure of performance).

be such as to lead to the conclusion that the other party no longer intends to be bound by the contract. Whether or not there has been a repudiatory breach is, however, highly fact-sensitive: the test is not easy to apply, and comparison with other cases is of limited value.[52]

(ii) Intention to renounce

The importance of this intention was emphasized in the case of *Freeth v Burr*,[53] where there was a failure on the part of the buyer to pay for one instalment of several deliveries of iron, under an erroneous impression that he was entitled to withhold payment as a set-off against damages for non-delivery of an earlier instalment. The seller was not discharged. Keating J said:[54] 'It is not a mere refusal or omission of one of the contracting parties to do something which he ought to do, that will justify the other in repudiating the contract; but there must be an absolute refusal to perform his part of the contract'.

Also in *Mersey Steel and Iron Co v Naylor, Benzon & Co*:[55]

NB bought from MS 5,000 tons of steel, to be delivered at the rate of 1,000 tons each month commencing in January 1881, payment to be made within 3 days of the receipt of the shipping documents. MS delivered part only of the first instalment in January, but delivered another in February. Shortly before payment for these was due, a petition was presented for the winding up of MS, whereupon NB refused to pay as it had been erroneously advised not to do so unless MS obtained the leave of the Court. MS informed NB that it would treat this refusal as breach, but NB continued to express its willingness to take delivery and to make the payments if possible.

The House of Lords held that MS was not entitled to treat itself as discharged. The Earl of Selborne LC said:[56]

I cannot ascribe to their [NB's] conduct, under these circumstances, the character of a renunciation of the contract, a repudiation of the contract, a refusal to fulfil the contract. It is just the reverse; the purchasers were desirous of fulfilling the contract; they were advised that there was a difficulty in the way, and they expressed anxiety that that difficulty should be as soon as possible removed.

In neither of these two cases did the breach, in the particular circumstances in which it had been committed, indicate, in the view taken by the Court, an intention in the party in default to throw up the contract altogether, so as to set the other party free.

---

[52] *Eminence Property Developments Ltd v Heaney*, above, n 50 at [62], [64].

[53] (1874) LR 9 CP 208, applied in *Aktion Maritime Corp of Liberia v S Kasmas & Brothers Ltd* [1987] 1 Lloyd's Rep 283, 306. See also *Mitsubushi Heavy Industries Ltd v Gulf Bank KSC* [1997] 1 Lloyd's Rep 343, 350, 354.

[54] (1874) LR 9 CP 208, 214. Note here that the word 'repudiating' is used in the sense of an election to discharge the contract. It is more normal to describe the guilty party as repudiating the contract: the innocent party discharges the contract by 'accepting the repudiation'.

[55] (1884) 9 App Cas 434. See also *Sweet & Maxwell Ltd v Universal News Services Ltd* [1964] 2 QB 699; *Alfred C Toepfer International GmbH v Itex Itagram Export SA* [1993] 1 Lloyd's Rep 360, 361.

[56] (1884) 9 App Cas 434, 441.

The contract-breaker's intention is assessed objectively, not subjectively; but his motive may be relevant if it is something, or it reflects something, of which the innocent party was, or a reasonable person in his or her position would have been, aware and throws light on the way the alleged repudiatory conduct would be viewed by such a reasonable person.[57] Moreover, a Court may be reluctant to find that there has been a renunciation where a party insists on performing the contract in a particular way which, although ultimately held to be a breach of contract, arose from a bona fide belief as to the construction of the contract which is also consistent with its continuance.[58] On the other hand, an unequivocal refusal, by words or conduct, to perform the contract will entitle the other party to be discharged from any further performance of its obligations even where the party who has failed to perform acted in good faith.[59] So, for example, if a buyer contracts to buy goods by instalments and agrees to pay cash for them, but then demands credit in respect of all future deliveries of the goods, the seller may refuse to make any further deliveries.[60] Similarly if, in breach of a contract of employment, a gardener insolently refuses to carry out instructions,[61] or a school teacher refuses to supervise school meals when required to do so,[62] the employer is justified in dismissing that person, that is, terminating the contract of employment.

Renunciation may take place either before performance is due or during performance itself.

(iii) Renunciation before performance is due: 'anticipatory breach'

The parties to a contract which is wholly executory have a right to something more than the performance when the time arrives. They have a right to the maintenance of the contractual relation right up to that time, as well as to a performance of the contract when due.

The renunciation of a contract by one of the parties before the time for performance has come does not, of itself, put an end to the contract, but the 'anticipatory breach' entitles the other to choose to be discharged and to sue at once for damages. A leading case upon this subject is *Hochster v De la Tour*:[63]

T engaged H on 12 April to enter into his service as a courier and to accompany him upon a tour; the employment was to commence on 1 June. On 11 May T wrote to H to inform him that his services would no longer be required. H at once brought an action, although the time for performance had not yet arrived.

The Court held that he was entitled to do so.

The rule has also been applied to situations where the performance is not absolute as in *Hochster v De la Tour*, but contingent. In that case a time was fixed for

---

[57] *Eminence Property Developments Ltd v Heaney*, above, n 50 at [63].

[58] *Vaswani v Italian Motors (Sales and Services) Ltd* [1996] 1 WLR 270. See also *Woodar Investment Development Ltd v Wimpey Construction UK Ltd* [1980] 1 WLR 277.

[59] *Federal Commerce & Navigation Co Ltd v Molena Alpha Inc* [1979] AC 757; *Farrant v The Woodroffe School* [1998] 2 ICR 184.

[60] *Withers v Reynolds* (1831) 2 B & Ad 882.
[61] *Pepper v Webb* [1969] 1 WLR 514.

[62] *Gorse v Durham CC* [1971] 1 WLR 775.
[63] (1853) 2 E & B 678.

performance, and before it arrived T renounced the contract, but in *Frost v Knight*,[64] performance was contingent upon an event which might not happen within the lifetime of the parties:

K, a bachelor, promised to marry F upon his father's death; but during his father's lifetime he renounced the contract.

F was held entitled to sue on the ground explained above. The principle of anticipatory breach was justified by Cockburn CJ as follows:[65]

The promisee has an inchoate right to the performance of the bargain, which becomes complete when the time for performance has arrived. *In the mean time he has a right to have the contract kept open as a subsisting and effective contract*. Its unimpaired and unimpeached efficacy may be essential to his interests.

The principle enables the innocent party to assert its rights speedily and so to minimize the damage which may be suffered from the breach.[66] Nevertheless, it is important to note that a party who has been guilty of an anticipatory breach by renunciation is accorded no privilege of withdrawing that renunciation once it has been accepted by the other party,[67] even though the guilty party tenders performance within the time originally fixed by the contract and even though the position of the other party has in no way changed as a result of the renunciation.

The promisee, however, has the right to continue to insist on the performance of the promise and to refuse to accept the renunciation. If this is done, the promisee loses the right to rely on the anticipatory breach and the contract remains in existence for the benefit and at the risk of both parties. Should anything occur subsequently to discharge the contract from other causes, the promisor, whose renunciation has been refused, may take advantage of such discharge. Thus in *Avery v Bowden*:[68]

A chartered his ship to B. It was agreed that the ship would sail to Odessa, and there take a cargo from B's agent, which was to be loaded within a certain number of days. The vessel reached Odessa, and her master demanded a cargo, but B's agent was unable to supply one. Nevertheless, the master of the ship continued to demand a cargo, but before the specified number of days had elapsed the Crimean War broke out between England and Russia and the performance of the contract became legally impossible. A afterwards sued for breach of the charterparty.

His action failed. If B's agent had positively informed the master that no cargo would be provided, and that there was no use in his remaining there any longer, the master might have treated this as an anticipatory breach and sailed away. A would then have had the right to sue at once upon the contract. But the Court found that as the conduct

---

[64] (1872) LR 7 Ex 111.   [65] *Ibid*, 114 (emphasis added). But see Vold (1928) 41 Harv LR 340.
[66] *Bunge SA v Nidera BV* [2015] UKSC 43, [2015] 3 All ER 1082 at [12].
[67] *Xenos v Danube, etc, Ry* (1863) 13 CBNS 824; but see *Aegnoussiotis Shipping Corp of Monrovia v A/S Kristian Jebsens Rederi of Bergen* [1977] 1 Lloyd's Rep 268, 276 (new contract).
[68] (1855) 5 E & B 714, (1856) 6 E & B 953. See also *Michael v Hart & Co* [1902] 1 KB 482; *Berners v Fleming* [1925] Ch 264.

of B's agent was not such as to constitute a renunciation of the contract there was therefore no breach committed by B before the contract was frustrated. Even, however, if there had been a renunciation of the contract, the Court considered that it could not be treated as a cause of action after the master still continued to insist upon having a cargo in fulfilment of the charterparty. Again, it has been held by the House of Lords[69] that where, following an anticipatory breach by charterers which was not accepted by the shipowners, the owners later failed to tender the vessel ready to load on time, the charterers were entitled to cancel the charterparty.

Despite the utility of the principle of 'anticipatory breach', the term itself is somewhat misleading. It suggests that the cause of action lies in the future breach that will occur on the date fixed for performance, which the innocent party is, in some sense, permitted to anticipate. But it is clear from the cases cited that, at any rate where the anticipatory breach consists of a renunciation of the contract, the breach is constituted by the renunciation itself, and, if this is accepted, the innocent party is immediately entitled to recover by way of damages the true value of the contractual rights which have been lost, subject to the innocent party's duty to mitigate.[70]

(iv) Renunciation during performance

If during the performance of a contract one of the parties by words or conduct unconditionally refuses to perform its side of the contract, the other party is forthwith entitled to be released from any further performance of its obligations, and to sue.

In *Cort v Ambergate etc Railway Co*:[71]

C contracted with the defendant to supply it with 3,900 tons of railway chairs, at a certain price, to be delivered in certain quantities at specified dates. After 1,787 tons had been delivered, the defendant requested C to deliver no more, as they would not be wanted. C brought an action upon the contract, averring that he was always ready and willing to perform his part, but had been prevented from doing so by the action of the defendant.

C obtained a verdict, and when the defendant moved for a new trial on the ground that he should have proved not merely that he was ready and willing to deliver, but an actual delivery, the Court rejected this submission. Since the contract had been renounced, C could maintain an action without manufacturing and tendering the rest of the goods.

(b) IMPOSSIBILITY CREATED BY ONE PARTY

If by the act or default of one party further commercial performance of the contract is made impossible,[72] although that party has not, by words or conduct, renounced the intention to fulfil it, the other party will be discharged.

---

[69] *Fercometal SARL v Mediterranean Shipping Co SA, The Simona* [1989] AC 788.
[70] *The Mihalis Angelos* [1971] 1 QB 164.   [71] (1851) 17 QB 127.
[72] If the impossibility arises through the occurrence of some external event, which radically alters the nature of the obligation (but not otherwise), the contract may be discharged by frustration: see above, pp 497, 500.

Renunciation is usually easier to establish because the innocent party need only show that the conduct of the promisor was such as to lead a reasonable person to believe that the promisor did not intend to perform the promise, whereas if reliance is placed on impossibility the innocent party must show that the contract was in fact impossible of performance due to the default of the promisor. But it is an independent ground for discharge, as can be seen from *Universal Cargo Carriers Corporation v Citati*:[73]

UCC chartered a ship to C who agreed to nominate a berth and a shipper, and to provide a cargo, all before a certain day. Three days before the due date C had done none of these things. Although C was willing to perform the contract if he could, UCC cancelled it and found another charterer.

Devlin J held that C had not renounced the contract, but, since he could not have performed before the delay became so long as to frustrate the commercial purpose of the contract, UCC was entitled to treat this inability to perform as discharging its obligations.

Here also the impossibility may be created either before performance is due or in the course of performance.

(i) Impossibility created before performance is due: anticipatory breach

If the act or default of a promisor which makes performance impossible occurs before the time for performance arrives, the effect is the same as though the promisor had renounced the contract at that time. Such impossibility need not be deliberately created: 'Anticipatory breach was not devised as a whip to be used for the chastisement of deliberate contract-breakers, but from which the shiftless, the dilatory, or the unfortunate are to be spared. It is not confined to any particular class of breach, deliberate or blameworthy or otherwise; it covers all breaches that are bound to happen'.[74]

The aggrieved party may sue at once. In *Lovelock v Franklyn*:[75]

F promised to assign to L within 7 years from the date of his promise, all his interest in a lease for the sum of £140. Before the end of 7 years he assigned his interest to another person.

It was held that L need not wait until the end of the seven years to bring an action. Lord Denman CJ stated:[76]

[L] has a right to say to [F]: 'You have placed yourself in a situation in which you cannot perform what you have promised; you promised to be ready during the period of seven years; and, during that period, I may at any time tender you the money and call for an assignment, and expect that you should keep yourself ready; but, if I now were to tender you the money, you would not be ready'. That is a breach of the contract.

---

[73] [1957] 2 QB 401 (aff'd in part [1957] 1 WLR 979 and revs'd in part [1958] 2 QB 254). See also *Sanko Steamship Co Ltd v Eacom Timber Sales Ltd* [1987] 1 Lloyd's Rep 487, 492.

[74] [1957] 2 QB 401, 438 (Devlin J).   [75] (1846) 8 QB 371.

[76] *Ibid*, 378. See also *Omnium D'Enterprises v Sutherland* [1919] 1 KB 618.

Similarly, in *Universal Cargo Carriers Corporation v Citati*,[77] the shipowners' cancellation of the contract was not premature. They were permitted to anticipate a breach which was in fact inevitable.

(ii) Impossibility created during performance

The rule is similar where the complete performance of the contract is made impossible by the act or default of one party. This is illustrated by the case of *O'Neil v Armstrong*:[78]

O'N, a British subject, was engaged by A, the captain of a warship owned by the Japanese Government, to act as a fireman on a voyage from the Tyne to Yokohama. In the course of the voyage the Japanese Government declared war on China. O'N was informed that performance of the contract would bring him under the penalties of the Foreign Enlistment Act 1870. He consequently left the ship, and sued A for the wages agreed upon.

It was held that he was entitled to succeed in his action, for the act of A's principal, the Japanese Government, had made his performance of the contract legally impossible.

It will be seen from this case that discharge by breach may occur, not only where one party disables itself from performing the contract, but also where it prevents completion of the contract by the other party.[79] The Courts may imply a term that the parties co-operate to ensure performance. A duty to co-operate cannot be imposed so as to compel a party to do something which the contract on its true construction relieved that party from doing, and cannot be used to compel a party to do something which that party is in fact unable to do.[80] But the Courts are often ready to imply a term that each party undertakes to do all that is necessary to secure performance of the contract.[81] Thus if a licence is required for the export of goods, and the buyer fails to provide the seller with the information necessary to obtain the licence, no action will lie against the seller for non-delivery.[82] In some situations, where performance has thus been prevented by the promisee, the contract is taken as satisfied and the promisor can sue for the full remuneration or price.[83] But in most cases the promisor will be forced to sue for damages for the breach, since the contract cannot be fulfilled without the co-operation of the party in default.[84]

---

[77] Above, n 73.   [78] [1895] 2 QB 418.

[79] See also *Ogdens Ltd v Nelson* [1905] AC 109. Cf *Bremer Vulkan v South India Shipping Co* [1981] AC 909 (both parties in breach).

[80] *North Sea Energy Holdings NV v Petroleum Authority of Thailand* [1999] 1 Lloyd's Rep 483, 492.

[81] *Stirling v Maitland* (1864) 5 B & S 840, 852; *Southern Foundries (1936) Ltd v Shirlaw* [1940] AC 701; *The Unique Mariner (No 2)* [1979] 1 Lloyd's Rep 37. Cf *Rhodes v Forwood* (1876) 1 App Cas 256; *Luxor (Eastbourne) Ltd v Cooper* [1941] AC 108. See Bateson [1960] JBL 187; Burrows (1968) 31 MLR 390.

[82] *Kyprianou v Cyprus Textiles Ltd* [1958] 2 Lloyd's Rep 60.

[83] *Mackay v Dick* (1881) 6 App Cas 256. See also *Metro Meat Ltd v Fares Rural Co Pty Ltd* [1985] 2 Lloyd's Rep 13.

[84] *Colley v Overseas Exporters* [1921] 3 KB 302. Contrast *White and Carter (Councils) Ltd v McGregor* [1962] AC 413, above, p 534 where no co-operation was necessary.

(c) FAILURE OF PERFORMANCE

Failure of performance, whether total or partial, is the most common ground for the discharge of a party by breach. But it is not every failure of performance by one party which entitles the other to be discharged from its own liabilities under it. In order to determine if this is so, it is necessary to ask a number of questions.

(i) Are the promises independent?

In certain circumstances, the obligations entered into by each party may be independent of each other in the sense that neither party can claim to be released from its promise by the failure of the other to perform its part. Put in another way, each party can enforce the obligations undertaken by the other even though it has not performed its own. For example, in the case of leases, a tenant's covenant to pay rent is independent of a landlord's covenant to repair; the tenant cannot withhold payment on the ground that the landlord has failed to repair the premises.[85] Again, a covenant by a husband in a separation deed to pay his wife maintenance has been said to be independent of any covenant on her part, for example not to molest him.[86] And, because of the involvement of third parties in documentary sales, the obligation of a buyer to pay when the shipping documents are tendered has been held to be independent of the seller's obligation to supply goods conforming to the contract.[87] But the tendency of the Courts is against construing a contract in this way unless the parties clearly intend to do so because such a construction means that both parties are inadequately protected from the risk of non-performance by the other.[88] Thus, in a contract for work or services, the obligation to pay would fall due although the work had not been done.

Normally, however, the obligations of each party will be regarded as *interdependent*. For example, an employee who has been wrongfully dismissed is not bound to observe a covenant in restraint of trade.[89] The clearest example of obligations which are dependent on each other arises if the parties agree that the performance of their respective promise shall be simultaneous, or at least that each shall be ready and willing to perform its promise at the same time. Then the obligation to perform each promise is dependent or conditional on this concurrence of readiness and willingness to perform the other; their mutual promises are *concurrent conditions*.

---

[85] *Taylor v Webb* [1937] 2 KB 283.

[86] *Fearon v Earl of Aylesford* (1884) 14 QBD 792, 800. See also *Winstone v Linn* (1823) 1 B & C 460 (contract of apprenticeship). Cf *Ellen v Topp* (1851) 6 Exch 424.

[87] *Gill & Duffus SA v Berger & Co* [1984] AC 382 (cif sale). See also *Vagres Comp. Maritima SA v Nissho-Iwai America Corp, The Karin Vatis* [1988] 2 Lloyd's Rep 330 (terms of contract rendered obligation to pay freight when cargo loaded independent of charterer's obligations).

[88] See also, above, pp 476–82.

[89] *General Billposting Co Ltd v Atkinson* [1909] AC 118. See also *Rock Refrigeration Ltd v Jones* [1997] 1 All ER 1, but cf the doubts of Phillips LJ at 18–19 and note that some primary obligations do continue after discharge, above, p 537, n 28; below, p 554.

Thus section 28 of the Sale of Goods Act 1979 provides that in a contract for the sale of goods:

Unless otherwise agreed, delivery of the goods and payment of the price are concurrent conditions, that is to say, the seller must be ready and willing to give possession of the goods to the buyer in exchange for the price and the buyer must be ready and willing to pay the price in exchange for possession of the goods.

Failure to tender the goods discharges the buyer from its obligation to pay the price; failure to tender the price discharges the seller from its obligation to deliver the goods.

(ii) Is the obligation 'entire' or 'divisible'?

It has already been pointed out in Chapter 12, Performance,[90] that certain obligations are 'entire' in the sense that the liability of one party is dependent upon the complete performance of the obligation by the other. Subject to the doctrine of substantial performance,[91] if A agrees to make a dress for B in return for a promise to pay for the dress on completion, anything less than complete performance by A will release B from her obligation to pay. It is immaterial how the failure to effect complete performance comes about. It may be due to a deliberate abandonment of the contract, to a negligent act or omission, or, as in *Cutter v Powell*,[92] to a simple misfortune occurring without any fault.

Entire obligations are, however, the exception rather than the rule. The obligations in most bilateral contracts are 'divisible' in the sense that the breach of any one or more of them will not necessarily constitute a ground of discharge. The contract may, for example, be a complex one, composed of a number of undertakings differing in character or importance; or it may be a promise to do a number of successive acts; or to do a single act which can be partly or defectively performed. A failure by one party precisely to perform its obligations under the contract will give a right of action in damages to the other; but it will not necessarily discharge the innocent party from the performance of its own obligations under the contract.

(iii) Is the term broken a condition?

Assuming that the obligations in the contract are divisible, and not entire, the question then arises whether the particular term which has been broken is a condition of the contract. From an historical point of view, the right of the innocent party to choose to be treated as discharged was said to turn upon the non-performance of a 'condition precedent' in the contract.[93] Performance by one party of that party's promise or 'covenant' was regarded as a condition precedent

---

[90] See above, p 477.   [91] See above, p 479.   [92] (1795) 6 Term R 320, above, p 477.

[93] *Pordage v Cole* (1669) 1 Wms Saund 319; *Kingston v Preston* (1773) 2 Doug 689, 691. The history of the expression is expounded in *Cehave NV v Bremer Handelsgesellschaft* [1976] QB 44, 57, 72; *United Scientific Holdings Ltd v Burnley BC* [1978] AC 904, 927. See also *Hurst v Bryk* [2002] 1 AC 185, 193 (Lord Millett); Dawson [1981] CLJ 83, 87.

to the liability of the other. The classification of contractual terms is dealt with in Chapter 5 of this book.[94] It was there noted that, today, a term will only be classified as a condition if it has been so categorized by statute (for instance by the Sale of Goods Act 1979) or by judicial decision, or if the parties have so agreed in their contract, either expressly or by implication.[95] Any breach of a condition will entitle the innocent party to choose to be treated as discharged.[96] It was also noted, however, that there has now emerged a category of 'innominate terms', the breach of which will not necessarily produce that effect.[97]

(iv) Does the breach go to 'the root of the contract'?

If the term broken is not a condition, but an innominate term, the right of the innocent party to choose to be treated as discharged from further performance will depend upon the nature and consequences of the breach. Differing terminology has been used by the Courts to describe the test to be applied, the most common being that the breach must go to 'the root of the contract'.[98] It has also been said that the breach must be 'fundamental',[99] that it must 'affect the very substance of the contract'[100] or 'frustrate the commercial purpose of the venture'.[101] The use of these and similar expressions emphasizes that the breach must be far-reaching in its effect in order to justify discharge, taking as the starting-point the benefit the injured party was intended to obtain from performance of the contract.[102] A test which is frequently applied is that stated by Diplock LJ in *Hongkong Fir Shipping Co Ltd v Kawasaki Kisen Kaisha Ltd*:[103] 'Does the occurrence of the event deprive the party who has further undertakings to perform of substantially the whole benefit which it was the intention of the parties as expressed in the contract

---

[94] Above, pp 148–58.   [95] Above, pp 155–8.

[96] Above, p 149. See, eg *Union Eagle Ltd v Golden Achievement Ltd* [1997] AC 514 (vendor entitled to terminate where purchaser tendered price 10 minutes late). In the case of a contract for the sale of goods a non-consumer buyer may not reject goods by reason of a breach of the statutory implied conditions by the seller as to description, quality or conformity with sample, where the breach is so slight that it would be unreasonable for him to reject them: the breach is then to be treated as breach of warranty, rather than breach of condition: Sale of Goods Act 1979, s 15A. See also Supply of Goods and Services Act 1982, ss 5A (non-consumer transfer of goods), 10A (non-consumer hire of goods).

[97] Above, p 154.

[98] *Mersey Steel & Iron Co v Naylor, Benzon & Co* (1884) 9 App Cas 434, 444; *Heyman v Darwins Ltd* [1942] AC 356, 397; *Suisse Atlantique Société d'Armement SA v NV Kolen Centrale* [1967] 1 AC 361, 422; *Cehave NV v Bremer Handelsgesellschaft* [1976] QB 44, 60, 73; *Federal Commerce & Navigation Co Ltd v Molena Alpha Inc* [1979] AC 757, 779.

[99] *Suisse Atlantique Société d'Armement SA v NV Kolen Centrale*, above, n 98, 397, 409–10, 421–2, 431; *Photo Production Ltd v Securicor Transport Ltd* [1980] AC 827, 849 (Lord Diplock).

[100] *Wallis, Son and Wells v Pratt and Haynes* [1910] 2 KB 1003, 1012.

[101] *MacAndrew v Chapple* (1866) LR 1 CP 643, 647, 648; *Jackson v Union Marine Insurance Co* (1874) LR 10 CP 125, 145, 147, 148; *Trade and Transport Inc v Iino Kaiun Kaisha Ltd* [1973] 1 WLR 210, 223.

[102] *Ampurius Nu Homes Holdings Ltd v Telford Homes (Creekside) Ltd* [2013] EWCA Civ 577, [2013] 4 All ER 377 at [51].

[103] [1962] 2 QB 26, 66; above, pp 154–5. See also *Photo Production Ltd v Securicor Transport Ltd* [1980] AC 827, 849.

that he should obtain as the consideration for performing those undertakings?'
In that case:

H chartered to K the *Hongkong Fir* for a period of 24 months, on terms that she was 'in every way fitted for ordinary cargo service'. The vessel was an old one, and by reason of its age needed to be maintained by an experienced, competent, careful, and adequate engine room staff. This H did not provide. The chief engineer was addicted to drink and inefficient, and the engine room complement inadequate, with the result that there were many serious breakdowns in machinery. In the first 7 months of the charter the ship was only eight and a half weeks at sea, the rest of the time being spent in breakdowns and repair to make the ship seaworthy; but this was eventually achieved. K refused to continue with the charterparty.

It was argued on behalf of K that the term as to seaworthiness was a condition of the contract, and that it was therefore entitled as of right to treat itself as discharged. This argument was not accepted by the Court of Appeal.[104] The Court then went on to hold, on the facts, that the delays which had already occurred, and the delay which was likely to occur, as a result of the vessel's unseaworthiness, and the conduct of H in taking steps to remedy the same, were not, when taken together, such as to deprive K of substantially the whole benefit which it was the intention of the parties K should obtain from further use of the ship under charterparty. K had therefore unjustifiably treated the contract as repudiated. It is to be noted that the court considers the position as at the date of purported termination of the contract, but taking into account any steps taken by the guilty party to remedy the accrued breach of contract, as well as likely future events, judged by reference to objective facts as at the date of purported termination.[105]

The same approach has been adopted with respect to contracts to deliver and pay for goods by instalments. If the seller makes defective deliveries in respect of one or more instalments, or the buyer neglects or refuses to take delivery of or pay for one or more instalments, this will not necessarily permit the innocent party to choose to be treated as discharged. The question will arise whether the breach is a repudiation of the whole contract or whether it is a severable breach giving rise to a claim for damages but not to a right to treat the whole contract as repudiated.[106] The breach or breaches may, of course, amount to an express or implied renunciation of the contract.[107] But if they amount only to a failure of performance, they must go to the root of the contract in order to justify discharge. Thus in *Simpson v Crippin*[108] it was agreed that 6,000 to 8,000 tons of coal should be delivered in equal monthly

---

[104] See above, p 155.

[105] *Ampurius Nu Homes Holdings Ltd v Telford Homes (Creekside) Ltd*, above, n 102 at [44] (delay of some months in construction of properties not sufficient to justify termination bearing in mind the ultimate objective was to grant 999-year leases).

[106] Sale of Goods Act 1979, s 31 (non-consumer contracts); see also Consumer Rights Act 2015, s 26 (similar provisions relating to consumer's entitlement to exercise right to reject for defective instalment deliveries).

[107] See above, p 540.   [108] (1872) LR 8 QB 14.

instalments during a period of 12 months, the buyer to send wagons to receive the coal; the buyer sent wagons for only 158 tons in the first month, but the seller was not held entitled to cancel the contract as the breach did not go 'to the whole root and consideration of the agreement'.

On the other hand, in *Honck v Muller*:[109]

H, in October 1879, bought from M 2,000 tons of pig iron to be delivered 'in November, 1879, or equally over November, December and January next at 6*d* per ton extra'. H failed to take delivery of any iron in November, but claimed to have delivery of one-third of the iron in December and one-third in January. M refused, and gave notice that he considered the contract discharged.

H brought an action for breach and failed, as a majority of the Court considered that his failure of performance was so substantial as to discharge M from further liability.[110]

In contracts for the sale and delivery of goods by instalments, the most relevant factors have been said to be, 'first, the ratio quantitatively which the breach bears to the contract as a whole, and secondly the degree of probability or improbability that such a breach will be repeated'.[111] The importance of the second factor was clearly emphasized by Bigham J in *Millar's Karri and Jarrah Co v Weddel*:[112]

If the breach is of such a kind, or takes place in such circumstances as reasonably to lead to the inference that similar breaches will be committed in relation to subsequent deliveries, the whole contract may there and then be regarded as repudiated and may be rescinded. If, for instance, a buyer fails to pay for one delivery in such circumstances as to lead to the inference that he will not be able to pay for subsequent deliveries; or if a seller delivers goods differing from the requirements of the contract, and does so in such circumstances as to lead to the inference that he cannot, or will not, deliver any other kind of goods in the future, the other contracting party will be under no obligation to wait to see what may happen; he can at once cancel the contract and rid himself of the difficulty.

It follows that, the further the parties have proceeded with the due performance of a contract, the less likely it is that one party will be able to claim that it has been discharged by a single breach.[113]

The right of discharge therefore depends on the answer to this question: Does the breach go so far to the root of the contract as to entitle the injured party to say, 'I have lost all that I cared to obtain under this contract; further performance cannot make good the prior default'?[114]

---

[109] (1881) 7 QBD 92. See also *Munro & Co Ltd v Meyer* [1930] 2 KB 312 (nearly half of goods seriously adulterated).
[110] *Maple Flock Co Ltd v Universal Furniture Products (Wembley) Ltd* [1934] 1 KB 148, 157 (Lord Hewart CJ).
[111] *Ibid.*   [112] (1909) 100 LT 128, 129.   [113] *Cornwall v Henson* [1900] 2 Ch 298, 304.
[114] Cited with approval in *Alkok v Grymek* (1966) 56 DLR (2d) 393 (Canada).

(v) Termination clauses

A contract may contain a clause setting out the circumstances and conditions upon which one party shall have the right to terminate by reason of the other party's breach. Such a clause may make clear that a particular term is a condition of the contract so that the rules of termination for breach of condition, discussed above, will then apply.[115] But the clause may be drafted more generally to provide a remedial regime (including the right for the innocent party to terminate the contract) for breach of contract in specified circumstances,[116] and it may refer to a standard of breach which is different from that which gives rise to the right to terminate at common law—such as where the breach is 'material', which has been held to cover breaches which are less than 'fundamental', but where it is more than trivial or minimal.[117] The party seeking to rely on such a clause must establish strictly that the clause entitles it to terminate in relation to the breach which has occurred,[118] and the Courts will not hold that the common law right to terminate for repudiatory breach has been excluded by an express termination clause without clear words showing such an intention.[119] Moreover, the exercise of the right to terminate under an express termination clause will not normally constitute affirmation of the contract so as to deprive the innocent party of the right to claim its remedies for breach at common law, at least where the clause provides a right to terminate at common law which corresponds to a right under the general law (eg because the breach goes to the root of the contract).[120]

3. CONSEQUENCES OF DISCHARGE

(a) RELEASE FROM FUTURE OBLIGATIONS

An innocent party who is entitled to, and does, choose to be treated as discharged by the other party's breach, is thereby released from further performance of those future obligations which remain still to be performed.[121] After such discharge the innocent party is not bound to accept, or pay for, any further performance by the party in breach. The duty of the party in default to perform future unperformed obligations likewise comes to an end, as does that party's right to perform them.

---

[115] *Union Eagle Ltd v Golden Achievement Ltd* [1997] AC 514.

[116] *Lombard North Central plc v Butterworth* [1987] QB 527;

[117] *Dalkia Utilities Services plc v Celtech International Ltd* [2006] EWHC 63 (Comm), [2006] 1 Lloyd's Rep 599.

[118] Cf *Rice v Great Yarmouth BC* (2001) 3 LGLR 4 (clause in long-term contract involving substantial investment, which allowed the defendant to terminate for 'a breach of any of the [claimant's] obligations' was construed as applying only to repudiatory breach); criticized by Whittaker, in Burrows and Peel (eds), *Contract Terms* (2007) 253.

[119] *Dalkia Utilities Services plc v Celtech International Ltd*, above, n 117; *Stocznia Gdynia SA v Gearbulk Holdings Ltd* [2009] EWCA Civ 75, [2010] QB 27 at [23].

[120] *Stocznia Gdynia SA v Gearbulk Holdings Ltd*, above, n 119 at [44].

[121] See Shea (1979) 42 MLR 623; Beatson (1981) 97 LQR 389; Rose (1981) 34 CLP 235; Law Com No 121, *Pecuniary Restitution on Breach of Contract* (1983).

(b) CONTRACT NOT RESCINDED *AB INITIO*

In the terminology employed in many of the cases, these consequences are often described as a 'rescission' of the contract; or it is stated that the contract is 'terminated' or 'put an end to' by the breach. But these expressions are somewhat misleading:

To say that the contract is rescinded or has come to an end or has ceased to exist may in individual cases convey the truth with sufficient accuracy, but the fuller expression that the injured party is thereby absolved from future performance of his obligations under the contract is a more exact description of the position. Strictly speaking, to say that on acceptance of the renunciation of the contract the contract is rescinded is incorrect.[122]

Certainly, this so-called rescission is quite different from rescission *ab initio*, such as may arise, for example, in cases of misrepresentation.[123] The contract is not set aside as from the beginning.

(c) ACCRUED OBLIGATIONS REMAIN

Although both parties are discharged from further performance of their obligations, rights are not divested which have already been unconditionally acquired. Rights and obligations which arise from the partial execution of the contract and causes of action which have accrued from its breach alike continue unaffected.[124] So, for instance, if a time charterparty of a ship is repudiated by the charterer, the shipowner can recover arrears of hire charges due but unpaid up to the date of the shipowner's acceptance of the repudiation.[125] Again, if building work is to be paid for by instalments, the builder can sue for any instalment due but unpaid at the time of discharge.[126]

It makes no difference in this respect whether the accrued obligation is in favour of the innocent or the guilty party. An employee who repudiates a contract of employment can nevertheless sue for wages earned before that time[127] and, following termination of a partnership agreement, it seems that the innocent partner remains liable for the accrued liabilities of the partnership, provided these were incurred when the innocent party was a partner.[128]

---

[122] *Heyman v Darwins Ltd* [1942] AC 356, 399 (Lord Porter). This statement was unanimously approved by the House of Lords in *Johnson v Agnew* [1980] AC 367. See also *Bank of Boston Connecticut v European Grain and Shipping Ltd* [1989] AC 1056, 1098–9 and *State Trading Corp of India Ltd v M Golodetz Ltd* [1989] 2 Lloyd's Rep 277, 286; *Howard-Jones v Tate* [2011] EWCA Civ 1330, [2012] 1 P & CR 11 at [15], [29].

[123] *Johnson v Agnew*, above, n 122, 393.

[124] *McDonald v Dennys Lascelles Ltd* (1933) 48 CLR 457, 476 (Dixon J) (Australia). But, once the contract has been discharged, equitable relief, eg an injunction, cannot be granted: *Walker v Standard Chartered Bank plc* [1992] BCLC 535.

[125] *Leslie Shipping Co v Welstead* [1921] 3 KB 420. See also *Chatterton v Maclean* [1951] 1 All ER 561 (hire-purchase).

[126] *Hyundai Heavy Industries Co Ltd v Papadopoulos* [1980] 1 WLR 1129 (HL).

[127] *Taylor v Laird* (1856) 25 LJ Ex 29. Cf Apportionment Act 1870, s 2.

[128] *Hurst v Bryk* [2002] 1 AC 185. See also Partnership Act 1890, s 9.

Admittedly, if money has been paid by one party to the other under the contract, and the consideration for the payment has wholly failed, the money may be recoverable in unjust enrichment by an action for money had and received.[129] But, in principle, accrued liabilities remain enforceable despite the discharge. Moreover, as we have seen,[130] only the primary obligations of the parties as a general rule come to an end. The primary obligations of the party in default are then replaced by a secondary obligation to pay compensation to the injured party for the breach. Note, however, certain primary obligations will survive discharge and continue to be enforceable. The continued enforcement of such obligations simply reflects the presumed intention of the parties. The best examples of obligations that survive are arbitration clauses and dispute resolution mechanisms.[131] In addition, there are clauses that may only come into operation upon discharge such as certain liquidated damages clauses. It has also been held that an obligation to pay a retainer for a specified period[132] and an agent's duty to provide records to its principal survive discharge.[133]

(d) RESTITUTIONARY CLAIMS

With respect to payments not yet due at the time of discharge, for example, for goods supplied or for services rendered under the contract, the innocent party can sue in unjust enrichment for restitution in the form of a reasonable price for the goods supplied (quantum valebat) or reasonable remuneration for the services rendered (quantum meruit),[134] or include them in his claim for damages for breach. Whether the guilty party has any claim will depend on whether the contract is entire or divisible. If it is entire, in principle no claim is possible.[135] But if it is divisible, the guilty party may be entitled to claim in respect of performance completed, subject to a counterclaim for damages by the innocent party in respect of loss suffered by the breach.

4. LOSS OF THE RIGHT OF DISCHARGE

The right of discharge may be lost by waiver, affirmation, acceptance, and operation of law. In addition, a party may be estopped from claiming to be entitled to treat a contract as discharged. This has been dealt with earlier in this book.[136]

---

[129] See below, p 621. [130] See above, p 552. [131] *Heyman v Darwins Ltd* [1942] AC 356.
[132] *Duffen v Frabo SpA* [2000] 1 Lloyd's Rep 180.
[133] *Yasuda Fire & Marine Insurance Co of Europe Ltd v Orion Marine Insurance Underwriting Agency Ltd* [1995] QB 174.
[134] See below, p 628. [135] See above, pp 476–8. But see below, p 623.
[136] See above, pp 159–60, 490–4.

FURTHER READING

SMITH, 'Anticipatory Breach of Contract' in Lomnicka and Morse (eds), *Contemporary Issues in Commercial Law* (London: Sweet & Maxwell, 1997) 175

WHITTAKER, 'Termination Clauses' in Burrows and Peel (eds), *Contract Terms* (Oxford: Oxford University Press, 2007) 253

LIU, 'The *White &Carter* Principle: A Restatement' (2011) 74 MLR 171

16

DISCHARGE BY
OPERATION OF LAW

There are rules of law which, operating upon certain sets of circumstances, will bring about the discharge of a contract, and these we will briefly consider.

1. MERGER

(a) ACCEPTANCE OF HIGHER SECURITY

If a higher security is accepted in place of a lower, the security which in the eye of the law is inferior in operative power,[1] in the absence of a contrary intention manifested by the parties, merges and is extinguished in the higher.

Thus, if two parties to a simple contract embody its contents in a deed which they both execute, the simple contract is thereby discharged. This most often happens in the case of a contract for the sale of land, the written agreement being merged and extinguished in the subsequent conveyance or transfer of the land which is executed as a deed.[2]

The rules governing this process may thus be summarized:

(1) The later security must be of higher efficacy than that which it is sought to replace. A negotiable instrument is not a higher security for the purposes of this rule,[3] although the giving of a negotiable instrument may constitute payment of a debt.[4]

(2) The subject-matter of the two securities must be the same, that is, they must secure the same obligation and be made between the same parties.[5]

---

[1] *Price v Moulton* (1851) 10 CB 561.
[2] *Knight Sugar Co Ltd v Alberta Ry and Irrigation Co* [1938] 1 All ER 266, 269–70. Cf *Tito v Waddell (No 2)* [1977] Ch 106, 284 (contrary intention).
[3] *Drake v Mitchell* (1803) 3 East 251.   [4] See above, p 471.
[5] *Twopenny v Young* (1824) 3 B & C 208; *Holmes v Bell* (1841) 3 M & G 213; *Hissett v Reading Roofing Co Ltd* [1969] 1 WLR 1757.

(b) RIGHTS VESTING IN SAME PERSON

The rights and liabilities under a contract are also extinguished if they become vested by assignment or otherwise in the same person and in the same right, for it is not possible to contract with oneself. So where a tenant for a term of years retains the lease and acquires the reversion, the lease merges in the reversion and is destroyed.[6] Similarly, a bill of exchange is discharged if the acceptor is or becomes the holder of it at or after its maturity in his own right.[7]

2. DISCHARGE BY JUDGMENT OF A COURT

A right of action arising from breach of contract is discharged by the judgment of a Court of Record[8] in the claimant's favour for the same demand. The right is thereby merged in the more solemn form of obligation called a Contract of Record. The result of legal proceedings taken upon a broken contract may be summarized as follows:

(a) EFFECT OF BRINGING ACTION

The bringing of an action has not itself any effect in discharging the right to bring the action. Another action may be brought for the same cause, although proceedings in such an action would, if they were merely vexatious, be struck out or stayed upon application to the summary jurisdiction of the Court.[9]

(b) EFFECT OF JUDGMENT FOR CLAIMANT

But when judgment is given in the claimant's favour, the cause of action is merged into matter of record, and only the judgment can be enforced.[10] Further, 'damages resulting from one and the same cause of action must be assessed and recovered once for all',[11] so that successive judgments cannot be obtained for different breaches of a single undertaking.[12]

---

[6] *Capital and Countries Bank Ltd v Rhodes* [1903] 1 Ch 631. By a rule of equity, however, the intentions of the parties may operate to prevent the occurrence of such merger. Under the provisions of the Law of Property Act 1925, s 185 the equitable rule now prevails in all cases.

[7] Bills of Exchange Act 1882, s 61.

[8] The county court is a court of record: County Courts Act 1984, s A1, added by Crime and Courts Act 2013, s 17(1).

[9] CPR rr 3.4(2), and 3.1(2)(f); cf County Courts Act 1984, s 35.

[10] *Kendall v Hamilton* (1879) 4 App Cas 504.

[11] *Brunsden v Humphrey* (1884) 14 QBD 141, 147 (Bowen LJ); *Furness, Withy & Co Ltd v Hall Ltd* (1909) 25 TLR 233.

[12] *Conquer v Boot* [1928] 2 KB 336. Cf *Overstone Ltd v Shipway* [1962] 1 WLR 117 (separate causes of action).

(c) EFFECT OF JUDGMENT FOR DEFENDANT

A person may be estopped from re-litigating in subsequent proceedings a cause of action in respect of which judgment was given against that person in earlier proceedings, or an issue raised and determined against him or her in such proceedings.[13] But, for such an estoppel to arise, certain conditions must be satisfied:[14] first, there must have been a final judgment on the merits[15] in the earlier proceedings by a Court of competent jurisdiction;[16] secondly, there must be identity of parties in the two sets of proceedings;[17] thirdly, there must be identity of subject-matter in the two proceedings.[18] Cause of action and issue estoppel are based upon the public interest in finality of litigation.[19]

3. ALTERATION OR CANCELLATION OF A WRITTEN INSTRUMENT

(a) RULE AS TO ALTERATION

If a deed or contract in writing is altered by addition or erasure, it is discharged, except as against a party making or assenting to the alteration, for 'no man shall be permitted to take the chance of committing a fraud, without running any risk of losing by the event, when it is detected'.[20]

This principle is subject to the following rules:

(1) The alteration must be made deliberately by the promisee or by one acting with the promisee's consent;[21] and even an alteration by a stranger while the instrument is in the custody of the promisee will have the same effect.[22] Earlier

---

[13] *Palmer v Temple* (1839) 9 A & E 508. This is also known as estoppel *per rem judicatam* which encompasses both cause of action estoppel and issue estoppel: *Thoday v Thoday* [1964] P 181, 197–8.

[14] *Carl Zeiss Stiftung v Rayner & Keeler Ltd (No 2)* [1967] 1 AC 853, 909, 910.

[15] *Hines v Birkbeck College (No 2)* [1992] Ch 33.

[16] *Midland Bank Trust Co Ltd v Green* [1980] Ch 590; *Hines v Birkbeck College (No 2)* [1992] Ch 33; *The European Gateway* [1987] QB 206.

[17] *Gleeson v J Wippell & Co Ltd* [1977] 1 WLR 510; *North West Water Ltd v Binnie & Partners* [1990] 3 All ER 547; *House of Spring Gardens Ltd v Waite* [1991] 1 QB 241, 252; *Talbot v Berkshire CC* [1994] QB 290, 296–7. Cf *Marginson v Blackburn BC* [1939] 2 KB 426; *C (a minor) v Hackney LBC* [1996] 1 WLR 789.

[18] *Haystead v Commissioner of Taxation* [1926] AC 155.

[19] *Republic of India v India Steamship Co Ltd* [1993] AC 410, 415; *ibid (No 2)* [1998] AC 878, 912; *Thrasyvoulou v Secretary of State for the Environment* [1990] 2 AC 273, 289. While a foreign judgment does not operate as a merger, under the Civil Jurisdiction and Judgments Act 1982, s 34, further proceedings are barred unless waived: [1993] AC 410, 423–4.

[20] *Master v Miller* (1791) 4 Term Rep 320, 329 (Lord Kenyon CJ).

[21] *Pattinson v Luckley* (1875) LR 10 Ex 330; *Hongkong & Shanghai Banking Corporation v Lo Lee Shi* [1928] AC 181. Cf *Co-operative Bank v Tipper* [1996] 4 All ER 366, 371 (pencilled alteration insufficient).

[22] *Pigot's Case* (1614) 11 Co Rep 26b; *Davidson v Cooper* (1844) 13 M & W 343.

editions of this book stated that this responsibility for the acts of officious burglars, could not be supported, but although described as 'a harsh and ancient common law doctrine', it is good law.[23]

(2) The alteration must be made without the consent of the other party, else it would operate as a new agreement.

(3) The alteration must be made in a material part. What amounts to a material alteration necessarily depends upon the character of the instrument, and it is possible for the character of an instrument to be affected by an alteration which does not touch the contractual rights set forth in it. In most cases, a material alteration will be one which imposes a greater liability on the promisor.[24]

(4) If the alteration is made not in the instrument which itself creates obligations, but in another written instrument designed to carry out the contract, or some aspect of it, the alteration does not automatically render the underlying transaction void. However, making a material alteration to such an instrument may itself amount to conduct which entitles the other party to treat it as discharged.[25]

(b) BILLS OF EXCHANGE

Section 64 of the Bills of Exchange Act 1882 provides that a bill shall not be avoided as against holder in due course, though it has been materially altered, if the alteration is not apparent, and the holder may enforce payment of it according to its original tenor.

(c) CANCELLATION AND LOSS

Intentional cancellation of a written instrument by the promisee also discharges the obligation, but the loss of the instrument only affects the rights of the parties insofar as it may occasion a difficulty of proof. In the case of bills of exchange and promissory notes, if the holder of the instrument loses it, *he* may require the drawer to give him another bill upon his giving an indemnity against possible claims.[26]

[23] *Goss v Chilcott* [1996] AC 788; *Co-operative Bank v Tipper*, above, n 21, 369. But the nullifying operation is confined to cases falling strictly within its ambit: *Farrow Mortgage Services Pty Ltd v Slade* (1996) 38 NSWLR 636, 640 (Australia).
[24] On the different position of alterations to bank notes, see *Suffell v Bank of England* (1882) 9 QBD 555.
[25] *Habibsons Bank Ltd v Standard Chartered Bank (Hong Kong) Ltd* [2010] EWCA Civ 1335, [2011] QB 943 at [34].
[26] Bills of Exchange Act 1882, s 69.

4. BANKRUPTCY

A contract is not discharged by bankruptcy of one of the parties to it;[27] but it effects a statutory release from debts and liabilities provable under the bankruptcy, when the bankrupt has obtained from the Court an order of discharge. It is sufficient to call attention to this mode of discharge, without entering into a discussion of the nature and effects of bankruptcy, or the provisions of the Insolvency Act 1986.

---

[27] *Re Edwards, ex p Chalmers* (1873) LR 8 Ch App 289; see below, p 713.

PART 5

REMEDIES FOR BREACH OF CONTRACT

17

DAMAGES

1. DAMAGES AND OTHER REMEDIES FOR BREACH OF CONTRACT

Where a party performing a contract does not do so to the standard required by the contract[1] or within the timeframe set, that party will breach the contract. Chapter 15 sets out the rules which govern the discharge of a contract by breach, and it now remains to consider the various remedies which are available apart from the entitlement of the innocent party in an appropriate case to be treated as discharged from further performance.

These remedies fall under three heads:[2]

(1) Every breach of contract entitles the injured party to damages. Damages are primarily concerned to compensate the injured party for the loss he or she has suffered.

(2) In certain circumstances the injured party may obtain the enforcement of the promise by an order for specific performance of the contract, an injunction to restrain its breach or for the payment of the sum due under the contract.

(3) In certain circumstances the parties to a contract that has been broken may be entitled to the return of money paid or restitution of the value of services rendered or goods transferred. These are restitutionary remedies for the independent cause of action of unjust enrichment. They are not remedies for the breach of contract. Exceptionally an injured party may be granted an award reflecting the gain made by the contract-breaker from the breach of contract. This is a restitutionary remedy for the breach of contract.

This and the following two chapters consider each of these remedies in turn, and a further chapter examines how they may be barred by lapse of time.

---

[1] The standard may be strict or may require only the exercise of reasonable care, above p 465.

[2] See Burrows, *Remedies for Torts and Breach of Contract* (3rd edn, 2004); Harris, Campbell, and Halson, *Remedies in Contract and Tort* (2nd edn, 2002); Treitel, *Remedies for Breach of Contract* (1988); Rowan, *Remedies for Breach of Contract* (2012).

It will be seen that the development of the law has been marked by a broadening approach to the concept of loss and thus in its ability to protect the claimant's interest in the performance by the other party of the contractual obligations. Except in the case of a debt, the repayment of which may be specifically enforced at common law by an award of the agreed sum, the common law remedy for breach of a contractual promise is that of damages. There has been increased sophistication in identifying and calculating economic interests and in recognizing intangible interests of no economic value but for which a contractor has paid, and in reflecting these in awards of damages. If the claimant's interest in the performance of the contractual obligations cannot adequately be protected by an award of damages, there has been greater willingness to order that the contract be specifically performed where this is possible and practicable.

In certain cases, for example professional negligence cases, there will be overlapping claims for damages in contract and in tort. The rules discussed in this section only apply to contractual damages. However, it should be borne in mind that in cases of overlap damages within the law of tort may present an alternative, and sometimes preferable, remedy.[3]

2. COMPENSATORY NATURE OF DAMAGES

(a) COMPENSATION FOR LOSS

Damages for breach of contract are normally designed to compensate for the damage, loss, or injury the claimant has suffered through that breach. A claimant who has not, in fact, suffered any loss by reason of the breach, is nevertheless entitled to a verdict, but the damages recoverable will be purely nominal (usually £2–£10).

Whereas physical losses are the most frequent subject of actions in tort, commercial (ie financial) losses are the most frequent subject of actions for breach of contract. However, as will be seen, damages for breach of contract are not necessarily limited to compensation of financial loss alone. Damages may also be awarded in contract to compensate for physical damage to the person or property, for the loss of an attribute of property (such as comfort or privacy) even where this has not affected its value, for inconvenience, and, in certain circumstances, for disappointment.

(b) DAMAGES ARE NOT PUNITIVE

Damages for breach of contract are given to compensate for loss suffered by the innocent party and not to punish the contract-breaker. 'Punitive' or 'exemplary' damages have no place in the law of contract.[4] Contractual damages cannot

---

[3] Above, p 26. See, eg, *Henderson v Merrett Syndicates Ltd* [1995] 2 AC 145; *Midland Bank Trust Co Ltd v Hett Stubbs & Kemp* [1979] Ch 384 (limitation).

[4] They may be recoverable in certain circumstances in tort: see *Rookes v Barnard* [1964] AC 1129, 1221; *Broome v Cassell & Co Ltd* [1972] AC 1027; *Kuddus v Chief Constable of Leicestershire Constabulary*

be used to punish, however outrageous the defendant's conduct. In *Addis v Gramophone Co Ltd*:[5]

A was employed by G as manager of their business in Calcutta at a salary together with a commission on trade done. G wrongfully dismissed A without giving him the required 6 months' notice.

The House of Lords held that, although A might recover a sum representing his salary for the period of notice and the commission he would have earned during that period, his employers were not to be penalized in damages for the humiliating and oppressive manner in which they had dismissed him.[6]

(c) DIFFICULTY OF ASSESSMENT NO BAR

Difficulty in assessing damages does not disentitle a claimant from having an attempt made to assess them, unless they depend on entirely speculative possibilities. This can be seen from the case of *Simpson v London and North Western Railway Company*,[7] where Simpson was deprived of the opportunity of exhibiting his products at an agricultural show. Although the ascertainment of damages was difficult, it was held that this was no reason for not giving any damages at all. Again, in *Chaplin v Hicks*,[8] a candidate in a beauty competition, who had successfully passed the earlier stages of the competition, was, in breach of contract, not allowed to compete in the later stages with 49 others from whom 12 winners were to be chosen. She was awarded substantial damages for the loss of the chance of being successful of which she had been wrongfully deprived. Similar considerations may affect the measure of damages in the cases where an offer to consider all conforming tenders is held to give rise to an enforceable obligation.[9] The value of the chance depends upon the number and type of contingencies upon which it depends.[10]

[2001] UKHL 29, [2002] 2 AC 122. For discussion of restitutionary damages in cases of 'cynical' breach, see below, pp 632–3, 637.

[5] [1909] AC 488, followed on this point but not others by *Malik v Bank of Credit & Commerce International SA* [1998] 1 AC 20, 50–1. See also *Co-operative Insurance Society Ltd v Argyll Stores (Holdings) Ltd* [1998] 1 AC 1, 15. Cf McBride (1995) 24 Anglo-American L Rev 369 and Cunnington (2006) 26 LS 369 for arguments that punitive damages should be available for breach of contract.

[6] See also *Malik v Bank of Credit & Commerce International SA* [1998] 1 AC 20, 51; *Johnson v Unisys Ltd* [1999] 1 All ER 854, 861, but note that the manner and circumstances of a dismissal may increase the claimant's financial loss: see below, p 569.

[7] (1876) 1 QBD 274.

[8] [1911] 2 KB 786. See also *Allied Maples Group v Simmons & Simmons* [1995] 1 WLR 1602; *Flame SA v Glory Wealth Shipping PTE Ltd, The Glory Wealth* [2013] EWHC 3153 (Comm), [2014] QB 1080 (both cases illustrating, in very different contexts, that uncertainty as to what the claimant, as opposed to a third party, would have done should be decided in an all-or-nothing way by applying a balance of probabilities test).

[9] *Blackpool and Fylde Aero Club Ltd v Blackpool BC* [1990] 1 WLR 1195, above, p 38, where the measure of damages was not considered.

[10] *Ministry of Defence v Wheeler* [1998] 1 WLR 637.

(d) THE DATE FOR ASSESSMENT

The date for the assessment of damages is normally thought to be the date when the cause of action arose: that is, the date of the breach of contract.[11] However, in some recent cases a more flexible approach has been adopted, in which a later date for assessment has been taken so as to enable compensation to be more accurately calculated (subject to not infringing the mitigation principle).[12] In *Golden Strait Corporation v Nippon Yusen Kubishika Kaisha, The Golden Victory:*[13]

After three years of a seven-year charterparty there was a repudiatory breach by the charterers. Fifteen months later, the Iraq war broke out which, under a war clause, would have entitled the charterers to terminate the contract in any event and it was assumed that, had the contract still been on foot, they would have done so.

The question that arose was whether damages should be assessed as at the date of breach on the basis of the value of a four-year remaining charterparty ignoring the outbreak of war, or as at the date of trial taking into account the known outbreak of war and hence on the basis of only a fifteen-month remaining charterparty. By a 3–2 majority (Lord Bingham and Lord Walker dissenting) it was held that damages should be assessed on the second basis. This is justified as more precisely measuring the claimant's known loss in a situation where the mitigation principle was essentially irrelevant because the claimant had not attempted to mitigate its loss by concluding a substitute charterparty for the four-year period. The minority preferred to adhere to the date of breach rule as promoting commercial certainty.

(e) COMPENSATION FOR INCONVENIENCE OR MENTAL DISTRESS

Contractual damages may be recovered for substantial physical inconvenience or discomfort arising from a breach. For example, where a family were transported by a railway company to the wrong station, with the result that they had to walk several miles home on a drizzling wet night,[14] and where a man, with his wife and child, was forced to live for two years in discomfort with his wife's parents owing to the failure of

---

[11] See, eg, *Dodd Properties (Kent) v Canterbury City Council* [1980] AC 174.

[12] See below pp 587–8.

[13] [2007] UKHL 12, [2007] 2 AC 353. The decision was emphatically upheld in *Bunge SA v Nidera BV* [2015] UKSC 43, [2015] 3 All ER 1082. The flawed view of some academics that the decision was wrong and that the minority was correct (see, eg, Stevens, 'Damages and the Right to Performance: *A Golden Victory* or Not?' in Neyers, Bronaugh, and Pitel (eds), *Exploring Contract Law* (2009) 171–98) can therefore be put to one side; as can the suggestion that it might not apply to cases where the contract provides for a single act of performance in contrast to several successive acts. See also, eg, the earlier case of *Johnson v Agnew* [1980] AC 367, which was applied in *Hooper v Oates* [2013] EWCA Civ 91, [2014] Ch 287. See generally Dyson and Kramer (2014) 130 LQR 259.

[14] *Hobbs v L & SW Ry* (1875) LR 10 QB 111.

a solicitor to take any effective steps to obtain possession of a house,[15] damages for the physical inconvenience were recovered.

Damages are not generally recoverable for 'any distress, frustration, anxiety, displeasure, vexation, tension or aggravation' caused by the breach even where it was in the contemplation of the parties that the breach would expose the parties to distress.[16] The reparation of such non-pecuniary, non-physical harm poses problems of incommensurability and subjectivity, and difficulties of proof.

There are, however, two exceptions to the general rule. Damages for mental distress can be awarded where the claimant's distress is directly consequential on physical inconvenience caused by the breach of contract.[17] They can also be awarded where an important purpose of the contract is to provide enjoyment or peace of mind, or to prevent distress.[18] In *Jarvis v Swans Tours Ltd*:[19]

J, a solicitor, was entitled to two weeks' paid holiday a year and booked with S Tours a 15-day Christmas winter sports holiday at a hotel in Switzerland. He did so on the faith of S's brochure which described the holiday as a 'house-party', and promised a variety of entertainments including excellent skiing, a yodeller evening, a bar, and afternoon tea and cakes. In the first week there were only 13 people at the hotel and in the second week he was entirely alone. The promised entertainments proved to be wholly inferior in quality in comparison with the description in the brochure.

The Court of Appeal held that J was entitled to damages consisting of the amount which he had paid for the holiday and an additional sum of some £60 to compensate him for the disappointment he had suffered. Similarly, damages were awarded for anxiety and distress suffered by a woman whose solicitors failed to take prompt and effective measures against a man who was pestering her,[20] by a

---

[15] *Bailey v Bullock* [1950] 2 All ER 1167. Noise can amount to physical inconvenience: *Farley v Skinner* [2001] UKHL 49, [2002] 2 AC 732 at [30], [60].

[16] *Watts v Morrow* [1991] 1 WLR 1421, 1445 (Bingham LJ). See also *Bliss v SE Thames RHA* [1987] ICR 700 (contract of employment); *Hayes v James & Charles Dodd* [1990] 2 All ER 815 (solicitor's contract to provide professional services); *Branchett v Beaney* [1992] 3 All ER 910 (covenant for quiet enjoyment of property); *Johnson v Gore Wood & Co* [2002] 2 AC 1 (claim for professional negligence against solicitor).

[17] *Perry v Sidney Phillips & Son* [1982] 1 WLR 1297 (anxiety and distress of living in a house in poor condition which had been bought in reliance on negligence in breach of contract in a surveyor's report); *Calabar Properties v Stitcher* [1984] 1 WLR 287 (unpleasantness of living in deteriorating premises until they became uninhabitable because of landlord's delay in repairing). But such damages should be 'modest': *Watts v Morrow* [1991] 1 WLR 1421, 1443, 1445. Cf Lord Cooke (dissenting) in *Johnson v Gore Wood & Co* [2002] 2 AC 1, 49 (distress due to poverty and changed way of life akin to that due to physical loss).

[18] *Ruxley Electronics & Constructions Ltd. v Forsyth* [1996] AC 344, 374 (Lord Lloyd) (cf Lord Mustill, *ibid*, 360–1); *Farley v Skinner* [2001] UKHL 49, [2002] 2 AC 732 at [28]; *Johnson v Gore Wood & Co* [2002] 2 AC 1, 37 (Lord Bingham). Lord Cooke, *ibid*, 49, considered that contracts for status such as membership of a trade union or club are also included.

[19] [1973] QB 233. See also *Jackson v Horizon Holidays Ltd* [1975] 1 WLR 1468. For the quantum of mental distress damages, see *Milner v Carnival plc* [2010] EWCA Civ 389, [2010] 3 All ER 701.

[20] *Heywood v Wellers* [1976] QB 446; *McLeish v Amoo-Gottfried & Co* The Times, 13 October 1995 (solicitor's negligence led to wrongful conviction). Cf *Cook v Swinfen* [1967] 1 WLR 457, 461; *Hayes v James & Charles Dodd* [1990] 2 All ER 815.

woman whose solicitors had failed to obtain proper financial relief in matrimonial proceedings,[21] by a bride when a photographer failed to keep his promise to be present and take photographs at her wedding,[22] and by children when a cemetery owner broke its contract to grant exclusive burial rights in a plot adjacent to that in which their parents were buried.[23] Such damages are compensatory in nature and are not designed to inflict retribution on the defendant for inflicting the harm.

Originally this exception only applied if 'the sole' object of the contract was to provide enjoyment or peace of mind, or to prevent distress.[24] Accordingly, a contract with an architect to design a house for a couple who contemplated that it would be their 'dream home' did not qualify.[25] This meant that the non-economic purposes of a party to a contract would be protected where they were the only purposes but would not be where there were also economic purposes, and to this extent part of the purposes of the contract were unenforceable.[26] It has, however, been held in *Farley v Skinner* that it suffices that the provision of peace of mind, or the prevention of distress is 'an important object' of the contract.[27] In that case:

F, a prospective purchaser of a house who wanted peace and quiet, employed a surveyor to report on the property and he was specifically requested to advise on whether the house might be affected by aircraft noise. The surveyor advised that it was unlikely that the property would suffer greatly from aircraft noise and F bought the house.[28] In fact, the house was near a navigation beacon used by aircraft waiting to land at Gatwick Airport and was substantially affected by noise.

It was held by the House of Lords that F was entitled to damages for the significant interference with his enjoyment of the property caused by the noise. But it was made clear that a contract for an ordinary survey report on a house would not fall within the exception: what made this case different was the specific request relating to the noise.

(f) LOSS OF REPUTATION

Although damages cannot be recovered in a contractual action for injury to reputation *per se*,[29] they may be where the loss of reputation caused by the

---

[21] *Dickinson v James Alexander & Co* (1990) 20 FLR 137.

[22] *Diesen v Samson* 1971 SLT (Sh Ct) 49.   [23] *Reed v Madon* [1989] Ch 408.

[24] *Watts v Morrow* [1991] 1 WLR 1421, 1445 (Bingham LJ).

[25] *Knott v Bolton* (1995) 45 Con LR 127 (overruled by *Farley v Skinner*).

[26] Capper (2000) 116 LQR 553, approved in *Farley v Skinner* [2001] UKHL 49, [2002] 2 AC 732 at [24], [51].

[27] *Farley v Skinner* [2001] UKHL 49, [2002] 2 AC 732. See also *Hamilton Jones v David & Snape* [2003] EWHC 3147 (Ch), [2004] 1 All ER 657 (mental distress damages awarded for loss of custody of claimant's children consequent on defendant solicitor's negligent failure to renew 'agency notifications' of the risk of the children being taken out of the jurisdiction by the claimant's former husband).

[28] The price F paid for the house coincided with its market value taking into account aircraft noise, so he had no claim for diminution of value.

[29] *Addis v Gramophone Co Ltd* [1909] AC 488.

breach of contract causes financial loss. In *Malik v Bank of Credit & Commerce International SA:*[30]

M and other relatively senior employees of BCCI, were made redundant following the bank's insolvency. They claimed that they were unable thereafter to obtain employment in the financial services industry because of the stigma attached to former employees of BCCI, and sought substantial compensation for this handicap in the labour market. For the purposes of the proceedings it was assumed that BCCI had carried on its business in a corrupt and dishonest manner, that this had become widely known, that M and the other employees were innocent of any involvement, were at a handicap in the labour market because of the stigma, and had suffered financial loss as a result.

The House of Lords held that contracts of employment contained an implied term of mutual trust and confidence so that the defendant was under an implied obligation not to carry on a dishonest or corrupt business, and that, in principle, financial loss in respect of damage to reputation caused by breach of this term is recoverable in a contractual action. It will, however, often be difficult to prove a handicap on the labour market.

The effect of this decision is to establish that financial loss resulting from a loss of reputation caused by a breach of contract is recoverable subject to standard contractual principles. The contrary statements in *Addis v Gramophone Co Ltd*[31] were explained in *Malik*'s case on the basis that the earlier case was decided before the development of the implied obligation of mutual trust and confidence so that the loss of reputation there had not been caused by a relevant breach of contract.[32] Having said that, it has been established that a claim for wrongful dismissal will still not trigger damages for loss of reputation.[33] This is, however, not because *Addis* is regarded as correctly reasoned but rather because the Courts are anxious not to undermine the statutory regime—and the levels of compensation laid down—for unfair dismissal.

Cases previously regarded as exceptional can now be seen as examples of the general rule. So, where a bank refuses to pay a customer's cheque when the customer is in credit, it will be liable in respect of any loss to the customer's trade reputation or credit-rating caused by the breach.[34] It is, moreover, no longer necessary to distinguish a breach of contract which causes injury to a reputation which a person already possesses from a breach of a specific undertaking to protect or enhance a person's reputation, for which damages were awarded prior to the decision in *Malik*'s case.[35] So, where a contract entitles an actor to be advertised as playing a leading part at a well-known music-hall, the actor may recover damages for the loss of publicity and for any injury that the failure to appear may cause to the actor's existing reputation.[36] In view of the

---

[30] [1998] 1 AC 20.   [31] [1909] AC 488, eg at 491 (Lord Loreburn).
[32] [1998] 1 AC 20, 38 (Lord Nicholls) and 51 (Lord Steyn).
[33] *Johnson v Unisys Ltd* [2001] UKHL 13, [2003] 1 AC 518; *Eastwood v Magnox Electric plc* [2004] UKHL 35, [2005] 1 AC 503; *Edwards v Chesterfield Royal Hospital NHS Foundation Trust* [2011] UKSC 58, [2012] 2 AC 22.
[34] *Kpohoror v Woolwich Building Society* [1996] 4 All ER 119, suggesting that a distinction between trade and personal transactions should no longer be made.
[35] *Clayton & Waller Ltd v Oliver* [1930] AC 209.
[36] *Marbe v George Edwardes (Daley's Theatre) Ltd* [1928] 1 KB 269, 281, 288.

assumed facts in *Malik*'s case, there was no need to deal with a breach of contract that causes non-financial loss, for instance distress and injured feelings resulting from loss of reputation, but the increased willingness to award contractual damages for such losses[37] suggests that this aspect of *Addis*'s case may also be ripe for reconsideration.

3. BASIS OF ASSESSMENT OF DAMAGES

The general principle that damages are compensatory in nature is nevertheless only a starting point, and the question must still be asked—when a contract is broken and action is brought upon it, how are we to arrive at the amount which the claimant, if successful, is entitled to recover in respect of its loss?

(a) THE 'PERFORMANCE' OR 'EXPECTATION' MEASURE

The object of an award of damages for breach of contract is to place the claimant, so far as money can do it, in the same situation, with respect to damages, as if the contract had been performed.[38] Claimants are thus enabled to recover damages in respect of the loss of gains of which they have been deprived by the breach. For example, if machinery is not delivered to a person or delivered late in breach of contract, that person will have a claim for loss of profits for being deprived of its use. A claim for loss of profits, however, is not peculiar to an action in contract, since a similar claim would lie if the machinery were damaged or destroyed by a tort. But the law of contract goes further and entitles claimants to damages for the loss of the bargained-for performance, that is to say, for the loss of the particular benefit which it was expected would be received by the contract which has been broken: an art dealer contracts to purchase a painting which is worth far more than the agreed price; a record company by contract obtains for a relatively modest sum the sole right to distribute the records of what proves to be a highly successful pop-group; a caterer obtains an extremely lucrative contract to cater for a banquet. In each case, if the contract is broken by the other party, the damages will be assessed by reference to the claimant's 'performance' or 'expectation' loss, consisting of what would have been received had the contract been duly performed.[39]

(i) Assessment by reference to contract terms

Damages must be assessed by reference to the terms of the contract sued upon, and the Court cannot take account of 'the expectations, however reasonable, of one contractor that the other will do something that it has assumed no legal obligation to do'.[40]

---

[37] For the conditions under which such an award will be made, see above, pp 567–8.

[38] *Robinson v Harman* (1848) 1 Exch 850, 855.

[39] See Fuller and Perdue (1936–37) 46 Yale LJ 52, 573; Taylor (1982) 45 MLR 139; Burrows (1983) 99 LQR 217; Friedmann (1995) 111 LQR 628; Coote [1997] CLJ 537. Cf Atiyah (1978) 94 LQR 193.

[40] *Lavarack v Woods of Colchester Ltd* [1967] 1 QB 278, 294. Cf *Horkulak v Cantor Fitzgerald International* [2004] EWCA Civ 1287, [2005] ICR 402.

Thus an employee who is wrongfully dismissed and sues the employer for breach of contract may be unable to recover contractual damages for the loss of 'fringe benefits' from the employment unless the employer has assumed a contractual obligation to provide those benefits.[41] Also, where the defendant has a choice of two methods of performance, damages will be assessed on the basis of the minimum legal obligation, that is, that the contract would have been performed by the method least onerous to the defendant and least beneficial to the claimant.[42]

(ii) Difference in value or 'cost of cure'

In many cases the assessment of the claimant's loss of bargain will be the difference in value between the performance received and that promised in the contract; 'difference in value'.[43] However, in appropriate circumstances, damages may be assessed on the basis of what it has cost or will cost the claimant to have the contract performed by a third party; the 'cost of cure'.[44] So if work contracted for is not performed or is performed badly, the claimant is entitled to the cost of substitute or remedial work to be carried out by a third party where it is possible to do so,[45] unless, in all the circumstances, this is unreasonable, as where the cost of cure is wholly disproportionate to any resulting benefit[46] or unless the claimant does not intend to have the work carried out.[47] In *Ruxley Electronics & Constructions Ltd v Forsyth*:[48]

F contracted with R for the construction of a swimming pool in his garden with a diving area 7 feet 6 inches deep at a price of £17,797. In breach of contract the diving area was

[41] *Lavarack v Woods of Colchester Ltd*, above, n 40.

[42] *Re Thornett & Fehr and Yuills Ltd* [1921] 1 KB 219; *Abraham v Herbert Reiach Ltd* [1922] 1 KB 477; *Bunge Corp v Tradax Export SA* [1981] 1 WLR 711. Cf *Paula Lee Ltd v Robert Zehil & Co Ltd* [1983] 2 All ER 390; *Lion Nathan Ltd v C-C Bottlers Ltd* [1996] 1 WLR 1438; *Durham Tees Valley Airport Ltd v BmiBaby Ltd* [2010] EWCA Civ 485, [2011] 1 Lloyd's Rep 68.

[43] See below, p 589; Landlord and Tenant Act 1927, s 18; Sale of Goods Act 1979, ss 50(3), 51(3), 53(3).

[44] *Jones v Herxheimer* [1950] 2 KB 106; *East Ham Corp v Bernard Sunley & Sons Ltd* [1966] AC 406, 434; *Tito v Waddell (No 2)* [1977] Ch 106, 329; *Radford v de Froberville* [1977] 1 WLR 1262, 1269-70; *Ruxley Electronics & Constructions Ltd v Forsyth* [1996] 1 AC 344. Where the 'cost of cure' is less than the reduction in value, the mitigation principle, below, p 555, will restrict the claimant to the former.

[45] Cf *Ward v Cannock Chase DC* [1985] 3 All ER 537 (a tort case where cost of cure was awarded subject to planning permission) and note that where a surveyor in breach of contract fails to identify defects in the property surveyed the prima facie measure is the diminution in the value of the property, not the cost of repairing it: *Phillips v Ward* [1956] 1 WLR 491; *Watts v Morrow* [1991] 1 WLR 1421; *Patel v Hooper & Jackson* [1999] 1 WLR 1792, 1801.

[46] *Ruxley Electronics & Constructions Ltd v Forsyth* [1996] 1 AC 344, 354, 361; *Sealace SS Co Ltd v Oceanvoice Ltd* [1991] 1 Lloyd's Rep 120; *Channel Island Ferries Ltd v Cenargo Navigation Ltd* [1994] 2 Lloyd's Rep 160, 167 (claimant's interest wholly financial). In principle 'benefit' should include non-monetary benefits such as bathroom tiles matching an existing colour scheme.

[47] *Ruxley Electronics & Constructions Ltd v Forsyth* [1996] 1 AC 344, 354, 359 (Lord Jauncey) and 372-3 (Lord Lloyd). See also *Tito v Waddell (No 2)* [1977] Ch 106, 317; *Radford v de Froberville* [1977] 1 WLR 1262, 1248; *Dean v Ainley* [1987] 1 WLR 1729 (Glidewell LJ and Sir George Waller); *Watts v Morrow* [1991] 1 WLR 1421; *Taylor v Hepworths Ltd* [1977] 1 WLR 659 (tort); *Southampton Container Terminals Ltd v Schiffahrtsgesellschaft Hansa Australia MBH & Co, The Maersk Colombo* [2001] EWCA Civ 717, [2001] 2 Lloyd's Rep 275 (tort). For Australia, see *De Cesare v Deluxe Motors Pty Ltd* (1996) 67 SALR 28, 33-5; *Tabcorp Holdings Ltd v Bowen Investments Pty Ltd* [2009] HCA 8.

[48] [1996] 1 AC 344, on which, see Coote [1997] CLJ 537; O'Sullivan, in Rose (ed), *Failure of Contracts* (1997) ch 1. See also *Harbutt's 'Plasticine' Ltd v Wayne Tank and Pump Co Ltd* [1970] 1 QB 447, 473.

only 6 feet 9 inches deep but was suitable for diving and there was no adverse effect on the market value of the pool. The estimated cost of rebuilding the pool to the specified depth was £21,560.

The House of Lords held that F was not entitled to the 'cost of cure'. In this case, the trial judge had found that F did not intend to rebuild the pool even if awarded the cost of so doing. It would also have been unreasonable to do so given the large disparity between the cost of so doing and the nil difference in value. However, it was held that as F had lost his personal preference for a deeper pool he was entitled to £2,500 for loss of amenity. This is best regarded as compensation for mental distress (ie loss of pleasure) as in the ruined holiday cases. Economists see this as a recognition of F's non-monetary 'consumer surplus'.[49] The decision has been said to be an example of the Courts taking steps to recognize and remedy a deficiency in the remedial regime for breach of contract where the claimant's loss is non-financial by giving fuller recognition to the performance interest as the basis of contractual damages.[50] In cases where there was never any question of being able to 'cure' the breach, for example where a carrier provided a low grade delivery service rather than the 'enhanced' service that was promised and paid for, it should, in principle, also be possible to put a figure to any non-monetary loss suffered.[51]

The increased willingness to award damages in such cases is a reflection of recognition that 'the principle of pacta sunt servanda would be eroded if the law did not take account of the fact that the consumer often demands specifications which, although not of economic value, have value to him'.[52]

(b) THE RELIANCE MEASURE

At first sight an alternative *basis* for the assessment of damages is that the claimant should recover its 'reliance loss', that is to say, expenses which it has incurred in preparing to perform or in part performance of the contract and which have been rendered futile by the breach. Even expenses incurred prior to, and in anticipation of, the making of the contract are recoverable, provided it was reasonably in the contemplation of the parties that they would be wasted if the contract was broken. Thus in *Anglia Television Ltd v Reed*,[53] the television company obtained damages in

---

[49] Harris, Ogus, and Phillips (1979) 95 LQR 58; Muris (1983) 12 JLS 379. See also Lord Bridge and Lord Mustill at 354, 360–1; Lord Lloyd, at 374, reserving his position but regarding it as compensation for F's disappointment.

[50] O'Sullivan, 'Reflections on the Role of Restitutionary Damages to Protect Contractual Expectations', unpublished but adopted in this context by Lord Goff and Lord Millett (dissenting) in *Alfred McAlpine Construction Ltd v Panatown Ltd* [2001] 1 AC 518, 548, 587.

[51] See Beale (1996) 112 LQR 205, discussing *White Arrow Express Ltd v Lamey's Distribution Ltd* (1995) 15 Tr LR 69.

[52] *Farley v Skinner* [2001] UKHL 49, [2002] 2 AC 732 at [21] (Lord Steyn); see also at [79]; *Ruxley Electronics & Constructions Ltd v Forsyth*, above, n 18, 360 (Lord Mustill).

[53] [1972] 1 QB 60. See also *Lloyd v Stanbury* [1971] 1 WLR 535.

respect of expenses of £2,750 which had been thrown away by reason of the defendant's refusal, in breach of contract, to play the leading part in a television play, even though the expenses had been incurred before the contract was made. A claimant may be compelled to claim damages for wasted expenses rather than for the loss of its bargain by reason of its inability to prove that financial benefit would have accrued to it had the contract been performed.[54]

If, however, the defendant can prove that the claimant would not have benefited financially had the contract been performed, the claimant will not be permitted to escape from a bad bargain by recovering as damages sums spent in reliance on the contract instead of loss of expectancy.[55] In such a case the reliance losses are considered to flow from entering into a losing contract and not from the defendant's breach.[56] A claimant who recovers for the loss of bargain cannot, as a general rule, combine a claim for reliance loss with one for loss of expectation so as to recover twice in respect of the same loss.[57] Thus damages for expenses rendered futile by the breach cannot be sought at the same time as damages for loss of profit, since such expenses would have had to be laid out in order to earn the profit claimed.

Although traditionally the reliance measure has been seen as an alternative basis to the expectation measure, the 'no escape from a bad bargain' and the recovery of pre-contractual expenses suggests that the reliance measure is better viewed as merely a *method* of assessing the claimant's expectation measure. That is, where the claimant has incurred reliance expenses it is given the benefit of a rebuttable presumption—and is thereby saved having to provide direct proof of the gains it would have made—that, if the contract had been performed, it would at the very least have made gains to cover its reliance expenses.[58] That this is the correct analysis of the reliance measure was made clear in *Omak Maritime Ltd v Mamola Challenger Co, The Mamola Challenger*:[59]

Charterers, under a long-term charterparty, repudiated that contract even though the contract was for them a good one with the charter rate being below the market rate (by about $7,500 per day). The owners accepted that repudiatory breach and thereby became able to trade the ship at the higher market rate. The owners nevertheless claimed substantial damages based on the expenses they had incurred in preparing to perform the charterparty.

The owners' argument was that they were entitled to the expenses incurred as reliance damages and that it was irrelevant to those damages that they had entirely mitigated

---

[54] *Anglia Television Ltd v Reed* [1972] 1 QB 60 (inability to prove what profits from TV play would have been); *McRae v Commonwealth Disposals Commission* (1950) 84 CLR 377 (value of ship to be salvaged too speculative; price paid and cost of salvage expedition recovered).
[55] *C & P Haulage v Middleton* [1983] 1 WLR 1461; *CCC (London) Films Ltd v Impact Quadrant Films Ltd* [1985] QB 16.
[56] Cf below, p 620 (restitutionary remedies can 'save' a claimant from a bad bargain).
[57] See *Cullinane v British 'Rema' Manufacturing Co Ltd* [1954] 1 QB 292, below, p 593.
[58] This is supported by the High Court of Australia in *Commonwealth of Australia v Amann Aviation Pty Ltd* (1991) 66 ALJR 123. See also McLauchlan [2007] NZLR 417; Burrows, *Remedies for Torts and Breach of Contract* (3rd edn, 2004) ch 5.
[59] [2010] EWHC 2026, [2011] 1 Lloyd's Rep 47, noted by McLauchlan (2011) 127 LQR 23.

the loss of hire because reliance damages were not concerned with the owners' position had the contract been performed. That argument of the owners was firmly rejected by Teare J. He made clear that reliance damages are not based on a separate principle from the expectation measure laid down by *Robinson v Harman*.[60] The expectation measure is the one and only compensatory measure to be applied so that, as the owners' loss assessed according to that measure had been entirely mitigated, there was no other loss to be compensated. The recovery of wasted reliance expense is merely an indirect method, supported by a reverse burden of proof, of applying that expectation measure.

4. CAUSATION

In order to establish a right to damages for a loss the claimant must show that the breach of contract caused the loss. Establishing 'but for' causation (ie that but for the breach of contract, the loss would not have been suffered) is not enough. Rather the breach of contract must be the 'effective' cause of the loss, as opposed to an event which merely gives the opportunity for the claimant to sustain the loss.[61] The Courts have treated the determination of whether a breach was the cause of the loss in a broad way, in the end turning to their 'commonsense'[62] in interpreting the facts. Accordingly, there are few rules of law that can be stated.

Where another event has also affected the fact situation, if that other event was *likely* to happen once the breach of contract had occurred it will generally not be held to break the chain of causation. In *Monarch Steamship Co Ltd v Karlshamms Oljefabriker (A/B)*[63] a voyage was delayed by the unseaworthiness of the vessel so that it arrived in European waters after the outbreak of the Second World War and was diverted by the Admiralty to Glasgow. It was held that the outbreak of war and the Admiralty's action did not break the chain of causation; the cause of the cargo-owners' loss was the defendant's breach of contract in failing to provide a seaworthy ship. But where that other event was *not likely* to happen once the breach of contract has occurred, the chain of causation may well be held to have been broken. Thus a breach of contract by a solicitor in wrongfully ceasing to act for a client gave rise to the opportunity for the client to sustain loss by acting without alternative legal advice and lodging a defective application, but was not the cause of such loss.[64]

---

[60] (1848) 1 Exch 850, 855.

[61] *Weld-Blundell v Stephens* [1920] AC 956; *Banco de Portugal v Waterlow & Sons Ltd* [1932] AC 452; *Compania Naviera Maropan S/A v Bowaters Lloyd Pulp & Paper Mills Ltd* [1955] 2 QB 68; *Quinn v Burch Bros (Builders) Ltd* [1966] 2 QB 370; *Galoo Ltd v Bright Grahame Murray* [1994] 1 WLR 1360; *Young v Purdy* [1997] PNLR 130; *Borealis AB v Geogas Trading SA* [2010] EWHC 2789 (Comm), [2011] 1 Lloyd's Rep 482.

[62] *Galoo Ltd v Bright Grahame Murray* [1994] 1 WLR 1360, 1374–5.

[63] [1949] AC 196. On the question of reducing damages for contributory negligence where the other event is the act of the claimant, see below, pp 594–5.

[64] *Young v Purdy* [1997] PNLR 130; *Galoo Ltd v Bright Grahame Murray* [1994] 1 WLR 1360. See also *South Australia Asset Management Co v York Montague Ltd* [1997] AC 191, 212–13 (Lord Hoffmann); cf, in the Court of Appeal, [1995] QB 375, 406, 420–1 (Bingham MR).

5. REMOTENESS

Where the test of causation is satisfied the law does not, however, compel the defendant to assume liability for all the loss which the claimant may have suffered as a consequence of the breach. Certain losses may be too 'remote', and for these the claimant is not entitled to compensation.

(a) THE BASIC TWO-BRANCHED RULE

The foundation of the law on this subject is contained in the judgment of Alderson B in the Court of Exchequer in the case of *Hadley v Baxendale*. Drawing on the civilian principle of foreseeability and Articles 1149–1151 of the French Civil Code, he stated that where the parties have made a contract which one of them has broken damages are recoverable: (1) when they are 'such as may fairly and reasonably be considered arising naturally, ie, according to the usual course of things' from the breach, or (2) when they are 'such as may reasonably be supposed to have been in the contemplation of both parties, at the time they made the contract, as the probable result of the breach of it.'[65] The effect of the second branch of the rule was explained by Alderson B as follows:[66]

[I]f the special circumstances under which the contract was actually made were communicated by the plaintiffs to the defendants, and thus known to both parties, the damages resulting from the breach of such a contract, which they would reasonably contemplate, would be the amount of injury which would ordinarily follow from a breach of contract under these special circumstances so known and communicated. But, on the other hand, if these special circumstances were wholly unknown to the party breaking the contract, he, at the most, could only be supposed to have had in his contemplation the amount of injury which would arise generally, and in the great multitude of cases not affected by any special circumstances, from such a breach of contract. For, had the special circumstances been known, the parties might have specially provided for the breach of contract by special terms as to the damages in that case; and of this advantage it would be very unjust to deprive them.

From this it will be seen that liability under the second branch of the rule will depend upon the special circumstances made known to the party in default at the time the contract was made. In the case in which these principles were formulated:

H's mill was stopped by the breakage of a crankshaft, and it was necessary to send the crankshaft to the makers as a pattern for a new one. The defendants, who were carriers, undertook to deliver the shaft to the makers, but the only information given to them was 'that the article to be carried was the broken shaft of a mill, and that H was the owner

---

[65] (1854) 9 Exch 341, 354. The French civil code, however, allows unforeseeable losses to be recovered where the breach is deliberate. *Hadley v Baxendale* and the English cases which have followed it do not distinguish between deliberate and non-deliberate breach.

[66] *Ibid*, 354, 355.

of the mill'.[67] By some neglect on their part the delivery of the shaft was delayed, and in consequence the mill could not be restarted until some time after it could otherwise have been. H lost profits which he would otherwise have made.

The question was whether this loss of profits ought to be taken into account in estimating the damages. Applying the principles quoted above, the Court pointed out that the circumstances communicated to the defendants did not show that a delay in the delivery of the shaft would entail loss of profits of the mill; H might have had another shaft, or there might have been some other defect in the machinery to cause the stoppage. Accordingly they could not recover for this loss because the Court stated[68] that:

[I]n the great multitude of cases of millers sending off broken shafts to third persons by a carrier under ordinary circumstances, such consequences would not, in all probability, have occurred; and these special circumstances were here never communicated by [H] to the defendants.

The rule was further considered in *Victoria Laundry (Windsor) Ltd v Newman Industries Ltd:*[69]

V, a launderer and dyer, wished to expand its business, and for this purpose entered into a contract with the defendant to purchase from it a new boiler. It was agreed that the boiler was to be delivered on 5 June, but when V sent to collect the boiler on that day it was informed that it had been damaged by a fall and was not ready. The boiler was not, in fact, delivered until November. In consequence of this delay, V lost the profits which it would have earned during this period, and, in particular, certain highly lucrative dyeing contracts which it could have obtained with the Ministry of Supply. V sued inter alia to recover these losses.

Streatfeild J held that V was not entitled to include in its measure of damages the loss of any business profits during the period of delay. His decision was reversed. Asquith LJ, delivering the judgment of the Court of Appeal, pointed out that the defendant knew before, and at the time of the contract, that V was a launderer and dyer and required the boiler for immediate use in its business. From the defendant's own technical experience, and from the business relations existing between the parties, the defendant must be presumed to have anticipated that some loss of profits would occur by reason of its delay. But in the absence of special knowledge on its part, the defendant could not reasonably foresee the additional losses suffered by V's inability to accept the highly lucrative dyeing contracts. The case was therefore to be referred to an Official Referee for a reassessment of the damages.

Although there are two branches to the rule in *Hadley v Baxendale*, in essence they both form a part of a single general principle. This was made clear by Asquith

---

[67] *Ibid*, 355 (Alderson B). It was stated by Asquith LJ in *Victoria Laundry (Windsor) Ltd v Newman Industries Ltd* [1949] 2 KB 528, 537, that the headnote is misleading in that it wrongly ascribes to the defendants knowledge that the mill was stopped for want of the shaft.

[68] (1854) 9 Exch 341, 356 (Alderson B).   [69] [1949] 2 KB 528.

LJ in the *Victoria Laundry* case[70] albeit that he used the terminology of the loss being reasonably foreseeable rather than reasonably contemplated. According to Asquith LJ, the general principle which governs both branches of the rule is that the aggrieved party is only entitled to recover such part of the loss actually resulting from the breach as was at the time of the contract reasonably foreseeable as liable to result from the breach. What was at that time reasonably so foreseeable depends on the knowledge then possessed by the parties or, at all events, by the party who later commits the breach. For this purpose, knowledge 'possessed' is of two kinds: one imputed, the other actual. Everyone, as a reasonable person, is taken to know the 'ordinary course of things' and consequently what loss is liable to result from a breach of contract in that ordinary course. This is the subject-matter of the first branch of the rule. But to this knowledge, which a contract-breaker is assumed to possess whether it is actually possessed or not, there may have to be added in a particular case knowledge which the claimant actually possesses, of special circumstances outside the 'ordinary course of things', of such a kind that a breach in those special circumstances would be liable to cause more loss.[71] Such a situation attracts the operation of the second branch of the rule and makes this additional loss recoverable. Under neither branch is it necessary that the contract-breaker should actually have asked what loss is liable to result from a breach. It suffices that, if the issue had been considered, the contract-breaker would as a reasonable person have concluded that the loss in question was liable to result.

The language of the judgment in the *Victoria Laundry* case was carefully considered in *Koufos v C Czarnikow Ltd, The Heron II*:[72]

The respondent, a sugar merchant, chartered the ship *Heron II* from the appellant to carry a cargo of sugar from Constanza to Basrah. The ship deviated without authority from the agreed voyage, with the result that the cargo was delayed. Owing to a fall in the market for sugar at Basrah, the respondent obtained £3,800 less for the sugar than the price obtainable when it should have been delivered.

The appellant contended that he was not liable for this sum as he had no special knowledge of the seasonal and other fluctuations of the sugar market. But the House of Lords held that a shipowner must be presumed to know that prices in a commodity market were liable to fluctuate, and judgment was given against him.

Asquith LJ's judgment in the *Victoria Laundry* case was described as 'a justifiable and valuable clarification of the principles which *Hadley v Baxendale* was intending to express' particularly in explaining that the phrase used by Alderson B—'in the contemplation of the parties ... as the probable result'—did not mean an odds on

---

[70] [1949] 2 KB 528, 539. See also *Koufos v C Czarnikow Ltd (The Heron II)* [1969] 1 AC 350, 385, 415; *The Pegase* [1981] 1 Lloyd's Rep 175, 182; *Khophraror v Woolwich Building Society* [1996] 4 All ER 119.

[71] Knowledge of special circumstances may, however, in some situations be such as to lead the parties to believe that the loss will be reduced: see *Biggin & Co Ltd v Permanite Ltd* [1951] 1 KB 422, 436; *Koufos v C Czarnikow Ltd* [1969] 1 AC 350, 416.

[72] [1969] 1 AC 350.

probability.[73] Nevertheless, there was some criticism of the way in which Asquith LJ formulated the general principle in terms of 'reasonable foresight' of the loss 'liable to result'. This, it was said, may engender confusion with the rule regarding remoteness of damage in tort,[74] where a defendant will be held responsible for damage which is reasonably foreseeable as liable to happen even if the risk is very small,[75] because it is said that normally in tort, unlike in contract, there is no opportunity for the injured party to protect itself against an unusual risk by informing the defendant.[76] Lord Reid and Lord Morris interpreted Alderson B's phrase as meaning the contemplation of a result which was 'not unlikely' to happen rather than an odds on probability;[77] and a majority of their Lordships distinguished the tort rule by requiring that the loss must be 'not very unusual and easily foreseeable',[78] or that there must be 'a real danger' or 'a serious possibility'[79] of its occurrence.

In *Jackson v Royal Bank of Scotland plc*[80] it was again stressed by the House of Lords that the contract remoteness test looks at the defendant's knowledge at the date the contract was made and not at the date of the breach of contract; and, as in *The Heron II*, it was explained that this is because it is at that date that the parties have the opportunity to draw attention to special circumstances outside the ordinary course of things and to limit their liability.

(b) THE IMPACT OF *THE ACHILLEAS*

The law on remoteness, as so far set out, has arguably been altered by the House of Lords in *Transfield Shipping Inc v Mercator Shipping Inc, The Achilleas*.[81]

Under a time charter, the defendant charterers should have redelivered the ship to the claimant owners by 2 May 2004. In breach of contract, they did not redeliver to the owners until 11 May. The owners had entered into a follow-on time charter (referred to as a follow-on 'fixture') under which they were bound to deliver the ship to the new charterers by 8 May. When they were unable to do so as a result of the defendants' breach, the owners renegotiated the follow-on fixture and, because rates had fallen, they agreed to reduce the rate of hire on that follow-on fixture from $39, 500 to $31,500, a loss of $8,000 a day.

---

[73] *Ibid*, 417. See also at 399, but contrast at 389, 390, 410–11, 424–5. In *R & H Hall Ltd v WH Pim (Junior) & Co Ltd* (1927) 33 Com Cas 324, 330 Lord Dunedin stated that 'probable' did not mean more than an even chance.

[74] *Overseas Tankship (UK) v Morts Dock and Engineering Co, The Wagon Mound* [1961] AC 388.

[75] *Koufos v C Czarnikow Ltd, The Heron II* [1969] 1 AC 350, 385–6, 389.

[76] *Ibid*, 385–6, 411, 422–3. See also *Jackson v Royal Bank of Scotland plc* [2005] UKHL 3, [2005] 1 WLR 377 at [36] (Lord Hope). But this suggests that where the parties to a tort claim are in a contractual or similar relationship there should be no difference in the remoteness tests. See below, p 582. See also Burrows, above, n 2, 54.

[77] *The Heron II*, above n 75, 388, 406. See also at 416–17 (Lord Pearce), 424 (Lord Upjohn).

[78] *Ibid*, 383.   [79] *Ibid*, 414–15, 425.   [80] [2005] UKHL 3, [2005] 1 WLR 377.

[81] [2008] UKHL 48, [2009] 1 AC 61. For criticism, see Peel (2009) 125 LQR 6; Wee [2010] LMCLQ 150; Stiggelbout [2012] LMCLQ 97; Burrows, in Davies and Pila (eds), *The Jurisprudence of Lord Hoffmann* (2015) ch 14. For support, see Kramer (2009) 125 LQR 408; Hoffmann (2010) 14 Edinburgh LR 47.

The defendants accepted that they were liable for damages of the difference between the market rate and the charter rate for the nine-day overrun period between 2 May and 11 May. That came to $158,301. However, the owners sought damages to cover the loss of $8,000 a day for the whole period of the follow-on fixture. That came to $1,364,584. It was held by the House of Lords that the owners' damages were limited to $158,301. The rest of the loss was too remote.

The reasoning of Lord Rodger and Baroness Hale differed sharply from that of Lord Hoffmann and Lord Hope. What makes it difficult to determine the *ratio* is that Lord Walker agreed with both lines of reasoning.

Lord Rodger and Baroness Hale applied the conventional remoteness test that has been set out above. The question they were therefore asking was whether it was reasonably contemplatable as a serious possibility at the time of contracting that, in the event of breach by late redelivery, a follow-on fixture might be lost. One would have thought that, on the facts, the answer to that would have been 'yes' so that the loss on the follow-on fixture would not have been too remote. However, the answer given was 'no' so that that loss was held to be too remote.

Lord Hoffmann and Lord Hope arrived at the same result by significantly different reasoning. In effect they departed from the conventional test for remoteness by adding to it a requirement that the defendant must have accepted liability or responsibility for the loss. Lord Hoffmann reasoned that the charterers had not accepted liability for the loss because the understanding of the shipping industry was that charterers were only liable for loss during the overrun period. Lord Hope thought that the charterers had not accepted liability for the loss because it was out of their control and unquantifiable.

The additional requirement insisted on by Lord Hoffmann and Lord Hope has thrown the law on remoteness in contract into confusion. As we shall see, the Courts have previously rejected the view that loss should be regarded as too remote unless the defendant has accepted liability for it as a term of the contract[82] and yet that appears to be very close to the reasoning of Lord Hoffmann and Lord Hope. It also seems doubtful whether leading decisions, such as *The Heron II*,[83] can be reconciled with their approach. Admittedly there have long been doubts about whether merely informing the claimant of the special risks involved is sufficient in all circumstances to make a defendant liable for the loss under the second branch of the rule in *Hadley v Baxendale*.[84] But that was not the issue in *The Achilleas*. Although their Lordships did not sharply distinguish between them, the facts clearly concerned the first branch of the rule in *Hadley v Baxendale* and not the second.[85] A further problem with the reasoning of Lord Hoffmann is that it is far from clear that he should have paid such deference to the apparent views of the shipping industry on a matter that had never previously been litigated and which,

---

[82] Below, p 586, especially n 118.   [83] Above, p 577.   [84] Below, p 586.
[85] See [2008] UKHL 48, [2009] 1 AC 61 at [6] (Lord Hoffmann) and at [93] (Baroness Hale).

applying the previously accepted law on remoteness, was based on a mistaken understanding of the law.

Lord Hoffmann saw remoteness as an aspect of construing the contract and he further drew in aid his approach in determining the scope of the duty of care in *South Australia Asset Management Corp v York Montague Ltd.*[86] The counter-argument to Lord Hoffmann's approach is that rules of remoteness are policy default rules of fairness set by the Courts albeit that they can be departed from by the contracting parties by express or implied terms. To treat the rules of remoteness as 'agreement-centred' is to put the matter the wrong way round and leads to 'construction' of the contract becoming a fictional mask for a decision that in reality is imposed on the parties.[87]

That the law of remoteness has been rendered less certain, and that *The Achilleas* is not to be confined to its own narrow sphere of shipping, is well illustrated by the most important case since *The Achilleas*. In *Supershield Ltd v Siemens Building Technologies FE Ltd,*[88] the Court of Appeal, in the context of deciding that a settlement reached by the parties was reasonable, has said that, while *Hadley v Baxendale* remains the standard rule and is grounded on policy, it can be displaced if, on examining the contract and the commercial background, the loss in question was within or outside the scope of the contractual duty. In other words, the approach in *The Achilleas* might displace the standard rule by making loss that would be recoverable under *Hadley v Baxendale* too remote (an 'exclusionary effect') or by making loss that would be non-recoverable under *Hadley v Baxendale* not too remote (an 'inclusionary effect'). On the facts, although it was unlikely that loss by flooding would occur as a consequence of the defendant's breach in failing properly to install a float valve in a fire-sprinkler water storage system—because normally the drains would have taken the overflow water but here the drains were blocked—that loss was thought not to be too remote because within the scope of the installer's duty. Although this is helpful in clarifying that *Hadley v Baxendale* basically remains good law and is the standard rule, it does show that it is far from clear what triggers the displacement of that standard rule.

---

[86] [1997] AC 191. That controversial decision was that, where there had been a fall in property prices, valuers who had negligently undervalued property were not liable to lenders, who had relied on that negligent undervaluation in lending money on the security of those properties, for losses greater than the difference between the represented value of the property and its actual value at the date of valuation. In the light of *The Achilleas*, it appears that Lord Hoffmann would regard that decision as correct because the market fall loss was too remote as being outside the scope of the duty assumed by the valuer. For criticism of *SAAMCO*, see Burrows, *Remedies for Torts and Breach of Contract* (3rd edn, 2004) 109–22.

[87] Robertson (2008) 28 LS 172 criticizes the agreement-centred approach of Kramer in Cohen and McKendrick (eds), *Comparative Remedies for Breach of Contract* (2004) 249. For the latter type of approach, see also Tettenborn (2007) 23 JCL 120. All three of these articles were cited by Lord Hoffmann in *The Achilleas*.

[88] [2010] EWCA Civ 7, [2010] 1 Lloyd's Rep 349. See also *Sylvia Shipping Co Ltd v Progress Bulk Carriers Ltd* [2010] EWHC 542 (Comm), [2010] 2 Lloyd's Rep 8 (the 'assumption of responsibility' approach in *The Achilleas* to be confined to exceptional cases where the orthodox approach would result in unquantifiable, unpredictable, disproportionate liability or a result contrary to clear market understanding and expectations).

(c) SHOULD THERE BE A DIFFERENCE BETWEEN THE TESTS OF REMOTENESS IN CONTRACT AND TORT?

We have seen from the reasoning of the House of Lords in *The Heron II* that, in the usual case where a tort claim is brought but the parties are not in a contractual relationship, the less strict *Wagon Mound* tort remoteness test is applied rather than the stricter contract remoteness test.[89] The interrelation of the tests for remoteness in contract and tort was further considered by the Court of Appeal in the context of physical damage in *H Parsons (Livestock) Ltd v Uttley Ingham & Co Ltd*.[90]

UI agreed to supply and erect on P's pig farm a bulk food storage hopper for the purpose of storing pig nuts for P's top grade pig herd. When the hopper was installed, UI failed to ensure that a ventilator at the top of the hopper was open, with the result that the pig nuts stored in it became mouldy. P fed the mouldy nuts to their pigs believing (as would normally be the case) that no harm could result. But the pigs suffered an attack of E coli, an intestinal infection triggered by feeding on the mouldy nuts, and 254 pigs died.

At first instance, Swanwick J held that the damage caused was not within the reasonable contemplation of the parties as a result of UI's breach of contract. The Court of Appeal reversed that decision. Lord Denning MR expressed the opinion[91] that the observations of the House of Lords in *Koufos v C Czarnikow Ltd* were limited to cases where a claimant was claiming for loss of profit or, at any rate, for economic loss. In his view, where the claim was for damages for personal injury or damage to property, or for resulting expenses to which the claimant had actually been put, the rule in contract was the same as that in tort, so that a defendant would be liable for any loss or damage which ought reasonably to have been foreseen at the time of the breach as a possible consequence, even if it was only a slight possibility.

A distinction between loss of profit and physical damage might be justified on the ground that a person is unlikely to consider the possibility of physical injury in advance and thus to disclose unusual risks.[92] However, Orr and Scarman LJJ, who held that the parties could have contemplated as 'a serious possibility' that the pigs might become ill as a result of the breach, considered that neither authority[93] nor principle supported a distinction in remoteness tests between loss of profit and physical damage. Nevertheless, Scarman LJ stated[94] that although the formulation of the remoteness test is not the same in tort and contract because the relationship of the parties in a contractual situation differs from that in tort, it would be absurd if the amount of damages recoverable were to depend upon whether the claimant's cause of action was in contract or in tort. In his opinion the difference between

---

[89] Above, p 578.   [90] [1978] QB 791.   [91] *Ibid*, 803–4.

[92] But this may not be the case for all types of contracts, eg a contract for medical services or for instruction in a sporting activity.

[93] The authority relied on by Lord Denning, *Ashington Piggeries Ltd v Christopher Hill Ltd* [1972] AC 441 and *Henry Kendall & Sons v William Lillico & Sons Ltd* [1969] 2 AC 31, in fact applied *Koufos v C Czarnikow Ltd* [1969] 1 AC 350, as, more recently, did *Kemp v Intasun Holidays Ltd* [1987] 2 FTLR 234 (asthmatic attack caused by dirty hotel room too remote).

[94] [1978] QB 791, 806–7. See also *Archer v Brown* [1985] QB 401, 418.

'reasonably foreseeable' (the test in tort) and 'reasonably contemplated' (the test in contract) was semantic, not substantial. This suggests that where there is a contractual relationship between the parties and concurrent liability in contract and tort there should, in principle, be no difference between the remoteness tests in contract and tort. Moreover, in *Wellesley Partners LLP v Withers LLP*[95] it was recently held by the Court of Appeal, after a full and enlightened consideration of the issues, that, because the defendant has assumed responsibility to the claimant under the contract or, put another way, the relevant risks have been allocated in the contract, the stricter 'contractual' remoteness test applies to a concurrent claim in the tort of negligence for pure economic loss by a client against a solicitor.

(d) TYPE OF DAMAGE

In the context of physical injury it is established that the word 'damage' refers to the type or kind of damage in question; it is not necessary for a claimant to go further and show contemplation of the exact nature of the damage that has arisen, or the amount of damage of the type or kind.[96] In principle the same should apply to cases of loss of profit,[97] but this is not easy to reconcile with the decision of the Court of Appeal in the *Victoria Laundry* case in which the 'ordinary' loss of profits were recovered but not that from the highly lucrative Ministry of Supply contracts.[98] In *Brown v KMR Services Ltd* Stuart-Smith LJ stated that, although categorization into types is difficult in the case of financial loss, loss of ordinary business profits is different *in type or kind* from loss flowing from a particular contract which gives rise to very high profits, whereas underwriting losses of a far larger magnitude than any contemplated were of the same *type* as those foreseeable.[99]

(e) DAMAGE ARISING IN THE USUAL COURSE OF THINGS

Although it would be incorrect to treat the two branches of the rule in *Hadley v Baxendale* as rigidly separate, it is helpful to examine the operation of each branch. Each may be regarded as covering a different degree of knowledge possessed by the contracting parties. The first branch of the rule in *Hadley v Baxendale* deals with such damage as may fairly and reasonably be considered arising naturally, that is, according to the usual course of things, from the breach of contract, as the probable result of the breach. It depends, as we have seen, on the knowledge which the parties are presumed to possess.

---

[95] [2015] EWCA Civ 1146. See also *Brown v KMR Services Ltd* [1995] 4 All ER 598. See generally Burrows, *Remedies for Torts and Breach of Contract* (3rd edn, 2004) pp 91–4; *McGregor on Damages* (19th edn, 2014) para 22–009.

[96] *Koufos v C Czarnikow Ltd*, above, n 72, 382, 383, 385–6, 417.

[97] *H Parsons (Livestock) Ltd v Uttley Ingham & Co Ltd* [1978] QB 791, 804, 813, *Wroth v Tyler* [1974] Ch 30, 60–2; *Transworld Oil Ltd v North Bay SS Corp* [1987] 2 Lloyd's Rep 173, 175 (relying on cases of physical injury); *Homsy v Murphy* (1997) 73 P & CR 26, 36, 45.

[98] Above, p 576. See also *Islamic Republic of Iran SS Lines v Ierax SS Co of Panama* [1991] 1 Lloyd's Rep 81, 85–6.

[99] [1995] 4 All ER 598, 620–1.

(i) Normal business position of parties

Damages will not be too remote if they flow from the normal business position of the parties, for the Court will assume that this is known to both of them. In *Monarch Steamship Co Ltd v Karlshamns Oljefabriker (A/B)*,[100] the facts of which are summarized above, as a result of the diversion of the delayed vessel to Glasgow the purchasers of the cargo of soya incurred expenses in having them forwarded to the contractual destination in Sweden.

The House of Lords held that the purchasers were entitled to recover this cost. Lord Wright pointed out that the question in all such cases must always be 'what reasonable business men must be taken to have contemplated as the natural or probable result if the contract was broken. As reasonable business men each must be taken to understand the ordinary practices and exigencies of the other's trade or business'.[101] In this case, the possibility of war must have been present in the minds of the parties, and experienced business people would know that one of the risks that would be consequent upon prolongation of the voyage at that time would be the diversion of the vessel by the order of the Admiralty. The cost of transhipment was therefore not too remote a consequence of the unseaworthiness of the ship.

(ii) Non-delivery or late delivery

The Sale of Goods Act 1979 contains statutory provisions for the standard assessment of damages for breach of a contract of sale which are founded on the first branch of the rule in *Hadley v Baxendale*, and these are considered later in this chapter.[102] But the first branch of the rule also applies where a seller fails to deliver or is late in delivering what is on the face of it obviously a profit-earning chattel, for instance, a merchant or passenger ship, or some essential part of such a ship.[103] In such cases the party injured will be entitled to recover the loss of profit which might reasonably be expected to arise if the contract were broken.[104]

In contracts for the carriage of goods, if, by default of a carrier, the goods which he has contracted to deliver are lost or delayed in transit, certain loss will ordinarily be assumed to have been suffered by the consignee as the natural and probable result of the breach. In the case of loss, the normal measure of damages is the market value of the goods at the time when they ought to have arrived, less the freight payable on safe delivery.[105] In the case of delay in delivering the goods, it is the difference between the market value of the goods on the day on which they ought to have arrived and their market value on the day on which they did arrive.[106]

---

[100] [1949] AC 196, above, p 543. Cf *Diamond v Campbell-Jones* [1961] Ch 22.

[101] [1949] AC 196, 224. See also *Bulk Oil v Sun International* [1984] 1 Lloyd's Rep 531, 544.

[102] Below, p 589.

[103] *Victoria Laundry (Windsor) Ltd v Newman Industries Ltd* [1949] 2 KB 528, 536 (Asquith LJ). See also *Fletcher v Tayleur* (1855) 17 CB 21; *Saint Lines v Richardsons Westgarth & Co* [1940] 2 KB 99.

[104] *Cory v Thames Ironworks & S.S. Co* (1868) LR 3 QB 181 (use of hull as coal store); *Fyffes Group Ltd v Reefer Express Lines Pty Ltd* [1996] 2 Lloyd's Rep 171, 203 (sub-charter of vessel on three-year time charter).

[105] *Rodocanachi v Milburn* (1886) 18 QBD 67, 76.

[106] *Wilson v Lancs & Yorks Ry* (1861) 9 CBNS 632; *Koufos v C Czarnikow Ltd*, above, n 72.

(iii) Exceptional loss not covered

On the other hand, the first branch of the rule in *Hadley v Baxendale* does not cover losses which are the consequence of special facts not known to the party in default at the time the agreement was made. In *Hadley v Baxendale* itself, H was unable to recover damages arising from the fact that they had only one shaft, and in *Victoria Laundry* V was unable to recover in respect of the exceptionally lucrative Ministry of Supply contracts because information about those facts had not been conveyed to the defendants. Again in *British Columbia etc Saw-Mill Co Ltd v Nettleship*:[107]

A number of cases of machinery intended for the erection of a sawmill at Vancouver were shipped on the defendant's vessel. The defendant failed to deliver one of the cases, but was unaware of the fact that it contained a material part without which the sawmill could not be erected at all. BC Saw-Mill claimed the cost of replacing the lost parts, and the loss incurred by the stoppage of its works during the time that the rest of the machinery remained useless owing to the absence of the lost parts.

It was held that the measure of damages was the cost of replacing the lost machinery at Vancouver only, and the Court said:[108]

The defendant is a carrier, and not a manufacturer of goods supplied for a particular purpose . . . He is not to be made liable for damages beyond what may fairly be presumed to have been contemplated by the parties at the time of entering into the contract. It must be something which could have been foreseen and reasonably expected, and to which he assented expressly or impliedly by entering into the contract.

This principle will exclude the recovery of damages in respect of loss of profit on actual or contemplated forward contracts where the carrier has no actual or imputed knowledge of these at the time of the contract. The loss of profit on such sales is too remote. An illustration is provided by *Horne v Midland Railway Company*:[109]

H being under contract to deliver military shoes in London for the French army at an unusually high price by a particular day, delivered them to the defendant to be carried, with notice of the contract only as to the date of delivery. The shoes were delayed in carriage, and were consequently rejected by the intending purchasers. H sought to recover, in addition to the ordinary loss for delay, the difference between the price at which the shoes were actually sold and the high price at which they would have been sold if they had been punctually delivered.

It was held that this damage was not recoverable unless it could be proved that the company was informed of the exceptional loss which H might suffer from an unpunctual delivery. Again, it has been held that a person who contracts to purchase land intending to resell it to an identified sub-purchaser at a profit will not be able

---

[107] (1868) LR 3 CP 499.   [108] (1868) LR 3 CP 499, 505 (Bovill CJ).
[109] (1873) LR 8 CP 131. Although this case was one of an exceptionally lucrative contract, the same principle applies to ordinary loss of profit: *Heskell v Continental Express* [1950] 1 All ER 1033.

to recover in respect of the loss of the sub-sale where the seller does not know of the purchaser's intention and purpose and the consequent exposure of the seller to the risk of such damage in the event of breach.[110]

(iv) Immaterial that breach not contemplated

In *Banco de Portugal v Waterlow & Sons Ltd*:[111]

W & Sons agreed to print for the Bank of Portugal a quantity of Portuguese banknotes of a particular type. They negligently delivered to one M, the head of an international band of criminals, some 580,000 of these notes, and these were subsequently put into circulation in Portugal. Upon discovery of the fraud, the Bank issued notices withdrawing from circulation all notes of that type, and undertook to exchange them for other notes. The Bank then brought an action against W & Sons claiming as damages for breach of contract the value of the notes exchanged, and the cost of printing the genuine notes withdrawn.

It was held by a majority of the House of Lords that these losses were recoverable. The damage suffered, although the result of a breach which could scarcely be said to have been in the contemplation of the parties at the time they made the contract, was nevertheless to be considered as flowing from the business positions of the parties and arising naturally from the breach.

(f) DAMAGE REASONABLY SUPPOSED TO BE IN THE CONTEMPLATION OF THE PARTIES

As we have seen, the application of this second branch of the rule depends upon the knowledge which the contract-breaker possesses at the time of the contract, of special circumstances outside the 'ordinary course of things', of such a kind that a breach in those circumstances will cause more loss. The question is whether the damage is such as may reasonably be supposed to have been in the contemplation of both parties, at the time they made the contract, as the probable result of the breach of it. So, in *Simpson v London and North Western Railway Company*:[112]

S, a manufacturer, was in the habit of sending specimens of his goods for exhibition to agricultural shows. After exhibiting in a show at Bedford, he entrusted some of his samples to an agent of the defendant company for carriage to a show-ground at Newcastle. On the consignment note he wrote: 'Must be at Newcastle Monday certain'. Owing to a default on the part of the company, the samples arrived late for the Newcastle show. S therefore claimed damages for his loss of profits at the show.

---

[110] *Seven Seas Properties v Al Essa (No 2)* [1993] 1 WLR 1083 (purchaser concealed purpose). See also *Seven Seas Properties v Al Essa* [1988] 1 WLR 1272, 1276.

[111] [1932] AC 452. See *The Portuguese Bank-note Case* by Sir Cecil Kisch for an exciting account of this case.

[112] (1876) 1 QBD 274.

It was held that the company was liable. The company's agent had knowledge of the special circumstances, that the goods were to be exhibited at the Newcastle show, and so should have contemplated that a delay in delivery might result in this loss.

It is usually said that 'bare knowledge' of the special circumstances surrounding the contract is sufficient to make the contract-breaker liable.[113] But there is some authority for the view that, in addition, the contract-breaker should either expressly or impliedly have contracted to assume liability for the exceptional loss. On this view, the mere communication to a party of the existence of special circumstances is not enough: there must be something to show that the contract was made *on the terms* that the defendant was to be liable for that loss.[114]

This view cannot be supported. No doubt a casual intimation would not suffice, for the special circumstances must be disclosed in such a manner as to render it a fair inference of fact that both parties contemplated the exceptional loss as a probable result of the breach. Thus in *Kemp v Intasun Holidays Ltd*:[115]

While booking a holiday Mrs K remarked to the travel agent that her husband was not present because he was suffering, as he sometimes did, from an asthma attack. In breach of contract Mr and Mrs K were accommodated for the first 30 hours of their holiday in a filthy and dusty room in an inferior hotel and Mr K had an asthma attack throughout the period. The trial judge awarded Mr K inter alia £800 for the consequences of having suffered an asthma attack due to the state of the alternative accommodation.

It was held by the Court of Appeal that this casual remark did not suffice to give the defendant the necessary degree of knowledge of special circumstances to make the defendant responsible for the consequences of the asthma attack he had suffered. What is necessary to enlarge the area of contemplation is that the special circumstances should be brought home to the party.[116] But, although one might interpret the reasoning of Lord Hoffmann and Lord Hope in *The Achilleas* as offering some support for this,[117] the Courts have expressly denied that it is necessary for there to be a term of the contract that the defendant is to be liable for that loss.[118]

---

[113] *Patrick v Russo-British Grain Export Co Ltd* [1972] 2 KB 535, 540 (Salter J).

[114] *British Columbia etc. Saw-Mill Co Ltd v Nettleship* (1868) LR 3 CP 499, 509; *Horne v Midland Ry* (1873) LR 8 CP 131, 141. See also *Victoria Laundry (Windsor) Ltd v Newman Industries Ltd* [1949] 2 KB 528, 538; *Seven Seas Properties v Al Essa (No 2)* [1993] 1 WLR 1083, 1088 (a party should not be exposed to risks of liability going beyond the first branch of *Hadley v Baxendale* without the opportunity of making an informed decision whether to accept such risk and whether to negotiate some exclusion from liability).

[115] [1987] 2 FTLR 234.

[116] See *Heywood v Wellers* [1976] 1 QB 446, 459 (Lord Denning MR) (tort). A much-discussed hypothetical example is of A booking a taxi for £50 with B, a taxi-driver. A explains to B when booking that it is essential for him to reach his specified destination on time as he is meeting a business client there to clinch a highly lucrative deal. In breach of contract, B takes the wrong route so that A arrives late at his destination. As a consequence A loses the lucrative deal (worth an estimated £10m net profit). Is A entitled to damages of £10m from B?

[117] Above, p 579.

[118] *Koufos v C Czarnikow Ltd, The Heron II* [1969] 1 AC 350, 422; *GKN Centrax Gears Ltd v Matbro Ltd* [1976] 2 Lloyd's Rep 555.

6. MITIGATION

A person who has suffered loss from a breach of contract must take any reasonable steps that are available to mitigate the extent of the damage caused by the breach.[119] The innocent party cannot claim to be compensated by the party in default for loss which is really due not to the breach but to its own failure to behave reasonably after the breach.[120] The underlying policy is the desirability of avoiding waste, in this context a loss which could have been avoided by reasonable action. It is often said that the law imposes 'a duty' on claimants to mitigate their loss. But this expression is misleading. The claimant cannot itself be sued for failure to comply with its duty; rather the consequence is simply that no damages are given for the avoidable loss.

(a) ACTING REASONABLY

An employee who is wrongfully dismissed must make reasonable efforts to obtain, and must accept an offer of, suitable alternative employment. A failure to do so may mean that the employee is, in certain circumstances, entitled to nominal damages only.[121] Again, where a seller wrongfully refuses to deliver goods due under a contract for the sale of goods, a buyer who fails to buy substitute goods which are available will be debarred from claiming any part of the damage which is due to the failure to do so.[122] A claimant may even be required to accept a reasonable offer from the defendant which would make good the loss or part of it.[123] But there is no obligation to do anything other than in the 'ordinary course of business'[124] and it is a question of fact in each case whether the claimant has acted as a reasonable person might have been expected to act. For example, there is no compulsion to accept goods of inferior quality[125] or to risk one's commercial reputation[126] or to embark upon complicated litigation[127] or to undergo an operation with the risk of surgical complications[128] in order to mitigate loss. The claimant need not take steps which it cannot financially

---

[119] Bridge (1989) 105 LQR 398.

[120] *British Westinghouse Electric Co Ltd v Underground Electric Rys Co of London Ltd* [1912] AC 673, 689.

[121] *Beckham v Drake* (1847–49) 2 HLC 579; *Shindler v Northern Raincoat Co Ltd* [1960] 1 WLR 1038; *Brace v Calder* [1895] 2 QB 253.

[122] *Kaines (UK) v Osterreichische Warenhandelsgesellschaft Austrowaren Gesellschaft mbH* [1993] 2 Lloyd's Rep 1 (in volatile market buyer must act quickly); *Coastal (Bermuda) Petroleum Ltd v VTT Vulcab Petroleum (No 2)* [1994] 2 Lloyd's Rep 629, 635.

[123] *Brace v Calder* [1895] 2 QB 253; *Payzu Ltd v Saunders* [1919] 2 KB 581; *Sotiros Shipping Inc v Sameiet Solholt* [1983] 1 Lloyd's Rep 605. Cf Bridge (1989) 105 LQR 398, 411 ff.

[124] *Dunkirk Colliery Co v Lever* (1878) 9 Ch D 20, 25.

[125] *Heaven & Kesterton Ltd v Et Francois Albiac & Cie* [1956] 2 Lloyd's Rep 316. See also *Strutt v Whitnell* [1975] 1 WLR 870.

[126] *James Finlay & Co Ltd v NV Kwik Hoo Tong HM* [1929] 1 KB 400; *London & South of England Building Society v Stone* [1983] 1 WLR 1242.

[127] *Pilkington v Wood* [1953] Ch 770.

[128] *Selvanayagam v University of West Indies* [1983] 1 WLR 585.

afford: that is, impecuniosity is an excuse for failure to mitigate.[129] In cases of wrongful dismissal, an employee is not compelled to accept re-employment if it involves lower status, if relations are irretrievably affected by the circumstances of dismissal (as where there has been a public charge of misconduct), or if it is likely to be less permanent than alternatives.[130]

A claimant who has taken unreasonable steps cannot hold the defendant liable for loss which has thus been suffered.[131] Again, the question of reasonableness is a question of fact. For example, it has been held reasonable to incur hire-purchase charges to replace a damaged rotor,[132] legal expenses in proceedings with a third party,[133] advertising to safeguard one's commercial reputation,[134] and voluntary expenses to meet the claimant's commercial (but legally unenforceable) obligations to the public.[135]

(b) COMPENSATING ADVANTAGES MAY REDUCE DAMAGES

Where a person mitigates loss and obtains a compensating advantage, the advantage will be deducted from the damages provided it arose directly from the breach and the act of mitigation and is not merely an 'indirect' or collateral benefit.[136] Thus where turbines which were less efficient than the contract specification and used more coal were replaced by turbines which resulted in an overall saving of coal over the whole period, the damages had to be reduced by the savings achieved.[137] But, where the benefit is independent of the act of mitigation, damages will not be reduced. Thus benefits from wholly independent transactions, for example sums due under an insurance policy, will not lead to a deduction.[138] The fact that replacement property bought is better than the original property, which was damaged as a consequence of the breach of contract, will not in itself reduce damages;[139] rather it must be shown that the claimant will derive a real pecuniary advantage from the better property.[140]

---

[129] *Clippens Oil Co Ltd v Edinburgh & District Water Trustees* [1907] AC 291, 303. See generally *Lagden v O'Connor* [2003] UKHL 64, [2004] 1 AC 1067.

[130] *Yetton v Eastwoods Froy Ltd* [1967] 1 WLR 104. Cf *Brace v Calder* [1895] 2 QB 253.

[131] *Sotiros Shipping Inc v Sameiet Solholt* [1983] 1 Lloyd's Rep 605, 608.

[132] *Bacon v Cooper (Metals) Ltd* [1982] 1 All ER 397.   [133] *The Antaios* [1981] 2 Lloyd's Rep 284, 299.

[134] *Holden Ltd v Bostock & Co Ltd* (1902) 18 TLR 317.

[135] *Banco de Portugal v Waterlow & Sons Ltd* [1932] AC 452, the facts of which are set out above, p 585.

[136] *British Westinghouse Co v Underground Electric Rys Co of London* [1912] AC 673; *Lavarack v Woods of Colchester* [1967] 1 QB 278; *Hussey v Eels* [1990] 2 QB 227; *Famosa SS Co Ltd. v Armada Bulk Carriers Ltd* [1994] 1 Lloyd's Rep 633, 637; *Dimond v Lovell* [2002] 1 AC 384; *Needler Financial Services Ltd v Taber* [2002] 3 All ER 501; *Primavera v Allied Dunbar Assurnace Plc* [2002] EWCA Civ 1327, [2003] PNLR 12; *Fulton Shipping Inc of Panama v Globalia Business Travel SAU of Spain* [2014] EWHC 1547 (Comm), [2014] 2 Lloyd's Rep 230.

[137] *British Westinghouse Co v Underground Electric Rys Co of London* [1912] AC 673. See Dyson [2012] LMCLQ 412.

[138] *Bradburn v GW Ry* (1874) LR 10 Ex 1; *Arab Bank plc v John D Wood Commercial Ltd* [2000] 1 WLR 857.

[139] *Bacon v Cooper (Metals) Ltd* [1982] 1 All ER 397. See also *Harbutt's Plasticine Ltd v Wayne Tank and Pump Co Ltd* [1970] 1 QB 447.

[140] *Voaden v Champion, The Baltic Surveyor* [2002] EWCA Civ 89, [2002] 1 Lloyd's Rep 623.

7. ASSESSMENT OF DAMAGES IN CONTRACTS FOR THE SALE OF GOODS

Useful illustrations of the application of the principles so far discussed are provided by the manner of assessment of damages in contracts for the sale of goods. For example, sections 50 and 51 of the Sale of Goods Act 1979 (the latter now applies only to non-consumer contracts for the sale of goods)[141] state that the measure of damages for non-acceptance or non-delivery of the goods is 'the estimated loss directly and naturally resulting, in the ordinary course of events, from the buyer's or seller's breach of contract'; and where there is an available market for the goods in question, this is prima facie to be ascertained by the difference between the contract price and the market or current price at the time when the goods ought to have been accepted or delivered, as the case may be, or, if no time was fixed, then at the time of the refusal to accept or deliver. The reason for this prima facie 'breach-date' rule[142] is that in a case of non-delivery by the seller the buyer may go into the market and buy alternative goods at the current price and, in a case of the buyer's failure to accept goods, the seller may take his goods into the market and obtain the current price for them.[143]

(a) NON-DELIVERY

Suppose that A promises to sell and deliver to B 1,000 tonnes of coal at £112 per tonne on 8 February. A fails to carry out its contract. On 8 February the market price of coal of that quality is £120 per tonne. B can recover as damages for non-delivery the difference between the contract price and the market price on that day, that is, £8 per tonne.[144]

Uncontemplated forward or sub-sales must ordinarily be disregarded. If, for instance, in the expectation of receiving the coal, B has contracted to sell a similar quantity to C at £117 per tonne, its damages will still be £8 (and not £5) per tonne, since it must normally go into the market in order to fulfil its contract with C.[145] And the same is true where the sub-sale is at a price higher than the market price at the date when delivery should be made.[146]

---

[141] By reason of the amendment of the 1979 Act by the Consumer Rights Act 2015.

[142] ss 50(3) and 51(3). For examples of its displacement, see *Van den Hurk v R Martens & Co Ltd* [1920] 1 KB 850 (sale of goods); *Johnson v Agnew* [1980] AC 367, 400–1 (sale of land). See generally Waddams (1981) 97 LQR 445 and above, p 566.

[143] *Barrow v Arnaud* (1846) 8 QB 604, 609 (Tindal CJ); *Kaines (UK) Ltd v Osterreichische Warrenhandelgesellschaft Austrowaren Gesellschaft mbH* [1993] 2 Lloyd's Rep 1 (in a volatile market this must be done at the first practical opportunity).

[144] s 51(3).   [145] Cf *Williams Bros v ET Agius Ltd* [1914] AC 510.

[146] *Great Western Ry v Redmayne* (1866) LR 1 CP 329. But contrast *Hall Ltd v Pim Junr & Co* (1928) 139 LT 50 and *Coastal International Trading Ltd v Maroil AG* [1988] 1 Lloyd's Rep 92 where it was contemplated that the buyer might resell the particular goods purchased.

(b) LATE DELIVERY

Where the seller is late in delivering the goods, the damage is normally the difference between the market value at the time they ought to have been delivered and the market value at the time when they actually were delivered.[147] Difficulties have arisen where the goods have been resold for more than their market value. In *Wertheim v Chicoutimi Pulp Co Ltd*:[148]

The seller was late in delivering the goods. The market price of the goods at the time when they ought to have been delivered was 70s per ton, and, at the time they were delivered, 42s 6d per ton. The normal measure of damages would therefore have been 27s 6d per ton, and this was the sum claimed by the buyer. But proof was adduced that he had actually sold the goods for 65s per ton.

The Judicial Committee of the Privy Council held that the seller could rely on this sale to reduce the damages to 5s per ton. Lord Atkinson considered that the prima facie market value rule was displaced where the sub-sale proves that the value of the goods to the buyer was more than their market value at the time of delivery and that to assess damages by reference to market value would allow the buyer to be 'compensated for a loss he never suffered'.[149] A possible counter-argument is that the buyer was not obliged to fulfil the subcontract by delivering the specific goods received.[150] The buyer would have been free to resell the goods at the time they ought to have been delivered at their then market price (70s per ton) and to procure other goods for the subcontract. In a falling market a buyer is likely to do this and, on the facts of *Wertheim's* case, to sell one lot at 70s per ton and to fulfil the 65s per ton sub-sale by buying in at the market price of 42s 6d per ton. The late delivery therefore deprived the buyer in that case of the opportunity to sell at the due date, a fact that was unaffected by the sub-sale.

(c) NON-ACCEPTANCE

Although the normal rule, as set out in section 50(3) of the Sale of Goods Act 1979 is that the measure of damages is the difference between the contract price and the market price on the day fixed for acceptance, in modern trading conditions the retail price is frequently that recommended by the manufacturers, so that there is no difference between the contract and the market price. The question then arises

---

[147] *Elbinger Aktiengesellschaft v Armstrong* (1874) LR 9 QB 473; Sale of Goods Act 1979, s 53(3).

[148] [1911] AC 301 approved in *Williams Bros v ET Agius Ltd* [1914] AC 510, 522. See also the reasoning in *Pagnan & Fratelli v Corsiba Industrial Agropacuaria* [1970] 1 WLR 1306.

[149] [1911] AC 301, 307–8.

[150] *Slater v Hoyle & Smith Ltd* [1920] 2 KB 11, 23 (Scrutton LJ). See also *Campbell Mostyn (Provisions) Ltd v Barnett Trading Co* [1954] 1 Lloyd's Rep 65. But in *Bence Graphics Ltd v Fasson UK Ltd* [1998] QB 87, *Slater's* case was not followed, it was stated that it 'should be reconsidered', and Auld LJ approved of *Wertheim's* case. For the *Bence Graphics* case, see below, pp 592–3.

whether a seller who is a dealer can recover its loss of profit on the sale. In *WL Thompson Ltd v Robinson (Gunmakers) Ltd*:[151]

The defendant contracted to buy a new Vanguard car from T. T was a car dealer and the price of the car was that fixed by the manufacturers, which it was unable to vary in any way. The defendant refused to accept the car, but T managed to persuade its wholesale suppliers to take the car back. T nevertheless claimed from the defendant the loss of its profit on the sale.

The defendant claimed that T was entitled to only nominal damages, there being no difference between the market price of the car and the contract price. Upjohn J refused to accept this contention. He held that section 50(3) of the Sale of Goods Act 1979 laid down only a prima facie rule, and that it was displaced by proof in this case that the supply of Vanguard cars currently exceeded demand. T therefore acted reasonably in returning the car to its suppliers, but it had sold one less Vanguard car than it would otherwise and so was entitled to claim its loss of profit on the transaction. It had therefore suffered a loss in the volume of its sales.[152]

On the other hand, in *Charter v Sullivan*,[153] the Court of Appeal held that a car dealer could recover only nominal damages for non-acceptance of a car when the state of the motor trade was such that he could sell all the cars he could get, and he in fact sold the vehicle in question within ten days of the failure to accept; here the breach did not result in loss in the volume of sales. Jenkins LJ went so far as to doubt whether it could be said that there was an 'available market' for the operation of the market price rule when goods could only be sold at a fixed retail price. But the Court was agreed that the dealer in this case could not be held to have made 'only one sale instead of two', since he was limited in the number of sales he could make by the fact that demand exceeded supply. The dealer had therefore suffered no loss of profit by the breach. The conclusion seems to be that loss of profit is not recoverable where demand exceeds supply, but can be recovered where supply equals or exceeds demand.[154]

A buyer who delays in accepting delivery is liable to the seller for any loss occasioned by the delay including for a reasonable charge for the care and custody of the goods.[155]

(d) BREACH OF WARRANTY

Where goods are delivered in breach of warranty, section 53 of the Sale of Goods Act 1979 (which now applies only to non-consumer contracts for the sale of goods)[156]

---

[151] [1955] Ch 177. Contrast *Lazenby Garages Ltd v Wright* [1976] 1 WLR 459 (second-hand BMW 'unique').

[152] On 'lost volume sellers', see Harris (1962) 60 Mich L Rev 577, 600–1; (1964) 18 Stan L Rev 66; Childres and Burgess (1973) 48 NYU L Rev 833. Cf economists' scepticism about an *assumption* of lost volume in the case of retail sales, Goetz and Scott (1979) 31 Stan L Rev 323, 355; Goldberg (1984) 57 S Cal Rev 283.

[153] [1957] 2 QB 117.   [154] See also *Re Vic Mill Ltd* [1913] 1 Ch 465.

[155] Sale of Goods Act 1979, s 37. Also under s 48(3) of the Act, an unpaid seller has the right to sell perishable goods, or any goods after notice, and to recover from the original buyer damages for any loss occasioned by the breach.

[156] By reason of the amendment of the 1979 Act by the Consumer Rights Act 2015.

provides a prima facie rule that the buyer is entitled to the difference between the value of the goods at the time of delivery to the buyer and the value which they would have had if they had fulfilled the warranty.

(i) Sub-sales

If it was within the reasonable contemplation of the parties at the time they made the contract that the goods would probably be re-sold to sub-purchasers on the same or substantially similar terms, either as they were or after manufacturing them into another product, the Court may have regard to the sub-sale. The buyer will, for example, be able to recover from the seller any damages which it has been forced to pay to those sub-purchasers together with any costs reasonably incurred in defending an action against him by them. Thus in *Hammond & Co v Bussey*:[157]

H, a shipping agent, contracted with B, a coal merchant, for the supply of a quantity of 'steam-coal' to be used in steamships, B knowing at the time of the contract that H was buying the coal for resale as fit for this purpose. H resold the coal, which was not fit for the purpose of steamships and they reasonably, but unsuccessfully, defended an action brought against them by their sub-purchaser.

It was held that H might recover not only the damages paid by it to its sub-purchaser, but the costs incurred in defending the action, for this damage came within the second branch of the rule in *Hadley v Baxendale*, B having had special knowledge of the probability of the subcontracts.

Where, however, the buyer has not been faced with claims by the sub-purchasers, it may not be able to recover from the seller for the difference between the value of the goods delivered and the value which they would have had if they had fulfilled the warranty. Thus in *Bence Graphics Ltd v Fasson UK Ltd*:[158]

B bought vinyl film from the defendant for some £564,300, and used it to manufacture decals which it then sold to companies to be used to identify bulk containers. It was a term of the contract that the decals should have a 'guaranteed minimum five year life' but due to a latent defect the vinyl film degraded prematurely and many of the decals became illegible. There were many complaints but only one claim, for which the defendant had compensated B. B returned some £22,000 worth of defective decals to the defendant, and the defendant conceded that B was entitled to be reimbursed for this. The lack of durability was found by the trial judge to render the vinyl film worthless, and he awarded B £564,300, being the difference between the value of the product had it fulfilled the warranty and its actual value. By the date of the trial, there was no possibility of further claims against B by its customers because the limitation period for such claims had expired.

A majority of the Court of Appeal allowed an appeal by the defendant, and held that since the parties contemplated that the vinyl film would be manufactured and

---

[157] (1887) 20 QBD 79. *Biggin & Co Ltd v Permanite Ltd* [1951] 2 KB 314. Cf *Coastal International Trading Ltd v Maroil AG* [1988] 1 Lloyd's Rep 92 (terms of sub-sale unusual so loss of profit irrecoverable).
[158] [1998] QB 87.

sold on, they contemplated that the measure of damages would be the claimant's liability to the ultimate users, thus displacing the prima facie measure of damages in section 53 of the Sale of Goods Act 1979. The majority cast doubt on the ignoring of the sub-sales in *Slater v Hoyle & Smith Ltd*.[159] This greater willingness to depart from the statutory prima facie rule has been criticized.[160] For example, it has been said that, had B's customers brought claims against B, the defendant would have undoubtedly been liable for the cost of meeting them so that the effect of the decision gave a defendant who delivered worthless goods a windfall gain, the benefit of the forbearance of a person's customers from claiming against him or her. However, it might be thought that this criticism sits uneasily with the rule, considered above, that in general a claimant may not recover for loss that has been avoided.[161]

(ii) Loss of profit

If, at the time of making the contract, the seller knew or may be presumed to have known that goods were to be used to produce a profit, and the breach of warranty precludes or reduces the profit likely to have been made, the buyer may recover damages for the loss of profit caused by the breach.[162] Such a buyer who brings an action for breach of warranty in respect of the quality or performance of goods sold to it cannot recover both the whole capital loss in the value of the goods and also the whole of the profit which it would have made by its use of them for this would be to allow the recovery of damages twice over. In *Cullinane v British 'Rema' Manufacturing Co Ltd*:[163]

C purchased from the defendants a clay pulverizing plant, warranted to be capable of pulverizing clay at the rate of six tons per hour. This warranty was not fulfilled, and C claimed as damages (a) the difference between the purchase price of the plant and its residual value, and (b) his loss of profits from the date of installation to the date of trial of the action.

The Court of Appeal held that these claims could not be cumulative but must be alternative because the profits would only have been made if the capital expenditure had been incurred. C could claim one or other, but not both.

---

[159] [1920] 2 KB 11. Auld LJ boldly said that *Slater* should be reconsidered. Otton LJ preferred to distinguish it because in that case, in contrast to *Bence*, the same goods were sub-sold without any manufacturing process and the defendant sellers did not know of the particular sub-sale.

[160] Treitel (1997) 113 LQR 188 prefers the reasoning in *Slater v Hoyle & Smith Ltd* [1920] 2 KB 11, which the Court of Appeal refused to follow. But cf *McGregor on Damages* (19th edn, 2014) para 23–069; Burrows, *Remedies for Torts and Breach of Contract* (3rd edn, 2004) 215–16.

[161] Above, p 588. The position would have been different if the limitation period for claims by B's customers had not expired, since it would have still been at risk of such a claim.

[162] *Richard Holden Ltd v Bostock & Co Ltd* (1902) 18 TLR 317.

[163] [1954] 1 QB 292. Cf *TC Industrial Plant Pty Ltd v Robert's (Queensland) Pty Ltd* [1964] ALR 1083 (Australia).

8. CLAIMANT'S CONTRIBUTORY NEGLIGENCE

(a) NO APPORTIONMENT AT COMMON LAW

As a general rule, where the claimant's loss has been caused partly by the defendant's breach of contract and partly by the claimant's own blameworthy conduct, the damages are not reduced[164] unless the claimant's conduct breaks the chain of causation[165] or constitutes a failure in the claimant's duty to mitigate its loss[166] or itself amounts to a breach of contract.[167]

(b) LAW REFORM (CONTRIBUTORY NEGLIGENCE) ACT 1945

The 1945 Act applies to reduce damages, where the claimant has been at fault in relation to his or her own damage. Damages are reduced proportionately taking into account both the causal potency and comparative blameworthiness of the parties' conduct.[168] The Act plainly applies to claims brought in tort. As regards breach of contract, the interpretation of the definition of 'fault' in the 1945 Act has led to a tripartite classification of claims.[169] The Act does not apply to the breach of a strict contractual duty (category one)[170] nor does it apply to the breach of a duty of care imposed by the contract which does not give rise to a liability in tort (category two).[171] However, the Act does apply to the breach of a duty of care imposed by the contract where there is concurrent liability in the tort of negligence, as where services are negligently rendered to a client by lawyers, builders or carriers (category three).[172]

---

[164] See generally Law Com No 219, *Contributory Negligence as a Defence in Contract* (1993).

[165] *Quinn v Burch Bros (Builders) Ltd* [1966] 2 QB 370; *Lambert v Lewis* [1982] AC 225; *Schering Agrochemicals Ltd v Reisbel NV SA* (1992, CA), noted by Burrows (1993) 109 LQR 175; *Beoco Ltd v Alfa Laval Co Ltd* [1995] QB 137; *County Ltd v Girozentrale Securities* [1996] 3 All ER 834; *Borealis AB v Geogas Trading SA* [2010] EWHC 2789 (Comm), [2011] 1 Lloyd's Rep 482. See above, p 574.

[166] See above pp 587–8.

[167] *Tennant Radiant Heat Ltd v Warrington Development Corp* [1988] 1 EGLR 41; *Harper v Ashton's Circus Pty Ltd* [1972] 2 NSWLR 395.

[168] See, eg, *Davies v Swan Motor Co (Swansea) Ltd* [1949] 2 KB 291, 326.

[169] This classification was first put forward by Hobhouse J, and confirmed by the Court of Appeal in *Forsikringsaktieselskapet Vesta v Butcher* [1986] 2 All ER 488, [1989] AC 852; aff'd on a different point [1989] AC 880, HL.

[170] *Schering Agrochemicals Ltd v Reisbel NVSA* (1992, CA), noted by Burrows (1993) 109 LQR 175; *Barclays Bank plc v Fairclough Building Ltd* [1995] QB 214.

[171] *Forsikringsaktieselskapet Vesta v Butcher* [1989] AC 852, 866; *Raflatac Ltd v Eade* [1999] 1 Lloyd's Rep 506. Cf *Clark Boyce v Mouat* [1992] 2 NZLR 559, 564, revs'd on other grounds [1994] 1 AC 428.

[172] *Forsikringsaktieselskapet Vesta v Butcher* [1989] AC 852; *UCB Bank plc v Hepherd Winstanley and Pugh* [1999] Lloyd's Rep PN 963. Cf the different conclusion of the High Court of Australia in *Astley v Austrust Ltd* (1999) 197 CLR 1 which has been criticized as being based on a mechanical, even formalistic construction of the legislation: Swanton (1999) 14 JCL 251, 260. It is not settled whether the 1945 Act applies where the claimant has a right of action in tort which is not co-extensive with the one it has in contract. The Law Commission concluded that the Act does not apply: Law Com No 219 (1993), para 3.29. Cf *Vacwell Engineering Co Ltd v BDH Chemicals Ltd* [1971] 1 QB 88 and *Bank of Nova Scotia v Hellenic Mutual War Risks*

While this position is not entirely logical, particularly in respect of breaches of contractual obligations to exercise reasonable care where the defendant's liability exists solely in contract, it has been argued that permitting apportionment in contract cases would allow Courts to vary an agreed allocation of risks. It has also been said that existing contract doctrines, in particular implied terms obliging claimants to take care for their own interests, mitigation, and causation, recognize and give effect to the principle that account should be taken of the fact that it is the claimant who is part author of the loss suffered. Those who take this view, while recognizing that these doctrines operate in an 'all or nothing' manner either allowing full recovery or no recovery, believe that apportionment would unduly undermine the certainty which is important in the English law of contract. The Law Commission accepted that this would be so in the (category one) case of a breach of a strict contractual duty but recommended that apportionment should be available in (category two) cases where the defendant is in breach of a purely contractual obligation to exercise reasonable care.[173] However, since the authoritative acceptance of concurrent liability in contract and tort,[174] it will be very rare for a case to fall within category two rather than category three so that the Law Commission's recommendation would, in practice, make very little difference to the law and has no prospect of being implemented.

9. THE TAX ELEMENT IN DAMAGES

Since damages are designed to compensate the claimant for the actual loss suffered and no more, any liability to pay tax may have to be taken into account. In *British Transport Commission v Gourley*,[175] where G claimed for loss of earnings arising out of personal injuries caused by negligence, the House of Lords held that damages awarded to G on the basis of his gross earnings before deduction of income tax and surtax (£37,720) should be reduced by the amount which he would have had to pay in tax. G was therefore left with a *net* sum of £6,695. This principle has subsequently been applied to contractual claims arising out of the wrongful dismissal of an employee[176] and to a claim for loss of profits on a contract for the purchase of goods.[177] Before it can be applied, however, two conditions must be satisfied: first, the earnings or

---

Association (Bermuda) Ltd [1988] 1 Lloyd's Rep 514, 555; [1990] 1 QB 818, revs'd on other grounds [1992] 1 AC 233, 266.

[173] Law Com No 219 (1993) Parts III and IV.

[174] *Henderson v Merrett Syndicates Ltd* [1995] 2 AC 145. See above, p 26.   [175] [1956] AC 185.

[176] *Beach v Reed Corrugated Cases Ltd* [1956] 1 WLR 807; *Re Houghton Main Colliery Co Ltd* [1959] 1 WLR 1219; *Phipps v Orthodox Unit Trusts Ltd* [1958] 1 QB 314. But under the Income Tax (Earnings and Pensions) Act 2003, ss 401–403, damages for wrongful dismissal are made taxable in the claimant's hands, save that tax is not chargeable on the first £30,000 of such payment. It has been held that the rule in *Gourley*'s case nevertheless continues to apply to the exempted amount: *Parsons v BNM Laboratories Ltd* [1964] 1 QB 95; *Bold v Brough, Nicholson & Hall Ltd* [1964] 1 WLR 201; *Lyndale Fashion Manufacturers v Rich* [1973] 1 WLR 73; *Shove v Downs Surgical plc* [1984] ICR 582.

[177] *Amstrad plc v Seagate Technology Inc* (1998) 86 BLR 34.

profits in respect of which the claim is made must be subject to tax; secondly, the sum awarded as damages must either not be subject to tax in the claimant's hands or, if it is, the tax payable on the damages must be taken into account in assessing the damages.

The first requirement means that the principle in *Gourley's* case does not apply to a claim in respect of the loss of a capital asset, for this would not have been subject to income tax.[178] The second excludes from its operation most claims for loss of profit, for sums awarded as damages for loss of profit are normally subject to tax (at the same rate) in the claimant's hands as part of the profits of his or her business.[179] The *Gourley* case itself has been the subject of considerable criticism. It is said, for example, that it has added needless complexity to the assessment of damages; and that the Courts treat damages for loss of earnings arising out of personal injuries as taxable income, whereas the Legislature exempts them, in part, from tax as being compensation for the loss of what may be called 'natural capital equipment'.[180] Nevertheless, the *Gourley* case is fully in accord with the avowed compensatory aim of damages and should, it is submitted, remain good law.[181]

10. INTEREST

Until recently, the position at common law was that the general loss of use of money (ie, interest) could not be awarded as damages for the late payment of money.[182] In general,[183] therefore, parties to a contract would have to rely either on a term of the contract, express or implied,[184] requiring the payment of interest or on the statutory power to award interest on debts and damages conferred by section 35A of the Senior Courts Act (formerly Supreme Court Act) 1981. That section enables the High Court[185] to include in any sum for which judgment is given simple (but not compound) interest at such rate as the Court thinks fit or as rules of Court may provide, on all or part of any part of the debt or damages for which judgment is given for all or any part of the period between the date when the cause of action arose and the date of the judgment. Further, if the debtor pays the debt after the institution of proceedings but before judgment, the

---

[178] *Hull & Co Ltd v Pearlberg* [1956] 1 WLR 244. Capital gains tax is to be disregarded.

[179] *Diamond v Campbell-Jones* [1961] Ch 22; *Dickinson v Jones Alexander* [1993] 2 FLR 521.

[180] See Baxter (1956) 19 MLR 373; Hall (1957) 73 LQR 212; Jolowicz [1959] CLJ 85; Tucker, *ibid*, 185; Bishop and Kay (1987) 103 LQR 211; Kerridge (1992) 108 LQR 433, 442–5.

[181] This was also the view of the Law Reform Committee in its 7th Report (1958), Cmd 501.

[182] *London, Chatham and Dover Railway Co v South Eastern Railway Co* [1893] AC 429; *President of India v La Pintada Co Nav* [1985] AC 104.

[183] Specific losses caused by not receiving money or receiving it late, such as interest charges paid on taking out a loan, have been recovered as 'special damages' where not too remote within the second rule in *Hadley v Baxendale* (1854) 9 Ex 341: *Wadsworth v Lydall* [1981] 1 WLR 598. Cf *President of India v Lips Maritime Corp, The Lips* [1988] AC 395 (currency exchange losses).

[184] *Re Marquis of Angelsey* [1901] 2 Ch 548.

[185] For the county court, see analogously the County Courts Act 1984, s 69.

Court has a similar power to award interest in respect of the period between the date when the cause of action arose and the date of payment.

However, the common law rule barring interest as damages was swept aside by the House of Lords, albeit arguably in *obiter dicta*, in *Sempra Metals Ltd v IRC*.[186] Interest, including compound interest, can now be awarded as damages where the loss of use, at the rate claimed, is proved and subject to the normal limitations, such as remoteness and the duty to mitigate.

The Late Payment of Commercial Debts (Interest) Act 1998 provides that it is an implied term in contracts for the supply of goods or services (other than consumer credit agreements or contracts intended to operate by way of security) where both parties are acting in the course of a business,[187] that any 'qualifying debt' created by the contract carries simple interest from the day after 'the relevant day'[188] at a rate prescribed by the Secretary of State.[189] The interest may be remitted, wholly or in part, because of the creditor's conduct.[190] Where the contract provides a 'substantial remedy' for late payment of the debt, the parties are permitted to oust or vary the right to statutory interest.[191] A remedy is to be regarded as 'substantial' unless it is insufficient for the purpose of compensating for or for deterring late payment, and it would not be 'fair or reasonable' to allow it to be relied on to oust or vary the right to statutory interest.[192]

Where the relationship between the creditor and the debtor is not purely contractual but also gives rise to equitable duties, for example where the parties are in a fiduciary relationship, interest, including not only simple interest but also compound interest, has long been recoverable in certain circumstances even in the absence of any agreement or custom to that effect.[193]

---

[186] [2007] UKHL 34, [2008] 1 AC 561.

[187] This includes a profession and the activities of government: s 2(1).

[188] The period from when the statutory interest runs—which turns on the definition of the 'relevant day'—is extremely complex. See on this *Ruttle Plant Ltd v Secretary of State for the Environment, Food and Rural Affairs (No 2)* [2008] EWHC 730 (TCC), [2009] 1 All ER (Comm) 73. The law is principally laid down in s 4 (and for advance payments in s 11) of the 1998 Act but complexity has been added by the amendments to s 4 by the Late Payment of Commercial Debts Regulations 2013 (SI 2013 No 395) and the Late Payment of Commercial Debts (Amendment) Regulations 2015 (SI 2015 No 1336). By s 4 it appears that where no date for payment has been agreed, the interest normally runs from 30 days after the date (which, for shorthand, may be referred to as the 'performance/notice date') on which the creditor performed or on which the debtor had notice of the amount of the debt, whichever is the later: but if the parties have agreed a date for payment, interest runs from the day after that date or, if earlier than the agreed payment date, 60 days from the performance/notice date (or if the debtor is a public authority 30 days from the performance/notice date). By reason of s 3(2) interest under this Act does not run after there is a judgment debt because then the Judgments Act 1838, s 17 applies.

[189] The rate of interest has been fixed at the base rate plus 8%: SI 2002 No 1675.

[190] s 5.   [191] ss 1(3) and 7–10.

[192] s 9. For an application of this, see *Yuanda (UK) Co Ltd v WW Gear Construction Ltd* [2010] EWHC 720 (TCC), [2011] 1 All ER (Comm) 550.

[193] *Wallersteiner v Moir (No 2)* [1975] QB 373, 388; *Re Fox, Walker & Co* (1880) 15 Ch D 400 (surety); *Mathew v TM Sutton Ltd* [1994] 1 WLR 1453 (pawnbroker). For a wider view of the equitable jurisdiction, see *Westdeutsche Landesbank Girozentrale v Islington LBC* [1996] AC 669, 695–6 (Lord Goff, dissenting) and 719–21, 735–6 (Lord Woolf, dissenting). Cf the majority, *ibid*, 717, 718–19, 737–41.

11. AGREED DAMAGES CLAUSES

(a) LIQUIDATED DAMAGES AND PENALTIES

The parties to a contract not infrequently make provision in the contract for the damages to be paid on a breach of contract. Such provision does not exclude the application of the general rule that damages for breach are intended to compensate for the actual loss sustained by the claimant. It is a question of the proper construction of the contract to decide whether a sum fixed by the parties, however they may have described it, is a 'penalty', in which case it cannot be recovered, or a genuine attempt to 'liquidate', that is to say, to reduce to certainty, prospective damages of an uncertain amount, in which case the sum will be recoverable.

The rule against penalties originated in equity which would relieve against penalties, cutting them down to the actual loss suffered, but was taken up and applied by the common law, and reinforced by statute.[194] Under the traditional test, enunciated in 1915 by Lord Dunedin in *Dunlop Pneumatic Tyre Co Ltd v New Garage and Motor Co Ltd*,[195] the Court will accept as liquidated damages the sum fixed by the parties if it is a genuine pre-estimate of the loss which seems likely to be caused if the breach provided for should occur.[196] The question is one of construction, to be decided upon the terms and inherent circumstances of each particular contract, judged as at the time of making the contract, not as at the time of breach.[197] Or, again, if, although it is not an estimate of the probable loss, the parties had fixed that sum because they were agreed in limiting the damages recoverable to an amount less than that which a breach would probably cause, it will similarly be accepted by the Court.[198]

The Supreme Court has recently reconsidered the law on penalties in the conjoined appeals in *Cavendish Square Holding BV v Talal El Makdessi* ('*Makdessi*') and *ParkingEye Ltd v Beavis* ('*ParkingEye*')[199] It was made clear that, even though a stipulated sum is not a genuine pre-estimate of loss, it is not a penalty if it protects a legitimate interest of the claimant in the performance of the contract and is not out of all proportion in doing so. In other words, the traditional focus on (non-excessive) compensation is only one of the legitimate interests that the claimant may protect. Lord Neuberger and Lord Sumption formulated the test as follows: 'The true test is

---

[194] 8 & 9 Will III, c 11 (an Act for the better preventing frivolous and vexatious Suits), s 8. For history, see *Wall v Rederiaktiebolaget Luggude* [1915] 3 KB 66, 72–3; Simpson (1966) 82 LQR 392.

[195] [1915] AC 79.

[196] There is some doubt about whether the loss that is the yardstick is actual or legally recoverable loss. In *Lansat Shipping Co Ltd v Glencore Grain BV, The Paragon* [2009] EWHC 551 (Comm), [2009] 1 Lloyd's Rep 659 at [22] Blair J thought that it was the legally recoverable loss. For the contrary view, see Burrows, *Remedies for Torts and Breach of Contract* (3rd edn, 2004) 446–7.

[197] *Dunlop Pneumatic Tyre Co Ltd v New Garage and Motor Co Ltd* [1915] AC 79; *Phillips Hong Kong Ltd v A-G of Hong Kong* (1993) 61 BLR 41 (PC).

[198] *Cellulose Acetate Silk Co Ltd v Widnes Foundry (1925) Ltd* [1933] AC 20.

[199] [2015] UKSC 67, [2015] 3 WLR 1373.

whether the impugned provision is a secondary obligation which imposes a detriment on the contract-breaker out of all proportion to any legitimate interest of the innocent party in the enforcement of the primary obligation.'[200] So, for example, on the facts of the cases, the legitimate interests included maintaining the goodwill of the company (in *Makdessi*) and encouraging the prompt turnover of car parking space and funding the claimant's business as car park managers (in *ParkingEye*). As the detriment on the defendant imposed by the clauses was not out of all proportion to those legitimate interests, the clauses were not penalties and were therefore enforceable.[201]

In clarifying the law in this way, the Supreme Court may be regarded as having built on the approach articulated in *Lordsvale Finance plc v Bank of Zambia*,[202] and followed in a number of subsequent cases.[203] In *Lordsvale*, Colman J said that a clause would be upheld if it was 'commercially justifiable, provided always that its dominant purpose was not to deter the other party from breach'. However, the Supreme Court stressed that it is unhelpful to regard deterrence as objectionable. It has replaced the notion of 'commercial justification' with an emphasis on protecting a legitimate interest and doing so proportionately.

Lord Dunedin's traditional 'genuine pre-estimate of loss' test will no doubt continue to be the usual means of determining whether a clause is a penalty or not, particularly in simple damages clauses in standard contracts.[204] But the important step taken by the Supreme Court is to make it clear that the underpinning and wider principle is one of legitimate interest and proportionality. The general trend appears to be one of upholding all but the most extreme clauses in commercial contracts.[205]

In construing the terms 'penalty' and 'liquidated damages' when inserted in a contract, the Courts will not be bound by the phraseology used, but will look to the substance rather than to the form. The parties may call the sum specified 'liquidated

---

[200] [2015] UKSC 67, [2015] 3 WLR 1373 at [32]. See also the similar formulations of Lord Mance at [152]; and Lord Hodge at [255] supported by Lord Toulson at [293].

[201] In *Makdessi*, Lords Neuberger and Sumption (with whom Lord Carnwath agreed) thought that the clauses were in any event primary, not secondary, obligations so that they fell outside the penalty jurisdiction (see below pp 602–3). But a majority (Lords Mance, Hodge, Clarke, and Toulson) took a different view on this point.

[202] [1996] QB 752, 764.

[203] eg *Cine Bes Filmcilik ve Yapimcilik v United International Pictures* [2003] EWCA Civ 1669; *Murray v Leisureplay plc* [2005] EWCA Civ 963, [2005] IRLR 946; *Euro London Appointments Ltd v Claessens International Ltd* [2006] EWCA Civ 385, [2006] 2 Lloyd's Rep 436; *M & J Polymers Ltd v Imerys Minerals Ltd* [2008] EWHC 344 (Comm), [2008] 1 Lloyd's Rep 541; *General Trading Company (Holdings) Ltd v Richmond Corp Ltd* [2008] EWHC 1479 (Comm), [2008] 2 Lloyd's Rep 475; *Lansat Shipping Co Ltd v Glencore Grain BV, The Paragon* [2009] EWCA Civ 855, [2009] 2 Lloyd's Rep 688.

[204] [2015] UKSC 67, [2015] 3 WLR 1373 at [22].

[205] See also *Phillips Hong Kong Ltd v A-G of Hong Kong* (1993) 61 BLR 41 (PC); *Alfred McAlpine Capital Projects Ltd v Tilebox Ltd* [2005] EWHC 281 (TCC), [2005] BLR 271 at [48]. For the advantages of such clauses, including avoiding difficulties of measuring loss and the inability of the penalty rule accurately to identify unfairness, leading to the argument that such clauses should be upheld subject to standard factors invalidating a contract or contract terms, see Goetz and Scott (1977) 77 Col L Rev 554; Rea (1984) 13 JLS 147; Downes, in Birks (ed), *Wrongs and Remedies in the Twenty-First Century* (1996) ch 11; Chen-Wishart, in the same publication, ch 12. But cf Fenton (1975/6) 51 Ind L Rev 189, 191–2.

damages' if they wish, but if the Court finds it to be a penalty, it will be treated as such. Conversely, if the parties had described the sum fixed as a 'penalty', but it turns out to be a genuine pre-estimate of the loss, it will be treated as liquidated damages.[206]

Alongside the common law rules, one must also now bear in mind in consumer contracts Part 2 of the Consumer Rights Act 2015.[207] This allows the Courts to protect consumers against unfair terms by, for example, holding that such terms are not binding on the consumer. One of the examples given of a term that may be unfair is one requiring any consumer who fails to fulfil his obligation to pay a disproportionately high sum in compensation.[208] In respect of sums payable on breach, it is likely that the 2015 Act will be construed so as to be consistent with the common law on liquidated damages and penalties. This is borne out by *ParkingEye Ltd v Beavis*[209] in which, for much the same reasons as relied on in deciding that the parking charge was not a penalty, it was decided that the term was fair (applying the now repealed Unfair Terms in Consumer Contracts Regulations 1999).

(b) APPLICATION OF THE TRADITIONAL TEST

The leading case on the traditional test is *Dunlop Pneumatic Tyre Co Ltd v New Garage and Motor Co Ltd*:[210]

The appellant sold motor tyre-covers, tyres, and tubes to the respondent which contracted not to resell them, or offer them for sale, at a price below the appellant's list prices and to pay the sum of £5 by way of liquidated damages for every breach of this agreement. The respondent sold a tyre-cover at less than the list price, and was sued by the appellant for liquidated damages for breach.

The House of Lords held that the sum fixed by the parties was a genuine pre-estimate of the loss which might ensue and not a penalty. In the course of his speech Lord Dunedin laid down the following rules:[211]

 (i) 'It will be held to be a penalty if the sum stipulated for is extravagant and unconscionable in amount in comparison with the greatest loss that could conceivably be proved to have followed from the breach.'

An illustration was provided by the Earl of Halsbury in an earlier case, where he said:[212]

For instance, if you agreed to build a house in a year, and agreed that if you did not build the house for £50, you were to pay a million of money as penalty, the extravagance of that would be at once apparent.

---

[206] *Cellulose Acetate Silk Co Ltd v Widnes Foundry (1925) Ltd* [1933] AC 20. See also *Union Eagle Ltd v Golden Achievement Ltd* [1997] AC 514; *Britvic Soft Drinks Ltd v Messer UK Ltd* [2002] 1 Lloyd's Rep 20.
[207] See above, pp 222–32.   [208] Sched 2, para 5.
[209] [2015] UKSC 67, [2015] 3 WLR 1373.   [210] [1915] AC 79.   [211] *Ibid*, 87.
[212] *Clydebank Engineering and Shipbuilding Co Ltd v Don Jose Ramos Yzquierdo y Castaneda* [1905] AC 6, 10.

The question is one of fact in each particular case.[213]

(ii) 'It will be held to be a penalty if the breach consists only in not paying a sum of money, and the sum stipulated is a sum greater than the sum which ought to have been paid.'

In *Kemble v Farren*:[214]

The defendant agreed to perform at the Covent Garden Theatre for four seasons at £3 6s 8d a night. The contract provided that if either party refused to fulfil the agreement or any part thereof, such party should pay to the other the sum of £1,000 as 'liquidated damages'. The defendant refused to perform during the second season.

It was held that the stipulation was penal. The obligation to pay £1,000 might have arisen upon a failure to pay £3 6s 8d and was therefore quite obviously a penalty. The most obvious example of this presumption is where a borrower of money promises to pay the lender an additional sum (over and above interest) if the money is not repaid by a fixed day. In contrast, 'accelerated payment' clauses, which are common in sales by instalments and leasing arrangements and which accelerate an *existing* liability to pay on default, are not invalid as penalties.[215]

(iii) 'There is a presumption (but no more) that it is a penalty when a single lump sum is made payable by way of compensation, on the occurrence of one or more of all of several events, some of which may occasion serious and others but trifling damage.'

An illustration is offered by *Ford Motor Co v Armstrong*:[216]

A retailer of motor-cars agreed with a manufacturer inter alia not to sell any one of the manufacturer's cars, or any part, below the listed price. For every breach of this agreement he was to pay £250, as 'agreed damages'.

A majority of the Court of Appeal held that this was a penalty. The defendant might have become bound to pay the sum of £250 for the breach of a term which would cause only trifling damage. Similarly, in *Kemble v Farren*, the same factor provided an additional reason for the Court to hold that the £1,000 was a penalty because that very large sum was to become immediately payable if 'the defendant had refused to conform to any usual regulation of the theatre, however minute or unimportant'.[217]

A single sum, as opposed to a sum proportioned to the seriousness of the breach (eg per week for delay or per item for items sold in breach of covenant), is presumed to be penal because one tests it against the least serious breach possible. The presumption

---

[213] In *Jeancharm Ltd v Barnet Football Club Ltd* [2003] EWCA Civ 58 (2003) 92 Con LR 26 a clause requiring the contract-breaker to pay interest that amounted to a rate of 260% was struck down as a penalty.

[214] (1829) 6 Bing 141.

[215] *Protector Loan Co v Grice* (1880) 5 QBD 529; *O'Dea v All States Leasing System Pty Ltd* (1983) 152 CLR 359; *The Angelic Star* [1988] 1 Lloyd's Rep 122.

[216] (1915) 31 TLR 267.   [217] (1829) 6 Bing 141, 148.

does not apply where the sum is payable for breach of a single obligation which can be broken in a number of ways, for example non-completion of a building contract.[218] Where it is difficult to estimate the loss and it is therefore uncertain that losses from one breach would be greater than those from another, a Court may hold that the presumption is rebutted. It may also be rebutted where it is clear that the contractual provision has sought to average out the probable losses from all the breaches provided, however, that the disparity is not too great.[219]

On the other hand:

> (iv) 'It is no obstacle to the sum stipulated being a genuine pre-estimate of damage, that the consequences of the breach are such as to make precise pre-estimation almost an impossibility.'

For example, in the *Dunlop Tyre* case itself, the stipulated sum of £5 could only, at the most, be a very rough and ready estimate of the possible damage which might be suffered if a trader undercut the manufacturer's listed price. In public works contracts, such as those for the construction of roads or tunnels, the nature of the loss may in part be non-financial and therefore be particularly difficult to evaluate: in *Phillips Hong Kong Ltd v Attorney-General of Hong Kong* a clause using a formula based on estimates, of the loss of return on the capital at a daily rate, the effect of the delay on related contracts, and increased costs, was said to be sensible.[220]

All these rules are no more than presumptions as to the intention of the parties; they may be rebutted by evidence of a contrary intention, appearing from a consideration of the contract as a whole.[221]

(c) NECESSITY FOR BREACH

At common law the question whether the sum of money or other performance[222] stipulated for is a penalty or liquidated damages can only arise when the event upon which it becomes payable is a *breach of the contract between the parties*.[223] It does

---

[218] *Law v Local Board of Redditch* [1892] 1 QB 127.

[219] *Dunlop Pneumatic Tyre Co Ltd v New Garage and Motor Co Ltd* [1915] AC 79, 99; *English Hop Growers v Dering* [1928] 2 KB 174.

[220] (1993) 61 BLR 41 (PC).

[221] *Pye v British Automobile Commercial Syndicate Ltd* [1906] 1 KB 425.

[222] *Jobson v Johnson* [1989] 1 WLR 1026 (transfer of shares); *General Trading Company (Holdings) Ltd v Richmond Corp Ltd* [2008] EWHC 1479 (Comm), [2008] 2 Lloyd's Rep 475 (clause entitling the buyer of shares, on the seller's breach by failing to procure a guarantee, to withhold payment of a sum otherwise due); *Cavendish Square Holdings BV v El Makdessi* [2015] UKSC 67 at [16], [157]–[159], [170], [230]–[233] (transfer of property), [69]–[73], [154], [170], [226]–[228] (withholding a sum otherwise due). For the forfeiture of money paid, see below, pp 625–7.

[223] *Export Credits Guarantee Department v Universal Oil Products Co* [1983] 1 WLR 399; *Cavendish Square Holdings BV v El Makdessi* [2015] UKSC 65 [12]–[13], [40]–[43], [239]–[241] (firmly rejecting the contrary view taken by the High Court of Australia in *Andrews v Australia and New Zealand Banking Group Ltd* [2012] HCA 30, (2012) 247 CLR 205). See also *Office of Fair Trading v Abbey National plc* [2008] EWHC 875 (Comm), [2008] 2 All ER (Comm) 625 at [295]–[323] (bank charges not payable on breach and therefore could not be penalties).

not therefore arise where the obligation is a true alternative mode of performing the contract.[224] However, it has been held that a 'take or pay' clause, whereby a buyer agreed to pay for a minimum quantity of goods per month whether it had ordered that minimum quantity or not, does fall within the scope of the rule against penalties although on the facts the clause in question was not a penalty.[225]

The distinction between clauses within and outside the penalty jurisdiction has given rise to litigation in the context of hire-purchase agreements. Finance companies sometimes provide that, in the event of termination of the agreement, not only shall they be entitled to take possession of the goods hired and to forfeit instalments already paid, but that the hirer shall also pay a certain sum as compensation for 'loss of profit on the transaction'. If the hiring is terminated as a result of a breach of the agreement by the hirer, the Courts may hold this payment to be a penalty.[226] But if it is terminated voluntarily by the hirer, or by his death or bankruptcy, so that there is no breach of the agreement, the question of a penalty or liquidated damages cannot arise.[227] At common law,[228] this may mean that it is more expensive for a hirer to terminate the agreement voluntarily than to repudiate and break the contract.

(d) AMOUNTS RECOVERABLE

Where the clause is a liquidated damages clause the claimant will recover the stipulated sum without being required to prove damage and irrespective of any actual damage, even where this is demonstrably smaller than the stipulated sum.[229] However, where the actual loss is greater, the claimant is limited to the stipulated sum. In *Cellulose Acetate Silk Co Ltd v Widnes Foundry (1925) Ltd*:

The appellant agreed to pay 'by way of penalty the sum of £20 per week for every week we exceed 18 weeks' in the completion of the delivery and erection of an acetone recovery plant. The work was completed 30 weeks late. Calculated on the agreed basis, the damages recoverable by the respondent on breach amounted to some £600, but its actual loss amounted to £5,850. It therefore claimed that it was entitled to disregard the penalty and to sue for the damages actually suffered.

---

[224] *Alder v Moore* [1961] 2 QB 57. See also *Golden Bay Realty v Orchard Investment* [1991] 1 WLR 981 (penalty rules not applicable to contract in statutory form).

[225] *M & J Polymers Ltd v Imerys Minerals Ltd* [2008] EWHC 344 (Comm), [2008] 1 Lloyd's Rep 541.

[226] *Bridge v Campbell Discount Co Ltd* [1962] AC 600; *Cooden Engineering Co Ltd v Stanford* [1953] 1 QB 86; *Financings Ltd v Baldock* [1963] 1 QB 887; *Lombard North Central plc v Butterworth* [1987] QB 527.

[227] *Bridge v Campbell Discount Co Ltd*, above, n 226, 613, 614, 625; cf Lord Denning at 631; *Goulston Discount Co v Harman* (1962) 106 SJ 369. See also *Alder v Moore* [1961] 2 QB 57; *Richco v AC Toepfer* [1991] 1 Lloyd's Rep 136.

[228] Contrast the Consumer Rights Act 2015, Sched 2, para 5. See also the Consumer Credit Act 1974, s 100 dealing with regulated hire-purchase and conditional sale agreements: where a debtor exercises its statutory right to terminate, its maximum liability, despite a higher agreed sum payable on termination (assuming it has taken reasonable care of the goods) is to pay what is needed to bring its payments up to half the purchase price, and the Court can further reduce this if the creditor's loss is less.

[229] *Wallis v Smith* (1882) 20 Ch D 243, 267.

It was, however, clear from the circumstances that the parties must have known that the damage which would be incurred might greatly exceed the stipulated sum. The House of Lords therefore held that the sum was not a penalty, but was liquidated damages and that damages must be limited to this agreed amount.[230]

Where a clause is held to be penal, the damages recoverable must be assessed in the usual way. Normally this will produce a lower award than the penalty. But it is possible for the claimant to recover a sum, equivalent to normal damages, that is greater than the stipulated penal sum.[231] It cannot be said that the clause has a penal effect in such circumstances and invalidating the penalty also means that a claimant who has acted unfairly by inserting a penal clause is treated more favourably than one whose clause is a genuine attempt to 'liquidate' prospective damages. However, this result can be seen as following from the principle that the validity of a clause is determined by reference to the time at which the contract is made.

FURTHER READING

FULLER and PERDUE, 'The Reliance Interest in Contract Damages' (1936) 46 Yale LJ 52, 373

OGUS, HARRIS, and PHILLIPS, 'Contract Remedies and the Consumer Surplus' (1979) 95 LQR 581

FRIEDMANN, 'The Performance Interest in Contract Damages' (1995) 111 LQR 628

CARTWRIGHT, 'Remoteness of Damage in Contract and Tort: a Reconsideration' [1996] CLJ 488

COOTE, 'Contract Damages, *Ruxley* and the Performance Interest' [1997] CLJ 537

BURROWS, 'Limitations on Compensation' in Burrows and Peel (eds), *Commercial Remedies* (Oxford: Oxford University Press, 2003) 27–43

KRAMER, 'An Agreement-Centred Approach to Remoteness and Contract Damages' in Cohen and McKendrick (eds), *Comparative Remedies for Breach of Contract* (Oxford: Hart Publishing, 2004) 249

CUNNINGTON, 'Should Punitive Damages be Part of the Judicial Arsenal in Contract Cases?' (2006) 26 LS 369

ROBERTSON, 'The Basis of the Remoteness Rule in Contract' (2008) 28 LS 172

PEARCE and HALSON, 'Damages for Breach of Contract: Compensation, Restitution, and Vindication' (2008) 28 OJLS 73

WEE, 'Contractual Interpretation and Remoteness' [2010] LMCLQ 150

---

[230] [1933] AC 20. See also *Diestal v Stevenson* [1906] 2 KB 345. Cf *AKT Reidar v Arcos* [1927] 1 KB 352 (unliquidated damages available in respect of breaches outside ambit of clause).

[231] *Wall v Rederiaktiebolaget Luggude* [1915] 3 KB 66; *Watts, Watts & Co v Mitsui* [1917] AC 227; *AMEV-UDC Finance Ltd v Austin* (1986) 162 CLR 344 (Australia). For criticism, see *Robophone Facilities v Blank* [1966] 1 WLR 1428, 1446; Law Com WP No 61 (1975), paras 46–8; Hudson (1974) 90 LQR 25, (1985) 101 LQR 480; Gordon (1974) 90 LQR 25.

HOFFMANN, '*The Achilleas*: Custom and Practice or Foreseeability?' (2010) Edinburgh LR 47

DYSON and KRAMER, 'There is No "Breach Date Rule": Mitigation, Difference in Value and Date of Assessment' (2014) 130 LQR 259

BURROWS, 'Lord Hoffmann and Remoteness in Contract' in Davies and Pila (eds), *The Jurisprudence of Lord Hoffmann* (Oxford: Hart Publishing, 2015) 251–67

18

SPECIFIC REMEDIES

Under certain circumstances, a contractual promise may be enforced directly. This may be by an action for the agreed sum, for instance the price it has been agreed would be paid for goods, by an order for specific performance of the obligation, or by an injunction to restrain the breach of a negative stipulation in a contract or to require the defendant to take positive steps to undo a breach of contract. These remedies have different historical roots, the claim for an agreed sum being, like damages, a common law remedy whereas specific performance and injunctions are equitable remedies which were once exclusively administered by the Court of Chancery.

1. ACTIONS FOR THE AGREED SUM

Where, for example, it is agreed to sell goods for a certain price, the seller may seek payment of the agreed price.[1] The claim, a liquidated claim for the precise sum, is for the payment of a debt. Although the award of an agreed sum orders the defendant to perform its positive contractual obligation to pay money, and in that sense is similar to specific performance, it is distinct from specific performance and does not attract the same bars.[2] The law of contract also draws a clear distinction between a claim for the agreed sum and a claim for damages for breach of contract. The claimant need prove no loss where the claim is for the payment of an agreed sum and rules, such as remoteness of damage and mitigation of loss, are irrelevant. However, a seller who suffers loss over and above the sum due may recover both the agreed sum and damages.[3]

An action for an agreed sum will not be available until the contractual duty to pay has arisen, whether expressly or impliedly.[4] Subject to any provision in the contract, in sale of goods, by section 49(1) and (2) of the Sale of Goods Act 1979 the seller is not entitled to the price unless the property in the goods has passed to the buyer[5] or

---

[1] Burrows, *Remedies for Torts and Breach of Contract* (3rd edn, 2004) ch 19.
[2] But this remedy was incorrectly treated as if it were specific performance and hence subject to, eg, a want of mutuality bar in *Ministry of Sound (Ireland) Ltd v World Online Ltd* [2003] EWHC 2178 (Ch), [2003] 2 All ER (Comm) 823.
[3] *Overstone Ltd v Shipway* [1962] 1 WLR 117. For interest on the agreed sum, including damages as interest, see above pp 596–7.
[4] *Mount v Oldham Corporation* [1973] QB 309 (implied term that school fees be paid in advance).
[5] *FG Wilson (Engineering) Ltd v John Holt & Co (Liverpool) Ltd* [2013] EWCA Civ 1232, [2014] 1 WLR 2365.

payment is due 'on a day certain irrespective of delivery'.[6] Where the goods have not been delivered, the seller's claim for the price depends on it being ready and willing to deliver.[7] The contractual duty to pay and the correlative right to payment may arise on entering the contract, as in the case of the deposits required in contracts for the sale of land[8] or during the course of performance, as in the case of hire in charterparties,[9] or progress payments in building contracts.[10] By the Apportionment Act 1870, all rents, annuities (including salaries and pensions), dividends, and other periodic payments in the nature of income shall be considered as accruing from day to day and are, subject to express contrary stipulation, apportionable in respect of time.[11]

Where the sum due is simply an advance payment of the price and was not required as security for due performance, the right to it is conditional upon subsequent completion of the contract. Where the contract is discharged before completion, the payment ceases to be due and the innocent party is relegated to its claim for damages.[12] Where the sum due is a deposit or other sum required as security for due performance of the contract, as a general rule it remains payable where the contract has been discharged.[13] It makes no difference whether the accrued obligation is one in favour of the innocent or the guilty party although a claim by the guilty party may be off-set by the innocent party's claim for damages. Thus, an employee who repudiates a contract of employment, can nevertheless sue for wages earned before that time.[14]

The effect of a repudiatory breach by the party who will become liable to pay the agreed sum but before the agreed sum has fallen due has been considered in the context of discharge.[15] *White and Carter (Councils) Ltd v McGregor*[16] established that an injured party who can perform without the co-operation of the contract-breaker[17]

---

[6] *Stein Forbes & Co Ltd v County Tailoring & Co Ltd* (1916) 86 LJKB 448 (provision for payment in cash 'against documents on arrival of steamer' means an action for the price can be brought before delivery of the goods).

[7] *Maclean v Dunn & Watkins* (1828) 6 LJ (OS) CP 184.

[8] *Howe v Smith* (1884) 27 Ch D 89.   [9] *Leslie Shipping Co v Welstead* [1921] 3 KB 420.

[10] *Hyundai Heavy Industries Co Ltd v Papadopoulos* [1980] 1 WLR 1129; *Stocznia Gdanska SA v Latvian Shipping Co*, [1998] 1 WLR 574 (ship-building contracts).

[11] By the Apportionment Act 1870, ss 2, 7.

[12] *Dies v British and International Mining and Finance Co Ltd* [1939] 1 KB 724, below, p 591; *McDonald v Dennys Lascelles* (1933) 48 CLR 457, 477; *Chinery v Viall* (1860) 5 H & N 288. On the position where the payment has been made, see below, pp 621–7.

[13] *Dies v British and International Mining and Finance Co Ltd* [1939] 1 KB 724. See also *Hinton v Sparkes* (1868) LR 3 CP 161, 166; *Damon Compania Naveria v Hapag Lloyd* [1985] 1 WLR 435, 451; *Rover International Ltd v Cannon Film Sales Ltd (No 3)* [1989] 1 WLR 912, 924–5; *Griffon Shipping LLC v Firodi Shipping Ltd, The Griffon* [2013] EWCA Civ 1567, [2014] 1 Lloyd's Rep 471. See further, above, pp 552–4 (consequences of discharge).

[14] *Taylor v Laird* (1856) 25 LJ Ex 329, above, p 42; Apportionment Act 1870, s 2. Cf *Boston Deep Sea Fishing and Ice Co v Ansell* (1888) 39 Ch D 339. Note the difference of opinion in *Moriarty v Regent's Garage & Engineering Co* [1921] 1 KB 423. Cf *ibid*, 434 (Lush J) and 448–9 (McCardie J).

[15] Above, Chapter 15.   [16] [1962] AC 413.

[17] This can include passive co-operation: *Hounslow London BC v Twickenham Garden Developments Ltd* [1971] Ch 233; *Ministry of Sound (Ireland) Ltd v World Online Ltd* [2003] EWHC (Ch) 2178, [2003] 2 All ER (Comm) 823.

almost unfettered option to hold the contract open, to perform, and to recover n once it becomes due. Admittedly Lord Reid indicated that that option is not available where it can be shown that the innocent party had 'no legitimate interest'[18] in performing the contract rather than claiming damages; and Kerr J subsequently expressed the same idea by saying that the innocent party could not hold the contract open to claim an agreed sum 'where damages would be an adequate remedy and where an election to keep the contract alive would be wholly unreasonable'.[19] However, this fetter on the innocent party's right to perform and create an entitlement to an agreed sum applies only in extreme cases.[20]

The almost unfettered option established by *White & Carter* may be said to uphold directly what the parties agreed in their contract and is consistent with the rejection in English law of a rule that contract remedies must be exercised reasonably. But it can be, and has been, criticized[21] as encouraging wasteful performance, as being inconsistent with the mitigation rule (which it is said should apply to actions for an agreed sum) and as giving what amounts to indirect specific performance of contracts which are not specifically enforceable. It is also noteworthy that the approach in *White & Carter* has not been applied in a number of other common law jurisdictions.[22]

2. SPECIFIC PERFORMANCE

An order for specific performance is one by which the Courts direct the defendant to perform the contract, and in accordance with its terms. By contrast to civil law systems which generally regard the innocent party's primary recourse as, in principle, to have the contract performed,[23] the jurisdiction to order specific performance is supplementary to the common law remedy of damages.

---

[18] [1962] AC 413, 431.

[19] *Gator Shipping Corp v Trans-Asiatic Oil Ltd SA, The Odenfeld* [1978] 2 Lloyd's Rep 357, 374.

[20] *Ibid; Clea Shipping Corp v Bulk Oil International Ltd, The Alaskan Trader* [1984] 1 All ER 129, 137; *Ocean Marine Navigation Ltd v Koch Carbon Inc, The Dynamic* [2003] EWHC 1936 (Comm), [2003] 2 Lloyd's Rep 693 at [23]; *Reichman v Beveridge* [2006] EWCA Civ 1659, [2007] 1 P & CR 20 at [41]; *Isabella Shipowner SA v Shagang Shipping Co Ltd, The Aquafaith* [2012] EWHC 1077 (Comm), [2012] 2 Lloyd's Rep 61 at [56]. For three cases where the exception was held to apply, see *Attica Sea Carriers Corp v Ferrostaal Poseidon Bulk Reederei GmbH, The Puerto Buitrago* [1976] 1 Lloyd's Rep 250 (interest not legitimate where cost of repairing ship exceeded the value of the ship when repaired); *Clea Shipping Corp v Bulk Oil International Ltd, The Alaskan Trader* [1984] 1 All ER 129 (which is controversial because the facts were not extreme); *MSC Mediterranean Shipping Co SA v Cottonex Anstalt* [2015] EWHC 283 (Comm), [2015] 1 Lloyd's Rep 359 (affirming a contract, so as to claim continuing demurrage in excess of income lost, held to be wholly unreasonable by Leggatt J who also controversially took the view that the 'no legitimate interest' or 'wholly unreasonable' qualification is an aspect of good faith in contractual dealings).

[21] Nienabar [1962] CLJ 213; Goodhart (1962) 78 LQR 263; Stoljar (1974) 9 Melb ULR 355, 368; Priestley (1990–91) 3 JCL 218. But cf (1962–66) 2 Adelaide LR 103; Tabachnik [1972] CLP 149, 164 ff.

[22] *Rockingham County v Luten Bridge Co* 35 F2d 301 (1929); ALI *Restatement, Contracts (2d)* para 253 (USA); *Asamera Oil Corp v Sea Oil Corp* [1979] 1 SCR 633 (Canada).

[23] Lando and Beale, *Principles of European Contract Law Parts I and II* (2000) 399–402. Although civil law systems may refuse specific performance on a variety of grounds which appear to be similar to those on which English Courts would also refuse the remedy, in practice civil law judges will order specific

(a) ADEQUACY OF DAMAGES

Specific performance will not be granted where damages provide adequate relief.[24] As we shall see, a main reason why damages are considered inadequate is because no substitute for the failed performance can be bought. But damages may also be inadequate where, for example, the contract provided for a series of regular payments but damages could only be sought as each payment fell due,[25] or, as discussed in Chapter 21, where the loss is suffered by a person who is not a party to the contract.[26] Sometimes the Courts have preferred to use different terminology than adequacy to explain the relationship between specific performance and damages. For example, it has been said that specific performance will be ordered if that remedy will 'do more perfect and complete justice than an award of damages.'[27] However, while some of the other bars to specific performance have been weakened in the modern law, so that an order of specific performance has become easier to obtain, it seems clear that no different underlying approach to the relationship between the two remedies has been heralded merely by such a change of terminology.

Should the inadequacy of damages requirement remain? Put another way, should specific performance remain a secondary remedy to damages? Two factors suggest that it should. First, specific performance, unlike damages, does not take account of the desirability of a claimant taking reasonable steps to mitigate its loss and granting specific performance avoids the policy of the mitigation rule. Secondly, there have been many improvements in the techniques for identifying and quantifying loss recoverable by damages.[28]

(i) Sale of goods in general

Where there has been a failure to supply goods, substitute goods can usually be bought so that damages are adequate. Specific performance has therefore only been awarded where the goods sold were in some sense unique, such as where they have special beauty, rarity, or interest,[29] so that substitutes cannot (easily) be bought. In contrast, specific performance has been refused where the chattel is 'an ordinary article of commerce' such as a piano or even a set of Hepplewhite chairs, as substitute goods can be obtained.[30]

---

performance in a wider range of circumstances than the English Courts. Cf *Co-operative Insurance Society Ltd v Argyll Stores (Holdings) Ltd* [1998] AC 1, 11–12.

[24] *Harnett v Yielding* (1805) 2 Sch & Lef 549, 553; *Ryan v Mutual Tontine Westminster Chambers Association* [1893] 1 Ch 116, 126; *South African Territories Ltd v Wallington* [1898] AC 309.

[25] *Beswick v Beswick* [1968] AC 58.

[26] *Ibid*, below, p 654. But not always, see *Co-operative Insurance Society Ltd v Argyll Stores (Holdings) Ltd* [1998] AC 1, 18, below, pp 613–14 (wrongful closure of 'anchor' supermarket in shopping centre caused losses to other tenants).

[27] *Tito v Waddell (No 2)* [1977] Ch 106, 322 (Megarry V-C). See also *Beswick v Beswick* [1968] AC 58, 77, 83, 88; *The Stena Nautica (No 2)* [1982] 2 Lloyd's Rep 336, 346–7.

[28] Burrows, *Remedies for Torts and Breach of Contract* (3rd edn, 2004) 472–5.

[29] *Holroyd v Marshall* (1862) 10 HL Cas 191, 209; *Falcke v Gray* (1859) 4 Drew 651, 658.

[30] *Whiteley Ltd v Hilt* [1918] 2 KB 808, 819; *Cohen v Roche* [1927] 1 KB 169. Cf *The Oro Chief* [1983] 2 Lloyd's Rep 509 (ship); *Record v Bell* [1991] 1 WLR 853, 862 (furniture in house separately sold to claimant).

Section 52 of the Sale of Goods Act 1979 (which now applies only to non-consumer contracts for the sale of goods)[31] provides that, in any action for breach of contract to deliver specific or ascertained goods, the Court may, if it thinks fit, direct that the contract shall be performed specifically, without giving the defendant the option of retaining the goods on payment of damages. This section has not, however, affected the law on specific performance. In particular, it does not mean that specific performance should be ordered simply because goods are specific or ascertained. And even in the case of a contract falling outside section 52 for the sale of generic goods, such as petrol or steel, specific performance may be ordered where scarcity of supplies means that substitutes are not available.[32]

(ii) Consumer contracts for the supply of goods, digital content, or services

There are special remedies provided for a consumer in Part 1 of the Consumer Rights Act 2015. By sections 19 and 23 and sections 42–43 of the Consumer Rights Act 2015 these include that a consumer, who has a contract for the supply of goods or digital content by a trader, has a right to the repair or replacement, within a reasonable time, of goods or digital content which do not conform to the contract terms (as defined in sections 19(1)–(2) and 42(1)) unless repair or replacement is impossible or disproportionate (compared to the other of those two rights). Similarly, by sections 54–55 of the 2015 Act, a consumer who has a contract for the supply of a service by a trader, has a right to require repeat performance, within a reasonable time and unless impossible, where the performance has not been in conformity with the contract terms (as defined in section 54(2)). By section 58 (which is headed 'powers of the courts'), the courts are expressly given the power to enforce these special remedies—the right to repair or replacement, or the right to repeat performance—by an order of specific performance.

It is important to appreciate that section 58 on specific performance, enforcing a consumer's statutory right to repair or replacement, or the right to repeat performance, represents a move away in this area from the normal requirement for specific performance that damages must be inadequate.[33] This is because section 58 appears to militate against the Courts applying the normal common law approach of denying specific performance unless damages are inadequate. Since the regime of consumer remedies in the 2015 Act is implementing an EC Directive it is perhaps not surprising that, in the primacy apparently afforded to specific performance, it reflects a civilian rather than a common law approach. It appears that (subject to the Court's discretion to decide that the exercise of another right is appropriate)[34] a Court should only refuse

---

[31] By reason of amendment of the 1979 Act by the Consumer Rights Act 2015.

[32] *Sky Petroleum Ltd v VIP Petroleum Ltd* [1974] 1 WLR 576 (scarcity due to oil embargo); *Howard E Perry v British Railways Board* [1980] 1 WLR 1375 (steel strike).

[33] See Harris (2003) 119 LQR 541 (referring to the original introduction of these provisions in relation to contracts for the supply of goods by the Sale and Supply of Goods to Consumers Regulations 2002 (SI 2002 No 3045)).

[34] Consumer Rights Act 2015, s 58(3).

specific performance (ordering repair or replacement of goods or digital content or ordering the repeat performance of services) if impossible or, as between repair and replacement, disproportionate to the other.[35] One may therefore regard the law on specific performance under the 2015 Act as departing not only from the adequacy of damages requirement but also, on the face of it, from several other of the bars to be discussed below (eg the bars concerning personal services, mutuality, constant supervision, and severe hardship to the defendant).

(iii) Sale of land

As a general rule, either party to a contract for the sale of land is entitled to sue for specific performance of the agreement.[36] As regards the vendor's obligation, the reason traditionally given for this is that each piece of land is unique and cannot readily be replaced in the market. And, as regards the purchaser's obligation to pay the price, the reasoning appears to be that the vendor should be entitled to a reciprocal remedy (not least because, by reason of the availability of specific performance, the purchaser acquires under the contract an immediate equitable interest in the land). The power of the Court to grant specific performance is not limited to those situations in which at law damages would be recoverable. Thus specific performance may be ordered in respect of an anticipatory breach of a contract for the sale of land in circumstances where the claimant, having elected to affirm the agreement, would have no immediate right of action for damages.[37]

(b) WANT OF MUTUALITY

In considering whether or not to entertain a claim for specific performance, the Court will take into account whether 'mutuality' exists between the parties. If one party were compelled to perform its obligations in accordance with the terms of the contract while the obligations of the other party under the contract, or some of them, remained unperformed, it might be unfair that the former party should be left to its remedy in damages if the latter party failed to perform any of its unperformed obligations.[38] At one time it was supposed that the Court would not grant specific performance to one party unless, at the time the contract was entered into, it could have been specifically enforced against that party by the other.[39] But this supposed rule was subject to a number of exceptions[40] and has since been exploded.[41] Lack of mutuality is now only relevant if, at the date of the hearing, the claimant has not

---

[35] Consumer Rights Act 2015, ss 23(3), 43(3), 55(3).

[36] *Sudbrook Trading Estate Ltd v Eggleton* [1983] 1 AC 444 478. In cases of misdescription by a vendor of land, eg where the area of the land is less than that stated in the contract, the purchaser may claim specific performance with an abatement of the purchase price to compensate for the misdescription: see Harpum [1981] CLJ 108.

[37] *Hasham v Zenab* [1960] AC 316; and see above, pp 542–4.

[38] *Price v Strange* [1978] Ch 337, 361.   [39] Fry, *Specific Performance* (6th edn, 1921) 219.

[40] Ames, *Lectures on Legal History* (1913) 370.   [41] *Price v Strange* [1978] Ch 337.

performed its obligations under the contract and could not be compelled for some reason to perform its unperformed obligations specifically.[42] Even where mutuality in this sense does not exist, the Court may possibly, in the exercise of its discretion, order specific performance if damages would be an adequate remedy to the defendant for any default on the claimant's part.[43]

(c) CONTRACTS OF PERSONAL SERVICE

The Court will not, in general, compel the performance of contracts which involve personal service.[44] In the case of contracts of employment, and as regards enforcing an employee's obligations, this principle is now embodied in legislation which provides that an employee shall not be compelled to perform a contract of employment.[45] The basis of this approach seems to be that to make one person serve another against his or her will would be improper and could 'turn contracts of service into contracts of slavery'.[46] But this does not explain why specific performance should not be ordered in favour of an employee against an employer and, on this side of the relationship, there have been departures from the general rule. So, for example, by declaration, a public official[47] and a university lecturer[48] may in effect be reinstated; certain statutes now enable a tribunal to make an order for re-engagement or reinstatement of an employee;[49] and, in exceptional circumstances, especially where there is no breakdown in mutual confidence, an injunction may be granted to restrain an employer from dismissing an employee even though this amounts to specific enforcement of the contract of employment.[50] In *Ashworth v Royal National Theatre*[51] it was held that specific performance would not be granted to require the National Theatre to continue employing musicians in the performance of the play *War Horse* because 'loss of confidence is fact-specific'[52] and there was 'clearly an absence of personal confidence on the part of the National Theatre which considered that the musicians could not contribute positively to the play'.[53] Cranston J stated that such an order would interfere

---

[42] *Ibid; Sutton v Sutton* [1984] Ch 184.   [43] *Price v Strange* [1978] Ch 337, 368.

[44] *Rigby v Connol* (1880) 14 Ch D 482, 487; *Scott v Rayment* (1868) LR 7 Eq 112 (partnership). But see above p 610 for specific performance being ordered under the Consumer Rights Act 2015, s 58, to enforce a consumer's right to repeat performance by a trader in a consumer contract for the supply of a service.

[45] Trade Union and Labour Relations (Consolidation) Act 1992, s 236. Cf *Stevenson v United Road Transport Union* [1977] ICR 893.

[46] *De Francesco v Barnum* (1890) 45 Ch D 430, 438.

[47] *Ridge v Baldwin* [1964] AC 40; *R v BBC, ex p Lavelle* [1983] 1 WLR 23. But cf *Chief Constable of North Wales Police v Evans* [1982] 1 WLR 1155, 1175–6; *R v East Berkshire HA, ex p Walsh* [1985] QB 152; *McLaren v Home Office* [1990] ICR 808.

[48] *Thomas v University of Bradford* [1987] AC 795, 824; *Pearce v University of Aston (No 2)* [1991] 2 All ER 469.

[49] Employment Rights Act 1996, ss 114–115, 130. See also Race Relations Act 1976, s 56.

[50] *Hill v CA Parsons & Co Ltd* [1972] Ch 305; *Irani v Southampton and SW Hampshire Health Authority* [1985] ICR 590; *Powell v Brent LBC* [1988] ICR 176; *Robb v Hammersmith and Fulham LBC* [1991] IRLR 72. Cf *Chappell v Times Newspapers Ltd* [1975] 1 WLR 482.

[51] [2014] EWHC 1176 (QB), [2014] 4 All ER 238.   [52] *Ibid* at [23].   [53] *Ibid* at [25].

with the National Theatre's right of artistic freedom under Article 10 of the European Convention on Human Rights to which the court must have particular regard.[54]

(d) UNCERTAINTY

The obligations in an agreement which it is sought to enforce may be so ill-defined, or what has to be done in order to comply with the order of the Court may not be capable of sufficient definition, that specific performance would in the circumstances be an unsuitable remedy. Thus a covenant to 'lay out £1,000 in building'[55] and a contract to construct 'a railway station' with nothing to indicate the nature, materials, style, dimensions, or anything else[56] have been held not to be specifically enforceable.

(e) CONSTANT SUPERVISION BY THE COURT

At one time it was said that an order for specific performance would not be granted if the Court would be required constantly to supervise the execution of the contract. Thus in *Ryan v Mutual Tontine Westminster Chambers Association*[57] the Court held that it could not grant specific performance of a covenant to maintain a resident porter in constant attendance at a block of flats for the benefit of the tenants as it was a contract which would require such supervision as the Court was not prepared to undertake. However, the impossibility for the Court to supervise the doing of the work has more recently been rejected as a ground for denying relief[58] and in *Posner v Scott-Lewis*[59] a covenant to employ a resident porter was specifically enforced. In the case of contracts which involve continuing or complex obligations, difficulties may arise in formulating with sufficient precision (having regard to the terms of the contract) what it is that the defendant must do to comply with the order for specific performance, any breach of which is punishable as a contempt of court. If those difficulties can be overcome, there is no reason why such a contract cannot be specifically enforced if damages would be an inadequate remedy.

A narrower approach was, however, taken by the House of Lords in *Co-operative Insurance Society Ltd v Argyll Stores (Holdings) Ltd*.[60] Their Lordships refused to order the specific performance of an undertaking in a lease (which had 19 years to run) to keep a supermarket 'open for retail trade during the usual hours of business'. A distinction was drawn between cases in which the order would require the party to achieve a result, for instance building or repairing a house, and those in which it would require the party to carry on an activity, such as to run a business

---

[54] *Ibid* at [27] and [33] and Human Rights Act 1998, s 12.

[55] *Moseley v Virgin* (1796) 3 Ves 184.

[56] *Wilson v Northampton and Banbury Ry Co* (1874) 9 Ch App 279.   [57] [1893] 1 Ch 116.

[58] *Shiloh Spinners Ltd v Harding* [1973] AC 691, 724 (Lord Wilberforce). See also the statements of Megarry V-C cited below, n 61.

[59] [1987] Ch 25. See also *Rainbow Estates v Tokenhold Ltd* [1999] Ch 64 (repairing covenant).

[60] [1998] AC 1. For criticism, see Burrows, *Remedies for Torts and Breach of Contract* (3rd edn, 2004) 480–1.

over an extended period of time. The more liberal approach was said to apply only to the first type of case[61] since, in the second type of case, there was a greater possibility of repeated applications to the Court to rule on whether the order would be breached. In the *Co-operative Insurance Society Ltd* case it was also said to be contrary to the long-standing and settled practice of the Court to order a person specifically to perform a contract to run a business,[62] and that the contract in that case did not define the obligation sufficiently precisely to make it capable of specific performance because it said nothing about the level of trade, the areas of trade, or the kind of trade.[63]

(f) CONDUCT AND HARDSHIP

Specific performance is a discretionary remedy. The Court has a choice in the matter and, although this does not mean that the choice will be exercised in an arbitrary or capricious manner, the Court can consider whether it would be fair to grant the remedy[64] and refuse it in circumstances which would not justify a refusal of the common law remedy of damages. 'He who comes to Equity must come with clean hands.' Thus the Court can take into account the fact that the claimant's conduct has been tricky or unfair,[65] or that the claimant has tried to take advantage of a mistake on the part of the defendant.[66] It can also take account of the conduct of the defendant,[67] and it can refuse specific performance if, to grant it, great hardship would be caused to the defendant.[68] The defendant's bad conduct may also induce the Court to grant the remedy where there has been a gross breach of personal faith or an attempt to use the threat of non-performance as blackmail.[69] But where the parties' interests are purely financial, acting 'with gross commercial cynicism' will not suffice.[70] These considerations are, of course, generally considered to be irrelevant at common law.[71]

---

[61] *Ibid*, 13–15. Lord Wilberforce's rejection of the nineteenth-century authorities in *Shiloh Spinners Ltd v Harding* [1973] AC 691, 724, was made in that context and Megarry V-C's statements in *CH Giles & Co Ltd v Morris* [1972] 1 WLR 307, 318 and *Tito v Waddell (No 2)* [1977] Ch 106, 321 were said to be based on incomplete analysis.

[62] [1998] AC 1, 13–15. See also below, n 68 (hardship to defendant).

[63] *Ibid*, 16–17.   [64] *Shell UK Ltd v Lostock Garages Ltd* [1976] 1 WLR 1187.

[65] *Mortlock v Buller* (1804) Ves 292; *Walters v Morgan* (1861) 3 De GF & J 718; *Sang Lee Investment Co v Wing Kwai Investment Co* (1983) 127 SJ 410.

[66] *Webster v Cecil* (1861) 30 Beav 62; above, p 288.

[67] *Sang Lee Investment Co v Wing Kwai Investment Co* (1983) 127 SJ 410.

[68] *Malins v Freeman* (1837) 2 Keen 25; *Denne v Light* (1857) 8 De GM & G 774; *Handley Page Ltd v Commissioners of Customs and Excise* [1970] 2 Lloyd's Rep 459; *Tito v Waddell (No 2)* [1977] Ch 106, 326; *Patel v Ali* [1984] Ch 283. But cf *Mountford v Scott* [1975] Ch 258; *Howard E Perry & Co v British Railways Board* [1980] 1 WLR 1375.

[69] *Co-operative Insurance Society Ltd v Argyll Stores (Holdings) Ltd* [1998] AC 1, 18 (Lord Hoffmann).

[70] *Ibid*.

[71] But see Friedmann, in Beatson and Friedmann (eds), *Good Faith and Fault in Contract Law* (1995) ch 16, and below, p 637 (right to recover the defendant's gain).

(g) MISCELLANEOUS

In addition to the above bars, the Court will also refuse specific performance where the interest to be transferred is merely transitory,[72] or where an entire obligation is specifically enforceable in part only.[73] Also contracts to appoint an arbitrator,[74] to convey the goodwill of a business without the business premises,[75] and to exercise a testamentary power of appointment[76] will not be specifically enforced.

3. INJUNCTIONS

Injunctions are either prohibitory or mandatory.[77] A prohibitory injunction may be granted to restrain the breach of a negative contract or of a negative stipulation in a contract. A mandatory injunction compels the positive performance of an act and may be used to restore the situation to what it was before the breach of contract.

(a) PROHIBITORY INJUNCTIONS

(i) General

Although the grant of an injunction is discretionary,[78] an injunction will normally be granted to restrain the breach of a negative contract or stipulation.[79] A negative contract or stipulation is one whereby a promisor covenants not to do something, for example, not to carry on a certain trade,[80] or to build on land,[81] or not to ring church bells early in the morning,[82] or not to ride a rival horse in 'The Derby'.[83] A negative stipulation, though not express, may be implied, for example, in the case of an exclusive dealing agreement relating to a particular product,[84] or an agreement to charter a ship to a particular person,[85] the injunction being granted to restrain the promisor from buying (or selling) the product elsewhere or chartering the ship to another.

---

[72] *Lavery v Pursell* (1888) 39 Ch D 508, 519 (tenancy for a year).

[73] *Ryan v Mutual Tontine Westminster Chambers Association* [1893] 1 Ch 116. Cf *Rainbow Estates Ltd v Tokenhold Ltd* [1999] Ch 64, 73.

[74] *Re Smith & Service and Nelson & Sons* (1890) 25 QBD 545.

[75] *Baxter v Connelly* (1820) 1 J & W 576. But see *Beswick v Beswick* [1968] AC 58, 89, 97.

[76] *Re Parkin* [1892] 3 Ch 510.

[77] On damages in lieu of an injunction, see below, p 619. On *interim* injunctions, see generally *American Cyanamid Co v Ethicon Ltd* [1975] AC 396.

[78] eg *Bankers Trust Co v PT Jakarta International Hotels and Development* [1999] 1 Lloyd's Rep 910, 911 (anti-suit injunction will only be granted where 'damages are manifestly an inadequate remedy').

[79] *Doherty v Allman* (1878) 3 App Cas 709, 720; *Araci v Fallon* [2011] EWCA Civ 668; *AB v CD* [2014] EWCA Civ 229, [2015] 1 WLR 771.

[80] *Nordenfelt v Maxim Nordenfelt Guns and Ammunition Co Ltd* [1894] AC 535.

[81] *Wrotham Park Estate Co v Parkside Homes Ltd* [1974] 1 WLR 798 (in relation to building that had been undertaken before the decision, see below, pp 630–1).

[82] *Martin v Nutkin* (1724) 2 Peere Wms 266.   [83] *Araci v Fallon* [2011] EWCA Civ 668.

[84] *Catt v Tourle* (1869) LR 4 Ch App 654; *Evans Marshall & Co Ltd v Bertola SA* [1973] 1 WLR 349.

[85] *Lord Strathcona SS Co v Dominion Coal Co* [1926] AC 108; *Associated Portland Cement Manufacturers Ltd v Teigland Shipping A/S* [1975] 1 Lloyd's Rep 581.

(ii) Indirect specific performance?

An injunction may be granted to restrain the breach of a negative stipulation in a contract even though the Court would not order specific performance of the positive stipulations contained in the same contract.[86] Also, it has been granted in cases where its effect may be to enforce performance of the contract, even though the contract is one which the Court might not normally specifically enforce. Thus in *Metropolitan Electric Supply Co Ltd v Ginder*,[87] an express promise by the defendant to take the whole of his supply of electricity from the Company was held to import a negative promise that he would take none from elsewhere, and an injunction was granted.

The question of whether a prohibitory injunction should be refused because it amounts to indirect specific performance of a contract that cannot be directly specifically enforced has been particularly raised in the context of contracts of personal service. As we have seen, in general contracts of personal service cannot be specifically enforced.[88] But the Courts have traditionally accepted that it is possible by means of an injunction to encourage performance in an oblique manner. In *Lumley v Wagner*,[89] for instance:

The defendant agreed to sing at the claimant's theatre, and during that season to sing nowhere else. She then made a contract with another person to sing at another theatre, and refused to perform her contract with the claimant.

The Court refused to order specific performance of her positive engagement to sing at the claimant's theatre, but granted an injunction to restrain the breach of her promise not to sing elsewhere.

The scope of the principle in *Lumley v Wagner* has, however, been confined by two restrictions. In the first place, although in certain instances an express positive promise implies a negative undertaking not to do anything which would interfere with the performance of this promise, the Courts have normally refused in contracts of personal service to enforce by injunction anything but an express stipulation not to do some specific thing. There must have been inserted in the contract itself an express negative stipulation, and the defendant must have acted in breach of that stipulation. Thus in *Mortimer v Beckett*,[90] a boxer, Joe Beckett, agreed with the claimant that he should have 'the sole arrangements of matching me for all my boxing contests and engagements during the period of the next seven years': afterwards he refused to be managed by the claimant. In terms, the contract contained no negative covenant, and so the Court held that an injunction could not be granted.

---

[86] *Lumley v Wagner* (1852) De GM & G 604; *Sky Petroleum Ltd v VIP Petroleum Ltd* [1974] 1 WLR 576; *Hill v CA Parsons & Co Ltd* [1972] Ch 305.

[87] [1901] 2 Ch 799.   [88] Above, p 612.   [89] (1852) 1 De GM & G 604.

[90] [1920] 1 Ch 571. See also *Whitwood Chemical Co v Hardman* [1891] 2 Ch 416. Cf *Hivac Ltd v Park Royal Scientific Instruments Ltd* [1946] Ch 169.

Secondly, an injunction will not be granted if its effect will be to compel the defendant to fulfil a contract for personal service or to abstain from any business whatsoever, for this would be to compel a contract-breaker to choose between specific performance and starvation. In *Ehrman v Bartholomew*,[91] therefore, where a traveller promised that he would serve a firm for ten years and would not, during that period, 'engage or employ himself in any other business', an injunction was refused, among other grounds, because to have granted it would have given him no real choice but to work for the firm. But if the employment is of a special kind, an injunction may be granted to restrain the defendant from doing similar work of that kind. So in *Warner Brothers Pictures Incorporated v Nelson*:[92]

A film actress, Mrs Nelson (professionally known as Bette Davis), agreed that she would render her exclusive services as an actress to the claimants for a three-year period, and would not during that period render any similar services to any other person *or engage in any other occupation*. In breach of these stipulations, she entered into an agreement to appear for another film company. The claimants sought an injunction to restrain her.

Branson J held that, although it was impossible to grant an injunction to prevent her from engaging in any other occupation as this would amount to specific performance, an injunction should be granted to restrain her from working as an actress for any other person for a period of up to three years. There were other spheres of activity which, if not so remunerative, would still be open to her, so that she would not be driven, although she might be encouraged, to perform the contract.[93] This has been criticized as implying that nothing short of idleness or starvation is compulsive and it has been said that Branson J's view that 'an actress of her then youth and soaring talent' might employ herself usefully and remuneratively in other spheres of activity for a period of up to three years appeared 'extraordinarily unrealistic'.[94] More recent cases have examined the practical realities of granting an injunction and have been more willing to infer compulsion where a longer term injunction was being sought. So in *Warren v Mendy*:[95]

There was a dispute over the management of the boxer, Nigel Benn. The case differed from the usual restrictive covenant case in that the injunction being sought by the claimant (Warren) was not against Benn for breach of contract but against another manager (Mendy) in a tort action for inducing breach of Benn's contract with the claimant. But as the claimant would have sought an injunction against anyone who arranged to manage Benn, the same principles were applicable as if the injunction had been sought against Benn for breach of contract.

---

[91] [1898] 1 Ch 671. [92] [1937] 1 KB 209. [93] *Ibid*, 217.

[94] *Warren v Mendy* [1989] 1 WLR 853, 865 (Nourse LJ).

[95] [1989] 1 WLR 853. See also *Page One Records Ltd v Britton* [1968] 1 WLR 157 (injunction not granted to restrain breach of management contract by pop group); *Young v Robson Rhodes* [1998] 3 All ER 524, 534–5.

The Court of Appeal refused the injunction on the ground that to grant it would constitute indirect specific performance of Benn's contract to be exclusively managed by the claimant for the three-year contract period.

On the other hand, *Warren v Mendy* was distinguished in *LauritzenCool AB v Lady Navigation Ltd*:[96]

In 1998 the defendant owners chartered two ships to the claimant charterers under a time charter that was due to run until 2010. The ships were part of a 'pool' managed by the claimants. Following a dispute the owners informed the charterers that they wished to withdraw the two ships from the pool: that is, they wished to pull out of the charterparty in respect of the two ships. Pending final arbitration, the charterers sought an interim injunction to restrain that alleged breach.

That injunction was granted. Although a time charter is a contract for personal services (the owner being required to provide the ship and services of the crew),[97] the Court of Appeal reasoned that it was acceptable to grant the injunction even though its practical effect would be to compel performance of the contract. *Warren v Mendy* was distinguished because the personal services in that case required very special skills and talents. But while that distinction may explain a greater willingness to order specific performance, it does not satisfactorily explain why the injunction granted did not indirectly amount to specific performance.

It has been assumed in the above discussion that the claimant wants the defendant to perform his or her positive contractual obligations. Where this is not so, for example where there is a restrictive covenant to take effect after termination of the defendant's employment[98] or where the claimant undertakes to pay the defendant and to give him his other contractual benefits even though the defendant does no work for him,[99] there is no question of an injunction amounting to indirect specific performance.

(b) MANDATORY INJUNCTIONS

An injunction may also be granted to restore the situation which would have prevailed but for the defendant's breach of contract, for example to put back a tenant wrongfully evicted by a landlord.[100] Such mandatory injunctions are not as readily granted as prohibitory injunctions[101] but the Court will intervene in this way where it is shown that the defendant has deliberately ridden roughshod over the claimant's rights[102]

---

[96] [2005] EWCA Civ 579, [2005] 1 WLR 3686.

[97] It was accepted in *The Scaptrade* [1983] 2 AC 694, per Lord Diplock, that specific performance will not be ordered of a time charter because it is a contract for personal services.

[98] As in, eg, *General Billposting Co Ltd v Atkinson* [1909] AC 118; *Credit Suisse Asset Management Ltd v Armstrong* [1996] ICR 882; *Rock Refrigeration Ltd v Jones* [1997] ICR 938.

[99] *Evening Standard Co Ltd v Henderson* [1987] IRLR 64; *Provident Financial Group plc v Hayward* [1989] 3 All ER 298. The defendant under such an arrangement is described as being on 'garden leave'.

[100] *Luganda v Service Hotels Ltd* [1969] 2 Ch 209.

[101] *Sharp v Harrison* [1922] 1 Ch 502, 512; *Shepherd Homes Ltd v Sandham* [1971] Ch 340.

[102] *Luganda v Service Hotels Ltd*, above, n 100; *Mortimer v Bailey* [2004] EWCA Civ 1514, [2005] 2 P & CR 9.

or that the claimant would be gravely prejudiced if the remedy were withheld.[103] At trial, specific performance, rather than a mandatory injunction, orders a defendant to perform its positive contractual obligations.[104]

4. EQUITABLE DAMAGES

Since Lord Cairns' Act 1858 there has been jurisdiction to grant damages either in addition to or in substitution for specific performance or an injunction.[105] Such damages—often referred to as equitable damages—are governed by the same principles as are damages at common law.[106] But in contrast to common law damages, damages in substitution for an injunction or specific performance may compensate for an anticipated, rather than just an accrued, cause of action.[107] They can also be awarded where an order for specific performance has been made and not complied with.[108]

FURTHER READING

Kronman, 'Specific Performance' (1978) 45 U Chicago LR 351

Schwartz, 'The Case for Specific Performance' (1979) 89 Yale LJ 271

---

[103] *Durell v Pritchard* (1865) LR 1 Ch App 244, 250; *Shepherd Homes Ltd v Sandham* [1971] Ch 340; *Wrotham Park Estate Co v Parkside Homes Ltd* [1974] 1 WLR 798.

[104] For *interim* mandatory injunctions enforcing positive contractual obligations, see *Nottingham Building Society v Eurodynamics Systems* [1993] FSR 468; *Zockoll Group Ltd v Mercury Communications Ltd* [1998] FSR 354.

[105] See now the Senior Courts Act 1981, ss 49, 50.

[106] *Johnson v Agnew* [1980] AC 367, 400 overruling *Wroth v Tyler* [1974] Ch 30.

[107] *Oakacre Ltd v Claire Cleaners (Holdings) Ltd* [1982] Ch 197; *Jaggard v Sawyer* [1995] 1 WLR 269.

[108] *Biggin v Minton* [1977] 1 WLR 701; *Johnson v Agnew* [1980] AC 367.

19

RESTITUTIONARY AWARDS

A person who pays money or renders services or supplies goods to the defendant pursuant to a contract which is discharged by breach may be entitled to restitution of the money paid or to restitution in the form of a reasonable remuneration for the services rendered (quantum meruit) or a reasonable price for the goods supplied (quantum valebat). These restitutionary remedies may be available not only to an innocent party but also, in certain situations, to a contract-breaker. These remedies may also be available in respect of money paid or non-money benefits rendered under other ineffective agreements including those that are void, illegal, discharged for frustration, or too uncertain to amount to contracts: such claims, which are outside the scope of this part of the book, since they do not follow a breach of contract, have been briefly considered in the chapters on ineffective contracts.[1] It should also be stressed that, even where the innocent party is seeking these remedies where the contract has been discharged for breach, the cause of action is not breach of contract but rather unjust enrichment with the relevant ground of unjust enrichment being, for example, total failure of consideration. A major advantage to an innocent party in seeking restitution after breach, rather than compensatory damages for the breach, is that restitution may enable the innocent party to escape from a bad bargain.[2]

In certain limited circumstances, the claimant may, by way of exception to the normal compensatory measure, be able to claim a restitutionary remedy (whether an account of profits or 'restitutionary damages') *for* the breach of contract (ie, the cause of action is breach of contract) to strip the profits the contract-breaker made from the breach. This will be advantageous where compensatory damages are limited or irrecoverable (perhaps because of the rules of remoteness or the mitigation principle), or where for some reason the innocent party finds it difficult to prove the loss suffered.[3]

---

[1] Above, pp 67, 71–3, 237, 246, 250, 261–5, 444–54, 525–32. See further Mitchell, Mitchell, and Watterson, *Goff and Jones on the Law of Unjust Enrichment* (8th edn, 2011) Part 5; Beatson, *The Use and Abuse of Unjust Enrichment* (1991) 1–11, ch 3; Burrows, *The Law of Restitution* (3rd edn, 2011) chs 14–15; Burrows, *A Restatement of the English Law of Unjust Enrichment* (2012) 86–92.

[2] *BP Exploration Co (Libya) Ltd v Hunt (No 2)* [1979] 1 WLR 783, 800, aff'd [1983] 2 AC 352; *Bush v Canfield* 2 Conn 485 (1818) (Connecticut). The limitation period may also be more favourable: see below, p 639.

[3] Above, p 565.

1. THE RECOVERY OF MONEY PAID

(a) RECOVERY BY THE INNOCENT PARTY

If one party is entitled to be treated as discharged from further performance of the contract by reason of the other party's breach, and does so, any money paid by that party to the other party under the contract can be recovered provided that the consideration for the payment has failed.[4] Strictly, the rule requires that the failure be *total*, but several factors indicate that the requirement of totality may be 'on the turn'. We shall first consider total failure, and then the recent developments.

(i) Total failure of consideration

In *Kwei Tek Chao v British Traders and Shippers Ltd*,[5] a case concerned with a cif contract for the sale of goods, Devlin J said:

If goods have been properly rejected, and the price has already been paid in advance, the proper way of recovering the money back is by an action for money paid on a consideration which has wholly failed, ie money had and received.

As well as the requirement that the failure of consideration be total, the party seeking repayment must have elected to accept the breach as discharging the contract.[6]

The need for a total failure of consideration is illustrated by *Hunt v Silk*:[7]

The claimant paid £10 to the defendant in return for a promise by the defendant to give him immediate possession of certain premises, to put them into repair, and to execute a lease of them in his favour within 10 days. The claimant obtained possession, but left soon afterwards when the defendant failed to carry out the rest of his promise; he also sued to recover the £10.

His action failed. It was held that, the contract having been in part performed, no part of the consideration could be recovered.

The common law has required the failure of consideration to be total for two main reasons.[8] First, the common law has set its face against apportionment, partly because one cannot assume that all parts of the payee's performance are equally valuable and that the contract price is earned incrementally. For example, in a contract to build a house, the preparation of the ground and the foundations on a difficult site may involve greater expense in either time or labour than the completion of the brickwork, the roof, and the interior. Secondly, in many cases the benefit the payer has received from the payee's part-performance cannot easily be valued in money. This is particularly

---

[4] See generally Wilmot-Smith [2013] CLJ 414.

[6] *Ibid*.

[5] [1954] 2 QB 459, 475.

[7] (1804) 5 East 449.

[8] *Whincup v Hughes* (1871) LR 6 CP 78, 81 (Bovill CJ). Birks, *An Introduction to the Law of Restitution* (revd edn, 1989) 242–4. For other justifications, see Law Com No 121, *Pecuniary Restitution on Breach of Contract* (1983), paras 3.8–3.10.

so where it consists of services. So, where a builder who has agreed to modernize a bathroom, abandons the contract after disconnecting the old fittings and removing some of them, it is not obvious what the benefit of such part performance is to the owner of the house,[9] who will have to pay another person to clear the room as well as having the trouble of finding another builder to complete the task.

Total failure of consideration occurs where none of the promised performance has been rendered.[10] Consideration in this context refers to performance by the payee of the contractual promise.[11] This means that any performance of the actual thing promised, as determined by the contract, is fatal to recovery. But in practice the concept of total failure of consideration has been applied somewhat arbitrarily, and has ignored real benefits received by the payer and significant detrimental reliance by the payee. For instance, in the case of a contract for the sale of goods,[12] or of hire purchase,[13] a failure by the seller to convey a good title to the goods in breach of the condition implied by statute[14] will constitute a total failure of consideration. Thus in *Rowland v Divall*:

R bought a motor-car from D for £334, repainted it and sold it on to a third party. It then turned out that the car had been stolen, although D had dealt with it in good faith. The police took possession of it on behalf of the true owner and R brought an action to recover from D the £334.

The Court of Appeal held that, since R 'had not received any part of that which he had contracted to receive—namely, the property and right to possession' of the car, there had been a total failure of consideration. He was entitled to recover the whole purchase price, notwithstanding that he and his sub-purchaser had had four months' use and enjoyment of the vehicle and that he could not restore the car to D.[15] Similarly, in *Butterworth v Kingsway Motors*[16] the hire-purchase price of a car (£1,275) was recovered although by the time the car, which had been used by the hire-purchaser for nearly a year, was returned it was worth only £800. Again in *Barber v NWS Bank plc*[17] a conditional purchaser was able to recover the purchase price of a car that had

---

[9] *Sumpter v Hedges* [1898] 1 QB 673, 514.

[10] *Fibrosa Spolka Akcyjna v Fairbairn Lawson Combe Barbour Ltd* [1943] AC 32; *Rover International v Cannon Film Sales Ltd (No 3)* [1989] 1 WLR 912; *Stocznia Gdanska SA v Latvian SS Co* [1998] 1 WLR 574.

[11] *Fibrosa Spolka Akcyjna v Fairbairn Lawson Combe Barbur Ltd* [1943] AC 32, 48. There is a wider meaning of failure of consideration that extends beyond non-performance of a contractual obligation to a failure of purpose or condition, whether promissory or not. That wider meaning was stressed by the High Court of Australia in *Roxborough v Rothmans of Pall Mall Ltd* (2001) 208 CLR 516 in which restitution was granted of money paid under a contract that had not been discharged.

[12] *Hudson v Robinson* (1816) 4 M & S 475; *Rowland v Divall* [1923] 2 KB 500.

[13] *Karflex Ltd v Poole* [1933] 2 KB 251; *Warman v Southern Counties Car Finance Corp Ltd* [1949] 2 KB 576.

[14] Above, pp 171–8.

[15] [1923] 2 KB 500, 504, 506–7. The principle has been both criticized and defended; see Law Reform Committee, Twelfth Report (Cmnd 2958, 1966); Law Com No 24, *Exemption Clauses in Contracts* (1969); Law Com No 160, *Sale and Supply of Goods* (1987), paras 6.1–5 (recommending no reform of the rule by requiring a buyer seeking to recover the price to make a money allowance in favour of the seller in respect of the use). Cf Torts (Interference with Goods) Act 1977, s 6(3).

[16] [1954] 1 WLR 1286.   [17] [1996] 1 WLR 641.

been used for 22 months before the defect in title was discovered and the contract terminated. In an action for damages, account would be taken of the benefit received by purchasers in these cases.[18] Similarly, there will be a total failure of consideration even though a buyer or hirer has incurred substantial reliance expenditure for the purpose of the contract[19] or where, although there has been partial performance by the payee, the Court is able to divide the contract and hold that there has been a total failure in relation to the parts not performed,[20] or can find that the parties have impliedly acknowledged that the consideration can be 'broken up' or apportioned.[21]

(ii) Partial failure of consideration

The willingness of the Court so to divide the contract may indicate dissatisfaction with the requirement of totality. We have seen that the requirement of totality can produce fine and sometimes arbitrary distinctions. In the case of frustrated contracts, dealt with in an earlier chapter,[22] the requirement of a total failure has been removed by statute so that money paid can be recovered even though there has only been a partial failure of consideration.[23] We shall also see that where a quantum meruit claim is made in respect of services rendered, the difficulty of valuing the work done is not regarded as an insurmountable bar to relief.

It may, moreover, be difficult to maintain the requirement that the failure be *total* now that the principle of unjust enrichment and the defence of change of position have been recognized in English law.[24] It has been said that 'if counter-restitution is relatively simple . . . insistence on total failure of consideration can be misleading and confusing',[25] and in *Goss v Chilcott*,[26] the Judicial Committee of the Privy Council relaxed the requirement that the failure be total by the use of apportionment. It was held that a loan could be apportioned between the principal sum lent and the interest, so that the receipt by the lender of interest did not prevent the lender recovering the principal sum lent, and the Court indicated that it would have been willing to apportion the principal sum itself so that partial repayment of the principal sum would not have prevented a restitutionary claim but would have merely reduced such a claim to the

[18] *Harling v Eddy* [1951] 2 KB 739, and above, p 588. But where a buyer has spent money on the goods while they are in its possession, damages may be the preferable remedy because this can be recovered in such an action but not in an action for the return of the price: *Mason v Burningham* [1949] 2 KB 545.

[19] *Fibrosa Spolka Akcyjna v Fairbairn Lawson Combe Barbour Ltd* [1943] AC 32, above, p 525 (work done by payees in manufacturing machines); *Rover International v Cannon Film Sales Ltd (No 3)* [1989] 1 WLR 912, 932, 936, 937 (expenditure in buying back films to fulfil terms of distributorship contract).

[20] *DO Ferguson v Sohl* (1992) 62 BLR 92 (building contract; total failure of consideration in respect of sum paid in excess of value of work done); *White Arrow Express Ltd v Lamey's Distribution Ltd* (1995) 15 Tr LR 69, noted Beale (1996) 112 LQR 205; *Baltic Shipping Co v Dillon* (1993) 176 CLR 344, 375 (High Court of Australia).

[21] *David Securities Pty Ltd v Commonwealth Bank of Australia* (1992) 175 CLR 353, 383.

[22] Above, Chapter 14.   [23] Above, p 526 (Law Reform (Frustrated Contracts) Act 1943, s 1(2)).

[24] *Lipkin Gorman v Karpnale Ltd* [1991] 2 AC 548.

[25] *David Securities Pty Ltd v Commonwealth Bank of Australia*, (1992) 175 CLR 353, 383 (High Court of Australia). 'Counter-restitution' means restitution *to the defendant* of any benefits received *by the claimant*.

[26] [1996] AC 788, 798.

balance of the loan. Moreover, support has been expressed in the House of Lords for the reformulation of the total failure of consideration rule.[27] Although these cases all concerned loans or other transactions in which the part-performance received by the payer consisted of money so that the problems of valuing non-monetary performance did not arise, it is submitted that, in principle, restitution should be available in all cases of a failure of consideration subject to giving counter-restitution.

(b) RECOVERY BY THE PARTY IN BREACH

It is similarly possible for the party who has broken the contract to recover from the innocent party money pre-paid by it. The recoverability of such payments partly depends on the construction of the contract and the purpose for which the payment is required. A distinction is drawn between deposits and other payments required as security for due performance on the one hand and advance payments of the price on the other.

(i) Advance payments of the contract price

Where the payment was not a deposit or otherwise required as security for due performance and where recovery was not otherwise expressly or impliedly precluded by the terms of the agreement (eg by express provision that it be forfeited) it may be recoverable. Thus in *Dies v British and International Mining and Finance Corporation Ltd*:[28]

The defendant contracted to sell rifles and ammunition to one Quintana at a total price of £270,000 of which £100,000 was paid before the agreed delivery date. Subsequently, in breach of contract, Quintana failed to take delivery or to pay the balance. The defendant elected to treat the contract as discharged but refused to return the £100,000. Quintana assigned his rights to the claimant, who brought an action to recover the money.

Stable J held that the claimant might recover it, less the amount of any damages suffered by the defendant through Quintana's breach of contract. It might seem strange, at first sight, that the party in breach should have succeeded. But as the judge pointed out, the defendant was 'amply protected', since it could set off its claim for damages against the sum sought to be recovered. Again, however, in the present state of the law, the consideration for the payment must have totally failed. So if the party in default has received a benefit from the subject-matter of the sale before the discharge, it cannot, subject to any equitable relief,[29] recover any part-payment made. Thus where a contract

---

[27] *Westdeutsche Landesbank Girozentrale v Islington LBC* [1996] AC 669, 682–3. See also Birks, *An Introduction to the Law of Restitution* (revd edn, 1989) 259–64; but cf Law Com No 121, *Pecuniary Restitution on Breach of Contract* (1983), paras 3.8–3.9 and *Stocznia Gdanska SA v Latvian SS Co* [1998] 1 WLR 574, 590.

[28] [1939] 1 KB 724. See also *McDonald v Dennys Lascelles Ltd* (1933) 48 CLR 457 (sale of land); *Rover International Ltd v Cannon Film Sales Ltd (No 3)* [1989] 1 WLR 912; Beatson, *The Use and Abuse of Unjust Enrichment* (1991) ch 3 (updating (1981) 97 LQR 389).

[29] See below, p 626.

for work and materials provides for payment of the purchase price by instalments, a contractor who is bound to incur expense as the work proceeds, will be entitled to retain any instalment paid if the other party repudiates the contract before completion of the work because, subject to a *de minimis* rule, the services rendered by the innocent party are to be regarded as part of the bargained-for performance and there is thus no total failure of consideration in such a contract once performance has commenced.[30]

(ii) Deposits and other payments as security for due performance

It is settled law that a sum paid by way of 'deposit' for the purchase of goods or land is security for completion of the contract by the buyer and cannot as a general rule be recovered if the buyer fails to perform its side of the contract.[31] Similarly, where the contract provides that on default instalments of the price already paid shall be forfeited, there will generally be no recovery.

The general rule that deposits and other payments required as security or subject to forfeiture clauses are irrecoverable is, however, subject to statutory and equitable exceptions. By section 49(2) of the Law of Property Act 1925 the Court has an unqualified discretion to order repayment of a deposit paid under a contract for the sale of land where the justice of the case requires it.[32] Another legislative exception can be found in the Consumer Rights Act 2015 which provides that a term which permits the trader 'to retain sums paid by the consumer where the consumer decides not to conclude or perform the contract, without providing for the consumer to receive compensation of an equivalent amount from the trader where the trader is the party cancelling the contract' may be unfair.[33] Secondly, where the provision for the forfeiture of the sum paid is penal and it is unconscionable for the payee to retain the money, equitable relief may be available.[34] Thus a person who purchases goods or land by instalments, or who hires goods in return for payment of rent, may be entitled to equitable relief against forfeiture of the property or purchase money if he defaults in prompt payment of the instalments or rent when due.[35] The principle is similar to that

---

[30] *Hyundai Heavy Industries Co Ltd v Papadopoulos* [1980] 1 WLR 1129; *Stocznia Gdanska SA v Latvian Shipping Co* [1998] 1 WLR 574. The case for relaxing the rule requiring that the failure of consideration be *total* is much weaker where the person seeking recovery is a contract-breaker: see above, p 476, in the context of the rule precluding recovery for part-performance of an entire obligation.

[31] *Howe v Smith* (1884) 27 Ch D 89. See generally Harpum [1984] CLJ 134; Beatson, *The Use and Abuse of Unjust Enrichment* (1991) 46–50, 76–7, 90–4.

[32] *Universal Corporation v Five Ways Properties Ltd* [1979] 1 All ER 552. Cf *James Macara Ltd v Barclay* [1945] 1 KB 148; *Midill (97PL) Ltd v Park Lane Estates Ltd* [2008] EWCA Civ 1227, [2009] 1 WLR 2460 (both cases indicating a somewhat narrow approach to the discretion).

[33] Consumer Rights Act 2015, Sched 2, para 4. See generally above, pp 222–32.

[34] See *Workers Trust & Merchant Bank Ltd v Dojap Investments Ltd* [1993] AC 573, where it was stated that the amount of the deposit has to be reasonable and that, as long usage established the reasonableness of a 10% deposit in sales of land, a larger deposit would, unless justified, be penal.

[35] *Stockloser v Johnson* [1954] 1 QB 476; *Shiloh Spinners Ltd v Harding* [1973] AC 691, 726–7 (Lord Simon). Cf Lord Wilberforce, *ibid*, 723–4. See also *Amble Assets LLP v Longbenton Foods Ltd* [2011] EWHC 3774 (Ch), [2012] 1 All ER (Comm) 764 at [62]–[82] (Andrew Sutcliffe QC, sitting as a Deputy High Court Judge regarded the test to be whether it was unconscionable to allow the forfeiture to take effect).

governing penalty clauses[36] but the law has treated the two situations as separate.[37] Plainly the 'genuine pre-estimate of loss' test does not apply to stipulations for security for due performance; 'the forfeiture rule looks at the position after the breach when the innocent party is enforcing the forfeiture'.[38] But in the light of its clarification that the underpinning principle for determining whether a clause is a penalty is one combining legitimate interest and proportionality, the Supreme Court in *Cavendish Square Holding BV v Talal El Makdessi* ('*Makdessi*') and *ParkingEye Ltd v Beavis*[39] has opened the way for clauses allowing the innocent party to retain pre-payments by the contract-breaker to be treated as penalties. *Obiter dicta* of the Supreme Court Justices also indicated that both the law on penalties and on relief against forfeiture may be applied to the same clause.[40]

The scope of the jurisdiction to relieve against forfeiture is somewhat uncertain.[41] It probably does not apply to those commercial contracts where speed and certainty are of paramount importance.[42] Although not entirely logical, it also appears that the Courts may only relieve against the forfeiture of proprietary or possessory interests as opposed to the forfeiture of 'mere contractual rights'.[43] This may, however, leave open the possibility of seeking relief where a contract is specifically enforceable and thus creates equitable rights, although in the case of breach of an essential condition as to time relief by way of specific performance is less likely to be given than relief by way of restitution, for example by repayment of retained money.[44] Apart from the uncertainty as to the scope of the equitable jurisdiction it is also possible, though unlikely, that the only form of relief available is to give the contract-breaker more time to perform the

---

[36] Above, pp 598–604. See *Public Works Commissioners v Hills* [1906] AC 368.

[37] *Linggi Plantations Ltd v Jagatheesan* (1972) 1 MLJ 89, 91 (Lord Hailsham LC); *Workers Trust & Merchant Bank Ltd v Dojap Investments Ltd* [1993] AC 573. It may sometimes be hard to say whether a contract is providing for forfeiture of money paid absolutely or for a penal liability: *Else (1982) Ltd v Parkland Holdings Ltd* [1994] 1 BCLC 130, 146.

[38] *Else (1982) Ltd v Parkland Holdings Ltd* [1994] 1 BCLC 130, 144 (Hoffmann LJ).

[39] [2015] UKSC 67, [2015] 3 WLR 1373 at [16]–[18], [156], [234]–[238]. See above pp 598–600.

[40] *Ibid* at [16]–[18], [156], [160]–[161], [230], [291].

[41] See, generally, Smith [2001] CLJ 178; Gullifer, in Burrows and Peel (eds), *Commercial Remedies* (2003) 191, 205–19.

[42] *The Laconia* [1977] AC 850; *Scandinavian Trading Tanker Co AB v Flota Petrolera Ecuatoriana, The Scaptrade* [1983] 2 AC 694; *Sport International Bussum BV v Inter-Footwear Ltd* [1984] 1 WLR 776; *Union Eagle Ltd v Golden Achievement Ltd* [1997] AC 514. Cf the broader approach of the High Court of Australia: *Legione v Hateley* (1983) 152 CLR 406; *Stern v McArthur* (1988) 165 CLR 489.

[43] *Scandinavian Trading Tanker Co AB v Flota Petrolera Ecuatoriana, The Scaptrade* [1983] 2 AC 694; *BICC plc v Burndy Corporation* [1985] Ch 232, 251–2; *Nutting v Baldwin* [1995] 1 WLR 201. See also *Transag Haulage Ltd v Leyland DAF Finance plc* [1994] 2 BCLC 88, 99; *Alf Vaughan & Co v Royscot Trust plc* [1999] 1 All ER (Comm) 856; *On Demand Information plc v Michael Gerson (Finance) plc* [2000] 4 All ER 734, CA, [2002] UKHL 13, [2003] 1 AC 368; *More OG Romsdal Flykesbatar AS v The Demise Charterers of the Ship Jutenheim, The Jutenheim* [2004] EWHC 671 (Comm), [2005] 1 Lloyd's Rep 181; *Celestial Aviation Trading 71 Ltd v Paramount Airways Private Ltd* [2010] EWHC 185, [2011] 1 Lloyd's Rep 9. Cf the broader dictum in *Workers Trust & Merchant Bank Ltd v Dojap Investments Ltd* [1993] AC 573, 578.

[44] *Union Eagle Ltd v Golden Achievement Ltd* [1997] AC 514; *Steedman v Drinkle* [1916] 1 AC 275. Cf. *Re Dagenham (Thames) Dock Co, ex p Hulse* (1873) LR 8 Ch App 1022 and the broader Australian approach: *Legione v Hateley* (1983) 152 CLR 406; *Stern v McArthur*, (1988) 165 CLR 489.

contract so that there will be no relief if it is clear that the contract-breaker will not be able to pay after such extension of time.[45]

In the exercise of the equitable jurisdiction account has been taken of whether the sum to be forfeited is much greater than the damage caused by the breach,[46] whether the party seeking relief had received a substantial part of the consideration for the payment,[47] whether there has been any fraud or sharp practice,[48] whether it is reasonable to require the party who is prima facie entitled to forfeiture to accept an alternative to the property it is sought to forfeit,[49] and whether relief would permit the evasion of a contractual obligation simply because the contract has turned out to be an unwise one.[50]

2. RESTITUTION IN RESPECT OF SERVICES OR GOODS

(a) INTRODUCTION

Sometimes a quantum meruit (or quantum valebat) claim is genuinely contractual.[51] That is, the remedy is given where there is a promise to pay for services (or goods) but no particular remuneration has been specified. The party performing the services is entitled at common law to a quantum meruit, that is, as much as the services are worth or, as it is generally described, a 'reasonable' sum.[52] The principle is statutorily embraced in section 8(2) of the Sale of Goods Act 1979, section 15(1) of the Supply of Goods and Services Act 1982, and section 51 of the Consumer Rights Act 2015, which provide that the buyer and the recipient of services must pay a reasonable price or charge.[53]

However, in many situations a quantum meruit (or quantum valebat) is a non-contractual remedy awarded to effect restitution of an unjust enrichment, including where there has been reasonable reliance by the claimant on the defendant's words

---

[45] *Stockloser v Johnson* [1954] 1 QB 476 (Romer LJ; cf Denning and Somervell LJJ); *Galbraith v Mitchenall Estates Ltd* [1965] 2 QB 473; *Starside Properties Ltd v Mustapha* [1974] 1 WLR 816; *BICC plc v Burndy Corporation* [1985] Ch 232; *Workers Trust and Merchant Bank Ltd v Dojap Investments Ltd* [1993] AC 573. See also *Jobson v Johnson* [1989] 1 All ER 621.

[46] *Stockloser v Johnson* [1954] 1 QB 476, 484, 490; *Transag Haulage Ltd v Leyland DAF Finance plc* [1994] 2 BCLC 88, 101–2.

[47] *Stockloser v Johnson* [1954] 1 QB 476, 484, 492. [48] *Ibid*, 495–6 (Romer LJ).

[49] *Shiloh Spinners Ltd v Harding* [1973] AC 691, 726–7; *Transag Haulage Ltd v Leyland DAF Finance plc* [1994] 2 BCLC 88, 101–2.

[50] *Galbraith v Mitchenall Estates Ltd* [1965] 2 QB 473; *Hyundai Ship Building and Heavy Industries Co Ltd v Pournaras* [1978] 2 Lloyd's Rep 502, 508–9.

[51] Winfield, *The Province of the Law of Tort* (1931) 157; (1947) 63 LQR 35; Birks, *An Introduction to the Law of Restitution* (1985) 275.

[52] *Steven v Bromley and* Son [1919] 2 KB 722; *Sir Lindsay Parkinson & Co Ltd v Commissioners of Works* [1949] 2 KB 632; *The 'Batis'* [1990] 1 Lloyd's Rep 345, 352.

[53] See above pp 66–7, 178.

or conduct.[54] There is no promise to pay, express or implied, and the obligation is imposed. We are here concerned with this non-contractual quantum meruit.

(b) RESTITUTIONARY CLAIMS BY THE INNOCENT PARTY

Where a contract has been broken in such a way as to entitle the innocent party to be treated as discharged, and it has elected to be so treated, it may sue on a quantum meruit for the value of the work done under the contract, as an alternative to bringing an action on the contract for damages. In such a case the quantum meruit claim arises in the law of restitution. Two cases provide possible illustrations of this remedy. In *Planché v Colburn*:[55]

The claimant had contracted to write a book on custom and ancient armour for a periodical publication, called the *Juvenile Library* to be published by the defendant. For this he was to receive the sum of £100 on completion. When he had completed half, but not the whole, of his volume, the defendant abandoned the publication.

The claimant was held entitled to retain a verdict for £50 which the jury had awarded him. Tindal CJ said:[56]

I agree that when a special contract is in existence and open, the plaintiff cannot sue on a quantum meruit: part of the question here, therefore, was whether the contract did exist or not. It distinctly appeared that the work was finally abandoned; and the jury found that no new contract had been entered into. Under these circumstances, the plaintiff ought not to lose the fruit of his labour.

Again, in *De Bernardy v Harding*:[57]

The defendant appointed the claimant his agent to advertise and sell tickets for seats to view the funeral of the Duke of Wellington, the claimant to receive a commission on the tickets sold. The defendant wrongfully revoked the claimant's authority after he had already incurred expenses in carrying out the contract.

It was held that the claimant was entitled to a quantum meruit for the work done.

(c) QUANTUM MERUIT COMPARED WITH DAMAGES

If the contract has not been discharged, the innocent party cannot use the quantum meruit remedy, but can only sue for damages. However, if the restitutionary remedy is available and the injured party chooses to sue on a quantum meruit, the principle

---

[54] Beatson, *The Use and Abuse of Unjust Enrichment* (1991) ch 2. Cf Birks, *An Introduction to the Law of Restitution* (revd edn, 1989) 265–76.

[55] (1831) 8 Bing 14.

[56] *Ibid*, 16. As no part of the book had been handed over, there is controversy as to whether the services were a benefit to the defendant and hence whether the case concerned *restitution* of an unjust *enrichment*.

[57] (1853) 8 Ex Ch 822. See also *Prickett v Badger* (1856) 1 CBNS 296; *Chandler Bros Ltd v Boswell* [1936] 3 All ER 179.

of assessment differs from that which is applied in assessing damages for breach of contract and the sum which the innocent party is entitled to recover may differ from that which is recoverable as damages:[58]

Suppose that by the terms of a contract A plc is to pave one mile of road for B plc for £100,000, payable on its completion. B repudiates the contract when A has done half of the work and A accepts that repudiation as discharging it from further performance of its obligations under the contract.

It is clear that A cannot claim the stipulated sum since the work has not been completed.[59] Should it claim damages, however, it will receive £100,000 less any saving on labour and materials. If, however, a quantum meruit is sought, A is asking to be paid the reasonable value of the work done. That is, it is seeking restitution of the unjust enrichment. Ordinarily, damages will be the more favourable remedy since the profit element in the transaction can then be recovered. But there might be special circumstances where, for instance, the contract price had been underestimated, or the costs of doing the work had risen considerably since the contract was made. In these circumstances it is arguable that a claimant may secure a higher measure by suing on a quantum meruit instead of for damages. Thus it has generally been held that relief by way of quantum meruit is not limited to a pro-ration of the contract price (in our example £50,000) or the contract price itself (in our example, £100,000).[60] Although this can be criticized as inconsistent with the contract and as reallocating contractual risks, pro-ration is difficult in a complex contract and may be unfair because it takes no account of fixed costs which may be incurred at the early stages of a contract or of economies of scale which may have affected the determination of the contract price but be lost on part performance.

Restriction to the contract price, while having some attractions on pragmatic grounds, would give the contract-breaker a proportion of the profits expected under the contract even though the contract has been discharged. It would also produce disequilibrium between the position of an innocent party who has only done a small proportion of the work before the contract is discharged, where the contract price limit would rarely apply, and a person who has done the bulk of the work, where the limit would be more likely to apply. So, in the example above, if the market value of half the work is in fact £200,000, the limit would not apply, and A would recover the true value of the work, £100,000, but if A has completed three-quarters of the job, it

---

[58] *Heyman v Darwins Ltd* [1942] AC 356, 398 (Lord Porter). See also *The Batis* [1990] 1 Lloyd's Rep 345, 353.

[59] See above, pp 476, 606.

[60] *Lodder v Slowey* (1900) 20 NZLR 321, 358, [1904] AC 442; *Boomer v Muir* 24 P 2d 570 (1933); *Newton Woodhouse v Trevor Toys Ltd*, 20 December 1991, CA; *Renard Constructions (ME) Pty Ltd v Minister for Public Works* (1992) 26 NSWLR 234. The contrary view was taken in *Taylor v Motability Finance Ltd* [2004] EWHC 2619 (QB) in which it was also held that restitution for work done could not be granted where the claimant had substantially performed the contract because then there was a claim for the agreed sum under the contract.

would apply and A would only recover £100,000 as the quantum meruit. On the other hand, it may be that some reference to the contract price ought to be applied as part of the standard exercise in the law of unjust enrichment of determining whether the particular defendant has been benefited. In other words, it is the value of the work to the particular defendant that one ought to be awarding and in determining that one would have expected the price under the contract to be relevant if lower than the market price.

(d) RESTITUTIONARY CLAIMS BY THE PARTY IN BREACH

Where the contractual obligations are entire the party in breach will have no entitlement to a restitutionary quantum meruit for past performance unless, perhaps, the other party freely accepted the work. In *Sumpter v Hedges*[61] the party in breach was held entitled to recover the value of materials left on the building site and used by the defendant who had a choice whether or not to use them to complete the building but not in respect of the partially completed building. This rule can work harshly where substantial benefits are conferred on an innocent party who has suffered no loss whatsoever from the breach of contract.[62] In one case it was suggested that a shipowner who deviated but delivered the goods at the port of discharge without injury or substantial delay would be entitled to reasonable remuneration.[63] Perhaps the best explanation is that the case was not really one of part-performance but one in which the goods' owner, in the end, got everything he had contracted for. Where, however, the innocent party has made it clear that anything other than full and precise performance is not wanted a quantum meruit will clearly not be awarded.[64]

3. AN ACCOUNT OF PROFITS OR DAMAGES MEASURED BY BENEFIT TO CONTRACT-BREAKER

(a) INTRODUCTION

A defendant may make a gain from a breach of contract as where a financier broke his contract to invest £15,000 in the claimant's timber business but instead invested it in a distillery which proved much more profitable;[65] or where a developer built more

---

[61] [1898] 1 QB 673 (for facts see above, p 481); *Bolton v Mahadeva* [1972] 1 WLR 1009. See, generally, McFarlane and Stevens (2002) 118 LQR 569.

[62] Law Com No 121, *Pecuniary Restitution on Breach of Contract* (1983) proposed reform but this was rejected by the Lord Chancellor; Law Com No 140, *19th Annual Report*, para 2.11.

[63] *Hain SS Co Ltd v Tate and Lyle Ltd* (1936) 41 Com Cas 350 (HL).

[64] *Wiluszynski v Tower Hamlets LBC* [1989] ICR 493. See also *British Telecommunications plc v Ticehurst* [1992] ICR 383. Cf *Miles v Wakefield MBC* [1987] AC 539. See also above, pp 478–9.

[65] *Teacher v Calder* (1899) 1 F 39.

houses on a site than was permitted by the contract and thereby made extra profit.[66] Alternatively, a defendant may gain by saving expense from its breach as where remedial work, for instance replacing soil or planting trees on the claimant's land, is not done.[67] The traditional approach, which remains the general rule, is that the gain to a defendant from a breach of contract is irrelevant.[68]

The defendant's gain has, however, been relevant in a number of situations in which a strict application of the principle that damages are compensatory would not do justice between the parties. In sales of land the defendant's gain is taken into account because the effect of the contract is that the purchaser has an equitable interest in the land and is accordingly entitled to the proceeds of any wrongful sale to a third party.[69] The defendant's gain will also be relevant where, in the context of a contractual relationship, there has been a breach of a duty of confidence[70] or a fiduciary duty.[71]

Prior to *A-G v Blake*,[72] the only direct exception to the rule against there being restitution for breach of contract—hence its description in *Blake* as a 'solitary beacon'[73]—was the principle established in *Wrotham Park Estate Co v Parkside Homes Ltd*.[74] Although the claim in question was for breach of a restrictive covenant, rather than an ordinary breach of contract, that is still in essence an action for breach of contract albeit one that depends on an equitable exception to privity of contract.

The defendants had built a number of houses on land in breach of a restrictive covenant enforceable in equity by the claimant neighbouring landowner. Brightman J refused an injunction ordering the demolition of the houses but held that, although the claimant's land had not been diminished in value, the defendants were liable to pay substantial damages assessed using a 'hypothetical bargain' approach. That is, he asked what would have been a reasonable contract price for the claimant to have accepted for relaxation of the covenant. In working out the price, the major factor taken into account was the defendants' profits from the housing development. That emphasis on the defendants' profits, in addition to Brightman J's acceptance that it was artificial to pretend that the claimant would ever have relaxed the covenant, means that the damages are most naturally viewed as restitutionary.[75] On a restitutionary analysis, the reasonable fee damages can be regarded as stripping the defendants of a fair proportion of their profits (assessed at 5%) or, perhaps, as the difference in use value to the defendant of its land with and without the restrictive covenant over it.

---

[66] *Surrey CC v Bredero Homes Ltd* [1993] 1 WLR 1361.

[67] *Tito v Waddell (No 2)* [1977] Ch 106.

[68] *A-G v Blake* [2001] 1 AC 268. See also *The Siboen* [1976] 1 Lloyd's Rep 293, 337; *Tito v Waddell (No 2)* [1977] Ch 106, 332; *Surrey CC v Bredero Homes Ltd* [1993] 1 WLR 1361.

[69] *Lake v Bayliss* [1974] 1 WLR 1073; *Tito v Waddell (No 2)* [1977] Ch 106, 332.

[70] *Peter Pan Manufacturing Corp v Corsets Silhouette Ltd* [1964] 1 WLR 96.

[71] See *Reading v A-G* [1951] AC 507. See also *Hospital Products Ltd v US Surgical Corp* (1984) 156 CLR 41 (Australia).

[72] [2001] 1 AC 268.   [73] *Ibid*, 283.   [74] [1974] 1 WLR 798.

[75] See, eg, Rotherham [2008] LMCLQ 25; Burrows, in Saidov and Cunnington (eds), *Contract Damages* (2008) ch 7.

Not everyone agrees that the *Wrotham Park* decision was an example of restitution for breach of contract. For example, applying their 'loss of opportunity to bargain' approach, Sharpe and Waddams argued that the case was simply explicable as awarding compensation for loss.[76] This can be criticized as fictional.[77] It was accepted that the claimant would never have relaxed the covenant.

Having said that, one can perhaps defend the view that the damages in *Wrotham Park* were compensatory on the basis that it was the loss of the opportunity to sell the right in the future that was being compensated; or that the claimant was being compensated for a non-pecuniary loss (ie the claimant valued the right so much—to protect the views over that land—that it would not have been willing to sell it).[78]

(b) *ATTORNEY-GENERAL V BLAKE*

The liability of a contract-breaker to account for gains made from the breach was considered afresh by the House of Lords in the leading case of *Attorney-General v Blake.*[79] B, a former member of the intelligence services, undertook not to divulge any official information gained as a result of his employment and broke the undertaking by publishing an autobiography. The Crown sought to recover the royalties he was to be paid by his publishers. Their Lordships confirmed that, in general, damages are measured by the claimant's loss, but held that in an exceptional case, where compensatory damages, specific enforcement, and injunction are inadequate or are not available, the Court can require the defendant to account to the claimant for profits received from a breach of contract even where the breach of contract does not involve the use of or interference with the claimant's property.

In determining whether to order an account of profits, the Court will have regard to all the circumstances, including the subject-matter of the contract, the purpose of the contractual provision which has been breached, the circumstances in which the breach occurred, the consequences of the breach, and the circumstances in which relief is being sought. Lord Nicholls of Birkenhead (with whom Lord Goff and Lord Browne-Wilkinson agreed) stated that 'a useful general guide, although not exhaustive, is whether the plaintiff had a legitimate interest in preventing the defendant's profit-making activity and, hence, in depriving him of his profit'.[80] The Crown was held to have such an interest in preventing B from profiting from breaches

---

[76] (1982) 2 OJLS 290, 292. See also Stoljar, (1989) 2 JCL 1, 4–5.

[77] In *Surrey County Council v Bredero Homes Ltd* [1993] 1 WLR 1361, 1369, Steyn LJ said, 'The plaintiff's argument that the *Wrotham Park* case can be justified on the basis of a loss of bargaining opportunity is a fiction. The object of the award in the *Wrotham Park* case was not to compensate the plaintiffs for financial injury, but to deprive the defendants of an unjustly acquired gain.' But these comments were expressly disagreed with by Millett LJ in *Jaggard v Sawyer* [1995] 1 WLR 269: in that case, which concerned damages for breach of covenant and trespass to land, the Court of Appeal applied compensatory 'hypothetical bargain' reasoning and rejected a restitutionary analysis.

[78] See above pp 566–8.   [79] *A-G v Blake* [2001] 1 AC 268.

[80] *Ibid*, 285. See also Lord Steyn at 292 (defendant's position closely analogous to that of a fiduciary).

of the undertaking in an autobiography. He was thus liable to account to the Crown for the royalties.

Their Lordships declined to give more specific guidance as to when an account of profits might be awarded for breach of contract. But they indicated that it would not in itself suffice that (a) the breach was cynical and deliberate;[81] (b) the breach enabled the defendant to enter into a more profitable contract elsewhere; and (c) by entering into a new and more profitable contract the defendant put it out of his power to perform the contract with the claimant.[82] Their Lordships did not, moreover, consider the two categories that had been suggested by the Court of Appeal in the *Blake* case for 'restitutionary damages'[83] were satisfactory. The first was the case of 'skimped' performance, where defendants fail to provide the full extent of the contracted services, as where a security firm which has agreed to guard premises using a stipulated number of guards uses a much smaller number and saves a considerable sum.[84] This was said not to fall within the scope of an account of profits as ordinarily understood and in any event, an account of profits was not needed in this context. Suppliers of inferior goods have to refund the difference in price as damages for breach of contract, and a similar approach should apply in cases where the defendant provided inferior and cheaper services than those contracted for.[85] The second category suggested by the Court of Appeal—where, as in *Blake*'s case, defendants profited by doing the very thing that they contracted not to do— was considered to be too widely defined because it embraced all express negative obligations.[86]

If an account of profits is to be awarded for breach of contract, it is the net profits from the breach that must be given up although, by analogy to cases awarding an account of profits for breach of fiduciary duty,[87] the Courts may give an allowance to the defendant for the skill and labour provided.

(c) DEVELOPMENTS SINCE *ATTORNEY-GENERAL V BLAKE*

The picture emerging since the case of *Blake* is that, while the award of an account of profits, stripping the defendant of all its wrongful net profits, has been extremely rare,

[81] Cf Birks [1987] LMCLQ 421 who suggested that gains should be recovered in all cases of cynical exploitation of breach for the purpose of making a gain so as to deter breaches of contract. This, however, would revolutionize contract remedies since in many cases, particularly commercial cases, the breach is in fact deliberate in the sense that it is knowingly done for commercial reasons. For instance, a seller of goods may choose to breach its contract and sell to a third party who is willing to pay a premium over and above the market price. Restitutionary awards made on this basis might also permit a claimant to evade the requirements of the mitigation rule.

[82] [2001] 1 AC 268, 286, 290, 293. See [1998] Ch 439, 457, 458 (CA).

[83] Lord Nicholls preferred (at 284) to avoid this term.

[84] See *City of New Orleans v Firemen's Charitable Association* 9 So 486 (1891). See also *White Arrow Express Ltd v Lamey's Distribution Ltd* (1995) 15 Tr LR 69; Beale (1996) 112 LQR 205.

[85] [2001] 1 AC 268, 286, 290, 291.   [86] *Ibid*, 286, 291.

[87] See, eg, *Boardman v Phipps* [1967] 2 AC 46.

the Courts have been increasingly willing to award 'Wrotham Park damages'[88]—best rationalized as restitutionary albeit often treated as compensatory[89]—in actions for breach of contract.

In only one subsequent case, Esso Petroleum Co Ltd v Niad,[90] has an account of profits been awarded for breach of contract. In that case Sir Andrew Morritt V-C decided that the claimants were entitled, at their election, to compensatory damages or an account of profits or a 'restitutionary remedy' for breach of contract.

Niad, who owned a petrol station, had entered into a pricing agreement (called 'Pricewatch') with Esso who supplied Niad with petrol. In breach of that agreement, Niad charged higher prices to its customers than had been agreed. This in turn meant that Niad was given 'price support' by Esso to which Niad was not entitled: that is, Niad paid less to Esso for its petrol than it would have done had Esso known that Niad was over-charging its customers.

Applying the case of Blake, Morritt V-C held that Esso was here entitled to an account of profits aimed at stripping away the gains Niad had made from breaking the contract. Compensatory damages were inadequate because it was almost impossible for Esso to establish that sales had been lost as a result of the breach by Niad. The breach undermined the whole Pricewatch scheme that Esso had agreed with all retailers in the area. Esso had complained to Niad on several occasions. And Esso had a legitimate interest in preventing Niad from profiting from its breach. Alternatively Morritt V-C said that Esso was entitled to a 'restitutionary remedy' for the amount of the price support that, in breach of contract, it had obtained from Esso.

Although the distinction between an account of profits and the so-called 'restitutionary remedy' is a difficult one to draw on these facts, the importance of the case is that it shows AG v Blake being applied, so as to award an account of profits, for breach of a commercial contract far removed from the peculiar facts of Blake's case itself. Some have criticized the decision for precisely that reason[91] although, as we shall see, it has subsequently been referred to, without disapproval, by the Court of Appeal.

While an account of profits has been extremely rare, there have been several cases in which the Courts have awarded 'Wrotham Park damages' for breach of contract

---

[88]   See above, pp 631–2. This refers to damages assessing using a hypothetical bargain between the parties according to which the defendant was released from its contractual obligation.

[89]   See, eg, Lane v O'Brien Homes Ltd [2004] EWHC 303 (QB) where the claimant was awarded damages based on a developer's estimated profit from building one house more than he was contractually entitled to build. The damages were treated as compensating the claimant's loss of opportunity to bargain. See also Chadwick LJ in WWF-World Fund for Nature v World Wrestling Federation Entertainment Inc [2007] EWCA Civ 286, [2008] 1 WLR 445 at [59]. The force of [59] is weakened because Chadwick LJ there treated an account of profits as belonging alongside 'Wrotham Park damages' as a flexible response to the need to 'compensate' the claimant for the wrong: but it cannot possibly be correct to regard an account of profits as compensatory rather than restitutionary.

[90]   22 November 2001, unreported, noted by Beatson (2002) 118 LQR 377.

[91]   McKendrick, in Burrows and Peel (eds), Commercial Remedies (2003) 93, 108–12.

since *A-G v Blake*. The most important of these has been *Experience Hendrix LLC v PPX Enterprises Inc.*[92]

The claimant, the estate of the rock star Jimi Hendrix, sued for breach of a contract made in 1973 between Jimi Hendrix and the defendant record company settling a dispute. Under the contract, the defendant was permitted to use certain master tapes but was required to deliver up others to Jimi Hendrix. In breach of that contract, the defendant used master tapes that should have been delivered up.

The claimant did not seek compensatory damages because the loss was too speculative to assess but sought an injunction, which was granted, and an account of profits, which was refused. However, *Wrotham Park* was applied in holding that the claimant was entitled to damages based not on compensating the claimant's loss but on what was a reasonable sum taking into account the gains made by the defendant from its use of the forbidden master tapes.

Although the Court of Appeal was not required to assess that reasonable sum, it considered that one-third of the defendant's royalties on the retail selling price of records made from the forbidden tapes would probably be an appropriate reasonable sum. Although there are passages where the judges referred to the damages as 'compensation', they are most naturally viewed as restitutionary being concerned to strip some, but not all, of the defendant's wrongful profits or to reverse the user value of the forbidden master tapes. That compensation was not principally in mind is consistent not only with counsel for the claimant's starting-point that the claimant was not seeking compensation for loss because that was too speculative to assess but also with the acceptance that the claimant would not have agreed to the defendant's use of those master tapes.[93] It is also consistent with the judges' emphasis on the profits made by the defendant in fixing the reasonable sum. Mance LJ said, '[I]f Lord Nicholls' general guide is a useful starting point in respect of an account of profits, it must be all the more so in respect of the lesser claim to a reasonable sum taking account of the defendant's profitable infringement'.[94] And in the words of Peter Gibson LJ:

In my judgment, because (1) there has been a deliberate breach by PPX of its contractual obligations for its own reward, (2) the claimant would have difficulty in establishing financial loss therefrom, and (3) the claimant has a legitimate interest in preventing PPX's profit-making activity carried out in breach of PPX's contractual obligations, the present case is a suitable one (as envisaged by Lord Nicholls) in which damages for breach of contract may be measured by the benefits gained by the wrongdoer from the breach. To avoid injustice I would require PPX to make a reasonable payment in respect of the benefit it has gained.'[95]

---

[92] [2003] EWCA Civ 323, [2003] 1 All ER (Comm) 830. See also *Lunn Poly Ltd v Liverpool and Lancashire Properties Ltd* [2006] EWCA Civ 430, [2006] 2 EGLR 29; *Pell Frischmann Engineering Ltd v Bow Valley Iran Ltd* [2009] UKPC 45, [2010] BLR 73; *Giedo Van der Garde BV v Force India Formula One Team Ltd* [2010] EWHC 2373 (QB) especially at [505]–[507]; *Primary Group (UK) Ltd v Royal Bank of Scotland* [2014] EWHC 1082, [2014] 2 All ER (Comm) 1121.

[93] See especially Peter Gibson LJ in [2003] EWCA Civ 323, [2003] 1 All ER (Comm) 830 at [57].

[94] [2003] EWCA Civ 323, [2003] 1 All ER (Comm) 830 at [35].   [95] *Ibid* at [58].

The Court stressed that the facts of this case were not as exceptional as those in *A-G v Blake* and it was for that reason that an account of profits, stripping the defendant of *all* its gains made from the breach of contract, was refused. In particular, although the defendant knew it was doing something which it had contracted not to do and to which the claimant would not have consented, the defendant was not close to being a fiduciary to the claimant and no issue analogous to national security was involved. The relationship was a straightforward commercial one. The Court of Appeal also referred to *Esso Petroleum v Niad* without disapproval but distinguished that decision on the ground that the contractual obligation broken had been central to the claimant's whole mode of operation and integrity which was not the position on the facts of this case.

It seems, therefore, that the Courts are more willing to award 'Wrotham Park damages' for breach of contract than they are an account of profits. This should not be a surprise. Even assuming that the former is, at least sometimes, concerned to effect restitution rather than compensation, it is a less extreme remedy than an account of profits. One can express this by saying that the former is concerned with a proportion of the profits made rather than with all the profits made (subject to an allowance for skill and effort).

Nevertheless it would appear that *both* restitutionary damages and an account of profits are exceptional remedies for breach of contract and are not as readily available as compensatory damages. It would seem therefore that an initial condition before either can be awarded is that standard remedies are 'inadequate'. However, it is not easy to pinpoint what 'inadequacy' here means. The concern might primarily be that difficulties of assessment, or bars to the recovery of certain types of damages, mean that compensatory damages will not put the claimant into as good a position as if the contract had been performed. In other words, compensatory damages (and specific remedies) will not properly protect the claimant's contractual expectations. In a case like *Surrey CC v Bredero Homes Ltd*[96] (on the facts of which, it may be suggested that, post-*Blake*, restitutionary damages would be awarded) and in *A-G v Blake* the claimants had non-financial expectations which would not be protected by compensatory damages; their interests were in protecting the environment or in protecting national security respectively. And in *Esso v Niad* and *Experience Hendrix*, while the claimants entered into the contract for financial reasons, the assessment of damages compensating their financial losses was highly problematic and prone to error. In contrast in standard commercial contracts, compensatory damages ought to be perfectly adequate.

Alternatively, 'inadequacy' might mean that the situation is one in which the courts wish to deter breach and yet standard remedies are thought inadequate to achieve that aim.

On either interpretation of the 'inadequacy' hurdle, it would seem that the measure of restitution will then turn on the extent to which (if at all) the courts consider that deterrence is justified. Stripping all profits is more of a deterrent than stripping some

---

[96] [1993] 1 WLR 1361: see above, p 631.

profits and it is therefore only in very exceptional cases, like *A-G v Blake*, that a full account of profits, rather than '*Wrotham Park* damages', is required. It may be that the more cynical the breach, the more likely the Courts are to wish to deter it. The breach was cynical in *A-G v Blake, Esso Petroleum v Niad*, and *Experience Hendrix LLC v PPX Enterprises Inc.* The same can be said, although restitution was refused, of the earlier case of *Surrey County Council v Bredero Homes*. But, as Lord Nicholls stressed, this is not a sufficient condition.[97] This is because there are many cynical breaches (eg where a party to a commercial contract of sale breaks it in order to enter into a more lucrative contract with someone else) that the law does not wish to deter.[98]

FURTHER READING

McKendrick, 'Breach of Contract, Restitution for Wrongs and Punishment' in Burrows and Peel (eds), *Commercial Remedies* (Oxford: Oxford University Press, 2003) 93

Rotherham, '"Wrotham Park Damages" and Account of Profits: Compensation or Restitution?' [2008] LMCLQ 25

Burrows, 'Are "Damages on the Wrotham Park Basis" Compensatory, Restitutionary or Neither?' in Saidov and Cunnington (eds), *Contract Damages* (Oxford: Hart Publishing, 2008) ch 7

---

[97] Above, p 633.
[98] See, eg *AB Corp v CD Company, The Sine Nomine* [2002] 1 Lloyd's Rep 805, noted by Beatson (2002) 118 LQR 377, in which an account of profits was refused by arbitrators for the withdrawal, and use of, a ship in breach of a charterparty.

20

LIMITATION OF ACTIONS

At common law, lapse of time does not affect contractual rights. But it is the policy of the law to discourage stale claims, because after a long period a defendant may not have the evidence to rebut such claims and should be in a position to know that after a given time an incident which might have led to a claim is finally closed. Accordingly, in the Limitation Act 1980, the Legislature has laid down certain periods of limitation after the expiry of which no action can be maintained.[1] Equity has developed a doctrine of laches, under which a claimant who has not shown reasonable diligence in prosecuting the claim may be barred from equitable relief.

1. LIMITATION ACT 1980

(a) THE GENERAL RULE

The Act provides that an action founded on a simple contract must be commenced within six years, and one created or secured by a deed, within 12 years, from the date on which the cause of action accrued.[2] In contract, the cause of action accrues, not, as in the tort of negligence, when the damage is suffered, but when the breach of contract takes place[3] or, in the case of an anticipatory breach, when the innocent party elects to treat the contract as terminated.[4] In the case of certain loans, however, the six-year period does not start to run unless and until a demand in writing for the repayment of the debt is made by or on behalf of the creditor.[5]

---

[1] For proposals for reform see Law Com Report No 270, *Limitation of Actions* (2001); Law Com No 316, Annual Report 2008–09 (2009) 60.

[2] Limitation Act 1980, ss 5, 8. But in the case of personal injuries arising from a breach of contract, ss 11 and 14 of the Act provide that the limitation period is to be three years from the date on which the cause of action accrued or the date of the claimant's knowledge (if later) of certain relevant facts: and that period may be disapplied at the Court's discretion under s 33. See also ss 12, 13, 14 (fatal accidents).

[3] *Battley v Faulkner* (1820) 3 B & Ald 288; *Short v M'Carthy* (1820) 3 B & Ald 626; *Howell v Young* (1826) 5 B & C 259. For accrual at the date of damage of a concurrent action in the tort of negligence, see, eg, *Midland Bank Trust Co Ltd v Hett, Stubbs & Kemp* [1979] Ch 384; *Forster v Outred & Co* [1982] 1 WLR 86; *Pirelli General Cable Works Ltd v Oscar Faber & Partners* [1983] 2 AC 1; *Bell v Peter Browne & Co* [1990] 2 QB 495; *Henderson v Merrett Syndicates Ltd* [1995] 2 AC 145.

[4] *Reeves v Butcher* [1891] 2 QB 509.   [5] Limitation Act 1980, s 6; *Boot v Boot* [1996] 2 FCR 713.

A distinction is drawn between a 'once and for all' breach and a 'continuing' breach. In the case of a continuing breach, such as of an obligation to repair a building, the promisor's duty is considered as persisting and as being forever renewed until that which has been promised has been done; 'a further breach arises in every successive moment of time during which the state or condition is not as promised, during which . . . the building is out of repair'.[6] In cases of continuing breaches the claimant will be able to recover in respect of that part of the breach which occurred within the six or, in the case of an obligation created or secured by a deed, 12 years before the action was brought.

It is no answer to a plea of limitation that the claimant was unaware or could not have been aware of the existence of the cause of action for breach of contract until after the expiry of the limitation period. The 'discoverability' rule for economic loss claims in the tort of negligence[7] does not apply to breach of contract.[8]

Where the action is for restitution of an unjust enrichment, the limitation period is normally six years from the accrual of the claimant's cause of action which normally accrues when the defendant is unjustly enriched whether by the receipt of money or otherwise.[9]

(b) PERSONS UNDER A DISABILITY

If on the date on which the cause of action accrued the person to whom it accrued was under a disability, that is, was a minor or lacked capacity within the meaning of the Mental Capacity Act 2005 to conduct legal proceedings,[10] the action may be brought within six years from the date when he or she ceased to be under the disability, or dies.[11] This enlargement of time does not apply when the disability supervenes after the right of action has already accrued, or where the same person is afflicted by successive disabilities (eg minority followed by insanity) separated by an interval in which he or she is under no disability.[12] Again, no extension is allowed when the right of action first accrues to a person not under a disability through whom the person under a disability claims.[13]

(c) EFFECT OF FRAUD, CONCEALMENT, AND MISTAKE

Where an action is based on the fraud of the defendant,[14] or where any fact relevant to the right of action has been deliberately concealed from the claimant by the

---

[6] *Larking v Great Western (Nepean) Gravel Ltd* (1940) 64 CLR 221, 236 (Dixon J) (High Court of Australia). See also the facts of *Midland Bank Trust Co Ltd v Hett, Stubbs & Kemp* [1979] Ch 384.

[7] Limitation Act 1980, ss 14A–14B.

[8] *Iron Trades Mutual Insurance Co Ltd v JK Buckenham Ltd* [1990] 1 All ER 808; *Société Commerciale de Réassurance v Eras International Ltd* [1992] 1 Lloyd's Rep 570.

[9] *Kleinwort Benson v South Tyneside MBC* [1994] 4 All ER 972, 978. See generally McLean [1989] CLJ 472; Burrows, *The Law of Restitution* (3rd edn, 2010) ch 22; Burrows, *A Restatement of the English Law of Unjust Enrichment* (2012) 143–9; Virgo, *The Principles of the Law of Restitution* (3rd edn, 2015) ch 29.

[10] Limitation Act 1980, s 38(2) (as amended). [11] Limitation Act 1980, s 28.

[12] *Purnell v Roche* [1927] 2 Ch 142. [13] Limitation Act 1980, s 28(2).

[14] *Beaman v ARTS Ltd* [1949] 1 KB 550; *Clef Aquitaine SARL v Laporte Materials (Barrow) Ltd* [2001] 1 QB 488; *Barnstaple Boat Co Ltd v Jones* [2007] EWCA Civ 727, [2008] 1 All ER 1124. It is submitted that an

defendant,[15] whether before or after the cause of action has accrued,[16] or where an action is for relief from the consequences of a mistake,[17] the period does not begin to run until the claimant has discovered the fraud, concealment, or mistake, or could with reasonable diligence have discovered it.[18] The 1980 Act further provides that a deliberate breach of duty in circumstances in which it is unlikely to be discovered for some time amounts to deliberate concealment of the facts involved in that breach of duty.[19] So, for example, if a builder fails to disclose the deliberate breach of a building contract by using defective bricks[20] or putting in inadequate foundations,[21] or if the vendors of a house knowingly fail to warn the purchaser of the risk of subsidence, when they are aware that the house has been built on a disused rubbish tip,[22] the running of the limitation period will be postponed until such time as the claimant discovers the concealment or could with reasonable diligence discover it.[23]

(d) ACKNOWLEDGEMENT AND PART PAYMENT

An acknowledgement or part payment of 'any debt or other liquidated pecuniary claim'[24] may extend the period of limitation. The 1980 Act provides[25] that in such a case the right shall be treated as having accrued on, and not before, the date of the acknowledgement or payment. Thus where A owes B the sum of £500, say, as the price of goods sold and delivered, B's remedy is barred after the passing of six years from the date on which payment became due. But if A, during that period, either acknowledges the debt and its legal liability to pay it[26] or makes a part payment on account of the debt,

---

action under the Misrepresentation Act 1967, s 2(1) does not fall within s 32(1)(a) of the 1980 Act despite the statutory fiction of fraud: above p 350.

[15] The leading case on the meaning of concealment is *Cave v Robinson Jarvis & Rolf* [2002] UKHL 18, [2003] 1 AC 384. See also *Williams v Fanshaw Porter & Hazelhurst* [2004] EWCA Civ 157, [2004] 1 WLR 3185.

[16] *Sheldon v RHM Outhwaite (Underwriting Agencies) Ltd* [1996] AC 102.

[17] This has been interpreted to mean that the mistake must be an element of the cause of action: *Phillips-Higgins v Harper* [1954] 1 QB 411; *Claimants in the Franked Investment Group Litigation v Revenue and Customs Commissioners* [2012] UKSC 19, [2012] 2 AC 337. The mistake can be a mistake of law resulting from a 'change' in the law: *Kleinwort Benson Ltd v Lincoln City Council* [1999] 2 AC 349.

[18] Limitation Act 1980, s 32. But this provision is not to affect the rights of third parties taking bona fide and for value.

[19] Limitation Act 1980, s 32(2).   [20] *Clark v Woor* [1965] 1 WLR 650.

[21] *Applegate v Moss* [1971] 1 QB 406.   [22] *King v Victor Parsons & Co* [1973] 1 WLR 29.

[23] Note, however, these cases were decided on the wording of the Limitation Act 1939, s 26(b), now repealed. But see generally on deliberate concealment *Cave v Robinson, Jarvis and Rolf* [2002] UKHL 18, [2003] 1 AC 384 (where the claim was for the tort of negligence).

[24] This includes a claim for a quantum meruit: *Phillips & Co v Bath Housing Co-operative Ltd* [2012] EWCA Civ 1591, [2013] 1 WLR 1479.

[25] s 29(5).

[26] *Surrendra Overseas Ltd v Government of Sri Lanka* [1977] 1 WLR 565; *Kamouh v Associated Electrical Industries International Ltd* [1980] QB 199; *Bradford and Bingley plc v Rashid* [2006] UKHL 37, [2006] 1 WLR 2066; *Habib Bank Ltd v Central Bank of Sudan* [2006] EWHC 1767 (Comm), [2007] 1 All ER (Comm) 53; *Lia Oil SA v ERG Petroli SpA* [2007] EWHC 505 (Comm), [2007] 2 Lloyd's Rep 509; *Ofulue v Bossert* [2009] UKHL 16, [2009] 1 AC 990.

time begins to run afresh from the date of the acknowledgement or part payment. The limitation period may thus be repeatedly extended. Once, however, it has expired, the right of action cannot subsequently be revived.[27] To be effective, an acknowledgement must be in writing and signed by the person making it or that person's agent, and either an acknowledgement or part payment must be made to the person or to the agent of the person whose claim is acknowledged or in respect of whose claim the payment is made.[28]

(e) STATUTE BARS REMEDY NOT RIGHT

The Act operates merely to bar the contractual remedy, but not to extinguish the right.[29] It is procedural and not substantive. Accordingly, a debtor who pays a statute-barred debt, cannot recover the money as money not due.[30] And if the debtor owes to the creditor certain debts some of which are, and some of which are not, statute-barred, the creditor is entitled to appropriate any payment made by the debtor to those debts which are statute-barred, unless the debtor at the time expressly indicates that he is discharging a debt which is still actionable.[31]

2. BARS TO EQUITABLE RELIEF: LACHES

(a) THE STATUTE APPLIED BY ANALOGY

The statutory periods of limitation for contract do not apply to claims for 'specific performance of a contract or for an injunction or for other equitable relief' except in so far as the Court may apply them by analogy.[32] The situations to which the statute will be applied by analogy are relatively few and, broadly, include those situations in which there is 'correspondence' between the remedies available at law and in equity, and equity is providing a remedy analogous to that which would have been available at law.

For example, it would appear that the statute will be applied by analogy to a claim for equitable compensation for dishonest assistance of a breach of fiduciary duty;[33] and the right to a final injunction will not be barred so long as the substantive legal right which it seeks to protect has not become barred (ie so long as the claimant

---

[27] Limitation Act 1980, s 29(7).   [28] Limitation Act 1980, s 30.

[29] *Royal Norwegian Government v Constant & Constant and Calcutta Marine Engineering Co Ltd* [1960] 2 Lloyd's Rep 431, 442; *Ronex Properties Ltd v John Laing Construction Ltd* [1982] 3 WLR 875, 879. But exceptionally delay may extinguish title to goods (Limitation Act 1980, s 3(2)) and unregistered land (Limitation Act 1980, s 17); and the right to damages for product liability under Part I of the Consumer Protection Act 1980 is extinguished by a ten-year long-stop (Limitation Act 1980, s 11A(3)).

[30] *Bize v Dickason* (1786) 1 Term R 286, 287.

[31] *Mills v Fowkes* (1830) 5 Bing NC 455.   [32] Limitation Act 1980, s 36(1).

[33] *Cattley v Pollard* [2006] EWHC 3130 (Ch), [2007] Ch 353. For the contrary (less persuasive) view, see *Statek Corp v Alford* [2008] EWHC 32 (Ch), [2008] BCC 266.

could still recover damages for infringement of the right).[34] In *P & O Nedlloyd BV v Arab Metals Co, The UB Tiger*[35] it was held, in a careful judgment by Moore-Bick LJ, that the usual contractual limitation period of six years does not apply by analogy under section 36(1) to a claim for specific performance.[36] This is because there is no directly equivalent remedy at common law to specific performance and because it is not even a requirement for specific performance that there be an existing breach of contract.[37] However, the doctrine of laches, discussed below, can apply.

(b) LACHES

Equitable claims or remedies to which the statute does not apply expressly or by analogy are subject to the equitable doctrine of laches.[38] Equity has always refused its aid to stale claims. Delay which is sufficient to deprive a person of the right to claim specific performance or injunction is known technically as 'laches'. This doctrine has been described in a well-known passage in the advice of the Privy Council in *Lindsay Petroleum Co v Hurd*,[39] as follows:

The doctrine of laches in Courts of Equity is not an arbitrary or a technical doctrine. Where it would be practically unjust to give a remedy, either because the party has, by his conduct, done that which might fairly be regarded as equivalent to a waiver of it, or where by his conduct and neglect he has, though perhaps not waiving that remedy, yet put the other party in a situation in which it would not be reasonable to place him if the remedy were afterwards to be asserted, in either of these cases lapse of time and delay are most material. But in every case, if an argument against relief, which otherwise would be just, is founded upon mere delay, that delay of course not amounting to a bar by any statute of limitations, the validity of that defence must be tried upon principles substantially equitable. Two circumstances, always important in such cases, are, the length of the delay and the nature of the acts done during the interval.

---

[34] *Fullwood v Fullwood* (1878) 9 Ch D 176. This was a tort case. There appears to be no example of this principle being applied where a final injunction is being sought for a breach of contract.

[35] [2006] EWCA Civ 1717, [2007] 1 WLR 2288.

[36] See Beatson, 'Limitation Periods and Specific Performance' in Lomnicka and Morse (eds), *Contemporary Issues in Commercial Law* (1997) 9–23.

[37] As shown in *Hasham v Zenab* [1960] AC 316.

[38] It is not clear whether laches can apply to bar an equitable remedy even where a statutory limitation period does apply. It may be that the best answer to this turns on whether the laches in question comprises mere delay or delay plus prejudice to the defendant. As regards the latter, there seems no reason why laches should not apply even within a statutory limitation period given that 'acquiescence' can so apply (as laid down in the Limitation Act 1980, s 36(2)). For this distinction as to the nature of the laches, see *obiter dicta* of Moore-Bick LJ in *P & O Nedlloyd BV v Arab Metals Co, The UB Tiger* [2006] EWCA Civ 1717, [2007] 1 WLR 2288 at [61].

[39] (1874) LR 5 PC 221, 239 (Lord Selborne). This was applied in *Fisher v Brooker* [2009] UKHL 41, [2009] 1 WLR 1764: it was not 'practically unjust' to grant a declaration of copyright despite 38 years' delay because there was no prejudice to the defendant (and, in any event, the relief sought was not 'equitable').

Delay may therefore bar equitable remedies such as claims for rescission,[40] rectification,[41] specific performance,[42] or for an interim injunction.[43] It has traditionally been said that the claimant must show himself to be 'ready, desirous, prompt and eager'[44] to assert his rights, and even a short lapse of time may, in certain circumstances,[45] be fatal. But in exceptional circumstances, as where the parties have been negotiating, a long lapse of time will not be fatal.[46]

[40] *Lindsay Petroleum Co v Hurd*, ibid; *Salt v Stratstone Specialist Ltd* [2015] EWCA Civ 745.

[41] *Beale v Kyte* [1907] 1 Ch 564.

[42] *Mills v Haywood* (1877) 6 Ch D 196; *P & O Nedlloyd BV v Arab Metals Co, The UB Tiger* [2006] EWCA Civ 1717, [2007] 1 WLR 2288. But delay does not bar specific performance ordering mere transfer of the legal estate where a party has taken possession of the property in reliance on that interest: *Williams v Greatrex* [1957] 1 WLR 31 (specific performance despite ten-year delay).

[43] *Great Western Ry v Oxford, Worcester and Wolverhampton Ry.* (1853) 3 De GM & G 341; *Shepherd Homes Ltd v Sandham* [1971] Ch 340 (four-month delay).

[44] *Milward v Earl of Thanet* (1801) 5 Ves 720n. Contrast *Lazard Bros & Co Ltd v Fairfield Properties Co (Mayfair) Ltd* (1977) 121 SJ 793.

[45] *Lehmann v McArthur* (1868) LR 3 Ch App 496 (short leasehold interest); *First National Reinsurance Co. Ltd v Greenfield* [1921] 2 KB 260 (shares). Cf *Jones v Jones* [1999] 1 WLR 1739 (mere delay in seeking relief does not signify acquiescence).

[46] *Southcomb v Bishop of Exeter* (1847) 6 Hare 213. See also *Tito v Waddell* [1977] Ch 106, 244–52 (specific performance refused 17 years after the breach of contract not because of delay but because of futility).

PART 6

LIMITS OF THE CONTRACTUAL OBLIGATION

21

THIRD PARTIES

1. INTRODUCTION

This chapter deals with the scope of a valid contract when formed, and the question, to whom does the obligation extend? This question must be considered under two separate headings: (1) the acquisition of rights by a third party, and (2) the imposition of liabilities upon a third party. At common law the general rule is that no one but the parties to a contract can be entitled under it, or bound by it. This principle is known as that of *privity of contract*.

Both aspects of this principle have long been subject to common law and statutory exceptions. But the first aspect, which prevented parties to a contract from enabling a third party to acquire rights under it, was subject to widespread criticism by judges, law reform bodies, and scholars.[1] Despite these criticisms it was reaffirmed on several occasions by the House of Lords in the late twentieth century. However, the criticisms were eventually heeded by the legislature. The Contracts (Rights of Third Parties) Act 1999, largely implementing a Law Commission report,[2] enables a third party to enforce a contract where the parties so intend.

While the 1999 Act creates a potentially 'general and wide-ranging exception'[3] to the first aspect of the privity principle, it does not abolish it and leaves it intact for cases not covered by the Act. It also preserves the statutory and common law exceptions to the rule.[4] A third party who is able to invoke one of these may be in a better position than one who relies on the 1999 Act.[5] The statutory and common law exceptions to the rule will also continue to be of importance because of the tendency of commercial contracts drafted since its enactment to exclude the Act. Moreover, the Act does not enable a contract term to be directly enforced against a third party and thus does not change the second aspect of the principle under which a burden cannot be imposed on a third party.[6] Accordingly, it remains necessary to consider the common law principle and the exceptions to and circumventions of it.

---

[1] Below, pp 657–8.

[2] Law Commission No 242, *Privity of Contract: Contracts for the Benefit of Third Parties* (1996), hereinafter 'Law Com No 242'.

[3] Law Com No 242, paras 5.16, 13.2.   [4] s 7(1).   [5] Below, pp 669, 675.

[6] Hansard HL Debs 11 January 1999, col 21 (Lord Irvine LC).

2. THE ACQUISITION OF CONTRACTUAL RIGHTS BY THIRD PARTIES

(a) THE DEVELOPMENT OF THE COMMON LAW RULE

If A and B make a contract in which A promises to do something or to refrain from doing something for the benefit of C, all three may be willing that C should have all the rights of an actual contracting party.[7] Thus A may promise to pay a sum of money[8] to, or perform a service for,[9] C. Alternatively, A may promise not to sue C, either at all[10] or in circumstances covered by an exclusion or limitation clause in the contract between A and B.[11] Many systems of law give effect to the intentions of those concerned but the rule of the English common law, now modified by the Contracts (Rights of Third Parties) Act 1999, is that a person who is not a party to a contract can neither sue on nor rely on defences based on that contract.

(i) A relative latecomer

This rule was not clearly established until the middle of the nineteenth century. There are earlier decisions permitting the third party, often a relative of the promisee[12] but not always,[13] to enforce the promise. The development of the rule of privity of contract was linked with that of the doctrine of consideration and the early cases used both strands of reasoning. In *Price v Easton*:[14]

WP owed Price £13. WP promised to work for E, and in return E undertook to discharge the debt to Price. The work was done by WP, but E did not pay the money to Price. Price sued E.

It was held that Price could not recover because he was not a party to the contract. However, the reasoning of the judges differed. Lord Denman CJ said that the claimant did not 'shew any consideration for the promise moving from him to the defendant',[15] while Littledale J said, 'No privity is shewn between the plaintiff and the defendant';[16] and Patteson J that there was 'no promise to the plaintiff alleged'.[17]

In *Tweddle v Atkinson*,[18] it was also held that no action could be brought by a non-party:

H and W married. After the marriage, X and Y, their respective fathers, made a contract by which they undertook that each should pay a sum of money to H, and that H should have

---

[7] Dowrick (1956) 19 MLR 374.   [8] *Beswick v Beswick* [1968] AC 58, below, p 649.

[9] *Jackson v Horizon Holidays Ltd* [1975] 1 WLR 1548, below, p 652 (provision of holiday accommodation).

[10] *Snelling v John Snelling Ltd* [1973] QB 87, below, p 655.

[11] *Scruttons v Midlands Silicones Ltd* [1962] AC 446, below, p 680.

[12] *Bourne v Mason* (1699) 1 Ventr 6; *Dutton v Poole* (1672) 2 Lev 210.

[13] *Marchington v Vernon* (1787) 1 Bos & P 101n (doubted in *Phillips v Bateman* (1812) 16 East 356); *Carnegie v Waugh* (1823) 1 LJ (OS) 89.

[14] (1833) 4 B & Ad 433.   [15] *Ibid*, 434.   [16] *Ibid*.

[17] *Ibid*, 435.   [18] (1861) 1 B & S 393; above, p 103.

power to sue for such sums. After the death of X and Y, H sued the executors of Y for the money promised to him.

Wightman J said:[19]

Some of the old decisions appear to support the proposition that a stranger to the consideration of a contract may maintain an action upon it, . . . But there is no modern case in which the proposition has been supported. On the contrary, it is now established *that no stranger to the consideration can take advantage of a contract, although made for his benefit.*

The modern rule is based on Lord Haldane's formulation in *Dunlop Pneumatic Tyre Co Ltd v Selfridge & Co Ltd*:[20]

[I]n the law of England certain principles are fundamental. One is that only a person who is a party to a contract can sue on it. Our law knows nothing of a *jus quaesitum tertio* arising by way of contract. Such a right may be conferred by way of property, as for example, under a trust, but it cannot be conferred on a stranger to a contract as a right to enforce the contract *in personam.*

The House of Lords reaffirmed the rule in several cases, notably in 1968 in *Beswick v Beswick*:[21]

B, a coal merchant, agreed to transfer the business to his nephew in return for a promise by the nephew to employ him as 'consultant' during his lifetime, and, after his death, to pay an annuity of £5 a week to his widow. On B's death, the nephew failed to pay the money to the widow. She brought an action against him in her personal capacity as the beneficiary of the contract, and also in her capacity as administratrix of her deceased husband's estate.

The House of Lords, applying the doctrine of privity, held that she was not entitled to enforce the obligation in her personal capacity because she was not a party to the contract (although she was able to sue as administratrix of the estate, that is, as her deceased husband's personal representative, being in that capacity a party to the contract).

(ii) Relationship with doctrine of consideration

Price v Easton and *Tweddle v Atkinson* might seem to rest solely on the rule that consideration must move from the promisee and it has been argued, therefore, that the privity rule is really no more than an application of the doctrine of consideration.[22] However, in *Dunlop Pneumatic Tyre Co Ltd v Selfridge & Co Ltd* Lord Haldane[23]

---

[19] *Ibid*, 397–8, emphasis added.   [20] [1915] AC 847, 853.

[21] [1968] AC 58, 72, 78, 83, 92, 95, 105. See also *Scruttons Ltd v Midland Silicones Ltd* [1962] AC 446; *The Eurymedon* [1975] AC 154; *Woodar Investment Development Ltd v Wimpey Construction (UK) Ltd* [1980] 1 WLR 277, 284, 291, 297, 300; *JH Rayner (Mincing Lane) Ltd v DTI* [1990] 2 AC 418, 479, 506; *White v Jones* [1995] 2 AC 207, 262–3, 266.

[22] Furmston (1960) 23 MLR 373; Smith, *The Law of Contract* (4th edn, 2002) 94.

[23] [1915] AC 847, 853.

distinguished the two and there is support for this in other cases.[24] Certainly in a broad sense privity and consideration may be said to reflect two logically separate issues of policy.[25] The first, primarily associated with the privity doctrine, relates to who can enforce a contract. The second, primarily associated with consideration, concerns the types of promises that can be enforced. Having said that, the closeness of the link between the two depends on the precise sense in which one is using the maxim 'consideration must move from the promisee'. This has been discussed in Chapter 4 above.[26] Suffice it to say here that, insofar as one means by that maxim that consideration must move *from the claimant* the maxim overlaps with, and is indistinguishable from, the doctrine of privity according to which only a party to a contract can enforce it.

(b) REMEDIES OF THE PROMISEE

Notwithstanding the fact that the third party cannot enforce the contract, the contract is binding between the parties to it. The remedies that may be available to the promisee if the promisor fails to perform the promise are only relevant where the promisee is able and willing to enforce the contract for the benefit of the third party. The widow in *Beswick v Beswick* would not have been able to obtain her annuity had Peter Beswick appointed his nephew the executor of his estate instead of the widow. There is no procedure by which an unwilling or unco-operative promisee can be compelled to institute proceedings on behalf of the third party.[27] The existence of a right of action in the promisee does not, in consequence, necessarily ensure that the third party will obtain damages or the performance promised in the contract. Even where the promisee seeks a remedy there are certain difficulties.

(i) Damages for loss sustained by the promisee

The general rule is that damages are for loss suffered by the claimant. Therefore, where the breach of contract consists of failure to perform in favour of the third party, the damages will, in principle, be nominal only.[28] Thus in *Beswick*

---

[24] *Vandepitte v Preferred Accident Insurance Corp of New York* [1933] AC 70, 79; *Scruttons Ltd v Midland Silicones Ltd* [1962] AC 446; *Kepong Prospecting Ltd v Schmidt* [1968] AC 810, 826. See also Atiyah, *Essays on Contract* (1986) 220; *KH Enterprise v Pioneer Container* [1994] 2 AC 324, 355; *White v Jones* [1995] 2 AC 207, 262–3; *Coulls v Bagot's Executor and Trustee Co Ltd* (1967) 119 CLR 460, 478, 486, 493; *Trident General Insurance Co Ltd v McNiece Bros Pty Ltd* (1988) 165 CLR 107, 164 (High Court of Australia); *London Drugs Ltd v Kuehene & Nagel International Ltd* [1992] 3 SCR 299, 417 (Supreme Court of Canada).

[25] Law Revision Committee, Sixth Interim Report 1937 (Cmnd 5449), para 37; Law Com CP No 121, *Privity of Contract: Contracts for the Benefit of Third Parties* (1991), para 2.9 and see (albeit more equivocally) Law Com No 242, Part VI.

[26] Above, pp 103–4.

[27] But see the suggestion that the third party be joined as a party to the action made by Lord Denning in *Beswick v Beswick* [1966] Ch 538, 554, and (in a different context) *Snelling v John Snelling Ltd* [1973] QB 87, below, p 621. Contrast *Gurtner v Circuit* [1968] 2 QB 587, 599, 606; *White v Jones* [1995] 2 AC 207, 267.

[28] See Coote's argument ([1997] CLJ 537, 549 ff) that Courts have confused loss of the enjoyments of the fruits of performance (which the promisee *has not* lost) and loss of the bargained-for contractual rights (which the promisee *has* lost).

v Beswick[29] the promisee's estate suffered no loss because the promise was to benefit the widow and not Peter Beswick (or his estate).[30] In some situations, however, including many commercial transactions, the promisee will suffer loss by reason of the breach, either because an obligation it owes to the third party is not discharged, as in *Price v Easton*,[31] or where the consequence is that the promisee comes under a legal obligation to the third party. In such cases substantial damages will, in principle,[32] be recoverable.

In principle, the promisee should also be able to recover substantial damages if, by reason of the breach of contract, the promisee (a) comes under a moral obligation to compensate the third party, though under no legal obligation to do so,[33] or, (b) voluntarily incurs expense in making good the default.[34] Thus if a vicar hires a coach for an outing for the choir, and the coach operator leaves the choir stranded half way, the vicar might recover substantial damages in respect of the taxi fares incurred in getting the choir home, whether the choir paid their own fares (in which case the vicar would recompense the choir from the damages recovered) or the vicar paid their fares for them.[35]

There may also be certain cases of contracts for the benefit of a third party where what might at first sight appear to be the third party's loss can in fact be analysed as the promisee's. One example, discussed below, is where the promisee contracts for a family holiday.[36]

(ii) Damages for loss sustained by the third party rejected as a general rule

The principle that as a general rule substantial damages can only be given for loss suffered by the claimant, applied by the House of Lords in *Beswick v Beswick*,[37] has been affirmed on several occasions since then. In *Woodar Investment Development Ltd v Wimpey Construction UK Ltd*:[38]

The defendants contracted to buy land from the claimants for £850,000. It was agreed that on completion £150,000 was to be paid by the defendants to a third party. The claimants sought damages for a repudiatory breach of the contract by the defendants.

A majority of the House of Lords held that the defendants had not repudiated the contract. But their Lordships agreed that, if the contract had been repudiated, the claimants could not, without showing that they had themselves suffered loss or were agents or trustees for the third party, have recovered damages for non-payment of the £150,000.

---

[29] [1968] AC 58.

[30] *Ibid*, 102 (Lord Upjohn). See also at 72, 78, 101. Cf Lord Pearce, at 88.

[31] (1833) 4 B & Ad 433, above, p 648.

[32] ie, subject to the ordinary rules, including those concerning remoteness and mitigation on which see above, pp 575 and 587.

[33] *Jackson v Watson* [1909] 2 KB 193; *Radford v de Froberville* [1977] 1 WLR 1262.

[34] It may be reasonable to make a voluntary payment; *Banco de Portugal v Waterlow & Sons Ltd* [1932] AC 452, above, p 588 (mitigation of damages). See also *Admiralty Commissioners v SS Amerika* [1917] AC 38, 61.

[35] An example given by Lord Denning MR in *Jackson v Horizon Holidays Ltd* [1975] 1 WLR 1468, 1472–3.

[36] Below, p 652.   [37] [1968] AC 58, 72, 78, 101.

[38] [1980] 1 WLR 277, 283–4, 291, 293, 297, 300.

In *Jackson v Horizon Holidays Ltd*[39] Lord Denning MR, with whom Orr LJ agreed, had stated that whenever a contract was made for the benefit of a third party and the third party suffered loss as a result of the failure of the promisor to perform the contract, the promisee could recover damages in respect of the loss sustained by the third party, holding the damages as money had and received to the use of the third party and paying them over. In that case:

J contracted with a travel company for the provision by the company of holiday accommodation for himself, his wife and two children. The accommodation provided fell below the standard required by the contract and the whole family suffered discomfort, vexation, inconvenience and distress. The trial judge awarded J £1,100 damages including £500 for his mental distress.

The Court of Appeal upheld the award. James LJ appeared to agree with the trial judge. Lord Denning MR said that, if regarded as only for the distress of the claimant himself, the award was excessive but held that the claimant could recover both for his loss and that of his family.

In *Woodar*'s case the House of Lords disapproved of this view[40] but it was said that the decision in *Jackson*'s case could be supported either on the ground that the claimant there was recovering damages in consequence of the loss which he had himself sustained[41] or as a case which called for 'special treatment'.[42] In view of its decision on the repudiation point it was not necessary for the House to make a decision on the damages point and it did not state any rule of law regarding the recovery of damages for the benefit of third parties. Nevertheless certain members of the House of Lords were strongly critical of the result produced by the combined effect of these two aspects of the privity of contract principle; neither the third party for whom the benefit was intended nor the promisee who contracted for it could recover damages for that which the promisor had agreed, but failed, to provide.

The hope was expressed that the House of Lords would soon have the opportunity of reconsidering this matter[43] but when the question again came before the House

---

[39] *Jackson v Horizon Holidays Ltd* [1975] 1 WLR 1468. Cf in tort, where voluntary services by the victim's carer are analysed as the carer's loss and damages are held on trust by the victim for the carer: *Cunningham v Harrison* [1973] QB 454; *Donnelly v Joyce* [1974] QB 454; *Housecroft v Burnett* [1986] 1 All ER 332, 343; *Hunt v Severs* [1994] AC 350, 363.

[40] Lord Denning had relied on a statement of Lush LJ in *Lloyd's v Harper* (1880) 16 Ch D 290, 321 which was made in the context of the 'trust of a promise' exception to the general rule; see below, p 672 and *Beswick v Beswick* [1968] AC 58, 101; *Woodar Investment Development Ltd v Wimpey Construction UK Ltd* [1980] 1 WLR 277, 283, 293–4, 297. The Package Travel, Package Holidays and Package Tours Regulations 1992 (SI 1992 No 3288), below p 677 now give the beneficiaries of package holidays a direct right of action.

[41] [1980] 1 WLR 277, 293, 297; *Jackson v Horizon Holidays Ltd* [1975] 1 WLR 1468, 1474 (James LJ).

[42] [1980] 1 WLR 277, 283, 291, 293. See also *Calabar Properties Ltd v Sticher* [1984] 1 WLR 287, 290 (tenant's damages included sum in respect of spouse's ill-health).

[43] *Ibid*, 291, 297–8, 300–1.

in *Linden Gardens Trust Ltd v Lenesta Sludge Disposals Ltd* and *St Martins Property Corporation Ltd v Sir Robert McAlpine Ltd*[44] and again in *Alfred McAlpine Construction Ltd v Panatown Ltd*,[45] the opportunity was not taken. In the *Linden Gardens* case the decision was that the case fell within the rationale of the exceptions to the general rule[46] and in *Alfred McAlpine Construction Ltd v Panatown Ltd* it was held that the exceptions did not apply where the third party has, as it was in that case, been given a direct contractual right against the promisor.[47]

(iii) Exceptionally third party's loss recoverable

What then are the exceptions to the general rule? A trustee-promisee may recover in respect of the beneficiary's loss,[48] an agent may recover in respect of the undisclosed principal's loss,[49] and a person with a limited interest in property who has taken out full insurance may recover the full amount of loss or damage.[50] Again, in a contract for the carriage of goods by sea, a consignor may recover substantial damages even where it has sold the goods and they are not at its risk provided it is not contemplated that the carrier would also be put into a direct contractual relationship with whomsoever might become the owner of the goods.[51] The last two exceptions concern commercial contracts about goods where the parties contemplate that the proprietary interests in the goods may be transferred after the contract has been entered into but before the breach which causes loss or damage to the goods. This principle has been held to apply to a contract for the development of land where the land was owned or occupied, or it was contemplated that the land was going to be owned or occupied, by third parties.[52] In such a case, where the third-party owner or occupier has no direct right to sue for breach of contract,[53] the contracting party can recover substantial damages as representing the third party's loss.

---

[44] [1994] AC 85, varying (1992) 57 BLR 57.

[45] [2001] 1 AC 518.

[46] [1994] AC 84, 114.

[47] [2001] 1 AC 518.

[48] *Lloyd's v Harper* (1880) 16 Ch D 290, 331 on which see below, p 672. See also *St Albans City and District Council v International Computers Ltd* [1996] 4 All ER 481, 489 (local authority recovered in respect of chargepayer's loss).

[49] *Allen v F O'Hearn & Co* [1937] AC 213, 218, below, pp 708–710, 715–716.

[50] *Waters v Monarch Fire and Life Assurance Co* (1856) 5 E & B 870; *Hepburn v A Tomlinson (Hauliers) Ltd* [1966] AC 451; Marine Insurance Act 1906, s 26(3). See also the right of the bailee, albeit in tort, in *The Winkfield* [1902] P 42 and the analogous fact situation in *Bovis International Inc v The Circle Limited Partnership* (1995) 49 Con LR 12.

[51] *Dunlop v Lambert* (1839) 6 Cl & F 600; *The Albazero* [1977] AC 774, 846–7. The direct contractual relationship, rendering the exception unnecessary, might be by the operation of the Carriage of Goods by Sea Act 1992 or by making a separate contract.

[52] *Linden Gardens Trust Ltd v Lenesta Sludge Disposals Ltd* and *St Martins Property Corporation Ltd v Sir Robert McAlpine Ltd* [1994] AC 85, 114–15 (contracting party owner of land); *Darlington BC v Wiltshier Northern Ltd* [1995] 1 WLR 68 (contracting party had no proprietary interest).

[53] *Alfred McAlpine Construction Ltd v Panatown Ltd* [2001] 1 AC 518 (exception did not apply because third party had direct contractual right).

(iv) Specific performance

The promisee may be able to obtain an order for specific performance against the promisor to compel him to carry out the promise in favour of the third party. Thus in *Beswick v Beswick*[54] the House of Lords held that the widow, in her capacity as personal representative of Peter Beswick (the promisee), could obtain specific performance of the promise in favour of herself as third party. As Lord Pearce explained: 'The estate (though not the widow personally) can enforce it'.[55]

Specific performance is, as has been seen, a discretionary equitable remedy which is not available as a matter of course. As a general rule, an order for specific performance will not be made against a defendant in any case where damages are an adequate and appropriate remedy,[56] where, had the positions been reversed, the claimant's undertaking could not have been specifically enforced, so 'mutuality' was lacking,[57] or where the contract has been discharged and is no longer in existence.[58] Contracts of personal service are normally not specifically enforceable;[59] and not all contractual undertakings are sufficiently precisely defined to be enforced specifically.[60]

In *Beswick v Beswick* an award of damages was considered inadequate and specific performance appropriate for a number of reasons. First, damages would not have taken account of the loss to the third party and would have been purely nominal.[61] Secondly, the defaulting promisor had received the full benefit of the contract by the completed transfer of the business.[62] Thirdly, had the business not been transferred, the defaulting promisor could have obtained specific performance of the promise.[63] Fourthly, specific performance was more appropriate for a promise to make a series of regular payments than a succession of actions for damages which would have had to have been brought as each payment fell due. It does not therefore follow that specific performance will necessarily be ordered in all cases where performance is to be made to a third party.

(v) Action for the agreed sum

Where money is promised to be paid to a third party, the contracting party to whom the promise is made has normally no claim whatsoever to the money which is properly due to the third party. It follows that the promisee cannot by means of an action for the agreed sum require the promisor to pay the agreed sum to the promisee.[64] However, although there is no clear support for this in the authorities,[65] it would seem that in

---

[54] [1968] AC 58.   [55] *Ibid*, 89.
[56] See above, p 609.   [57] See above, p 611.
[58] *Woodar Investment Development Ltd v Wimpey Construction UK Ltd* [1980] 1 WLR 277, 300.
[59] See above, p 612.
[60] *Forster v Silvermere Gold and Equestrian Centre* (1981) 125 SJ 397, above, p 613.
[61] Above, p 650.   [62] [1968] AC 58, 83, 89, 97.   [63] *Ibid*, 89 (Lord Pearce).
[64] *Re Stapleton-Bretherton* [1941] Ch 482; *Re Schebsman* [1944] Ch 83; *Coulls v Bagot's Executor and Trustee Co Ltd* (1967) 119 CLR 460, 502; *Beswick v Beswick* [1968] AC 58, 94, 96. Cf *Re Sinclair's Life Policy* [1938] Ch 799.
[65] Passages in *Beswick v Beswick* [1968] AC 58, 81, 88, 97 may be thought to suggest that the administratrix could sue for arrears to be paid *to the widow* in her personal capacity.

principle the promisee should be able to bring an action for the agreed sum to enforce payment to the third party. This is simply to enforce the promise made.

(vi) Recovery of money paid

Where a contract is made for the benefit of a third party and the promisee has paid money to the promisor in consideration of a promise which the promisor has totally failed to perform, the promisee will be entitled to recover the money as paid on a consideration which has totally failed. This remedy for restitution of an unjust enrichment, which might be less advantageous than damages or specific performance, would not be available in the present state of the law if the promisor had partly performed the promise, as there would not be a total failure of consideration.[66]

(vii) Injunction

Where the promisor, either expressly or by necessary implication, promises not to sue a third party, the third party, as a stranger to the contract, cannot rely directly on the terms of the contract as a defence to any action brought by the promisor.[67] But the promisee may obtain an injunction enforcing the negative promise or a declaration that the promise is binding on the promisor thereby effectively preventing the promisor from suing the third party. In *Snelling v John Snelling Ltd*:[68]

Three brothers were shareholders and directors of a family company which owed each of them considerable sums of money. Differences arose between them, and, as part of an effort to settle these, they made a contract, agreeing, *inter alia*, that, in the event of any director resigning, he would immediately forfeit all moneys due to him from the company. Subsequently, one brother (Brian) resigned his directorship and brought an action against the company for payment of the money owed to him. His two brothers applied to be, and were, joined as co-defendants to the action, and they counterclaimed for a declaration that the sums due to Brian from the company had been forfeited.

The question arose whether the company, which was not a party to the agreement, could rely on it. In principle, it could not do so, and so Brian would be entitled to judgment on his claim. The two brothers would, however, also be entitled to a declaration that the provisions of the agreement were binding on Brian. In the view of Ormrod J the resulting situation was absurd, and he held that the proper order to make was to dismiss Brian's claim. The reality of the situation was that Brian's claim had failed since his two brothers had succeeded in their counterclaim, and the order of the Court should reflect that fact. It would therefore seem that, where all parties are before the Court, the Court may stay[69] or dismiss a claim brought by a contracting party against a third party whom the other contracting party has promised not to sue.

---

[66] See above, p 621.   [67] See below, p 679 (exemption clauses).   [68] [1973] QB 87.
[69] This power is now in Senior Courts Act (formerly Supreme Court Act) 1981, s 49(2). But contrast *Gore v Van der Lann* [1967] 2 QB 31.

It has been said that for the Court to exercise its power to stay or dismiss a claim, the promisee must have a sufficient interest,[70] such as a legal or equitable right to protect,[71] and must be able to show a real possibility of prejudice to himself, for example by being exposed to an action by the third party.[72] In *Snelling*'s case the promisees were not subject to this kind of 'legal' prejudice since they would not have been exposed to an action by the company. However, they would have been commercially and financially prejudiced by any deterioration in the company's financial position, as would have occurred had Brian's action succeeded.

(c) RATIONALE AND APPRAISAL OF THE COMMON LAW RULE

(i) Justification of rule

The case for the common law rule that a third party cannot enforce a contract rests on a number of factors. First, although consideration has been provided for the promise, it has not been provided by the third party. Secondly, it would be unjust if a person could sue on a contract but not be sued upon the contract.[73] Thirdly, if third parties could enforce contracts made for their benefit, the rights of the contracting parties to vary or terminate such contracts would be affected. Fourthly, it is undesirable for the promisor to be liable to two actions from both the promisor and the third party, and the privity rule limits the potential liability of a contracting party to a wide range of possible third-party claimants.[74] The Law Commission did not regard any of these explanations as convincing justifications of the rule.[75]

Those who favour the common law rule[76] also point out that it is not absolute. The Courts and the Legislature have created exceptions and circumventions to avoid perceived injustice. These are considered below.[77] In some, particularly those based on statute, the third-party rule is simply overridden. In others the third-party claimant does not need to rely on the contract but is able to have recourse to other areas of the law and to rely on a property right, a possessory right, or is able to sue in tort.[78] Alternatively, the third party may be able to establish a collateral contract with the promisor.[79] Other exceptions to and circumventions of the rule may be seen in

---

[70] *Gore v Van der Lann* [1967] 2 QB 31.

[71] *European Asian Bank v Punjab & Sind Bank* [1982] 2 Lloyd's Rep, 356, 369.

[72] *The Elbe Maru* [1978] 1 Lloyd's Rep 206. Cf *The Chevalier Roze* [1983] 2 Lloyd's Rep 438, 443; *The Starsin* [2001] 1 Lloyd's Rep 437, 461–2.

[73] *Tweddle v Atkinson* (1861) 1 B & S 393, 398; *London Drugs Ltd v Kuehene & Nagel International Ltd* [1992] 3 SCR 299, 418, 440 (Canada). But see above, p 32 for the position in the case of unilateral contracts.

[74] *Trident General Insurance Co Ltd v McNiece Bros Pt. Ltd* (1988) 165 CLR 107, 121–2 (Australia).

[75] *Privity of Contract: Contracts for the Benefit of Third Parties*, Law Com CP No 121 (1991), para 4.4; Law Com No 242, para 3.1.

[76] Kincaid (1994) 8 JCL 51; (1999) 12 JCL 47; (2000) 116 LQR 43; Smith (1997) 17 OJLS 643; Stevens (2004) 120 LQR 292.

[77] See below, pp 671–86.   [78] See below, pp 679 (tort), 671, 677 (property).

[79] See generally, above, p 146 and, on exemption clauses and third parties, below, p 682.

assignment,[80] agency (including the doctrine of the undisclosed principal),[81] transfer on death,[82] and bankruptcy.[83]

(ii) Criticism of rule

The considerable criticism of the principle that a third party cannot acquire rights under a contract has been noted. Its desirability as a matter of policy has been questioned by judges,[84] law reform bodies,[85] and commentators.[86] Its pedigree has also been criticized on the ground that it was doubtful that the nineteenth-century cases on which it is based in fact established its existence and that it was only a rule of procedure.[87] It is said that it serves only to defeat the intentions of the contracting parties and the legitimate expectations of the third party, who may have organized its affairs on the faith of the contract; that it undermines the social interest of the community in the security of bargains; and that it is commercially inconvenient.[88] In the standard situation the person who has suffered the loss cannot sue, while the person who has suffered no loss can sue but may be able to obtain only nominal damages.[89] Where the object of the contract is to benefit the third party, the effect of this is tantamount to ruling that the object of the contract is unenforceable. The exceptions and circumventions are complicated and not always available, particularly to those who do not have access to sophisticated legal advice. Moreover, their technicality has led to artificiality and uncertainty.

(iii) Reform

The right of a third party to sue on a contract made for its benefit is recognized by the law of Scotland and the legal systems of the United States. It has also been introduced by statute in several Commonwealth jurisdictions[90] while in others the privity doctrine has been modified judicially.[91] In England, the Courts, while criticizing the

---

[80] See below, Chapter 22.   [81] See below, Chapter 23.

[82] See below, p 713.   [83] See below, p 713.

[84] *Scruttons Ltd v Midland Silicones Ltd* [1962] AC 446, 467–8; *Beswick v Beswick* [1968] AC 58, 72; *Woodar Investment Development Ltd v Wimpey Construction UK Ltd* [1980] 1 WLR 277, 291, 297–8, 300; *Forster v Silvermere Gold and Equestrian Centre* (1981) 125 SJ 397; *Swain v The Law Society* [1983] 1 AC 598, 611; *Darlington BC v Wiltshier Northern Ltd* [1995] 1 WLR 68, 73, 76.

[85] Law Revision Committee Sixth Interim Report (Cmnd 5449); Law Com No 242.

[86] Corbin (1930) 46 LQR 12; Furmston (1960) 23 MLR 373; Flannigan (1987) 103 LQR 564; Andrews (1988) 8 LS 14; Adams & Brownsword (1990) 10 LS 12. Cf Kincaid [1989] CLJ 243, (1994) 8 JCL 51, (2000) 116 LQR 43; Smith (1997) 17 OJLS 643; Stevens (2004) 120 LQR 292.

[87] *Drive Yourself Hire Co (London) Ltd v Strutt* [1954] 1 QB 250, 273; *Beswick v Beswick* [1968] Ch 538, 553–4, 557 (Lord Denning MR, a particularly vigorous critic).

[88] For difficulties in construction and insurance contracts, see Law Com No 242, paras 3.10–3.27.

[89] Above, p 650.

[90] Western Australia, Queensland, and New Zealand. For a summary of this legislation, see Law Com No 242, Appendix B, and for a summary of the position in other legal systems, including Scotland, the United States, France, and Germany, see the Appendix to Law Com CP No 121 (1991).

[91] *London Drugs Ltd v Kuehene & Nagel International Ltd* [1992] 3 SCR 299, (Canada), below, p 650 (exemption clauses); *Trident General Insurance Co Ltd v NcNiece Bros Pty Ltd* (1988) 165 CLR 107 (Australia).

principle that a third party cannot acquire rights under a contract, indicated that a radical change in the common law, such as abrogation of the principle, should be introduced by legislation.[92] This reluctance stemmed from the nature of the third-party rule itself, which some saw as a 'fundamental' rule and which, in Anson's words, 'seems to flow from the very conception we form of contract'.[93] As such, it fixed 'a reference point for the development of subsidiary rules', here the rules of trust, agency, and estoppel. Those who took this view considered that it was not possible to abrogate the rule without leaving open major issues of policy, which it was not appropriate for Courts to decide.[94]

As long ago as 1937 the Law Revision Committee recommended that where a contract by its express terms purports to confer a benefit directly on a third party, the third party should be entitled to enforce the provision in its own name.[95] Although widely supported, the recommendation was not implemented because of the outbreak of the Second World War.[96] In 1991 the Law Commission returned to the subject and in 1996 it recommended that the rule should be reformed so as to enable contracting parties to confer a right to enforce the contract on a third party.[97] The Law Commission saw its proposals 'as achieving at a stroke and with certainty and clarity what a progressive House of Lords might well itself have brought about over the course of time', and as not cutting across the underpinning principles of the common law.[98]

While the simple recognition of some form of third-party right might be uncontroversial, the determination of its precise extent is not. The most important difficulties concern the test of enforceable benefit, the validity of defences that would have been available had the promisee sued, and whether the contracting parties should have power to vary or cancel the contract. The way that these issues are dealt with by the Contracts (Rights of Third Parties) Act 1999, which substantially implemented the Law Commission's Report,[99] is considered in the next section.

---

[92] *Scruttons Ltd v Midland Silicones Ltd* [1962] AC 446, 467–8; *Beswick v Beswick* [1968] AC 58, 72; *Woodar Investment Development Ltd v Wimpey Construction UK Ltd* [1980] 1 WLR 277, 291, 297–8, 300. But cf *KH Enterprise v Pioneer Container* [1994] 2 AC 324, 335; *Darlington BC v Wiltshier Northern Ltd* [1995] 1 WLR 68. Cf *The Mahkutai* [1996] AC 650, 665.

[93] *Principles of the Law of Contract* (1879) 195.

[94] See Brennan and Deane JJ's minority judgments in *Trident General Insurance Co Ltd v McNiece Bros Pty Ltd* (1988) 165 CLR 107, 128, 131–2, 134, 140–1, 142–5 and Beatson (1992) 44 CLP 1.

[95] Sixth Interim Report (Cmnd 5449), para 48.

[96] See further Beatson (1992) 44 CLP 1, 10–15.

[97] Law Com No 242, paras 3.29, 3.32, including (see now s 1(6) of the 1999 Act) the right to rely on clauses limiting or excluding the third party's liability to a contracting party. See Adams, Beyleveld, and Brownsword (1997) 60 MLR 238.

[98] Law Com No 242, para 1.10.

[99] s 6(2)–(4), exempting contracts of employment and the contract contained in a company's articles from the Act, is not based on recommendations of the Law Commission and s 8, on arbitration clauses, differs from the Draft Bill attached to the Commission's Report.

(d) THE CONTRACTS (RIGHTS OF THIRD PARTIES) AC

(i) Introduction

The Contracts (Rights of Third Parties) Act 1999 enables the parties
to make it enforceable by a third party.[100] It enables a third party bo
enforce a positive provision in the contract, such as a promise to pay mo
rely on an exemption or limitation clause in its favour as a defence.[101] The Act thus
removes the limit on the autonomy of the parties represented by the first rule of the
privity principle. It is fundamental to the scheme of the Act that the parties to the
contract control both whether a third party has an enforceable right and, if so,
the extent of such right.[102] The third party's rights are thus derived from the parties'
intentions as embodied in the contract. But they are distinct from, and additional to,
the rights of the promisee, which the promisee retains.[103] The existing statutory and
common law exceptions, by which the third party has rights, are preserved.[104] These
are considered later in this chapter.[105] It will be seen that some of the common law
and statutory exceptions give third parties more secure rights than those given by
the 1999 Act.

(ii) The scope of the Act

Although it is general, certain types of contract are not affected by the Act. The
common law position for contracts in the constitution of a company, binding on
the company and its members under section 33 of the Companies Act 2006, is
preserved by section 6(2) of the 1999 Act. Moreover, section 6(3) prevents third
parties from relying on the 1999 Act to enforce terms in contracts of employment
and similar contracts purporting to enable them to sue an employee, a worker, or
an agency worker.[106]

A second category of contracts is excluded from the 1999 Act because they are
subject to an alternative legislative regime recognizing and regulating third-party
rights which might otherwise be undermined. Bills of exchange, promissory notes,
and negotiable instruments are excluded by section 6(1). Contracts of carriage subject
either to the Carriage of Goods by Sea Act 1992 or international conventions governing
carriage by road, air, and rail to which the United Kingdom is party are, subject to one

---

[100] For commentary on the Act see Andrews [2001] CLJ 353; Bridge (2001) 5 Edin L Rev 85; Burrows
[2000] LMCLQ 540; MacMillan (2000) 63 MLR 721; Roe (2000) 63 MLR 887; Merkin, *Privity of Contract*
(2000) ch 5 (usefully containing the Law Commission consultation paper, report, and the Parliamentary
debates on the bill in appendices). For criticism of the Act, see Stevens (2004) 120 LQR 292. For an assessment
of the Act ten years on from its enactment, see Beale, in Burrows and Peel (eds), *Contract Formation and
Parties* (2010) ch 11.

[101] s 1(6).   [102] s 1(4).   [103] s 4.

[104] s 7(1). See Law Com No 242, paras 12.1–12.2. But note the position of negotiable instruments and
certain contracts of carriage, below, pp 659–60.

[105] Below, 671–86.

[106] As defined by the National Minimum Wage Act 1998, ss 54 and 34–35. See Hansard HL Debs
11 January 1999, col 21 (Lord Irvine LC)

qualification, excluded by section 6(5). The qualification is that a third party may avail itself of an exclusion or limitation of liability in such a contract.[107] Contracts by way of charterparties are not excluded.[108]

In the case of negotiable instruments, only third parties who are 'holders' of the instrument can sue[109] whereas, if the 1999 Act applied, this would have opened up the possibility of others suing. In the case of contracts of carriage, where third parties are given the right to enforce the contract under the Carriage of Goods by Sea Act 1992 they also take some or all of the burdens, whereas under the 1999 Act the third party takes only the benefits.[110] Moreover, under section 2(1) of the 1992 Act, 'all rights of suit' are transferred to the third party[111] so that, unlike under the 1999 Act, the promisee is left with no rights of enforcement.

(iii) The tests of enforceability

The 1999 Act contains two tests of enforceability. By section 1:

(1) Subject to the provisions of this Act, a person who is not a party to a contract (a 'third party') may in his own right enforce a term of the contract if—

(a) the contract expressly provides that he may, or

(b) subject to subsection (2), the term purports to confer a benefit on him.

(2) Subsection (1)(b) does not apply if on a proper construction of the contract it appears that the parties did not intend the term to be enforceable by the third party.

(3) The third party must be expressly identified in the contract by name, as a member of a class or as answering a particular description, but need not be in existence when the contract is entered into.

Each of the two tests will be considered in turn.

(a) Express provision. Section 1(1)(a) of the 1999 Act provides a simple and certain test: a third party acquires an enforceable right where the contract contains an express provision to that effect. Section 1(3) provides that the third party must be expressly identified in the contract by name, class or description.[112] Identification in the course of negotiations does not suffice. But the third party need not be in existence when the contract is made. Accordingly, a contracting party's present and future employees and subcontractors may qualify, as may unborn children.[113] Third parties who qualify under section 1(1)(a) may enforce a contractual term (including an exclusion or

---

[107] s 6(5).   [108] See the definitions in ss 6(6) and (7) of the 1999 Act.

[109] Bills of Exchange Act 1882.

[110] See Law Com No 242, paras 12.7–12.16.   [111] See below, 676–7.

[112] In the similarly worded New Zealand legislation, the words 'or nominee' may not sufficiently identify the third party (*Karangahape Road International Village Ltd v Holloway* [1989] 1 NZLR 83) and may be insufficient to indicate an intention to create an enforceable right in the nominee (*Field v Filton* [1988] 1 NZLR 482). But cf *Rattrays Wholesale Ltd v Meredyth Young and A'Court Ltd* [1997] 2 NZLR 363.

[113] Law Com No 242, paras 8.1–8.16.

limitation clause) even if they are not intended to be the beneficiaries of the term, as where they are trustees.[114]

The Law Revision Committee had recommended that this should be the only way that a third party could acquire an enforceable right.[115] But, while a requirement of express contractual provision is conducive to certainty, it means that the intentions of contracting parties (including those reflected in trade practice or by the principles governing implied terms)[116] will not always be recognized. Nor would it cover the facts of many of the cases where the privity doctrine caused a problem, such as *Beswick v Beswick*.[117] For these reasons, and because requiring express contractual provision would 'operate to the disadvantage of those who do not have the benefit of (good) legal advice',[118] the Law Commission concluded that there should also be a second test of enforceability to cover situations where the parties do not expressly contract to confer a legal right on the third party.

(b) Term purporting to confer a benefit on an expressly identified third party. The effect of section 1(1)(b) and section 1(2) is in general terms to provide for what the Law Commission and the Lord Chancellor described as a rebuttable presumption in favour of there being a third-party right where a contractual term purports to confer a benefit on a third party expressly identified by name, class, or description.[119] This will be rebutted where, on the proper construction of the contract as a whole, that is, including the surrounding circumstances,[120] the parties do not intend the third party to have a right to enforce it.

It has been suggested that the words 'purport to confer a benefit' mean that the presumption in section 1(1)(b) is triggered only where the third party is to receive a benefit directly from the promisor,[121] but this is not entirely clear from the words of the Act or the Law Commission's report.[122]

The approach of the 1999 Act should avoid a problem which has arisen in the United States where an 'intention to benefit' test has been used. That test has led to difficult distinctions between the 'intended beneficiary' and the 'incidental beneficiary': the latter is the third party who benefits *incidentally* by the performance of a contract by others.[123] Where A contracts with B to construct a new road on B's land, C, whose adjoining land would be enhanced in value by the building of the road, while deriving a factual benefit from the performance of the contract made between A and B, is merely an incidental beneficiary of the contract, the primary benefit of which is conferred

---

[114] Law Com No 242, para 7.12 ff.

[115] Law Com No 242, paras 8.1–8.16.   [116] Sixth Interim Report (Cmnd 5449).

[117] [1968] AC 58, above, p 654. See Law Com. No 242, para 7.11.   [118] Law Com No 242, para 7.11.

[119] Law Com No 242, para 7.17; Hansard HL Debs, 2 February 1999, col 1425. The identification requirement in s 1(3), above p 660, also applies to s 1(1)(b).

[120] See above, p 179.   [121] Burrows [2000] LMCLQ 540, 544.

[122] Cf the example in Law Com No 242, paras 7.33, 7.51, based on the facts of *Green v Russell* [1959] 2 QB 226, below, p 663.

[123] ALI *Restatement, Contracts* (1932) paras 133(1) and 147; ALI *Restatement, Contracts (2d)* (1981) para 302. See Prince (1985) 25 Boston College L Rev 919, 934–7, 979.

upon B. Moreover, while the road may be intended for the benefit of all road-users, it is unlikely that the parties intend that road-users should have a right of action in the event of a delay in construction.

It is clear that the 1999 Act does not enable either C or other road-users to enforce the terms of the contract between A and B. Again, a standard liability insurance policy indemnifying the assured against liability to third parties is plainly for the benefit of those who may make claims against the assured. But, in general, payment is to be made to the assured and the term so providing purports to confer a benefit on the assured. It is accordingly difficult to say that the term purports to confer a benefit on a person with a claim against the assured.[124]

The Law Commission illustrated the application of the test now contained in section 1(1)(b) by reference to a number of hypothetical situations and some of the celebrated cases in which the first aspect of the privity principle has caused difficulty.[125] A selection is set out below. First, there are cases or situations in which the Commission considered the third party would be able to enforce the term on the basis of what is now section 1(1)(b).

(1) In *Beswick v Beswick*[126] the contract gave Mrs Beswick, who was expressly named, a presumed right of enforceability because the nephew promised to confer the benefit (the annuity payments) on her. As there was no indication in the contract that the parties did not intend her to enforce the term, she would have been able to enforce it under section 1(1)(b).

(2) B takes out a policy of insurance with A Ltd to cover her employees against medical expenses. The policy provides that payments under it will be made directly to ill employees or, at the discretion of A Ltd, to the provider of the medical services in discharge of an employee's liability. C, an employee, becomes ill and requires hospitalization. Meanwhile B disappears. C seeks to sue as a beneficiary of B's contract of insurance with A Ltd. In the absence of some contrary indication in the contract triggering section 1(2), C would be able to do so. A Ltd has promised to confer a benefit (direct payment or the discharge of C's liability) on C, who is expressly identified by class.[127]

(3) B Ltd, the owner of land, takes out a liability insurance policy with A Ltd, an insurance company, whereby A Ltd agrees to indemnify B Ltd and B's subsidiary companies, contractors, and subcontractors. C, one of B Ltd's contractors, incurs liability while carrying out work for B Ltd. C seeks to sue as a beneficiary of B's contract of insurance with A Ltd. In the absence of some contrary indication in the contract triggering section 1(2), C would be able

---

[124] Merkin, *Privity of Contract* (2000) 105; Burrows [2000] LMCLQ 540, 544–5.
[125] Law Com No 242, paras 7.28–7.51. For other examples see Burrows [2000] LMCLQ 540, 552–3.
[126] [1968] AC 58, above, p 654. See Law Com No 242, para 7.46.　　　[127] Law Com No 242, para 7.32.

to do so. The contract purported to confer a benefit on C, who is expressly identified by class.[128]

(4) B Ltd takes out a personal accident insurance policy with A Ltd to cover its employees against accidents. By the terms of the policy, payments are to be made to B Ltd. C, an employee, is injured and B Ltd is insolvent. The Commission considered this a difficult case because it is arguable that, since payment is to be made to B Ltd, it is difficult to say that under the contract A purports to confer a benefit on C so as to bring section 1(1)(b) into operation. But it concluded that, once received by B Ltd, the money is held on trust for C, so that the contract does purport to confer a benefit on C and the provision that the money be paid to B Ltd would not show that the parties did not intend C to be able to enforce the term because channelling the money in this way is a matter of administrative convenience.[129]

Secondly, there are those cases or situations in which the Commission considered that the third party would not be able to rely on section 1(1)(b). The first is the clear case where the parties expressly provide that the third party is to have no rights, or where the intention to benefit the third party is not known to one of the parties (illustration (5)). It is also likely to be the case where the third party is an incidental beneficiary of the contract (illustration (6)), or where the transaction is part of a customary chain of contracts which gives the third party a contractual claim against someone else (illustrations (7) and (8)).

(5) On Mr and Mrs C's marriage, their wealthy relative B buys an expensive set of china dishes as a wedding gift from A Ltd, a well-known department store. The china is delivered to B, who sends it to Mr and Mrs C. The glazing is defective and after two weeks of use the pattern is fading badly. Mr and Mrs C could not sue A Ltd under the 1999 Act since the contract between A Ltd and B does not purport to confer a benefit on them and they are not identified in the contract.[130] The position would be different if B had made it clear to A Ltd when purchasing the china that it was a gift and A Ltd agreed to deliver it to Mr and Mrs C's home. In such circumstances the Commission concluded that A Ltd would have promised to confer a benefit (china of satisfactory quality) on Mr and Mrs C, who have been expressly identified by name.[131]

---

[128] Law Com No 242, para 7.50, broadly the facts of *Trident General Insurance Co Ltd v McNiece Bros Pty Ltd* (1988) 165 CLR 107 (High Court of Australia).

[129] Law Com No 242, paras 7.33, 7.51, broadly the facts of *Green v Russell* [1959] 2 QB 226. See Pearce LJ, *ibid*, 246–7.

[130] Based on the example in Law Com No 242, para 7.42. On the rejection of a special test for consumers, see Law Com No 242, para 7.54.

[131] Based on the example in Law Com No 242, para 7.41.

(6) In *White v Jones*[132] a firm of solicitors, A, contracted with B to draw up a will benefiting C but, as a result of the solicitors' negligence, the will was never drawn up. Although the intended legatee is expressly designated as a beneficiary, the contract is not one in which the solicitor promises the testator to confer a benefit on the third party, the intended legatee, but one by which the solicitor is to enable the testator to do so. The relevant contractual beneficiary is the testator who intends to confer on the third party the benefit of his assets after death and not the benefit of the solicitor's promise to draft the will. Accordingly, the contract does not fall within section 1(1)(b) of the 1999 Act. The intended legatee, however, has a claim in tort against the solicitors.[133]

(7) C, the owner of property, contracted with B Ltd for the erection of a factory. The contract entitled C to nominate subcontractors and B Ltd made a contract with A, a nominated flooring subcontractor. The floor was defective. The Commission considered that in such a case, even if A's obligations, including the obligation to use reasonable care in laying the floor, purported to benefit C, who was expressly identified, C would not be able to sue A under section 1(1)(b). It considered that the presumption of an enforceable right would be rebutted because A's subcontract was part of a wider chain of contracts, under which C's rights for breach of A's obligations, were to lie against B Ltd, the head contractor.[134]

(8) A person who purchases goods from a retailer against whom he has a claim under the contract of sale is, in general, unlikely to be able to rely on section 1(1)(b) to sue the manufacturer of the goods for breach of the manufacturer's contract with the retailer.[135]

As regards cases in which the 1999 Act has been considered, we shall consider two cases in which the second test of enforceability was held to be satisfied and two in which it was held not to be satisfied.

In *Nisshin Shipping Co Ltd v Cleaves & Co Ltd*:[136]

A chartering broker (Cleaves) had negotiated a number of charterparties on behalf of the shipowners (Nisshin). In each of the charterparties, Nisshin agreed with the charterers to pay Cleaves its commission. In each charterparty, there was also an arbitration clause by which the parties agreed to refer all disputes arising out of the contract to arbitration.

Colman J held that, applying the second test of enforceability, Cleaves had the right as a third party under the 1999 Act, to enforce Nisshin's promise to pay it commission;

---

[132] [1995] 2 AC 207.

[133] See Law Com No 242, paras 7.19–7.27, 7.48. Because there was a claim in tort (on which see below, p 679), the Commission was content (Law Com No 242, para 7.25) to leave these cases outside its proposed third-party right although 'at a theoretical level' it preferred the view that the right of the prospective beneficiaries more properly belongs within the realm of contract than tort: Law Com No 242, para 7.27.

[134] Law Com No 242, para 7.47, the facts of *Junior Books Co Ltd v Veitchi Co Ltd* [1983] 1 AC 520. The owner successfully sued the subcontractor in tort in respect of the economic loss suffered. Macmillan (2000) 63 MLR 721, 725 considers the view that the presumption of enforceability was rebutted to involve a certain circularity.

[135] See Law Com No 242, para 7.54.   [136] [2003] EWHC 2602, [2004] 1 Lloyd's Rep 38.

and that it was entitled, and indeed bound (as a condition of enforcement), to enforce that right by arbitration. The most difficult argument facing Colman J was that, as the contract had not provided for arbitration by the third party, so the parties could not have intended the third party to have a right of enforceability. The contracting parties could only have intended either a right of enforceability by arbitration (which they had not provided for) or no right of enforceability at all. Colman J rejected that argument by accepting that the parties could have intended the third party to have a right of enforceability by court action. In any event, he went on to hold that the third party, by reason of the elaborate provisions on arbitration in section 8 of the 1999 Act, *did* have the right to enforce payment of the commission by arbitration (and indeed was bound to do so, applying a 'conditional benefit' analysis).[137]

In *Laemthong International Lines Company Ltd v Artis, The Laemthong Glory (No 2):*[138]

By a contractual letter of indemnity given by the receivers (ie buyers) of sugar to the charterers of the ship carrying the sugar, the receivers promised to indemnify the charterers against loss sustained by them. Under clause 1 of the letter of indemnity, the promise was to indemnify the charterers and their 'servants and agents' against loss caused by releasing the goods without the bill of lading. Under clause 3 the promise was to provide security for the ship's release, and to indemnify the charterers against loss caused, if the ship was arrested in connection with the delivery of the cargo. The ship was arrested by a bank for non-payment to it in relation to the cargo.

The question at issue was whether the third-party shipowners could enforce clause 3 of the letter of indemnity given by the receivers to the charterers. The Court of Appeal held that, applying the second test of enforceability, they could. In deciding that the letter of indemnity purported to confer a benefit upon the shipowners, the term 'agents' in clause 1 was construed as referring to the shipowners and as applying equally to clause 3. Moreover, although the charterers had also given a direct letter of indemnity to the shipowners, so that there was a chain of contracts, this was thought on the facts not to rebut the presumption under section 1(1)(b). In contrast to the chain of contracts in the context of construction or sales, the third-party right would not here cut across a legal framework that has customarily been employed.

In *Avraamides v Colwill:*[139]

On the takeover of a company (B) by a partnership (A), A agreed to 'pay any liabilities properly incurred' by B. B had a liability to C. On B's insolvency, C sought to enforce that liabilities clause against A.

---

[137] For further analysis of s 8, see *AES Ust-Kamenogvok Hydropower Plant v Ust-K* [2010] EWHC 772 (Comm), [2010] 2 Lloyds' Rep 493 at [26]–[32] (aff'd without discussing this point at [2013] UKSC 35, [2013] 1 WLR 1889); *Fortress Value Recovery Fund v Blue Skye Special Opportunities Fund* [2013] EWCA Civ 367, [2013] 1 WLR 3466.

[138] [2005] EWCA Civ 519, [2005] 1 Lloyd's Rep 688. See also *Great Eastern Shipping Co Ltd v Far East Chartering, The Jag Ravi* [2011] EWHC 1372 (Comm), [2011] 2 Lloyd's Rep 309; *Starlight Shipping Co v Allianz Marine & Aviation Versicherungs AG* [2014] EWHC 3068 (Comm), [2014] 2 Lloyd's Rep 579.

[139] [2006] EWCA Civ 1533, [2007] BLR 76.

It was held that the second test of enforceability was not satisfied not least because C had not been expressly identified in the liabilities clause so that the requirement of section 1(3) was not met.

Finally, in *Dolphin Maritime & Aviation Services Ltd v Sveriges Angfartygs Assurans Forening*:[140]

A cargo of scrap steel was damaged in a collision at sea. The insurers of the cargo paid the cargo-owners for the damage and hence took over their rights to recover compensation from the relevant ship. The insurers instructed the claimant (Dolphin) as their agent to recover the compensation. The interests of the ship were represented by the defendant P & I Club. The defendant gave a letter of undertaking (LOU) to the insurers promising that, in return for the non-arrest of the ship, the defendant would pay the claimant, on the cargo-interest's behalf, such sums as might be held, or agreed, to be owing by the owners of the ship for the damage. Subsequently the defendant paid the insurers $8.5 million directly.

The claimant argued that, by reason of the Contracts (Rights of Third Parties) Act 1999, it was entitled to be paid the $8.5 million under the terms of the LOU and that it could then deduct its commission from that before accounting for it to the insurers. That argument failed. The LOU did not 'purport to benefit' the claimant under section 1(1)(b). Payment to the claimant was merely the means by which the defendant's obligation to the insurers was to be discharged and the intended beneficiaries were the insurers not their agent. In any event, under section 1(2), on a proper construction of the contract, the parties to the LOU did not intend the term to be enforceable by the claimant.

(iv) The nature of the rights under the Act

(a) The third party's rights.   The third party's rights are derived from the parties' intentions as embodied in the contract and are supplementary to rights the third party has under the common law or other statutes. But, as will be seen in the discussion of defences and variation and cancellation below, the third party entitled to sue under the 1999 Act does not specifically step into the shoes of the promisee and is not treated as a party to the contract.[141]

By section 1(5), a third party who has a right to enforce a contractual provision under the 1999 Act will be able to claim any remedy for breach of contract given by the Courts that would have been available if he had been a party to the contract. Accordingly, while the third party may claim damages for its own loss, an award of an agreed sum, specific performance, and an injunction, the Act does not permit him or her to terminate the contract since termination is a self-help remedy, or to claim restitution of money paid or a restitutionary quantum meruit, since those are

---

[140] [2009] EWHC 716 (Comm), [2009] 2 Lloyd's Rep 123.
[141] Save for the limited purposes set out in ss 1(5) and 3(4), see the next paragraph and below, p 668.

not remedies for breach of contract.[142] Where the third party seeks damages, it would appear that rules, such as those concerning remoteness and mitigation, will be applied by reference to the position of the third party rather than the contracting party, so that, for example, it would be the third party's loss that had to be contemplated.[143]

Section 1(4) contains an important limitation on the third party's rights. A third party has no right to enforce a term 'otherwise than subject to and in accordance with any other relevant terms of the contract'. In this way, although the Act does not change the rule whereby parties to a contract cannot generally impose an obligation upon a third party, if the benefit conferred is qualified or subject to a condition, the third party cannot ignore the qualification or condition.

The distinction between the imposition of a burden and the conferral of a conditional benefit is easy to draw where the condition does not require any performance by the third party, for example where the contract states that the benefit is conditional on the third party reaching a certain age or where the contract contains a clause exempting or limiting the promisor's liability to the third party. Where, however, the condition requires performance by the third party, for example the grant of a right of way over a path subject to a condition that the third party keeps the path in repair, the distinction may be less easy to draw. In order to avoid the possibility of the third party being overall worse off by being given the right to enforce, the Commission considered that in such a case the third party should be bound by the condition in the limited sense that the promisor can use the condition as the basis of a defence or set-off to a claim by the third party to enforce the contract.[144]

(b) The promisee's rights. The third party's rights are distinct from the rights of the promisee, which are preserved by the provision in section 4 that section 1 'does not affect any right of the promisee to enforce any term of the contract'.[145]

(c) Avoidance of double liability. Since, unless otherwise agreed between the contracting parties, both the promisee and the third party have independent and concurrent rights to sue, the Law Commission was concerned to protect the promisor against double liability. This is not a problem where the promisee either recovers nominal damages or is granted specific performance of the obligation to benefit the third party. The Commission considered that it is also not a problem where the third party first recovers damages because then the promisee will be left with no corresponding loss outstanding. In the occasional cases in which the promisee has suffered personal loss which is independent of the third party's loss, the promisee should be entitled to sue for that loss in its own name.[146] That leaves the situation in

---

[142] Law Com No 242, para 3.33.
[143] An amendment to make this clear was rejected as unnecessary: Hansard HL Deb, 27 May 1999, col 1052.
[144] Law Com No 242, para 10.27.   [145] On damages in such cases, see above, pp 650–3.
[146] Andrews [2001] CLJ 353, 371.

which the promisee has recovered substantial damages and the third party then brings an action in reliance on section 1.[147] Section 5 of the 1999 Act provides that in any such action by the third party the Court or arbitral tribunal shall reduce any award to the third party to such extent as it thinks appropriate to take account of the sum recovered by the promisee.

(v) Defences

(a) Defences that would have been available against the promisee.   Section 3(2) of the Act provides that the rights of the third party are subject to the entitlement of the promisor to raise any defence or set-off which arise out of or in connection with the contract and which would have been available against the promisee.[148] Counterclaims are excluded because a counterclaim may exceed the value of the third party's claim and thus impose a burden on the third party.[149] 'Defences' include matters which render the contract void (such as mistake), voidable (such as misrepresentation), or which have led to the contract being discharged (such as serious breach or frustration). But the Law Commission did not consider that personal bars on the promisee, such as inequitable conduct by the promisee which would bar a claim by him for specific performance or a failure to mitigate his loss, should automatically bar or restrict the third party's remedy.[150]

That is the default position. The Act enables the parties to the contract by an express term either to enlarge the defences available to the promisor to include all defences available against the promisee whether or not they arise out of or are connected with the contract,[151] or to preclude the promisor from raising any defence available against the promisee.[152]

(b) Defences that would have been available had the third party been a party to the contract.   By section 3(4) the third party's claim is also subject to the defences, set-offs, and counterclaims (not arising from the contract) that would have been available to the promisor had the third party been a party to the contract. Again, the parties may expressly contract out of this. Section 3(5) enables the parties to provide that such defences, set-offs, and counterclaims are not to be available in a claim by the third party.

(vi) Variation and rescission

Perhaps the most difficult question in deciding on the precise extent of a third-party right is when the contracting parties should have power to vary or cancel the contract by agreement. A balance has to be struck between preserving the freedom of the

---

[147] But of the two situations envisaged in s 5, that in s 5(a) no longer raises the 'double liability' problem because, according to *Alfred McAlpine Construction Ltd v Panatown Ltd* [2001] 1 AC 518, a promisee cannot recover a third party's loss where the third party has its own contractual right against the promisor. Such a contractual right is precisely what is given to the third party under the 1999 Act.

[148] Law Com No 242, para 10.12. Cf Law Revision Committee, Cmnd 5449, para 47.

[149] Law Com No 242, para 10.10.   [150] Law Com No 242, para 10.2.

[151] 1999 Act, s 3(3).   [152] 1999 Act, s 3(5).

contracting parties to implement their intentions at any particular time and allowing the creation of effective third-party rights so that a third party can arrange its affairs with some certainty.[153]

(a) The range of solutions. The matter has not been satisfactorily solved in certain jurisdictions which recognize third-party rights.[154] The Law Revision Committee considered that third-party rights should be subject to cancellation of the contract by the contracting parties at any time before the third party had adopted the contract either expressly or by conduct. But this notion lacks precision and may lead to Courts presuming that there has been acceptance.[155] In New Zealand, variation is allowed until the third party has materially altered his position in reliance on the contract.[156] In certain cases, such as contracts of insurance[157] and possibly other contracts which expressly name a third party, it is even arguable that the third party's rights should not be subject to cancellation unless the contract expressly provides for this.

The Law Commission sought to balance the freedom of the contracting parties to implement their intentions with the need to create effective third-party rights by having a statutory scheme as the 'default' arrangement but allowing the parties to vary it by express provision in the contract. The Commission considered that reliance should be the primary test for the crystallization of the third party's rights but that there should also be an alternative test of acceptance to enable a third party who has successfully communicated its assent to the promisor to be secure in its entitlement without having to show reliance.

(b) Section 2(1) of the Act. Section 2(1) of the Act gives effect to the Law Commission's recommendations. It provides that the contracting parties' right to vary or rescind the contract by agreement should be lost in two situations. First, where the third party has relied on the term and the promisor is aware of such reliance or could reasonably have foreseen that the third party would rely on it.[158] The third party will have to prove that it has relied on the term. Secondly, the right to rescind is lost where the third party has communicated its assent to the term by words or conduct[159] to the promisor.[160] Communication of the acceptance to the promisee will not suffice and by section 2(2)(b) if sent by post the acceptance shall not be regarded as communicated to the promisor until received by him; the Law Commission considered that it would be inappropriate to apply the postal acceptance rule.[161]

---

[153] Law Com No 242, para 9.8.

[154] In Scotland, while *Carmichael v Carmichael's Executrix* 1920 SC (HL) 195 suggests the right becomes irrevocable when brought to the notice of the third party, the position is unclear; McCormick [1970] Jur Rev 228, 236; Scot Law Com Memorandum No 38 (1977).

[155] Law Com CP No 121 (1991), paras 4.32, 5.31; Law Com No 242, para 9.17.

[156] New Zealand Contracts (Privity) Act 1982, s 5, set out in Appendix B to Law Com No 242. See also ALI *Restatement, Contracts (2d)* para 311.

[157] As in the case of the Married Women's Property Act 1882, s 11, below, p 676.

[158] s 2(1)(b) and (c). See Law Com No 242, paras 9.26–9.30.

[159] s 2(2)(a).   [160] s 2(1)(a). See Law Com No 242, paras 9.20, 9.26.

[161] Law Com No 242, para 9.20. On postal acceptance, see above, p 48.

(c) Contractual provision.   The Commission's recognition of the autonomy of the parties resulted in it recommending that the contracting parties be able expressly to reserve the right to vary or rescind the third party's right without the third party's consent irrespective of reliance or acceptance by the third party; or to provide that, for rescission or variation, the third party's consent is needed in specified circumstances (including that the third party's consent is *always* needed)[162] instead of, and irrespective of, whether there has been reliance or acceptance.[163] These are enacted in section 2(3) (a) and (b) of the 1999 Act.

(d) Discretion to dispense with the third party's consent.   Where the consent of a third party is, or may be, required for any variation or rescission of the term by agreement, a Court or arbitral tribunal has power to dispense with such consent in three limited situations. First, where consent cannot be obtained because the third party's whereabouts cannot reasonably be ascertained.[164] Secondly, where the third party is mentally incapable of giving his consent.[165] Thirdly, where it cannot reasonably be ascertained whether or not the third party has in fact relied on the term.[166] This limited conferral of discretion is designed to allow the contracting parties to escape from being unreasonably 'locked in' to a contract that confers a right on a third party.

(vii) The relationship with the Unfair Contract Terms Act 1977

Say a third party is given a right under the 1999 Act but there is an exclusion or limitation clause in the contract (valid as between the promisor and promisee) which excludes or limits the promisor's contractual liability to the third party. Might that exclusion or limitation clause be struck down as unreasonable under the Unfair Contract Terms Act 1977? To ensure that the answer to this question is 'no'—which the Law Commission thought important in reassuring contracting parties that their intentions do govern[167]—section 7(2) of the 1999 Act lays down that section 2(2) of UCTA 1977 does not apply in this situation. It was thought unnecessary to curtail the operation of any other section of UCTA or of the Unfair Terms in Consumer Contracts Regulations 1999 (now Part 2 of the Consumer Rights Act 2015) because they could not apply in any event where a third party is seeking to enforce its rights.[168]

(viii) The meaning of 'contract' under the 1999 Act

The term 'contract' was not defined in the 1999 Act. The better view is that, in accordance with our general understanding of what a contract is,[169] it includes both simple contracts (contracts supported by consideration) and contracts made by deed.[170]

---

[162] Law Com No 242, paras 9.45–9.47, are unclear on this point. But the broad wording of s 2(3) clearly allows for this.

[163] Law Com No 242, paras 9.37–9.42.   [164] s 2(4)(a).   [165] s 2(4)(b).

[166] s 2(5).   [167] Law Com No 242, para 13.10, point (viii).

[168] Law Com No 242, para 13.10, point (x) and para 13.12.   [169] Above, pp 2, 79.

[170] This is supported by s 7(3) of the 1999 Act in the references made to the Limitation Act 1980.

(e) ASSIGNMENT AND AGENCY

Assignment and agency (especially the doctrine of the undisclosed principal), may be viewed as exceptions to the benefit or *rights* side of privity (and are also, with the exception of voluntary assignment, exceptions to the burden side of privity). They are dealt with in Chapters 22 to 23 and will not be discussed further in this chapter.

(f) TRUSTS OF CONTRACTUAL RIGHTS

(i) Rights based on equitable property not contract

Equity allows a third party to enforce a contract where it can be construed as creating a completely constituted trust of the contractual right, also known as a trust of the promise. However, as Lord Haldane stated in *Dunlop v Selfridge*,[171] the rights do not arise by way of contract but are based on the third party's equitable proprietary interest in the subject matter of the contract and the right of the equitable owner to enforce the trust in his favour. Property may be tangible or intangible[172] and certain rights under a contract, 'choses in action', constitute an important example of intangible property.[173]

Thus a promisee under a contract, either at the time when the contract is made or thereafter, may constitute a trust of the right to which the promisee is entitled in favour of a third party which is enforceable in equity.[174] The subject of the trust, the contractual right to money or property,[175] is at law vested in the trustee, that is to say, in the promisee under the contract.

As with the enforcement of equitable rights in general, the person having the legal right in the thing demanded, in this case the promisee who has thus become a trustee, must in general be a party to the action. 'The trustee then can take steps to enforce performance to the beneficiary by the other contracting party as in the case of other equitable rights. The action should be in the name of the trustee. If, however, the trustee refuses to sue, the beneficiary can sue, joining the trustee as defendant'.[176] A trustee who sues on behalf of the third party may recover not merely nominal damages representing the trustee's own meagre interest in the performance of the contract, but the whole loss suffered by the beneficiary.[177]

---

[171] [1915] AC 847, 853; above, p 649.
[172] Lawson and Rudden, *The Law of Property* (3rd edn, 2003) ch 2.   [173] *Ibid*, 26–8. Below, p 661.
[174] Williston (1902) 15 Harvard LR 767; Corbin (1930) 46 LQR 12; Glanville Williams (1944) 7 MLR 123; Barton (1975) 91 LQR 236; Rickett (1979) 32 CLP 1; Law Com No 242, paras 2.8–2.9.
[175] Cf *Southern Water Authority v Carey* [1985] 2 All ER 1077, 1083 (no trust of the benefit of an exemption clause).
[176] *Vandepitte v Preferred Accident Insurance Corporation of New York* [1933] AC 70, 79.
[177] *Lloyd's v Harper* (1880) 16 Ch D 290.

Although this equitable principle was first enunciated in the eighteenth century by Lord Hardwicke,[178] the important developments occurred in the nineteenth century. Thus in *Lloyd's v Harper*:[179]

H, whose son was about to be elected a member of Lloyd's, wrote to the committee guaranteeing his son's solvency. When the son became insolvent, Lloyd's claimed against the father on behalf of members who had suffered thereby, and also on behalf of some outsiders.

It was held that the creditors were entitled to the benefit of the contract made, since the committee had entered into it as trustee for all those who had suffered by the insolvency of the son.

The principle was applied by the House of Lords in *Les Affréteurs Réunis Société Anonyme v Leopold Walford (London) Ltd*:[180]

In a charterparty made between the appellant, the owner of a steamship, and a firm of charterers, the appellant promised to pay a commission of 3 per cent on the gross amount of hire to the respondent, the broker who had negotiated the contract of charterparty. It failed to pay, and the respondent sued to obtain its commission.

The respondent was not a party to the contract. Although it would not normally be entitled to any rights under it, it was the practice for a charterer, if necessary, to sue the shipowner for the amount of a broker's commission *as trustee for the broker*. Here the action had been brought by the broker, but by consent it was treated as brought by the charterers as trustees for the broker. The House of Lords recognized the practice and gave judgment in the broker's favour.

(ii) Intention to create trust

To establish a trust of the promise it is necessary to establish that the promisee intended to enter the contract as trustee but, in the absence of express words,[181] there is no satisfactory test to determine whether the requisite intention exists. The consequence is uncertainty.[182]

The different judicial approaches to the question at different stages of the doctrine have led to a complicated body of case law which is not possible to reconcile. *Lloyds v Harper* and *Walford's* case may suggest that it is possible to infer an intention to create a trust solely from the intention to benefit the third party and, as such, the device of a trust could be fictionally employed as a way round the privity rule.[183] However, the approach of the Courts in more recent times has been stricter. It is said that the intention to constitute the trust must be affirmatively proved by substantial evidence,[184] in part

---

[178] *Tomlinson v Gill* (1756) Amb 330.

[179] (1880) 16 Ch D 290. See also *Fletcher v Fletcher* (1844) 4 Hare 67.

[180] [1919] AC 801. For the approach to this situation under the Contracts (Rights of Third Parties) Act 1999, see *Nisshin Shipping Co Ltd v Cleaves & Co Ltd* [2003] EWHC 2602, [2004] 1 Lloyd's Rep 38; above, p 664 and below p 675.

[181] *Fletcher v Fletcher* (1844) 4 Hare 67.   [182] Glanville Williams (1944) 7 MLR 123.

[183] Corbin (1930) 46 LQR 12, 17; Lord Wright (1939) 55 LQR 189, 208 (a 'cumbrous fiction').

[184] *Vandepitte v Preferred Accident Insurance Corp of New York* [1933] AC 70, 80.

because the presence of a trust renders the contract immutable where the parties might otherwise wish to be free to vary it.[185] Thus it will be more difficult to establish a trust where the intention to benefit the third party is not irrevocable,[186] where the contract consists of a complex package of benefits and burdens,[187] or where the third party may not need the benefit.[188]

An example of the differences of approach is provided by the contrast between *Re Flavell*[189] and *Re Schebsman*.[190] In *Re Flavell*:

Partnership articles provided that, in the event of the death of one of the partners, an annuity out of the firm's net profits each year was to be paid to his widow or children as he should appoint and, in default of appointment, to his widow.

It was held that the executors of the deceased partner were trustees for the widow under this contract, and that she was entitled to be paid the promised sums. But in *Re Schebsman*:

In 1940 S's employment was terminated, and, in consideration of his retirement, the company agreed to pay him the sum of £5,500 by instalments. If he died before the completion of the payments to him they were to be paid to his widow and daughter. S later became bankrupt, and then died. His trustee in bankruptcy claimed to intercept the sums being paid to his widow, on the ground that S himself could have intercepted them, and so they were available for his creditors.

The Court refused to hold that the contract created a trust in favour of the widow and daughter; they had therefore no enforceable right to the money. But the company was free to perform its obligation if it so wished, and, if it did so, neither S nor his trustee in bankruptcy could intercept the money and put it in his own pocket. Accordingly, the claim failed. Du Parcq LJ said:[191]

It is true that, by the use possibly of unguarded language, a person may create a trust, as Monsieur Jourdain talked prose, without knowing it, but unless an intention to create a trust is clearly to be collected from the language used and the circumstances of the case, I think that the Court ought not to be astute to discover indications of such an intention. I have little doubt that in the present case both parties (and certainly the debtor) intended to keep alive their common law right to vary consensually the terms of the obligation undertaken by the company, and if circumstances had changed in the debtor's life-time injustice might have been done by holding that a trust had been created and that those terms were accordingly unalterable.

---

[185] *Re Schebsman* [1944] Ch 83, 104; *Green v Russell* [1959] 2 QB 226, 241.

[186] *Re Sinclair's Life Policy* [1938] Ch 799.

[187] *Vandepitte v Preferred Accident Insurance Corp of New York* [1933] AC 70, 81; *Swain v The Law Society* [1983] 1 AC 598, 612; *Southern Water Authority v Carey* [1985] 2 All ER 1077, 1083.

[188] *Vandepitte v Preferred Accident Insurance Corp of New York* [1933] AC 70, 80 (contracting party liable for infant third party's torts); *Swain v The Law Society* [1983] 1 AC 598, 612, 621 (third-party beneficiary accorded direct action against promisor by statute).

[189] (1883) 25 Ch D 89.   [190] [1944] Ch 83.   [191] [1944] Ch 83, 104.

Similar contrasts can be found in the approach of the Courts to contracts of insurance. Thus while in some cases such contracts have been held to create a trust in favour of third parties,[192] in others they have not.[193] In this context too it would appear that English Courts no longer favour the device of a trust of a contractual right. It has been stated in Australian decisions that this may be too cautious and that there is 'considerable scope for the development of trusts' particularly in the context of insurance policies for the benefit of third persons.[194] One recent English case also indicates less hostility.[195] However, the dominant approach is exemplified by the decision of the Judicial Committee of the Privy Council in *Vandepitte v Preferred Accident Insurance Corporation of New York*[196] on appeal from British Columbia:

B insured his car with the respondent. The contract of insurance was stated to cover not only B himself, but all persons driving the car with his consent. B's daughter, while driving it with his consent, knocked down and injured the appellant, V. She was successfully sued in negligence by V, but the judgment was unsatisfied. By the British Columbia Insurance Act, an injured person could, in such circumstances, avail himself of any rights possessed by the driver of the vehicle against the insurance company. V therefore brought an action against the respondent under this Act.

In order to succeed, he had to establish that the daughter had some rights against the company under the policy, and he could only do this by showing that a trust had been created for her benefit. The Judicial Committee was not satisfied that this was B's intention. First, as British Columbia law provided that a father was liable for the torts of his minor children living with the family, B would 'naturally expect' any claim to be against him.[197] Secondly, a trust was not appropriate for a contract, such as insurance which imposes 'serious duties and obligations . . . on any person claiming to be insured, which necessarily involve consent and privity of contract'.[198]

The strict approach to the requirement of intention means that, other than where a trust of the promise is expressly created by the draftsman, or where the finding of a trust is established by binding authority, it will now be rare for the Courts to find that a contract for the benefit of a third party creates a trust of the promise.[199]

---

[192] *Royal Exchange Assurance v Hope* [1928] Ch 179; *Re Webb* [1941] Ch 225; *Re Foster's Policy* [1966] 1 WLR 222. See also *Williams v Baltic Insurance Association of London Ltd* [1924] 2 KB 282.

[193] *Re Englebach's Estate* [1924] 2 Ch 348; *Clay's Policy of Assurance* [1937] 2 All ER 548; *Re Sinclair's Life Policy* [1938] Ch 799; *Green v Russell* [1959] 2 QB 226; *Swain v The Law Society* [1983] 1 AC 598; *McCamley v Cammell Laird Shipbuilders Ltd* [1990] 1 WLR 963, 969.

[194] *Trident General Insurance Co Ltd v NcNiece Bros Pty Ltd* (1988) 165 CLR 107, 166 (Toohey J). See also ibid, 120–1, 146–51, 156; *Wilson v Darling Island Stevedoring and Lighterage Co* (1956) 95 CLR 43, 67.

[195] *Darlington BC v Wiltshier (Northern) Ltd* [1995] 1 WLR 68, 75, 81 (a constructive trust). Cf Law Com No 242, para 2.9.

[196] [1933] AC 70. Cf *Williams v Baltic Insurance Association of London Ltd* [1924] 2 KB 282; Road Traffic Act 1988, s 148(7).

[197] [1933] AC 70, 80.   [198] *Ibid*, 81.

[199] For a rare example, see *Burton v FX Music Ltd* [1999] EMLR 826, 840–1 (trust of promise to pay royalties due under a music distribution agreement).

(iii) Relationship to rights under the 1999 Act

Any incentive to strain to find the necessary intention to create a trust in this context has been weakened still further by the Contract (Rights of Third Parties) Act 1999, which provides a straightforward non-fictional way of upholding the rights of third parties. In the *Nisshin Shipping Co Ltd v Cleaves & Co Ltd*,[200] Colman J held that the finding of a trust of the promise, in line with the binding authority of the *Les Affréteurs Réunis Société Anonyme v Leopold Walford (London) Ltd*,[201] did not preclude the conferral of rights on the third-party broker under the 1999 Act; and that the Act provided a more natural and direct approach to enforcement of the broker's right to commission than the 'cumbrous fiction'[202] of the trust of the promise. He particularly had in mind the procedural disadvantage that it is necessary in an action based on a trust of the promise for the promisee to be joined in the action, whereas under the 1999 Act this is unnecessary.[203] This indicates that, in time, the trust of the promise may wither away as an exception to privity.

Having said that, and while it is clearly more difficult for a third party to establish a trust of a contractual promise for the third party's benefit than to establish a right to enforce the promise under the 1999 Act, the third party's rights under the 1999 Act may be more limited because, subject to section 2, they can be altered or extinguished by the agreement of the contracting parties whereas the third party's rights under a trust of a promise are irrevocable.

(g) MISCELLANEOUS STATUTORY EXCEPTIONS TO PRIVITY

We have seen that the Contracts (Rights of Third Parties) Act 1999 is a wide-ranging statutory exception to privity on its benefit side. But there have been many statutes conferring rights on third rights to enforce specific types of contract (particularly insurance contracts). We here refer to a few of them as illustrations.

(i) Road traffic insurance

Under section 148(7) of the Road Traffic Act 1988, the person issuing a policy of insurance against death or bodily injury to third parties in accordance with the requirements of the Act is made liable to indemnify not only the persons taking out the policy, but 'the person or classes of persons specified in the policy in respect of any liability which the policy purports to cover'. This means that the driver of a motor vehicle is entitled to the benefit of an insurance policy made with an insurance company by the owner of the vehicle and which purports to cover the driver.[204] The Act also permits an injured third party to proceed directly against the insurance company on obtaining judgment against the assured.[205] It precludes the insurer

---

[200] [2003] EWHC 2602, [2004] 1 Lloyd's Rep 38; above, p 664.

[201] [1919] 1 AC 801; above, p 672.   [202] Citing at [31] Lord Wright, above n 183.

[203] Although, applying the normal approach in Civil Procedure Rules, r 19.2, the Court has a discretion to join other parties where desirable to do so.

[204] *Tattersall v Drysdale* [1935] 2 KB 174.   [205] Road Traffic Act 1988, ss 151–3.

relying on various defences which would have been available in a claim by the assured.[206] Victims of road accidents are also protected by agreements entered into between the Secretary of State and the Motor Insurers' Bureau.[207] These are designed to compensate those injured by untraced ('hit and run') drivers and by uninsured drivers. Where the victim claims against the Bureau in respect of injuries sustained, as it is the policy of the Bureau not to raise the defence that the victim is not a party to the agreement between it and the Secretary of State,[208] the victim may proceed and even obtain judgment.[209]

(ii) Third Parties (Rights Against Insurers) Act 1930

Under the Third Parties (Rights against Insurers) Act 1930 a third party, who has a claim against a defendant who has taken out insurance against liability to third parties, can claim against the insurer where the defendant has become, inter alia, insolvent either before or after incurring the liability to the third party. The Third Parties (Rights against Insurers) Act 2010 will, if and when it is brought into force, remove a number of restrictions in the 1930 Act and enable the third party to resolve all issues relating to a claim in a single set of proceedings against the insurer.[210]

(iii) Life assurance

Section 11 of the Married Women's Property Act 1882 allows a husband to effect an insurance on his life for the benefit of his wife and children. A wife, too, may effect an insurance on her own life for the benefit of her husband and children. By section 11, such an insurance creates a trust in favour of the objects of the policy, and does not form part of the assured's estate. The Law Revision Committee proposed that this be extended to all life, endowment, and education policies which name a beneficiary[211] but the Law Commission considered that this would only be sensible as part of a general review of insurance.[212] Nevertheless, those named as beneficiaries under such policies may have a right to enforce them by virtue of the 1999 Act, albeit subject to the limits set out in it, in particular those in sections 2 and 3.

(iv) Carriage of goods by sea

Under the Carriage of Goods by Sea Act 1992, a person may have transferred to him rights under a contract for the carriage of goods by sea to which he was not an original party. So, for example, the lawful holder of a bill of lading has transferred to him the rights under the contract which is contained in, or evidenced by, that bill of lading.[213]

---

[206] Road Traffic Act 1988, ss 148, 152. Cf 1999 Act, s 3 above, p 668.

[207] For interpretation of the 1998 agreement, see *White v White* [2001] UKHL 99, [2001] 1 WLR 481.

[208] *Hardy v Motor Insurers' Bureau* [1964] 2 QB 745, 757; *Gurtner v Circuit* [1968] 2 QB 587, 599.

[209] But see the criticism voiced by Lord Dilhorne in *Albert v Motor Insurers' Bureau* [1972] AC 301, 320.

[210] The 2010 Act is based on Law Commission Report No 272 (2001) *Third Parties—Rights against Insurers*. There are amendments to the 2010 Act contained in the Insurance Act 2015.

[211] Sixth Interim Report 1937, Cmnd 5449, para 49.   [212] Law Com No 242, para 12.26.

[213] s 2(1)(a). By s 2(5), the rights of the original party are extinguished by the transfer so that the effect is the same as an assignment.

Such a person may also be subject to the liabilities under the original contract: for example, if he takes or demands delivery of the goods.[214] But as regards the liabilities, the original party remains liable so that there is no transfer of liability as such.[215]

(v) Package holidays

Where a consumer makes a contract for the provision of a package holiday, the beneficiaries of that contract (eg family members and others who go on the holiday) are given direct contractual rights against the organizer and the retailer even where they are not parties to the contract.[216]

(h) CONTRACTS CONCERNING LAND

(i) Covenants

The benefit (and burden) of the landlord's and the tenant's covenants in a lease, as long as they are not personal, will run upon an assignment of the lease or of the reversion.[217] Also, under the rule in *Tulk v Moxhay*,[218] a vendor of freehold land may attach to the land sold restrictive covenants as to its future use (eg that no buildings shall be erected on the land). Provided that the covenant was imposed for the benefit of neighbouring land, any subsequent owner of that land may enforce the covenant if he shows that the benefit of the covenant has become annexed to the land,[219] has been assigned to him, or that its benefit has passed to him under a building scheme.[220] Third parties may thus acquire rights under a covenant to which they were not privy. These rules, however, are simply rules applicable to rights over land.[221]

(ii) Law of Property Act 1925, section 56(1)

A more controversial exception is provided by section 56(1) of the Law of Property Act 1925, which states:

A person may take an immediate or other interest in land or other property, or the benefit of any condition, right of entry, covenant or agreement over or respecting land or other property, although he may not be named as a party to the conveyance or other instrument.

---

[214] s 3(1)(a).   [215] s 3(3).

[216] Package Travel, Package Holidays and Package Tours Regulations 1992 (SI 1992 No 3288), regs 2 and 15, implementing EEC Council Directive 90/314, 1990 OJ L 158/59. See also *Jackson v Horizon Holidays Ltd* [1975] 1 WLR 1468, above, p 652.

[217] Landlord and Tenant (Covenants) Act 1995, s 3 (covenants in post-1995 leases). For pre-1996 leases, the covenant must 'touch and concern the land': *Spencer's Case* (1583) 5 Co Rep 16a; Law of Property Act 1925, ss 141, 142.

[218] (1848) 2 Ph 774; see below, p 688.

[219] In *Federated Homes Ltd v Mill Lodge Properties Ltd* [1980] 1 WLR 594 Brightman LJ indicated this could take place automatically without express words.

[220] See the Law of Property Act 1925, s 78(1) and also *Smith and Snipes Hall Farm Ltd v River Douglas Catchment Board* [1949] 2 KB 500.

[221] See generally, Harpum, Bridge, and Dixon, *Megarry & Wade's Law of Real Property* (8th edn, 2012) ch 32.

The word 'property' is defined in the Act, unless the context otherwise requires, as including 'any thing in action, and any interest in real or personal property'.[222]

The scope of this sub-section has long been debated.[223] In the view of some it is merely a conveyancing provision and applies only to land; but others, in particular Lord Denning, interpreted it much more widely.[224] There has also been considerable doubt as to who can properly rely on it. In its terms the sub-section is wide enough to permit any person who might conceive it of 'benefit' to take advantage of a covenant or agreement made by others, but such could scarcely have been the intention of the legislature. Accordingly, the Courts have construed it in a more limited fashion. In *White v Bijou Mansions Ltd* Simonds J said that the only person who could rely on section 56 is one who, although not expressly named, the instrument purports to grant something to, or covenant with.[225]

This, which we may call the orthodox meaning, however, does not assist a person who is not a party to a contract but wishes to sue on that contract. The agreement is not 'made with him', nor does it 'grant something to him' since the sub-section does not give to the non-party a right to the performance of a contract if, apart from the sub-section, that person has no such right.[226] The sub-section did not create any fresh rights to sue under a contract, but only assisted the protection of rights shown to exist.

In *Beswick v Beswick*[227] the House of Lords held unanimously that the context of section 56(1) required that a limited interpretation should be given to the word 'property', but there was no agreement as to what that interpretation should be. Lord Guest thought that it meant land,[228] but Lord Upjohn did not accept that the word was limited to an interest in real property.[229] There was similar disagreement about the orthodox meaning of the scope of the sub-section.[230] And Lord Upjohn expressed the view, based on historical grounds, that the words 'conveyance or other instrument' were confined to documents *inter partes* and under seal.[231] These differences of opinion have yet to be resolved,[232] and the enactment of the 1999 Act with its wider scope for third-party enforcement may mean that they will not be. It is, however, clear that section 56(1) does not apply to a simple promise by A to B to pay a sum of money to C.

---

[222] s 205(1)(xx).

[223] See Elliott (1956) 20 Conv (NS) 43, 114; Andrews (1959) 23 Conv (NS) 179; Furmston (1960) 23 MLR 373, 380–5; Ellinger (1963) 26 MLR 396; Wade [1964] CLJ 66.

[224] See *Smith and Snipes Hall Farm Ltd v River Douglas Catchment Board* [1949] 2 KB 500, 517; *Drive Yourself Hire Co (London) Ltd v Strutt* [1954] 1 QB 250, 274; *Beswick v Beswick* [1966] Ch 538.

[225] [1937] Ch 610, 625. See also (on appeal) [1938] Ch 351, 365; *Re Ecclesiastical Commissioners for England's Conveyance* [1936] Ch 430; *Amsprop Trading Ltd v Harris Distribution Ltd* [1997] 1 WLR 1025. Contrast *Stromdale and Ball Ltd v Burden* [1952] Ch 223.

[226] *Re Miller's Agreement* [1947] Ch 615. See also *Re Foster* [1938] 3 All ER 357; *Re Sinclair's Life Policy* [1938] Ch 799; *Green v Russell* [1959] 2 QB 226; *Scruttons Ltd v Midland Silicones Ltd* [1962] AC 446.

[227] [1968] AC 58.   [228] *Ibid*, 87.

[229] *Ibid*, 105, with whom Lord Pearce agreed (at 94).   [230] *Ibid*, 74–5, 81, 87, 94, 106.

[231] *Ibid*, 107, with whom Lord Pearce agreed (at 94). See also Lord Reid at 76–7.

[232] In *Lyus v Prowsa* [1982] 1 WLR 1044, 1049 and *Amsprop Trading Ltd v Harris Distribution Ltd* [1997] 1 WLR 1025 the orthodox meaning was considered correct.

(i) CONTRACTS GIVING RISE TO TORTIOUS DUTIES OF CARE TO THIRD PARTIES

The tort of negligence sometimes entitles a claimant, who has suffered injury or loss, to sue a defendant who was performing a contract with another party. So, for example, in *Donoghue v Stevenson*[233] the claimant was held to be owed a duty of care by a manufacturer in relation to injury caused by a defective product supplied by the manufacturer under a contract with the distributor or retailer. In that very general sense, the standard application of the tort of negligence evades the doctrine of privity of contract.

However, in some more limited situations, liability for pure economic loss in the tort of negligence more obviously represents an exception to privity in that, arguably, it is tantamount to enforcement of a contract by a third-party beneficiary. For example, in *Ross v Caunters*[234] and *White v Jones*[235] solicitors, who had contracted with a testator to draw up wills benefiting third parties, were held liable in tort to the third parties where, as a result of their negligence, in the first case the will was executed in such a way as to invalidate the gift, and in the second case it was never drawn up. In these cases the relationship created by the contract gave rise to a duty of care to a third party who was thus able to sue the contracting party in tort in a situation where no loss was suffered by the testator's estate.[236]

It has been noted[237] that these cases do not fall within section 1(1)(b) of the 1999 Act. Although the intended legatee is expressly designated as a beneficiary, the contract is not one in which the solicitor promises the testator to confer a benefit on the third party, the intended legatee, but one by which the solicitor is to enable the testator to do so.[238] The direct contractual beneficiary is the testator who intended to confer on the third party the benefit of his assets after death and not the benefit of the solicitor's promise to draft the will. Given that the legatees were incidental beneficiaries, a solution through the tort of negligence seems appropriate.

(j) THIRD PARTIES TAKING THE BENEFIT OF EXEMPTION CLAUSES

(i) Introduction

Say a contracting party (A) has sought to exempt persons who are not parties to the contract, for example, its employees or subcontractors who participate in the performance of the contract from liability to the other party to the contract (B).[239]

---

[233] [1932] AC 562.   [234] [1980] Ch 287.

[235] [1995] 2 AC 207. See Weir (1995) 111 LQR 357. See further *Hill v Van Erp* (1997) 142 ALR 687 (Australia). See generally Barker (1994) 14 OJLS 137; Markesinis (1987) 103 LQR 354; Macmillan (2000) 63 MLR 721, 724.

[236] *Carr-Glyn v Frearsons* [1997] 2 All ER 614, 623–4, 628.   [237] Above, p 664.

[238] *White v Jones* [1995] 2 AC 207, 262–3, 273; *Gartside v Sheffield, Young & Ellis* [1983] NZLR 37, 42, 49.

[239] See Law Com No 242, paras 2.19–2.35.

A's employees and subcontractors, although not in a contractual relationship with B, may nevertheless be under duties to B imposed by the law of tort. If the employees or independent contractors are not able to rely on the exemption clause as a defence to a tort action by B, they in turn may have a right to be indemnified by A. Even where there is no right to be indemnified, A may, particularly in the case of employees, nevertheless agree to meet the damages awarded to B.[240] In both cases the risk is ultimately borne by A, thus defeating the purpose of the exemption clause. Whether or not it is A who ends up paying, permitting B to succeed against the employees or independent contractors will in many cases upset the allocation of risks and consequent pattern of insurance in the transaction, since A and its employees and independent contractors will have expected B to insure against the relevant loss and not done so themselves.[241]

Despite this, prior to the Contracts (Rights of Third Parties) Act 1999, such attempts by third parties to rely on exemption clauses encountered great difficulties, primarily because A's employees or subcontractors were not parties to the contract. The tension between the doctrine of privity of contract and the commercial expectations of those who take part in multiparty transactions produced a very complicated body of law. At times the Courts applied the doctrine and prevented a defendant from relying on an exemption clause. At other times, and particularly more recently, they have been willing to circumvent the doctrine and even to contemplate some form of modification or exception to it with regard to exemption clauses.

(ii) Privity applied

The operation of the doctrine of privity in such cases will first be considered. In *Scruttons Ltd v Midland Silicones Ltd*:[242]

A drum of chemicals was shipped from New York to London and consigned to the respondents upon the terms of a bill of lading which exempted the carriers from liability in excess of $500 (£179) per package. The drum was damaged by the negligence of the appellants, a firm of stevedores employed by the carriers, and the damage amounted to £593. The consignees sued the stevedores in the tort of negligence for that damage. Although the stevedores were not a party to the bill of lading, nor expressly mentioned therein, they claimed to be entitled to the benefit of the clause limiting liability.

In the House of Lords, Lord Denning (dissenting) considered that the stevedores were protected by an accepted principle of the law of tort, that of voluntary assumption of risk, since the consignees had assented to the limitation of liability. But the majority of

---

[240] *Adler v Dickson* [1955] 1 QB 158.

[241] eg where there is a limitation clause, the non-party performer would be expected to insure up to the limit and the contracting party (B) beyond that: see *Scruttons Ltd v Midland Silicones Ltd* [1962] AC 446, where the non-party stevedores only agreed to take out insurance in excess of a $500 limitation where that limitation did not apply: Lord Denning at 481–2. See also *The Mahkutai* [1996] AC 650; *London Drugs Ltd v Kuehene & Nagel International Ltd* [1992] 3 SCR 299, 423 (Iacobucci J) (Canada); *Fraser River Pile & Dredge Ltd v Can-Dive Services Ltd* [2000] 1 Lloyd's Rep 199 (third party able to enforce waiver of subrogation clause).

[242] [1962] AC 446.

their Lordships unequivocally reasserted the doctrine of privity of contract. They held that the stevedores could not claim the benefit of an exemption clause in a contract to which they were not a party.[243]

At one time the proposition was advanced that where a contract contained an exemption clause, any employee or agent while performing the contract was entitled to the same immunity from liability as the employer or principal.[244] But this principle of 'vicarious immunity' was rejected by the House of Lords in *Scruttons Ltd v Midland Silicones*.[245]

(iii) Privity avoided

Exemption clauses are unambiguously brought within the 1999 Act[246] so that effect can now be given to the commercial expectations of those who take part in multiparty transactions. The Act thus sweeps 'away the technicalities applying to the enforcement by expressly designated third parties of exclusion clauses'.[247]

Nevertheless, discussion of the complex common law position remains necessary. First, the common law applies to contracts made before 11 May 2000 and disputes concerning such contracts will continue to come before the Courts for some time. Moreover, there may be cases in which the 1999 Act does not apply or in which, if it does, it will be advantageous for a person to rely on the common law.

There are a number of ways in which the doctrine of privity may be avoided at common law. The willingness of the Courts to do so has varied. The application of the doctrine in some cases can be seen as part of the process by which Courts sought to alleviate the position of those affected by onerous terms,[248] for instance clauses seeking to exclude liability for personal injury resulting from negligence, now prohibited by statute.[249] The reluctance to save negligent people from the normal consequences of their fault, however, extended beyond such cases and may have influenced the decision in *Scruttons Ltd v Midland Silicones Ltd*[250] Since that decision, the perceived need to support established commercial practice and to avoid redistributing the risks of transactions has led to greater judicial dissatisfaction with the operation of privity in such situations and a greater willingness to avoid the operation of the doctrine.

---

[243] Article IV *bis* (2) of the Hague-Visby Rules, contained in the Schedule to the Carriage of Goods by Sea Act 1971, now extends protection to the servants and agents (but not independent contractors) of the carrier in respect of loss or damage to goods covered by a contract of carriage of goods by sea to which the Rules apply.

[244] *Elder Dempster & Co Ltd v Peterson, Zochonis & Co Ltd* [1924] AC 522, 534 (Viscount Cave). See also at 548 (Viscount Finlay) and [1923] 1 KB 436, 441 (Scrutton LJ).

[245] [1962] AC 446.

[246] 1999 Act, s 1(6). This includes such clauses in contracts of carriage which are otherwise excluded from the 1999 Act by s 6(5).

[247] Law Com No 242, paras 2.35, 3.32.   [248] Above, p 172.

[249] *Cosgrove v Horsfall* (1945) 62 TLR 140; *Adler v Dickson* [1955] 1 QB 158; and *Genys v Matthews* [1966] 1 WLR 758 concerned such clauses. See now the Unfair Contract Terms Act 1977, s 2 and the Consumer Rights Act 2015, s 65.

[250] See [1962] AC 446, 472 (Viscount Simonds), relying on *Wilson v Darling Island Stevedoring & Lighterage Co Ltd* (1956) 95 CLR 43, 78 (Fullagar J). See also *The Mahkutai* [1996] AC 650, 660 (Lord Goff).

There are two methods of avoiding the privity doctrine at common law; these may be termed the 'direct contractual relationship' route and the 'negating the tortious duty' route. The contractual route involves the identification of a second contract between the claimant (B) and the person wishing to rely on the exemption clause. The second route is based on the exemption clause showing that the claimant (B), in its contract with A, assumed the risk of damage or loss resulting from the negligence of the defendant so as to qualify or negate the defendant's tortious duty of care to it. In its wider form this was not favoured by the majority in *Scruttons Ltd v Midland Silicones Ltd* but has since attracted some support.[251] One should also not forget that the promisee may be willing to intervene in the proceedings to protect the defendant. So, where the contract containing the exemption clause can be construed as a promise by the claimant not to sue the third-party defendant, if the promisee intervenes in the proceedings to protect the defendant, the Court may stay or dismiss the claim.[252]

(a) Finding a direct contractual relationship.   The Courts may be able to imply that a party (A) to a contract containing an exemption clause which is intended to benefit third parties such as its employees or subcontractors was either acting as agent for the third parties or as agent for the other party to the contract (B) so as to create a direct contractual relationship (in particular by means of a unilateral contract) between B and the employees or subcontractors.

This device was first employed during the nineteenth century, when England was (as it is again) covered by a network of small railway companies and a contract made with one might entitle the holder of a ticket to travel on one or more of them. In such circumstances, the passenger was not allowed to say that only the company which was a party to the primary agreement was protected by the exemption clauses contained in it. The Courts were ready to find either that the contracting company was acting as agent for the other companies,[253] or that it was acting as agent for the passenger.[254] The passenger was thus brought into a direct contractual relationship with the other companies. In reliance on the principle of agency many enterprises have framed contractual clauses designed to protect their employees and subcontractors from liability.

In *Scruttons Ltd v Midland Silicones Ltd,*[255] the House of Lords left open the question whether the stevedores could have been protected if the carriers had contracted as agents on their behalf. Lord Reid said:[256]

I can see a possibility of success of the agency argument if (first) the bill of lading makes it clear that the stevedore is intended to be protected by the provisions in it which limit liability, (secondly) the bill of lading makes it clear that the carrier, in addition to contracting for these provisions on his own behalf, is also contracting as agent for the stevedore that these provisions should apply to the stevedore, (thirdly) the carrier has authority to do that, or

---

[251] See *Pacific Associates v Baxter* [1990] 1 QB 933, 1011 (Purchas LJ); *Norwich CC v Harvey* [1989] 1 WLR 828; *Marc Rich & Co AG v Bishop Rock Marine Co Ltd, The 'Nicholas H'* [1996] AC 211, 239–40 (Lord Steyn).
[252] See above, p 655.   [253] *Hall v NE Ry* (1875) LR 10 QB 437, 442.
[254] *Ibid*, 443.   [255] [1962] AC 446; above, p 680.   [256] *Ibid*, 474.

perhaps later ratification by the stevedore would suffice, and (fourthly) that any difficulties about consideration moving from the stevedore were overcome.

These conditions set out in *Scruttons Ltd v Midland Silicones Ltd* were held to have been satisfied in *New Zealand Shipping Co Ltd v AM Satterthwaite & Co Ltd, The Eurymedon*,[257] where the bill of lading contained a clause by which the carrier, as agent of the stevedore, stipulated that both he and the stevedore should be entitled to the limitation of liability contained in the bill. The Judicial Committee of the Privy Council held that the stevedore had furnished consideration by unloading the goods under its contract with the carrier.[258] The contract was, however, only established by somewhat artificially[259] identifying an offer to the stevedore in the contract between the carrier and the shipper.[260] That is, the offer was treated as being the offer of a unilateral contract under which the owner excluded or limited the liability of the stevedore in return for the stevedore unloading the goods. This technical approach will not be possible in all cases. The carrier may not have authority to act as agent of the stevedore and, although in the majority of cases this may be solved by recourse to the principle of ratification,[261] this may not always be possible.[262] Again, the company seeking the benefit of the exemption clause will only be held to have furnished consideration where it is performing the contract containing the exemption clause.[263] More fundamentally, the exclusion clause may not refer to the employee or subcontractor.[264]

Although, in cases of the carriage of goods by sea, it has been said that stevedores and others performing the contract would normally be protected and that Courts should not search for 'fine distinctions' which would diminish this general position,[265] this approach has not been applied in other contexts.[266] It is in such contexts that the 1999 Act is likely to make a real difference. It is, moreover, inevitable, even in carriage of goods by sea, 'so long as the principle continues to be understood to rest upon an enforceable contract as between the cargo owners and the stevedores entered into through the agency of the shipowner . . . that technical points of contract and agency law will continue to be invoked'.[267]

---

[257] [1975] AC 154.   [258] See above, p 112.

[259] See Reynolds (1974) 90 LQR 301; Coote (1974) 37 MLR 453; Battersby (1978) 28 U of Tor LJ 75.

[260] The claimant was in fact the consignee not the shipper. It would be party to the offer made by the shipper to the stevedore either by statute (then the Bills of Lading Act 1855, now the Carriage of Goods by Sea Act 1992, s 2) or by presenting the bill of lading to the ship and requesting delivery of the goods thereunder: *Brandt v Liverpool Brazil & River Plate Navigation Co Ltd* [1924] 1 KB 575.

[261] *The Mahkutai* [1996] AC 650.

[262] *The Suleyman Stalskiy* [1976] 2 Lloyd's Rep 609 (Sup Ct of British Columbia); *Lummus Co Ltd v East African Harbours Corp* [1978] 1 Lloyd's Rep 317, 322–3 (High Ct of Kenya).

[263] *Raymond Burke Motors Ltd v The Mersey Docks and Harbour Co* [1986] 1 Lloyd's Rep 155 (goods damaged while they were being stored and not during loading or unloading).

[264] eg in *London Drugs Ltd v Kuehene & Nagel International Ltd* [1992] 3 SCR 299 the clause did not refer to warehouseman's employees. Cf Contracts (Rights of Third Parties) Act 1999, s 1(3).

[265] *Port Jackson Stevedoring Pty Ltd v Salmond and Spraggon (Australia) Pty Ltd* [1981] 1 WLR 138, 144 (Lord Wilberforce). See Reynolds (1979) 95 LQR 183; Coote [1981] CLJ 13.

[266] *Southern Water Authority v Carey* [1985] 2 All ER 1077, 1084 (construction); *Kendall v Morgan* The Times, 2 December 1980 (employment).

[267] *The Mahkutai* [1996] AC 650, 664 (Lord Goff).

The approach in *The Eurymedon* was approved by the House of Lords in *Homburg Houtimport BV v Agrosin Private Ltd, The Starsin*:[268]

The claimants were owners of a cargo of timber who had entered into a contract of carriage with the charterers of a ship. Under that contract, they excluded liability for negligent stowage. In their action in the tort of negligence against the shipowners, who were the actual performing carriers, one question was whether the shipowners could take the benefit of that exclusion.

While approving *The Eurymedon*,[269] the House of Lords held that it was inapplicable to these facts. This was because to allow the actual performing carriers to take the benefit of the exclusion clause would undermine the Hague-Visby Rules (given legislative force by the Carriage of Goods Act 1971) which, in a contract of carriage, invalidate the exclusion clause in question.

(b) Negating the tortious duty.   The majority in *Scruttons Ltd v Midland Silicones Ltd*[270] rejected Lord Denning's powerful reasoning based on the general defence to actions in tort where a claimant has voluntarily consented to take the risk of a loss or injury. But a defendant who is sued in tort may rely on an exclusion clause in a contract to which the claimant but not the defendant is a party as restricting or excluding the duty of care that it would otherwise owe to the claimant. Where this is so the defendant is taking the benefit of an exemption clause in a contract to which it is not a party.

So, in *Pacific Associates Inc v Baxter*[271] a consultant engineer successfully defended a claim for negligence by the contractor by relying on a term of the contract between the employer and the contractor which provided that neither the engineer nor any of his staff 'shall be in any way personally liable for the acts or obligations under the Contract . . .'. Purchas LJ said:

The presence of such an exclusion clause, while not directly binding between the parties, cannot be excluded from a general consideration of the contractual structure against which the contractor demonstrates reliance on, and the engineer accepts responsibility for, a duty in tort, if any, arising out of the proximity established between them by the existence of that very contract.[272]

The contractual structure may be relevant even where there is no express provision seeking to exempt the third party.

In *Norwich CC v Harvey*:[273]

A building was damaged by fire as a result of the negligence of a roofing subcontractor. The main contract provided that the building owner was to bear the risk of damage by fire and

---

[268] [2003] UKHL 12, [2004] 1 AC 715.

[269] There are clear analyses by Lord Hoffmann at [93], by Lord Hobhouse at [149]–[153] and, especially helpful, by Lord Millett at [196]–[197]. Cf Lord Bingham at [34] who talks of a bilateral contract.

[270] [1962] AC 446. See also *Leigh & Sillavan Ltd v Aliakmon SS Co Ltd* [1986] AC 785, 817 (Lord Brandon) but cf Robert Goff LJ [1985] QB 350, 399. Cf also the cases considered below.

[271] [1990] 1 QB 993. See also *Southern Water Authority v Carey* [1985] 2 All ER 1077.

[272] [1990] 1 QB 993, 1022–3.   [273] [1989] 1 WLR 828.

the subcontractor contracted on the same terms and conditions as in the main contract. The owner of the building brought an action against the subcontractor.

It was held that, although there was no direct contractual relationship between the owner and the subcontractor, nevertheless they had both contracted with the main contractor on the basis that the owner had assumed the risk of damage by fire and the subcontractor owed no duty in respect of the damage which occurred. It is not, however, necessary for the defendant's contract to contain the exemption clause; what is important is whether the recognition of a duty of care by the defendant would outflank the contractual structure governing dealings between the claimant and others.[274]

(c) A general common law exception for the benefit of exemption clauses? The commercial inconvenience that results from the application of the doctrine of privity in the context of exemption clauses has led to the recognition by the Supreme Court of Canada of a wide exception whereby employees and subcontractors acting in the course of their employment and performing the services provided for in the main contract can rely on an exemption clause in that contract which is intended to protect them.[275]

Prior to the enactment of the 1999 Act there were indications that the artificiality and technical nature of the approach based on New Zealand Shipping Co Ltd v AM Satterthwaite, The Eurymedon[276] inclined senior judges to regard the development started in that decision as not yet complete. They appeared to be prepared to recognize a fully fledged exception to the doctrine of privity where a contract clearly provides that (for example) independent contractors such as stevedores are to have the benefit of exceptions and limitations contained in that contract.[277] The case for such recognition is that the reasons for and justifications of the privity doctrine do not apply where a third party seeks to rely on a contractual provision as a defence; there is an identity of interest between the contracting party and the third party as far as the performance of the contracting party's contractual obligations is concerned, and it is commercially undesirable to allow a person to circumvent a contractual exclusion clause and thus redistribute the contractual

---

[274] Marc Rich & Co AG v Bishop Rock Marine Co Ltd, The Nicholas H [1996] AC 211, 239–40 (Lord Steyn) (if the cargo owner recovered from the defendant, a classification society, the cost of insuring against such claims would be passed on to shipowners and the contractual structure governing dealings between shipowners and cargo owners and the limitation of shipowners' liability would be destroyed). See also Henderson v Merrett Syndicates Ltd [1995] 2 AC 145, 197.

[275] London Drugs Ltd v Kuehene & Nagel International Ltd [1992] 3 SCR 299. It may be more problematic to establish a clear intention to extend the protection of an exemption clause to an independent contractor than to an employee; ibid, 441. See also Fraser River Pile & Dredge Ltd v Can-Dive Services Ltd [2000] 1 Lloyd's Rep 199 (third party able to enforce waiver of subrogation clause).

[276] [1975] AC 154, above, p 648.

[277] The Mahkutai [1996] AC 650, 665 (but the exclusive jurisdiction clause was held not to be intended to benefit third parties). See also Dresser UK Ltd v Falcongate Freight Management Ltd [1992] 1 QB 502, 511 (Bingham LJ) (describing the principle of bailment on terms as 'a pragmatic legal recognition of commercial reality'); Law Com CP No 121 (1991), paras 4.8–4.12; Law Com No 242, para 2.19 ff.

allocation of risk by suing the employee or subcontractor of the other party to the contract.[278]

It is important to realize, however, that the wide Canadian common law exception goes further in the context to which it applies than the 1999 Act. This is because, contrary to the 1999 Act, the Canadian exception does not require the third party to be expressly identified by name, class or description.[279] In the light of that, the English Courts may consider it inappropriate to adopt the Canadian exception.[280] On the other hand, the Law Commission, as we shall now see, indicated that it did not want its reform to curtail further development of the common law.

(k) FURTHER DEVELOPMENT OF THE COMMON LAW

The traditional reluctance of English Courts to reform the third party rule has been noted.[281] What is the effect of the enactment of the Contracts (Rights of Third Parties) Act 1999 on further development of the common law?[282]

The Law Commission stated that it intended that legislation based on its recommendations, which it described as 'relatively conservative and moderate' should not hamper the judicial development of third-party rights where the Courts decide that in a particular sphere the reform did not go far enough.[283] It is submitted that this cannot mean that, in situations in which the 'intention that the third party should enforce the contract' test is not satisfied, Courts should have no regard to the existence of the 1999 Act and its policy and should continue to develop the common law in the same way as they would have done without the 1999 Act. So, for example, it would seem inappropriate to build on the suggestion, based on dicta in *Darlington BC v Wilshier (Northern) Ltd*[284] that, despite an unpromising history, the trust of a promise should be deployed as a way of granting a right of action to a third party.

In contrast, it may be appropriate for the Courts in a particular context to identify some common law principle other than the intention of the parties upon which to rest third-party rights of suit, for instance 'reasonable reliance'. Moreover, there seems no good reason why the 1999 Act should prevent Courts, after careful consideration, accepting the Canadian exception adopted in the *London Drugs* case,[285] albeit that that exception applies a wider intention test than that under the 1999 Act.[286] It may also be appropriate for there to be judicial development where, as in the case of the

---

[278] *London Drugs Ltd v Kuehene & Nagel International Ltd* [1992] 3 SCR 299, 440–7. For these reasons and justifications, see above, pp 679–80 and *Privity of Contract: Contracts for the Benefit of Third Parties* Law Com CP No 121 (1991), para 4.3; Law Com No 242, paras 2.33–2.35.

[279] s 1(3), above, p 660.

[280] Cf *Alfred McAlpine Construction Ltd v Panatown Ltd* [2001] 1 AC 518, 535 (Lord Clyde).

[281] Above, pp 657–8.   [282] See Beatson (2001) 117 LQR 106.

[283] Law Com No 242, para 5.11. See also paras 5.15, 12.1. See, eg, the exception for exemption clauses developed by the Supreme Court of Canada in *London Drugs Ltd v Kuehene & Nagel International Ltd* [1992] 3 SCR 299.

[284] [1995] 1 WLR 68, 75, 81.   [285] [1992] 3 SCR 299.   [286] See above, n 279.

promisee's remedies in contracts for the benefit of third parties, this has expressly been left to the common law.[287]

3. THE IMPOSITION OF CONTRACTUAL LIABILITIES UPON THIRD PARTIES

(a) INTRODUCTION

As a general rule, two persons cannot, by any contract into which they may enter, thereby impose contractual liabilities upon a third party.

This principle may be illustrated by reference to building contracts, where a person (the employer) engages a contractor to carry out certain building work. The contractor frequently subcontracts parts of the work to subcontractors. A subcontractor has no cause of action against the employer for the price of work done or materials supplied under the subcontract, since the employer is not a party to that contract.[288] Even if the employer has nominated the subcontractor and taken the benefit of the subcontractor's work, the employer will not be liable to the subcontractor for the price, as there is no privity of contract between them. Conversely, the employer has no claim in contract[289] against the subcontractor,[290] since the subcontractor is not a party to the main contract between the employer and the contractor.

Further, the principle of privity of contract normally prevents a person from being bound by an exemption clause contained in a contract to which it is not a party.

This is not to deny that third parties may be legally affected by contracts to which they are not parties. For example, a person who knowingly interferes with contractual rights may be liable for an 'economic tort'; the contractual creation of *proprietary* rights (in land or personal property) bind most third parties who deal with the property; and a contractual obligation to keep information confidential can sometimes render a third party liable for the equitable wrong of breach of confidence.

There are also a few exceptions where a third party is liable *in contract* for breach of the duty created by a contract to which it is not a party. Agency is considered in Chapter 23 and transfer by death and bankruptcy in Chapter 22. In this chapter, we consider covenants concerning land and the controversial issue as to whether a similar approach applies to contracts concerning chattels. We also look at situations where exemption clauses have been held to bind third parties.

---

[287] Law Com No 242, paras 5.12–5.17. See *Alfred McAlpine Construction Ltd v Panatown Ltd* [2001] 1 AC 518, 551–2 (Lord Goff), 590 (Lord Millett) (both dissenting). Cf Lord Clyde at 535.

[288] *Hampton v Glamorgan CC* [1917] AC 13. See also *Schmaling v Tomlinson* (1815) 6 Taunt 147 (principal and sub-agent).

[289] But a claim may lie in tort.　　　　[290] Unless there is a collateral warranty: see above, p 145.

(b) COVENANTS CONCERNING LAND

Certain kinds of covenants concerning land are enforceable against third parties whether or not there is notice. If A leases land to B, there is privity of contract between them. But covenants in a lease which have reference to the subject-matter of the lease will be enforceable, not only between A and B, but against assignees of the lease or of the reversion.[291]

Also, under the rule in *Tulk v Moxhay*,[292] the burden of covenants restricting the use to which land may be put can 'run with the land'. In that case:

T, who owned houses in Leicester Square, sold the garden in the centre of the square to E. E covenanted to maintain the land sold as a garden and not to build on it. The land was sold several times before being purchased by the defendant with notice of the covenant. The defendant proposed to build on the land and T sought an injunction to restrain him.

The injunction was granted. The defendant was not permitted to use the land in a manner inconsistent with the covenant entered into by E. The ground for the decision was the defendant's *notice* of the covenant at the time of the purchase.[293] But in subsequent cases the principle in *Tulk v Moxhay* has undergone a considerable change. It must now be shown that the covenant was imposed for the benefit of neighbouring land owned by the person seeking to enforce it and that the benefit of the covenant has passed to that person.[294] The right of a person entitled to the benefit of the covenant to prevent the inconsistent use has taken on a proprietary quality, an 'equitable interest'[295] in the land burdened by the covenant. A subsequent purchaser of that land buys it subject to the equitable interest and with the burden of the interest attached.[296]

(c) CONTRACTS CONCERNING CHATTELS

The question arises as to whether an analogous approach applies to contracts concerning chattels.

In *De Mattos v Gibson* Knight Bruce LJ said:

Reason and justice seem to prescribe that, at least as a general rule, where a man, by gift or purchase, acquires property from another, with knowledge of a previous contract, lawfully and for valuable consideration made by him with a third person, to use and employ the property for a particular purpose in a specified manner, the acquirer shall not, to the material damage of the third person, in opposition to the contract and inconsistently with it, use and employ the property in a manner not allowable to the giver or seller.[297]

---

[291] See above p 677, n 217.   [292] (1848) 2 Ph 774.

[293] The doctrine of notice no longer applies to such covenants, which must now be protected by registration if they are to bind a purchaser of the land: Land Charges Act 1972, ss 2(5), 4(6) (unregistered land); Land Registration Act 2002, ss 28, 29 (registered land).

[294] *London CC v Allen* [1914] 3 KB 642; see above, p 677.

[295] *Re Nisbet and Potts' Contract* [1905] 1 Ch 391, 398, [1906] 1 Ch 386, 403, 405.

[296] *Rogers v Hosegood* [1900] 2 Ch 388, 407.   [297] (1858) 4 De G & J 276, 282.

In *Lord Strathcona Steamship Co Ltd v Dominion Coal Co Ltd*:[298]

The D Co had a long-term time charterparty of a ship. The owners sold the ship, which eventually came into the possession of the LS Co, who took it with notice of the charterparty and on the understanding that the agreement should be honoured. They did not honour the agreement, and, when sued by the charterers, D Co pleaded that they were not bound by the charterparty as there was no privity of contract between them.

The Judicial Committee of the Privy Council upheld the decision of the Courts in Nova Scotia granting the charterers an injunction restraining the LS Co from using the ship inconsistently with the charterparty. The Board relied upon the dictum of Knight Bruce LJ in *De Mattos v Gibson* quoted above.[299] The case was said to fall under the rule in *Tulk v Moxhay* relating to the use of land: whether the subject-matter was land or a chattel, the principle is the same: 'the remedy is a remedy in equity by way of injunction against acts inconsistent with the covenant, with notice of which the land was acquired'.[300]

This reasoning has, however, been the subject of considerable criticism,[301] and it has been said that the case was wrongly decided.[302] In the first place, it is argued that reliance should not have been placed on the dictum of Knight Bruce LJ. In *De Mattos v Gibson* an interim injunction was granted to restrain the mortgagee of a ship, who had acquired his mortgage with knowledge of an existing voyage charterparty, from interfering with the performance of the charter. Knight Bruce LJ's reasoning did not, however, form part of the concurring judgment of Turner LJ and has been doubted.[303] When the case came before Lord Chelmsford LC,[304] a final injunction was refused.[305] Although the Lord Chancellor expressed the opinion that the mortgagee was bound to abstain from any act which would have the immediate effect of preventing performance of the charter, he appeared to do so on the ground that any right to an injunction was based on an extension of the principle whereby a person who knowingly induces one party to break his contract with another is liable to that other in tort in respect of any loss which may have been suffered by the breach.[306]

Secondly, insofar as the Judicial Committee in the *Strathcona* case drew an analogy with the rule in *Tulk v Moxhay*, this too will not bear examination. We have seen that the *Tulk v Moxhay* rule is now dependent upon the ownership of neighbouring land for the benefit of which the covenant was imposed: the person seeking to enforce the covenant must have a continuing proprietary interest in its enforcement.[307] But

---

[298] [1926] AC 108.   [299] Above, p 688.   [300] [1926] AC 108, 119.

[301] *Greenhalgh v Mallard* [1943] 2 All ER 234, 239.

[302] *Port Line Ltd v Ben Line Steamers Ltd* [1958] 2 QB 146, 168.

[303] *London CC v Allen* [1914] 3 KB 642, 658; *Barker v Stickney* [1919] 1 KB 121, 132.

[304] (1859) 4 De G & J 288.

[305] On the ground that the mortgagee had not interfered with performance of the charter until it was evident that the shipowner was wholly unable to perform it (at *ibid*, 299–300).

[306] *Lumley v Gye* (1853) 3 E & B 216. See also Wade (1926) 42 LQR 139; *The Lord Strathcona* [1925] P 143; below, p 690, n 310.

[307] See above, p 677.

a charterer under a voyage or time charterparty (even if of long duration) only has a personal right that the shipowner should continue to use the ship to perform the services which he has covenanted to perform. The charterer has no proprietary interest in the subject-matter of the contract, the ship.[308]

Although the principle stated by Knight Bruce LJ in *De Mattos v Gibson* was subsequently applied in cases of the mortgage of ships subject to a charterparty,[309] these are open to the same criticisms. The better view is that any right of the charterer to an injunction to restrain a use of the ship inconsistent with his charterparty arises if, but only if, the conduct of the purchaser is such as to constitute the tort of knowing interference with the charterer's contractual rights.[310]

There may, moreover, be alternative explanations for the decision in the *Strathcona* case. One is that there was an implied contract between the third party and the charterers, or a 'novation' of the original agreement,[311] for the Board pointed out: 'This is not a mere case of notice of the existence of a covenant affecting the use of the property sold, but it is the case of the acceptance of their property expressly *sub conditione*'.[312] Alternatively, there may be some ground for saying that the third party was in the position of a 'constructive trustee'[313] with obligations which a Court of Equity would not permit it to violate.[314]

With these reservations in mind, we have now to consider the scope of the decision. This was considered in *Port Line Ltd v Ben Line Steamers Ltd*:[315]

The ship *Port Stephens* was chartered to Port Line by its owner, Silver Line Ltd, on a time charter for 30 months from March 1955. In February 1956, Silver Line sold the ship to the defendant, it being agreed that the defendant should immediately charter the ship back to Silver Line by demise in order that it might fulfil its contract with Port Line. Unfortunately, this second charterparty contained the term that 'If the ship be requisitioned this charter shall thereupon cease', although no such clause appeared in the original time charterparty. The defendant was unaware of this disparity. In August 1956 the ship was requisitioned by the Crown, and as a result Port Line lost the use of the ship. Its claim against Silver Line was settled, but it then brought an action against the defendant to recover the whole or part

---

[308] *Port Line Ltd v Ben Line Steamers Ltd* [1958] 2 QB 146, 166 (Diplock J). Unless it is a charterparty by demise, when the charter could be said to acquire a 'possessory interest' in the vessel: see *Baumwoll Manufacturer Von Carl Scheibler v Furness* [1893] AC 8. See also *Lorentzen v White Shipping Co Ltd* (1943) 74 Ll LR 161.

[309] *Messageries Imperiales v Baines* (1863) 7 LT 763; *The Celtic King* [1894] P 175.

[310] *Lumley v Wagner* (1852) 1 De GM & G 604. See also *Torquay Hotel Co Ltd v Cousins* [1969] 2 Ch 106; *Acrow Ltd v Rex Chainbelt Inc* [1971] 1 WLR 1676; *Law Debenture Trust Corp v Ural Caspian Oil Corp Ltd* [1995] Ch 152. In *Swiss Bank Corp v Lloyd's Bank Ltd* [1979] Ch 548, 573 (revs'd [1982] AC 584), Browne-Wilkinson J stated that the principle of Knight Bruce LJ represented 'the counterpart in equity of the tort of knowing interference with contractual rights'. But although they may cover the same ground they are doctrinally distinct and subject to different requirements: see Cohen-Grabelsky (1982) 45 MLR 241, 265–7; Gardner (1982) 98 LQR 279, 289–93; Tettenborn [1982] CLJ 58, 82.

[311] See below, p 712.   [312] [1926] AC 108, 116.   [313] Cf above, p 671.

[314] [1926] AC 108, 125. See also *Swiss Bank Corp v Lloyd's Bank Ltd* [1979] Ch 548, 573 (revs'd [1982] AC 584).

[315] [1958] 2 QB 146.

of the compensation received by the defendant from the Crown in respect of the period of requisition.

Diplock J stated that the *Strathcona* case was wrongly decided but held that, even if it was correct, Port Line could not bring its claim within its principles, as the defendant had no knowledge at the time of its purchase of Port Line's rights under the time charter. The principle in the *Strathcona* case thus only applies where there is actual knowledge by the subsequent purchaser at the time of the purchase of the charterer's rights.[316] Constructive notice is insufficient.[317] Moreover, Diplock J considered that, even if notice had been shown, (a) the defendant was not in breach of duty to Port Line since it was not by its act that the vessel during the period of requisition was used inconsistently with the terms of Port Line's charter—it was by act of the Crown by title paramount—and (b) Port Line was not entitled to any remedy against the defendant except an injunction to restrain the defendant from using the vessel in a manner inconsistent with the terms of the charter.[318]

The charterer cannot obtain specific performance of the contract,[319] nor, it seems, damages or monetary compensation.[320] It would also seem that the Court will not be prepared to grant an injunction if the situation is such that, in any case, the vendor was incapable of further performing the charterparty,[321] or if, in the case of the mortgage of a vessel, the charter is such as substantially to impair the security.[322]

There is even more doubt as to whether the principle stated by Knight Bruce LJ in *De Mattos v Gibson*, and the decision in the *Strathcona* case, would apply to contracts under which the owner of a particular chattel, other than a ship, undertakes to use the chattel to perform its obligations to the other contracting party: for example, where the owner of a costly machine[323] agrees to use the machine to manufacture goods for the other party over a certain period. In *De Mattos v Gibson* Lord Chelmsford LC stressed that 'a vessel engaged under a charterparty ought to be regarded as a chattel of peculiar value to the charterer',[324] and it has been said that the *Strathcona* decision may be confined to 'the very special case of a ship under charterparty'.[325] Nevertheless, there would seem to be no reason why the immediate purchaser of a chattel should not be restrained by injunction if it commits or threatens to commit the tort of knowing

---

[316] [1958] 2 QB 146, 168.

[317] The doctrine of constructive notice does not apply to chattels (*Joseph v Lyons* (1884) 15 QBD 280, 287) nor to the contents of documents in commercial transactions (*Manchester Trust v Furness* [1895] 2 QB 539, 545).

[318] *Port Line Ltd v Ben Line Steamers Ltd* [1958] 2 QB 146, 167.

[319] *De Mattos v Gibson* (1859) 4 De G & J 277, 297.

[320] Although the form of the order made in the *Strathcona* case would seem to indicate that damages could be awarded, cf *Port Line Ltd v Ben Line Steamers Ltd* [1958] 2 QB 146, 169; *Law Debenture Trust Corp v Ural Caspian Oil Corp Ltd* [1993] 1 WLR 138, 144; revs'd on another ground [1995] Ch 152.

[321] *Lord Strathcona* [1925] P 143. See also above, p 689, n 305.   [322] *The Celtic King* [1894] P 175.

[323] *De Mattos v Gibson* (1858) 4 De G & J 276, 283 (Knight Bruce LJ).

[324] (1859) 4 De G & J 288, 299.

[325] *Clore v Theatrical Properties Ltd* [1936] 3 All ER 483, 490 (Lord Wright MR).

interference with such a contract.[326] The same would probably apply to any covenant by the owner of a chattel to use[327] or not to use[328] the chattel in a particular manner. But the relief granted against the third-party purchaser would depend upon the fact of tortious interference, and not upon notice of any 'interest' in the chattel.

Moreover, it is highly unlikely that any covenant affecting the use of a chattel would be held to 'run with the goods', so as to bind all persons who subsequently purchased the chattel with notice of the covenant.[329] There are good reasons why land-owners should be entitled to prevent neighbouring land from being put to a use that would be prejudicial to their property. But no such reasons would justify the imposition of incumbrances on chattels.[330]

(d) EXEMPTION CLAUSES BINDING THIRD PARTIES

An exemption clause will, as a general rule, only operate so as to take away the rights of the contracting parties, and not those of third parties who suffer injury or damage. In *Haseldine v CA Daw & Son Ltd*:[331]

The owners of a block of flats employed the defendant engineers to repair a lift in the building. Owing to their negligence, the lift was badly repaired and H, a visitor to the premises, was injured when the lift fell to the bottom of the lift-shaft.

The defendant was held liable in tort for negligence. Goddard LJ said:[332]

It is, however, argued that it is not right that a repairer who, as in the present case, has stipulated with the person who employs him that he shall not be liable for accidents, should none the less be made liable to a third person. The answer to this argument is that the duty to the third party does not arise out of the contract, but independently of it.

Nevertheless it has been held that a third party may be bound by an exemption clause where that clause relates to goods that have been bailed by the third party.

Bailment involves the transfer of possession (or an agreement to transfer possession) of goods to a person (the 'bailee') who holds (or agrees to hold) the goods either for

---

[326] See Cohen-Grabelsky (1982) 45 MLR 241; Gardner (1982) 98 LQR 279; Tettenborn [1982] CLJ 58.

[327] *Sefton v Tophams Ltd* [1965] Ch 1140 (land). But see *Clarke v Price* (1819) 2 Wils Ch 157; *Haywood v Brunswick Permanent Benefit Building Soc* (1876) 3 Ch D 694.

[328] *British Motor Trade Association v Salvadori* [1949] Ch 556 (covenant not to resell chattel). See also *Esso Petroleum Co Ltd v Kingswood Motors (Addlestone) Ltd* [1974] QB 142 (land); *Law Debenture Trust Corp v Ural Caspian Oil Corp Ltd* [1995] Ch 152 (shares).

[329] *Taddy v Sterious & Co* [1904] 1 Ch 354; *McGruther v Pitcher* [1904] 2 Ch 306; above, p 688.

[330] The position is different where there are competing 'proprietary' claims to the same goods. The starting point in resolving such title conflicts is *nemo dat quod non habet* ('one cannot give what one does not have'). But there are numerous exceptions to that which often protect a bona fide purchaser for value without notice.

[331] [1941] 2 KB 343. By the Occupiers Liability Act 1957, s 3(1), a contract made by an occupier of premises may increase its liability to non-parties beyond the common duty of care but may not reduce it below that duty. Cf, at common law, *Fosbroke-Hobbes v Airwork Ltd* [1937] 1 All ER 108, 112.

[332] [1941] 2 KB 343, 379.

or at the direction of the bailor, to whom they will be returned.[333] The hirer of a car is a bailee as is the dry cleaning firm which takes in a customer's clothes for cleaning. In many situations there will be a series of bailments and the question is whether, if the ultimate sub-bailee loses or damages the goods and is sued by the bailor either in tort or for breach of duties arising from the bailment,[334] it can rely on the terms of the contract it made with its immediate bailor as a defence. In *Morris v CW Martin & Sons Ltd*:[335]

Morris sent a mink stole to a furrier to be cleaned. The furrier did not clean furs himself, so, with Morris's consent, he delivered it for cleaning to the defendant, one of whose servants later stole it. The contract between the furrier and the defendant contained an exemption clause, on which the defendant sought to rely when sued by Morris.

On the facts the exemption clause was held, as a matter of construction, not to apply but Lord Denning MR said that, had it applied, in principle the defendant could have relied on it. Morris would be bound by the conditions if she had expressly or impliedly consented to the furrier making a sub-bailment containing those conditions. Since she had agreed that the furrier should send the stole to the defendant, she impliedly consented to his making a contract for cleaning on the terms current in the trade.[336]

In *KH Enterprise v Pioneer Container*[337] this principle was applied to a contract for the carriage of goods by sea:

KHE contracted for the carriage of goods from Taiwan to Hong Kong. The carrier was permitted to sub-contract 'on any terms' and did so to the defendant who took possession of the goods under bills of lading providing that any dispute was exclusively to be determined in Taiwan. The goods were lost and KHE sued in Hong Kong, contending that it was not bound by the exclusive jurisdiction clause because there was no contract between it and the defendants.

The Judicial Committee of the Privy Council stated that a person who voluntarily takes another person's goods into its custody holds them as bailee of that person (the owner) even if it does so without the owner's consent, but can only invoke the terms of the sub-bailment under which it received the goods from an intermediate bailee (the carrier) as qualifying its responsibility if the owner consented to them.[338] It held that consent to subcontract and therefore to sub-bail 'on any terms' was wide enough to constitute express consent to the clause and KHE was bound by it.

---

[333] *Palmer on Bailment* (3rd edn, 2009).
[334] For instance, only to deal with the goods in the manner authorized.   [335] [1966] 1 QB 716.
[336] *Ibid*, 729. See also Salmon LJ at 741. See also *Singer Co (UK) Ltd v Tees and Hartlepool Port Authority* [1988] 2 Lloyd's Rep 164; *The Captain Gregos (No 2)* [1990] 2 Lloyd's Rep 395, 405.
[337] [1994] 2 AC 324.
[338] *Ibid*, 342, disapproving *Johnson Matthey & Co Ltd v Constantine Terminals Ltd* [1976] 2 Lloyd's Rep 215. The principles in *The Pioneer Container* were applied in *Sonicare International Ltd v East Anglia Freight Terminal Ltd* [1997] 2 Lloyd's Rep 48 and *Spectra International plc v Hayesoak Ltd* [1997] 1 Lloyd's Rep 153.

Privity questions may also be avoided by the implication of a contract between the claimant and the third party. In *Pyrene Co Ltd v Scindia Navigation Co Ltd:*[339]

P sold to ISD in India certain fire-tenders 'fob London'. The defendant agreed with ISD to carry the tenders to India. The contract of carriage contained a clause limiting the liability of the defendant to £200. Owing to the negligence of the defendant, a tender was damaged while being loaded. But since it had not yet crossed the ship's side, it was still at P's risk. P made good the damage and sued the defendant for the loss, which amounted to more than £900.

Devlin J held that P was bound by the exemption clause. Although it was not a party to the contract of carriage, it was entitled to the benefits of the contract and had in consequence also to accept its liabilities. But this approach would constitute a wide-ranging exception to privity and has not subsequently found favour. In the *Midland Silicones* case it was stated that this decision could be supported 'only upon the facts of the case, which may well have justified the implication of a contract between the parties'.[340] It may therefore be an example of an implied contract, that is to say, all three parties intended P to participate in the contract of affreightment.

(e) THE CONTRACTS (RIGHTS OF THIRD PARTIES) ACT 1999

The Contracts (Rights of Third Parties) Act 1999 Act does not affect the principle that a third party to a contract cannot be subjected to a liability, or the burden of an exemption clause, in that contract.[341] This must be distinguished from the clarification in the Act that a benefit being enforced may be conditional. So, by section 1(4), a third party who wishes to enforce a term conferring a benefit on him or her can only do so subject to and in accordance with any other terms of the contract. Those other terms may impose burdens and conditions upon the enjoyment of any benefit.

FURTHER READING

COOTE, 'Consideration and the Joint Promisee' [1978] CLJ 301

FLANNIGAN, 'Privity—The End of an Era (Error)' (1987) 103 LQR 564

SMITH, 'Contracts for the Benefit of Third Parties: in Defence of the Third Party Rule' (1997) 17 OJLS 643

MACMILLAN, 'A Birthday Present for Lord Denning: The Contracts (Rights of Third Parties) Act 1999' (2000) 63 MLR 721

---

[339] [1954] 2 QB 402.

[340] [1962] AC 466, 471 (Viscount Simonds), and see at 470 where *Elder Dempster & Co Ltd v Paterson, Zochonis & Co Ltd* [1924] AC 522 was similarly explained. See also *Hispanica de Petroleos SA v Vencedora Oceanica SA, The Kapetan Markos NL (No 2)* [1987] 2 Lloyd's Rep 321, 331; *Comp Portorafti Comm SA v Ultramar Panama Inc, The Captain Gregos (No 2)* [1990] 2 Lloyd's Rep 395, 401–3.

[341] Hansard HL Debs 11 January 1999, col 21 (Lord Irvine LC).

Burrows, 'Contracts (Rights of Third Parties) Act 1999 and its implications for Commercial Contracts' [2000] LMCLQ 540

Burrows, 'No Damages for a Third Party's Loss' (2001) 1 Ox Univ Commonwealth LJ 107

Coote, 'The Performance Interest, Panatown and the Problem of Loss' (2001) 117 LQR 81

Treitel, *Some Landmarks of Twentieth Century Contract Law* (Oxford: Clarendon Press, 2002) ch 2

Stevens, 'The Contracts (Rights of Third Parties) Act 1999' (2004) 120 LQR 292

Beale, 'A Review of the Contracts (Rights of Third Parties) Act 1999' in Burrows and Peel (eds), *Contract Formation and Parties* (Oxford: Oxford University Press, 2010) 225

22

ASSIGNMENT

The benefit of a contract may, in certain circumstances, be transferred to a third party. This chapter considers assignment, that is to say, the transfer to C of B's contractual rights against A by means of an agreement between B (the assignor) and C (the assignee) irrespective of A's (the debtor's) consent.[1] After examining assignment, we will distinguish it from several similar concepts: vicarious performance, novation, and the transfer of rights and liabilities by operation of law on death and bankruptcy.

1. ASSIGNMENT

(a) NO ASSIGNMENT AT COMMON LAW

At common law the benefit of a contract could not be assigned so as to enable the assignee to bring an action upon it in its own name. This rule was sometimes expressed by the phrase 'a chose in action is not assignable'.

'"Choses in action" is a known legal expression used to describe all personal rights of property which can only be claimed or enforced by action, and not by taking physical possession.'[2] The contrasted term in a classification of types of personal property is 'chose in possession', which refers to tangible personal property, that is, goods. A chose in action is intangible personal property, that is, property that does not physically exist and cannot be physically possessed. A chose in action includes not only debts and all other contractual rights but rights to tort damages, intellectual property rights, shares, and equitable rights in a trust fund.[3] We are concerned here, however, only with the assignment of contractual rights.

The only exceptions to the no assignment rule allowed by the common law were assignments by or to the Crown.[4] The common law also recognized the law merchant by which rights to payment of a sum of money embodied in a negotiable instrument

---

[1] See generally Smith and Leslie, *The Law of Assignment* (2nd edn, 2013).

[2] *Torkington v Magee* [1902] 2 KB 427, 430 (Channell J); revs'd [1903] 1 KB 644.

[3] In *Investors Compensation Scheme Ltd v West Bromwich Building Society* [1998] 1 WLR 896 the House of Lords clarified that a right to rescind a mortgage is not a chose in action or part of a chose in action (and an owner cannot therefore assign a right to rescission separately from his property).

[4] *Master v Miller* (1791) 4 Term Rep 320, 340.

could be transferred by transfer of the instrument to a holder for value.[5] The reason for the non-recognition of assignments of choses in action seems to have been that the common law judges feared that to permit assignments would both undermine the doctrine of privity of contract and encourage unnecessary litigation and maintenance and champerty.[6] But even at common law it was (and still is) possible for the right to sue on a contract to be transferred to a third party by other, albeit cumbrous and unsatisfactory, means.

In the first place, the contracting party could give to the third party a power of attorney and thus enable the third party to sue the debtor as the contracting party's representative.[7]

Secondly, the contracting party could allow the third party to sue the debtor in the contracting party's name, taking from the third party an indemnity against costs.

Thirdly, with the consent and co-operation of the debtor, the contracting party could effect a transfer by means of a substituted agreement, or 'novation'.[8]

(b) ASSIGNMENT IN EQUITY: THE HISTORICAL BACKGROUND

Equity would permit the assignment of a chose in action, including debts and other contractual rights, whether such chose was equitable or legal.

(i) Equitable choses

An *equitable* chose is one which, before 1875, could only be enforced in the Court of Chancery, such as a share in a trust fund, a legacy, or a reversionary interest under a will. Where there was an assignment of an equitable chose, the assignee was allowed to proceed in its own name, and only an assignor who retained an interest in the action (eg if the assignment was not absolute but conditional) had to be made a party to it.[9] The reason for this was that since there was no claim that might be asserted by an action at law, the Court of Chancery had exclusive jurisdiction over the whole transaction; there was therefore no risk that the trustees of the fund (ie the debtors) would be exposed to a second action at law by the assignor.

(ii) Legal choses

A *legal* chose in action is one which, before 1875, could be enforced by an action at law, for example, a right under a contract, such as a debt or a claim under a policy of insurance. Equity would recognize the assignment of a legal chose in action, but had here to proceed more carefully. If equity itself enforced the claim of the assignee, that would not prevent the assignor from bringing an action at law; and the debtor would

---

[5] See the previous edition of this work, pp 677–82.

[6] *Lampert's Case* (1612) 10 Co Rep 46b, 48a; *Fitzroy v Cave* [1905] 2 KB 364, 372.

[7] *Re Bowden* [1936] Ch 71, 74.   [8] See below, p 712.

[9] *Goodson v Ellisson* (1827) 3 Russ. 583; *Cator v Croydon Canal Co* (1841) 4 Y & C Ex 593; *Donaldson v Donaldson* (1854) Kay 711.

have been put to the inconvenience of resorting to equity to restrain the assignor from enforcing the judgment on the ground that the assignee had already recovered in equity. Consequently, the Court of Chancery did not in the ordinary case enforce the assignee's claim. What it did was to infer from the assignment a duty on the assignor to exercise the right for the benefit of the assignee. On receiving a proper indemnity against costs, the assignor's duty was to permit the assignee to use the assignor's name so that the assignee might bring an action at law. If necessary, it would enforce this duty.[10] So whenever a legal chose in action was assigned in equity—and it could not be assigned otherwise—the action in a Court of law was brought in the assignor's name.[11] This was primarily in the interests of the party liable, so that it was not susceptible to more than one action; and partly in the interests of the assignor, who might dispute the assignment if he thought fit.

Since the Judicature Act 1873 an assignment in equity will be recognized by all divisions of the High Courts of Justice, whether it be of a legal or equitable chose in action. But the rules relating to such assignments (including the use of the assignor's name) are based on those in operation before the passing of the Act. These rules are examined in detail below, but it is first necessary to examine section 136(1) of the Law of Property Act 1925[12] which provides a form of statutory assignment.

(c) ASSIGNMENT UNDER THE LAW OF PROPERTY ACT 1925

By section 136(1) of the Law of Property Act 1925:

Any absolute assignment by writing under the hand of the assignor (not purporting to be by way of charge only) of any debt or other legal thing in action, of which express notice in writing has been given to the debtor, trustee or other person from whom the assignor would have been able to claim such debt or thing in action, is effectual in law (subject to equities having priority over the right of the assignee) to pass and transfer from the date of such notice—

(a) the legal right to such debt or thing in action;

(b) all legal and other remedies for the same; and

(c) the power to give a good discharge for the same without the concurrence of the assignor.

The effect of this section, provided the conditions laid down in it are fulfilled, is to allow the assignee to sue the debtor in its own name.[13]

---

[10] *Hammond v Messenger* (1838) 9 Sim 327.

[11] See, however, the statement of practice by Buller J in *Master v Miller* (1791) 4 Term Rep 320, 341, which shows that a Court of law did not always insist on the rule.

[12] This replaced and substantially reenacted the Judicature Act 1873, s 25(6). Other statutes have created specific further exceptions to the rule that there can be no assignment at law. For example, by the Policies of Assurance Act 1867, s 1 and by the Marine Insurance Act 1906, s 50(2), policies of life and marine insurance can be assigned, but the former Act requires notice to be given by the assignee to the insurance company. Stock and shares in a company are transferable under the Companies Act 2006, s 544 and the Stock Transfer Act 1963, and assignments of patents and copyright are regulated by the Patents Act 1977, ss 30 and 32 and the Copyright, Designs and Patents Act 1988, ss 90 and 94.

[13] *Warner Bros Records Inc v Rollgreen Ltd* [1976] QB 430. The assignee's right is subject to the right of a debtor who receives notice of a disputed assignment to call upon the persons giving notice to interplead.

This sub-section is merely machinery; it enables an action to be brought by the assignee in his own name in cases where previously he would have sued in the assignor's name, but only where he could so sue.[14]

It is necessary to examine the words of the section in some detail.

(i) 'Absolute' and not a charge

The Act requires the assignment to be 'absolute', that is, unconditional. This means that it must be an assignment of a sum due or about to become due, not of an amount which is dependent on any question as to the state of accounts between assignor and assignee. An assignment by way of charge is one which merely gives a right to payment out of a particular fund, and does not transfer the fund to the assignee.

If the assignment is to take effect or to cease upon the happening of a future uncertain event, so that the original debtor is uncertain as to the person in whom the right to receive the money is vested, it is not absolute. Thus in *Durham Brothers v Robertson*:[15]

A building contractor wrote to the claimants in the following terms: 'Re Building Contract, South Lambert Road. In consideration of money advanced from time to time we hereby charge the sum of £1,080, being the price . . . due to us from [the defendant] on the completion of the above buildings as security for advances, and we hereby assign our interest in the above-mentioned sum until the money with added interest be repaid to you'.

It was held that the assignment was not within the section. It was purporting to be by way of charge and so did not transfer the whole debt to the claimants unconditionally, but only until the advances were repaid. The defendant could not be sure that he was paying his debt to the right person without knowing the state of accounts between the assignor and assignee.

A further illustration is furnished by *Jones v Humphreys*:[16]

A schoolmaster, in consideration of a loan to him of £15, assigned to the claimant so much and such part of his income, salary and other emoluments from his employers as should be necessary and requisite for repayment of the sum borrowed (with interest) or of any further or other sums in which he might thereafter become indebted to the claimant.

It was held that this was not an absolute assignment, but was a mere security purporting to be by way of a charge. Even the assignment of a definite part of an existing debt, for example part of a sum deposited in a bank account,[17] is not absolute, but merely a charge upon the whole debt;[18] for otherwise it would be in the power of the original

---

[14] *Torkington v Magee* [1902] 2 KB 427, 435 (Channell J); *Marchant v Morton, Down & Co* [1901] 2 KB 829, 832.

[15] [1898] 1 QB 765. See also *Raiffeisen Zentralbank Österreich AG v Five Star General Trading LLC* [2001] EWCA Civ 68, [2001] QB 825.

[16] [1902] 1 KB 10. See also *Court Line Ltd v Akt Gøtaverken* [1984] 1 Lloyd's Rep 283.

[17] *Deposit Protection Board v Dalia* [1994] 2 AC 367.

[18] *Williams v Atlantic Assurance Co* [1933] 1 KB 81.

creditor 'to split up the single legal cause of action for the debt into as many separate legal causes of action as he might think fit',[19] thus obviously prejudicing the position of the debtor. But an assignment which passes the entire interest of the assignor in the debt (ie, it is a mortgage rather than a charge) is absolute despite the fact that it contains a proviso for redemption and reassignment on repayment.[20] The assignment cannot prejudice the debtor, who will receive notice first of the assignment, and then of the reassignment, if one is made. The debtor will always know to whom the debt is owed. There may, too, be an absolute assignment of a debt arising out of an existing contract, even though it does not become payable until a date later than the assignment.[21] All contracted rights are vested from the moment the contract is made, even if they are not presently enforceable.[22]

(ii) 'Writing'

The assignment must be in writing and signed by the assignor; signature by an agent may be insufficient.[23]

(iii) 'Notice'

The Act requires that notice in writing should be given to the debtor (although it does not specify which party must give the notice). This requirement has been strictly construed so that in a case where the debtor was unable to read and it was therefore thought useless to give him written notice, though the assignment was read over to him and understood by him, there was held to be no legal assignment.[24] The written notice, however, need not be in any particular form, provided that it sufficiently indicates the fact of the assignment.[25] The notice takes effect when it is received by the debtor.[26]

(iv) Consideration

An assignment under the Act does not require the assignee to have furnished consideration.[27]

(v) Rights assignable

The Act refers to 'any debt or other legal thing in action'.[28] This expression is not, as might appear at first sight, confined to legal choses in action, which were enforceable

---

[19] *Durham Brothers v Robertson* [1898] 1 QB 765, 774 (Chitty LJ); *Forster v Baker* [1910] 2 KB 636. See Hall [1959] CLJ 99.

[20] *Tancred v Delagoa Bay and East Africa Ry* (1889) 23 QBD 239. See also, eg, *Bexhill UK Ltd v Razzaq* [2012] EWCA Civ 1376 at [42]–[56].

[21] *G & T Earle Ltd v Hemsworth RDC* (1928) 44 TLR 758; *Care SS Corp v Latin American SS Corp* [1983] QB 1005.

[22] *Marathon Electrical Mfg Corp v Mashreqbank PSC* [1997] CLC 1090, approving Oditah, *Legal Aspects of Receivables Financing* (1991) 28–9.

[23] *Wilson v Wallani* (1880) 5 Ex D 155.   [24] *Hockley v Goldstein* (1922) 90 LJ KB 111.

[25] *Denny, Gasquet & Metcalfe v Conklin* [1913] 3 KB 177.

[26] *Holt v Heatherfield Trust Ltd* [1942] 2 KB 1.   [27] *Re Westerton* [1919] 2 Ch 104.

[28] See, eg *King v Victoria Insurance Co Ltd* [1896] AC 250; *Investors Compensation Scheme v West Bromwich BS* [1998] 1 WLR 896.

only in a Court of Common Law, but extends to choses in equity as well; that is, rights which a Court of Equity would have dealt with as being assignable.[29]

A 'legal thing in action' may therefore be defined as any right the assignment of which a Court of law or equity would, before the Judicature Act, have recognized or enforced.

(d) EQUITABLE ASSIGNMENT

We have seen that assignment was possible in equity but not at common law.[30] An assignment which does not comply with one or more of the requirements of section 136(1) of the Law of Property Act 1925 (eg because it is by way of charge or because no written notice has been given to the debtor) may still be a perfectly good and valid equitable assignment. 'The statute does not forbid or destroy equitable assignments or impair their efficacy in the slightest degree.'[31] But whereas a statutory assignee acquires a legal title to the chose assigned, an assignee in equity does not do so.[32] Thus a statutory assignee is entitled to bring an action without the necessity of joining the assignor as a party to the action, but an assignee in equity will not always enjoy this right.

(i) Joinder of the assignor

If the chose in action is *equitable*, the assignee is entitled to sue without joining the assignor as a party unless the assignor still has some interest in the suit.[33] This may arise where there is still some question of accounts outstanding between the assignor and the assignee, or where the assignment consists of a charge upon a trust fund. In such a case the parties interested must be made parties to the action so that the Court may make a final adjudication binding them all.

If the chose in action is *legal*, the assignee cannot normally recover damages or other relief without joining the assignor as a party to the action, if the assignor is willing as co-claimant, if not, as co-defendant.[34] Moreover the *assignor* of part of a debt cannot recover the balance in excess of the sum assigned without joining the assignee.[35] Attempts have been made to justify these requirements on the ground that they serve to protect the debtor who might otherwise pay the debt to the wrong person,[36] and that they allow an assignor who wishes to dispute the assignment to

---

[29] *Re Pain* [1919] 1 Ch 38; *Torkington v Magee* [1902] 2 KB 427, 430, revs'd on other grounds [1903] 1 KB 646.

[30] See above, pp 696–8.

[31] *Brandt's Sons & Co v Dunlop Rubber Co Ltd* [1905] AC 454, 461 (Lord Macnaghten). See also *Raiffeisen Zentralbank Österreich AG v Five Star General Trading LLC* [2001] EWCA Civ 68, [2001] QB 825.

[32] *Warner Bros. Records Inc v Rollgreen Ltd* [1976] QB 430.   [33] See above p 697.

[34] *Brandt's Sons & Co v Dunlop Rubber Co Ltd* [1905] AC 454; *Performing Right Society Ltd v London Theatre of Varieties Ltd* [1924] AC 1; *Williams v Atlantic Assurance Co* [1933] 1 KB 81; *The Aiolos* [1983] 2 Lloyd's Rep 25; *Weddell v JA Pearce & Major* [1988] Ch 26; *Three Rivers DC v Bank of England* [1996] QB 292; *Raiffeisen Zentralbank Österreich AG v Five Star General Trading LLC* [2001] EWCA Civ 68, [2001] QB 825 at [60].

[35] *Walter & Sullivan Ltd v J Murphy & Sons Ltd* [1955] 1 QB 584.   [36] *Ibid*, 588 (Parker LJ).

do so.[37] But the first reason is only relevant where the assignor retains an interest in the chose, and the second would apply even in the case of a statutory assignment, where the assignee is entitled to sue alone. Where the assignor retains no interest in the chose in action and the assignment only fails to be statutory, for example because it was not in writing or because no notice has been given, a requirement that the assignor be made a party to the proceedings would seem to serve no useful purpose.[38]

(ii) Form

No particular form is necessary for an equitable assignment, and, except where the interest assigned is an equitable interest or trust within section 53(1) of the Law of Property Act 1925,[39] it need not even be in writing. It may be addressed to the debtor or to the assignee. If it is addressed to the debtor:

It may be couched in the language of command. It may be a courteous request. It may assume the form of mere permission. The language is immaterial if the meaning is plain. All that is necessary is that the debtor should be given to understand that the debt has been made over by the creditor to some third person.[40]

In *Thomas v Harris*,[41] it was addressed to the assignee:

A father handed to his son certain insurance policies on his life with the request that the son should erect a tombstone in his memory, using the policy monies for this purpose. No notice was given to the insurance company.

It was held that, by this informal act, the father had assigned the policies to his son by way of charge for the cost of the tombstone. There was a valid equitable assignment.

While no formalities are required, it has been said in recent cases that there must be 'an outward expression by the assignor of his intention to make an immediate disposition of the subject matter of the assignment'.[42]

(iii) Notice

No notice to the debtor is necessary; the assignment is effective as between assignor and assignee from the moment it is made.[43] Notice is nevertheless *advisable* for several

---

[37] *Durham Brothers v Robertson* [1898] 1 QB 765, 770 (Chitty LJ).

[38] *The Aiolos* [1983] 2 Lloyd's Rep 25, 33–4; *Weddell v J A Pearce & Major* [1988] Ch 26, 40–1; *Raiffeisen Zentralbank Österreich AG v Five Star General Trading LLC* [2001] EWCA Civ 68, [2001] QB 825 at [60].

[39] *Grey v IRC* [1960] AC 1; *Oughtred v IRC* [1960] AC 206. Cf *Vandervell v IRC* [1967] 2 AC 291; *Neville v Wilson* [1997] Ch 144.

[40] *Brandt's Sons & Co v Dunlop Rubber Co Ltd* [1905] AC 454, 462 (Lord Macnaghten). See also *Allied Carpets Group Plc v MacFarlane* [2002] EWHC 1155, [2002] PNLR 38; *Burridge v MPH Soccer Management Ltd* [2011] EWCA Civ 835. But the assignment must either have been made by prior arrangement with, or be communicated to, the assignee: *Re Hamilton* (1921) 124 LT 737.

[41] [1947] 1 All ER 444.

[42] *Phelps v Spon-Smith & Co* [2001] BPIR 326 at [33]; *Coulter v Chief of Dorset Police* [2003] EWHC 3391 (Ch), [2004] 1 WLR 1425; *Finlan v Eyton Morris Winfield* [2007] EWHC 914 (Ch), [2007] 4 All ER 143.

[43] *Brandt's Sons & Co v Dunlop Rubber Co Ltd* [1905] AC 454, 462.

reasons. In the first place, the assignment will not bind the debtor until notice has been received, not necessarily in writing, of the assignment. So, if, before notice, the debtor pays the assignor, that is a good discharge of the debt[44] but if the debtor pays the assignor after notice that is no answer to a claim by the assignee.[45] Secondly, notice to the debtor is necessary to establish priority under the rule in *Dearle v Hall*, which we shall deal with later.[46] Thirdly, notice to the debtor will prevent the debtor from setting up new equities which may mature after the receipt of the notice.

(iv) Consideration

The question whether, as between assignor and assignee, consideration is necessary in an equitable assignment is a difficult one.[47] Equity will not assist a volunteer, and it has been said that 'for every equitable assignment . . . there must be consideration. If there be no consideration, there can be no equitable assignment'.[48] This statement is, however, much too wide, and it is by no means true to say that value is required in every case.

Valuable consideration for this purpose may consist in any consideration sufficient to support a simple contract.[49] Thus if A assigns to B the benefit of a contract in satisfaction of a debt owed by A to B, this is good consideration for the assignment. Similarly, if the assignment is by way of security for an existing debt in such circumstances that a forbearance to sue will be implied on the part of the assignee, this is sufficient to give the assignee a right to sue the debtor.[50] If consideration has been furnished by the assignee, no problem will arise; it is where the assignment is gratuitous that some doubt exists.

It is well established that a mere *agreement* to assign a chose in action must, like other contracts, have consideration to support it; if it is gratuitous, it is unenforceable.[51] An assignment of a future chose in action therefore requires consideration.[52] A future chose in action is a mere expectancy which may or may not materialize, such as a share of a trust fund which will be received only if an uncertain event occurs,[53] damages in an action which is still pending,[54] or the right to payments falling due under contracts not yet made.[55] Such an assignment can only operate as a contract to assign when

---

[44] *Stocks v Dobson* (1853) 4 De GM & G 15.

[45] *Deposit Protection Board v Dalia* [1994] 2 AC 367, 387 (CA), revs'd on other grounds, *ibid*.

[46] Below, pp 707–8.

[47] For a discussion of this subject see Megarry (1943) 59 LQR 58; Hollond (1943) 59 LQR 129; Sheridan (1955) 33 Can Bar Rev 284; Hall [1959] CLJ 99; Marshall, *The Assignment of Choses in Action* (1950) 109; Smith and Leslie, *The Law of Assignment* (2nd edn, 2013) paras 13.79–13.84.

[48] *Glegg v Bromley* [1912] 3 KB 474, 491 (Parker J).

[49] *Currie v Misa* (1875) LR 10 Ex 153; *Leask v Scott* (1877) 2 QBD 376, (1943) 59 LQR 208.

[50] *Glegg v Bromley* [1912] 3 KB 474.   [51] *Re McArdle* [1951] Ch 669.

[52] *Tailby v Official Receiver* (1888) 13 App Cas 523.

[53] *Re Ellenborough* [1903] 1 Ch 697. See also *Norman v Federal Commissioner of Taxation* (1963) 109 CLR 9 (future interest and dividends).

[54] *Glegg v Bromley* [1912] 3 KB 474.

[55] *E Pfeiffer Weinkellerei-Weineinkauf GmbH & Co v Arbuthnot Factors Ltd* [1988] 1 WLR 150; *Annangel Glory Comp Nav SA v M Golodetz, Middle East Marketing Corp Ltd* [1988] 1 Lloyd's Rep 45.

the subject-matter comes into existence, for 'nothing passes even in equity until the property comes into present existence';[56] it is therefore unenforceable unless value has been given.

But just as it is possible to make a gift of a chattel, so also it is possible to make a gift of (ie to transfer without consideration) a chose in action, provided that the transfer is effected in whatever manner is necessary for a transfer of that particular chose. Such a transfer, however, must, as it is said, be 'complete and perfect', for if anything remains to be done by the donor in order to give effect to the donor's intention, the gift will fail. Equity will not intervene to perfect an imperfect gift.[57] The question of consideration in equitable assignments turns, therefore, on whether any act remains to be done by the assignor in order to perfect the assignment; the assignor must have made every effort to complete the transaction.[58]

If the subject-matter assigned is an equitable chose in action, the assignment is complete when the assignor has unequivocally, even though informally, expressed an intention that the chose should henceforth belong to the assignee.[59] The assignee is then, as we have seen, in a position to enforce the right to the chose without more ado: 'such an assignment without any valuable consideration is not a mere agreement but is an actual transfer of the equitable right'.[60] But if the subject of the assignment is a legal chose in action, can a merely equitable assignment of it be said to be complete and perfect given that a statutory assignment could have been made which would have entitled the assignee to sue in its own name? That is the question on which the law is still not altogether clear. But as noted,[61] it is not now necessary for the assignee to ask the Court to compel the assignor to join as co-claimant, for an unwilling assignor can be made a defendant. In the result, an equitable assignee of a legal chose in action is able to enforce the rights under the contract against the debtor without seeking the aid either of the assignor or of the Court. In that sense the assignor has done all those things which it and only it could do[62] and there seems no reason why the assignment should not be regarded as complete and perfect without consideration.[63]

There may, of course, be other reasons why a particular equitable assignment is not complete and perfect, for example because the assignor fails to complete the transfer

---

[56] *Glegg v Bromley* [1912] 3 KB 474, 490 (Parker J).

[57] A similar principle is that in *Milroy v Lord* (1862) 4 De GF & J 264, 274. See also *Pennington v Waine* [2002] EWCA Civ 227, [2002] 1 WLR 2075.

[58] *Fortescue v Barnett* (1834) 3 My & K 36, (1943) 59 LQR 58, 61, 129; *Kekewich v Manning* (1851) 1 De F M & G 176, [1959] CLJ 99.

[59] *Voyle v Hughes* (1954) 2 Sm & G 18; *Re Wale* [1956] 1 WLR 1346; cf *Re Earl of Lucan* (1890) 45 Ch D 470 where an assignment which failed to create a complete and perfect charge on a reversionary interest was held to be unenforceable for want of consideration.

[60] *Voyle v Hughes* (1954) 2 Sm & G 18; *Letts v IRC* [1957] 1 WLR 201.   [61] Above, p 701.

[62] *Corin v Patton* (1990) 169 CLR 540 (High Court of Australia). Cf *Olsson v Dyson* (1969) 120 CLR 365.

[63] *Holt v Heatherfield Trust Ltd* [1942] 2 KB 1; *Harding v Harding* (1886) 17 QBD 442; *Re Patrick* [1891] 1 Ch 82; *Re Griffin* [1899] 1 Ch 408; *German v Yates* (1915) 32 TLR 52; *Re Rose* [1952] Ch 499; *Pulley v Public Trustee* [1956] NZLR 771; *Mascall v Mascall* (1984) 50 P & CR 119.

of shares or stock in the sole recognized form,[64] or because the necessary consent of a third party to the transfer has not been obtained.[65] But the better view is that, as between assignor and assignee, an equitable assignment of an existing chose in action, whether legal or equitable, is not rendered ineffective merely because there is no consideration.

(v) Transfer of rights?

The conventional view is that an equitable assignment, like a statutory assignment, involves a transfer of rights from the assignor to the assignee. However, this orthodox position has recently been challenged.[66] It has been argued that equitable assignment, as distinct from statutory assignment, does not involve any *transfer* of rights. Rather the assignee in equity is given new rights by the assignor in respect of the rights of the assignor which are still retained by the assignor: that is, the assignee's rights encumber the assignor's rights but the assignor's rights are not transferred. In effect, the assignor holds its rights on trust for the assignee. Although this theory runs counter to the prevailing view that all assignments involve a transfer and that an assignment in equity and a trust are different concepts, it does have the merit of providing a substantive reason, rather than a somewhat vague procedural explanation, for why the assignor must (at least normally) be joined to the assignee's action: that is, as the assignor retains the relevant rights it follows that the assignee's action must be brought in the assignor's name.

(e) ASSIGNEE TAKES 'SUBJECT TO EQUITIES'

Whether the assignment of a chose in action is statutory[67] or equitable,[68] the assignee takes 'subject to equities', that is, subject to all such defences as might have prevailed against the assignor. An assignee of contractual rights must therefore take care to ascertain the exact nature and extent of those rights; for no more than the assignor has to give can be taken and an assignee cannot be exempt from the effect of transactions by which the assignor may have lessened or invalidated the rights assigned.

(i) Claims arising out of contract assigned

The debtor is entitled to raise, by way of defence to an action brought by the assignee, all claims that directly arise out of the contract or transaction which forms the subject-matter of the assignment, whether such claims accrue before or after notice of the assignment is received. So, for example, despite the fact that the assignee is wholly

---

[64] *Milroy v Lord* (1862) 4 De GF & J 264. But such an 'assignment' could nevertheless take effect as a declaration of trust.

[65] *Re Fry* [1946] 312.   [66] Edelman and Elliott (2015) 131 LQR 228.

[67] The wording of the Law of Property Act 1925, s 136 is 'subject to equities having priority over the right of the assignee': see above, p 698.

[68] *Mangles v Dixon* (1852) 3 HLC 702, 731; *Crouch v Crédit Foncier of England* (1873) LR 8 QB 374, 380.

innocent and has given value for the contractual rights assigned, the debtor can rescind the contract on the ground that it was induced to enter into it by the fraud of the assignor[69] or set off a claim for unliquidated damages for breach of the contract by the assignor,[70] or obtain a stay where the assignor's action would have been stayed for failure to pay the costs of an earlier action.[71]

But a debtor with a tort claim against the assignor cannot set that claim up against an innocent assignee. The debtor is restricted to claims which arise out of the contract itself and do not exist independently of it. For instance, while, as we have seen, the debtor can assert a right to rescind a contract because of the fraud of the assignor, a claim for damages for fraud cannot be asserted by the debtor in proceedings by the assignee. Thus in *Stoddart v Union Trust*:[72]

The Union Trust were fraudulently induced by one Price to buy a newspaper called 'Football Chat' for the sum of £1,000, of which £200 was to be paid immediately, and the balance of £800 by instalments. Price assigned this £800 to the claimant, Stoddart, who took in good faith without knowledge of the fraud. When sued by Stoddart, the Union Trust pleaded that they had sustained damage exceeding £800 and that therefore no money was owed by them.

The Court of Appeal rejected this contention and held that the Union Trust could not set off their claim for damages against the assignee. Kennedy LJ said:[73]

The defendants are claiming damages for the fraud which induced them to enter into the contract on the footing that they are liable under it, and at the same time seeking to repudiate their obligation under it. The claim for damages is a personal claim against the wrong-doer; it is something dehors the contract.

The debtor may also not recover from the assignee hire paid to the assignee, even though the hire was to be repaid by the assignor to the debtor if unearned.[74]

(ii) Claims arising out of other transactions

Where a claim arises out of a contract or transaction other than the one which forms the subject-matter of the assignment, the debtor can set off such a claim against the assignee if but only if the claim accrues[75] *before the debtor has notice of the assignment.* An example is where money on deposit with a bank is assigned, but the bank has a claim against the assignor for taking up and paying bills of exchange.[76] The effect of notice is, therefore, in this case to prevent the debtor from setting up against the assignee any fresh equities which may mature. 'After notice of assignment of a chose

---

[69] *Graham v Johnson* (1869) LR 8 Eq 36; *Banco Santander SA v Bayfern Ltd* [2000] 1 All ER (Comm) 776 (letter of credit).

[70] *Young v Kitchin* (1878) 3 Ex D 127; *Newfoundland Government v Newfoundland Ry* (1888) 13 App Cas 199. See also *Bank of Boston Connecticut v European Grain and Shipping Ltd* [1989] AC 1056 (if debtor's claim against assignor could not be set off against debt, it cannot be set off against assignee).

[71] *Sinclair v British Telecommunications plc* [2000] 2 All ER 461, 469.   [72] [1912] 1 KB 181.

[73] *Ibid*, 194.   [74] *Pan Ocean Shipping Co Ltd v Creditcorp Ltd* [1994] 1 WLR 161.

[75] *Business Computers Ltd v Anglo-African Leasing Ltd* [1977] 1 WLR 578.

[76] *Re Pinto Leite and Nephews* [1929] 1 Ch 221.

in action the debtor cannot by payment or otherwise do anything to take away or diminish the rights of the assignee as they stood at the time of the notice'.[77]

(iii) Assignee cannot recover more than assignor

A further aspect of the idea that an assignee takes an assignment 'subject to equities' is the principle that an assignee cannot recover more from the debtor than the assignor could have done had there been no assignment.[78] In recent years, the principle has given rise to particular difficulties where damaged or defective buildings have been sold along with the assignment of claims in contract or tort relating to the building. But the problem of damages disappearing into some 'legal black hole' has now been solved by the Court of Appeal's clarification in *Offer-Hoar v Larkstore Ltd*[79] that, in applying in this context the principle that the assignee cannot recover more than the assignor, one should be asking what damages the assignor could itself have recovered had there been no assignment and *had there been no transfer of the land* to the assignee. Substantial damages were therefore recoverable by the assignee where an assignor had sold its land to an assignee along with, or prior to, the assignment of the relevant cause of action relating to the land.

The problem has, in any event, normally been circumvented because of the Courts' recognition that, where a third party is, or will become, owner of the defective or damaged property, there is an exception to the general rule that a contracting party can recover damages only for its own loss and not the loss of the third party.[80] Where the exception applies, the contracting party (the assignor) is entitled to substantial damages for the loss suffered by the third party (the assignee): by the same token, there is no question of an award of substantial damages to the assignee infringing the principle that the assignee cannot recover more than the assignor.

(f) PRIORITIES

It may happen that an assignor makes two or more assignments of the same chose in action (whether statutory or equitable) to different assignees. If the fund is insufficient to meet all the claims, a problem of their respective priorities will arise. The rule is that *assignments have priority according to the priority of notice*.[81] The successive assignees of an obligation rank as to their title, not according to the dates at which the creditor assigned the contractual rights to them respectively, but according to the dates at which notice was given to the party to be charged. This rule is generally known as the

---

[77] *Roxburghe v Cox* (1881) 17 Ch D 520, 526 (James LJ).

[78] *Dawson v Great Northern & City Railway Co* [1905] 1 KB 260.

[79] [2006] EWCA Civ 1079, [2006] 1 WLR 2926. This was applied in *Landfast (Anglia) Ltd v Cameron Taylor One Ltd* [2008] EWHC 343 (TCC), (2008) 117 Con LR 53.

[80] *Linden Gardens Trust Ltd v Lenesta Sludge Disposals Ltd* [1994] 1 AC 85; *Darlington BC v Wiltshier Northern Ltd* [1995] 1 WLR 68; *Alfred McAlpine Construction Ltd v Panatown Ltd* [2001] 1 AC 518. The exception is based on *Dunlop v Lambert* (1839) 6 Cl & F 600 and *The Albazero* [1977] AC 774. See above, p 653.

[81] *Marchant v Morton, Down & Co* [1901] 2 KB 829.

rule in *Dearle v Hall*.[82] The reason lying behind it seems to be that, by failing to give notice to the debtor, the first assignee has enabled the assignor to make a second, and possibly fraudulent, assignment to the subsequent assignee. Accordingly, even though the first assignee's assignment was first in time, it ought to be postponed to the later assignment.

But the first assignee will only be postponed to a subsequent assignment of which prior notice has been given, if, at the time of the first assignment, the second assignee had no knowledge of the previous assignment.[83] A second assignee who had such knowledge could scarcely claim to have been misled.

Except where the interest assigned is an equitable interest in land or in personalty, when the notice must be in writing,[84] no special form is required for a notice to gain priority. Provided it is clear and unequivocal, and brought home to the party charged, oral notice is sufficient. Even a notice in a newspaper read by the debtor has been held to suffice.[85] If the interest assigned is an equitable interest in a trust fund, it is advisable to give notice to all the trustees in order to be perfectly safe; otherwise notice given to one trustee alone may determine with his death or resignation.[86]

(g) RIGHTS NOT ASSIGNABLE

Some choses in action are not assignable, and not every right which arises under or out of a contract can be assigned. These restrictions apply to both statutory and equitable assignments.

(i) Assignment prohibited by contract

In the first place, the contract itself may expressly provide that the rights arising under it, or some of them, shall not be assignable. In such a case, a purported assignment of those rights will be invalid as against the debtor,[87] although it may be effective as between assignor and assignee[88] and enable the assignee to sue the assignor for breach of contract.[89] It has also been held that a clause prohibiting

---

[82] (1823) 3 Russ 1. See generally *E Pfeiffer Weinkellerei-Weinenkauf GmbH & Co v Arbuthnot Factors Ltd* [1988] 1 WLR 150; Beale, Bridge, Gullifer, and Lomnicka, *The Law of Security and Title-Based Financing* (2nd edn, 2012) paras 14.09–14.20; Smith and Leslie, *The Law of Assignment* (2nd edn, 2013) paras 27.48–27.105; Oditah (1989) 9 OJLS 513; De Lacy [1999] Conv 311.

[83] *Re Holmes* (1885) 29 Ch D 786. [84] Law of Property Act 1925, s 137(3).

[85] *Lloyd v Banks* (1868) LR 3 Ch App 488. [86] *Re Phillips' Trusts* [1903] 1 Ch 183.

[87] *Helstan Securities Ltd v Hertfordshire CC* [1978] 3 All ER 262; *Linden Gardens Trust Ltd v Lenesta Sludge Disposals Ltd* [1994] 1 AC 85, 103; *Hendry v Chartsearch Ltd* [1998] CLC 1382; *British Energy Power & Energy Trading Ltd v Credit Suisse* [2007] EWHC 1428 (Comm), [2007] 2 Lloyd's Rep 427; *Ruttle Plant Ltd v Secretary of State for the Environment and Rural Affairs* [2007] EWHC 2870 (TCC), [2008] 2 All ER (Comm) 264; Goode (1979) 42 MLR 553; Allcock [1983] CLJ 328; Turner [2008] LMCLQ 306; Goode [2009] LMCLQ 330; Akseli [2009] JBL 650; Tolhurst and Carter [2014] CLJ 405.

[88] *Re Turcan* (1888) 40 Ch D 5; *Re Westerton* [1919] 2 Ch 104. Contrast *Spellman v Spellman* [1961] 1 WLR 921, 928, but cf at 925.

[89] *R v Chester & North Wales Legal Aid Office, ex p Queensferry Ltd* [1998] 2 BCLC 436; *Bawejem Ltd v MC Fabrications Ltd* [1999] 1 All ER (Comm) 377.

assignment does not necessarily prohibit a declaration of trust in favour of a third party.[90]

(ii) Bare right of action

Secondly, it is said that by reason of the rules against champerty and maintenance[91] a mere right to sue for damages (a 'bare right of action') cannot be assigned.[92] However, rights of action arising out of or incidental to rights of property can be assigned with the property transferred. Thus the purchaser of an estate was permitted to sue for damages for breaches of covenant committed by the vendor's tenants before the sale,[93] and the purchaser of land injuriously affected by a railway was permitted to claim compensation in respect of damages already sustained.[94] Again, a debt, as opposed to a mere right to sue for damages, is assignable:[95] the practice of 'selling' debts to debt-collecting agencies ('factoring') could not be carried on if the law were otherwise. Further, in *Trendtex Trading Corporation v Crédit Suisse*,[96] the House of Lords made it clear that even an assignment of a bare right of action may be upheld if the assignee has a 'genuine commercial interest' in taking the assignment. An assignment to an insurer, who has indemnified the insured under a policy of insurance, of the insured's right of action has been held valid on the ground that the insurer has a legitimate interest in recouping the loss sustained by paying out on the policy.[97] Likewise, an assignee who has financed the transaction giving rise to the right of action assigned will have a legitimate commercial interest in taking the assignment if its sole object is to enable the assignee to recoup its loss on the transaction.[98]

On the other hand, in the *Trendtex* case, the purchase with a view to profit of a right of action arising out of the breach and repudiation of a letter of credit was held to be invalid in English law as 'savouring of maintenance', since it involved trafficking in litigation.[99] But where the assignee has a genuine commercial interest an assignment by a party unable to fund litigation to recover damages for breach of contract to a

---

[90] *Don King Productions Inc v Warren* [2000] Ch 291; *Barbados Trust Co Ltd v Bank of Zambia* [2007] EWCA Civ 148, [2007] 1 Lloyd's Rep 494, noted by Smith (2008) 124 LQR 517; *Co-operative Group Ltd v Birse Developments Ltd* [2014] EWHC 530 (TCC), [2014] BLR 359.

[91] See above, p 422. This principle is unaffected by the abolition of the torts and crimes of champerty and maintenance: see Criminal Law Act 1967, s 14(2).

[92] *De Hoghton v Money* (1866) LR 2 Ch App 164; *May v Lane* (1894) 64 LJ QB 236; *Torkington v McGee* [1902] 2 KB 427, 433 (decision rvs'd [1903] 1 KB 644); *Defries v Milne* [1913] 1 Ch 98. Cf *Glegg v Bromley* [1912] 3 KB 474 (fruits of action).

[93] *Defries v Milne* [1913] 1 Ch 98; *Ellis v Torrington* [1920] 1 KB 399.

[94] *Dawson v GN & City Ry* [1905] 1 KB 260.

[95] *Ellis v Torrington* [1920] 1 KB 399, 411; *Camdex International Ltd v Bank of Zambia* [1998] QB 22.

[96] [1982] AC 679, 694, 696, 697, 703. For criticism of the *Trendtex* test and a call for a reconsideration of this area of the law so that assignments of rights to compensation are recognized as valid, subject to a few specific exceptions, see Tettenborn [2007] LMCLQ 392.

[97] *Compania Colombiana de Seguros v Pacific Steam Navigation Co* [1965] 1 QB 101.

[98] *Trendtex Trading Cpn v Crédit Suisse*, above, n 96, 694, 696, 697, 703 (but not if the object is to sell on to and divide the 'spoils' with a subsequent assignee).

[99] See also *Re Trepca Mines Ltd (No 2)* [1963] Ch 199; *Laurent v Sale & Co* [1963] 1 WLR 829; *Re Oasis Merchandising Services Ltd* [1998] Ch 170.

person who can, where the object and effect of the assignment is to enable the litigation to be funded, is not contrary to public policy or unlawful[100] unless there is an obvious disproportion between the assignee's true interest and what it bargained to receive under the assignment.[101] In *Simpson v Norfolk & Norwich University Hospital NHS Trust*[102] it was held, after a detailed consideration of the issue, that while an action for damages for personal injury is capable of being assigned, the claimant in the case had no legitimate interest in the claim (applying the *Trendtex* test) and the assignment plainly savoured of champerty. The assignment was therefore void.

(iii) Personal relationship

Thirdly, where there is a relationship of personal confidence between the parties, or their personal qualifications are of the essence of a contract, one party cannot assign the right to the performance of the obligations of the other, since to do so would be to alter the nature of the contract without the other's consent.

So, for example, a cake manufacturer was held not to be able to assign the right to be supplied with 'all the eggs he should require for manufacturing purposes for one year' to a new company on the amalgamation of the business.[103] What the supplier had undertaken to do was to supply all the eggs that the manufacturer, and not all that any other person or company, should require. Moreover, the manufacturer had undertaken not to buy eggs elsewhere and this introduced a personal element which was most material to the contract. This undertaking would not be binding on the assignee, so that the supplier would be deprived of its benefit. For a similar reason, a motor insurance policy cannot be assigned to the purchaser if the car is sold, unless the insurance company consents to the assignment, for that would be to 'thrust a new assured upon a company against its will'.[104] On the other hand, where it appears from the nature of the contract that no special personal considerations are involved, so that it can make no difference to the party on whom an obligation rests whether the performance is rendered for the original contracting party or another, then the right to the performance of an obligation may be assigned.[105] Moreover, as noted, the fact that a contract is non-assignable has been held not to preclude the making of a declaration of trust of the benefit of the contract for a third party.[106]

The paradigm example of a personal contract is a contract of employment but, although at common law an employer could not assign its rights under contracts of employment with employees if it transferred the business without consent,[107] the

---

[100] *Norglen Ltd v Reeds Rains Prudential Ltd* [1999] 2 AC 1; *Circuit Systems Ltd v Zuken-Redac (UK) Ltd* [1997] 1 WLR 721.

[101] *Advanced Technology Structures Ltd v Cray Valley Products Ltd* [1993] BCLC 723.

[102] [2011] EWCA Civ 904, [2012] QB 640.   [103] *Kemp v Baerselman* [1906] 2 KB 604.

[104] *Peters v General Accident and Life Assurance Corp Ltd* [1937] 4 All ER 628, 633 (Goddard J).

[105] *Tolhurst v Associated Portland Cement Manufacturers (1900) Ltd* [1903] AC 414; *Shayler v Woolf* [1946] Ch 320.

[106] *Don King Productions Inc v Warren* [2000] Ch 291.

[107] *Nokes v Doncaster Amalgamated Collieries Ltd* [1940] AC 1014, 1026; *Newns v British Airways* (1992) 21 IRLR 575, 576.

position has been altered by legislation. On transfers of a business by sale, other disposition or by operation of law (eg on insolvency), there is a statutory novation by which all rights, powers, duties, and liabilities under a contract of employment operate between the employee and the transferee[108] unless the employee gives notice that he or she objects to being employed by the transferee.

(iv) Miscellaneous

Finally, for reasons of public policy, no assignment may be made of the salary of a public officer paid out of national funds (eg of a civil servant's pay),[109] of maintenance granted to a wife,[110] or of benefits under social security legislation.[111]

(h) LIABILITIES CANNOT BE ASSIGNED

The burden of a contract can never be assigned without the consent of the other party to the contract.[112] Everybody has a right to choose who should perform a contractual obligation for him so that a promisee should not be compelled, by reason of an agreement between the promisor and a third party, to accept any but the promisor as the person liable on the promise.

The rule is illustrated by the case of *Robson and Sharpe v Drummond*:[113]

S hired a carriage to D for 5 years, undertaking to paint it every year and to keep it in repair. R was the partner of S, but the contract was made with S alone. After 3 years S retired from business, and D was informed that R was thenceforth answerable for the painting and repair of the carriage and would receive the payments. D refused to deal with R, and returned the carriage.

It was held that he was entitled to do so. Lord Tenterden stated:[114]

[T]he defendant may have been induced to enter into this contract by reason of the personal confidence which he reposed in [S], and therefore have agreed to pay money in advance. The . . . defendant had a right to object to its being performed by any other person, and to say that he contracted with [S] alone, and not with any other person.

Parke J stated that D 'had a right to have the benefit of the judgment and taste of [S] to the end of the contract'.[115]

Although liabilities cannot be assigned, the 'conditional benefit' principle means that rights assigned may themselves be qualified or conditional, the condition being that certain restrictions be observed or certain obligations assumed.[116] In such situations,

---

[108] Transfer of Undertakings (Protection of Employment) Regulations 2006 (SI 2006 No 246).
[109] See above, p 419.   [110] *Re Robinson* (1884) 27 Ch D 160.
[111] eg Social Security Administration Act 1992, s 187.
[112] *Linden Gardens Trust Ltd v Lenesta Sludge Disposals Ltd* [1994] 1 AC 85, 103.
[113] (1831) 2 B & Ad 303.   [114] *Ibid*, 307.   [115] *Ibid*, 308.
[116] *Tolhurst v Associated Portland Cement Manufacturers Ltd* [1903] AC 414; *Tito v Waddell (No 2)* [1977] Ch 106, 290–307. See also *Pan Ocean Shipping Co Ltd v Creditcorp Ltd, The Trident Beauty* [1994] 1 WLR 161, 171.

an assignee who takes the benefit of the contract must also bear the burden.[117] The question whether a contract creates a conditional benefit is one of construction.[118]

2. VICARIOUS PERFORMANCE

At first sight, an exception to the rule that there can be no assignment of liabilities is that there may be circumstances which make it permissible for a contracting party to perform its side of the contract by getting someone else to do in a satisfactory fashion the work for which the contract provides. If A undertakes to do work for B which needs no special skill, and it does not appear that A has been selected with reference to any personal qualification, B cannot complain if A sub-contracts the work to an equally competent subcontractor. Such cases are sometimes loosely referred to as assignments of a contractual liability, but they are really instances of the *vicarious performance* of a contract. This is because the original contracting party remains liable on the contract and, as a rule, is the only person entitled to sue for payment. This is clearly stated by Lord Greene MR in *Davies v Collins*:[119]

In many contracts all that is stipulated for is that the work shall be done and the actual hand to do it need not be that of the contracting party himself; the other party will be bound to accept performance carried out by somebody else. The contracting party, of course, is the only party who remains liable. He cannot assign his liability to a subcontractor, but his liability in those cases is to see that the work is done, and if it is not properly done he is liable. It is quite a mistake to regard that as an assignment of the contract; it is not.

The circumstances in which a contract may be vicariously performed, which are similar to those which determine whether a contractual right is assignable, are discussed in Chapter 12.

3. NOVATION

Another way by which the benefit or burden of a contract may be transferred to a third party is with the co-operation of all the parties.

If A owes M £100, and M owes X £100, it may be agreed between all three that A shall pay X instead of M, which thus terminates M's legal relationship with either party. In such a case the consideration for A's promise to pay X is the discharge by X of M's debt; for M's discharge of A, the promise of A to pay X; for X's discharge of M, the discharge by M of A's debt to M.

This is in effect the rescission of one contract and the substitution of a new one in which the same acts are to be performed by different parties. This is called a novation and

---

[117] For doubt cast on a wide 'pure principle of benefit and burden', see *Rhone v Stephens* [1994] 2 AC 130.
[118] *Tito v Waddell (No 2)* [1997] Ch 106, 302.
[119] [1945] 1 All ER 247, 249. See also *Stewart v Reavell's Garage* [1952] 2 QB 545.

it can only take place by an agreement supported by consideration[120] between all the parties. Novation is not, therefore, 'compulsory';[121] and precisely because it involves the consent of all three parties it cannot properly be regarded as an assignment.

As novation is different from assignment, it follows that the rule that assignment is 'subject to equities' does not apply to novation. Say, for example, a contract was induced by a misrepresentation and there has then been an assignment by the person making the misrepresentation: the debtor can rely on the misrepresentation vis-à-vis the assignee. In contrast, it is irrelevant to a novation that the original contract was induced by a misrepresentation. Once there has been a novation, the original contract has been extinguished and with it the power to rescind for the original misrepresentation.

4. ASSIGNMENT BY OPERATION OF LAW

So far we have dealt with the voluntary assignment by parties to a contract of the benefit of the contract. But rules of law may also operate to transfer these rights, or contractual liabilities, from one to another. Two areas are here considered: death and bankruptcy.

(a) THE EFFECT OF DEATH

The general rule is that rights and liabilities under a contract pass, on the death of a party to the contract, to his or her personal representatives. They can, therefore, both sue, and be sued,[122] on the contract made by the deceased.

But performance of such contracts as depend upon the personal service or skill of the deceased cannot be demanded of personal representatives, nor can they insist upon offering such performance, though they can sue for money earned by the deceased and unpaid at the time of the death.[123] Contracts of agency and of personal service expire with the death of either of the parties to them; thus an apprenticeship contract is terminated by the death of the master, and no claim to the services of the apprentice survives to the executor or administrator.[124]

(b) BANKRUPTCY

Bankruptcy is regulated by the Insolvency Act 1986. Proceedings commence with the filing of a petition for a bankruptcy order either by a creditor alleging acts of bankruptcy against the debtor or by the debtor alleging inability to pay

---

[120] *Commissioners of Customs and Excise v Diners Club Ltd* [1988] 2 All ER 1016, 1023, aff'd [1989] 1 WLR 1196.

[121] Approved in *Re United Railways of the Havana and Regla Warehouses Ltd* [1960] Ch 52, 84, revs'd in part on other grounds *sub nom Tomkinson v First Pennsylvania Banking and Trust Co* [1961] AC 1007.

[122] But only to the extent of the assets of the estate.

[123] *Stubbs v Holywell Railway Co* (1867) LR 2 Ex 311.   [124] *Baxter v Burfield* (1746) 2 Stra 1266.

the debts.[125] Where the grounds of the petition are established the Court may, in an appropriate case, appoint an insolvency practitioner to ascertain whether the debtor is willing to make a proposal for a voluntary arrangement and a meeting of the creditors should be summoned.[126]

If the creditors decide not to accept a composition or scheme of arrangement, the Court makes a bankruptcy order and a trustee is appointed. To the trustee passes 'all property belonging to or vested in the bankrupt at the commencement of the bankruptcy',[127] or property which may be acquired by or has devolved upon the bankrupt since the commencement of the bankruptcy.[128] The object of the laws of bankruptcy is that 'every beneficial interest which the bankrupt has shall be disposed of for the benefit of his creditors'.[129] It suffices to note that:

(1) Where any part of the property of the bankrupt consists of a chose in action, it is deemed to have been assigned to the trustee.[130]

(2) The trustee may disclaim, and so discharge, unprofitable contracts.[131]

(3) The trustee is excluded from suing for personal injuries arising out of breaches of contract, such as injuries to reputation or credit.[132]

(4) Executory contracts personal to the bankrupt do not pass.[133]

The trustee, as statutory assignee of the bankrupt's choses in action, is in one respect in a more favourable position than an ordinary assignee. If a chose in action has been assigned by the bankrupt *before* the bankruptcy took place, the assignment will be void as against the trustee if (i) it is of a future chose in action for which the consideration is not supplied until after the commencement of the bankruptcy[134] or (ii) it is a general assignment of book debts by a trader and has not been registered under the Bills of Sale Act 1878.[135]

---

[125] Insolvency Act 1986, ss 264–72. Cf the Enterprise and Regulatory Reform Act 2013, which has not yet been brought into force.

[126] Insolvency Act 1986, ss 273–4.

[127] Insolvency Act 1986, s 283(1). 'Property' includes 'things in action': *ibid*, s 436. Between the date of the order and the appointment of the trustee the official receiver is under a duty to act as receiver and manager of the estate: *ibid*, s 287.

[128] Insolvency Act 1986, s 307.   [129] *Smith v Coffin* (1795) 2 H Bl 444, 461.

[130] Insolvency Act 1986, s 311(4). Where there is a cross-claim what is assigned is a claim to the net balance: *ibid*, s 323; *Stein v Blake* [1996] AC 243.

[131] Insolvency Act 1986, s 315. An administrative receiver of a company becomes liable on any contract of employment 'adopted' by him: *ibid*, s 44; *Powdrill v Watson* [1995] 2 All ER 65.

[132] *Wilson v United Counties Bank* [1920] AC 102 (credit); *Re Kavanagh* [1949] 2 All ER 264, aff'd [1950] 1 All ER 39n (reputation). Cf *Beckham v Drake* (1849) 2 HLC 579 (wrongful dismissal). See *Heath v Tang* [1993] 1 WLR 1421.

[133] *Gibson v Carruthers* (1841) 8 M & W 321 (contract to marry); *Lucas v Moncrieff* (1905) 21 TLR 683 (contract to publish book).

[134] *Wilmot v Alton* [1897] 1 QB 17; *Re Collins* [1925] Ch 556; *Re de Marney* [1943] Ch 126. Cf *Re Davis & Co* (1888) 22 QBD 193; *Re Trytel* [1952] 2 TLR 32.

[135] Insolvency Act 1986, s 344.

23

AGENCY

Agency is the relationship which exists where one person (the principal) authorizes another (the agent) to act on its behalf and the agent agrees to do so.[1] Although agency can be relevant in various areas of the law (eg tort and unjust enrichment), this book is solely concerned with the agent making contracts with others for a principal.

For an agent to act on behalf of its principal in making contracts with other parties, the agent must have the principal's authority. Where a (bilateral) contract is concluded by an agent for its principal, the principal can both sue and be sued on the contract (although, if the agent's authority is merely ostensible, rather than actual, the principal cannot sue unless it has ratified the contract). So, one *could* argue that the whole law of agency in contract is an exception to, or a way round, the doctrine of privity.[2] The principal, albeit in one sense a stranger to the contract concluded by its agent, is able to sue and be sued on that contract.

However, in most circumstances, one can say without any fiction that the principal, not the agent, is the party to the contract concluded by the agent. Indeed in most circumstances the agent will not be named in the contract and will drop out of the picture once the contract has been concluded. But that is generally not the case where one has an undisclosed principal: that is, where the other party has not been informed, and hence does not know, that she is dealing with an agent rather than with a principal.[3] Where the principal is undisclosed, the agent usually does not drop out of the picture: in general, the agent, as well as the principal, can sue and be sued on the contract. Therefore, it is artificial to say that the principal, not the agent, is the party to the contract. Where the principal is undisclosed, the other party has no knowledge of the principal's existence and may find that she is in a contractual relationship with someone of whom she has never heard and with whom she never intended to contract.

It follows that, whatever one says about agency where there is a disclosed principal, agency where the principal is undisclosed is clearly an exception to, or way of avoiding, the doctrine of privity, Indeed, it avoids not only the benefit side of privity but also the burden side: the undisclosed principal can both sue, and be sued by, the other party.

---

[1] The leading textbook on this subject is *Bowstead and Reynolds on Agency* (20th edn, 2014). See generally Dowrick (1954) 17 MLR 24; McMeel (2000) 116 LQR 387. See also the ALI, *Restatement, Agency* (3d, 2006).

[2] See above, p 671.   [3] See below, pp 724–6.

Even when confined to contracts, this chapter is not concerned with all the relevant law on agency which includes, for example, the fiduciary duties owed by the agent to the principal, how one terminates an agency, and the rights of commercial agents in the event of termination under the Commercial Agents (Council Directive) Regulations 1993.[4] Instead, the focus is on understanding how agency may be regarded as an exception to, or a way round, the privity doctrine. The relevant material will be divided into two parts: first, the creation of agency; and, secondly, the effects of agency in respect of the contractual relations between the principal and the third party and between the agent and the third party.

1. MODES OF CREATION

Agency may be created in any one of three main ways:[5]

(1) by an actual authority to contract given by the principal to the agent;

(2) by the principal's ratification of a contract entered into by the agent on the principal's behalf but without its authority (ie, the authority is retrospectively conferred);

(3) by an ostensible authority conferred by the principal on the agent even though no actual authority has been given.

In the first two cases, the principal can sue and be sued by the third party and rights and duties also arise between the principal and the agent. In the last case, the principal can be sued but cannot always sue. We shall deal with each of these in turn.

(a) ACTUAL AUTHORITY

Actual authority to contract may be express or implied.

Normally the authority given by a principal to its agent is an express authority enabling the latter to bind the former by acts done within the scope of that authority. Such authority may, in general, be given orally. But in some cases it is necessary that the authority should be given in a special form. First, in order that an agent may make a binding contract by deed, it is necessary that authority should normally be given in a deed.[6] Certain transactions, for example, conveyances of land, must still be made by deed.[7] Secondly, the Law of Property Act 1925,[8] which requires the creation or

---

[4] SI 1993 No 3053.

[5] This chapter does not consider the law on 'agency of necessity': for that law, see the previous edition of this book at pp 694–696.

[6] *Bowstead and Reynolds on Agency* (20th edn, 2014) Art 10.

[7] See above, p 82. On formalities for the creation of powers of attorney, see Powers of Attorney Act 1971, s 1; Mental Capacity Act 2005, s 9.

[8] ss 53(1), 54. This is to be contrasted with a contract for the disposition of an interest in land: *McLaughlin v Duffill* [2008] EWCA Civ 1627, [2010] Ch 1.

disposition of any equitable interest, or interest in land, to be in writing, signed by the grantor or the grantor's agent, lays down that in such case the agent shall be authorized in writing.

The authority of an agent may also be implied.[9] But such implied authority can be negatived by an express limitation. In most cases implied authority is said to be *incidental* to an express authority or *required* due to the circumstances of the case. The category of implied authority also includes *usual* and *customary* authority. Generally, agents have the authority *usually* possessed by agents in their position. Therefore if an agent is authorized to conduct a particular trade or business, or to perform certain duties, that agent has implied authority to do such acts as are usual in the trade or business, or ordinarily incidental to the due performance of the duties. In addition, every agent has implied authority to act in accordance with the reasonable customs and usages of the particular place, trade, or market where the agent is employed, for example, the London Stock Exchange.[10]

(b) RATIFICATION

Even if the agent enters into a contract without the authority of the principal, the principal may subsequently ratify, that is to say, adopt the benefit and liabilities of a contract made on the principal's behalf.

This may occur in one of two ways. First, when A, though contracting as P's agent, and having P in contemplation as the principal, was not at the time of the contract P's agent in fact, as no precedent authority had been received. Secondly, when A was in fact P's agent at the time of making the contract, but exceeded the authority which P had given. In either case a ratification duly made places the parties in exactly the same position in which they would have been if A had P's authority at the time the contract was made. It is said to 'relate back' to the time of contracting and to have a retrospective effect.[11] An unauthorized acceptance may therefore be ratified even though the offer has in the meantime been withdrawn. So in *Bolton Partners v Lambert*:[12]

The managing director of a company, purporting to act as agent on the company's behalf, but without its authority, accepted an offer by the defendant for the purchase of some sugar works belonging to them. The defendant then withdrew his offer, but the company ratified the manager's acceptance.

It was held that the defendant was bound. The ratification related back to the time of the agent's acceptance and so prevented the defendant subsequently revoking the offer. But there can be no true ratification where an agent purports to accept an offer 'subject to ratification'. In such a case the so-called ratification would itself be an acceptance of

---

[9] *Freeman & Lockyer v Buckhurst Park Properties (Mangal) Ltd* [1964] 2 QB 480, 502; *Hely-Hutchinson v Brayhead Ltd* [1968] 1 QB 549.
[10] *Pollock v Stables* (1848) 12 QB 765.
[11] *Wilson v Tumman* (1843) 6 M & G 236, 242 (Tindal CJ) 242.   [12] (1888) 41 Ch D 295.

the offer of the other party, which may be withdrawn at any time before the so-called ratification takes place.[13]

The following rules govern ratification:

(i) The agent must purport to act as an agent for a disclosed principal

An individual may not conclude a contract on its own behalf and then transfer it to someone else under colour of ratification. The individual must contract as agent at the time of the contract, and an undisclosed principal, that is, a principal who is not disclosed by the agent to the third party at the time of contracting, may not step in and ratify acts done by the agent in excess of what had previously been authorized.[14] In *Keighley, Maxsted & Co v Durant*:[15]

A corn merchant was authorised to buy wheat at a certain price on a joint account for himself and KM. Acting in excess of his authority, he purchased wheat at a higher price from D, but in his own name. KM next day ratified the transaction, but later failed to take delivery of the wheat. D brought an action against KM for breach.

The action failed. The corn merchant had contracted in his own name without mentioning that KM was his principal. Any purported ratification by KM was therefore ineffective, and KM was consequently under no contractual obligation to D.

On the other hand, if this requirement is satisfied, it makes no difference that the agent's act was a fraud on the principal. So where an agent, without authority, and fraudulently, entered into a contract for the sale of wheat in the principal's name, but intending to take the benefit of it, the principal could nevertheless ratify and adopt the contract and hold the buyers to their bargain.[16] But a forged signature cannot be ratified, for one who forges the signature of another is not an agent. The forger does not act for another; but rather personates the person whose signature has been forged.[17]

(ii) The principal must be in existence

To ratify the contract, the intended principal must have been in existence, and ascertainable, at the time that the contract was made. It is not necessary for the principal to be named as long as he or she is ascertainable.[18]

This rule is important in its bearing on the liabilities of companies for the contracts made by the promoters on their behalf before they are formed. In *Kelner v Baxter*:[19]

The promoters of an unformed company entered into a contract on its behalf, which the company when duly incorporated, ratified. It went into liquidation and the promoters, who

---

[13] *Watson v Davies* [1931] 1 Ch 455; *Warehousing & Forwarding Co of East Africa Ltd v Jafferali & Sons Ltd* [1964] AC 1.

[14] Cf *Welsh Development Agency v Export Finance Co Ltd* [1992] BCLC 148, 159, 173, 182 (this principle is qualified by the maxim *id certum est quod certum reddi potest*, ie that which is capable of being made certain is to be treated as certain).

[15] [1901] AC 240.   [16] *Re Tiedemann and Ledermann Frères* [1899] 2 QB 66.

[17] *Brook v Hook* (1871) LR 6 Ex 89.

[18] *National Oilwell (UK) Ltd v Davy Offshore Ltd* [1993] 2 Lloyd's Rep 582, 592–7.

[19] (1866) LR 2 CP 174. See also *Natal Land and Colonization Co Ltd v Pauline Colliery and Development Syndicate Ltd* [1904] AC 120.

had contracted as agents, were sued upon the contract. They pleaded that the liability had passed, by ratification, to the company, and no longer attached to them.

The Court rejected this argument. Willes J said:[20]

Could the company become liable by a mere ratification? Clearly not. Ratification can only be by a person ascertained at the time of the act done,—by a person in existence either actually or in contemplation of law; as in the case of assignees of bankrupts and administrators, whose title, for the protection of the estate, vests by relation.

This limitation might work hardship to solicitors and others who are called in to do the preliminary work leading to the formation of a company as they will have no right of action against the company when formed. But as the above case shows, and as embodied in statute,[21] they will normally be able to assert a right of action against the agent (the promoter) in such cases, since the agent will be considered to have incurred personal liability on the contract.

(iii) Capacity of the principal to contract

'At the time the act was done the agent must have had a competent principal.'[22] Thus, if an agent enters into a contract on behalf of a principal who is, at the time, incapable of making it, no ratification is possible.[23]

(iv) Manner of ratification

The principal who accepts the contract made by a person whom the principal thereby undertakes to regard as its agent, may accept by words or conduct. The principal may avow responsibility for the act of the agent, or take the benefit of the contract, or otherwise by acquiescence in what is done create a presumption of authority. In the absence of an express avowal, however, the ratification must be founded on a full knowledge of the facts,[24] and the principal must have had the option whether to accept or to refuse the contract.[25] Otherwise it will be unenforceable against the principal. It is not, however, necessary for the ratification to be communicated to the third party.[26]

(v) Time and retrospectivity of ratification

The general rule is that the effect of ratification is retrospective so that the agent is treated as having had the relevant authority at the time it purported to make the

---

[20] (1866) LR 2 CP 174, 184.

[21] Companies Act 2006, s 51(1), which replaces Companies Act 1985, s 36C(1). See below, p 729. In *Braymist Ltd v Wise Finance Co Ltd* [2002] EWCA Civ 127, [2002] Ch 273 it was held that this statutory provision meant that the agent was not only liable on the contract but entitled to enforce it.

[22] *Firth v Staines* [1897] 2 QB 70, 75 (Wright J).

[23] *Ashbury Railway Carriage and Iron Co v Riche* (1875) LR 7 HL 653 (*ultra vires* contract); *Boston Deep Sea Fishing and Ice Co Ltd v Farnham* [1957] 1 WLR 1051 (alien enemy).

[24] *La Banque Jacques-Cartier v La Banque d'Epargne de Montréal* (1887) 13 App Cas 111.

[25] *Forman & Co Pty Ltd v Ship 'Liddesdale'* [1900] AC 190, above, p 481.

[26] *Shell Co of Australia Ltd v Nat Shipping Bagging Services Ltd, The Kilmun* [1988] 2 Lloyd's Rep 1, 11. See also *Pagnan SpA v Feed Products Ltd* [1987] 2 Lloyd's Rep 601.

contract. So an offer accepted without authority by an agent can be later ratified by a principal even though at that later time the other party, to the principal's knowledge, has withdrawn its offer.[27]

An exception to that general rule is that 'an estate once vested cannot be divested, nor can an act lawful at the time of its performance be rendered unlawful by the doctrine of ratification'.[28] Similarly the traditional rule for non-marine insurance, albeit controversial, is that a contract of insurance made by an agent without the principal's authority cannot be ratified after the principal has become aware that the event insured against has in fact occurred.[29]

Subject to any express time limit for ratification fixed by the parties and, assuming that a time fixed for performance by the other party has not expired, the principal has a reasonable time to ratify after acquiring notice of the unauthorized act.[30]

(c) OSTENSIBLE AUTHORITY

The principal may, by words or conduct, create an inference that an agent has authority to act on behalf of the principal even though no authority exists in fact. In such a case, if the agent contracts within the limits of the apparent authority, although without any actual authority, the principal will be bound to third parties by the agent's acts.

(i) Requirements

This doctrine of apparent authority, or ostensible authority as it is usually called, is really an application of the principle of estoppel, for estoppel means only that a person is not permitted to resist an inference which can reasonably be drawn from that person's words or conduct. Thus where one person expressly or impliedly represents another to have authority to act as agent, so that a third party reasonably believes the person who is so held out to possess that authority and deals with that person in reliance on the representation so made, the person making the representation will be bound to the same extent as if actual authority had in fact been conferred.[31] The person

---

[27] *Bolton Partners v Lambert* (1881) 41 Ch D 295: see above, p 717. See also *Presentaciones Musicales SA v Secunda* [1994] Ch 271 (the unauthorized commencement of legal proceedings within the limitation period by an agent could be ratified by the principal outside the limitation period); *The Borvigilant* [2002] EWHC 1759 (Admlty), [2002] 2 Lloyd's Rep 631.

[28] *Bolton Partners v Lambert* (1881) 41 Ch D 295, 307 (Cotton LJ).

[29] *Grover & Grover v Matthews* [1910] 2 KB 401. The contrary rule applies to marine insurance (see Marine Insurance Act 1906, s 86; *Williams v North China Insurance Co* (1876) 1 CPD 757): in *obiter dicta* in *National Oilwell (UK) Ltd v Davy Offshore Ltd* [1983] 2 Lloyd's Rep 582, 607–8, Colman J expressed the strong view that the rule in marine insurance should be extended to non-marine insurance.

[30] *Re Portuguese Consolidated Copper Mines* (1890) 45 Ch D 16; *Bedford Insurance Co Ltd v Instituto de Resseguros do Brasil* [1985] QB 966, 987.

[31] For a clear general statement of the law, see *Freeman & Lockyer v Buckhurst Park Properties (Mangal) Ltd* [1964] 2 QB 480, 503–4 (Diplock LJ). For examples of factual situations in which ostensible authority may exist, see *Egyptian Intl Foreign Trade Co v Soplex Wholesale Supplies Ltd, The Raffaella* [1985] 2 Lloyd's Rep 36; *Shearson Lehman Hutton Inc v MacLaine, Watson & Co Ltd (No 2)* [1988] 1 WLR 16; *Polish SS Co v AJ Williams Fuels (Overseas Sales) Ltd, The Suwalki* [1989] 1 Lloyd's Rep 511. A person negotiating a contract on

making the representation is estopped from denying the ostensible authority which was thus created.

It is, however, important to note three things. First, the representation must be made by *the principal*. Ostensible authority cannot be created simply by a representation by the agent.[32] Secondly, subject to certain exceptions discussed below,[33] the third party must rely on a representation of the agent's authority to act *as agent*. The doctrine cannot apply where the third party does not know or believe that person to be an agent, for example, if the existence of the principal is unknown to the third party.[34] Thirdly, the agent's want of authority must be *unknown* to the third party.[35]

(ii) Never any authority

These requirements mean that there will seldom be ostensible authority where a person has never at any time had authority to contract. But that there can be an exceptional case is exemplified by *Freeman & Lockyer v Buckhurst Park Properties (Mangal) Ltd*:[36]

The articles of a company contained power to appoint a managing director. With the knowledge and approval of the board of directors, K acted as managing director, although he was never appointed to this post. K instructed the claimants, a firm of architects, to do certain work for the company. The company disclaimed liability for payment for this work on the ground that K had no authority to contract on the company's behalf.

The Court of Appeal held that, although K had no actual authority to employ the claimants, the company had created an ostensible authority by its conduct in permitting him to act as managing director to the knowledge of the board. Any act done within the usual ambit of that ostensible authority was therefore binding on the company.

(iii) Limited or revoked authority

The doctrine of ostensible authority is more likely to apply where an authorized agent goes beyond the limits of his actual authority, yet acts within an authority which he is

---

behalf of a company but known not to have authority to bind the company may, nevertheless, have ostensible authority to communicate that those with authority to bind the company have approved the contract in question: *First Energy (UK) Ltd v Hungarian International Bank Ltd* [1993] 2 Lloyd's Rep 194 distinguishing *Armagas Ltd v Mundogas SA, The Ocean Frost* [1986] AC 717.

[32] *A-G for Ceylon v Silva* [1953] AC 461, 479; *Freeman & Lockyer v Buckhurst Park Properties (Mangal) Ltd* [1964] 2 QB 480, 505; *British Bank of the Middle East v Sun Life Assurance Co of Canada (UK) Ltd* [1983] 2 Lloyd's Rep 9; *First Sport Ltd v Barclays Bank plc* [1993] 1 WLR 1229; *First Energy (UK) Ltd v Hungarian Int'l Bank Ltd* [1993] 2 Lloyd's Rep 194.

[33] See below, p 722.

[34] *Farquharson Bros v King & Co* [1902] AC 325; *Freeman & Lockyer v Buckhurst Park Properties (Mangal) Ltd* [1964] 2 QB 480, 503.

[35] See *Armagas Ltd v Mundogas SA* [1986] 1 AC 717, 777–9.

[36] [1964] 2 QB 480. But see now Companies Act 2006, s 39(1), and above, p 249 (*ultra vires* contracts).

made to appear to possess.[37] In particular, where a principal has publicly allowed the agent to assume an authority, that authority cannot be revoked privately. The principal will be bound by the acts of the agent if the principal has given other persons reason to suppose that they are done with authority.

Thus an employer who habitually allows employees to purchase goods on credit[38] or a husband who takes upon himself the liability in respect of his wife's past dealings with suppliers of goods or services[39] 'holds out' the employees or wife as agent. They will be liable on such contracts unless and until they actually make known to the supplier the fact that the agency has been determined.

(iv) Partnership

Every partner is an agent of the firm and of the other partners for the business of the partnership; this is simply a case of implied authority. But any act done by a partner for carrying on in the usual way business of a kind carried on by the firm binds the firm and the other partners, even if the partner so acting has in fact no authority to act for the firm in the particular matter, unless the person with whom the partner is dealing either knows that person has no authority, or does not know or believe that person to be a partner.[40] Moreover, a partner who retires from a firm may still be liable for partnership debts contracted after retirement. A person dealing with a firm after a change in its constitution is entitled to treat all apparent members of the old firm as still being members of the firm until that person has notice of the change.[41] The retiring partner will be estopped from denying the continuation of that authority,[42] except where he was not known to be a partner by the person dealing with the firm.[43]

(d) USUAL AUTHORITY?

There are a number of cases which appear to establish that, in certain circumstances, a principal may be liable for the unauthorized acts of an agent, even though the third party did not rely upon any representation by the principal of the agent's authority to act as agent. In these cases, the existence of the principal was unknown to the third party, so that it could not be said that the principal held out the agent to

---

[37] *Todd v Robinson* (1825) 1 Ry & M 217; *Summers v Solomon* (1857) 7 E & B 879; *Manchester Trust v Furness* [1895] 2 QB 539; *AMB Generali Holding AG v SEB Trygg Liv Holding AB* [2005] EWCA Civ 1237, [2006] 1 WLR 2276.

[38] *Summers v Solomon*, above n 37.

[39] *Drew v Nunn* (1879) 4 QBD 661; *Jetley v Hill* (1884) Cab & El 239. See also *Ryan v Sams* (1848) 12 QB 460 (mistress).

[40] Partnership Act 1890, s 5. See also s 8. See further, *United Bank of Kuwait Ltd v Hammoud* [1988] 1 WLR 1051.

[41] Partnership Act 1890, s 36(1). Under s 36(2), notice in the *London Gazette* is sufficient notice as to persons who had no dealings with the firm before the change; otherwise express notice is required.

[42] *Scarf v Jardine* (1882) 7 App Cas 345, 349.   [43] Partnership Act 1890, s 36(3).

have authority to act as agent and was estopped. The apparent rule to be extracted from them is as follows: an undisclosed principal who employs an agent to conduct business is liable for any act of the agent which is incidental to or usual in that business, although such act may have been forbidden by the principal. The leading example is *Watteau v Fenwick*:[44]

F, a firm of brewers, bought a pub from H, but kept him on as manager, and his name appeared above the door. They instructed H not to buy cigars although it was usual for such a business to deal in cigars. H bought some cigars on credit from W, who thought H was the owner of the business and gave credit to him personally. On discovering that he was employed by F, W sued F for the price of the cigars.

It was held that F was liable. Wills J rejected the argument that a principal could only be bound where there had been a holding out of authority—which could not be said of this case where the person supplying the goods knew nothing of the existence of the principal. 'The principal', he said,[45] 'is liable for all the acts of the agent which are within the authority usually confided to an agent of that character, notwithstanding limitations as between the principal and the agent, put upon that authority'.

This case is anomalous, and has been criticized as such.[46] One attempt made to explain it and similar cases is that they are cases of 'usual authority'. But as noted above,[47] the usual authority of an agent is normally merely an example of implied authority, which could be negatived by an express limitation. If this and similar cases[48] are rightly decided, which seems unlikely, they are perhaps best regarded as examples of the operation of a quasi-tortious principle whereby an employer is rendered vicariously liable for the acts of an agent if done in the course of the agent's employment.

2. EFFECTS OF AGENCY

As has been explained, we are concerned in this chapter with the effects of agency in respect of the contractual relations between the principal and the third party[49] and between the agent and the third party.[50]

---

[44] [1893] 1 QB 346.　　　　　　　　　　　　　　　　[45] *Ibid*, 348.

[46] *Rhodian River Shipping SA v Halla Maritime Corporation* [1984] 1 Lloyd's Rep 373, 378–9 (Bingham LJ); *Sign-o-Lite Plastics Ltd v Metropolitan Life Insurance Co* (1990) 73 DLR (4th) 541 (British Columbian CA). See also Hornby [1961] CLJ 239; Fridman (1991) 70 Can Bar Rev 329.

[47] Above, p 717.

[48] It is not unique: see *Edmunds v Bushell and Jones* (1865) LR 1 QB. 97. For further examples, see Powell, *The Law of Agency* (2nd edn, 1961) 72 ff.

[49] For a principal's liability in tort (whether the tort of deceit or negligence or under the Misrepresentation Act 1967, s 2(1)) for the misrepresentation of its agent, see the previous edition of this book, pp 710–711.

[50] For the relations between the principal and the agent, see the previous edition of this book at pp 701–707.

(a) THE CONTRACTUAL RELATIONS BETWEEN THE PRINCIPAL AND THE THIRD PARTY

(i) The general position

When a principal endows an agent with actual authority to contract, the principal is bound, as regards third parties, by all acts of the agent which are done within the limits of that authority. This rule is often expressed in the maxim, *Qui facit per alium, facit per se*, a person who acts through another acts in person.

The same rule applies where the agent is acting within its ostensible authority.[51] The principal will be liable to third parties even though the agent has acted for its own benefit and in fraud of the principal.[52] Where, however, the third party dealing with the agent is aware that the agent is acting for its own benefit, or where the circumstances of the transaction are such as to put the third party on enquiry, the principal is not bound.[53]

A principal also acquires rights against a third party under a contract entered into by an agent on its behalf where the agent has acted within the limits of its actual authority. But a principal does not acquire rights (as opposed to liabilities) against the third party by reason of ostensible authority because that doctrine is based on a representation by the principal. In other words, a principal must ratify a contract entered into without authority before it can acquire rights (as opposed to liabilities) against the third party.

(ii) Undisclosed principal

Normally, where an agent acts on behalf of a principal whose existence, at the time the contract is made, is not disclosed, that 'undisclosed principal' can sue and be sued under the contract; and the agent does not drop out[54] so that there is a contract between the undisclosed principal and agent on the one hand and the third party on the other.[55] This doctrine of the undisclosed principal is peculiar to English law,[56] and has sometimes been criticized as an anomaly, since it runs counter to the principles of privity of contract.[57] But it serves a useful commercial purpose.[58] Moreover, it is subject to the qualification that the authority must have been in existence at the time the contract was made: in other words, it is not possible to ratify a contract unless the principal is named therein, or is at any rate identifiable. Otherwise it would be open to any stranger to intervene and sue.[59]

---

[51]　Above, p 720.　　　　　[52]　*Hambro v Burnand* [1904] 2 KB 10. See also Watts (2001) 117 LQR 300.
[53]　*Reckitt v Burnett, Pembroke & Slater Ltd* [1929] AC 176.
[54]　*Bowstead and Reynolds on Agency* (20th edn, 2014) para 9–012. See below, pp 726, 730.
[55]　*Welsh Development Agency v Export Finance Co* [1992] BCLC 148, 173, 182.
[56]　Lando and Beale, *Principles of European Contract Law Parts I and II* (2000) 221.
[57]　Pollock (1888) 3 LQR 359; Ames, *Lectures on Legal History* (1913) 453. Cf Goodhart and Harrison (1932) 4 CLJ 320; Tan Cheng-Han (2004) 120 LQR 480. In continental systems the absence of the doctrine of privity of contract makes such a principle commercially unnecessary. Cf Müller-Freienfels (1953) 16 MLR 299.
[58]　See *Siu Yin Kwan v Eastern Insurance Co Ltd* [1994] 2 AC 199, 207.
[59]　*Keighley, Maxsted & Co v Durant* [1901] AC 240; above, p 718.

But the right of the undisclosed principal to intervene as a contracting party is subject to certain limitations.

First, intervention is excluded if the contract is in terms which import that the agent is the real and only principal, for then the idea of agency is incompatible with the terms of the contract. Thus, in *Humble v Hunter*,[60] where an agent in making a charterparty described himself therein as 'owner' of the ship, it was held that evidence was not admissible to prove that another person was the real owner and that he was merely acting as agent on his behalf. His principal could not intervene, nor could he be sued. On the other hand, where the agent was described as 'charterer',[61] 'landlord',[62] 'tenant',[63] 'disponent owner',[64] and 'employer'[65] evidence has been admitted to show who the real principal was. It appears that in modern law intervention of the principal will only be excluded by descriptive words where such intervention would clearly be inconsistent with the object and intent of the contract.[66]

Secondly, where the personality of the agent is of such importance that the contract must be taken to have been made with that person alone, no one else can interpose and adopt the contract.[67] For example, in the case where there is an agreement to write a book,[68] or to underwrite shares in a company,[69] or to purchase goods subject to a right of set-off,[70] if the agent contracts in its own name without disclosure of the agency, the principal cannot intervene. Of course, if the third party subsequently discovers the identity of the principal, and with an opportunity of affirming or rejecting the contract, elects to affirm it, as, for example, by retaining goods purchased, the third party will be bound to the principal, but not otherwise.[71]

In any case, a person who contracts with an agent, honestly and reasonably believing the agent to be the principal party to the transaction, is entitled to set up against the principal, when discovered, any set-off which is available against the agent, and which accrued before the person knew that the party with whom the contract was made

---

[60] (1848) 12 QB 310. See also *Formby v Formby* (1910) 102 LT 116 ('proprietor'); *Asty Maritime Co Ltd and Panagiotis Stravelakis v Rocco Guiseppe & Figli, SNC, The Astyanax* [1985] 2 Lloyd's Rep 109 ('disponent owner').

[61] *Fred Drughorn Ltd v Rederiaktiebolaget Transatlantic* [1919] AC 203.

[62] *Epps v Rothnie* [1945] KB 562.   [63] *Danziger v Thompson* [1944] KB 654.

[64] *O/Y Wasa SS Co v Newspaper Pulp and Wood Exports* (1949) 82 Ll LR 936. Cf *Asty Maritime Co Ltd and Panagiotis Stravelakis v Rocco Guiseppe & Figli, SNC, The Astyanax* [1985] 2 Lloyd's Rep 109.

[65] *Ferryways NV v Associated British Ports, The Humber Way* [2008] EWHC 225 (Comm), [2008] 2 All ER (Comm) 504.

[66] See eg *JH Rayner (Mincing Lane) Ltd v Department of Trade and Industry* [1989] Ch 72, 190–1; *Welsh Development Agency v Export Finance Co* [1992] BCLC 148, 159; *Siu Yin Kwan v Eastern Insurance Co Ltd* [1994] 2 AC 199, 209; *Rolls-Royce Power Engineering plc v Ricardo Consulting Engineers* Ltd [2003] EWHC 2871, [2004] 2 All ER (Comm) 129; *Ferryways NV v Associated British Ports, The Humber Way* [2008] EWHC 225, [2008] 2 All ER (Comm) 504.

[67] *Said v Butt* [1920] 3 KB 497, above, p 294. Cf *Dyster v Randall & Sons* [1926] Ch 932.

[68] *Boulton v Jones* (1857) 2 H & N 564, 566 (Bramwell B).

[69] *Collins v Associated Greyhound Racecourses Ltd* [1930] 1 Ch 1.

[70] *Boulton v Jones* (1857) 2 H & N 564, above, p 290; *Greer v Downs Supply Co* [1927] 2 KB 28.

[71] *Greer v Downs Supply Co* [1927] 2 KB 28, 33.

was in fact an agent.[72] This rule rests upon the doctrine of estoppel.[73] But a person who has not been misled cannot claim such a set-off. So in a case where a man dealt with brokers whom he knew to be in the habit of selling, sometimes as brokers for principals, and sometimes on their own account, he could not set off his indebtedness to the brokers against his debt to the principal.[74]

Upon discovering the principal, the other contracting party may elect to sue either the agent or the principal. Any act which unequivocally indicates the adoption of either principal or agent as the party liable determines the election, and the contracting party cannot afterwards sue the other.[75]

A contract for the sale or other disposition of land must be in writing 'signed *by or on behalf* of each party to the contract'.[76] Although, as we have noted, the contract to which the undisclosed principal is a party is considered not to be separate from the contract between the agent and the other party,[77] the sub-section would seem to preclude an undisclosed or an unnamed principal from suing or being sued on contracts signed by their agents.[78] But the Law Commission's Working Paper stated that 'plainly agents should be permitted to sign on behalf of the parties' and that it was intended to 'let the ordinary principles of agency operate',[79] and the Commission's Report indicates that its recommendations were made on this basis.[80] So, it is arguable that, as was the case before the enactment of the 1989 Act,[81] an agent signs 'on behalf of' the principal whenever the contract is signed with authority and the agent intends to act on behalf of the principal.

(iii) Settlement with the agent

It often happens that either the principal or the third party incurs a debt to the other under a contract made through an agent and the principal or the third party thereupon settles with the agent, intending that the agent should pay across the money and so discharge the debt. Sometimes, however, the agent fails to do so, and makes away with the money or becomes bankrupt. Is the debtor then liable to pay over again? The answer will depend on whether it is the principal or the third party who is making the payment.

Where the principal pays the agent, the general rule is that the principal is not discharged.[82] But where there are indications that the third party looks to the agent

---

[72] *Isberg v Bowden* (1853) 8 Exch 852, 859; *Montagu v Forwood* [1893] 2 QB 350.

[73] *Cooke v Eshelby* (1887) 12 App Cas 271, 278 (Lord Watson).

[74] *Cooke v Eshelby* (1887) 12 App Cas 271.

[75] *Scarf v Jardine* (1882) 7 App Cas 345. Cf *Clarkson Booker Ltd v Andjel* [1964] 2 QB 775; *Pyxis Special Shipping Co Ltd v Dritsas & Kaglis Bros Ltd* [1978] 2 Lloyd's Rep 380 (institution of legal proceedings not conclusive). See Reynolds (1970) 86 LQR 318.

[76] Law of Property (Miscellaneous Provisions) Act 1989, s 2(3), above, p 90.

[77] *Welsh Development Agency v Export Finance Co*, above, n 55.

[78] See *Bowstead and Reynolds on Agency* (20th edn, 2014) para 8–004.

[79] Law Com WP No 92 (1985), para 5.16.   [80] Law Com No 164 (1987), para 4.8.

[81] *Basma v Weekes* [1950] AC 441, 454, on the Law of Property Act 1925, s 40.

[82] *Irvine & Co v Watson & Sons* (1880) 5 QBD 414.

alone for payment and in consequence the principal settles with the agent,[83] or where the third party's conduct leads the principal to suppose that the debt has already been paid,[84] the third party is estopped from claiming to be paid over again. Normally, however, this is not the case. Where the third party knows that the agent is contracting on behalf of a principal, this indicates that the third party did not look exclusively to the agent for payment.[85] It is necessary to show conduct by the third party which would estop it from proceeding against the principal, or a custom of the trade to this effect.

It was laid down in *Armstrong v Stokes*[86] that, if an undisclosed principal pays the agent for the price of goods sold to it, and the existence of the undisclosed principal is then discovered, the seller cannot sue the undisclosed principal. This decision proceeded on the ground that a demand for payment could not be made from 'those who were only discovered to be principals after they had fairly paid the price to those whom the vendor believed to be the principals, and to whom alone the vendor gave credit'.[87] But this case is contrary to earlier authority,[88] and it was subsequently criticized by the Court of Appeal.[89] No estoppel could legitimately arise since the seller was unaware of the undisclosed principal's existence, and thus could not have induced it to settle with the agent. It may therefore be that it does not represent the law.

If it is the third party who settles with the agent, again the general rule is that the third party is not discharged. The reason for this is that an agent who is authorized to sell is not necessarily authorized to accept the purchase money.[90] Payment, however, to an agent who has such authority, either from an express mandate of the principal or in the ordinary course of business, will constitute a good discharge.[91] It would also seem that where the principal is undisclosed, payment to the agent before disclosure would be effective, for the principal has led the third party to believe that the agent is dealing on its own account.[92]

(b) THE CONTRACTUAL RELATIONS BETWEEN THE AGENT AND THE THIRD PARTY

An agent who is employed to establish privity of contract between the principal and a third party, in most instances will acquire no rights and incur no liabilities in respect of the contract which is entered in the capacity of agent. But 'it is not the law that, if a principal is liable, his agent cannot be',[93] and the agent may be found to have undertaken personal liability.[94] It is therefore our first task to discover the circumstances in which an agent may be under a personal contractual liability.

[83] *Smith v Ferrand* (1827) 7 B & C 191.
[84] *Wyatt v Marquis of Hertford* (1802) 3 East 147.
[85] *Irvine & Co v Watson & Sons* (1880) 5 QBD 414.
[86] (1872) LR 7 QB 598.
[87] *Ibid*, 610.
[88] *Heald v Kenworthy* (1855) 10 Exch 739, 745.
[89] *Irvine & Co v Watson & Sons* (1880) 5 QBD 414, 417 (Bramwell LJ).
[90] *Butwick v Grant* [1924] 2 KB 483.
[91] *Howard v Chapman* (1831) 4 C & P 508; *International Sponge Importers v Watt* [1911] AC 279.
[92] *Curlewis v Birkbeck* (1863) 3 F & F 894. Cf *Drakeford v Piercy* (1866) 7 B & S 515.
[93] *Yeung Kai Yung v Hong Kong and Shanghai Banking Corp* [1981] AC 787, 795 (Lord Scarman).
[94] See Reynolds (1969) 85 LQR 92.

(i) Personal contractual liability of the agent

Where an agent contracts, as agent, for a disclosed principal, so that the other party to the contract looks through the agent to a principal, it may be laid down, as a general rule, that the agent drops out of the transaction as soon as the contract is made. The agent acquires neither rights nor liabilities. But there are several situations in which the agent is personally liable.

(a) Agent undertakes liability

Whether the agent has undertaken personal liability depends on the proper construction to be put upon the conduct of the parties where the contract is oral, or upon the wording of the document and the surrounding circumstances if it is written.[95] There is nothing to prevent both principal and agent being severally liable on, and entitled to enforce, a contract which the agent has made on behalf of the principal, if that was the intention of the parties.[96] The agent may, for example, expressly or impliedly undertake liability for payment,[97] or may be considered to have done so by trade usage.[98] Or the document in which the contract is written may give no indication that the agent was acting as such, although both parties knew this to be the case: 'Where a person signs a contract in his own name, without qualification, he is prima facie to be deemed to be a person contracting personally: and, in order to prevent this liability from attaching, it must be apparent from the other portions of the document that he did not intend to bind himself as principal'.[99]

(b) Agent party to a deed

An agent who is party to a deed is bound thereby even though described as agent,[100] except possibly where the agent is acting under a power of attorney.[101]

(c) Negotiable instruments

An agent who signs as party to a negotiable instrument, such as a bill of exchange or promissory note, either as drawer, indorser, or acceptor, will be personally liable

---

[95] *Chapman v Smith* [1907] 2 Ch 97, 103. See also *Elpis Maritime Co Ltd v Marti Chartering Co Inc, The Maria D* [1992] 1 AC 21; *Punjab National Bank v De Boinville* [1992] 1 WLR 1138, 1155.

[96] *The Swan* [1968] 1 Lloyd's Rep 5, 13–14.

[97] *Hall v Ashurst* (1833) 1 C & M 714; *Rusholme & Bolton, etc Ltd v SG Read & Co* [1955] 1 WLR 146; *Format International Security Printers Ltd v Mosden* [1975] 1 Lloyd's Rep 37; *Fraser v Equitorial Shipping Co Ltd* [1979] 1 Lloyd's Rep 103.

[98] *Fleet v Murton* (1871) LR 7 QB 126; *Perishables Transport Co v Spyropoulos* [1964] 2 Lloyd's Rep 379.

[99] *2 Smith's Leading Cases* (12th edn, 1915) 379; *HO Brandt & Co v HN Morris & Co Ltd* [1917] 2 KB 784; *Hichens Harrison Woolston & Co v Jackson* [1943] AC 266, 273; *Tudor Marine Ltd v Tradax Export SA* [1976] 2 Lloyd's Rep 134. Cf *The Santa Carina* [1977] 1 Lloyd's Rep 478 (oral contract); *Seatrade Gronigen BV v Geest Industries Ltd* [1996] 2 Lloyd's Rep 375 (signature had to be read in conjunction with other parts of document).

[100] *Appleton v Binks* (1804) 5 East 148.

[101] Powers of Attorney Act 1971, s 7(1), as amended by the Law of Property (Miscellaneous Provisions) Act 1989 and SI 2005 No 1906. This exception probably only applies where the principal is named in the deed: *Harmer v Armstrong* [1934] Ch 65.

even though words which describe the agent as such, or as filling a representative character, are added to the signature.[102] The agent must go even further and indicate clearly that the signature is only on the principal's behalf. Thus the addition of the words 'receiver',[103] 'executor',[104] or 'director'[105] will not necessarily relieve the agent of liability; but such expressions as 'for and on behalf of X as agent', or *'per pro'* will do so.[106]

(d) Foreign principal

Although there is no rule of law to the effect that an agent who contracts on behalf of a foreign principal will be personally liable, the fact that a principal is a foreigner may be of some weight in determining whether the mutual intention of the third party and the agent was that the agent should be personally liable to be sued as well as the principal, particularly if credit has been extended by the third party.[107]

(e) Principal not in existence

An agent who contracts on behalf of a non-existent principal (eg a company before it has been incorporated) risks incurring personal liability on the contract so made.[108] At common law this was a question of construction. While the Court may assume that the agent making the contract would be personally liable,[109] there was no rule of law that an agent is automatically a party whenever there is no principal capable of being bound by the agreement.[110] The construction of the particular contract, and the signature on the contract may show that it was made with the principal alone, so that the agent acquires neither rights[111] nor liabilities[112] under the contract. Section 51(1) of the Companies Act 2006, however, provides that a contract which purports to be made by or on behalf of a company at a time when the company has not been formed has effect, subject to any agreement to the contrary, as one made with the person purporting to act for the company or as agent for it, and he is personally liable on the contract accordingly. This provision applies whatever the form of the signature, that is, whether the agent signs on behalf of the company or as the company itself.[113] Moreover, the agent can sue as well as be sued.[114]

---

[102] Bills of Exchange Act 1882, s 26. Cf *ibid*, s 17. See also Companies Act 2006, s 83. Cf *Bondina v Rollaway Shower Blinds Ltd* [1986] 1 WLR 517.

[103] *Kettle v Dunster and Wakefield* (1927) 43 TLR 770.

[104] *Liverpool Bank v Walker* (1859) 4 De G & J 24.   [105] *Elliott v Bax-Ironside* [1925] 2 KB 301.

[106] *Ibid*, 307 (Scrutton LJ); Bills of Exchange Act 1882, ss 25, 31(5).

[107] *Teheran-Europe Co Ltd v ST Belton (Tractors) Ltd* [1968] 2 QB 545, 558.

[108] *Kelner v Baxter* (1866) LR 2 CP 174, above, p 718.   [109] *Ibid*, 185 (Willes J).

[110] *Black v Smallwood* (1966) 117 CLR 52 (Australia).

[111] *Newborne v Sensolid (Great Britain) Ltd* [1954] 1 QB 45.

[112] *Hollman v Pullin* (1884) 1 Cab & El 254.   [113] *Phonogram Ltd v Lane* [1982] QB 938.

[114] *Braymist Ltd v Wise Finance Co Ltd* [2002] EWCA Civ 127, [2002] Ch 273.

(f) Unnamed principal

An agent who contracts as agent, but does *not* disclose the name of the principal, is also, as a rule, not personally liable on the contract which is made. Yet here too, as where the name of the principal is disclosed, the matter is one of construction.[115] But, although there is a prima facie rule that the agent drops out of the transaction, the terms of the contract or trade usage may again indicate a contrary intention.[116]

(ii) 'Agent' acting as principal

Is it possible for a person who has purported to contract as agent for an unnamed principal, to state that he or she is in fact the real principal? The answer is that this is possible, for if the other party to the contract was willing to take the liability of an unknown person, it is hard to suppose that the agent was the one person in the world with whom the other party was unwilling to contract. At any rate, the character or the solvency of the unnamed principal could not have induced the contract. Thus in *Schmaltz v Avery*:[117]

S entered into a contract of charterparty with D. S described themselves as 'agents of the freighter', and it was provided in the contract that, since they were contracting 'on behalf of another party', all personal liability on their part should cease when the cargo was shipped. They then revealed themselves as principals and sought to enforce the charterparty.

It was held that they were entitled to do so. In this case, the 'agent' was allowed to sue on the contract, and by the same token ought similarly to incur liability under it.

(iii) Undisclosed principal

If the agent acts on behalf of a principal whose existence is not at the time disclosed (the 'undisclosed principal'),[118] the other contracting party, when discovering the true facts, is entitled to elect whether to treat the principal or the agent as liable.

The reason for this rule is plain. If T enters into a contract with A, T is entitled at all events to treat A, the party with whom T supposed the contract was made, as liable. If T subsequently discovers that A is in fact the representative of P, T is entitled to choose whether to accept the actual state of things, and treat P as liable, or whether to adhere to the supposed state of things upon which the contract was entered, and continue to treat A as liable.

The liability of the agent continues until the other contracting party has done some act which unequivocally indicates that it regards the principal as the party solely liable.[119]

---

[115] *Fleet v Murton* (1871) LR 7 QB 126, 131.

[116] *Southwell v Bowditch* (1876) 1 CPD 374, 376; *Hichens, Harrison Woolston & Co v Jackson & Sons* [1943] AC 266; *Perishables Transport Co v N Spyropoulos (London) Ltd* [1964] 2 Lloyd's Rep 379.

[117] (1851) 16 QB 655. See also *Harper & Co v Vigers* [1909] 2 KB 549. Cf *Sharman v Brandt* (1871) LR 6 QB 720.

[118] See above, p 724.   [119] See above, p 726.

(iv) Unauthorized acts of the agent: breach of warranty of authority

Where a person purports to act as agent for a disclosed principal but without any authority to do so, the party who was thus induced to enter into a contract has a contractual action against the agent for breach of warranty of authority (as well as possible claims for the tort of deceit[120] or negligence).[121] A warranty of authority is an implied promise on the part of the professed agent that, in consideration of the other party entering into the contract, the professed agent warrants the existence of a principal and that the contract is within the authority conferred by that principal.[122]

This rule applies not only to transactions or representations which would result in contract, but also to any representation of authority whereby one induces another to act detrimentally.[123] It is immaterial that the agent had no knowledge or means of knowledge that it was acting without authority, for 'moral innocence, so far as the person who has been induced to contract is concerned, in no way aids that person or alleviates the inconvenience and damage which he sustains'.[124] The warranty is, moreover, a continuing warranty, and therefore the agent is liable even though the authority, though valid at the time of the contract, has, unknown to the agent, been determined, as by the death or mental incapacity of the principal.

---

[120] *Polhill v Walter* (1832) 3 B & Ad 114; above, p 342.

[121] *Hedley Byrne & Co Ltd v Heller & Partners Ltd* [1964] AC 465, 532.

[122] *Collen v Wright* (1857) 8 E & B 647; *Penn v Bristol and West Building Society* [1997] 1 WLR 1356; *AMB Generali Holding AG v SEB Trygg Liv Holding AB* [2005] EWCA Civ 1237, [2006] 1 WLR 2276 at [60].

[123] *Starkey v Bank of England* [1903] AC 114.

[124] *Collen v Wright* (1857) 8 E & B 647, 657 (Willes J). See also *Suart v Haigh* (1893) 9 TLR 488; *Yonge v Toynbee* [1910] 1 KB 215.

INDEX